IRENE C. FOUNTAS
GAY SU PINNELL

The FOUNTAS and PINNELL
LEVELED BOOK LIST K-8

Heinemann
Portsmouth, NH

Heinemann
A division of Reed Elsevier Inc.
361 Hanover Street
Portsmouth, NH 03801-3912
www.heinemann.com

Offices and agents throughout the world

Library of Congress Cataloging-in-Publication Data

Fountas, Irene C.
       The Fountas & Pinnell leveled book list K-8 / Irene C. Fountas, Gay Su Pinnell.-- 2006-2008 ed.
       p. cm.
Includes bibliographical references.
ISBN 0-325-00819-1 (alk. paper)
1. Reading (Elementary) 2. Reading (Middle school) 3. Children--Books and reading. 4. Effective teaching.
I. Title: Fountas and Pinnell leveled book list K-8. II. Title: Leveled book list K-8. III. Pinnell, Gay Su. IV. Title.
  LB1573.F638 2006
    372.41--dc22
                              2005033254

Production: Michael Cirone
Cover design: Lisa Fowler
Typesetter: Technologies 'N Typography
Manufacturing: Jamie Carter

Printed in the United States of America on acid-free paper
10 09 08 07 06   VP   2 3 4 5

TABLE OF CONTENTS

INTRODUCTION TO THE BOOK LIST iv

EVALUATION RESPONSE FOR TEXT GRADIENT vi

THE LISTS
ORGANIZED ALPHABETICALLY BY **BOOK TITLE** 1
ORGANIZED BY **BOOK LEVEL** 365

APPENDIX A
PUBLISHER AND DISTRIBUTOR INFORMATION 729

INTRODUCTION TO THE BOOK LIST

All teachers want their students to be successful, confident readers. This process begins with sensitive, responsive reading instruction, an understanding of how books support the "learning to read" process, and access to a sufficient quantity of high-quality books at appropriate instructional levels. In our books *Guided Reading: Good First Teaching for All Children* (Heinemann, 1996) and *Guiding Readers and Writers: Teaching Comprehension, Genre, and Content Literacy* (Heinemann, 2001) we describe a comprehensive language and literacy framework designed to help students develop a broad and integrated range of reading, writing, and language abilities.

Then in *Leveled Books K–8: Matching Texts to Readers for Effective Teaching* (Heinemann, 2006) we focus on the texts you will need to support a rich environment for literacy teaching and learning, beginning with a description of the most effective ways to use books in the classroom. That book also describes our gradient of leveled texts and its uses. We encourage the use of leveled books for instruction in guided reading. Our levels will help you make good choices for students at various stages of reading development.

This book—*The Fountas and Pinnell Leveled Book List, K–8*—is a reference resource of over 18,000 titles that have been through an in-depth analysis by teams of experts who are experienced in analyzing features of texts as well as in teaching guided reading. The list includes a wide variety of genres and formats, fiction and nonfiction. Of course, we can't possibly level every book published. As you get to know books at our levels, talk with colleagues about the books you have that are not yet part of this list and assign them a tentative level.

The leveling process is ongoing, including constant review and revision as books are used by teachers in the classroom. "Leveling" is not an exact science. A level is an approximation, not an absolute designation; not all books on a level are precisely alike. There are many variables to take into account in determining text difficulty. A text's demands and supports cannot be reduced to a mathematical formula. The concepts of "easier" and "harder" must always be understood in relation to the complex and interrelated text factors that we describe in *Leveled Books K–8*. What's more, myriad student factors have an impact on text readability as well. The readability of a text is influenced by the background knowledge required of the reader to understand the text, the reader's facility with word solving, the number of complex sentences embedded in the text, and so on. The specialized process of determining text difficulty is a challenge worthy of our time because the more we learn about texts, the better we understand their demands on the individual readers we teach—the first step in matching books to readers.

The most current book list can be found at *www.fountasandpinnellleveledbooks.com*. This online version of the book list is updated monthly with new titles as well as corrections and revisions to existing titles as they are needed. The web site also includes a wide variety of other resources to support your work in the classroom, including video clips of teaching in guided reading.

Book collections continually evolve. You build your collection slowly over time as you test books with students. We hope our gradient and book list will help you select texts that are "just right" for your readers.

How to Use the Book List

The list is sorted two ways: by book title and by book level. Both listings are alphabetical and the tabs along the page edge make it possible to quickly turn to the listing you want to use.

As you will see, there are six columns on each page. The contents of each column are described below.

❑ **Title:** The first column indicates the title of the book. Books are placed alphabetically by the first word of the title—unless it is *a, an,* or *the*, in which case the article follows the title. Titles beginning with a numeral are placed at the beginning of the list.

❏ **Level:** The second column indicates the level assigned to the book, from A to Z. We use the letter A to indicate the easiest books to read and the letter Z to identify the most challenging books. More detailed descriptions of the text features of each level can be found in *Leveled Books K–8.* Two other abbreviations are used in this column:

- *WB - Wordless Books:* Books without any words in them at all (books that tell a story only in pictures) are excellent for the development of oral language and so are included in our list. However, they are not "leveled" in the same sense that the other books in the list are leveled.

- *LB - Label Books:* These are books with only one word or a very short phrase on every page. As with Wordless Books, we find leveling these books inappropriate. We do not recommend label books for use in guided reading.

❏ **Genre:** The third column indicates the type of book, or genre. Genre is a term that means type of text. We have classified each book as one genre though you will find there are some books that have elements of more than one. With the wealth and variety of children's books available today, it is sometimes difficult to make a designation of genre for a particular text. A text may have some features of an informational text, such as describing a series of actions; but the characters in the illustrations may be animals talking or getting dressed like people. In this case, the text would be fantasy. In this list, if material in the text or illustrations has elements of fantasy, the book is classified as fantasy. In addition, there are many "hybrid texts" that combine elements of fiction and nonfiction; for example, a group of fictional children might visit a museum and learn a great deal about fossils. The text would be realistic fiction but would provide authentic information to the reader. Where any part of the text is fiction, we have designated it as fiction. You will want to analyze texts carefully, however, to take advantage of all the text characteristics and learning opportunities.

The following codes are used to indicate genre:

- *TL - Traditional Literature*
- *RF - Realistic Fiction*
- *HF - Historical Fiction*
- *SF - Science Fiction*
- *F - Fantasy*
- *B - Biography (includes autobiography and memoir)*
- *I - Information Book*

❏ **Words:** The fourth column provides the number of words appearing in the book. Note: "250+" indicates the book contains more than 250 words.

❏ **Author/Series:** The fifth column provides the name of the author or specific reading series.

❏ **Publisher/Distributor:** The sixth column indicates the publisher's or distributor's name. A list of addresses and phone numbers for each publisher or distributor of reading series and collections can be found in Appendix A. Trade books listed with the author's name are available from a variety of distributors.

❏ Finally, you'll notice that some books are marked with an ✱ (asterisk). This indicates that the book is a collection of short stories. Some collections are ones where each story in the book is completely independent of the others. In other collections, the stories are interrelated in some way.

The true test of any leveling system, of course, is using the texts with students over time. We have included a form on the following page, **Evaluation Response for Text Gradient,** to gather more information about the books on our list and to provide you the opportunity to suggest new books for leveling. We want teachers in many different geographic areas to test the books and provide feedback based on their use with students in guided reading. We invite you to send feedback to us at any time. As the online database and this book are revised, we will take your comments and suggestions into consideration.

Evaluation Response for Text Gradient

Directions: Since any text gradient is always in the process of construction as it is used with varying groups of children, we expect our list to change every year. We encourage you to try the levels with your students and to provide feedback based on your own experiences. Please suggest changes to existing book levels and suggest new books for the list. Please provide the information requested below.

Name: _____ Grade Level You Teach: _____

Telephone: (   ) _____ E-mail address: _____

Address (street, city, state): _____

Book Evaluated:

Book Title: _____

Level: A B C D E F G H I J K L M N O P Q R S T U V W X Y Z

Author: _____

Publisher: _____

This book is:

_____ A book listed on the gradient that I have evaluated with my class.
(Complete SECTION A and make comments in SECTION C.)

_____ A book listed on the gradient that I am recommending as a benchmark for a level.
(Complete SECTION A and make comments in SECTION C.)

_____ A new book that I suggest adding to the collection.
(Complete SECTION B and make comments in SECTION C.)

SECTION A: (for an evaluation of a book currently included in the list)

Is it appropriately placed on the level (explain)? _____
To what level should the book be moved?
A B C D E F G H I J K L M N O P Q R S T U V W X Y Z

Are there points of difficulty that make it harder than it seems? _____

_____

Is the text supportive in ways that might not be noticeable when examining the superficial characteristics?

_____

SECTION B: (for the recommendation of a new book) Indicate recommended level:

How does this book support readers at this level? _____

_____

What challenges does it offer? _____

_____

SECTION C: Please place additional comments on the back or on another sheet.

Mail or fax (603-431-7840) this form to:
Leveled Book List Suggestions
c/o Heinemann
361 Hanover Street
Portsmouth, NH 03801-3912

Book List

(ORGANIZED BY TITLE)

TITLE	LEVEL	GENRE	WORD COUNT	AUTHOR / SERIES	PUBLISHER / DISTRIBUTOR
1 Is for One	E	F	82	Bookshop	Mondo
1 Potato 2 Potato	N	I	250+	Literacy 2000	Rigby
1, 2, 3 in the Box	B	RF	23	Tarlow, Ellen	Scholastic
1, 2, Kangaroo	LB	F	54	Reading Corners	Pearson Learning Group
10 Cats	LB	RF	13	Leveled Readers Language Support	Houghton Mifflin
100 Days	B	RF	16	Bebop Books	Lee & Low Books Inc.
100 Years Ago	E	I	119	Learn to Read	Creative Teaching Press
100 Years Ago	H	I	135	Twig	Wright Group/McGraw Hill
1000 Facts about Space	X	I	250+	Beasant, Pam	Scholastic
12 Again	V	F	250+	Corbett, Sue	Penguin Group
13 Ghosts: Strange But True Stories	X	F	250+	Osborne, Will	Scholastic
13th Floor, The: A Ghost Story	U	F	250+	Fleischman, Sid	Bantam
15 Facts about Atoms	S	I	654	Independent Readers Science	Houghton Mifflin
15 Facts about Snakes	K	I	347	Rigby Focus	Rigby
15 Facts about Stars	W	I	1652	Independent Readers Science	Houghton Mifflin
15 Facts about the Solar System	P	I	474	Independent Readers Science	Houghton Mifflin
18th Emergency, The	R	RF	250+	Byars, Betsy	Bantam
1980s, The	R	I	1144	Leveled Readers Social Studies	Houghton Mifflin
2 of Everything	I	RF	217	Talking Point Series	Pearson Learning Group
20 Pennies	E	RF	212	Teacher's Choice Series	Pearson Learning Group
26 Fairmount Avenue	N	B	250+	DePaola, Tomie	Putnam
3-2-1 Blast-Off	I	RF	291	Talking Point Series	Pearson Learning Group
40 Nights to Knowing the Sky	Z	I	250+	Schaaf, Fred	Henry Holt & Co.
5 Novels	V	F	250+	Pinkwater, Daniel	Farrar, Straus and Giroux
52 Days by Camel: My Sahara Adventure	T	I	250+	Raskin, Lawrie	Annick Press
7 Facts About the Weather	I	I	231	Leveled Readers Science	Houghton Mifflin
7 Uses for Air	B	I	46	Independent Readers Science	Houghton Mifflin
7 Ways to Get Energy	J	I	193	Independent Readers Science	Houghton Mifflin
89th Kitten, The	O	RF	250+	Nilsson, Eleanor	Scholastic
Abarat	Z	F	250+	Barker, Clive	HarperCollins
Abby	M	RF	250+	Hanel, Wolfram	North-South Books
ABC I Like Me!	H	F	136	Carlson, Nancy	Puffin Books
ABC Who's Got Me?	E	F	40	Instant Readers	Harcourt School Publishers
Abe Lincoln: Log Cabin To White House	Z	B	250+	North, Sterling	Random House
Abe Lincoln's Hat	M	B	250+	Brenner, Martha	Random House
Abel's Island	T	F	250+	Steig, William	Farrar, Straus and Giroux
Abigail Adams, Patriot	U	B	2288	Leveled Readers Social Studies	Houghton Mifflin
Abigail Adams: Girl of Colonial Days	R	B	250+	Wagoner, Jean Brown	Aladdin
About 100 Years Ago	I	I	250+	Yellow Umbrella Books	Red Brick Learning
About How Many?	M	I	250+	Early Connections	Benchmark Education
About The B'nai Bagels	T	RF	250+	Konigsburg, E. L.	Dell
Above and Below	F	I	128	Sunshine	Wright Group/McGraw Hill
Abracadabra	L	RF	372	Reading Unlimited	Pearson Learning Group
Abracadabra Kid, The	X	B	250+	Fleischman, Sid	Beech Tree Books
Abraham Lincoln	L	B	235	Famous Americans	Capstone Press
Abraham Lincoln	N	B	235	First Biographies	Capstone Press
Abraham Lincoln	U	B	250+	Profiles of the Presidents	Compass Point Books
Abraham Lincoln	U	B	250+	Let Freedom Ring	Red Brick Learning
Abraham Lincoln	Q	B	250+	Gross, Ruth Belov	Scholastic

* Collection of short stories

TITLE	LEVEL	GENRE	WORD COUNT	AUTHOR / SERIES	PUBLISHER / DISTRIBUTOR
Abraham Lincoln	O	B	250+	Early Biographies	Compass Point Books
Abraham Lincoln	S	B	250+	Parin d'Aulaire, Ingri & Edgar	Bantam
Abraham Lincoln: Lawyer, President, Emancipator	M	B	250+	Biographies	Picture Window Books
Abraham Lincoln: President of a Divided Country	O	B	250+	Greene, Carol	Children's Press
Abraham Lincoln: The Great Emancipator	R	B	250+	Stevenson, Augusta	Aladdin
Abraham's Battle: A Novel of Gettysburg	T	HF	250+	Banks, Sara Harrell	Atheneum
Absent Author, The	N	RF	250+	Roy, Ron	Random House
Absolutely Normal Chaos	V	RF	250+	Creech, Sharon	HarperTrophy
Absolutely Not!	E	F	199	Story Steps	Rigby
Absolutely True Story, The: How I Visited Yellowstone Park With the Terrible Rupes	R	RF	250+	Roberts, Willo Davis	Aladdin
Acceptable Time, An	X	F	250+	L'Engle, Madeleine	Laurel-Leaf Books
Accident Prone	P	RF	250+	Bookweb	Rigby
Accident, The	H	RF	313	Foundations	Wright Group/McGraw Hill
Accidental Angel (Secret Sisters)	P	RF	250+	Byrd, Sandra	WaterBrook Press
Accidents	D	RF	35	Visions	Wright Group/McGraw Hill
Ace: The Very Important Pig	R	F	250+	King-Smith, Dick	Alfred A. Knopf
Achilles	W	I	250+	World Mythology	Capstone Press
Acid Rain	Y	I	1702	Independent Readers Science	Houghton Mifflin
Acid Rain	L	I	368	Wonder World	Wright Group/McGraw Hill
A-Counting We Will Go	E	RF	191	Learn to Read	Creative Teaching Press
Across Five Aprils	Z	HF	250+	Hunt, Irene	Follett
Across the Lines	W	HF	250+	Reeder, Carolyn	Avon Camelot
Across the Seasons	C	I	75	Early Connections	Benchmark Education
Across the Stream	F	F	94	Ginsburg, Mirra	Morrow
Ad Break	P	RF	250+	Bookweb	Rigby
Adam Canfield of the Slash	U	RF	250+	Winerip, Michael	Candlewick Press
Adam Joshua Capers: Halloween Monster	N	RF	250+	Smith, Janice Lee	HarperTrophy
*Adam Joshua Capers: Kid Next Door, The	N	RF	250+	Smith, Janice Lee	HarperTrophy
*Adam Joshua Capers: Monster in the Third	N	RF	250+	Smith, Janice Lee	HarperTrophy
Adam Joshua Capers: Nelson in Love	N	RF	250+	Smith, Janice Lee	HarperTrophy
Adam Joshua Capers: Show-and-Tell War, The	N	RF	250+	Smith, Janice Lee	HarperTrophy
Adam Joshua Capers: Superkid!	N	RF	250+	Smith, Janice Lee	HarperTrophy
Adam Joshua Capers: Turkey Trouble	N	RF	250+	Smith, Janice Lee	HarperTrophy
Adam of the Road	W	HF	250+	Gray, Elizabeth Janet	Scholastic
Add It Up	J	RF	311	Story Box	Wright Group/McGraw Hill
Add the Animals	D	I	74	Early Connections	Benchmark Education
Addie Meets Max	J	RF	250+	Robins, Joan	Harper & Row
Addie's Bad Day	J	RF	566	Robins, Joan	HarperTrophy
Addie's Dakota Winter	T	RF	250+	Lawlor, Laurie	Pocket Books
Adding Arctic Animals	I	I	120	Yellow Umbrella Books	Red Brick Learning
Adding It Up at the Zoo	G	I	250+	Yellow Umbrella Books	Red Brick Learning
Addition Annie	G	RF	30	Rookie Readers	Children's Press
Addy Learns a Lesson: A School Story	Q	HF	250+	The American Girls Collection	Pleasant Company
Addy Saves the Day: A Summer Story	Q	HF	250+	The American Girls Collection	Pleasant Company
Addy's Surprise: A Christmas Story	Q	HF	250+	The American Girls Collection	Pleasant Company
Adios, Anna	N	RF	250+	Giff, Patricia Reilly	Bantam
Adios, Coyote	K	F	250+	Rigby Literacy	Rigby
Admiral Perry	T	B	2451	Independent Readers Social Studies	Houghton Mifflin
Adventure In Alaska	O	I	250+	Kramer, S. A.	Random House
Adventure Vacations	M	I	250+	Rigby Literacy	Rigby

* Collection of short stories

TITLE	LEVEL	GENRE	WORD COUNT	AUTHOR / SERIES	PUBLISHER / DISTRIBUTOR
Adventures of a Kite	L	F	33	Jellybeans	Rigby
*Adventures of Ali Baba Bernstein, The	O	RF	250+	Hurwitz, Johanna	Scholastic
Adventures of George Washington, The	N	B	250+	Davidson, Margaret	Scholastic
Adventures of Granny Gatman, The	L	RF	250+	Meadows, Graham	Pearson Learning Group
Adventures of Huckleberry Finn, The	Z	HF	250+	Twain, Mark	Scholastic
Adventures of Max and Ned, The	N	F	250+	Little Celebrations	Pearson Learning Group
Adventures of Ratman	M	F	250+	Weiss, Ellen; Freidman, Mel	Random House
Adventures of Snail at School	J	F	250+	Stadler, John	HarperTrophy
Adventures of Spider, The	R	TL	250+	Arkhurst, Joyce C.	Scholastic
Adventures of the Buried Treasure, The	L	F	250+	McArthur, Nancy	Scholastic
Adventures of the Shark Lady	Q	I	250+	McGovern, Ann	Scholastic
Adventures of Tom Sawyer, The	Z	HF	250+	Twain, Mark	Scholastic
*Aesop & Company: With Scenes from His Legendary Life	O	TL	250+	Bader, Barbara	Houghton Mifflin
Afghanistan	P	I	250+	Fact Finders	Capstone Press
Africa	N	I	250+	Continents	Capstone Press
African Giants	M	I	250+	World Quest Adventures	World Quest Learning
African Hunting Dog, The	M	I	250+	Sunshine	Wright Group/McGraw Hill
*African-American Scientists	O	B	250+	St. John, Jetty	Red Brick Learning
African-Americans in the Colonies	U	I	250+	We The People	Compass Point Books
African-Americans in the Old West	V	I	250+	Cornerstones of Freedom	Children's Press
African-Americans in the Thirteen Colonies	V	I	250+	Cornerstones of Freedom	Children's Press
After Goldilocks	E	F	44	Instant Readers	Harcourt School Publishers
After School	H	RF	199	Foundations	Wright Group/McGraw Hill
After School	D	I	58	Sunshine	Wright Group/McGraw Hill
After the Dancing Days	W	HF	250+	Rostkowski, Margaret I.	HarperTrophy
After the Flood	G	RF	210	PM Extensions-Green	Rigby
After the Goat Man	R	RF	250+	Byars, Betsy	Puffin Books
After the Rain	Z	RF	250+	Mazer, Norma Fox	Avon
After the War	W	HF	250+	Matas, Carol	Aladdin
Afternoon of the Elves	S	F	250+	Lisle, Janet Taylor	Scholastic
Afternoon on the Amazon	M	F	250+	Osborne, Mary Pope	Random House
Against the Odds	P	I	250+	Layden, Joe	Scholastic
Against the Odds	R	I	250+	Wildcats	Wright Group/McGraw Hill
Against the Rules	R	RF	250+	Costello, Emily	Dell
Aggressive In-Line Skating	R	I	250+	X-Sports	Capstone Press
Agnes Macphail: Canada's Champion of the Poor	U	B	2412	Independent Readers Social Studies	Houghton Mifflin
Agnes the Sheep	R	F	250+	Taylor, William	Bantam
Agua, Agua, Agua	H	TL	94	Little Celebrations	Pearson Learning Group
Ah Liang's Gift	J	RF	352	Sunshine	Wright Group/McGraw Hill
Ah, Treasure	F	F	19	Voyages	SRA/McGraw Hill
Ah-Choo	WB	F	N/A	Mayer, Mercer	Dial Books
Ah-choo!	J	RF	291	Samuels, Aurora	Sadlier-Oxford
Ahyoka and the Talking Leaves	S	HF	250+	Roop, Peter & Connie	Beech Tree Books
Air: Outside, Inside, and All Around	M	I	250+	Amazing Science	Picture Window Books
Airborne	X	I	250+	iOpeners	Pearson Learning Group
Aircraft Carriers	T	I	250+	Land and Sea	Capstone Press
Aircraft Carriers	K	I	124	Mighty Machines	Capstone Press
Airplane, The	B	RF	21	Sunshine	Wright Group/McGraw Hill
Airplanes	F	I	60	Pebble Books	Capstone Press
Airplanes	M	I	250+	Transportation	Compass Point Books
Airport	I	I	116	Barton, Byron	HarperCollins
Ajeemah and his Son	S	HF	250+	Berry, James	HarperTrophy

TITLE	LEVEL	GENRE	WORD COUNT	AUTHOR / SERIES	PUBLISHER / DISTRIBUTOR
Aki's Special Gift	H	RF	240	Leveled Readers Language Support	Houghton Mifflin
Aksum: Heart of Ancient Ethiopia	X	I	2568	Independent Readers Social Studies	Houghton Mifflin
Alabama	R	I	250+	This Land Is Your Land	Compass Point Books
Alabama	S	I	250+	Land of Liberty	Red Brick Learning
Aladdin & the Magic Lamp	J	TL	851	Traditional Tales	Pearson Learning Group
Alas My Albatross is Molting	T	I	250+	Literacy 2000	Rigby
Alaska	R	I	250+	This Land Is Your Land	Compass Point Books
Alaska	S	I	250+	Land of Liberty	Red Brick Learning
Albert Einstein	P	B	250+	Early Biographies	Compass Point Books
Albert the Albatross	I	F	191	Hoff, Syd	HarperCollins
Alcatraz	V	I	250+	Cornerstones of Freedom	Bantam
Aldo Ice Cream	O	RF	250+	Hurwitz, Johanna	Penguin Group
Aldo Peanut Butter	O	RF	250+	Hurwitz, Johanna	Penguin Group
Alex Rodriguez	T	B	250+	Sports Heroes	Red Brick Learning
Alexander and the Stallion	M	HF	434	Books for Young Learners	Richard C. Owen
Alexander and the Wind-Up Mouse	L	F	250+	Lionni, Leo	Scholastic
Alexander Ant Cools Off	F	F	76	Little Books	Sadlier-Oxford
Alexander Graham Bell	P	B	250+	Bridgestone Books	Red Brick Learning
Alexander Graham Bell	M	B	250+	Rosen Real Readers	Rosen Publishing Group
Alexander Graham Bell	X	B	250+	The Canadians	Fitzhenry & Whiteside
Alexander Graham Bell	N	B	250+	First Biographies	Red Brick Learning
Alexander Graham Bell and the Telephone	P	B	250+	Windows on Literacy	National Geographic
Alexander Graham Bell: An Inventive Life	U	B	250+	MacLeod, Elizabeth	Kids Can Press Ltd.
Alfie's Gift	L	F	250+	Literacy 2000	Rigby
Alfred	F	RF	54	Voyages	SRA/McGraw Hill
Alfred the Curious	O	RF	250+	PM Emerald	Rigby
Algonquin, The	V	I	3436	Leveled Readers Social Studies	Houghton Mifflin
*Ali Baba Bernstein, Lost and Found	O	RF	250+	Hurwitz, Johanna	Avon
Alice in Rapture: Sort of	U	RF	250+	Naylor, Phyllis Reynolds	Aladdin
Alice in Wonderland	V	F	250+	Carroll, Lewis	Scholastic
Alice the Brave	U	RF	250+	Naylor, Phyllis Reynolds	Aladdin
Alice: Alice Alone	U	RF	250+	Naylor, Phyllis Reynolds	Simon & Schuster
Alice's Diary, Living With Diabetes	S	I	250+	Gibson, Marie	Pacific Learning
Alida's Song	Y	RF	250+	Paulsen, Gary	Random House
Alien at the Zoo	E	F	85	Sunshine	Wright Group/McGraw Hill
Alien in the Classroom	N	F	250+	Keene, Carolyn	Pocket Books
Alien Plant and Animal Invaders	V	I	3318	Leveled Readers Science	Houghton Mifflin
Alien Vacation	F	F	105	Instant Readers	Harcourt School Publishers
Alien Visitors and Abductions	Z	I	250+	Innes, Brian	Steck-Vaughn
Alien, The	H	F	177	Windmill Books	Rigby
Aliens Ate My Homework	Q	F	250+	Coville, Bruce	Pocket Books
Aliens Don't Wear Braces	M	F	250+	Dadey, Debbie; Jones, Marcia Thornton	Scholastic
Aliens for Breakfast	M	F	250+	Etra, Jonathan; Spinner, Stephanie	Random House
Aliens for Dinner	M	F	250+	Spinner, Stephanie	Random House
Aliens for Lunch	M	F	250+	Spinner, Stephanie; Etra, Jonathan	Random House
Aliens on the Lawn	H	F	175	Windmill Books	Rigby
Ali's Story	H	RF	236	Sunshine	Wright Group/McGraw Hill
Alison Wendlebury	J	RF	250+	Literacy 2000	Rigby
Alison's Puppy	K	RF	250+	Bauer, Marion Dane	Hyperion

* Collection of short stories

TITLE	LEVEL	GENRE	WORD COUNT	AUTHOR / SERIES	PUBLISHER / DISTRIBUTOR
Alison's Wings	K	RF	250+	Bauer, Marion Dane	Hyperion
All About Ants	H	I	214	Rosen Real Readers	Rosen Publishing Group
All About Apples	E	I	35	Rosen Real Readers	Rosen Publishing Group
All About Bats	J	I	250+	Ready Readers	Modern Curriculum
All About Bears	N	I	250+	Voyages	SRA/McGraw Hill
All About Bicycles	L	I	250+	Sunshine	Wright Group/McGraw Hill
All About Bikes	O	I	250+	iOpeners	Pearson Learning Group
All About Cats and Kittens	N	I	250+	Neye, Emily	Grosset & Dunlap
All About Codes	Q	I	250+	Riley, Gail Blasser	Steck-Vaughn
All About Deer	Q	I	250+	Arnosky, Jim	Scholastic
All About Dinosaurs	C	I	34	Teacher's Choice Series	Pearson Learning Group
All About Drums	M	I	250+	Rosen Real Readers	Rosen Publishing Group
All About Eggs	P	I	250+	Sunshine	Wright Group/McGraw Hill
All About Frogs	Q	I	250+	Arnosky, Jim	Scholastic
All About Me	L	I	250+	iOpeners	Pearson Learning Group
All About Me!	J	RF	250+	Pacific Literacy	Pacific Learning
All About Money	O	I	250+	Let's See	Compass Point Books
All About Owls	Q	I	250+	Arnosky, Jim	Scholastic
All About Plants	L	I	250+	Home Connection Collection	Rigby
All About Potbellied Pigs	M	I	250+	Rigby Literacy	Rigby
All About Rattlesnakes	Q	I	250+	Aronsky, Jim	Scholastic
All About Sam	Q	RF	250+	Lowry, Lois	Bantam
All About Seeds	Q	I	250+	Berger, Melvin	Scholastic
All About Stacy	L	RF	250+	Giff, Patricia Reilly	Bantam
All About Things People Do	K	I	250+	Rice, Melanie & Chris	Scholastic
All About You	G	I	250+	Anholt, Catherine & Laurence	Scholastic
All Alone in the Universe	S	RF	250+	Perkins, Lynne Rae	Greenwillow
All American Girl	Y	RF	250+	Cabot, Meg	HarperCollins
All Around Our Country	E	I	112	Hutchins, Jeannie	Scholastic
All But Alice	U	RF	250+	Naylor, Phyllis Reynolds	Dell
All by Myself	H	RF	215	Cambridge Reading	Pearson Learning Group
All By Myself	E	RF	105	Foundations	Wright Group/McGraw Hill
All By Myself	E	F	157	Mayer, Mercer	Golden
All Dressed Up	H	RF	137	Voyages	SRA/McGraw Hill
All Dressed Up	B	RF	38	Visions	Wright Group/McGraw Hill
All Fall Down	L	I	206	Spyglass Books	Compass Point Books
All Fall Down	B	F	23	Instant Readers	Harcourt School Publishers
All Fall Down	C	F	72	Wildsmith, Brian	Oxford University Press
All for the Better: A Story of El Barrio	R	RF	250+	Mohr, Nicholasa	Steck-Vaughn
All From a Bottle	N	F	250+	Phonics and Friends	Hampton-Brown
All I Did	E	RF	83	Instant Readers	Harcourt School Publishers
All Is Well	R	HF	250+	Litchman, Kristin Embry	Bantam
All Join In	D	F	38	Literacy 2000	Rigby
All Kinds of Animals	O	I	250+	It's Science	Children's Press
All Kinds of Books	E	I	77	Canizares, Susan; Chessen, Betsey	Scholastic
All Kinds of Eyes	I	I	128	Pacific Literacy	Pacific Learning
All Kinds of Eyes	L	I	250+	Discovery World	Rigby
All Kinds of Farms	G	I	146	Yellow Umbrella Books	Red Brick Learning
All Kinds of Fish	D	F	37	Instant Readers	Harcourt School Publishers
All Kinds of Flowers	L	I	250+	Turner, Teresa	Steck-Vaughn
All Kinds of Food	D	I	72	Learn to Read	Creative Teaching Press
All Kinds of Food	D	RF	72	Carousel Readers	Pearson Learning Group
All Kinds of Maps	N	I	163	Windows on Literacy	National Geographic
All Kinds of Museums	N	I	250+	Ramsey, Joe	Wright Group/McGraw Hill

* Collection of short stories

TITLE	LEVEL	GENRE	WORD COUNT	AUTHOR / SERIES	PUBLISHER / DISTRIBUTOR
All Kinds of People: What Makes Us Different	J	I	250+	Spyglass Books	Compass Point Books
All Kinds of Rocks	G	RF	136	Instant Readers	Harcourt School Publishers
All Kinds of Things	B	I	24	Pacific Literacy	Pacific Learning
All Kinds of Wheels	E	I	76	Pair-It Books	Steck-Vaughn
All Mixed Up	G	F	105	Little Books	Sadlier-Oxford
All Night Long	E	RF	65	Visions	Wright Group/McGraw Hill
All of Me	B	RF	25	Literacy 2000	Rigby
All Over Me!	LB	RF	24	Pair-It Books	Steck-Vaughn
All Over the World	E	RF	82	Jones, D.	Continental Press
All Pigs Are Beautiful	N	I	250+	King-Smith, Dick	Candlewick Press
All Pull Together	D	F	69	Home Connection Collection	Rigby
All the World's a Stage	O	I	250+	Literacy Tree	Rigby
All Through the Week with Cat and Dog	C	F	91	Learn to Read	Creative Teaching Press
All Through the Year	F	I	261	Visions	Wright Group/McGraw Hill
All Tutus Should Be Pink	I	RF	243	Brownrigg, Sheri	Scholastic
All Wet!	B	I	28	Ready Readers	Pearson Learning Group
Allen Jay and the Underground Railroad	O	HF	250+	Brill, Marlene Targ	Carolrhoda Books
Allen Say, Writer and Artist	K	B	219	Leveled Readers Social Studies	Houghton Mifflin
Alley Cat	C	RF	30	Books for Young Learners	Richard C. Owen
Allie's Basketball Dream	K	RF	250+	Barber, Barbara E.; Ligasan, Darryl	Scholastic
Allie's Basketball Dream	K	RF	250+	Soar To Success	Houghton Mifflin
Alligator Alley	M	RF	250+	Schultz, Irene	Wright Group/McGraw Hill
Alligator in the Bathtub	N	F	628	Leveled Readers	Houghton Mifflin
Alligator Mouse and Other Disasters	K	F	250+	Voyages	SRA/McGraw Hill
Alligator Shoes	G	F	122	Dorros, Arthur	Dutton
*Alligator Tails and Crocodile Cakes	K	F	250+	Moon, Nicola	Wright Group/McGraw Hill
Alligator, The	M	I	250+	Crewe, Sabrina	Steck-Vaughn
Alligators & Crocodiles	U	I	250+	The Untamed World	Steck-Vaughn
Alligators All Around	LB	F	59	Sendak, Maurice	HarperCollins
All-of-a-Kind Family	Q	RF	250+	Taylor, Sydney	Bantam
Allosaurus	M	I	250+	Discovering Dinosaurs	Capstone Press
All-Pro Biographies: Dan Marino	P	B	250+	Stewart, Mark	Children's Press
All-Pro Biographies: Gwen Torrence	P	B	250+	Stewart, Mark	Children's Press
All-Star Fever	M	RF	250+	Christopher, Matt	Little, Brown & Co.
Alma Flor Ada, Storyteller	F	B	75	Leveled Readers Language Support	Houghton Mifflin
Alma Flor Ada: From a Family of Storytellers	G	B	75	Leveled Readers	Houghton Mifflin
Almost Home	T	RF	250+	Baskin, Nora Raleigh	Little, Brown & Co.
Almost Starring Skinnybones	O	RF	250+	Park, Barbara	Random House
Alone and Together	H	RF	292	Early Connections	Benchmark Education
Alone in the Storm	R	RF	250+	Leveled Readers Language Support	Houghton Mifflin
Along Came Greedy Cat	G	F	166	Pacific Literacy	Pacific Learning
Along Comes Jake	C	RF	86	Sunshine	Wright Group/McGraw Hill
Alphabet Game, The	H	F	272	Story Basket	Wright Group/McGraw Hill
Alphabet Race, The	C	F	7	Visions	Wright Group/McGraw Hill
Alphabet, The	R	I	250+	Literacy 2000	Rigby
Alroy's Very Nearly Clean Bedroom	O	RF	250+	SupaDoopers	Sundance
*Altogether, One at a Time	S	RF	250+	Konigsburg, E. L.	Simon & Schuster
Alvin Ailey	P	B	250+	Pinkney, Andrea Davis	Hyperion
Alvin Ailey, an American Dancer	N	B	326	Vocabulary Readers	Houghton Mifflin
Always Elephant: A Traditional Tale	M	TL	250+	Rigby Literacy	Rigby
Always My Dad	N	RF	250+	Wyeth, Sharon Dennis	Alfred A. Knopf

* Collection of short stories

TITLE	LEVEL	GENRE	WORD COUNT	AUTHOR / SERIES	PUBLISHER / DISTRIBUTOR
Am I Ready Now?	C	RF	41	Visions	Wright Group/McGraw Hill
Amalia and the Grasshopper	K	RF	392	Tello, Jerry; Krupinski, Loretta	Scholastic
Amanda Joins the Circus	R	F	250+	Avi	Bantam
Amanda Miranda	Y	HF	250+	Peck, Richard	Penguin Group
*Amanda Pig and Her Big Brother Oliver	L	F	250+	Van Leeuwen, Jean	Puffin Books
Amanda's Bear	G	F	154	Reading Corners	Pearson Learning Group
Amaze Us!	T	I	250+	Wildcats	Wright Group/McGraw Hill
Amazing Adaptations	O	I	453	Independent Readers Science	Houghton Mifflin
Amazing Amoeba, The	X	I	1290	Independent Readers Science	Houghton Mifflin
Amazing Animal Rescue Team, The	Q	I	250+	Blankenhorn, Rebecca	Steck-Vaughn
Amazing Ant, The	M	I	250+	Story Box	Wright Group/McGraw Hill
Amazing Birds of the Rain Forest	M	I	250+	Daniel, Claire	Steck-Vaughn
*Amazing But True Sports Stories	Q	I	250+	Hollander, Phyllis & Zander	Scholastic
Amazing Earthworm, The	I	I	169	Leveled Readers Language Support	Houghton Mifflin
Amazing Egg, The	J	I	220	Spyglass Books	Compass Point Books
Amazing Eggs	J	I	250+	Discovery World	Rigby
Amazing Fish, The	G	TL	167	Pair-It Books	Steck-Vaughn
Amazing Hands	K	I	250+	Rigby Literacy	Rigby
Amazing Impossible Erie Canal, The	S	I	250+	Harness, Cheryl	Simon & Schuster
Amazing Journeys	P	I	250+	Literacy 2000	Rigby
Amazing Magnets	C	I	53	Twig	Wright Group/McGraw Hill
Amazing Maze, The	J	RF	334	Foundations	Wright Group/McGraw Hill
Amazing Mr. Mulch, The	L	F	250+	Cambridge Reading	Pearson Learning Group
Amazing Popple Seed, The	G	F	113	Read Alongs	Rigby
Amazing Race, The	A	RF	28	Smart Starts	Rigby
Amazing Rocks	T	I	1894	Leveled Readers Science	Houghton Mifflin
Amazing Silkworm, The	M	I	250+	Windows on Literacy	National Geographic
Amazing Skyscrapers	S	I	2047	Independent Readers Social Studies	Houghton Mifflin
Amazing Spiders	Q	I	250+	Eyewitness Juniors	Alfred A. Knopf
Amazing Trains	L	I	482	Pair-It Books	Steck-Vaughn
Amazon, The	N	I	250+	Early Connections	Benchmark Education
Amber Brown Goes Fourth	N	RF	250+	Danziger, Paula	Scholastic
Amber Brown is Feeling Blue	N	RF	250+	Danziger, Paula	Scholastic
Amber Brown is Green with Envy	N	RF	250+	Danziger, Paula	Scholastic
Amber Brown is Not a Crayon	N	RF	250+	Danziger, Paula	Scholastic
Amber Brown Sees Red	N	RF	250+	Danziger, Paula	Scholastic
Amber Brown Wants Extra Credit	N	RF	250+	Danziger, Paula	Scholastic
Amber Cat, The	P	RF	250+	McKay, Hilary	Simon & Schuster
Amber Spyglass, The	Z	F	250+	Pullman, Phillip	Alfred A. Knopf
Ambulance	I	I	116	Pebble Books	Capstone Press
Ambulances	J	I	119	Mighty Machines	Capstone Press
Amelia Bedelia	L	F	250+	Parish, Peggy	HarperTrophy
Amelia Bedelia and the Baby	L	F	250+	Parish, Peggy	Harper & Row
Amelia Bedelia and the Surprise Shower	L	F	250+	Parish, Peggy	Harper & Row
Amelia Bedelia Goes Camping	L	F	250+	Parish, Peggy	Avon Camelot
Amelia Bedelia Helps Out	L	F	250+	Parish, Peggy	Avon Camelot
Amelia Bedelia's Family Album	L	F	250+	Parish, Peggy	Avon
Amelia Earhart	Q	B	250+	Literacy Tree	Rigby
Amelia Earhart	P	B	250+	Parlin, John	Bantam
Amelia Earhart	P	B	250+	Rosenthal, Marilyn; Freeman, Daniel	Red Brick Learning
Amelia Earhart: Challenging the Skies	S	B	250+	Sloate, Susan	Fawcett Columbine

* Collection of short stories

TITLE	LEVEL	GENRE	WORD COUNT	AUTHOR / SERIES	PUBLISHER / DISTRIBUTOR
Amelia Earhart: Courage in the Sky	S	B	250+	Kerby, Mona	Puffin Books
Amelia Earhart: Flying for Adventure	S	B	250+	Wade, Mary Dodson	The Millbrook Press
Amelia Earhart: Young Aviator	R	B	250+	Gormley, Beatrice	Aladdin
Amelia's Road	O	RF	250+	Soar To Success	Houghton Mifflin
*America Street: A Multicultural Anthology of Stories	R	RF	250+	Mazer, Anne	Persea Books
America: A Dream	R	HF	1620	Leveled Readers	Houghton Mifflin
American Alligator, The	R	I	250+	Potts, Steve	Red Brick Learning
American Beginnings: You're Right There!	P	HF	250+	Navigators Drama Series	Benchmark Education
American Bison, The	R	I	250+	Potts, Steve	Red Brick Learning
*American Dragons: Twenty-Five Asian American Voices	Z	RF	250+	Yep, Laurence	HarperTrophy
American Dream, An	Q	HF	250+	Leveled Readers Language Support	Houghton Mifflin
*American Eyes: New Asian-American Short Stories for Young Adults	Z	RF	250+	Carlson, Lori M.	Ballantine Books
American Flag, The	Q	I	250+	Let's See	Compass Point Books
American Flag, The	N	I	250+	American Symbols	Capstone Press
American Flag, The	N	I	250+	A True Book	Children's Press
American Heroes	M	I	189	Phonics Readers	Compass Point Books
American Plague, An	Z	I	250+	Murphy, Jim	Clarion
American Revolution, The	T	I	250+	Bliven, Bruce, Jr.	Random House
American Revolution, The	V	I	250+	Carter, Alden R.	Franklin Watts
Americans of the Midwest: The Potawatomi	P	I	701	Leveled Readers Social Studies	Houghton Mifflin
America's Birthplace: Independence Hall	K	RF	249	Leveled Readers Social Studies	Houghton Mifflin
America's First City: Caral	X	I	2654	Independent Readers Social Studies	Houghton Mifflin
America's First Traitor: Benedict Arnold Betrays the Colonies	S	I	250+	Headlines from History	Rosen Publishing Group
America's Most Wanted Fifth-Graders	R	RF	250+	Lawrence, Jan; Raskin, Linda	Scholastic
Amigo	O	F	250+	Baylor, Byrd	Aladdin
Among the Betrayed	Z	SF	250+	Haddix, Margaret Peterson	Simon & Schuster
Among the Flowers	M	I	250+	Look Once Look Again	Creative Teaching Press
Among the Hidden	Z	SF	250+	Haddix, Margaret Peterson	Aladdin
Among the Volcanoes	Y	RF	250+	Castaneda, Omar S.	Bantam
Amos and the Alien	R	F	250+	Paulsen, Gary	Bantam
Amos Binder, Secret Agent	R	F	250+	Paulsen, Gary	Bantam
Amos Fortune: Free Man	V	HF	250+	Yates, Elizabeth	Puffin Books
Amos Gets Famous	R	F	250+	Paulsen, Gary	Bantam
Amos Gets Married	R	F	250+	Paulsen, Gary	Bantam
Amos Goes Bananas	R	F	250+	Paulsen, Gary	Bantam
Amos's Killer Concert Caper	R	F	250+	Paulsen, Gary	Bantam
Amphibians	M	I	250+	First Facts	Capstone Press
Amphibious Ships	T	I	250+	Land and Sea	Capstone Press
Amy Goes to School	D	RF	89	Literacy Tree	Rigby
Amy Loves the Snow	F	RF	127	Hoban, Julia	Scholastic
Amy Loves the Sun	F	RF	122	Hoban, Julia	Scholastic
Amy Loves the Wind	F	RF	116	Hoban, Julia	Scholastic
Amy's True Prize	Q	HF	250+	The Little Women Journals	Avon
Amy's Water Wings	K	F	250+	Lighthouse	Rigby
An Wang: A Mind for Computers	R	B	3495	Leveled Readers Science	Houghton Mifflin
Anak the Brave	L	F	250+	Sunshine	Wright Group/McGraw Hill
Anansi Does the Impossible	O	TL	250+	Aardema, Verna	Simon & Schuster
Anansi's Narrow Waist	I	TL	157	Little Celebrations	Pearson Learning Group

* Collection of short stories

TITLE	LEVEL	GENRE	WORD COUNT	AUTHOR / SERIES	PUBLISHER / DISTRIBUTOR
Anastasia Again!	Q	RF	250+	Lowry, Lois	Bantam
Anastasia At This Address	Q	RF	250+	Lowry, Lois	Bantam
Anastasia At Your Service	Q	RF	250+	Lowry, Lois	Bantam
Anastasia Has the Answers	Q	RF	250+	Lowry, Lois	Bantam
Anastasia Krupnik	Q	RF	250+	Lowry, Lois	Bantam
Anastasia On Her Own	Q	RF	250+	Lowry, Lois	Bantam
Anastasia, Absolutely	Q	RF	250+	Lowry, Lois	Bantam
Anastasia, Ask Your Analyst	Q	RF	250+	Lowry, Lois	Bantam
Anastasia's Chosen Career	Q	RF	250+	Lowry, Lois	Bantam
Ancient Baghdad: City at the Crossroads of Trade	W	I	1989	Leveled Readers	Houghton Mifflin
Ancient Egypt	W	I	250+	Let's See	Compass Point Books
Ancient Egypt	U	I	250+	Make It Work!	World Book
Ancient Greece	W	I	250+	Let's See	Compass Point Books
Ancient Greece	S	I	250+	Journey Into Civilization	Chelsea House
Ancient Greeks	Q	I	250+	Worldwise	Grolier Press
Ancient Heritage: The Arab-American Minority, An	Z	I	250+	Ashabranner, Brent	HarperCollins
Ancient Indochina	W	I	2456	Independent Readers Social Studies	Houghton Mifflin
Ancient Mesopotamia	W	I	250+	Let's See	Compass Point Books
Ancient Romans	Q	I	250+	Worldwise	Grolier Press
Ancient Rome	W	I	250+	Let's See	Compass Point Books
And Billy Went Out to Play	I	RF	227	Bookshop	Mondo
And Grandpa Sat on Friday	K	RF	250+	Voyages	SRA/McGraw Hill
And I Mean it Stanley	J	RF	184	Bonsall, Crosby	HarperCollins
. . . and Now Miguel	Z	RF	250+	Krumgold, Joseph	Scholastic
And One For All	V	RF	250+	Nelson, Theresa	Dell
And Still the Turtle Watched	Q	RF	250+	MacGill-Callahan, Sheila	Penguin Group
And the Teacher Got Mad	H	RF	109	City Kids	Rigby
And the Teacher Smiled	H	RF	86	City Kids	Rigby
And Then It Was Sugar	N	RF	250+	Story Vines	Wright Group/McGraw Hill
And Then There Were Birds	L	TL	156	Books for Young Learners	Richard C. Owen
And Then What Happened, Paul Revere?	R	B	250+	Fritz, Jean	Bantam
Andi's Wool	H	I	107	Books for Young Learners	Richard C. Owen
Andrew Carnegie	P	B	530	Leveled Readers Social Studies	Houghton Mifflin
Andrew Carnegie: Builder of Libraries	P	B	250+	Community Builders	Children's Press
Andrew Jackson	U	B	250+	Profiles of the Presidents	Compass Point Books
Andrew Johnson	U	B	250+	Profiles of the Presidents	Compass Point Books
Andrew's Angry Words	M	F	250+	Lachner, Dorothea	North-South Books
Androcles and the Lion	L	TL	250+	PM Tales and Plays-Silver	Rigby
Andy (That's my Name)	H	F	104	DePaola, Tomie	Aladdin
Andy and Tamika	N	RF	250+	Adler, David A.	Harcourt Trade
Angel and the Soldier Boy, The	WB	F	N/A	Collington, Peter	Alfred A. Knopf
Angel Factory, The	X	SF	250+	Blacker, Terence	Simon & Schuster
Angel for Solomon Singer, An	T	RF	250+	Rylant, Cynthia	Orchard Books
Angel Island and the Land of Promise	V	I	2595	Independent Readers Social Studies	Houghton Mifflin
Angel Park Hoopstars: Nothing But Net	O	RF	250+	Hughes, Dean	Alfred A. Knopf
Angel Park Hoopstars: Point Guard	O	RF	250+	Hughes, Dean	Alfred A. Knopf
Angel Park Soccer Stars: Backup Goalie	O	RF	250+	Hughes, Dean	Random House
Angel Park Soccer Stars: Defense!	O	RF	250+	Hughes, Dean	Alfred A. Knopf
Angel Park Soccer Stars: Psyched!	O	RF	250+	Hughes, Dean	Random House
Angel Park Soccer Stars: Total Soccer	O	RF	250+	Hughes, Dean	Alfred A. Knopf

* Collection of short stories

TITLE	LEVEL	GENRE	WORD COUNT	AUTHOR / SERIES	PUBLISHER / DISTRIBUTOR
Angel Park Soccer Stars: Victory Goal	O	RF	250+	Hughes, Dean	Alfred A. Knopf
Angelina Trueheart and the Fox	I	RF	228	Voyages	SRA/McGraw Hill
*Angels and Other Strangers	T	RF	250+	Paterson, Katherine	HarperTrophy
Angels Don't Know Karate	M	F	250+	Dadey, Debbie; Jones, Marcia Thornton	Scholastic
Angel's Mother's Boyfriend	O	RF	250+	Delton, Judy	Houghton Mifflin
Angels on the Roof	Z	RF	250+	Moore, Martha	Bantam Doubleday Dell
*Angry Bull and Other Cases, The	O	RF	250+	Simon, Seymour	Avon
Angry Old Woman, The	E	F	126	Adventures in Reading	Pearson Learning Group
Angus and the Cat	I	F	250+	Flack, Marjorie	Viking
Angus Thought He Was Big	G	F	58	Giant Step Readers	Educational Insights
Angus, Thongs and Full-Frontal Snogging: Confessions of Georgia Nicolson	Z	RF	250+	Rennison, Louise	HarperCollins
Animal Actions	I	I	190	Home Connection Collection	Rigby
Animal Adventures	M	RF	250+	Navigators Fiction Series	Benchmark Education
Animal Adventures	N	HF	250+	Little House	HarperTrophy
Animal Advertisements	N	F	250+	Sails	Rigby
Animal Armor	I	I	155	Windows on Literacy	National Geographic
Animal Babies	B	I	114	Little Red Readers	Sundance
Animal Babies	E	I	114	Rookie Readers	Children's Press
Animal Babies	R	I	250+	Kalman, Bobbie	Crabtree
Animal Babies	F	I	131	Twig	Wright Group/McGraw Hill
Animal Band, The	K	TL	250+	PM Tales and Plays-Purple	Rigby
Animal Behaviorists	P	B	250+	Navigators Biography Series	Benchmark Education
Animal Builders	I	I	148	Little Celebrations	Pearson Learning Group
Animal Champions	O	I	250+	Jones, Teri Crawford	Pearson Learning Group
Animal Communication	N	I	250+	Cambridge Reading	Pearson Learning Group
Animal Coverings	E	I	153	Early Connections	Benchmark Education
Animal Crackers	D	F	194	Bookshop	Mondo
Animal Dazzlers: The Role of Brilliant Colors in Nature	T	I	250+	Collard, Sneed B.	Franklin Watts
Animal Ears	I	I	250+	Yellow Umbrella Books	Red Brick Learning
Animal Ears	N	I	250+	Look Once Look Again	Creative Teaching Press
Animal Eyes	M	I	250+	Look Once Look Again	Creative Teaching Press
Animal Farm	Z	F	250+	Orwell, George	Harcourt Trade
Animal Farmers	N	I	250+	Literacy Tree	Rigby
Animal Fathers	N	I	250+	Literacy 2000 Satellites	Rigby
Animal Feathers and Fur	M	I	250+	Look Once Look Again	Creative Teaching Press
Animal Feet	I	I	166	Rigby Literacy	Rigby
Animal Fibers	I	I	440	Science	Wright Group/McGraw Hill
Animal Friends	N	I	250+	Literacy 2000	Rigby
Animal Groups	I	I	265	Early Connections	Benchmark Education
Animal Habitats	B	I	73	Little Celebrations	Pearson Learning Group
Animal Habitats	B	I	73	Little Red Readers	Sundance
Animal Hiding Places	O	I	250+	Windows on Literacy	National Geographic
Animal Homes	K	I	193	Pair-It Books	Steck-Vaughn
Animal Homes	B	I	48	Little Red Readers	Sundance
Animal Homes	B	I	48	Early Connections	Benchmark Education
Animal Homes	D	I	53	Instant Readers	Harcourt School Publishers
Animal Homes	G	I	193	PM Plus Nonfiction	Rigby
Animal Hospital	G	RF	193	Sunshine	Wright Group/McGraw Hill
Animal Hospital, The	B	I	24	Windows on Literacy	National Geographic
Animal Inventions	G	I	80	Sunshine	Wright Group/McGraw Hill
Animal Legs	B	I	37	Discovery World	Rigby

TITLE	LEVEL	GENRE	WORD COUNT	AUTHOR / SERIES	PUBLISHER / DISTRIBUTOR
Animal Look-Alikes	O	I	250+	iOpeners	Pearson Learning Group
Animal Messengers	I	I	116	Discovery Links	Newbridge
Animal Moms and Dads	E	I	121	Tarlow, Ellen	Scholastic
Animal Mouths	M	I	250+	Look Once Look Again	Creative Teaching Press
Animal Mummies of Ancient Egpyt	W	I	2896	Independent Readers Social Studies	Houghton Mifflin
Animal Mysteries	L	I	250+	Rigby Literacy	Rigby
Animal Neighbors	Q	I	250+	Orbit Double Takes	Pacific Learning
Animal Neighbors	I	I	250	Vocabulary Readers	Houghton Mifflin
Animal Noises	D	I	56	Little Red Readers	Sundance
Animal Noses	M	I	250+	Look Once Look Again	Creative Teaching Press
Animal Pals	E	I	111	Cherrington, Janelle	Scholastic
Animal Patterns	F	I	130	Yellow Umbrella Books	Capstone Press
Animal Pets	L	I	250+	Sunshine	Wright Group/McGraw Hill
Animal Reports	L	I	277	Little Red Readers	Sundance
Animal Sculpture	LB	I	24	Canizares, Susan; Chanko, Pamela	Scholastic
Animal Senses	J	I	224	Spyglass Books	Compass Point Books
Animal Senses	M	I	250+	Cambridge Reading	Pearson Learning Group
Animal Shapes	H	I	133	Rigby Focus	Rigby
Animal Shapes	D	I	14	Wildsmith, Brian	Oxford University Press
Animal Shelters	N	I	250+	Bookshop	Mondo
Animal Skeletons	G	I	91	Alphakids	Sundance
Animal Skin and Scales	N	I	250+	Look Once Look Again	Creative Teaching Press
Animal Sounds	C	I	21	Visions	Wright Group/McGraw Hill
*Animal Stories	Q	F	250+	King-Smith, Dick	Penguin Group
*Animal Stories by Young Writers	R	F	250+	Rubel, William; Mandel, Gerry	Tricycle Press
Animal Stretches	C	RF	35	Little Celebrations	Pearson Learning Group
Animal Tails	N	I	250+	Look Once Look Again	Creative Teaching Press
Animal Tails	L	I	250+	Lighthouse	Rigby
Animal Trackers, The	M	I	333	Independent Readers Science	Houghton Mifflin
Animal Tracks	L	I	250+	Dorros, Arthur	Scholastic
Animal Tracks	D	I	152	Wonder World	Wright Group/McGraw Hill
Animal Tricks	H	F	102	Wildsmith, Brian	Merrimak
Animal Walk, The	B	RF	39	Rigby Literacy	Rigby
Animal Worlds	E	I	94	Early Connections	Benchmark Education
Animal Wrestlers, The	J	TL	338	Cambridge Reading	Pearson Learning Group
Animal, the Vegetable, and John D. Jones, The	R	RF	250+	Byars, Betsy	Bantam
Animals	LB	I	14	Instant Readers	Harcourt School Publishers
Animals	D	I	70	Foundations	Wright Group/McGraw Hill
Animals	A	I	28	Smart Starts	Rigby
Animals and Air	M	I	250+	Sunshine	Wright Group/McGraw Hill
Animals and Their Babies	E	I	166	Early Connections	Benchmark Education
Animals and Their Teeth	K	I	510	Sunshine	Wright Group/McGraw Hill
Animals and Their Young	N	I	484	Kratky, Lada Josefa	Hampton-Brown
Animals at Night	C	I	35	Windows on Literacy	National Geographic
Animals at Night	L	I	520	Leveled Readers	Houghton Mifflin
Animals at Night	I	I	215	First Start	Troll Associates
Animals at School	I	I	250+	Early Transitional, Set 1	Pioneer Valley
Animals at the Mall	D	F	39	Teacher's Choice Series	Pearson Learning Group
Animals at the Zoo	F	I	158	First Start	Troll Associates
Animals at Work	M	I	250+	Home Connection Collection	Rigby
Animals Build	H	I	129	Discovery Links	Newbridge
Animals Building Homes	L	I	250+	Animal Behavior	Capstone Press
Animals Communicating	M	I	250+	First Facts	Capstone Press

* Collection of short stories

TITLE	LEVEL	GENRE	WORD COUNT	AUTHOR / SERIES	PUBLISHER / DISTRIBUTOR
Animals Eat	C	I	27	We Do Too Series	Pearson Learning Group
Animals' Eyes and Ears	K	I	411	Early Connections	Benchmark Education
Animals Finding Food	L	I	250+	Animal Behavor	Capstone Press
Animals from Long Ago	G	I	141	Discovery Links	Newbridge
Animals from the Past	N	I	304	Independent Readers Science	Houghton Mifflin
Animals Grow	I	I	152	Wonder World	Wright Group/McGraw Hill
Animals Have Babies	C	I	42	We Do Too Series	Pearson Learning Group
Animals Have Homes	C	I	31	We Do Too Series	Pearson Learning Group
Animals Hide	D	I	55	Discovery Links	Newbridge
Animals Hide and Seek	C	I	56	Twig	Wright Group/McGraw Hill
Animals Hiding	B	I	61	Bookshop	Mondo
Animals I Like to Feed	C	I	38	Little Red Readers	Sundance
Animals in Danger	M	I	250+	Pair-It Books	Steck-Vaughn
Animals in the Desert	D	I	31	Carousel Readers	Pearson Learning Group
Animals in the Fall	E	I	34	Pebble Books	Capstone Press
Animals in the Rain Forest	C	I	33	Vocabulary Readers	Houghton Mifflin
Animals in Winter	L	I	250+	Soar To Success	Houghton Mifflin
Animals in Winter	C	I	42	Rosen Real Readers	Rosen Publishing Group
Animals Keep Warm	C	I	25	We Do Too Series	Pearson Learning Group
Animals Live Everywhere	H	I	250+	Phonics and Friends	Hampton-Brown
Animals Love the Fair	E	F	43	Literacy 2000	Rigby
Animals Make Noises	C	I	19	We Do Too Series	Pearson Learning Group
Animals Nearby	O	I	943	Leveled Readers Science	Houghton Mifflin
Animals of Alaska	S	I	517	Vocabulary Readers	Houghton Mifflin
Animals of Alaska	J	I	147	Rosen Real Readers	Rosen Publishing Group
Animals of Long Ago	N	I	250+	Ring, Susan	Scholastic
Animals of the Amazon	R	I	683	Vocabulary Readers	Houghton Mifflin
Animals of the Ice and Snow	O	I	250+	Literacy 2000	Rigby
Animals of the Savanna	M	I	250+	Rosen Real Readers	Rosen Publishing Group
Animals of the Tropical Forest	M	I	250+	Rosen Real Readers	Rosen Publishing Group
Animals of the Tropical Rain Forest	M	I	250+	Sunshine	Wright Group/McGraw Hill
Animals of the Tundra	N	I	250+	Little Celebrations	Pearson Learning Group
Animals on the Loose	M	F	642	Leveled Readers	Houghton Mifflin
Animals on the Move	K	I	145	Planet Earth	Rigby
Animals Play	C	I	27	We Do Too Series	Pearson Learning Group
Animals Raising Offspring	L	I	250+	Animal Behavior	Capstone Press
Animals Say	M	F	250+	Sails	Rigby
Animals Sleeping	L	I	250+	Animal Behavior	Capstone Press
Animals Sleeping	B	RF	61	Bookshop	Mondo
Animals Staying Safe	L	I	250+	First Facts	Capstone Press
Animals Talk, Too	N	I	250+	Literacy 2000	Rigby
Animals That Work	A	I	14	Foundations	Wright Group/McGraw Hill
Animals Went to Bed, The	B	F	32	Smart Starts	Rigby
Animals With Backbones	M	I	177	Windows on Literacy	National Geographic
Animated Illusions	S	I	250+	Sunshine	Wright Group/McGraw Hill
Animorphs	U	F	250+	Applegate, K. A.	Scholastic
Ankylosaurus	M	I	250+	Discovering Dinosaurs	Capstone Press
Anna Allen Faces the White Dragon	P	I	250+	Leveled Readers Language Support	Houghton Mifflin
Anna and the King	V	HF	250+	Landon, Margaret	HarperTrophy
Anna Is Still Here	V	HF	250+	Vos, Ida	Puffin Books
Anna, Grandpa, and the Big Storm	N	RF	250+	Stevens, Carla	Penguin Group
Annabel	H	RF	251	Story Basket	Wright Group/McGraw Hill

TITLE	LEVEL	GENRE	WORD COUNT	AUTHOR / SERIES	PUBLISHER / DISTRIBUTOR
Annabel the Actress Starring in Gorilla My Dreams	L	RF	250+	Conford, Ellen	Simon & Schuster
Anna's Big Day	D	RF	73	Sun Sprouts	ETA/Cuisenaire
Anna's Sandwich	C	RF	33	Windmill Books	Rigby
Anna's Tree	I	RF	213	Windmill Books	Rigby
Anne Bradstreet	R	B	548	Independent Readers Science	Houghton Mifflin
Anne Frank	S	B	250+	Epstein, Rachel	Franklin Watts
Anne Frank Remembered: The Story of the Woman Who Helped Hide the Frank Family	Y	B	250+	Gies, Miep	Simon & Schuster
Anne Frank: Beyond the Diary	X	I	250+	Van der Rol, Ruud; Verhoeven, Rian	Puffin Books
Anne Frank: Life in Hiding	W	B	250+	Hurwitz, Johanna	Avon
Anne Frank: The Diary of a Young Girl	Y	B	250+	Frank, Anne	Bantam
Anne of Green Gables	V	RF	250+	Montgomery, L. M.	Scholastic
Annie Bananie Moves To Barry Avenue	L	RF	250+	Komaiko, Leah	Bantam
Annie John	Z	RF	250+	Kincaid, Jamaica	Farrar, Straus and Giroux
Annie Oakley	R	B	250+	Wilson, Ellen	Aladdin
Annie's Pet	J	RF	250+	Bank Street	Bantam
Annie's Secret Diary	M	RF	250+	Little Celebrations	Pearson Learning Group
Anno's USA	WB	I	N/A	Mitsumaso, Anna	Philomel Books
Another Day, Another Challenge	L	RF	250+	Literacy 2000	Rigby
Another Point of View	P	RF	250+	Wildcats	Wright Group/McGraw Hill
Ansel Adams, Photographer	R	B	1763	Leveled Readers Social Studies	Houghton Mifflin
Answer the Phone, Fiona!	G	RF	119	Lighthouse	Rigby
Ant	O	I	250+	Chinery, Michael	Troll Associates
Ant and the Dove, The	I	TL	250+	PM Plus Story Books	Rigby
*Ant and the Dove, The	G	TL	173	New Way Blue	Steck-Vaughn
Ant and the Grasshopper, The	J	TL	250+	PM Plus Story Books	Rigby
Ant and the Grasshopper, The	L	TL	250+	Little Celebrations	Pearson Learning Group
Ant and the Grasshopper, The	J	TL	250+	Story Steps	Rigby
Ant and the Grasshopper, The	I	TL	231	Aesop's Fables	Pearson Learning Group
Ant and the Grasshopper, The: A Play	I	TL	250+	Literacy Tree	Rigby
Ant Cities	O	I	250+	Dorros, Arthur	HarperCollins
Ant City	J	RF	393	PM Turquoise	Rigby
Ant, The	D	F	48	Ray's Readers	Outside the Box
Ant, The	E	F	97	Ready Readers	Pearson Learning Group
Antarctic Adventure, An	M	I	296	Vocabulary Readers	Houghton Mifflin
Antarctic Diary	M	I	250+	Voyages	SRA/McGraw Hill
Antarctic Penguins	N	I	250+	PM Animal Facts: Silver	Rigby
Antarctic Seals	N	I	250+	PM Animal Facts: Silver	Rigby
Antarctica	T	I	250+	Literacy 2000	Rigby
Antarctica	N	I	250+	Continents	Capstone Press
Antarctica	L	I	250+	Read-About Geography	Children's Press
Antarctica	L	I	250+	Fowler, Allan	Scholastic
Antarctica	L	RF	250+	Soar To Success	Houghton Mifflin
Antarctica: Ice-Covered Continent	N	I	250+	Phonics and Friends	Hampton-Brown
Antarctica: The Last Great Wilderness	O	I	250+	Rigby Literacy	Rigby
Anthony Burns: Defeat and Triumph of a Fugitive Slave	Y	B	250+	Hamilton, Virginia	Alfred A. Knopf
Anthony's Unhappy Birthday	K	RF	560	Leveled Readers	Houghton Mifflin
Antonia Novello: Doctor for the Nation	K	B	204	Independent Readers Science	Houghton Mifflin
Ants	N	I	250+	Nature's Friends	Compass Point Books
Ants	E	I	50	Pebble Books	Capstone Press
Ants	N	I	250+	Daronco, Mickey; Presti, Lori	Benchmark Education

* Collection of short stories

Organized Alphabetically by Book Title

TITLE	LEVEL	GENRE	WORD COUNT	AUTHOR / SERIES	PUBLISHER / DISTRIBUTOR
Ants	B	I	16	Discovery Links	Newbridge
Ants	H	I	94	Pebble Plus	Red Brick Learning
Ants	H	I	250+	Sunshine	Wright Group/McGraw Hill
Ants	G	I	94	Wonder World	Wright Group/McGraw Hill
Ants and Grasshoppers, The	J	F	250+	The Wright Skills	Wright Group/McGraw Hill
Ants and the Grasshoppers, The	G	TL	144	New Way Blue	Steck-Vaughn
Ants and Their Nests	J	I	150	Animal Homes	Capstone Press
Ants Aren't Antisocial	S	I	250+	Action Packs	Rigby
Ants Everywhere	C	RF	24	Visions	Wright Group/McGraw Hill
Ants Go Marching, The	J	TL	250+	Traditional Songs	Picture Window Books
Ants Love Picnics, Too	B	F	27	Literacy 2000	Rigby
Ants on a Picnic	C	F	35	Joy Readers	Pearson Learning Group
Ants, Ants, Ants	E	I	131	Sunshine	Wright Group/McGraw Hill
Anyone Can have a Pet	K	RF	503	PM Plus Story Books	Rigby
Anywhere Everywhere Bus, The	K	F	250+	Home Connection Collection	Rigby
Apache Indian Community, An	O	I	250+	Rosen Real Readers	Rosen Publishing Group
Apache Indians, The	P	I	250+	Lund, Bill	Red Brick Learning
Apache, The	R	I	250+	First Reports	Compass Point Books
Apache, The: Nomadic Hunters of the Southwest	S	I	250+	American Indian Nations	Capstone Press
Aphrodite's Blessings	Z	TL	250+	McLaren, Clemence	Atheneum
Apple Bird, The	WB	F	N/A	Wildsmith, Brian	Oxford University Press
Apple Farm, The	E	RF	95	Ready Readers	Pearson Learning Group
Apple Floats, An	D	I	35	Science	Outside the Box
Apple Man, The	P	F	1094	Leveled Readers	Houghton Mifflin
Apple Picking	B	RF	44	Bookshop	Mondo
Apple Pie Family, The	E	RF	72	Pair-It Books	Steck-Vaughn
Apple Pie Tree, The	K	I	250+	Zoe Hall	Scholastic
Apple Star, The	C	RF	33	First Stories	Pacific Learning
Apple Thief, The	G	F	62	Voyages	SRA/McGraw Hill
Apple Tree	I	RF	110	Book Bank	Wright Group/McGraw Hill
Apple Tree	G	RF	198	Literacy Tree	Rigby
Apple Tree Apple Tree	G	RF	340	Blocksma, Mary	Children's Press
Apple Tree, The	J	I	160	Sunshine	Wright Group/McGraw Hill
Apple Trees	D	I	62	Pebble Books	Capstone Press
Apples	LB	I	23	Berger, Samantha; Chessen, Betsey	Scholastic
Apples	C	I	45	Williams, Deborah	Kaeden Books
Apples and More Apples	E	I	97	Pair-It Books	Steck-Vaughn
Apples and Pumpkins	I	RF	185	Rockwell, Ann	Scholastic
Apples for America	P	B	824	Leveled Readers	Houghton Mifflin
Apples!	J	RF	503	Cambridge Reading	Pearson Learning Group
Appointment with Action	P	RF	250+	Wildcats	Wright Group/McGraw Hill
Apprenticeship of Lucas Whitaker, The	U	HF	250+	DeFelice, Cynthia	Avon
April Fool's Day Mystery, The	M	RF	250+	Soar To Success	Houghton Mifflin
April Morning	X	HF	250+	Fast, Howard	Bantam
April Who? April Fools	I	RF	197	Sunshine	Wright Group/McGraw Hill
Apron Annie in the Garden	G	RF	153	Learn to Read	Creative Teaching Press
Apron Annie's Pies	G	RF	167	Learn to Read	Creative Teaching Press
Apsaalooke (Crow) Nation, The	P	I	250+	Native Peoples	Red Brick Learning
Aquarium, The	LB	I	24	KinderReaders	Rigby
Aquarium, The	LB	I	18	Kloes, Carol	Kaeden Books
Arapaho, The: Hunters of the Great Plains	S	I	250+	American Indian Nations	Capstone Press
Archaeologists Dig for Clues	P	I	250+	Duke, Kate	HarperCollins

* Collection of short stories

TITLE	LEVEL	GENRE	WORD COUNT	AUTHOR / SERIES	PUBLISHER / DISTRIBUTOR
Arctic	R	I	250+	The Heinle Reading Library	Thomson Learning
Arctic Babies	P	I	250+	Darling, Kathy	Scholastic
Arctic Food Web, The	P	I	250+	Rigby Literacy	Rigby
Arctic Investigations: Exploring the Frozen Ocean	T	I	250+	Young, Karen Romano	Steck-Vaughn
Arctic Journey	I	I	198	Sunshine	Wright Group/McGraw Hill
Arctic Life	M	I	250+	Robinson, F. R.	Steck-Vaughn
Arctic Tundra	M	I	250+	Forman, Michael H.	Children's Press
Are All The Giants Dead?	V	F	250+	Norton, Mary	Harcourt Trade
Are They Look-Alikes?	I	I	194	Independent Readers Science	Houghton Mifflin
Are We Hurting the Earth?	K	I	363	Early Connections	Benchmark Education
Are We There Yet?	F	RF	127	Teacher's Choice Series	Pearson Learning Group
Are You a Ladybug?	F	I	116	Sunshine	Wright Group/McGraw Hill
Are You Afraid of . . .?	B	I	18	Little Celebrations	Pearson Learning Group
Are You My Mommy?	F	F	112	Dijs, Carla	Simon & Schuster
Are You My Mother?	I	F	250+	Eastman, Philip D.	Random House
Are You the New Principal?	E	RF	120	Teacher's Choice Series	Pearson Learning Group
Are You There, Bear?	F	F	42	Maris, Ron	Greenwillow
Are You There, God? It's Me, Margaret.	T	RF	250+	Blume, Judy	Bantam
Are You There?	D	F	81	Sun Sprouts	ETA/Cuisenaire
Arguments	K	F	398	Read Alongs	Rigby
Ariel of the Sea	U	F	250+	Calhoun, Dia	Winslow Press
Arizona	S	I	250+	Land of Liberty	Red Brick Learning
Ark, The	O	HF	250+	Geisert, Arthur	Houghton Mifflin
Arkadians, The	W	F	250+	Alexander, Lloyd	Puffin Books
Arkansas	R	I	250+	This Land Is Your Land	Compass Point Books
Arkansas	S	I	250+	Land of Liberty	Red Brick Learning
Arky, the Dinosaur With Feathers	K	HF	529	PM Plus Story Books	Rigby
Arlington National Cemetery	V	I	250+	Cornerstones of Freedom	Bantam
Armadillo	M	RF	134	Books for Young Learners	Richard C. Owen
Armadillo, The	L	I	250+	Sunshine	Wright Group/McGraw Hill
Armadillo, The	R	I	250+	Potts, Steve	Red Brick Learning
Armando Asked, "Why?"	I	RF	250+	Ready Set Read	Steck-Vaughn
Armies of Ants	M	I	250+	Retan, Walter	Scholastic
Arnold Lobel: Words and Pictures Together	L	B	375	Leveled Readers	Houghton Mifflin
Around and About	E	RF	209	Sun Sprouts	ETA/Cuisenaire
Around and Around	B	I	72	PM Plus Nonfiction	Rigby
Around My School	E	I	60	Exploring History & Geography	Rigby
Around the Neighborhood	E	I	74	Pair-It Books	Steck-Vaughn
Around the World in a Hundred Years: From Henry the Navigator to Magellan	W	I	250+	Fritz, Jean	Putnam & Grosset
Around-the-World Lunch, The	K	RF	250+	Canetti, Yanitzia	Steck-Vaughn
Art Around the World	J	I	239	Early Connections	Benchmark Education
Art Around the World	M	I	250+	Discovery World	Rigby
Art Class, The	H	RF	240	Leveled Readers	Houghton Mifflin
Art in Sub-Saharan Africa	W	I	2877	Independent Readers Social Studies	Houghton Mifflin
Art Lesson, The	M	B	246	DePaola, Tomie	Putnam
Art Riddle Contest, The	Q	RF	250+	Medearis, Angela Shelf	Steck-Vaughn
Artemis Fowl	Y	F	250+	Colfer, Eoin	Hyperion
Artemis Fowl: The Arctic Incident	Y	F	250+	Colfer, Eoin	Hyperion
Artful Stories	P	I	250+	Rigby Literacy	Rigby
Arthur Accused!	M	F	250+	Brown, Marc	Little, Brown & Co.
Arthur and the Big Blow-Up	M	F	250+	Brown, Marc	Little, Brown & Co.

TITLE	LEVEL	GENRE	WORD COUNT	AUTHOR / SERIES	PUBLISHER / DISTRIBUTOR
Arthur and the Cootie-Catcher	M	F	250+	Brown, Marc	Little, Brown & Co.
Arthur and the Crunch Cereal Contest	M	F	250+	Brown, Marc	Little, Brown & Co.
Arthur and the Lost Diary	M	F	250+	Brown, Marc	Little, Brown & Co.
Arthur and the Poetry Contest	M	F	250+	Brown, Marc	Little, Brown & Co.
Arthur and the Popularity Test	M	F	250+	Brown, Marc	Little, Brown & Co.
Arthur and the Scare-Your-Pants-Off Club	M	F	250+	Brown, Marc	Little, Brown & Co.
Arthur and the TL Contest	M	F	250+	Brown, Marc	Little, Brown & Co.
Arthur Makes the Team	M	F	250+	Brown, Marc	Little, Brown & Co.
Arthur Rocks with BINKY	M	F	250+	Brown, Marc	Little, Brown & Co.
Arthur, For the Very First Time	R	RF	250+	MacLachlan, Patricia	Bantam
Arthur's Baby	K	F	250+	Brown, Marc	Scholastic
Arthur's Back to School Day	K	F	250+	Hoban, Lillian	HarperTrophy
Arthur's Camp-Out	K	F	250+	Hoban, Lillian	HarperTrophy
Arthur's Christmas Cookies	K	F	250+	Hoban, Lillian	HarperTrophy
Arthur's Eyes	K	F	250+	Brown, Marc	Scholastic
Arthur's Funny Money	K	F	250+	Hoban, Lillian	HarperTrophy
Arthur's Great Big Valentine	K	F	250+	Hoban, Lillian	HarperTrophy
Arthur's Honey Bear	K	F	250+	Hoban, Lillian	HarperCollins
Arthur's Loose Tooth	K	F	250+	Hoban, Lillian	HarperCollins
Arthur's Mystery Envelope	M	F	250+	Brown, Marc	Little, Brown & Co.
Arthur's Pen Pal	K	F	250+	Hoban, Lillian	HarperCollins
Arthur's Prize Reader	K	F	250+	Hoban, Lillian	HarperTrophy
Artist in the Woods	G	F	228	Seedlings	Continental Press
Artist, The	F	F	83	Books for Young Learners	Richard C. Owen
*Artists and Their Art	Q	I	250+	Medearis, Michael	Steck-Vaughn
Arturo's Baton	L	RF	250+	Soar To Success	Houghton Mifflin
As Fast as a Fox	D	RF	69	Ready Readers	Pearson Learning Group
Ashes for Gold	K	TL	250+	Folk Tales	Mondo
Ashes of Roses	Y	HF	250+	Auch, Mary Jane	Random House
Ashley's World Record	L	F	250+	Little Celebrations	Pearson Learning Group
Asia	N	I	250+	Continents	Capstone Press
Ask Einstein!	N	RF	250+	Trussell-Cullen, Alan	Pacific Learning
Ask Mr. Bear	J	F	613	Flack, Marjorie	Macmillan
Ask Nicely	F	F	110	Literacy 2000	Rigby
Asleep	C	RF	26	Joy Readers	Pearson Learning Group
Asli's Story	S	I	250+	Jansen, Adrienne	Pacific Learning
Assassination of Abraham Lincoln, The	V	B	250+	Cornerstones of Freedom	Children's Press
Assassination of John F. Kennedy, The	V	B	250+	Cornerstones of Freedom	Children's Press
Assassination of Martin Luther King, Jr., The	V	B	250+	Cornerstones of Freedom	Children's Press
Assembly Line, The	M	I	501	Leveled Readers Social Studies	Houghton Mifflin
Asteroid, The	M	F	752	PM Gold	Rigby
Asteroids	P	I	250+	The Galaxy	Red Brick Learning
Astronaut	B	I	22	Hoenecke, Karen	Kaeden Books
Astronaut Adventure	C	F	41	Phonics and Friends	Hampton-Brown
Astronaut, The	B	RF	30	Sunshine	Wright Group/McGraw Hill
Astronauts	I	I	118	Phonics Readers	Compass Point Books
Astronauts	I	I	171	Wonder World	Wright Group/McGraw Hill
Astronauts	M	I	250+	Deedrick, Tami	Red Brick Learning
Astronauts at Work	N	I	250+	Explore Space	Red Brick Learning
Astronauts in Space	J	I	135	Windows on Literacy	National Geographic
Astronauts Take Flight	Q	I	250+	iOpeners	Pearson Learning Group
Astronauts, The	F	F	112	Foundations	Wright Group/McGraw Hill
At 1600 Pennsylvania Avenue	O	I	250+	Wirth, Crystal	Scholastic
At Christmas	C	RF	26	Visions	Wright Group/McGraw Hill

TITLE	LEVEL	GENRE	WORD COUNT	AUTHOR / SERIES	PUBLISHER / DISTRIBUTOR
At Grandma's House	D	RF	66	Teacher's Choice Series	Pearson Learning Group
At Grandma's House	E	RF	118	Handprints D, Set 1	Educator's Publishing Service
At Her Majesty's Request: An African Princess in Victorian England	X	HF	250+	Myers, Walter Dean	Scholastic
At Home and at School	B	I	32	Leveled Readers Social Studies	Houghton Mifflin
At Home Around the World	F	I	82	Rosen Real Readers	Rosen Publishing Group
At Home in Space	V	I	2547	Leveled Readers	Houghton Mifflin
At Home on the Prairie	N	I	436	Vocabulary Readers	Houghton Mifflin
At Last!	D	RF	41	Rigby Literacy	Rigby
At My Grandfather's	G	RF	63	City Stories	Rigby
At My School	B	I	43	Little Books for Early Readers	University of Maine
At Night	D	RF	21	Literacy Tree	Rigby
At School	B	I	29	Vocabulary Readers	Houghton Mifflin
At School	A	I	28	Little Books for Early Readers	University of Maine
At School	LB	I	12	Rise & Shine	Hampton-Brown
At School	B	I	23	Sunshine	Wright Group/McGraw Hill
At School	G	I	250+	Yellow Umbrella Books	Red Brick Learning
At the Airport	B	I	42	Leveled Readers Social Studies	Houghton Mifflin
At the Art Museum	M	I	250+	Rosen Real Readers	Rosen Publishing Group
At the Ballpark	H	RF	105	Sunshine	Wright Group/McGraw Hill
At the Barbershop	F	RF	179	Visions	Wright Group/McGraw Hill
At the Beach	LB	RF	15	Rigby Literacy	Rigby
At the Beach	B	I	30	Discovery Links	Newbridge
At the Beach	B	I	74	Leveled Readers Emergent	Houghton Mifflin
At the Beach	E	RF	43	Literacy 2000	Rigby
At the Beach	E	RF	85	Oxford Reading Tree	Oxford University Press
At the Beach	C	I	74	Sun Sprouts	ETA/Cuisenaire
At the Car Wash	E	RF	143	Visions	Wright Group/McGraw Hill
At the Coal Mine	L	I	317	Rigby Focus	Rigby
At the Doctor	J	I	250+	Story Starter	Wright Group/McGraw Hill
At the Edge of the Sea	M	I	693	Sunshine	Wright Group/McGraw Hill
At the End of the Day	L	RF	250+	Pacific Literacy	Pacific Learning
At the Fair	D	RF	175	Sunshine	Wright Group/McGraw Hill
At the Fair	C	RF	58	Rise & Shine	Hampton-Brown
At the Fair	D	I	116	Little Red Readers	Sundance
At the Fair	LB	I	14	Little Books for Early Readers	University of Maine
At the Farm	C	I	52	Little Red Readers	Sundance
At the Farm	M	I	250+	Look Once Look Again	Creative Teaching Press
At the Game	G	F	85	City Stories	Rigby
At the Horse Show	D	I	24	Books for Young Learners	Richard C. Owen
At the Ice Cream Shop	C	I	35	Vocabulary Readers	Houghton Mifflin
At the Lake	C	RF	23	KinderReaders	Rigby
At the Lake	I	RF	176	Books for Young Learners	Richard C. Owen
At the Library	F	F	31	Little Celebrations	Pearson Learning Group
At the Library	C	I	69	PM Starters	Rigby
At the Museum	B	RF	28	Ready Readers	Pearson Learning Group
At the Ocean	A	I	29	Little Books for Early Readers	University of Maine
At the Ocean	C	RF	26	Early Emergent	Pioneer Valley
At the Park	C	I	40	Harry's Math Books	Outside the Box
At the Park	F	I	30	Yellow Umbrella Books	Capstone Press
At the Park	F	RF	163	Early Connections	Benchmark Education
At the Park	D	I	37	Hoenecke, Karen	Kaeden Books
At the Park	D	I	91	Little Red Readers	Sundance

* Collection of short stories

TITLE	LEVEL	GENRE	WORD COUNT	AUTHOR / SERIES	PUBLISHER / DISTRIBUTOR
At the Park	E	RF	29	Oxford Reading Tree	Oxford University Press
At the Park	D	RF	74	Teacher's Choice Series	Pearson Learning Group
At the Park	C	I	32	Bebop Books	Lee & Low Books Inc.
At the Pet Store	I	I	177	Foundations	Wright Group/McGraw Hill
At the Playground	B	I	54	Little Books for Early Readers	University of Maine
At the Playground	C	I	86	Little Red Readers	Sundance
At the Playground	LB	I	25	Visions	Wright Group/McGraw Hill
At the Playground	LB	I	8	Windows on Literacy	National Geographic
At the Playground	G	I	151	Discovery Links	Newbridge
At the Pond	E	I	55	Vocabulary Readers	Houghton Mifflin
At the Pond	B	RF	51	Leveled Readers Science	Houghton Mifflin
At the Pond	M	I	250+	Look Once Look Again	Creative Teaching Press
At the Pool	A	I	29	Vocabulary Readers	Houghton Mifflin
At the Pool	F	RF	87	Oxford Reading Tree	Oxford University Press
At the Pool	C	I	64	Foundations	Wright Group/McGraw Hill
At the Post Office	H	RF	100	City Stories	Rigby
At the Root of It	Q	I	250+	iOpeners	Pearson Learning Group
At the Science Center	H	I	158	Discovery Links	Newbridge
At the Seashore	N	I	250+	Look Once Look Again	Creative Teaching Press
At the Seaside	E	RF	85	Oxford Reading Tree	Oxford University Press
At the Store	LB	I	14	Visions	Wright Group/McGraw Hill
At the Store	B	I	21	Read-More Books	Pearson Learning Group
At the Supermarket	C	RF	60	Little Readers	Houghton Mifflin
At the Supermarket	C	I	60	Little Red Readers	Sundance
At the Supermarket	D	I	29	Read-More Books	Pearson Learning Group
At the Toy Store	C	I	35	PM Plus Nonfiction	Rigby
At the Toyshop	D	RF	41	Home Connection Collection	Rigby
At the Track	E	RF	122	Ready Readers	Pearson Learning Group
At the Truckstop	LB	RF	25	Kloes, Carol	Kaeden Books
At the Vet	D	RF	83	Leveled Readers	Houghton Mifflin
At the Water Hole	D	I	70	Little Red Readers	Sundance
At the Water Hole	K	I	236	Foundations	Wright Group/McGraw Hill
At the Wildlife Park	B	I	34	Little Red Readers	Sundance
At the Zoo	E	I	54	Vocabulary Readers	Houghton Mifflin
At the Zoo	B	I	40	PM Starters	Rigby
At the Zoo	D	RF	116	Predictable Storybooks	SRA/McGraw Hill
At the Zoo	M	I	250+	Look Once Look Again	Creative Teaching Press
At the Zoo	C	I	73	Little Red Readers	Sundance
At the Zoo	B	RF	54	Little Readers	Houghton Mifflin
At the Zoo	D	RF	37	Little Celebrations	Pearson Learning Group
At the Zoo	B	I	40	Leveled Readers Emergent	Houghton Mifflin
At the Zoo	B	RF	29	Kloes, Carol	Kaeden Books
At the Zoo	B	I	40	Early Connections	Benchmark Education
At Work	B	I	29	Bookshop	Mondo
At Work	B	I	54	Independent Readers Social Studies	Houghton Mifflin
At Work	C	I	29	Geist, Ellen	Scholastic
Athena	W	I	250+	World Mythology	Capstone Press
Atoms	V	I	250+	Simply Science	Compass Point Books
Attaboy, Sam	P	RF	250+	Lowry, Lois	Bantam
Attack and Defense	Q	I	250+	Explorers	Wright Group/McGraw Hill
Attack of the Giant Squirrel!	N	F	653	Leveled Readers	Houghton Mifflin
Atul's Christmas Hamster	I	I	250+	Cambridge Reading	Pearson Learning Group
Aung San Suu Kyi	V	B	1980	Leveled Readers Social Studies	Houghton Mifflin

* Collection of short stories

TITLE	LEVEL	GENRE	WORD COUNT	AUTHOR / SERIES	PUBLISHER / DISTRIBUTOR
Aunt Clara Brown: Official Pioneer	P	B	250+	Lowery, Linda	Lerner Publishing
Aunt Eater Loves a Mystery	J	F	250+	Cushman, Doug	HarperTrophy
Aunt Eater's Mystery Christmas	J	F	250+	Cushman, Doug	HarperTrophy
Aunt Eater's Mystery Vacation	J	F	250+	Cushman, Doug	HarperTrophy
Aunt Flossie's Hats (and Crab Cakes Later)	M	RF	250+	Howard, Elizabeth	Scholastic
Aunt Jessie	G	RF	114	Literacy 2000	Rigby
Aunt Louisa Is Coming for Lunch	G	RF	118	Windmill Books	Rigby
Aunt Wilhelmina's Will	L	RF	250+	Voyages	SRA/McGraw Hill
Auntie Maria and the Cat	D	RF	215	Sunshine	Wright Group/McGraw Hill
Aunts	D	I	49	Pebble Books	Capstone Press
Austere Academy, The	V	F	250+	Snicket, Lemony	Scholastic
Australia	N	I	250+	Continents	Capstone Press
Australia	H	I	27	Chessen, Betsey; Chanko, Pamela	Scholastic
Australia	N	I	250+	A True Book	Children's Press
Australia	U	I	250+	Countries and Cultures	Red Brick Learning
Australia	O	I	250+	Countries of the World	Red Brick Learning
Australia	Q	I	250+	First Reports	Compass Point Books
Author on My Street, The	J	RF	260	Books for Young Learners	Richard C. Owen
Auto Mechanics	M	I	250+	Boraas, Tracey	Red Brick Learning
Autumn	M	I	225	Pebble Books	Red Brick Learning
Autumn Leaves	G	RF	84	Voyages	SRA/McGraw Hill
Autumn Leaves	A	I	17	Pebble Books	Capstone Press
Autumn Street	V	HF	250+	Lowry, Lois	Bantam
Avalanche!	L	I	250+	Rosen Real Readers	Rosen Publishing Group
Avi	T	B	250+	Markham, Lois	Learning Works, The
Avion My Uncle Flew, The	Y	RF	250+	Fisher, Cyrus	Penguin Group
Awake and Dreaming	S	F	250+	Person, Kit	Puffin Books
Away Went the Hat	I	F	260	New Way Green	Steck-Vaughn
Awful Mess, The	H	RF	58	Rockwell, Anne	Four Winds
Awful Waffles	G	F	296	Williams, D. H.	Continental Press
Awfully Short for the Fourth Grade	Q	RF	250+	Woodruff, Elvira	Bantam
Awumpalema	L	TL	250+	Literacy 2000	Rigby
Awww	C	RF	35	Little Celebrations	Pearson Learning Group
A-Z Fascinating Facts About Animals	R	I	250+	Literacy 2000	Rigby
Baba Nangko	P	F	250+	Voyages	SRA/McGraw Hill
Baba Yaga	K	TL	250+	Literacy 2000	Rigby
Baba Yaga: A Russian Folktale	N	TL	250+	Phinney, Margaret Y.	Mondo
Babe Didrikson: Athlete of the Century	R	B	250+	Knudson, R. Rozanne	Bantam
Babe Ruth: One of Baseball's Greatest	R	B	250+	Van Riper, Guernsey	Aladdin
Babe the Gallant Pig	R	F	250+	King-Smith, Dick	Random House
Babies	D	I	42	Canizares, Susan; Chanko, Pamela	Scholastic
Babies on the Move	LB	I	30	Canizares, Susan; Moreton, Daniel	Scholastic
Baboon Troops	M	I	250+	Sails	Rigby
Baby	A	RF	29	Instant Readers	Harcourt School Publishers
Baby	A	I	28	Little Books for Early Readers	University of Maine
Baby	A	I	24	PM Plus Starters	Rigby
Baby	T	RF	250+	MacLachlan, Patricia	Language for Learning Assoc.
Baby Animal Zoo	O	I	250+	Martin, Ann M.	Scholastic
Baby Animals	A	I	24	Vocabulary Readers	Houghton Mifflin
Baby Animals	E	I	109	Rigby Focus	Rigby
Baby Animals	B	I	44	Reading Corners	Pearson Learning Group
Baby Animals	D	I	78	Foundations	Wright Group/McGraw Hill
Baby Animals	D	I	41	Discovery Links	Newbridge

TITLE	LEVEL	GENRE	WORD COUNT	AUTHOR / SERIES	PUBLISHER / DISTRIBUTOR
Baby Animals	B	I	89	Rigby Literacy	Rigby
Baby Animals at Home	C	I	64	Twig	Wright Group/McGraw Hill
Baby Animals Learn	C	I	52	Chanko, Pamela; Berger, Samantha	Scholastic
Baby at Our House, The	H	RF	93	Foundations	Wright Group/McGraw Hill
Baby Bear Climbs a Tree	F	F	147	PM Plus Story Books	Rigby
Baby Bear Goes Fishing	E	F	112	PM Story Books	Rigby
Baby Bear's Hiding Place	F	F	187	PM Plus Story Books	Rigby
Baby Bear's Present	F	F	206	PM Story Books	Rigby
Baby Bear's Ride	WB	F	N/A	Ready Readers	Pearson Learning Group
Baby Bear's Toys	A	F	35	Phonics and Friends	Hampton-Brown
Baby Birds	D	I	51	Pebble Books	Capstone Press
Baby Birds	D	I	37	Windows on Literacy	National Geographic
Baby Brother, The	I	RF	131	Voyages	SRA/McGraw Hill
Baby Can Ride	C	I	67	Leveled Readers Emergent	Houghton Mifflin
Baby Chimp	A	RF	14	Twig	Wright Group/McGraw Hill
Baby Elephant Gets Lost	D	F	90	Foundations	Wright Group/McGraw Hill
Baby Elephant's New Bike	G	F	187	Foundations	Wright Group/McGraw Hill
Baby Elephant's Sneeze	F	F	78	Foundations	Wright Group/McGraw Hill
Baby Food	C	RF	21	Dunn, Tansy	Scholastic
Baby Gets Dressed	LB	RF	16	Sunshine	Wright Group/McGraw Hill
Baby Grand, the Moon in July, and Me, The	P	RF	250+	Barnes, Joyce Annette	Penguin Group
Baby Hippo	D	RF	117	PM Extensions-Yellow	Rigby
Baby in the Cart	C	RF	84	Foundations	Wright Group/McGraw Hill
Baby Island	P	RF	250+	Brink, Carol Ryrie	Simon & Schuster
Baby Lamb's First Drink	C	F	64	PM Story Books	Rigby
Baby Monkey	I	F	250+	Reading Unlimited	Pearson Learning Group
Baby Owls, The	C	RF	90	PM Extensions-Red	Rigby
Baby Panda	D	RF	97	PM Plus Story Books	Rigby
Baby Says	LB	RF	26	Steptoe, John	Morrow
Baby Shark, The	D	I	49	Windows on Literacy	National Geographic
Baby Sister for Frances, A	K	F	250+	Hoban, Lillian	Scholastic
Baby Wakes Up	C	RF	50	PM Plus Story Books	Rigby
Baby Whale Rescue: The True Story of J.J.	P	I	250+	Arnold, Caroline; Hewett, Richard	Troll Associates
Baby Whales Drink Milk	M	I	250+	Soar To Success	Houghton Mifflin
Baby Writer	I	RF	182	Stepping Stones	Nelson/Michaels Assoc.
Baby, The	E	RF	60	Burningham, John	Crowell
Baby's Birthday	D	RF	53	Literacy 2000	Rigby
Baby's Dinner	E	RF	26	Literacy 2000	Rigby
Baby-Sitter Burglaries, The	S	RF	250+	Keene, Carolyn	Pocket Books
Babysitter, The	H	RF	243	PM Extensions-Green	Rigby
Baby-Sitter, The	E	RF	69	Oxford Reading Tree	Oxford University Press
Baby-Sitters Club Mystery: Beware, Dawn!	O	RF	250+	Martin, Ann M.	Scholastic
Baby-Sitters Club Mystery: Claudia, Clue in the Photograph	O	RF	250+	Martin, Ann M.	Scholastic
Baby-Sitters Club Mystery: Claudia, Mystery at the Museum	O	RF	250+	Martin, Ann M.	Scholastic
Baby-Sitters Club Mystery: Claudia, Recipe for Danger	O	RF	250+	Martin, Ann M.	Scholastic
Baby-Sitters Club Mystery: Dawn, Disappearing Dogs	O	RF	250+	Martin, Ann M.	Scholastic
Baby-Sitters Club Mystery: Dawn, Halloween Mystery	O	RF	250+	Martin, Ann M.	Scholastic
Baby-Sitters Club Mystery: Dawn, Surfer Ghost	O	RF	250+	Martin, Ann M.	Scholastic

* Collection of short stories

TITLE	LEVEL	GENRE	WORD COUNT	AUTHOR / SERIES	PUBLISHER / DISTRIBUTOR
Baby-Sitters Club Mystery: Jessi, Jewel Thieves	O	RF	250+	Martin, Ann M.	Scholastic
Baby-Sitters Club Mystery: Kristy, Haunted Mansion	O	RF	250+	Martin, Ann M.	Scholastic
Baby-Sitters Club Mystery: Kristy, Missing Child	O	RF	250+	Martin, Ann M.	Scholastic
Baby-Sitters Club Mystery: Kristy, Missing Fortune	O	RF	250+	Martin, Ann M.	Scholastic
Baby-Sitters Club Mystery: Kristy, Vampires	O	RF	250+	Martin, Ann M.	Scholastic
Baby-Sitters Club Mystery: Mallory, Ghost Cat	O	RF	250+	Martin, Ann M.	Scholastic
Baby-Sitters Club Mystery: Mary Anne, Library Mystery	O	RF	250+	Martin, Ann M.	Scholastic
Baby-Sitters Club Mystery: Mary Anne, Secret in the Attic	O	RF	250+	Martin, Ann M.	Scholastic
Baby-Sitters Club Mystery: Mary Anne, Zoo Mystery	O	RF	250+	Martin, Ann M.	Scholastic
Baby-Sitters Club Mystery: Mystery at Claudia's House	O	RF	250+	Martin, Ann M.	Scholastic
Baby-Sitters Club Mystery: Stacey and the Mystery Money	O	RF	250+	Martin, Ann M.	Scholastic
Baby-Sitters Club Mystery: Stacey, Haunted Masquerade	O	RF	250+	Martin, Ann M.	Scholastic
Baby-Sitters Club Mystery: Stacey, Missing Ring	O	RF	250+	Martin, Ann M.	Scholastic
Baby-Sitters Club Mystery: Stacey, Mystery at the Empty House	O	RF	250+	Martin, Ann M.	Scholastic
Baby-Sitters Club Mystery: Stacey, Mystery at the Mall	O	RF	250+	Martin, Ann M.	Scholastic
Baby-Sitters Club Special Edition, The: Readers' Request	O	RF	250+	Martin, Ann M.	Scholastic
Baby-Sitters Club: Abby and the Best Kid Ever	O	RF	250+	Martin, Ann M.	Scholastic
Baby-Sitters Club: Abby, the Bad Sport	O	RF	250+	Martin, Ann M.	Scholastic
Baby-Sitters Club: Claudia and the Bad Joke	O	RF	250+	Martin, Ann M.	Scholastic
Baby-Sitters Club: Claudia and the Little Liar	O	RF	250+	Martin, Ann M.	Scholastic
Baby-Sitters Club: Claudia and the New Girl	O	RF	250+	Martin, Ann M.	Scholastic
Baby-Sitters Club: Claudia and the Phantom Phone Calls	O	RF	250+	Martin, Ann M.	Scholastic
Baby-Sitters Club: Dawn and Too Many Sitters	O	RF	250+	Martin, Ann M.	Scholastic
Baby-Sitters Club: Dawn's Big Move	O	RF	250+	Martin, Ann M.	Scholastic
Baby-Sitters Club: Dawn's Wicked Stepsister	O	RF	250+	Martin, Ann M.	Scholastic
Baby-Sitters Club: Get Well Soon, Mallory	O	RF	250+	Martin, Ann M.	Scholastic
Baby-Sitters Club: Ghost at Dawn's House, The	O	RF	250+	Martin, Ann M.	Scholastic
Baby-Sitters Club: Good-bye Stacey, Good-bye	O	RF	250+	Martin, Ann M.	Scholastic
Baby-Sitters Club: Hello, Mallory	O	RF	250+	Martin, Ann M.	Scholastic
Baby-Sitters Club: Jessi and the Bad Baby-Sitter	O	RF	250+	Martin, Ann M.	Scholastic
Baby-Sitters Club: Jessi and the Superbrat	O	RF	250+	Martin, Ann M.	Scholastic
Baby-Sitters Club: Jessi Ramsey, Pet-sitter	O	RF	250+	Martin, Ann M.	Scholastic
Baby-Sitters Club: Kristy and the Snobs	O	RF	250+	Martin, Ann M.	Scholastic
Baby-Sitters Club: Kristy's Big Day	O	RF	250+	Martin, Ann M.	Scholastic
Baby-Sitters Club: Kristy's Great Idea	O	RF	250+	Martin, Ann M.	Scholastic
Baby-Sitters Club: Mary Anne and Camp BSC	O	RF	250+	Martin, Ann M.	Scholastic
Baby-Sitters Club: Mary Anne Saves the Day	O	RF	250+	Martin, Ann M.	Scholastic
Baby-Sitters Club: Welcome to the BSC, Abby	O	RF	250+	Martin, Ann M.	Scholastic
Baby-Sitter's Little Sister	O	RF	250+	Martin, Ann M.	Scholastic
Baby-Sitter's Little Sister : Karen's Accident	O	RF	250+	Martin, Ann M.	Scholastic
Baby-Sitter's Little Sister : Karen's Big Fight	O	RF	250+	Martin, Ann M.	Scholastic
Baby-Sitter's Little Sister : Karen's Big Sister	O	RF	250+	Martin, Ann M.	Scholastic

* Collection of short stories

TITLE	LEVEL	GENRE	WORD COUNT	AUTHOR / SERIES	PUBLISHER / DISTRIBUTOR
Baby-Sitter's Little Sister : Karen's Copycat	O	RF	250+	Martin, Ann M.	Scholastic
Baby-Sitter's Little Sister : Karen's Dinosaur	O	RF	250+	Martin, Ann M.	Scholastic
Baby-Sitter's Little Sister : Karen's Monsters	O	RF	250+	Martin, Ann M.	Scholastic
Baby-Sitter's Little Sister: Karen's Campout	O	RF	250+	Martin, Ann M.	Scholastic
Baby-Sitter's Little Sister: Karen's Mystery, Super Special	O	RF	250+	Martin, Ann M.	Scholastic
Baby-Sitter's Little Sister: Karen's Nanny	O	RF	250+	Martin, Ann M.	Scholastic
Baby-Sitter's Little Sister: Karen's Stepmother	O	RF	250+	Martin, Ann M.	Scholastic
Baby-Sitter's Little Sister: Karen's Two Families	O	RF	250+	Martin, Ann M.	Scholastic
Baby-Snatcher	Z	RF	250+	Terris, Susan	Scholastic
Back and Forth	E	I	54	Pebble Books	Capstone Press
Back Home	O	RF	250+	Pinkney, Gloria Jean	Penguin Group
Back To The Day Lincoln Was Shot!	S	I	250+	Gormley, Beatrice	Scholastic
Back to the Dentist	M	RF	199	City Kids	Rigby
Back To The Titanic!	S	F	250+	Gormley, Beatrice	Scholastic
Backhoes	J	I	118	Pebble Plus	Capstone Press
Backstage	I	I	250+	Twig	Wright Group/McGraw Hill
Backward Bird Dog, The	R	F	250+	Wallace, Bill	Bantam
Backyard Angel	O	RF	250+	Delton, Judy	Houghton Mifflin
Backyard Camp-Out	L	RF	628	Leveled Readers	Houghton Mifflin
Backyard Hunter: The Praying Mantis	P	I	250+	Lavies, Bianca	Penguin Group
Backyard Zoo	G	I	167	Ready Readers	Pearson Learning Group
Bacon Saturday Mornings	K	RF	365	Books for Young Learners	Richard C. Owen
Bad Beginning, The	V	F	250+	Snicket, Lemony	HarperTrophy
Bad Boy, Billy	G	RF	129	Cambridge Reading	Pearson Learning Group
Bad Dad List, The	M	RF	250+	Kenna, Anna	Pacific Learning
Bad Day for Ballet	N	RF	250+	Keene, Carolyn	Pocket Books
Bad Day for Benjamin, A	L	RF	250+	Reading Unlimited	Pearson Learning Group
Bad Day, The	D	RF	93	Teacher's Choice Series	Pearson Learning Group
Bad Dream, The	E	RF	88	Teacher's Choice Series	Pearson Learning Group
Bad Girls	U	RF	250+	Voigt, Cynthia	Scholastic
Bad Hair Day	E	RF	113	Teacher's Choice Series	Pearson Learning Group
Bad Luck of King Fred, The	O	F	250+	Literacy Tree	Rigby
Bad Spell for the Worst Witch, A	P	F	250+	Murphy, Jill	Puffin Books
Bad, Badder, Baddest	U	RF	250+	Voigt, Cynthia	Scholastic
Badger in the Basement	Q	RF	250+	Daniels, Lucy	Barron's Educational
Badgers	L	I	250+	Bridgestone Books	Capstone Press
Bad-Luck Penny, The	L	F	250+	O'Connor, Jane	Grosset & Dunlap
Bagels for Kids	O	I	250+	Pacific Literacy	Pacific Learning
Bags, Cans, Pots, and Pans	C	RF	56	Ready Readers	Pearson Learning Group
*Bake a Cake and other stories	C	RF	94	Story Steps	Rigby
Baked Beans	K	I	221	Lighthouse	Rigby
Baked Potatoes	D	RF	73	Book Bank	Wright Group/McGraw Hill
Bakers	M	I	250+	Deedrick, Tami	Red Brick Learning
Baking	D	I	27	Harry's Math Books	Outside the Box
Baking a Cake	LB	I	7	Windows on Literacy	National Geographic
Baking Bread	L	I	426	How-To Series	Benchmark Education
Baking Bread	F	I	70	Windows on Literacy	National Geographic
Baking Day	C	F	35	Windmill Books	Rigby
Balancing	C	I	46	Twig	Wright Group/McGraw Hill
Balcony Garden	G	I	258	Storyteller Nonfiction	Wright Group/McGraw Hill
Bald Bandit, The	N	RF	250+	Roy, Ron	Random House
Bald Eagle Free Again!, The	P	I	250+	Young Readers' Series	Barron's Educational
Bald Eagle Is Back, The	W	I	2691	Leveled Readers	Houghton Mifflin

* Collection of short stories

TITLE	LEVEL	GENRE	WORD COUNT	AUTHOR / SERIES	PUBLISHER / DISTRIBUTOR
Bald Eagle, The	N	I	250+	American Symbols	Capstone Press
Bald Eagle, The	R	I	250+	Potts, Steve	Red Brick Learning
Bald Eagle, The	N	I	250+	A True Book	Children's Press
Bald Eagles	Q	I	250+	Action Packs	Rigby
Ball Bounced, The	D	F	33	Tafuri, Nancy	Morrow
Ball Game	B	RF	16	Literacy 2000	Rigby
Ball Game, A	D	I	72	Carousel Readers	Pearson Learning Group
Ball Game, The	E	RF	45	Packard, David	Scholastic
Ball Games	B	RF	44	PM Starters	Rigby
Ball, The	C	RF	40	KinderReaders	Rigby
Ballad of Robin Hood, The	P	HF	250+	Literacy 2000	Rigby
Ballad of the Civil War, A	T	HF	250+	Stolz, Mary	HarperTrophy
Ballerina Girl	D	RF	77	My First Reader	Grolier Press
Balloon Ride	A	F	32	Early Connections	Benchmark Education
Balloon, The	D	F	64	Carousel Readers	Pearson Learning Group
Balloons	I	I	211	Independent Readers Science	Houghton Mifflin
Balloons	B	I	55	Early Emergent	Pioneer Valley
Balloons	M	I	57	iOpeners	Pearson Learning Group
Balloons	WB	RF	N/A	Rigby Literacy	Rigby
Balloons	B	RF	57	PM Plus Starters	Rigby
Balloons!	D	F	56	Storyteller-First Snow	Wright Group/McGraw Hill
Balloons, The	LB	RF	19	Sunshine	Wright Group/McGraw Hill
Balls	C	I	33	Windows on Literacy	National Geographic
Ballyhoo!	F	F	124	Story Basket	Wright Group/McGraw Hill
Balto and the Great Race	P	RF	250+	Kimmel, Elizabeth Cody	Random House
Bambi: A Life in the Woods	T	F	250+	Salten, Felix	Aladdin
Banana Monster, The	D	F	54	Joy Readers	Pearson Learning Group
Banana Shake	C	RF	44	Book Bank	Wright Group/McGraw Hill
Band of Brave Men, A	X	I	250+	iOpeners	Pearson Learning Group
Band, The	C	RF	31	Voyages	SRA/McGraw Hill
Band, The	C	I	33	Sun Sprouts	ETA/Cuisenaire
Bandages	F	F	139	Moskowitz, Ellen	Kaeden Books
Bandit Moon	V	HF	250+	Fleischman, Sid	Dell Yearling
Bang	F	F	55	Literacy 2000	Rigby
Banished, The	W	F	250+	Levin, Betty	William Morrow
*Bank Robbery and Jack and the Beanstalk, The	L	TL	250+	New Way Literature	Steck-Vaughn
Bank Tellers	M	I	250+	Community Workers	Compass Point Books
Barbara Esbensen: Words into Pictures	R	B	1043	Leveled Readers	Houghton Mifflin
Barbara McClintock	V	B	1926	Independent Readers Science	Houghton Mifflin
Barbecue, The	LB	RF	14	Sunshine	Wright Group/McGraw Hill
Bare Feet	B	RF	40	Visions	Wright Group/McGraw Hill
Barefoot: Escape on the Underground Railroad	S	HF	250+	Edwards, Pamela Duncan	HarperTrophy
Bargain For Frances, A	K	F	250+	Hoban, Russell	HarperTrophy
Bargains for Everyone	P	RF	1025	Leveled Readers	Houghton Mifflin
Barn Dance	C	F	47	Story Box	Wright Group/McGraw Hill
Barn Dance, The	B	RF	46	Leveled Readers Emergent	Houghton Mifflin
Barn Party	K	F	250+	O'Brien, Claire	Wright Group/McGraw Hill
Barn, The	T	RF	250+	Avi	Avon
Barnaby Bullfrog	F	F	121	Seedlings	Continental Press
Barnaby's Birthday	J	RF	214	Voyages	SRA/McGraw Hill
Barnaby's New House, The	G	RF	135	Literacy 2000	Rigby
Barney	P	RF	250+	Literacy 2000	Rigby
Barney Bear Gets Dressed	D	F	38	Learn to Read	Creative Teaching Press
Barney Bear, World Traveler	H	F	65	Learn to Read	Creative Teaching Press

* Collection of short stories

TITLE	LEVEL	GENRE	WORD COUNT	AUTHOR / SERIES	PUBLISHER / DISTRIBUTOR
Barney's Horse	I	HF	250+	Hoff, Syd	HarperTrophy
Barney's Lovely Lunch	K	RF	330	Windmill Books	Rigby
Barnyard Baseball	C	F	19	Pair-It Books	Steck-Vaughn
Barnyard Math with Farmer Fred	G	RF	139	Learn to Read	Creative Teaching Press
Barnyard Song	F	TL	196	PM Readalongs	Rigby
Baron: Rescue Dog	I	RF	120	Books for Young Learners	Richard C. Owen
Barrel in the Basement, The	R	F	250+	Wallace, Barbara Brooks	Aladdin
Barrel of Gold, A	K	F	251	Story Box	Wright Group/McGraw Hill
Barry and Bennie	H	F	251	Little Celebrations	Pearson Learning Group
Bart's Amazing Charts	N	RF	250+	Ochiltree, Dianne	Scholastic
Baseball	B	RF	14	Sunshine	Wright Group/McGraw Hill
Baseball Ballerina	J	RF	250+	Cristaldi, Kathryn	Random House
Baseball Birthday Party, The	J	RF	250+	Prager, Annabelle	Random House
Baseball Fever	O	RF	250+	Hurwitz, Johanna	William Morrow
Baseball Flyhawk	M	RF	250+	Christopher, Matt	Little, Brown & Co.
Baseball for Fun	S	I	250+	Sports for Fun	Compass Point Books
Baseball Fun	E	RF	51	Geddes, Diana	Kaeden Books
Baseball Game, The	I	F	211	Foundations	Wright Group/McGraw Hill
Baseball Heroes, The	M	RF	250+	Schultz, Irene	Wright Group/McGraw Hill
*Baseball in April and Other Stories	U	RF	250+	Soto, Gary	Harcourt Trade
Baseball in the Barrios	P	I	250+	Horenstein, Henry	Harcourt Trade
Baseball Math	N	I	250+	Early Connections	Benchmark Education
Baseball Megastars	O	I	250+	Weber, Bruce	Scholastic
Baseball Pals	M	RF	250+	Christopher, Matt	Little, Brown & Co.
*Baseball Pitching Challenge and Other Cases, The	O	RF	250+	Simon, Seymour	Avon
Baseball Saved Us	O	HF	250+	Mochizuki, Ken	Scholastic
*Baseball's Best: Five True Stories	O	B	250+	Step into Reading	Random House
*Baseball's Greatest Pitchers	P	B	250+	Kramer, S. A.	Random House
Basket Counts, The	M	RF	250+	Christopher, Matt	Little, Brown & Co.
Basket Full of Surprises, A	B	RF	43	Little Books	Sadlier-Oxford
Basket of Beethoven	S	RF	250+	Currie, Susan	Fitzhenry & Whiteside
Basketball	I	I	159	Ready Readers	Pearson Learning Group
Basketball	B	I	20	Wonder World	Wright Group/McGraw Hill
Basketball	C	RF	23	Visions	Wright Group/McGraw Hill
Basketball for Fun	S	I	250+	Sports for Fun	Compass Point Books
Basketball Game, The	L	RF	607	Leveled Readers Science	Houghton Mifflin
Bat 6	Z	HF	250+	Wolff, Virginia Euwer	Scholastic
Bat Bones and Spider Stew	K	RF	250+	Poploff, Michelle	Bantam
Bath Day for Brutus	K	RF	347	Little Red Readers	Sundance
Bath for a Beagle	D	RF	102	First Start	Troll Associates
Bath for Patches, A	E	RF	89	Carousel Readers	Pearson Learning Group
Bath Time	C	I	23	Wonder World	Wright Group/McGraw Hill
Bath Time	B	I	44	Bebop Books	Lee & Low Books Inc.
Bath, The	LB	RF	14	Ready Readers	Pearson Learning Group
Bath, The	B	RF	28	Smart Starts	Rigby
Bat-Poet, The	S	F	250+	Jarrell, Randall	HarperCollins
Bats	M	I	250+	PM Animal Facts: Gold	Rigby
Bats	O	I	250+	Gibbons, Gail	Holiday House
Bats	O	I	250+	Holmes, Kevin J.	Red Brick Learning
Bats	P	I	250+	Literacy 2000	Rigby
Bats	I	I	162	Phonics Readers	Compass Point Books
Bats and Burglars	N	RF	250+	First Flight	Fitzhenry & Whiteside
Bats at Bat	D	F	36	Pair-It Books	Steck-Vaughn

* Collection of short stories

TITLE	LEVEL	GENRE	WORD COUNT	AUTHOR / SERIES	PUBLISHER / DISTRIBUTOR
Bat's Night Out	L	RF	172	Books for Young Learners	Richard C. Owen
Bats Out the Window	O	RF	250+	First Flight	Fitzhenry & Whiteside
Bats, Bats, Bats	E	I	33	Pair-It Books	Steck-Vaughn
Bats, Bats, Bats	D	I	29	Rosen Real Readers	Rosen Publishing Group
Bats, The	C	I	21	Twig	Wright Group/McGraw Hill
Bats: The Amazing Upside-Downers	S	I	250+	A First Book	Franklin Watts
Batter Up	G	RF	183	Adventures in Reading	Pearson Learning Group
Batter Up	C	I	8	Bebop Books	Lee & Low Books Inc.
Batter Up!	C	RF	39	Bookshop	Mondo
Batteries	G	I	105	Early Connections	Benchmark Education
Battle for Iwo Jima, The	W	I	250+	Cornerstones of Freedom	Children's Press
Battle for Survival, The	P	I	250+	Sunshine	Wright Group/McGraw Hill
Battle for the Castle, The	P	F	250+	Winthrop, Elizabeth	Yearling
Battle of Chancellorsville, The	V	I	250+	Cornerstones of Freedom	Children's Press
Battle of Leyte, The	U	I	974	Leveled Readers Social Studies	Houghton Mifflin
Battle of the Alamo, The	V	I	250+	Cornerstones of Freedom	Children's Press
Battle of the Little Bighorn, The	V	I	250+	Cornerstones of Freedom	Children's Press
Battle of Words, A	O	RF	250+	Literacy 2000	Rigby
Battle of Yorktown, The	V	I	250+	Let Freedom Ring	Red Brick Learning
Battles of Lexington & Concord, The	T	I	250+	We The People	Compass Point Books
Battles of Lexington and Concord, The	V	I	250+	Let Freedom Ring	Red Brick Learning
Battleships	T	I	250+	Land and Sea	Capstone Press
Bay Run, The	C	RF	80	Foundations	Wright Group/McGraw Hill
Be a Clown	C	I	29	The Candid Collection	Pearson Learning Group
Be a Good Friend!	J	I	250+	Spyglass Books	Compass Point Books
Be a Good Sport!	J	I	250+	Spyglass Books	Compass Point Books
Be A Perfect Person In Just Three Days!	N	RF	250+	Manes, Stephen	Dell
Be a Plant Scientist	L	I	250+	Paul, Michele	Wright Group/McGraw Hill
Be Careful, Matthew!	F	RF	80	Sunshine	Wright Group/McGraw Hill
Be Quiet	B	RF	25	Smart Starts	Rigby
Be Quiet	A	RF	25	Literacy 2000	Rigby
Be Ready at Eight	K	F	250+	Parish, Peggy	Simon & Schuster
Be Safe on Your Bike	J	I	250+	Rosen Real Readers	Rosen Publishing Group
Beach Creatures	H	I	231	Pair-It Books	Steck-Vaughn
Beach House, The	F	RF	164	PM Plus Story Books	Rigby
Beach, The	D	RF	38	Book Bank	Wright Group/McGraw Hill
Beach, The	A	I	16	Little Celebrations	Pearson Learning Group
Beacons of Light: Lighthouses	O	I	250+	Gibbons, Gail	Scholastic
Beads	C	I	16	Instant Readers	Harcourt School Publishers
Beak Book, The	D	I	48	Chanko, Pamela	Scholastic
Beaks	G	I	125	Discovery Links	Newbridge
Beaks and Feet	J	I	234	Alphakids	Sundance
Bean	N	I	250+	Life Cycles	Creative Teaching Press
Bean Bag That Mom Made, The	I	RF	270	Tadpoles	Rigby
Beanbag	K	RF	250+	Literacy 2000	Rigby
Beans	B	I	35	Pebble Books	Capstone Press
Beans on the Roof	L	RF	250+	Byars, Betsy	Bantam
Bear and the Bees, The	J	TL	250+	PM Plus Story Books	Rigby
Bear and the Trolls, The	L	TL	250+	PM Tales and Plays-Silver	Rigby
Bear at the Beach	K	F	250+	Carmichael, Clay	North-South Books
Bear Called Paddington, A	T	F	250+	Bond, Michael	Bantam
Bear Collection, The	N	I	250+	PM Ruby	Rigby
Bear Eats Fish, A	C	I	44	Windows on Literacy	National Geographic
Bear Escape, The	D	F	42	Pair-It Books	Steck-Vaughn

* Collection of short stories

TITLE	LEVEL	GENRE	WORD COUNT	AUTHOR / SERIES	PUBLISHER / DISTRIBUTOR
Bear Facts	E	I	41	Pair-It Books	Steck-Vaughn
Bear For Miguel, A	K	RF	250+	Alphin, Elaine Marie	HarperTrophy
Bear Goes to Town	K	F	250+	Browne, Anthony	Doubleday Books
Bear Hunt	F	RF	146	Lighthouse	Rigby
Bear Lived in a Cave, A	D	I	102	Little Red Readers	Sundance
Bear Needs a Place to Climb, A	B	I	49	Independent Readers Science	Houghton Mifflin
Bear Shadow	J	F	489	Asch, Frank	Simon & Schuster
Bear That Heard Crying, The	P	HF	250+	Kinsey-Warnock, Natalie; Kinsey, Helen	Penguin Group
Bear, The	LB	I	17	Carousel Earlybirds	Pearson Learning Group
Bear, The	M	I	250+	Life Cycles	Steck-Vaughn
Bear, The: An American Folk Song	K	F	250+	Bookshop	Mondo
Bears	B	I	59	Storyteller Nonfiction	Wright Group/McGraw Hill
Bears	P	I	3286	Leveled Readers Science	Houghton Mifflin
Bears	O	I	59	Holmes, Kevin J.	Red Brick Learning
Bears	D	F	56	Joy Readers	Pearson Learning Group
Bears and the Magpie, The	G	F	205	PM Plus Story Books	Rigby
Bears and Their Dens	J	I	131	Animal Homes	Capstone Press
Bears are Curious	J	I	250+	Milton, Joyce	Random House
Bear's Ball	A	F	32	Sun Sprouts	ETA/Cuisenaire
Bear's Bargain	J	F	250+	Asch, Frank	Scholastic
Bear's Bicycle, The	I	F	185	McLeod, Emilie	Little, Brown & Co.
Bear's Christmas	M	F	250+	Berenstain, Stan & Jan	Random House
Bear's Diet	L	RF	652	PM Gold	Rigby
Bears Have Cubs	M	I	250+	Animals and Their Young	Compass Point Books
Bears' House, The	T	RF	250+	Sachs, Marilyn	Puffin Books
Bears in the Night	D	F	108	Berenstain, Stan & Jan	Random House
Bears On Hemlock Mountain, The	M	RF	250+	Dalgliesh, Alice	Aladdin
Bears on Wheels	D	F	89	Berenstain, Stan & Jan	Random House
Bears' Picnic	M	F	250+	Berenstain, Stan & Jan	Random House
Bears' Picnic, The	D	F	61	Story Box	Wright Group/McGraw Hill
Bear's Tale, The	H	TL	155	Books for Young Learners	Richard C. Owen
Bear's Year, A	J	I	213	Phonics Readers	Compass Point Books
Bears, Bears Everywhere	D	F	52	Rookie Readers	Children's Press
Bears, Bears, Bears	I	F	250+	Little Readers	Houghton Mifflin
Bears, Bears, Bears	E	F	250+	Story Steps	Rigby
Bears, Bears, Bears	D	RF	76	Step-By-Step Series	Pearson Learning Group
Bears, Bears, Everywhere	E	F	67	Learn to Read	Creative Teaching Press
Bearstone	V	RF	250+	Hobbs, Will	Hearst
Beast	X	F	250+	Napoli, Donna Jo	Atheneum
Beast and the Halloween Horror	M	RF	250+	Giff, Patricia Reilly	Bantam
Beast in Ms. Rooney's Room, The	M	RF	250+	Giff, Patricia Reilly	Bantam
Beat This	D	RF	79	Ready Readers	Pearson Learning Group
Beating Diabetes	S	I	250+	Orbit Double Takes	Pacific Learning
Beating the Drought	M	RF	250+	Noonan, Diana	Pacific Learning
Beating the Heat, Desert Style	W	I	1874	Leveled Readers	Houghton Mifflin
Beatles, The	N	B	250+	Venezia, Mike	Children's Press
Beatrix Potter	O	B	250+	Wallner, Alexandra	Holiday House
Beatrix Potter	J	B	135	iOpeners	Pearson Learning Group
Beauregard the Cat	M	RF	250+	Bookshop	Mondo
Beautiful Bugs	E	I	70	Fleming, Maria	Scholastic
Beautiful Flowers	B	I	28	Wonder World	Wright Group/McGraw Hill
Beautiful Land: A Story of the Oklahoma Land Rush	S	I	250+	Antle, Nancy	Penguin Group

* Collection of short stories

TITLE	LEVEL	GENRE	WORD COUNT	AUTHOR / SERIES	PUBLISHER / DISTRIBUTOR
Beautiful Pig	J	F	423	Read Alongs	Rigby
Beauty	V	RF	250+	Wallace, Bill	Holiday House
Beauty and the Beast	K	TL	250+	Sunshine	Wright Group/McGraw Hill
Beauty and the Beast	K	TL	250+	PM Tales and Plays-Gold	Rigby
Beaver Engineers	N	I	250+	Reeder, Tracey	Wright Group/McGraw Hill
Beaver Tale, A	E	I	228	Twig	Wright Group/McGraw Hill
Beaver, The	M	I	250+	Crewe, Sabrina	Steck-Vaughn
Beavers	N	I	250+	Bookshop	Mondo
Beavers and Their Lodges	J	I	121	Pebble Plus	Capstone Press
Beavers Beware!	K	I	250+	Bank Street	Bantam
Because a Little Bug Went Ka-Choo	I	F	250+	Stone, Rosetta	Random House
Because Daddy Did My Hair	I	RF	214	Teacher's Choice Series	Pearson Learning Group
Because I'm Little	B	RF	51	Home Connection Collection	Rigby
Because of Walter	N	RF	250+	Action Packs	Rigby
Because of Winn-Dixie	R	RF	250+	DiCamillo, Kate	Candlewick Press
Becoming a Butterfly	H	I	83	Rosen Real Readers	Rosen Publishing Group
Becoming a Citizen	P	I	209	Vocabulary Readers	Houghton Mifflin
Becoming A Real Hero	T	B	1650	Leveled Readers	Houghton Mifflin
Becoming Joe DiMaggio	T	HF	250+	Testa, Maria	Candlewick Press
Bed Rest	E	I	34	Rhythm 'N' Rhyme Readers	Pearson Learning Group
Beds	C	I	44	Interaction	Rigby
Bedtime	C	RF	83	PM Plus Story Books	Rigby
Bedtime	C	RF	23	Books for Young Learners	Richard C. Owen
Bedtime at Aunt Carmen's	K	RF	250	Ready Readers	Pearson Learning Group
Bedtime for Bear	C	F	12	Instant Readers	Harcourt School Publishers
Bedtime for Frances	K	F	250+	Hoban, Russell	Scholastic
Bedtime Fun	B	RF	46	Bebop Books	Lee & Low Books Inc.
Bedtime Story, A	K	RF	250+	Bookshop	Mondo
Bee My Valentine!	H	RF	250+	Cohen, Miriam	Bantam
Bee, The	C	RF	26	Story Box	Wright Group/McGraw Hill
Bee, The	M	I	250+	Crewe, Sabrina	Steck-Vaughn
Beekeeper, The	M	I	250+	Literacy 2000	Rigby
Beeman Interview	N	F	250+	Sails	Rigby
Beep, Beep	F	F	51	Start to Read	School Zone
Beep, Beep, Beep	D	F	86	Foundations	Wright Group/McGraw Hill
Bees	N	I	250+	Nature's Friends	Compass Point Books
Bees	O	I	250+	Holmes, Kevin J.	Red Brick Learning
Bees	N	I	250+	A True Book	Children's Press
Bees and Their Hives	J	I	112	Animal Homes	Capstone Press
Bees Buzzed, The	B	RF	41	Science	Outside the Box
Bee's Home, A	K	I	127	Salem, Lynn	Continental Press
Bees on Trees	H	F	250+	Sunshine	Wright Group/McGraw Hill
Beethoven Lives Upstairs	S	I	250+	Nichol, Barbara	Orchard Books
Beetles	C	I	36	Science	Outside the Box
Beetles	N	I	250+	Minibeasts	Franklin Watts
Beetles	D	I	39	Pebble Books	Capstone Press
Beetles, Lightly Toasted	Q	RF	250+	Naylor, Phyllis Reynolds	Bantam
Beezus & Ramona	O	RF	250+	Cleary, Beverly	Avon
Before I Go to School	B	I	71	Storyteller-First Snow	Wright Group/McGraw Hill
Before the Fridge	G	I	88	Seedlings	Continental Press
Beginnings of Sports	R	I	250+	PM Nonfiction-Ruby	Rigby
Behind Rebel Lines	T	HF	250+	Reit, Seymour	Harcourt Trade
Behind The Bedroom Wall	V	HF	250+	Williams, Laura E.	Milkweed Editions
Behind the Couch	N	F	250+	Gerstein, Mordicai	Hyperion

TITLE	LEVEL	GENRE	WORD COUNT	AUTHOR / SERIES	PUBLISHER / DISTRIBUTOR
Behind the Rocks	E	RF	50	Wonder World	Wright Group/McGraw Hill
Behind the Scenes	R	I	250+	Literacy 2000	Rigby
Behind the Scenes with Sammy	N	I	250+	Little Celebrations	Pearson Learning Group
Being Danny's Dog	U	RF	250+	Naylor, Phyllis Reynolds	Aladdin
Being Friends	C	I	21	Rosen Real Readers	Rosen Publishing Group
Bell, the Book, and the Spellbinder, The	S	F	250+	Strickland, Brad	Puffin Books
Bella and Rosie Play Hide and Seek	D	RF	118	Bella and Rosie Series	Pioneer Valley
Bella Is a Bad Dog	H	RF	132	Bella and Rosie Series	Pioneer Valley
Bella's Birthday	C	RF	59	Bella and Rosie Series	Pioneer Valley
Belle Prater's Boy	V	RF	250+	White, Ruth	Bantam
Below the Green Pond	N	I	250+	Read All About It	Steck-Vaughn
Ben and Me	S	HF	250+	Lawson, Robert	Little, Brown & Co.
Ben and the Bear	I	F	250+	Riddell, Chris	Harper & Row
Ben and the Cold	C	RF	76	Sun Sprouts	ETA/Cuisenaire
Ben at the Theme Park	F	RF	214	Sun Sprouts	ETA/Cuisenaire
Ben Ate It	E	RF	130	Teacher's Choice Series	Pearson Learning Group
Ben Franklin of Old Philadelphia	U	B	250+	Cousins, Margaret	Random House
Ben Franklin Remembers	P	B	493	Vocabulary Readers	Houghton Mifflin
Ben Franklin: Scientist	J	I	266	Leveled Readers Science	Houghton Mifflin
Ben Franklin's Fire Company	I	I	147	Leveled Readers Language Support	Houghton Mifflin
Ben Lost a Tooth	E	I	31	iOpeners	Pearson Learning Group
Ben Runs	C	RF	66	Sun Sprouts	ETA/Cuisenaire
Ben the Bold	C	RF	71	Literacy 2000	Rigby
Bend and Stretch: Learning About Your Bones and Muscles	M	I	250+	Amazing Body	Picture Window Books
Bend, Stretch, and Leap	J	RF	250+	PM Plus Story Books	Rigby
Beneath Earth's Surface	O	I	250+	Rosen Real Readers	Rosen Publishing Group
Benedict Arnold at Saratoga	Y	HF	2151	Leveled Readers	Houghton Mifflin
Benjamin Banneker: An American Scientist	K	B	374	Leveled Readers Science	Houghton Mifflin
Benjamin Franklin	U	B	250+	Kent, Deborah	Scholastic
Benjamin Franklin	N	B	250+	Pebble Books	Capstone Press
Benjamin Franklin	N	B	250+	Biography	Benchmark Education
Benjamin Franklin: A Man with Many Jobs	O	B	250+	Greene, Carol	Children's Press
Benjamin Franklin: A Scientist by Nature	X	B	2095	Leveled Readers	Houghton Mifflin
Benjamin Franklin: American Inventor	N	B	250+	Rosen Real Readers	Rosen Publishing Group
Benjamin Franklin: Writer, Inventor, Statesman	M	B	250+	Biographies	Picture Window Books
Benjamin Franklin: Young Printer	R	B	250+	Stevenson, Augusta	Aladdin
Benjamin Harrison	U	B	250+	Profiles of the Presidents	Compass Point Books
Benji's Pup	I	RF	439	Evangeline Nicholas Collection	Wright Group/McGraw Hill
Bennie	A	RF	29	Ray's Readers	Outside the Box
Benny Bakes a Cake	I	RF	250+	Rice, Eve	Greenwillow
Benny's Baby Brother	E	RF	89	Start to Read	School Zone
Benny's School Trip	G	RF	217	Pair-It Books	Steck-Vaughn
Ben's Amazing Birthday	L	RF	250+	Cambridge Reading	Pearson Learning Group
Ben's Banana	C	F	60	Foundations	Wright Group/McGraw Hill
Ben's Bath	C	RF	56	Sun Sprouts	ETA/Cuisenaire
Ben's Colors	C	RF	75	Sun Sprouts	ETA/Cuisenaire
Ben's Dad	E	RF	102	PM Story Books	Rigby
Ben's Dream	WB	F	N/A	Van Allsburg, Chris	Houghton Mifflin
Ben's Fun Box	D	RF	63	New Way Red	Steck-Vaughn
Ben's New Trick	F	RF	219	Ready Readers	Pearson Learning Group
Ben's Pets	C	RF	30	Ready Readers	Pearson Learning Group
Ben's Red Car	B	RF	49	PM Starters	Rigby

* Collection of short stories

TITLE	LEVEL	GENRE	WORD COUNT	AUTHOR / SERIES	PUBLISHER / DISTRIBUTOR
Ben's Teddy Bear	D	RF	68	PM Story Books	Rigby
Ben's Tooth	H	RF	197	PM Story Books	Rigby
Ben's Treasure Hunt	D	RF	72	PM Story Books	Rigby
Ben's Tune	N	RF	250+	PM Ruby	Rigby
*Beowulf	U	TL	250+	Literacy 2000	Rigby
Berenstain Bear Scouts and the Coughing Catfish	M	F	250+	Berenstain, Stan & Jan	Scholastic
Berenstain Bear Scouts, The: Ghost Versus Ghost	M	F	250+	Berenstain, Stan & Jan	Scholastic
Berenstain Bears and the Ghost of the Auto Graveyard, The	M	F	250+	Berenstain, Stan & Jan	Random House
Berenstain Bears and the Missing Honey	M	F	531	Berenstain, Stan & Jan	Random House
Berlin Wall, The	V	I	2050	Independent Readers Social Studies	Houghton Mifflin
Berlioz The Bear	N	F	250+	Brett, Jan	Scholastic
Bermuda Triangle, The	Q	I	250+	The Unexplained	Capstone Press
Bermuda Triangle, The	Z	I	250+	Innes, Brian	Steck-Vaughn
Bernardo de Gálvez	W	B	1818	Leveled Readers	Houghton Mifflin
Berta: A Remarkable Dog	N	RF	250+	Lottridge, Celia Barker	Groundwood Books
Bertie the Bear	I	F	250+	Allen, Pamela	Coward
Bessie Coleman	O	B	250+	Brager, Bruce	Scholastic
Bessie Coleman: Queen of the Sky	K	B	229	Sunshine	Wright Group/McGraw Hill
Bess's Log Cabin Quilt	P	HF	250+	Love, D. Anne	Bantam
Best Friends	WB	RF	N/A	Books for Young Learners	Richard C. Owen
Best Bad Thing, The	T	RF	250+	Uchida, Yoshiko	Aladdin
Best Birthday Gift Ever, The	I	RF	249	Talking Point Series	Pearson Learning Group
Best Birthday Mole Ever Had, The	E	F	252	Ready Readers	Pearson Learning Group
Best Birthday Present, The	K	RF	250+	Literacy 2000	Rigby
Best Boat, The	J	I	690	Leveled Readers Science	Houghton Mifflin
Best Book for Terry Lee, The	I	RF	250+	Literacy Tree	Rigby
Best Cake, The	F	RF	162	PM Story Books	Rigby
Best Car For Us, The	I	I	161	Windows on Literacy	National Geographic
Best Children in the World, The	F	F	148	Story Box	Wright Group/McGraw Hill
Best Class Trip, The	F	RF	214	Leveled Readers	Houghton Mifflin
Best Clown in Town, The	L	RF	250+	Bradley, Tom	Pearson Learning Group
Best Detective, The	N	RF	250+	Keene, Carolyn	Pocket Books
Best Dog in the Whole World, The	K	RF	250+	Sunshine	Wright Group/McGraw Hill
Best Enemies	P	RF	250+	Leverich, Kathleen	Beech Tree Books
Best Enemies Again	P	RF	250+	Leverich, Kathleen	Alfred A. Knopf
Best Enemies Forever	P	RF	250+	Leverich, Kathleen	William Morrow
Best Fish Ever, The	O	RF	884	Leveled Readers	Houghton Mifflin
Best Friends	D	RF	15	Instant Readers	Harcourt School Publishers
Best Friends	F	HF	127	Learn to Read	Creative Teaching Press
Best Friends	B	I	28	Bebop Books	Lee & Low Books Inc.
Best Friends	E	RF	31	Fitros, Pamela	Kaeden Books
Best Friends	D	RF	68	Little Readers	Houghton Mifflin
Best Friends	C	I	43	Rosen Real Readers	Rosen Publishing Group
Best Friends	C	RF	34	Windows on Literacy	National Geographic
B-E-S-T Friends	L	RF	250+	Giff, Patricia Reilly	Bantam
Best Friends Don't Fight	M	RF	250+	Bookshop	Mondo
Best Friends for Frances	K	F	250+	Hoban, Russell	HarperTrophy
Best Guess, The	I	RF	241	Foundations	Wright Group/McGraw Hill
Best Hats, The	G	RF	201	PM Plus Story Books	Rigby
Best Job for Scooter, The	J	RF	580	Leveled Readers	Houghton Mifflin

* Collection of short stories

TITLE	LEVEL	GENRE	WORD COUNT	AUTHOR / SERIES	PUBLISHER / DISTRIBUTOR
Best Little Monkeys in the World, The	J	F	250+	Standiford, Natalie	Random House
Best Nest	J	F	250+	Eastman, Philip D.	Random House
Best Older Sister, The	L	RF	250+	Choi, Sook Nyul	Bantam
Best Part, The	K	RF	250+	PM Story Books-Silver	Rigby
Best Pet, The	J	RF	250+	Lighthouse	Rigby
Best Place, The	C	RF	61	Literacy 2000	Rigby
Best Place, The	C	F	77	Leveled Readers	Houghton Mifflin
Best Places, The	D	RF	68	Ready Readers	Pearson Learning Group
Best Present, The	G	RF	146	Rigby Literacy	Rigby
Best Ranger, The	K	RF	396	Leveled Readers	Houghton Mifflin
Best School Year Ever, The	P	RF	250+	Robinson, Barbara	HarperTrophy
Best Teacher in the World, The	K	RF	250+	Chardiet, Bernice	Scholastic
Best Thing About Food, The	F	I	132	Twig	Wright Group/McGraw Hill
Best Way to Play, The	K	I	250+	Cosby, Bill	Scholastic
Best Wishes	O	B	250+	Rylant, Cynthia	Richard C. Owen
Best Wishes for Eddie	M	RF	250+	Nayer, Judy	Pearson Learning Group
Best Worst Day, The	L	RF	250+	Graves, Bonnie	Hyperion
Best-Loved Doll, The	L	RF	250+	Caudill, Rebecca	Henry Holt & Co.
Beth's Bed	E	RF	81	Supersonics	Rigby
Beth's Snow Dancer	Q	HF	250+	The Little Women Journals	Avon
Betsy and Tacy Go Downtown	Q	HF	250+	Lovelace, Maud Hart	HarperTrophy
Betsy and Tacy Go Over the Big Hill	Q	HF	250+	Lovelace, Maud Hart	HarperTrophy
Betsy and Tacy: 60th Anniversary Edition	Q	HF	250+	Lovelace, Maud Hart	HarperTrophy
Betsy and the Boys	P	RF	250+	Haywood, Carolyn	Harcourt Trade
Betsy Ross	L	B	250+	Pebble Books	Red Brick Learning
Betsy Ross: Designer of Our Flag	R	B	250+	Weil, Ann	Aladdin
Betsy the Babysitter	F	RF	115	First Start	Troll Associates
Better Brown Stories, The	T	F	250+	Ahlberg, Allan	Penguin Group
Better Life, A	T	RF	1066	Independent Readers Social Studies	Houghton Mifflin
Better Look, A	H	I	106	Windows on Literacy	National Geographic
Better Than TV	J	RF	250+	Miller, Sara Swan	Bantam
*Between Earth and Sky: Legends of Native American Sacred Places	Z	TL	250+	Bruchac, Joseph	Voyager Books
Between the Dragon and the Eagle	W	HF	250+	Schneider, Mical	Carolrhoda Books
Between the Tides	E	I	52	Wonder World	Wright Group/McGraw Hill
Beware!	N	RF	250+	Cartwright, Pauline	Pacific Learning
Beware, Princess Elizabeth	Y	HF	250+	Meyer, Carolyn	Harcourt Trade
Beyond Belief	Z	I	250+	Steiger, Brad	Scholastic
Beyond Providence	X	RF	250+	Schnur, Steven	OSI
Beyond the Beyond	Q	I	250+	Wildcats	Wright Group/McGraw Hill
Beyond the Black Hole	Q	SF	250+	Bookweb	Rigby
Beyond the Burning Lands	U	F	250+	Christopher, John	Aladdin
Beyond the Mango Tree	V	RF	250+	Zemser, Amy Bronwen	HarperTrophy
Beyond the Myth: The Story of Joan of Arc	Z	B	250+	Brooks, Polly Schoyer	Houghton Mifflin
Beyond the Western Sea, Book II: Lord Kirkle's Money	V	HF	250+	Avi	Avon Camelot
BFG, The	U	F	250+	Dahl, Roald	Penguin Group
Bicentennial Gift, The	T	RF	1906	Leveled Readers	Houghton Mifflin
Bicycle Book, The	O	I	250+	PM Nonfiction-Emerald	Rigby
Bicycle for Rosaura, A	M	F	250+	Soar To Success	Houghton Mifflin
Bicycle Man, The	P	RF	250+	Say, Allen	Houghton Mifflin
Bicycle Patrol Officers	S	I	250+	Law Enforcement	Capstone Press
Bicycle Rider	O	B	250+	Scioscia, Mary	HarperTrophy

* Collection of short stories

TITLE	LEVEL	GENRE	WORD COUNT	AUTHOR / SERIES	PUBLISHER / DISTRIBUTOR
Bicycle, The	Q	I	250+	Great Inventions	Capstone Press
Bicycle, The	C	F	29	Story Box	Wright Group/McGraw Hill
Bicycles	M	I	250+	Windows on Literacy	National Geographic
Biff's Aeroplane	E	RF	64	Oxford Reading Tree	Oxford University Press
Big Al	L	F	250+	Yoshi, Andrew C.	Scholastic
Big and Green	D	I	12	Wonder World	Wright Group/McGraw Hill
Big and Little	WB	I	N/A	Vocabulary Readers	Houghton Mifflin
Big and Little	B	RF	21	Foundations	Wright Group/McGraw Hill
Big and Little	B	I	38	Rigby Literacy	Rigby
Big and Little	C	I	36	Sunshine	Wright Group/McGraw Hill
Big and Little	C	I	66	Little Readers	Houghton Mifflin
Big and Little	D	F	92	Joy Readers	Pearson Learning Group
Big and Little	B	F	40	Carousel Earlybirds	Pearson Learning Group
Big and Little	LB	I	24	KinderReaders	Rigby
Big and Little	LB	I	59	Berger, Samantha; Chanko, Pamela	Scholastic
Big and Little	B	I	68	PM Plus Starters	Rigby
Big and Little	C	I	56	Early Connections	Benchmark Education
Big and Little Dinosaurs	E	I	50	Planet Earth	Rigby
Big Bad Rex	I	I	176	Erickson, Betty	Continental Press
Big Bad Wolf, The	I	RF	250+	PM Plus Story Books	Rigby
Big Balloon Festival, The	L	RF	625	PM Gold	Rigby
Big Balloon Race, The	K	RF	250+	Coerr, Eleanor	HarperTrophy
Big Barn, The	C	RF	81	Teacher's Choice Series	Pearson Learning Group
Big Bed, The	I	RF	346	Pacific Literacy	Pacific Learning
Big Beet, The	L	F	250+	Ready Readers	Pearson Learning Group
Big Ben	E	RF	100	Real Kids Readers	Millbrook Press
Big Bird's Copycat Day	F	F	232	Lerner, Sharon	Random House
Big Black Bears	F	I	43	Rosen Real Readers	Rosen Publishing Group
Big Boo Bird, The	C	F	66	Joy Readers	Pearson Learning Group
Big Box, The	H	RF	183	New Way Green	Steck-Vaughn
Big Box, The	D	F	81	Leveled Readers	Houghton Mifflin
Big Boy	O	TL	250+	Mollel, Tololwa M.	Houghton Mifflin
Big Bradley	D	F	30	Ray's Readers	Outside the Box
Big Bulgy Fat Black Slugs	M	F	250+	Stepping Stones	Nelson/Michaels Assoc.
Big Cat Trouble	N	RF	250+	World Quest Adventures	World Quest Learning
Big Cat, Little Cat	B	I	61	Rigby Focus	Rigby
Big Cat, The	D	RF	41	Ready Readers	Pearson Learning Group
Big Catch, The	K	RF	250+	Literacy 2000	Rigby
Big Chase, The	A	F	14	Foundations	Wright Group/McGraw Hill
Big Chase, The	M	F	250+	SupaDoopers	Sundance
Big Chief of the Neverwoz, The	H	F	250+	Little Celebrations	Pearson Learning Group
Big Crocodile, The	G	F	61	Little Celebrations	Pearson Learning Group
Big Dipper and You, The	Q	I	250+	Krupp, E. C.	Mulberry Books
Big Dipper, The	M	I	585	Leveled Readers Science	Houghton Mifflin
Big Dog, Little Dog	I	F	265	Eastman, Philip D.	Random House
Big Egg	E	F	103	Coxe, Molly	Random House
BIG Elephants	D	I	41	Rosen Real Readers	Rosen Publishing Group
Big Enough	C	RF	49	Visions	Wright Group/McGraw Hill
Big Family, The	H	RF	250+	Sunshine	Wright Group/McGraw Hill
Big Fat Worm, The	G	F	250+	Van Laan, Nancy	Random House
Big Fish Little Fish	K	TL	250+	Folk Tales	Wright Group/McGraw Hill
Big Fish, The	N	RF	250+	Sunshine	Wright Group/McGraw Hill
Big Fish, The	M	RF	301	Yukish, Joe	Kaeden Books

* Collection of short stories

TITLE	LEVEL	GENRE	WORD COUNT	AUTHOR / SERIES	PUBLISHER / DISTRIBUTOR
Big Fish, The	C	RF	82	Early Emergent	Pioneer Valley
Big Foot	X	I	250+	The Unexplained	Capstone Press
Big Friend, Little Friend	E	RF	56	Greenfield, Eloise	Houghton Mifflin
Big Game, The	H	RF	69	Pacific Literacy	Pacific Learning
Big Gold Mountain	N	RF	250+	Bookweb	Rigby
Big Green Caterpillar, The	J	RF	161	Literacy 2000	Rigby
Big Gust, The	N	F	650	Leveled Readers	Houghton Mifflin
Big Hill, The	C	F	55	PM Plus Story Books	Rigby
Big Hill, The	D	F	19	Story Box	Wright Group/McGraw Hill
Big Hole, The	E	RF	150	Developing Books	Pioneer Valley
Big Hungry Bear, The	I	F	148	Wood, Don & Audrey	Scholastic
Big Hush, The	I	RF	281	Story Box	Wright Group/McGraw Hill
Big Kick, The	C	RF	67	PM Story Books	Rigby
Big Laugh, The	I	F	152	Sunshine	Wright Group/McGraw Hill
Big Lie, The: A True Story	T	B	250+	Leitner, Isabella	Scholastic
Big Long Animal Song	C	F	29	Little Celebrations	Pearson Learning Group
Big Mama and Grandma Ghana	J	RF	250+	Medearis, A. Shelf	Scholastic
Big Mammals	B	I	42	Little Red Readers	Sundance
Big Max	J	F	250+	Platt, Kin	HarperTrophy
Big Mix-Up, The	G	F	70	City Stories	Rigby
Big or Little?	B	I	35	Bebop Books	Lee & Low Books Inc.
Big or Little?	I	RF	250+	Stinson, Kathy	Pearson Learning Group
Big or Small?	B	I	30	Yellow Umbrella Books	Red Brick Learning
Big Orange Spot, The	L	F	250+	Pinkwater, Daniel Manus	Scholastic
Big Picture, The	R	I	250+	Bennett, Mary	Pacific Learning
Big Pig, Little Pig	E	F	54	Little Celebrations	Pearson Learning Group
Big Prize, The	K	F	401	Adventures in Reading	Pearson Learning Group
Big Race, The	N	F	250+	Pye, Trevor	Pacific Learning
Big Race, The	H	RF	250+	Home Connection Collection	School Zone
Big Race, The	L	RF	250+	Pattrick, Steve	Rigby
Big Red Apple, The	H	F	250+	Momentum Literacy Program	Troll Associates
Big Red Fire Engine	G	F	158	First Start	Troll Associates
Big Red Tomatoes	I	I	168	Windows on Literacy	National Geographic
Big Rigs	M	I	250+	Transportation	Compass Point Books
Big Rocks, Little Rocks	E	I	180	Early Connections	Benchmark Education
Big Roundup, The	G	I	121	Wonder World	Wright Group/McGraw Hill
Big Sea Animals	B	I	79	PM Plus Starters	Rigby
Big Seed, The	E	RF	83	New Way	Steck-Vaughn
Big Shrink, The	L	F	250+	Cambridge Reading	Pearson Learning Group
Big Sister	C	RF	44	Visions	Wright Group/McGraw Hill
Big Sneeze, The	D	F	112	Foundations	Wright Group/McGraw Hill
Big Sneeze, The	K	F	131	Brown, Ruth	Lothrop
Big Snow, The	E	RF	150	Developing Books	Pioneer Valley
Big Snow, The	J	I	150	Early Connections	Benchmark Education
Big Snowball Fight	C	RF	15	Bebop Books	Lee & Low Books Inc.
Big Storm, The	Q	I	250+	Hiscock, Bruce	Aladdin
Big Surprise, The	H	RF	123	Pacific Literacy	Pacific Learning
Big Tease, The	I	RF	250+	Story Box	Wright Group/McGraw Hill
Big Tennis Match, A	I	I	122	Vocabulary Readers	Houghton Mifflin
Big Things	A	I	33	PM Starters	Rigby
Big Toe Robbery, The	N	F	250+	PM Ruby	Rigby
Big Toe, The	E	F	123	Story Box	Wright Group/McGraw Hill
Big Tug	D	F	80	Leveled Readers	Houghton Mifflin
Big Wave, The	Q	RF	250+	Buck, Pearl S.	Scholastic

* Collection of short stories

TITLE	LEVEL	GENRE	WORD COUNT	AUTHOR / SERIES	PUBLISHER / DISTRIBUTOR
Big Yellow Castle, The	E	RF	135	PM Plus Story Books	Rigby
Big, Bad Cook, The	J	TL	250+	Literacy Tree	Rigby
Big, Big Box, A	B	RF	35	Ready Readers	Pearson Learning Group
Big, Big Trucks	H	I	162	School Zone	School Zone
Big, Bigger, Biggest	C	I	31	Windows on Literacy	National Geographic
Big, Brown Box, The	E	RF	93	Voyages	SRA/McGraw Hill
Big, Fat, Wide Mouth	G	F	183	Story Box	Wright Group/McGraw Hill
Big, Hit, The	D	RF	120	PM Plus Story Books	Rigby
Big, Small, or Just Right?	C	F	40	Leveled Readers Language Support	Houghton Mifflin
Bigfoot Doesn't Square Dance	M	F	250+	Dadey, Debbie; Jones, Marcia Thornton	Scholastic
Bigger and Bigger	C	I	49	Twig	Wright Group/McGraw Hill
Bigger Burger, A	I	RF	253	Story Box	Wright Group/McGraw Hill
Bigger or Smaller?	F	I	112	Sunshine	Wright Group/McGraw Hill
Bigger Than? Smaller Than?	D	I	123	Early Connections	Benchmark Education
Biggest Bear in the Woods, The	K	F	250+	Little Celebrations	Pearson Learning Group
Biggest Cake in the World, The	F	F	120	Pacific Literacy	Pacific Learning
Biggest Fish, The	I	RF	254	PM Story Books-Orange	Rigby
Biggest Klutz in Fifth Grade, The	V	RF	250+	Wallace, Bill	Simon & Schuster
Biggest Pool of All, The	K	RF	250+	Sunshine	Wright Group/McGraw Hill
Biggest Sandwich Ever, The	E	F	87	Pair-It Books	Steck-Vaughn
Big-Hearted Monkey and the Crocodile, The	K	TL	250+	World Quest Adventures	World Quest Learning
Big-Hearted Monkey and the Lion, The	K	TL	250+	World Quest Adventures	World Quest Learning
Bighorn Sheep, The	R	I	250+	Mattern, Joanne	Red Brick Learning
Bike For Alex, A	I	RF	250+	PM Plus Story Books	Rigby
Bike for Brad, A	K	RF	510	PM Story Books	Rigby
Bike Lesson	I	F	250+	Berenstain, Stan & Jan	Random House
Bike Parade, The	LB	RF	16	Literacy 2000	Rigby
Bike Ride, The	D	RF	100	Emergent	Pioneer Valley
Bike Ride, The	D	RF	72	Leveled Readers Language Support	Houghton Mifflin
Bike That Spike Likes, The	E	RF	91	Ready Readers	Pearson Learning Group
Bike Trip, The	D	RF	60	Leveled Readers	Houghton Mifflin
Bike, The	LB	I	14	Twig	Wright Group/McGraw Hill
Bikes	F	I	133	Discovery Links	Newbridge
Bikes	G	RF	156	Foundations	Wright Group/McGraw Hill
Bill	I	RF	166	Sunshine	Wright Group/McGraw Hill
Bill and Ted at the Store	D	F	50	Joy Readers	Pearson Learning Group
Bill Clinton: Forty-Second President of the U.S.	O	B	250+	Greene, Carol	Children's Press
Bill Cosby: The Changing Black Image	X	B	250+	Rosenberg, Robert	Millbrook Press
Bill Cosby's Little Bill: The Best Way to Play	L	F	250+	Cosby, Bill	Scholastic
Bill Gates: Helping People Use Computers	P	B	250+	Community Builders	Children's Press
Bill of Rights, The	D	I	364	Independent Readers Social Studies	Houghton Mifflin
Bill of Rights, The	V	I	250+	Cornerstones of Freedom	Bantam
Bill of Rights, The	N	I	250+	A True Book	Children's Press
Bill Pickett, Rodeo King	V	B	3134	Leveled Readers	Houghton Mifflin
Billie the Hippo	N	I	250+	Pacific Literacy	Pacific Learning
Billie's Book	F	I	110	Sunshine	Wright Group/McGraw Hill
Bill's Baby	E	RF	41	Tadpoles	Rigby
Bill's Trip	E	RF	77	Dominie Phonics Reader	Pearson Learning Group
Billy at School	F	RF	163	PM Plus Story Books	Rigby
Billy Can Count	D	RF	122	PM Plus Story Books	Rigby

* Collection of short stories

TITLE	LEVEL	GENRE	WORD COUNT	AUTHOR / SERIES	PUBLISHER / DISTRIBUTOR
Billy Goats Gruff	F	TL	381	Hunia, Fran	Ladybird Books
Billy Is Hiding	D	RF	97	PM Plus Story Books	Rigby
Billy Magee's New Car	J	RF	391	Foundations	Wright Group/McGraw Hill
Billy the Ghost and Me	L	F	250+	Greer, Gery; Ruddick, Bob	HarperTrophy
Billy's Box	G	F	207	Cambridge Reading	Pearson Learning Group
Billy's Truck Diary	N	I	250+	Sunshine	Wright Group/McGraw Hill
Bingo	D	TL	179	PM Readalongs	Rigby
B-I-N-G-O	C	RF	41	Tiger Cub	Peguis
Bingo Goes to School	F	RF	171	PM Plus Story Books	Rigby
Bingo's Birthday	E	RF	116	PM Plus Story Books	Rigby
Bingo's Ice-Cream Cone	D	RF	88	PM Plus Story Books	Rigby
Biodiversity Hotspots	Y	I	250+	Independent Readers Science	Houghton Mifflin
Biography of Faith Ringgold, A	J	B	132	Vocabulary Readers	Houghton Mifflin
Biomes	V	I	1420	Independent Readers Science	Houghton Mifflin
Birchbark House, The	T	HF	250+	Erdrich, Louise	Hyperion
Bird Barn, The	I	I	241	Foundations	Wright Group/McGraw Hill
Bird Beaks	I	I	180	Wonder World	Wright Group/McGraw Hill
Bird Behavior: Living Together	M	I	631	Sunshine	Wright Group/McGraw Hill
Bird Chain, The	M	F	250+	Voyages	SRA/McGraw Hill
Bird Eggs	F	I	50	Pebble Books	Capstone Press
Bird Families	F	I	60	Pebble Books	Capstone Press
Bird Feeder, The	C	I	31	Storyteller-First Snow	Wright Group/McGraw Hill
Bird Feeder, The	D	I	55	Coulton, Mia	Kaeden Books
Bird Feeder, The	C	RF	40	Sun Sprouts	ETA/Cuisenaire
Bird Flies By, A	E	I	87	Windows on Literacy	National Geographic
Bird for You, A: Caring for Your Bird	M	I	250+	Pet Care	Picture Window Books
Bird Has Feathers, A	C	I	27	Science	Outside the Box
Bird in the Basket, The	M	RF	250+	Beveridge, Barbara	Pacific Learning
Bird Lady, The	J	I	250+	Story Steps	Rigby
Bird Nests	F	I	78	Pebble Books	Capstone Press
Bird on the Bus, A	E	RF	115	Leveled Readers	Houghton Mifflin
Bird Race	I	TL	195	Leveled Readers	Houghton Mifflin
Bird Song	I	F	99	Storyteller-Night Crickets	Wright Group/McGraw Hill
Bird Table, The	H	RF	166	Book Bank	Wright Group/McGraw Hill
Bird Talk: Kok, Kok	B	F	42	Little Celebrations	Pearson Learning Group
Bird That Could Think, The	I	F	250+	PM Plus Story Books	Rigby
Bird Watching	J	RF	475	PM Plus Story Books	Rigby
Birds	D	I	39	All About Pets	Red Brick Learning
Birds	LB	I	12	Vocabulary Readers	Houghton Mifflin
Birds	N	I	250+	Nature's Friends	Compass Point Books
Birds	F	I	54	Birds Series	Pearson Learning Group
Birds	M	I	68	First Facts	Capstone Press
Birds	F	I	50	Literacy 2000	Rigby
Birds	B	I	18	Rigby Focus	Rigby
Birds	F	I	68	Windows on Literacy	National Geographic
Birds and How They Grow	N	I	250+	National Geographic Society	National Geographic
Birds and Their Nests	J	I	175	Animal Homes	Capstone Press
Birds at My Barn, The	L	RF	230	Books for Young Learners	Richard C. Owen
Birds At My Feeder	R	I	250+	Kalman, Bobbie	Crabtree
Bird's Bad Day	C	F	36	Instant Readers	Harcourt School Publishers
Birds Need Trees	D	I	63	Teacher's Choice Series	Pearson Learning Group
Birds' Nests	J	I	111	Wonder World	Wright Group/McGraw Hill
Birds of a Feather	N	RF	250+	Literacy 2000	Rigby
Birds of Prey	S	I	250+	Peterson Field Guides	Houghton Mifflin

TITLE	LEVEL	GENRE	WORD COUNT	AUTHOR / SERIES	PUBLISHER / DISTRIBUTOR
Birds of Prey	O	I	250+	Woolley, M.; Pigdon, K.	Mondo
Birds of Prey: A Look at Daytime Raptors	U	I	250+	Collard III, Sneed B.	Franklin Watts
Birds of the City	M	I	840	Sunshine	Wright Group/McGraw Hill
Birds on Stage	H	F	153	Romay, Saturnino	Scholastic
Birds, Bees, and Sailing Ships	I	F	243	Sunshine	Wright Group/McGraw Hill
Bird's-Eye View	J	RF	393	PM Turquoise	Rigby
Bird's-Eye View, A	K	I	250+	People, Spaces & Places	Rand McNally
Bird-Watching	S	I	250+	iOpeners	Pearson Learning Group
Birdwoman Interview	M	RF	250+	Sails	Rigby
Birthday	N	RF	250+	Steptoe, John	Henry Holt & Co.
Birthday Balloons	D	F	104	Rigby Literacy	Rigby
Birthday Balloons	F	RF	182	PM Extensions-Blue	Rigby
Birthday Bear	D	F	91	Sun Sprouts	ETA/Cuisenaire
Birthday Bike for Brimhall, A	K	RF	250+	Delton, Judy	Bantam
Birthday Bird, The	F	RF	82	Books for Young Learners	Richard C. Owen
Birthday Book	H	RF	93	Storybox	Wright Group/McGraw Hill
Birthday Bug, The	B	RF	53	Story Steps	Rigby
Birthday Cake	D	RF	27	Literacy 2000	Rigby
Birthday Cake for Ben, A	C	RF	59	PM Extensions-Red	Rigby
Birthday Cake, The	LB	F	22	Sunshine	Wright Group/McGraw Hill
Birthday Cake, The	H	F	201	Story Box	Wright Group/McGraw Hill
Birthday Cake, The	G	RF	107	Rigby Focus	Rigby
Birthday Candles	C	RF	52	Carousel Readers	Pearson Learning Group
Birthday Celebrations	E	I	111	Early Connections	Benchmark Education
Birthday Dig, The	R	F	1216	Leveled Readers	Houghton Mifflin
Birthday Disaster	Q	RF	250+	Literacy 2000	Rigby
Birthday Dog	I	RF	250+	Sunshine	Wright Group/McGraw Hill
Birthday for Frances, A	K	F	250+	Hoban, Russell	Scholastic
Birthday in the Woods, A	F	F	199	Salem, Lynn; Stewart, Josie	Continental Press
Birthday Party for Cornelius, A	N	RF	250+	Leveled Readers Language Support	Houghton Mifflin
Birthday Party, A	C	RF	47	Early Emergent	Pioneer Valley
Birthday Party, The	O	F	797	Leveled Readers	Houghton Mifflin
Birthday Party, The	LB	I	16	Rise & Shine	Hampton-Brown
Birthday Party, The	A	RF	15	Sunshine	Wright Group/McGraw Hill
Birthday Present, The	E	F	86	Leveled Readers Language Support	Houghton Mifflin
Birthday Presents	F	RF	162	PM Plus Story Books	Rigby
Birthday Room, The	V	RF	250+	Henkes, Kevin	William Morrow
Birthday Surprise	H	RF	265	Leveled Readers	Houghton Mifflin
Birthday Surprise, A	H	RF	157	Developing Books, Set 2	Pioneer Valley
*Birthday Surprises: Ten Great Stories to Unwrap	R	RF	250+	Hurwitz, Johanna	William Morrow
Birthday Wishes	L	RF	250+	Voyages	SRA/McGraw Hill
Birthday, A	C	F	39	New Way	Steck-Vaughn
Birthday, The	C	RF	30	Harry's Math Books	Outside the Box
Birthday, The	A	I	23	Little Books for Early Readers	University of Maine
Birthdays	C	RF	59	Foundations	Wright Group/McGraw Hill
Birthdays	K	I	59	Purkis, Sallie	Nelson/Michaels Assoc.
Birthdays	I	I	147	Sunshine	Wright Group/McGraw Hill
Birthdays Around the World	M	I	250+	Early Connections	Benchmark Education
Biscuit	F	RF	132	Capucilli, Alyssa Satin	HarperTrophy
Biscuit Finds a Friend	F	RF	114	Capucilli, Alyssa Satin	HarperTrophy
Bison Are Back!, The	P	RF	743	Leveled Readers	Houghton Mifflin

* Collection of short stories

TITLE	LEVEL	GENRE	WORD COUNT	AUTHOR / SERIES	PUBLISHER / DISTRIBUTOR
Bite of the Gold Bug, The: A Story of the Alaskan Gold Rush	S	I	250+	DeClements, Barthe	Penguin Group
Black and White	C	I	32	Voyages	SRA/McGraw Hill
Black and White	D	I	77	Storyteller Nonfiction	Wright Group/McGraw Hill
Black Bear Cub	L	F	250+	Lind, Alan	Scholastic
Black Bears	E	I	50	Pebble Books	Capstone Press
Black Boy	Z	RF	250+	Wright, Richard	HarperPerennial
Black Diamond: Story of the Negro Baseball Leagues	Q	I	250+	McKissack, Patricia & Fred	Scholastic
Black Eagles: African Americans in Aviation	X	B	250+	Haskins, Jim	Scholastic
Black Elk: A Man with a Vision	N	B	250+	Rookie Biographies	Children's Press
Black Gold	R	RF	250+	Henry, Marguerite	Aladdin
Black Hearts in Battersea	V	HF	250+	Aiken, Joan	Houghton Mifflin
*Black Heroes of the American Revolution	X	B	250+	Davis, Burke	Harcourt Trade
Black Holes	N	I	250+	A True Book	Children's Press
Black Kitten, The	E	RF	115	Handprints C, Set 2	Educator's Publishing Service
Black Pearl, The	X	RF	250+	O'Dell, Scott	Bantam
*Black Pioneers of Science and Invention	Y	B	250+	Haber, Louis	Harcourt Trade
Black Stallion, The	T	RF	250+	Farley, Walter	Language for Learning Assoc.
Black Star, Bright Dawn	V	RF	250+	O'Dell, Scott	Ballantine Books
Black Swan's Breakfast	G	RF	147	Book Bank	Wright Group/McGraw Hill
Black Velvet Mystery, The	N	RF	250+	Keene, Carolyn	Pocket Books
Black: Seeing Black All Around Us	L	I	250+	Colors	Capstone Press
Black-and-White Ruffed Lemurs	H	I	94	Seedlings	Continental Press
Blackberries	D	F	107	PM Story Books	Rigby
Blackberries in the Dark	N	RF	250+	Jukes, Mavis	Alfred A. Knopf
Blackbirds	L	I	250+	Sunshine	Wright Group/McGraw Hill
Blackbird's Nest	G	RF	71	Pacific Literacy	Pacific Learning
Blackboard Bear	J	F	117	Alexander, Martha	Penguin Group
Black-Eyed Susan	Q	HF	250+	Armstrong, Jennifer	Alfred A. Knopf
Blackfeet, The	R	I	250+	First Reports	Compass Point Books
Blackfeet, The: People of the Dark Moccasins	S	I	250+	American Indian Nations	Capstone Press
Blackout!	P	RF	250+	Bookweb	Rigby
Blackwater Swamp	T	RF	250+	Wallace, Bill	Language for Learning Assoc.
Blair's Deer	K	RF	250+	Phonics and Friends	Hampton-Brown
Blanche Bruce of Mississippi	K	B	413	Leveled Readers Social Studies	Houghton Mifflin
Blanket, The	E	RF	65	Burningham, John	Crowell
Blast Off with Ellen Ochoa!	M	B	250+	Greetings	Rigby
Blast Off!	N	I	250+	Home Connection Collection	Rigby
Blast Off!	F	I	95	Ready Readers	Pearson Learning Group
Blast to the Past	N	SF	250+	Orbit Chapter Books	Pacific Literacy
Bless Me, Ultima	Z	RF	250+	Anaya, Rudolfo	Warner Books
Blimps	N	I	250+	A True Book	Children's Press
Blind Men and the Elephant, The	K	TL	250+	Backstein, Karen	Scholastic
Blind Outlaw, The	P	RF	250+	Rounds, Glen	Scholastic
Blister	S	RF	250+	Shreve, Susan	Scholastic
Blizzard	S	HF	250+	Duey, Kathleen	Simon & Schuster
Blizzards!	M	HF	250+	Hopping, Lorraine Jean	Scholastic
Block Party, The	H	I	127	Learn to Read	Creative Teaching Press
Blocks	C	RF	60	Early Emergent	Pioneer Valley
Blood	J	I	241	Twig	Wright Group/McGraw Hill

* Collection of short stories

TITLE	LEVEL	GENRE	WORD COUNT	AUTHOR / SERIES	PUBLISHER / DISTRIBUTOR
Bloomability	V	RF	250+	Creech, Sharon	HarperCollins
Blossom	J	F	225	Voyages	SRA/McGraw Hill
Blossom Promise, A	R	RF	250+	Byars, Betsy	Bantam
Blossoms and the Green Phantom, The	R	RF	250+	Byars, Betsy	Dell
Blossom's Babies	I	F	250+	Book Bus	Creative Edge
Blossoms Meet the Vulture Lady, The	R	RF	250+	Byars, Betsy	Bantam
Blow, Wind, Blow!	D	RF	114	Story Steps	Rigby
Blowing in the Wind	T	I	250+	Literacy 2000	Rigby
Blubber	T	RF	250+	Blume, Judy	Bantam
Blue Bug and the Bullies	D	F	18	Poulet, Virginia	Children's Press
Blue Bug Goes to School	D	F	57	Poulet, Virginia	Children's Press
Blue Bug Goes to the Library	F	F	59	Poulet, Virginia	Children's Press
Blue Bug's Book of Colors	E	F	49	Poulet, Virginia	Children's Press
Blue Bug's Vegetable Garden	D	F	27	Poulet, Virginia	Children's Press
Blue Day	C	RF	35	Literacy 2000	Rigby
Blue Door, The	X	HF	250+	Rinaldi, Ann	Scholastic
Blue Heron	W	RF	250+	Avi	Avon
*Blue Hill Meadows, The	M	RF	250+	Rylant, Cynthia	Harcourt Trade
Blue Ice	U	RF	250+	Salata, Estelle	Fitzhenry & Whiteside
Blue Jay, The	H	RF	173	Little Readers	Houghton Mifflin
Blue Kangaroo, The	H	F	361	Leveled Readers	Houghton Mifflin
Blue Layer, The	N	I	250+	Voyages	SRA/McGraw Hill
Blue Lollipops	G	RF	250	Stepping Stones	Nelson/Michaels Assoc.
Blue Mittens, The	I	RF	250+	Mann, Rachel	Scholastic
Blue Ribbon Blues	M	RF	250+	Spinelli, Jerry	Random House
Blue Sue	G	F	121	Ready Readers	Pearson Learning Group
Blue Sword, The	Y	F	250+	McKinley, Robin	Puffin Books
Blue Whales	U	I	250+	The Untamed World	Steck-Vaughn
Blue Willow	V	RF	250+	Gates, Doris	Puffin Books
Blue: Seeing Blue All Around Us	L	I	250+	Colors	Capstone Press
Blueberries for Sal	M	RF	250+	McCloskey, Robert	Scholastic
Blueberries from Maine	A	RF	28	Little Books for Early Readers	University of Maine
Blueberry Muffins	D	RF	191	Story Box	Wright Group/McGraw Hill
Bluebird Out My Window	L	RF	633	Leveled Readers Science	Houghton Mifflin
Blue-Eyed Daisy, A	W	RF	250+	Rylant, Cynthia	Simon & Schuster
BMX Billy	G	RF	93	Literacy 2000	Rigby
BMX Freestyle	M	I	250+	Blazers	Capstone Press
BMX Racing	S	I	250+	X-Sports	Capstone Press
Bo and Peter	C	RF	44	Franco, Betsy	Scholastic
Bo Peep's Sheep	C	TL	39	Pair-It Books	Steck-Vaughn
Boa Constrictors	J	I	250+	Rain Forest Animals	Red Brick Learning
Boards and More	I	RF	250+	Phonics Readers Plus	Steck-Vaughn
Boat Trip, The	D	F	70	Carousel Earlybirds	Pearson Learning Group
Boat, The	A	RF	28	Sunshine	Wright Group/McGraw Hill
Boat, The	LB	RF	14	Pacific Literacy	Pacific Learning
Boats	D	I	57	Twig	Wright Group/McGraw Hill
Boats	M	I	250+	Transportation	Compass Point Books
Boats	G	I	84	Rockwell, Anne	Penguin Group
Boats	C	I	100	Pebble Books	Capstone Press
Boats Afloat	M	I	752	Sunshine	Wright Group/McGraw Hill
Boats, Boats, Boats	D	I	44	My First Reader	Grolier Press
Bobbie and the Baby	D	RF	62	Rigby Literacy	Rigby
Bobbie and the Kite	WB	RF	N/A	Rigby Literacy	Rigby
Bobbie and the Monster	B	RF	24	Rigby Literacy	Rigby

* Collection of short stories

TITLE	LEVEL	GENRE	WORD COUNT	AUTHOR / SERIES	PUBLISHER / DISTRIBUTOR
Bobbie and the Parade	C	RF	49	Rigby Literacy	Rigby
Bobbie and the Play	F	RF	164	Rigby Literacy	Rigby
Bobbie Goes on Vacation	F	RF	240	Rigby Literacy	Rigby
Bobbie's Airplane	E	RF	64	Oxford Reading Tree	Oxford University Press
Bobbie's New Coat	F	RF	189	Rigby Literacy	Rigby
Bobby's Zoo	E	RF	54	Rookie Readers	Children's Press
Bobo's Magic Wishes	L	F	250+	Little Readers	Houghton Mifflin
Body Battles	P	I	250+	Gelman, Rita G.	Scholastic
Body Numbers	K	I	250+	Discovery World	Rigby
Body Parts Work Together	I	I	119	Instant Readers	Harcourt School Publishers
Bogeymen Don't Play Football	M	F	250+	Dadey, Debbie; Jones, Marcia Thornton	Scholastic
Boggart and the Monster, The	U	F	250+	Cooper, Susan	Aladdin
Boggart, The	U	F	250+	Cooper, Susan	Simon & Schuster
Boggywooga	I	F	274	Sunshine	Wright Group/McGraw Hill
Bogle's Card	H	F	244	Sunshine	Wright Group/McGraw Hill
Bogle's Feet	I	F	280	Sunshine	Wright Group/McGraw Hill
Bomb Detection Squads	S	I	250+	Law Enforcement	Capstone Press
Bomb, The	Z	HF	250+	Taylor, Theodore	Avon
Bonanza Girl	T	RF	250+	Beatty, Patricia	Scholastic
Bone Dance	X	RF	250+	Brooks, Martha	Random House
Bone Museum, The	M	RF	250+	Sunshine	Wright Group/McGraw Hill
Bone Tree, The	N	F	250+	Voyages	SRA/McGraw Hill
Bones	C	I	56	Rigby Literacy	Rigby
Bones	J	I	182	Rigby Focus	Rigby
Bones for Lunch	K	F	221	Sunshine	Wright Group/McGraw Hill
Bonnie on the Beach	H	RF	198	Little Readers	Houghton Mifflin
Bony-Legs	K	F	250+	Cole, Joanna	Scholastic
Boodil My Dog	Q	RF	250+	Lindenbaum, Pija	Henry Holt & Co.
Boogie-Woogie Man, The	D	F	101	Story Box	Wright Group/McGraw Hill
Boogly, The	E	F	61	Literacy 2000	Rigby
Boo-Hoo	E	F	149	Story Box	Wright Group/McGraw Hill
Book About Planets and Stars, A	R	I	250+	Reigot, Betty Polisar	Scholastic
Book About Your Skeleton, A	M	I	250+	Gross, Ruth Belov	Scholastic
Book Club, The	H	RF	247	Leveled Readers Language Support	Houghton Mifflin
*Book of Black Heroes from A to Z	P	B	250+	Hudson, Wade; Wesley, Valerie Wilson	Scholastic
Book of Hours, A	O	I	250+	Cambridge Reading	Pearson Learning Group
Book of Monsters, The	P	I	250+	Sunshine	Wright Group/McGraw Hill
*Book of Monsters: Tales to Give You the Creeps	T	F	250+	Coville, Bruce	Scholastic
*Book of Spine Tinglers: Tales To Make You Shiver	T	F	250+	Coville, Bruce	Scholastic
Book of Three, The	U	F	250+	Alexander, Lloyd	Bantam
Book Week	E	RF	71	Oxford Reading Tree	Oxford University Press
Booker T. Washington	M	B	250+	Schaefer, Lola M.	Steck-Vaughn
Books	C	RF	21	Beginning Literacy	Scholastic
Books	B	I	21	Smart Starts	Rigby
Books	B	RF	29	Sunshine	Wright Group/McGraw Hill
Bookstore Cat	I	RF	207	Little Readers	Houghton Mifflin
Bookworm Who Hatched, A	O	B	250+	Aardema, Verna	Richard C. Owen
Boom Boom Bay!	D	RF	130	Phonics and Friends	Hampton-Brown
Boom!	N	I	250+	Gutner, Howard	Scholastic
Boomtowns of the West	S	I	250+	Kalman, Bobbie	Crabtree

* Collection of short stories

TITLE	LEVEL	GENRE	WORD COUNT	AUTHOR / SERIES	PUBLISHER / DISTRIBUTOR
Boonsville Bombers, The	N	RF	250+	Herzig, Alison	Puffin Books
Boot Balancers Wanted	O	F	250+	Sails	Rigby
Bootlace Soup	J	TL	250+	Voyages	SRA/McGraw Hill
Boots	C	RF	57	Schreiber, Anne; Doughty, Arbo	Scholastic
Boots and Shoes	E	F	68	Cooper, Anne	Kaeden Books
Boots for the King	D	F	93	Sun Sprouts	ETA/Cuisenaire
Boots for Toots	C	F	41	Pacific Literacy	Pacific Learning
Bootscooting	B	I	38	First Stories	Pacific Learning
Bootsie Barker Ballerina	K	F	250+	Bottner, Barbara	HarperTrophy
Boring Day, The	D	RF	81	Emergent Books	Pioneer Valley
Boring Old Bed	I	RF	211	Sunshine	Wright Group/McGraw Hill
Boring Old Bed	J	F	250+	Lighthouse	Rigby
Boris Bad Enough	G	F	167	Kraus, Robert	Simon & Schuster
Born To Trot	R	RF	250+	Henry, Marguerite	Aladdin
Borning Room, The	Y	HF	250+	Fleischman, Paul	HarperCollins
Borreguita and the Coyote	O	TL	250+	Aardema, Verna	Scholastic
Borrowers, The	S	F	250+	Norton, Mary	Harcourt Trade
Boss	C	F	48	Foundations	Wright Group/McGraw Hill
Boss For A Day	I	RF	250+	DePaola, Tomie	Grosset & Dunlap
Bossy and Wag	D	F	63	Sun Sprouts	ETA/Cuisenaire
Bossy Bettina	F	RF	97	Literacy 2000	Rigby
Boston Coffee Party, The	L	HF	250+	Rappaport, Doreen	HarperCollins
Boston Massacre, The	V	I	250+	Let Freedom Ring	Red Brick Learning
Boston Massacre, The: Five Colonists Killed by British Soldiers	S	I	250+	Headlines from History	Rosen Publishing Group
Boston Tea Party, The	V	I	250+	Let Freedom Ring	Red Brick Learning
Boston Tea Party, The	T	I	250+	We The People	Compass Point Books
Boston Tea Party, The	V	I	250+	Cornerstones of Freedom	Children's Press
Boston Tea Party, The: Angry Colonists Dump British Tea	S	I	250+	Headlines from History	Rosen Publishing Group
Boston Tea Party: Rebellion in the Colonies	T	I	250+	Adventures in Colonial America	Troll Associates
Bot's Bits	G	F	99	Supersonics	Rigby
Botticelli	R	B	250+	Venezia, Mike	Children's Press
Bottle Garden, A	E	I	52	Wonder World	Wright Group/McGraw Hill
Bottles, Boxes, and Bins	C	I	36	Twig	Wright Group/McGraw Hill
*Bound for the North Star: True Stories of Fugitive Slaves	Z	B	250+	Fradin, Dennis Brindell	Houghton Mifflin
Boundless Grace	M	RF	250+	Hoffman, Mary	Scholastic
Bouquet, The	A	RF	38	Carousel Earlybirds	Pearson Learning Group
Bow Down, Shadrach	R	RF	250+	Cowley, Joy	Wright Group/McGraw Hill
Bowman's Store: A Journey to Myself	Z	B	250+	Bruchac, Joseph	Lee & Low Books Inc.
Box Can Be Many Things, A	E	RF	51	Rookie Readers	Children's Press
Box of Butterflies, A	K	RF	250+	Leveled Readers Language Support	Houghton Mifflin
Box, The	A	RF	31	First Stories	Pacific Learning
Box, The	C	RF	30	Leveled Readers Language Support	Houghton Mifflin
Boxcar Children Return, The	O	RF	250+	Warner, Gertrude Chandler	Albert Whitman & Co.
Boxcar Children Special: The Mystery at Snowflake Inn	O	RF	250+	Warner, Gertrude Chandler	Albert Whitman & Co.
Boxcar Children Special: The Mystery at the Ballpark	O	RF	250+	Warner, Gertrude Chandler	Albert Whitman & Co.
Boxcar Children Special: The Mystery at the Fair	O	RF	250+	Warner, Gertrude Chandler	Albert Whitman & Co.

TITLE	LEVEL	GENRE	WORD COUNT	AUTHOR / SERIES	PUBLISHER / DISTRIBUTOR
Boxcar Children Special: The Pilgrim Village Mystery	O	RF	250+	Warner, Gertrude Chandler	Albert Whitman & Co.
Boxcar Children: Amusement Park Mystery, The	O	RF	250+	Warner, Gertrude Chandler	Albert Whitman & Co.
Boxcar Children: Animal Shelter Mystery, The	O	RF	250+	Warner, Gertrude Chandler	Albert Whitman & Co.
Boxcar Children: Basketball Mystery, The	O	RF	250+	Warner, Gertrude Chandler	Albert Whitman & Co.
Boxcar Children: Benny Uncovers a Mystery	O	RF	250+	Warner, Gertrude Chandler	Albert Whitman & Co.
Boxcar Children: Bicycle Mystery	O	RF	250+	Warner, Gertrude Chandler	Albert Whitman & Co.
Boxcar Children: Black Pearl Mystery, The	O	RF	250+	Warner, Gertrude Chandler	Albert Whitman & Co.
Boxcar Children: Blue Bay Mystery	O	RF	250+	Warner, Gertrude Chandler	Albert Whitman & Co.
Boxcar Children: Boxcar Children, The	O	RF	250+	Warner, Gertrude Chandler	Albert Whitman & Co.
Boxcar Children: Bus Station Mystery	O	RF	250+	Warner, Gertrude Chandler	Albert Whitman & Co.
Boxcar Children: Caboose Mystery	O	RF	250+	Warner, Gertrude Chandler	Albert Whitman & Co.
Boxcar Children: Camp-Out Mystery, The	O	RF	250+	Warner, Gertrude Chandler	Albert Whitman & Co.
Boxcar Children: Canoe Trip Mystery, The	O	RF	250+	Warner, Gertrude Chandler	Albert Whitman & Co.
Boxcar Children: Castle Mystery, The	O	RF	250+	Warner, Gertrude Chandler	Albert Whitman & Co.
Boxcar Children: Cereal Box Mystery, The	O	RF	250+	Warner, Gertrude Chandler	Albert Whitman & Co.
Boxcar Children: Chocolate Sundae Mystery, The	O	RF	250+	Warner, Gertrude Chandler	Albert Whitman & Co.
Boxcar Children: Deserted Library Mystery, The	O	RF	250+	Warner, Gertrude Chandler	Albert Whitman & Co.
Boxcar Children: Dinosaur Mystery, The	O	RF	250+	Warner, Gertrude Chandler	Albert Whitman & Co.
Boxcar Children: Disappearing Friend Mystery, The	O	RF	250+	Warner, Gertrude Chandler	Albert Whitman & Co.
Boxcar Children: Firehouse Mystery, The	O	RF	250+	Warner, Gertrude Chandler	Albert Whitman & Co.
Boxcar Children: Ghost Ship Mystery, The	O	RF	250+	Warner, Gertrude Chandler	Albert Whitman & Co.
Boxcar Children: Growling Bear Mystery, The	O	RF	250+	Warner, Gertrude Chandler	Albert Whitman & Co.
Boxcar Children: Haunted Cabin Mystery, The	O	RF	250+	Warner, Gertrude Chandler	Albert Whitman & Co.
Boxcar Children: Lighthouse Mystery, The	O	RF	250+	Warner, Gertrude Chandler	Albert Whitman & Co.
Boxcar Children: Mike's Mystery	O	RF	250+	Warner, Gertrude Chandler	Albert Whitman & Co.
Boxcar Children: Mountain Top Mystery	O	RF	250+	Warner, Gertrude Chandler	Albert Whitman & Co.
Boxcar Children: Mystery at Snowflake Inn, The	O	RF	250+	Warner, Gertrude Chandler	Albert Whitman & Co.
Boxcar Children: Mystery at the Alamo, The	O	RF	250+	Warner, Gertrude Chandler	Albert Whitman & Co.
Boxcar Children: Mystery at the Ballpark, The	O	RF	250+	Warner, Gertrude Chandler	Albert Whitman & Co.
Boxcar Children: Mystery at the Dog Show, The	O	RF	250+	Warner, Gertrude Chandler	Albert Whitman & Co.
Boxcar Children: Mystery at the Fair	O	RF	250+	Warner, Gertrude Chandler	Albert Whitman & Co.
Boxcar Children: Mystery Behind the Wall	O	RF	250+	Warner, Gertrude Chandler	Albert Whitman & Co.
Boxcar Children: Mystery Bookstore, The	O	RF	250+	Warner, Gertrude Chandler	Albert Whitman & Co.
Boxcar Children: Mystery Cruise, The	O	RF	250+	Warner, Gertrude Chandler	Albert Whitman & Co.
Boxcar Children: Mystery Girl, The	O	RF	250+	Warner, Gertrude Chandler	Albert Whitman & Co.
Boxcar Children: Mystery Horse, The	O	RF	250+	Warner, Gertrude Chandler	Albert Whitman & Co.
Boxcar Children: Mystery in San Francisco, The	O	RF	250+	Warner, Gertrude Chandler	Albert Whitman & Co.
Boxcar Children: Mystery in the Cave, The	O	RF	250+	Warner, Gertrude Chandler	Albert Whitman & Co.
Boxcar Children: Mystery in the Old Attic, The	O	RF	250+	Warner, Gertrude Chandler	Albert Whitman & Co.
Boxcar Children: Mystery in the Sand	O	RF	250+	Warner, Gertrude Chandler	Albert Whitman & Co.
Boxcar Children: Mystery in Washington, DC, The	O	RF	250+	Warner, Gertrude Chandler	Albert Whitman & Co.
Boxcar Children: Mystery of the Hidden Beach	O	RF	250+	Warner, Gertrude Chandler	Albert Whitman & Co.
Boxcar Children: Mystery of the Lost Mine, The	O	RF	250+	Warner, Gertrude Chandler	Albert Whitman & Co.
Boxcar Children: Mystery of the Lost Village, The	O	RF	250+	Warner, Gertrude Chandler	Albert Whitman & Co.
Boxcar Children: Mystery of the Missing Cat, The	O	RF	250+	Warner, Gertrude Chandler	Albert Whitman & Co.
Boxcar Children: Mystery of the Mixed-Up Zoo, The	O	RF	250+	Warner, Gertrude Chandler	Albert Whitman & Co.

* Collection of short stories

TITLE	LEVEL	GENRE	WORD COUNT	AUTHOR / SERIES	PUBLISHER / DISTRIBUTOR
Boxcar Children: Mystery of the Stolen Boxcar, The	O	RF	250+	Warner, Gertrude Chandler	Albert Whitman & Co.
Boxcar Children: Mystery of the Stolen Music, The	O	RF	250+	Warner, Gertrude Chandler	Albert Whitman & Co.
Boxcar Children: Mystery on Stage, The	O	RF	250+	Warner, Gertrude Chandler	Albert Whitman & Co.
Boxcar Children: Mystery on the Train, The	O	RF	250+	Warner, Gertrude Chandler	Albert Whitman & Co.
Boxcar Children: Mystery Ranch	O	RF	250+	Warner, Gertrude Chandler	Albert Whitman & Co.
Boxcar Children: Outer Space Mystery, The	O	RF	250+	Warner, Gertrude Chandler	Albert Whitman & Co.
Boxcar Children: Pizza Mystery, The	O	RF	250+	Warner, Gertrude Chandler	Albert Whitman & Co.
Boxcar Children: Schoolhouse Mystery	O	RF	250+	Warner, Gertrude Chandler	Albert Whitman & Co.
Boxcar Children: Snowbound Mystery	O	RF	250+	Warner, Gertrude Chandler	Albert Whitman & Co.
Boxcar Children: Soccer Mystery, The	O	RF	250+	Warner, Gertrude Chandler	Albert Whitman & Co.
Boxcar Children: Surprise Island	O	RF	250+	Warner, Gertrude Chandler	Albert Whitman & Co.
Boxcar Children: Woodshed Mystery, The	O	RF	250+	Warner, Gertrude Chandler	Albert Whitman & Co.
Boxcar Children: Yellow House Mystery, The	O	RF	250+	Warner, Gertrude Chandler	Albert Whitman & Co.
Boxes	E	F	103	Foundations	Wright Group/McGraw Hill
Boxes	H	F	153	Literacy 2000	Rigby
Boxes of Fun	D	RF	95	Story Steps	Rigby
Boxes, Boxes, Boxes	E	RF	63	Stewart, Josie; Salem, Lynn	Continental Press
Boy	T	B	250+	Dahl, Roald	Puffin Books
Boy and His Donkey, A	K	F	250+	Literacy 2000	Rigby
Boy and the Elk Dogs, The	T	TL	1688	Leveled Readers	Houghton Mifflin
Boy and the Lion, The	H	TL	166	Aesop	Wright Group/McGraw Hill
Boy and the Wolf, The	I	TL	200	Book Bank	Wright Group/McGraw Hill
Boy Called Slow, A	S	B	250+	Bruchac, Joseph	Putnam & Grosset
Boy in the Doghouse, A	N	RF	250+	Duffey, Betsy	Simon & Schuster
Boy Named Boomer, A	K	B	250+	Esiason, Boomer	Scholastic
Boy of the Three-Year Nap, The	N	TL	250+	Soar To Success	Houghton Mifflin
Boy Who Ate Dog Biscuits, The	N	RF	250+	Sachs, Betsy	Random House
Boy Who Cried Bigfoot, The	N	F	250+	The Zack Files	Grosset & Dunlap
Boy Who Cried Wolf, The	H	TL	324	Sunshine	Wright Group/McGraw Hill
Boy Who Cried Wolf, The	K	TL	250+	PM Tales and Plays-Purple	Rigby
Boy Who Cried Wolf, The	J	TL	140	Littledale, Freya	Scholastic
Boy Who Cried Wolf, The	L	TL	250+	Literacy Tree	Rigby
Boy Who Cried Wolf, The	J	TL	460	Aesop's Fables	Pearson Learning Group
Boy Who Lost His Face, The	R	RF	250+	Sachar, Louis	Alfred A. Knopf
Boy Who Owned the School, The	U	RF	250+	Paulsen, Gary	Bantam
Boy Who Reversed Himself, The	Y	SF	250+	Sleator, William	Puffin Books
Boy Who Saved Baseball, The	U	RF	250+	Ritter, John H.	Penguin Group
Boy Who Stretched to the Sky, The	M	F	463	Book Bank	Wright Group/McGraw Hill
Boy Who Tried to Hide, The	I	TL	219	Storyteller-Night Crickets	Wright Group/McGraw Hill
Boy Who Turned Into a T.V. Set, The	L	F	250+	Manes, Stephen	Avon Camelot
Boy Who Went to the North Wind, The	L	TL	250+	Literacy 2000	Rigby
Boy, a Dog, and a Frog, A	WB	F	N/A	Mayer, Mercer	Dial Books
Boys Against Girls	S	RF	250+	Naylor, Phyllis Reynolds	Bantam
Boys and Girls	D	RF	62	Williams, Deborah	Kaeden Books
Boys Start the War and the Girls Get Even, The	S	RF	250+	Naylor, Phyllis Reynolds	Bantam
*Boys Who Rocked the World: From King Tut to Tiger Woods	U	B	250+	Carlsmith, L.; Mann, B.; McCann, M. R.; & Strelow, E.	Beyond Words
*Boys Will Be	X	I	250+	Brooks, Bruce	Hyperion
Boy's Will, A	S	HF	250+	Haugaard, Erik Christian	Houghton Mifflin
Bozo	H	RF	94	Wonder World	Wright Group/McGraw Hill
Bozo the Clone	N	SF	250+	The Zack Files	Grosset & Dunlap
Bracelet, The	R	HF	250+	Uchida, Yoshiko	Philomel Books

TITLE	LEVEL	GENRE	WORD COUNT	AUTHOR / SERIES	PUBLISHER / DISTRIBUTOR
Brachiosaurus	M	I	250+	Discovering Dinosaurs	Capstone Press
Brachiosaurus	N	I	250+	Discovering Dinosaurs	Red Brick Learning
Brachiosaurus in the River	L	F	200	Wesley & The Dinosaurs	Wright Group/McGraw Hill
Brad and Butter Play Ball!	N	RF	250+	Hughes, Dean	William Morrow
Brady	V	HF	250+	Fritz, Jean	Puffin Books
Braids	D	RF	24	Visions	Wright Group/McGraw Hill
Braids for Naya	G	RF	89	City Stories	Rigby
Brain	V	I	250+	You And Your Body	Troll Associates
Brain-in-a-Box	M	F	250+	Matthews, Steve	Sundance
*Brainstorm!: The Stories of Twenty American Kid Inventors	P	B	250+	Tucker, Tom	Farrar, Straus and Giroux
Brand New Butterfly, A	L	I	186	Literacy 2000	Rigby
Brandon's New School	F	RF	163	Developing Books, Set 3	Pioneer Valley
Brave As	P	RF	250+	Marriott, Janice	Pacific Learning
Brave Ben	K	RF	162	Literacy 2000	Rigby
Brave Father Mouse	E	RF	92	PM Story Books	Rigby
Brave Irene	S	F	250+	Steig, William	Farrar, Straus and Giroux
Brave Little Mouse	I	F	249	Story Steps	Rigby
Brave Little Tailor, The	J	TL	250+	PM Tales and Plays Turquoise	Rigby
Brave Little Tailor, The: A German Folktale	O	TL	660	Leveled Readers	Houghton Mifflin
Brave Maddie Egg	M	RF	250+	Standiford, Natalie	Random House
Brave Past, A	V	I	1931	Leveled Readers	Houghton Mifflin
Brave Pilot, A	U	B	660	Vocabulary Readers	Houghton Mifflin
Brave Triceratops	G	F	178	PM Story Books	Rigby
Bravest Dog Ever, The: The True Story of Balto	L	I	250+	Standiford, Natalie	Random House
Bravo Amelia Bedelia!	L	F	250+	Parish, Herman	Avon
Brazil	P	I	250+	Fact Finders	Capstone Press
Brazil	N	I	250+	A True Book	Children's Press
Brazil	O	I	250+	Dahl, Michael	Red Brick Learning
Brazil	Q	I	250+	First Reports	Compass Point Books
Bread	D	RF	69	Sunshine	Wright Group/McGraw Hill
Bread and Jam for Frances	K	F	250+	Hoban, Russell	Scholastic
Bread and Roses: How an Orphan Girl Helped American Women Win the Vote	R	I	250+	Navigators Fiction Series	Benchmark Education
Bread for the Ducks	D	RF	109	PM Plus Story Books	Rigby
Bread, Bread, Bread	F	I	95	Morris, Ann	Scholastic
Break with Charity, A: A Story About the Salem Witch Trials	X	HF	250+	Rinaldi, Ann	Harcourt Trade
Breakfast	D	RF	23	Voyages	SRA/McGraw Hill
Breakfast	C	I	37	Little Books for Early Readers	University of Maine
Breakfast	C	RF	35	Foundations	Wright Group/McGraw Hill
Breakfast Around the World	J	I	101	Twig	Wright Group/McGraw Hill
Breakfast Around the World	S	I	1894	Leveled Readers Social Studies	Houghton Mifflin
Breakfast at the Farm	B	RF	56	Bookshop	Mondo
*Breakfast Bird and Other Animal Stories	M	F	250+	Bookshop	Mondo
Breakfast for Bears	I	F	477	Leveled Readers	Houghton Mifflin
Breakfast for Pickles	C	RF	62	Pickles the Dog Series	Pioneer Valley
Breakfast in Bed	C	RF	10	Voyages	SRA/McGraw Hill
Breakfast in Bed	G	RF	36	Tadpoles	Rigby
Breakfast on the Farm	D	I	73	Storyteller Nonfiction	Wright Group/McGraw Hill
Breakfast Time	G	F	250+	Bookshop	Mondo
Breakfast with John	C	RF	29	Books for Young Learners	Richard C. Owen
Breath of Air, A	T	I	1356	Leveled Readers Science	Houghton Mifflin
Breath of Fresh Air, A	P	RF	961	Leveled Readers	Houghton Mifflin

* Collection of short stories

TITLE	LEVEL	GENRE	WORD COUNT	AUTHOR / SERIES	PUBLISHER / DISTRIBUTOR
Breath of the Dragon	P	RF	250+	Giles, Gail	Bantam
Breathe In, Breathe Out: Learning About Your Lungs	M	I	250+	Amazing Body	Picture Window Books
Breathing	L	I	106	Bookshop	Mondo
Breathing Under Water	C	I	39	Sunshine	Wright Group/McGraw Hill
Breathing Underwater: Adventures in Chemistry	Y	RF	1752	Leveled Readers Science	Houghton Mifflin
Bremen-Town Musicians, The	K	TL	741	Gross, Ruth Belov	Scholastic
Brendan the Navigator: A History Mystery about the Discovery of America	R	I	250+	Fritz, Jean	Penguin Group
Brenda's Birthday	A	RF	18	Story Box	Wright Group/McGraw Hill
Brenda's Private Swing	K	RF	250+	Chardiet, Bernice; Maccarone, Grace	Scholastic
Brian's Brilliant Career	P	RF	250+	Literacy 2000	Rigby
Brian's Song	Z	I	250+	Blinn, William	Bantam
Brian's Winter	R	RF	250+	Paulsen, Gary	Bantam
Bricks, Wood, and Stones	D	I	54	Windows on Literacy	National Geographic
Bridge to Terabithia	T	RF	250+	Paterson, Katherine	HarperTrophy
Bridge, The	M	I	250+	Cambridge Reading	Pearson Learning Group
Bridge, The	B	F	32	Story Box	Wright Group/McGraw Hill
Bridges	D	RF	62	Seedlings	Continental Press
Bridges	N	I	250+	Wildcats	Wright Group/McGraw Hill
Bridges	D	I	49	Canizares, Susan; Moreton, Daniel	Scholastic
Bridging Beyond	X	F	250+	Duble, Kathleen Benner	Penguin Group
Bridging the Gap	Q	I	250+	Miller, Steve	Pacific Learning
Bright Idea, A	X	I	250+	iOpeners	Pearson Learning Group
Bright Ideas	Q	I	250+	Explorers	Wright Group/McGraw Hill
Bright Lights and Shadowy Shapes	L	I	250+	Spyglass Books	Compass Point Books
Bright Paddles	P	HF	250+	Downi, Mary Alice	Fitzhenry & Whiteside
Bright Shadow	T	F	250+	Avi	Aladdin
Brighty of the Grand Canyon	R	RF	250+	Henry, Marguerite	Aladdin
Brigid Beware	L	RF	250+	Leverich, Kathleen	Random House
Brigid Bewitched	L	RF	250+	Leverich, Kathleen	Random House
Brigid the Bad	L	RF	250+	Leverich, Kathleen	Random House
Brilliant Bugologist, The	N	RF	250+	Orbit Chapter Books	Pacific Literacy
Bring Me Your Horses	J	I	250+	Phonics and Friends	Hampton-Brown
Bringing the Rain to Kapiti Plain	J	TL	739	Aardema, Verna	Scholastic
Bringing the Sea Back Home	L	F	250+	Literacy 2000	Rigby
Bringing Up Baby Chimp	N	I	495	Independent Readers Science	Houghton Mifflin
Brinker's Isle	T	RF	2475	Leveled Readers	Houghton Mifflin
Brith The Terrible	M	F	250+	Literacy 2000	Rigby
Broccoli Tapes, The	S	RF	250+	Slepian, Jan	Scholastic
Broken Blade, The	T	HF	250+	Durbin, William	Yearling
Broken Bones	J	I	250+	Sunshine Books	Wright Group/McGraw Hill
Broken Bridge, The	Z	RF	250+	Pullman, Philip	Alfred A. Knopf
Broken Flower Pot, The	G	RF	203	PM Plus Story Books	Rigby
Broken Plate, The	I	RF	198	Foundations	Wright Group/McGraw Hill
Broken Window	G	RF	136	New Way Blue	Steck-Vaughn
*Broken Window and Other Cases, The	O	RF	250+	Simon, Seymour	Avon
Bronco Charlie and the Pony Express	U	B	1824	Leveled Readers	Houghton Mifflin
Bronze Bow, The	U	HF	250+	Speare, Elizabeth George	Houghton Mifflin
Brooke and Her Crayons	H	RF	283	Leveled Readers	Houghton Mifflin
Brookfield Days	N	HF	250+	Little House	HarperTrophy
Brooklyn Bridge: Eighth Wonder of the World, The	Z	I	3473	Leveled Readers	Houghton Mifflin

TITLE	LEVEL	GENRE	WORD COUNT	AUTHOR / SERIES	PUBLISHER / DISTRIBUTOR
Brother To Shadows	Z	SF	250+	Norton, Andre	Avon
Brothers	E	I	65	Talk About Books	Pearson Learning Group
Brothers	B	I	36	Pebble Books	Capstone Press
Brothers are Forever	L	RF	536	Leveled Readers	Houghton Mifflin
Brown Bear Figures it Out!	K	F	250+	Phonics and Friends	Hampton-Brown
Brown Bear, Brown Bear	C	F	185	Martin, Bill	Henry Holt & Co.
Brown Bears	E	I	45	Pebble Books	Capstone Press
Brown Bears	K	I	250+	PM Animal Facts: Turquoise	Rigby
Brown Cow Frowned, The	F	F	102	Seedlings	Continental Press
Brown Mouse Gets Some Corn	F	F	158	PM Plus Story Books	Rigby
Brown Mouse Plays a Trick	F	F	155	PM Plus Story Books	Rigby
Brown Sunshine of Sawdust Valley	O	RF	250+	Henry, Marguerite	Aladdin
Brown: Seeing Brown All Around Us	L	I	250+	Colors	Capstone Press
Brownie	C	RF	38	Hooker, Karen	Continental Press
Brownie Math	I	I	206	Rosen Real Readers	Rosen Publishing Group
Bruises	Z	RF	250+	De Vries, Anke	Bantam
Bruno's Birthday	E	RF	32	Literacy 2000	Rigby
Brushes	E	I	109	Rigby Literacy	Rigby
Brushing Well	D	I	42	Pebble Books	Capstone Press
Brutus Learns to Fetch	F	RF	155	Little Red Readers	Sundance
Bryce Canyon National Park	N	I	250+	A True Book	Children's Press
Bubble Gum	H	RF	66	City Kids	Rigby
Bubble Gum	B	RF	21	Carousel Readers	Pearson Learning Group
Bubble Gum Can Be Trouble	E	RF	147	Visions	Wright Group/McGraw Hill
Bubbles	C	RF	31	Sunshine	Wright Group/McGraw Hill
Bubbles	M	I	250+	Cambridge Reading	Pearson Learning Group
Bubbles	C	I	34	Discovery Links	Newbridge
Bubbles	C	RF	33	Literacy 2000	Rigby
Bubbles	I	RF	236	Leveled Readers Science	Houghton Mifflin
Bubbles Everywhere	C	I	41	Twig	Wright Group/McGraw Hill
Bubbling Crocodile	K	F	250+	Pacific Literacy	Pacific Learning
Buck Leonard, Baseball Hero	Q	B	250+	Leveled Readers Language Support	Houghton Mifflin
Buck Leonard, Baseball's Greatest Gentleman	R	B	1419	Leveled Readers	Houghton Mifflin
Buck Stops Here, The	T	I	250+	Provensen, Alice	OSI
Buckle My Shoe	C	RF	31	Sunshine	Wright Group/McGraw Hill
Bud, Not Buddy	T	RF	250+	Curtis, Christopher Paul	Random House
Buddha Boy	X	RF	250+	Koja, Kathe	Puffin Books
Buddies	F	F	177	Instant Readers	Harcourt School Publishers
Buddy	Q	RF	1522	Leveled Readers	Houghton Mifflin
Buddy: The First Seeing Eye Dog	M	I	250+	Moore, Eva	Scholastic
Budgie's Dream	J	F	250+	Story Starter	Wright Group/McGraw Hill
Buds and Blossoms: A Book About Flowers	M	I	250+	Growing Things	Picture Window Books
Buffalo Before Breakfast	M	F	250+	Osborne, Mary Pope	Random House
Buffalo Bill and the Pony Express	K	B	250+	Coerr, Eleanor	HarperTrophy
Buffalo Bill's Wild West Show	V	B	1750	Leveled Readers	Houghton Mifflin
Buffalo Gal	U	RF	250+	Wallace, Bill	Simon & Schuster
Buffalo Woman	N	TL	250+	Goble, Paul	Aladdin
Buffalo, The	M	I	250+	Crewe, Sabrina	Steck-Vaughn
Buffy	B	F	28	Literacy 2000	Rigby
Buffy's Tricks	G	RF	97	Literacy 2000	Rigby
Bug Bus, The	K	F	250+	Sunshine	Wright Group/McGraw Hill
Bug Off!	L	F	250+	Dussling, Jennifer	Grosset & Dunlap
Bug Party	F	I	131	Twig	Wright Group/McGraw Hill

* Collection of short stories

TITLE	LEVEL	GENRE	WORD COUNT	AUTHOR / SERIES	PUBLISHER / DISTRIBUTOR
Bug Watching	B	I	25	Twig	Wright Group/McGraw Hill
Bug, a Bear, and a Boy, A	F	F	250+	McPhail, David	Scholastic
Buggy Riddles	I	F	221	Little Books	Sadlier-Oxford
Bug-head and Me	M	RF	250+	Rigby Literacy	Rigby
Bugs	O	I	250+	Parker, Nancy Winslow; Wright, Joan Richards	Mulberry Books
Bugs and Other Insects	O	I	250+	Kalman, Bobbie	Crabtree
*Bugs And Other Stories	F	RF	250+	Story Steps	Rigby
Bugs for Breakfast	F	F	158	PM Plus Story Books	Rigby
Bugs on the Menu	M	I	250+	Sails	Rigby
Bugs!	L	I	250+	Phonics and Friends	Hampton-Brown
Bugs!	C	F	32	Rookie Readers	Children's Press
Build It Strong!	M	I	250+	First Science	Children's Press
Build Your Own Weather Station	I	I	250	Leveled Readers Science	Houghton Mifflin
Build Your Own Web Site	X	I	250+	iOpeners	Pearson Learning Group
Build, Build, Build	M	I	470	Sunshine	Wright Group/McGraw Hill
Building a Case	N	I	379	Vocabulary Readers	Houghton Mifflin
Building a Castle	L	I	250+	Early Connections	Benchmark Education
Building a Dream: Mary Bethune's School	R	B	250+	Kelso, Richard	Steck-Vaughn
Building a House	G	I	197	PM Plus Nonfiction	Rigby
Building a House	H	I	83	Barton, Byron	Morrow
Building an Ice Hotel	U	I	250+	iOpeners	Pearson Learning Group
Building Bridges	S	I	250+	Navigators Science Series	Benchmark Education
Building Bridges	V	I	250+	iOpeners	Pearson Learning Group
Building Homes, Building Hope	O	I	250+	Bovez, Marcie	Wright Group/McGraw Hill
Building Lady Liberty	K	I	450	Leveled Readers Social Studies	Houghton Mifflin
Building Shapes	G	I	30	Canizares, Susan; Berger, Samantha	Scholastic
Building Strong Bridges	M	I	250+	Twig	Wright Group/McGraw Hill
Building the Capital City	V	I	250+	Cornerstones of Freedom	Bantam
Building the Hoover Dam	W	I	1878	Leveled Readers Science	Houghton Mifflin
Building the Railroad	K	I	250+	Twig	Wright Group/McGraw Hill
Building Things	F	I	24	Sunshine	Wright Group/McGraw Hill
Building with Blocks	LB	RF	20	Sunshine	Wright Group/McGraw Hill
Buildings	C	I	61	Chessen, Betsy; Chanko, Pamela	Scholastic
Buildings	F	I	85	Leveled Readers Science	Houghton Mifflin
Buildings on My Street	F	RF	109	Foundations	Wright Group/McGraw Hill
Built for Speed Aircraft	T	I	250+	Graham, Ian	Steck-Vaughn
Bull Harris and the Purple Ooze	M	RF	250+	SupaDoopers	Sundance
Bull in a China Shop, A	K	F	250+	Literacy 2000	Rigby
Bull Run	Y	HF	250+	Fleischman, Paul	HarperCollins
Bulldog George	K	RF	250+	Voyages	SRA/McGraw Hill
Bulldozer, The	D	I	48	Sunshine	Wright Group/McGraw Hill
Bulldozers	I	I	94	Pebble Plus	Capstone Press
Bull's-eye!	F	RF	87	Oxford Reading Tree	Oxford University Press
Bully Bear	F	F	139	Rigby Literacy	Rigby
Bully for You, Teddy Roosevelt!	X	B	250+	Fritz, Jean	Penguin Group
Bully of Barkham Street	R	RF	250+	Stolz, Mary	HarperTrophy
Bully, The	L	RF	250+	PM Story Books	Rigby
Bumble Bear	F	F	89	Start to Read	School Zone
Bumble Bee	D	I	53	Pacific Literacy	Pacific Learning
Bumble Bees	I	I	123	Bugs, Bugs, Bugs	Capstone Press
Bumble Bees	E	I	56	Pebble Books	Capstone Press
Bump	F	I	217	Sun Sprouts	ETA/Cuisenaire

TITLE	LEVEL	GENRE	WORD COUNT	AUTHOR / SERIES	PUBLISHER / DISTRIBUTOR
Bump!	C	F	12	KinderReaders	Rigby
Bump, Bump, Bump	D	RF	51	Cat on the Mat	Oxford University Press
Bumper Cars, The	C	RF	94	PM Extensions-Red	Rigby
Bumpity, Bumpity, Bump	F	RF	62	Parker, Carol	Continental Press
Bumps in the Night	L	F	250+	Allard, Harry	Bantam
Bun, The	I	TL	421	Storyteller-Moon Rising	Wright Group/McGraw Hill
Bundle Up!	B	RF	35	Science	Outside the Box
Bungy 70528	O	RF	250+	Belcher, Angie	Pacific Learning
Bunker's Cove	S	I	1125	Leveled Readers	Houghton Mifflin
Bunnicula	Q	F	250+	Howe, James	Avon
Bunnicula Strikes Again!	Q	F	250+	Howe, James	Simon & Schuster
Bunnies in the Bathroom	Q	RF	250+	Baglio, Ben M.	Scholastic
Bunny Hop, The	I	F	250+	Slater, Teddy	Scholastic
Bunny Magic	I	RF	176	Books for Young Learners	Richard C. Owen
Bunny Opposites	B	F	14	Pair-It Books	Steck-Vaughn
Bunny Runs Away	K	F	250+	Chardiet, Bernice; Maccarone, Grace	Scholastic
Bunny, Bunny	D	F	40	My First Reader	Grolier Press
Bunny's Recess	A	I	35	Little Books for Early Readers	University of Maine
Bunrakkit	K	F	250+	Sunshine	Wright Group/McGraw Hill
Burger Time	L	I	250+	Voyages	SRA/McGraw Hill
Buried Eye, The	M	F	250+	Schultz, Irene	Wright Group/McGraw Hill
Burps, Boogers, and Bad Breath	K	I	246	Spyglass Books	Compass Point Books
Burrows	E	I	51	Storyteller-Setting Sun	Wright Group/McGraw Hill
Burrows, Tunnels, and Chambers	N	I	250+	Sails	Rigby
Bus Ride, The	C	F	164	Little Celebrations	Pearson Learning Group
Bus Ride, The	F	RF	99	Storyteller-Setting Sun	Wright Group/McGraw Hill
Bus Ride, The	C	F	175	Reading Unlimited	Pearson Learning Group
Bus Stop, The	G	RF	110	Hellen, Nancy	Orchard Books
Bus, The	C	I	46	Twig	Wright Group/McGraw Hill
Bush Bunyip, The	J	F	250+	Bookshop	Mondo
Bush Tucker	M	I	250+	Sunshine	Wright Group/McGraw Hill
Bushfire in the Koala Reserve	K	RF	250+	PM Plus Story Books	Rigby
Buster	C	I	36	Twig	Wright Group/McGraw Hill
Buster	M	F	250+	Bookshop	Mondo
Buster Baxter, Cat Saver	M	F	250+	Brown, Marc	Little, Brown & Co.
Buster Makes the Grade	M	F	250+	Brown, Marc	Little, Brown & Co.
Buster McCluster	E	F	71	Wonder World	Wright Group/McGraw Hill
Buster McCluster has Chicken Pox	E	RF	77	Wonder World	Wright Group/McGraw Hill
Buster the Balloon	E	F	70	Mathtales	Mimosa
Buster's Dino Dilemma	M	F	250+	Brown, Marc	Little, Brown & Co.
Busy Baby	J	RF	250+	Sunshine	Wright Group/McGraw Hill
Busy Beavers	K	RF	80	Dabcovich, Lydia	Scholastic
Busy Beavers, The	I	RF	362	PM Story Books-Orange	Rigby
Busy Bees	LB	RF	12	Voyages	SRA/McGraw Hill
Busy Bees	M	I	514	Leveled Readers	Houghton Mifflin
Busy Bees	K	I	177	Rosen Real Readers	Rosen Publishing Group
Busy Bird	LB	F	14	Pacific Literacy	Pacific Learning
Busy Dad	A	RF	24	Mom and Dad Series	Pioneer Valley
Busy Guy, A	K	RF	72	Rookie Readers	Children's Press
Busy Mosquito, The	C	F	112	Foundations	Wright Group/McGraw Hill
Busy People	C	RF	40	Little Celebrations	Pearson Learning Group
Busy Street	E	RF	67	Tadpoles	Rigby
Busy Week, A	D	RF	49	Pair-It Books	Steck-Vaughn

* Collection of short stories

TITLE	LEVEL	GENRE	WORD COUNT	AUTHOR / SERIES	PUBLISHER / DISTRIBUTOR
*Busybody Nora	N	RF	250+	Hurwitz, Johanna	Penguin Group
But Granny Did!	D	RF	58	Voyages	SRA/McGraw Hill
But I Knew Better	H	RF	242	Home Connection Collection	Rigby
But I'll Be Back Again	V	B	250+	Rylant, Cynthia	Beech Tree Books
Butch, the Outdoor Cat	E	RF	65	Carousel Readers	Pearson Learning Group
Buttercup Moon	F	RF	61	Book Bank	Wright Group/McGraw Hill
Butterflies	I	I	94	Bugs, Bugs, Bugs	Capstone Press
Butterflies	C	I	16	Instant Readers	Harcourt School Publishers
Butterflies	E	I	41	Pebble Books	Capstone Press
Butterflies	O	I	250+	Nature's Friends	Compass Point Books
Butterflies	O	I	250+	Holmes, Kevin J.	Red Brick Learning
Butterflies and Moths	N	I	250+	Kalman, Bobbie	Crabtree
Butterflies and Moths	L	I	250+	Early Connections	Benchmark Education
Butterflies in My Garden	G	RF	177	Bookshop	Mondo
Butterflies of the Sea	L	I	250+	Swartz, Stanley L.	Pearson Learning Group
Butterflies!	O	I	725	Leveled Readers	Houghton Mifflin
Butterfly and Me, The	F	RF	41	Reading Links	Steck-Vaughn
Butterfly Colors	F	I	52	Pebble Books	Capstone Press
Butterfly Day	K	RF	250+	Pacific Literacy	Pacific Learning
Butterfly Eggs	F	I	57	Pebble Books	Capstone Press
Butterfly Farm Burglar, The	M	RF	250+	Schultz, Irene	Wright Group/McGraw Hill
Butterfly Pyramid, The	N	TL	250+	Story Vines	Wright Group/McGraw Hill
Butterfly, The	C	I	21	Science	Outside the Box
Butterfly, The	M	I	250+	Crewe, Sabrina	Steck-Vaughn
Butterfly's Life, A	K	I	250+	Burke, Melissa Blackwell	Steck-Vaughn
Button Soup	K	RF	250+	Bank Street	Bantam
Buttons	C	RF	81	First Stories	Pacific Learning
Buttons Buttons	LB	I	26	Learn to Read	Creative Teaching Press
Buttons for General Washington	M	HF	250+	Roop, Peter & Connie	Carolrhoda Books
Buzby	J	F	250+	Hoban, Julia	HarperTrophy
Buzz Is Part of a Bee, A	E	RF	56	Rookie Readers	Children's Press
Buzz Said the Bee	G	F	62	Lewison, Wendy	Scholastic
Buzz, Buzz, Buzz	H	F	162	Barton, Byron	Macmillan
Buzzing Bees	LB	RF	69	Mathtales	Mimosa
Buzzing Flies	C	RF	45	Sunshine	Wright Group/McGraw Hill
Buzzzzzz Said the Bee	G	F	147	Hello Reader	Scholastic
By E-mail with Love	Q	RF	250+	Leveled Readers	Houghton Mifflin
By Lakes and Rivers	N	I	250+	Animal Trackers	Crabtree
By Myself or with My Friends	E	RF	200	Learn to Read	Creative Teaching Press
By the Great Horn Spoon!	V	HF	250+	Fleischman, Sid	Little, Brown & Co.
By the Seashore	N	I	250+	Animal Trackers	Crabtree
By the Shores of Silver Lake	Q	HF	250+	Wilder, Laura Ingalls	HarperTrophy
By the Stream	E	RF	73	Oxford Reading Tree	Oxford University Press
By the Tree	D	RF	75	Ready Readers	Pearson Learning Group
Bye, Bye, Bali Kai	U	RF	250+	Luger, Harriett	OSI
C. W. Post: A Pioneer in His Time	X	B	2121	Leveled Readers	Houghton Mifflin
Cabbage Caterpillar	I	F	221	Sunshine	Wright Group/McGraw Hill
Cabbage Princess, The	K	TL	250+	Literacy 2000	Rigby
Cabin Faced West, The	R	HF	250+	Fritz, Jean	Bantam
Cabin in the Hills, The	J	RF	349	PM Turquoise	Rigby
Cabot: John Cabot and the Journey to North America	U	B	250+	Exploring the World	Compass Point Books
Cactus Town	C	RF	43	Sunshine	Wright Group/McGraw Hill
Cactuses	K	I	237	Windows on Literacy	National Geographic

* Collection of short stories

TITLE	LEVEL	GENRE	WORD COUNT	AUTHOR / SERIES	PUBLISHER / DISTRIBUTOR
Caddie Woodlawn	R	HF	250+	Brink, Carol Ryrie	Bantam
Cage, The	Z	B	250+	Sender, Ruth Minsky	Simon & Schuster
Cajun Country	S	I	2013	Leveled Readers Social Studies	Houghton Mifflin
Cake for Mom, A	D	RF	63	Home Connection Collection	Rigby
Cake That Mack Ate, The	H	TL	189	Robart, Rose; Kovalski, Maryann	Little, Brown & Co.
Cake Walk	M	RF	250+	Books for Young Learners	Richard C. Owen
Cake, The	M	RF	250+	Read Alongs	Rigby
Cake, The	E	RF	250+	Story Steps	Rigby
Cake, The	C	I	40	Sun Sprouts	ETA/Cuisenaire
Calamity Kate	Q	RF	250+	Deary, Terry	HarperTrophy
Caleb's Choice	S	HF	250+	Wisler, Clifton G.	Penguin Group
Calico Bush	W	HF	250+	Field, Rachel	Simon & Schuster
Calico Captive	S	HF	250+	Speare, Elizabeth George	Yearling
Calico Cat at School	G	F	86	Charles, Donald	Children's Press
Calico Cat at the Zoo	F	F	88	Charles, Donald	Children's Press
Calico Cat Meets Bookworm	G	F	90	Charles, Donald	Children's Press
Calico Cat's Rainbow	E	F	78	Charles, Donald	Children's Press
Calico the Cat	F	F	82	Charles, Donald	Children's Press
California	Q	I	250+	One Nation	Capstone Press
California	R	I	250+	This Land Is Your Land	Compass Point Books
California	S	I	250+	Land of Liberty	Red Brick Learning
California	T	I	250+	Sea To Shining Sea	Children's Press
California Gold Rush, The	T	I	250+	We The People	Compass Point Books
California Gold Rush, The	T	I	250+	McNeer, May	Random House
California Gold Rush, The	V	I	250+	Let Freedom Ring	Red Brick Learning
California Gold Rush, The	V	I	250+	Cornerstones of Freedom	Children's Press
California or Bust!	N	HF	250+	Stamper, Judith	Scholastic
Call 911	C	I	22	Twig	Wright Group/McGraw Hill
Call It Courage	X	RF	250+	Sperry, Armstrong	Aladdin
Call Me Francis Tucket	V	HF	250+	Paulsen, Gary	Yearling
Call Me Ruth	R	RF	250+	Sachs, Marilyn	Beech Tree Books
Call Mr. Vasquez, He'll Fix It!	K	I	250+	Our Neighborhood	Children's Press
Call of the Selkie	Q	RF	250+	Action Packs	Rigby
Call of the Wild	Y	RF	250+	London, Jack	Signet Classics
Calvin Coolidge	U	B	250+	Profiles of the Presidents	Compass Point Books
Cam Jansen and the Chocolate Fudge Mystery	L	RF	250+	Adler, David A.	Puffin Books
Cam Jansen and the Ghostly Mystery	L	RF	250+	Adler, David A.	Puffin Books
Cam Jansen and the Mystery at the Haunted House	L	RF	250+	Adler, David A.	Puffin Books
Cam Jansen and the Mystery at the Monkey House	L	RF	250+	Adler, David A.	Puffin Books
Cam Jansen and the Mystery of Flight 54	L	RF	250+	Adler, David A.	Puffin Books
Cam Jansen and the Mystery of the Babe Ruth Baseball	L	RF	250+	Adler, David A.	Puffin Books
Cam Jansen and the Mystery of the Carnival Prize	L	RF	250+	Adler, David A.	Puffin Books
Cam Jansen and the Mystery of the Circus Clown	L	RF	250+	Adler, David A.	Puffin Books
Cam Jansen and the Mystery of the Dinosaur Bones	L	RF	250+	Adler, David A.	Puffin Books
Cam Jansen and the Mystery of the Gold Coins	L	RF	250+	Adler, David A.	Puffin Books
Cam Jansen and the Mystery of the Monkey House	L	RF	250+	Adler, David A.	Puffin Books

* Collection of short stories

TITLE	LEVEL	GENRE	WORD COUNT	AUTHOR / SERIES	PUBLISHER / DISTRIBUTOR
Cam Jansen and the Mystery of the Monster Movie	L	RF	250+	Adler, David A.	Puffin Books
Cam Jansen and the Mystery of the Stolen Corn Popper	L	RF	250+	Adler, David A.	Puffin Books
Cam Jansen and the Mystery of the Stolen Diamonds	L	RF	250+	Adler, David A.	Puffin Books
Cam Jansen and the Mystery of the Television Dog	L	RF	250+	Adler, David A.	Puffin Books
Cam Jansen and the Mystery of the U.F.O.	L	RF	250+	Adler, David A.	Puffin Books
Cam Jansen and the Scary Snake Mystery	L	RF	250+	Adler, David A.	Puffin Books
Cam Jansen and the Triceratops Pops Mystery	L	RF	250+	Adler, David A.	Puffin Books
Camel Ben	F	RF	32	Books for Young Learners	Richard C. Owen
Camel Called Bump-Along, A	K	F	373	Evangeline Nicholas Collection	Wright Group/McGraw Hill
Camels: Ships of the Desert	T	I	667	Vocabulary Readers	Houghton Mifflin
Camera, The	Q	I	250+	Great Inventions	Capstone Press
Cameras on the Battlefield: Photos of War	W	I	250+	High Five Reading	Red Brick Learning
Camouflage	M	I	250+	Cambridge Reading	Pearson Learning Group
Camouflage	K	I	202	Rigby Focus	Rigby
Camouflage	H	I	154	Sunshine	Wright Group/McGraw Hill
Camp Big Paw	J	RF	250+	Cushman, Doug	HarperTrophy
Camp Knock Knock	K	RF	250+	Duffey, Betsy	Bantam
Camp Knock Knock Mystery, The	K	RF	250+	Duffey, Betsy	Bantam
Camp Sink or Swim	M	RF	250+	Davis, Gibbs	Random House
Camping	E	RF	264	Sunshine	Wright Group/McGraw Hill
Camping	B	RF	19	Literacy 2000	Rigby
Camping	F	RF	71	Leveled Readers	Houghton Mifflin
Camping	D	RF	64	Hooker, Karen	Kaeden Books
Camping	C	RF	49	Foundations	Wright Group/McGraw Hill
Camping Out	E	RF	141	Visions	Wright Group/McGraw Hill
Camping Outside	F	RF	95	Book Bank	Wright Group/McGraw Hill
Camping Trip, The	E	RF	71	Leveled Readers Language Support	Houghton Mifflin
Camping with Claudine	K	RF	250+	Literacy 2000	Rigby
Camping with Our Dad	L	RF	250+	Sunshine	Wright Group/McGraw Hill
Can a Cow Hop?	D	I	40	Ready Readers	Pearson Learning Group
Can Do, Jenny Archer	M	RF	250+	Conford, Ellen	Random House
Can I Have a Dinosaur?	L	RF	250+	Literacy 2000	Rigby
Can I Have a Lick?	C	RF	69	Carousel Readers	Pearson Learning Group
Can I Have a Pet?	A	RF	36	Bebop Books	Lee & Low Books Inc.
Can I Help?	F	F	250	Janovitz, Marilyn	North-South Books
Can I Play Outside?	H	RF	121	Literacy 2000	Rigby
Can I Play?	C	F	30	The Book Project	Sundance
Can It Rain Cats and Dogs?	R	I	250+	Berger, Melvin & Gilda	Scholastic
Can We Go?	C	RF	25	Cherrington, Janelle	Scholastic
Can You Do This?	B	F	20	The Book Project	Sundance
Can You Eat a Fraction?	M	I	250+	Yellow Umbrella Books	Capstone Press
Can You Find It?	B	I	34	Ready Readers	Pearson Learning Group
Can You Find the Pattern?	D	I	113	Visions	Wright Group/McGraw Hill
Can You Fly?	C	I	51	Foundations	Wright Group/McGraw Hill
Can You Guess?	K	I	196	Yellow Umbrella Books	Capstone Press
Can You Imagine?	O	B	250+	McKissack, Patricia	Richard C. Owen
Can You Read a Map?	C	F	38	Learn to Read	Creative Teaching Press
Can You See An Insect?	J	I	171	Windows on Literacy	National Geographic
Can You See Me?	C	I	48	Foundations	Wright Group/McGraw Hill

* Collection of short stories

| --- | --- | --- | --- | --- | --- |
Can You See the Eggs?	C	I	87	PM Starters	Rigby
Canada	P	I	250+	Fact Finders	Capstone Press
Canada	H	I	68	Canizares, Susan; Berger, Samantha	Scholastic
Canada	Q	I	250+	First Reports	Compass Point Books
Canada	O	I	250+	Dahl, Michael	Red Brick Learning
Canada Celebrates Multiculturalism	T	I	250+	Kalman, Bobbie	Crabtree
Canada Geese Quilt, The	P	RF	250+	Kinsey-Warnock, Natalie	Bantam
Canada: The Culture	T	I	250+	Kalman, Bobbie	Crabtree
Canada: The Land	T	I	250+	Kalman, Bobbie	Crabtree
Canada: The People	T	I	250+	Kalman, Bobbie	Crabtree
Canary Caper, The	N	RF	250+	Roy, Ron	Random House
Candlelight	G	RF	231	PM Story Books	Rigby
Candlelight Service	O	RF	250+	Literacy 2000	Rigby
Candy Corn Contest, The	L	RF	250+	Giff, Patricia Reilly	Bantam
Candy Creations from the "Candy Queen"	N	I	250+	Bookshop	Mondo
Candy, the Old Car	H	F	234	PM Plus Story Books	Rigby
Cannonball Chris	L	RF	250+	Marzollo, J.	Random House
Canoe Diary	O	I	250+	Bishop, Nic	Pacific Learning
Canoeing	S	I	250+	The Great Outdoors	Red Brick Learning
Can't You Make Them Behave, King George?	R	I	250+	Fritz, Jean	Putnam & Grosset
Can't You See We're Reading?	D	RF	71	Stepping Stones	Nelson/Michaels Assoc.
Canyons	V	F	250+	Paulsen, Gary	Laurel-Leaf Books
Cape of Rushes, The	M	TL	250+	Cambridge Reading	Pearson Learning Group
Capitol, The	V	I	250+	Cornerstones of Freedom	Bantam
Caps for Sale	K	F	675	Slobodkina, Esphyr	Harper & Row
Capsize!	P	RF	250+	Bookweb	Rigby
Captain Bluefin's Underwater Ride	J	I	250+	Phonics Readers Plus	Steck-Vaughn
Captain B's Boat	G	F	158	Sunshine	Wright Group/McGraw Hill
Captain Bumble	K	F	510	Story Box	Wright Group/McGraw Hill
Captain Cat	H	F	250+	Hoff, Syd	HarperTrophy
Captain Felonius	L	F	250+	Literacy 2000	Rigby
Captain Grey	U	HF	250+	Avi	HarperTrophy
Captain Orinocos Onion	K	RF	250+	Voyages	SRA/McGraw Hill
Car Accident, The	F	RF	161	Foundations	Wright Group/McGraw Hill
Car Followed Us, A	D	RF	54	Books for Young Learners	Richard C. Owen
Car Ride, The	A	RF	41	Little Red Readers	Sundance
Car Trouble	L	RF	724	PM Gold	Rigby
Car Wash, The	G	I	98	Windows on Literacy	National Geographic
Caravan Boy	X	HF	3258	Leveled Readers	Houghton Mifflin
Cardboard Box, A	K	TL	250+	Ready to Read	Pacific Learning
Careful Crocodile, The	I	HF	271	PM Story Books-Orange	Rigby
Caribbean Cats	M	RF	250+	Books for Young Learners	Richard C. Owen
Caribou (Reindeer)	N	I	250+	PM Animal Facts: Silver	Rigby
Caribou Journey, A	Q	I	250+	Miller, Debbie S.	Little, Brown & Co.
Caring	L	I	250+	Character Education	Red Brick Learning
Caring	C	I	47	Interaction	Rigby
Caring for Earth	H	I	80	Windows on Literacy	National Geographic
Caring for Our Lizard	G	I	133	Learn to Read	Creative Teaching Press
Caring for Our Pets	C	I	74	Early Connections	Benchmark Education
Caring For Your Pets	I	I	175	Community Workers	Picture Window Books
Carl Goes Shopping	WB	F	N/A	Day, Alexandra	Green Tiger Press
Carl Goes to Daycare	WB	F	N/A	Day, Alexandra	Green Tiger Press
Carla Gets a Pet	I	RF	250+	Ready Readers	Pearson Learning Group

* Collection of short stories

TITLE	LEVEL	GENRE	WORD COUNT	AUTHOR / SERIES	PUBLISHER / DISTRIBUTOR
Carla's Breakfast	G	RF	225	Harper, Leslie	Kaeden Books
Carla's Corner	J	RF	646	Leveled Readers	Houghton Mifflin
Carla's Ribbons	G	RF	212	Harper, Leslie	Kaeden Books
Carla's Wheels	I	RF	200	Story Box	Wright Group/McGraw Hill
Carlita Ropes the Twister	L	F	363	Pair-It Books	Steck-Vaughn
Carlos and his Friends	M	RF	250+	Sunflower	Intercultural Center for Research in Education
Carl's Afternoon in the Park	WB	F	N/A	Day, Alexandra	Green Tiger Press
Carl's Birthday	WB	F	N/A	Day, Alexandra	Green Tiger Press
Carl's High Jump	K	RF	250+	PM Plus Story Books	Rigby
Carmen's Colors	LB	RF	14	Bebop Books	Lee & Low Books Inc.
Carmen's Star Party	J	RF	250+	Phonics and Friends	Hampton-Brown
Carnival	P	I	250+	Holidays and Festivals	Compass Point Books
Carnival Horse, The	K	RF	499	PM Plus Story Books	Rigby
Carnival, The	F	RF	82	Oxford Reading Tree	Oxford University Press
Carnivals Around the World	I	I	116	Lighthouse	Rigby
Carnivorous Carnival, The	V	F	250+	Snicket, Lemony	Scholastic
Carole: The Inside Story	R	RF	250+	Bryant, Bonnie	Skylark
Carolina Crow Girl	T	F	250+	Hobbs, Valerie	Puffin Books
Carpenters	L	I	250+	Community Workers	Compass Point Books
Carpenters	M	I	250+	Community Helpers	Red Brick Learning
Carrot Seed, The	G	F	101	Krauss, Ruth	Harper & Row
Carrot Soup	H	TL	142	Literacy Tree	Rigby
Carrot, The	C	F	48	Leveled Readers Language Support	Houghton Mifflin
Carrots	B	I	51	Pebble Books	Capstone Press
Carrots Don't Talk!	J	F	250+	Ready Readers	Pearson Learning Group
Carrots, Peas, and Beans	F	RF	142	Sunshine	Wright Group/McGraw Hill
Carry on, Mr. Bowditch	Y	B	250+	Latham, Jean Lee	Houghton Mifflin
Carry-Out Food	D	RF	56	Tadpoles	Rigby
Cars	Q	I	250+	Early Connections	Benchmark Education
Cars	C	I	30	Little Readers	Houghton Mifflin
Cars	F	I	72	Rockwell, Anne	Dutton
Cars	B	I	30	Little Readers	Houghton Mifflin
Cars	A	I	18	Pebble Books	Capstone Press
Cars!	F	I	56	Independent Readers Social Studies	Houghton Mifflin
Cartier: Jacques Cartier in Search of the Northwest Passage	U	B	250+	Exploring the World	Compass Point Books
Cartoonist, The	S	RF	250+	Byars, Betsy	Puffin Books
Carved in Stone: Borglum and Mount Rushmore	W	I	2997	Leveled Readers	Houghton Mifflin
Case for Jenny Archer, A	M	RF	250+	Conford, Ellen	Random House
Case of Capital Intrigue, The	S	RF	250+	Keene, Carolyn	Pocket Books
Case of Hermie the Missing Hamster, The	N	RF	250+	Preller, James	Scholastic
Case of the Captured Queen	S	RF	250+	Keene, Carolyn	Pocket Books
Case of the Cat's Meow, The	K	RF	250+	Bonsall, Crosby	HarperTrophy
Case of the Christmas Snowman, The	N	RF	250+	Preller, James	Scholastic
Case of the Cool-Itch Kid, The	L	RF	250+	Giff, Patricia Reilly	Bantam
Case of the Dangerous Solution, The	S	RF	250+	Keene, Carolyn	Pocket Books
Case of the Dirty Bird, The	O	RF	250+	Paulsen, Gary	Bantam
Case of the Disappearing Bones	N	RF	250+	SupaDoopers	Sundance
Case of the Double Cross, The	K	RF	250+	Bonsall, Crosby	HarperTrophy
Case of the Dumb Bells, The	K	RF	250+	Bonsall, Crosby	HarperTrophy
Case of the Elevator Duck, The	M	RF	250+	Berends, Polly Berrien	Random House

* Collection of short stories

TITLE	LEVEL	GENRE	WORD COUNT	AUTHOR / SERIES	PUBLISHER / DISTRIBUTOR
Case of the Floating Crime, The	S	RF	250+	Keene, Carolyn	Pocket Books
Case of the Furry Thing, The	G	RF	267	Ready Readers	Pearson Learning Group
Case of the Hungry Stranger, The	K	RF	1358	Bonsall, Crosby	HarperTrophy
Case of the Invisible Cat, The	Q	RF	250+	Parker, A. E.	Scholastic
Case of the Lion Dance	U	RF	250+	Yep, Laurence	HarperTrophy
Case of the Measled Cowboy, The	P	F	250+	Erickson, John R.	Puffin Books
Case of the Midnight Rustler, The	P	F	250+	Erickson, John R.	Puffin Books
Case of the Missing Cat, The	P	F	250+	Erickson, John R.	Puffin Books
Case of the Missing Cutthroats, The	S	RF	250+	George, Jean Craighead	HarperTrophy
Case of the Missing Key, The	P	F	1198	Leveled Readers	Houghton Mifflin
Case of the Missing Snacks, The	J	RF	454	Sunshine	Wright Group/McGraw Hill
Case of the Nervous Newsboy, The	N	RF	250+	Hildick, E. W.	Sundance
Case of the Sabotaged School Play, The	R	RF	250+	Singer, Marilyn	Bantam
Case of the Scaredy Cats, The	K	RF	250+	Bonsall, Crosby	HarperTrophy
Case of the Secret Valentine, The	N	RF	250+	Preller, James	Scholastic
Case of the Spooky Sleepover, The	N	RF	250+	Preller, James	Scholastic
Case of the Stolen Baseball Cards, The	N	RF	250+	Preller, James	Scholastic
Case of the Twin Teddy Bears, The	S	RF	250+	Keene, Carolyn	Pocket Books
Case of the Two Masked Robbers, The	K	F	250+	Hoban, Lillian	HarperTrophy
Casey's Case	Q	RF	250+	Literacy 2000	Rigby
Casey's Code	Q	RF	250+	Riley, Gail Blasser	Steck-Vaughn
Cass Becomes a Star	L	B	250+	Literacy 2000	Rigby
Cassidy's Magic	S	F	250+	Literacy 2000	Rigby
Cassie Binegar	T	RF	250+	MacLachlan, Patricia	HarperTrophy
Cassie's Castle	L	RF	250+	Rigby Literacy	Rigby
Castle	E	I	37	Exploring History & Geography	Rigby
Castle	X	I	250+	Macaulay, David	Scholastic
Castle in the Attic, The	R	F	250+	Winthrop, Elizabeth	Bantam
Castle of Llyr, The	W	F	250+	Alexander, Lloyd	Dell
Cat and Dog	C	F	71	Learn to Read	Creative Teaching Press
Cat and Dog	B	RF	41	Leveled Readers	Houghton Mifflin
Cat and Dog at School	F	F	101	Learn to Read	Creative Teaching Press
Cat and Dog Go Shopping	G	F	127	Learn to Read	Creative Teaching Press
Cat and Dog Make the Best, Biggest, Most Wonderful Cheese Sandwich	G	F	250+	Learn to Read	Creative Teaching Press
Cat and Dog: The Super Snack	F	F	161	Learn to Read	Creative Teaching Press
Cat and Mouse	B	F	75	PM Starters	Rigby
Cat and Rat	M	TL	250+	Young, Ed	Henry Holt & Co.
Cat and Rat Fall Out	J	TL	250+	Lighthouse	Rigby
Cat and the King, The	D	F	30	Literacy 2000	Rigby
Cat and the Mice, The	I	F	526	Book Bank	Wright Group/McGraw Hill
Cat at School?, A	D	RF	58	Independent Readers Social Studies	Houghton Mifflin
Cat Ate My Gymsuit, The	U	RF	250+	Danziger, Paula	Putnam & Grosset
Cat Burglar of Pethaven Drive, The	N	F	250+	Literacy 2000	Rigby
Cat Burglar, The	M	RF	250+	Krailing, Tessa	Barron's Educational
Cat Called Tim, A	L	RF	250+	New Way Literature	Steck-Vaughn
Cat Called, The	B	F	18	Ray's Readers	Outside the Box
Cat Came Back, The	I	TL	250+	Little Celebrations	Pearson Learning Group
Cat Came Back, The	B	TL	22	Ready Readers	Pearson Learning Group
Cat Chat	F	F	85	Ready Readers	Pearson Learning Group
Cat Concert	J	F	250+	Literacy 2000	Rigby
Cat Crazy	O	RF	250+	Baglio, Ben M.	Scholastic
Cat for Keeps, A	L	RF	250+	Cambridge Reading	Pearson Learning Group

* Collection of short stories

TITLE	LEVEL	GENRE	WORD COUNT	AUTHOR / SERIES	PUBLISHER / DISTRIBUTOR
Cat for You, A: Caring for Your Cat	M	I	250+	Pet Care	Picture Window Books
Cat Games	E	F	229	Ziefert, Harriet	Puffin Books
Cat Goes Fiddle-i-fee	F	TL	333	Galdone, Paul	Houghton Mifflin
Cat in the Hat	J	F	250+	Seuss, Dr.	Random House
Cat in the Tree, A	F	F	79	Oxford Reading Tree	Oxford University Press
Cat on the Mat	B	F	37	Wildsmith, Brian	Oxford University Press
Cat on the Move	A	F	30	Phonics and Friends	Hampton-Brown
Cat on the Roof	H	RF	250+	Story Box	Wright Group/McGraw Hill
Cat Prints	C	RF	25	Pair-It Books	Steck-Vaughn
Cat Running	U	RF	250+	Snyder, Zilpha Keatley	Bantam
Cat Tails	D	I	40	Books for Young Learners	Richard C. Owen
Cat Talk	N	I	250+	Long, Don	Pacific Learning
Cat That Broke the Rules, The	G	F	192	Ready Readers	Pearson Learning Group
Cat That Sat, The	D	RF	66	Start to Read	School Zone
Cat Traps	D	F	93	Coxe, Molly	Random House
Cat Walk	R	F	250+	Stolz, Mary	Bantam
Cat Whispers	H	RF	250+	Rigby Literacy	Rigby
Cat Who Loved Red, The	D	F	63	Salem, Lynn; Stewart, Josie	Continental Press
Cat Who Went To Heaven, The	S	F	250+	Coatsworth, Elizabeth	Aladdin
Cat Who Wore a Pot on Her Head, The	N	F	250+	Slepian, Jan; Seidler, Ann	Scholastic
Cat with No Tail, The	I	TL	137	Books for Young Learners	Richard C. Owen
Cat!	S	I	250+	Kroll, Virginia L.	Dawn
Cat, The	A	I	42	Little Books for Early Readers	University of Maine
Cat, The	C	RF	23	Smart Starts	Rigby
Cat, The	A	I	28	Leveled Readers Science	Houghton Mifflin
Catalyst	Z	RF	250+	Anderson, Laurie Halse	Penguin Group
Catch It, Marvin	E	RF	61	Windmill Books	Rigby
Catch Me If You Can!: The Roadrunner	M	I	250+	Chukran, Bobbi A.	Wright Group/McGraw Hill
Catch That Frog	E	F	131	Reading Unlimited	Pearson Learning Group
Catch That Pass!	M	RF	250+	Christopher, Matt	Little, Brown & Co.
Catch the Cookie	J	F	250+	Little Celebrations	Pearson Learning Group
Catcher With a Glass Arm	M	RF	250+	Christopher, Matt	Little, Brown & Co.
Catcher's Mask, The	M	RF	250+	Christopher, Matt	Little, Brown & Co.
Catching	B	I	35	Teacher's Choice Series	Pearson Learning Group
Catching Sunlight: A Book About Leaves	M	I	250+	Growing Things	Picture Window Books
Catching Some Respect	T	RF	3009	Leveled Readers	Houghton Mifflin
*Catching the Sun	M	TL	250+	Paul, Michele	Wright Group/McGraw Hill
Catching the Wind	N	I	250+	iOpeners	Pearson Learning Group
Caterpillars	N	I	250+	Minibeasts	Franklin Watts
Caterpillars	M	I	114	Bookshop	Mondo
Caterpillars	P	I	250+	Mini Pets	Steck-Vaughn
Caterpillars	F	I	54	Pebble Books	Capstone Press
Caterpillar's Adventure	F	F	69	Story Box	Wright Group/McGraw Hill
Catherine the Counter	E	RF	86	Sunshine	Wright Group/McGraw Hill
Catherine, Called Birdy	X	HF	250+	Cushman, Karen	Clarion
Cats	A	I	24	Vocabulary Readers	Houghton Mifflin
Cats	D	I	43	All About Pets	Red Brick Learning
Cats	J	I	250+	PM Animal Facts: Orange	Rigby
Cats	C	I	45	Williams, Deborah	Kaeden Books
Cats	I	I	137	Wonder World	Wright Group/McGraw Hill
Cats and Kittens	F	I	44	Reading Unlimited	Pearson Learning Group
Cats and Mice	H	F	51	Gelman, Rita	Scholastic
*Cats and Other Stories	J	F	250+	Story Steps	Rigby
Cats' Burglar, The	K	F	250+	Parish, Peggy	Hearst

* Collection of short stories

TITLE	LEVEL	GENRE	WORD COUNT	AUTHOR / SERIES	PUBLISHER / DISTRIBUTOR
Cat's Day, A	B	I	23	Twig	Wright Group/McGraw Hill
Cat's Diary	M	F	250+	Sails	Rigby
Cats Everywhere	F	RF	51	Books for Young Learners	Richard C. Owen
Cats Have Kittens	M	I	250+	Animals and Their Young	Compass Point Books
Cat's Meow, The	O	F	250+	Soto, Gary	Scholastic
Cats of the Night	K	RF	379	Book Bank	Wright Group/McGraw Hill
Cats on the Farm	H	I	71	Pebble Books	Red Brick Learning
Cat's Party	F	F	39	Sunshine	Wright Group/McGraw Hill
Cat's Surprise Party	I	F	376	Leveled Readers	Houghton Mifflin
Cat's Trip	G	F	158	Ready Readers	Pearson Learning Group
Cat's Whiskers, A	I	I	250+	Windows on Literacy	National Geographic
Cats, Cats, Cats	G	RF	217	Story Basket	Wright Group/McGraw Hill
Cats, Cats, Cats	Q	I	250+	Literacy 2000	Rigby
Cats, Cats, Cats	B	I	14	Pair-It Books	Steck-Vaughn
Catten, The	K	F	769	Jellybeans	Rigby
Cattle	L	I	250+	PM Animal Facts: Purple	Rigby
Catwings	N	F	250+	Le Guin, Ursula K.	Scholastic
Catwings Return	N	F	250+	Le Guin, Ursula K.	Scholastic
Caught by the Sea	N	RF	250+	Keating, Rosemary	Pacific Learning
Caught in a Flash	P	I	250+	Bishop, Nic	Pacific Learning
Caught in the Storm	H	RF	250+	Home Connection Collection	Rigby
Cave Creatures	Q	I	872	Independent Readers Science	Houghton Mifflin
Cave, The	C	RF	67	Book Bank	Wright Group/McGraw Hill
Caves	G	I	79	Seedlings	Continental Press
Caves	R	I	250+	The Wonders of our World	Crabtree
Caves	M	I	250+	Discovery World	Rigby
Caves	R	I	250+	Wood, Jenny	Scholastic
Caves and Caverns	O	I	250+	Gibbons, Gail	Harcourt Trade
Cay, The	V	HF	250+	Taylor, Theodore	Avon
CD and the Giant Cat	V	SF	250+	Action Packs	Rigby
Cecil the Caterpillar	E	F	130	Lighthouse	Rigby
Ceiling of Stars, A	U	RF	250+	Creel, Ann Howard	Pleasant Company
Celebrate Art	M	I	228	Twig	Wright Group/McGraw Hill
Celebrating Chanukah: Eight Nights	J	I	188	Learn to Read	Creative Teaching Press
Celebrating Chinese New Year: Nick's New Year	J	I	142	Learn to Read	Creative Teaching Press
Celebrating Christmas: Christmas Decorations	J	I	165	Learn to Read	Creative Teaching Press
Celebrating Cinco de Mayo: Fiesta Time!	J	I	41	Learn to Read	Creative Teaching Press
Celebrating Easter: The Easter Egg Hunt	J	I	166	Learn to Read	Creative Teaching Press
Celebrating Father's Day: Father's Day is for Special People	F	RF	115	Learn to Read	Creative Teaching Press
Celebrating Martin Luther King, Jr. Day: Dreaming of Change	J	I	152	Learn to Read	Creative Teaching Press
Celebrating Mother's Day: Mom's Memory Box	E	F	100	Learn to Read	Creative Teaching Press
Celebrating Patriotic Holidays: Honoring America	H	I	175	Learn to Read	Creative Teaching Press
Celebrating President's Day	H	I	181	Learn to Read	Creative Teaching Press
Celebrating Thanksgiving: Giving Thanks	F	I	145	Learn to Read	Creative Teaching Press
Celebrating Valentine's Day: My Special Valentines	F	RF	137	Learn to Read	Creative Teaching Press
Celebrations	G	I	37	Berger, Samantha; Moreton, Daniel	Scholastic
Celebrations	G	I	107	Storyteller-Moon Rising	Wright Group/McGraw Hill
Celebrations	L	I	199	Yellow Umbrella Books	Capstone Press
Celebrations Around the World	J	I	205	Early Connections	Benchmark Education

TITLE	LEVEL	GENRE	WORD COUNT	AUTHOR / SERIES	PUBLISHER / DISTRIBUTOR
Celery Stalks at Midnight, The	R	F	250+	Howe, James	Atheneum
Celia	K	RF	182	Leveled Readers	Houghton Mifflin
Celia and Ali	I	RF	137	Leveled Readers Language Support	Houghton Mifflin
Cells	R	I	1649	Leveled Readers Science	Houghton Mifflin
Cells	J	I	96	Wonder World	Wright Group/McGraw Hill
Cement Tent	G	F	358	First Start	Troll Associates
Center Court Sting	M	RF	250+	Christopher, Matt	Little, Brown & Co.
*Centerburg Tales: More Adventures of Homer Price	Q	RF	250+	McCloskey, Robert	Puffin Books
Centerfield Ballhawk	M	RF	250+	Christopher, Matt	Little, Brown & Co.
Cesar Chavez	Y	B	250+	Rodriguez, Consuelo	Chelsea House
Cesar Chavez	L	B	262	Pebble Books	Capstone Press
Cesar Chavez	Y	B	2023	Leveled Readers	Houghton Mifflin
Cesar Chavez	M	B	295	Independent Readers Social Studies	Houghton Mifflin
Cesar Chavez	P	B	262	Davis, Lucile	Red Brick Learning
Cesar Chavez	N	B	262	Biography	Benchmark Education
Chad and the Big Egg	F	F	204	Leveled Readers	Houghton Mifflin
Chair For My Mother, A	M	RF	250+	Williams, Vera B.	Scholastic
Chalk Box Kid, The	N	RF	250+	Bulla, Clyde Robert	Random House
Chalk Talk	C	I	69	Storyteller-First Snow	Wright Group/McGraw Hill
Challenge at Second Base	M	RF	250+	Christopher, Matt	Little, Brown & Co.
Chameleons	L	I	201	Twig	Wright Group/McGraw Hill
Champ	I	RF	274	Story Box	Wright Group/McGraw Hill
Champion Billy Mills	P	B	725	Leveled Readers	Houghton Mifflin
Champions	C	I	13	Twig	Wright Group/McGraw Hill
Chancy and the Grand Rascal	R	F	250+	Fleischman, Sid	Beech Tree Books
Change for Zoe, A	K	RF	250+	Home Connection Collection	Rigby
Change The Locks	S	RF	250+	French, Simon	Scholastic
Changes	WB	I	N/A	Book Bank	Wright Group/McGraw Hill
Changes Around Us	J	I	176	Instant Readers	Harcourt School Publishers
Changes for Addy	Q	HF	250+	The American Girls Collection	Pleasant Company
Changes For Addy: A Winter Story	Q	HF	250+	The American Girls Collection	Pleasant Company
Changes For Felicity: A Winter Story	Q	HF	250+	The American Girls Collection	Pleasant Company
Changes For Josefina: A Winter Story	Q	HF	250+	The American Girls Collection	Pleasant Company
Changes For Kirsten: A Winter Story	Q	HF	250+	The American Girls Collection	Pleasant Company
Changes For Molly: A Winter Story	Q	HF	250+	The American Girls Collection	Pleasant Company
Changes For Samantha: A Winter Story	Q	HF	250+	The American Girls Collection	Pleasant Company
Changes in Seasons	I	I	250+	Phonics Readers Plus	Steck-Vaughn
Changes, Changes	WB	I	N/A	Hutchins, Pat	Aladdin
Changing Caterpillar, The	G	I	56	Books for Young Learners	Richard C. Owen
Changing Colors	M	I	247	Vocabulary Readers	Houghton Mifflin
Changing Colors	B	I	16	Pair-It Books	Steck-Vaughn
Changing Earth, The	P	I	250+	iOpeners	Pearson Learning Group
Changing Land, The	I	I	64	Pacific Literacy	Pacific Learning
Changing Schools	F	RF	53	City Stories	Rigby
Changing Seasons	S	I	1936	Leveled Readers Science	Houghton Mifflin
Changing Shape	I	I	143	Rigby Literacy	Rigby
Changing Shores	O	I	250+	iOpeners	Pearson Learning Group
Changing the Rules	S	RF	1908	Leveled Readers	Houghton Mifflin
Changing Times	Q	RF	250+	Treasured Horses Collection	Scholastic
Changing Weather	G	I	145	Early Connections	Benchmark Education
Chang's Paper Pony	L	RF	250+	Coerr, Eleanor	HarperTrophy

---

* Collection of short stories

TITLE	LEVEL	GENRE	WORD COUNT	AUTHOR / SERIES	PUBLISHER / DISTRIBUTOR
Chano	H	RF	124	Literacy 2000	Rigby
Chaos in the Kitchen	K	F	250+	Home Connection Collection	Rigby
Charlemagne and the Holy Roman Empire	Y	B	3083	Leveled Readers Social Studies	Houghton Mifflin
Charles	C	RF	48	Learn to Read	Creative Teaching Press
Charles Lindbergh	O	B	250+	Early Biographies	Compass Point Books
Charles M. Schulz	L	B	186	First Biographies	Red Brick Learning
Charley Skedaddle	U	HF	250+	Beatty, Patricia	Troll Associates
Charlie	L	F	250+	Literacy 2000	Rigby
Charlie and the Chocolate Factory	R	F	250+	Dahl, Roald	Bantam
Charlie and the Great Glass Elevator	R	F	250+	Dahl, Roald	Bantam
Charlie Best	J	F	250+	Voyages	SRA/McGraw Hill
Charlie Is a Chicken	P	RF	250+	Smith, Jane Denitz	HarperTrophy
Charlie Malarkey and the Singing Moose	R	F	250+	Kennedy, William & Brendan	Puffin Books
Charlie Needs a Cloak	I	HF	187	DePaola, Tomie	Prentice-Hall
Charlie Strong and his favourite song	G	RF	120	Breakthrough	Longman/Bow
Charlie Takes a Shot	W	RF	2507	Leveled Readers	Houghton Mifflin
Charlie the Bridesmaid	K	RF	250+	Rigby Literacy	Rigby
Charlie's Black Hen	E	RF	89	Seedlings	Continental Press
Charlie's P.E. Gear	E	RF	102	Lighthouse	Rigby
Charlotte's Web	R	F	250+	White, E. B.	HarperTrophy
Charlotte's Web Page	P	RF	250+	Action Packs	Rigby
Charters of Freedom	Y	I	2738	Independent Readers Social Studies	Houghton Mifflin
Charting Your Course	T	I	250+	iOpeners	Pearson Learning Group
Chase, The	F	F	85	Oxford Reading Tree	Oxford University Press
Chasing Redbird	V	RF	250+	Creech, Sharon	HarperCollins
Chasing the Train	P	HF	768	Leveled Readers	Houghton Mifflin
Chasing Tornadoes	P	I	250+	Gold, Becky	Pearson Learning Group
Chasing Tornadoes!	P	I	250+	Rigby Literacy	Rigby
Cheerful King, The	K	F	351	Little Books	Sadlier-Oxford
Cheerleading for Fun!	S	I	250+	Activities for Fun	Compass Point Books
Cheese, Please?	C	RF	62	Story Steps	Rigby
Cheetahs	G	RF	140	Seedlings	Continental Press
Chefs	L	I	250+	Community Workers	Compass Point Books
Chen's Christmas Tree	E	RF	166	Developing Books	Pioneer Valley
Cherokee Indians, The	P	I	250+	Lund, Bill	Red Brick Learning
Cherokee Little People, The: A Native American Tale	I	TL	250+	Rigby Literacy	Rigby
Cherokee, The	R	I	250+	First Reports	Compass Point Books
Cherokee, The: Native Basket Weavers	R	I	250+	America's First Peoples	Capstone Press
Cherries and Cherry Pits	M	RF	250+	Williams, Vera B.	Houghton Mifflin
Cherry Blossoms Everywhere	M	I	370	Independent Readers Social Studies	Houghton Mifflin
Chesapeake Bay	R	I	1192	Leveled Readers Social Studies	Houghton Mifflin
Chester A. Arthur	U	B	250+	Profiles of the Presidents	Compass Point Books
Chester Cricket's New Home	S	F	250+	Selden, George	Bantam
Chester Cricket's Pigeon Ride	S	F	250+	Selden, George	Bantam
Chester the Wizard	M	F	250+	Reading Unlimited	Pearson Learning Group
Chester's Good Idea	M	B	250+	Leveled Readers Language Support	Houghton Mifflin
Chew, Chew, Chew	C	RF	24	Literacy 2000	Rigby
Cheyenne, The	R	I	250+	First Reports	Compass Point Books
Cheyenne, The	N	I	250+	A New True Book	Children's Press
Chicago Fire, The	P	I	250+	Gutner, Howard	Scholastic

* Collection of short stories

TITLE	LEVEL	GENRE	WORD COUNT	AUTHOR / SERIES	PUBLISHER / DISTRIBUTOR
Chicago Winds	K	I	173	Evangeline Nicholas Collection	Wright Group/McGraw Hill
Chick and the Duckling, The	D	F	112	Ginsburg, Mirra	Macmillan
Chick Challenge	O	RF	250+	Baglio, Ben M.	Scholastic
Chicken	M	I	250+	Life Cycles	Creative Teaching Press
Chicken and Egg Chores	C	RF	27	Little Books for Early Readers	University of Maine
Chicken and the Egg, The	E	I	68	Sun Sprouts	ETA/Cuisenaire
Chicken Feed	E	RF	67	Joy Readers	Pearson Learning Group
Chicken for Dinner	C	RF	27	Story Box	Wright Group/McGraw Hill
Chicken in the Middle of the Road	J	RF	250+	Bookshop	Mondo
Chicken Licken	H	TL	233	Supersonics	Rigby
Chicken Licken	I	TL	346	Sunshine	Wright Group/McGraw Hill
Chicken Little	L	TL	587	Traditional Tales & More	Rigby
Chicken Little	I	TL	250+	PM Traditional Tales-Orange	Rigby
Chicken Little	E	TL	107	Sunshine	Wright Group/McGraw Hill
Chicken Pox	H	RF	220	Little Readers	Houghton Mifflin
Chicken Soup	B	I	38	Fitros, Pamela	Kaeden Books
Chicken Soup with Rice	M	F	310	Sendak, Maurice	HarperCollins
Chicken Sunday	N	RF	250+	Polacco, Patricia	Scholastic
Chickens	L	I	250+	PM Animal Facts: Purple	Rigby
Chickens	B	I	24	Pebble Books	Capstone Press
Chickens	D	I	23	Books for Young Learners	Richard C. Owen
Chickens	G	I	105	Bookshop	Mondo
Chickens Are Here!, The	D	I	50	Vocabulary Readers	Houghton Mifflin
Chickens Aren't the Only Ones	K	I	250+	Heller, Ruth	Scholastic
Chickens Have Chicks	M	I	250+	Animals and Their Young	Compass Point Books
Chickens on the Farm	F	I	68	Vocabulary Readers	Houghton Mifflin
Chickens on the Farm	G	I	59	Pebble Books	Capstone Press
Chickens On Vacation	G	F	169	Seedlings	Continental Press
Chick-in-a-Box	K	RF	250+	Voyages	SRA/McGraw Hill
Chicks Don't Say Quack	D	F	86	Sun Sprouts	ETA/Cuisenaire
Chick's Walk	A	F	14	Story Box	Wright Group/McGraw Hill
Chief Great Raven	N	TL	250+	Orbit Double Takes	Pacific Learning
Chief Joseph	Y	B	2199	Leveled Readers	Houghton Mifflin
Chief Joseph of the Nez Percé	P	B	250+	McAuliffe, Bill	Red Brick Learning
Child in Prison Camp, A	X	HF	250+	Takashima, Shizuye	Tundra Books
Child of the Owl	W	RF	250+	Yep, Laurence	HarperTrophy
Child of the Wolves	U	RF	250+	Hall, Elizabeth	Bantam
Children	C	I	45	Pebble Books	Capstone Press
Children Around the World	P	I	250+	Rigby Focus	Rigby
Children Around the World	M	I	250+	People, Spaces & Places	Rand McNally
Children as Young Scientists	K	I	393	Early Connections	Benchmark Education
Children at Play	F	I	101	Little Red Readers	Sundance
Children of Ancient Greece	P	I	250+	Rosen Real Readers	Rosen Publishing Group
*Children of Christmas: Stories for the Season	R	RF	250+	Rylant, Cynthia	Orchard Books
Children of Clay: A Family of Pueblo Potters	S	I	250+	Swentzell, Rina	Lerner Publishing
Children of Green Knowe, The	T	F	250+	Boston, L. M.	Harcourt Trade
Children of Sierra Leone, The	J	I	142	Books For Young Learners	Richard C. Owen
Children of the Dust Bowl	Y	I	250+	Stanley, Jerry	Crown
*Children of the Earth and Sky	P	I	250+	Krensky, Stephen	Scholastic
Children of the Fire	P	HF	250+	Robinet, Harriette	Aladdin
Children of the Longhouse	S	HF	250+	Bruchac, Joseph	Penguin Group
Children of the River	X	RF	250+	Crew, Linda	Bantam
Children of the Sierra Madre, The	U	I	250+	Staub, Frank	Carolrhoda Books
Children of the Wild West	X	I	250+	Freedman, Russell	Clarion

TITLE	LEVEL	GENRE	WORD COUNT	AUTHOR / SERIES	PUBLISHER / DISTRIBUTOR
Children's Clothing of the 1800's	S	I	250+	Historic Communities	Crabtree
Child's Day, A	T	I	250+	Historic Communities	Crabtree
Child's Day, A	C	RF	34	Sunshine	Wright Group/McGraw Hill
Child's Portrait of Shakespeare, A	Q	B	250+	Burdett, Lois	Firefly Books
Childtimes: A Three-Generation Memoir	X	B	250+	Greenfield, Eloise; Little, Lessie Jones	HarperTrophy
Chile	Q	I	250+	First Reports	Compass Point Books
Chili for Lindy	J	RF	250+	Leveled Readers Language Support	Houghton Mifflin
Chili Pepper Pinata, The	H	RF	257	Story Box	Wright Group/McGraw Hill
Chill Wind	Z	RF	250+	McDonald, Janet	Farrar, Straus and Giroux
Chimp Communities	U	I	1618	Leveled Readers Science	Houghton Mifflin
Chimpanzees	M	I	250+	The Wild World of Animals	Capstone Press
Chimpanzees	S	I	1605	Leveled Readers Science	Houghton Mifflin
China	P	I	250+	Fact Finders	Capstone Press
China	O	I	250+	Many Cultures, One World	Capstone Press
China	N	I	250+	A True Book	Children's Press
China	Q	I	250+	First Reports	Compass Point Books
China	O	I	250+	Dahl, Michael	Red Brick Learning
China Teacup, The	M	F	250+	Voyages	SRA/McGraw Hill
China: The Culture	T	I	250+	Kalman, Bobbie	Crabtree
China: The Land	T	I	250+	Kalman, Bobbie	Crabtree
China: The People	T	I	250+	Kalman, Bobbie	Crabtree
China's Amazing Buildings	T	I	498	Vocabulary Readers	Houghton Mifflin
China's Bravest Girl: The Legend of Hua Mu Lan	O	TL	250+	Chin, Charlie	Children's Press
China's Huang River	S	I	2036	Independent Readers Social Studies	Houghton Mifflin
Chinese Foods and Recipes	P	I	250+	Rosen Real Readers	Rosen Publishing Group
Chinese Kites	A	I	15	Twig	Wright Group/McGraw Hill
Chinese New Year	F	I	79	Vocabulary Readers	Houghton Mifflin
Chinese New Year	O	I	250+	Holidays and Festivals	Compass Point Books
Chinese New Year	D	I	33	Pacific Literacy	Pacific Learning
Chinese New Year, The	J	TL	250+	Troughton, Joanna	Pearson Learning Group
Chipmunk at Hollow Tree Lane	K	F	250+	Sherrow, Victoria	Scholastic
Chip's Dad	K	RF	250+	Rigby Literacy	Rigby
Chisholm Trail, The	V	I	250+	Cornerstones of Freedom	Bantam
Chloe the Chameleon	F	F	250+	Warren, Celia	Scholastic
Chocolate	N	I	250+	What's For Lunch?	Children's Press
Chocolate	L	I	191	Windows on Literacy	National Geographic
Chocolate by Hershey: A Story about Milton S. Hershey	R	B	250+	Burford, Betty	Carolrhoda Books
Chocolate Cake, The	J	RF	250+	PM Plus Story Books	Rigby
Chocolate Cake, The	B	RF	23	Story Box	Wright Group/McGraw Hill
Chocolate Chip Cookies	LB	I	12	Preiss, Leah Palmer	Henry Holt & Co.
Chocolate Chip Cookies	B	I	32	Ready Readers	Pearson Learning Group
Chocolate Fever	O	F	250+	Smith, Robert	Bantam
Chocolate Flier, The	R	I	250+	Action Packs	Rigby
Chocolate Touch, The	N	F	250+	Catling, Patrick Skene	Bantam
Chocolate Trail, The	N	I	250+	Rigby Focus	Rigby
Chocolate!	P	I	250+	Action Packs	Rigby
Chocolate, Chocolate, Chocolate	E	RF	106	Visions	Wright Group/McGraw Hill
Chocolate-Chip Muffins	J	RF	204	Sunshine	Wright Group/McGraw Hill
Chocolate-Covered Contest, The	S	RF	250+	Keene, Carolyn	Pocket Books
Choice for Sarah, A	K	RF	250+	PM Plus Story Books	Rigby

* Collection of short stories

TITLE	LEVEL	GENRE	WORD COUNT	AUTHOR / SERIES	PUBLISHER / DISTRIBUTOR
Chomp	L	I	250+	Berger, Melvin	Scholastic
Chook, Chook	E	RF	42	Sunshine	Wright Group/McGraw Hill
Choose Me!	H	F	204	Reading Corners	Pearson Learning Group
Choosing a Puppy	E	RF	158	PM Extensions-Yellow	Rigby
Choosing Up Sides	V	RF	250+	Ritter, John H.	Puffin Books
Chop, Simmer, Season	LB	I	21	Brandenburg, Alexa	OSI
Chores	D	RF	50	Windows on Literacy	National Geographic
Christa McAuliffe	M	B	250+	Explore Space!	Capstone Press
Christa McAuliffe: Teacher in Space	W	B	250+	Naden, Corinne J.; Blue, Rose	Millbrook Press
Christina's Ghost	R	F	250+	Wright, Betty Ren	Bantam
Christmas	O	I	250+	Holidays and Festivals	Compass Point Books
Christmas	P	I	250+	Let's See	Compass Point Books
Christmas	F	I	106	Fiesta Holiday Series	Pearson Learning Group
Christmas	J	I	106	Pebble Books	Capstone Press
Christmas	LB	I	16	Smart Start	Rigby
Christmas Carol, A	U	F	250+	Dickens, Charles	Scholastic
Christmas in the Big Woods	J	HF	250+	Wilder, Laura Ingalls	HarperCollins
Christmas Santa Almost Missed, The	G	F	158	First Start	Troll Associates
Christmas Shopping	E	RF	48	Literacy 2000	Rigby
Christmas Spurs, The	R	RF	250+	Wallace, Bill	Bantam
Christmas Surprise	G	RF	145	First Start	Troll Associates
Christmas Tree, The	F	RF	163	PM StoryBooks	Rigby
Christmas: Why We Celebrate It the Way We Do	P	I	250+	Hintz, Martin & Kate	Red Brick Learning
Christopher Columbus	M	B	250+	First Biographies	Red Brick Learning
Christopher Columbus: A Great Explorer	O	B	250+	Greene, Carol	Children's Press
Christopher Reeve: Still a Hero	R	B	250+	Leveled Readers Language Support	Houghton Mifflin
Christy's First Dive	J	RF	250+	Leveled Readers Language Support	Houghton Mifflin
Chug the Tractor	F	F	203	PM Story Books	Rigby
Church	LB	I	17	Visions	Wright Group/McGraw Hill
Cicadas	J	I	87	Pebble Books	Red Brick Learning
Cinco de Mayo	O	I	250+	Holidays and Festivals	Compass Point Books
Cinco de Mayo	E	I	120	Fiesta Holiday Series	Pearson Learning Group
Cinderella	J	TL	250+	Jumbled Tumbled Tales & Rhymes	Rigby
Cinderella	I	TL	580	Traditional Tales	Pearson Learning Group
Cinderella	K	TL	250+	Once Upon a Time	Wright Group/McGraw Hill
Cinderella	K	TL	250+	PM Tales and Plays-Gold	Rigby
Cinderella Dressed in Yellow	E	F	81	Learn to Read	Creative Teaching Press
*Cinderella's Big Night and Other Fractured Fairy Tales	P	TL	250+	Action Packs	Rigby
Circle of Gold	R	RF	250+	Boyd, Candy Dawson	Bantam
Circle of Quiet, A	Z	B	250+	L'Engle, Madeleine	HarperCollins
Circle of Time, A	Y	RF	250+	Montes, Marisa	Harcourt Trade
Circle Unbroken, A	V	HF	250+	Leveled Readers Language Support	Houghton Mifflin
Circles: Seeing Circles All Around Us	L	I	198	Shapes	Capstone Press
Circuit, The	Z	HF	250+	Francisco, Jimenez	University of New Mexico
Circular Movement	E	I	43	Pebble Books	Capstone Press
Circulatory System, The	M	I	171	Human Body Systems	Red Brick Learning
Circulatory System, The	N	I	250+	A True Book	Children's Press
Circus	B	I	20	Twig	Wright Group/McGraw Hill
Circus Book, The	I	I	250+	Reading Unlimited	Pearson Learning Group
Circus Clown, The	A	RF	31	Literacy 2000	Rigby

* Collection of short stories

TITLE	LEVEL	GENRE	WORD COUNT	AUTHOR / SERIES	PUBLISHER / DISTRIBUTOR
Circus Fun	G	RF	219	Momentum Literacy Program	Troll Associates
Circus Mystery, The	M	RF	250+	Schultz, Irene	Wright Group/McGraw Hill
Circus Train, The	A	F	48	Little Red Readers	Sundance
Circus, The	WB	I	N/A	Carle, Eric	HarperCollins
Circus, The	LB	I	31	Literacy 2000	Rigby
Circus, The	D	RF	42	Wonder World	Wright Group/McGraw Hill
Cities Around the World	M	I	250+	Pair-It Books	Steck-Vaughn
Cities of Splendor: The Facts and the Fables	R	TL	250+	Landscapes of Legend	Children's Press
Cities Then, Cities Now	M	I	406	Leveled Readers Social Studies	Houghton Mifflin
Cities: The Building of America	Q	I	250+	Thompson, Gare	Children's Press
Cities: Then and Now	O	I	250+	People, Spaces & Places	Rand McNally
Citizens of the World	T	I	2642	Independent Readers Social Studies	Houghton Mifflin
City and the Country, The	B	I	48	Leveled Readers Emergent	Houghton Mifflin
City Animals	G	RF	102	Higgins, Malcom	Houghton Mifflin
City Buildings	G	I	133	Discovery Links	Newbridge
City Bus, The	B	RF	21	Visions	Wright Group/McGraw Hill
City by the Lake	N	I	250+	Early Connections	Benchmark Education
City Cat and the Country Cat, The	E	F	152	Ready Readers	Pearson Learning Group
City Garden, A	G	RF	77	City Stories	Rigby
City Green	L	RF	250+	DiSalvo-Ryan, DyAnne	Scholastic
City Life	C	I	32	Rosen Real Readers	Rosen Publishing Group
City Life and Country Life	E	F	66	Moriarty, Julie	Scholastic
City Lights	N	RF	250+	Orbit Double Takes	Pacific Learning
City Lights	LB	RF	16	Visions	Wright Group/McGraw Hill
City Mouse and Country Mouse	D	TL	87	Learn to Read	Creative Teaching Press
City Mouse-Country Mouse	J	TL	198	Wallner, John	Scholastic
City Noises	D	RF	37	Instant Readers	Harcourt School Publishers
City of Ember, The	W	F	250+	DuPrau, Jeanne	Random House
City of Gold & Lead, The	V	F	250+	Christopher, John	Aladdin
City on a Lake, The	R	I	642	Vocabulary Readers	Houghton Mifflin
City Park, A	I	RF	59	Leveled Readers	Houghton Mifflin
City Scenes	E	RF	24	Pacific Literacy	Pacific Learning
City Senses	C	I	85	Twig	Wright Group/McGraw Hill
City Shapes	G	I	177	Yellow Umbrella Books	Red Brick Learning
City Sights	G	I	250+	Phonics and Friends	Hampton-Brown
City Sounds	G	RF	142	Marzollo, Jean	Scholastic
City Storm	E	I	180	Twig	Wright Group/McGraw Hill
City Through the Ages	U	I	250+	Steele, Philip	Troll Associates
Civil Rights Marches	V	I	250+	Cornerstones of Freedom	Children's Press
Civil War on Sunday	M	F	250+	Osborne, Mary Pope	Random House
Clap for the Show	I	RF	250+	Phonics and Friends	Hampton-Brown
Clap Your Hands!	B	I	22	Pair-It Books	Steck-Vaughn
Clara and the Bookwagon	K	RF	250+	Levinson, Nancy Smiler	HarperTrophy
Clara Barton	M	B	320	Independent Readers Social Studies	Houghton Mifflin
Clara Barton	P	B	250+	Photo-Illustrated Biographies	Red Brick Learning
Clara Barton: Angel of the Battlefield	M	B	250+	Rosen Real Readers	Rosen Publishing Group
Clara Barton: Founder of the American Red Cross	R	B	250+	Stevenson, Augusta	Aladdin
Clarence the Crocodile	L	F	250+	New Way Literature	Steck-Vaughn
Class Calender	H	I	81	Windows on Literacy	National Geographic
Class Clown	O	RF	250+	Hurwitz, Johanna	Scholastic
Class Play with Ms. Vanilla, A	I	RF	234	Ehrlich, Fred	Puffin Books

* Collection of short stories

TITLE	LEVEL	GENRE	WORD COUNT	AUTHOR / SERIES	PUBLISHER / DISTRIBUTOR
Class Play, The	J	RF	250+	Little Readers	Houghton Mifflin
Class President	O	RF	250+	Hurwitz, Johanna	Scholastic
Class Rules	G	RF	143	Windows on Literacy	National Geographic
Class Teddy Bear	F	RF	106	Windows on Literacy	National Geographic
Class Trip to the Cave of Doom	Q	F	250+	McMullan, Kate	Grosset & Dunlap
Classroom Caterpillars, The	H	RF	216	PM Plus Story Books	Rigby
Claudine's Concert	L	RF	250+	Literacy 2000	Rigby
Clay	M	I	250+	First Facts	Capstone Press
Clay Art	F	I	62	Chanko, Pamela; Chessen, Betsey	Scholastic
Clay Creatures	I	I	213	Rigby Literacy	Rigby
Clay Dog, The	L	HF	250+	Lighthouse	Rigby
Clay Marble, The	V	RF	250+	Ho, Minfong	Farrar, Straus and Giroux
Clay Things, Play Things	J	I	250+	Phonics Readers	Scholastic
Clay Today!	C	RF	37	Learn to Read	Creative Teaching Press
Clean Air	P	I	250+	Independent Readers Social Studies	Houghton Mifflin
Clean and Clear	P	I	806	Independent Readers Social Studies	Houghton Mifflin
Clean and Healthy	I	I	199	Rosen Real Readers	Rosen Publishing Group
Clean Beaches	I	I	155	Early Connections	Benchmark Education
Clean House for Mole and Mouse, A	H	F	201	Ziefert, Harriet	Scholastic
Clean Machine, The	L	RF	250+	Home Connection Collection	Rigby
Clean Out the Fridge, Fred	I	F	250+	Popcorn	Sundance
Clean Up Your Room	B	RF	35	Visions	Wright Group/McGraw Hill
Cleaning Day	C	RF	26	Bebop Books	Lee & Low Books Inc.
Cleaning My Room	I	I	189	Early Connections	Benchmark Education
Cleaning Teeth	D	I	37	Wonder World	Wright Group/McGraw Hill
Cleaning Up	A	I	26	Early Connections	Benchmark Education
Cleaning Up the Park	H	I	153	Home Connection Collection	Rigby
Clean-Up Day	H	RF	179	Instant Readers	Harcourt School Publishers
Clean-Up Time	F	RF	226	Handprints D, Set 1	Educator's Publishing Service
Clearing the Dust	V	HF	2327	Leveled Readers	Houghton Mifflin
Clementine	L	TL	101	Traditional Songs	Picture Window Books
Cleopatra	T	B	250+	Stanley, Diane; Vennema, Peter	Mulberry Books
Cleopatra	W	B	2055	Independent Readers Social Studies	Houghton Mifflin
Cleopatra	X	B	250+	Green, Robert	Franklin Watts
Clever Bird	K	F	250+	Little Celebrations	Pearson Learning Group
Clever Brown Mouse	G	F	199	PM Plus Story Books	Rigby
Clever Fox	D	RF	114	PM Plus Story Books	Rigby
Clever Hamburger	K	F	560	Jellybeans	Rigby
Clever Happy Monkey	C	F	28	Joy Readers	Pearson Learning Group
Clever Little Bird	D	F	73	Storyteller-Setting Sun	Wright Group/McGraw Hill
Clever Mr. Brown	K	F	397	Story Box	Wright Group/McGraw Hill
Clever Penguins, The	G	I	174	PM Story Books	Rigby
Clever Tortoise, The	H	TL	202	Cambridge Reading	Pearson Learning Group
Clever, Crow, The	H	TL	223	PM Plus Story Books	Rigby
Click	E	RF	41	Books for Young Learners	Richard C. Owen
Click!	G	RF	250+	Foundations	Wright Group/McGraw Hill
Cliff Can't Come	F	RF	276	Leveled Readers	Houghton Mifflin
Clifford Can	E	F	55	Blevins, Wiley	Scholastic
Clifford, the Big Red Dog	K	F	241	Bridwell, Norman	Scholastic
Clifford, The Firehouse Dog	K	F	250+	Bridwell, Norman	Scholastic

TITLE	LEVEL	GENRE	WORD COUNT	AUTHOR / SERIES	PUBLISHER / DISTRIBUTOR
Clifford, the Small Red Puppy	K	F	499	Bridwell, Norman	Scholastic
Clifford's First Halloween	K	F	250+	Bridwell, Norman	Scholastic
Climbing	B	I	48	PM Starters	Rigby
Climbing	C	F	34	Literacy 2000	Rigby
Climbing Everest	W	I	250+	iOpeners	Pearson Learning Group
Climbing the Continents: Everest, McKinley, Kilimanjaro	W	I	3847	Leveled Readers Social Studies	Houghton Mifflin
Cloak of the Wind	O	HF	250+	Voyages in Time	Wright Group/McGraw Hill
Clock That Couldn't Tell Time, The	H	F	310	Carousel Readers	Pearson Learning Group
Clock Watch	B	I	76	Early Connections	Benchmark Education
Clocks and More Clocks	J	RF	374	Hutchins, Pat	Scholastic
Clockwork	Z	F	250+	Pullman, Philip	Scholastic
Close Call, A	M	RF	250+	Kenna, Anna	Pacific Learning
Close to Home: A Story of the Polio Epidemic	R	I	250+	Weaver, Lydia	Bantam
Close Your Eyes	E	RF	131	Foundations	Wright Group/McGraw Hill
Closer and Closer	LB	I	13	Twig	Wright Group/McGraw Hill
Closet in the Hall, The	D	F	84	Wonder World	Wright Group/McGraw Hill
Closet Under the Stairs, The	I	RF	214	Story Box	Wright Group/McGraw Hill
Clothes	F	I	103	Talk About Books	Pearson Learning Group
Clothes	L	I	386	Wonder World	Wright Group/McGraw Hill
Clothes	C	I	25	Interaction	Rigby
Clothes	D	RF	63	Voyages	SRA/McGraw Hill
Clothes & Crafts in Ancient Egypt	T	I	250+	Balkwill, Richard	Dillon Press
Clothes & Crafts in Ancient Greece	T	I	250+	Steele, Philip	Dillon Press
Clothes & Crafts in Aztec Times	T	I	250+	Dawson, Imogen	Dillon Press
Clothes & Crafts in Roman Times	T	I	250+	Steele, Philip	Dillon Press
Clothes & Crafts in the Middle Ages	T	I	250+	Dawson, Imogen	Dillon Press
Clothes & Crafts in Victorian Times	T	I	250+	Steele, Philip	Dillon Press
Clothes Around the World	J	I	214	Vocabulary Readers	Houghton Mifflin
Cloud Book, The	N	I	250+	DePaola, Tomie	Scholastic
Cloud Catcher	P	F	250+	Action Packs	Rigby
Clouds	C	RF	44	Science	Outside the Box
Clouds	J	I	204	Independent Readers Science	Houghton Mifflin
Clouds	A	RF	47	Bookshop	Mondo
Clouds	I	I	249	Pebble Books	Capstone Press
Clouds	J	I	40	Early Connections	Benchmark Education
Clouds	B	RF	42	Voyages	SRA/McGraw Hill
Clouds	H	I	132	Twig	Wright Group/McGraw Hill
Clouds	L	I	40	iOpeners	Pearson Learning Group
Clouds	N	I	250+	Literacy 2000	Rigby
Clouds	H	I	108	Sunshine	Wright Group/McGraw Hill
Clouds	D	RF	40	Costain, Meredith	Scholastic
Clouds	C	I	67	Handprints C, Set 1	Educator's Publishing Service
Clouds of Terror	L	HF	250+	Welsh, Catherine A.	Carolrhoda Books
Clouds of Terror	L	HF	250+	Soar To Success	Houghton Mifflin
Clouds, Rain, and Fog	K	I	488	Sunshine	Wright Group/McGraw Hill
Cloudy With a Chance of Meatballs	M	F	250+	Barrett, Judi	Atheneum
Clown	WB	I	N/A	Blake, Quentin	Henry Holt & Co.
Clown and Elephant	C	F	38	Story Box	Wright Group/McGraw Hill
Clown Around	F	F	67	Early Readers	Compass Point Books
Clown Face	LB	RF	14	Twig	Wright Group/McGraw Hill
Clown Fish	J	I	123	Pebble Plus	Capstone Press
Clown in the Well, The	D	F	140	Story Box	Wright Group/McGraw Hill

* Collection of short stories

TITLE	LEVEL	GENRE	WORD COUNT	AUTHOR / SERIES	PUBLISHER / DISTRIBUTOR
Clown, The	LB	I	13	Smart Starts	Rigby
Clown, The	LB	I	29	Urmston, Kathleen; Evans, Karen	Kaeden Books
Clown, The	LB	I	31	First Stories	Pacific Learning
Clubhouse, The	K	RF	659	PM Gold	Rigby
Cluck! Quack! Moo!	F	RF	209	Sun Sprouts	ETA/Cuisenaire
Clucky	I	F	250+	PM Plus Story Books	Rigby
Clue at the Zoo, The	L	RF	250+	Giff, Patricia Reilly	Bantam
Clue Club, The	M	RF	660	Leveled Readers	Houghton Mifflin
Clue in the Castle, The	M	RF	250+	Schultz, Irene	Wright Group/McGraw Hill
Clue in the Glue, The	N	RF	250+	Keene, Carolyn	Pocket Books
Clue of the Gold Doubloons, The	S	RF	250+	Keene, Carolyn	Pocket Books
Clue, Jr.: The Case of the Chocolate Fingerprints	O	RF	250+	Hinter, Parker C.	Scholastic
Clues in the Woods	M	RF	250+	Parrish, Peggy	Bantam
Clyde Klutter's Room	I	F	146	Sunshine	Wright Group/McGraw Hill
Clyde Tombaugh and the Search for Planet X	N	B	250+	Wetterer, Margaret K.	Carolrhoda Books
Coach Amos	R	RF	250+	Paulsen, Gary	Bantam
Coal Miner's Son, A	U	RF	2652	Leveled Readers Science	Houghton Mifflin
Coast to Coast	N	I	250+	People, Spaces & Places	Rand McNally
Coat Full of Bubbles, A	G	F	72	Books for Young Learners	Richard C. Owen
Coats	A	I	32	Ray's Readers	Outside the Box
Cobwebs, Elephants, and Stars	M	F	779	Sunshine	Wright Group/McGraw Hill
Cock-A-Doodle-Do	F	RF	160	Brandenberg, Franz	Greenwillow
Cockroaches	I	I	60	Pebble Books	Red Brick Learning
Coconut Lunches	J	RF	564	Sunshine	Wright Group/McGraw Hill
Coconut Seed or Fruit?	N	I	250+	iOpeners	Pearson Learning Group
Cocoons and Cases	C	I	59	Rigby Literacy	Rigby
Coco's Bell	H	RF	224	PM Plus Story Books	Rigby
Code that No One Broke, The	L	I	90	Independent Readers Social Studies	Houghton Mifflin
Codes and Signals	N	I	250+	Cambridge Reading	Pearson Learning Group
Coin Magic	L	I	250+	How-To Series	Benchmark Education
Cold and Hot	B	RF	24	Bebop Books	Lee & Low Books Inc.
Cold As Ice	T	RF	250+	Keene, Carolyn	Pocket Books
Cold Day, A	E	I	71	Pebble Books	Capstone Press
Cold Day, The	F	RF	80	Oxford Reading Tree	Oxford University Press
Cold Shoulder Road	V	RF	250+	Aiken, Joan	Bantam
Colibri	W	RF	250+	Cameron, Ann	Farrar, Straus and Giroux
Colin Powell	K	B	250+	Welcome Books	Children's Press
Colin Powell, American Leader	H	B	77	Leveled Readers Social Studies	Houghton Mifflin
Colin Powell: Straight to the Top	S	B	250+	Blue, Rose; Naden, Corinne J.	The Millbrook Press
Collecting Badges	J	I	250+	Stepping Stones	Nelson/Michaels Assoc.
Collecting Cones	I	I	127	Wonder World	Wright Group/McGraw Hill
Collecting Leaves	K	I	250+	Stepping Stones	Nelson/Michaels Assoc.
Collecting Shapes	J	I	250+	Stepping Stones	Nelson/Michaels Assoc.
Collecting Things Is Fun!	G	RF	134	Learn to Read	Creative Teaching Press
Collections	J	RF	250+	Voyages	SRA/McGraw Hill
Collections	E	RF	54	Ballinger, Margaret; Gosset, Rachel	Scholastic
Colonial Crafts	T	I	250+	Historic Communities	Crabtree
Colonial Families	K	I	250+	Rosen Real Readers	Rosen Publishing Group
Colonial Life	T	I	250+	Historic Communities	Crabtree
Colonial Teachers	L	I	250+	Rosen Real Readers	Rosen Publishing Group
Colonial Times from A to Z	T	I	250+	Kalman, Bobbie	Crabtree
Colonial Town, A: Williamsburg	T	I	250+	Historic Communities	Crabtree

| --- | --- | --- | --- | --- | --- |
Colony of Massachusetts, The	T	I	250+	The Library of the Thirteen Colonies and The Lost Colony	Rosen Publishing Group
Colony of New York, The	T	I	250+	The Library of the Thirteen Colonies and The Lost Colony	Rosen Publishing Group
Colony of Pennsylvania, The	T	I	250+	The Library of the Thirteen Colonies and The Lost Colony	Rosen Publishing Group
Colony of Virginia, The	T	I	250+	The Library of the Thirteen Colonies and The Lost Colony	Rosen Publishing Group
Color	M	I	250+	Early Connections	Benchmark Education
Color It My Way	G	RF	123	Story Steps	Rigby
Color of His Own, A	I	F	239	Lionni, Leo	Scholastic
Color of Light, The	M	I	558	Leveled Readers Science	Houghton Mifflin
Color Wizard, The	J	F	250+	Bank Street	Bantam
Colorado	T	I	250+	Sea To Shining Sea	Children's Press
Colorado	S	I	250+	Land of Liberty	Red Brick Learning
Colorado	R	I	250+	This Land Is Your Land	Compass Point Books
Colorful Animals	M	I	250+	Sunshine	Wright Group/McGraw Hill
Colorful Facts	N	I	561	Leveled Readers Science	Houghton Mifflin
Colorful Ghost, The	E	F	135	TOTTS	Tott Publications
Colors	LB	I	6	Vocabulary Readers	Houghton Mifflin
Colors	B	I	38	Science	Outside the Box
Colors	A	I	9	Little Red Readers	Sundance
Colors	LB	I	9	Leveled Readers Language Support	Houghton Mifflin
Colors	F	I	198	Foundations	Wright Group/McGraw Hill
Colors at the Zoo	B	I	59	Little Books	Sadlier-Oxford
Colors in the City	LB	I	61	Urmston, Kathleen; Evans, Karen	Kaeden Books
Colors of Australia	P	I	250+	Colors of the World	Carolrhoda Books
Colors of Germany	P	I	250+	Colors of the World	Carolrhoda Books
Colors of Ghana	P	I	250+	Colors of the World	Carolrhoda Books
Colors of Horses	E	I	49	Brand, Mona	Kaeden Books
Colors of India	P	I	250+	Colors of the World	Carolrhoda Books
Colors of Kenya	P	I	250+	Colors of the World	Carolrhoda Books
Colors of Mexico	P	I	250+	Colors of the World	Carolrhoda Books
Colors of My Day, The	F	I	147	Learn to Read	Creative Teaching Press
Colours	LB	I	8	Pienkowski, Jan	Penguin Group
Columbia	U	I	250+	Countries and Cultures	Red Brick Learning
Comanche Indians, The	P	I	250+	Lund, Bill	Red Brick Learning
Combat Rescue Helicopters: The MH-53 Pave Lows	R	I	250+	War Planes	Red Brick Learning
Come and Have Fun	I	F	250+	Hurd, Edith Thacher	HarperCollins
Come and Have Fun	A	F	49	KinderReaders	Rigby
Come and Play	B	F	34	Interaction	Rigby
Come and Play	B	F	104	Bookshop	Mondo
Come and Play	D	F	104	Story Steps	Rigby
Come and Play, Cats!	C	RF	45	Early Emergent	Pioneer Valley
Come and Play, Sarah!	D	RF	49	Sunshine	Wright Group/McGraw Hill
Come and See!	G	RF	134	Foundations	Wright Group/McGraw Hill
Come Back, Amelia Bedelia	L	F	250+	Parish, Peggy	Harper & Row
Come Back, Pip!	J	RF	355	PM Plus Story Books	Rigby
Come for a Swim!	F	RF	129	Sunshine	Wright Group/McGraw Hill
Come Here Spinner!	K	F	250+	Foundations	Wright Group/McGraw Hill
Come In!	B	F	20	The Book Project	Sundance
Come Meet Some Seals	I	I	118	Little Books	Sadlier-Oxford

* Collection of short stories

TITLE	LEVEL	GENRE	WORD COUNT	AUTHOR / SERIES	PUBLISHER / DISTRIBUTOR
Come Morning	V	HF	250+	Guccione, Leslie Davis	Lerner Publishing
Come On Down	K	I	250+	World Quest Adventures	World Quest Learning
Come On Up	A	F	16	KinderReaders	Rigby
Come On!	B	RF	22	Sunshine	Wright Group/McGraw Hill
Come On, Mom	D	RF	56	New Way	Steck-Vaughn
Come On, Tim	G	RF	198	PM Story Books	Rigby
Come Out and Play Little Mouse	H	F	198	Kraus, Robert	Morrow
Come Play With Me	D	RF	69	Leveled Readers	Houghton Mifflin
Come Play With Me	C	F	36	Little Readers	Houghton Mifflin
Come Sing, Jimmy Jo	V	RF	250+	Paterson, Katherine	Penguin Group
Come to My House	C	F	56	Joy Readers	Pearson Learning Group
Come to My House!	F	RF	131	Sunshine	Wright Group/McGraw Hill
Come to My Party	D	RF	84	Windows on Literacy	National Geographic
Come with Me	C	RF	25	Story Box	Wright Group/McGraw Hill
Come! Sit! Speak!	H	RF	57	Rookie Readers	Children's Press
Comeback Challenge, The	M	RF	250+	Christopher, Matt	Little, Brown & Co.
Comeback Dog, The	O	RF	250+	Thomas, Jane Resh	Bantam
Comets	P	I	250+	The Galaxy	Red Brick Learning
Comets	U	I	250+	A First Book	Franklin Watts
Comets and Meteor Showers	N	I	250+	A True Book	Children's Press
Comets, Asteroids, and Meteoroids	S	I	250+	Our Solar System	Compass Point Books
Coming Home	U	HF	1920	Leveled Readers	Houghton Mifflin
Coming to America	L	I	185	Vocabulary Readers	Houghton Mifflin
Commander Toad and the Big Black Hole	K	F	250+	Yolen, Jane	Putnam & Grosset
Commander Toad and the Dis-Asteroid	K	F	250+	Yolen, Jane	Putnam & Grosset
Commander Toad and the Intergalactic Spy	K	F	250+	Yolen, Jane	Putnam & Grosset
Commander Toad and the Planet of the Grapes	K	F	250+	Yolen, Jane	Putnam & Grosset
Commander Toad and the Space Pirates	K	F	250+	Yolen, Jane	Putnam & Grosset
Commander Toad And The Voyage Home	K	F	250+	Yolen, Jane	Putnam & Grosset
Commander Toad in Space	K	F	250+	Yolen, Jane	Scholastic
Communication	N	I	250+	Literacy 2000	Rigby
Communities	E	I	59	Wonder World	Wright Group/McGraw Hill
Communities	I	I	42	Yellow Umbrella Books	Red Brick Learning
Communities	D	I	42	Pebble Books	Capstone Press
Community Jobs	I	I	207	Early Connections	Benchmark Education
Commuter	M	I	343	Independent Readers Social Studies	Houghton Mifflin
Computer Buttons	I	F	250+	Sunshine	Wright Group/McGraw Hill
Computer Error	L	F	250+	Rigby Literacy	Rigby
Computer Evidence	Q	I	250+	Forensic Crime Solvers	Capstone Press
Computer Game, The	D	RF	75	Rigby Literacy	Rigby
Computer Nut, The	R	SF	250+	Byars, Betsy	Bantam
Computers Are for Everyone	K	I	464	Sunshine	Wright Group/McGraw Hill
Comstock Lode, The	U	I	2086	Leveled Readers Social Studies	Houghton Mifflin
Conceived in Liberty: The Gettysburg Address	X	I	2069	Leveled Readers	Houghton Mifflin
Concert Night	K	RF	250+	Literacy 2000	Rigby
Concrete	K	I	123	Books for Young Learners	Richard C. Owen
Concrete Jungle	L	RF	250+	Pacific Literacy	Pacific Learning
Concrete Mixers	K	I	110	Pebble Books	Capstone Press
Confucius: The Golden Rule	Y	HF	250+	Russell Freedman	Scholastic
Congress	N	I	250+	A True Book	Children's Press
Congress and Parliament	W	I	1803	Leveled Readers Social Studies	Houghton Mifflin
Congress of the United States, The	W	I	250+	American Civics	Red Brick Learning
Connecticut	R	I	250+	This Land Is Your Land	Compass Point Books

* Collection of short stories

TITLE	LEVEL	GENRE	WORD COUNT	AUTHOR / SERIES	PUBLISHER / DISTRIBUTOR
Connecticut	T	I	250+	Sea To Shining Sea	Children's Press
Connecticut	S	I	250+	Land of Liberty	Red Brick Learning
Connecting to the Internet	O	I	250+	Rigby Literacy	Rigby
Connie's Dance	M	RF	361	Windmill Books	Rigby
Consideration	L	I	250+	Character Education	Red Brick Learning
Constantinople in the Center of the World	Z	I	2840	Independent Readers Social Studies	Houghton Mifflin
Constellations	P	I	250+	Bridgestone Books	Capstone Press
Constellations	N	I	250+	A True Book	Children's Press
Constitution, The	V	I	250+	Cornerstones of Freedom	Children's Press
Constitution, The	N	I	250+	A True Book	Children's Press
Constitutional Convention, The	T	I	1267	Leveled Readers Social Studies	Houghton Mifflin
Construction Workers	M	I	250+	Deedrick, Tami	Red Brick Learning
Contemporary Age, The	R	I	250+	Journey Through History	Barron's Educational
Contender, The	Z	RF	250+	Lipsythe, Robert	HarperTrophy
Contest, The	K	RF	250+	PM Plus Story Books	Rigby
Continents, The	M	I	250+	Spyglass Books	Compass Point Books
Conversation Club, The	L	F	250+	Stanley, Diane	Aladdin
Coo Coo Caroo	G	F	57	Books for Young Learners	Richard C. Owen
Cook: Captain James Cook Charts the Pacific Ocean	U	B	250+	Exploring the World	Compass Point Books
Cookcamp, The	S	RF	250+	Paulsen, Gary	Bantam
Cookie Count!	M	I	250+	Early Connections	Benchmark Education
Cookie Jar, The	G	RF	106	Sunshine	Wright Group/McGraw Hill
Cookies	LB	I	15	Twig	Wright Group/McGraw Hill
Cookies	D	RF	18	Little Celebrations	Pearson Learning Group
Cookies to Share	E	RF	45	Pair-It Books	Steck-Vaughn
Cookie's Week	F	RF	84	Ward, Cindy	Putnam
Cooking at School	G	RF	68	City Kids	Rigby
Cooking Contest, The	K	RF	904	Early Connections	Benchmark Education
Cooking Dinner	G	I	86	Windows on Literacy	National Geographic
*Cooking Pot	L	TL	250+	The Story Box	Rigby
Cooking Pot, The	F	F	132	Sunshine	Wright Group/McGraw Hill
Cooking Spaghetti	I	RF	150	City Kids	Rigby
Cooking Thanksgiving Dinner	E	RF	126	Early Emergent	Pioneer Valley
Cook-Out, The	E	RF	78	Oxford Reading Tree	Oxford University Press
Cool	L	RF	137	Books for Young Learners	Richard C. Owen
Cool Cat, A	O	RF	250+	Leveled Readers	Houghton Mifflin
Cool Customs	K	I	250+	Spyglass Books	Compass Point Books
Cool in the Summer	E	I	63	Windows on Literacy	National Geographic
Cool Off	C	RF	37	Bookshop	Mondo
Cool School	O	F	250+	Sails	Rigby
Cool School, A	G	RF	138	City Stories	Rigby
Cool Tools	K	I	250+	Spyglass Books	Compass Point Books
Cool Treasure, The	N	RF	250+	Orbit Chapter Books	Pacific Literacy
Coolest Rock, The	L	I	250+	Chanek, Sherilin	Hampton-Brown
Cooling Off	D	RF	104	Reading Corners	Pearson Learning Group
Cooped Up	K	RF	250+	Pacific Literacy	Pacific Learning
Copán: City of the Maya	Z	I	3688	Leveled Readers	Houghton Mifflin
Copper Lady, The	M	HF	250+	Ross, Alice & Kent	Carolrhoda Books
Copycat	C	F	54	Story Box	Wright Group/McGraw Hill
Cora at Camp	M	RF	250+	Leveled Readers Language Support	Houghton Mifflin
Cora at Camp Blue Waters	N	RF	772	Leveled Readers	Houghton Mifflin

* Collection of short stories

TITLE	LEVEL	GENRE	WORD COUNT	AUTHOR / SERIES	PUBLISHER / DISTRIBUTOR
Coral	K	I	250+	Marine Life For Young Readers	Pearson Learning Group
Coral Reef	P	I	250+	Habitats	Children's Press
Coral Reef Hunters	N	I	250+	Soar To Success	Houghton Mifflin
Coral Reef, A	I	I	153	Rigby Focus	Rigby
Coral Reef, The	H	I	186	Discovery Links	Newbridge
Coral Reef: Inside Australia's Great Barrier Reef	P	I	250+	Cambridge Reading	Pearson Learning Group
Coral Reefs	Q	I	250+	First Reports	Compass Point Books
Coraline	W	F	250+	Gaiman, Neil	HarperCollins
Corals	K	I	133	Under the Sea	Capstone Press
Corals	G	I	51	Pebble Books	Capstone Press
Corduroy	K	F	250+	Freeman, Don	Scholastic
Corey's Christmas Wish	M	RF	250+	Pony Tails	Skylark
Corn	K	I	221	Windows on Literacy	National Geographic
Corn Husk Doll, The	K	RF	250+	Schiller, Melissa	Scholastic
Corn Is Maize: The Gift of the Indians	O	I	250+	Aliki	Steck-Vaughn
Corn: An American Indian Gift	M	I	690	Pair-It Books	Steck-Vaughn
Corn: From Table to Table	H	I	171	Discovery Links	Newbridge
Corner of the Universe, A	Y	RF	250+	Martin, Ann M.	Scholastic
Coronado and the Cities of Gold	Y	B	2051	Leveled Readers	Houghton Mifflin
Coronado: Francisco Vasquez de Coronado Explores the Southwest	U	B	250+	Exploring the World	Compass Point Books
Coronado's Golden Quest	R	F	250+	Weisberg, Barbara	Steck-Vaughn
Corrie's Important Decision	V	I	250+	Leveled Readers Language Support	Houghton Mifflin
Corrie's Secret	W	I	1726	Leveled Readers	Houghton Mifflin
Corvettes	T	I	250+	Gronvall, Kal	Red Brick Learning
Cosmic Joker, The	Z	I	250+	Innes, Brian	Steck-Vaughn
Costume Parade, The	E	RF	57	Learn to Read	Creative Teaching Press
Costume Party	C	RF	64	Early Connections	Benchmark Education
Costume Party	A	RF	32	Joy Readers	Pearson Learning Group
Costume Party, The	B	RF	15	Sunshine	Wright Group/McGraw Hill
Costume Party, The	J	RF	145	City Kids	Rigby
Costumes	C	RF	23	Oxford Reading Tree	Oxford University Press
Costumes	C	I	36	Pebble Books	Capstone Press
Cottle Street	N	RF	250+	Action Packs	Rigby
Cotton Comes From Plants	K	I	161	Windows on Literacy	National Geographic
Cotton Plant to Cotton Shirt	L	I	250+	Schaefer, Lola M.	Benchmark Education
Cougars	R	I	250+	Predators in the Wild	Capstone Press
Could It Be?	J	RF	250+	Bank Street	Bantam
Could We Live on the Moon?	O	I	250+	iOpeners	Pearson Learning Group
Count and See	WB	I	N/A	Hoban, Tana	Macmillan
Count Karlstein	Y	F	250+	Pullman, Philip	Alfred A. Knopf
Count on Your Body	K	I	250+	Rigby Literacy	Rigby
Count the Animals	LB	I	10	Windows on Literacy	National Geographic
Count with Me	A	I	49	Little Books	Sadlier-Oxford
Count Your Chickens	G	I	123	Yellow Umbrella Books	Red Brick Learning
Count Your Money with the Polk Street School	M	RF	250+	Giff, Patricia Reilly	Bantam
Count!	H	RF	70	Fleming, Denise	Scholastic
Countdown	G	F	70	Literacy Tree	Rigby
Countdown: a play	J	F	250+	Story Box	Wright Group/McGraw Hill
Counterfeit Tackle, The	M	RF	250+	Christopher, Matt	Little, Brown & Co.
Countess Veronica	Q	RF	250+	Robinson, Nancy K.	Scholastic
Counting Around Town	D	RF	84	Early Connections	Benchmark Education
Counting Insects	K	I	230	Early Connections	Benchmark Education

TITLE	LEVEL	GENRE	WORD COUNT	AUTHOR / SERIES	PUBLISHER / DISTRIBUTOR
Counting Many Ways	J	I	250+	Yellow Umbrella Books	Capstone Press
Counting Money	G	I	122	Early Connections	Benchmark Education
Counting My Collections	F	I	126	Early Connections	Benchmark Education
Counting One to Five	B	I	64	Early Connections	Benchmark Education
Counting Seeds	C	I	63	Early Connections	Benchmark Education
Counting Stars	F	I	144	Early Connections	Benchmark Education
Country Fair	J	HF	250+	Wilder, Laura Ingalls	HarperCollins
Country Family	G	RF	262	Instant Readers	Harcourt School Publishers
Courage of Helen Keller, The	N	B	250+	Rosen Real Readers	Rosen Publishing Group
Courage of Sarah Noble, The	O	HF	250+	Dalgliesh, Alice	Aladdin
Courtney's Twos	C	RF	30	Harry's Math Books	Outside the Box
Cousin Kira	J	RF	250+	Sunshine	Wright Group/McGraw Hill
Cousins	D	I	41	Pebble Books	Capstone Press
Cousins	T	RF	250+	Hamilton, Virginia	Language for Learning Assoc.
Cousins in the Castle	U	F	250+	Wallace, Barbara Brooks	Aladdin
Covers	E	RF	30	Little Celebrations	Pearson Learning Group
Cow	O	I	250+	Older, Jules	Charlesbridge
Cow in the Garden and Other Stories, The	H	F	158	New Way Literature	Steck-Vaughn
*Cow of No Color, The: Riddle Stories and Justice Tales From Around the World	U	TL	250+	Jaffe, Nina; Zeitlin, Steve	Henry Holt & Co.
Cow Up a Tree	H	F	215	Read Alongs	Rigby
Cowboy Jake	I	RF	174	Sunshine	Wright Group/McGraw Hill
Cowboy Trade, The	S	I	250+	Rounds, Glen	Holiday House
Cowboy, The	C	RF	35	Step-By-Step Series	Pearson Learning Group
Cowboys	T	I	250+	Sandler, Martin W.	HarperTrophy
Cowboys of the Wild West	X	I	250+	Freedman, Russell	Clarion
Cowpokes and Desperadoes	O	RF	250+	Paulsen, Gary	Bantam
Cows Have Calves	M	I	250+	Animals and Their Young	Compass Point Books
Cows in the Garden	G	F	163	PM Story Books	Rigby
Cows on the Farm	G	I	56	Pebble Books	Capstone Press
Coyote Girl	M	TL	250+	Cambridge Reading	Pearson Learning Group
*Coyote in Trouble	L	TL	250+	Beveridge, Barbara	Pacific Learning
*Coyote Not-So-Clever	N	TL	250+	Beveridge, Barbara	Pacific Learning
Coyote Plants a Peach Tree	I	TL	233	Books for Young Learners	Richard C. Owen
Coyote, The	R	I	250+	Mattern, Joanne	Red Brick Learning
Coyotes	L	I	250+	Story Box	Wright Group/McGraw Hill
Crab at the Bottom of the Sea, The	H	TL	141	Literacy 2000	Rigby
Crabbing Time	I	RF	75	Books for Young Learners	Richard C. Owen
Crabs	E	I	46	Pebble Books	Capstone Press
Crabs	L	I	501	Sunshine	Wright Group/McGraw Hill
Crabs	M	I	272	Wonder World	Wright Group/McGraw Hill
Crabs on a Rock	D	RF	77	Sun Sprouts	ETA/Cuisenaire
Crabs, Shrimp & Lobsters	L	I	322	Marine Life For Young Readers	Pearson Learning Group
Cracker Jack, The	D	F	25	Sunshine	Wright Group/McGraw Hill
Cracker Jackson	T	RF	250+	Byars, Betsy	Puffin Books
CrackerJack Halfback	M	RF	250+	Christopher, Matt	Little, Brown & Co.
Cracking the Code	Z	I	3314	Leveled Readers Science	Houghton Mifflin
Craft Makers	A	I	24	Early Connections	Benchmark Education
Crafts	G	I	50	Chessen, Betsey; Chanko, Pamela	Scholastic
Crafts and Games Around the World	U	I	250+	iOpeners	Pearson Learning Group
Crafty Jackal	L	TL	250+	Folk Tales	Wright Group/McGraw Hill
Cranberries: Fruit of the Bogs	T	I	250+	Burns, Diane L.	Carolrhoda Books
Crane Wife, The	M	F	620	Pair-It Books	Steck-Vaughn

TITLE	LEVEL	GENRE	WORD COUNT	AUTHOR / SERIES	PUBLISHER / DISTRIBUTOR
Cranes	N	I	250+	Cole, Sally	Wright Group/McGraw Hill
Cranes	K	I	105	Pebble Books	Capstone Press
Crash	V	RF	250+	Spinelli, Jerry	Alfred A. Knopf
Crash	A	RF	29	First Stories	Pacific Learning
Crawl, Caterpillar, Crawl!	C	RF	24	Pair-It Books	Steck-Vaughn
Crayola Counting Book, The	G	I	102	Learn to Read	Creative Teaching Press
Crazy Cats	A	I	42	Little Books for Early Readers	University of Maine
Crazy Fish	T	RF	250+	Mazer, Norma Fox	Avon
Crazy Horse	S	I	515	Vocabulary Readers	Houghton Mifflin
Crazy Lady!	U	RF	250+	Conly, Jane Leslie	HarperCollins
Crazy Quilt, The	G	RF	148	Little Readers	Houghton Mifflin
Crazy Quilt, The	G	F	148	Little Celebrations	Pearson Learning Group
*Creature from Beneath the Ice and Other Cases, The	O	RF	250+	Simon, Seymour	Avon
Creature of Cassidy's Creek, The	N	RF	250+	PM Emerald	Rigby
Creatures of the Dark	N	I	250+	Literacy 2000	Rigby
Creatures of the Night	M	I	250+	Murdock & Ray	Mondo
Creatures of the Night	M	I	250+	Rigby Focus	Rigby
Creatures of the Reef	S	I	250+	Belcher, Angie	Pacific Learning
Creek, The: Farmers of the Southeast	S	I	250+	American Indian Nations	Capstone Press
Creep Show	L	F	250+	Dussling, Jennifer	Grosset & Dunlap
Creepy Caterpillar	E	F	118	Little Readers	Houghton Mifflin
Creepy Crawlies	F	I	35	Voyages	SRA/McGraw Hill
Creepy Crawlies	P	I	250+	Literacy 2000	Rigby
Creepy Crawlies	B	RF	38	Carousel Earlybirds	Pearson Learning Group
Creepy Creatures	Q	I	250+	Explorers	Wright Group/McGraw Hill
*Cricket Boy and Other Stories, The	L	TL	250+	New Way Literature	Steck-Vaughn
Cricket in Times Square, The	S	F	250+	Selden, George	Bantam
Crickets	H	I	89	Pebble Plus	Red Brick Learning
Crickets	D	I	48	Pebble Books	Capstone Press
Crickets on the Go	D	F	56	Little Celebrations	Pearson Learning Group
Crime At the Chat Café	S	RF	250+	Keene, Carolyn	Pocket Books
Crime for Christmas, A	S	RF	250+	Keene, Carolyn	Pocket Books
Crime in the Queen's Court	S	RF	250+	Keene, Carolyn	Pocket Books
Crime Scene Clues	X	I	250+	Independent Readers Science	Houghton Mifflin
*Crinkum Crankum	M	F	250+	Pacific Literacy	Pacific Learning
Crispin: The Cross of Lead	W	HF	250+	Avi	Hyperion
Crispus Attucks: Black Leader of Colonial Patriots	R	B	250+	Millender, Dharathula H.	Aladdin
Critter Race	G	F	118	Reese, Bob	Children's Press
Crocodile and a Whale, A	E	RF	127	PM Plus Story Books	Rigby
Crocodile in the Garden, A	L	F	250+	Ready to Read	Pacific Learning
Crocodile in the Library, A	L	F	250+	Pacific Literacy	Pacific Learning
Crocodile Lake	K	F	322	Pacific Literacy	Pacific Learning
Crocodiles	L	I	250+	Sunshine	Wright Group/McGraw Hill
Crocodile's Christmas Jandals, The	L	F	250+	Pacific Literacy	Pacific Learning
Crocodilians	O	I	250+	Literacy 2000	Rigby
Crocodilians	U	I	250+	Short, Joan; Bird, Bettina	Mondo
Crocodilians: Reminders of the Age of Dinosaurs	S	I	250+	A First Book	Franklin Watts
Crosby Crocodile's Disguise	K	F	250+	LIteracy 2000	Rigby
Cross-Country Race	C	RF	33	Windmill Books	Rigby
Cross-Country Race, The	H	RF	246	PM Story Books	Rigby
Crossing Borders Stories of Immigrants	T	I	250+	iOpeners	Pearson Learning Group
Crossing Jordan	X	RF	250+	Fogelin, Adrian	Peachtree

* Collection of short stories

TITLE	LEVEL	GENRE	WORD COUNT	AUTHOR / SERIES	PUBLISHER / DISTRIBUTOR
Crossing the Atlantic: One Family's Story	N	I	250+	iOpeners	Pearson Learning Group
Crossing the Creek	C	F	35	Learn to Read	Creative Teaching Press
Crossing the Street	G	RF	142	City Stories	Rigby
Crow and the Pitcher, The	I	TL	265	Aesop's Fables	Pearson Learning Group
*Crowded Dock and Other Cases, The	O	RF	250+	Simon, Seymour	Avon
Crowfoot	X	B	250+	The Canadians	Fitzhenry & Whiteside
Cruisers	T	I	250+	Land and Sea	Capstone Press
Crunchy Munchy	G	F	189	Bookshop	Mondo
Cry of the Crow, The	S	RF	250+	George, Jean Craighead	HarperTrophy
*Crying Rocks and Other Cases, The	O	RF	250+	Simon, Seymour	Avon
Crystal Unicorn, The	N	RF	250+	PM Emerald	Rigby
Cuauhtemoc, the Last Aztec Ruler	S	B	1598	Leveled Readers Social Studies	Houghton Mifflin
Cub in the Cupboard	Q	RF	250+	Baglio, Ben M.	Scholastic
Cuba	O	I	250+	Mara, William P.	Red Brick Learning
Cuba 15	W	RF	250+	Osa, Nancy	Delacorte
Cubby's Gum	J	F	250+	Ready Readers	Pearson Learning Group
Cuckoo Child, The	Q	F	250+	King-Smith, Dick	Hyperion
Cuckoo's Sacrifice, The: A Tale From the Yucatán	T	F	1900	Leveled Readers	Houghton Mifflin
Culpepper's Canyon	O	RF	250+	Paulsen, Gary	Bantam
Cumberland Gap, The	S	I	1262	Leveled Readers Social Studies	Houghton Mifflin
Cunning Creatures	K	I	250+	Home Connection Collection	Rigby
Cupboard Full of Summer, A	J	RF	234	Pacific Literacy	Pacific Learning
Cupcakes	E	F	68	Leveled Readers	Houghton Mifflin
Cupids Don't Flip Hamburgers	M	F	250+	Dadey, Debbie; Jones, Marcia Thornton	Scholastic
Curious Cat	E	F	95	Little Celebrations	Pearson Learning Group
Curious George Rides a Bike	J	F	250+	Rey, Margaret	Scholastic
Curious Kat	P	RF	250+	Leveled Readers	Houghton Mifflin
Curly and His Friends	LB	RF	15	Rigby Literacy	Rigby
Curly and the Cherries	WB	RF	N/A	Rigby Literacy	Rigby
Curly Finds a Home	B	F	30	Rigby Literacy	Rigby
Curly Is Hungry	C	F	41	Rigby Literacy	Rigby
Curly to the Rescue	E	F	107	Rigby Literacy	Rigby
Curlylocks and the Three Bears: A Play	F	TL	194	Rigby Literacy	Rigby
Current in Your Home, The	T	I	554	Leveled Readers Science	Houghton Mifflin
Curse of Being Pharaoh, The	P	RF	250+	Marriott, Janice	Pacific Learning
Curse of the Cobweb Queen, The	L	F	250+	Hayes, Geoffrey	Random House
Curse of the Squirrel, The	N	F	250+	Yep, Laurence	Random House
Custard	E	RF	82	Wonder World	Wright Group/McGraw Hill
Custodians	M	I	250+	Community Helpers	Red Brick Learning
Customs Service	S	I	250+	Law Enforcement	Capstone Press
*Cut From the Same Cloth: American Women of Myth, Legend, and Tall Tale	T	TL	250+	San Souci, Robert D.	Puffin Books
Cutting and Sticking	K	RF	250+	Cambridge Reading	Pearson Learning Group
Cutting Machines	G	I	132	Sunshine Books	Wright Group/McGraw Hill
Cutting Our Food	B	I	40	Early Connections	Benchmark Education
Cyberspace	S	SF	250+	Wildcats	Wright Group/McGraw Hill
Cybil War, The	S	RF	250+	Byars, Betsy	Scholastic
Cyclops Doesn't Roller-Skate	M	F	250+	Dadey, Debbie; Jones, Marcia Thornton	Scholastic
Cynthia Rylant, Author	J	B	137	Vocabulary Readers	Houghton Mifflin
Da Gama: Vasco da Gama Sails Around the Cape of Good Hope	U	B	250+	Exploring the World	Compass Point Books

TITLE	LEVEL	GENRE	WORD COUNT	AUTHOR / SERIES	PUBLISHER / DISTRIBUTOR
Da Vinci	R	B	250+	Venezia, Mike	Children's Press
Dabble Duck	K	RF	250+	Ellis, Anne Leo	HarperTrophy
Dabbling in Dough	K	I	250+	Book Bank	Wright Group/McGraw Hill
Dad	A	I	24	PM Starters	Rigby
Dad	B	RF	21	Little Readers	Houghton Mifflin
Dad and Beth Clean Up	E	RF	113	Book Bus	Creative Edge
Dad and I	C	RF	59	Rise & Shine	Hampton-Brown
Dad and the Mosquito	I	RF	246	Sunshine	Wright Group/McGraw Hill
Dad Cooks Breakfast	H	RF	195	Windmill Books	Rigby
Dad Didn't Mind at All	F	RF	134	Literacy 2000	Rigby
Dad Goes to School	A	RF	43	Mom and Dad Series	Pioneer Valley
Dad Still Smiles	M	RF	212	Books for Young Learners	Richard C. Owen
Daddy Saved the Day	M	RF	250+	Greetings	Rigby
Daddy Works Out	D	RF	39	Visions	Wright Group/McGraw Hill
Dad's Bathtime	E	RF	114	Literacy Tree	Rigby
Dad's Bike	E	RF	52	Literacy 2000	Rigby
Dad's Garden	D	RF	25	Literacy 2000	Rigby
Dad's Headache	F	RF	86	Sunshine	Wright Group/McGraw Hill
Dad's New Path	F	RF	218	Foundations	Wright Group/McGraw Hill
Dad's Pasta	L	RF	250+	Sails	Rigby
Dad's Promise	L	RF	250+	Cambridge Reading	Pearson Learning Group
Dad's Shirt	F	RF	38	Joy Readers	Pearson Learning Group
Dad's Surprise	J	RF	202	Foundations	Wright Group/McGraw Hill
Dad's Turkey Sandwich	A	RF	26	Mom and Dad Series	Pioneer Valley
Daily Life in a Plains Indian Village: 1868	U	I	250+	Terry, Michael Bad Hand	Clarion
Daily Meow, The	M	F	250+	Sails	Rigby
Dairy Group, The	H	I	97	Pebble Books	Red Brick Learning
Daisy	J	RF	250+	Stepping Stones	Nelson/Michaels Assoc.
Daisy Divine, Dancing Dog	M	F	763	Leveled Readers	Houghton Mifflin
Dalmatians	I	RF	70	Salem, Lynn	Continental Press
Dalmations	E	I	70	Seedlings	Continental Press
Dame Shirley and the Gold Rush	R	B	250+	Rawls, Jim	Steck-Vaughn
Dan and Dan	E	RF	96	Real Kids Readers	Millbrook Press
Dan Gets Dressed	B	RF	42	Story Box	Wright Group/McGraw Hill
Dan Goes Home	E	F	153	Story Basket	Wright Group/McGraw Hill
Dan the Dunce	J	TL	539	Tales from Hans Andersen	Wright Group/McGraw Hill
Dan the Flying Man	C	F	60	Story Box	Wright Group/McGraw Hill
Dance at Grandpa's	J	HF	250+	Wilder, Laura Ingalls	HarperCollins
Dance for Fun!	S	I	250+	Activities for Fun	Compass Point Books
Dance My Dance	L	TL	250+	Foundations	Wright Group/McGraw Hill
Dance Wth Rosie	N	RF	250+	Giff, Patricia Reilly	Penguin Group
Dance, The	C	F	35	Learn to Read	Creative Teaching Press
Dances We Do, The	G	I	131	Twig	Wright Group/McGraw Hill
Dancin' Down	I	RF	193	Evangeline Nicholas Collection	Wright Group/McGraw Hill
Dancing	E	I	42	Instant Readers	Harcourt School Publishers
Dancing	D	I	27	Canizares, Susan; Chessen, Betsey	Scholastic
Dancing	C	RF	38	Visions	Wright Group/McGraw Hill
Dancing Around the World	T	I	250+	iOpeners	Pearson Learning Group
Dancing Carl	U	RF	250+	Paulsen, Gary	Aladdin
Dancing Dinosaurs	E	F	45	Little Celebrations	Pearson Learning Group
Dancing Dragon, The	I	F	236	Bookshop	Mondo
Dancing Fly, The	F	F	108	Sunshine	Wright Group/McGraw Hill
Dancing in Soot	L	RF	250+	Cambridge Reading	Pearson Learning Group
Dancing in the Cadillac Light	T	HF	250+	Holt, Kimberly Willis	G.P. Putnam's Sons

TITLE	LEVEL	GENRE	WORD COUNT	AUTHOR / SERIES	PUBLISHER / DISTRIBUTOR
Dancing on the Edge	Z	RF	250+	Nolan, Han	Harcourt School Publishers
Dancing Shoes	B	F	23	Literacy 2000	Rigby
Dancing to the River	J	TL	250+	Cambridge Reading	Pearson Learning Group
Dancing with Jacques	P	HF	250+	Voyages in Time	Wright Group/McGraw Hill
Dancing with Manatees	N	I	250+	McNulty, Faith	Scholastic
Dancing with the Indians	M	HF	250+	Medearis, Angela	Scholastic
Dandelion, The	E	RF	99	Sunshine	Wright Group/McGraw Hill
Dandelions and Other Stories	H	F	250+	Story Steps	Rigby
Danger	C	RF	66	Story Box	Wright Group/McGraw Hill
Danger Guys	N	RF	250+	Abbott, Tony	HarperTrophy
Danger Guys Blast Off	N	RF	250+	Abbott, Tony	HarperTrophy
Danger Guys on Ice	N	RF	250+	Abbott, Tony	HarperTrophy
Danger In Quicksand Swamp	W	RF	250+	Wallace, Bill	Simon & Schuster
Danger in the Parking Lot	J	RF	250+	PM Plus Story Books	Rigby
Danger on Midnight River	O	RF	250+	Paulsen, Gary	Bantam
Danger on Panther Peak	R	RF	250+	Wallace, Bill	Pocket Books
Danger on Parade	T	RF	250+	Keene, Carolyn	Pocket Books
Danger, Landslides!	Q	I	250+	Leveled Readers Language Support	Houghton Mifflin
Dangerous Animals	R	I	250+	Explorers	Wright Group/McGraw Hill
*Dangerous Comet and Other Cases, The	O	RF	250+	Simon, Seymour	Avon
Dangerous Droughts	L	I	250+	Rosen Real Readers	Rosen Publishing Group
Dangerous Waters	Q	I	250+	Leveled Readers	Houghton Mifflin
Dangerous Wishes	U	F	250+	Sleator, William	Penguin Group
Daniel	F	RF	161	Literacy 2000	Rigby
Daniel Boone: Man of the Forests	O	B	250+	Greene, Carol	Children's Press
Daniel Inouye: Hero from Hawaii	W	B	3114	Leveled Readers	Houghton Mifflin
Daniel Inouye: Senator from Hawaii	P	B	799	Leveled Readers Social Studies	Houghton Mifflin
Daniel's Basketball Team	E	RF	80	Carousel Readers	Pearson Learning Group
Daniel's Dog	K	RF	250+	Bogart, Jo Allen	Scholastic
Daniel's Duck	K	RF	250+	Bulla, Clyde Robert	HarperTrophy
Danny and Abby Are Friends	E	RF	109	Coulter, Mia	Maryruth Books
Danny and Bee's Safety Rules	F	RF	106	Coulter, Mia	Maryruth Books
Danny and the Dinosaur	J	F	250+	Hoff, Syd	Scholastic
Danny and the Dinosaur Go to Camp	H	F	250+	Hoff, Syd	HarperTrophy
Danny and the Four Seasons	C	RF	55	Coulter, Mia	Maryruth Books
Danny Gets Fit	E	RF	177	Coulter, Mia	Maryruth Books
Danny Looks for Abby	F	RF	120	Coulter, Mia	Maryruth Books
Danny, Champion of the World	T	RF	250+	Dahl, Roald	Language for Learning Assoc.
Danny's Big Jump	L	RF	250+	Reeder, Tracey	Wright Group/McGraw Hill
Danny's Desert Rats	X	RF	250+	Naylor, Phyllis Reynolds	Aladdin
Danny's Dollars	D	RF	88	Reading Corners	Pearson Learning Group
Danny's Five Senses	D	RF	52	Coulter, Mia	Maryruth Books
Danny's Groundhog Day	F	RF	126	Coulter, Mia	Maryruth Books
Danny's New Toy	E	RF	70	Coulter, Mia	Maryruth Books
Dan's Box	G	F	105	Cambridge Reading	Pearson Learning Group
Dan's Old Van	H	F	145	Supersonics	Rigby
Darby	T	HF	250+	Fuqua, Jonathon Scott	Candlewick Press
Darcy and Gran Don't Like Babies	K	RF	250+	Cutler, Jane	Scholastic
Daring Rescue of Marlon the Swimming Pig, The	P	F	250+	Saunders, S.	Random House
Dark and Full of Secrets	N	RF	250+	Carrick, Carol	Houghton Mifflin
Dark and Stormy Night, A	G	F	160	Little Red Readers	Sundance

* Collection of short stories

Dark Is Rising, The	X	F	250+	Cooper, Susan	Macmillan
Dark Night, Sleepy Night	F	I	123	Ziefert, Harriet	Puffin Books
Dark Side of the Creek, The	M	RF	250+	Harlow, Joan Hiatt	Wright Group/McGraw Hill
Dark Stairs	V	RF	250+	Byars, Betsy	Puffin Books
Dark, Dark Tale, A	F	F	115	Brown, Ruth	Penguin Group
*Dark-Thirty: Southern Tales of the Supernatural	R	F	250+	McKissack, Patricia C.	Alfred A. Knopf
Darryl the Doorman	F	RF	85	City Stories	Rigby
Dash, the Young Meerkat	K	RF	250+	PM Plus Story Books	Rigby
Daughter of the Mountains	V	HF	250+	Rankin, Louise	Penguin Group
Daughter of the Sun	H	RF	210	Storyteller-Night Crickets	Wright Group/McGraw Hill
Daughter of Venice	X	HF	250+	Napoli, Donna Jo	Random House
Daughters of Liberty	S	B	1620	Independent Readers Social Studies	Houghton Mifflin
David McCord: Poet	Q	B	407	Vocabulary Readers	Houghton Mifflin
David Wiggles	F	RF	54	City Stories	Rigby
Davin	R	F	250+	Gordon, Dan; Gordon, Zaki	Bantam
Davy Crockett	P	B	250+	Photo-Illustrated Biographies	Red Brick Learning
Davy Crockett and the Wild Cat	H	F	148	Instant Readers	Harcourt School Publishers
Davy Crockett: Frontier Hero	V	B	2127	Leveled Readers	Houghton Mifflin
Dawn of Fear	X	HF	250+	Cooper, Susan	Simon & Schuster
Day and Night	M	TL	250+	Orbit Chapter Books	Pacific Learning
Day and Night	D	I	102	Twig	Wright Group/McGraw Hill
Day and Night	G	I	115	Discovery Links	Newbridge
Day at Rainbow Lake, A	I	I	250+	Phonics Readers Plus	Steck-Vaughn
Day at School, A	A	I	21	Leveled Readers Emergent	Houghton Mifflin
Day at School, A	C	RF	38	Sunshine	Wright Group/McGraw Hill
Day at the Fair, A	B	RF	42	Bebop Books	Lee & Low Books Inc.
Day at the Races, A	M	RF	250+	Michaels, Eric	Pearson Learning Group
Day at the Races, A	H	RF	85	Bauer, Roger	Kaeden Books
Day Buzzy Stopped Being Busy, The	G	F	147	First Start	Troll Associates
Day for J. J. and Me, A	M	RF	371	Evangeline Nicholas Collection	Wright Group/McGraw Hill
Day I Had to Play with My Sister, The	G	RF	139	Bonsall, Crosby	HarperCollins
Day I Lost My Bus Pass, The	J	RF	131	City Kids	Rigby
Day I Tore My Shorts, The	I	RF	209	City Kids	Rigby
Day in Japan, A	G	I	54	Moreton, Daniel; Berger, Samantha	Scholastic
Day in Space, A	L	SF	250+	Lord, Suzanne; Epstein, Jolie	Scholastic
Day in the Life of a Colonial Cabinetmaker, A	S	I	250+	The Library of Living and Working in Colonial Times	Rosen Publishing Group
Day in the Life of a Colonial Dressmaker, A	S	I	250+	The Library of Living and Working in Colonial Times	Rosen Publishing Group
Day in the Life of a Colonial Glassblower, A	S	I	250+	The Library of Living and Working in Colonial Times	Rosen Publishing Group
Day in the Life of a Colonial Sea Captain, A	S	I	250+	The Library of Living and Working in Colonial Times	Rosen Publishing Group
Day in the Life of a Colonial Soldier, A	S	I	250+	The Library of Living and Working in Colonial Times	Rosen Publishing Group
Day in the Life of a Colonial Surveyor, A	S	I	250+	The Library of Living and Working in Colonial Times	Rosen Publishing Group
Day in the Life of a Garbage Collector, A	K	I	250+	First Facts	Capstone Press
Day in the Life of a Librarian, A	L	I	250+	First Facts	Capstone Press
Day in the Life of a Zoo Keeper, A	L	I	250+	First Facts	Capstone Press
Day in the Life of the Great Plains, A	Q	I	1287	Leveled Readers Social Studies	Houghton Mifflin

TITLE	LEVEL	GENRE	WORD COUNT	AUTHOR / SERIES	PUBLISHER / DISTRIBUTOR
Day in Town, A	K	RF	206	Story Box	Wright Group/McGraw Hill
Day It Rained Forever, The: A Story of the Johnstown Flood	S	I	250+	Gross, Virginia T.	Penguin Group
Day Jimmy's Boa Ate the Wash, The	K	F	250+	Noble, Trinka H.	Scholastic
Day Martin Luther King, Jr., Died, The	M	RF	250+	Story Vines	Wright Group/McGraw Hill
Day Martin Luther King, Jr., Was Shot, The	Y	B	250+	Haskins, Jim	Scholastic
Day Miss Francie Got Skunked, The	N	RF	250+	DeFord, Diane	Pearson Learning Group
Day No Pigs Would Die, A	Z	HF	250+	Peck, Robert Newton	Random House
Day of Ahmed's Secret, A	M	RF	250+	Heide, Florence Perry; Gilliland, Judith Heide	Scholastic
Day of Pleasure, A: Stories of a Boy Growing Up in Warsaw	W	B	250+	Singer, Isaac Bashevis	Farrar, Straus and Giroux
Day of the Blizzard	Q	I	250+	Moskin, Marietta	Scholastic
Day of the Dead, The	I	RF	250+	Greetings	Rigby
Day of the Dragon King	M	F	250+	Osborne, Mary Pope	Random House
Day of the Rain, The	L	F	250+	Cowley, Joy	Pearson Learning Group
Day of the Snow, The	L	F	250+	Cowley, Joy	Pearson Learning Group
Day of the Tornadoes	P	I	552	Vocabulary Readers	Houghton Mifflin
Day of the Wind, The	L	F	250+	Cowley, Joy	Pearson Learning Group
Day Shopping, A	E	RF	157	Foundations	Wright Group/McGraw Hill
Day the Earth Shook, The	T	I	1889	Leveled Readers Science	Houghton Mifflin
Day the Fifth Grade Disappeared, The	Q	F	250+	Fields, Terri	Scholastic
Day the Gorilla Came to School, The	I	RF	293	Sunshine	Wright Group/McGraw Hill
Day the Sky Fell Down, The	H	F	226	Lighthouse	Rigby
Day the Sky Turned Green, The	M	F	250+	Reeves, Barbara	Pearson Learning Group
Day the Women Got the Vote, The: A Photo History of the Women's Rights Movement	Y	B	250+	Sullivan, George	Scholastic
Day With a Mail Carrier, A	J	I	187	Welcome Books	Children's Press
Day With a Mechanic, A	J	I	147	Welcome Books	Children's Press
Day with Emily Emeryboard	K	F	250+	Foundations	Wright Group/McGraw Hill
Day with Firefighters, A	H	I	171	Welcome Books	Children's Press
Day with My Dad, A	C	RF	88	Fiesta Series	Pearson Learning Group
Day with Paramedics, A	F	I	147	Kottke, Jan	Scholastic
Day with the Mayor, A	N	RF	704	Leveled Readers Social Studies	Houghton Mifflin
Day with Wilbur Robinson, A	N	RF	250+	Joyce, William	HarperTrophy
Day with Your Dog, A	C	I	32	Rosen Real Readers	Rosen Publishing Group
Day, A	H	I	134	The Calendar	Capstone Press
Days at the Beach	E	I	85	Sun Sprouts	ETA/Cuisenaire
Days of Adventure	E	F	47	Bookshop	Mondo
Days of Courage: The Little Rock Story	R	I	250+	Kelso, Richard	Steck-Vaughn
Days to Remember	R	I	250+	iOpeners	Pearson Learning Group
*Days With Frog and Toad	K	F	250+	Lobel, Arnold	HarperTrophy
Dayton and the Happy Tree	M	RF	1237	Sunshine	Wright Group/McGraw Hill
De Soto: Hernando de Soto Explores the Southeast	U	B	250+	Exploring the World	Compass Point Books
Dead Girls Don't Write Letters	W	RF	250+	Giles, Gail	Millbrook Press
Dead Letter	S	RF	250+	Byars, Betsy	Puffin Books
Deadbolts and Dinkles	N	RF	250+	Tapp, Kathy Kennedy	Mondo
Deadly Dungeon, The	N	RF	250+	Roy, Ron	Random House
Dear Butterflies . . .	L	RF	414	Leveled Readers	Houghton Mifflin
Dear Diary	N	RF	250+	Literacy 2000 Satellites	Rigby
Dear Future	Q	RF	250+	Literacy 2000	Rigby
Dear Grandma	M	I	264	Storyteller Nonfiction	Wright Group/McGraw Hill
Dear Levi: Letters from the Overland Trail	T	HF	250+	Woodruff, Elvira	Alfred A. Knopf

* Collection of short stories

TITLE	LEVEL	GENRE	WORD COUNT	AUTHOR / SERIES	PUBLISHER / DISTRIBUTOR
Dear Mabel!	H	RF	138	Little Celebrations	Pearson Learning Group
Dear Mr. Henshaw	Q	RF	250+	Cleary, Beverly	HarperCollins
Dear Prime Minister	O	I	250+	Roberts, Chris	Fitzhenry & Whiteside
Dear Santa	B	F	50	Literacy 2000	Rigby
Dear Tom	H	RF	153	Wonder World	Wright Group/McGraw Hill
Dear Zoo	F	F	115	Campbell, Rod	Macmillan
Death Valley	S	HF	250+	Duey, Kathleen; Bale, Karen A.	Simon & Schuster
Death's Door	V	RF	250+	Byars, Betsy	Puffin Books
Deborah Sampson, Soldier of the American Revolution	P	B	250+	Leveled Readers Language Support	Houghton Mifflin
Deborah Sampson: Soldier of the Revolution	S	B	1207	Leveled Readers	Houghton Mifflin
Debra's Dog	H	F	157	Tadpoles	Rigby
Deb's Secret Wish and Other Stories	H	F	250+	New Way Literature	Steck-Vaughn
December Secrets	L	RF	250+	Giff, Patricia Reilly	Bantam
Declaration of Independence and Benjamin Franklin of Pennsylvania, The	R	B	250+	Framers of the Declaration of Independence	Rosen Publishing Group
Declaration of Independence and John Adams of Massachusetts, The	R	B	250+	Framers of the Declaration of Independence	Rosen Publishing Group
Declaration of Independence and Richard Henry Lee of Virginia, The	R	B	250+	Framers of the Declaration of Independence	Rosen Publishing Group
Declaration of Independence and Robert Livingston of New York, The	R	B	250+	Framers of the Declaration of Independence	Rosen Publishing Group
Declaration of Independence and Roger Sherman of Connecticut, The	R	B	250+	Framers of the Declaration of Independence	Rosen Publishing Group
Declaration of Independence and Thomas Jefferson of Virginia, The	R	B	250+	Framers of the Declaration of Independence	Rosen Publishing Group
Declaration of Independence, The	V	I	250+	Cornerstones of Freedom	Children's Press
Declaration of Independence, The	V	I	250+	Let Freedom Ring	Red Brick Learning
Declaration of Independence, The	N	I	250+	A True Book	Children's Press
Declaration of Independence, The	T	I	250+	We The People	Compass Point Books
Dede and the Dinosaur	K	F	232	Cumpiano, Ina	Hampton-Brown
DeDe Takes Charge!	O	RF	250+	Hurwitz, Johanna	Morrow
Dee and Me	G	RF	189	Ready Readers	Pearson Learning Group
Deep Blue Lake, A	V	I	2270	Leveled Readers	Houghton Mifflin
Deep in the Forest	WB	TL	N/A	Turkle, Brinton	Dutton
Deep in the Woods	E	RF	164	Carousel Readers	Pearson Learning Group
Deep Sea, The	G	I	152	Ready Readers	Pearson Learning Group
Deer and the Crocodile, The	G	F	178	Literacy 2000	Rigby
Deer Have Fawns	M	I	250+	Animals and Their Young	Compass Point Books
Deer in the Wood, The	J	HF	250+	Wilder, Laura Ingalls	HarperCollins
Defenders, The	T	B	250+	McGovern, Ann	Language for Learning Assoc.
Definitely Cool	X	RF	250+	Wilkinson, Brenda	Scholastic
Definitely Different	I	RF	102	Voyages	SRA/McGraw Hill
Definitely, Positively, Absolutely NO!	D	F	147	Story Basket	Wright Group/McGraw Hill
Delaware	R	I	250+	This Land Is Your Land	Compass Point Books
Delaware	T	I	250+	Sea to Shining Sea	Children's Press
Delaware	S	I	250+	Land of Liberty	Red Brick Learning
Delaware	T	I	250+	Hello U.S.A.	Lerner Publishing
Delaware People, The	P	I	250+	Native Peoples	Red Brick Learning
Delivering Your Mail: Book About Mail Carriers, A	H	I	120	Community Workers	Picture Window Books
Demolition	V	I	250+	iOpeners	Pearson Learning Group
Dennis Tito: First Space Tourist	Q	I	250+	Rosen Real Readers	Rosen Publishing Group

TITLE	LEVEL	GENRE	WORD COUNT	AUTHOR / SERIES	PUBLISHER / DISTRIBUTOR
Dentist, The	G	I	201	PM Nonfiction-Blue	Rigby
Dentists	M	I	250+	Ready, Dee	Red Brick Learning
Deputy Dan and the Bank Robbers	L	RF	250+	Rosenbloom, Joseph	Random House
Deputy Dan Gets His Man	L	RF	250+	Rosenbloom, Joseph	Random House
Desert Animals	I	I	134	Spyglass Books	Compass Point Books
Desert Animals	K	I	195	Rosen Real Readers	Rosen Publishing Group
Desert Birds	N	I	250+	A New True Book	Children's Press
Desert Dance	G	RF	184	Little Celebrations	Pearson Learning Group
Desert Day	C	I	23	Twig	Wright Group/McGraw Hill
Desert Friends	E	I	48	Ray's Readers	Outside the Box
Desert Giant: The World of the Saguaro Cactus	L	I	250+	Bash, Barbara	Scholastic
Desert Life	K	I	129	Independent Readers Science	Houghton Mifflin
Desert Life	N	I	250+	Mann, Rachel	Scholastic
Desert Machine, The	K	I	202	Sunshine	Wright Group/McGraw Hill
Desert Rain	K	I	214	Windows on Literacy	National Geographic
Desert Run, The	P	I	250+	Bonallack, John	Pacific Learning
Desert Treasure	M	RF	250+	Pair-It Books	Steck-Vaughn
Desert, The	C	I	34	Carousel Readers	Pearson Learning Group
Desert: Inside Australia's Simpson Desert	P	I	250+	Cambridge Reading	Pearson Learning Group
Deserts	K	I	212	Early Connections	Benchmark Education
Deserts	Q	I	250+	First Reports	Compass Point Books
Deserts	O	I	250+	Gibbons, Gail	Holiday House
Deserts	N	I	250+	Habitats of the World	Pearson Learning Group
Deserts	M	I	250+	PM Plus Nonfiction	Rigby
Deserts	R	I	250+	The Wonders of our World	Crabtree
Deserts	N	I	250+	A True Book	Children's Press
Deserts of the World	Q	I	1288	Leveled Readers Science	Houghton Mifflin
Designs	E	I	15	Little Celebrations	Pearson Learning Group
Destination Disaster	P	RF	250+	Action Packs	Rigby
Destroyers	T	I	250+	Land and Sea	Capstone Press
*Detective Dinosaur	J	F	250+	Skofield, James	HarperTrophy
Detective Dog and the Search for Cat	E	F	142	Learn to Read	Creative Teaching Press
Detective Max	LB	RF	32	Pair-It Books	Steck-Vaughn
*Detective Stories	Z	RF	250+	Pullman, Philip	Kingfisher
Devil's Arithmetic, The	Y	F	250+	Yolen, Jane	Puffin Books
Devil's Bridge	R	RF	250+	DeFelice, Cynthia	Avon
Devil's Highway, The	T	HF	250+	Applegate, Stan	Peachtree
DeWitt and Lila Wallace: Charity for All	P	B	250+	Community Builders	Children's Press
Diamond Champs, The	M	RF	250+	Christopher, Matt	Little, Brown & Co.
Diamond of Doom, The	M	RF	250+	Schultz, Irene	Wright Group/McGraw Hill
Diana	W	I	250+	World Mythology	Capstone Press
Diana Made Dinner	E	RF	81	Carousel Readers	Pearson Learning Group
Diary of a Honeybee	L	I	250+	Literacy 2000	Rigby
Diary of a Hurricane	S	RF	3402	Leveled Readers Science	Houghton Mifflin
Diary of a Pioneer Boy	Q	HF	250+	Massie, Elizabeth	Steck-Vaughn
Diary of a Sunflower	L	I	250+	Story Steps	Rigby
Diary of Anne Frank, The	Y	B	250+	Frank, Anne	Pocket Books
Dicey's Song	X	RF	250+	Voigt, Cynthia	Ballantine Books
Dick Whittington	L	TL	250+	PM Tales and Plays-Silver	Rigby
Did You Carry The Flag Today, Charley?	N	RF	250+	Caudill, Rebecca	Bantam
Did You Hear Wind Sing Your Name?	N	TL	182	Bookshop	Mondo
Did You Know?	G	I	22	Learn to Read	Creative Teaching Press
Did You Know?	L	I	250+	Sunshine	Wright Group/McGraw Hill
Did you say, "Fire"?	G	F	158	Pacific Literacy	Pacific Learning

* Collection of short stories

TITLE	LEVEL	GENRE	WORD COUNT	AUTHOR / SERIES	PUBLISHER / DISTRIBUTOR
Diddle Diddle Dumpling	E	F	54	Seedlings	Continental Press
Diego Rivera	R	B	250+	Venezia, Mike	Children's Press
Diego Rivera	O	B	250+	First Biographies	Steck-Vaughn
Diego Rivera: An Artist's Life	L	B	250+	Pair-It Books	Steck-Vaughn
Different Beat, A	U	RF	250+	Boyd, Candy Dawson	Penguin Group
Different Dragons	O	RF	250+	Little, Jean	Penguin Group
Different Faces from Different Places	I	I	148	Twig	Wright Group/McGraw Hill
Different Homes Around the World	K	I	200	Rigby Literacy	Rigby
Different Seasons	B	I	37	Leveled Readers Science	Houghton Mifflin
Different Tune, A	G	F	86	Start to Read	School Zone
Difficult Day, The	J	RF	304	Read Alongs	Rigby
Dig	C	F	20	KinderReaders	Rigby
Dig In	I	I	96	iOpeners	Pearson Learning Group
Dig, Dig	A	RF	12	Cat on the Mat	Oxford University Press
Digby	I	RF	250+	Little Readers	Houghton Mifflin
*Digby and Kate	K	F	250+	Baker, Barbara	Puffin Easy-to-Read
Digestive System, The	L	I	173	Human Body Systems	Red Brick Learning
Digestive System, The	N	I	250+	A True Book	Children's Press
Digging Dinosaurs	P	I	250+	Nayer, Judy	Pearson Learning Group
Digging to China	H	F	108	Books for Young Learners	Richard C. Owen
Digging Up Tyrannosaurus Rex	P	I	250+	Horner, John; Lessem, Don	Crown
Dilly Duck and Dally Duck	D	F	139	PM Plus Story Books	Rigby
Dingoes at Dinnertime	M	F	250+	Osborne, Mary Pope	Random House
Dinner	A	F	21	KinderReaders	Rigby
Dinner by Five	F	RF	215	Ready Readers	Pearson Learning Group
Dinner!	LB	RF	19	Sunshine	Wright Group/McGraw Hill
Dinosaur	B	I	17	Science	Outside the Box
Dinosaur	M	I	250+	Cambridge Reading	Pearson Learning Group
Dinosaur Babies	L	I	250+	Penner, Lucille Recht	Random House
Dinosaur Chase, The	I	HF	240	PM Story Books-Orange	Rigby
Dinosaur Connection, The	O	I	250+	Literacy Tree	Rigby
Dinosaur Dance, The	B	F	52	Little Books	Sadlier-Oxford
Dinosaur Days	K	RF	250+	Ready Readers	Pearson Learning Group
Dinosaur Days	L	I	250+	Milton, Joyce	Random House
Dinosaur Detective	O	I	250+	Wildcats	Wright Group/McGraw Hill
Dinosaur Detectives	K	F	250+	Pacific Literacy	Pacific Learning
Dinosaur Discovery	I	I	250+	Story Steps	Rigby
Dinosaur Fan, The	F	F	125	Windmill Books	Rigby
Dinosaur Fun Facts	E	I	84	Pair-It Books	Steck-Vaughn
Dinosaur Girl	N	RF	250+	Literacy Tree	Rigby
Dinosaur Hunt, The	G	RF	155	Rigby Literacy	Rigby
Dinosaur Hunt, The	G	F	131	Windmill Books	Rigby
Dinosaur Hunters	L	I	250+	McMullan, Kate	Random House
Dinosaur Hunting	N	I	579	Leveled Readers Science	Houghton Mifflin
Dinosaur in Trouble	G	F	121	First Start	Troll Associates
Dinosaur Named Sue, A	P	F	250+	Robinson, Fay	Scholastic
Dinosaur on the Motorway	K	F	231	Wesley and the Dinosaurs	Wright Group/McGraw Hill
Dinosaur Party	B	F	27	Smart Starts	Rigby
Dinosaur Reports	L	I	324	Little Red Readers	Sundance
Dinosaur Show and Tell	G	RF	212	Pair-It Books	Steck-Vaughn
Dinosaur Time	K	I	250+	Parish, Peggy	HarperTrophy
Dinosaur Times	D	RF	43	Sunshine	Wright Group/McGraw Hill
Dinosaur Who Lived in My Backyard, The	I	F	250+	Hennessy, Brendan G.	Scholastic
Dinosaur Zoo, The	J	F	250+	Literacy Tree	Rigby

* Collection of short stories

TITLE	LEVEL	GENRE	WORD COUNT	AUTHOR / SERIES	PUBLISHER / DISTRIBUTOR
Dinosaur, The	A	F	14	Sunshine	Wright Group/McGraw Hill
Dinosaur, The	F	F	131	Joy Readers	Pearson Learning Group
Dinosaurs	E	I	37	Instant Readers	Harcourt School Publishers
Dinosaurs	K	I	193	Bookshop	Mondo
Dinosaurs	H	I	117	Sunshine	Wright Group/McGraw Hill
Dinosaurs	M	I	250+	Gibbons, Gail	Holiday House
Dinosaurs	F	I	115	Maccarone, Grace	Scholastic
Dinosaurs & Other Reptiles	I	I	123	Planet Earth	Rigby
Dinosaurs Before Dark	M	F	250+	Osborne, Mary Pope	Random House
Dinosaur's Cold, The	J	F	244	Literacy 2000	Rigby
Dinosaurs Dance	E	F	17	Rookie Readers	Children's Press
Dinosaurs Dancing	F	F	115	Learn to Read	Creative Teaching Press
Dinosaurs Galore	D	F	34	Eaton, Audrey; Kennedy, Jane	Continental Press
Dinosaurs on the Motorway	K	F	250+	Wesley & the Dinosaurs	Wright Group/McGraw Hill
Dinosaurs, Dinosaurs	G	I	96	Barton, Byron	HarperCollins
Diplodocus	N	I	250+	Discovering Dinosaurs	Red Brick Learning
Dipplidocus in the Garden, A	K	F	210	Wesley and the Dinosaurs	Wright Group/McGraw Hill
Dippy Dinner Drippers, The	H	F	181	Sunshine	Wright Group/McGraw Hill
Dirt Bike Racer	M	RF	250+	Christopher, Matt	Little, Brown & Co.
Dirt Bike Runaway	M	RF	250+	Christopher, Matt	Little, Brown & Co.
Dirt Bikes	M	I	250+	Blazers	Capstone Press
Dirt: The Scoop on Soil	M	I	250+	Amazing Science	Picture Window Books
Dirty Beasts	O	F	250+	Dahl, Roald	Penguin Group
Dirty Larry	D	RF	53	Rookie Readers	Children's Press
Dirty Socks Don't Win Games	R	RF	250+	Marney, Dean	Scholastic
Disability Rights Movement, The	W	I	250+	Cornerstones of Freedom	Children's Press
Disappearing Acts	S	RF	250+	Byars, Betsy	Puffin Books
Disappearing Bike Shop, The	Q	SF	250+	Woodruff, Elvira	Bantam
*Disappearing Cookies and Other Cases, The	O	RF	250+	Simon, Seymour	Avon
*Disappearing Ice Cream and Other Cases, The	O	RF	250+	Simon, Seymour	Avon
*Disappearing Snowball and Other Cases, The	O	RF	250+	Simon, Seymour	Avon
Disaster of the Hindenburg, The: The Last Flight of the Greatest Airship Ever Built	Z	I	250+	Tanaka, Shelley	Scholastic
Disaster, The	R	RF	1309	Leveled Readers	Houghton Mifflin
Discovering Dinosaurs	K	I	211	Spyglass Books	Compass Point Books
Discovering Dinosaurs	M	F	335	Little Books	Sadlier-Oxford
Discovering Jupiter: The Amazing Collision in Space	T	I	250+	Berger, Melvin	Scholastic
Discovering the Past	S	I	250+	Literacy 2000	Rigby
Discovering the Titanic	O	I	250+	Trumbore, Cindy	Pearson Learning Group
Discovery of the Americas, The	S	I	250+	Maestro, Betsy & Giulio	William Morrow
Dishy-Washy	E	F	92	Story Basket	Wright Group/McGraw Hill
*Distant Stars and Other Cases, The	O	RF	250+	Simon, Seymour	Avon
Ditching School	J	RF	128	City Kids	Rigby
Dive In!	F	RF	133	Ready Readers	Pearson Learning Group
Dive to the Deep Ocean: Voyages of Exploration and Discovery	W	I	250+	Kovacs, Deborah	Steck-Vaughn
Dive!: My Adventures in the Deep Frontier	V	B	250+	Earle, Sylvia A.	Scholastic
Dive, The	K	RF	488	Leveled Readers	Houghton Mifflin
Diver, The	B	RF	30	Sunshine	Wright Group/McGraw Hill
Divers' Dream	P	I	250+	Pacific Literacy	Pacific Learning
Divers of the Deep Sea	S	I	250+	Windows on Literacy	National Geographic
Divers, The	C	I	25	Wonder World	Wright Group/McGraw Hill
Diving	G	RF	164	Story Box	Wright Group/McGraw Hill

* Collection of short stories

TITLE	LEVEL	GENRE	WORD COUNT	AUTHOR / SERIES	PUBLISHER / DISTRIBUTOR
Diving at the Pool	M	RF	519	PM Plus Story Books	Rigby
Diving for Treasure	M	I	284	Books for Young Learners	Richard C. Owen
Dizzy Lizzy	E	RF	37	Literacy 2000	Rigby
Do Animals Live in Plants?	F	I	56	Instant Readers	Harcourt School Publishers
Do Bears Buzz?: A Book About Animal Sounds	M	I	250+	Animals All Around	Picture Window Books
Do Bees Make Butter?: A Book About Things Animals Make	M	I	250+	Animals All Around	Picture Window Books
Do Cows Eat Cake?: A Book About What Animals Eat	M	I	250+	Animals All Around	Picture Window Books
Do Dogs Make Dessert?: A Book About How Animals Help Humans	M	I	250+	Animals All Around	Picture Window Books
Do Ducks Live in the Desert?: A Book About Where Animals Live	M	I	250+	Animals All Around	Picture Window Books
Do Frogs Have Fur?: A Book About Animal Coats and Coverings	M	I	250+	Animals All Around	Picture Window Books
Do Goldfish Gallop?: A Book About Animal Movement	M	I	250+	Animals All Around	Picture Window Books
Do Ladybugs Go to School?	E	F	75	Visions	Wright Group/McGraw Hill
Do Not Open This Book!	F	F	134	Story Basket	Wright Group/McGraw Hill
Do Parrots Have Pillows?: A Book About Where Animals Sleep	M	I	250+	Animals All Around	Picture Window Books
Do Penguins Have Puppies?: A Book About Animal Babies	M	I	250+	Animals All Around	Picture Window Books
Do Salamanders Spit?: A Book About How Animals Protect Themselves	M	I	250+	Animals All Around	Picture Window Books
Do Squirrels Swarm?: A Book About Animal Groups	M	I	250+	Animals All Around	Picture Window Books
Do Stars Have Points?	R	I	250+	Berger, Melvin & Gilda	Scholastic
Do That, Do This!	H	RF	151	Supersonics	Rigby
Do The Funky Pickle	U	RF	250+	Spinelli, Jerry	Scholastic
Do Tornadoes Really Twist?	S	I	250+	Berger, Melvin	Scholastic
Do We Need It? Do We Want It?	G	I	111	Early Connections	Benchmark Education
Do Whales Have Wings?: A Book About Animal Bodies	M	I	250+	Animals All Around	Picture Window Books
Do You Know Me?	Q	RF	250+	Farmer, Nancy	Penguin Group
Do You Like Cats?	K	I	250+	Bank Street	Bantam
Do You Like Grapes?	B	RF	31	Science	Outside the Box
Do You Like My Pet?	A	F	35	Phonics and Friends	Hampton-Brown
Do You Remember When?	D	RF	198	Visions	Wright Group/McGraw Hill
Do You Want to be My Friend?	A	F	8	Carle, Eric	Penguin Group
Doctor Boondoggle	D	F	51	Story Box	Wright Group/McGraw Hill
Doctor Foster	D	F	68	Seedlings	Continental Press
Doctor Has the Flu, The	H	RF	106	Ready Readers	Pearson Learning Group
Doctor, The	G	I	179	PM Nonfiction-Blue	Rigby
Doctors	L	I	250+	Community Workers	Compass Point Books
Doctors	M	I	250+	Ready, Dee	Red Brick Learning
Doctor's Busy Day, A	L	I	250+	Rosen Real Readers	Rosen Publishing Group
Doctor's Office, The	K	I	272	Pebble Books	Capstone Press
Does a Kangaroo Have a Mother Too?	F	I	214	Carle, Eric	Scholastic
Does a Penguin Have Fur?	D	RF	74	Rigby Literacy	Rigby
Does Third Grade Last Forever?	O	RF	250+	Schanback, Mindy	Troll Associates
Dog	B	RF	37	Pacific Literacy	Pacific Learning
Dog and Cat	F	RF	62	My First Reader	Grolier Press
Dog and the Bone, The	E	TL	67	Leveled Readers	Houghton Mifflin

* Collection of short stories

TITLE	LEVEL	GENRE	WORD COUNT	AUTHOR / SERIES	PUBLISHER / DISTRIBUTOR
Dog Called Bear, A	K	RF	438	PM Story Books	Rigby
Dog Called Kitty, A	R	RF	250+	Wallace, Bill	Pocket Books
Dog Called Mischief, A	D	RF	42	Cat on the Mat	Oxford University Press
Dog Day!, A	LB	RF	21	Smart Starts	Rigby
Dog Family, The	J	I	250+	Story Steps	Rigby
Dog for Mrs. Muddle Mud-Puddle, A	H	F	194	Story Box	Wright Group/McGraw Hill
Dog for You, A: Caring for Your Dog	M	I	250+	Pet Care	Picture Window Books
Dog From Outer Space, The	I	SF	250+	Lighthouse	Rigby
Dog I Share, The	N	RF	250+	Marriott, Janice	Pacific Learning
Dog in The Freezer, The	W	F	250+	Mazer, Harry	Simon & Schuster
Dog Named Honey, A	F	I	46	iOpeners	Pearson Learning Group
Dog on Barkham Street, A	R	RF	250+	Stolz, Mary	HarperTrophy
Dog School	A	RF	11	TOTTS	Tott Publications
Dog School	I	RF	224	Story Steps	Rigby
Dog Show, The	K	RF	250+	Cambridge Reading	Pearson Learning Group
Dog Show, The	F	I	131	Foundations	Wright Group/McGraw Hill
Dog that Pitched a No-Hitter, The	L	F	250+	Christopher, Matt	Little, Brown & Co.
Dog that Stole Football Plays, The	L	F	250+	Christopher, Matt	Little, Brown & Co.
Dog that Stole Home, The	L	F	250+	Christopher, Matt	Little, Brown & Co.
Dog Went for a Walk	D	RF	51	Voyages	SRA/McGraw Hill
Dog Who Wanted to Be a Tiger!, The	M	F	250+	Little Celebrations	Pearson Learning Group
Dog Years	R	RF	250+	Warner, Sally	Alfred A. Knopf
Dog, The	G	RF	56	Burningham, John	Crowell
Dog-Gone Hollywood	L	F	250+	Sharmat, Marjorie Weinman	Random House
Doggy Dare	O	RF	250+	Baglio, Ben M.	Scholastic
Dogs	D	I	44	All About Pets	Red Brick Learning
Dogs	J	I	250+	PM Animal Facts: Orange	Rigby
Dogs	B	RF	27	Levin, Amy	Scholastic
Dogs	F	I	116	Foundations	Wright Group/McGraw Hill
Dogs	I	I	116	Hutchins, Pat	Wright Group/McGraw Hill
Dogs Are My Favorite Things	J	RF	246	Bookshop	Mondo
Dogs at School	F	F	94	Books for Young Learners	Richard C. Owen
Dogs at Work	J	I	250+	Little Readers	Houghton Mifflin
Dog's Best Friend, A	M	RF	647	Pair-It Books	Steck-Vaughn
Dog's Diary	M	F	250+	Sails	Rigby
Dogs Dogs Dogs	R	I	250+	Literacy 2000	Rigby
Dogs Don't Tell Jokes	O	RF	250+	Sachar, Louis	Alfred A. Knopf
Dogs Have Puppies	M	I	250+	Animals and Their Young	Compass Point Books
Dogs Learn Every Day	C	I	38	Vocabulary Readers	Houghton Mifflin
Dog's Life, A	WB	I	N/A	Windows on Literacy	National Geographic
Dogs Love to Play Ball	I	F	159	Books for Young Learners	Richard C. Owen
Dogs on the Farm	I	I	85	Pebble Books	Red Brick Learning
Dog's Party	I	F	628	Leveled Readers	Houghton Mifflin
Dogsong	V	RF	250+	Paulsen, Gary	Simon & Schuster
Dogstar	J	F	250+	Literacy 2000	Rigby
Doing Jobs Together	F	RF	194	Early Connections	Benchmark Education
Doing My Job	H	I	188	Early Connections	Benchmark Education
Doing the Dishes	L	RF	136	City Kids	Rigby
Dollar, The	K	RF	169	Books for Young Learners	Richard C. Owen
Dolley Madison, First Lady	L	B	330	Leveled Readers Social Studies	Houghton Mifflin
Dolley Madison: First Lady	T	B	250+	Let Freedom Ring	Capstone Press
Dollhouse Murders, The	S	RF	250+	Wright, Betty Ren	Scholastic
Doll's House, The	R	RF	250+	Godden, Rumer	Penguin Group
Dolly Madison, First Lady	J	B	250+	Leveled Readers Social Studies	Houghton Mifflin

* Collection of short stories

TITLE	LEVEL	GENRE	WORD COUNT	AUTHOR / SERIES	PUBLISHER / DISTRIBUTOR
Dolly's Car	H	RF	192	Handprints C, Set 2	Educator's Publishing Service
Dolores Huerta, Civil Rights Leader	U	B	1655	Leveled Readers Social Studies	Houghton Mifflin
Dolphin	L	I	250+	Morris, Robert A.	HarperTrophy
Dolphin Adventure	P	RF	250+	Grover, Wayne	Beech Tree Books
Dolphin on the Wall, The	K	RF	250+	PM Story Books-Silver	Rigby
Dolphin Treasure	P	RF	250+	Grover, Wayne	Beech Tree Books
Dolphin, The	P	I	250+	Animal Close-Ups	Charlesbridge
Dolphins	U	I	250+	The Heinle Reading Library	Thomson Learning
Dolphins	O	I	250+	Holmes, Kevin J.	Red Brick Learning
Dolphins	K	I	111	Bookshop	Mondo
Dolphins	N	I	250+	Kalman, Bobbie	Crabtree
Dolphins	I	I	44	Pebble Books	Red Brick Learning
Dolphins	J	I	111	Wonder World	Wright Group/McGraw Hill
Dolphins	I	I	250+	Pebble Plus	Capstone Press
Dolphins at Daybreak	M	F	250+	Osborne, Mary Pope	Random House
Dolphin's First Day: The Story of a Bottlenose Dolphin	N	I	250+	Zoehfeld, Kathleen Weidnetz	Scholastic
Dolphins!	L	I	250+	Bokoske, Sharon	Random House
Dolphins!	L	I	250+	Bokoske, Sharon; Davidson, M.	Random House
Dolphins, The	L	RF	721	PM Gold	Rigby
Dominic	R	F	250+	Steig, William	Farrar, Straus and Giroux
Dominoes	P	I	250+	Games Around the World	Compass Point Books
Dom's Handplant	L	RF	250+	Literacy 2000	Rigby
Donald's Garden	K	RF	250+	Reading Unlimited	Pearson Learning Group
Donavan's Word Jar	N	RF	250	DeGross, Monalisa	HarperCollins
Donkey	M	F	250+	Literacy 2000	Rigby
Donkey in the Lion's Skin, The	G	TL	213	PM Plus Story Books	Rigby
Donkey in the Lion's Skin, The	G	TL	56	Aesop	Wright Group/McGraw Hill
Donkey Rescue	M	RF	250+	Krailing, Tessa	Barron's Educational
Donkey Work	H	I	129	Wonder World	Wright Group/McGraw Hill
Donkeys	M	I	250+	Voyages	SRA/McGraw Hill
Donkey's Tale, The	J	TL	250+	Bank Street	Bantam
Donna O'Neeshuck Was Chased By Some Cows	L	RF	250+	Grossman, Bill	HarperTrophy
Donner Party, The	Q	HF	250+	Werther, Scott P.	Scholastic
Don't Be Late	D	F	111	Gibson, Akimi	Scholastic
Don't Be Late!	L	RF	250+	Cambridge Reading	Pearson Learning Group
Don't Be My Valentine: A Classroom Mystery	J	RF	250+	Lexau, Joan M.	HarperTrophy
Don't Be Silly	E	F	76	Teacher's Choice Series	Pearson Learning Group
Don't Bug Me!	T	RF	2224	Leveled Readers	Houghton Mifflin
Don't Call Me Beanhead!	N	RF	250+	Wojciechowski, Susan	Candlewick Press
Don't Cut Down This Tree	G	F	129	Voyages	SRA/McGraw Hill
Don't Eat the Stick	I	F	250+	Sunshine	Wright Group/McGraw Hill
Don't Eat Too Much Turkey	J	TL	250+	Cohen, Miriam	Bantam
Don't Forget	E	RF	80	Literacy Tree	Rigby
Don't Forget Fun	L	RF	250+	Little Celebrations	Pearson Learning Group
Don't Forget the Bacon	M	RF	174	Hutchins, Pat	Puffin Books
Don't Interrupt!	I	RF	225	Windmill Books	Rigby
Don't Leave Anything Behind!	C	RF	26	Literacy 2000	Rigby
Don't Let Ted Have Bubble Gum!	I	RF	250+	Phonics Readers Plus	Steck-Vaughn
Don't Let the Cat Out!	F	RF	109	Independent Readers Social Studies	Houghton Mifflin
Don't Panic!	E	RF	122	Book Bank	Wright Group/McGraw Hill
Don't Splash Me!	A	RF	24	Windmill	Wright Group/McGraw Hill

TITLE	LEVEL	GENRE	WORD COUNT	AUTHOR / SERIES	PUBLISHER / DISTRIBUTOR
*Don't Split the Pole: Tales of Down-Home Folk Wisdom	S	RF	250+	Tate, Eleanora E.	Bantam
Don't Stomp on That Bug	I	I	250+	Rigby Literacy	Rigby
Don't Talk to Strangers	E	I	157	Rosen Real Readers	Rosen Publishing Group
Don't Tell!	G	RF	82	Little Books	Sadlier-Oxford
Don't Throw It Away!	F	I	90	Wonder World	Wright Group/McGraw Hill
Don't Throw Your Spinach	I	RF	155	Story Box	Wright Group/McGraw Hill
Don't Touch	I	RF	250+	Kline, Suzy	Penguin Group
Don't Touch It, Lily	K	F	250+	Popcorn	Sundance
Don't Wake the Baby	B	RF	18	Literacy 2000	Rigby
Don't Worry	J	RF	339	Literacy 2000	Rigby
Don't You Laugh at Me!	E	F	167	Sunshine	Wright Group/McGraw Hill
Doodler, The	T	RF	2012	Leveled Readers	Houghton Mifflin
Doomed Queen Anne	Z	HF	250+	Meyer, Carolyn	Harcourt Trade
Door in the Wall, The	U	HF	250+	De Angeli, Marguerite	Bantam
Doorbell Rang, The	J	RF	283	Hutchins, Pat	Greenwillow
Dorothea Dix: Social Reformer	T	B	250+	Let Freedom Ring	Capstone Press
Double Danger	P	F	250+	Hager, Mandy	Pacific Learning
Double Dutch	E	RF	191	Visions	Wright Group/McGraw Hill
Double Life of Pocahontas, The	U	B	250+	Fritz, Jean	Language for Learning Assoc.
Double Play at Short	M	RF	250+	Christopher, Matt	Little, Brown & Co.
Double Switch	M	RF	250+	Noonan, Diana	Pacific Learning
Double Trouble	L	RF	250+	Sunshine	Wright Group/McGraw Hill
Double Trouble	Q	RF	250+	Leveled Readers Language Support	Houghton Mifflin
Double Trouble	M	TL	250+	Literacy 2000	Rigby
Douglas Fir	O	I	250+	Davis, Wendy	Children's Press
Douglas Florian	K	B	250+	Leveled Readers Language Support	Houghton Mifflin
Douglas Florian, Poet and Artist	M	B	484	Leveled Readers	Houghton Mifflin
Dove Isabeau	T	F	250+	Yolen, Jane	OSI
Do-Whacky-Do	H	F	249	Read Alongs	Rigby
Down at the River	E	RF	51	Pacific Literacy	Pacific Learning
Down at the Billabong	F	RF	93	Voyages	SRA/McGraw Hill
Down By the Bay	E	RF	121	Little Celebrations	Pearson Learning Group
Down by the Pond	I	I	118	Story Box	Wright Group/McGraw Hill
Down By the Sea	G	RF	173	PM Plus Story Books	Rigby
Down By the Stream	E	I	97	Independent Readers Science	Houghton Mifflin
Down by the Swamp	F	RF	50	Little Celebrations	Pearson Learning Group
Down in the Woods	I	F	155	Storyteller-Moon Rising	Wright Group/McGraw Hill
Down on the Farm	E	F	244	Learn to Read	Creative Teaching Press
Down on the Ice	P	I	250+	Alchin, Rupert	Pacific Learning
Down the Hill	C	RF	32	KinderReaders	Rigby
Down the Hill	C	RF	94	New Way Red	Steck-Vaughn
Down the Street	E	RF	66	Little Celebrations	Pearson Learning Group
Down the Well	E	F	200	Sun Sprouts	ETA/Cuisenaire
Down to a Sunless Sea: The Strange World of Hydrothermal Vents	W	I	250+	Madin, Kate	Steck-Vaughn
Down to Town	A	F	26	Sunshine	Wright Group/McGraw Hill
Downtown Lost & Found	E	F	55	New Reader Series	Bungalo Books
Dozen Dizzy Dogs, A	G	F	157	Bank Street	Bantam
Dozen Dogs, A	F	F	228	Ziefert, Harriet	Random House
Dozen Eggs, A	LB	RF	14	Harry's Math Books	Outside the Box

* Collection of short stories

TITLE	LEVEL	GENRE	WORD COUNT	AUTHOR / SERIES	PUBLISHER / DISTRIBUTOR
Dr. Charles Drew and the Blood Banks	S	B	1515	Independent Readers Science	Houghton Mifflin
Dr. Green	G	RF	141	Little Readers	Houghton Mifflin
Dr. Jekyll, Orthodontist	N	RF	250+	The Zack Files	Grosset & Dunlap
Dr. MacTavish's Creature	N	RF	250+	PM Emerald	Rigby
Dr. Quinn, Medicine Woman	T	B	250+	McKenna, Colleen O'Shaughnessy	Language for Learning Assoc.
Dr. Seuss	L	B	184	First Biographies	Red Brick Learning
Dr. Seuss and His Stories	N	B	250+	Colgon, Kari	Wright Group/McGraw Hill
Dracula Doesn't Drink Lemonade	M	F	250+	Dadey, Debbie; Jones, Marcia Thornton	Scholastic
Dragon	I	F	161	Pacific Literacy	Pacific Learning
Dragon Bones	O	F	250+	Hindman, Paul	Random House
Dragon Breath	L	F	250+	O'Connor, Jane	Grosset & Dunlap
Dragon Cauldron	W	F	250+	Yep, Laurence	HarperCollins
Dragon Chronicles, The: Dragon's Milk	V	F	250+	Fletcher, Susan	Aladdin
Dragon Feet	K	F	153	Books For Young Learners	Richard C. Owen
Dragon Fire	P	F	250+	Cowley, Joy	Pacific Learning
Dragon for Sale	Q	F	250+	MacDonald, Marianne	Troll Associates
Dragon Gets By	I	F	250+	Pilkey, Dave	Orchard Books
*Dragon Hunt, The	F	F	53	New Way Red	Steck-Vaughn
Dragon in the Family, A	Q	F	250+	Koller, Jackie French	Pocket Books
Dragon in the Ghetto Caper, The	T	RF	250+	Konigsburg, E. L.	Aladdin
*Dragon King's Palace, The	T	TL	250+	Literacy 2000	Rigby
Dragon of Krakow, The: A Polish Folktale	L	TL	366	Leveled Readers	Houghton Mifflin
Dragon of the Lost Sea	W	F	250+	Yep, Laurence	HarperCollins
Dragon Parade: A Chinese New Year Story	O	I	250+	Chin, Steven A.	Steck-Vaughn
Dragon Prince, The: A Chinese Beauty and the Beast Tale	P	TL	250+	Yep, Laurence	HarperCollins
Dragon Quest	Q	F	250+	Koller, Jackie French	Pocket Books
Dragon Slayer	P	F	250+	Cowley, Joy	Pacific Learning
Dragon Steel	W	F	250+	Yep, Laurence	HarperCollins
Dragon Trouble	Q	F	250+	Koller, Jackie French	Pocket Books
Dragon Trouble	N	F	250+	SupaDoopers	Sundance
Dragon War	W	F	250+	Yep, Laurence	HarperCollins
Dragon Who Came to Dinner, The	K	F	250+	The Wright Skills	Wright Group/McGraw Hill
Dragon Who Had the Measles, The	J	F	250+	Literacy 2000	Rigby
Dragon with a Cold	J	F	250+	Sunshine	Wright Group/McGraw Hill
Dragon!	E	F	68	Wonder World	Wright Group/McGraw Hill
Dragon, The	I	F	250+	Story Box	Wright Group/McGraw Hill
Dragon, The	C	F	130	Sunshine	Wright Group/McGraw Hill
Dragonflies	G	I	53	Books for Young Learners	Richard C. Owen
Dragonflies	E	I	39	Pebble Books	Capstone Press
Dragonflies Are Super Bugs	G	I	101	Seedlings	Continental Press
*Dragonfly Dreams and Other Dreams	I	F	250+	Story Steps	Rigby
Dragonling, The	Q	F	250+	Koller, Jackie French	Pocket Books
Dragons and Kings	Q	F	250+	Koller, Jackie French	Pocket Books
Dragon's Birthday, The	K	F	250+	Literacy 2000	Rigby
Dragon's Blood	X	F	250+	Yolen, Jane	Harcourt Trade
Dragon's Coming After You, The	H	F	156	Voyages	SRA/McGraw Hill
Dragons Don't Cook Pizza	M	F	250+	Dadey, Debbie; Jones, Marcia Thornton	Scholastic
Dragons Don't Read Books	M	RF	250+	Bookshop	Mondo
Dragon's Dream	C	F	34	Learn to Read	Creative Teaching Press
Dragon's Fat Cat	I	F	250+	Pilkey, Dave	Orchard Books

* Collection of short stories

TITLE	LEVEL	GENRE	WORD COUNT	AUTHOR / SERIES	PUBLISHER / DISTRIBUTOR
Dragons Galore	N	F	250+	Wildcats	Wright Group/McGraw Hill
Dragon's Gate	W	HF	250+	Yep, Laurence	HarperCollins
Dragon's Halloween	I	F	250+	Pilkey, Dave	Orchard Books
Dragon's Lunch	F	F	85	Ready Readers	Pearson Learning Group
Dragon's Merry Christmas	I	F	250+	Pilkey, Dave	Orchard Books
Dragons of Blueland, The	L	F	250+	Gannett, Ruth	Random House
Dragons of Krad	Q	F	250+	Koller, Jackie French	Pocket Books
Dragon's Scales, The	J	F	250+	Albee, Sarah	Random House
Dragonsong	V	F	250+	McCaffrey, Anne	Bantam
Dragonwings	W	HF	250+	Yep, Lawrence	HarperTrophy
Dragsters	M	I	250+	Blazers	Capstone Press
Dragsters	T	I	250+	The World's Fastest	Red Brick Learning
Drat That Cat!	I	F	250+	Cambridge Reading	Pearson Learning Group
Draw Me a Story	P	B	250+	Winter, Max	Scholastic
Drawbridge	E	I	29	Books for Young Learners	Richard C. Owen
Dreadful Future of Blossom Culp, The	U	SF	250+	Peck, Richard	Bantam
Dream Around the World	G	F	138	Instant Readers	Harcourt School Publishers
Dream Boat	M	RF	250+	Action Packs	Rigby
Dream Catcher	M	TL	159	Books for Young Learners	Richard C. Owen
Dream Catchers	M	RF	176	Storyteller-Night Crickets	Wright Group/McGraw Hill
Dream Come True, A	O	B	250+	Hurwitz, Johanna	Richard C. Owen
Dream Eater, The	N	F	250+	Garrison, Christian	Aladdin
Dream Horse	C	F	47	Pair-It Books	Steck-Vaughn
Dream in the Wishing Well	H	F	250+	Van Allen, Roach	SRA/McGraw Hill
Dream of Flight, The	O	I	250+	Rigby Focus	Rigby
Dream Team, The	I	RF	250+	Lighthouse	Rigby
Dream Weaver	W	HF	3045	Leveled Readers	Houghton Mifflin
Dream, The	F	RF	54	Oxford Reading Tree	Oxford University Press
Dreaming	B	RF	23	Smart Starts	Rigby
Dreaming in Black and White	Z	HF	250+	Jung, Reinhardt	Penguin Group
Dreams	E	RF	93	Book Bank	Wright Group/McGraw Hill
Dreams	G	RF	98	Sunshine	Wright Group/McGraw Hill
Dred Scott Decision, The	X	I	250+	Cornerstones of Freedom	Children's Press
Dress Up	D	RF	80	Carousel Readers	Pearson Learning Group
Dressed-Up Sammy	E	F	91	Urmston, Kathleen; Evans, Karen	Kaeden Books
Dressing Up	A	RF	12	Jellybeans	Rigby
Dressing Up	LB	RF	12	Sunshine	Wright Group/McGraw Hill
Dressing Up	I	RF	222	Stepping Stones	Nelson/Michaels Assoc.
Dressing Up	B	RF	25	Smart Starts	Rigby
Dressing Up	C	RF	31	Literacy 2000	Rigby
Dressing Up	A	F	32	PM Starters	Rigby
Dressing-up Box, The	C	RF	61	Book Bank	Wright Group/McGraw Hill
Dress-Up Corner, The	H	RF	68	City Kids	Rigby
Drew and the Homeboy Question	U	RF	250+	Armstrong, Robb	HarperTrophy
Drinking Gourd, The	M	HF	250+	Monjo, F. N.	HarperTrophy
Drinking Water	H	I	79	Pebble Books	Red Brick Learning
Driscoll and the Singing Fish	Q	F	1005	Leveled Readers	Houghton Mifflin
Drive-By	W	RF	250+	Ewing, Lynne	HarperCollins
Driving Mom Crazy	H	RF	131	City Stories	Rigby
Driving on Mars	T	I	936	Leveled Readers	Houghton Mifflin
Drought Marker, The	M	F	250+	Literacy 2000	Rigby
Droughts	Q	I	250+	Natural Disasters	Red Brick Learning
Drum Beats On, The	O	I	250+	Cherrington, Janelle	Scholastic
Drum Dancers: An Inuit Story	Q	RF	873	Leveled Readers	Houghton Mifflin

* Collection of short stories

TITLE	LEVEL	GENRE	WORD COUNT	AUTHOR / SERIES	PUBLISHER / DISTRIBUTOR
Drum, The	D	TL	117	Instant Readers	Harcourt School Publishers
Drummer Boy, The	S	I	1164	Leveled Readers	Houghton Mifflin
Drummer Hoff	J	TL	173	Emberly, Barbara	Prentice-Hall
Drummers, The	H	RF	80	Gould, Carol	Kaeden Books
Dry and Snug and Warm	G	RF	64	Book Bank	Wright Group/McGraw Hill
Drylongso	V	RF	250+	Hamilton, Virginia	Harcourt Trade
Duck and Hen	H	F	193	Sunshine	Wright Group/McGraw Hill
Duck Goes to the Farm	J	F	373	Leveled Readers	Houghton Mifflin
Duck in the Gun, The	M	F	250+	Literacy 2000	Rigby
Duck Magic	N	I	250+	Literacy 2000 Satellites	Rigby
Duck Pond, The	G	RF	276	Leveled Readers	Houghton Mifflin
Duck with the Broken Wing, The	F	RF	189	PM Extensions-Blue	Rigby
Duck, Duck, Goose!	E	F	92	My First Reader	Grolier Press
Duckling Diary	O	RF	250+	Baglio, Ben M.	Scholastic
Ducks	D	F	94	Story Box	Wright Group/McGraw Hill
Ducks Crossing	M	RF	250+	Wilson, Trevor	Pacific Learning
Ducks Have Ducklings	M	I	250+	Animals and Their Young	Compass Point Books
Ducks on the Farm	I	I	91	Pebble Books	Red Brick Learning
Ducks on the Run	I	RF	250+	PM Plus Story Books	Rigby
Duke Ellington: A Life in Music	Q	B	905	Leveled Readers	Houghton Mifflin
Duke Ellington: Man of Music	P	B	250+	Leveled Readers Language Support	Houghton Mifflin
Duke the Mule	H	F	59	Easy Phonics Readers	Teacher Created Materials
Dump Trucks	I	I	119	Pebble Plus	Capstone Press
Dumpsideary Jelly	H	RF	250+	Momentum Literacy Program	Troll Associates
Dunc and Amos and the Red Tattoos	R	RF	250+	Paulsen, Gary	Bantam
Dunc and Amos Go to the Dogs	R	RF	250+	Paulsen, Gary	Bantam
Dunc and Amos Hit the Big Top	R	RF	250+	Paulsen, Gary	Bantam
Dunc and Amos Meet the Slasher	R	RF	250+	Paulsen, Gary	Bantam
Dunc and the Flaming Ghost	R	F	250+	Paulsen, Gary	Bantam
Dunc and the Greased Sticks of Doom	R	RF	250+	Paulsen, Gary	Bantam
Dunc and the Haunted Castle	R	RF	250+	Paulsen, Gary	Bantam
Dunc and the Scam Artists	R	RF	250+	Paulsen, Gary	Bantam
Dunc Breaks the Record	R	RF	250+	Paulsen, Gary	Bantam
Dunc Gets Tweaked	R	RF	250+	Paulsen, Gary	Bantam
Dunc's Doll	R	RF	250+	Paulsen, Gary	Bantam
Dunc's Dump	R	RF	250+	Paulsen, Gary	Bantam
Dunc's Halloween	R	RF	250+	Paulsen, Gary	Bantam
Dunc's Undercover Christmas	R	RF	250+	Paulsen, Gary	Bantam
Dunkin' Dazza's Daring Dribble	O	RF	250+	SupaDoopers	Sundance
Dunkin' Dazza's Soaring Slammer	O	RF	250+	SupaDoopers	Sundance
DuSable - Chicago's First Citizen	T	B	1522	Leveled Readers Social Studies	Houghton Mifflin
Dust Bowl, The	P	I	1204	Leveled Readers Social Studies	Houghton Mifflin
Dust from Old Bones	X	HF	250+	Forrester, Sandra	William Morrow
Dustland	V	F	250+	Hamilton, Virginia	Scholastic
Dwight D. Eisenhower	U	B	250+	Profiles of the Presidents	Compass Point Books
Dynamic Duos	P	F	250+	Moore, David	Scholastic
*E is for Elisa	N	RF	250+	Hurwitz, Johanna	Puffin Books
Each Peach, Pear, Plum	G	TL	115	Ahlberg, Allan & Janet	Penguin Group
Eagle Feathers	N	TL	250+	Story Vines	Wright Group/McGraw Hill
Eagle Flies High, An	G	I	142	Ready Readers	Pearson Learning Group
Eagle Has Landed, The	O	I	250+	Merchant, Peter	Scholastic
Eagle in the Sky	L	RF	250+	Little Celebrations	Pearson Learning Group
Eagle Song	S	RF	250+	Bruchac, Joseph	Puffin Books

* Collection of short stories

TITLE	LEVEL	GENRE	WORD COUNT	AUTHOR / SERIES	PUBLISHER / DISTRIBUTOR
Eagle Watchers	N	RF	765	Leveled Readers	Houghton Mifflin
*Eagle's Reflection and Other Northwest Coast Stories	P	TL	250+	Challenger, James Robert	Heritage House
Eagles: Birds of Prey	M	I	250+	The Wild World of Animals	Red Brick Learning
Ear Book	E	I	119	Perkins, Al	Random House
Ear, the Eye, and the Arm, The	Y	SF	250+	Farmer, Nancy	Puffin Books
Early American Industrial Revolution, 1793-1850, The	V	I	250+	Let Freedom Ring	Capstone Press
Early Bird's Alarm Clock, The	J	F	250+	Daniel, Claire	Steck-Vaughn
Early in the Morning	D	RF	55	Rise & Shine	Hampton-Brown
Early in the Morning	C	RF	56	Windows on Literacy	National Geographic
Early Inventions	M	I	250+	Rigby Focus	Rigby
Early Winter, An	T	RF	250+	Bauer, Marion Dane	Houghton Mifflin
Earning Money	O	I	250+	Let's See	Compass Point Books
Earning Money	L	I	250+	First Facts	Capstone Press
Ears	C	I	37	Rise & Shine	Hampton-Brown
Ears	E	I	74	Rigby Literacy	Rigby
Earth	S	I	250+	Our Solar System	Compass Point Books
Earth	N	I	250+	A True Book	Children's Press
Earth and Moon	G	I	250	Sunshine	Wright Group/McGraw Hill
Earth at Risk	V	I	250+	Sunshine	Wright Group/McGraw Hill
Earth Is Mostly Ocean, The	M	I	250+	Rookie Read About Science	Children's Press
Earth on Turtle's Back, The	L	TL	508	Early Connections	Benchmark Education
Earth to Matthew	U	RF	250+	Danziger, Paula	PaperStar
Earth, The	H	I	112	Windows on Literacy	National Geographic
Earthborn	Z	F	250+	Card, Orson Scott	Tor
Earthfall	Z	F	250+	Card, Orson Scott	Tor
Earthlings in Space	U	SF	250+	Sunshine	Wright Group/McGraw Hill
Earthmovers	J	I	121	Pebble Plus	Capstone Press
Earthquake	M	RF	415	Jellybeans	Rigby
Earthquake	E	RF	40	Wonder World	Wright Group/McGraw Hill
Earthquake	S	HF	250+	Duey, Kathleen; Bale, Karen A.	Simon & Schuster
Earthquake Alaska	U	HF	2192	Leveled Readers	Houghton Mifflin
Earthquake in the Third Grade	N	RF	250+	Myers, Laurie	Clarion
Earthquake Terror	X	RF	250+	Kehret, Peg	Puffin Books
Earthquake!	N	RF	250+	Bookweb	Rigby
Earthquake!	S	I	2075	Leveled Readers Science	Houghton Mifflin
Earthquake!	S	HF	2376	Leveled Readers	Houghton Mifflin
Earthquake!: A Story of Old San Francisco	S	I	250+	Kudlinski, Kathleen V.	Penguin Group
Earthquake!: San Francisco, 1906	R	I	250+	Wilson, Kate	Steck-Vaughn
Earthquakes	R	I	250+	The Wonders of our World	Crabtree
Earthquakes	O	I	250+	Branley, Franklyn M.	HarperCollins
Earthquakes	R	I	250+	Explorers	Wright Group/McGraw Hill
Earthquakes	T	I	250+	Simon, Seymour	Mulberry Books
Earthquakes	N	I	250+	A True Book	Children's Press
Earthquakes and Tsunamis	O	I	250+	PM Plus Story Books	Rigby
Earth's Land and Water	J	I	234	Yellow Umbrella Books	Capstone Press
Earthworm, The	H	I	157	Wonder World	Wright Group/McGraw Hill
Earthworms	O	I	250+	Holmes, Kevin J.	Red Brick Learning
Earthworms	K	I	212	Rigby Focus	Rigby
Earthworms	J	I	185	Leveled Readers	Houghton Mifflin
Earthworm's Life, An	L	I	250+	Himmelman, John	Scholastic
Earthworm's Life, An	L	I	250+	Nature Up Close	Children's Press
East of the Sun & West of the Moon	P	TL	250+	Mayer, Mercer	Aladdin

* Collection of short stories

TITLE	LEVEL	GENRE	WORD COUNT	AUTHOR / SERIES	PUBLISHER / DISTRIBUTOR
East of the Sun and West of the Moon	R	TL	250+	Hague, Kathleen & Michael	Harcourt Trade
Easter	E	I	112	Fiesta Holiday Series	Pearson Learning Group
Easter Bunny that Ate My Sister, The	Q	F	250+	Marney, Dean	Scholastic
Easter Bunny's Lost Egg	G	F	174	First Start	Troll Associates
Easter Island: Giant Stone Statues Tell of a Rich and Tragic Past	W	I	250+	Arnold, Caroline	Houghton Mifflin
Eat and Run!	L	I	289	Vocabulary Readers	Houghton Mifflin
Eat It, Print It	B	I	70	Rigby Literacy	Rigby
Eat Right, Feel Good	K	I	250+	Rosen Real Readers	Rosen Publishing Group
Eat Up!	G	RF	95	Sunshine	Wright Group/McGraw Hill
Eat Up, Gemma	I	RF	463	Hayes, Sarah	Sundance
Eat Your Broccoli	D	RF	72	Books for Young Learners	Richard C. Owen
Eat Your Peas, Louise	E	RF	83	Rookie Readers	Children's Press
Eat Your Vegetables	J	I	157	iOpeners	Pearson Learning Group
Eat!	M	RF	250+	Kroll, Steven	Hyperion
Eating	A	RF	29	Foundations	Wright Group/McGraw Hill
Eating Apples	A	I	17	Pebble Books	Capstone Press
Eating Breakfast	B	I	18	Rosen Real Readers	Rosen Publishing Group
Eating Lunch at School	I	RF	170	City Kids	Rigby
Eating Out	C	RF	31	Sunshine	Wright Group/McGraw Hill
Eating Right	H	I	151	Pebble Books	Red Brick Learning
Eating Well	H	I	124	Yellow Umbrella Books	Red Brick Learning
Ebenezer and the Sneeze	D	RF	77	Story Box	Wright Group/McGraw Hill
Echohawk	X	HF	250+	Durrant, Lynda	Bantam
Eclipses: Nature's Blackouts	T	I	250+	Aronson, Billy	Franklin Watts
Ed and Me	L	RF	250+	McPhail, David	OSI
Eddie and the Fire Engine	P	RF	250+	Haywood, Carolyn	Beech Tree Books
Edgar Badger's Balloon Day	K	F	864	Kulling, Monica	Mondo
Edgar Badger's Butterfly Day	K	F	250+	Kulling, Monica	Mondo
Edgar Badger's Fishing Day	K	F	250+	Kulling, Monica	Mondo
Edgar Badger's Fix-it Day	K	F	250+	Kulling, Monica	Mondo
Edmond Went Splash	B	F	69	First Stories	Pacific Learning
Educating Arthur	J	F	250+	Soar To Success	Houghton Mifflin
Edward's Night Light	M	RF	622	Reading Corners	Pearson Learning Group
Edwin and Emily	K	RF	250+	Williams, Suzanne	Hyperion
Eek!	D	F	103	Lester the Lion Series	Pioneer Valley
Eek! Look at This!	C	I	66	Rigby Literacy	Rigby
Eency Weency Spider	I	F	250+	Bank Street	Bantam
Eenie, Meanie, Murphy, NO!	S	RF	250+	McKenna, Colleen O'Shaughnessy	Scholastic
Eeny, Meeny, Miney Mole	M	F	250+	Yolen, Jane	OSI
Effie	K	F	250+	Allison, Beverly	Scholastic
Egg	K	F	250+	Logan, Dick	Cypress
Egg Saga, The	N	RF	250+	Sails	Rigby
Egg To Chick	J	I	250+	Selsam, Millicent E.	HarperTrophy
Egg, The	C	F	48	Joy Readers	Pearson Learning Group
Eggs	L	I	250+	Rigby Literacy	Rigby
Eggs	C	I	30	Windows on Literacy	National Geographic
Eggs and Baby Birds	M	I	539	Sunshine	Wright Group/McGraw Hill
Eggs for Breakfast	D	I	126	PM Nonfiction-Red	Rigby
Eggs!	B	RF	28	Ready Readers	Pearson Learning Group
Eggs, Eggs, Eggs	J	I	188	Wonder World	Wright Group/McGraw Hill
Eggs, Larvae, and Flies	K	I	450	Sunshine	Wright Group/McGraw Hill
Eggshell Garden, The	LB	RF	14	Sunshine	Wright Group/McGraw Hill
Egypt	P	I	250+	Fact Finders	Capstone Press

* Collection of short stories

TITLE	LEVEL	GENRE	WORD COUNT	AUTHOR / SERIES	PUBLISHER / DISTRIBUTOR
Egypt	Q	I	250+	First Reports	Compass Point Books
Egypt Game, The	X	RF	250+	Snyder, Zilpha Keatley	Bantam
Egypt: The Culture	U	I	250+	Kalman, Bobbie	Crabtree
Egypt: The Land	U	I	250+	Kalman, Bobbie	Crabtree
Egypt: The People	U	I	250+	Kalman, Bobbie	Crabtree
Egyptian Town	U	I	250+	Steedman, Scott	Franklin Watts
Eight Friends in All	D	RF	64	Ready Readers	Pearson Learning Group
Eileen Collins: First Woman in Space	V	B	2488	Leveled Readers	Houghton Mifflin
Einstein, Father of Physics	Z	B	250+	Independent Readers Science	Houghton Mifflin
Einstein: Champion of the World	N	RF	250+	Trussell-Cullen, Alan	Pacific Learning
*EL Bronx Remembered	Z	RF	250+	Mohr, Nicholas	HarperTrophy
El Chino	P	B	250+	Say, Allen	Houghton Mifflin
El Greco	R	B	250+	Venezia, Mike	Children's Press
El Sid and the Flea	V	RF	2632	Leveled Readers	Houghton Mifflin
Elaine	J	B	250+	Stepping Stones	Nelson/Michaels Assoc.
Elaine and the Flying Frog	M	RF	250+	Chang, Heidi	Scholastic
Elbert's Bad Word	M	RF	250+	Wood, Audrey	Harcourt Trade
Eleanor	S	B	250+	Cooney, Barbara	Puffin Books
Eleanor Everywhere: The Life of Eleanor Roosevelt	O	B	250+	Step into Reading	Random House
Eleanor Roosevelt	P	B	250+	Early Biographies	Compass Point Books
Eleanor Roosevelt	P	B	250+	Davis, Lucile	Red Brick Learning
Eleanor Roosevelt	U	B	250+	Blevins, Wiley	Scholastic
Eleanor Roosevelt	N	B	250+	Pebble Books	Capstone Press
Eleanor Roosevelt: A Life of Discovery	W	B	250+	Freedman, Russell	Clarion
Eleanor Roosevelt: Fighter for Social Justice	O	B	250+	Childhood of Famous Americans	Aladdin
Eleanor Roosevelt: First Lady of the World	R	B	250+	Faber, Doris	Penguin Group
Election Connection	T	I	250+	Ring, Susan	Chronicle Books
Election Day	H	RF	250+	McNamara, Margaret	Aladdin
Elections in the United States	W	I	250+	American Civics	Red Brick Learning
*Electric Spark and Other Cases, The	O	RF	250+	Simon, Seymour	Avon
Electricity	O	I	250+	Winkelman, Barbara Gaines	Wright Group/McGraw Hill
Electricity Makes Things Work	N	I	250+	PM Plus Nonfiction	Rigby
Electricity: Bulbs, Batteries, and Sparks	N	I	250+	Amazing Science	Picture Window Books
*Electrifying Cows and Other Cases, The	O	RF	250+	Simon, Seymour	Avon
Elements in Nature	V	I	1001	Leveled Readers Science	Houghton Mifflin
Elements, The	V	I	841	Leveled Readers Science	Houghton Mifflin
Elena in America	O	HF	575	Leveled Readers	Houghton Mifflin
Elena Makes Tortillas	A	I	18	Pacific Literacy	Pacific Learning
Elena's Two Homes	M	HF	250+	Leveled Readers Language Support	Houghton Mifflin
Elephant and Envelope	G	F	158	Start to Read	School Zone
Elephant and the Bad Baby, The	J	F	250+	Hayes, Sarah	Sundance
Elephant for the Holidays, An	I	F	118	Sunshine	Wright Group/McGraw Hill
Elephant in the House, An	J	F	546	Read Alongs	Rigby
Elephant in Trouble	H	F	98	First Start	Troll Associates
Elephant Play	E	F	35	Sun Sprouts	ETA/Cuisenaire
Elephant Rescue	J	RF	250+	Leveled Readers Language Support	Houghton Mifflin
Elephant Tricks	F	F	147	Sun Sprouts	ETA/Cuisenaire
Elephant Walk	C	F	44	Sunshine	Wright Group/McGraw Hill
Elephant Walk	C	RF	50	Rigby Literacy	Rigby
Elephants	I	I	224	Foundations	Wright Group/McGraw Hill
Elephants	N	I	250+	Meadows, Graham; Vial, Claire	Pearson Learning Group

TITLE	LEVEL	GENRE	WORD COUNT	AUTHOR / SERIES	PUBLISHER / DISTRIBUTOR
Elephants	C	F	224	Phonics and Friends	Hampton-Brown
Elephants	K	I	250+	PM Animal Facts: Turquoise	Rigby
Elephants	U	I	250+	The Untamed World	Steck-Vaughn
Elephants Are Coming, The	E	F	138	Little Readers	Houghton Mifflin
Elephant's Trunk, An	C	F	31	Little Celebrations	Pearson Learning Group
Elephant's Trunk, An	D	I	49	Windows on Literacy	National Geographic
Elephant's Trunk, The	E	I	60	Seedlings	Continental Press
Elevator	D	F	90	Story Box	Wright Group/McGraw Hill
Eleven Kids, One Summer	O	RF	250+	Martin, Ann M.	Scholastic
Eli Whitney: American Inventor	T	B	250+	Let Freedom Ring	Capstone Press
Elijah McCoy	U	B	250+	Independent Readers Science	Houghton Mifflin
*Elisa in the Middle	N	RF	250+	Hurwitz, Johanna	Penguin Group
Elisha Otis's Ups and Downs	U	I	1759	Leveled Readers	Houghton Mifflin
Eliza Pinckney	M	B	325	Independent Readers Social Studies	Houghton Mifflin
Eliza the Hypnotizer	M	RF	250+	Granger, Michele	Scholastic
Elizabeth Blackwell: First Woman Doctor	O	B	250+	Greene, Carol	Children's Press
Elizabeth Blackwell: Girl Doctor	O	B	250+	Henry, Joanne Landers	Simon & Schuster
Elizabeth Cady Stanton	P	B	250+	Davis, Lucile	Red Brick Learning
Elizabeth the First: Queen of England	O	B	250+	Greene, Carol	Children's Press
Elizabite: Adventures of a Carnivorous Plant	K	F	250+	Rey, H. A.	Houghton Mifflin
Ella Enchanted	U	F	250+	Carson Levine, Gail	HarperTrophy
Ella Minnow Pea	Z	F	250+	Dunn, Mark	MacAdam/Cage Publishing
Ella's Time Line	H	RF	101	Windows on Literacy	National Geographic
Ellen Ochoa	L	B	250+	Biography	Benchmark Education
Ellen Ochoa	N	B	703	Leveled Readers Science	Houghton Mifflin
Ellen Ochoa	G	B	250+	Welcome Books	Children's Press
Ellen Ochoa, Astronaut	M	B	726	Leveled Readers Science	Houghton Mifflin
Ellen Tebbits	P	RF	250+	Cleary, Beverly	Dell
Ellie	Z	RF	250+	Borntrager, Mary Christner	Herald Press
Ellie Brader Hates Mr. G.	R	RF	250+	Johnston, Janet	Pocket Books
Ellis Island	N	I	250+	Early Connections	Benchmark Education
Ellis Island	U	I	250+	We The People	Compass Point Books
Ellis Island	N	I	263	Independent Readers Social Studies	Houghton Mifflin
Ellis Island	V	I	250+	Cornerstones of Freedom	Children's Press
Ellis Island	N	I	250+	A True Book	Children's Press
Ellis Island: Welcome to America	P	I	250+	Rosen Real Readers	Rosen Publishing Group
Elmer and the Dragon	M	F	250+	Gannett, Ruth	Random House
Eloise Greenfield: Poetry to Grow On	P	B	886	Leveled Readers	Houghton Mifflin
Eloise Greenfield: The Music of Poetry	O	B	250+	Leveled Readers Language Support	Houghton Mifflin
Elves and the Shoemaker, The	J	TL	300	PM Tales and Plays-Turquoise	Rigby
Elves and the Shoemaker, The: A Tale by the Brothers Grimm	K	TL	250+	Rigby Literacy	Rigby
*Elves and the Shoemaker, The	K	TL	622	New Way Orange	Steck-Vaughn
Elves Don't Wear Hard Hats	M	F	250+	Dadey, Debbie; Jones, Marcia Thornton	Scholastic
Elvis the Turnip and Me	N	F	250+	The Zack Files	Gosset & Dunlap
Emancipation Proclamation, The	V	I	250+	Cornerstones of Freedom	Children's Press
Emerald Cathedral, The	V	I	1983	Leveled Readers	Houghton Mifflin
Emergency Vehicles	K	I	250+	PM Plus	Rigby
Emil	J	RF	250+	Stepping Stones	Nelson/Michaels Assoc.
Emilio and the River	J	RF	403	Sunshine	Wright Group/McGraw Hill

* Collection of short stories

TITLE	LEVEL	GENRE	WORD COUNT	AUTHOR / SERIES	PUBLISHER / DISTRIBUTOR
Emily and Alice	L	RF	250+	Champion, Joyce	Harcourt Trade
Emily Arrow Promises to Do Better This Year	M	RF	250+	Giff, Patricia Reilly	Bantam
Emily at School	L	RF	250+	Williams, Suzanne	Hyperion
Emily Can't Sleep	F	RF	124	Early Emergent, Set 2	Pioneer Valley
Emily Carr	X	B	250+	The Canadians	Fitzhenry & Whiteside
Emily Dickinson: American Poet	O	B	250+	Greene, Carol	Children's Press
Emily Eyefinger	M	F	250+	Ball, Duncan	Aladdin
Emily Loved Yellow	I	RF	99	Sunshine	Wright Group/McGraw Hill
Emily Murphy	X	B	250+	The Canadians	Fitzhenry & Whiteside
Emily's Babysitter	C	RF	67	Emergent	Pioneer Valley
Emily's Runaway Imagination	P	F	250+	Cleary, Beverly	Avon Camelot
Emma	L	RF	250+	Kesselman, Wendy	HarperTrophy
Emma Rides on the Erie Canal	T	HF	1904	Leveled Readers	Houghton Mifflin
Emma, the Birthday Clown	M	RF	1887	Sunshine	Wright Group/McGraw Hill
Emma's Emu	N	F	250+	First Flight	Fitzhenry & Whiteside
Emma's Problem	H	RF	190	Literacy 2000	Rigby
Emperor and the Nightingale, The	L	TL	250+	Literacy 2000	Rigby
Emperor's New Clothes, The	J	TL	250+	Rigby Literacy	Rigby
Emperor's New Clothes, The	J	TL	571	Tales from Hans Andersen	Wright Group/McGraw Hill
Empire Builders	T	I	250+	Rigby Focus	Rigby
Empty Envelope, The	N	RF	250+	Roy, Ron	Random House
Empty Lot, The	M	RF	606	Leveled Readers	Houghton Mifflin
Emu Who Wanted to Be a Horse, The	J	F	250+	Voyages	SRA/McGraw Hill
Enchanted Horse, The	R	F	250+	Nabb, Magdalen	Hyperion
*Encyclopedia Brown Boy Detective	P	RF	250+	Sobol, Donald J.	Bantam
*Encyclopedia Brown Carries On	P	RF	250+	Sobol, Donald J.	Bantam
*Encyclopedia Brown Finds the Clues	P	RF	250+	Sobol, Donald J.	Bantam
*Encyclopedia Brown Gets His Man	P	RF	250+	Sobol, Donald J.	Bantam
*Encyclopedia Brown Keeps the Peace	P	RF	250+	Sobol, Donald J.	Bantam
*Encyclopedia Brown Lends a Hand	P	RF	250+	Sobol, Donald J.	Bantam
*Encyclopedia Brown Saves the Day	P	RF	250+	Sobol, Donald J.	Bantam
*Encyclopedia Brown Sets the Pace	P	RF	250+	Sobol, Donald J.	Bantam
*Encyclopedia Brown Shows the Way	P	RF	250+	Sobol, Donald J.	Bantam
*Encyclopedia Brown Solves Them All	P	RF	250+	Sobol, Donald J.	Bantam
Encyclopedia Brown Takes the Cake	P	RF	250+	Sobol, Donald J.	Bantam
*Encyclopedia Brown Takes the Case	P	RF	250+	Sobol, Donald J.	Bantam
*Encyclopedia Brown Tracks Them Down	P	RF	250+	Sobol, Donald J.	Bantam
*Encyclopedia Brown: Case of Pablo's Nose	P	RF	250+	Sobol, Donald J.	Scholastic
*Encyclopedia Brown: Case of the Dead Eagles	P	RF	250+	Sobol, Donald J.	Bantam
*Encyclopedia Brown: Case of the Disgusting Sneakers	P	RF	250+	Sobol, Donald J.	Bantam
*Encyclopedia Brown: Case of the Midnight Visitor	P	RF	250+	Sobol, Donald J.	Bantam
*Encyclopedia Brown: Case of the Mysterious Handprints	P	RF	250+	Sobol, Donald J.	Bantam
*Encyclopedia Brown: Case of the Secret Pitch	P	RF	250+	Sobol, Donald J.	Bantam
*Encyclopedia Brown: Case of the Sleeping Dog	P	RF	250+	Sobol, Donald J.	Scholastic
*Encyclopedia Brown: Case of the Slippery Salamander	P	RF	250+	Sobol, Donald J.	Scholastic
*Encyclopedia Brown: Case of the Treasure Hunt	P	RF	250+	Sobol, Donald J.	Bantam
*Encyclopedia Brown: Case of the Two Spies	P	RF	250+	Sobol, Donald J.	Bantam
Encyclopedia Brown's Book of Strange But True Crimes	P	RF	250+	Sobol, Donald J.; Sobol, Rose	Scholastic

* Collection of short stories

TITLE	LEVEL	GENRE	WORD COUNT	AUTHOR / SERIES	PUBLISHER / DISTRIBUTOR
Encyclopedia of a Rain Forest	O	I	250+	Rigby Literacy	Rigby
Encyclopedia of Tiny Creatures	J	I	250+	Discovery World	Rigby
End of the Ice Age, The	U	I	2221	Independent Readers Science	Houghton Mifflin
End, The	C	RF	106	Tiger Cub	Peguis
Endangered Animals	K	I	148	Early Connections	Benchmark Education
Endangered Animals	N	I	250+	A New True Book	Children's Press
Endangered Desert Animals	R	I	250+	Taylor, Dave	Crabtree
Endangered Forest Animals	R	I	250+	Taylor, Dave	Crabtree
Endangered Grassland Animals	R	I	250+	Taylor, Dave	Crabtree
Endangered Island Animals	R	I	250+	Taylor, Dave	Crabtree
Endangered Mountain Animals	R	I	250+	Taylor, Dave	Crabtree
Endangered Ocean Animals	R	I	250+	Taylor, Dave	Crabtree
Endangered Savannah Animals	R	I	250+	Taylor, Dave	Crabtree
Endangered Wetland Animals	R	I	250+	Taylor, Dave	Crabtree
Endless Puzzle, The	J	RF	416	Leveled Readers	Houghton Mifflin
Endless Steppe, The	Y	B	250+	Hautzig, Esther	HarperTrophy
Endurance: Shackleton's Antarctic Expedition	S	I	250+	Marriott, Janice	Pacific Learning
Endurance: Shipwreck and Survival on a Sea of Ice	T	I	250+	High Five Reading	Red Brick Learning
Energy	M	I	250+	First Facts	Capstone Press
Energy: Heat, Light, and Fuel	M	I	250+	Amazing Science	Picture Window Books
Engelbert the Hero	H	F	113	Little Celebrations	Pearson Learning Group
Engelbert's Exercises	E	F	23	Little Celebrations	Pearson Learning Group
Engines	E	I	81	Sunshine	Wright Group/McGraw Hill
England	P	I	250+	Fact Finders	Capstone Press
England	O	I	250+	Many Cultures, One World	Capstone Press
England	Q	I	250+	First Reports	Compass Point Books
Enormous Crocodile, The	N	F	250+	Dahl, Roald	Penguin Group
Enormous Egg, The	C	F	52	Learn to Read	Creative Teaching Press
Enormous Egg, The	R	F	250+	Butterworth, Oliver	Little, Brown & Co.
Enormous Turnip, The	H	TL	431	Hunia, Fran	Ladybird Books
Enormous Watermelon, The	H	TL	304	Traditional Tales & More	Rigby
Environmentally Friendly World	L	F	929	Early Connections	Benchmark Education
Eric's Birthday	H	RF	77	City Stories	Rigby
Erik and the Three Goats	H	F	257	Ready Readers	Pearson Learning Group
Er-Lang and the Suns: A Tale from China	M	TL	250+	Folk Tales	Mondo
Erosion	L	I	300	Independent Readers Social Studies	Houghton Mifflin
Erosion	M	I	250+	Schaefer, Lola	Benchmark Education
Errol the Peril	Q	F	250+	Literacy 2000	Rigby
Ersatz Elevator, The	V	F	250+	Snicket, Lemony	Scholastic
Eruption	R	I	250+	Wildcats	Wright Group/McGraw Hill
Escalator, The	A	RF	23	Story Box	Wright Group/McGraw Hill
Escape from Death Valley	M	I	419	Books for Young Learners	Richard C. Owen
Escape From Slavery: Five Journeys to Freedom	Q	B	250+	Rappaport, Doreen	HarperTrophy
Escape from the Comics	Q	RF	250+	Bookweb	Rigby
Escape to Canada	P	I	513	Vocabulary Readers	Houghton Mifflin
Escape to Freedom	V	HF	250+	Davis, Ossie	Puffin Books
Escape!	N	SF	250+	Cartwright, Pauline	Pacific Learning
ESP TV	R	SF	250+	Rodgers, Mary	HarperTrophy
Esperanza Rising	V	HF	250+	Ryan, Pam Munoz	Scholastic
Eureka! It's an Airplane	T	I	250+	Bendick, Jeanne	Scholastic
Eureka! It's Television!	T	I	250+	Bendick, Jeanne & Robert	Scholastic
Eureka! Stories of Everyday Inventions	P	I	250+	Literacy 2000	Rigby

* Collection of short stories

TITLE	LEVEL	GENRE	WORD COUNT	AUTHOR / SERIES	PUBLISHER / DISTRIBUTOR
Europe	N	I	250+	Continents	Capstone Press
Europe: Geography of Conquest	X	I	1830	Leveled Readers Social Studies	Houghton Mifflin
Eva	Z	F	250+	Dickenson, Eva	Laurel-Leaf Books
Eva the Beekeeper	J	I	250+	iOpeners	Pearson Learning Group
Eve Shops	F	RF	146	Ready Readers	Pearson Learning Group
Even Steven and Odd Todd	K	F	250+	Cristaldi, Kathryn	Scholastic
Evening Song	L	RF	115	Books for Young Learners	Richard C. Owen
Everest Challenge	Q	I	489	Vocabulary Readers	Houghton Mifflin
Everglades	T	I	250+	George, Jean Craighead	HarperTrophy
Everglades, The	M	I	250+	Early Connections	Benchmark Education
Every Bird Has a Beak	E	I	49	Birds Series	Pearson Learning Group
Every Bird Has Feathers	E	I	50	Birds Series	Pearson Learning Group
Every Bird has Two Feet	E	I	46	Birds Series	Pearson Learning Group
Every Body Tells a Story	R	I	250+	Explorers	Wright Group/McGraw Hill
Every Cat	F	RF	91	Instant Readers	Harcourt School Publishers
Every Day But Sunday	E	RF	83	Home Connection Collection	Rigby
Every Flower is Beautiful	K	TL	250+	Turner, Teresa	Steck-Vaughn
*Every Living Thing	R	RF	250+	Rylant, Cynthia	Aladdin
Every Monday	C	F	52	Pair-It Books	Steck-Vaughn
Every Morning	A	I	30	Twig	Wright Group/McGraw Hill
Every Mother Bird Builds a Nest	E	I	62	Birds Series	Pearson Learning Group
Every Shape and Size	G	I	97	Wonder World	Wright Group/McGraw Hill
Everybody Cooks Rice	M	I	250+	Dooley, Norah	Scholastic
Everybody Dances	T	I	250+	Literacy 2000	Rigby
Everybody Eats Bread	J	I	241	Literacy 2000	Rigby
Everybody Says	G	RF	70	Rookie Readers	Children's Press
Everybody Wears Braids	B	RF	30	Bebop Books	Lee & Low Books Inc.
Everyday Forces	M	I	250+	Discovery World	Rigby
Everyday Machines	J	I	188	Rigby Focus	Rigby
Everyday Math	D	I	102	Early Connections	Benchmark Education
Everyday Patterns	F	I	110	Early Connections	Benchmark Education
Everyone Eats	C	I	44	Discovery Links	Newbridge
Everyone Eats Bread	G	I	139	Yellow Umbrella Books	Red Brick Learning
Everyone Else's Parents Said Yes	U	RF	250+	Danziger, Paula	PaperStar
Everyone Is a Scientist	I	I	197	Yellow Umbrella Books	Red Brick Learning
Everyone is Reading	H	RF	225	Cambridge Reading	Pearson Learning Group
Everyone Knows About Cars	L	I	176	Bookshop	Mondo
Everyone Says Sh-h-h!	E	RF	93	Rigby Literacy	Rigby
Everyone Uses Math	G	I	211	Yellow Umbrella Books	Red Brick Learning
Everyone Wears Wool	A	I	21	Pair-It Books	Steck-Vaughn
Everything Cat: What Kids Really Want to Know About Cats	R	I	250+	Crisp, Marty	NorthWord Press
Everything Changes	L	I	250+	Discovery World	Rigby
Everything Is Matter!	L	I	226	Yellow Umbrella Books	Capstone Press
Everything on a Waffle	V	RF	250+	Horvath, Polly	Farrar, Straus and Giroux
Everywhere	R	RF	250+	Brooks, Bruce	Scholastic
Everywhere You Look	H	I	191	Sunshine	Wright Group/McGraw Hill
Evil Queen Tut and the Great Ant Pyramids	N	F	250+	The Zack Files	Grosset & Dunlap
Evvy's Civil War	X	HF	250+	Brenaman, Miriam	Putnam
Excuses, Excuses	E	RF	104	Tadpoles	Rigby
Exercise Time	O	F	250+	Sails	Rigby
Exotic Tropical Fish	L	I	250+	Swartz, Stanley L.	Pearson Learning Group
Expect the Unexpected	Q	I	250+	Orbit Double Takes	Pacific Learning
Experiment with Movement	Q	I	250+	Murphy, Bryan	Scholastic

* Collection of short stories

TITLE	LEVEL	GENRE	WORD COUNT	AUTHOR / SERIES	PUBLISHER / DISTRIBUTOR
Experiment with Water	Q	I	250+	Murphy, Bryan	Scholastic
Exploration and Conquest: The Americas After Columbus, 1500-1620	T	I	250+	Maestro, Betsy & Giulio	William Morrow
Explore Your World	V	I	250+	iOpeners	Pearson Learning Group
Explorer, The	F	RF	73	City Stories	Rigby
Explorers: Searching for Adventure	M	I	250+	Pair-It Books	Steck-Vaughn
*Explorers: Women in Profile	T	B	250+	Hacker, Carolotta	Crabtree
Exploring a Park	H	I	65	Vocabulary Readers	Houghton Mifflin
Exploring an Ocean Tide Pool	W	I	250+	Bendick, Jeanne	Henry Holt & Co.
Exploring Freshwater Habitats	P	I	250+	Snowball, Diane	Mondo
Exploring Land Habitats	P	I	250+	Phinney, Margaret Yatsevitch	Mondo
Exploring National Parks	L	I	250+	Rigby Literacy	Rigby
Exploring Saltwater Habitats	P	I	250+	Smith, Sue	Mondo
Exploring Saturn	L	I	250+	Rosen Real Readers	Rosen Publishing Group
Exploring Space	R	I	250+	Explorers	Wright Group/McGraw Hill
Exploring Space	I	I	250+	Sunshine Books	Wright Group/McGraw Hill
Exploring the Grand Canyon	Q	I	250+	Rosen Real Readers	Rosen Publishing Group
Exploring the Titanic	Q	I	250+	Ballard, Robert D.	Scholastic
Exploring Tree Habitats	P	I	250+	Seifert, Patti	Mondo
Exploring with Lewis and Clark	O	I	250+	People, Spaces & Places	Rand McNally
Expressway Jewels	M	RF	368	Evangeline Nicholas Collection	Wright Group/McGraw Hill
Extinct	S	I	2101	Leveled Readers Science	Houghton Mifflin
*Extraordinary American Indians	W	B	250+	Avery, Susan; Skinner, Linda	Children's Press
*Extraordinary Black Americans: From Colonial to Contemporary Times	W	B	250+	Altman, Susan	Children's Press
*Extraordinary Jewish Americans	W	B	250+	Brooks, Philip	Children's Press
Extraordinary Life, An: The Story of a Monarch Butterfly	V	I	250+	Pringle, Laurence	Orchard Books
*Extraordinary People with Disabilities	W	B	250+	Kent, Deborah; Quinlan, Kathryn A.	Children's Press
*Extraordinary Women in Politics	W	B	250+	Gulatta, Charles	Children's Press
*Extraordinary Women Journalists	W	B	250+	Price-Groff, Claire	Children's Press
*Extraordinary Women of Medicine	W	B	250+	Stille, Darlene R.	Children's Press
*Extraordinary Women of the American West	W	B	250+	Alter, Judy	Children's Press
*Extraordinary Women Scientists	W	B	250+	Stille, Darlene R.	Children's Press
*Extraordinary Young People	W	B	250+	Brill, Marlene Targ	Children's Press
Extreme Lives	N	I	250+	Wildcats	Wright Group/McGraw Hill
Extreme Sports	R	I	250+	PM Nonfiction-Ruby	Rigby
Extreme Sports	P	I	250+	Wildcats	Wright Group/McGraw Hill
Eye in the Sky	P	F	250+	Marriott, Janice	Pacific Learning
Eye Spy	P	I	250+	Wildcats	Wright Group/McGraw Hill
Eyes	C	I	64	Wonder World	Wright Group/McGraw Hill
Eyes are Everywhere	E	I	131	Ready Readers	Pearson Learning Group
Eyes in the Sky	R	I	250+	Literacy 2000	Rigby
Eyes of the Amaryllis, The	V	RF	250+	Babbitt, Natalie	Farrar, Straus and Giroux
F is for Fabuloso	W	RF	250+	Lee, Marie G.	Avon
Fab Four from Liverpool, The	U	B	1862	Leveled Readers	Houghton Mifflin
Fables	D	I	40	Vocabulary Readers	Houghton Mifflin
*Fables	N	TL	250+	Lobel, Arnold	HarperCollins
*Fables by Aesop	K	TL	250+	Reading Unlimited	Pearson Learning Group
Fabulous Animal Families	K	I	250+	Home Connection Collection	Rigby
Fabulous Fish	K	I	178	Rigby Focus	Rigby
Fabulous Freckles	K	RF	250+	Literacy 2000	Rigby
Fabulous Fruits	D	I	121	Fiesta Series	Pearson Learning Group

* Collection of short stories

TITLE	LEVEL	GENRE	WORD COUNT	AUTHOR / SERIES	PUBLISHER / DISTRIBUTOR
Fabulous Principal Pie, The	G	F	250+	Start to Read	School Zone
*Fabulous Spotted Egg, The	T	TL	250+	Literacy 2000	Rigby
Face in the Dark, The	D	RF	64	Storyteller-Setting Sun	Wright Group/McGraw Hill
Face on the Milk Carton, The	Y	RF	250+	Cooney, Caroline B.	Bantam Doubleday Dell
Face Painting	G	RF	90	Wonder World	Wright Group/McGraw Hill
Face Sandwich, The	LB	RF	16	Sunshine	Wright Group/McGraw Hill
Face to Face	P	RF	250+	Bookweb	Rigby
Face to Face	W	RF	250+	Bauer, Marion Dane	Bantam
Face-Off	O	RF	250+	Christopher, Matt	Little, Brown & Co.
Faces	B	RF	27	Sunshine	Wright Group/McGraw Hill
Faces	D	I	250+	Little Celebrations	Pearson Learning Group
Faces of Mount Rushmore	D	I	36	Leveled Readers Social Studies	Houghton Mifflin
Facing the Flood	Q	RF	250+	Kleinhenz, Sydnie Meltzer	Steck-Vaughn
Facing West: A Story of the Oregon Trail	S	I	250+	Kudlinski, Kathleen V.	Penguin Group
Factory Through the Ages	U	I	250+	Steele, Philip	Troll Associates
Facts About Earthquakes	O	I	250+	Rosen Real Readers	Rosen Publishing Group
Facts About Forest Fires	J	I	250+	Rosen Real Readers	Rosen Publishing Group
Facts About Magnets	L	I	237	Leveled Readers Science	Houghton Mifflin
Facts About Tornadoes	L	I	250+	Rosen Real Readers	Rosen Publishing Group
Facts and Fictions of Minna Pratt, The	U	RF	250+	MacLachlan, Patricia	HarperTrophy
Facts and Fun About the Presidents	S	I	250+	Sullivan, George	Scholastic
Fair Day	J	RF	184	City Kids	Rigby
Fair Swap, A	K	TL	250+	PM Story Books-Silver	Rigby
Fair, The	A	RF	40	First Stories	Pacific Learning
Faith's Journey	S	HF	1263	Leveled Readers	Houghton Mifflin
Falcon, The	N	RF	250+	PM Emerald	Rigby
Falcon's Feathers, The	N	RF	250+	Roy, Ron	Random House
Falcons Nest on Skyscrapers	P	I	250+	Soar To Success	Houghton Mifflin
Fall	B	I	12	Discovery Links	Newbridge
Fall	A	I	22	Little Books for Early Readers	University of Maine
Fall	E	I	73	Sunshine	Wright Group/McGraw Hill
Fall Colors	D	I	23	Windows on Literacy	National Geographic
Fall Harvest	LB	I	16	Little Books for Early Readers	University of Maine
Fall Harvest	E	I	39	Pebble Books	Capstone Press
Fall Leaves	J	I	222	Leveled Readers	Houghton Mifflin
Fall of Tenochtitlan	X	I	3489	Leveled Readers Social Studies	Houghton Mifflin
Falling Off a Log	Q	RF	1290	Leveled Readers	Houghton Mifflin
Families	J	F	184	Storyteller-Night Crickets	Wright Group/McGraw Hill
Families	F	I	132	Twig	Wright Group/McGraw Hill
Families	F	I	159	Yellow Umbrella Books	Capstone Press
Families	C	I	32	Rosen Real Readers	Rosen Publishing Group
Families	D	I	60	Pebble Books	Capstone Press
Families	B	I	49	Interaction	Rigby
Families	H	I	160	Early Connections	Benchmark Education
Families	LB	I	8	Windows on Literacy	National Geographic
Families and Feasts	I	I	196	PM Plus Nonfiction	Rigby
Families Are Different	K	RF	250+	Pellegrini, Nina	Scholastic
Families of 1608 Ash Street, The	L	RF	571	Leveled Readers	Houghton Mifflin
Families of the Deep Blue Sea	P	I	250+	Mallory, Kenneth	Charlesbridge
Families Share	E	RF	72	Learn to Read	Creative Teaching Press
Family Bike Ride	C	RF	55	Handprints C, Set 1	Educator's Publishing Service
Family Counts	B	RF	19	Rise & Shine	Hampton-Brown
Family Dinner	Q	RF	250+	Cutler, Jane	Farrar, Straus and Giroux

TITLE	LEVEL	GENRE	WORD COUNT	AUTHOR / SERIES	PUBLISHER / DISTRIBUTOR
Family Names	D	RF	36	Visions	Wright Group/McGraw Hill
Family of Beavers, A	J	RF	141	Books for Young Learners	Richard C. Owen
Family of Five, A	C	F	26	Pair-It Books	Steck-Vaughn
Family on Lake Street, The	F	RF	159	Teacher's Choice Series	Pearson Learning Group
Family Pets	C	I	37	Pebble Books	Capstone Press
Family Photos	F	RF	106	Literacy 2000	Rigby
Family Picnic	B	RF	18	Bebop Books	Lee & Low Books Inc.
Family Picture, A	R	RF	1570	Leveled Readers	Houghton Mifflin
Family Reunion	G	RF	243	Visions	Wright Group/McGraw Hill
Family Soccer	D	RF	55	Geddes, Diana	Kaeden Books
Family Table, The	J	RF	274	Leveled Readers Language Support	Houghton Mifflin
Family Time	B	I	16	Pair-It Books	Steck-Vaughn
Family Tree	S	RF	250+	Ayres, Katherine	Bantam
Family Tree, The	K	RF	250+	PM Plus Story Books	Rigby
Family Tree, The	G	F	213	Ready Readers	Pearson Learning Group
Family Under the Bridge, The	R	RF	250+	Savage Carlson, Natalie	Scholastic
Family Work and Fun	B	I	38	Little Red Readers	Sundance
Family, The	E	RF	55	Sunshine	Wright Group/McGraw Hill
*Famous Animals	Q	I	250+	Literacy Tree	Rigby
*Famous Children	O	I	250+	Literacy 2000	Rigby
Famous Feet	E	F	34	Instant Readers	Harcourt School Publishers
Famous Friendships	Z	I	2538	Independent Readers Social Studies	Houghton Mifflin
Famous Rocks	Q	I	578	Independent Readers Science	Houghton Mifflin
Fancy Dress Parade, The	H	RF	171	Stepping Stones	Nelson/Michaels Assoc.
Fancy Feet	L	RF	250+	Giff, Patricia Reilly	Bantam
Fanfare for Food	O	I	497	Vocabulary Readers	Houghton Mifflin
Fangs and Me	N	RF	250+	Gilmore, Rachna	Fitzhenry & Whiteside
Fans and Umbrellas	E	TL	107	Joy Readers	Pearson Learning Group
Fantail, Fantail	D	F	67	Pacific Literacy	Pacific Learning
Fantastic Animal Features	Q	I	250+	Parker, Heather	Steck-Vaughn
Fantastic Cake, The	E	RF	169	Story Box	Wright Group/McGraw Hill
Fantastic Fungi	K	I	234	Rigby Focus	Rigby
Fantastic Mr. Fox	P	F	250+	Dahl, Roald	Penguin Group
Fantastic Pumpkin, The	H	F	216	Rigby Literacy	Rigby
Fantastic Washing Machine	J	F	250+	Sunshine	Wright Group/McGraw Hill
*Fantastic Water Pot and Other Cases, The	O	RF	250+	Simon, Seymour	Avon
Far Away Moon	G	I	80	Pacific Literacy	Pacific Learning
Farewell to Manzanar	Z	B	250+	Houston, Jeanne; Houston, James D.	Houghton Mifflin
Farley Frog	B	F	33	Pair-It Books	Steck-Vaughn
Farm Alarm	E	F	103	Early Connections	Benchmark Education
Farm Animals	A	I	24	Vocabulary Readers	Houghton Mifflin
Farm Animals	A	I	28		Belle Rivers Readers
Farm Chores	D	RF	35	Early Emergent, Set 4	Pioneer Valley
Farm Concert, The	C	F	74	Story Box	Wright Group/McGraw Hill
Farm Day	D	F	36	Little Celebrations	Pearson Learning Group
Farm for Wild Animals, A	K	I	161	Vocabulary Readers	Houghton Mifflin
Farm Friends	K	I	197	Spyglass Books	Compass Point Books
Farm in Spring, The	C	I	69	PM Starters	Rigby
Farm Life Long Ago	L	I	436	Pair-It Books	Steck-Vaughn
Farm Through the Ages	U	I	250+	Steele, Philip	Troll Associates
Farm Work	D	F	80	Early Connections	Benchmark Education

* Collection of short stories

| --- | --- | --- | --- | --- | --- |
Farm, A	A	I	28	Little Books for Early Readers	University of Maine
Farm, The	B	I	79	Leveled Readers Emergent	Houghton Mifflin
Farm, The	B	I	21	Sunshine	Wright Group/McGraw Hill
Farm, The	LB	I	14	Smart Starts	Rigby
Farm, The	LB	I	14	Ready Readers	Pearson Learning Group
Farm, The	I	I	228	Pebble Books	Capstone Press
Farm, The	A	I	42	Little Readers	Houghton Mifflin
Farm, The	A	I	28	Little Books for Early Readers	University of Maine
Farm, The	LB	I	14	Literacy 2000	Rigby
Farmer and His Two Lazy Sons, The	I	TL	250+	Aesop's Fables	Pearson Learning Group
Farmer and the Skunk	E	F	139	Tiger Cub	Peguis
Farmer Boy	Q	HF	250+	Wilder, Laura Ingalls	HarperTrophy
Farmer Boy Birthday, A	J	HF	250+	Wilder, Laura Ingalls	HarperCollins
Farmer Boy Days	M	HF	250+	Wilder, Laura Ingalls	HarperTrophy
Farmer Brown and Dapple Gray	J	RF	166	Books for Young Learners	Richard C. Owen
Farmer Brown's Garden	C	F	48	Windmill Books	Rigby
Farmer Didn't Wake Up, The	F	F	185	Learn to Read	Creative Teaching Press
Farmer Had a Pig, A	G	TL	149	Tiger Cub	Peguis
Farmer in the Dell	E	F	114	Parkinson, Kathy	Whitman
farmer in the dell, The	F	TL	159	PM Readalongs	Rigby
Farmer in the Dell, The	K	TL	250+	Traditional Songs	Picture Window Books
Farmer in the Soup, The	K	TL	250+	Littledale, Freya	Scholastic
Farmer Joe's Hot Day	J	F	406	Richards, Nancy W.	Scholastic
Farmer Mike	E	RF	52	Leveled Readers	Houghton Mifflin
Farmer Upsy-Daisy	E	F	129	Start to Read	School Zone
Farmers	M	I	250+	Ready, Dee	Red Brick Learning
Farmers	M	I	250+	Community Workers	Compass Point Books
Farmer's Journey, The	M	RF	250+	Little Celebrations	Pearson Learning Group
Farms	N	I	606	Wonders	Hampton-Brown
Farms	F	I	153	Foundations	Wright Group/McGraw Hill
Farms	F	RF	102	Sunshine	Wright Group/McGraw Hill
Farmyard Fiasco, A	H	F	186	Book Bank	Wright Group/McGraw Hill
*Far-Out Frisbee and Other Cases, The	O	RF	250+	Simon, Seymour	Avon
Farthest Shore, The	Z	F	250+	Le Guin, Ursula	Bantam
Fascinating Faces	J	I	99	Literacy Tree	Rigby
Fascinating Families	O	I	717	Leveled Readers	Houghton Mifflin
Fasi Sings and Fasi's Fish	I	RF	204	Pacific Literacy	Pacific Learning
Fast and Faster	B	I	24	Windows on Literacy	National Geographic
*Fast and Funny	J	RF	1499	Story Box	Wright Group/McGraw Hill
Fast Athletes	C	I	104	Careers Series	Benchmark Education
Fast Food	E	RF	112	Foundations	Wright Group/McGraw Hill
Fast Food for Butterflies	I	I	170	Storyteller-Moon Rising	Wright Group/McGraw Hill
Fast Machines	D	RF	146	Foundations	Wright Group/McGraw Hill
Fast Sam, Cool Clyde, and Stuff	Y	RF	250+	Myers, Walter Dean	Puffin Books
Fast, Faster, Fastest	C	I	66	Twig	Wright Group/McGraw Hill
Fast, Not Last	H	F	233	Sunshine	Wright Group/McGraw Hill
Fast-Draw Freddie	D	F	50	Rookie Readers	Children's Press
Faster! Faster!	H	F	285	Leveled Readers	Houghton Mifflin
Fastest Gazelle, The	E	RF	146	Literacy 2000	Rigby
*Fastest Ketchup in the Cafeteria and Other Cases, The	O	RF	250+	Simon, Seymour	Avon
Fat Cat	I	TL	250+	Kent, Jack	Scholastic
Fat Cat Sat on the Mat, The	G	F	250+	Karlin, Nurit	HarperTrophy
Fat Cat Tompkin	I	F	196	Voyages	SRA/McGraw Hill

* Collection of short stories

TITLE	LEVEL	GENRE	WORD COUNT	AUTHOR / SERIES	PUBLISHER / DISTRIBUTOR
Fat Pig, The	I	TL	250+	Tiger Cub	Peguis
Father Bear Comes Home	I	F	331	Minarik, Else H.	HarperCollins
Father Bear Goes Fishing	D	F	98	PM Story Books	Rigby
Father Bear's Surprise	H	RF	224	PM Extensions-Green	Rigby
Father Eusebio Francisco Kino: Changing the Colonial Southwest	W	I	2436	Independent Readers Science	Houghton Mifflin
Father Fights Back: Franklin Delano Roosevelt and Polio	M	B	250+	Twig	Wright Group/McGraw Hill
*Father Water, Mother Woods	V	RF	250+	Paulsen, Gary	Bantam
Father Who Walked on Hands	K	RF	344	Literacy 2000	Rigby
Fathers	B	I	26	Pebble Books	Capstone Press
Father's Arcane Daughter	V	RF	250+	Konigsburg, E. L.	Aladdin
Fats, Oils, and Sweets	I	I	190	The Food Guide Pyramid	Capstone Press
Favorite Games Around the World	Q	I	250+	Sunshine	Wright Group/McGraw Hill
*Favorite Greek Myths	Y	TL	250+	Pope, Mary Osborne	Scholastic
Favorite Medieval Tales	S	TL	250+	Pope, Mary Osborne	Scholastic
Fawn in the Forest, The	H	RF	227	PM Plus Story Books	Rigby
Fear of White Water	S	RF	250+	Leveled Readers Language Support	Houghton Mifflin
*Fearless Explorer and Other Cases, The	O	RF	250+	Simon, Seymour	Avon
Feast, The	E	F	58	Leveled Readers	Houghton Mifflin
Feathers and Flight	I	I	790	Sunshine	Wright Group/McGraw Hill
Feathers and Flight	Q	I	250+	Explorers	Wright Group/McGraw Hill
*Feathery Fables	P	TL	250+	Action Packs	Rigby
Feed Me! An Aesop Fable	I	TL	250+	Bank Street	Bantam
Feeding	A	I	40	Sun Sprouts	ETA/Cuisenaire
Feeding the Baby	C	I	51	Home Connection Collection	Rigby
Feeding the Lambs	H	RF	61	PM Plus Nonfiction	Rigby
Feeding Time	C	RF	55	Carousel Readers	Pearson Learning Group
Feeding Time at the Zoo	D	RF	73	Windmill Books	Rigby
Feel the Power: Energy All Around	K	I	250+	Spyglass Books	Compass Point Books
Feeling Angry	F	I	70	Emotions	Red Brick Learning
Feeling Funny	J	F	250+	Sunshine	Wright Group/McGraw Hill
Feeling Happy	F	I	57	Emotions	Red Brick Learning
Feeling Sad	F	I	62	Emotions	Red Brick Learning
Feeling Scared	F	I	62	Emotions	Red Brick Learning
Feelings	P	I	250+	Sunshine	Wright Group/McGraw Hill
Feelings	LB	I	12	Canizares, Susan	Scholastic
Feelings	A	I	24	Windows on Literacy	National Geographic
Feelings	D	RF	39	Rise & Shine	Hampton-Brown
Feet	H	F	76	Book Bank	Wright Group/McGraw Hill
Feet	D	RF	18	Story Box	Wright Group/McGraw Hill
Feet	A	I	14	Foundations	Wright Group/McGraw Hill
Feet!	LB	I	28	Ray's Readers	Outside the Box
Feisty Old Woman Who Lived in the Cozy Cave	J	F	301	Foundations	Wright Group/McGraw Hill
Felicia the Critic	P	RF	250+	Conford, Ellen	Little, Brown & Co.
Felicity Learns a Lesson	Q	HF	250+	The American Girls Collection	Pleasant Company
Felicity Saves the Day	Q	HF	250+	The American Girls Collection	Pleasant Company
Felicity's Surprise	Q	HF	250+	The American Girls Collection	Pleasant Company
Felita	P	RF	250+	Mohr, Nicholas	Dell
Felix, the Very Hungry Fish	C	F	32	Little Books	Sadlier-Oxford
Fence, The	B	F	44	Bookshop	Mondo
Fergus and Bridey	K	F	250+	Little Celebrations	Pearson Learning Group
Fern and Burt	H	F	250+	Ready Readers	Pearson Learning Group

* Collection of short stories

TITLE	LEVEL	GENRE	WORD COUNT	AUTHOR / SERIES	PUBLISHER / DISTRIBUTOR
Fernitickles	R	HF	250+	Literacy 2000	Rigby
Fern's Purple Birthday	I	F	250+	Phonics Readers Plus	Steck-Vaughn
Ferret Fun	O	RF	250+	Baglio, Ben M.	Scholastic
Ferret In The Bedroom, Lizards In The Fridge	T	RF	250+	Wallace, Bill	Language for learning Assoc.
Ferry, The	C	RF	27	Sunshine	Wright Group/McGraw Hill
Festival Foods Around the World	M	I	250+	Stull, Becky	Steck-Vaughn
Festival Fun	N	I	250+	Wildcats	Wright Group/McGraw Hill
Festival in Valencia	L	RF	301	Leveled Readers	Houghton Mifflin
Festival, the	B	I	37	Windows on Literacy	National Geographic
Festival, The	D	I	146	Fiesta Series	Pearson Learning Group
Festivals	F	I	40	Berger, Samantha; Chanko, Pamela	Scholastic
Fever 1793	Z	HF	250+	Anderson, Laurie Halse	Simon & Schuster
Fibers from Plants	I	I	392	Sunshine	Wright Group/McGraw Hill
Fibers Made by People	M	I	442	Sunshine	Wright Group/McGraw Hill
*Fiddle and the Gun, The	M	F	250+	Literacy 2000	Rigby
Fiesta Time	C	I	28	Little Celebrations	Pearson Learning Group
Fiesta!	M	I	250+	Festivals and Holidays	Children's Press
Fifth Grade: Here Comes Trouble	S	RF	250+	McKenna, Colleen O'Shaughnessy	Scholastic
Fig Pudding	R	RF	250+	Fletcher, Ralph	Clarion
Figaro	K	F	250+	Voyages	SRA/McGraw Hill
Fight in the Schoolyard, The	K	RF	129	City Kids	Rigby
Fight on the Hill, The	I	F	336	Read Alongs	Rigby
Fighter Planes	K	I	115	Mighty Machines	Capstone Press
Fighting Fire With Fire	M	I	250+	Rigby Literacy	Rigby
Fighting Fires Then and Now	L	I	381	Leveled Readers	Houghton Mifflin
Fighting Fish	O	I	250+	Life Cycles	Creative Teaching Press
Fighting Ground, The	V	HF	250+	Avi	HarperTrophy
Fighting Tackle	M	RF	250+	Christopher, Matt	Little, Brown & Co.
Figure in the Shadows, The	S	F	250+	Bellairs, John	Penguin Group
Fiji Flood, The	M	F	250+	Schultz, Irene	Wright Group/McGraw Hill
Filbert the Fly	C	F	28	Literacy 2000	Rigby
Final Freedom, The	V	RF	250+	Wallace, Bill	Pocket Books
*Finch Family Summer	M	F	250+	Sunshine	Wright Group/McGraw Hill
Finches' Fabulous Furnace, The	O	F	250+	Drury, Roger	Scholastic
Find a Caterpillar	E	I	102	Book Bank	Wright Group/McGraw Hill
Find A Stranger, Say Goodbye	X	RF	250+	Lowry, Lois	Dell
Find It	C	RF	63	Carousel Earlybirds	Pearson Learning Group
Find Out About It!	T	I	250+	iOpeners	Pearson Learning Group
FInd the Prize	E	RF	39	Independent Readers Social Studies	Houghton Mifflin
Find the Wild Animal	F	I	108	Foley, Cate	Scholastic
Find Yourself a Friend	F	RF	261	Visions	Wright Group/McGraw Hill
Finding a Way: Six Historic U.S. Routes	W	I	250+	iOpeners	Pearson Learning Group
Finding a Wooly Mammoth	F	I	120	Independent Readers Science	Houghton Mifflin
Finding Buck McHenry	S	RF	250+	Slote, Alfred	Scholastic
Finding Gold	N	I	848	Leveled Readers Science	Houghton Mifflin
Finding Out About the Past	H	I	155	Windows on Literacy	National Geographic
Finding Providence: The Story of Roger Williams	P	B	250+	Avi	HarperTrophy
Finding the Titanic	Q	I	250+	Ballard, Robert D.	Scholastic
Finding Your Way	R	I	250+	Bonallack, John	Pacific Learning
Fine Lines	O	B	250+	Heller, Ruth	Richard C. Owen
Finger Puppet, The	B	RF	18	Sunshine	Wright Group/McGraw Hill

* Collection of short stories

TITLE	LEVEL	GENRE	WORD COUNT	AUTHOR / SERIES	PUBLISHER / DISTRIBUTOR
Finger Puppets, Finger Plays	I	I	268	Storyteller-Night Crickets	Wright Group/McGraw Hill
Fingerprint Family	C	I	24	Rigby Literacy	Rigby
Fins, Wings, and Legs	J	I	250+	iOpeners	Pearson Learning Group
Fire	S	HF	250+	Duey, Kathleen; Bale, Karen A.	Simon & Schuster
Fire and Water	E	TL	127	Story Box	Wright Group/McGraw Hill
Fire and Wind	L	TL	250+	PM Story Books-Silver	Rigby
Fire at the Triangle Factory	P	HF	250+	Littlefield, Holly	Carolrhoda Books
Fire at the Zoo, A	I	F	229	Sunshine	Wright Group/McGraw Hill
Fire Boats	I	I	188	Pebble Books	Capstone Press
Fire Bug Connection, The	S	RF	250+	George, Jean Craighead	HarperTrophy
Fire Cat, The	J	F	250+	Averill, Esther	HarperTrophy
Fire Engines	I	I	184	Pebble Books	Capstone Press
Fire Fighters	L	I	250+	Community Workers	Compass Point Books
Fire Fighters	M	I	250+	Ready, Dee	Red Brick Learning
Fire in the Hills	Y	RF	250+	Myers, Anna	Puffin Books
Fire in the Sky	R	HF	250+	Ransom, Candice F.	Carolrhoda Books
Fire in the Wind	U	RF	250+	Levin, Betty	Beech Tree Books
Fire on Toytown Hill, The	F	F	166	PM Plus Story Books	Rigby
Fire Safety Day	M	RF	749	Leveled Readers	Houghton Mifflin
Fire Station, The	J	I	237	Pebble Books	Capstone Press
Fire Trucks	J	I	127	Mighty Machines	Capstone Press
Fire Trucks	M	I	250+	Transportation	Compass Point Books
Fire!	K	F	250+	Rigby Literacy	Rigby
Fire! Fire!	O	I	250+	Wildcats	Wright Group/McGraw Hill
Fire! Fire!	E	RF	164	PM Story Books	Rigby
Fire! in Yellowstone: A True Adventure	O	I	250+	Soar To Success	Houghton Mifflin
Fire! The Beginnings of the Labor Movement	R	HF	250+	Goldin, Barbara Diamond	Puffin Books
*Fire-Bird, The	U	TL	250+	Literacy 2000	Rigby
Firefighter Wears a Helmet, A	F	I	79	Windows on Literacy	National Geographic
Firefighters	E	RF	250+	Bookshop	Mondo
Firefighters	L	I	250+	Mitten, Christopher	Scholastic
Fireflies	E	I	57	Vocabulary Readers	Houghton Mifflin
Fireflies	E	I	49	Pebble Books	Capstone Press
Fireflies in the Night	M	I	250+	Hawes, Judy	HarperTrophy
Fireflies!	L	I	250+	Twig	Wright Group/McGraw Hill
Firefly Named Torchy, A	L	F	250+	Waber, Bernard	Houghton Mifflin
Firehouse Sal	F	RF	52	Rookie Readers	Children's Press
Firelight Secrets	O	RF	250+	PM Ruby	Rigby
Firetalking	O	B	250+	Polacco, Patricia	Richard C. Owen
Fireworks	C	RF	29	Joy Readers	Pearson Learning Group
Fireworks!	P	I	889	Leveled Readers Science	Houghton Mifflin
First Aid	F	I	44	Canizares, Susan; Chanko, Pamela	Scholastic
First Americans, The	O	I	250+	People, Spaces & Places	Rand McNally
First and Last	C	I	44	Teacher's Choice Series	Pearson Learning Group
First Apple	N	RF	250+	Russell, Ching Yueng	Penguin Group
First Art Class, The	G	RF	250+	Leveled Readers Language Support	Houghton Mifflin
First Book About Africa: An Introduction for Young Readers	Q	I	250+	Ellis, Veronica Freeman	Just Us Books
First Day Back at School	H	RF	132	City Kids	Rigby
First Day For Carlos	P	RF	764	Leveled Readers	Houghton Mifflin
First Day of School	LB	RF	16	Visions	Wright Group/McGraw Hill
First Day of School	D	RF	60	Carousel Readers	Pearson Learning Group
First Day of School, The	A	RF	28	Bookshop	Mondo

* Collection of short stories

TITLE	LEVEL	GENRE	WORD COUNT	AUTHOR / SERIES	PUBLISHER / DISTRIBUTOR
First Family on Mars, The	P	SF	250+	Orbit Double Takes	Pacific Learning
First Family: The Roosevelts	U	B	2374	Independent Readers Social Studies	Houghton Mifflin
First Fire Company, The	J	I	182	Leveled Readers	Houghton Mifflin
First Fire, The	K	F	250+	Little Celebrations	Pearson Learning Group
First Fire: A Traditional Native American Tale	K	TL	250+	Rigby Literacy	Rigby
First Flight	K	B	250+	Shea, George	HarperTrophy
First Flight	J	RF	250+	PM Plus Story Books	Rigby
First Four Years, The	R	HF	250+	Wilder, Laura Ingalls	HarperTrophy
First Grade Takes a Test	J	RF	250+	Cohen, Miriam	Bantam
First Hot-Air Balloons, The	M	I	250+	Moore, Philip	Wright Group/McGraw Hill
First Humans, The	U	I	1814	Leveled Readers Social Studies	Houghton Mifflin
First in Line	D	RF	77	Teacher's Choice Series	Pearson Learning Group
First Journeys	X	I	250+	iOpeners	Pearson Learning Group
First Ladies	U	B	250+	Cornerstones of Freedom	Children's Press
*First Ladies of the White House	U	B	250+	Skarmeas, Nancy	Ideals Publications Inc.
*First Ladies: Women Who Called the White House Home	U	B	250+	Gormley, Beatrice	Scholastic
First Morning, The	N	TL	250+	Literacy 2000	Rigby
First On The Moon	Y	I	250+	Hehner, Barbara	Hyperion/Madison Press
First Snow	WB	RF	N/A	McCully, Emily Arnold	Harper & Row
First Thanksgiving, The	R	I	250+	The Library of the Pilgrims	Rosen Publishing Group
First Things	N	RF	250+	Stepping Stones	Nelson/Michaels Assoc.
First Things	LB	RF	18	Home Connection Collection	Rigby
First Woman Doctor, The	T	B	250+	Rachel Baker	Scholastic
First, Take the Flour	L	I	186	Rigby Literacy	Rigby
First-Aid Handbook	S	I	250+	iOpeners	Pearson Learning Group
Fish	D	I	34	All About Pets	Red Brick Learning
Fish	L	I	250+	Rigby Literacy	Rigby
Fish	D	I	58	Wonder World	Wright Group/McGraw Hill
Fish	O	I	250+	Nature's Friends	Compass Point Books
Fish	M	I	250+	First Facts	Capstone Press
Fish	L	I	298	Marine Life For Young Readers	Pearson Learning Group
Fish	D	I	58	Sun Sprouts	ETA/Cuisenaire
Fish and the Cat, The	C	F	91	Sun Sprouts	ETA/Cuisenaire
Fish Bowl, The	C	I	48	Sun Sprouts	ETA/Cuisenaire
Fish Colors	LB	I	6	Vocabulary Readers	Houghton Mifflin
Fish Face	M	RF	250+	Giff, Patricia Reilly	Bantam
Fish for Sale	K	RF	250+	SupaDoopers	Sundance
Fish for You: Caring for Your Fish	M	I	250+	Pet Care	Picture Window Books
Fish from the Rainbow	I	F	239	Sunshine	Wright Group/McGraw Hill
Fish Picture, A	B	RF	58	First Stories	Pacific Learning
Fish Print	B	I	25	Bebop Books	Lee & Low Books Inc.
Fish Stew for Supper	C	I	56	First Stories	Pacific Learning
Fish that Hide	L	I	250+	Swartz, Stanley L.	Pearson Learning Group
Fishing	C	RF	15	Instant Readers	Harcourt School Publishers
Fishing	C	RF	35	Story Box	Wright Group/McGraw Hill
Fishing	G	RF	180	Foundations	Wright Group/McGraw Hill
Fishing	C	I	35	KinderReaders	Rigby
Fishing	C	RF	63	PM Starters	Rigby
Fishing	E	RF	47	Wonder World	Wright Group/McGraw Hill
Fishing	D	RF	48	Yukish, Joe	Kaeden Books
Fishing	B	I	41	Little Books for Early Readers	University of Maine
Fishing Contest, The	E	RF	84	Literacy Tree	Rigby

* Collection of short stories

TITLE	LEVEL	GENRE	WORD COUNT	AUTHOR / SERIES	PUBLISHER / DISTRIBUTOR
Fishing Family	L	I	281	Independent Readers Science	Houghton Mifflin
Fishing Off the Wharf	M	RF	274	Pacific Literacy	Pacific Learning
Fishing Trip, The	K	RF	250+	PM Plus Story Books	Rigby
Fishy Alphabet Story	F	F	126	Wylie, Joanne & David	Children's Press
Fishy Color Story	D	F	142	Wylie, Joanne & David	Children's Press
Fishy Mystery, The	N	RF	250+	Orbit Chapter Books	Pacific Literacy
Fishy Scales	I	F	107	Mathtales	Mimosa
Fishy Story, A	C	F	102	Pair-It Books	Steck-Vaughn
Fishy Story, A	L	F	174	Books for Young Learners	Richard C. Owen
Fishy, Flashy Fourth, The	M	RF	250+	Schultz, Irene	Wright Group/McGraw Hill
Fitness	C	F	60	Foundations	Wright Group/McGraw Hill
Five Beans	H	I	197	Sun Sprouts	ETA/Cuisenaire
*Five Brave Explorers	Q	B	250+	Hudson, Wade	Scholastic
*Five Brilliant Scientists	Q	B	250+	Steward, Susan McKinney	Scholastic
Five Days to Go!	K	RF	250+	Rigby Literacy	Rigby
Five Ducks	D	RF	89	Joy Readers	Pearson Learning Group
*Five Funny Frights	K	RF	250+	Bauer, Judith	Scholastic
Five Funny Uncles	I	RF	269	Story Box	Wright Group/McGraw Hill
Five Little Dinosaurs	E	F	113	Ready Readers	Pearson Learning Group
Five Little Monkeys	G	F	160	Cambridge Reading	Pearson Learning Group
Five Little Monkeys	F	F	81	Bookshop	Mondo
Five Little Monkeys Going to the Zoo	E	F	201	Valerie Cutteridge's First Grade	Continental Press
Five Little Monkeys Jumping on the Bed	E	TL	200	Christelow, Eileen	Houghton Mifflin
Five Little Monsters	D	F	146	Learn to Read	Creative Teaching Press
Five Little Monsters Went to School	E	F	65	Learn to Read	Creative Teaching Press
Five Little Speckled Frogs	G	RF	180	Tiger Cub	Peguis
*Five Notable Inventors	Q	B	250+	Hudson, Wade	Scholastic
Five Senses	D	RF	101	Sun Sprouts	ETA/Cuisenaire
Five Senses, The	K	I	280	Story Box	Wright Group/McGraw Hill
Five Senses, The	C	I	53	Rigby Focus	Rigby
Five Silly Fishermen	G	TL	250+	Edwards, Roberta	Random House
*Five True Dog Stories	M	I	250+	Davidson, Margaret	Scholastic
*Five True Horse Stories	M	I	250+	Davidson, Margaret	Scholastic
Five-Dog Night, The	P	RF	250+	Christelow, Eileen	Clarion
Fix It	I	F	171	McPhail, David	Penguin Group
Fix It, Fox	E	F	62	Ready Readers	Pearson Learning Group
Fizz and Splutter	E	F	92	Story Box	Wright Group/McGraw Hill
Fizzkid the Inventor	J	F	250+	Rigby Literacy	Rigby
Flag Day	L	I	116	National Holidays	Red Brick Learning
Flag For All, A	I	RF	250+	Rookie Choices	Children's Press
Flag For Our Country, A	N	I	250+	Spencer, Eve	Steck-Vaughn
Flags	U	I	250+	iOpeners	Pearson Learning Group
Flags	R	I	250+	Action Packs	Rigby
Flags Everywhere!	B	I	25	Independent Readers Social Studies	Houghton Mifflin
Flakes and Flurries: A Book About Snow	M	I	250+	Amazing Science	Picture Window Books
Flaming Arrows	T	HF	250+	Steele, William O.	Harcourt Trade
Flamingos	N	I	250+	Cole, Sally	Wright Group/McGraw Hill
Flash Flood!	O	I	1784	Independent Readers Science	Houghton Mifflin
Flashlights	J	I	250+	Sunshine Books	Wright Group/McGraw Hill
Flat Hat, The	C	I	24	KinderReaders	Rigby
Flat Stanley	M	F	250+	Brown, Jeff	HarperTrophy
Flatboat Mondays	U	I	2452	Independent Readers Social Studies	Houghton Mifflin

* Collection of short stories

TITLE	LEVEL	GENRE	WORD COUNT	AUTHOR / SERIES	PUBLISHER / DISTRIBUTOR
Flavors and Fragrances	T	I	1987	Leveled Readers Science	Houghton Mifflin
Flea Story, A	L	F	250+	Lionni, Leo	Scholastic
Fledgling, The	U	F	250+	Langton, Jane	Scholastic
Flicking the Switch	O	I	250+	Pacific Literacy	Pacific Learning
Flies	N	I	250+	A True Book	Children's Press
Flies	F	I	56	Pebble Books	Capstone Press
Flight #116 Is Down!	Z	RF	250+	Cooney, Caroline B.	Scholastic
Flight Deck	C	I	30	Wonder World	Wright Group/McGraw Hill
Flight of the Union, The	L	B	250+	White, Tekla	Carolrhoda Books
Flight: The Journey of Charles Lindbergh	R	I	250+	Burleigh, Robert	Putnam & Grosset
Flip Flop	G	RF	70	Books for Young Learners	Richard C. Owen
Flip, Flap, Flop	I	F	252	Sunshine	Wright Group/McGraw Hill
Flipped	U	RF	250+	Van Draanen, Wendelin	Random House
Flip's Trick	H	RF	134	Ready Readers	Pearson Learning Group
Floating	K	RF	250+	Sunshine	Wright Group/McGraw Hill
Floating	C	I	29	Little Blue Readers	Sundance
Floating and Paddling	N	I	250+	Strebor, Leon	Wright Group/McGraw Hill
Floating and Sinking	H	I	168	Sunshine	Wright Group/McGraw Hill
Floating and Sinking	J	I	168	Bookshop	Mondo
Floating and Sinking	J	I	221	Alphakids	Sundance
Floating Markets of Bangkok, The	L	I	250+	Sunshine	Wright Group/McGraw Hill
Floating on Air	Q	F	1332	Leveled Readers	Houghton Mifflin
Flood	H	RF	170	Story Box	Wright Group/McGraw Hill
Flood	S	HF	250+	Duey, Kathleen; Bale, Karen A.	Simon & Schuster
Flood!	K	RF	250+	Rigby Literacy	Rigby
Flood, The	H	RF	237	PM Story Books	Rigby
Flood, The	I	I	138	Wonder World	Wright Group/McGraw Hill
Floods	N	I	250+	A True Book	Children's Press
Floods	R	I	1142	Leveled Readers	Houghton Mifflin
Floppy the Hero	F	F	74	Oxford Reading Tree	Oxford University Press
Floppy's Bath	E	F	55	Oxford Reading Tree	Oxford University Press
Flora, a Friend for the Animals	J	RF	337	Sunshine	Wright Group/McGraw Hill
Florence Griffith-Joyner: Olympic Champion	K	B	184	Leveled Readers	Houghton Mifflin
Florence Griffith-Joyner: Olympic Runner	J	B	184	Leveled Readers Language Support	Houghton Mifflin
Florence Kelley	P	B	250+	Saller, Carol	Carolrhoda Books
Florence Nightingale	P	B	250+	Davis, Lucile	Red Brick Learning
Florence Nightingale	N	B	228	Pebble Books	Capstone Press
Florida	Q	I	250+	One Nation	Capstone Press
Florida	S	I	250+	Land of Liberty	Red Brick Learning
Florida	R	I	250+	This Land Is Your Land	Compass Point Books
Flossie and the Fox	O	F	250+	McKissack, Patricia	Scholastic
Flour	K	I	174	Wonder World	Wright Group/McGraw Hill
Flower Box, The	LB	I	14	Twig	Wright Group/McGraw Hill
Flower Girl, The	C	RF	90	PM Extensions-Red	Rigby
Flower Girls # 1: Violet	L	RF	250+	Leverich, Kathleen	HarperTrophy
Flower Girls # 2: Daisy	L	RF	250+	Leverich, Kathleen	HarperTrophy
Flower Girls # 3: Heather	L	RF	250+	Leverich, Kathleen	HarperTrophy
Flower Girls # 4: Rose	L	RF	250+	Leverich, Kathleen	HarperTrophy
Flower of Sheba, The	L	TL	250+	Orgel, Doris; Schecter, Ellen	Bantam
Flowers	A	I	27	Bookshop	Mondo
Flowers	A	I	27	Hoenecke, Karen	Kaeden Books
Flowers	L	I	270	Pebble Books	Capstone Press
Flowers For Algernon	Z	RF	250+	Keyes, Daniel	Harcourt Trade

* Collection of short stories

TITLE	LEVEL	GENRE	WORD COUNT	AUTHOR / SERIES	PUBLISHER / DISTRIBUTOR
Flowers for Grandma	LB	RF	8	Windows on Literacy	National Geographic
Flowers for Mom	E	RF	88	Carousel Readers	Pearson Learning Group
Flowers for Mrs. Falepau	M	RF	857	Book Bank	Wright Group/McGraw Hill
Flowers Have Colors	B	I	29	Cherrington, Janelle	Scholastic
Flows & Quakes and Spinning Winds	K	I	250+	Home Connection Collection	Rigby
Fluffy Chicks	E	RF	50	Book Bank	Wright Group/McGraw Hill
Fluffy's Trip	K	F	250+	Sunshine	Wright Group/McGraw Hill
Flunking of Joshua T. Bates, The	Q	RF	250+	Shreve, Susan	Alfred A. Knopf
Fly Away Home	I	I	250+	Wonder World	Wright Group/McGraw Hill
Fly Away, Children	S	I	548	Vocabulary Readers	Houghton Mifflin
Fly High	B	RF	24	Visions	Wright Group/McGraw Hill
Fly Homer Fly	N	F	250+	Peet, Bill	Houghton Mifflin
Fly Trap	L	F	250+	Anastasio, Dina	Grosset & Dunlap
Fly, Butterfly	F	I	49	Discovery Links	Newbridge
Fly, The	D	F	78	Story Steps	Rigby
Fly-away Umbrella, The	M	F	250+	Voyages	SRA/McGraw Hill
Flyers	I	RF	250+	Rigby Literacy	Rigby
Fly-Fishing with Grandpa	O	RF	1029	Leveled Readers	Houghton Mifflin
Flying	C	F	26	Story Box	Wright Group/McGraw Hill
Flying	C	I	49	Crews, Donald	Mulberry Books
Flying Ace: The Story of Amelia Earhart	Q	B	250+	Eyewitness Readers	DK Publishing
Flying and Floating	B	I	64	Little Red Readers	Sundance
Flying Fingers	K	RF	250+	Literacy 2000	Rigby
Flying Fish, The	H	RF	215	PM Extensions-Green	Rigby
Flying Flea, Callie, and Me, The	S	F	250+	Wallace, Carol & Bill	Pocket Books
Flying Football, The	I	RF	250+	Cambridge Reading	Pearson Learning Group
*Flying Free: America's First Black Aviators	T	B	250+	Hart, Philip S.	Lerner Publishing
Flying High	R	RF	250+	Orbit Double Takes	Pacific Learning
Flying High	F	RF	250+	Predictable Storybooks	SRA/McGraw Hill
Flying Lessons	W	HF	250+	Matthews, Kezi	Cricket Books
Flying Saucer	I	RF	250+	Phonics Readers Plus	Steck-Vaughn
Flying Solo	S	RF	250+	Fletcher, Ralph	Bantam
Flying Trunk,The	M	TL	644	Tales from Hans Andersen	Wright Group/McGraw Hill
*Flying With the Eagle, Racing the Great Bear: Stories from Native North America	U	TL	250+	Bruchac, Joseph	Troll Associates
*Flying-Saucer People and Other Cases, The	O	RF	250+	Simon, Seymour	Avon
Folk Dancer	C	I	36	The Candid Collection	Pearson Learning Group
*Folktales from Asia	O	TL	250+	Bookshop	Mondo
Folktales from China	N	TL	250+	Lawson, Barbara	Scholastic
Follow a River	L	I	198	iOpeners	Pearson Learning Group
Follow Me!	I	F	250+	Ziefert, Harriet	Puffin Books
Follow Me, Be a Bee	K	I	428	Independent Readers Science	Houghton Mifflin
Follow My Leader	H	RF	96	Cambridge Reading	Pearson Learning Group
Follow That Fin!: Studying Dolphin Behavior	T	I	250+	Samuels, Amy	Steck-Vaughn
Follow That Fish	K	F	250+	Bank Street	Bantam
Follow That Spy!	P	RF	250+	Action Packs	Rigby
Follow the Applachian Trail	I	I	129	Leveled Readers Social Studies	Houghton Mifflin
Follow the Leader	D	RF	75	Teacher's Choice Series	Pearson Learning Group
Follow the Leader	B	RF	32	Independent Readers Social Studies	Houghton Mifflin
Follow the Leader	C	RF	62	First Stories	Pacific Learning
Follow the Leader	B	RF	15	Windmill	Wright Group/McGraw Hill
Follow the Sun	D	RF	60	Leveled Readers Science	Houghton Mifflin
Food & Feasts Between the Two World Wars	T	I	250+	Steele, Philip	Dillon Press

TITLE	LEVEL	GENRE	WORD COUNT	AUTHOR / SERIES	PUBLISHER / DISTRIBUTOR
Food & Feasts In Ancient Egypt	T	I	250+	Balkwill, Richard	Dillon Press
Food & Feasts In Ancient Greece	T	I	250+	Steele, Philip	Dillon Press
Food & Feasts In Ancient Rome	T	I	250+	Steele, Philip	Dillon Press
Food & Feasts In the Middle Ages	T	I	250+	Dawson, Imogen	Dillon Press
Food & Feasts In Tudor Times	T	I	250+	Balkwill, Richard	Dillon Press
Food & Feasts With the Aztecs	T	I	250+	Dawson, Imogen	Dillon Press
Food & Feasts With the Vikings	T	I	250+	Martell, Hazel	Dillon Press
Food and Festivals: Israel	O	I	250+	Randall, Ronne	Steck-Vaughn
Food and Festivals: Italy	O	I	250+	Pirotta, Saviour	Steck-Vaughn
Food and Recipes of the Pilgrims	R	I	250+	Cooking Throughout American History	Rosen Publishing Group
Food and Recipes of the Thirteen Colonies	R	I	250+	Cooking Throughout American History	Rosen Publishing Group
Food and Recipes of the Westward Expansion	R	I	250+	Cooking Throughout American History	Rosen Publishing Group
Food Around the World	I	I	298	Early Connections	Benchmark Education
Food Chains	O	I	677	Leveled Readers Science	Houghton Mifflin
Food Comes From Farms	F	I	75	Windows on Literacy	National Geographic
Food for Healthy Teeth	E	I	40	Pebble Books	Capstone Press
Food for Thought	I	I	250+	Yellow Umbrella Books	Red Brick Learning
Food for You	F	I	85	Leveled Readers Science	Houghton Mifflin
Food Found All Around	L	I	220	Spyglass Books	Compass Point Books
Food From Another Country	H	I	91	Windows on Literacy	National Geographic
Food from Plants	D	RF	66	Rigby Literacy	Rigby
Food from the Farm	D	RF	78	Home Connection Collection	Rigby
Food Is Fun	H	RF	250+	PM Plus Poetry	Rigby
Food Journey, The	K	I	116	Home Connection Collection	Rigby
Food Pyramid, The	L	I	155	Spyglass Books	Compass Point Books
Food Service Workers	M	I	250+	Community Helpers	Red Brick Learning
Food to Eat	B	I	29	Little Readers	Houghton Mifflin
Food Trappers	I	I	165	Wonder World	Wright Group/McGraw Hill
Foolish Goose	F	F	141	Start To Read	School Zone
Foolish Gretel	O	TL	250+	Armstrong, Jennifer	Random House
Foot Book	E	F	108	Seuss, Dr.	Random House
Football	B	I	28	Visions	Wright Group/McGraw Hill
Football Fever	H	RF	51	Pacific Literacy	Pacific Learning
Football for Fun	S	I	250+	Sports for Fun	Compass Point Books
Football Friends	L	RF	250+	Marzollo, Jean, Dan & Dave	Scholastic
Football Fugitive	M	RF	250+	Christopher, Matt	Little, Brown & Co.
Footprints	G	RF	96	Literacy Tree	Rigby
Footprints	C	I	69	Rigby Focus	Rigby
Footprints	H	RF	96	Book Bus	Creative Edge
Footprints in the Snow	D	RF	39	Benjamin, Cynthia	Scholastic
For Breakfast	LB	I	22	Visions	Wright Group/McGraw Hill
For My Birthday	B	RF	48	Lighthouse	Rigby
For The Life of Laetitia	Y	RF	250+	Hodge, Merle	Farrar, Straus and Giroux
For the Love of Pooch	N	RF	250+	Literacy 2000	Rigby
For the Love of Turtles	M	RF	250+	Greetings	Rigby
For the Love of Turtles	N	RF	250+	Greetings	Rigby
Forced Out	O	I	889	Independent Readers Science	Houghton Mifflin
Forest Community, A	Q	I	250+	Massie, Elizabeth	Steck-Vaughn
Forest Fire!	O	I	769	Leveled Readers Science	Houghton Mifflin
Forest Fires: Run for Your Life!	T	I	250+	Bookshop	Mondo
Forest Mammals	R	I	250+	Kalman, Bobbie	Crabtree

* Collection of short stories

TITLE	LEVEL	GENRE	WORD COUNT	AUTHOR / SERIES	PUBLISHER / DISTRIBUTOR
Forest, The	L	I	250+	Cambridge Reading	Pearson Learning Group
Forests	N	I	250+	Habitats of the World	Pearson Learning Group
Forests	M	I	250+	PM Plus Nonfiction	Rigby
Forests	R	I	250+	The Wonders of Our World	Crabtree
Forest's Life, A: From Meadow to Mature Woodland	T	I	250+	A First Book	Franklin Watts
Forests, Grasslands, Deserts	M	I	250+	People, Spaces & Places	Rand McNally
Forever Amber Brown	N	RF	250+	Danziger, Paula	Scholastic
Forever Friends	X	RF	250+	Boyd, Candy Dawson	Puffin Books
Forged By Fire	Z	RF	250+	Draper, Sharon M.	Aladdin
Forget It!	L	RF	250+	Rigby Literacy	Rigby
Forgetful Fran	J	RF	250+	Sunshine	Wright Group/McGraw Hill
Forgetful Fred	E	RF	78	Tadpoles	Rigby
Forgiveness	M	I	250+	Character Education	Red Brick Learning
Forgotten Door, The	T	SF	250+	Key, Alexander	Language for Learning Assoc.
Forgotten Heroes, The: The Story of the Buffalo Soldiers	X	I	250+	Cox, Clinton	Scholastic
Forgotten Hiding Place, The	M	RF	250+	Schultz, Irene	Wright Group/McGraw Hill
Forgotten Princess, The	L	TL	250+	Literacy 2000	Rigby
Fort Life	T	I	250+	Historic Communities	Crabtree
Fort Sumter	V	I	250+	Cornerstones of Freedom	Children's Press
Fort Sumter: Where the Civil War Began	Q	I	250+	Rosen Real Readers	Rosen Publishing Group
Fortune Branches Out, A	R	RF	250+	Mahy, Margaret	Bantam
*Fortune's Friend: Tales of Rivalry and Riches	Q	TL	250+	Literacy 2000	Rigby
Fortune-Tellers, The	O	TL	250+	Alexander, Lloyd	Puffin Books
Forty-Three Cats	K	RF	232	Sunshine	Wright Group/McGraw Hill
Fossil Fuels	M	I	250+	Rigby Focus	Rigby
Fossil Hunters, The	J	I	207	Instant Readers	Harcourt School Publishers
Fossil Hunting	L	I	170	Rigby Focus	Rigby
Fossil Seekers	U	I	250+	iOpeners	Pearson Learning Group
Fossils	P	I	250+	Simply Science	Compass Point Books
Fossils	L	I	250+	Early Connections	Benchmark Education
Fossils	K	I	238	Windows on Literacy	National Geographic
Fossils	R	I	1272	Leveled Readers Science	Houghton Mifflin
Fossils Alive!	Q	I	250+	Daniel, Claire	Steck-Vaughn
Fossils Tell of Long Ago	O	I	250+	Soar To Success	Houghton Mifflin
Fossils: Pictures from the Past	Q	I	250+	Daniel, Claire	Steck-Vaughn
Foster's War	V	HF	250+	Reeder, Carolyn	Scholastic
Foul Play on the Sidelines	R	RF	250+	Costello, Emily	Dell
Fountains of Life: The Story of Deep-Sea Vents	S	I	250+	A First Book	Franklin Watts
Four A's, The	Q	RF	250+	Wildcats	Wright Group/McGraw Hill
Four Cheerful Chipmunks	H	F	250+	Phonics and Friends	Hampton-Brown
Four Days in the Life of Zoe Coznaut	L	SF	250+	Foundations	Wright Group/McGraw Hill
Four Faces in Rock	M	I	300	Early Connections	Benchmark Education
*Four Friends and Other Stories, The	L	TL	250+	New Way Literature	Steck-Vaughn
Four Getters and Arf, The	G	F	123	Little Celebrations	Pearson Learning Group
Four Great Cities	W	I	250+	iOpeners	Pearson Learning Group
Four Great Inventions of Ancient China	W	I	2534	Independent Readers Social Studies	Houghton Mifflin
Four Ice Creams	C	RF	61	PM Starters	Rigby
*Four on the Shore	J	F	250+	Marshall, Edward	Puffin Books
Four Seasons, The	E	I	154	Early Connections	Benchmark Education
Four Seasons, The	C	RF	20	Learn to Read	Creative Teaching Press

* Collection of short stories

TITLE	LEVEL	GENRE	WORD COUNT	AUTHOR / SERIES	PUBLISHER / DISTRIBUTOR
Four Seasons, The	S	I	1820	Leveled Readers Science	Houghton Mifflin
Four Very Big Beans	E	RF	79	Instant Readers	Harcourt School Publishers
*Four-Legged Friends	N	TL	250+	Literacy 2000	Rigby
Fourth Grade Celebrity	Q	RF	250+	Giff, Patricia Reilly	Bantam
Fourth Grade Is a Jinx	P	RF	250+	McKenna, Colleen	Scholastic
Fourth Grade Wizards, The	Q	RF	250+	DeClements, Barthe	Penguin Group
Fourth Little Pig, The	K	TL	250+	Ready Set Read	Steck-Vaughn
Fourth of July, The	I	I	153	Rosen Real Readers	Rosen Publishing Group
Fourth of July, The	B	I	17	Windows on Literacy	National Geographic
Fourth of July, The	G	I	120	Fiesta Holiday Series	Pearson Learning Group
Fourth of July, The	F	I	153	Ready Readers	Pearson Learning Group
Fourth-Graders Don't Believe In Witches	P	F	250+	Fields, Terri	Scholastic
*Fox All Week	J	F	250+	Marshall, Edward	Puffin Books
Fox and Crow, The	H	TL	201	Alphakids	Sundance
*Fox and His Friends	J	F	250+	Marshall, Edward	Puffin Books
Fox and the Crow, The	J	F	240	Instant Readers	Harcourt School Publishers
Fox and The Crow, The	K	TL	250+	Ready Readers	Pearson Learning Group
Fox and the Crow, The	I	TL	250+	Aesop's Fables	Pearson Learning Group
Fox and the Crow, The	M	TL	614	Leveled Readers	Houghton Mifflin
Fox and the Crow, The	J	TL	250+	PM Plus Story Books	Rigby
Fox and the Goat, The	J	TL	365	Aesop's Fables	Pearson Learning Group
Fox and the Grapes, The	G	TL	60	Jumbled Tumbled Tales & Rhymes	Rigby
Fox and the Little Red Hen, The	L	TL	250+	Traditional Tales & More	Rigby
Fox and the Stork	H	F	149	New Way Blue	Steck-Vaughn
*Fox at School	J	F	250+	Marshall, Edward	Puffin Books
*Fox Be Nimble	J	F	250+	Marshall, James	Puffin Books
Fox Fables	J	F	250+	Sunshine	Wright Group/McGraw Hill
*Fox In Love	J	F	250+	Marshall, Edward	Puffin Books
Fox in the Frost	Q	RF	250+	Baglio, Ben M.	Scholastic
Fox Lives Here, A	I	I	160	Ready Readers	Pearson Learning Group
*Fox on Stage	J	F	250+	Marshall, James	Puffin Books
Fox on the Box, The	C	RF	36	Start to Read	School Zone
Fox on the Box, The	C	RF	36	Little Readers	Houghton Mifflin
Fox on the Job	J	F	250+	Marshall, James	Puffin Books
*Fox on Wheels	J	F	250+	Marshall, Edward	Puffin Books
*Fox Outfoxed	J	F	250+	Marshall, James	Puffin Books
Fox Steals Home, The	M	RF	250+	Christopher, Matt	Little, Brown & Co.
Fox Who Foxed, The	H	F	212	PM Story Books	Rigby
Fox, The	C	RF	24	Books for Young Learners	Richard C. Owen
Foxes	M	I	250+	PM Animal Facts: Gold	Rigby
Foxes and Their Dens	J	I	146	Pebble Plus	Capstone Press
Foxes: Clever Hunters	M	I	250+	The Wild World of Animals	Red Brick Learning
Fox's Box	D	I	72	Dominie Phonics Reader	Pearson Learning Group
Fractions: Making Fair Shares	M	I	250+	Exploring Math	Capstone Press
Fraidy Cats	J	F	250+	Krensky, Stephen	Scholastic
France	P	I	250+	Fact Finders	Capstone Press
France	O	I	250+	Dahl, Michael	Red Brick Learning
France	U	I	250+	Countries and Cultures	Red Brick Learning
Frances Hodgson Burnett: Beyond the Secret Garden	U	B	250+	Carpenter, Angelica Shirley; Shirley, Jean	Lerner Publishing
Frances the Fairy Dressmaker	L	F	736	Early Connections	Benchmark Education
Francie	W	RF	250+	English, Karen	Farrar, Straus and Giroux
Francis Scott Key and "The Star-Spangled Banner"	M	I	250+	Bookshop	Mondo

* Collection of short stories

TITLE	LEVEL	GENRE	WORD COUNT	AUTHOR / SERIES	PUBLISHER / DISTRIBUTOR
Francis Scott Key: Patriotic Poet	T	B	250+	Let Freedom Ring	Capstone Press
Francisco Goya	R	B	250+	Venezia, Mike	Children's Press
Francisco's Collection	H	RF	250+	Pacific Literacy	Pacific Learning
Frank and Sam's Summer at Aramoana	M	RF	250+	Voyages	SRA/McGraw Hill
Frank Lloyd Wright	O	B	346	Independent Readers Social Studies	Houghton Mifflin
Frank The Fish Gets His Wish	J	F	250+	Appleton-Smith, Laura	Flyleaf Publishing
Frankenstein Doesn't Plant Petunias	M	F	250+	Dadey, Debbie; Jones, Marcia Thornton	Scholastic
Frankenstein Doesn't Slam Hockey Pucks	M	F	250+	Dadey, Debbie; Jones, Marcia Thornton	Scholastic
Frankenstein Moved on to the 4th Floor	M	RF	250+	Levy, Elizabeth	Harper & Row
Franklin Chang-Diaz in Space	M	B	250	Vocabulary Readers	Houghton Mifflin
Franklin D. Roosevelt	N	B	223	Pebble Books	Capstone Press
Franklin D. Roosevelt	U	B	250+	Profiles of the Presidents	Compass Point Books
Franklin Delano Roosevelt	W	B	250+	Freedman, Russell	Clarion
Franklin Goes To School	K	F	250+	Bourgeois, Paulette; Clark, Brenda	Scholastic
Franklin Pierce	U	B	250+	Profiles of the Presidents	Compass Point Books
Franklin Plays the Game	K	F	250+	Bourgeois, Paulette; Clark, Brenda	Scholastic
Freak the Mighty	W	RF	250+	Philbrick, Rodman	Scholastic
Freaky Friday	R	F	250+	Rodgers, Mary	HarperTrophy
Freckle Juice	M	RF	250+	Blume, Judy	Bantam
Fred Fixes a Faucet	I	F	250+	Popcorn	Sundance
Fred Goes Shopping	I	F	250+	Popcorn	Sundance
Fred Joins the Band	I	F	250+	Popcorn	Sundance
Fred Said	D	RF	35	Sunshine	Wright Group/McGraw Hill
Freddie the Frog	D	F	132	First Start	Troll Associates
Freddie the Frog	G	F	250+	Supersonics	Rigby
Freddie's Spaghetti	F	RF	250+	Doyle, Charlotte	Random House
Freddy Frog's Note	H	F	253	Ready Readers	Pearson Learning Group
Freddy's Train Ride	K	RF	573	Pair-It Books	Steck-Vaughn
Frederick Douglass	P	B	250+	Early Biographies	Compass Point Books
Frederick Douglass	M	B	250+	First Biographies	Red Brick Learning
Frederick Douglass	P	B	250+	McLoone, Margo	Red Brick Learning
Frederick Douglass: Fights For Freedom	M	B	250+	Davidson, Margaret	Language for Learning Assoc.
Frederick Douglass: His Story Made History	U	B	2008	Leveled Readers	Houghton Mifflin
Frederick Douglass: The Last Days of Slavery	R	B	250+	Miller, William	Lee & Low Books Inc.
Fred's Big Lunch	I	F	250+	Popcorn	Sundance
Fred's Cold	I	F	250+	Popcorn	Sundance
Fred's Little Snack	I	F	250+	Popcorn	Sundance
Fred's Polka-Dot Sock	I	F	250+	Popcorn	Sundance
Fred's Weekend	I	F	250+	Popcorn	Sundance
Free Black Communities in the Time of Slavery	W	I	3120	Leveled Readers Social Studies	Houghton Mifflin
Free Fall	Q	I	250+	Basalaj, Kathy	Pacific Learning
Free Fall	WB	F	N/A	Wiesner, David	Lothrop, Lee & Shepard
Free to Fly	E	RF	96	Gibson, Kathleen	Continental Press
Freedom	L	RF	250+	Rigby Literacy	Rigby
Freedom Crossing	R	HF	250+	Clark, Margaret Goff	Scholastic
Freedom Fighters: The Massachusetts 54th Regiment	V	I	2052	Leveled Readers Social Studies	Houghton Mifflin
Freedom Quilt	M	HF	300	Books for Young Learners	Richard C. Owen

TITLE	LEVEL	GENRE	WORD COUNT	AUTHOR / SERIES	PUBLISHER / DISTRIBUTOR
Freedom Songs	T	HF	250+	Moore, Yvette	Language for Learning Assoc.
Freedom Train	T	B	250+	Sterling, Dorothy	Scholastic
Freeze Tag	G	RF	112	City Stories	Rigby
Freeze, Goldilocks!	M	F	250+	Pacific Literacy	Pacific Learning
Freight Trains	M	I	250+	Transportation	Compass Point Books
Fresh Air	O	RF	250+	Leveled Readers Language Support	Houghton Mifflin
Fresh Fall Leaves	E	RF	50	Franco, Betsy	Scholastic
Freshwater Giants: Hippopatamus, River Dolphins, and Manatees	S	I	250+	Perry, Phyllis J.	Franklin Watts
Freshwater Habitats	N	I	250+	Habitats of the World	Pearson Learning Group
Freshwater Pond, A	T	I	250+	Small Worlds	Crabtree
Freshwater Seas: The Great Lakes	S	I	1905	Independent Readers Social Studies	Houghton Mifflin
Frida Kahlo	R	B	250+	Venezia, Mike	Children's Press
Frida María: A Story of the Old Southwest	M	RF	250+	Lattimore, Deborah Nourse	Harcourt Trade
Friedrich	Z	HF	250+	Richter, Hans Peter	Puffin Books
Friend for Dragon, A	I	F	250+	Pilkey, Dave	Orchard Books
Friend for Kate, A	I	RF	250+	Cambridge Reading	Pearson Learning Group
Friend for Little White Rabbit	E	F	113	PM Story Books	Rigby
Friend for Max, A	G	RF	228	PM Plus Story Books	Rigby
Friend for Me, A	A	I	48	First Stories	Pacific Learning
Friend, A	G	RF	57	Literacy 2000	Rigby
Friendliness	L	I	250+	Character Education	Red Brick Learning
Friendly Crocodile, The	I	F	218	Hiris, Monica	Kaeden Books
Friendly Snowman	F	F	134	First Start	Troll Associates
Friendly Snowman	F	F	144	Joyce, William	Scholastic
Friends	D	I	60	Sun Sprouts	ETA/Cuisenaire
Friends	F	RF	57	Bookshop	Mondo
Friends	I	I	313	Early Connections	Benchmark Education
Friends	D	I	134	Fiesta Series	Pearson Learning Group
Friends	A	I	21	Leveled Readers Emergent	Houghton Mifflin
Friends	G	RF	250+	Well-Being Series	Pearson Learning Group
Friends	B	RF	36	Little Readers	Houghton Mifflin
Friends	G	RF	195	Reading Unlimited	Pearson Learning Group
Friends	B	I	21	Rigby Literacy	Rigby
Friends and Competitors	X	B	2333	Leveled Readers	Houghton Mifflin
Friends are Forever	K	F	585	Literacy 2000	Rigby
Friends Forever	K	RF	559	Leveled Readers	Houghton Mifflin
Friends Forever	I	TL	250+	Ready Readers	Pearson Learning Group
Friends Go Together	D	RF	36	Pair-It Books	Steck-Vaughn
Friends Online	I	RF	318	Leveled Readers	Houghton Mifflin
Friends or Enemies?	R	I	250+	Leveled Readers Language Support	Houghton Mifflin
Friends Share	C	I	34	Vocabulary Readers	Houghton Mifflin
Friends, The	T	RF	250+	Yumoto, Kazumi	Yearling
Friends, The	Z	RF	250+	Guy, Rosa	Bantam
Friendship and the Gold Cadillac, The	S	HF	250+	Taylor, Mildred	Bantam
Friendship Garden, The	K	RF	250+	Little Celebrations	Pearson Learning Group
Friendship in Action	O	I	250+	Literacy Tree	Rigby
Friendship Pact, The	Q	RF	250+	Pfeffer, Susan Beth	Scholastic
Friendship Salad	D	RF	42	Instant Readers	Harcourt School Publishers
Friendship, The	S	HF	250+	Taylor, Mildred	Puffin Books

* Collection of short stories

TITLE	LEVEL	GENRE	WORD COUNT	AUTHOR / SERIES	PUBLISHER / DISTRIBUTOR
Frightened	B	F	42	Story Box	Wright Group/McGraw Hill
Frightful's Mountain	U	RF	250+	George, Jean Craighead	Puffin Books
Frindle	R	RF	250+	Clements, Andrew	Aladdin
Frito Jumps In	D	RF	34	Step-By-Step Series	Pearson Learning Group
Frog and the Fly, The	D	F	33	Cat on the Mat	Oxford University Press
*Frog and Toad All Year	K	F	250+	Little Readers	Houghton Mifflin
*Frog and Toad Are Friends	K	F	250+	Lobel, Arnold	Harper & Row
Frog and Toad Together	K	F	1927	Lobel, Arnold	HarperCollins
Frog and Toad Together	K	F	250+	Little Readers	Houghton Mifflin
Frog Goes to Dinner	WB	F	N/A	Mayer, Mercer	Dial Books
Frog Has a Sticky Tongue, A	H	I	176	Windows on Literacy	National Geographic
Frog on His Own	WB	F	N/A	Mayer, Mercer	Dial Books
Frog or Toad?	I	I	241	Ready Readers	Pearson Learning Group
Frog Prince, The	K	TL	250+	Tarcov, Edith H.	Scholastic
Frog Prince, The	I	TL	572	Traditional Tales	Pearson Learning Group
Frog Prince, The	I	TL	250+	Jumbled Tumbled Tales & Rhymes	Rigby
Frog Princess, The	K	TL	206	Literacy 2000	Rigby
Frog Report, The	K	I	184	Rigby Focus	Rigby
Frog Who Thought He Was A Horse, The	L	F	250+	Literacy 2000	Rigby
Frog Who Would Be King, The	N	TL	250+	Walker, Kate	Mondo
Frog, The	M	I	250+	Crewe, Sabrina	Steck-Vaughn
Froggy Learns to Swim	J	F	250+	London, Jonathan	Scholastic
Froggy Tale, A	I	F	250+	Literacy 2000	Rigby
Frogs	K	I	311	Wonder World	Wright Group/McGraw Hill
Frogs	K	I	170	Windows on Literacy	National Geographic
Frogs	A	I	13	Twig	Wright Group/McGraw Hill
Frogs	G	I	100	Storyteller-First Snow	Wright Group/McGraw Hill
Frogs	D	I	28	Pebble Books	Capstone Press
Frogs	C	I	34	Pair-It Books	Steck-Vaughn
Frogs	N	I	250+	Nature's Friends	Compass Point Books
Frogs	C	F	36	Joy Readers	Pearson Learning Group
Frogs	O	I	250+	Holmes, Kevin J.	Red Brick Learning
Frogs	N	I	250+	Bookshop	Mondo
Frogs and Toads	P	I	250+	Crabapples	Crabtree
Frogs Can Jump	C	I	41	Book Bank	Wright Group/McGraw Hill
Frog's Day	E	F	101	Instant Readers	Harcourt School Publishers
Frog's Lunch	E	F	89	Lillegard, Dee	Scholastic
Frogs of Betts, The	N	RF	250+	SupaDoopers	Sundance
Frogs on a Log	D	F	75	Teacher's Choice Series	Pearson Learning Group
From a Tree	K	I	351	Rigby Focus	Rigby
From Acorn to Oak Tree	I	I	199	Welcome Books	Children's Press
From Apples to Applesauce	M	I	250+	First Facts	Capstone Press
From Axes to Zippers: Simple Machines	Q	I	250+	Navigators Social Studies Series	Benchmark Education
From Barbadoes to Brooklyn: The Story of Shirley Chisholm	S	B	2374	Leveled Readers Social Studies	Houghton Mifflin
From Blossom to Fruit	E	I	44	Pebble Books	Capstone Press
From Bud to Blossom	D	I	40	Pebble Books	Capstone Press
From Camel Cart to Canoe	L	I	250+	Sunshine	Wright Group/McGraw Hill
From Caves to Canvas	V	I	250+	Navigators Social Studies Series	Benchmark Education
From Cotton Plant to Cotton Shirt	L	I	250+	Schaefer, Lola M.	Benchmark Education
From Cow to Milk Carton	M	I	250+	Miles, Annie	Wright Group/McGraw Hill
From Egg to Robin	D	I	31	Canizares, Susan; Chessen, Betsey	Scholastic
From Farm to Store	J	I	181	Phonics Readers	Compass Point Books
From Field to Florist	I	I	142	Windows on Literacy	National Geographic

* Collection of short stories

TITLE	LEVEL	GENRE	WORD COUNT	AUTHOR / SERIES	PUBLISHER / DISTRIBUTOR
From Here to There	M	I	250+	Sails	Rigby
From Here to There	G	I	179	Yellow Umbrella Books	Red Brick Learning
From Here to There: Transportation Timelines	P	I	250+	Discovery World	Rigby
From Hive to Home	J	I	200	Windows on Literacy	National Geographic
From Idea to Law: The Legislative Process	S	I	1625	Leveled Readers Social Studies	Houghton Mifflin
From Maple Trees to Maple Syrup	M	I	250+	First Facts	Capstone Press
From Milk to Ice Cream	M	I	250+	First Facts	Capstone Press
From Oranges to Orange Juice	M	I	250+	First Facts	Capstone Press
From Paper Airplanes to Outer Space	O	B	250+	Simon, Seymour	Richard C. Owen
From Peanuts to Peanut Butter	M	I	250+	First Facts	Capstone Press
From Rocks to Sand: The Story of a Beach	J	I	224	Wonder World	Wright Group/McGraw Hill
From Seed to Plant	M	I	250+	Gibbons, Gail	Holiday House
From Seed to Pumpkin	F	I	148	Kottke, Jan	Scholastic
From Sheep to Sweater	B	I	28	Tarlow, Ellen	Scholastic
From Sky to Sea	H	I	40	Pacific Literacy	Pacific Learning
From the Air	E	I	107	Wonder World	Wright Group/McGraw Hill
From the Earth	J	I	186	Discovery Links	Newbridge
From the Farm to the Table	D	I	26	Rosen Real Readers	Rosen Publishing Group
From the Mixed-up Files of Mrs. Basil E. Frankweiler	S	RF	250+	Konigsburg, E. L.	Bantam
From the Mountain to the Ocean	K	I	99	Independent Readers Social Studies	Houghton Mifflin
From the Notebooks of Melanin Sun	Z	RF	250+	Woodson, Jacqueline	Scholastic
From the Skyscraper	E	I	82	Windows on Literacy	National Geographic
From Wheat to Bread	M	I	250+	First Facts	Capstone Press
Frost in the Night, A: A Girlhood on the Eve of the Third Reich	X	B	250+	Baer, Edith	Sunburst
Frown, The	K	RF	228	Read Alongs	Rigby
Frozen Man	T	I	250+	Getz, David	Henry Holt & Co.
Frozen Music	L	TL	432	Books for Young Learners	Richard C. Owen
Fruit	B	I	20	Rise & Shine	Hampton-Brown
Fruit	A	I	28	Leveled Readers Emergent	Houghton Mifflin
Fruit Facts	E	I	198	Rosen Real Readers	Rosen Publishing Group
Fruit Group, The	M	I	96	Pebble Books	Red Brick Learning
Fruit Pops	H	I	89	Windows on Literacy	National Geographic
Fruit Salad	B	I	24	Early Emergent	Pioneer Valley
Fruit Salad	D	I	18	Hoenecke, Karen	Kaeden Books
Fruit Salad	LB	I	15	Literacy 2000	Rigby
Fruit Salad	A	I	37	Sun Sprouts	ETA/Cuisenaire
Fruit Salad	LB	I	7	Windows on Literacy	National Geographic
Fruit Salad	D	I	37	Wonder World	Wright Group/McGraw Hill
Fruit Trees	B	I	24	Visions	Wright Group/McGraw Hill
Fudge	O	RF	250+	Graeber, Charlotte Towner	Simon & Schuster
Fudge-a-Mania	Q	RF	250+	Blume, Judy	Bantam
Full House: Club Stephanie	Q	RF	250+	Herman, Gail	Pocket Books
Full House; Stephanie	Q	RF	250+	Herman, Gail	Pocket Books
Fun	D	RF	45	Yannone, Deborah	Kaeden Books
Fun and Food to Eat	D	F	68	Leveled Readers Language Support	Houghton Mifflin
Fun and Games, Then and Now	C	I	42	Independent Readers Social Studies	Houghton Mifflin
Fun at Camp	H	RF	178	First Start	Troll Associates
Fun at School	C	RF	50	Foundations	Wright Group/McGraw Hill
Fun at the Amusement Park	G	RF	176	Frankford, Marilyn	Kaeden Books

* Collection of short stories

TITLE	LEVEL	GENRE	WORD COUNT	AUTHOR / SERIES	PUBLISHER / DISTRIBUTOR
Fun at the Beach	E	RF	88	Rigby Focus	Rigby
Fun Facts About Fossils	S	I	1129	Leveled Readers Science	Houghton Mifflin
Fun Food	C	I	29	Home Connection Collection	Rigby
Fun in the Mud	G	RF	182	Foundations	Wright Group/McGraw Hill
Fun in the Snow	H	RF	132	Bella and Rosie Series	Pioneer Valley
Fun in the Snow	D	I	76	Leveled Readers	Houghton Mifflin
Fun on the Slide	C	RF	37	Early Emergent	Pioneer Valley
Fun Place to Eat, A	E	RF	90	Ready Readers	Pearson Learning Group
Fun Things to Make and Do	I	I	250+	Discovery World	Rigby
Fun with Fingerprints	K	I	250+	How-To Series	Benchmark Education
Fun with Fingerprints	M	I	250+	Sokoloff, Myka-Lynne	Wright Group/McGraw Hill
Fun with Fractions	P	I	250+	Rosen Real Readers	Rosen Publishing Group
Fun with Friends	B	RF	18	Rise & Shine	Hampton-Brown
Fun With Friends	A	RF	21	Bookshop	Mondo
Fun with Hats	B	F	38	Bookshop	Mondo
Fun With Magnets	M	I	250+	Early Connections	Benchmark Education
Fun with Magnets	D	I	38	Rosen Real Readers	Rosen Publishing Group
Fun with Magnets	L	I	394	Rigby Focus	Rigby
Fun with Mo and Toots	C	F	41	Pacific Literacy	Pacific Learning
Fun With Plaster	H	I	150	Rigby Focus	Rigby
Fun With Shadows	M	I	250+	iOpeners	Pearson Learning Group
Fun with Simple Machines	C	RF	28	Tarlow, Ellen	Scholastic
Fun Zone	N	F	250+	Sails	Rigby
Fun, Fun, Fun	D	I	71	Leveled Readers	Houghton Mifflin
Funny Bananas: The Mystery in the Museum	N	RF	250+	McHargue, Georgess	Dell
Funny Bones	J	F	250+	Ahlberg, Allan & Janet	Viking
Funny Faces and Funny Places	D	I	45	Ready Readers	Pearson Learning Group
Funny Fish Story	E	F	152	Rookie Readers	Children's Press
Funny Man, A	E	F	244	Jensen, Patricia	Scholastic
Funny Old Man and the Funny Old Woman, The	M	F	250+	Bookshop	Mondo
Funny Talk and More	I	F	250+	Bookshop	Mondo
Funny, Funny Clown Face, The	M	F	250+	Sunshine	Wright Group/McGraw Hill
Fur	D	RF	32	Mark, Jan	Harper & Row
Fur Traders of New France	X	I	2576	Independent Readers Social Studies	Houghton Mifflin
Fur, Feathers, and Flippers: How Animals Live Where They Do	T	I	250+	Lauber, Patricia	Scholastic
Fur, Feathers, Scales, Skin	H	I	173	Discovery Links	Newbridge
Furry	B	I	19	Little Celebrations	Pearson Learning Group
Fussy Wolf	D	F	60	Sun Sprouts	ETA/Cuisenaire
*Future-Telling Lady and Other Stories, The	S	RF	250+	Berry, James	HarperTrophy
Fuzz and the Glass Eye	M	RF	250+	Literacy Tree	Rigby
Fuzz, Feathers, Fur	E	I	131	Twig	Wright Group/McGraw Hill
Gabby and the Christmas Tree	G	F	113	Developing Books, Set 2	Pioneer Valley
Gabby Is Hungry	C	RF	78	Emergent	Pioneer Valley
Gabby Runs Away	G	RF	223	Developing Books, Set 1	Pioneer Valley
Gabby Visits Buster	B	RF	39	Early Emergent	Pioneer Valley
Gadget War, The	N	RF	250+	Duffey, Betsy	Penguin Group
Gail & Me	L	RF	250+	Literacy 2000	Rigby
Gail Devers: A Runner's Dream	M	B	250+	Pair-It Books	Steck-Vaughn
Galapagos Giants	P	I	250+	Orbit Double Takes	Pacific Learning
Galapagos Islands, The	R	I	250+	Rosen Real Readers	Rosen Publishing Group
Galaxies	N	I	250+	A True Book	Children's Press
Galaxies	T	I	250+	Simon, Seymour	Mulberry Books

* Collection of short stories

TITLE	LEVEL	GENRE	WORD COUNT	AUTHOR / SERIES	PUBLISHER / DISTRIBUTOR
Galileo Galilee, Astronomer	Q	B	455	Independent Readers Science	Houghton Mifflin
Galileo, Messenger of Modern Science	Z	B	3428	Leveled Readers	Houghton Mifflin
Galileo: Man of Science	R	B	250+	Rosen Real Readers	Rosen Publishing Group
Gallo and Zorro	J	F	369	Literacy 2000	Rigby
Game for Jamie, A	M	RF	572	Sunshine	Wright Group/McGraw Hill
Games	A	F	28	KinderReaders	Rigby
Games	C	RF	69	Berger, Samantha; Moreton, Daniel	Scholastic
Games	B	I	28	Berger, Samantha; Moreton, Daniel	Scholastic
Games from Long Ago	T	I	250+	Historic Communities	Crabtree
Games We Play	J	I	250+	PM Plus Nonfiction	Rigby
Gampy's Lamps	P	RF	1296	Leveled Readers	Houghton Mifflin
Gannets	L	I	250+	Sunshine	Wright Group/McGraw Hill
Garage Sale, The	D	RF	44	Harry's Math Books	Outside the Box
Garbage	C	I	51	Wonder World	Wright Group/McGraw Hill
Garbage Collectors	M	I	250+	Deedrick, Tami	Red Brick Learning
Garden Birthday	LB	F	15	Instant Readers	Harcourt School Publishers
Garden Colors	B	F	15	Pair-It Books	Steck-Vaughn
Garden in Your Bedroom, A	O	I	250+	Sunshine	Wright Group/McGraw Hill
Garden of Eden Motel, The	W	RF	250+	Hamilton, Morse	William Morrow
Garden on Green Street, The	L	RF	250+	Meish Goldish	Scholastic
Garden Tools	J	I	165	Spyglass Books	Compass Point Books
Garden, A	A	I	40	Foundations	Wright Group/McGraw Hill
Garden, The	LB	I	14	Instant Readers	Harcourt School Publishers
Garden, The	B	RF	63	Leveled Readers Emergent	Houghton Mifflin
Garden, The	G	RF	21	Hoenecke, Karen	Kaeden Books
Gardening	D	RF	77	Foundations	Wright Group/McGraw Hill
Gardens on Green Street, The	I	RF	174	TOTTS	Tott Publications
Garfield and the Beast in the Basement	Q	F	250+	Davis, Jim	Troll Associates
Garfield and the Mysterious Mummy	Q	F	250+	Davis, Jim	Troll Associates
Gargoyles Don't Drive School Buses	M	F	250+	Dadey, Debbie; Jones, Marcia Thornton	Scholastic
Gargoyles On Guard	K	I	269	Books for Young Learners	Richard C. Owen
Gary Soto	Y	B	2464	Leveled Readers	Houghton Mifflin
Gasp!	L	F	250+	Bookshop	Mondo
*Gaston the Giant	K	F	331	New Way Orange	Steck-Vaughn
Gathering Blue	X	F	250+	Lowry, Lois	Houghton Mifflin
Gathering of Days, A: A New England Girl's Journal, 1830-32	U	HF	250+	Blos, Joan	Aladdin
*Gathering of Flowers, A	Z	RF	250+	Thomas, Joyce Carol	HarperTrophy
Gathering, The	V	F	250+	Hamilton, Virginia	OSI
Gathering: A Northwoods Counting Book	Q	I	250+	Bowen, Betsy	Houghton Mifflin
Gator Girls, The	L	F	250+	Calmenson, Stephanie & Cole	Beech Tree Books
Gecko's Story	F	F	61	Books for Young Learners	Richard C. Owen
Geese on the Farm	I	I	69	On the Farm	Red Brick Learning
General Butterfingers	O	RF	250+	Gardiner, John Reynolds	Puffin Books
Genghis Khan: A Dog Star is Born	L	RF	250+	Sharmat, Marjorie Weinman	Random House
Genies Don't Ride Bicycles	M	F	250+	Dadey, Debbie; Jones, Marcia Thornton	Scholastic
Gentle Annie: The True Story of a Civil War Nurse	R	I	250+	Shura, Mary Frances	Scholastic
Gentlehands	Z	RF	250+	Kerr, M. E.	HarperTrophy

* Collection of short stories

TITLE	LEVEL	GENRE	WORD COUNT	AUTHOR / SERIES	PUBLISHER / DISTRIBUTOR
Gentleman Outlaw and Me - Eli, The: A Story of the Old West	T	HF	250+	Hahn, Mary Downing	Avon Camelot
Geoffrey the Dinosaur	D	F	36	Sunshine	Wright Group/McGraw Hill
Geographic Information Systems: Locating Ourselves	T	I	1493	Leveled Readers Social Studies	Houghton Mifflin
Geography of an Empire: Ancient Rome	X	I	2392	Independent Readers Social Studies	Houghton Mifflin
Geography of War, The: The Battle of Salamis	Y	I	2877	Independent Readers Social Studies	Houghton Mifflin
George and Martha	L	F	250+	Marshall, James	Houghton Mifflin
George and Martha Back in Town	L	F	250+	Marshall, James	Houghton Mifflin
George and Martha Encore	L	F	250+	Marshall, James	Houghton Mifflin
George and Martha One Fine Day	L	F	250+	Marshall, James	Houghton Mifflin
George and Martha Rise and Shine	L	F	250+	Marshall, James	Houghton Mifflin
George and Martha Round and Round	L	F	250+	Marshall, James	Houghton Mifflin
George and the Whopper	L	F	250+	Rigby Literacy	Rigby
George Armstrong Custer	P	B	250+	Early Biographies	Compass Point Books
George at the Zoo	H	F	250+	Voyages	SRA/McGraw Hill
George Catlin, Frontier Painter	Y	B	3371	Leveled Readers	Houghton Mifflin
George H. W. Bush	U	B	250+	Profiles of the Presidents	Compass Point Books
George Handel	R	B	250+	Venezia, Mike	Children's Press
George Rogers Clark and the American Revolution in the Midwest	V	B	2534	Leveled Readers Social Studies	Houghton Mifflin
George Shrinks	H	F	114	Joyce, William	Scholastic
George the Drummer Boy	K	HF	250+	Benchley, Nathaniel	HarperTrophy
George W. Bush	U	B	250+	Profiles of the Presidents	Compass Point Books
George Washington	L	B	270	Pebble Books	Capstone Press
George Washington	E	B	69	Independent Readers Social Studies	Houghton Mifflin
George Washington	O	B	250+	Early Biographies	Compass Point Books
George Washington	U	B	250+	Profiles of the Presidents	Compass Point Books
George Washington Carver	M	B	521	Leveled Readers	Houghton Mifflin
George Washington Carver	P	B	250+	McLoone, Margo	Red Brick Learning
George Washington Carver	M	B	250+	Biography	Benchmark Education
George Washington Carver	N	B	224	Pebble Books	Capstone Press
George Washington Carver: Scientist and Teacher	O	B	250+	Greene, Carol	Children's Press
George Washington Elected: How America's First President Was Chosen	S	I	250+	Headlines from History	Rosen Publishing Group
George Washington: A Picture Book Biography	R	B	250+	Giblin, James Cross	Scholastic
George Washington: Farmer, Soldier, President	M	B	250+	Biographies	Picture Window Books
George Washington: First President of the U.S.	N	B	250+	Rookie Biographies	Children's Press
George Washington: Our First President	M	B	200	Rosen Real Readers	Rosen Publishing Group
George Washington: The Man Who Would Not Be King	U	B	250+	Krensky, Stephen	Scholastic
George Washington: Young Leader	O	B	250+	Childhood of Famous Americans	Aladdin
George Washington: Young Leader	R	B	250+	Santrey, Laurence	Troll Associates
George Washington's Breakfast	P	B	250+	Fritz, Jean	Putnam & Grosset
George Washington's Mother	M	B	250+	Fritz, Jean	Scholastic
George Washington's Socks	T	B	250+	Woodruff, Elvira	Language for Learning Assoc.
George's Marvelous Medicine	P	F	250+	Dahl, Roald	Penguin Group
George's Show and Tell	E	RF	133	Early Emergent	Pioneer Valley
George's Story	G	RF	133	Developing Books	Pioneer Valley

TITLE	LEVEL	GENRE	WORD COUNT	AUTHOR / SERIES	PUBLISHER / DISTRIBUTOR
Georgia	T	I	250+	Sea to Shining Sea	Children's Press
Georgia	S	I	250+	Land of Liberty	Red Brick Learning
Georgia	T	I	250+	LaDoux, Rita C.	Lerner Publishing
Georgia	Q	I	250+	One Nation	Capstone Press
Georgia	R	I	250+	This Land Is Your Land	Compass Point Books
Georgia O'Keeffe	R	B	250+	Venezia, Mike	Children's Press
Georgia O'Keeffe	M	B	250+	Lowery, Linda	Carolrhoda Books
Gerald R. Ford	U	B	250+	Profiles of the Presidents	Compass Point Books
Geraldine's Big Snow	I	RF	250+	Keller, Holly	Scholastic
Gerard Giraffe: Private Investigator	M	F	250+	Foundations	Wright Group/McGraw Hill
Gerbil Genius	O	RF	250+	Baglio, Ben M.	Scholastic
Gerbilitis	P	RF	250+	Spinner, Stephanie; Weiss, Ellen	HarperTrophy
Gerbilitis	P	RF	250+	Soar To Success	Houghton Mifflin
Germany	P	I	250+	Fact Finders	Capstone Press
Germany	Q	I	250+	First Reports	Compass Point Books
Germany	O	I	250+	Dahl, Michael	Red Brick Learning
Germs	L	I	250+	Twig	Wright Group/McGraw Hill
Germs! Germs! Germs!	L	F	250+	Katz, Bobbi	Scholastic
Geronimo	U	B	1903	Leveled Readers Social Studies	Houghton Mifflin
Gertie's Green Thumb	O	F	250+	Dexter, Catherine	Dell
Get A Grip, Pip!	P	RF	250+	Literacy 2000	Rigby
Get Lost Becka!	E	RF	102	Start to Read	School Zone
Get Lost!	F	RF	219	Foundations	Wright Group/McGraw Hill
Get on Board: The Story of the Underground Railroad	V	I	250+	Haskins, Jim	Scholastic
Get On Out of Here, Philip Hall	Y	RF	250+	Greene, Bette	Puffin Books
Get Ready to Race	H	F	98	Instant Readers	Harcourt School Publishers
Get Set and Go	J	F	250+	Real Reading	Steck-Vaughn
Get the Ball, Slim	E	RF	94	Real Kids Readers	Millbrook Press
Get the Message	J	I	110	iOpeners	Pearson Learning Group
Getting Around	F	I	182	Chessen, Betsey; Moreton, Daniel	Scholastic
Getting Around	H	I	211	Momentum Literacy Program	Troll Associates
Getting Cold! Getting Hot!	K	RF	753	Sunshine	Wright Group/McGraw Hill
Getting Dressed	LB	RF	16	Sunshine	Wright Group/McGraw Hill
Getting Dressed	B	RF	40	Carousel Earlybirds	Pearson Learning Group
Getting Fit	C	I	15	Wonder World	Wright Group/McGraw Hill
Getting Glasses	G	I	82	Wonder World	Wright Group/McGraw Hill
Getting Home	A	I	24	Windows on Literacy	National Geographic
Getting Lincoln's Goat	V	RF	250+	Goldman, E. M.	Bantam
Getting Near to Baby	V	RF	250+	Couloumbis, Audrey	Penguin Group
Getting Ready	B	I	29	Little Books for Early Readers	University of Maine
Getting Ready	WB	I	N/A	Windows on Literacy	National Geographic
Getting Ready for School	E	RF	109	Foundations	Wright Group/McGraw Hill
Getting Ready for School	C	I	109	Little Red Readers	Sundance
Getting Ready for the Ball	C	F	27	Literacy 2000	Rigby
Getting Rid of Katherine	Q	RF	250+	Wright, Betty Ren	Troll Associates
Getting the Mail	G	RF	213	Voyages	SRA/McGraw Hill
Getting There	B	I	36	Wonder World	Wright Group/McGraw Hill
Getting To Know Sharks	K	I	379	Little Books	Sadlier-Oxford
Gettysburg Address, The	V	I	250+	Cornerstones of Freedom	Children's Press
Gettysburg Address, The	T	I	250+	Lincoln, Abraham	Houghton Mifflin
Get-Up Machine, The	I	F	115	Sunshine	Wright Group/McGraw Hill
Geysers: When Earth Roars	U	I	250+	A First Book	Franklin Watts
Ghana	O	I	250+	Davis, Lucile	Red Brick Learning

* Collection of short stories

TITLE	LEVEL	GENRE	WORD COUNT	AUTHOR / SERIES	PUBLISHER / DISTRIBUTOR
Ghana: Ancient Empire	Y	I	2070	Leveled Readers Social Studies	Houghton Mifflin
Ghost and the Sausage, The	I	F	250+	Story Box	Wright Group/McGraw Hill
Ghost Belonged to Me, The	V	F	250+	Peck, Richard	Penguin Group
Ghost Cadet	T	SF	250+	Alphin, Elaine Marie	Language for Learning Assoc.
Ghost Canoe	X	HF	250+	Hobbs, Will	Avon Books
Ghost Comes Calling, The	Q	F	250+	Wright, Betty	Scholastic
Ghost Dog	M	F	250+	Allen, Eleanor	Scholastic
Ghost Fox, The	P	F	250+	Yep, Laurence	Scholastic
Ghost in Tent 19, The	M	F	250+	O'Connor, Jim	Random House
Ghost in the Tokaido Inn, The	U	F	250+	Hoobler, Dorothy & Thomas	Penguin Group
Ghost Named Wanda, A	N	F	250+	The Zack Files	Grosset & Dunlap
Ghost of Popcorn Hill, The	N	F	250+	Wright, Betty Ren	Scholastic
Ghost On Saturday Night, The	Q	F	250+	Fleischman, Sid	Beech Tree Books
Ghost School	M	F	250+	Clifford, Eth	Scholastic
Ghost Town at Sundown	M	F	250+	Osborne, Mary Pope	Random House
Ghost Town Treasure	M	RF	250+	Bulla, Clyde Robert	Penguin Group
Ghost Tree, The	K	RF	250+	Voyages	SRA/McGraw Hill
Ghost Twins: Mystery at Kickingbird Lake	P	F	250+	Regan, Diane Curtis	Scholastic
Ghost, The	A	RF	26	Story Box	Wright Group/McGraw Hill
Ghostmobile, The	S	F	250+	Tapp, Kathy Kennedy	Scholastic
Ghosts	X	I	250+	The Unexplained	Capstone Press
Ghosts Beneath Our Feet	R	F	250+	Wright, Betty Ren	Scholastic
Ghosts Don't Eat Potato Chips	M	F	250+	Dadey, Debbie; Jones, Marcia Thornton	Scholastic
Ghosts of Flight 401	Z	I	250+	Innes, Brian	Steck-Vaughn
Ghosts' Secret, The	D	F	79	TOTTS	Tott Publications
*Ghosts!: Ghostly Tales from Folklore	J	TL	250+	Schwartz, Alvin	HarperTrophy
Ghouls Don't Scoop Ice Cream	M	F	250+	Dadey, Debbie; Jones, Marcia Thornton	Scholastic
Giant and the Boy, The	C	F	44	Sunshine	Wright Group/McGraw Hill
Giant and the Frippit, The	H	F	250+	Rigby Literacy	Rigby
Giant Balloons	J	I	185	Rigby Focus	Rigby
Giant Bugs Were Real!	I	I	54	Seedlings	Continental Press
Giant Games	K	F	250+	Phonics and Friends	Hampton-Brown
Giant Gingerbread Man, The	G	TL	248	Alphakids	Sundance
Giant Grass	J	I	250+	Story Steps	Rigby
Giant Humanlike Beasts	Z	I	250+	Innes, Brian	Steck-Vaughn
Giant in the Bed, The	H	F	253	New Way Green	Steck-Vaughn
Giant in the Forest, A	J	F	250+	Reading Unlimited	Pearson Learning Group
Giant Jack's Boots	M	F	420	Book Bank	Wright Group/McGraw Hill
Giant Jam Sandwich, The	K	F	250+	Vernon Lord, John	Houghton Mifflin
Giant Jumperee, The: A Play	J	F	250+	Rigby Literacy	Rigby
Giant Pandas	U	I	250+	The Untamed World	Steck-Vaughn
Giant Pandas	G	I	72	Pebble Books	Capstone Press
Giant Pandas: Gifts from China	I	I	250+	Rookie Read-About Science	Children's Press
Giant Rock of Yosemite, The: A Sierra Miwok Tale	Q	F	1028	Leveled Readers	Houghton Mifflin
Giant Seeds, The	K	RF	507	PM Plus Story Books	Rigby
Giant -Sized Day, A	I	F	245	Ready Readers	Pearson Learning Group
*Giant Soup	J	F	419	Pacific Literacy	Pacific Learning
Giant, The	M	F	250+	Voyages	SRA/McGraw Hill
Giant, The	LB	F	20	Joy Readers	Pearson Learning Group
Giants	F	F	52	Blaxland, Wendy	Scholastic

* Collection of short stories

TITLE	LEVEL	GENRE	WORD COUNT	AUTHOR / SERIES	PUBLISHER / DISTRIBUTOR
Giant's Boy, The	H	F	89	Sunshine	Wright Group/McGraw Hill
Giant's Breakfast, The	B	F	42	Literacy 2000	Rigby
Giant's Cake	M	F	250+	Learning Media	Mondo
Giant's Cake, The	H	F	162	Literacy 2000	Rigby
Giant's Day Out, The	B	F	26	Smart Starts	Rigby
Giants Don't Go Snowboarding	M	F	250+	Dadey, Debbie; Jones, Marcia Thornton	Scholastic
Giant's Job, The	H	F	180	Stewart, Josie; Salem, Lynn	Continental Press
Giant's Pizza, The	C	RF	28	Joy Readers	Pearson Learning Group
Giant's Rice, The	C	F	28	Joy Readers	Pearson Learning Group
Giant's Stew, The	I	F	259	Sunshine	Wright Group/McGraw Hill
Giants, Monsters & Mythical Beasts	O	I	250+	Literacy 2000	Rigby
Giant-Size Hamburger, A	C	F	38	Wonder World	Wright Group/McGraw Hill
Gib Rides Home	V	RF	250+	Snyder, Zilpha Keatley	Bantam
Gibbon Island	K	RF	444	PM Plus Story Books	Rigby
Giddy Up	C	RF	49	Cat on the Mat	Oxford University Press
Giddyoocha	I	F	297	Story Box	Wright Group/McGraw Hill
Gift for Mama, A	N	RF	250+	Hautzig, Esther	Penguin Group
Gift for Yoshi, A	J	RF	282	Leveled Readers	Houghton Mifflin
*Gift From Zeus, A: Sixteen Favorite Myths	X	TL	250+	Steig, Jeanne	HarperCollins
Gift of Crayons, A	G	RF	226	Leveled Readers Language Support	Houghton Mifflin
Gift of Light, The: A Japanese Myth	Y	TL	2018	Leveled Readers	Houghton Mifflin
Gift of the Girl Who Couldn't Hear, The	U	RF	250+	Shreve, Susan	Beech Tree Books
Gift of the Pirate Queen, The	S	RF	250+	Giff, Patricia Reilly	Yearling
Gift to Share, A	K	RF	544	Pair-It Books	Steck-Vaughn
Gift, The	N	TL	250+	Story Vines	Wright Group/McGraw Hill
Gift, The	WB	RF	N/A	Prater, J.	Wright Group/McGraw Hill
Gift-Giver, The	S	RF	250+	Hansen, Joyce	Houghton Mifflin
Gifts for Dad	H	RF	178	Urmston, Kathleen; Evans, Karen	Kaeden Books
Gifts for Everyone	B	F	35	Rigby Literacy	Rigby
Gifts of the Dineh	Q	RF	1301	Leveled Readers	Houghton Mifflin
Gifts to Make	K	I	509	Pair-It Books	Steck-Vaughn
Gifts, The	B	RF	34	Story Box	Wright Group/McGraw Hill
*Gigantic Ants and Other Cases, The	O	RF	250+	Simon, Seymour	Avon
Gigantic Bell, The	K	TL	250+	PM Plus Story Books	Rigby
Gigantic George	H	F	224	Little Celebrations	Pearson Learning Group
Giggle Box, The	E	F	176	Story Box	Wright Group/McGraw Hill
Gillian's Nines	C	RF	29	Harry's Math Books	Outside the Box
Ginger	I	RF	232	Little Readers	Houghton Mifflin
Ginger	D	RF	43	Parker, Ant	Mondo
Ginger Brown: The Nobody Boy	L	RF	250+	Wyeth, Sharon Dennis	Random House
Ginger Brown: Too Many Houses	L	RF	250+	Wyeth, Sharon Dennis	Random House
Ginger Pye	U	RF	250+	Estes, Eleanor	Scholastic
Gingerbread Boy	F	TL	137	New Way Red	Steck-Vaughn
Gingerbread Boy, The	G	TL	250+	Ziefert, Harriet	Puffin Books
Gingerbread Boy, The	L	TL	1097	Galdone, Paul	Clarion
Gingerbread Man	I	TL	250+	Hunia, Fran	Ladybird Books
Gingerbread Man, The	E	F	79	Instant Readers	Harcourt School Publishers
Gingerbread Man, The	G	TL	139	Cambridge Reading	Pearson Learning Group
Gingerbread Man, The	I	TL	250+	Tiger Cub	Peguis
Gingerbread Man, The	F	TL	180	Little Readers	Houghton Mifflin
Gingerbread Man, The	H	TL	197	Sunshine	Wright Group/McGraw Hill
Gingerbread Man, The	I	TL	180	Rose, Rita	Scholastic

* Collection of short stories

TITLE	LEVEL	GENRE	WORD COUNT	AUTHOR / SERIES	PUBLISHER / DISTRIBUTOR
Gingerbread Man, The	J	TL	535	Traditional Tales & More	Rigby
Gingerbread Man, The	I	TL	544	Traditional Tales	Pearson Learning Group
Gingerbread Man, The	H	TL	250+	Literacy 2000	Rigby
Gingerbread Men, The	D	I	37	Sunshine	Wright Group/McGraw Hill
Ginger's War	N	HF	250+	Daniel, Lea	Wright Group/McGraw Hill
Giraffe and the Pelly and Me, The	P	F	250+	Dahl, Roald	Penguin Group
Giraffe Made Her Laugh, The	E	F	70	Learn to Read	Creative Teaching Press
Giraffe, The	P	I	250+	Animal Close-Ups	Charlesbridge
Giraffes	N	I	250+	Meadows, Graham; Vial, Claire	Pearson Learning Group
Giraffes	P	I	250+	Crabapples	Crabtree
Giraffes	O	I	250+	Reeder, Tracey	Wright Group/McGraw Hill
Giraffe's Sad Tale (With a Happy Ending)	H	F	250+	Alma Flor Ada	Hampton-Brown
Girl Called Al, A	P	RF	250+	Greene, Constance C.	Puffin Books
Girl Called Boy, A	U	F	250+	Hurmence, Belinda	Clarion
Girl From Yamhill, A	W	B	250+	Cleary, Beverly	Bantam
Girl in the Golden Bower, The	Q	TL	250+	Yolen, Jane	Little, Brown & Co.
Girl In the Window, The	U	RF	250+	Yeo, Wilma	Scholastic
Girl Named Disaster, A	X	RF	250+	Farmer, Nancy	Penguin Group
Girl Named Helen Keller, A	K	B	250+	Lundell, Margo	Scholastic
Girl Who Chased Away Sorrow, The: The Diary of Sarah Nita, a Navajo Girl	T	HF	250+	Turner, Ann	Scholastic
Girl Who Climbed to the Moon, The	L	F	604	Sunshine	Wright Group/McGraw Hill
Girl Who Knew it All, The	Q	RF	250+	Giff, Patricia Reilly	Bantam
Girl Who Loved Meerkats, The	M	F	250+	World Quest Adventures	World Quest Learning
Girl Who Loved the Wind, The	Q	TL	250+	Yolen, Jane	HarperTrophy
*Girl Who Married the Moon, The: Tales from Native North America	U	TL	250+	Bruchac, Joseph; Ross, Gayle	Troll Associates
Girl Who Owned a City, The	X	F	250+	Nelson, O. T.	Laurel-Leaf Books
Girl With the Silver Eyes, The	U	F	250+	Roberts, Willo Davis	Scholastic
Girls of Many Lands	W	HF	250+	Croutier, Alev Lytle	Pleasant Company
*Girls to the Rescue, Book #3	Q	RF	250+	Lansky, Bruce	Meadowbrook Press
*Girls to the Rescue, Book #4	Q	RF	250+	Lansky, Bruce	Meadowbrook Press
*Girls to the Rescue, Book #6	Q	RF	250+	Lansky, Bruce	Meadowbrook Press
Girl-Son, The	R	HF	250+	Neuberger, Anne E.	Carolrhoda Books
Give Me a Hug	B	RF	28	Sunshine	Wright Group/McGraw Hill
Giver, The	Y	F	250+	Lowry, Lois	Bantam
Gizmos' Party, The	J	F	250+	Rigby Literacy	Rigby
Gizmos' Trip, The	J	F	250+	Rigby Literacy	Rigby
Glaciers	V	I	2117	Leveled Readers Social Studies	Houghton Mifflin
Glaciers	T	I	250+	Gallant, Roy A.	Franklin Watts
Gladly, Here I Come	R	RF	250+	Cowley, Joy	Wright Group/McGraw Hill
Gladys and Max Love Bob	M	RF	459	Book Bank	Wright Group/McGraw Hill
Glass	M	I	250+	First Facts	Capstone Press
Glass	G	I	112	Rigby Focus	Rigby
Glass Café, The	Z	RF	250+	Paulsen, Gary	Random House
Glass Slipper for Rosie, A	N	RF	250+	Giff, Patricia Reilly	Penguin Group
Glasses	D	RF	19	Visions	Wright Group/McGraw Hill
Glenda	P	F	250+	Udry, Janice May	HarperTrophy
Glenda Glinka: Witch-At-Large	P	F	250+	Udry, Janice May	HarperTrophy
Glenda the Lion	E	F	88	Ready Readers	Pearson Learning Group
Glitter Trouble	C	RF	32	Learn to Read	Creative Teaching Press
Global Alert	Q	I	250+	Navigators Social Studies Series	Benchmark Education
Global Energy	Y	I	2359	Independent Readers Science	Houghton Mifflin

* Collection of short stories

TITLE	LEVEL	GENRE	WORD COUNT	AUTHOR / SERIES	PUBLISHER / DISTRIBUTOR
Glorious Days, Dreadful Days: The Battle of Bunker Hill	R	I	250+	Kirby, Philippa	Steck-Vaughn
Glorious Flight, The: Across the Channel with Louis Blériot	O	B	250+	Provensen, Alice & Martin	Puffin Books
Glory Field, The	X	HF	250+	Myers, Walter Dean	Scholastic
Glory Girl, The	S	RF	250+	Byars, Betsy	Penguin Group
Gloves	E	RF	103	Story Box	Wright Group/McGraw Hill
Glow from Lighthouse Cove, The	S	RF	2501	Leveled Readers	Houghton Mifflin
Gluepots	K	RF	205	Book Bank	Wright Group/McGraw Hill
Glumly	Q	F	250+	Literacy 2000	Rigby
Gnu Named Blue, A	K	F	250+	Phonics and Friends	Hampton-Brown
Go and Hush the Baby	K	RF	250+	Byars, Betsy	Viking
Go Annie, Go!	K	RF	250+	Pacific Literacy	Pacific Learning
Go Away Dog	I	RF	250+	Nodset, Joan	HarperCollins
Go Away, Tooth Decay	T	I	250+	Leveled Readers Language Support	Houghton Mifflin
Go Back to Sleep	E	RF	74	Literacy 2000	Rigby
Go Dog Go	E	F	250+	Eastman, Philip D.	Random House
Go Free or Die: A Story About Harriet Tubman	R	B	250+	Ferris, Jeri	Carolrhoda Books
Go Sea It!	A	I	16	Little Celebrations	Pearson Learning Group
Go Teddy!	B	I	27	Windows on Literacy	National Geographic
Go to Bed!	D	RF	45	Joy Readers	Pearson Learning Group
Go!	D	RF	44	Little Readers	Houghton Mifflin
Go, Go, Go	A	I	23	Little Books for Early Readers	University of Maine
Go, Go, Go	A	RF	17	Story Box	Wright Group/McGraw Hill
Goal!	H	RF	232	Lighthouse	Rigby
Goat in the Chile Patch, The	H	TL	250+	Kratky, Lada Josefa	Hampton-Brown
Goat in the Garden	Q	RF	250+	Baglio, Ben M.	Scholastic
*Goat Monster and Other Stories, The	L	F	250+	New Way Literature	Steck-Vaughn
Goat Who Wouldn't Come Home, The	G	F	184	Seedlings	Continental Press
Goat, The	C	RF	17	KinderReaders	Rigby
Goats	L	I	250+	PM Animal Facts: Purple	Rigby
Goats in the Turnip Field, The	I	TL	250+	PM Plus Story Books	Rigby
Goats on the Farm	I	I	67	Pebble Books	Red Brick Learning
Gobble! Gobble! Munch!	F	F	64	Rhythm 'N' Rhyme Readers	Pearson Learning Group
Gobble, Gobble, Gone	D	F	58	Little Celebrations	Pearson Learning Group
Goblins Don't Play Video Games	M	RF	250+	Dadey, Debbie; Jones, Marcia Thornton	Scholastic
Go-cart Day	K	RF	165	City Kids	Rigby
Go-cart Team, The	O	I	250+	PM Nonfiction-Emerald	Rigby
Go-cart, The	E	RF	47	Oxford Reading Tree	Oxford University Press
Go-carts, The	B	RF	46	PM Starters	Rigby
Godzilla Ate My Homework	O	F	250+	Jones, Marcia	Scholastic
Goggly Gookers	H	F	100	Story Basket	Wright Group/McGraw Hill
Goha and His Donkey	I	F	114	Books for Young Learners	Richard C. Owen
Going Back to Harlem	P	I	522	Vocabulary Readers	Houghton Mifflin
Going Fishing	G	RF	117	Cambridge Reading	Pearson Learning Group
Going Fishing	F	F	240	Leveled Readers	Houghton Mifflin
Going Fishing	E	RF	26	Literacy 2000	Rigby
Going Fishing	I	RF	250+	Momentum Literacy Program	Troll Associates
Going Fishing	B	F	22	Ready Readers	Pearson Learning Group
Going Fishing	C	RF	30	Visions	Wright Group/McGraw Hill
Going Fishing	F	RF	26	Voyages	SRA/McGraw Hill
Going Fishing	I	I	161	Windows on Literacy	National Geographic

TITLE	LEVEL	GENRE	WORD COUNT	AUTHOR / SERIES	PUBLISHER / DISTRIBUTOR
Going for a Ride	B	I	67	Leveled Readers Emergent	Houghton Mifflin
Going for a Ride	C	RF	52	Early Emergent	Pioneer Valley
Going for a Ride	B	RF	40	Little Books for Early Readers	University of Maine
Going for a Walk	F	RF	82	DeRegniers, Beatrice Schenk	Harper & Row
Going for Gold!	P	B	250+	Eyewitness Readers	DK Publishing
Going Here and There	D	RF	124	Early Connections	Benchmark Education
Going Home	T	RF	250+	Mohr, Nicholas	Penguin Group
Going in the Car	B	RF	24	Sunshine	Wright Group/McGraw Hill
Going Lobstering	O	I	250+	Pallotta, Jerry; Bolster, Rob	Charlesbridge
Going on a Field Trip	I	RF	288	Visions	Wright Group/McGraw Hill
Going on Vacation	A	I	40	PM Plus Starters	Rigby
Going Out	B	RF	48	PM Plus Starters	Rigby
Going Out	A	F	42	KinderReaders	Rigby
Going Out	D	RF	94	Foundations	Wright Group/McGraw Hill
Going Outside	M	F	118	Voyages	SRA/McGraw Hill
Going Places	B	F	49	First Stories	Pacific Learning
Going Places	K	I	410	Early Connections	Benchmark Education
Going Places	C	I	32	Rosen Real Readers	Rosen Publishing Group
Going Shopping	F	RF	99	Leveled Readers Social Studies	Houghton Mifflin
Going Shopping	B	RF	31	Rigby Literacy	Rigby
Going Shopping	F	I	112	Bookshop	Mondo
Going Shopping	D	RF	92	Carousel Readers	Pearson Learning Group
Going Solo	T	I	250+	iOpeners	Pearson Learning Group
Going Solo	T	B	250+	Dahl, Roald	Puffin Books
Going Swimming	J	RF	210	City Kids	Rigby
Going the Distance	T	RF	1626	Leveled Readers	Houghton Mifflin
Going to a Football Game	I	RF	131	City Kids	Rigby
Going to America	N	RF	250+	Orbit Chapter Books	Pacific Literacy
Going to America	K	HF	250+	Leveled Readers Language Support	Houghton Mifflin
Going to Be a Butterfly	L	I	250+	Sunshine	Wright Group/McGraw Hill
Going to Grandma's	I	RF	250+	Read by Reading	Scholastic
Going to Grandpa's	C	RF	37	Frankford, Marilyn	Kaeden Books
Going to Lucy's House	E	RF	151	Sunshine	Wright Group/McGraw Hill
Going to School	H	RF	250	Cambridge Reading	Pearson Learning Group
Going to School	O	I	21	iOpeners	Pearson Learning Group
Going to School	F	I	171	Foundations	Wright Group/McGraw Hill
Going to School	LB	RF	21	Smart Starts	Rigby
Going to School	A	RF	28	Leveled Readers Emergent	Houghton Mifflin
Going to School	C	I	30	Windows on Literacy	National Geographic
Going to School	C	I	50	Sunshine	Wright Group/McGraw Hill
Going to School	C	I	43	Story Box	Wright Group/McGraw Hill
Going to the Bank	J	I	317	Foundations	Wright Group/McGraw Hill
Going to the Beach	C	RF	75	Carousel Readers	Pearson Learning Group
Going to the Beach	LB	RF	30	Pacific Literacy	Pacific Learning
Going to the Beach	E	I	30	Little Red Readers	Sundance
Going to the City	J	I	250+	People, Spaces & Places	Rand McNally
Going to the Dentist	F	I	122	Pebble Books	Capstone Press
Going to the Doctor	F	RF	101	City Stories	Rigby
Going to the Hairdresser	J	I	227	Foundations	Wright Group/McGraw Hill
Going to the Hospital	H	RF	335	Foundations	Wright Group/McGraw Hill
Going to the Park	C	RF	41	Home Connection Collection	Rigby
Going to the Park with Grandaddy	C	RF	30	Visions	Wright Group/McGraw Hill
Going to the Pool	D	RF	55	Pair-It Books	Steck-Vaughn

TITLE	LEVEL	GENRE	WORD COUNT	AUTHOR / SERIES	PUBLISHER / DISTRIBUTOR
Going to the Symphony	G	I	132	Twig	Wright Group/McGraw Hill
Going to the Vet	D	I	46	Sunshine	Wright Group/McGraw Hill
Going to Town	J	HF	250+	Wilder, Laura Ingalls	HarperCollins
Going to Town With Mom and Dad	D	RF	85	Early Connections	Benchmark Education
Going Up and Down	B	RF	51	Early Emergent	Pioneer Valley
Going Up the Mountain	K	I	251	Windows on Literacy	National Geographic
Going Up?	B	F	26	Little Celebrations	Pearson Learning Group
Going West	N	I	428	Vocabulary Readers	Houghton Mifflin
Going West	O	HF	250+	Van Leeuwen, Jean	Penguin Group
Going West	J	HF	250+	Wilder, Laura Ingalls	HarperCollins
Going West: Trials and Tradeoffs	S	I	2572	Independent Readers Social Studies	Houghton Mifflin
Gold Cadillac, The	S	HF	250+	Taylor, Mildred D.	Puffin Books
Gold Dust Kids, The	N	HF	250+	Dionetti, Michelle	Wright Group/McGraw Hill
Gold Dust Letters, The	S	RF	250+	Lisle, Janet Taylor	Avon Camelot
Gold Fever!	N	HF	250+	Step into Reading	Random House
Golden Compass, The	Z	F	250+	Pullman, Philip	Ballantine Books
Golden Dragon	J	F	250+	Supersonics	Rigby
Golden Games	Q	I	250+	Zemanski, Stella	Scholastic
Golden Goblet, The	V	RF	250+	McGraw, Eloise Jarvis	Scholastic
Golden Goose, The	L	TL	731	Sunshine	Wright Group/McGraw Hill
Golden Goose, The	M	TL	250+	Literacy 2000	Rigby
Golden Land, The	L	HF	505	Leveled Readers	Houghton Mifflin
Golden Lasso, The	H	F	250+	Home Connection Collection	Rigby
Golden Locket, The	M	F	250+	Greene, Carol	OSI
Golden Sword of Dragonwalk	Q	F	250+	Stine, R. L.	Scholastic
Goldfish	J	I	250+	PM Animal Facts: Orange	Rigby
Goldfish Charlie and the Case of the Missing Planet	R	SF	250+	Mazer, Anne	Troll Associates
Goldilocks	G	TL	244	Sunshine	Wright Group/McGraw Hill
Goldilocks	C	TL	19	Tarlow, Ellen	Scholastic
Goldilocks	I	TL	250+	Jumbled Tumbled Tales & Rhymes	Rigby
Goldilocks and the Three Bears	C	TL	54	Little Books	Sadlier-Oxford
Goldilocks and the Three Bears	K	TL	250+	New Way Literature	Steck-Vaughn
Goldilocks and the Three Bears	K	TL	250+	Once Upon a Time	Wright Group/McGraw Hill
Goldilocks and The Three Bears	H	TL	250+	PM Tales and Plays-Turquoise	Rigby
Goldilocks and the Three Bears	G	TL	265	Storyteller Nonfiction	Wright Group/McGraw Hill
Goldilocks and the Three Bears	H	TL	250+	Traditional Tales & More	Rigby
Goldilocks and the Three Bears	E	TL	184	Hunia, Fran	Ladybird Books
Goldilocks and the Three Bears	G	TL	250+	Literacy Tree	Rigby
Goldilocks Comes Back	F	TL	134	Pair-It Books	Steck-Vaughn
Goldsworthy and Mort Blast Off	L	F	250+	Little Celebrations	Pearson Learning Group
Golf for Fun!	S	I	250+	Sports for Fun	Compass Point Books
Goliath and the Burglar	L	RF	250+	Dicks, Terrance	Barron's Educational
Goliath and the Buried Treasure	L	RF	250+	Dicks, Terrance	Barron's Educational
Goliath and the Cub Scouts	L	RF	250+	Dicks, Terrance	Barron's Educational
Goliath at the Dog Show	L	RF	250+	Dicks, Terrance	Barron's Educational
Goliath at the Seaside	L	RF	250+	Dicks, Terrance	Barron's Educational
Goliath Goes to Summer School	L	RF	250+	Dicks, Terrance	Barron's Educational
Goliath on Vacation	L	RF	250+	Dicks, Terrance	Barron's Educational
Goliath's Birthday	L	RF	250+	Dicks, Terrance	Barron's Educational
Goliath's Christmas	L	RF	250+	Dicks, Terrance	Barron's Educational
Goliath's Easter Parade	L	RF	250+	Dicks, Terrance	Barron's Educational
Golly Sisters Go West, The	K	RF	250+	Byars, Betsy	HarperTrophy

* Collection of short stories

TITLE	LEVEL	GENRE	WORD COUNT	AUTHOR / SERIES	PUBLISHER / DISTRIBUTOR
Golly Sisters Ride Again, The	K	RF	250+	Byars, Betsy	HarperTrophy
*Gone Fishing	G	RF	180	Long, Erlene	Houghton Mifflin
*Gone from Home	W	RF	250+	Johnson, Angela	Alfred A. Knopf
Gone-Away Lake	V	RF	250+	Enright, Elizabeth	Harcourt Trade
Gonna Bird, The	H	F	209	Storyteller-Night Crickets	Wright Group/McGraw Hill
Good As New	L	RF	250+	Douglass, Barbara	Scholastic
Good Bad Cat, The	D	RF	65	Start to Read	School Zone
Good Bad Cat, The	D	RF	65	Little Readers	Houghton Mifflin
Good Boy, Andrew!	E	RF	85	Literacy 2000	Rigby
*Good Catch!, A	E	RF	191	New Way Red	Steck-Vaughn
Good Choices for Cat and Dog	E	F	97	Learn to Read	Creative Teaching Press
Good Dessert, A	J	F	250+	Leveled Readers Language Support	Houghton Mifflin
Good Dog	C	RF	43	Sun Sprouts	ETA/Cuisenaire
Good Dog, Bonita	N	RF	250+	Giff, Patricia Reilly	Bantam
Good Dog, Carl	WB	F	N/A	Day, Alexandra	Green Tiger Press
Good Dog, Carl	WB	RF	N/A	Day, Alexandra	Simon & Schuster
Good Dog, The	S	F	250+	Avi	Simon & Schuster
Good Driving, Amelia Bedelia	L	F	250+	Parish, Peggy	Harper & Row
Good Food	F	I	78	Leveled Readers Science	Houghton Mifflin
Good for You	D	F	44	Sunshine	Wright Group/McGraw Hill
Good Girl	B	F	18	Ready Readers	Pearson Learning Group
Good Grief . . . Third Grade	O	RF	250+	McKenna, Colleen	Scholastic
Good Home, A	C	F	77	Leveled Readers Language Support	Houghton Mifflin
Good Idea, A	H	RF	250+	Leveled Readers Language Support	Houghton Mifflin
Good Knee for a Cat, A	I	RF	205	Pacific Literacy	Pacific Learning
Good Luck Elephant	I	F	171	Sunshine	Wright Group/McGraw Hill
Good Manners	H	RF	222	Well-Being Series	Dominie Press
Good Master, The	S	RF	250+	Seredy, Kate	Scholastic
Good Morning Isabel	G	RF	143	Literacy 2000	Rigby
Good Morning Mrs. Martin	K	F	156	Book Bank	Wright Group/McGraw Hill
Good Morning!	C	F	51	Science	Outside the Box
Good Morning, Monday	H	RF	77	Keenan, Sheila	Scholastic
Good Morning, Who's Snoring?	E	F	127	Story Steps	Rigby
Good News	I	TL	250+	Brenner, Barbara	Bantam
Good Night	M	RF	753	Leveled Readers	Houghton Mifflin
Good Night	E	RF	114	Start to Read	School Zone
Good Night Sky	D	RF	32	Seedlings	Continental Press
Good Night!	D	F	73	Leveled Readers Language Support	Houghton Mifflin
Good Night, City Lights	F	RF	74	City Stories	Rigby
Good Night, Little Brother	F	RF	69	Literacy 2000	Rigby
Good Night, Little Bug	D	F	54	Ready Readers	Pearson Learning Group
Good Night, Little Kitten	D	F	78	My First Reader	Grolier Press
Good Night, Mr. Tom	Z	HF	250+	Magorian, Michelle	HarperTrophy
Good Night's Sleep, A	P	RF	1091	Leveled Readers	Houghton Mifflin
Good Old Mom	C	RF	34	Oxford Reading Tree	Oxford University Press
Good Place for a City, A	N	I	194	Windows on Literacy	National Geographic
Good Place to Live, A	G	I	97	Windows on Literacy	National Geographic
Good Sports	H	I	206	Foundations	Wright Group/McGraw Hill
Good to Eat	H	I	152	Rigby Focus	Rigby
Good to Eat	B	I	31	Twig	Wright Group/McGraw Hill

* Collection of short stories

TITLE	LEVEL	GENRE	WORD COUNT	AUTHOR / SERIES	PUBLISHER / DISTRIBUTOR
Good Vibrations: Experimenting with Sound	K	I	250+	Rigby Literacy	Rigby
Good Work, Amelia Bedelia	L	F	250+	Parish, Peggy	Avon Camelot
Good, the Bad, and Everything Else, The	R	RF	250+	Action Packs	Rigby
Goodbye Gabby	I	RF	400	Early Transitional, Set 1	Pioneer Valley
Goodbye Goose	L	F	264	Books for Young Learners	Richard C. Owen
Good-Bye Marianne	T	B	250+	Watts, Irene N.	Tundra Books
Good-Bye My Wishing Star	S	RF	250+	Grove, Vicki	Scholastic
Good-bye Perky	E	RF	54	Twig	Wright Group/McGraw Hill
Good-bye Summer, Hello Fall	H	I	169	Ready Readers	Pearson Learning Group
Goodbye to Angel Island	R	HF	1055	Leveled Readers	Houghton Mifflin
Good-Bye, Billy Radish	V	HF	250+	Skurzynski, Gloria	Aladdin
Good-Bye, Chicken Little	Q	RF	250+	Byars, Betsy	HarperTrophy
Good-Bye, Fox	D	F	27	Instant Readers	Harcourt School Publishers
Good-Bye, Lucy	D	RF	60	Sunshine	Wright Group/McGraw Hill
Good-Bye, Vietnam	V	RF	250+	Whelan, Gloria	Alfred A. Knopf
Good-bye, Zoo	C	RF	48	Ready Readers	Pearson Learning Group
Good-for-Nothing Dog, The	M	RF	250+	Schultz, Irene	Wright Group/McGraw Hill
Goodness Gracious	I	I	190	Literacy 2000	Rigby
Goodnight	D	RF	83	Voyages	SRA/McGraw Hill
Goodnight Bobbie	LB	RF	15	Rigby Literacy	Rigby
Goodnight Goodnight	H	F	185	Literacy Tree	Rigby
Goodnight Moon	H	F	130	Brown, Margaret Wise	HarperCollins
Goodnight Peter	G	RF	107	Windmill	Wright Group/McGraw Hill
Goodnight!	D	RF	61	Joy Readers	Pearson Learning Group
Goodnight, Gorilla	LB	F	25	Rothmann, Peggy	Putnam
Goodnight, Owl	I	F	181	Hutchins, Pat	Aladdin
Goodnight, Owl!	I	F	196	Hutchins, Pat	Macmillan
Goody Hall	V	RF	250+	Babbitt, Natalie	Farrar, Straus and Giroux
Gooey Chewy Contest, The	L	F	1512	Goldsmith, Howard	Mondo
Goose Chase	D	F	43	Ready Readers	Pearson Learning Group
Goose on the Loose	Q	RF	250+	Baglio, Ben M.	Scholastic
Goose That Laid the Golden Egg, The	G	TL	73	Aesop	Wright Group/McGraw Hill
Goose Who Acted Like a Cow, The	J	F	250+	Phonics & Friends	Hampton-Brown
Gooseberry Park	P	F	250+	Rylant, Cynthia	Scholastic
Goosebumps: It Came From Beneath the Sink	T	F	250+	Stine, R. L.	Language for Learning Assoc.
Goose's Gold, The	N	RF	250+	Roy, Ron	Random House
Gorganzola Zombies in the Park	O	F	250+	Levy, Elizabeth	HarperTrophy
Gorgo Meets Her Match	K	HF	453	PM Story Books	Rigby
Gorilla Families	L	I	250+	Rosen Real Readers	Rosen Publishing Group
Gorilla Games	B	F	27	Phonics and Friends	Hampton-Brown
Gorilla Guardian	L	RF	250+	World Quest Adventures	World Quest Learning
Gorillas	H	I	185	Seedlings	Continental Press
Gorillas	T	I	250+	Burgel, Paul H.; Hartwig, M.	Carolrhoda Books
Gorillas	J	I	250+	Pebble Books	Red Brick Learning
Gorillas	I	I	185	Stewart, Josie	Continental Press
Gorillas	U	I	250+	The Untamed World	Steck-Vaughn
Gorillas: Gentle Giants on the Forest	L	I	250+	Milton, Joyce	Random House
Gotcha Box, The	A	RF	30	Story Box	Wright Group/McGraw Hill
Grab Bag, The	C	RF	85	PM Plus Story Books	Rigby
Grab Hands and Run	V	RF	250+	Temple, Frances	HarperTrophy
Grab It!	C	RF	45	Leveled Readers Language Support	Houghton Mifflin
Grabbing Bird, The	L	F	250+	Cambridge Reading	Pearson Learning Group

* Collection of short stories

TITLE	LEVEL	GENRE	WORD COUNT	AUTHOR / SERIES	PUBLISHER / DISTRIBUTOR
Grace	U	HF	250+	Walsh, Jill Paton	Farrar, Straus and Giroux
Grace the Pirate	O	F	250+	Lasky, Kathryn	Hyperion
Grace's Letter to Lincoln	P	HF	250+	Roop, Peter & Connie	Hyperion
Gracie's Cat	I	RF	250+	Cambridge Reading	Pearson Learning Group
Graffiti	I	RF	168	Sunshine	Wright Group/McGraw Hill
Graham Hawkes: Underwater Pilot	U	B	1492	Leveled Readers	Houghton Mifflin
Grain Group, The	H	I	108	Pebble Books	Red Brick Learning
Grain of Rice, A	P	TL	250+	Pittman, Helena Clare	Bantam
Gram's Hat	D	RF	76	Leveled Readers	Houghton Mifflin
Grams, Her Boyfriend, My Family, and Me	U	RF	250+	Derby, Pat	Sunburst
Grand Canyon Journey, A: Tracing Time in Stone	W	I	250+	A First Book	Franklin Watts
Grand Coulee Dam, The	Q	I	793	Leveled Readers Social Studies	Houghton Mifflin
Grand Escape, The	S	F	250+	Naylor, Phyllis Reynolds	Bantam
*Grand Mothers: Poems, Reminiscences, and Short Stories About Keepers of Our Traditions	Y	B	250+	Giovanni, Nikki	Henry Holt & Co.
Grand Trees of America: Our State and Champion Trees	T	I	250+	Jorgenson, Lisa	Roberts Rinehart
Grandad	L	RF	250+	Literacy 2000	Rigby
Grandad's Dinosaur	K	F	250+	Girling, Brough	Wright Group/McGraw Hill
Grandad's Mask	K	RF	250+	PM Turquoise	Rigby
Grandfather Horned Toad	K	F	250+	Little Celebrations	Pearson Learning Group
Grandfathers	C	I	41	Pebble Books	Capstone Press
Grandfather's Ghost	M	F	250+	Sunshine	Wright Group/McGraw Hill
Grandfather's Mask	I	RF	245	Leveled Readers Language Support	Houghton Mifflin
Grandma and Me	D	I	68	Sun Sprouts	ETA/Cuisenaire
Grandma and the Pirate	F	RF	105	Lloyd, David	Crown
Grandma Carol's Plant	I	RF	250+	Home Connection Collection	Rigby
Grandma J	I	RF	170	Instant Readers	Harcourt School Publishers
Grandma Mixup, The	K	RF	250+	Little Readers	Houghton Mifflin
Grandma Mix-Up, The	K	RF	250+	McCully, Emily Arnold	HarperTrophy
Grandma Moses	N	B	250+	Biography	Benchmark Education
Grandma Moses: Painter of Rural America	T	B	250+	O'Neal, Zibby	Penguin Group
Grandma Moves In	I	RF	250+	Greetings	Rigby
Grandmas At Bat	K	RF	250+	McCully, Emily Arnold	HarperTrophy
Grandmas at the Lake	K	RF	250+	McCully, Emily Arnold	HarperTrophy
Grandma's Bicycle	G	RF	74	Read Alongs	Rigby
Grandma's Cane	H	RF	250+	Story Box	Wright Group/McGraw Hill
Grandma's Cookie Cutters	K	RF	577	Leveled Readers	Houghton Mifflin
Grandma's Garden	K	I	340	Rigby Focus	Rigby
Grandma's Heart	K	I	90	Wonder World	Wright Group/McGraw Hill
Grandma's Letter	D	RF	67	Foundations	Wright Group/McGraw Hill
Grandma's Memories	F	RF	102	Literacy 2000	Rigby
Grandma's Pictures of The Past	J	RF	250+	Home Connection Collection	Rigby
Grandma's Present	F	RF	191	Foundations	Wright Group/McGraw Hill
Grandma's Stick	H	RF	250+	Story Box	Wright Group/McGraw Hill
Grandma's Table	K	RF	287	Leveled Readers	Houghton Mifflin
Grandmother	E	RF	60	Joy Readers	Pearson Learning Group
Grandmother and I	C	RF	53	Home Connection Collection	Rigby
Grandmother Is Tired	C	RF	31	Joy Readers	Pearson Learning Group
Grandmothers	C	I	50	Pebble Books	Capstone Press
Grandpa	E	RF	70	Sunshine	Wright Group/McGraw Hill
Grandpa	C	RF	61	Rigby Literacy	Rigby

* Collection of short stories

TITLE	LEVEL	GENRE	WORD COUNT	AUTHOR / SERIES	PUBLISHER / DISTRIBUTOR
Grandpa and I	C	RF	40	Home Connection Collection	Rigby
Grandpa and Me	D	I	36	Sun Sprouts	ETA/Cuisenaire
*Grandpa at the Beach	J	F	250+	Lewis, Rob	Mondo
*Grandpa Comes To Stay	J	F	1083	Lewis, Rob	Mondo
Grandpa Knits Hats	E	RF	55	Wonder World	Wright Group/McGraw Hill
Grandpa Snored	F	RF	51	Literacy 2000	Rigby
Grandpa, Grandma, and the Tractor	H	RF	220	Ready Readers	Pearson Learning Group
Grandpa, Grandpa	G	RF	122	Story Box	Wright Group/McGraw Hill
Grandparents Are Fun!	H	I	216	Leveled Readers Language Support	Houghton Mifflin
Grandparents Are Great	I	I	257	Leveled Readers	Houghton Mifflin
Grandpa's Baseball Card	P	RF	1022	Leveled Readers	Houghton Mifflin
Grandpa's Birthday	J	RF	250+	Literacy 2000	Rigby
Grandpa's Boat	E	RF	108	Developing Books	Pioneer Valley
Grandpa's Candy Store	F	RF	65	Books for Young Learners	Richard C. Owen
Grandpa's Clues	F	RF	198	Rigby Literacy	Rigby
Grandpa's Cookies	F	F	193	Little Readers	Houghton Mifflin
Grandpa's Face	Q	RF	250+	Greenfield, Eloise	Putnam & Grosset
Grandpa's Garden Shed	G	I	68	Windows on Literacy	National Geographic
Grandpa's Lemonade	G	RF	138	Storyteller Nonfiction	Wright Group/McGraw Hill
Grandpa's Mountain	T	RF	250+	Reeder, Carolyn	Avon Camelot
Grandpa's Rail Tales	T	F	1730	Leveled Readers	Houghton Mifflin
Grandpa's Special Present	I	RF	286	Foundations	Wright Group/McGraw Hill
Grandpa's Train	E	RF	69	Early Emergent, Set 3	Pioneer Valley
Grandpa's Visit	C	RF	38	Vocabulary Readers	Houghton Mifflin
Granny and the Desperadoes	J	RF	250+	Parish, Peggy	Simon & Schuster
Granny Bundle's Boring Walk	H	RF	250+	Stepping Stones	Nelson/Michaels Assoc.
Granny's Teeth	H	RF	169	Cambridge Reading	Pearson Learning Group
Granny's Visit	E	RF	144	Leveled Readers Language Support	Houghton Mifflin
Grant Wood	R	B	250+	Venezia, Mike	Children's Press
Graph It	K	I	250+	Yellow Umbrella Books	Capstone Press
Grass Circles Mystery, The	K	F	250+	Talking Points	Pearson Learning Group
Grass Is for Goats	D	RF	84	Joy Readers	Pearson Learning Group
Grasshopper and the Ants	K	TL	452	Sunshine	Wright Group/McGraw Hill
Grasshopper on the Road	K	F	250+	Lobel, Arnold	HarperTrophy
Grasshoppers	N	I	250+	Nature's Friends	Compass Point Books
Grasshoppers	F	I	50	Pebble Books	Capstone Press
Grasshoppers	H	I	84	Pebble Plus	Red Brick Learning
Grasslands	Q	I	250+	First Reports	Compass Point Books
Grasslands	N	I	250+	A True Book	Children's Press
Gratefully Yours	T	HF	250+	Buchanan, Jane	Puffin Books
*Graven Images: Three Stories by Paul Fleischman	U	F	250+	Fleischman, Paul	HarperTrophy
Gravity	O	I	250+	Early Connections	Benchmark Education
Gravity	D	I	33	Wonder World	Wright Group/McGraw Hill
Gravity and the Solar System	O	I	250+	PM Plus Story Books	Rigby
Gravity: Simple Experiments for Young Scientists	T	I	250+	White, Larry	Millbrook Press
Gray Blanket, The: Rabbits in Australia	V	I	1878	Leveled Readers Social Studies	Houghton Mifflin
*Gray Heroes Elder Tales from Around the World	Z	TL	250+	Yolen, Jane	Penguin Group
*Great African Americans in Business	T	B	250+	Rediger, Pat	Crabtree
*Great African Americans in Civil Rights	T	B	250+	Rediger, Pat	Crabtree

* Collection of short stories

TITLE	LEVEL	GENRE	WORD COUNT	AUTHOR / SERIES	PUBLISHER / DISTRIBUTOR
*Great African Americans in Entertainment	T	B	250+	Rediger, Pat	Crabtree
*Great African Americans in Film	T	B	250+	Parker, Janice	Crabtree
*Great African Americans in Government	T	B	250+	Dudley, Karen	Crabtree
*Great African Americans in History	T	B	250+	Hacker, Carlotta	Crabtree
*Great African Americans in Jazz	T	B	250+	Hacker, Carlotta	Crabtree
*Great African Americans in Literature	T	B	250+	Rediger, Pat	Crabtree
*Great African Americans in Music	T	B	250+	Rediger, Pat	Crabtree
*Great African Americans in Sports	T	B	250+	Rediger, Pat	Crabtree
*Great African Americans in the Arts	T	B	250+	Hacker, Carlotta	Crabtree
*Great African Americans in the Olympics	T	B	250+	Hunter, Shaun	Crabtree
Great Apes, The	S	I	250+	A First Book	Franklin Watts
Great Attitude, A	F	B	196	Learn to Read	Creative Teaching Press
Great Bean Race, The	K	RF	295	Pacific Literacy	Pacific Learning
Great Big Enormous Turnip, The	H	TL	317	Reading Unlimited	Pearson Learning Group
Great Big Enormous Turnip, The	H	TL	250+	Tolstoi, Aleksei; Nikolaevich, Graf	Watts
Great Brain at the Academy, The	T	RF	250+	Fitzgerald, John D.	Yearling
Great Brain Does It Again, The	T	RF	250+	Fitzgerald, John D.	Yearling
Great Brain Reforms, The	T	RF	250+	Fitzgerald, John D.	Yearling
Great Brain, The	T	RF	250+	Fitzgerald, John D.	Language for Learning Assoc.
Great Bug Hunt, The	G	RF	96	Rookie Readers	Children's Press
Great Car Race, The	E	F	162	Carousel Readers	Pearson Learning Group
Great Chicago Fire, 1871, The	Z	HF	250+	Massie, Elizabeth	Pocket Books
Great Day	G	RF	161	Alphakids	Sundance
Great Day for Snorkeling, A	K	RF	238	Leveled Readers	Houghton Mifflin
Great Day for Up	J	F	180	Seuss, Dr.	Random House
Great Depression, The	X	I	250+	Cornerstones of Freedom	Children's Press
Great Dimpole Oak, The	S	RF	250+	Lisle, Janet Taylor	Puffin Books
Great Dinosaur Hunt, The	M	F	250+	Schultz, Irene	Wright Group/McGraw Hill
Great Dinosaur Race, The	L	F	250+	Popcorn	Sundance
Great Dog Wash, The	O	RF	250+	Rigby Focus	Rigby
Great Enormous Hamburger, The	B	F	36	Sunshine	Wright Group/McGraw Hill
Great Escape, The	L	RF	250+	Rigby Literacy	Rigby
*Great Escapes of World War II	Z	I	250+	Sullivan, George	Scholastic
Great Expectations	S	HF	250+	Bullseye Step Into Classics	Random House
Great Explorations	T	HF	250+	Neufeld, David	Scholastic
Great Genghis Khan Look-Alike Contest, The	L	RF	250+	Sharmat, Marjorie Weinman	Random House
Great Ghosts	L	F	250+	Cohen, Daniel	Scholastic
Great Gilly Hopkins, The	S	RF	250+	Paterson, Katherine	Hearst
Great Great Grandfather's Railroad	J	HF	250+	Sunshine Books	Wright Group/McGraw Hill
Great Green Place, The	K	I	242	Story Box	Wright Group/McGraw Hill
Great Grumbler and the Wonder Tree, The	K	F	250+	Mahy, Margaret	Pacific Learning
Great Houdini, The: World Famous Magician and Escape Artist	M	B	250+	Kulling, Monica	Random House
Great Ice Battle, The	M	F	250+	Abbott, Tony	Scholastic
Great Interactive Dream Machine, The	Y	SF	250+	Peck, Richard	Puffin Books
Great Invention, The	H	RF	108	City Stories	Rigby
Great Inventions and Where They Came From	P	I	250+	Navigators Social Studies Series	Benchmark Education
Great Inventor, A: An Wang	J	B	207	Leveled Readers Social Studies	Houghton Mifflin
Great Kapok Tree, The	R	I	250+	Cherry, Lynne	Scholastic
Great Little Madison, The	X	B	250+	Fritz, Jean	G.P. Putnam's Sons
Great Migration, The	R	I	250+	Lawrence, Jacob	HarperCollins
Great Ocean, The	K	I	250+	Spyglass Books	Compass Point Books
Great Pumpkin, The	I	F	239	Sunshine	Wright Group/McGraw Hill

* Collection of short stories

TITLE	LEVEL	GENRE	WORD COUNT	AUTHOR / SERIES	PUBLISHER / DISTRIBUTOR
Great Pyramid, The	S	I	250+	Windows on Literacy	National Geographic
Great Quarterback Switch, The	M	RF	250+	Christopher, Matt	Little, Brown & Co.
Great Race, The	G	F	250+	McPhail, David	Scholastic
Great Riddle Mystery, The	M	RF	250+	MacClean, James R.	Pearson Learning Group
Great Snake Escape, The	J	F	250+	Coxe, Molly	HarperTrophy
Great Snakes!	I	I	161	Robinson, Fay	Scholastic
Great Sporting Events	R	I	250+	PM Nonfiction-Ruby	Rigby
Great Wall of China, The	N	I	141	Vocabulary Readers	Houghton Mifflin
Great Wall of China, The	Q	I	250+	Fisher, Leonard Everett	Aladdin
Great Wall of China, The	Q	I	250+	Rosen Real Readers	Rosen Publishing Group
Great Whales: The Gentle Giants	W	I	250+	Lauber, Patricia	Henry Holt & Co.
Great Wheel, The	U	RF	250+	Lawson, Robert	Scholastic
Great White Sharks	F	I	98	Pair-It Books	Steck-Vaughn
Great White Sharks	U	I	250+	The Untamed World	Steck-Vaughn
Great, Big, Giant Turnip, The	J	TL	610	Early Connections	Benchmark Education
Greatest Binnie in the World, The	M	RF	709	Sunshine	Wright Group/McGraw Hill
Greatest Electrician in the World, The	W	B	1926	Leveled Readers	Houghton Mifflin
Greatest of All, The: A Japanese Folktale	L	TL	250+	Kimmel, Eric A.	Holiday House
Greatest, The	R	I	250+	Literacy 2000	Rigby
Great-Grandpa	G	RF	130	Voyages	SRA/McGraw Hill
Great-Grandpa's In The Litter Box	N	F	250+	The Zack Files	Grosset & Dunlap
Greece	W	I	250+	Countries and Cultures	Capstone Press
Greece: The Culture	U	I	250+	Kalman, Bobbie	Crabtree
Greece: The Land	U	I	250+	Kalman, Bobbie	Crabtree
Greece: The People	U	I	250+	Kalman, Bobbie	Crabtree
Greedy Cat	G	F	166	Pacific Literacy	Pacific Learning
Greedy Cat and the Birthday Cake	M	F	250+	Cowley, Joy	Pacific Learning
Greedy Cat Is Hungry	D	RF	103	Pacific Literacy	Pacific Learning
Greedy Cat's Breakfast	E	F	53	Story Basket	Wright Group/McGraw Hill
Greedy Crows, The	M	TL	250+	Story Vines	Wright Group/McGraw Hill
Greedy Dog, The	H	F	148	New Way Blue	Steck-Vaughn
Greedy Goat, The	L	TL	250+	Bookshop	Mondo
Greedy Gray Octopus, The	G	F	195	Tadpoles	Rigby
Greedy King, The	J	RF	250+	Lighthouse	Rigby
Greek and Roman Eras, The	R	I	250+	Journey Through History	Barron's Educational
Greeks, The	M	I	250+	Footsteps in Time	Children's Press
Green and Growing: A Book About Plants	M	I	250+	Growing Things	Picture Window Books
Green Bananas	F	F	49	Tadpoles	Rigby
Green Book, The	V	F	250+	Walsh, Jill Paton	Farrar, Straus and Giroux
Green Dragon, The	I	F	131	Sunshine	Wright Group/McGraw Hill
Green Dragons, The	J	RF	250+	PM Story Books	Rigby
Green Eggs and Ham	J	F	250+	Seuss, Dr.	Random House
Green Eyes	F	RF	111	Literacy 2000	Rigby
Green Footprints	E	RF	42	Literacy 2000	Rigby
Green Grass	B	F	26	Story Box	Wright Group/McGraw Hill
Green Grass Grows All Around, The	H	TL	144	Instant Readers	Harcourt School Publishers
Green Grasshoppers	K	F	229	Sunshine	Wright Group/McGraw Hill
Green Green Green	E	F	218	Instant Readers	Harcourt School Publishers
Green Means Go	D	I	25	Yellow Umbrella Books	Red Brick Learning
Green Plants	H	RF	213	Foundations	Wright Group/McGraw Hill
Green Snake	N	I	250+	Life Cycles	Creative Teaching Press
Green Snake, The	D	I	131	Twig	Wright Group/McGraw Hill
Green Thumbs	Q	I	250+	Literacy 2000	Rigby
Green Thumbs, Everyone	N	RF	250+	Giff, Patricia Reilly	Bantam

* Collection of short stories

TITLE	LEVEL	GENRE	WORD COUNT	AUTHOR / SERIES	PUBLISHER / DISTRIBUTOR
Green with Red Spots Horrible	N	RF	250+	SupaDoopers	Sundance
Green, Green	D	RF	114	Little Readers	Houghton Mifflin
Green: Seeing Green All Around Us	L	I	250+	Colors	Capstone Press
Greenwitch	X	F	250+	Cooper, Susan	Scholastic
Gregor the Grumblesome Giant	G	F	212	Literacy 2000	Rigby
Gregory, the Mean Dragon	I	F	250+	Phonics and Friends	Hampton-Brown
Gregory, the Terrible Eater	L	F	250+	Sharmat, Marjorie Weinman	Scholastic
Gregory's Dog	C	RF	23	Cat on the Mat	Oxford University Press
Gregory's Garden	F	RF	70	Cat on the Mat	Oxford University Press
Greg's Microscope	K	I	250+	Selsam, Millicent E.	HarperTrophy
Gremlins Don't Chew Bubble Gum	M	F	250+	Dadey, Debbie; Jones, Marcia Thornton	Scholastic
Grey King, The	X	F	250+	Cooper, Susan	Simon & Schuster
Grey Lady and the Strawberry Snatcher, The	WB	F	N/A	Bang, Molly	Aladdin
Gribblegrot from Outer Space, The	N	F	250+	Literacy 2000 Satellites	Rigby
Griffin, the School Cat	I	RF	160	Sunshine	Wright Group/McGraw Hill
Grilled Cheese Sandwich	G	I	61	Windows on Literacy	National Geographic
Grim Grotto, The	V	F	250+	Snicket, Lemony	HarperCollins
Gristmill, The	T	I	250+	Historic Communities	Crabtree
Grizzly and the Bumble-Bee	I	F	183	Sunshine	Wright Group/McGraw Hill
Grizzly Bear, The	R	I	250+	Potts, Steve	Red Brick Learning
Grizzly Bears	R	I	250+	Predators in the Wild	Red Brick Learning
Grizzly Bears	N	I	250+	Woolley, M.; Pigdon, K.	Mondo
*Grizzly Mistake and Other Cases, The	O	RF	250+	Simon, Seymour	Avon
Grizzwold	I	F	250+	Hoff, Syd	HarperTrophy
Grocery Shopping	D	RF	34	Yannone, Deborah	Kaeden Books
Grover Cleveland	U	B	250+	Profiles of the Presidents	Compass Point Books
Grow a Plant Inch by Inch	H	I	142	Rosen Real Readers	Rosen Publishing Group
Grow, Seed, Grow	E	I	36	Discovery Links	Newbridge
Growin'	R	RF	250+	Grimes, Nikki	Puffin Books
Growing	C	I	42	Story Steps	Rigby
Growing	B	I	23	Windmill	Wright Group/McGraw Hill
Growing a Kitchen Garden	O	I	250+	Navigators Fiction Series	Benchmark Education
Growing a Plant	G	I	115	Discovery World	Rigby
Growing a Plant	C	I	43	Early Connections	Benchmark Education
Growing Ideas	O	B	250+	Van Leeuwen, Jean	Richard C. Owen
Growing Older	I	I	216	Early Connections	Benchmark Education
Growing Radishes and Carrots	I	I	125	Bookshop	Mondo
Growing Sprouts and Eva's Sprout Diary	J	RF	250+	Voyages	SRA/McGraw Hill
Growing Tomatoes	G	I	87	Alphakids	Sundance
Growing Tomatoes	M	I	626	Leveled Readers Science	Houghton Mifflin
Growing Up	P	I	250+	It's Science	Children's Press
Growing Up in Coal Country	X	I	250+	Bartoletti, Susan Campbell	Houghton Mifflin
Growing Up Is Fun	C	I	87	The Candid Collection	Pearson Learning Group
*Growing Up Stories	T	RF	250+	Byars, Betsy	Kingfisher
Growing Up, Up, Up Book	F	RF	120	First Start	Troll Associates
Grown-ups Say the Silliest Things	J	F	250+	Lighthouse	Rigby
Gruff Brothers, The	I	TL	250+	Hooks, William H.	Bantam
Grumbles, Growls, and Roars	F	I	133	Twig	Wright Group/McGraw Hill
Grump, The	F	RF	73	Literacy 2000	Rigby
Grumputer, The	G	F	235	Story Basket	Wright Group/McGraw Hill
Grumpy Elephant	E	F	100	Story Box	Wright Group/McGraw Hill
Grumpy Grizzly	C	RF	40	Learn to Read	Creative Teaching Press
Guard Dog Diggory	L	RF	250+	Pacific Literacy	Pacific Learning

TITLE	LEVEL	GENRE	WORD COUNT	AUTHOR / SERIES	PUBLISHER / DISTRIBUTOR
Guard the House, Sam!	G	RF	46	Rookie Readers	Children's Press
Guardian of the Dark	W	F	250+	Spencer, Bev	Scholastic
Guardians of Ga'Hoole: The Journey	V	F	250+	Lasky, Kathryn	Scholastic
Guatemala	O	I	250+	Dahl, Michael	Red Brick Learning
Guess How Many	N	I	250+	Rosen Real Readers	Rosen Publishing Group
Guess How Many I Have	A	I	24	Early Connections	Benchmark Education
Guess What Kind of Ball	E	RF	219	Urmston, Kathleen; Evans, Karen	Kaeden Books
Guess What the Moon Saw?	C	RF	38	Home Connection Collection	Rigby
Guess What the Sun Saw?	C	RF	36	Home Connection Collection	Rigby
Guess What Today Is?	I	F	250+	Popcorn	Sundance
Guess What!	E	RF	28	Literacy 2000	Rigby
Guess What?	E	RF	120	Foundations	Wright Group/McGraw Hill
Guess Who?	L	I	250+	Home Connection Collection	Rigby
Guess Who's Coming to Dinner?	F	RF	130	Literacy 2000	Rigby
Guessing Jar, The	K	I	395	Early Connections	Benchmark Education
Guests	T	HF	250+	Dorris, Michael	Hyperion
Guide Dog, The	K	I	338	Foundations	Wright Group/McGraw Hill
Guide Dogs	H	I	107	Rosen Real Readers	Rosen Publishing Group
Guinea Pig for You, A: Caring for Your Guinea Pig	M	I	250+	Pet Care	Picture Window Books
Guinea Pig Gang	O	RF	250+	Baglio, Ben M.	Scholastic
Guinea Pig Grass	I	RF	140	Literacy 2000	Rigby
Guinea Pigs	C	I	34	Sun Sprouts	ETA/Cuisenaire
Guinea Pigs	J	I	250+	PM Animal Facts: Orange	Rigby
Guinea Pigs	S	I	250+	Hansen, Elvig	Carolrhoda Books
Guinea Pigs	E	I	250+	Pebble Books	Capstone Press
Gulf	X	F	250+	Westfall, Robert	Scholastic
Gulliver's Stories	Q	F	250+	Dolch, E. W.; Marguerite, P.	Scholastic
Gulp!	D	F	103	Story Box	Wright Group/McGraw Hill
Gum on the Drum, The	E	F	41	Start to Read	School Zone
Gumby Shop, The	I	F	359	Read Alongs	Rigby
Gumshoe Goose Private Eye	K	F	250+	Kwitz, Mary DeBall	Puffin Books
Gung Hay Fat Choy	N	I	250+	Behrens, June	Children's Press
Gunpowder and Tea	W	HF	3290	Leveled Readers	Houghton Mifflin
Gurgles and Growls: Learning About Your Stomach	L	I	250+	Amazing Body	Picture Window Books
Gus and Grandpa	J	RF	250+	Mills, Claudia	Sunburst
Gusts and Gales: A Book About Wind	M	I	250+	Amazing Science	Picture Window Books
Gwen Torrence	P	B	250+	Stewart, Mark	Children's Press
Gwendolyn Brooks: A Life of Poetry	R	B	811	Leveled Readers	Houghton Mifflin
Gypsy Game, The	U	RF	250+	Snyder, Zilpha Keatly	Yearling
Habibi	V	B	250+	Nye, Naomi Shihab	Simon & Schuster
Habitat Is Where We Live, A	F	I	132	Twig	Wright Group/McGraw Hill
Habitat Rescue	O	I	250+	Navigators Fiction Series	Benchmark Education
Haddie's Caps	D	F	90	Ready Readers	Pearson Learning Group
Hades	W	I	250+	World Mythology	Capstone Press
Ha-Ha Party, The	J	RF	250	Sunshine	Wright Group/McGraw Hill
Hailstorm, The	J	RF	386	PM Turquoise	Rigby
Hair	A	RF	32	Carousel Earlybirds	Pearson Learning Group
Hair	B	I	37	Foundations	Wright Group/McGraw Hill
Hair	C	RF	35	Little Celebrations	Pearson Learning Group
Hair	C	I	60	Sun Sprouts	ETA/Cuisenaire
Hair Party, The	J	RF	250+	Literacy 2000	Rigby
Haircut, The	D	RF	27	Hartley, Susan; Armstrong, Shane	Scholastic

TITLE	LEVEL	GENRE	WORD COUNT	AUTHOR / SERIES	PUBLISHER / DISTRIBUTOR
Hairdresser, The	G	I	164	PM Nonfiction-Blue	Rigby
Hairy Bear	G	F	109	Story Box	Wright Group/McGraw Hill
Hairy Harry	G	I	92	Windows on Literacy	National Geographic
Hairy Little Critters	O	I	250+	Literacy Tree	Rigby
Haiti	U	I	250+	Countries and Cultures	Red Brick Learning
Half for You, Half for Me	K	TL	399	Literacy 2000	Rigby
Halloween	O	I	250+	Holidays and Festivals	Compass Point Books
Halloween	P	I	250+	Let's See	Compass Point Books
Halloween	E	I	128	Fiesta Holiday Series	Pearson Learning Group
Halloween	D	RF	32	Visions	Wright Group/McGraw Hill
Halloween	C	RF	87	Handprints C, Set 1	Educator's Publishing Service
Halloween	J	I	32	Pebble Books	Capstone Press
Halloween	B	RF	44	Story Box	Wright Group/McGraw Hill
Halloween Danny	E	F	51	Coulter, Mia	Maryruth Books
*Halloween Horror and Other Cases, The	O	RF	250+	Simon, Seymour	Avon
Halloween Mask for Monster	C	F	38	Mueller, Virginia	Whitman
Halloween Parade	F	RF	101	Ziefert, Harriet	Puffin Books
Halloween: Why We Celebrate It the Way We Do	P	I	250+	Hintz, Martin & Kate	Red Brick Learning
Hamburger	H	RF	49	City Kids	Rigby
Hamlet the Hamster	G	RF	189	Breakthrough	Longman/Bow
Hammurabi and the Glory of Mesopotamia	Y	B	2564	Independent Readers Social Studies	Houghton Mifflin
Hamster Hotel	O	RF	250+	Baglio, Ben M.	Scholastic
Hamster in a Handbasket	Q	RF	250+	Baglio, Ben M.	Scholastic
Hamster of the Baskervilles, The: A Chet Gecko Mystery	T	F	250+	Hale, Bruce	Harcourt Trade
Hamsters	D	I	39	All About Pets	Red Brick Learning
Hana's Suitcase	Y	I	250+	Levine, Karen	Albert Whitman & Co.
Hand Me Downs, The	G	RF	156	Little Readers	Houghton Mifflin
Hand Tools	M	I	367	Wonder World	Wright Group/McGraw Hill
Hand, Hand, Fingers, Thumb	J	F	250+	Perkins, Al	Random House
Handful of Time, A	U	F	250+	Pearson, Kit	Puffin Books
Hands	C	RF	39	Literacy 2000	Rigby
Hands	B	I	15	Twig	Wright Group/McGraw Hill
Hands at Work	C	I	50	Windows on Literacy	National Geographic
Hands Up, Wolf	L	F	250+	Pacific Literacy	Pacific Learning
Hands, Hands, Hands	B	RF	17	Little Celebrations	Pearson Learning Group
Hands, Hands, Hands	F	I	85	Bookshop	Mondo
Handy Dragon, A	H	F	159	Literacy 2000	Rigby
Hang a Left at Venus	N	F	250+	The Zack Files	Grosset & Dunlap
Hang in there, Oscar Martin!	N	RF	250+	Noonan, Diana	Pacific Learning
Hanged Man, The	Z	RF	250+	Block, Francesca Lia	HarperCollins
Hannah	I	RF	250+	Stepping Stones	Nelson/Michaels Assoc.
Hannah	N	RF	250+	Whelan, Gloria	Random House
Hannah and Her Dad	J	RF	250+	Voyages	SRA/McGraw Hill
Hannah and the Angels	Q	F	250+	Lowery, Linda	Random House
Hannah Brown, Union Army Spy	V	HF	2231	Leveled Readers	Houghton Mifflin
Hannah of Fairfield	Q	HF	250+	Pioneer Daughters	Puffin Books
Hannah's Fancy Notions: A Story of Industrial New England	R	HF	250+	Ross, Pat	Penguin Group
Hannah's Halloween	LB	I	14	Little Books for Early Readers	University of Maine
Hannah's Helping Hands	Q	HF	250+	Van Leeuwen, Jean	Puffin Books
Hannah's Hiccups	G	RF	196	Home Connection Collection	Rigby

TITLE	LEVEL	GENRE	WORD COUNT	AUTHOR / SERIES	PUBLISHER / DISTRIBUTOR
Hannah's Winter of Hope	Q	HF	250+	Van Leeuwen, Jean	Puffin Books
Hanna's Butterfly	I	RF	158	Start to Read	School Zone
Hannibal	T	B	250+	Green, Robert	Franklin Watts
Hans Christian Andersen: Prince of Storytellers	N	B	250+	Rookie Biographies	Children's Press
Hansel and Gretel	K	TL	250+	Enrichment	Wright Group/McGraw Hill
Hansel and Gretel	G	TL	451	Hunia, Fran	Ladybird Books
Hanukkah	N	I	250+	Festivals and Holidays	Children's Press
Hanukkah	P	I	250+	Let's See	Compass Point Books
Hanukkah Party, The	I	RF	250+	Early Transitional, Set 1	Pioneer Valley
Happily Ever After	O	F	250+	Quindlen, Anna	Penguin Group
Happy 100th Day!	C	RF	35	Little Celebrations	Pearson Learning Group
Happy Accidents!	Q	I	250+	Action Packs	Rigby
Happy and Sad	I	F	232	Sunshine	Wright Group/McGraw Hill
Happy Birthday	G	RF	130	First Start	Troll Associates
Happy Birthday	C	F	26	Instant Readers	Harcourt School Publishers
Happy Birthday Book, The	P	I	250+	Sunshine	Wright Group/McGraw Hill
Happy Birthday!	C	RF	28	Literacy 2000	Rigby
Happy Birthday, Addy!	Q	HF	250+	The American Girls Collection	Pleasant Company
Happy Birthday, Anna, Sorpresa!	N	RF	250+	Giff, Patricia Reilly	Bantam
Happy Birthday, Brother!	A	I	24	Vocabulary Readers	Houghton Mifflin
Happy Birthday, Danny and the Dinosaur	H	F	250+	Little Readers	Houghton Mifflin
Happy Birthday, Danny and the Dinosaur!	H	F	250+	Hoff, Syd	HarperTrophy
Happy Birthday, Dear Duck	K	F	250+	Bunting, Eve	Clarion
Happy Birthday, Duckling	I	I	154	Literacy Tree	Rigby
Happy Birthday, Estela!	LB	RF	30	Pacific Literacy	Pacific Learning
Happy Birthday, Felicity!	Q	HF	250+	The American Girls Collection	Pleasant Company
Happy Birthday, Frog	C	F	87	Story Box	Wright Group/McGraw Hill
Happy Birthday, Josefina!	Q	HF	250+	The American Girls Collection	Pleasant Company
Happy Birthday, Kirsten!	Q	HF	250+	The American Girls Collection	Pleasant Company
Happy Birthday, Martin Luther King	L	B	250+	Marzollo, Jean	Scholastic
Happy Birthday, Molly!	Q	HF	250+	The American Girls Collection	Pleasant Company
Happy Birthday, Moon	L	F	345	Asch, Frank	Simon & Schuster
Happy Birthday, Mrs. Boedecker	L	RF	250+	Little Celebrations	Pearson Learning Group
Happy Birthday, Sam	I	RF	213	Hutchins, Pat	Greenwillow
Happy Birthday, Sam!	I	RF	258	Leveled Readers	Houghton Mifflin
Happy Birthday, Samantha!	Q	HF	250+	The American Girls Collection	Pleasant Company
Happy Café, The	I	RF	238	Story Box	Wright Group/McGraw Hill
Happy Egg	E	F	210	Kraus, Robert	Scholastic
Happy Endings	I	F	213	Sunshine	Wright Group/McGraw Hill
Happy Face, Sad Face	C	I	77	Foundations	Wright Group/McGraw Hill
Happy Faces	H	RF	210	Reading Unlimited	Pearson Learning Group
Happy Holidays	B	I	27	Teacher's Choice Series	Pearson Learning Group
Happy Jack	F	F	99	First Start	Troll Associates
Happy Monkey in the Shed	C	F	30	Joy Readers	Pearson Learning Group
Happy Monkey's Peanuts	D	F	63	Joy Readers	Pearson Learning Group
Happy Mother's Day!	G	RF	101	Teacher's Choice Series	Pearson Learning Group
Happy New Year!	M	I	114	Independent Readers Social Studies	Houghton Mifflin
Happy Pets, Healthy Pets	H	I	98	Spyglass Books	Compass Point Books
Happy Valentine's Day, Miss Hildy!	K	RF	250+	Grambling, Lois	Random House
Harbour, The	M	I	250+	Cambridge Reading	Pearson Learning Group
Hard at Work	B	RF	66	Early Emergent	Pioneer Valley
Hard Drive to Short	M	RF	250+	Christopher, Matt	Little, Brown & Co.
Hard Workers	J	I	186	Phonics Readers	Compass Point Books

* Collection of short stories

TITLE	LEVEL	GENRE	WORD COUNT	AUTHOR / SERIES	PUBLISHER / DISTRIBUTOR
Hare and the Tortoise, The	K	TL	250+	Literacy 2000	Rigby
Hare and the Tortoise, The	J	TL	587	Aesop's Fables	Pearson Learning Group
Hare and the Tortoise, The	K	TL	250+	PM Tales and Plays-Purple	Rigby
Hare's Big Tug-of-War	I	TL	207	Instant Readers	Harcourt School Publishers
Harlem Globetrotters, The: Clown Princes of Basketball	T	I	250+	High Five Reading	Red Brick Learning
Harold and the Purple Crayon	K	F	660	Johnson, Crockett	Harper & Row
Harold's Flyaway Kite	G	F	166	First Start	Troll Associates
Harriet Beecher Stowe and the Beecher Preachers	X	B	250+	Fritz, Jean	Penguin Group
Harriet the Spy	T	RF	250+	Fitzhugh, Louise	HarperCollins
Harriet Tubman	O	B	250+	Early Biographies	Compass Point Books
Harriet Tubman	U	B	250+	Let Freedom Ring	Red Brick Learning
Harriet Tubman	P	B	250+	McLoone, Margo	Red Brick Learning
Harriet Tubman	N	B	239	Pebble Books	Capstone Press
Harriet Tubman and the Underground Railroad	X	B	2159	Leveled Readers	Houghton Mifflin
Harriet Tubman: A Lesson in Bravery	M	B	250+	Rosen Real Readers	Rosen Publishing Group
Harriet Tubman: A Woman of Courage	K	B	170	Independent Readers Social Studies	Houghton Mifflin
Harriet's Hare	O	F	250+	King-Smith, Dick	Alfred A. Knopf
Harris and Me	V	RF	250+	Paulsen, Gary	Bantam
Harry and Chicken	S	F	250+	Sheldon, Dyan	Candlewick Press
Harry and the Lady Next Door	J	F	250+	Zion, Gene	HarperTrophy
Harry and Willy and Carrothead	K	RF	250+	Caseley, Judith	Scholastic
Harry Cat's Pet Puppy	R	F	250+	Selden, George	Bantam
Harry Gets Ready for School	G	F	170	Ziefert, Harriet	Puffin Books
Harry Goes to Day Camp	F	F	250+	Ziefert, James	Puffin Books
Harry Goes to Fun Land	F	F	166	Ziefert, Harriet	Puffin Books
Harry Hates Shopping!	K	F	250+	Armitage, Ronda & David	Scholastic
Harry Houdini: Master of Magic	R	B	250+	Kraske, Robert	Scholastic
Harry Houdini: Wonderdog!	N	RF	250+	Taylor, William	Pacific Learning
Harry Houdini: Young Magician	O	B	250+	Childhood of Famous Americans	Aladdin
Harry On Vacation	S	SF	250+	Sheldon, Dyan	Candlewick Press
Harry Potter and the Chamber of Secrets	V	F	250+	Rowling, J. K.	Scholastic
Harry Potter and the Goblet of Fire	W	F	250+	Rowling, J. K.	Scholastic
Harry Potter and the Half-Blood Prince	W	F	250+	Rowling, J. K.	Scholastic
Harry Potter and the Order of the Phoenix	W	F	250+	Rowling, J. K.	Scholastic
Harry Potter and the Prisoner of Azkaban	V	F	250+	Rowling, J. K.	Scholastic
Harry Potter and the Sorcerer's Stone	V	F	250+	Rowling, J. K.	Scholastic
Harry S. Truman	U	B	250+	Profiles of the Presidents	Compass Point Books
Harry Takes a Bath	G	F	132	Ziefert, Harriet	Puffin Books
Harry the Explorer	S	F	250+	Sheldon, Dyan	Candlewick Press
Harry's Hat	B	RF	45	Little Books	Sadlier-Oxford
Harry's Hats	D	F	49	Teacher's Choice Series	Pearson Learning Group
Harry's House	F	RF	83	Medearis, Angela; Keeter, Susan	Scholastic
Harry's Mad	P	F	250+	King-Smith, Dick	Alfred A. Knopf
Harvest Festivals	O	I	250+	Windows on Literacy	National Geographic
Harvest Time	J	I	228	Spyglass Books	Compass Point Books
Harvest Time	H	I	184	Yellow Umbrella Books	Red Brick Learning
Hat Came Back, The	K	RF	250+	Literacy 2000	Rigby
Hat Trick	C	RF	38	Literacy 2000	Rigby
Hat, The	LB	F	12	Ready Readers	Pearson Learning Group
Hatchet	R	RF	250+	Paulsen, Gary	Aladdin
Hatching Chickens at School	H	RF	94	City Kids	Rigby

* Collection of short stories

TITLE	LEVEL	GENRE	WORD COUNT	AUTHOR / SERIES	PUBLISHER / DISTRIBUTOR
Hats	C	RF	35	Joy Readers	Pearson Learning Group
Hats	C	RF	43	Little Readers	Houghton Mifflin
Hats	C	I	27	Twig	Wright Group/McGraw Hill
Hats	LB	I	46	Williams, Deborah	Kaeden Books
Hats	F	I	114	Wonder World	Wright Group/McGraw Hill
Hats	F	I	88	Talk About Books	Pearson Learning Group
Hats Around the World	B	I	59	Charlesworth, Liza	Scholastic
Hats for the Carnival	H	RF	231	Lighthouse	Rigby
Hats!	E	RF	59	Early Readers	Compass Point Books
Hats!	C	F	28	Learn to Read	Creative Teaching Press
Hatshepsut and Nerfertiti: Egyptian Queens	X	B	2135	Leveled Readers Social Studies	Houghton Mifflin
Hatshepsut Egypt's Woman King	Y	I	250+	iOpeners	Pearson Learning Group
Hattie and the Fox	I	TL	321	Fox, Mem	Bradbury/Trumpet
Hatupatu and the Birdwoman	J	F	250+	Story Box	Wright Group/McGraw Hill
Hau Kola Hello Friend	O	B	250+	Goble, Paul	Richard C. Owen
Haunted	Q	F	250+	Ragged Island Mysteries	Wright Group/McGraw Hill
Haunted Bike, The	L	F	250+	Herman, Gail	Grosset & Dunlap
Haunted Halloween, The	M	F	250+	Schultz, Irene	Wright Group/McGraw Hill
Haunted House, The	E	F	77	Story Box	Wright Group/McGraw Hill
Haunting of Grade Three, The	O	RF	250+	Maccarone, Grace	Scholastic
Have a Cookout	A	RF	21	Little Books for Early Readers	University of Maine
Have Numbers, Will Travel	WB	I	N/A	Gosset, Rachel	Scholastic
Have You Ever Found a Beetle?	F	I	94	Voyages	SRA/McGraw Hill
Have You Got Everything, Colin?	D	RF	72	Rigby Literacy	Rigby
Have You Seen a Javelina?	K	F	250+	Literacy 2000	Rigby
Have You Seen Birds?	K	I	250+	Oppenheim, Joanne; Reid, Barbara	Scholastic
Have You Seen Hyacinth Macaw?	R	RF	250+	Giff, Patricia Reilly	Dell
Have You Seen Joe?	D	RF	57	Home Connection Collection	Rigby
Have You Seen My Cat?	B	F	93	Carle, Eric	Putnam
Have You Seen My Duckling?	WB	F	N/A	Tafuri, Nancy	Greenwillow
Have You Seen the Crocodile?	F	F	150	West, Colin	Harper & Row
Have You Seen the Tooth Fairy?	E	RF	187	Visions	Wright Group/McGraw Hill
Have You Seen?	C	RF	38	Literacy 2000	Rigby
Having a Haircut	J	RF	298	City Kids	Rigby
Having Fun	D	I	78	Windows on Literacy	National Geographic
Having Fun	B	RF	35	Early Emergent	Pioneer Valley
Having My Hair Washed	I	RF	171	City Kids	Rigby
Hawaii	R	I	250+	This Land Is Your Land	Compass Point Books
Hawaii	S	I	250+	Land of Liberty	Red Brick Learning
Hawaii	T	I	250+	Sea to Shining Sea	Children's Press
Hawaii	L	I	240	Windows on Literacy	National Geographic
Hawaii: The Aloha State	Q	I	250+	Rosen Real Readers	Rosen Publishing Group
Hawaiian Magic	R	I	250+	Morris, Rod	Pacific Learning
Hawkers' Amazing Machines, The: A Play	K	F	250+	Phonics and Friends	Hampton-Brown
Hawks	R	I	250+	Predators in the Wild	Red Brick Learning
Hawks	F	RF	87	Seedlings	Continental Press
Hay for Ambrosia	G	I	86	Pacific Literacy	Pacific Learning
Hay Making	F	I	62	Wonder World	Wright Group/McGraw Hill
Haymeadow, The	T	RF	250+	Paulsen, Gary	Dell
Haystack, The	L	RF	250+	Cambridge Reading	Pearson Learning Group
He Bear, She Bear	J	F	250+	Berenstain, Stan & Jan	Random House
He Who Listens	K	RF	250+	Literacy 2000	Rigby
Head For the Hills!	O	I	250+	Walker, Paul Robert	Random House

* Collection of short stories

TITLE	LEVEL	GENRE	WORD COUNT	AUTHOR / SERIES	PUBLISHER / DISTRIBUTOR
Head Full of Notions, A: A Story about Robert Fulton	S	B	250+	Russell Bowen, Andy	Carolrhoda Books
Headache, The	B	RF	20	Oxford Reading Tree	Oxford University Press
Headfirst into the Oatmeal	L	F	250+	Rigby Literacy	Rigby
Headless Horseman, The	L	TL	250+	Standiford, Natalie	Random House
Headlines from Space	Q	I	250+	Rigby Focus	Rigby
Heads and Tails	LB	I	29	Windmill Books	Rigby
Healthy Food	I	I	162	PM Plus Nonfiction	Rigby
Healthy Visit, A	E	I	44	New Way Red	Steck-Vaughn
Hear Our Stories	Y	I	250+	iOpeners	Pearson Learning Group
Hearing	J	I	107	Pebble Books	Capstone Press
Heartbeat	W	RF	250+	Creech, Sharon	HarperCollins
Heart's Blood	X	F	250+	Yolen, Jane	Harcourt Trade
Heat	I	I	203	Early Connections	Benchmark Education
Heat all Around	E	I	120	Leveled Readers Science	Houghton Mifflin
Heat and Eat!	C	I	79	Independent Readers Science	Houghton Mifflin
Heat Changes Things	G	I	101	Instant Readers	Harcourt School Publishers
Heat Changes Things	E	I	46	Windows on Literacy	National Geographic
Heat Is On, The	U	I	250+	Tanaka, Shelley	Firefly Books
Heather and the Pink Poodles	Q	RF	250+	Engle, Marion	Magic Attic
Heather at the Barre	Q	RF	250+	Sinykin, Sheri Cooper	Magic Attic
Heather Goes to Hollywood	Q	RF	250+	Sinykin, Sheri Cooper	Magic Attic
Heather Takes the Reins	Q	RF	250+	Sinykin, Sheri Cooper	Magic Attic
Heather, Belle of the Ball	Q	RF	250+	Sinykin, Sheri Cooper	Magic Attic
Heather's Book	K	RF	250+	Ready Readers	Pearson Learning Group
Heather's Story	R	I	250+	Orbit Double Takes	Pacific Learning
*Heavy Weight and Other Cases, The	O	RF	250+	Simon, Seymour	Avon
Heavyweights	O	I	250+	Paul, Michele	Wright Group/McGraw Hill
Hedgehog Bakes a Cake	J	F	250+	Bank Street	Bantam
Hedgehog Day	I	I	121	Seedlings	Continental Press
Hedgehog in the Hall	Q	RF	250+	Daniels, Lucy	Barron's Educational
Hedgehog Is Hungry	C	RF	48	PM Story Books	Rigby
Helen Keller	P	B	250+	Photo-Illustrated Biographies	Red Brick Learning
Helen Keller	N	B	250+	Davidson, Margaret	Scholastic
Helen Keller: A Light For The Blind	R	B	250+	Kudlinski, Kathleen V.	Penguin Group
Helen Keller: Courage in the Dark	N	B	250+	Hurwitz, Johanna	Random House
Helen Keller: Crusader for the Blind and Deaf	P	B	250+	Graff, Stewart & Polly Anne	Bantam
Helen Keller: From Tragedy to Triumph	O	B	250+	Childhood of Famous Americans	Aladdin
Helen Keller's Teacher	N	B	250+	Davidson, Margaret	Scholastic
Helen's Job	A	RF	24	Phonics and Friends	Hampton-Brown
Helga's Secret	J	RF	250+	Rigby Literacy	Rigby
Helicopter Over Hawaii	LB	I	21	Twig	Wright Group/McGraw Hill
Helicopters	N	I	250+	A True Book	Children's Press
Helicopters	T	I	250+	The World's Fastest	Red Brick Learning
Hello	C	F	63	Story Box	Wright Group/McGraw Hill
Hello Chick!	D	I	54	Leveled Readers Language Support	Houghton Mifflin
Hello Creatures!	K	I	250+	Literacy 2000	Rigby
Hello Flower	B	RF	20	Bebop Books	Lee & Low Books Inc.
Hello Goodbye	B	F	29	Literacy 2000	Rigby
Hello Puppet	C	I	26	Voyages	SRA/McGraw Hill
Hello!	F	I	17	Chessen, Betsey; Bergen, Samantha	Scholastic
Hello, Cat: You Need a Hat	I	F	250+	Gelman, Rita	Scholastic

* Collection of short stories

TITLE	LEVEL	GENRE	WORD COUNT	AUTHOR / SERIES	PUBLISHER / DISTRIBUTOR
Hello, Dad!	D	RF	16	Pacific Literacy	Pacific Learning
Hello, Doctor	F	RF	44	Rookie Reader	Children's Press
Hello, First Grade	I	RF	250+	Ryder, Joanne	Troll Associates
Hello, Friend	C	F	39	Instant Readers	Harcourt School Publishers
Hello, Hello, Hello	E	RF	56	Sunshine	Wright Group/McGraw Hill
Hello, Little Chick!	D	I	56	Leveled Readers	Houghton Mifflin
*Hello, Mrs. Piggle-Wiggle	O	F	250+	MacDonald, Betty	HarperTrophy
Hello, My Name Is Scrambled Eggs	R	RF	250+	Gilson, Jamie	Pocket Books
Hello, Peter-Bonjour, Remy	L	F	250+	Little Celebrations	Pearson Learning Group
Help for Rosie	H	RF	165	Bella and Rosie Series	Pioneer Valley
Help Is on the Way	Q	I	372	Vocabulary Readers	Houghton Mifflin
Help Me	H	TL	196	Story Box	Wright Group/McGraw Hill
Help Me	D	RF	107	Emergent	Pioneer Valley
Help Me!	C	F	55	New Way Red	Steck-Vaughn
Help with the Herd	T	RF	1830	Leveled Readers	Houghton Mifflin
Help!	H	RF	82	Giant Step Readers	Educational Insights
Help!	C	I	57	Reading Corners	Pearson Learning Group
Help!	C	RF	57	Rigby Literacy	Rigby
Help! Help!	LB	RF	14	Joy Readers	Pearson Learning Group
Help! I'm a Prisoner in the Library	Q	RF	250+	Clifford, Eth	Scholastic
Help! I'm Stuck!	J	F	250+	Little Celebrations	Pearson Learning Group
Help! I'm Trapped in an Alien's Body	Q	F	250+	Strasser, Todd	Scholastic
Help! I'm Trapped in My Lunch Lady's Body	Q	F	250+	Strasser, Todd	Scholastic
Help! I'm Trapped in My Teacher's Body	Q	F	250+	Strasser, Todd	Scholastic
Help! I'm Trapped in Obedience School	Q	F	250+	Strasser, Todd	Scholastic
Help! I'm Trapped in Obedience School Again	Q	F	250+	Strasser, Todd	Scholastic
Help! I'm Trapped in Santa's Body	Q	F	250+	Strasser, Todd	Scholastic
Help! I'm Trapped in the First Day of School	Q	F	250+	Strasser, Todd	Scholastic
Help! I'm Trapped in the First Day of Summer Camp	Q	F	250+	Strasser, Todd	Scholastic
Help! I'm Trapped in the President's Body	Q	F	250+	Strasser, Todd	Scholastic
"Help!" Said Jed	C	TL	35	Instant Readers	Harcourt School Publishers
Helpful Becky	J	RF	250+	Phonics Readers Plus	Steck-Vaughn
Helpful Change, A	L	RF	250+	Behr, Alexandra	Hampton-Brown
*Helpful Harry and Other Stories	L	RF	250+	New Way Literature	Steck-Vaughn
Helpful or Harmful?	O	I	250+	Orbit Double Takes	Pacific Learning
Helping	F	RF	79	Bookshop	Mondo
Helping	D	RF	79	Joy Readers	Pearson Learning Group
Helping	F	RF	103	Well-Being Series	Pearson Learning Group
Helping Dad	C	RF	34	Sunshine	Wright Group/McGraw Hill
Helping Mom and Dad	E	RF	121	Learn to Read	Creative Teaching Press
Helping My Dad	D	RF	90	Teacher's Choice Series	Pearson Learning Group
Helping Out	L	RF	317	Independent Readers Social Studies	Houghton Mifflin
Helping the Hoiho	S	I	250+	Literacy 2000	Rigby
Helping Wild Animals	R	I	582	Vocabulary Readers	Houghton Mifflin
Helping You	D	I	53	Interaction	Rigby
Helping You Heal	H	I	145	Community Workers	Picture Window Books
Helping You Learn: Book About Teachers, A	H	I	147	Community Workers	Picture Window Books
Hen Can, A	E	F	159	Tiger Cub	Peguis
Hen, The Rooster, and the Bean, The	I	TL	250+	Kratky, Lada Josefa	Hampton-Brown
Henny Penny	H	TL	292	New Way Green	Steck-Vaughn
Henny Penny	I	TL	250+	Zimmerman, H. Werner	Scholastic
Henny Penny	I	TL	582	Galdone, Paul	Clarion

* Collection of short stories

TITLE	LEVEL	GENRE	WORD COUNT	AUTHOR / SERIES	PUBLISHER / DISTRIBUTOR
Henri de Toulouse-Lautrec	R	B	250+	Venezia, Mike	Children's Press
Henri Matisse	R	B	250+	Venezia, Mike	Children's Press
Henri Rousseau	T	B	250+	Rabott, Ernest	HarperTrophy
Henry	F	F	141	Instant Readers	Harcourt School Publishers
Henry	T	RF	250+	Bawden, Nina	Bantam
Henry	E	RF	77	Books for Young Learners	Richard C. Owen
Henry and Beezus	O	RF	250+	Cleary, Beverly	Avon
Henry and Mudge and Annie's Good Move	J	RF	250+	Rylant, Cynthia	Aladdin
Henry and Mudge and the Bedtime Thumps	J	RF	250+	Rylant, Cynthia	Aladdin
Henry and Mudge and the Best Day of All	J	RF	250+	Rylant, Cynthia	Aladdin
Henry and Mudge and the Careful Cousin	J	RF	250+	Rylant, Cynthia	Aladdin
Henry and Mudge and the Forever Sea	J	RF	250+	Rylant, Cynthia	Aladdin
Henry and Mudge and the Happy Cat	J	RF	250+	Rylant, Cynthia	Aladdin
Henry and Mudge and the Long Weekend	J	RF	250+	Rylant, Cynthia	Aladdin
Henry and Mudge and the Sneaky Crackers	J	RF	250+	Rylant, Cynthia	Aladdin
Henry and Mudge and the Snowman Plan	J	RF	250+	Rylant, Cynthia	Aladdin
Henry and Mudge and the Starry Night	J	RF	250+	Rylant, Cynthia	Aladdin
Henry and Mudge and the Wild Wind	J	RF	250+	Rylant, Cynthia	Aladdin
Henry and Mudge Get the Cold Shivers	J	RF	250+	Rylant, Cynthia	Aladdin
Henry and Mudge in Puddle Trouble	J	RF	250+	Rylant, Cynthia	Aladdin
Henry and Mudge in the Family Trees	J	RF	250+	Rylant, Cynthia	Aladdin
Henry and Mudge in the Green Time	J	RF	250+	Rylant, Cynthia	Aladdin
Henry and Mudge in the Sparkle Days	J	RF	250+	Rylant, Cynthia	Aladdin
Henry and Mudge Take the Big Test	J	RF	250+	Rylant, Cynthia	Aladdin
Henry and Mudge Under the Yellow Moon	J	RF	250+	Rylant, Cynthia	Aladdin
Henry and Mudge: The First Book	J	RF	250+	Rylant, Cynthia	Aladdin
Henry and Ribsy	O	RF	250+	Cleary, Beverly	Hearst
Henry and the Clubhouse	O	RF	250+	Cleary, Beverly	Avon
Henry and the Fox	K	RF	388	Leveled Readers	Houghton Mifflin
Henry and the Helicopter	D	RF	58	Literacy 2000	Rigby
Henry and the Paper Route	O	RF	250+	Cleary, Beverly	Hearst
Henry Ford: Young Man with Ideas	O	B	250+	Childhood of Famous Americans	Aladdin
Henry Gonzales, U.S. Representative	N	B	491	Leveled Readers Social Studies	Houghton Mifflin
Henry Huggins	O	RF	250+	Cleary, Beverly	Avon
Henry Reed, Inc.	X	F	250+	Robertson, Keith	Puffin Books
Henry Runs Away	F	RF	150	Books for Young Learners	Richard C. Owen
Henry's Busy Day	E	F	112	Campbell, Rod	Penguin Group
Henry's Choice	M	RF	527	Reading Unlimited	Pearson Learning Group
Henry's New Friend	I	RF	250+	Leveled Readers Language Support	Houghton Mifflin
Henry's Tricks	H	RF	162	Books for Young Learners	Richard C. Owen
Her Piano Sang: A Story About Clara Schumann	R	B	250+	Allman, Barbara	Carolrhoda Books
Her Seven Brothers	O	TL	250+	Goble, Paul	Aladdin
Herbert Hoover	U	B	250+	Profiles of the Presidents	Compass Point Books
Herbie Jones	N	RF	250+	Kline, Suzy	Penguin Group
Herbie Jones and Hamburger Head	N	RF	250+	Kline, Suzy	Penguin Group
Herbie Jones and the Birthday Showdown	N	RF	250+	Kline, Suzy	Penguin Group
Herbie Jones and the Class Gift	N	RF	250+	Kline, Suzy	Penguin Group
Herbie Jones and the Dark Attic	N	RF	250+	Kline, Suzy	Puffin Books
Herbie Jones and the Monster Ball	N	RF	250+	Kline, Suzy	Penguin Group
Hercules	W	I	250+	World Mythology	Capstone Press
Hercules and Other Greek Legends	T	TL	250+	Wildcats	Wright Group/McGraw Hill
Hercules Doesn't Pull Teeth	M	F	250+	Dadey, Debbie; Jones, Marcia Thornton	Scholastic

* Collection of short stories

TITLE	LEVEL	GENRE	WORD COUNT	AUTHOR / SERIES	PUBLISHER / DISTRIBUTOR
Here are My Hands	H	I	127	Bobber Book	SRA/McGraw Hill
Here Come the Bison	L	I	212	Sunshine	Wright Group/McGraw Hill
Here Come the Shapes	E	F	118	PM Plus Story Books	Rigby
Here Comes a Bus	F	F	171	Ziefert, Harriet	Penguin Group
Here Comes Annette!	E	RF	143	Voyages	SRA/McGraw Hill
Here Comes Everyone	F	RF	78	Cambridge Reading	Pearson Learning Group
Here Comes Kate!	J	RF	250+	Real Reading	Steck-Vaughn
Here Comes Little Chimp	D	F	69	PM Plus Story Books	Rigby
*Here Comes McBroom	O	F	250+	Fleischman, Sid	Beech Tree Books
Here Comes the Bus	B	RF	21	Bebop Books	Lee & Low Books Inc.
Here Comes the Cat	LB	RF	24	Asch, Frank	Scholastic
Here Comes the Parade!	B	RF	32	Pair-It Books	Steck-Vaughn
Here Comes the Rain!	C	I	47	Little Books	Sadlier-Oxford
Here Comes the Strikeout	K	RF	250+	Kessler, Leonard	HarperTrophy
Here Comes the Strikeout	I	RF	250+	Little Readers	Houghton Mifflin
Here Comes Winter	G	RF	134	First Start	Troll Associates
Here I Am!	B	RF	36	First Stories	Pacific Learning
Here Is . . .	B	I	49	Carousel Earlybirds	Pearson Learning Group
Here Is a Box	B	I	91	Rigby Literacy	Rigby
Here Is a Carrot	C	I	96	Foundations	Wright Group/McGraw Hill
Here Is a Seed	C	RF	23	Science	Outside the Box
Here Is Hen	A	F	21	Leveled Readers Language Support	Houghton Mifflin
*Here There Be Dragons	Y	F	250+	Yolen, Jane	Harcourt Trade
*Here There Be Witches	Y	F	250+	Yolen, Jane	Harcourt Trade
Here We All Are	N	B	250+	DePaola, Tomie	Penguin Group
Here we go round the mulberry bush	F	TL	208	PM Readalongs	Rigby
Here We Go Round the Mulberry Bush	D	RF	187	Little Readers	Houghton Mifflin
Here's a House	C	I	45	Windmill	Wright Group/McGraw Hill
Here's Bobby's World! How a TV Cartoon Is	L	I	250+	Little Celebrations	Pearson Learning Group
Here's Skipper	B	RF	28	Salem, Lynn; Stewart, Josie	Continental Press
Here's to Hats	L	I	250+	Sunshine	Wright Group/McGraw Hill
Here's to You, Rachel Robinson	T	RF	250+	Blume, Judy	Bantam
Here's What I Made	C	RF	38	Literacy 2000	Rigby
Herman Henry's Dog	I	F	250+	Little Readers	Houghton Mifflin
Herman the Helper	J	F	94	Kraus, Robert	Simon & Schuster
Herman the Helper Lends a Hand	F	F	198	Kraus, Robert	Windmill
Herman's Tooth	H	F	210	Foundations	Wright Group/McGraw Hill
Hermie the Crab	J	RF	250+	PM Plus Story Books	Rigby
Hermit Crab	E	I	111	PM Story Books	Rigby
Hermit Crab, The	G	RF	119	Sunshine	Wright Group/McGraw Hill
Hero and the Crown, The	Z	F	250+	McKinley, Robin	Puffin Books
Hero in the Mirror, The	M	RF	250+	Rigby Literacy	Rigby
Heroes	N	I	250+	Wildcats	Wright Group/McGraw Hill
Heroes & Idealists	U	B	250+	Real Lives	Troll Associates
Heros and Heroines	S	I	250+	Literacy 2000	Rigby
Hey Coach!	C	RF	37	TOTTS	Tott Publications
Hey Diddle Diddle	D	F	53	Seedlings	Continental Press
Hey There, Bear!	C	F	39	Little Celebrations	Pearson Learning Group
*Hey World, Here I Am!	S	RF	250+	Little, Jean	HarperTrophy
Hey, Al	N	F	250+	Yorinks, Arthur	Farrar, Straus and Giroux
Hey, Diddle, Diddle!	D	TL	30	Sunshine	Wright Group/McGraw Hill
Hey, New Kid!	N	RF	250+	Duffey, Betsy	Penguin Group
Hi Clouds	E	F	142	Rookie Reader	Children's Press

* Collection of short stories

TITLE	LEVEL	GENRE	WORD COUNT	AUTHOR / SERIES	PUBLISHER / DISTRIBUTOR
Hi Dog	D	RF	137	Ready Readers	Pearson Learning Group
Hiawatha, American Leader	M	B	535	Leveled Readers Social Studies	Houghton Mifflin
Hiccups	I	F	250+	Bookshop	Mondo
Hiccups for Elephant	I	F	250+	Preller, James	Scholastic
Hiccups for Hippo	I	F	100	Sunshine	Wright Group/McGraw Hill
Hiccups Would Not Stop, The	H	F	177	Ready Readers	Pearson Learning Group
Hickory Dickory Dock	D	F	20	Instant Readers	Harcourt School Publishers
Hickory, Dickory Pizza Clock	C	F	92	Little Celebrations	Pearson Learning Group
Hidden Hand, The	M	RF	250+	Schultz, Irene	Wright Group/McGraw Hill
Hidden World	R	I	250+	Explorers	Wright Group/McGraw Hill
Hide & Seek	H	I	138	Wonder World	Wright Group/McGraw Hill
Hide and Seek	K	I	250+	World Quest Adventures	World Quest Learning
Hide and Seek	I	I	250+	Phonics and Friends	Hampton-Brown
Hide and Seek	E	F	60	Instant Readers	Harcourt School Publishers
Hide and Seek	D	RF	49	New Way Red	Steck-Vaughn
Hide and Seek	B	RF	38	Literacy 2000	Rigby
Hide and Seek	D	F	63	Brown, Roberta; Carey, Sue	Scholastic
Hide and Seek	H	RF	215	Foundations	Wright Group/McGraw Hill
Hide and Seek	D	RF	108	PM Extensions-Red	Rigby
Hide and Seek	A	F	38	Smart Starts	Rigby
Hide and Seek	D	RF	49	Start to Read	School Zone
Hide and Seek	E	F	228	Sun Sprouts	ETA/Cuisenaire
Hide to Survive	L	I	250+	Home Connection Collection	Rigby
Hide!	C	F	81	Sun Sprouts	ETA/Cuisenaire
Hide, Spider!	G	F	179	Momentum Literacy Program	Troll Associates
Hide-and-Go-Seek	C	F	66	First Stories	Pacific Learning
Hide-and-Seek	H	F	546	Leveled Readers	Houghton Mifflin
Hide-and-Seek	H	F	250+	Momentum Literacy Program	Troll Associates
Hide-and-Seek All Week	I	RF	250+	DePaola, Tomie	Grosset & Dunlap
*Hide-and-Seek with Grandpa	J	F	250+	Lewis, Rob	Mondo
Hi-De-Hi	E	F	110	Little Celebrations	Pearson Learning Group
Hiders, The	M	I	250+	Sails	Rigby
Hiding	E	I	97	Foundations	Wright Group/McGraw Hill
Hiding	A	F	28	KinderReaders	Rigby
Hiding in Plain Sight	I	I	173	Instant Readers	Harcourt School Publishers
Hiding Places	J	I	250+	Storyteller-Night Crickets	Wright Group/McGraw Hill
High Flying	R	I	250+	Explorers	Wright Group/McGraw Hill
High Tide	X	I	2084	Independent Readers Science	Houghton Mifflin
High Wire	N	RF	250+	Orbit Double Takes	Pacific Learning
High-Flying Contest, The: An African American	N	F	639	Leveled Readers	Houghton Mifflin
High-Water Heroes	T	RF	2242	Leveled Readers	Houghton Mifflin
Highway Turtles, The	K	RF	250+	PM Plus Story Books	Rigby
Hike at Day Camp, The	C	RF	32	Visions	Wright Group/McGraw Hill
Hiking with Dad	H	RF	189	Wonder World	Wright Group/McGraw Hill
Hilary and the Lions	M	F	250+	Desaix, Frank	Farrar, Straus and Giroux
Hill of Fire	L	RF	1099	Lewis, Thomas P.	HarperCollins
Hillary Rodham Clinton: A New Kind of First Lady	S	B	250+	Guernsey, JoAnn Bren	Lerner Publishing
Hindu Holiday	P	I	494	Independent Readers Social Studies	Houghton Mifflin
Hippo from Another Planet	M	F	250+	Little Celebrations	Pearson Learning Group
Hippo in June's Tub, A	H	F	85	Little Books	Sadlier-Oxford
Hippo Pot and Hippo Tot	G	F	88	Supersonics	Rigby
Hippopotamus Ate the Teacher, A	J	F	250+	Thaler, Mike	Avon

* Collection of short stories

TITLE	LEVEL	GENRE	WORD COUNT	AUTHOR / SERIES	PUBLISHER / DISTRIBUTOR
Hippos	K	I	250+	PM Animal Facts: Turquoise	Rigby
Hippos	H	I	117	Story Steps	Rigby
Hippo's Hiccups	G	F	208	Literacy 2000	Rigby
Hiram Fong, Hawaii's First Senator	S	B	1726	Leveled Readers Social Studies	Houghton Mifflin
Hiroshima	S	HF	250+	Yep, Laurence	Scholastic
His Majesty the King	J	F	250+	Little Celebrations	Pearson Learning Group
Hispaniola: Island of Two Nations	T	I	1871	Independent Readers Social Studies	Houghton Mifflin
History Behind the Holidays	N	I	250+	Early Connections	Benchmark Education
History Nook, The	O	SF	250+	Phonics and Friends	Hampton-Brown
History of Electricity, A	S	I	794	Leveled Readers Science	Houghton Mifflin
History of Machines, The	O	I	250+	Home Connection Collection	Rigby
History of the Blues, The	S	I	250+	Rosen Real Readers	Rosen Publishing Group
History Walk	M	RF	250+	Pacific Literacy	Pacific Learning
Hit By a Blade	K	RF	250+	Foundations	Wright Group/McGraw Hill
Hit-Away Kid, The	M	RF	250+	Christopher, Matt	Little, Brown & Co.
Hitty: Her First Hundred Years	U	F	250+	Field, Rachel	Aladdin
*Ho Yi the Archer and Other Classic Chinese Tales	X	TL	250+	Fu, Shelley	Linnet Books
Ho, Ho, Benjamin, Feliz Navidad	N	RF	250+	Giff, Patricia Reilly	Bantam
Hoang Anh: A Vietnamese-American Boy	T	B	250+	Hoyt-Goldsmith, Diane	Scholastic
Hobbit, The	Z	F	250+	Tolkien, J.R.R.	Ballantine Books
Hobby: The Young Merlin Trilogy	V	F	250+	Yolen, Jane	Scholastic
Hobnob the Troll	H	F	165	Supersonics	Rigby
Hobson Family Vacation, The	H	RF	250+	Momentum Literacy Program	Troll Associates
Hockey for Fun!	S	I	250+	Sports for Fun	Compass Point Books
Hockey Practice	G	RF	134	Geddes, Diana	Kaeden Books
Hocus Pocus	M	I	250+	Wildcats	Wright Group/McGraw Hill
Hogboggit, The	D	RF	65	Pacific Literacy	Pacific Learning
Hoiho's Chicks	D	I	38	Pacific Literacy	Pacific Learning
Hoketichee and the Manatee	I	RF	113	Books for Young Learners	Richard C. Owen
Hole in Harry's Pocket, The	I	RF	250+	Little Readers	Houghton Mifflin
Hole in the Hedge, The	F	F	188	Sunshine	Wright Group/McGraw Hill
Hole in the Hill, The	N	RF	250+	Action Packs	Rigby
Hole Is A Great Home, A	F	RF	236	Phonics and Friends	Hampton-Brown
Holes	V	RF	250+	Sachar, Louis	Random House
Holidays	J	I	191	Windows on Literacy	National Geographic
Holidays at Our Home	I	RF	88	Leveled Readers Social Studies	Houghton Mifflin
Holly & Mac	N	RF	250+	SupaDoopers	Sundance
Home	M	RF	250+	Voyages	SRA/McGraw Hill
Home at Last	D	F	94	Sun Sprouts	ETA/Cuisenaire
Home Crafts	T	I	250+	Historic Communities	Crabtree
Home for a Dog, A	G	RF	146	Book Bus	Creative Edge
Home for a Puppy	G	RF	194	First Start	Troll Associates
Home for Diggory, A	K	RF	250+	Pacific Literacy	Pacific Learning
Home for Little Teddy, A	D	F	153	PM Extensions-Red	Rigby
Home for Mindy, A	H	I	250+	Rigby Literacy	Rigby
Home for Star and Patches, A	J	RF	250+	PM Plus Story Books	Rigby
Home for the Howl-idays	S	F	250+	Regan, Diane Curtis	Scholastic
Home in the Sky	K	RF	250+	Baker, Jeannie	Scholastic
Home Run, The	E	RF	92	Teacher's Choice Series	Pearson Learning Group
Home Sweet Home	E	I	172	Roffey, Maureen	Bodley
Home Sweet Home	N	I	250+	Literacy 2000	Rigby
Home Sweet Home, Goodbye	R	RF	250+	Stowe, Cynthia	Scholastic

TITLE	LEVEL	GENRE	WORD COUNT	AUTHOR / SERIES	PUBLISHER / DISTRIBUTOR
Home, A	D	I	40	Instant Readers	Harcourt School Publishers
Home: A Journey Through America	R	I	250+	Locker, Thomas	Voyager Books
Homecoming	X	RF	250+	Voigt, Cynthia	Ballantine Books
Homegirl on the Range (Sister Sister)	S	RF	250+	Quin-Harkin, Janet	Pocket Books
Homeless Bird	X	RF	250+	Whelan, Gloria	HarperCollins
*Homer Price	Q	RF	250+	McCloskey, Robert	Puffin Books
Homes	I	I	244	Yellow Umbrella Books	Red Brick Learning
Homes	B	I	63	Bookshop	Mondo
Homes	D	I	42	Rise & Shine	Hampton-Brown
Homes	C	I	69	Storyteller Nonfiction	Wright Group/McGraw Hill
Homes Are for Living	M	I	417	Cumpiano, Ina	Hampton-Brown
Homes Around the World	D	I	192	iOpeners	Pearson Learning Group
Homes Around the World	I	I	192	Rigby Focus	Rigby
Homes Around the World	C	I	73	Early Connections	Benchmark Education
Homes for People	B	I	40	Early Connections	Benchmark Education
Homesick, My Own Story	X	B	250+	Fritz, Jean	Penguin Group
Hometown Turtles	P	RF	1175	Leveled Readers	Houghton Mifflin
Homework	F	RF	57	City Stories	Rigby
Honesty	L	I	250+	Character Education	Red Brick Learning
Honey Bees	D	I	41	Pebble Books	Capstone Press
Honey Bees	M	I	250+	Kahkonen, Sharon	Steck-Vaughn
Honey Bees and Flowers	G	I	67	Pebble Books	Capstone Press
Honey Bees and Hives	E	I	58	Pebble Books	Capstone Press
Honey Bees and Honey	F	I	57	Pebble Books	Capstone Press
Honey for Baby Bear	F	F	200	PM Story Books	Rigby
Honey Hunt	E	RF	63	Sunshine	Wright Group/McGraw Hill
Honey Tree, The	L	F	250+	Literacy 2000	Rigby
Honey, My Rabbit	E	RF	56	Voyages	SRA/McGraw Hill
Honk!	B	F	36	Bookshop	Mondo
Honorable Prison, The	W	HF	250+	Becerra de Jenkins, Lyll	Penguin Group
Hoofprints	D	RF	62	Teacher's Choice Series	Pearson Learning Group
Hoop Dancers	L	I	250+	Phonics and Friends	Hampton-Brown
Hoops	X	RF	250+	Myers, Walter Dean	Bantam
Hoopstars: Go to the Hoop!	M	RF	250+	Hughes, Dean	Random House
Hooray for Midsommar!	J	RF	250+	Greetings	Rigby
Hooray for Snail	F	F	102	Stadler, John	HarperCollins
Hooray for Snow	D	RF	15	Voyages	SRA/McGraw Hill
Hooray for the Golly Sisters!	K	RF	250+	Byars, Betsy	HarperTrophy
Hoot	W	RF	250+	Hiaasen, Carl	Alfred A. Knopf
Hop and Stop	C	RF	35	Books for Young Learners	Richard C. Owen
Hop on Pop	J	F	250+	Seuss, Dr.	Random House
Hop to it, Minty!	O	RF	250+	PM Ruby	Rigby
Hop, Skip, Run	E	RF	109	Real Kids Readers	Millbrook Press
Hope Not	D	RF	83	Salem, Lynn; Stewart, Josie	Continental Press
Hope Was Here	W	RF	250+	Bauer, Joan	G.P. Putnam's Sons
Hopi, The	P	I	250+	Native Peoples	Red Brick Learning
Hopscotch	P	I	250+	Games Around the World	Compass Point Books
Horace	D	F	56	Story Box	Wright Group/McGraw Hill
Horatio Whale	J	F	165	Book Bus	Creative Edge
Horns, Scales, Claws, and Tales	I	I	208	Story Steps	Rigby
*Horrakapotchkin	M	F	250+	Pacific Literacy	Pacific Learning
Horrible Big Black Bug, The	D	RF	50	Tadpoles	Rigby
Horrible Harry and the Ant Invasion	L	RF	250+	Kline, Suzy	Scholastic
Horrible Harry and the Christmas Surprise	L	RF	250+	Kline, Suzy	Scholastic

* Collection of short stories

TITLE	LEVEL	GENRE	WORD COUNT	AUTHOR / SERIES	PUBLISHER / DISTRIBUTOR
Horrible Harry and the Drop of Doom	L	RF	250+	Kline, Suzy	Puffin Books
Horrible Harry and the Dungeon	L	RF	250+	Kline, Suzy	Penguin Group
Horrible Harry and the Green Slime	L	RF	250+	Kline, Suzy	Penguin Group
Horrible Harry and the Kickball Wedding	L	RF	250+	Kline, Suzy	Penguin Group
Horrible Harry and the Purple People	L	F	250+	Kline, Suzy	Puffin Books
Horrible Harry in Room 2B	L	RF	250+	Kline, Suzy	Penguin Group
Horrible Harry Moves Up to Third Grade	L	RF	250+	Kline, Suzy	Puffin Books
Horrible Harry's Secret	L	RF	250+	Kline, Suzy	Penguin Group
Horrible Thing with Hairy Feet	H	TL	208	Read Alongs	Rigby
Horrible Urktar of Or, The	G	F	143	Sunshine	Wright Group/McGraw Hill
Horrie the Hoarder	K	RF	250+	Voyages	SRA/McGraw Hill
Horrors of the Haunted Museum	Q	RF	250+	Stine, R. L.	Scholastic
Horse	M	I	250+	Life Cycles	Creative Teaching Press
Horse and His Boy, The	T	F	250+	Lewis, C. S.	Collier Books
Horse and the Bell, The	J	TL	250+	PM Plus Story Books	Rigby
*Horse and the Donkey, The	I	F	382	New Way Green	Steck-Vaughn
Horse Called Sky, A	M	RF	250+	Leveled Readers Language Support	Houghton Mifflin
Horse Feathers	D	I	41	Pair-It Books	Steck-Vaughn
Horse in Harry's Room, The	J	F	425	Hoff, Syd	HarperCollins
Horse Power	O	I	250+	Pacific Literacy	Pacific Learning
Horse, of Course, The	Q	I	250+	Action Packs	Rigby
Horseback Riding for Fun!	S	I	250+	Activities for Fun	Compass Point Books
Horses	D	I	43	All About Pets	Red Brick Learning
Horses	F	I	131	Twig	Wright Group/McGraw Hill
Horses	N	I	250+	A New True Book	Children's Press
Horses	P	I	250+	Crabapples	Crabtree
Horses	E	I	131	Pebble Books	Capstone Press
Horses	L	I	250+	PM Animal Facts: Purple	Rigby
Horses Have Foals	M	I	250+	Animals and Their Young	Compass Point Books
Horse's Hiccups	F	F	83	Storyteller-Moon Rising	Wright Group/McGraw Hill
Horses of the Air	N	I	250+	Little Celebrations	Pearson Learning Group
Horses of the Sea	P	I	250+	Rigby Literacy	Rigby
Horses on the Farm	I	I	120	Pebble Books	Red Brick Learning
Hospital Party, The	H	RF	237	PM Plus Story Books	Rigby
Hospitals	L	I	177	Bookshop	Mondo
Hostile Hospital, The	V	F	250+	Snicket, Lemony	Scholastic
Hot Air Balloons	L	I	479	Pair-It Books	Steck-Vaughn
Hot and Cold	C	I	47	Windows on Literacy	National Geographic
Hot and Cold Summer	O	RF	250+	Hurwitz, Johanna	Scholastic
Hot and Cold Weather	K	I	922	Sunshine	Wright Group/McGraw Hill
Hot Day, A	E	I	61	Pebble Books	Capstone Press
Hot Dogs	I	RF	196	City Kids	Rigby
Hot Dogs (Sausages)	C	RF	84	PM Story Books	Rigby
Hot Fudge Hero	L	RF	250+	Brisson, Pat	Henry Holt & Co.
Hot Potato and Cold Potato	C	I	77	Foundations	Wright Group/McGraw Hill
Hot Rod Harry	E	RF	66	Rookie Readers	Children's Press
Hot Sidewalks	C	RF	28	Visions	Wright Group/McGraw Hill
Hot Sunny Days	F	I	122	PM Plus Nonfiction	Rigby
Hot Surprise, A	H	RF	162	Rigby Literacy	Rigby
Houdini's Last Trick	O	B	250+	Hass, Elizabeth	Random House
Hour of the Olympics	M	F	250+	Osborne, Mary Pope	Random House
House	WB	I	N/A	Felix, Monique	Stewart, Tabori & Chang
House	C	I	47	Little Celebrations	Pearson Learning Group

TITLE	LEVEL	GENRE	WORD COUNT	AUTHOR / SERIES	PUBLISHER / DISTRIBUTOR
House Book, The	LB	I	17	Windows on Literacy	National Geographic
House Cleaning	LB	RF	19	Book Bank	Wright Group/McGraw Hill
House for a Mouse, A	LB	F	21	Pacific Literacy	Pacific Learning
House for Hickory, A	H	F	174	Bookshop	Mondo
House for Little Red	F	RF	78	Just Beginning	Modern Curriculum
House for Me, A	C	I	71	Twig	Wright Group/McGraw Hill
House for Sergin, A	M	RF	250+	Greetings	Rigby
House Gobbaleen, The	P	F	250+	Alexander, Lloyd	Penguin Group
House Hunting	G	RF	223	PM Story Books	Rigby
House in the Snow, The	S	RF	250+	Engh, M. J.	Scholastic
House in the Tree, The	F	RF	202	PM Story Books	Rigby
House of Dies Drear	V	HF	250+	Hamilton, Virginia	Aladdin
House of Mirrors, The	M	F	250+	Weaver, Betty-May	Wright Group/McGraw Hill
House of Stairs	Z	F	250+	Sleator, William	Puffin Books
House of the Horrible Ghosts	M	F	250+	Hayes, Geoffrey	Random House
House of Wings, The	R	RF	250+	Byars, Betsy	Penguin Group
House on Mango Street, The	W	RF	250+	Cisneros, Sandra	Alfred A. Knopf
House on the Hill, The	F	F	189	PM Plus Story Books	Rigby
House on Walenska Street, The	N	RF	250+	Herman, Charlotte	Penguin Group
House Spider's Life, A	K	I	230	Himmelman, John	Scholastic
House that Jack Built, The	I	TL	201	Cat on the Mat	Oxford University Press
House that Jack Built, The	J	TL	250+	Peppe, Rodney	Delacorte
House That Jack's Friends Built, The	J	RF	254	Pair-It Books	Steck-Vaughn
House that Stood on Booker Hill, The	J	RF	250+	Ready Readers	Pearson Learning Group
House Through the Ages	U	I	250+	Steele, Philip	Troll Associates
House with a Clock in its Walls, The	S	F	250+	Bellairs, John	Penguin Group
House, A	A	I	32	PM Starters One	Rigby
Houses	G	I	51	Learn to Read	Creative Teaching Press
Houses	M	I	279	Wonder World	Wright Group/McGraw Hill
Houses	I	I	103	Windows on Literacy	National Geographic
Houses	C	RF	38	Windmill	Wright Group/McGraw Hill
Houses	C	I	64	Story Box	Wright Group/McGraw Hill
Houses	B	I	64	Rigby Literacy	Rigby
Houses	C	I	35	Little Celebrations	Pearson Learning Group
Houses and Homes	G	RF	250+	PM Plus Poetry	Rigby
Houses That Move	K	I	250+	Voyages	SRA/McGraw Hill
How 100 Dandelions Grew	E	I	173	Instant Readers	Harcourt School Publishers
How a Book is Made	N	I	250+	Aliki	Harper & Row
How a Frog Grows	I	I	136	Phonics Readers	Compass Point Books
How a House is Built	M	I	250+	Gibbons, Gail	Scholastic
How a Plant Grows	O	I	250+	Kalman, Bobbie	Crabtree
How a Volcano is Formed	M	I	135	Wonder World	Wright Group/McGraw Hill
*How Angel Peterson Got His Name: And Other Outrageous Tales About Extreme Sports	U	RF	250+	Paulsen, Gary	Random House
How Animals Hide	F	I	98	Wonder World	Wright Group/McGraw Hill
How Animals Move	G	I	132	Discovery Links	Newbridge
How Animals Move	L	I	132	Discovery World	Rigby
How Animals Move	L	I	250+	First Facts	Capstone Press
How Animals Move Around	L	I	593	PM Plus Nonfiction	Rigby
How Ants Live	I	I	159	Sunshine	Wright Group/McGraw Hill
How Are Magnets Used?	I	I	166	Windows on Literacy	National Geographic
How Are We the Same?	D	I	100	Teacher's Choice Series	Pearson Learning Group
How Bat Learned to Fly	H	TL	168	Storyteller-Night Crickets	Wright Group/McGraw Hill
How Big Is a Foot?	K	F	250+	Myller, Rolf	Bantam

* Collection of short stories

TITLE	LEVEL	GENRE	WORD COUNT	AUTHOR / SERIES	PUBLISHER / DISTRIBUTOR
How Big Is Big?	F	I	158	Ziefert, Harriet	Puffin Books
How Big Is It?	J	RF	250+	Lighthouse	Rigby
How Big? How Much?	H	I	134	Hutchins, Jeannie	Scholastic
How Birds Live	I	I	1090	Sunshine	Wright Group/McGraw Hill
How Bullfrog Found His Sound	M	F	250+	Michaels, Eric	Pearson Learning Group
How Can I Help?	E	RF	73	Learn to Read	Creative Teaching Press
How Can I Help?	D	I	65	Questions & Answers	Pearson Learning Group
How Can We See in the Dark?	H	I	157	Sunshine	Wright Group/McGraw Hill
How Can You Fix It?	B	I	56	Rigby Literacy	Rigby
How Chocolate Is Made	L	I	250+	Lighthouse	Rigby
How Did the Lights Go Out? The Story of the New York City Blackout	R	I	1175	Independent Readers Science	Houghton Mifflin
How Did This City Grow?	M	I	250+	Schaefer, Lola M.	Benchmark Education
How Do Airplanes Fly?	Q	I	250+	Rosen Real Readers	Rosen Publishing Group
How Do Animals Stay Alive?	I	I	193	Early Connections	Benchmark Education
How Do Fish Live?	I	I	1242	Sunshine	Wright Group/McGraw Hill
How Do Flies Walk Upside Down?	R	I	250+	Berger, Melvin & Gilda	Scholastic
How Do Frogs Grow?	G	I	42	Discovery Links	Newbridge
How Do Frogs Swallow with Their Eyes?	R	I	250+	Berger, Melvin	Scholastic
How Do I Feel?	D	I	64	Questions & Answers	Pearson Learning Group
How Do I Put It On?	H	I	168	Watanabe, Shiego	Penguin Group
How Do Plants Get Food?	L	I	250+	Goldish, Meish	Steck-Vaughn
How Do Plants Grow?	L	I	250+	Rosen Real Readers	Rosen Publishing Group
How Do Seeds Travel?	J	I	179	Windows on Literacy	National Geographic
How Do Trees Grow?	L	I	250+	Rosen Real Readers	Rosen Publishing Group
How Do You Feel Today?	L	I	250+	Rosen Real Readers	Rosen Publishing Group
How Do You Make a Bubble?	G	RF	250+	Hooks, William H.	Bantam
How Do You Measure a Dinosaur?	M	F	257	Pacific Literacy	Pacific Learning
How Do You Say Hello to A Ghost?	F	F	149	Tiger Cub	Peguis
How Does a Plant Grow?	I	I	115	Instant Readers	Harcourt School Publishers
How Does It Breathe?	K	I	250+	Home Connection Collection	Rigby
How Does It Feel?	LB	I	11	Windows on Literacy	National Geographic
How Does It Grow?	L	I	250+	Home Connection Collection	Rigby
How Does My Bike Work?	J	I	127	Windows on Literacy	National Geographic
How Does My Garden Grow?	H	I	73	Windows on Literacy	National Geographic
How Does Sound Travel?	J	I	148	Instant Readers	Harcourt School Publishers
How Does This Sound?	L	I	260	Independent Readers Science	Houghton Mifflin
How Does Your Salad Grow?	H	I	136	Alexander, Francie	Scholastic
How Dog Lost His Bone	E	TL	100	Leveled Readers Language Support	Houghton Mifflin
How Far Is It?	L	I	250+	Rosen Real Readers	Rosen Publishing Group
How Far Will I Fly?	F	RF	94	Oyama, Sachi	Scholastic
How Fire Came to Earth	K	TL	250+	Literacy 2000	Rigby
How Flamingos Came to Have Red Legs: A South American Folk Tale	M	TL	250+	Jensen, Ned	Wright Group/McGraw Hill
How Flexible Are You?	M	I	250+	Marks, Ashley	Wright Group/McGraw Hill
How Flies Live	I	I	448	Sunshine	Wright Group/McGraw Hill
How Flowers Grow	E	I	68	Rosen Real Readers	Rosen Publishing Group
How Goods Are Moved	K	I	250+	People, Spaces & Places	Rand McNally
How Grandmother Spider Got the Sun	J	TL	115	Little Readers	Houghton Mifflin
How Has It Changed?	D	I	103	Rigby Literacy	Rigby
How Have I Grown	G	RF	235	Reid, Mary	Scholastic
How I Came to Be a Writer	W	B	250+	Naylor, Phyllis Reynolds	Scholastic
How I Fixed the Year 1000 Problem	N	F	250+	The Zack Files	Grosset & Dunlap

* Collection of short stories

TITLE	LEVEL	GENRE	WORD COUNT	AUTHOR / SERIES	PUBLISHER / DISTRIBUTOR
How I Go	F	I	138	Early Connections	Benchmark Education
How I Met Archie	M	RF	250+	Kenna, Anna	Pacific Learning
How I Met Einstein: A Character Comes to Life	S	I	250+	Trussell-Cullen, Alan	Pacific Learning
How I Move	A	RF	21	Leveled Readers Science	Houghton Mifflin
How I Went from Bad to Verse	N	F	250+	The Zack Files	Grosset & Dunlap
How Is a Crayon Made?	P	I	250+	Oz, Charles	Scholastic
How Kittens Grow	L	I	250+	Selsam, Millicent E.	Scholastic
How Leaves Change Color	M	I	250+	Rosen Real Readers	Rosen Publishing Group
How Lizard Lost His Colors	J	TL	197	Literacy Tree	Rigby
How Long Do Animals Live?	D	I	65	Pacific Literacy	Pacific Learning
How Long Is a Foot?	M	I	250+	Twig	Wright Group/McGraw Hill
How Machines Help	D	I	143	Sunshine	Wright Group/McGraw Hill
How Many Animals?	A	I	25	Vocabulary Readers	Houghton Mifflin
How Many Ants?	E	RF	35	Rookie Readers	Children's Press
How Many Are Left?	I	I	225	Early Connections	Benchmark Education
How Many Bugs in a Box?	LB	F	126	Carter, David	Simon & Schuster
How Many Can Play?	D	I	46	Canizares, Susan; Chessen, Betsey	Scholastic
How Many Days to America?: A Thanksgiving Story	S	I	250+	Bunting, Eve	Houghton Mifflin
How Many Ducks?	F	F	88	Chapman, Cindy	Scholastic
How Many Fish?	B	F	30	Gosset, Rachel; Ballinger, Margaret	Scholastic
How Many Frogs?	C	I	44	Leveled Readers Language Support	Houghton Mifflin
How Many Hot Dogs?	E	I	115	Story Box	Wright Group/McGraw Hill
How Many Jelly Beans	B	RF	61	Phonics and Friends	Hampton-Brown
How Many Kittens?	C	I	37	Twig	Wright Group/McGraw Hill
How Many Legs?	B	I	19	Windmill	Wright Group/McGraw Hill
How Many Legs?	C	F	47	Science	Outside the Box
How Many Legs?	E	I	104	Early Connections	Benchmark Education
How Many Legs?	D	I	74	Bookshop	Mondo
How Many Monkeys?	B	F	16	Pair-It Books	Steck-Vaughn
How Many Pets?	D	RF	37	Bookshop	Mondo
How Many Seeds?	E	I	42	Pair-It Books	Steck-Vaughn
How Many?	C	I	45	Learn to Read	Creative Teaching Press
How Many?	E	I	147	Early Connections	Benchmark Education
How Much Does This Hold?	K	RF	179	Coulton, Mia	Kaeden Books
How Much Is That Guinea Pig in the Window?	L	RF	250+	Rocklin, Joanne	Scholastic
How My Family Lives in America	O	I	250+	Kuklin, Susan	Aladdin
How My Pet Grew	I	RF	235	Leveled Readers Science	Houghton Mifflin
How News Travels	M	I	250+	PM Plus Nonfiction	Rigby
How Owl Changed His Hoot	I	TL	227	Sunshine	Wright Group/McGraw Hill
How People Got Wisdom: An Ashanti Tale	N	TL	891	Leveled Readers	Houghton Mifflin
How People Move Around	L	I	541	PM Plus Nonfiction	Rigby
How Spider Tricked Snake	K	TL	250+	Real Reading	Steck-Vaughn
How Spiders Got Eight Legs	L	F	884	Pair-It Books	Steck-Vaughn
How Spiders Live	F	I	145	Sunshine	Wright Group/McGraw Hill
How the Animals Got Their Tails	L	TL	250+	Cambridge Reading	Pearson Learning Group
How the Chick Tricked the Fox	G	F	167	Ready Readers	Pearson Learning Group
How the Donosaurs Disappeared	L	I	250+	Rosen Real Readers	Rosen Publishing Group
How the Giraffe Became a Giraffe	M	TL	648	Sunshine	Wright Group/McGraw Hill
How the Mouse Got Brown Teeth	I	F	250+	Bookshop	Mondo
How the Rattlesnake Got Its Rattle	L	TL	1006	Pair-It Books	Steck-Vaughn
How the Sky Got Its Stars	G	TL	208	Instant Readers	Harcourt School Publishers

* Collection of short stories

TITLE	LEVEL	GENRE	WORD COUNT	AUTHOR / SERIES	PUBLISHER / DISTRIBUTOR
*How the Tortoise Got His Shell and Other Stories	K	TL	250+	New Way Literature	Steck-Vaughn
How the Water Got to the Plains	L	TL	250+	Home Connection Collection	Rigby
How Things Move	H	I	214	Yellow Umbrella Books	Red Brick Learning
How Things Work	R	I	250+	Explorers	Wright Group/McGraw Hill
How To Be Cool in the Third Grade	N	RF	250+	Duffey, Betsy	Penguin Group
How to Be Healthy	K	I	250+	Rosen Real Readers	Rosen Publishing Group
How To Choose a Pet	L	I	250+	Discovery World	Rigby
How to Clean a Dinosaur	G	F	208	Windmill Books	Rigby
How To Cook Scones	J	I	250+	Bookshop	Mondo
How To Eat Fried Worms	R	RF	250+	Rockwell, Thomas	Bantam
How to Grow a Plant	E	I	172	Visions	Wright Group/McGraw Hill
How To Grow Crystals	P	I	250+	Bookshop	Mondo
How to Make a Bird Feeder	D	I	80	Rigby Literacy	Rigby
How to Make a Card	G	I	69	Urmston, Kathleen; Evans, Karen	Kaeden Books
How to Make a Crocodile	H	F	62	Little Books	Sadlier-Oxford
How to Make a Hen House	B	I	25	Ready Readers	Pearson Learning Group
How to Make a Hot Dog	C	I	48	Story Box	Wright Group/McGraw Hill
How To Make a Kite	M	I	250+	Reeder, Paul	Wright Group/McGraw Hill
How to Make a Lion Mask	G	I	133	Instant Readers	Harcourt School Publishers
How to Make a Mud Pie	H	RF	127	Little Readers	Houghton Mifflin
How to Make a Mudpie	A	I	32	Learn to Read	Creative Teaching Press
How to Make a Salad	A	I	12	Vocabulary Readers	Houghton Mifflin
How to Make a Sandwich	C	I	27	Visions	Wright Group/McGraw Hill
How to Make a Sun Hat	E	I	87	Home Connection Collection	Rigby
How to Make a Wind Sock	B	F	20	Tarlow, Ellen	Scholastic
How to Make Can Stilts	C	I	28	Story Box	Wright Group/McGraw Hill
How to Make Cheese Muffins	K	I	220	Voyages	SRA/McGraw Hill
How To Make Salsa	J	I	192	Bookshop	Mondo
How to Make Snack Mix	C	I	47	Oppenlander, Meredith	Kaeden Books
How to Make Sock Puppets	H	I	229	Bookshop	Mondo
How to Ride a Giraffe	I	F	191	Little Readers	Houghton Mifflin
How To Speak Dolphin in Three Easy Lessons	N	F	250+	The Zack Files	Grosset & Dunlap
How to Stay Safe at Home and On-Line	M	I	250+	Rosen Real Readers	Rosen Publishing Group
How to Weigh an Elephant	K	F	390	Pacific Literacy	Pacific Learning
How Turtle Got His Tail	H	F	248	Rigby Literacy	Rigby
How Turtle Raced Beaver	J	TL	182	Literacy 2000	Rigby
How We Make Music	H	I	104	Rosen Real Readers	Rosen Publishing Group
How We Vote	L	I	314	Independent Readers Social Studies	Houghton Mifflin
How Will I Get to Grandma's House?	D	F	103	Blevins, Wiley	Scholastic
How Wisdom Came to the World: An Ashanti Tale	M	TL	250+	Khan, Benjamin	Houghton Mifflin
Howard Carter: Searching for King Tut	W	B	250+	Ford, Barbara	W. H. Freeman & Co.
Howie Has a Stomachache	E	F	100	Moore, Johnny R.	Continental Press
Howie Merton and the Magic Dust	M	F	250+	Reeves, Faye Couch	Random House
Howliday Inn	P	F	250+	Howe, James	Atheneum
Howling at the Hauntly's	M	RF	250+	Dadey, Debbie; Jones, Marcia Thornton	Scholastic
*Howling Dog and Other Cases, The	O	RF	250+	Simon, Seymour	Avon
How's the Weather	B	I	29	Learn to Read	Creative Teaching Press
How's the Weather?	N	I	250+	Berger, Melvin & Gilda	Ideals Children's Books
Hubble Space Telescope, The	N	I	250+	A True Book	Children's Press
Huberta the Hiking Hippo	L	RF	250+	Literacy 2000	Rigby

* Collection of short stories

TITLE	LEVEL	GENRE	WORD COUNT	AUTHOR / SERIES	PUBLISHER / DISTRIBUTOR
Hudson: Henry Hudson Searches for a Passage to Asia	U	B	250+	Exploring the World	Compass Point Books
Hue Boy	M	RF	250+	Mitchell, Rita Phillips	Penguin Group
Hug Bug	F	F	65	Start to Read	School Zone
Hug Is Warm, A	C	F	60	Sunshine	Wright Group/McGraw Hill
Huge Carrot, The	D	F	50	Leveled Readers	Houghton Mifflin
Huggles Breakfast	LB	F	14	Sunshine	Wright Group/McGraw Hill
Huggles Can Juggle	LB	F	15	Sunshine	Wright Group/McGraw Hill
Huggles Goes Away	LB	F	14	Sunshine	Wright Group/McGraw Hill
Huggly, Snuggly Pets	F	RF	142	Giant Step Readers	Educational Insights
Hugo Hogget: Story Based on an Ecuadoran Legend	K	TL	528	Cumpiano, Ina	Hampton-Brown
Hullabaloo at the Zoo	G	F	172	Lighthouse	Rigby
Human Body Math	T	I	250+	Navigators Math Series	Benchmark Education
Human Body, The	Q	I	250+	Explorers	Wright Group/McGraw Hill
Hummingbird	N	I	250+	Life Cycles	Creative Teaching Press
Hummingbird Garden	K	RF	252	Story Box	Wright Group/McGraw Hill
Humongous Cat, The	I	F	250+	Sunshine	Wright Group/McGraw Hill
Humpback Whale, The	S	I	250+	Frahm, Randy	Red Brick Learning
Humpback Whales	E	I	48	Pair-It Books	Steck-Vaughn
Humpback Whales	F	I	72	Ready Readers	Pearson Learning Group
Humphrey	M	RF	250+	Literacy Tree	Rigby
Humpity-Bump!	C	F	36	Little Celebrations	Pearson Learning Group
Humpty Dumpty	D	F	28	Instant Readers	Harcourt School Publishers
Humpty Dumpty	C	F	42	Seedlings	Continental Press
Humpty Dumpty	D	TL	26	Jumbled Tumbled Tales & Rhymes	Rigby
Humpty Dumpty	D	TL	27	Peppe, Rodney	Penguin Group
Hundred Dresses, The	O	RF	250+	Estes, Eleanor	Scholastic
Hundred Hugs, A	I	F	229	Sunshine	Wright Group/McGraw Hill
Hundred Penny Box, The	P	RF	250+	Mathis, Sharon Bell	Puffin Books
Hungry Animals	G	I	127	Little Readers	Houghton Mifflin
Hungry Bear	C	F	22	Smart Starts	Rigby
Hungry Chickens, The	G	F	107	Literacy Tree	Rigby
Hungry Farmer, The	E	RF	149	Learn to Read	Creative Teaching Press
Hungry Fox, The	E	F	158	Early Connections	Benchmark Education
Hungry Fox, The	LB	I	12	Rigby Literacy	Rigby
Hungry Giant, The	F	F	183	Story Box	Wright Group/McGraw Hill
Hungry Giant's Birthday Cake, The	G	F	241	Story Basket	Wright Group/McGraw Hill
Hungry Giant's Lunch, The	F	F	140	Story Box	Wright Group/McGraw Hill
Hungry Giant's Soup, The	G	F	42	Story Basket	Wright Group/McGraw Hill
Hungry Goat, The	D	F	30	Ray's Readers	Outside the Box
Hungry Goat, The	C	F	33	Rise & Shine	Hampton-Brown
Hungry Happy Monkey	E	F	77	Joy Readers	Pearson Learning Group
Hungry Hedgehog	C	F	79	Story Steps	Rigby
Hungry Horse	E	RF	35	Literacy 2000	Rigby
Hungry Kitten	C	F	50	Teacher's Choice Series	Pearson Learning Group
Hungry Kitten, The	D	F	95	PM Story Books	Rigby
Hungry Monster	I	F	241	Story Box	Wright Group/McGraw Hill
Hungry Red Hawk, A	K	I	2312	Independent Readers Science	Houghton Mifflin
Hungry Sea Star, The	I	I	69	Books for Young Learners	Richard C. Owen
Hungry Turtle	F	I	173	Handprints D, Set 1	Educator's Publishing Service
Hungry, Hungry Jack	I	RF	173	Lighthouse	Rigby
Hungry, Hungry Sharks	L	I	250+	Cole, Joanna	Random House

* Collection of short stories

TITLE	LEVEL	GENRE	WORD COUNT	AUTHOR / SERIES	PUBLISHER / DISTRIBUTOR
Hunt for Clues, A	G	RF	157	Ready Readers	Pearson Learning Group
Hunt for Pirate Gold, The	M	F	250+	Schultz, Irene	Wright Group/McGraw Hill
Hunted, The	O	I	250+	Rigby Focus	Rigby
Hunter and the Animals, The	WB	RF	N/A	DePaola, Tomie	Holiday House
Hunting Sharks	M	I	250+	Pull Ahead Books	Lerner Publishing
Hunting the Horned Lizard	R	I	250+	Bishop, Nic	Pacific Learning
Hunting with My Camera	S	I	250+	Literacy 2000	Rigby
Hup Pups	F	F	89	Supersonics	Rigby
Hurdles and Jumps	M	I	250+	Reeder, Tracey	Wright Group/McGraw Hill
*Hurray For Ali Baba Bernstein	O	RF	250+	Hurwitz, Johanna	Scholastic
Hurricane	S	HF	250+	Duey, Kathleen; Bale, Karen A.	Simon & Schuster
Hurricane	D	RF	36	Joy Readers	Pearson Learning Group
Hurricane Diary	T	RF	3392	Leveled Readers Science	Houghton Mifflin
*Hurricane Machine and Other Cases, The	O	RF	250+	Simon, Seymour	Avon
Hurricane Music	Y	RF	2564	Leveled Readers	Houghton Mifflin
Hurricane Opal: Into the Storm	U	RF	1931	Leveled Readers	Houghton Mifflin
Hurricanes	T	I	250+	iOpeners	Pearson Learning Group
Hurricanes & Tornadoes	R	I	250+	The Wonders of our World	Crabtree
Hurricanes and Storms	M	I	250+	Rosen Real Readers	Rosen Publishing Group
Hurricanes!	N	I	250+	Hopping, Jean	Scholastic
Hurry Squirrel!	E	RF	72	Start to Read	School Zone
Hurry Up	D	RF	49	Voyages	SRA/McGraw Hill
Hush Up!	L	F	250+	Little Celebrations	Pearson Learning Group
Hushtown: A Peaceful Community	Q	RF	250+	Massie, Elizabeth	Steck-Vaughn
Hut in the Old Tree, The	I	RF	250+	PM Plus Story Books	Rigby
Huzzard Buzzard	F	F	112	Reese, Bob	Children's Press
Hyenas	O	I	250+	Holmes, Kevin J.	Red Brick Learning
*Hypnotized Frog and Other Cases, The	O	RF	250+	Simon, Seymour	Avon
Hyrax of Top-Knot Island, The	S	I	1762	Leveled Readers	Houghton Mifflin
Hyrax, The: An Interesting Puzzle	R	I	250+	Leveled Readers Language Support	Houghton Mifflin
I Am	B	RF	32	Seedlings	Continental Press
I Am	A	RF	21	Klein, Adria	Scholastic
I Am	B	RF	32	Little Readers	Houghton Mifflin
I Am	D	RF	27	Rookie Readers	Children's Press
I Am . . .	A	RF	20	Sunshine	Wright Group/McGraw Hill
I Am a Bookworm	C	F	32	Sunshine	Wright Group/McGraw Hill
I Am a Dentist	C	I	20	Read-More Books	Pearson Learning Group
I Am a Drummer	E	I	32	iOpeners	Pearson Learning Group
I Am a Fireman	D	I	45	Read-More Books	Pearson Learning Group
I Am a Gypsy Pot	K	F	220	Evangeline Nicholas Collection	Wright Group/McGraw Hill
I Am a Photographer	E	I	32	Read-More Books	Pearson Learning Group
I Am a Rock	J	I	250+	Marzollo, Jean	Scholastic
I Am a Star	B	RF	32	Little Readers	Houghton Mifflin
I Am a Star	I	I	195	Marzollo, Jean	Scholastic
I Am A Star: Child of the Holocaust	W	I	250+	Auerbacher, Inge	Penguin Group
I Am a Train Driver	D	I	32	Read-More Books	Pearson Learning Group
I Am an American: A True Story of Japanese Internment	Z	HF	250+	Stanley, Jerry	Scholastic
I Am an Artist	C	I	30	Rosen Real Readers	Rosen Publishing Group
I Am an Explorer	D	RF	32	Rookie Readers	Children's Press
I Am Busy	C	RF	43	Windows on Literacy	National Geographic
I Am Cold	E	RF	136	Foundations	Wright Group/McGraw Hill
I Am Frightened	B	RF	41	Story Box	Wright Group/McGraw Hill

* Collection of short stories

TITLE	LEVEL	GENRE	WORD COUNT	AUTHOR / SERIES	PUBLISHER / DISTRIBUTOR
I Am Generous	G	I	89	Pebble Books	Capstone Press
I Am Going	B	RF	31	Sun Sprouts	ETA/Cuisenaire
I Am Hot	E	RF	123	Foundations	Wright Group/McGraw Hill
I Am Jumping	A	RF	24	Sun Sprouts	ETA/Cuisenaire
I Am King!	E	F	57	My First Reader	Grolier Press
I Am Not Afraid	K	RF	250+	Mann, Kenny	Bantam
I Am Patriotic	H	I	76	Pebble Books	Red Brick Learning
I Am Planet Earth	G	I	124	Marzollo, Jean	Scholastic
I Am Polite	G	I	76	Pebble Books	Capstone Press
I Am Regina	U	HF	250+	Keehn, Sally	Bantam
I Am Rosa Parks	O	B	250+	Parks, Rosa	Dial Books
I Am Running	A	I	24	PM Plus Starters	Rigby
I Am Special	C	RF	38	Learn to Read	Creative Teaching Press
I Am Thankful	A	RF	42	Carousel Earlybirds	Pearson Learning Group
I Am the Cheese	Z	RF	250+	Cormier, Robert	Laurel-Leaf Books
I Am the Ice Worm	S	F	250+	Easley, Mary Ann	Yearling
I Am Tolerant	H	I	132	Pebble Books	Red Brick Learning
I Am Water	A	I	25	Independent Readers Science	Houghton Mifflin
I Bought My Lunch Today	I	I	90	City Kids	Rigby
I Can	B	RF	21	New Way	Steck-Vaughn
I Can	B	RF	54	Little Readers	Houghton Mifflin
I Can	A	RF	21	Carousel Earlybirds	Pearson Learning Group
I Can	C	RF	27	Visions	Wright Group/McGraw Hill
I Can	B	RF	40	Ready Readers	Pearson Learning Group
I Can Be Anything	E	RF	242	Pair-It Books	Steck-Vaughn
I Can Breathe Underwater	G	RF	44	Windows on Literacy	National Geographic
I Can Build a House	D	I	52	Watanabe, Shiego	Viking
I Can Change Things!	A	RF	29	Leveled Readers Science	Houghton Mifflin
I Can Dig	C	I	45	Can You Do This?	SRA/McGraw Hill
I Can Do Anything!	C	RF	21	Sunshine	Wright Group/McGraw Hill
I Can Do It	I	RF	200	Bookshop	Mondo
I Can Do It Myself	C	RF	37	Literacy 2000	Rigby
I Can Do It Myself	E	RF	150	Visions	Wright Group/McGraw Hill
I Can Do It!	D	RF	74	Early Learning Modules	Steck-Vaughn
I Can Do It, I Really Can	G	RF	195	Teacher's Choice Series	Pearson Learning Group
I Can Do Many Things	C	RF	43	Carousel Readers	Pearson Learning Group
I Can Draw	C	RF	37	Learn to Read	Creative Teaching Press
I Can Draw	C	RF	75	Carousel Earlybirds	Pearson Learning Group
I Can Draw	A	I	33	Sun Sprouts	ETA/Cuisenaire
I Can Eat	C	I	51	Can You Do This?	SRA/McGraw Hill
I Can Find	E	I	131	Teacher's Choice Series	Pearson Learning Group
I Can Fly	F	F	107	Carousel Readers	Pearson Learning Group
I Can Fly	B	F	21	Sunshine	Wright Group/McGraw Hill
I Can Fly	C	F	68	Lighthouse	Rigby
I Can Hear	A	RF	32	TOTTS	Tott Publications
I Can Help	D	RF	65	Teacher's Choice Series	Pearson Learning Group
I Can Hop. Can You?	B	I	41	Independent Readers Science	Houghton Mifflin
I Can Jump	C	F	40	Sunshine	Wright Group/McGraw Hill
I Can Make Music	B	I	41	Little Red Readers	Sundance
I Can Make You Red	B	F	43	The Book Project	Sundance
I Can Measure an Elephant	R	I	521	Independent Readers Science	Houghton Mifflin
I Can Move!	A	I	18	Vocabulary Readers	Houghton Mifflin
I Can Move!	B	I	39	Leveled Readers Science	Houghton Mifflin
I Can Paint	A	RF	35	Book Bank	Wright Group/McGraw Hill

* Collection of short stories

TITLE	LEVEL	GENRE	WORD COUNT	AUTHOR / SERIES	PUBLISHER / DISTRIBUTOR
I Can Paint a Picture	C	I	26	Rosen Real Readers	Rosen Publishing Group
I Can Play	C	I	45	Can You Do This?	SRA/McGraw Hill
I Can Play	B	RF	32	Handprints B	Educator's Publishing Service
I Can Play Tangram	E	I	99	Pacific Literacy	Pacific Learning
I Can Push	A	RF	29	Bookshop	Mondo
I Can Read	A	I	35	Learn to Read	Creative Teaching Press
I Can Read	A	RF	35	Pacific Literacy	Pacific Learning
I Can Read	C	RF	38	Teacher's Choice Series	Pearson Learning Group
I Can Read Anything	C	F	42	Sunshine	Wright Group/McGraw Hill
I Can Read with My Eyes Shut	J	F	250+	Seuss, Dr.	Random House
I Can Read! I Can Read!	L	RF	250+	Little Celebrations	Pearson Learning Group
I Can Ride	C	I	66	Can You Do This?	SRA/McGraw Hill
I Can Ride	A	I	66	Sun Sprouts	ETA/Cuisenaire
I Can See	A	I	35	Independent Readers Science	Houghton Mifflin
I Can See	E	RF	38	Cervantes, Jesus	Scholastic
I Can See	B	RF	36	Rigby Focus	Rigby
I Can See	A	F	40	Carousel Earlybirds	Pearson Learning Group
I Can See My Shadow	F	I	55	Windows on Literacy	National Geographic
I Can See the Leaves	K	RF	368	Pacific Literacy	Pacific Learning
I Can See You	D	RF	66	Sun Sprouts	ETA/Cuisenaire
I Can Spell Dinosaur	F	RF	82	Predictable Storybooks	SRA/McGraw Hill
I Can Squeak	E	RF	154	Windmill	Wright Group/McGraw Hill
I Can Swim	D	RF	61	Ready Readers	Pearson Learning Group
I Can Take Care of the Earth	C	I	72	Independent Readers Science	Houghton Mifflin
I Can Talk with My Hands	G	RF	146	Learn to Read	Creative Teaching Press
I Can Taste	C	I	31	Teacher's Choice Series	Pearson Learning Group
I Can Use a Computer	D	RF	52	Teacher's Choice Series	Pearson Learning Group
I Can Wash	C	RF	66	Carousel Earlybirds	Pearson Learning Group
I Can Write	A	RF	40	Learn to Read	Pacific Learning
I Can Write, Can You?	B	RF	30	Stewart, Josie; Salem, Lynn	Continental Press
I Can!	F	I	131	Twig	Wright Group/McGraw Hill
I Can't Find It!	WB	RF	N/A	Rigby Literacy	Rigby
I Can't Open It!	E	F	76	Rigby Literacy	Rigby
I Can't Said the Ant	M	F	250+	Cameron, Polly	Scholastic
I Can't See	C	RF	36	Little Celebrations	Pearson Learning Group
I Can't Sleep	D	F	71	Learn to Read	Creative Teaching Press
I Can't Wait to Read	H	RF	185	Adventures in Reading	Pearson Learning Group
I Care: American Reformers	S	I	914	Independent Readers Social Studies	Houghton Mifflin
I Climb	C	I	57	This Is the Way I Go	SRA/McGraw Hill
I Could Be	D	RF	71	Sun Sprouts	ETA/Cuisenaire
I Could Be	B	RF	40	Visions	Wright Group/McGraw Hill
I Crawl	C	I	56	This Is the Way I Go	SRA/McGraw Hill
I Did It!	E	RF	213	Handprints D, Set 1	Educator's Publishing Service
I Did That!	I	RF	250+	Momentum Literacy Program	Troll Associates
I Do Not Like Peas	D	RF	32	Visions	Wright Group/McGraw Hill
I Don't Believe It!	L	RF	250+	Home Connection Collection	Rigby
I Don't Care	H	F	250+	Reading Friends	Pearson Learning Group
I Don't Care!	H	RF	250	TOTTS	Tott Publications
I Don't Like Peas	F	RF	89	Start to Read	School Zone
I Don't Think It's Fair	G	RF	147	Teacher's Choice Series	Pearson Learning Group
I Double Dare You	S	RF	1910	Leveled Readers	Houghton Mifflin

* Collection of short stories

TITLE	LEVEL	GENRE	WORD COUNT	AUTHOR / SERIES	PUBLISHER / DISTRIBUTOR
I Dream	K	RF	583	Sunshine	Wright Group/McGraw Hill
I Dress Up Like Mama	C	RF	35	Visions	Wright Group/McGraw Hill
I Eat Leaves	C	I	47	Bookshop	Mondo
I Feel Cold	C	RF	57	Home Connection Collection	Rigby
I Feel Hot	C	RF	58	Home Connection Collection	Rigby
I Feel Sick	A	RF	15	Science	Outside the Box
I Fixed Breakfast	H	RF	176	Teacher's Choice Series	Pearson Learning Group
I Fly	C	I	57	This Is the Way I Go	SRA/McGraw Hill
I Found a Can	C	I	33	Twig	Wright Group/McGraw Hill
I Get Ready for School	C	RF	37	Visions	Wright Group/McGraw Hill
I Get the Creeps	K	RF	250+	Reading Corners	Pearson Learning Group
I Get Tired	B	RF	37	Carousel Earlybirds	Pearson Learning Group
I Go to Gymnastics	D	I	58	Sun Sprouts	ETA/Cuisenaire
I Go, Go, Go	B	F	21	Sunshine	Wright Group/McGraw Hill
I Got a Goldfish	E	F	92	Ready Readers	Pearson Learning Group
I Grow Too!	C	I	30	Start to Read	School Zone
I Hadn't Meant to Tell You This	Z	RF	250+	Woodson, Jacqueline	Bantam
I Hate Camping	M	RF	250+	Petersen, P. J.	Penguin Group
I Hate Company	M	RF	250+	Petersen, P. J.	Penguin Group
I Hate English	L	RF	250+	Levine, Ellen	Scholastic
I Hate My Best Friend	L	RF	250+	Rosner, Ruth	Hyperion
I Have a Dream	Q	B	250+	Davidson, Margaret	Scholastic
I Have a Home	E	RF	79	Sunshine	Wright Group/McGraw Hill
I Have a New Baby Brother	F	F	163	Learn to Read	Creative Teaching Press
I Have a Paper Route	I	I	90	City Kids	Rigby
I Have a Pet	B	RF	35	Reading Corners	Pearson Learning Group
I Have a Question, Grandma	G	RF	124	Literacy 2000	Rigby
I Have a Watch!	C	RF	60	Williams, Deborah	Kaeden Books
I Have Another Language	F	RF	92	Instant Readers	Harcourt School Publishers
I Have Feelings!	J	F	250+	Book Shop	Mondo
I Have Lived a Thousand Years	Y	B	250+	Bitton-Jackson, Livia	Simon & Schuster
I Have Shoes	C	RF	24	Visions	Wright Group/McGraw Hill
I Hear!	A	I	33	Early Connections	Benchmark Education
I Heard the Owl Call My Name	Z	RF	250+	Craven, Margaret	Random House
I Help My Dad	A	I	24	Windows on Literacy	National Geographic
I Jump	C	I	56	This Is the Way I Go	SRA/McGraw Hill
I Know a Lady	L	RF	221	Zolotow, Charlotte	Penguin Group
I Know an Old Lady	K	TL	250+	Traditional Songs	Picture Window Books
I Know an Old Lady	H	F	82	Readalong Rhythms	Wright Group/McGraw Hill
I Know Karate	E	RF	62	Packard, Mary	Scholastic
I Know That Tune!	F	RF	201	Foundations	Wright Group/McGraw Hill
I Know That!	I	I	99	Sunshine	Wright Group/McGraw Hill
I Know, I Know!	U	RF	1820	Leveled Readers	Houghton Mifflin
I Like	C	RF	24	Literacy 2000	Rigby
I Like	A	RF	24	Sunshine	Wright Group/McGraw Hill
I Like	B	RF	53	Early Connections	Benchmark Education
I Like Apples	A	RF	12	Windows on Literacy	National Geographic
I Like Balloons	A	RF	27	Reading Corners	Pearson Learning Group
I Like Being Outdoors	WB	I	N/A	Windows on Literacy	National Geographic
I Like Bikes	A	I	24	Sun Sprouts	ETA/Cuisenaire
I Like Books	D	F	168	Browne, Anthony	Random House
I Like Cheese	G	I	105	Welcome Books	Children's Press
I Like Dogs	C	RF	35	Rigby Literacy	Rigby
I Like Fruit	LB	RF	18	Visions	Wright Group/McGraw Hill

* Collection of short stories

TITLE	LEVEL	GENRE	WORD COUNT	AUTHOR / SERIES	PUBLISHER / DISTRIBUTOR
I Like Green	B	F	28	The Book Project	Sundance
I Like Green	C	RF	47	Literacy 2000	Rigby
I Like It When . . .	E	RF	82	Ready Set Read	Steck-Vaughn
I Like Me	A	RF	31	Visions	Wright Group/McGraw Hill
I Like Mess	E	RF	74	Real Kids Readers	Millbrook Press
I Like My Picture!	D	RF	160	Teacher's Choice Series	Pearson Learning Group
I Like Painting	C	RF	42	Little Red Readers	Sundance
I Like Rice	B	I	36	First Stories	Pacific Learning
I Like Shapes	LB	RF	21	Armstrong, Shane	Scholastic
I Like Shopping	J	RF	287	Sunshine	Wright Group/McGraw Hill
I Like to Count	C	RF	40	Ready Readers	Pearson Learning Group
I Like to Eat	A	RF	41	Reading Corners	Pearson Learning Group
I Like to Eat	C	RF	56	Sunshine	Wright Group/McGraw Hill
I Like to Find Things	C	I	40	Sunshine	Wright Group/McGraw Hill
I Like to Help	B	RF	46	Little Books for Early Readers	University of Maine
I Like to Jump	C	F	50	Rigby Literacy	Rigby
I Like to Paint	A	RF	29	Reading Corners	Pearson Learning Group
I Like to Play	C	RF	50	Carousel Readers	Pearson Learning Group
I Like to Read	B	RF	49	Little Books for Early Readers	University of Maine
I Like to Read	A	RF	44	Early Emergent	Pioneer Valley
I Like to Ride	C	RF	72	Little Readers	Houghton Mifflin
I Like to Write	C	RF	62	Carousel Readers	Pearson Learning Group
I Like Worms!	D	F	213	Sunshine	Wright Group/McGraw Hill
I Listen	F	RF	84	Windows on Literacy	National Geographic
I Live in a House	D	I	51	Read-More Books	Pearson Learning Group
I Live in an Apartment	D	I	41	Read-More Books	Pearson Learning Group
I Live in an Apartment Building	I	I	111	City Kids	Rigby
I Live in the Rockies	L	I	259	Windows on Literacy	National Geographic
I Live on a Farm	C	I	42	Read-More Books	Pearson Learning Group
I Love a Parade	C	I	38	Yellow Umbrella Books	Red Brick Learning
I Love Bugs	C	RF	40	Bookshop	Mondo
I Love Camping	E	RF	83	Carousel Readers	Pearson Learning Group
I Love Camping	B	RF	34	Early Emergent	Pioneer Valley
I Love Cats	I	RF	104	Bookshop	Mondo
I Love Cats	E	RF	116	Rookie Readers	Children's Press
I Love Chickens	D	F	67	Story Box	Wright Group/McGraw Hill
I Love Fishing	D	RF	37	Rookie Readers	Children's Press
I Love Guinea Pigs	O	I	250+	King-Smith, Dick	Candlewick Press
I Love Ladybugs	C	RF	68	Van Allen, Roach	Wright Group/McGraw Hill
I Love Mud and Mud Loves Me	D	RF	121	Stephens, Vicki	Scholastic
I Love Music	C	RF	41	Carousel Readers	Pearson Learning Group
I Love My Family	B	RF	34	Foundations	Wright Group/McGraw Hill
I Love My Family	B	RF	31	Sunshine	Wright Group/McGraw Hill
I Love My Grandma	D	RF	36	Rise & Shine	Hampton-Brown
I Love the Beach	M	I	250+	Literacy 2000	Rigby
I Love to Sneeze	J	F	250+	Bank Street	Bantam
I Love You	E	F	121	Teacher's Choice Series	Pearson Learning Group
I Make Clay Pots	C	I	29	Bebop Books	Lee & Low Books Inc.
I Meowed	D	RF	58	Books for Young Learners	Richard C. Owen
I Need . . .	C	RF	23	Ray's Readers	Outside the Box
I Need a Book	F	RF	113	Sunshine	Wright Group/McGraw Hill
I Need a Rest	F	RF	119	Home Connection Collection	Rigby
I Need Glasses: My Visit to the Optometrist	M	RF	250+	Bookshop	Mondo
I Need to Clean My Room	F	RF	157	Learn to Read	Creative Teaching Press

* Collection of short stories

TITLE	LEVEL	GENRE	WORD COUNT	AUTHOR / SERIES	PUBLISHER / DISTRIBUTOR
I Paint	A	RF	22	Bookshop	Mondo
I Paint	A	I	22	Literacy 2000	Rigby
I Picked a Flower	C	RF	33	Science	Outside the Box
I Play Soccer	J	RF	97	City Kids	Rigby
I Play Soccer	C	RF	31	Bebop Books	Lee & Low Books Inc.
I Read	A	RF	38	Reading Corners	Pearson Learning Group
I Read Signs	LB	I	12	Hoban, Tana	Greenwillow
I Read Symbols	LB	I	14	Hoban, Tana	Greenwillow
I Remember	C	RF	26	Literacy 2000	Rigby
I Ride the Waves	I	RF	61	Books for Young Learners	Richard C. Owen
I Rode a Horse of Milk White Jade	V	HF	250+	Wilson, Diane Lee	HarperTrophy
I Run	B	RF	22	Carousel Earlybirds	Pearson Learning Group
I Run	C	I	56	This Is the Way I Go	SRA/McGraw Hill
I Said to Sam	M	F	250+	Molnar, Gwen	Scholastic
I Saw a Dinosaur	E	F	98	Book Bus	Creative Edge
I Saw a Dinosaur	G	F	55	Literacy 2000	Rigby
I Saw a Sign	F	RF	100	Literacy Tree	Rigby
I Saw the Boston Tea Party	J	HF	273	Independent Readers Social Studies	Houghton Mifflin
I Saw You in the Bathtub	J	TL	250+	Schwartz, Alvin	HarperTrophy
I See	B	F	29	Bookshop	Mondo
I See	A	I	32	Early Connections	Benchmark Education
I See	A	I	32	Sun Sprouts	ETA/Cuisenaire
I See	C	RF	29	Teacher's Choice Series	Pearson Learning Group
I See Animals Hiding	M	I	250+	Arnosky, Jim	Scholastic
I See Bugs	A	I	30	Blevins, Wiley	Scholastic
I See Colors	B	RF	50	Little Readers	Houghton Mifflin
I See Colors	B	I	23	Learn to Read	Creative Teaching Press
I See Fish	B	I	45	Curry, Don L.	Scholastic
I See Flags	C	I	31	Blevins, Wiley	Scholastic
I See Monkeys	C	RF	39	Williams, Deborah	Kaeden Books
I See Patterns	A	I	42	Learn to Read	Creative Teaching Press
I See Patterns	C	I	43	Yellow Umbrella Books	Red Brick Learning
I See Shapes	B	I	37	Learn to Read	Creative Teaching Press
I See Spring!	A	I	18	Vocabulary Readers	Houghton Mifflin
I See Tails!	B	I	42	Rise & Shine	Hampton-Brown
I See You	C	I	56	Twig	Wright Group/McGraw Hill
I Shop with My Daddy	G	RF	131	Maccarone, Grace	Scholastic
I Smell Smoke!	E	RF	49	Sunshine	Wright Group/McGraw Hill
I Spy	B	RF	30	Story Steps	Rigby
I Spy	C	RF	29	Literacy Tree	Rigby
I Spy	A	RF	31	Lighthouse	Rigby
I Spy a Fly	I	I	132	Wonder World	Wright Group/McGraw Hill
I Swim	C	I	57	This Is the Way I Go	SRA/McGraw Hill
I Take Care of My Dog	WB	RF	N/A	Rigby Literacy	Rigby
I Thought I Couldn't	C	RF	40	Visions	Wright Group/McGraw Hill
I Try to Be a Good Person	H	RF	192	Learn to Read	Creative Teaching Press
I Walk and Read	LB	I	16	Hoban, Tana	Greenwillow
I Want a Dog	F	RF	192	Sun Sprouts	ETA/Cuisenaire
I Want a Pet	C	RF	46	Little Readers	Houghton Mifflin
I Want a Pet	C	RF	46	Start to Read	School Zone
I Want a Red Ball	B	F	29	The Book Project	Sundance
I Want Ice Cream	C	RF	18	Story Box	Wright Group/McGraw Hill
I Want My Own Room!	LB	RF	25	Visions	Wright Group/McGraw Hill

* Collection of short stories

TITLE	LEVEL	GENRE	WORD COUNT	AUTHOR / SERIES	PUBLISHER / DISTRIBUTOR
I Want to be a Ballerina	D	RF	66	Teacher's Choice Series	Pearson Learning Group
I Want to Be a Clown	F	RF	82	Start to Read	School Zone
I Want to Be an Astronaut	I	RF	79	Barton, Byron	HarperCollins
I Want to Be...	B	F	46	The Book Project	Sundance
I Want to Go Camping	I	RF	407	Leveled Readers	Houghton Mifflin
I Was a Sixth Grade Alien	S	F	250+	Coville, Bruce	Pocket Books
I Was a Third Grade Science Project	N	RF	250+	Auch, Mary Jane	Yearling
I Was at the Zoo	J	I	250+	Literacy Tree	Rigby
I Was Just About To Go To Bed	E	RF	107	Instant Readers	Harcourt School Publishers
I Was So Mad	J	RF	232	Mayer, Mercer	Donovan
I Was Walking Down the Road	H	F	299	Barchas, Sarah	Scholastic
I Wash	B	RF	33	First Stories	Pacific Learning
I Went to the Beach	C	RF	25	Books for Young Learners	Richard C. Owen
I Went to the Dentist	K	RF	152	City Kids	Rigby
I Went to the Movies	J	RF	120	City Kids	Rigby
I Went to Visit a Friend One Day	F	F	111	Voyages	SRA/McGraw Hill
I Went Walking	C	RF	105	Williams, Sue	Harcourt Trade
I Will Plant You a Lilac Tree: A Memoir of a Schindler's List Survivor	Z	B	250+	Hillman, Laura	Atheneum
I Wish I Had a Dinosaur	D	F	46	Little Celebrations	Pearson Learning Group
I Wish I Was Sick Too	G	RF	94	Brandenburg, Franz	Morrow
I Wonder	C	RF	49	Little Celebrations	Pearson Learning Group
I Wonder	F	RF	67	Sunshine	Wright Group/McGraw Hill
I Wonder Why	E	RF	73	Foundations	Wright Group/McGraw Hill
I Wonder Why Snakes Shed Their Skins and Other Questions About Reptiles	O	I	250+	O'Neill, Amanda	Scholastic
I Wonder Why the Sky is Blue	O	I	250+	Rosen Real Readers	Rosen Publishing Group
I Wonder Why?	F	I	95	Wonder World	Wright Group/McGraw Hill
I Work at Night	D	RF	49	Windows on Literacy	National Geographic
I Write	B	RF	40	Little Books for Early Readers	University of Maine
I Write	C	RF	19	Sunshine	Wright Group/McGraw Hill
I Write for the Newspaper	I	I	145	Rosen Real Readers	Rosen Publishing Group
I, Amber Brown	N	RF	250+	Danziger, Paula	Scholastic
I. M. Pei	M	B	250+	Biography	Benchmark Education
Ibis: A True Whale Story	K	I	250+	Himmelman, John	Scholastic
Ice	I	I	92	Windows on Literacy	National Geographic
Ice Age Safari	P	I	250+	Rigby Focus	Rigby
Ice Cream	C	RF	49	Sunshine	Wright Group/McGraw Hill
Ice Cream for You	J	I	214	Windows on Literacy	National Geographic
*Ice Dove and Other Stories, The	M	RF	250+	deAnda, Diane	Arte Publico
Ice Fishing	H	I	140	Ready Readers	Pearson Learning Group
Ice Fishing	S	I	250+	The Great Outdoors	Red Brick Learning
Ice Is . . . Whee!	D	RF	59	Rookie Readers	Children's Press
Ice Magic	M	RF	250+	Christopher, Matt	Little, Brown & Co.
Ice Man, The: A Traditional Native American Tale	L	TL	250+	Rigby Literacy	Rigby
Ice Mummy: The Discovery of a 5,000-Year-Old Man	P	I	250+	Dubowski, Mark & Cathy East	Random House
Ice on the Move	K	I	362	Rigby Focus	Rigby
Ice Storms	Q	I	250+	Natural Disasters	Red Brick Learning
Iceberg Hermit, The	X	RF	250+	Roth, Arthur	Scholastic
Iceberg Rescue	N	I	464	Leveled Readers	Houghton Mifflin
Icebergs	L	I	250+	Sunshine	Wright Group/McGraw Hill
Ice-Cream Factory, The	I	I	250+	Rigby Literacy	Rigby

* Collection of short stories

TITLE	LEVEL	GENRE	WORD COUNT	AUTHOR / SERIES	PUBLISHER / DISTRIBUTOR
Ice-Cream Stick	B	RF	35	Story Box	Wright Group/McGraw Hill
Iceman	Z	RF	250+	Lynch, Chris	HarperCollins
Ichthyosaurus	N	I	250+	Discovering Dinosaurs	Red Brick Learning
*Icy Question and Other Cases, The	O	RF	250+	Simon, Seymour	Avon
Ida Lewis and the Lighthouse	S	I	973	Leveled Readers	Houghton Mifflin
Idaho	R	I	250+	This Land Is Your Land	Compass Point Books
Idaho	S	I	250+	Land of Liberty	Red Brick Learning
Iditarod: Dogsled Race Across Alaska	Q	I	250+	Fuerst, Jeffery B.	Wright Group/McGraw Hill
If	H	F	83	Sunshine	Wright Group/McGraw Hill
If a Tree Could Talk	G	F	62	Learn to Read	Creative Teaching Press
If Animals Came to School	F	F	125	Learn to Read	Creative Teaching Press
If Anything Ever Goes Wrong at the Zoo	L	F	250+	Hendrick, Mary Jean	Harcourt Trade
If Dogs Ruled the World	J	F	250+	McNulty, Faith	Scholastic
If Germs Were Purple	D	F	53	Carousel Readers	Pearson Learning Group
If Horses Could Talk!	E	RF	32	Teacher's Choice Series	Pearson Learning Group
If I Forget, You Remember	V	RF	250+	Williams, Carol Lynch	Bantam
If I Had an Alligator	H	F	214	Mayer, Mercer	Dial Books
If I Had an Elephant	F	F	90	Teacher's Choice Series	Pearson Learning Group
If I Were a Penguin	H	RF	159	Goeneil, Heidi	Little, Brown & Co.
If I Were an Ant	I	F	51	Rookie Readers	Children's Press
If I Were You	E	RF	77	Wildsmith, Brian	Oxford University Press
If We Could Do What the Animals Do	G	F	188	Learn to Read	Creative Teaching Press
If You Give A Moose A Muffin	K	F	250+	Numeroff, Laura Joffe	HarperCollins
If You Give A Mouse A Cookie	K	F	291	Numeroff, Laura Joffe	HarperCollins
If You Grew Up with Abraham Lincoln	Q	I	250+	McGovern, Ann	Scholastic
If You Grew Up with George Washington	Q	I	250+	Gross, Ruth Belov	Scholastic
If You Like Strawberries, Don't Read this Book	H	RF	101	Literacy 2000	Rigby
If You Lived 100 Years Ago	Q	I	250+	McGovern, Ann	Scholastic
If You Lived at the Time of Martin Luther King	Q	I	250+	Levine, Ellen	Scholastic
If You Lived at the Time of the American Revolution	Q	I	250+	Moore, Kay	Scholastic
If You Lived at the Time of the Civil War	Q	I	250+	Moore, Kay	Scholastic
If You Lived at the Time of the Great San Francisco Earthquake	Q	I	250+	Levine, Ellen	Scholastic
If You Lived in Colonial Times	Q	I	250+	McGovern, Ann	Scholastic
If you Lived in the Alaska Territory	Q	I	250+	Levinson, Nancy Smiler	Scholastic
If You Lived with the Cherokee	Q	I	250+	Roop, Peter & Connie	Scholastic
If You Lived with the Hopi	Q	I	250+	Kamma, Anne	Scholastic
If You Lived with the Iroquois	Q	I	250+	Levine, Ellen	Scholastic
If You Lived with the Sioux Indians	Q	I	250+	McGovern, Ann	Scholastic
If You Meet a Dragon	C	F	31	Story Box	Wright Group/McGraw Hill
If You Miss Your Bus	F	F	160	Leveled Readers	Houghton Mifflin
If You Sailed on the Mayflower in 1620	Q	I	250+	McGovern, Ann	Scholastic
If You Traveled on the Underground Railroad	Q	I	250+	Levine, Ellen	Scholastic
If You Traveled West in a Covered Wagon	Q	I	250+	Levine, Ellen	Scholastic
If You Were a Bat	F	F	78	Instant Readers	Harcourt School Publishers
If You Were There in 1492: Everyday Life in the Time of Columbus	U	I	250+	Brenner, Barbara	Aladdin
If You Were There When They Signed the Constitution	Q	I	250+	Levy, Elizabeth	Scholastic
If Your Name was Changed at Ellis Island	Q	I	250+	Levine, Ellen	Scholastic
Iggie's House	R	RF	250+	Blume, Judy	Bantam
Iggy Iguana's Trip	B	F	43	Phonics and Friends	Hampton-Brown
Iguanodon	M	I	250+	Discovering Dinosaurs	Capstone Press

* Collection of short stories

TITLE	LEVEL	GENRE	WORD COUNT	AUTHOR / SERIES	PUBLISHER / DISTRIBUTOR
I'll Be a Pirate	E	F	53	Eifrig, Kate	Kaeden Books
I'll Make You a Card	G	RF	180	Early Readers	Compass Point Books
I'll Run Away	D	RF	53	Home Connection Collection	Rigby
Illinois	Q	I	250+	One Nation	Capstone Press
Illinois	S	I	250+	Land of Liberty	Red Brick Learning
I'm a Caterpillar	G	I	169	Marzollo, Jean	Scholastic
I'm a Chef	M	I	250+	Literacy 2000	Rigby
I'm a Good Reader	H	RF	188	Carousel Readers	Pearson Learning Group
I'm a Little Seed	D	F	30	Pair-It Books	Steck-Vaughn
I'm a Seed	G	F	181	Marzollo, Jean	Scholastic
I'm an Artist	N	I	250+	Literacy 2000	Rigby
I'm an Astronaut	H	F	162	Voyages	SRA/McGraw Hill
I'm an Entrepreneur	N	B	501	Independent Readers Social Studies	Houghton Mifflin
I'm Bigger Than You!	C	F	48	Sunshine	Wright Group/McGraw Hill
I'm Brave	D	RF	51	Sunshine	Wright Group/McGraw Hill
I'm Glad I'm Me	F	RF	147	Windmill Books	Rigby
I'm Glad to Say	H	RF	165	Sunshine	Wright Group/McGraw Hill
I'm Hungry	B	I	25	Fitros, Pamela	Kaeden Books
I'm Hungry	D	RF	84	Tuer, Judy	Scholastic
I'm Hungry	C	RF	37	Visions	Wright Group/McGraw Hill
I'm King of the Castle	F	F	184	Watanabe, Shigeo	Philomel Books
I'm King of the Mountain	G	F	285	Pacific Literacy	Pacific Learning
I'm Looking for My Hat	F	RF	89	Book Bank	Wright Group/McGraw Hill
I'm No One Else But Me	M	RF	1010	Book Bank	Wright Group/McGraw Hill
I'm Not, I'm Not	C	RF	19	Windmill	Wright Group/McGraw Hill
I'm Out of My Body . . . Please Leave a Message	N	F	250+	The Zack Files	Grosset & Dunlap
I'm Red	B	F	25	The Book Project	Sundance
I'm Sick Today	H	RF	150	Carousel Readers	Pearson Learning Group
I'm So Hungry and Other Plays	M	F	250+	Orbit Chapter Books	Pacific Learning
I'm Telling	E	RF	71	Teacher's Choice Series	Pearson Learning Group
Images of Nikki Grimes, The	Y	B	1974	Leveled Readers	Houghton Mifflin
Imagine That	J	F	250+	Story Box	Wright Group/McGraw Hill
Imagine This, James Robert	P	F	250+	Action Packs	Rigby
Immigrants	T	I	250+	Sandler, Martin W.	HarperTrophy
Immigrants: Coming to America	R	I	250+	Thompson, Gare	Children's Press
Imogene's Antlers	L	F	191	Small, David	Scholastic
*Impossible Bend and Other Cases, The	O	RF	250+	Simon, Seymour	Avon
Impossible Bridge, The	N	I	250+	Pacific Literacy	Pacific Learning
Imran and the Watch	J	RF	415	Cambridge Reading	Pearson Learning Group
*In a Dark, Dark Room	J	TL	250+	Schwartz, Alvin	HarperTrophy
In a Dark, Dark Wood	E	TL	168	Carter, David	Simon & Schuster Trade
In a Dark, Dark Wood	E	F	81	Story Box	Wright Group/McGraw Hill
In a Faraway Forest	K	F	347	Kratky, Lada Josefa	Hampton-Brown
In a Muddle	G	RF	93	Voyages	SRA/McGraw Hill
In a New Land	L	HF	378	Sunshine	Wright Group/McGraw Hill
In a Painting	E	I	52	Canizares, Susan; Moreton, Daniel	Scholastic
In a Pickle	M	RF	250+	SupaDoopers	Sundance
In a Town	E	RF	47	Little Celebrations	Pearson Learning Group
In a Tree	M	I	250+	Look Once Look Again	Creative Teaching Press
In Aunt Lucy's Kitchen	M	RF	250+	Rylant, Cynthia	Aladdin
In City Gardens	L	I	250+	Little Celebrations	Pearson Learning Group
In Danger	M	I	250+	Home Connection Collection	Rigby
In Grandma Rita's Garden	K	RF	191	Books for Young Learners	Richard C. Owen

* Collection of short stories

TITLE	LEVEL	GENRE	WORD COUNT	AUTHOR / SERIES	PUBLISHER / DISTRIBUTOR
In Grandma's Garden	H	RF	244	Sunshine	Wright Group/McGraw Hill
In Hiding, Animals Under Cover	L	I	250+	Burke, Melissa Blackwell	Steck-Vaughn
In My Backyard	LB	RF	18	Visions	Wright Group/McGraw Hill
In My Bag	H	RF	237	Windows on Literacy	National Geographic
In My Bed	C	RF	57	Literacy 2000	Rigby
In My Bucket	F	RF	94	Carousel Readers	Pearson Learning Group
In My Desert	D	I	24	Little Celebrations	Pearson Learning Group
In My Family	D	RF	61	Windows on Literacy	National Geographic
In My Garden	C	RF	36	Carousel Readers	Pearson Learning Group
In My Garden	B	RF	35	Bookshop	Mondo
In My Garden	I	I	250+	Momentum Literacy Program	Troll Associates
In My Head	G	RF	74	Voyages	SRA/McGraw Hill
In My Pocket	B	RF	34	Instant Readers	Harcourt School Publishers
In My Pocket	E	RF	195	Carousel Readers	Pearson Learning Group
In My Pocket	A	I	28	Sun Sprouts	ETA/Cuisenaire
In My Room	C	F	44	Literacy 2000	Rigby
In My Room	D	RF	58	Seedlings	Continental Press
In My School	A	I	27	Little Books for Early Readers	University of Maine
In My Toolbox	B	I	36	Foundations	Wright Group/McGraw Hill
In Nonna's Kitchen	C	I	32	Home Connection Collection	Rigby
In Our Classroom	F	I	89	Windows on Literacy	National Geographic
In Our Classroom	A	I	33	PM Plus Starters	Rigby
In Our Country	F	I	63	Canizares, Susan; Moreton, Daniel	Scholastic
In Ravi's Fort	C	RF	78	Lighthouse	Rigby
In Search of Something Delicious	G	F	202	Seedlings	Continental Press
In Search of the Grand Canyon	W	I	250+	Fraser, Mary Ann	Henry Holt & Co.
In Search of the Great Bears	S	I	250+	Literacy 2000	Rigby
In Search of Treasure	L	TL	250+	PM Story Books	Rigby
*In Short: A Collection of Brief Creative Nonfiction	Z	I	250+	Kitchen, J.; Jones, M. P.	W. W. Norton
In Spring	B	I	15	Discovery Links	Newbridge
In Spring	B	I	34	Science	Outside the Box
In Summer	D	I	36	Discovery Links	Newbridge
In the Afternoon	H	I	156	PM Nonfiction-Green	Rigby
In the Air	B	I	20	Sunshine	Wright Group/McGraw Hill
In the Arctic	C	I	43	Science	Outside the Box
In the Backyard	H	F	197	Little Celebrations	Pearson Learning Group
In the Bank	H	I	140	Independent Readers Social Studies	Houghton Mifflin
In the Barn	D	I	38	Vocabulary Readers	Houghton Mifflin
In the Barrio	J	RF	130	Ada, Alma Flor	Scholastic
In the Bathroom	B	RF	24	Smart Starts	Rigby
In the Box	C	RF	64	Leveled Readers Emergent	Houghton Mifflin
In the Box	C	RF	33	Phonics and Friends	Hampton-Brown
In the Box	D	I	36	Sun Sprouts	ETA/Cuisenaire
In the Box	B	F	64	The Book Project	Sundance
In the Car	B	RF	32	First Stories	Pacific Learning
In the Chicken Coop	D	I	56	Twig	Wright Group/McGraw Hill
In the City	LB	RF	22	Home Connection Collection	Rigby
In the City	C	RF	45	Pasternac, Susana	Scholastic
In the City	C	RF	50	Rise & Shine	Hampton-Brown
In the City of Rome	J	TL	250+	Literacy 2000	Rigby
In the Clouds	M	RF	250+	Literacy 2000	Rigby
In the Country	D	I	54	Vocabulary Readers	Houghton Mifflin

TITLE	LEVEL	GENRE	WORD COUNT	AUTHOR / SERIES	PUBLISHER / DISTRIBUTOR
In the Country	D	RF	21	Home Connection Collection	Rigby
In the Country, In the City	B	I	71	Rigby Literacy	Rigby
In the Dark Forest	C	I	24	Pacific Literacy	Pacific Learning
In the Days of the Dinosaur	V	I	3182	Leveled Readers Science	Houghton Mifflin
In the Days of the Dinosaurs: Arky, the Dinosaur With Feathers	K	HF	250+	PM Plus Story Books	Rigby
In the Desert	M	I	250+	Look Once Look Again	Creative Teaching Press
In the Desert	D	I	51	Pacific Literacy	Pacific Learning
In the Desert	D	I	62	Sunshine	Wright Group/McGraw Hill
In the Dinosaur's Paw	M	RF	250+	Giff, Patricia Reilly	Bantam
In the Fast Lane	R	I	250+	Literacy 2000	Rigby
In the Forest	N	I	250+	Look Once Look Again	Creative Teaching Press
In the Forest	C	F	71	Schiller, Melissa	Scholastic
In the Forest	B	I	38	Science	Outside the Box
In the Forest	C	RF	42	Twig	Wright Group/McGraw Hill
In the Forest	G	RF	95	Voyages	SRA/McGraw Hill
In the Forest	L	I	581	Leveled Readers	Houghton Mifflin
In the Garden	D	I	90	Literacy 2000	Rigby
In the Garden	M	I	250+	Look Once Look Again	Creative Teaching Press
In the Garden	WB	I	N/A	Windows on Literacy	National Geographic
In the Garden	A	I	32	PM Plus Starters	Rigby
In The Garden	E	I	N/A	Sun Sprouts	ETA/Cuisenaire
In the Hen House	G	RF	82	Oppenlander, Meredith	Kaeden Books
In the Kitchen	C	I	16	Canizares, Susan; Chessen, Betsey	Scholastic
In the Land of the Polar Bear	J	RF	250+	Robinson, F. R.	Steck-Vaughn
In the Line of Fire: Eight Women War Spies	U	B	250+	Sullivan, George	Scholastic
In the Meadow	M	I	250+	Look Once Look Again	Creative Teaching Press
In the Middle of the Night	I	RF	250+	Sunshine	Wright Group/McGraw Hill
In the Mirror	B	RF	26	Story Box	Wright Group/McGraw Hill
In the Morning	H	I	218	PM Nonfiction-Green	Rigby
In the Mountains	U	I	250+	iOpeners	Pearson Learning Group
In the Mountains	LB	I	14	Twig	Wright Group/McGraw Hill
In the News	Q	I	250+	Wildcats	Wright Group/McGraw Hill
In the Park	D	RF	65	Foundations	Wright Group/McGraw Hill
In the Park	F	I	96	Literacy 2000	Rigby
In the Park	M	I	250+	Look Once Look Again	Creative Teaching Press
In the Path of Lewis & Clark: Traveling the Missouri	V	I	250+	Lourie, Peter	Silver Burdett Press
In the Rain	B	F	19	Ready Readers	Pearson Learning Group
In the Rain Forest	E	I	57	Twig	Wright Group/McGraw Hill
In the Rain Forest	Q	I	250+	Wildcats	Wright Group/McGraw Hill
In the Sea	B	I	41	Little Red Readers	Sundance
In the Sea	C	I	41	Sunshine	Wright Group/McGraw Hill
In the Shade of the Nispero Tree	S	HF	250+	Bernier-Grand, Carmen T.	Orchard Books
In the Shopping Cart	A	I	24	PM Starters	Rigby
In the Sky	B	I	42	Little Red Readers	Sundance
In the Supermarket	A	RF	24	Smart Starts	Rigby
In the Teacup	A	F	35	KinderReaders	Rigby
In the Toy Shop	C	F	29	The Book Project	Sundance
In the Tree	B	RF	48	Leveled Readers Emergent	Houghton Mifflin
In the Tree	B	I	36	Windows on Literacy	National Geographic
In the Treetops	M	I	250+	Woolley, M.; Pigdon, K.	Mondo
In the Van	C	RF	55	Leveled Readers	Houghton Mifflin

* Collection of short stories

TITLE	LEVEL	GENRE	WORD COUNT	AUTHOR / SERIES	PUBLISHER / DISTRIBUTOR
In the Woods	WB	I	N/A	Christini, Ermanno; Puricelli, Luigi	Scholastic
In the Woods	B	I	48	Bookshop	Mondo
In the Woods	B	F	25	Gibson, Akimi	Scholastic
In the Woods	G	I	304	Reading Corners	Pearson Learning Group
In the Yard	F	RF	40	Early Readers	Compass Point Books
In the Yard	D	RF	88	Rigby Literacy	Rigby
In the Year of the Boar and Jackie Robinson	S	HF	250+	Lord, Bette Bao	HarperTrophy
In Times Long Ago	G	I	196	Learn to Read	Creative Teaching Press
In Went Goldilocks	C	TL	30	Literacy 2000	Rigby
In-Between Days, The	P	RF	250+	Bunting, Eve	HarperTrophy
Incident at Hawk's Hill	V	F	250+	Eckert, Allen W.	Little, Brown & Co.
*Incredible Animal Adventures	N	I	250+	George, Jean Craighead	HarperCollins
Incredible Creatures	P	I	250+	Explorers	Wright Group/McGraw Hill
Incredible Insects	M	I	250+	Sunshine	Wright Group/McGraw Hill
Incredible Journey, The	V	F	250+	Burnford, Sheila	Bantam
Incredible Places	P	I	250+	Wildcats	Wright Group/McGraw Hill
Incredible Shrinking Kid, The	P	F	250+	Abbott, Tony	Scholastic
*Incredible Shrinking Machine and Other Cases, The	O	RF	250+	Simon, Seymour	Avon
Incredible, Edible Plants	L	I	250+	Early Connections	Benchmark Education
Independence Day	L	I	182	Pebble Books	Red Brick Learning
Independence Hall	I	I	77	Leveled Readers	Houghton Mifflin
India	Q	I	250+	First Reports	Compass Point Books
India	W	I	250+	Countries and Cultures	Capstone Press
India	O	I	250+	Dahl, Michael	Red Brick Learning
Indian in the Cupboard, The	R	F	250+	Banks, Lynne Reid	Avon
Indian School, The	P	RF	250+	Whelan, Gloria	HarperTrophy
Indian Winter, An	U	I	250+	Freedman, Russell	Scholastic
Indiana	R	I	250+	This Land Is Your Land	Compass Point Books
Indiana	S	I	250+	Land of Liberty	Red Brick Learning
*Indian-Head Pennies and Other Cases, The	O	RF	250+	Simon, Seymour	Avon
Indonesia	O	I	250+	Countries of the World	Red Brick Learning
Indy Cars	T	I	250+	The World's Fastest	Red Brick Learning
In-Line Skates, The	F	RF	137	Foundations	Wright Group/McGraw Hill
Inn Keeper's Apprentice	Z	B	250+	Say, Allen	Penguin Group
Insect and Spider	C	F	50	Science	Outside the Box
Insect-Eaters	J	I	213	Rigby Focus	Rigby
Insects	N	I	250+	A New True Book	Children's Press
Insects	U	I	250+	Bird, Bettina; Short, Joan	Mondo
Insects	M	I	250+	First Facts	Capstone Press
Insects	J	I	171	MacLulich, Carolyn	Scholastic
Insects	G	I	107	Rigby Focus	Rigby
Insects & Spiders	U	TL	250+	World Book Looks at Science	World Book
Insects & Spiders	R	I	250+	Worldwise	Franklin Watts
Insects All Around	K	I	229	Early Connections	Benchmark Education
Insects That Bother Us	G	I	87	Foundations	Wright Group/McGraw Hill
Inside a Cell	S	I	1651	Leveled Readers Science	Houghton Mifflin
Inside a Rain Forest	M	I	353	Pair-It Books	Steck-Vaughn
Inside an Ant Colony	K	I	250+	Rookie Read-About Science	Children's Press
Inside or Outside?	E	RF	57	Literacy 2000	Rigby
Inside School	A	I	35	Little Books for Early Readers	University of Maine
Inside Story, The	E	RF	43	Teacher's Choice Series	Pearson Learning Group
Inside the Sun	O	I	250+	Rosen Real Readers	Rosen Publishing Group

* Collection of short stories

TITLE	LEVEL	GENRE	WORD COUNT	AUTHOR / SERIES	PUBLISHER / DISTRIBUTOR
Inside, Outside, Upside Down	E	F	118	Berenstain, Stan & Jan	Random House
Inside-Outside Book of London, The	WB	I	N/A	Monro, Roxie	Dutton
Inside-Outside Book of Washington, DC	WB	I	N/A	Monro, Roxie	Dutton
Inspector Grub and the Fizzer-X Spy	N	RF	250+	Bookweb	Rigby
Inspector Grub and the Gourmet Mystery	Q	F	250+	Bookweb	Rigby
*Instead of Three Wishes: Magical Short Stories	Y	F	250+	Turner, Megan Whalen	Penguin Group
International Day	D	I	47	Home Connection Collection	Rigby
Interrupting The Big Sleep	P	RF	250+	Marriott, Janice	Pacific Learning
Interruptions	F	F	81	Bookshop	Mondo
Into Space	J	I	250+	Momentum Literacy Program	Troll Associates
Into the Eye of a Hurricane	T	I	2712	Leveled Readers Science	Houghton Mifflin
Into the Jungle: Searching for the Rare Mountain Gorilla	L	I	250+	World Quest Adventures	World Quest Learning
Introducing the Euro	W	I	1930	Leveled Readers Social Studies	Houghton Mifflin
Invaders!	Y	I	3289	Leveled Readers	Houghton Mifflin
Inventing the Telephone	L	I	250+	iOpeners	Pearson Learning Group
Inventive Mind of Jules Verne, The	X	B	1828	Leveled Readers	Houghton Mifflin
Inventors	T	I	250+	Sandler, Martin W.	HarperTrophy
Inventor's Diary, The	M	RF	271	Pacific Literacy	Pacific Learning
Inventors: Making Things Better	M	I	250+	Pair-It Books	Steck-Vaughn
Invincible Louisa	Z	B	250+	Meigs, Cornelia	Scholastic
Invisible	I	F	111	Read Alongs	Rigby
Invisible Dog, The	M	F	250+	King-Smith, Dick	Alfred A. Knopf
Invisible in the Third Grade	M	RF	250+	Cuyler, Margery	Scholastic
Invisible Spy, The	J	F	227	Foundations	Wright Group/McGraw Hill
Invisible Stanley	O	F	250+	Brown, Jeff	HarperTrophy
Iowa	R	I	250+	This Land Is Your Land	Compass Point Books
Iowa	S	I	250+	Land of Liberty	Red Brick Learning
Iowa	T	I	250+	Sea to Shining Sea	Children's Press
Iqbal	X	RF	250+	D'Adamo, Francesco	Atheneum
Iraq	P	I	250+	Fact Finders	Capstone Press
Ireland	W	I	250+	Countries and Cultures	Capstone Press
Irniq and the Eagles	M	TL	250+	Orbit Chapter Books	Pacific Learning
Iron Giant, The	O	SF	250+	Hughes, Ted	Alfred A. Knopf
Iron Horse, The	A	F	21	Smart Starts	Rigby
Iron Ring, The	W	F	250+	Alexander, Lloyd	Puffin Books
Ironman	Z	RF	250+	Crutcher, Chris	Laurel-Leaf Books
Iroquois Indians, The	P	I	250+	Lund, Bill	Red Brick Learning
Iroquois League, The	Q	I	250+	Rosen Real Readers	Rosen Publishing Group
Iroquois, The	R	I	250+	First Reports	Compass Point Books
Irrational Season, The	Z	B	250+	L'Engle, Madeleine	HarperCollins
Irritating Irma	N	F	250+	Literacy 2000	Rigby
Is a Dollar Enough?	D	RF	75	Visions	Wright Group/McGraw Hill
Is Anyone Home?	F	RF	65	Maris, Ron	Greenwillow
Is it a Fish?	K	I	606	Sunshine	Wright Group/McGraw Hill
Is it a Fruit?	G	I	101	Rigby Literacy	Rigby
Is It Alive?	C	RF	26	Learn to Read	Creative Teaching Press
Is it almost ready?	C	RF	53	Book Bus	Creative Edge
Is It Floating?	E	I	146	Sunshine	Wright Group/McGraw Hill
Is It Hot? Is It Not?	C	I	30	Phonics Readers	Compass Point Books
Is It Metal?	C	I	19	Rigby Focus	Rigby
Is It Red? Is It Yellow? Is It Blue?	WB	F	N/A	Hoban, Tana	Greenwillow
Is it Rough? Is it Smooth?	D	I	45	Rosen Real Readers	Rosen Publishing Group
Is It Time Yet?	G	RF	162	Foundations	Wright Group/McGraw Hill

* Collection of short stories

TITLE	LEVEL	GENRE	WORD COUNT	AUTHOR / SERIES	PUBLISHER / DISTRIBUTOR
Is It Time?	C	RF	52	Campbell, J. G.	Scholastic
Is Jim In?	F	RF	106	Supersonics	Rigby
Is That a Bear?	H	RF	225	Sunshine	Wright Group/McGraw Hill
Is the Spaghetti Ready?	E	F	80	New Reader Series	Bungalo Books
Is the Wise Owl Wise?	I	F	250+	Rigby Literacy	Rigby
Is There Life in Outer Space	O	I	250+	Branley, Franklyn M.	HarperCollins
Is This a Monster?	C	F	93	Bookshop	Mondo
Is This My Dinner?	I	F	162	Black/Fry	Whitman
Is This You?	F	RF	250+	Krauss, Ruth	Scholastic
Is Tomorrow My Birthday?	E	RF	87	Blaxland, Wendy	Scholastic
Is Your Mama a Llama?	L	F	250+	Guarino, Deborah	Scholastic
Is Your Pail Full?	F	RF	162	Mishica, Clare	Continental Press
Isabella: A Wish for Miguel	Q	HF	250+	Childhood Journeys	Aladdin
Ishi's Tale of Lizard	P	TL	250+	Hinton, Leanne; Roth, Susan L.	Farrar, Straus and Giroux
Island Baby	M	RF	250+	Keller, Holly	Scholastic
Island Far From Home, An	W	HF	250+	Donahue, John	Carolrhoda Books
Island Keeper	T	RF	250+	Mazer, Harry	Language for Learning Assoc.
Island Life	R	I	250+	iOpeners	Pearson Learning Group
*Island Like You, An: Stories of the Barrio	Z	RF	250+	Cofer, Judith Ortiz	Penguin Group
Island of the Blue Dolphins	V	HF	250+	O'Dell, Scott	Bantam
Island of the Skog, The	M	F	250+	Kellogg, Steven	Dial Books
Island of Wingo, The	N	F	250+	Sails	Rigby
Island on Bird Street, The	X	HF	250+	Orlev, Uri	Houghton Mifflin
Island Picnic, The	H	RF	236	PM Story Books	Rigby
Island to Island	K	RF	250+	Ready to Read	Pacific Learning
Island, The	R	RF	250+	Paulsen, Gary	Bantam
Island, The	D	RF	24	Wildsmith, Brian	Oxford University Press
Islander, The	T	F	250+	Rylant, Cynthia	Random House
Isn't It Cool?	R	I	250+	Action Packs	Rigby
Israel	O	I	250+	Thoennes, Kristin	Red Brick Learning
It Came From Ohio!: My Life as a Writer	R	B	250+	Stine, R. L.	Scholastic
It Came Through the Wall	O	F	1182	Healey, Tim	Mondo
It Can Fly	LB	I	8	Windows on Literacy	National Geographic
It Could Be Worse	E	F	108	Home Connection Collection	Rigby
It Didn't Frighten Me	D	F	250+	Bookshop	Mondo
It Is Halloween!	I	RF	250+	Appleton-Smith, Laura	Flyleaf Publishing
It Is Raining	F	I	56	PM Plus Nonfiction	Rigby
It Looked Like Split Milk	E	RF	172	Shaw, Charles	Harper & Row
It Must Be Clay	H	I	173	Independent Readers Science	Houghton Mifflin
It Smells Like Friday	L	F	250+	Popcorn	Sundance
It Sounds Like Music	D	I	56	Pair-It Books	Steck-Vaughn
It Started As a Seed	F	I	126	Learn to Read	Creative Teaching Press
It Started As an Egg	G	I	179	Learn to Read	Creative Teaching Press
It Starts as a Seed	E	I	36	Rosen Real Readers	Rosen Publishing Group
It Takes A Village	L	RF	250+	Cowen-Fletcher, J.	Scholastic
It Takes All Kinds	N	I	250+	Voyages	SRA/McGraw Hill
It Takes Time to Grow	H	RF	57	Sunshine	Wright Group/McGraw Hill
*It Was On Fire When I Lay Down On It	Z	I	250+	Fulghum, Robert	Ballantine Books
It Wasn't My Fault	L	RF	250+	Lester, Helen	Houghton Mifflin
It Would Be Fun!	F	F	203	Start to Read	School Zone
Italy	Q	I	250+	First Reports	Compass Point Books
Italy	H	I	34	Canizares, Susan; Chessen, Betsey	Scholastic
Italy	O	I	250+	Thoennes, Kristin	Red Brick Learning

* Collection of short stories

TITLE	LEVEL	GENRE	WORD COUNT	AUTHOR / SERIES	PUBLISHER / DISTRIBUTOR
Itch! Itch!	C	RF	76	Bookshop	Mondo
Itchy, Itchy Chicken Pox	F	RF	131	Maccarone, Grace	Scholastic
It'll Be All Right on the Night!	Q	I	250+	Quinn, Pat	Pacific Learning
It's a Bit Tricky	G	RF	250+	Home Connection Collection	Rigby
It's a Blizzard!	L	I	250+	Rosen Real Readers	Rosen Publishing Group
It's a Fiesta, Benjamin	N	RF	250+	Giff, Patricia Reilly	Bantam
It's a Frog's Life	Q	I	250+	Literacy 2000 Satellites	Rigby
It's a Gift	H	I	156	Lighthouse	Rigby
It's a Good Thing That There Are Insects	H	I	250+	Fowler, Allan	Scholastic
It's a Mammal!	Q	I	250+	iOpeners	Pearson Learning Group
It's a Party	D	I	24	Berger, Samantha; Moreton, Daniel	Scholastic
It's a Zoo!	H	RF	100	City Stories	Rigby
It's About Time	B	I	39	Twig	Wright Group/McGraw Hill
It's About Time	K	I	250+	Yellow Umbrella Books	Capstone Press
It's About Time	M	I	481	Storyteller Nonfiction	Wright Group/McGraw Hill
It's All in the Soil	Q	I	250+	iOpeners	Pearson Learning Group
It's All in Your Mind, James Robert	P	F	250+	Literacy 2000	Rigby
It's Alright to Cry	F	RF	138	Teacher's Choice Series	Pearson Learning Group
It's Broken	E	RF	88	Dominie Phonics Reader	Pearson Learning Group
It's Cold Where I Live	H	RF	98	Windows on Literacy	National Geographic
It's Dinner Time	WB	I	N/A	Windows on Literacy	National Geographic
It's Easy!	O	RF	250+	Leveled Readers Language Support	Houghton Mifflin
It's Electric!	T	I	250+	Rosen Real Readers	Rosen Publishing Group
It's Football Time	C	RF	24	Geddes, Diana	Kaeden Books
It's Fun to Exercise	J	I	250+	Rosen Real Readers	Rosen Publishing Group
It's Game Day	D	RF	65	Salem, Lynn; Stewart, Josie	Continental Press
It's George!	H	RF	250+	Cohen, Miriam	Bantam
It's Halloween!	K	RF	250+	Prelutsky, Jack	Scholastic
It's Hot	D	RF	54	Ready Readers	Pearson Learning Group
It's in the Air	Z	I	2025	Independent Readers Science	Houghton Mifflin
It's Just a Trick	O	RF	250+	Literacy 2000	Rigby
It's Magic	H	F	204	Start to Read	School Zone
It's Melting	C	RF	16	Learn to Read	Creative Teaching Press
It's Mine!	P	F	250+	Lionni, Leo	Scholastic
It's My Bread	B	F	43	Pacific Literacy	Pacific Learning
It's New, It's Improved, It's Terrible!	Q	RF	250+	Manes, Stephen	Bantam
It's Noisy at Night	E	RF	80	Wonder World	Wright Group/McGraw Hill
It's Not All Ancient History	Y	I	250+	iOpeners	Pearson Learning Group
It's Not Easy Being a Bunny	I	F	250+	Sadler, Marilyn	Random House
It's Not Easy Being George	S	RF	250+	Smith, Janice Lee	HarperTrophy
It's Not Fair	F	RF	51	Tadpoles	Rigby
It's Not the End of the World	T	RF	250+	Blume, Judy	Dell
It's Not the Same	I	RF	250+	Sunshine	Wright Group/McGraw Hill
It's Raining	E	I	86	Teacher's Choice Series	Pearson Learning Group
It's Raining!	C	I	32	Pair-It Books	Steck-Vaughn
It's Snowing!	J	I	193	Find Out Readers	Continental Press
It's Spring	A	I	24	Vocabulary Readers	Houghton Mifflin
It's Spring!	H	F	124	Berger, Samantha; Chanko, Pamela	Scholastic
It's Taco Time	F	I	56	Teacher's Choice Series	Pearson Learning Group
It's the Fashion	S	I	250+	Literacy 2000	Rigby
It's Time for Bed	E	RF	126	Visions	Wright Group/McGraw Hill

* Collection of short stories

TITLE	LEVEL	GENRE	WORD COUNT	AUTHOR / SERIES	PUBLISHER / DISTRIBUTOR
It's Time to Get Up	E	RF	143	Visions	Wright Group/McGraw Hill
It's Time!	H	I	175	Yellow Umbrella Books	Red Brick Learning
It's Time!	A	I	24	Early Connections	Benchmark Education
It's Too Loud	C	I	53	Independent Readers Science	Houghton Mifflin
I've Been Working on the Railroad	J	TL	250+	Traditional Songs	Picture Window Books
I've Got New Sneakers	H	RF	111	City Kids	Rigby
I've Lost My Boot	C	RF	18	Windmill	Wright Group/McGraw Hill
Ivy's Journal: A Trip to the Yucatán	R	RF	250+	Bookshop	Mondo
Izzy, Willy-Nilly	X	RF	250+	Voigt, Cynthia	Aladdin
J. T.	Q	RF	250+	Wagner, Jane	Bantam
J: My Name Is Jess	C	RF	61	Little Books	Sadlier-Oxford
Jace, Mace, and the Big Race	F	RF	124	Start to Read	School Zone
Jack	D	TL	11	Jumbled Tumbled Tales & Rhymes	Rigby
Jack & the Beanstalk	I	TL	250+	Literacy 2000	Rigby
Jack and Billy	C	RF	50	PM Plus Story Books	Rigby
Jack and Billy and Rose	G	RF	179	PM Plus Story Books	Rigby
Jack and Chug	I	F	337	PM Story Books-Orange	Rigby
Jack and Jill	D	F	40	Seedlings	Continental Press
Jack and Jill	D	TL	25	Jumbled Tumbled Tales & Rhymes	Rigby
Jack and Jill	E	TL	51	Sunshine	Wright Group/McGraw Hill
Jack and the Beanstalk	K	TL	250+	Weisner, David	Scholastic
Jack and the Beanstalk	I	TL	250+	Literacy 2000	Rigby
Jack and the Beanstalk	H	TL	170	Sunshine	Wright Group/McGraw Hill
Jack and the Beanstalk	K	TL	901	Hunia, Fran	Ladybird Books
Jack and the Magic Harp	K	TL	250+	PM Tales and Plays-Gold	Rigby
Jack DePert at the Supermarket	G	RF	188	Wonder World	Wright Group/McGraw Hill
Jack in the Box	I	F	250+	Storybox	Wright Group/McGraw Hill
Jack Plays the Violin	H	RF	250+	Schultz, Jessica	Scholastic
Jackaroo	Y	RF	250+	Voigt, Cynthia	Scholastic
Jackets	C	RF	42	Joy Readers	Pearson Learning Group
Jackie Robinson	N	B	250+	Soar To Success	Houghton Mifflin
Jackie Robinson	O	B	250+	Early Biographies	Compass Point Books
Jackie Robinson and the Breaking of the Color Barrier	S	B	250+	Shorto, Russell	Millbrook Press
Jackie Robinson and the Story of All-Black Baseball	N	I	250+	O'Connor, Jim	Random House
Jackie Robinson Breaks the Color Line	V	B	250+	Cornerstones of Freedom	Children's Press
Jackie Robinson: Baseball's First Black Major Leaguer	O	B	250+	Greene, Carol	Children's Press
Jackie's New Friend	F	I	168	O'Connor, C. M.	Continental Press
Jack-in-the-Box	B	RF	34	Literacy 2000	Rigby
Jack-O-Lantern	B	I	37	Twig	Wright Group/McGraw Hill
Jack-O-Lanterns	D	I	47	Pebble Books	Capstone Press
Jacks	P	I	250+	Games Around the World	Compass Point Books
Jacks and More Jacks	F	F	79	Little Celebrations	Pearson Learning Group
Jack's Birthday	C	RF	89	PM Plus Story Books	Rigby
Jack's Boat	I	I	172	Windows on Literacy	National Geographic
*Jack's New Power: Stories From a Caribbean Year	W	RF	250+	Gantos, Jack	Sunburst
Jack's New Skates	E	RF	148	Developing Books	Pioneer Valley
Jack's Pack	C	I	22	KinderReaders	Rigby
Jackson's Monster	I	F	250+	Little Readers	Houghton Mifflin
Jacob Have I Loved	X	RF	250+	Paterson, Katherine	HarperTrophy
Jacob Two-Two and the Dinosaur	P	F	250+	Richler, Mordecai	Tundra Books

* Collection of short stories

| --- | --- | --- | --- | --- | --- |
Jacob Two-Two Meets the Hooded Fang	P	F	250+	Richler, Mordecai	Seal Books
Jacob's Day	F	RF	51	Windows on Literacy	National Geographic
Jacob's Rescue: A Holocaust Story	Y	HF	250+	Drucker, M.; Halperin, M.	Bantam
Jacques Cousteau	L	B	250+	Biography	Benchmark Education
Jade Emperor and the Four Dragons, The	K	TL	250+	Lighthouse	Rigby
Jade Green	Z	F	250+	Naylor, Phyllis Reynolds	Simon & Schuster
Jaguar Attack!	P	RF	250+	Bookweb	Rigby
Jaguars	O	I	250+	First Reports	Compass Point Books
Jaguars	U	I	250+	Green, Michael	Red Brick Learning
Jaguars	J	I	78	Pebble Books	Red Brick Learning
Jaime Escalante, A Great Teacher	M	B	273	Independent Readers Social Studies	Houghton Mifflin
Jake	A	I	35	Little Books for Early Readers	University of Maine
Jake and the Copycats	J	RF	250+	Rocklin, Joanne	Bantam
Jake Can Play	B	RF	42	Little Books for Early Readers	University of Maine
Jake Greenthumb	J	F	250+	Bookshop	Mondo
Jake Makes a Map	D	RF	55	Leveled Readers	Houghton Mifflin
Jake the Snake	K	F	250+	Supersonics	Rigby
Jake Was a Pirate	M	F	250+	Voyages	SRA/McGraw Hill
Jake's First Word	H	RF	204	Books for Young Learners	Richard C. Owen
Jake's Map	C	RF	63	Leveled Readers Language Support	Houghton Mifflin
Jamaica and Brianna	K	RF	250+	Little Readers	Houghton Mifflin
Jamaica's Find	K	RF	250+	Havill, Juanita	Scholastic
Jamall's City Garden	I	I	250+	Rigby Literacy	Rigby
Jamberry	J	F	111	Degen, Bruce	Harper & Row
James A. Garfield	U	B	250+	Profiles of the Presidents	Compass Point Books
James and the Giant Peach	Q	F	250+	Dahl, Roald	Penguin Group
James Buchanan	U	B	250+	Profiles of the Presidents	Compass Point Books
James Earl Carter, Jr.	U	B	250+	Profiles of the Presidents	Compass Point Books
James Is Hiding	A	RF	24	Windmill	Wright Group/McGraw Hill
James K. Polk	U	B	250+	Profiles of the Presidents	Compass Point Books
James Madison	U	B	250+	Profiles of the Presidents	Compass Point Books
James Madison: Founding Father	Q	B	250+	Rosen Real Readers	Rosen Publishing Group
James Monroe	U	B	250+	Profiles of the Presidents	Compass Point Books
Jamestown Colony, The	T	I	250+	We The People	Compass Point Books
Jamestown Colony, The	V	I	250+	Cornerstones of Freedom	Children's Press
Jamestown: New World Adventure	T	I	250+	Adventures in Colonial America	Troll Associates
Jan and the Jacket	E	RF	74	Oxford Reading Tree	Oxford University Press
Jan Can Juggle	B	RF	25	Ready Readers	Pearson Learning Group
Jan Matzeliger, Inventor	T	B	1916	Leveled Readers Science	Houghton Mifflin
Jane Addams	O	B	586	Leveled Readers Social Studies	Houghton Mifflin
Jane Addams	P	B	250+	Community Builders	Children's Press
Jane and the Beanstalk	Q	TL	1534	Leveled Readers	Houghton Mifflin
Jane Goodall	N	B	250+	Pebble Books	Capstone Press
Jane Goodall	E	B	183	Leveled Readers Science	Houghton Mifflin
Jane Goodall	N	B	250+	Biography	Benchmark Education
Jane Goodall and the Chimps	L	B	250+	Twig	Wright Group/McGraw Hill
Jane Goodall and the Wild Chimpanzees	L	B	250+	Birnbaum, Bette	Steck-Vaughn
Jane Goodall: Living With Chimpanzees	M	I	250+	Rigby Literacy	Rigby
Jane Goodall: Living With Chimpanzees	E	B	162	Leveled Readers Science	Houghton Mifflin
Jane Mt. Pleasant	H	B	134	Leveled Readers Science	Houghton Mifflin
Jane's Car	F	RF	121	PM Story Books	Rigby
Jane's Mansion	N	I	250+	Literacy 2000	Rigby

* Collection of short stories

TITLE	LEVEL	GENRE	WORD COUNT	AUTHOR / SERIES	PUBLISHER / DISTRIBUTOR
Jan's New Fan	C	RF	34	KinderReaders	Rigby
Japan	P	I	250+	Fact Finders	Capstone Press
Japan	O	I	250+	Many Cultures, One World	Capstone Press
Japan	O	I	250+	Countries of the World	Red Brick Learning
Japan	M	I	488	Pair-It Books	Steck-Vaughn
Japan	Q	I	250+	First Reports	Compass Point Books
Japan	N	I	250+	A True Book	Children's Press
Japanese Garden, The	K	RF	250+	PM Plus Story Books	Rigby
Jar of Dreams, A	R	RF	250+	Uchida, Yoshiko	Aladdin
Jasmine's Duck	H	RF	207	Lighthouse	Rigby
Jason and the Aliens Down the Street	O	F	250+	Greer, Greg; Ruddick, Bob	HarperTrophy
Jason Kidd Story, The	P	RF	250+	Moore, David	Scholastic
Jason's Bus Ride	G	F	117	Ziefert, Harriet	Penguin Group
Jason's Gold	T	HF	250+	Hobbs, Will	William Morrow
Jasper	F	RF	107	Books for Young Learners	Richard C. Owen
Jazmin's Notebook	Z	RF	250+	Grimes, Nikki	Penguin Group
Jazz Great	U	RF	3296	Leveled Readers	Houghton Mifflin
Jazz Kid, The	Y	RF	250+	Lincoln Collier, James	Penguin Group
Jazz Man, The	T	RF	250+	Weik, Mary Hays	Simon & Schuster
Jazz, Pizzazz, and the Silver Threads	P	RF	250+	Quattlebaum, Mary	Bantam
Jean Craighead George	S	B	250+	Cary, Alice	Learning Works, The
Jean Fritz Comes Home	X	B	2268	Leveled Readers	Houghton Mifflin
Jeb's Barn	G	RF	86	Little Celebrations	Pearson Learning Group
Jefferson Davis	U	B	250+	Let Freedom Ring	Red Brick Learning
Jeff's Magnets	I	I	168	Instant Readers	Harcourt School Publishers
Jelly Beans	M	I	250+	Stadler, Charlotte	Benchmark Education
Jellybean Tree, The	H	F	231	Sunshine	Wright Group/McGraw Hill
Jellyfish	I	I	58	Pebble Books	Red Brick Learning
Jellyfish	J	I	95	Pebble Plus	Capstone Press
Jenius: The Amazing Guinea Pig	N	F	250+	King-Smith, Dick	Hyperion
Jennifer Pockets	I	RF	205	Book Bank	Wright Group/McGraw Hill
Jennifer, Hecate, Macbeth, William McKinley, and Me, Elizabeth	R	RF	250+	Konigsburg, E. L.	Yearling
Jennifer, Too	L	RF	250+	Havill, Juanita	Hyperion
Jenny and the Cornstalk	L	TL	890	Pair-It Books	Steck-Vaughn
Jenny Archer to the Rescue	M	RF	250+	Conford, Ellen	Little, Brown & Co.
Jenny Archer, Author	M	RF	250+	Conford, Ellen	Little, Brown & Co.
Jenny in Bed	D	RF	76	Lighthouse	Rigby
Jenny Lives on Hunter Street	H	RF	141	Book Bank	Wright Group/McGraw Hill
Jenny's Garden	E	RF	45	Leveled Readers Science	Houghton Mifflin
Jen's Best Gift Ever	I	RF	250+	Appleton-Smith, Laura	Flyleaf Publishing
Jeremy Thatcher, Dragon Hatcher	R	F	250+	Coville, Bruce	Aladdin
Jeremy's Cake	F	RF	97	Storyteller-Moon Rising	Wright Group/McGraw Hill
Jericho	T	RF	250+	Hickman, Janet	Hearst
Jericho Walls	V	HF	250+	Collier, Kristi	Henry Holt & Co.
Jericho's Journey	U	RF	250+	Wisler, G. Clifton	Penguin Group
Jerry on the Line	R	RF	250+	Seabrooke, Brenda	Puffin Books
Jess in the Snow	E	RF	109	Handprints C, Set 2	Educator's Publishing Service
Jesse	Y	RF	250+	Soto, Gary	Scholastic
Jesse Jackson	P	B	250+	Simon, Charnan	Children's Press
Jesse Owens: Olympic Hero	P	B	250+	Sabin, Francene	Troll Associates
Jessica in the Dark	I	RF	362	PM Story Books-Orange	Rigby
Jessica's Dress-Ups	F	RF	130	Voyages	SRA/McGraw Hill

* Collection of short stories

TITLE	LEVEL	GENRE	WORD COUNT	AUTHOR / SERIES	PUBLISHER / DISTRIBUTOR
Jessie's Flower	G	F	132	Read Alongs	Rigby
Jets and the Rockets, The	J	RF	250+	PM Plus Story Books	Rigby
Jewel of the Desert	V	HF	2994	Leveled Readers	Houghton Mifflin
Jigaree, The	E	F	128	Story Box	Wright Group/McGraw Hill
Jigsaw Jones Mystery: The Case of the Christmas Snowman	M	RF	250+	Ruller, James	Scholastic
Jill Jumps	C	F	35	Ray's Readers	Outside the Box
Jillian Jiggs	J	RF	250+	Gilman, Phoebe	Scholastic
Jilly the Kid	M	RF	250+	Krailing, Tessa	Barron's Educational
Jim Abbott: Making the Most of It	X	B	2451	Leveled Readers	Houghton Mifflin
Jim Meets the Thing	I	F	250+	Cohen, Miriam	Bantam
Jim Morrison	Z	B	250+	Rock Music Library	Capstone Press
Jim Ugly	Q	RF	250+	Fleischman, Sid	Bantam
Jimmy	D	RF	83	Foundations	Wright Group/McGraw Hill
Jimmy Lee Did It	J	RF	250+	Cummings, Pat	Lothrop
Jimmy Parker's New Job	J	RF	250+	Voyages	SRA/McGraw Hill
Jimmy the Gymnast	K	RF	250+	Foundations	Wright Group/McGraw Hill
Jimmy's Birthday Balloon	F	RF	95	Foundations	Wright Group/McGraw Hill
Jimmy's Goal	E	RF	159	Foundations	Wright Group/McGraw Hill
Jim's Dog Muffins	K	RF	250+	Cohen, Miriam	Bantam
Jim's Trumpet	H	RF	304	Sunshine	Wright Group/McGraw Hill
Jim's Visit to Kim	G	RF	149	Ready Readers	Pearson Learning Group
Jingo Django	V	RF	250+	Fleischman, Sid	Bantam
Jinx	Z	RF	250+	Wild, Margaret	Walker & Company
Jip the Pirate	F	F	142	New Way Blue	Steck-Vaughn
Jip: His Story	V	HF	250+	Paterson, Katherine	Penguin Group
*JJ Rabbit and the Monster	K	F	250+	Moon, Nicola	Wright Group/McGraw Hill
Jo and the Spider	D	RF	78	Sun Sprouts	ETA/Cuisenaire
Jo Jo Winnie Again	O	RF	250+	Sachs, Marilyn	Dutton
Jo Jo's Flying Side Kick	M	RF	250+	Soar To Success	Houghton Mifflin
Jo the Model Maker	K	I	250+	Lighthouse	Rigby
Joan's Garden	B	F	34	Sun Sprouts	ETA/Cuisenaire
Joan's Hat	F	F	174	Sun Sprouts	ETA/Cuisenaire
Job for Giant Jim, A	I	RF	298	Sunshine	Wright Group/McGraw Hill
Job for Jenny Archer, A	M	RF	250+	Conford, Ellen	Random House
Job for You, A	D	I	56	Independent Readers Social Studies	Houghton Mifflin
Jobs	D	I	71	Leveled Readers	Houghton Mifflin
Jobs	I	I	112	Canizares, Susan; Chessen, Betsey	Scholastic
Jobs	B	I	29	Bookshop	Mondo
Jobs	E	F	112	Benger, Wendy	Kaeden Books
Jobs Around Town	A	I	31	Leveled Readers Social Studies	Houghton Mifflin
Jobs at Home	C	I	35	Leveled Readers Language Support	Houghton Mifflin
Jobs For Dogs	H	I	188	Rigby Focus	Rigby
Jobs Up High	C	I	62	Early Connections	Benchmark Education
Jobs: Making and Helping	E	I	63	Windows on Literacy	National Geographic
Jock Jerome	E	F	99	Voyages	SRA/McGraw Hill
Joe and Betsy the Dinosaur	K	F	250+	Hoban, Lillian	HarperTrophy
Joe and the BMX Bike	E	RF	91	Oxford Reading Tree	Oxford University Press
Joe and the Mouse	F	RF	138	Oxford Reading Tree	Oxford University Press
Joe Cocker Spaniel	N	RF	250+	SupaDoopers	Sundance
Joe Joe	LB	RF	22	Montezinos, Nina	McElderry
Joe Makes a House	G	RF	174	PM Plus Story Books	Rigby

* Collection of short stories

TITLE	LEVEL	GENRE	WORD COUNT	AUTHOR / SERIES	PUBLISHER / DISTRIBUTOR
Joe's Blue Shoes	G	RF	130	Books for Young Learners	Richard C. Owen
Joe's Father	E	RF	138	Book Bank	Wright Group/McGraw Hill
Joe's Pizza Parlor	I	RF	113	City Stories	Rigby
Joey	G	RF	243	PM Extensions-Green	Rigby
Joey Pigza Loses Control	T	RF	250+	Gantos, Jack	Farrar, Straus and Giroux
Joey Pigza Swallowed the Key	T	RF	250+	Gantos, Jack	HarperTrophy
Joey's Head	L	F	250+	Cretan, G.	Simon & Schuster
Joey's Rowboat	H	RF	83	Little Books	Sadlier-Oxford
Jog, Frog, Jog	F	F	72	Start to Read	School Zone
Johann Sebastian Bach: Great Man of Music	O	B	250+	Greene, Carol	Children's Press
John & Abigail Adams: An American Love Story	W	B	250+	St. George, Judith	Scholastic
John A. Macdonald	X	B	250+	The Canadians	Fitzhenry & Whiteside
John Adams	S	B	250+	Photo-Illustrated Biographies	Red Brick Learning
John Adams	U	B	250+	Profiles of the Presidents	Compass Point Books
John Adams and the Boston Massacre	Y	I	2307	Leveled Readers	Houghton Mifflin
John Chapman: The Man Who Was Johnny	N	B	250+	Rookie Biographies	Children's Press
John Charles and Jessie Fremont: Pathfinders of the West	V	B	2453	Leveled Readers Social Studies	Houghton Mifflin
John F. Kennedy	L	B	250+	Pebble Books	Red Brick Learning
John F. Kennedy	N	B	250+	Pebble Books	Capstone Press
John F. Kennedy	U	B	250+	Profiles of the Presidents	Compass Point Books
John F. Kennedy	V	B	250+	World Leaders: Past and Present	Chelsea House
John F. Kennedy: America's Youngest President	O	B	250+	Childhood of Famous Americans	Aladdin
John Glenn	M	B	250+	Explore Space!	Capstone Press
John H. Johnson, Business Leader	K	B	130	Independent Readers Social Studies	Houghton Mifflin
John Henry	N	TL	250+	Tall Tales	Compass Point Books
John Henry and the Steam Drill	Q	F	1203	Leveled Readers	Houghton Mifflin
John James Audubon	M	B	250+	Biography	Benchmark Education
John James Audubon, American Painter	M	B	538	Leveled Readers Social Studies	Houghton Mifflin
John James Audubon: Wildlife Artist	V	B	250+	A First Book	Franklin Watts
John Lennon	Z	B	250+	Rock Music Library	Capstone Press
John Muir: Man of the Wild Places	N	B	250+	Rookie Biographies	Children's Press
John Paul Jones and the Battle at Sea	W	B	2095	Independent Readers Social Studies	Houghton Mifflin
John Peter Zenger and Freedom of the Press	V	B	2213	Leveled Readers Social Studies	Houghton Mifflin
John Philip Sousa: The March King	N	B	250+	Rookie Biographies	Children's Press
John Quincy Adams	U	B	250+	Profiles of the Presidents	Compass Point Books
John Tyler	U	B	250+	Profiles of the Presidents	Compass Point Books
Johnny Appleseed	O	B	622	Leveled Readers	Houghton Mifflin
Johnny Appleseed	K	TL	250+	Moore, Eva	Scholastic
Johnny Appleseed	N	TL	250+	Tall Tales	Compass Point Books
Johnny Appleseed	M	B	250+	First Biographies	Red Brick Learning
Johnny Kelley's Tale	X	HF	2162	Leveled Readers	Houghton Mifflin
Johnny Lion's Book	J	F	250+	Hurd, Edith Thacher	HarperCollins
Johnny Lion's Rubber Boots	F	F	80	Hurd, Edith Thacher	HarperCollins
Johnny Long Legs	M	RF	250+	Christopher, Matt	Little, Brown & Co.
Johnny Tremain	Z	HF	250+	Forbes, Esther	Bantam Doubleday Dell
Jojo and the Robot	J	F	250+	Sunshine	Wright Group/McGraw Hill
Joke Book, The	H	I	143	Vocabulary Readers	Houghton Mifflin
Joke, The	H	F	186	Little Readers	Houghton Mifflin
Jokers	H	F	190	Breakthrough	Longman/Bow
Jokes and Riddles	O	I	250+	Literacy 2000	Rigby
Jolly Jumping Jelly Beans	E	F	121	Sunshine	Wright Group/McGraw Hill

* Collection of short stories

Jolly Roger and the Treasure	E	F	129	PM Plus Story Books	Rigby
Jolly Roger, the Pirate	D	F	138	PM Extensions-Yellow	Rigby
Jon Scieszka Gets Kids Reading	Q	B	1155	Leveled Readers	Houghton Mifflin
Jon Sleeps On	G	RF	147	Little Red Readers	Sundance
Jonathan and His Mommy	L	RF	250+	Smalls, Irene	Scholastic
Jonathan Buys a Present	J	RF	353	PM Story Books-Turquoise	Rigby
Jordan and the Northside Reps	K	RF	250+	PM Story Books-Silver	Rigby
Jordan at the Big Game	I	RF	250+	PM Plus Story Books	Rigby
Jordan Is Hiding	A	RF	24	Little Books for Early Readers	University of Maine
Jordan's Catch	J	RF	250+	PM Story Books	Rigby
Jordan's Lucky Day	K	RF	466	PM Story Books-Turquoise	Rigby
Jordan's Soccer Ball	G	RF	210	PM Plus Story Books	Rigby
Jordan's Zoo	G	RF	90	City Stories	Rigby
Jo's Troubled Heart	Q	HF	250+	The Little Women Journals	Avon
Josefina Learns a Lesson	Q	HF	250+	The American Girls Collection	Pleasant Company
Josefina Saves the Day	Q	HF	250+	The American Girls Collection	Pleasant Company
Josefina Story Quilt	L	F	250+	Coerr, Eleanor	HarperTrophy
Josefina's Surprise	Q	HF	250+	The American Girls Collection	Pleasant Company
Joseph Brant: Iroquois Leader in the Revolution	Y	B	1743	Leveled Readers	Houghton Mifflin
Joseph: 1861 - A Rumble of War	V	HF	250+	Pryor, Bonnie	Avon
Josephine's Imagination	L	RF	250+	Dobrin, Arnold	Scholastic
Joshua James Likes Trucks	C	RF	50	Rookie Readers	Children's Press
Joshua Poole and Sunrise	L	RF	250+	Rigby Literacy	Rigby
Joshua T. Bates	Q	RF	250+	Shreve, Susan	Alfred A. Knopf
Joshua T. Bates in Trouble Again	Q	RF	250+	Shreve, Susan	Alfred A. Knopf
Joshua T. Bates Takes Charge	Q	RF	250+	Shreve, Susan	Alfred A. Knopf
Josie Cleans Up	I	RF	213	Little Readers	Houghton Mifflin
Journal of Douglas Allen Deeds, The: The Donner Party Expedition, 1846	U	HF	250+	My Name is America	Scholastic
Journal of Patrick Seamus Flaherty, The	Z	HF	250+	White, Ellen Emerson	Scholastic
Journal, The: Dear Future II	Q	SF	250+	Literacy 2000	Rigby
Journey	S	RF	250+	MacLachlan, Patricia	Yearling
Journey Home	V	RF	250+	Uchida, Yoshika	Aladdin
Journey Home, The	S	RF	250+	Holland, Isabelle	Scholastic
Journey Into Terror	U	RF	250+	Wallace, Bill	Simon & Schuster
Journey of a Butterfly, The	P	I	250+	Scrace, Carolyn	Scholastic
Journey Outside	V	F	250+	Steele, Mary Q.	Penguin Group
Journey to a Free Town	S	HF	1747	Leveled Readers	Houghton Mifflin
Journey to a New Land	M	HF	250+	Rigby Literacy	Rigby
Journey to a New Land: An Oral History	R	B	250+	Bookshop	Mondo
Journey to America	U	HF	250+	Levitin, Sonia	Simon & Schuster
Journey to an 800 Number	V	RF	250+	Konigsburg, E. L.	Aladdin
Journey to Ellis Island: How My Father Came to America	T	B	250+	Bierman, Carol	Scholastic
Journey to Jo'burg	S	HF	250+	Naidoo, Beverly	HarperTrophy
Journey to Kansas	R	HF	250+	Leveled Readers Language Support	Houghton Mifflin
Journey to Mars	T	I	644	Vocabulary Readers	Houghton Mifflin
Journey to Nowhere	T	HF	250+	Auch, Mary Jane	Bantam
Journey to the Center of the Earth, A	X	SF	250+	Verne, Jules	HarperCollins
Journey to the New World	S	HF	250+	Action Packs	Rigby
Journey to the Undersea Gardens	Q	I	250+	iOpeners	Pearson Learning Group
Journey to Topaz	U	HF	250+	Uchida, Yoshiko	Creative Arts Book Co.
Journey West, The	N	I	250+	Rigby Literacy	Rigby

* Collection of short stories

TITLE	LEVEL	GENRE	WORD COUNT	AUTHOR / SERIES	PUBLISHER / DISTRIBUTOR
Journeys of Sojourner Truth, The	R	B	1217	Leveled Readers Social Studies	Houghton Mifflin
Joy Crowley Writes	K	B	250+	Sunshine	Wright Group/McGraw Hill
Joy of Making Music, The	N	I	280	Vocabulary Readers	Houghton Mifflin
Joy's Great Idea	M	RF	250+	Ellis, Veronica Freeman	Houghton Mifflin
Juan	H	RF	77	City Kids	Rigby
Juan Bobo	E	TL	55	Leveled Readers	Houghton Mifflin
Juan Ponce De Leon	Q	B	250+	Biographies-Great Explorers	Capstone Press
Juan's Three Wishes	V	F	1842	Leveled Readers	Houghton Mifflin
Judge Rabbit Helps the Fish	N	TL	250+	Story Vines	Wright Group/McGraw Hill
Judy Moody	L	RF	250+	McDonald, Megan	Candlewick Press
Judy Moody Saves the World	L	RF	250+	McDonald, Megan	Candlewick Press
Juggling	P	I	250+	Games Around the World	Compass Point Books
Juggling	LB	RF	15	Rigby Literacy	Rigby
Juicy Peach	C	RF	18	Bebop Books	Lee & Low Books Inc.
Julia Alvarez: One Author, Two Cultures	Q	B	1029	Leveled Readers	Houghton Mifflin
Julian, Dream Doctor	N	RF	250+	Cameron, Ann	Random House
Julian, Secret Agent	N	RF	250+	Cameron, Ann	Random House
Julian's Glorious Summer	N	RF	250+	Cameron, Ann	Random House
Julia's Lists	D	RF	47	Little Celebrations	Pearson Learning Group
Julie	U	RF	250+	George, Jean Craighead	HarperTrophy
Julie Krone	Y	B	250+	The Achievers	Lerner Publishing
Julie of the Wolves	U	RF	250+	George, Jean Craighead	HarperCollins
Julie Rescues Big Mack	M	RF	250+	Voyages	SRA/McGraw Hill
Julie's Mornings	K	F	250+	Ready Readers	Pearson Learning Group
Julie's Wolf Pack	U	RF	250+	George, Jean Craighead	HarperTrophy
July 4th	C	RF	20	Instant Readers	Harcourt School Publishers
Jumbaroo, The	H	F	173	Story Basket	Wright Group/McGraw Hill
Jumble Power	L	F	250+	Cambridge Reading	Pearson Learning Group
Jumble Sale, The	E	RF	81	Oxford Reading Tree	Oxford University Press
Jumbo	E	RF	133	PM Plus Story Books	Rigby
Jump and Swim	H	RF	293	Leveled Readers	Houghton Mifflin
Jump and Thump!	C	RF	18	Home Connection Collection	Rigby
Jump Ball!: You Can Play Basketball	M	I	250+	Game Day	Picture Window Books
Jump in the Pool, A	H	RF	243	Leveled Readers Language Support	Houghton Mifflin
Jump Jets: The AV-88 Harriers	R	I	250+	War Planes	Red Brick Learning
Jump Right In	D	RF	50	Ready Readers	Pearson Learning Group
Jump Rope	B	RF	18	Bebop Books	Lee & Low Books Inc.
Jump Rope, The	H	RF	241	PM Plus Story Books	Rigby
Jump Ship to Freedom	U	HF	250+	Collier, James & Christopher	Bantam
Jump the Broom	L	RF	119	Books For Young Learners	Richard C. Owen
*Jump!: The Adventures of Brer Rabbit	T	TL	250+	Harris, Joel Chandler	OSI
Jump, Frog	C	F	33	Stewart, Josie; Salem, Lynn	Continental Press
Jump, Jump, Jump	I	F	236	Sunshine	Wright Group/McGraw Hill
Jump, Jump, Kangaroo	B	F	31	Story Box	Wright Group/McGraw Hill
Jumper	E	RF	125	Literacy Tree	Rigby
Jumpers	B	F	21	Sunshine	Wright Group/McGraw Hill
Jumping Into Nothing	M	RF	250+	Willner-Pardo, Gina	Houghton Mifflin
Jumping into the Flames	P	I	675	Vocabulary Readers	Houghton Mifflin
Jumping Jack	J	F	250+	Rigby Literacy	Rigby
Jumping Shoes	C	RF	34	Joy Readers	Pearson Learning Group
Jumping Spider	O	I	250+	Life Cycles	Creative Teaching Press
Jumprope	D	RF	31	Visions	Wright Group/McGraw Hill

* Collection of short stories

TITLE	LEVEL	GENRE	WORD COUNT	AUTHOR / SERIES	PUBLISHER / DISTRIBUTOR
June Bacon-Bercey: A Meteorologist Talks About the Weather	K	I	192	Leveled Readers Science	Houghton Mifflin
Junebug	Q	RF	250+	Mead, Alice	Bantam
Juneteenth: Celebrating the End of Slavery	Q	I	250+	Rosen Real Readers	Rosen Publishing Group
Jungle Book, The	U	F	250+	Kipling, Rudyard	Scholastic
Jungle Frogs	G	F	195	PM Plus Story Books	Rigby
Jungle Life	K	I	268	Spyglass Books	Compass Point Books
Jungle Parade: A Singing Game	D	F	105	Little Celebrations	Pearson Learning Group
Jungle Spots	B	F	28	Little Celebrations	Pearson Learning Group
Jungle Sun, The	M	F	250+	Sails	Rigby
Jungle Tiger Cat	G	F	120	Frankford, Marilyn	Kaeden Books
Jungle Walk	WB	RF	N/A	Tafuri, Nancy	Greenwillow
Junie B. Jones and a Little Monkey Business	M	RF	250+	Park, Barbara	Random House
Junie B. Jones and Her Big Fat Mouth	M	RF	250+	Park, Barbara	Random House
Junie B. Jones and Some Sneaky Peeky Spying	M	RF	250+	Park, Barbara	Random House
Junie B. Jones and that Meanie Jim's Birthday	M	RF	250+	Park, Barbara	Random House
Junie B. Jones and the Mushy Gushy Valentine	M	RF	250+	Park, Barbara	Random House
Junie B. Jones and the Stupid Smelly Bus	M	RF	250+	Park, Barbara	Random House
Junie B. Jones and the Yucky Blucky Fruitcake	M	RF	250+	Park, Barbara	Random House
Junie B. Jones Has a Monster Under Her Bed	M	RF	250+	Park, Barbara	Random House
Junie B. Jones Has a Peep in Her Pocket	M	RF	250+	Park, Barbara	Random House
Junie B. Jones is (almost) a Flower Girl	M	RF	250+	Park, Barbara	Random House
Junie B. Jones Is a Beauty Shop Guy	M	RF	250+	Park, Barbara	Random House
Junie B. Jones Is a Party Animal	M	RF	250+	Park, Barbara	Random House
Junie B. Jones Is Not a Crook	M	RF	250+	Park, Barbara	Random House
Junie B. Jones Loves Handsome Warren	M	RF	250+	Park, Barbara	Random House
Junie B. Jones Smells Something Fishy	M	RF	250+	Park, Barbara	Random House
Junior Gymnasts: Katie's Big Move	M	RF	250+	Slater, Teddy	Scholastic
Junk Box, The	C	RF	54	Windmill Books	Rigby
Junk into Art	K	RF	587	Leveled Readers	Houghton Mifflin
Junkpile Robot, The	L	F	250+	Ready Readers	Pearson Learning Group
Junkyard Dog, The	N	RF	250+	PM Emerald	Rigby
Juno Loves Barney	I	RF	249	Voyages	SRA/McGraw Hill
Jupiter	P	I	250+	Bridgestone Books	Capstone Press
Jupiter	N	I	250+	A True Book	Children's Press
Jupiter	S	I	250+	Our Solar System	Compass Point Books
Jupiter Spiders and Other Scary Creatures	K	SF	250+	Popcorn	Sundance
Just a Few Words, Mr. Lincoln	N	I	250+	Fritz, Jean	Putnam
Just a Mess	I	F	206	Mayer, Mercer	Donovan
Just a Seed	E	I	74	Blaxland, Wendy	Scholastic
Just Add Water	C	I	41	Discovery World	Rigby
Just As Long As We're Together	T	RF	250+	Blume, Judy	Bantam
Just Call Me Stupid	R	RF	250+	Birdseye, Tom	Puffin Books
Just Ella	Y	F	250+	Haddix, Margaret Peterson	Simon & Schuster
Just Enough	G	RF	107	Salem, Lynn; Stewart, Josie	Continental Press
Just for Fun	J	F	250+	Literacy 2000	Rigby
Just for You	G	F	160	Mayer, Mercer	Donovan
Just Grandma and Me	I	F	186	Mayer, Mercer	Donovan
Just Graph It!	G	I	156	Learn to Read	Creative Teaching Press
Just Hanging Around	J	I	223	Storyteller-Night Crickets	Wright Group/McGraw Hill
Just in Passing	WB	RF	N/A	Bonners, Susan	Lothrop, Lee & Shepard
Just Juice	Q	RF	250+	Hesse, Karen	Scholastic
Just Like Dad	D	RF	44	Hiris, Monica	Kaeden Books
Just Like Daddy	F	F	93	Asch, Frank	Simon & Schuster

* Collection of short stories

TITLE	LEVEL	GENRE	WORD COUNT	AUTHOR / SERIES	PUBLISHER / DISTRIBUTOR
Just Like Everyone Else	I	RF	250+	Kuskin, Karla	HarperCollins
Just Like Grandpa	E	RF	81	Literacy 2000	Rigby
Just Like Grandpa	C	RF	49	Little Celebrations	Pearson Learning Group
Just Like Me	G	RF	108	Learn to Read	Creative Teaching Press
Just Like Me	F	RF	86	First Start	Troll Associates
Just Like Me	E	RF	138	Rookie Readers	Children's Press
*Just Like Me	J	F	2154	Story Box	Wright Group/McGraw Hill
Just Like Me!	D	RF	62	Sunshine	Wright Group/McGraw Hill
Just Like Mom and Dad	O	I	1099	Leveled Readers Science	Houghton Mifflin
Just Like My Grandpa	D	RF	48	Rise & Shine	Hampton-Brown
Just Like Us	E	RF	55	Ready Readers	Pearson Learning Group
Just Like You!	C	F	28	Instant Readers	Harcourt School Publishers
Just Look at You	B	RF	16	Sunshine	Wright Group/McGraw Hill
Just Me	C	RF	51	Literacy 2000	Rigby
Just Me and My Babysitter	H	F	182	Mayer, Mercer	Donovan
Just Me and My Dad	H	F	161	Mayer, Mercer	Donovan
Just Me and My Puppy	H	F	190	Mayer, Mercer	Donovan
Just My Luck	G	RF	136	Literacy 2000	Rigby
Just One Fish Would Do	I	RF	250+	Home Connection Collection	Rigby
Just One Guinea Pig	I	RF	339	PM Story Books-Orange	Rigby
Just Plain Cat	O	RF	250+	Robinson, Nancy K.	Scholastic
Just Right for the Night	E	RF	69	Voyages	SRA/McGraw Hill
Just Right!	C	F	75	Leveled Readers	Houghton Mifflin
Just Right!	G	RF	105	Sunshine	Wright Group/McGraw Hill
Just Tell Me When We're Dead!	O	RF	250+	Clifford, Eth	Scholastic
Just the Bee's Knees	K	I	250+	Story Steps	Rigby
Just This Once	H	F	252	Sunshine	Wright Group/McGraw Hill
Just Us Women	J	RF	250+	Caines, Jeannette	Scholastic
Justin and the Best Biscuits in the World	P	RF	250+	Pitts, Walter & Mildred	Alfred A. Knopf
Justin Morgan Had a Horse	R	HF	250+	Henry, Marguerite	Scholastic
Just-Right House, The	F	F	201	Leveled Readers	Houghton Mifflin
K. C. at the Bat	U	F	1939	Leveled Readers	Houghton Mifflin
Kalpana Chawla, Astronaut	T	B	250+	Independent Readers Science	Houghton Mifflin
Kalulu's Pumpkins	K	F	250+	Rigby Literacy	Rigby
Kandake, The: Queens of Kush	X	I	2040	Independent Readers Social Studies	Houghton Mifflin
Kangaroo from Wooloomooloo	H	F	254	Jellybeans	Rigby
Kangaroo in the Kitchen	D	F	72	Ready Readers	Pearson Learning Group
Kangaroo, The	M	I	250+	Crewe, Sabrina	Steck-Vaughn
Kangaroos	N	I	250+	A New True Book	Children's Press
Kangaroos	K	I	250+	PM Animal Facts: Turquoise	Rigby
Kangaroos Have Joeys	M	I	250+	Animals and Their Young	Compass Point Books
Kangaroos in the Land Down Under	M	I	250+	Rosen Real Readers	Rosen Publishing Group
Kansas	R	I	250+	This Land Is Your Land	Compass Point Books
Kansas	S	I	250+	Land of Liberty	Red Brick Learning
Kantjil and Tiger	M	TL	250+	Story Vines	Wright Group/McGraw Hill
Karina	D	RF	40	Step-By-Step Series	Pearson Learning Group
Kat the Curious	R	RF	1723	Leveled Readers	Houghton Mifflin
Katarina	X	HF	250+	Winter, Kathryn	Scholastic
Kate Shelley and the Midnight Express	M	B	250+	Wetterer, Margaret	Carolrhoda Books
Katherine Dunham, Black Dancer	N	B	250+	Rookie Biographies	Children's Press
Katherine Paterson	S	B	250+	Cary, Alice	Learning Works, The
Katie Couldn't	F	RF	176	Rookie Readers	Children's Press
Katie Did It	G	RF	105	Rookie Readers	Children's Press

* Collection of short stories

TITLE	LEVEL	GENRE	WORD COUNT	AUTHOR / SERIES	PUBLISHER / DISTRIBUTOR
Katie's Butterfly	H	RF	222	PM Plus Story Books	Rigby
Katie's Caterpillar	E	RF	149	PM Plus Story Books	Rigby
Katy and the Big Snow	L	F	250+	Burton, Virginia L.	Scholastic
Katydids	E	I	20	Books for Young Learners	Richard C. Owen
Katydid's Life, A	M	I	250+	Twig	Wright Group/McGraw Hill
Kayaking	Q	I	250+	Lund, Bill	Red Brick Learning
Kayaking at Blue Lake	J	RF	250+	PM Plus Story Books	Rigby
Kay's Birthday	C	RF	26	KinderReaders	Rigby
Keelboat Annie	N	TL	250+	Johnson, Janet P.	Troll Associates
Keep Calm!	Q	RF	250+	Bookweb	Rigby
Keep Ms. Sugarman in the Fourth Grade	M	RF	250+	Levy, Elizabeth	HarperTrophy
Keep Out!	B	RF	19	Ready Readers	Pearson Learning Group
Keep Out: Our Dog Buries What It Can't Eat	P	RF	250+	Beale, Fleur	Pacific Learning
Keep Smiling Through	V	RF	250+	Rinaldi, Ann	Harcourt Trade
Keep the Beat	D	RF	48	Little Celebrations	Pearson Learning Group
Keep the Lights Burning Abbie	K	HF	250+	Roop, Peter & Connie	Scholastic
Keep Your Eye On Amanda!	R	F	250+	Avi	Avon
Keeping Baby Animals Safe	C	I	56	Little Books	Sadlier-Oxford
Keeping Clean	WB	I	N/A	Windows on Literacy	National Geographic
Keeping Cool	D	I	18	Foundations	Wright Group/McGraw Hill
Keeping Cool	C	I	18	Pacific Literacy	Pacific Learning
Keeping Days, The	Z	HF	250+	Johnston, Norma	Puffin Books
Keeping Fit!	E	F	36	Little Celebrations	Pearson Learning Group
Keeping Room, The	V	HF	250+	Myers, Anna	Puffin Books
Keeping Score	J	I	240	Early Connections	Benchmark Education
Keeping Tadpoles	N	I	250+	Discovery World	Rigby
Keeping Time	J	I	231	Early Connections	Benchmark Education
Keeping Warm in Winter	P	I	516	Vocabulary Readers	Houghton Mifflin
Keeping Warm! Keeping Cool!	K	I	946	Sunshine	Wright Group/McGraw Hill
Keeping Water Clean	I	I	117	Pebble Books	Red Brick Learning
Keeping You Healthy	I	I	185	Community Workers	Picture Window Books
Keeping You Safe: Book About Police Officers, A	I	I	112	Community Workers	Picture Window Books
Keisha Discovers Harlem	Q	RF	250+	Lewis, Zoe	Magic Attic
Keisha Leads the Way: Magic Attic Club	Q	RF	250+	Reed, Teresa	Magic Attic
Keisha the Fairy Snow Queen: Magic Attic Club	Q	RF	250+	Reed, Teresa	Magic Attic
Keisha to the Rescue: Magic Attic Club	Q	RF	250+	Reed, Teresa	Magic Attic
Keisha's Maze Mystery: Magic Attic Club	Q	RF	250+	Benson, Lauren	Magic Attic
Kelly's Trip	L	RF	250	Sunshine	Wright Group/McGraw Hill
Ken Griffey, Jr. & Ken Griffey, Sr.	T	B	250+	Star Families	Crestwood House
Kenji's Haircut	D	RF	105	Lighthouse	Rigby
Kenny and the Little Kickers	J	F	250+	Mareollo, Claudio	Scholastic
Kenny's Big Present	H	RF	181	Leveled Readers	Houghton Mifflin
Kensuke's Kingdom	V	RF	250+	Morpurgo, Michael	Scholastic
Kentucky	S	I	250+	Land of Liberty	Red Brick Learning
Kentucky	R	I	250+	This Land Is Your Land	Compass Point Books
Kenya	Q	I	250+	First Reports	Compass Point Books
Kenya	O	I	250+	Dahl, Michael	Red Brick Learning
Kermit and Robin's Scary Story	J	F	250+	Muntean, Michaela	Puffin Books
Kerplunk!	J	I	250	Spyglass Books	Compass Point Books
Kerri Strug: Heart of Gold	L	B	250+	Strug, K.; Brown, G.	Scholastic
Kerry	K	RF	250+	PM Story Books-Silver	Rigby
Kerry's Double	K	RF	250+	PM Story Books-Silver	Rigby
Ketchup Deal, The	P	F	250+	Marriott, Janice	Pacific Learning
Kevin Counts	D	RF	83	Seedlings	Continental Press

* Collection of short stories

TITLE	LEVEL	GENRE	WORD COUNT	AUTHOR / SERIES	PUBLISHER / DISTRIBUTOR
Key to Maps, The	K	I	222	Windows on Literacy	National Geographic
Key to the Playhouse, The	O	RF	250+	York, Carol	Scholastic
Key to the Treasure	N	RF	250+	Parish, Peggy	Bantam
Keys	B	I	31	Ready Readers	Pearson Learning Group
Khyber Pass, The	W	I	1993	Leveled Readers Social Studies	Houghton Mifflin
Kick, Pass, and Run	J	RF	250+	Kessler, Leonard	HarperTrophy
Kick-a-Lot Shoes, The	H	F	433	Story Box	Wright Group/McGraw Hill
Kickball	F	RF	148	Handprints D, Set 1	Educator's Publishing Service
Kickboxing	S	I	250+	X-Sports	Capstone Press
Kid Heroes of the Environment	Q	I	250+	Dee, Catherine	Scholastic
Kid in the Red Jacket, The	O	RF	250+	Park, Barbara	Random House
Kid Next Door, The	N	RF	250+	Smith, Janice Lee	HarperTrophy
Kid Power	P	RF	250+	Pfeffer, Susan Beth	Scholastic
Kid Who Only Hit Homers, The	M	RF	250+	Christopher, Matt	Little, Brown & Co.
Kid Who Ran For President, The	T	RF	250+	Gutman, Dan	Language for Learning Assoc.
Kids at Our School	I	RF	107	City Kids	Rigby
Kids at Work: Lewis Hine and the Crusade Against Child Labor	T	B	250+	Freedman, Russell	Clarion
Kids Can Cook	M	I	250+	Literacy 2000	Rigby
Kids from Quiller's Bend	P	RF	250+	Action Packs	Rigby
Kids' Guide to Family Reunions, A	O	I	351	Vocabulary Readers	Houghton Mifflin
Kids in Ms. Colman's Class: Author Day	M	RF	250+	Martin, Ann M.	Scholastic
Kids in Pioneer Times	Q	I	250+	Kids Throughout History	Rosen Publishing Group
Kids in the Circus	L	I	250+	Robinson, Fay	Wright Group/McGraw Hill
Kids Rule!	O	I	250+	Bookshop	Mondo
Kids Say	N	F	250+	Sails	Rigby
Killer Bees	S	I	250+	Blau, Melinda	Steck-Vaughn
Killer Whales	R	I	250+	Predators in the Wild	Red Brick Learning
Kilmer's Pet Monster	L	RF	250+	Dadey, Debbie; Jones, Marcia Thornton	Scholastic
Kind Child, The	I	RF	250+	Hechinger, Nancy	Scholastic
Kind of Thief, A	U	RF	250+	Alcock, Vivien	Bantam
*Kind Prince and Rupert, The	L	F	250+	New Way Literature	Steck-Vaughn
Kindergarten	D	RF	118	Carousel Readers	Pearson Learning Group
Kindest Family, The	K	TL	536	PM Plus Story Books	Rigby
Kindling, The (Fire-Us Trilogy: Book 1)	Y	SF	250+	Armstrong, Jennifer; Butcher, Nancy	HarperCollins
King Arthur	M	F	250+	Brown, Marc	Little, Brown & Co.
King Beast's Birthday	L	F	250+	Literacy 2000	Rigby
King Emmett the Second	R	RF	250+	Stolz, Mary	Bantam
King Glitter and the Stars	J	F	318	Talking Point Series	Pearson Learning Group
King Max	Q	F	250+	King-Smith, Dick	Troll Associates
King Midas and the Golden Touch	K	TL	721	PM Gold	Rigby
King Midas and the Golden Touch	J	TL	250+	Traditional Tales	Pearson Learning Group
King of Shadows	Z	F	250+	Cooper, Susan	McElderry
King of the Birds, The	J	F	250+	Rigby Literacy	Rigby
King of the Sky	J	RF	250+	Foundations	Wright Group/McGraw Hill
King of the Wind	R	HF	250+	Henry, Marguerite	Aladdin
King Who Could Knit, The	J	F	250+	The Wright Skills	Wright Group/McGraw Hill
King Who Had Dirty Feet, The: A Play	M	TL	250+	Rigby Literacy	Rigby
King Who Loved to Dance, The	F	F	82	Instant Readers	Harcourt School Publishers
King, the Mice, and the Cheese, The	K	F	250+	Gurney, Nancy	Random House

* Collection of short stories

TITLE	LEVEL	GENRE	WORD COUNT	AUTHOR / SERIES	PUBLISHER / DISTRIBUTOR
Kingdom of Kush, The	Z	I	3395	Leveled Readers	Houghton Mifflin
Kingfisher's Gift, The	W	F	250+	Beckhorn, Susan Williams	Penguin Group
King's Birthday, The	B	F	35	Ray's Readers	Outside the Box
*King's Dream and Sammy's New Yellow Sweater, The	L	TL	250+	New Way Literature	Steck-Vaughn
King's Equal, The	O	TL	250+	Paterson, Katherine	HarperTrophy
King's Job	F	F	155	Handprints C, Set 2	Educator's Publishing Service
King's Pudding, The	I	F	214	Literacy Tree	Rigby
*King's Race and Other Stories, The	L	F	250+	New Way Literature	Steck-Vaughn
King's Ring, The	C	F	38	KinderReaders	Rigby
King's Slippers, The	E	F	107	Sun Sprouts	ETA/Cuisenaire
King's Surprise, The	D	F	54	Stewart, Josie; Salem, Lynn	Continental Press
Kink the Mink	C	F	18	KinderReaders	Rigby
Kip and Tip	C	I	24	KinderReaders	Rigby
Kipper's Birthday	E	RF	64	Oxford Reading Tree	Oxford University Press
Kirsten Learns a Lesson	Q	HF	250+	The American Girls Collection	Pleasant Company
Kirsten Saves the Day	Q	HF	250+	The American Girls Collection	Pleasant Company
Kirsten's Surprise	Q	HF	250+	The American Girls Collection	Pleasant Company
Kiss for Little Bear, A	H	F	250+	Minarik, Else H.	HarperTrophy
Kiss the Dust	W	RF	250+	Laird, Elizabeth	Penguin Group
Kit Finds a Mitt	H	RF	198	Leveled Readers	Houghton Mifflin
Kitchen Rules	J	I	153	Windows on Literacy	National Geographic
Kitchen Science	M	I	250+	Windows on Literacy	National Geographic
Kitchen Science	P	I	958	Independent Readers Science	Houghton Mifflin
Kitchen Tools	E	I	104	Foundations	Wright Group/McGraw Hill
Kitchen, The	T	I	250+	Historic Communities	Crabtree
Kite and the Butterflies, The	I	F	364	Book Bank	Wright Group/McGraw Hill
Kite Dance	E	RF	65	Danforth, Audrey	Continental Press
Kite That Flew Away, The	H	RF	279	Ready Readers	Pearson Learning Group
Kite That Got Away, The	I	RF	250+	PM Plus Story Books	Rigby
Kite, The	D	RF	59	My First Reader	Grolier Press
Kites	C	RF	41	Joy Readers	Pearson Learning Group
Kites	C	RF	42	Ling, Bettina	Scholastic
Kites	N	I	250+	Literacy 2000	Rigby
Kites	O	I	250+	PM Nonfiction-Emerald	Rigby
Kites	B	F	41	Phonics and Friends	Hampton-Brown
Kitesurfing	O	I	250+	Sails	Rigby
Kit's Castle	L	RF	250+	Powling, Chris	Wright Group/McGraw Hill
Kit's Wilderness	Y	RF	250+	Almond, David	Random House
Kitten Chased a Fly	C	RF	57	Windmill	Wright Group/McGraw Hill
Kitten Crowd	O	RF	250+	Baglio, Ben M.	Scholastic
Kitten in the Cold	Q	RF	250+	Baglio, Ben M.	Scholastic
Kitten Is a Baby Cat, A	D	I	64	Blevins, Wiley	Scholastic
Kitten That Won First Prize, The	Q	RF	250+	Baglio, Ben M.	Scholastic
Kitten, The	A	RF	40	Sun Sprouts	ETA/Cuisenaire
Kittens	B	RF	33	Curry, Don L.	Scholastic
Kittens	G	I	107	Discovery Links	Newbridge
Kittens	C	RF	22	Literacy 2000	Rigby
Kittens in the Kitchen	Q	RF	250+	Daniels, Lucy	Barron's Educational
Kitty and the Birds	C	F	64	PM Story Books	Rigby
Kitty Cat	C	RF	57	PM Plus Story Books	Rigby
Kitty Cat and Fat Cat	D	F	98	PM Plus Story Books	Rigby
Kitty Cat and the Fish	D	F	73	PM Plus Story Books	Rigby

* Collection of short stories

TITLE	LEVEL	GENRE	WORD COUNT	AUTHOR / SERIES	PUBLISHER / DISTRIBUTOR
Kitty Cat and the Paint Can	F	F	165	PM Plus Story Books	Rigby
Kitty Cat Plays Inside	E	F	134	PM Plus Story Books	Rigby
Kitzikuba	G	F	198	Story Basket	Wright Group/McGraw Hill
Klondike Gold Rush, The	S	I	250+	A First Book	Franklin Watts
Knee Knock Rise	S	F	250+	Babbitt, Natalie	Farrar, Straus and Giroux
Knife, The	N	RF	250+	Cartwright, Pauline	Pacific Learning
Knight at Dawn, The	M	F	250+	Osborne, Mary Pope	Random House
Knightly News	P	RF	250+	Kenna, Anna	Pacific Learning
Knights & Armor	Q	I	250+	Worldwise	Grolier Press
Knights Don't Teach Piano	M	F	250+	Dadey, Debbie; Jones, Marcia Thornton	Scholastic
Knights in Shining Armor	O	I	250+	Gibbons, Gail	Little, Brown & Co.
Knit, Knit, Knit, Knit	J	F	250+	Literacy 2000	Rigby
Knitwits	Q	RF	250+	Taylor, William	Scholastic
Knobby Knuckles, Knobby Knees	I	F	236	Sunshine	Wright Group/McGraw Hill
Knock! Knock!	K	RF	250+	Carter, Jackie	Scholastic
Knock, Knock	E	RF	96	Leveled Readers	Houghton Mifflin
Knock, Knock	C	F	56	Little Celebrations	Pearson Learning Group
*Knot in the Grain (and Other Stories)	X	F	250+	McKinley, Robin	HarperTrophy
Knots in My Yo-yo String: The Autobiography of a Kid	U	B	250+	Spinelli, Jerry	Alfred A. Knopf
Knots on a Counting Rope	P	RF	250+	Martin, Jr., B.; Archambault, J.	Henry Holt & Co.
Know Where to Go	M	I	250+	Pacific Literacy	Pacific Learning
Know Your Birthday Manners	D	F	38	Instant Readers	Harcourt School Publishers
Know-Nothing Birthday, A	K	RF	250+	Spirn, Michele Sobel	HarperTrophy
Know-Nothings, The	K	RF	250+	Spirn, Michele Sobel	HarperTrophy
Koala Bears	D	I	37	Rosen Real Readers	Rosen Publishing Group
Koala Is Not a Bear, A	P	I	250+	Crabapples	Crabtree
Koalas	E	I	36	Literacy 2000	Rigby
Koalas	N	I	250+	A New True Book	Children's Press
Koalas	F	I	45	Pebble Books	Capstone Press
Kobe Bryant	T	B	250+	Sports Heroes	Red Brick Learning
Koi's Python	P	RF	250+	Moore, Miriam	Hyperion
Komodo Dragons	R	I	250+	Predators in the Wild	Red Brick Learning
Korka the Mighty Elf	H	F	250+	Rigby Literacy	Rigby
Korky Paul: Biography of an Illustrator	M	B	250+	Discovery World	Rigby
Koya DeLaney and the Good Girl Blues	P	RF	250+	Greenfield, Eloise	Scholastic
Krakus and the Dragon: A Polish Folktale	J	TL	250+	Leveled Readers Language Support	Houghton Mifflin
Kristy and the Walking Disaster	O	RF	250+	Martin, Ann M.	Scholastic
Kurt Cobain	Z	B	250+	Rock Music Library	Capstone Press
Kwanzaa	K	I	225	Visions	Wright Group/McGraw Hill
Kwanzaa	O	I	250+	Chocolate, Deborah M. Newton	Children's Press
Kwasi: A Storysong	J	RF	250+	Greetings	Rigby
Kyle's First Kwanzaa	L	RF	250+	Little Celebrations	Pearson Learning Group
La Causa: The Migrant Farmworkers' Story	U	I	250+	deRuiz, Dana Catharine	Steck-Vaughn
La Salle: La Salle and the Mississippi River	U	B	250+	Exploring the World	Compass Point Books
Labor Day	L	I	125	National Holidays	Red Brick Learning
Lacey's Loud Voice	L	RF	589	Leveled Readers	Houghton Mifflin
Lad Who Went to the North Wind, The	J	F	250+	Bookshop	Mondo
"Ladies and Gentlemen"	G	RF	120	Early Readers	Compass Point Books
Lady Bird Johnson	Q	B	250+	Simon, Charnan	Children's Press
Lady Liberty	J	I	229	Twig	Wright Group/McGraw Hill
Lady with the Alligator Purse	F	F	218	Wescott, Nadine Bernard	Little, Brown & Co.

TITLE	LEVEL	GENRE	WORD COUNT	AUTHOR / SERIES	PUBLISHER / DISTRIBUTOR
Lady with the Hat, The	Z	HF	250+	Orlev, Uri	Penguin Group
Ladybug	N	I	250+	Life Cycles	Creative Teaching Press
Ladybug and the Legislature, The	O	I	484	Independent Readers Social Studies	Houghton Mifflin
Ladybug, The	O	I	250+	Crewe, Sabrina	Steck-Vaughn
Ladybug, The	O	I	250+	Exploring History & Geography	Rigby
Ladybugs	N	I	250+	Minibeasts	Franklin Watts
Ladybugs	N	I	250+	Nature's Friends	Compass Point Books
Ladybugs	D	I	42	Pebble Books	Capstone Press
Ladybugs	G	I	250+	Pebble Plus	Red Brick Learning
Lake Critter Journal	O	RF	250+	Little Celebrations	Pearson Learning Group
Lake of Secrets	V	RF	250+	Little, Lael	Henry Holt & Co.
Lake, The	G	I	53	Windows on Literacy	National Geographic
Lamb in the Laundry	Q	RF	250+	Baglio, Ben M.	Scholastic
Lamb Lessons	O	RF	250+	Baglio, Ben M.	Scholastic
Lamborghinis	U	I	250+	Green, Michael	Red Brick Learning
Lamp from the Warlock's Tomb, The	S	F	250+	Bellairs, John	Puffin Books
Lampfish of Twill, The	U	F	250+	Lisle, Janet Taylor	Scholastic
Lan Xang, Kingdom of the Million Elephants	Y	I	2056	Leveled Readers Social Studies	Houghton Mifflin
Land and Water	K	I	106	Independent Readers Social Studies	Houghton Mifflin
Land I Lost, The	P	I	250+	Nhuong, Huynh Quang	HarperTrophy
Land of the Dragons	P	I	250+	Morris, Rod	Pacific Learning
Land of the Great Big "No!"	L	RF	250+	Trussell-Cullen, Alan	Pearson Learning Group
Land, The	Z	HF	250+	Taylor, Mildred D.	Penguin Group
Landry News, The	R	RF	250+	Clements, Andrew	Simon & Schuster
Lands of the Rainforest	T	I	1698	Leveled Readers Social Studies	Houghton Mifflin
Landslides	R	I	1127	Leveled Readers	Houghton Mifflin
Landslides	Q	I	250+	Natural Disasters	Red Brick Learning
Landslides, Slumps & Creep	U	I	250+	A First Book	Franklin Watts
Langston Hughes	L	B	168	Vocabulary Readers	Houghton Mifflin
Langston Hughes: An Illustrated Edition	X	B	250+	Meltzer, Milton	Millbrook Press
Langston Hughes: Young Black Poet	O	B	250+	Childhood of Famous Americans	Aladdin
Larry and the Cookie	E	RF	56	Rookie Readers	Children's Press
Lasers	V	I	250+	Sunshine	Wright Group/McGraw Hill
Last Book in the Universe, The	W	SF	250+	Philbrick, Rodman	Scholastic
Last Chance for Magic	P	F	250+	Chew, Ruth	Scholastic
Last Game, The	G	RF	89	Start to Read	School Zone
Last Look	P	RF	250+	Bulla, Clyde Robert	Puffin Books
Last One In Is a Rotten Egg	J	RF	250+	Kessler, Leonard	HarperTrophy
Last Puppy, The	K	F	244	Asch, Frank	Simon & Schuster
Last Summer with Maizon	Q	RF	250+	Woodson, Jacqueline	G.P. Putnam's Sons
Late for Soccer (Football)	F	RF	185	PM Story Books	Rigby
Late One Night	D	RF	97	Mader, Jan	Kaeden Books
Later	D	RF	106	Teacher's Choice Series	Pearson Learning Group
Later, Gator	R	RF	250+	Yep, Laurence	Hyperion
Later, Rover	G	RF	200	Ziefert, Harriet	Puffin Books
Laughing Cake, The	G	F	89	Reading Corners	Pearson Learning Group
Laughing Hyena	I	F	250+	Lighthouse	Rigby
Laughing Place, The	K	F	250+	Story Steps	Rigby
Laughter Is the Best Medicine	P	I	250+	Literacy Tree	Rigby
Laundromat, The	B	RF	25	Visions	Wright Group/McGraw Hill
Laundromat, The	D	RF	25	Sunshine	Wright Group/McGraw Hill
Laundry Day	C	RF	28	Bebop Books	Lee & Low Books Inc.

* Collection of short stories

TITLE	LEVEL	GENRE	WORD COUNT	AUTHOR / SERIES	PUBLISHER / DISTRIBUTOR
Laura and Mr. Edwards	M	HF	250+	Wilder, Laura Ingalls	HarperTrophy
Laura and Nellie	M	HF	250+	Wilder, Laura Ingalls	HarperTrophy
Laura Ingalls Wilder	L	B	250+	Biography	Benchmark Education
Laura Ingalls Wilder	P	B	250+	Blair, Gwenda; Allen, Thomas	Lerner Publishing
Laura Ingalls Wilder	O	B	250+	Allen, Thomas B.	Putnam
Laura Ingalls Wilder, Pioneer Girl	R	B	250+	Stine, Megan	Bantam
Laura Ingalls Wilder: A Biography	R	B	250+	Anderson, William	HarperTrophy
Laura Ingalls Wilder: An Author's Story	N	B	250+	Glasscock, Sarah	Steck-Vaughn
Laura Ingalls Wilder: Author of the Little House Books	O	B	250+	Greene, Carol	Children's Press
Laura Ingalls Wilder: Growing Up in the Little House	P	B	250+	Giff, Patricia Reilly	Puffin Books
Laura's Ma	M	HF	250+	Wilder, Laura Ingalls	HarperTrophy
Laura's Pa	M	HF	250+	Wilder, Laura Ingalls	HarperTrophy
Lavender	O	RF	250+	Hesse, Karen	Henry Holt & Co.
Lavender the Library Cat	K	RF	418	Jellybeans	Rigby
Law and Order	K	I	250+	Spyglass Books	Compass Point Books
Lazy Bones Jones	P	F	250+	Welch, Sheila Kelly	Pacific Learning
Lazy Fox	I	F	268	Leveled Readers	Houghton Mifflin
Lazy Jackal, The	M	F	561	Sunshine	Wright Group/McGraw Hill
Lazy Lions, Lucky Lambs	M	RF	250+	Giff, Patricia Reilly	Bantam
Lazy Mary	D	RF	191	Story Box	Wright Group/McGraw Hill
Lazy Pig, The	C	F	78	PM Story Books	Rigby
Leaders of the People	U	B	250+	Real Lives	Troll Associates
Leaders: People Who Make a Difference	R	B	250+	You Are There	Children's Press
Leaf Boats, The	E	RF	132	PM Plus Story Books	Rigby
Leaf Rain	F	RF	82	Book Bank	Wright Group/McGraw Hill
Leaf Raker, The	M	RF	250+	Voyages	SRA/McGraw Hill
Leafcutter Ant, The	H	I	77	Vocabulary Readers	Houghton Mifflin
Leafy Sea Dragons	F	I	183	Sun Sprouts	ETA/Cuisenaire
Leap Frog	WB	RF	N/A	Ready to Read	Pacific Learning
Leaping Lena	L	F	250+	Rigby Literacy	Rigby
Leaping Lizards	M	I	250+	Stadler, Charlotte	Benchmark Education
Learning About Clouds	D	I	18	Rosen Real Readers	Rosen Publishing Group
Learning About Leaves	D	I	37	Rosen Real Readers	Rosen Publishing Group
Learning About Rain	E	I	26	Rosen Real Readers	Rosen Publishing Group
Learning About Sand	E	I	42	Rosen Real Readers	Rosen Publishing Group
Learning About Snow	F	I	42	Rosen Real Readers	Rosen Publishing Group
Learning About the Library	I	I	164	Rosen Real Readers	Rosen Publishing Group
Learning from Fossils	Q	I	3234	Leveled Readers Science	Houghton Mifflin
Learning New Things	H	RF	156	Foundations	Wright Group/McGraw Hill
Learning to Swim	I	RF	234	My World	Steck-Vaughn
Leave It to Beavers	F	RF	102	Leveled Readers Science	Houghton Mifflin
Leaves	K	I	236	Pebble Books	Capstone Press
Leaves	I	I	250+	Momentum Literacy Program	Troll Associates
Leaves	C	I	29	Hoenecke, Karen	Kaeden Books
Leaves, Fruits, Seeds, and Roots	C	I	26	Pacific Literacy	Pacific Learning
*Leaving Home	Z	RF	250+	Keillor, Garrison	Penguin Group
*Leaving Home: 15 Distinguished Authors Explore Personal Journeys	Z	RF	250+	Rochman, Hazel; McCampbell, Darlene	HarperTrophy
Left Behind	L	RF	250+	Carrick, Carol	Clarion
Left, Right	G	RF	182	Sunshine	Wright Group/McGraw Hill
Leftovers, The: Catch Flies!	N	RF	250+	Howard, Tristan	Scholastic
Leftovers, The: Fast Break	N	RF	250+	Howard, Tristan	Scholastic

* Collection of short stories

TITLE	LEVEL	GENRE	WORD COUNT	AUTHOR / SERIES	PUBLISHER / DISTRIBUTOR
Leftovers, The: Get Jammed	N	RF	250+	Howard, Tristan	Scholastic
Leftovers, The: Reach Their Goal	N	RF	250+	Howard, Tristan	Scholastic
Leftovers, The: Strike Out!	N	RF	250+	Howard, Tristan	Scholastic
Leftovers, The: Use Their Heads!	N	RF	250+	Howard, Tristan	Scholastic
Legend of the Bluebonnet, The	O	TL	250+	DePaola, Tomie	Scholastic
Legend of the Hummingbird, The	K	TL	250+	Folk Tales	Mondo
Legend of the Indian Paintbrush, The	O	TL	250+	DePaola, Tomie	Scholastic
Legend of the Red Bird, The	K	TL	389	Sunshine	Wright Group/McGraw Hill
Legendary Places	N	I	250+	Wildcats	Wright Group/McGraw Hill
*Legends	S	TL	250+	Goodman, R.; Pierce, R.; Wagner, Betty Jane	Houghton Mifflin
Legs	LB	I	21	Twig	Wright Group/McGraw Hill
Legs	D	I	21	Literacy 2000	Rigby
Legs	B	F	15	Gosset, Rachel; Ballinger, Margaret	Scholastic
Legs, Legs, Legs	C	I	36	Wonder World	Wright Group/McGraw Hill
Leif Eriksson	Q	B	250+	Biographies-Great Explorers	Capstone Press
Lemon Tree, The	D	RF	28	Harry's Math Books	Outside the Box
Lemonade	F	F	140	Learn to Read	Creative Teaching Press
Lemonade Stand, The	G	RF	148	City Stories	Rigby
Lemonade Trick, The	Q	RF	250+	Corbett, Scott	Scholastic
Lemurs	M	I	250+	The Wild World of Animals	Capstone Press
Lend a Hand	E	I	26	iOpeners	Pearson Learning Group
Lend a Hand	K	F	250+	Kratky, Lada	Hampton-Brown
Lenny and Tweek	K	F	250+	Bookshop	Mondo
Lentil	M	RF	250+	McCloskey, Robert	Scholastic
Leo and Lester	L	F	250+	Bookshop	Mondo
Leo the Late Bloomer	I	F	164	Kraus, Robert	Simon & Schuster
Leonard Bernstein	R	B	250+	Venezia, Mike	Children's Press
Leonardo da Vinci	S	B	250+	Masterpieces: Artists and Their Works	Capstone Press
Leonardo da Vinci	T	B	1776	Leveled Readers Science	Houghton Mifflin
Leon's Story	T	B	250+	Tillage, Leon Walter	Farrar, Straus and Giroux
Leontyne Price: Opera Superstar	N	B	250+	Williams, Sylvia B.	Children's Press
Leprechauns Don't Play Basketball	M	F	250+	Dadey, Debbie; Jones, Marcia Thornton	Scholastic
Lesson, The	H	RF	133	Cummings, Pat	Scholastic
Lester's Bedtime	B	F	39	Lester the Lion Series	Pioneer Valley
Lester's Haircut	I	F	250+	Lester the Lion Series	Pioneer Valley
Lester's Song	H	F	250+	Lester the Lion Series	Pioneer Valley
*Let Me In	I	TL	1814	Story Box	Wright Group/McGraw Hill
Let the Circle Be Unbroken	X	HF	250+	Taylor, Mildred D.	Penguin Group
Let's All Dance!	G	I	148	Vocabulary Readers	Houghton Mifflin
Let's Bake	G	I	195	Discovery Links	Newbridge
Let's Be Enemies	J	RF	250+	Sendak, Maurice	Harper & Row
Let's Be Friends	D	I	23	Pair-It Books	Steck-Vaughn
Let's Brush Our Teeth	F	I	78	Rosen Real Readers	Rosen Publishing Group
Let's Build a Playground	O	I	250+	Myers, Edward	Pearson Learning Group
Let's Build a Tower	LB	RF	15	Literacy 2000	Rigby
Let's Celebrate	C	I	33	Rise & Shine	Hampton-Brown
Let's Draw!	F	I	21	Rosen Real Readers	Rosen Publishing Group
Let's Eat	E	RF	63	Teacher's Choice Series	Pearson Learning Group
Let's Eat: Foods of Our World	K	I	250+	Spyglass Books	Compass Point Books
Let's Find Out about Money	O	I	250+	Barabas, Kathy	Scholastic

* Collection of short stories

TITLE	LEVEL	GENRE	WORD COUNT	AUTHOR / SERIES	PUBLISHER / DISTRIBUTOR
Let's Get a Pet	F	RF	22	Jellybeans	Rigby
Let's Get Dressed: What People Wear	K	I	250+	Spyglass Books	Compass Point Books
Let's Get Moving	M	I	250+	Literacy 2000	Rigby
Let's Go	B	I	81	Early Connections	Benchmark Education
Let's Go	A	RF	32	Reading Corners	Pearson Learning Group
Let's Go	C	RF	30	Windmill	Wright Group/McGraw Hill
Let's Go Camping	E	I	44	Vocabulary Readers	Houghton Mifflin
Let's Go Camping and Other Stories	H	F	250+	New Way Literature	Steck-Vaughn
Let's Go Downtown	F	RF	85	City Stories	Rigby
Let's Go Fishing	M	RF	250+	Voyages	SRA/McGraw Hill
Let's Go Marching	E	RF	94	Ready Readers	Pearson Learning Group
Let's Go Rock Climbing!	I	I	128	Vocabulary Readers	Houghton Mifflin
Let's Go Rock Collecting	N	I	250+	Soar To Success	Houghton Mifflin
Let's Go Shopping	C	I	34	Rise & Shine	Hampton-Brown
Let's Go to a Fair	F	I	139	Welcome Books	Children's Press
Let's Go to a Museum	E	RF	181	Blevins, Wiley	Scholastic
Let's Go to the Bank	I	I	233	Rosen Real Readers	Rosen Publishing Group
Let's Go to the Supermarket	I	I	198	Rosen Real Readers	Rosen Publishing Group
Let's Go to the Theater!	N	I	320	Vocabulary Readers	Houghton Mifflin
Let's Go!	A	I	30	Vocabulary Readers	Houghton Mifflin
Let's Go, Philadelphia!	M	RF	250+	Giff, Patricia Reilly	Bantam
Let's Grab It!	D	RF	60	Leveled Readers	Houghton Mifflin
Let's Graph	M	I	239	Yellow Umbrella Books	Capstone Press
Let's Graph It!	S	I	250+	Rosen Real Readers	Rosen Publishing Group
Let's Have a Swim	C	F	74	Sunshine	Wright Group/McGraw Hill
Let's Look After Our World	L	I	250+	Sunshine	Wright Group/McGraw Hill
Let's Look at Leopards	H	I	155	Rosen Real Readers	Rosen Publishing Group
Let's Look at Rocks	I	I	186	Yellow Umbrella Books	Red Brick Learning
Let's Look at Venus	L	I	250+	Rosen Real Readers	Rosen Publishing Group
Let's Look Outside	B	I	38	Early Connections	Benchmark Education
Let's Make a Kite	J	I	250+	Book Shop	Mondo
Let's Make Butter	I	I	224	Yellow Umbrella Books	Red Brick Learning
Let's Make Music	J	I	220	iOpeners	Pearson Learning Group
Let's Make Something New	G	I	116	Discovery Links	Newbridge
Let's Measure It!	D	F	100	Learn to Read	Creative Teaching Press
Let's Move!	B	RF	29	Ready Readers	Pearson Learning Group
Let's Paint	C	RF	51	Rise & Shine	Hampton-Brown
Let's Play	B	RF	40	Little Books for Early Readers	University of Maine
Let's Play Ball	C	F	68	New Way Red	Steck-Vaughn
Let's Play Basketball	E	RF	46	Geddes, Diana	Kaeden Books
Let's Play Games Around the World	O	I	250+	iOpeners	Pearson Learning Group
Let's Play Today	D	RF	68	Leveled Readers Language Support	Houghton Mifflin
Let's Pretend	C	RF	82	PM Plus Story Books	Rigby
Let's Pretend	B	RF	40	Home Connection Collection	Rigby
Let's Take a Trip	H	F	178	Leveled Readers	Houghton Mifflin
Let's Take Care of the Earth	E	I	121	Learn to Read	Creative Teaching Press
Let's Take the Bus	H	RF	250+	Real Reading	Steck-Vaughn
Let's Talk: How We Communicate	K	I	250+	Spyglass Books	Compass Point Books
Let's Visit the Moon	E	F	130	Instant Readers	Harcourt School Publishers
Let's Wash Up	F	I	69	Rosen Real Readers	Rosen Publishing Group
Letter Carriers	L	I	250+	Community Workers	Compass Point Books
Letter from Fish Bay, A	N	B	250+	Cowley, Joy	Pacific Learning
Letter From Phoenix Farm, A	O	B	250+	Yolen, Jane	Richard C. Owen

TITLE	LEVEL	GENRE	WORD COUNT	AUTHOR / SERIES	PUBLISHER / DISTRIBUTOR
Letter to a Friend	L	I	250+	Early Connections	Benchmark Education
Letter to Amy, A	K	RF	250+	Keats, Ezra Jack	Harper & Row
Letter to Mrs. Roosevelt, A	R	HF	250+	DeYoung, C. Coco	Delacorte
Letter, The	LB	RF	15	Twig	Wright Group/McGraw Hill
Letter, the Witch, and the Ring, The	S	F	250+	Bellairs, John	Penguin Group
Letters for Mr. James	H	RF	203	Sunshine	Wright Group/McGraw Hill
Letters From a Mill Town	T	HF	1662	Leveled Readers Social Studies	Houghton Mifflin
Letters From a Slave Girl: The Story of Harriet Jacobs	X	HF	250+	Lyons, Mary E.	Simon & Schuster
Letters From Camp: A Mystery	V	RF	250+	Klise, Kate	HarperTrophy
Letters from Rifka	S	HF	250+	Hesse, Karen	Puffin Books
Letters from the Sea	S	I	250+	Voyages in Time	Wright Group/McGraw Hill
Letters to Cupid	Z	RF	250+	Lantz, Francess	Pleasant Company
Letters to Julia	W	RF	250+	Holmes, Barbara Ware	HarperTrophy
Letting Swift River Go	M	HF	250+	Yolen, Jane	Little, Brown & Co.
Levi Sings	C	RF	29	Teacher's Choice Series	Pearson Learning Group
Lewis & Clark: Explorers of the American West	S	I	250+	Kroll, Steven	Holiday House
Lewis and Clark	Q	B	250+	Biographies-Great Explorers	Capstone Press
Lewis and Clark	V	B	250+	Cornerstones of Freedom	Children's Press
Lewis and Clark	T	HF	250+	Sullivan, George	Scholastic
Lewis and Clark Expedition, The	T	I	250+	We The People	Compass Point Books
Lewis and Clark Expedition, The	V	I	250+	Let Freedom Ring	Red Brick Learning
Lewis and Clark's Voyage of Discovery	S	I	250+	The Library of the Westward Expansion	Rosen Publishing Group
Lexington and Concord	V	I	250+	Cornerstones of Freedom	Children's Press
Liar, Liar Pants on Fire	I	RF	250+	Cohen, Miriam	Bantam
Liar, Liar, Pants on Fire	O	RF	250+	Korman, Gordon	Scholastic
Liberty Bell, The	N	I	250+	American Symbols	Capstone Press
Liberty Bell, The	V	I	250+	Cornerstones of Freedom	Children's Press
Librarians	L	I	250+	Community Workers	Compass Point Books
Librarians	M	I	250+	Ready, Dee	Red Brick Learning
Library Card, The	R	RF	250+	Spinelli, Jerry	Scholastic
Library Day	J	F	250+	Sunshine	Wright Group/McGraw Hill
Library of Congress, The	V	I	250+	Cornerstones of Freedom	Children's Press
Library, The	D	RF	96	Emergent	Pioneer Valley
Library, The	C	RF	33	Carousel Readers	Pearson Learning Group
License Plates	J	RF	411	PM Turquoise	Rigby
Licken Chicken	I	TL	250+	Tiger Cub	Peguis
Lid, The	G	RF	111	Books for Young Learners	Richard C. Owen
Lid, The	I	F	111	Books for Young Learners	Richard C. Owen
Life and Death of Martin Luther King, Jr.,The	Y	B	250+	Haskins, James	Beech Tree Books
Life and Words of Martin Luther King, Jr., The	W	B	250+	Peck, Ira	Scholastic
Life at Plimouth	L	I	210	Leveled Readers Social Studies	Houghton Mifflin
Life at the Bottom of the Sea	U	I	250+	Leveled Readers Language Support	Houghton Mifflin
Life Cycle of a Butterfly, The	J	I	211	Pebble Books	Red Brick Learning
Life Cycle of a Cat, The	J	I	108	Pebble Books	Red Brick Learning
Life Cycle of a Chicken, The	J	I	214	Pebble Books	Red Brick Learning
Life Cycle of a Dog, The	J	I	110	Pebble Books	Red Brick Learning
Life Cycle of a Frog, The	J	I	218	Pebble Books	Red Brick Learning
Life Cycle of a Whale, The	J	I	209	Pebble Books	Red Brick Learning
Life in a Coral Reef	L	I	250+	Rosen Real Readers	Rosen Publishing Group
Life in Colonial America	L	I	405	Leveled Readers Social Studies	Houghton Mifflin
Life in the Arctic	M	I	250+	Rosen Real Readers	Rosen Publishing Group

* Collection of short stories

TITLE	LEVEL	GENRE	WORD COUNT	AUTHOR / SERIES	PUBLISHER / DISTRIBUTOR
Life In the Arctic	K	I	293	Leveled Readers Science	Houghton Mifflin
Life in the City	J	I	307	Early Connections	Benchmark Education
Life in the City	E	RF	184	Handprints D, Set 1	Educator's Publishing Service
Life in the Desert	L	I	250+	Sails	Rigby
Life in the Desert	M	I	250+	Pair-It Books	Steck-Vaughn
Life in the Mangroves	I	I	172	Home Connection Collection	Rigby
Life in the Ocean	M	I	250+	Windows on Literacy	National Geographic
Life in the Ocean Depths	T	I	2165	Leveled Readers Science	Houghton Mifflin
Life in the Oceans: Animals, People, Plants	T	I	250+	Baker, Lucy	Scholastic
Life in the Rain Forest	L	I	250+	Rosen Real Readers	Rosen Publishing Group
Life in the Rain Forests: Animals, People, Plants	T	I	250+	Baker, Lucy	Scholastic
Life in the Sahara	U	I	1804	Leveled Readers Social Studies	Houghton Mifflin
Life in the Sahara	U	I	250+	Leveled Readers Social Studies	Houghton Mifflin
Life Long Ago	K	I	250+	Spyglass Books	Compass Point Books
Life of a Bean, The	J	I	201	Independent Readers Science	Houghton Mifflin
Life of a Butterfly, The	E	I	46	Vocabulary Readers	Houghton Mifflin
Life of a Dollar Bill, The	N	I	301	Leveled Readers Social Studies	Houghton Mifflin
Life of a Lion, The	E	I	28	Rosen Real Readers	Rosen Publishing Group
Life of a Miner	T	I	250+	Life in the Old West	Crabtree
Life of Abraham Lincoln, The	M	B	250+	Rosen Real Readers	Rosen Publishing Group
Life on a Farm	A	I	24	Early Connections	Benchmark Education
Life on a Plantation	T	I	250+	Historic Communities	Crabtree
Life on a Wagon Train	Q	I	250+	Rosen Real Readers	Rosen Publishing Group
Life on the Serengeti	V	I	1811	Independent Readers Science	Houghton Mifflin
Lifeboat in Space	Z	I	3358	Leveled Readers	Houghton Mifflin
Lifeguards	M	I	250+	Community Helpers	Red Brick Learning
Lift Off!	G	I	121	Pair-It Books	Steck-Vaughn
Lift the Sky Up	H	RF	133	Little Celebrations	Pearson Learning Group
Lift the Sky Up	H	RF	133	Little Readers	Houghton Mifflin
Lift-Off!	I	SF	141	Pacific Literacy	Pacific Learning
Light	J	I	250+	Momentum Literacy Program	Troll Associates
Light	C	I	30	Twig	Wright Group/McGraw Hill
Light	J	I	150	Early Connections	Benchmark Education
Light and Shade	X	I	250+	iOpeners	Pearson Learning Group
Light and Shadow	G	I	138	Discovery Links	Newbridge
Light at Tern Rock, The	N	RF	250+	Sauer, Julia L.	Scholastic
Light in the Forest, The	Y	HF	250+	Richter, Conrad	Random House
Light in the Storm, A	T	HF	250+	Hesse, Karen	Scholastic
Light: Shadows, Mirrors, and Rainbows	M	I	250+	Amazing Science	Picture Window Books
Lighthouse Children, The	I	F	250+	Hoff, Syd	HarperTrophy
Lighthouse Mermaid, The	M	F	250+	Karr, Kathleen	Hyperion
Lightning	L	I	279	Pebble Books	Capstone Press
Lightning	S	I	1110	Leveled Readers	Houghton Mifflin
Lightning	T	I	250+	Kramer, Stephen	Carolrhoda Books
Lightning Liz	F	F	41	Rookie Readers	Children's Press
Lights at Night	LB	I	33	Pacific Literacy	Pacific Learning
Lights Go On	C	I	45	Windows on Literacy	National Geographic
Lights On!	S	I	1450	Independent Readers Science	Houghton Mifflin
*Lightweight Rocket and Other Cases, The	O	RF	250+	Simon, Seymour	Avon
Like Jake and Me	O	RF	250+	Jukes, Mavis	Alfred A. Knopf
Like Me	D	RF	20	Book Bank	Wright Group/McGraw Hill
Like My Daddy	E	RF	129	Visions	Wright Group/McGraw Hill
Lila the Fair	L	RF	250+	Social Studies Connects	The Kane Press

* Collection of short stories

TITLE	LEVEL	GENRE	WORD COUNT	AUTHOR / SERIES	PUBLISHER / DISTRIBUTOR
Lilacs, Lotuses, and Ladybugs	L	RF	402	Evangeline Nicholas Collection	Wright Group/McGraw Hill
Lili the Brave	N	RF	250+	Armstrong, Jennifer	Random House
Lili's Breakfast	F	RF	156	Storyteller-Setting Sun	Wright Group/McGraw Hill
Lillian the Librarian	I	RF	315	Seedlings	Continental Press
Lilly-Lolly-Little-Legs	H	RF	129	Literacy 2000	Rigby
Lily and Miss Liberty	N	HF	250+	Stephens, Carla	Scholastic
Lily's Crossing	S	HF	250+	Giff, Patricia Reilly	Delacorte
Limestone Caves	N	I	250+	A First Book	Franklin Watts
Limestone Caves	N	I	250+	Davis, Gary	Children's Press
Lincoln Memorial, The	Q	I	250+	National Landmarks	Red Brick Learning
Lincoln Memorial, The	V	I	250+	Cornerstones of Freedom	Children's Press
Lincoln: A Photobiography	V	B	250+	Freedman, Russell	Clarion
Lincoln-Douglas Debates, The	W	I	250+	Cornerstones of Freedom	Children's Press
Ling's New Friend	F	RF	164	Sun Sprouts	ETA/Cuisenaire
Lin's Backpack	C	RF	49	Little Celebrations	Pearson Learning Group
Lion and the Mouse	E	TL	87	Herman, Gail	Random House
Lion and the Mouse, The	E	SF	91	Cambridge Reading	Pearson Learning Group
Lion and the Mouse, The	G	TL	250	Traditional Tales & More	Rigby
Lion and the Mouse, The	G	TL	125	PM Story Books	Rigby
Lion and the Mouse, The	I	TL	499	Aesop's Fables	Pearson Learning Group
Lion and The Mouse, The	G	TL	250	Literacy 2000	Rigby
Lion and the Mouse, The	J	TL	325	Little Books	Sadlier-Oxford
Lion and the Mouse, The	J	TL	285	Sunshine	Wright Group/McGraw Hill
Lion and the Mouse, The	K	TL	557	Pair-It Books	Steck-Vaughn
*Lion and the Mouse, The	F	TL	115	New Way Red	Steck-Vaughn
Lion and the Rabbit, The	F	TL	99	PM Story Books	Rigby
Lion Dancer: Ernie Wan's Chinese New Year	N	B	250+	Waters, Kate; Slovenz-Low, Madeline	Scholastic
Lion in the Night, The	J	F	250+	Momentum Literacy Program	Troll Associates
Lion Roars, The	I	RF	270	Ready Readers	Pearson Learning Group
Lion Talk	I	I	216	Storyteller-Night Crickets	Wright Group/McGraw Hill
*Lion Tamer's Daughter And Other Stories, The	Z	F	250+	Dickinson, Peter	Laurel-Leaf Books
Lion to Guard Us, A	P	HF	250+	Bulla, Clyde Robert	HarperTrophy
Lion, the Witch, and the Wardrobe, The	T	F	250+	Lewis, C. S.	HarperTrophy
Lionel and Amelia	L	F	250+	Bookshop	Mondo
*Lionel and His Friends	K	RF	250+	Krensky, Stephen	Puffin Books
*Lionel and Louise	K	RF	250+	Krensky, Stephen	Puffin Books
*Lionel at Large	K	RF	250+	Krensky, Stephen	Puffin Books
*Lionel In The Fall	K	RF	250+	Krensky, Stephen	Puffin Books
*Lionel In The Spring	K	RF	250+	Krensky, Stephen	Puffin Books
*Lionel In The Summer	K	RF	250+	Krensky, Stephen	Puffin Books
*Lionel In The Winter	K	RF	250+	Krensky, Stephen	Puffin Books
Lions	O	I	250+	Holmes, Kevin J.	Red Brick Learning
Lions	N	I	250+	Meadows, Graham; Vial, Claire	Pearson Learning Group
Lions	L	I	644	Pair-It Books	Steck-Vaughn
Lions & Tigers	K	I	250+	PM Animals in the Wild-Yellow	Rigby
Lions and the Water Buffaloes, The	I	RF	250+	PM Plus Story Books	Rigby
Lions and Tigers	K	I	250+	PM Animal Facts: Turquoise	Rigby
Lions at Lunchtime	M	F	250+	Osborne, Mary Pope	Random House
Lion's Dinner, The	E	F	111	Rigby Literacy	Rigby
Lion's Lunch	F	F	201	Lighthouse	Rigby
Lion's Tail, The	F	F	147	Reading Unlimited	Pearson Learning Group
Lisa's Diary	L	RF	250+	Home Connection Collection	Rigby
Lisa's Ices	G	RF	106	City Stories	Rigby

* Collection of short stories

TITLE	LEVEL	GENRE	WORD COUNT	AUTHOR / SERIES	PUBLISHER / DISTRIBUTOR
Lise Meitner	Y	B	3362	Leveled Readers Science	Houghton Mifflin
Listen	D	RF	35	Visions	Wright Group/McGraw Hill
*Listen Children: An Anthology of Black Literature	U	RF	250+	Strickland, Dorothy S.	Bantam
Listen to Me	G	RF	47	Rookie Readers	Children's Press
Listening in Bed	M	RF	116	Book Bank	Wright Group/McGraw Hill
Listening to Crickets: A Story about Rachel Carson	R	HF	250+	Ransom, Candice F.	Carolrhoda Books
Little Adventure, A	J	RF	250+	PM Story Books-Silver	Rigby
Little and Big	C	I	57	Little Red Readers	Sundance
Little Ant, The: A Folktale From New Mexico	J	TL	250+	Costigan, Shirleyann	Hampton-Brown
Little Bear	J	F	1664	Minarik, Else H.	HarperCollins
Little Bear	D	F	77	My First Reader	Grolier Press
Little Bears	A	I	37	Bookshop	Mondo
Little Bear's Friend	J	F	250+	Minarik, Else H.	HarperTrophy
Little Bear's Visit	J	F	250+	Minarik, Else H.	HarperTrophy
Little Bike, The	C	F	29	Joy Readers	Pearson Learning Group
Little Bill	L	RF	250+	Cosby, Bill	Scholastic
Little Bird	E	TL	42	Sunshine	Wright Group/McGraw Hill
Little Bit Hotter Can't Hurt, A	L	RF	466	Leveled Readers	Houghton Mifflin
Little Black: A Pony	J	RF	250+	Farley, Walter	Random House
Little Blue and Little Yellow	J	F	250+	Lionni, Leo	Scholastic
Little Blue Big Blue	K	RF	250+	Rigby Literacy	Rigby
Little Blue Horse, The	I	RF	250+	PM Plus Story Books	Rigby
Little Book of Street Rods, The	H	I	79	Books for Young Learners	Richard C. Owen
Little Bo-Peep	C	F	48	Seedlings	Continental Press
Little Boy and the Balloon Man	E	F	16	Tiger Cub	Peguis
Little Boy Blue	D	TL	32	Sunshine	Wright Group/McGraw Hill
*Little Boy with Three Names and Other Short Stories	S	TL	250+	Clark, Ann Nolan	Kiva Publishing
Little Brother	C	RF	31	Story Box	Wright Group/McGraw Hill
Little Brother	A	RF	14	Sunshine	Wright Group/McGraw Hill
Little Brother's Haircut	J	RF	250+	Story Box	Wright Group/McGraw Hill
Little Brown House	H	RF	266	Jellybeans	Rigby
Little Brown Jay, The: A Tale from India	K	TL	366	Claire, Elizabeth	Mondo
Little Bulldozer	E	F	170	PM Story Books	Rigby
Little Bulldozer Helps Again	F	F	197	PM Extensions-Blue	Rigby
Little Car	F	F	181	Sunshine	Wright Group/McGraw Hill
Little Caribou	N	I	250+	Fox-Davies, Sarah	Candlewick Press
Little Cats	P	I	250+	Crabapples	Crabtree
Little Chick's Friend Duckling	I	F	572	Kwitz, Mary Deball	HarperTrophy
Little Chicks Sing, The	E	F	52	Instant Readers	Harcourt School Publishers
Little Chief	K	F	250+	Hoff, Syd	HarperCollins
Little Chimp	C	F	50	PM Plus Story Books	Rigby
Little Chimp and Baby Chimp	E	F	184	PM Plus Story Books	Rigby
Little Chimp and Big Chimp	C	RF	66	PM Plus Story Books	Rigby
Little Chimp and the Bees	F	F	160	PM Plus Story Books	Rigby
Little Chimp and the Termites	H	F	192	PM Plus Story Books	Rigby
Little Chimp Runs Away	D	F	104	PM Plus Story Books	Rigby
Little Clearing in the Woods	Q	HF	250+	Wilkes, Maria D.	HarperTrophy
Little Cousins' Visit, The	C	RF	123	Emergent	Pioneer Valley
Little Critters	I	RF	127	Books for Young Learners	Richard C. Owen
*Little Dancer and Other Short Stories, The	K	F	250+	New Way Literature	Steck-Vaughn
Little Danny Dinosaur	G	F	195	First Start	Troll Associates

* Collection of short stories

TITLE	LEVEL	GENRE	WORD COUNT	AUTHOR / SERIES	PUBLISHER / DISTRIBUTOR
Little Dinosaur	K	F	250+	Voyages	SRA/McGraw Hill
Little Dinosaur Escapes	J	HF	389	PM Turquoise	Rigby
Little Dutch Boy, The	J	TL	250+	Jumbled Tumbled Tales & Rhymes	Rigby
Little Elephant	G	F	192	New Way Blue	Steck-Vaughn
Little Farm in the Ozarks	R	HF	250+	MacBride, Roger Lea	HarperTrophy
Little Firefighter, The	M	RF	867	Sunshine	Wright Group/McGraw Hill
Little Fireman	J	RF	250+	Brown, Margaret Wise	HarperCollins
Little Fish	C	F	192	Tiger Cub	Peguis
Little Fish that Got Away	I	F	250+	Cook, Bernadine	Scholastic
Little Frog, Big Pond	J	F	250+	The Wright Skills	Wright Group/McGraw Hill
Little Frog's Monster Story	E	F	144	Ready Readers	Pearson Learning Group
Little Frogs of Puerto Rico, The	J	RF	143	Books for Young Learners	Richard C. Owen
Little Ghost Goes to School	G	F	210	TOTTS	Tott Publications
Little Ghost's Baby Brother	G	F	221	TOTTS	Tott Publications
Little Ghost's Vacation	G	F	118	TOTTS	Tott Publications
Little Girl and Her Beetle, The	I	TL	250+	Literacy 2000	Rigby
Little Gorilla	J	F	167	Bornstein, Ruth	Clarion
Little Green Dandelion, A	H	RF	191	Books for Young Learners	Richard C. Owen
Little Green Frog	F	F	121	Learn to Read	Creative Teaching Press
Little Green Man Visits a Farm, The	E	F	183	Learn to Read	Creative Teaching Press
Little Half Chick	K	F	250+	Literacy Tree	Rigby
Little Hawk's New Name	M	HF	250+	Bolognese, Don	Scholastic
Little Hearts	C	RF	44	Story Box	Wright Group/McGraw Hill
Little Hen, The	D	F	107	Ready Readers	Pearson Learning Group
Little House	LB	F	14	Ready Readers	Pearson Learning Group
Little House Birthday, A	J	HF	250+	Wilder, Laura Ingalls	HarperCollins
Little House by Boston Bay	Q	HF	250+	Wiley, Melissa	HarperTrophy
Little House Farm Days	M	HF	250+	Wilder, Laura Ingalls	HarperTrophy
Little House Friends	M	HF	250+	Wilder, Laura Ingalls	HarperTrophy
Little House in Brookfield	Q	HF	250+	Wilkes, Maria D.	HarperTrophy
Little House in the Big Woods	Q	HF	250+	Wilder, Laura Ingalls	HarperTrophy
Little House in the Highlands	Q	HF	250+	Wiley, Melissa	HarperTrophy
Little House on Rocky Ridge	R	HF	250+	MacBride, Roger Lea	HarperTrophy
Little House on the Prairie	Q	HF	250+	Wilder, Laura Ingalls	HarperTrophy
Little House, The	I	TL	391	Pacific Literacy	Pacific Learning
Little Icicle	O	RF	250+	Szymanski, Lois	Avon Camelot
Little Jack Horner	D	TL	29	Jumbled Tumbled Tales & Rhymes	Rigby
Little Kid	H	F	169	Literacy 2000	Rigby
Little Kittens	B	F	27	Ready Readers	Pearson Learning Group
Little Knight, The	K	F	250+	Reading Unlimited	Pearson Learning Group
Little Lady, The	C	RF	37	Ray's Readers	Outside the Box
*Little Leaf's Journey and the Lost Tooth, The	K	F	564	New Way Orange	Steck-Vaughn
Little Lefty	M	RF	250+	Christopher, Matt	Little, Brown & Co.
Little Lion, The	A	I	29	Phonics and Friends	Hampton-Brown
Little Meanie's Lunch	D	F	90	Story Box	Wright Group/McGraw Hill
Little Miss Muffet	D	RF	59	Seedlings	Continental Press
Little Miss Muffet	D	TL	26	Jumbled Tumbled Tales & Rhymes	Rigby
Little Miss Muffet	F	TL	146	Literacy 2000	Rigby
Little Miss Stoneybrook and Dawn	O	RF	250+	Martin, Ann M.	Scholastic
Little Monkey	I	F	250+	Alphakids	Sundance
Little Monkey Is Stuck	E	F	251	Foundations	Wright Group/McGraw Hill
Little Monkeys	A	I	21	Windows on Literacy	National Geographic
Little Mouse	C	F	59	Handprints B	Educator's Publishing Service

* Collection of short stories

TITLE	LEVEL	GENRE	WORD COUNT	AUTHOR / SERIES	PUBLISHER / DISTRIBUTOR
Little Mouse's Trail Tale	I	F	250+	Bookshop	Mondo
Little Number Stories: Addition	G	I	154	Learn to Read	Creative Teaching Press
Little Number Stories: Subtraction	G	I	133	Learn to Read	Creative Teaching Press
Little Old Lady Who Danced on the Moon, The	M	RF	711	Sunshine	Wright Group/McGraw Hill
Little One Inch	K	TL	384	Gibson, Akimi	Scholastic
Little Overcoat, The	F	TL	237	Bookshop	Mondo
Little Painter of Sabana Grande, The	M	RF	250+	Soar To Success	Houghton Mifflin
Little Panda	G	F	143	Books for Young Learners	Richard C. Owen
Little Panda, The	D	I	40	Windows on Literacy	National Geographic
*Little Pear	O	HF	250+	Lattimore, Eleanor F.	Harcourt Trade
*Little Pear and His Friends	O	HF	250+	Lattimore, Eleanor F.	Harcourt Trade
Little Penguin's Tale	L	F	250+	Wood, Audrey	Scholastic
Little Pickle	WB	F	N/A	Collington, Peter	Dutton
Little Pig	C	F	63	Story Box	Wright Group/McGraw Hill
Little Polar Bear and the Brave Little Hare	K	F	250+	de Beer, Hans	North-South Books
Little Prairie House, A	J	HF	250+	Wilder, Laura Ingalls	HarperCollins
Little Prince, The	X	F	250+	De Saint-Exupery, Antoine	Harcourt Trade
Little Princess	E	F	99	Seedlings	Continental Press
Little Princess, A	L	RF	250+	All Aboard Reading	Grosset & Dunlap
Little Puffer Fish	H	F	133	Books for Young Learners	Richard C. Owen
Little Puppy Rap	I	F	211	Sunshine	Wright Group/McGraw Hill
Little Rabbit Is Sad	D	F	97	Williams, Deborah	Kaeden Books
Little Rabbit Who Wanted Red Wings, The	H	F	364	Seedlings	Continental Press
Little Red and the Wolf	I	TL	316	Pair-It Books	Steck-Vaughn
Little Red Bus, The	H	RF	222	PM Story Books	Rigby
Little Red Hen	H	TL	255	New Way Green	Steck-Vaughn
Little Red Hen	I	TL	250+	Hunia, Fran	Ladybird Books
Little Red Hen, The	G	TL	250+	Cambridge Reading	Pearson Learning Group
Little Red Hen, The	I	TL	226	Sunshine	Wright Group/McGraw Hill
Little Red Hen, The	B	TL	96	Folk Tales	Pioneer Valley
Little Red Hen, The	I	TL	250+	Literacy 2000	Rigby
Little Red Hen, The	G	TL	256	Storyteller-Moon Rising	Wright Group/McGraw Hill
Little Red Hen, The	H	TL	375	Traditional Tales	Pearson Learning Group
Little Red Hen, The	B	TL	87	Windmill	Wright Group/McGraw Hill
Little Red Hen, The	G	TL	250+	Ziefert, Harriet	Puffin Books
Little Red Hen, The	I	TL	250+	PM Traditional Tales Orange	Rigby
Little Red Pig, The	G	F	214	Ready Readers	Pearson Learning Group
Little Red Riding Hood	H	TL	250+	Hunia, Fran	Ladybird Books
Little Red Riding Hood	G	TL	140	Sun Sprouts	ETA/Cuisenaire
Little Red Riding Hood	K	TL	250+	Story Steps	Rigby
Little Red Riding Hood	I	TL	250+	Jumbled Tumbled Tales & Rhymes	Rigby
Little Red Riding Hood	WB	TL	N/A	Goodall, John	McElderry
Little Red Riding Hood	G	TL	140	Folk Tales	Pioneer Valley
Little Red Riding Hood	K	TL	250+	Enrichment	Wright Group/McGraw Hill
Little Red Riding Hood	E	TL	140	Bookshop	Mondo
Little Red Riding Hood	J	TL	250+	PM Tales and Plays-Turquoise	Rigby
Little Runner of the Longhouse	K	HF	250+	Baker, Betty	HarperTrophy
Little Sea Pony, The	N	F	250+	Cresswell, Helen	HarperTrophy
Little Seed, A	B	I	18	Smart Starts	Rigby
Little Shopping, A	M	RF	250+	Rylant, Cynthia	Aladdin
Little Sister	C	RF	40	Mitchell, Robin	Scholastic
Little Snowman, The	C	RF	59	PM Extensions-Red	Rigby
Little Soup's Birthday	K	RF	250+	Peck, Robert Newton	Bantam

* Collection of short stories

TITLE	LEVEL	GENRE	WORD COUNT	AUTHOR / SERIES	PUBLISHER / DISTRIBUTOR
Little Sparrow, The: A Cinderella Story From Italy	O	TL	795	Leveled Readers	Houghton Mifflin
Little Spider, The	K	F	250+	Literacy 2000	Rigby
Little Swan	M	RF	250+	Geras, Adele	Random House
Little Things	A	I	33	PM Starters	Rigby
Little Tin Soldier, The	M	TL	766	Tales from Hans Andersen	Wright Group/McGraw Hill
Little Tommy Tucker	E	TL	30	Jumbled Tumbled Tales & Rhymes	Rigby
Little Town at the Crossroads	Q	HF	250+	Wilkes, Maria D.	HarperTrophy
Little Town in the Ozarks	R	HF	250+	MacBride, Roger Lea	HarperTrophy
Little Town on the Prairie	Q	HF	250+	Wilder, Laura Ingalls	HarperTrophy
Little Tuppen	I	TL	250+	Galdone, Paul	Houghton Mifflin
Little Turtle	WB	RF	N/A	Books for Young Learners	Richard C. Owen
Little Vampire and the Midnight Bear	L	F	250+	Kwitz, Mary DeBall	Puffin Books
Little Walrus Rising	K	F	250+	Young, Carol	Scholastic
Little Whale, The	M	F	1057	Sunshine	Wright Group/McGraw Hill
Little White Hen, The	E	F	159	PM Plus Story Books	Rigby
Little Witch Goes to School	K	F	250+	Hautzig, Deborah	Random House
Little Witch's Big Night	K	F	250+	Hautzig, Deborah	Random House
Little Women	Z	HF	250+	Alcott, Louisa May	Aladdin
Little Women	M	HF	250+	Bullseye	Random House
Little Work Plane, The	I	F	250+	PM Plus Story Books	Rigby
Little Yellow Chicken, The	I	F	322	Sunshine	Wright Group/McGraw Hill
Little Yellow Chicken's House, The	F	F	287	Story Basket	Wright Group/McGraw Hill
Little Zoot	E	F	33	Little Celebrations	Pearson Learning Group
Little, Little Man, The	M	F	741	Book Bank	Wright Group/McGraw Hill
Littles and the Great Halloween Scare, The	M	F	250+	Peterson, John	Scholastic
Littles and the Lost Children, The	M	F	250+	Peterson, John	Scholastic
Littles and the Terrible Tiny Kid, The	M	F	250+	Peterson, John	Scholastic
Littles and the Trash Tinies, The	M	F	250+	Peterson, John	Scholastic
Littles Give a Party, The	M	F	250+	Peterson, John	Scholastic
Littles Go Exploring, The	M	F	250+	Peterson, John	Scholastic
Littles Go to School, The	M	F	250+	Peterson, John	Scholastic
Littles Have a Wedding, The	M	F	250+	Peterson, John	Scholastic
Littles Take a Trip, The	M	F	250+	Peterson, John	Scholastic
Littles to the Rescue, The	M	F	250+	Peterson, John	Scholastic
Littles, The	M	F	250+	Peterson, John	Scholastic
Living and Growing	J	I	250+	PM Plus Nonfiction	Rigby
Living History	V	I	250+	iOpeners	Pearson Learning Group
Living in Hard Times	S	I	594	Vocabulary Readers	Houghton Mifflin
Living in Harsh Lands	X	I	250+	iOpeners	Pearson Learning Group
Living in Space	U	I	250+	Leveled Readers Language Support	Houghton Mifflin
Living in Space	O	I	250+	Nayer, Judy	Pearson Learning Group
Living in the Sky	K	RF	328	Sunshine	Wright Group/McGraw Hill
Living on the Farm	D	I	155	Early Connections	Benchmark Education
Living or Nonliving	B	I	27	Instant Readers	Harcourt School Publishers
Living Rain Forest, The	S	I	250+	Bishop, Nic	Pacific Learning
Living Things	C	I	57	Independent Readers Science	Houghton Mifflin
Living Things	C	I	43	Leveled Readers Science	Houghton Mifflin
Living Things	G	I	151	Rosen Real Readers	Rosen Publishing Group
Living Things Need Food	H	I	66	Windows on Literacy	National Geographic
Living Things Need Water	C	I	26	Windows on Literacy	National Geographic
Living Through a Natural Disaster	W	I	250+	iOpeners	Pearson Learning Group
*Living Up The Street	Y	RF	250+	Soto, Gary	Bantam

* Collection of short stories

TITLE	LEVEL	GENRE	WORD COUNT	AUTHOR / SERIES	PUBLISHER / DISTRIBUTOR
Living With Others	J	I	250+	PM Plus Nonfiction	Rigby
Living with Salties	P	I	250+	Orbit Double Takes	Pacific Learning
Lizard	E	RF	80	Foundations	Wright Group/McGraw Hill
Lizard Loses His Tail	D	RF	54	PM Story Books	Rigby
Lizard Music	T	F	250+	Pinkwater, D. Manus	Bantam
Lizard on a Stick	C	RF	38	Wonder World	Wright Group/McGraw Hill
Lizards	L	I	356	Wonder World	Wright Group/McGraw Hill
Lizards and Salamanders	M	I	250+	Reading Unlimited	Pearson Learning Group
Lizards and Snakes	O	I	250+	Rigby Literacy	Rigby
Lizard's Grandmother	J	F	336	Sunshine	Wright Group/McGraw Hill
Lizard's Song	M	TL	250+	Voyages	SRA/McGraw Hill
Lizzie's Lizard	L	I	289	Storyteller Nonfiction	Wright Group/McGraw Hill
Lizzie's Lunch	I	F	118	Literacy Tree	Rigby
Llama in the Family, A	O	RF	250+	Hurwitz, Johanna	Scholastic
Llama Pajamas	N	RF	250+	Clymer, Susan	Scholastic
Loading the Airplane	G	RF	140	Windows on Literacy	National Geographic
Lobster Fishing at Dawn	I	I	194	Ready Readers	Pearson Learning Group
Lobstering	LB	I	14	Little Books for Early Readers	University of Maine
Lobster's Tale, A	W	I	2114	Leveled Readers	Houghton Mifflin
*Local News	W	RF	250+	Soto, Gary	Scholastic
Loch Ness Monster Mystery, The	S	I	250+	Literacy 2000	Rigby
Loch Ness Monster, The	Q	I	250+	The Unexplained	Capstone Press
Lock the Gate!	D	RF	41	Leveled Readers	Houghton Mifflin
Locked In	H	RF	228	PM Plus Story Books	Rigby
Locked in the Library!	M	F	250+	Brown, Marc	Little, Brown & Co.
Locked Out	G	RF	15	PM Story Books	Rigby
Locked Out!	B	RF	15	Twig	Wright Group/McGraw Hill
Locomotion	V	RF	250+	Woodson, Jacqueline	Penguin Group
Log Cabin in the Woods	R	HF	250+	Henry, Joanne Landers	Scholastic
Log Garfish	M	TL	114	Books for Young Learners	Richard C. Owen
Log Hotel	J	RF	261	Schreiber, Anne	Scholastic
Log Hotel, The	A	F	22	Little Celebrations	Pearson Learning Group
Log, The	C	RF	29	New Way Red	Steck-Vaughn
Lois Lowry	T	B	250+	Markham, Lois	Learning Works, The
Lola and Miss Kitty	H	RF	250+	Little Readers	Houghton Mifflin
Lollipop	G	F	59	Watson, Wendy	Crowell
Lollipop Please, A	H	RF	73	Literacy 2000	Rigby
Lon Po Po: A Red-Riding Hood Story from China	S	TL	250+	Young, Ed	Scholastic
Lone Wolf	Y	RF	2697	Leveled Readers	Houghton Mifflin
Lonely Bull, The	E	F	116	Pacific Literacy	Pacific Learning
Lonely Dragon, The	J	F	250+	Momentum Literacy Program	Troll Associates
Lonely Giant, The	K	F	449	Literacy 2000	Rigby
Long Ago	D	I	105	Early Connections	Benchmark Education
Long Ago and Far Away	T	I	250+	Wildcats	Wright Group/McGraw Hill
Long Ago and Today	D	I	72	Learn to Read	Creative Teaching Press
Long and Short	I	F	228	Sunshine	Wright Group/McGraw Hill
Long Arrow and the Elk Dogs	Q	TL	250+	Leveled Readers Language Support	Houghton Mifflin
Long Grass of Tumbledown Road	M	F	283	Read Alongs	Rigby
Long Shot for Paul	M	RF	250+	Christopher, Matt	Little, Brown & Co.
Long Walk Home, The	P	RF	250+	Action Packs	Rigby
Long Walk, A	E	I	131	Twig	Wright Group/McGraw Hill
Long Way from Chicago, A	V	HF	250+	Peck, Richard	Puffin Books

* Collection of short stories

TITLE	LEVEL	GENRE	WORD COUNT	AUTHOR / SERIES	PUBLISHER / DISTRIBUTOR
Long Way to a New Land, A	L	HF	250+	Sandin, Joan	HarperTrophy
Long Way to Go, A	R	I	250+	O'Neal, Zibby	Penguin Group
Long Way Westward, The	L	HF	250+	Sandin, Joan	HarperTrophy
Long Winter, The	Q	HF	250+	Wilder, Laura Ingalls	HarperTrophy
Long, Long Ago	M	I	250+	Literacy 2000	Rigby
Long, Long Tail, The	B	F	33	Sunshine	Wright Group/McGraw Hill
Longest Noodle in the World, The	D	F	66	Joy Readers	Pearson Learning Group
Long-Lost Friends, The	M	RF	250+	Schultz, Irene	Wright Group/McGraw Hill
Look	A	F	20	Sunshine	Wright Group/McGraw Hill
Look Again	C	I	47	Bookshop	Mondo
Look and See	G	I	208	Learn to Read	Creative Teaching Press
Look at Australia, A	M	I	250+	Pebble Books	Red Brick Learning
Look at Both Sides	K	I	236	Yellow Umbrella Books	Capstone Press
Look at Canada, A	M	I	250+	Pebble Books	Red Brick Learning
Look at China, A	M	I	178	Pebble Books	Capstone Press
Look at Conor	A	RF	27	Little Books for Early Readers	University of Maine
Look at Danny	C	RF	39	Coulter, Mia	Macmillan
Look at Dogs, A	M	I	551	Pair-It Books	Steck-Vaughn
Look at France, A	M	I	250+	Pebble Books	Red Brick Learning
Look at Japan, A	M	I	250+	Pebble Books	Red Brick Learning
Look at Kenya, A	M	I	161	Pebble Books	Capstone Press
Look at Kyle	B	I	46	Little Books for Early Readers	University of Maine
Look at Lady Liberty, A	M	B	250+	Rosen Real Readers	Rosen Publishing Group
Look at Me	C	RF	62	Early Connections	Benchmark Education
Look at Me	B	RF	48	PM Starters	Rigby
Look at Me	LB	I	13	Windows on Literacy	National Geographic
Look at Me	LB	I	17	Little Books for Early Readers	University of Maine
Look at Me	D	RF	67	Carousel Readers	Pearson Learning Group
Look at Me	F	RF	104	Literacy 2000	Rigby
Look at Me!	B	RF	35	Lighthouse	Rigby
Look at Me!	A	F	27	KinderReaders	Rigby
Look at Me!	A	RF	27	Leveled Readers Emergent	Houghton Mifflin
Look at Mexico, A	M	I	159	Pebble Books	Capstone Press
Look at Minerals, A: From Galena to Gold	S	I	250+	A First Book	Franklin Watts
Look at My Weaving	C	I	69	First Stories	Pacific Learning
Look at Pickles	B	RF	90	Pickles the Dog Series	Pioneer Valley
Look at Rocks, A: From Coal to Kimerlite	S	I	250+	A First Book	Franklin Watts
Look at Russia, A	M	I	161	Pebble Books	Capstone Press
Look at Snakes, A	M	I	250+	Pair-It Books	Steck-Vaughn
Look at Spiders, A	M	I	785	Pair-It-Books	Steck-Vaughn
Look at the Animals	B	I	64	Early Connections	Benchmark Education
Look at the Calendar, A	H	I	139	Rosen Real Readers	Rosen Publishing Group
Look at the Garden	A	I	43	Windmill Books	Rigby
Look at the House	B	F	53	PM Plus Starters	Rigby
Look at the Lizard	A	I	33	Bookshop	Mondo
Look at the Moon	N	I	250+	Bookshop	Mondo
Look at the Ocean, A	B	I	50	Little Books for Early Readers	University of Maine
Look at the Stars	H	I	144	Rigby Focus	Rigby
Look at the Tree	B	I	22	Windows on Literacy	National Geographic
Look at This	B	I	57	Carousel Earlybirds	Pearson Learning Group
Look at This Mess!	C	RF	50	First Stories	Pacific Learning
Look Closer	A	I	21	Ready Readers	Pearson Learning Group
Look Down Low	F	I	66	Early Readers	Compass Point Books
Look Down!	B	I	51	Early Connections	Benchmark Education

* Collection of short stories

TITLE	LEVEL	GENRE	WORD COUNT	AUTHOR / SERIES	PUBLISHER / DISTRIBUTOR
Look for Me	F	I	208	Little Readers	Houghton Mifflin
Look for Me	D	RF	71	Story Box	Wright Group/McGraw Hill
Look Here!	E	RF	67	Wonder World	Wright Group/McGraw Hill
Look in Mom's Purse	D	RF	60	Carousel Readers	Pearson Learning Group
Look in the Garden	G	RF	208	PM Plus Story Books	Rigby
Look Inside	J	I	168	Storyteller Nonfiction	Wright Group/McGraw Hill
Look into Space, A	D	I	71	Discovery World	Rigby
Look Out for Bingo	E	RF	138	PM Plus Story Books	Rigby
Look Out For Your Tail	J	F	250+	Literacy 2000	Rigby
Look Out the Window	C	RF	67	Story Steps	Rigby
Look Out!	D	F	53	Sunshine	Wright Group/McGraw Hill
Look Out!	I	RF	250+	PM Plus Story Books	Rigby
Look Out!	B	F	15	Literacy 2000	Rigby
Look Out, Dan!	B	F	34	Story Box	Wright Group/McGraw Hill
Look Out, Fish!	C	F	65	Lighthouse	Rigby
Look Out, Washington D.C.!	O	RF	250+	Giff, Patricia Reilly	Bantam
Look Up	E	I	44	Little Celebrations	Pearson Learning Group
Look Up	R	I	250+	iOpeners	Pearson Learning Group
Look Up, Look Down	D	I	165	PM Nonfiction-Red	Rigby
Look What Came from China	O	I	250+	Harvey, Miles	Franklin Watts
Look What Came from Egypt	O	I	250+	Harvey, Miles	Franklin Watts
Look What Came from France	O	I	250+	Harvey, Miles	Franklin Watts
Look What Came from Italy	O	I	250+	Harvey, Miles	Franklin Watts
Look What Came from Mexico	O	I	250+	Harvey, Miles	Franklin Watts
Look What Came from Russia	O	I	250+	Harvey, Miles	Franklin Watts
Look What Came from the United States	O	I	250+	Davis, Kevin	Franklin Watts
Look What I Can Do	WB	F	N/A	Aruego, Jose	Macmillan
Look What I Can Read!	E	RF	49	Instant Readers	Harcourt School Publishers
Look What I Found!	B	RF	29	Science	Outside the Box
Look What I Found!	B	RF	29	Lighthouse	Rigby
Look What I Made!	M	I	250+	Literacy 2000	Rigby
Look What You Can Make!	G	I	203	Story Steps	Rigby
Look Who's Playing First Base	M	RF	250+	Christopher, Matt	Little, Brown & Co.
Look Who's Talking!	L	I	250+	Rigby Literacy	Rigby
Look!	C	RF	43	Little Celebrations	Pearson Learning Group
Look! Bugs!	C	I	32	Seedlings	Continental Press
Look! I Can Read!	F	RF	124	Hood, Susan	Grosset & Dunlap
Look! Now Look!	B	I	9	Rigby Literacy	Rigby
Look! Snow!	LB	RF	14	Montezinos, Nina	McElderry
Look, Bear	D	F	51	Sun Sprouts	ETA/Cuisenaire
Look, Listen, and Learn	E	I	49	Canizares, Susan; Chanko, Pamela	Scholastic
Look, Listen, Taste, Touch, and Smell: Learning About Your Five Senses	M	I	250+	Amazing Body	Picture Window Books
Look, We Can Fly Too	I	F	250+	Phonics Readers Plus	Steck-Vaughn
Look-Alike Animals	I	I	130	Bernard, Robin	Scholastic
Look-Alike Animals	H	I	130	Bernard, Robin	Scholastic
Looking After a Dog	C	I	58	Sun Sprouts	ETA/Cuisenaire
Looking After Baby	E	I	143	Storyteller Nonfiction	Wright Group/McGraw Hill
Looking After Grandpa	D	RF	91	Foundations	Wright Group/McGraw Hill
Looking after Suzie	G	RF	209	Well-Being Series	Dominie Press
Looking at Animals in Cold Places	O	I	250+	Butterfield, Moira	Steck-Vaughn
Looking at Animals in Hot Places	N	I	250+	Butterfield, Moira	Steck-Vaughn
Looking at Animals in the Ocean	O	I	250+	Butterfield, Moira	Steck-Vaughn
Looking at Ants	I	I	250+	Yellow Umbrella Books	Red Brick Learning

* Collection of short stories

TITLE	LEVEL	GENRE	WORD COUNT	AUTHOR / SERIES	PUBLISHER / DISTRIBUTOR
Looking at Baby Animals	E	I	54	Teacher's Choice Series	Pearson Learning Group
Looking at Cities	E	I	30	iOpeners	Pearson Learning Group
Looking at Insects	L	I	250+	Discovery World	Rigby
Looking at Low Tide	M	RF	642	Leveled Readers	Houghton Mifflin
Looking at Maps and Globes	K	I	250+	Brederson, Carmen	Scholastic
Looking at Our World	I	I	188	Early Connections	Benchmark Education
Looking at Plants	C	I	44	Leveled Readers Science	Houghton Mifflin
Looking at Shapes	G	I	235	Yellow Umbrella Books	Red Brick Learning
Looking Back: A Book of Memories	X	B	250+	Lowry, Lois	Delacorte
Looking Down	E	I	130	Early Connections	Benchmark Education
Looking Down	B	RF	64	First Stories	Pacific Learning
Looking Down	C	RF	70	PM Starters	Rigby
Looking for a Letter	F	RF	223	New Way Green	Steck-Vaughn
Looking for a New House	I	RF	250+	Windows on Literacy	National Geographic
Looking for Angus	H	F	99	Ready Readers	Pearson Learning Group
Looking for Bears	H	RF	80	Books for Young Learners	Richard C. Owen
Looking for Birds	D	I	74	Leveled Readers	Houghton Mifflin
Looking for Buddy	N	RF	250+	Leveled Readers Language Support	Houghton Mifflin
Looking for Dad	M	RF	250+	SupaDoopers	Sundance
Looking for Eggs	C	RF	47	Windmill Books	Rigby
Looking for Frogs	D	I	50	Leveled Readers	Houghton Mifflin
Looking for Halloween	LB	RF	49	Urmston, Kathleen; Evans, Karen	Kaeden Books
Looking for Lions	L	I	250+	World Quest Adventures	World Quest Learning
Looking for Luke	I	RF	250+	Sunshine	Wright Group/McGraw Hill
Looking for Numbers	D	I	91	Early Connections	Benchmark Education
Looking For Patterns	J	I	160	Early Connections	Benchmark Education
Looking for Shapes	K	I	289	Early Connections	Benchmark Education
Looking for the Queen	O	I	250+	Frederick, Shirley	Hampton-Brown
Looking into Space	L	I	345	Early Connections	Benchmark Education
Looking the Part	X	I	2322	Leveled Readers	Houghton Mifflin
Looking Through a Telescope	K	I	250+	Rookie Read-About Science	Children's Press
Looks Like Rain!	C	RF	24	Science	Outside the Box
Loose Bolts	O	SF	250+	Neufeld, David	Wright Group/McGraw Hill
Loose Laces	L	RF	209	Reading Unlimited	Pearson Learning Group
Loose Tooth	B	RF	51	Bebop Books	Lee & Low Books Inc.
Loose Tooth, The	H	RF	112	Breakthrough	Longman/Bow
Lord Mount Dragon, The	M	TL	250+	Cambridge Reading	Pearson Learning Group
Lord of the Rings, The	Z	F	250+	Tolkien, J.R.R.	Houghton Mifflin
Loser	U	RF	250+	Spinelli, Jerry	HarperCollins
Losing Joe's Place	Y	RF	250+	Korman, Gordon	Scholastic
Lost	E	RF	29	Sun Sprouts	ETA/Cuisenaire
Lost	A	RF	29	TOTTS	Tott Publications
Lost	C	RF	38	Story Box	Wright Group/McGraw Hill
Lost	E	RF	82	Literacy Tree	Rigby
Lost and Found	G	F	55	Instant Readers	Harcourt School Publishers
*Lost and Found	D	RF	55	New Way Red	Steck-Vaughn
Lost and Found	D	RF	64	Carousel Readers	Pearson Learning Group
Lost and Found Game, The	M	RF	250+	Nayer, Judy	Pearson Learning Group
Lost at the Fun Park	F	RF	192	PM Extensions-Blue	Rigby
Lost at the White House: A 1909 Easter Story	L	HF	250+	Griest, Lisa	Carolrhoda Books
Lost Cat!	E	RF	156	Bookshop	Mondo
Lost Children, The	M	TL	250+	Goble, Paul	Aladdin
Lost Colony of Roanoke, The	T	I	1081	Leveled Readers Social Studies	Houghton Mifflin

* Collection of short stories

TITLE	LEVEL	GENRE	WORD COUNT	AUTHOR / SERIES	PUBLISHER / DISTRIBUTOR
*Lost Continent and Other Cases, The	O	RF	250+	Simon, Seymour	Avon
Lost Flower Children, The	Q	RF	250+	Lisle, Janet Taylor	Philomel Books
Lost Garden, The	W	B	250+	Yep, Laurence	Beech Tree Books
Lost Glove, The	D	RF	105	Foundations	Wright Group/McGraw Hill
*Lost Hikers and Other Cases, The	O	RF	250+	Simon, Seymour	Avon
Lost in Cyberspace	Y	SF	250+	Peck, Richard	Puffin Books
Lost in Space	M	SF	250+	Pacific Literacy	Pacific Learning
Lost in the Dark	Q	I	250+	Orbit Double Takes	Pacific Learning
Lost in the Fog	D	F	59	Ready Readers	Pearson Learning Group
Lost in the Forest	K	RF	250+	Robinson, Fay	Wright Group/McGraw Hill
Lost in the Forest	I	HF	298	PM Story Books-Orange	Rigby
Lost in the Museum	I	RF	250+	Cohen, Miriam	Bantam
Lost in the Wilderness!	Q	I	660	Vocabulary Readers	Houghton Mifflin
Lost in the Woods	D	RF	120	Bella and Rosie Series	Pioneer Valley
Lost Keys, The	G	RF	223	PM Plus Story Books	Rigby
Lost Lake, The	M	RF	250+	Soar To Success	Houghton Mifflin
Lost Mother, The	E	RF	112	Alphakids	Sundance
Lost on a Mountain in Maine	R	RF	250+	Fendler, Donn	Peter Smith Publications
Lost Sandals, The	N	RF	250+	Bennett, Jean	Pacific Learning
Lost Sheep, The	I	F	219	Little Readers	Houghton Mifflin
Lost Socks	F	RF	159	PM Plus Story Books	Rigby
Lost Star: The Story of Amelia Earhart	T	B	250+	Lauber, Patricia	Language for Learning Assoc.
Lost World of the Olmec	V	I	2149	Independent Readers Social Studies	Houghton Mifflin
Lost!	D	RF	57	Harry's Math Books	Outside the Box
Lost!	B	RF	18	Smart Starts	Rigby
Lost!	C	RF	57	Harry's Math Books	Outside the Box
Lost!	L	F	57	Home Connection Collection	Rigby
Lot Happened Today, A	I	RF	193	Ready Readers	Pearson Learning Group
Lots and Lots of Stairs	B	RF	33	Little Books for Early Readers	University of Maine
Lots of Balloons	F	RF	72	Early Readers	Compass Point Books
Lots of Caps	G	F	205	New Way Blue	Steck-Vaughn
Lots of Dogs	C	I	68	Teacher's Choice Series	Pearson Learning Group
Lots of Dolls!	C	I	61	The Candid Collection	Pearson Learning Group
Lots of Things	B	RF	23	Reading Corners	Pearson Learning Group
Lots of Toys	B	I	47	Carousel Earlybirds	Pearson Learning Group
Lottie Goat & Donny Goat	H	F	145	Ready Readers	Pearson Learning Group
Lotus Seed, The	P	HF	250+	Garland, Sherry	Harcourt Trade
Lou Gehrig: One of Baseball's Greatest	O	B	250+	Childhood of Famous Americans	Aladdin
Loud Sounds, Quiet Sounds	B	I	26	Rosen Real Readers/Red	Rosen Publishing Group
Louis Agassiz Fuertes, Painter of the Bird	L	B	250+	Independent Readers Science	Houghton Mifflin
Louis Armstrong	Z	B	250+	Brown, Sandford	Franklin Watts
Louis Braille	G	B	132	Independent Readers Science	Houghton Mifflin
Louis Braille: Boy Who Invented Books for the Blind	N	B	250+	Davidson, Margaret	Scholastic
Louis Pasteur	N	B	250+	Biography	Benchmark Education
Louis Riel	X	B	250+	The Canadians	Fitzhenry & Whiteside
Louisa May Alcott: Young Novelist	O	B	250+	Childhood of Famous Americans	Aladdin
Louisiana	R	I	250+	This Land Is Your Land	Compass Point Books
Louisiana	S	I	250+	Land of Liberty	Red Brick Learning
Louisiana Purchase, The	V	I	250+	Cornerstones of Freedom	Children's Press
Louisiana Purchase, The	V	I	250+	Let Freedom Ring	Red Brick Learning
Love from Your Friend, Hannah	Y	HF	250+	Skolsky, Mindy Warshaw	HarperTrophy

* Collection of short stories

TITLE	LEVEL	GENRE	WORD COUNT	AUTHOR / SERIES	PUBLISHER / DISTRIBUTOR
Love Is	LB	RF	11	Visions	Wright Group/McGraw Hill
Love Me, Love My Broccoli	S	RF	250+	Peters, Julie Anne	Avon Camelot
Love That Dog	T	RF	250+	Creech, Sharon	HarperCollins
Love You, Soldier	R	HF	250+	Hest, Amy	Puffin Books
Love, from the Fifth-Grade Celebrity	Q	RF	250+	Giff, Patricia Reilly	Bantam
Lucky Baseball Bat, The	M	RF	250+	Christopher, Matt	Little, Brown & Co.
Lucky Candlesticks, The	N	RF	764	Leveled Readers	Houghton Mifflin
Lucky Day for Little Dinosaur, A	F	HF	135	PM Extensions-Yellow	Rigby
Lucky Duck, The	E	F	73	Ready Readers	Pearson Learning Group
Lucky Feather, The	L	F	250+	Literacy 2000	Rigby
Lucky Goes to Dog School	E	RF	127	PM Story Books	Rigby
Lucky Last Luke	M	RF	250+	Clark, Margaret	Sundance
Lucky Stars	L	RF	250+	Adler, David A.	Random House
Lucky Stone, The	P	RF	250+	Clifton, Lucille	Bantam
Lucky We Have a Station Wagon	F	RF	259	Foundations	Wright Group/McGraw Hill
Lucy Meets a Dragon	L	F	250+	Literacy 2000	Rigby
Lucy Takes A Holiday	M	F	250+	Bookshop	Mondo
Lucy's Box	E	F	108	Cambridge Reading	Pearson Learning Group
Lucy's Sore Knee	F	RF	93	Windmill	Wright Group/McGraw Hill
Ludwig van Beethoven: Musical Pioneer	N	B	250+	Rookie Biographies	Children's Press
Luis Alvarez	S	B	871	Leveled Readers Science	Houghton Mifflin
Luis Rodriguez	S	B	250+	Schwartz, Michael	Steck-Vaughn
Luis W. Alvarez	R	B	250+	Hispanic Stories	Steck-Vaughn
Luke's Adventures	H	F	98	City Stories	Rigby
Luke's Bully	N	RF	250+	Winthrop, Elizabeth	Puffin Books
Luke's Go-cart	L	RF	656	PM Gold	Rigby
Lulu Goes to Witch School	K	F	250+	O'Connor, Jane	HarperTrophy
Lumberjacks	M	I	255	Vocabulary Readers	Houghton Mifflin
Lump in My Bed, A	D	RF	48	Book Bank	Wright Group/McGraw Hill
Lumpy Rug	D	RF	86	Dominie Phonics Reader	Pearson Learning Group
Luna	L	F	371	Leveled Readers	Houghton Mifflin
Lunch	F	RF	156	Urmston, Kathleen; Evans, Karen	Kaeden Books
Lunch	C	RF	42	Harry's Math Books	Outside the Box
Lunch at the Joy House Café	K	RF	250+	Blackaby, Susan	Hampton-Brown
Lunch at the Pond	E	F	146	Foundations	Wright Group/McGraw Hill
Lunch at the Zoo	B	RF	64	Blaxland, Wendy; Brimage, C.	Scholastic
Lunch at the Zoo	A	RF	32	Bookshop	Mondo
Lunch Bunch, The	I	I	169	Storyteller-Moon Rising	Wright Group/McGraw Hill
Lunch in Space	G	RF	156	Instant Readers	Harcourt School Publishers
Lunch Orders	C	RF	18	Tadpoles	Rigby
Lunch Room, The	M	F	259	Leveled Readers	Houghton Mifflin
Lunch Time	C	RF	69	Carousel Readers	Pearson Learning Group
Lunch with Cat and Dog	F	F	122	Learn to Read	Creative Teaching Press
Lunchbox Mystery, The	N	RF	250+	Lohans, Alison	Scholastic
Lunchbox, The	H	RF	90	Pacific Literacy	Pacific Learning
Lunchroom, The	F	RF	80	City Stories	Rigby
Lunchtime	D	RF	82	Rigby Literacy	Rigby
Lunchtime at the Zoo	B	RF	53	First Stories	Pacific Learning
Luther Burbank	O	B	250+	Faber, Doris	Garrard Publishing Co.
Lyddie	V	HF	250+	Paterson, Katherine	Penguin Group
Lydia and Her Cat	G	RF	77	Oxford Reading Tree	Oxford University Press
Lydia and Her Garden	G	RF	88	Oxford Reading Tree	Oxford University Press
Lydia and Her Kitten	G	RF	77	Oxford Reading Tree	Oxford University Press
Lydia and the Ducks	G	RF	87	Oxford Reading Tree	Oxford University Press

* Collection of short stories

TITLE	LEVEL	GENRE	WORD COUNT	AUTHOR / SERIES	PUBLISHER / DISTRIBUTOR
Lydia and the Letters	F	RF	84	Oxford Reading Tree	Oxford University Press
Lydia and the Present	F	RF	77	Oxford Reading Tree	Oxford University Press
Lydia at the Shops	G	RF	72	Oxford Reading Tree	Oxford University Press
Lying as Still as I Can	L	RF	250+	Greetings	Rigby
Lyla and the New Piano	D	F	85	Lester the Lion Series	Pioneer Valley
Lyndon Baines Johnson	U	B	250+	Profiles of the Presidents	Compass Point Books
M & M and The Bad News Babies	K	RF	250+	Ross, Pat	Penguin Group
M & M and the Big Bag	K	RF	250+	Ross, Pat	Penguin Group
M & M and the Halloween Monster	K	RF	250+	Ross, Pat	Penguin Group
M & M and the Haunted House Game	K	RF	250+	Ross, Pat	Penguin Group
M & M and the Mummy Mess	K	RF	250+	Ross, Pat	Penguin Group
M & M and the Santa Secrets	K	RF	250+	Ross, Pat	Penguin Group
M & M and the Super Child Afternoon	K	RF	250+	Ross, Pat	Penguin Group
M. C. Higgins the Great	X	RF	250+	Hamilton, Virginia	Macmillan
Ma and Pa Dracula	O	F	250+	Martin, Ann M.	Scholastic
MacGregors and the MacDougalls, The	N	RF	250+	Bookweb	Rigby
Machines	C	I	36	Little Celebrations	Pearson Learning Group
Machines	J	I	44	Sunshine Books	Wright Group/McGraw Hill
Machines	E	I	44	Twig	Wright Group/McGraw Hill
Machines at Work	H	I	101	Little Red Readers	Sundance
Machines in the Home	N	I	250+	Home Connection Collection	Rigby
Machines Make Fun Rides	I	I	182	Windows on Literacy	National Geographic
Machines That Fly	I	I	111	Windows on Literacy	National Geographic
Mack's Big Day	L	RF	464	PM Plus Story Books	Rigby
Mad Scientist, The	M	F	250+	Schultz, Irene	Wright Group/McGraw Hill
Mad Scientist's Secret, The	P	SF	250+	Miller, Marvin	Scholastic
Madame C. J. Walker	Q	B	494	Independent Readers Social Studies	Houghton Mifflin
Made with Glass	F	I	106	Cherrington, Janelle	Scholastic
Madeline	K	F	250+	Bemelmans, Ludwig	Scholastic
Madeline's Rescue	K	F	250+	Bemelmans, Ludwig	Scholastic
Made's Birthday	L	RF	250+	Little Celebrations	Pearson Learning Group
Mae Jemison	M	B	250+	Explore Space!	Capstone Press
Mae Jemison	R	B	250+	Bookshop	Mondo
Mae Jemison: Making Dreams Come True	N	B	540	Leveled Readers	Houghton Mifflin
Mae-Nerd	C	F	44	Teacher's Choice Series	Pearson Learning Group
Magellan: Ferdinand Magellan and the First Trip Around the World	U	B	250+	Exploring the World	Compass Point Books
Maggie Moves Away	H	RF	327	Adventures in Reading	Pearson Learning Group
Maggie's Pets	I	RF	250+	Early Transitional, Set 1	Pioneer Valley
Magic All Around	L	F	250+	Literacy 2000	Rigby
Magic Box, The	K	F	250+	Brenner, Barbara	Bantam
Magic Finger, The	N	F	250+	Dahl, Roald	Penguin Group
Magic Fish, The	J	TL	250+	Rylant, Cynthia	Scholastic
Magic Fish, The	L	TL	870	Littledale, Freya	Scholastic
Magic Food	C	F	26	Smart Starts	Rigby
Magic Machine, The	C	F	163	Sunshine	Wright Group/McGraw Hill
Magic Money	L	RF	250+	Adler, David A.	Random House
Magic Money Box, The	E	I	71	Learn to Read	Creative Teaching Press
Magic Moscow, The	P	RF	250+	Pinkwater, Daniel	Aladdin
Magic Noodle Show, The	N	RF	250+	Orbit Chapter Books	Pacific Literacy
Magic Passport, The	N	F	250+	Navigators Fiction Series	Benchmark Education
Magic Pear Tree, The	I	TL	207	Little Celebrations	Pearson Learning Group
Magic Porridge Pot, The	L	TL	497	Sunshine	Wright Group/McGraw Hill

* Collection of short stories

TITLE	LEVEL	GENRE	WORD COUNT	AUTHOR / SERIES	PUBLISHER / DISTRIBUTOR
Magic Porridge Pot, The	I	TL	321	New Way Orange	Steck-Vaughn
Magic Ride, The	M	F	170	Book Bank	Wright Group/McGraw Hill
Magic School Bus	P	F	250+	Cole, Joanna; Degen, Bruce	Scholastic
Magic School Bus and the Electric Field Trip, The	P	F	250+	Cole, Joanna; Degen, Bruce	Scholastic
Magic School Bus Answers Questions, The	P	F	250+	Cole, Joanna; Degen, Bruce	Scholastic
Magic School Bus At the Waterworks, The	P	F	250+	Cole, Joanna; Degen, Bruce	Scholastic
Magic School Bus Blows Its Top, The	P	F	250+	Cole, Joanna; Degen, Bruce	Scholastic
Magic School Bus Briefcase, The	P	F	250+	Cole, Joanna; Degen, Bruce	Scholastic
Magic School Bus Butterfly and the Bog Beast, The	P	F	250+	Cole, Joanna; Degen, Bruce	Scholastic
Magic School Bus Explores the Senses, The	P	F	250+	Cole, Joanna; Degen, Bruce	Scholastic
Magic School Bus Explores the World of Animals, The	P	F	250+	Cole, Joanna; Degen, Bruce	Scholastic
Magic School Bus Gets a Bright Idea, The	P	F	250+	Cole, Joanna; Degen, Bruce	Scholastic
Magic School Bus Gets All Dried Up, The	P	F	250+	Cole, Joanna; Degen, Bruce	Scholastic
Magic School Bus Gets Ants in Its Pants, The	P	F	250+	Cole, Joanna; Degen, Bruce	Scholastic
Magic School Bus Gets Baked in a Cake, The	P	F	250+	Cole, Joanna; Degen, Bruce	Scholastic
Magic School Bus Gets Cold Feet, The	P	F	250+	Cole, Joanna; Degen, Bruce	Scholastic
Magic School Bus Gets Eaten, The	P	F	250+	Cole, Joanna; Degen, Bruce	Scholastic
Magic School Bus Gets Programmed, The	P	F	250+	Cole, Joanna; Degen, Bruce	Scholastic
Magic School Bus Goes Upstream, The	I	F	250+	Cole, Joanna; Degen, Bruce	Scholastic
Magic School Bus Going Batty, The	P	F	250+	Cole, Joanna; Degen, Bruce	Scholastic
Magic School Bus Hops Home, The	P	F	250+	Cole, Joanna; Degen, Bruce	Scholastic
Magic School Bus in a Pickle, The	P	F	250+	Cole, Joanna; Degen, Bruce	Scholastic
Magic School Bus in the Arctic, The	P	F	250+	Cole, Joanna; Degen, Bruce	Scholastic
Magic School Bus in the Haunted Museum, The	P	F	250+	Cole, Joanna; Degen, Bruce	Scholastic
Magic School Bus in the Rain Forest, The	P	F	250+	Cole, Joanna; Degen, Bruce	Scholastic
Magic School Bus in the Time of the Dinosaurs, The	P	F	250+	Cole, Joanna; Degen, Bruce	Scholastic
Magic School Bus Inside a Beehive, The	P	F	250+	Cole, Joanna; Degen, Bruce	Scholastic
Magic School Bus Inside a Hurricane, The	P	F	250+	Cole, Joanna; Degen, Bruce	Scholastic
Magic School Bus Inside Ralphie, The	P	F	250+	Cole, Joanna; Degen, Bruce	Scholastic
Magic School Bus Inside the Earth, The	P	F	250+	Cole, Joanna; Degen, Bruce	Scholastic
Magic School Bus Inside the Human Body, The	I	F	250+	Cole, Joanna; Degen, Bruce	Scholastic
Magic School Bus Kicks Up a Storm, The	M	F	250+	Cole, Joanna; Degen, Bruce	Scholastic
Magic School Bus Liz Sorts It Out, The	P	F	250+	Cole, Joanna; Degen, Bruce	Scholastic
Magic School Bus Lost in the Solar System, The	P	F	250+	Cole, Joanna; Degen, Bruce	Scholastic
Magic School Bus Makes a Rainbow, The	P	F	250+	Cole, Joanna; Degen, Bruce	Scholastic
Magic School Bus Meets the Rot Squad, The	P	F	250+	Cole, Joanna; Degen, Bruce	Scholastic
Magic School Bus on the Ocean Floor, The	P	F	250+	Cole, Joanna; Degen, Bruce	Scholastic
Magic School Bus Out of This World, The	P	F	250+	Cole, Joanna; Degen, Bruce	Scholastic
Magic School Bus Plants Seeds, The	P	F	250+	Cole, Joanna; Degen, Bruce	Scholastic
Magic School Bus Plays Ball, The	P	F	250+	Cole, Joanna; Degen, Bruce	Scholastic
Magic School Bus Science Explorations, The	P	F	250+	Cole, Joanna; Degen, Bruce	Scholastic
Magic School Bus Search for the Missing Bones, The	P	F	250+	Cole, Joanna; Degen, Bruce	Scholastic
Magic School Bus Sees Stars, The	P	F	250+	Cole, Joanna; Degen, Bruce	Scholastic
Magic School Bus Shows and Tells, The	P	F	250+	Cole, Joanna; Degen, Bruce	Scholastic
Magic School Bus Space Explorers, The	P	F	250+	Cole, Joanna; Degen, Bruce	Scholastic
Magic School Bus Spins a Web, The	P	F	250+	Cole, Joanna; Degen, Bruce	Scholastic
Magic School Bus Takes a Dive, The	P	F	250+	Cole, Joanna; Degen, Bruce	Scholastic
Magic School Bus Taking Flight, The	P	F	250+	Cole, Joanna; Degen, Bruce	Scholastic
Magic School Bus The Truth About Bats, The	P	F	250+	Cole, Joanna; Degen, Bruce	Scholastic

* Collection of short stories

TITLE	LEVEL	GENRE	WORD COUNT	AUTHOR / SERIES	PUBLISHER / DISTRIBUTOR
Magic School Bus The Wild Whale Watch, The	P	F	250+	Cole, Joanna; Degen, Bruce	Scholastic
Magic School Bus Twister Trouble, The	P	F	250+	Cole, Joanna; Degen, Bruce	Scholastic
Magic School Bus Ups and Downs, The	P	F	250+	Cole, Joanna; Degen, Bruce	Scholastic
Magic School Bus Visits the Planets, The	P	F	250+	Cole, Joanna; Degen, Bruce	Scholastic
Magic School Bus Wet All Over, The	P	F	250+	Cole, Joanna; Degen, Bruce	Scholastic
Magic Squad and the Dog of Great Potential, The	P	RF	250+	Quattlebaum, Mary	Bantam
Magic Store, The	I	RF	203	Sunshine	Wright Group/McGraw Hill
Magic Sword, The	L	F	250+	Cambridge Reading	Pearson Learning Group
Magic Tricks	P	I	250+	Games Around the World	Compass Point Books
Magic Wand, The	E	F	100	Start to Read	School Zone
Magic Wheel, The	P	I	250+	Voyages	SRA/McGraw Hill
Magic!	LB	RF	23	Twig	Wright Group/McGraw Hill
Magical Adventures of Pretty Pearl, The	W	F	250+	Hamilton, Virginia	HarperTrophy
Magician's House, A	I	F	214	Sunshine	Wright Group/McGraw Hill
Magician's Lunch	I	F	272	Jellybeans	Rigby
Magician's Nephew, The	T	F	250+	Lewis, C. S.	HarperTrophy
Magnet Book, The	T	I	250+	Levine, Shar; Johnstone, Leslie	Sterling
Magnet Fishing Game	A	I	28	How-To Series	Benchmark Education
Magnet Time	I	I	212	Independent Readers Science	Houghton Mifflin
Magnet, The	D	I	115	Sun Sprouts	ETA/Cuisenaire
Magnets	B	I	28	Seedlings	Continental Press
Magnets	G	I	71	Phonics Readers	Compass Point Books
Magnets	C	I	55	Early Connections	Benchmark Education
Magnets	F	I	79	Sunshine	Wright Group/McGraw Hill
Magnets	J	I	259	Windows on Literacy	National Geographic
Magnets	E	I	52	Discovery Links	Newbridge
Magnets in Medicine	Y	I	2083	Leveled Readers Science	Houghton Mifflin
Magnets: Pulling Together, Pushing Apart	M	I	250+	Amazing Science	Picture Window Books
Magnifying Glass, The	C	I	45	Foundations	Wright Group/McGraw Hill
Magpie's Baking Day	F	F	132	PM Story Books	Rigby
Magpie's Tail, The	L	F	543	Pacific Literacy	Pacific Learning
Mai Li's Surprise	F	RF	63	Books for Young Learners	Richard C. Owen
Mail Came Today, The	C	RF	35	Carousel Readers	Pearson Learning Group
Mail Carriers	M	I	250+	Ready, Dee	Red Brick Learning
Mail Myself to You	E	RF	60	Little Celebrations	Pearson Learning Group
Mailman Mario & His Boris-Busters	L	RF	250+	Parker, John	Pearson Learning Group
Main Street	F	I	87	Leveled Readers Social Studies	Houghton Mifflin
Maine	R	I	250+	This Land Is Your Land	Compass Point Books
Maine	S	I	250+	Land of Liberty	Red Brick Learning
Mai's Big Surprise	J	RF	250+	The Wright Skills	Wright Group/McGraw Hill
Maisie's Race	L	RF	250+	Mawter, Jeni	Wright Group/McGraw Hill
Major Jump	B	F	21	Sunshine	Wright Group/McGraw Hill
Make a "Talking" Card	H	I	165	Sunshine	Wright Group/McGraw Hill
Make A Bird Feeder	D	I	62	How-To Series	Benchmark Education
Make a Boat That Floats	I	I	126	Book Bank	Wright Group/McGraw Hill
Make a Bottle Garden	L	I	250+	Lighthouse	Rigby
Make a Bottle Orchestra	J	I	250	Sunshine	Wright Group/McGraw Hill
Make a Cloud, Measure the Wind	M	I	250+	Reimer, Luther	Wright Group/McGraw Hill
Make a Dinosaur	H	I	208	Sun Sprouts	ETA/Cuisenaire
Make a Drum	C	I	29	Early Connections	Benchmark Education
Make a Glider	G	I	57	Storyteller-Setting Sun	Wright Group/McGraw Hill
Make a Guitar	J	I	540	Sunshine	Wright Group/McGraw Hill
Make a House	F	I	41	iOpeners	Pearson Learning Group

TITLE	LEVEL	GENRE	WORD COUNT	AUTHOR / SERIES	PUBLISHER / DISTRIBUTOR
Make A Kite	F	I	49	Story Steps	Rigby
Make a Lei	F	I	39	Pacific Literacy	Pacific Learning
Make a Monster	E	I	31	Windows on Literacy	National Geographic
Make a Necklace	E	I	106	How-To Series	Benchmark Education
Make a Paper Airplane	J	I	158	How-To Series	Benchmark Education
Make a Pinata	C	I	16	Little Celebrations	Pearson Learning Group
Make a Pinata	I	I	152	Windows on Literacy	National Geographic
Make a Plan of Your Classroom	E	I	94	How-To Series	Benchmark Education
Make a Rainbow Fish	G	I	139	Sun Sprouts	ETA/Cuisenaire
Make a Safety Puppet	E	I	107	How-To Series	Benchmark Education
Make a Salad Face	F	I	82	Voyages	SRA/McGraw Hill
Make a Shake and a Bakeless Cake	L	I	250+	Cole, Sally	Wright Group/McGraw Hill
Make a Sundial	K	I	250+	How-To Series	Benchmark Education
Make a Tune	J	I	246	Kratky, Lada	Hampton-Brown
Make a Turkey	C	I	14	Bebop Books	Lee & Low Books Inc.
Make a Valentine	D	RF	33	Bookshop	Mondo
Make A Wish, Molly	O	RF	250+	Cohen, Barbara	Bantam
Make a Worm Farm	E	I	98	Sun Sprouts	ETA/Cuisenaire
Make an Animal Mobile	H	I	116	How-to Series	Benchmark Education
Make an Island	J	I	199	How-To Series	Benchmark Education
Make Dinosaur Eggs	I	I	188	Sunshine	Wright Group/McGraw Hill
Make It Move!	N	I	215	Yellow Umbrella Books	Capstone Press
Make It Move!	E	I	29	Canizares, Susan; Chessen, Betsey	Scholastic
Make It Spin	D	I	18	Pacific Literacy	Pacific Learning
Make It!	A	RF	21	Phonics and Friends	Hampton-Brown
Make It! Ship It!	K	I	250+	Spyglass Books	Compass Point Books
Make It, Wear It	P	I	250+	iOpeners	Pearson Learning Group
Make Lemonade	Z	RF	250+	Wolff, Virginia Euwer	Scholastic
Make Like a Tree and Leave	U	RF	250+	Danziger, Paula	PaperStar
Make Masks for a Play	J	I	540	Sunshine	Wright Group/McGraw Hill
Make Mini Movies	I	I	309	Sunshine	Wright Group/McGraw Hill
Make Prints and Patterns	K	I	454	Sunshine	Wright Group/McGraw Hill
*Make Room For Elisa	N	RF	250+	Hurwitz, Johanna	Penguin Group
Make Things That Move	O	I	250+	Sunshine	Wright Group/McGraw Hill
Make Way For Ducklings	L	RF	250+	McCloskey, Robert	Puffin Books
Make Way for Sam Houston	X	B	250+	Fritz, Jean	Putnam & Grosset
Make Your Own Party	I	I	314	Sunshine	Wright Group/McGraw Hill
Make Your Own Terrarium	P	I	1380	Leveled Readers Science	Houghton Mifflin
Making a Bird	B	I	32	PM Plus Nonfiction	Rigby
Making a Bug Habitat	K	I	250+	How-To Series	Benchmark Education
Making a Cake	G	I	125	Little Red Readers	Sundance
Making a Cat and a Mouse	D	I	121	PM Plus Nonfiction	Rigby
Making a Caterpillar	E	I	115	PM Plus Nonfiction	Rigby
Making a Dinosaur	B	I	32	PM Plus Nonfiction	Rigby
Making a Garden	A	RF	28	Foundations	Wright Group/McGraw Hill
Making a Hat	C	I	24	Windows on Literacy	National Geographic
Making a House	C	I	89	Early Connections	Benchmark Education
Making a Magazine	O	I	496	Vocabulary Readers	Houghton Mifflin
Making a Map	L	I	293	Rigby Focus	Rigby
Making a Marionette	J	I	250+	Early Connections	Benchmark Education
Making a Marionette	K	I	349	How-To Series	Benchmark Education
Making a Memory	D	I	53	Ballinger, Margaret	Scholastic
Making a Mural	H	I	128	Vocabulary Readers	Houghton Mifflin
Making a Plate	H	I	183	Ready Readers	Pearson Learning Group

* Collection of short stories

TITLE	LEVEL	GENRE	WORD COUNT	AUTHOR / SERIES	PUBLISHER / DISTRIBUTOR
Making a Rabbit	B	I	32	PM Plus Nonfiction	Rigby
Making a Terrarium	L	I	250+	How-To Series	Benchmark Education
Making a Toy House	G	I	132	PM Plus Nonfiction	Rigby
Making a Weather Station	M	I	250+	How-To Series	Benchmark Education
Making Art	J	I	250+	Rosen Real Readers	Rosen Publishing Group
Making Breakfast	F	I	59	Windows on Literacy	National Geographic
Making Caterpillars and Butterflies	I	I	162	Literacy 2000	Rigby
Making Clay	O	I	792	Leveled Readers Science	Houghton Mifflin
Making Collages	J	I	250+	Bookshop	Mondo
Making Concrete	I	I	136	Alphakids	Sundance
Making Crafts From Around the World	O	I	250+	Navigators Fiction Series	Benchmark Education
Making Flavors and Fragrances	S	I	2032	Leveled Readers Science	Houghton Mifflin
Making Friends	J	RF	214	Foundations	Wright Group/McGraw Hill
Making Friends on Beacon Street	M	RF	250+	Literacy 2000	Rigby
Making Ice Cream	J	I	176	How-To Series	Benchmark Education
Making It Go?	F	I	106	Independent Readers Science	Houghton Mifflin
Making Lily Laugh!	M	RF	250+	Dreyer, Ellen	Pearson Learning Group
Making Money	I	I	129	Yellow Umbrella Books	Red Brick Learning
Making Money	H	I	129	Rosen Real Readers	Rosen Publishing Group
Making Mount Rushmore	M	I	250+	Twig	Wright Group/McGraw Hill
Making Mountains	B	I	35	Gosset, Rachel; Ballinger, Margaret	Scholastic
Making Movies	LB	I	43	Sunshine	Wright Group/McGraw Hill
Making Music	H	RF	71	Early Reader	Compass Point Books
Making Music	C	I	35	Wonder World	Wright Group/McGraw Hill
Making Music	K	I	174	Windows on Literacy	National Geographic
Making Oatmeal	E	I	38	Interaction	Rigby
Making Pancakes	D	RF	39	Carousel Readers	Pearson Learning Group
Making Paper	H	I	128	Rigby Focus	Rigby
Making Party Food	I	I	221	PM Plus Nonfiction	Rigby
Making Patterns	L	I	250+	Early Connections	Benchmark Education
Making Patterns	C	I	30	Twig	Wright Group/McGraw Hill
Making Pictures	G	I	132	Vocabulary Readers	Houghton Mifflin
Making Pictures	B	RF	48	Foundations	Wright Group/McGraw Hill
Making Pop-ups	N	I	250+	Bookshop	Mondo
Making Pop-ups	O	I	250+	Brian, Janeen	Mondo
Making Raisins	E	I	35	Windows on Literacy	National Geographic
Making Sense of Your Senses	P	I	250+	Navigators Science Series	Benchmark Education
Making Shapes	H	I	206	Early Connections	Benchmark Education
Making Shapes	K	I	250+	Yellow Umbrella Books	Capstone Press
Making Soup	C	RF	77	Leveled Readers Emergent	Houghton Mifflin
Making Things	D	RF	64	Foundations	Wright Group/McGraw Hill
Making Tortillas	H	I	104	Windows on Literacy	National Geographic
Malawi: Keeper of the Trees	D	I	250+	Little Celebrations	Pearson Learning Group
Malcolm Magpie	F	I	126	Storyteller-Setting Sun	Wright Group/McGraw Hill
Malka	Z	HF	250+	Pressler, Mirjam	Philomel Books
Mall Mystery, The	M	F	250+	Schultz, Irene	Wright Group/McGraw Hill
Mama and Kit Go Away	D	F	84	Leveled Readers	Houghton Mifflin
Mama Cut My Hair	H	RF	134	Books for Young Learners	Richard C. Owen
Mama Goes to School	D	RF	47	Visions	Wright Group/McGraw Hill
Mama Hen, Come Quick	C	F	35	Ready Readers	Pearson Learning Group
Mama, Let's Dance	W	RF	250+	Hermes, Patricia	Scholastic
Mama's Llamas	J	F	159	Books for Young Learners	Richard C. Owen
Mammals	N	I	250+	Simply Science	Compass Point Books

TITLE	LEVEL	GENRE	WORD COUNT	AUTHOR / SERIES	PUBLISHER / DISTRIBUTOR
Mammals	M	I	134	First Facts	Capstone Press
Mammals	H	I	134	Yellow Umbrella Books	Red Brick Learning
Mammals of the Sea	Q	I	250+	Explorers	Wright Group/McGraw Hill
Mammoth Mistake, A	K	RF	250+	Rigby Literacy	Rigby
Mammoths: Ice-Age Giants	Z	I	250+	Agenbroad, Dr. Larry D.; Nelson, Lisa	Lerner Publishing
Man from Mars, The	K	SF	250+	Popcorn	Sundance
Man From The Sky	S	RF	250+	Avi	Beech Tree Books
Man in the Moon and Other Moon Tales, The	N	RF	322	Independent Readers Science	Houghton Mifflin
Man in the Moon, The	H	I	173	Pair-It-Books	Steck-Vaughn
Man Out at First	M	RF	250+	Christopher, Matt	Little, Brown & Co.
Man Who Kept His Heart in a Bucket, The	S	TL	250+	Levitin, Sonia	Penguin Group
Man Who Paints Nature, The	O	B	250+	Locker, Thomas	Richard C. Owen
Man Who Rode the Tiger, The	L	TL	250+	PM Story Books	Rigby
Man Who Tricked a Ghost, The	N	TL	250+	Yep, Laurence	Troll Associates
Man Who Was Poe, The	T	B	250+	Avi	Avon
Man, the Boy, and the Donkey, The	I	TL	234	Story Box	Wright Group/McGraw Hill
Manatee Winter	K	RF	250+	Zoehfeld, Kathleen Weidnetz	Scholastic
Manatee, The	V	I	250+	Silverstein, A.; Nunn, L.	The Millbrook Press
Manatees	G	I	73	Pebble Books	Red Brick Learning
Manatees and Dugongs	M	I	250+	Cole, Sally	Wright Group/McGraw Hill
Mango Tree, The	E	F	163	Sun Sprouts	ETA/Cuisenaire
Manhattan Project, The: the Race to the Atomic Bomb	Y	I	2925	Leveled Readers Science	Houghton Mifflin
Maniac Magee	W	RF	250+	Spinelli, Jerry	Scholastic
Manly Ferry Pigeon, The	K	RF	250+	Sunshine	Wright Group/McGraw Hill
Manners at a Friend's Home	L	I	250+	First Facts	Capstone Press
Manners at a Restaurant	L	I	250+	First Facts	Capstone Press
Manners at the Library	L	I	250+	First Facts	Capstone Press
Manners in the Classroom	L	I	250+	First Facts	Capstone Press
Manners of a Pig, The	I	F	250+	Bookshop	Mondo
Manners on the Playground	L	I	250+	First Facts	Capstone Press
Manners on the Telephone	L	I	250+	First Facts	Capstone Press
Manners Please	C	RF	27	Pair-It-Books	Steck-Vaughn
Mansion in the Mist, The	S	F	250+	Bellairs, John	Puffin Books
Mantu the Elephant	K	F	250+	Rigby Literacy	Rigby
Manual of House Monsters, A	O	F	250+	Marijanovic, Stanislav	Mondo
Many Friends, Many Languages	D	I	98	Fiesta Series	Pearson Learning Group
Many Happy Returns: A Review of Recycling	R	I	250+	Literacy 2000	Rigby
Many Kinds of Birds	I	I	290	Leveled Readers	Houghton Mifflin
Many Thousand Gone: African Americans From Slavery to Freedom	X	TL	250+	Hamilton, Virginia	Alfred A. Knopf
Many Waters	V	F	250+	L'Engle, Madeleine	Bantam
Many Ways to 100	I	I	250+	Yellow Umbrella Books	Red Brick Learning
Map Book, The	F	I	144	Sunshine	Wright Group/McGraw Hill
Map Mysteries	M	I	250+	Home Connection Collection	Rigby
Maple Thanksgiving, The	L	F	250+	Little Celebrations	Pearson Learning Group
Maple Tree	O	I	250+	Life Cycles	Creative Teaching Press
Maple Trees	F	I	118	Pebble Books	Capstone Press
Mapping North America	M	I	148	Windows on Literacy	National Geographic
Mapping Our World	K	I	250+	Spyglass Books	Compass Point Books
Maps	Q	I	250+	Rigby Focus	Rigby
Maps	G	I	99	Learn to Read	Creative Teaching Press
Maps	K	I	150	Phonics Readers	Compass Point Books

* Collection of short stories

TITLE	LEVEL	GENRE	WORD COUNT	AUTHOR / SERIES	PUBLISHER / DISTRIBUTOR
Maps	G	I	142	Early Connections	Benchmark Education
Maps and Codes	P	I	250+	Wildcats	Wright Group/McGraw Hill
Maps and Our World	Q	I	250+	Explorers	Wright Group/McGraw Hill
Maps Show Us the Way	H	I	94	Rosen Real Readers	Rosen Publishing Group
Maps, Maps, Maps	E	I	47	Rosen Real Readers	Rosen Publishing Group
Marble Patch, The	J	RF	250+	PM Story Books	Rigby
Marbles	P	I	250+	Games Around the World	Compass Point Books
Marcella	L	RF	250+	Literacy 2000	Rigby
March Along with Me	D	F	56	Literacy 2000	Rigby
March for Freedom	J	I	132	Twig	Wright Group/McGraw Hill
March on Washington, The	P	I	304	Vocabulary Readers	Houghton Mifflin
March, March, Marching	D	RF	60	Teacher's Choice Series	Pearson Learning Group
Marching Band	LB	RF	35	Urmston, Kathleen; Evans, Karen	Kaeden Books
Marching to Freedom: The Story of Martin Luther King, Jr.	P	B	250+	Milton, Joyce	Bantam
Marcie's Birthday Dig	Q	RF	250+	Leveled Readers Language Support	Houghton Mifflin
Marco Polo: Marco Polo and the Silk Road to China	U	B	250+	Exploring the World	Compass Point Books
Marco Saves Grandpa	I	RF	232	Foundations	Wright Group/McGraw Hill
Mardi Gras	H	I	84	Vocabulary Readers	Houghton Mifflin
Mare for Young Wolf, A	L	HF	250+	Shefelman, Janice	Random House
Margaret Bourke-White	O	B	250+	Welch, Catherine	Carolrhoda Books
Margaret Bourke-White: A Photographer's Life	P	B	250+	Keller, Emily	Lerner Publishing
Margaret Bourke-White: Life Through the Lens	X	B	3041	Leveled Readers	Houghton Mifflin
Margaret Mahy	L	B	250+	Sunshine	Wright Group/McGraw Hill
Margaret Wise Brown	O	B	250+	Greene, Carol	Children's Press
Margarito's Carvings	L	I	250+	Little Celebrations	Pearson Learning Group
Maria	I	RF	72	City Kids	Rigby
Maria Goes to School	E	RF	174	Foundations	Wright Group/McGraw Hill
Maria Mitchell	O	B	291	Independent Readers Science	Houghton Mifflin
Maria Tallchief	R	B	250+	Native American Stories	Steck-Vaughn
Maria Tallchief	E	B	48	Independent Readers Social Studies	Houghton Mifflin
Maria: A Christmas Story	R	RF	250+	Taylor, Theodore	Avon Camelot
Marian Anderson: Singer	V	B	250+	American Women of Achievement	Chelsea House
Marian Wright Edelman: For Every Child	S	B	2406	Leveled Readers	Houghton Mifflin
Maria's House	F	RF	138	Seedlings	Continental Press
Marie Curie	S	B	1924	Independent Readers Science	Houghton Mifflin
Marie Curie	N	B	182	Pebble Books	Capstone Press
Marie Curie	O	B	250+	Early Biographies	Compass Point Books
Marie Mitchell	O	B	250+	Independent Readers Science	Houghton Mifflin
Marie: Summer in the Country	Q	HF	250+	Girlhood Journeys	Aladdin
Mariel of Redwall	Z	F	250+	Jacques, Brian	Avon
Marie-Maud Becomes a Citizen	L	RF	563	Leveled Readers Social Studies	Houghton Mifflin
Marigold and Grandma On The Town	J	F	250+	Calmenson, Stephanie	HarperTrophy
Marigolds for Dona Remedios	M	RF	250+	Story Vines	Wright Group/McGraw Hill
Marina Silva: Conserving the Rain Forest	N	B	812	Leveled Readers Science	Houghton Mifflin
Mario Mixwell	M	B	250+	Reimer, Luther	Wright Group/McGraw Hill
Mario Molina: Above the Clouds	X	B	2464	Leveled Readers Science	Houghton Mifflin
Marion Anderson, American Hero	M	B	645	Leveled Readers Social Studies	Houghton Mifflin
Marion Jones: Quest for Gold	R	B	1337	Leveled Readers	Houghton Mifflin
Mario's Mayan Journey	P	F	250+	Bookshop	Mondo
Marjorie Harris Carr	O	B	546	Leveled Readers Science	Houghton Mifflin

* Collection of short stories

TITLE	LEVEL	GENRE	WORD COUNT	AUTHOR / SERIES	PUBLISHER / DISTRIBUTOR
Marjorie Stoneman Douglas	N	B	294	Independent Readers Social Studies	Houghton Mifflin
Mark McGuire, Home Run King	P	B	250+	Leveled Readers Language Support	Houghton Mifflin
Mark McGwire: Home Run Hero	Q	B	960	Leveled Readers	Houghton Mifflin
Mark Twain	W	B	250+	Cox, Clinton	Scholastic
Mark Twain: Young Writer	O	B	250+	Childhood of Famous Americans	Aladdin
Market Day for Mrs. Wordy	J	RF	177	Sunshine	Wright Group/McGraw Hill
Market, The	D	RF	48	Joy Readers	Pearson Learning Group
Marketplace, The	E	RF	58	Visions	Wright Group/McGraw Hill
Markets	D	I	44	Chanko, Pamela; Berger, Samantha	Scholastic
Marks in the Sand	F	I	121	Windows on Literacy	National Geographic
Mark's Monster	I	F	250+	Reading Unlimited	Pearson Learning Group
Marlfox: A Novel of Redwall	Z	F	250+	Jacques, Brian	Ace Books
Marmalade's Nap	F	F	57	Wheeler, Cindy	Alfred A. Knopf
Marmalade's Snowy Day	F	F	61	Wheeler, Cindy	Alfred A. Knopf
Marrying Malcolm Murgatroyd	T	RF	250+	Farrell, Mame	Sunburst
Mars	W	I	250+	World Mythology	Capstone Press
Mars	S	I	250+	Our Solar System	Compass Point Books
Mars	L	I	220	Rigby Focus	Rigby
Mars, Our Closest Neighbor	S	I	1366	Leveled Readers Science	Houghton Mifflin
Mars: Mysteries of the Red Planet	X	I	3297	Leveled Readers	Houghton Mifflin
Mars: The Red Planet	L	I	250+	Rosen Real Readers	Rosen Publishing Group
Martha Graham, Modern Dancer	P	B	982	Leveled Readers	Houghton Mifflin
Martha Washington: America's First First Lady	O	B	250+	Childhood of Famous Americans	Aladdin
Martial Arts	R	I	250+	Malane, Donna	Pacific Learning
Martial Arts for Fun!	S	I	250+	Activities for Fun	Compass Point Books
Martian Goo	E	F	65	Salem, Lynn; Stewart, Josie	Continental Press
Martians Are People, Too	N	F	250+	Navigators Fiction Series	Benchmark Education
Martians Don't Take Temperatures	M	F	250+	Dadey, Debbie; Jones, Marcia Thornton	Scholastic
Martin and the Teacher's Pets	K	RF	250+	Chardiet, Bernice; Maccarone, Grace	Scholastic
Martin and the Tooth Fairy	K	RF	250+	Chardiet, Bernice; Maccarone, Grace	Scholastic
Martin Luther King	T	B	250+	Bray, Rosemary L.	William Morrow
Martin Luther King Day	L	I	250+	Lowery, Linda	Scholastic
Martin Luther King, Jr.	P	B	250+	Photo-Illustrated Biographies	Red Brick Learning
Martin Luther King, Jr.	O	B	250+	Rookie Biographies	Children's Press
Martin Luther King, Jr.	L	B	290	Pebble Books	Capstone Press
Martin Luther King, Jr. and the March Toward Freedom	R	B	250+	Hakim, Rita	The Millbrook Press
Martin Luther King, Jr. Day	K	I	138	Pebble Books	Capstone Press
Martin Luther King, Jr., A Man Who Changed Things	O	B	250+	Greene, Carol	Children's Press
Martin Luther King, Jr.: Preacher, Freedom Fighter, Peacemaker	M	B	250+	Biographies	Picture Window Books
Martin Luther King, Jr.: Young Man with a Dream	O	B	250+	Childhood of Famous Americans	Aladdin
Martin Van Buren	U	B	250+	Profiles of the Presidents	Compass Point Books
Martin's Mice	P	F	250+	King-Smith, Dick	Alfred A. Knopf
Martin's Mighty Hit	M	RF	390	Windmill Books	Rigby
Marvella and the Moon	F	F	250+	Bookshop	Mondo

TITLE	LEVEL	GENRE	WORD COUNT	AUTHOR / SERIES	PUBLISHER / DISTRIBUTOR
Marvelous Mammals	F	I	99	Independent Readers Science	Houghton Mifflin
Marvelous Me	F	F	29	Literacy 2000	Rigby
Marvelous Menus	N	F	250+	Sails	Rigby
Marvelous Metals	U	I	1616	Independent Readers Science	Houghton Mifflin
Marvelous Treasure, The	M	RF	481	Sunshine	Wright Group/McGraw Hill
Marvin and the Mean Words	M	RF	250+	Kline, Suzy	PaperStar
Marvin One Too Many	J	RF	250+	Paterson, Katherine	HarperCollins
Marvin Redpost (Class President)	M	RF	250+	Sachar, Louis	Random House
Marvin Redpost, Super Fast, Out of Control!	M	RF	250+	Sachar, Louis	Random House
Marvin Redpost: A Flying Birthday Cake?	M	RF	250+	Sachar, Louis	Random House
Marvin Redpost: Alone in His Teacher's House	M	RF	250+	Sachar, Louis	Random House
Marvin Redpost: Is He a Girl?	M	RF	250+	Sachar, Louis	Random House
Marvin Redpost: Kidnapped at Birth?	M	RF	250+	Sachar, Louis	Random House
Marvin Redpost: Why Pick on Me?	M	RF	250+	Sachar, Louis	Random House
Marvin's Birthday	K	RF	250+	Pacific Literacy	Pacific Learning
Marvin's Manners	E	RF	32	Pair-It Books	Steck-Vaughn
Mary Anning, Fossil Hunter	R	B	1307	Independent Readers Science	Houghton Mifflin
Mary by Myself	Q	F	250+	Smith, Jane Denitz	HarperTrophy
Mary Cassatt	S	B	250+	Masterpieces: Artists and Their Works	Capstone Press
Mary Leakey	W	B	2174	Leveled Readers Social Studies	Houghton Mifflin
Mary Marony and the Chocolate Surprise	M	RF	250+	Kline, Suzy	Bantam
Mary Marony and the Snake	M	RF	250+	Kline, Suzy	Bantam
Mary Marony Hides Out	M	RF	250+	Kline, Suzy	Bantam
Mary Marony, Mummy Girl	M	RF	250+	Kline, Suzy	Bantam
Mary McLeod Bethune	O	B	250+	Greenfield, Eloise	HarperTrophy
Mary McLeod Bethune	U	B	250+	Cornerstones of Freedom	Children's Press
Mary McLeod Bethune - Voice of Black Hope	S	B	250+	Meltzer, Milton	Puffin Books
*Mary on Horseback	Q	RF	250+	Wells, Rosemary	Puffin Books
Mary Todd Lincoln: Girl of the Bluegrass	O	B	250+	Childhood of Famous Americans	Aladdin
Mary Wore Her Red Dress	D	F	170	Peek, Merle	Clarion
Mary, Mary	D	TL	21	Jumbled Tumbled Tales & Rhymes	Rigby
Maryland	S	I	250+	Land of Liberty	Red Brick Learning
Maryland	R	I	250+	This Land Is Your Land	Compass Point Books
Mask Book, The	L	I	217	Twig	Wright Group/McGraw Hill
Mask Makers, The	K	RF	242	Leveled Readers	Houghton Mifflin
Mask, The	E	I	45	Pair-It Books	Steck-Vaughn
Masks	M	I	250+	Literacy 2000	Rigby
Masks	C	I	41	Pebble Books	Capstone Press
Masks	E	I	62	Wonder World	Wright Group/McGraw Hill
Massachusetts	S	I	250+	Land of Liberty	Red Brick Learning
Massachusetts	R	I	250+	This Land Is Your Land	Compass Point Books
Master Puppeteer, The	X	HF	250+	Paterson, Katherine	HarperCollins
Matchbox Collection, A	K	I	250+	Stepping Stones	Nelson/Michaels Assoc.
Matchbox, The	S	HF	250+	Literacy 2000	Rigby
Matchlock Gun, The	P	HF	250+	Edmonds, Walter D.	Putnam & Grosset
Materials	L	I	250+	Discovery World	Rigby
Math at the Store	G	I	127	Amato, William	Scholastic
Math Bee, The	P	B	795	Leveled Readers	Houghton Mifflin
Math Chat: A Glossary of Terms	M	I	250+	Twig	Wright Group/McGraw Hill
Math Counts	L	I	250+	Pluckrose, Henry	Scholastic
Math in the Garden	R	I	250+	Navigators Math Series	Benchmark Education
Math Is Everywhere	F	I	95	Sunshine	Wright Group/McGraw Hill
Math on the Moon	O	I	250+	Navigators Fiction Series	Benchmark Education

TITLE	LEVEL	GENRE	WORD COUNT	AUTHOR / SERIES	PUBLISHER / DISTRIBUTOR
Math to Munch On	T	I	250+	Navigators Math Series	Benchmark Education
Math Wiz, The	N	RF	250+	Duffey, Betsy	Penguin Group
Mathew Brady: Civil War Photographer	T	B	250+	A First Book	Franklin Watts
Matilda	S	F	250+	Dahl, Roald	Penguin Group
Matilda Bone	X	HF	250+	Cushman, Karen	Clarion
Matilda's Plans	O	F	250+	Sails	Rigby
Matisse	S	B	250+	Masterpieces: Artists and Their Works	Capstone Press
Matsumura's Ice Sculpture	I	I	94	iOpeners	Pearson Learning Group
Matt Drives the Car	D	RF	136	Early Emergent, Set 3	Pioneer Valley
Matter	N	I	250+	Our Physical World	Capstone Press
Matter of Balance, A	L	B	250+	Voyages	SRA/McGraw Hill
Matter of Conscience, A: The Trial of Anne Hutchinson	U	I	250+	Nichols, Joan Kane	Steck-Vaughn
Matter: See It, Touch It, Taste It, Smell It	N	I	250+	Amazing Science	Picture Window Books
Matthew and Tilly	L	RF	250+	Jones, Rebecca C.	Penguin Group
Matthew Henson	L	B	250+	Biography	Benchmark Education
Matthew Henson: Arctic Explorer	O	B	250+	Podojil, Catherine	Wright Group/McGraw Hill
Matthew Likes to Read	J	RF	144	Pacific Literacy	Pacific Learning
Matthew the Magician	E	RF	116	Learn to Read	Creative Teaching Press
Matthew's Meadow	V	RF	250+	Bliss, Corinne Demas	OSI
Matthew's Tantrum	J	RF	250+	Literacy 2000	Rigby
Mattimeo: A Tale from Redwall	Z	F	250+	Jacques, Brian	Avon
Maui and the Sun	I	TL	267	Story Box	Wright Group/McGraw Hill
Maui and the Sun	M	TL	359	Pacific Literacy	Pacific Learning
Maura's Angel	X	F	250+	Banks, Lynne Reid	Avon
Maurice Sendak	L	B	201	First Biographies	Red Brick Learning
Max	J	RF	234	Isadora, Rachel	Macmillan
Max and Jake	G	RF	212	PM Plus Story Books	Rigby
Max and Me and the Time Machine	T	SF	250+	Greer, Gery; Ruddick, Bob	HarperTrophy
Max and Mintie	K	F	250+	Home Connection Collection	Rigby
Max and the Birdhouse	G	RF	190	PM Plus Story Books	Rigby
Max and the Clouds	E	F	211	Sun Sprouts	ETA/Cuisenaire
Max and the Little Plant	E	RF	134	PM Plus Story Books	Rigby
Max Comes Home	A	RF	24	First Stories	Pacific Learning
Max Gets Ready	C	RF	48	Rigby Literacy	Rigby
Max Goes Fishing	E	RF	147	PM Plus Story Books	Rigby
Max in a Tree	D	F	86	Sun Sprouts	ETA/Cuisenaire
Max is a Star!	F	RF	160	Leveled Readers Language Support	Houghton Mifflin
Max Jumps	B	F	37	Sun Sprouts	ETA/Cuisenaire
Max Malone and the Great Cereal Rip-off	N	RF	250+	Herman, Charlotte	Henry Holt & Co.
Max Malone Makes a Million	N	RF	250+	Herman, Charlotte	Henry Holt & Co.
Max Malone the Magnificent	N	RF	250+	Herman, Charlotte	Scholastic
Max Malone, Superstar	N	RF	250+	Herman, Charlotte	Scholastic
Max on a Hill	E	F	80	Sun Sprouts	ETA/Cuisenaire
Max on Ice	E	F	219	Sun Sprouts	ETA/Cuisenaire
Max Rides His Bike	E	RF	143	PM Plus Story Books	Rigby
Max the Man Mountain	Q	RF	250+	McFarlane, Peter	HarperCollins
Max the Mighty	W	RF	250+	Philbrick, Rodman	Scholastic
Max the Pet Show Star	G	RF	175	Leveled Readers	Houghton Mifflin
Max Visits London	K	RF	250+	Leveled Readers Language Support	Houghton Mifflin
Maxie, Rosie, and Earl - Partners in Grime	O	RF	250+	Park, Barbara	Random House

* Collection of short stories

TITLE	LEVEL	GENRE	WORD COUNT	AUTHOR / SERIES	PUBLISHER / DISTRIBUTOR
Max's Box	B	RF	43	Little Celebrations	Pearson Learning Group
Max's Glasses	L	RF	250+	Navigators Fiction Series	Benchmark Education
May Chinn: The Best Medicine	U	B	250+	Butts, Ellen; Schwartz, Joyce	W. H. Freeman & Co.
May I Stay Home Today?	E	RF	73	Tadpoles	Rigby
Maya Angelou: Greeting the Morning	W	B	250+	King, Sarah E.	The Millbrook Press
Maya Angelou: Journey of the Heart	W	B	250+	Pettit, Jayne	Puffin Books
Maya, The	R	I	250+	First Reports	Compass Point Books
Maya, The	N	I	250+	A New True Book	Children's Press
Maya, The	S	I	250+	Journey Into Civilization	Chelsea House
Maybe I'll Be	D	F	49	Carousel Readers	Pearson Learning Group
Maybe Yes, Maybe No, Maybe Maybe	M	RF	250+	Patron, Susan	Bantam
Mayflower, The	R	I	250+	The Library of the Pilgrims	Rosen Publishing Group
Mayors	L	I	250+	Community Workers	Compass Point Books
Maze, The	V	RF	250+	Hobbs, Will	Morrow Junior Books
Mazes Are Amazing!	K	I	220	Vocabulary Readers	Houghton Mifflin
*McBroom's Wonderful One-Acre Farm	O	RF	250+	Fleischman, Sid	Beech Tree Books
McBungle's African Safari	I	F	336	Traditional Tales & More	Rigby
McGinty's Friend	L	F	250+	Sails	Rigby
Me	C	RF	41	Reading Corners	Pearson Learning Group
Me	A	I	24	PM Starters	Rigby
Me (boy)	C	I	34	Tonon, Terry	Kaeden Books
Me (girl)	C	I	34	Tonon, Terry	Kaeden Books
Me and My Dog	F	RF	115	Sunshine	Wright Group/McGraw Hill
Me and My Little Brain	T	RF	250+	Fitzgerald, John D.	Dell
Me and My Pup	C	RF	34	Leveled Readers Language Support	Houghton Mifflin
Me and My Shadow	H	F	247	Momentum Literacy Program	Troll Associates
Me Too	K	RF	136	Mayer, Mercer	Donovan
Me Too!	G	F	200	Bookshop	Mondo
Me Too!	D	F	70	Sunshine	Wright Group/McGraw Hill
Me, Mop, and the Moondance Kid	S	RF	250+	Myers, Walter Dean	Bantam
Mean Giant, The	C	F	69	Sun Sprouts	ETA/Cuisenaire
Meanest Thing to Say, The	K	RF	250+	Cosby, Bill	Scholastic
Meanies	F	F	158	Story Box	Wright Group/McGraw Hill
Meanies Came to School, The	E	RF	135	Story Basket	Wright Group/McGraw Hill
Meanies' Trick, The	E	F	93	Story Box	Wright Group/McGraw Hill
Measure	L	I	229	Spyglass Books	Compass Point Books
Measure It	C	I	56	Twig	Wright Group/McGraw Hill
Measure the Motion	H	I	146	Leveled Readers Science	Houghton Mifflin
Measure Up!	K	I	303	Early Connections	Benchmark Education
Measurement Mysteries	G	I	124	Learn to Read	Creative Teaching Press
Measuring Motion	H	I	113	Leveled Readers Science	Houghton Mifflin
Measuring the Weather	R	I	250+	Gaynor, Bill	Pacific Learning
Measuring Time	E	I	217	Early Connections	Benchmark Education
Measuring Tools	M	I	250+	Daronco, Mickey; Presti, Lori	Benchmark Education
Measuring Weather	E	I	99	Independent Readers Science	Houghton Mifflin
Meat and Protein Group, The	H	I	117	Pebble Books	Red Brick Learning
Meat Eaters, Plant Eaters	K	I	156	Planet Earth	Rigby
Meat Pies	D	I	21	Bebop Books	Lee & Low Books Inc.
Medal for Molly, A	N	RF	250+	PM Emerald	Rigby
Medal for Nickie, A	K	RF	262	Sunshine	Wright Group/McGraw Hill
Medical Pioneers	P	B	250+	Navigators Biography Series	Benchmark Education
Medieval Feast, A	Q	I	250+	Aliki	HarperCollins
Medieval Town	Q	I	250+	Worldwise	Grolier Press

* Collection of short stories

TITLE	LEVEL	GENRE	WORD COUNT	AUTHOR / SERIES	PUBLISHER / DISTRIBUTOR
Medusa	W	I	250+	World Mythology	Capstone Press
Meerkat Chat	L	I	250+	Story Steps	Rigby
Meerkats	O	I	250+	Weaver, Robyn	Red Brick Learning
Meet a Community Helper	D	RF	41	Independent Readers Social Studies	Houghton Mifflin
Meet Abraham Lincoln	O	B	250+	Cary, Barbara	Step-Up Books
Meet Addy	Q	HF	250+	The American Girls Collection	Pleasant Company
Meet an Author: Laura Kvasnosky	E	B	54	Sunshine	Wright Group/McGraw Hill
Meet Benjamin Franklin	O	B	250+	Scarf, Maggi	Step-Up Books
Meet Calliope Day	R	F	250+	Haddad, Charles	Random House
Meet Erdene	P	I	250+	iOpeners	Pearson Learning Group
Meet Felicity	Q	HF	250+	The American Girls Collection	Pleasant Company
Meet Firefighter Jen	I	I	250+	Rosen Real Readers	Rosen Publishing Group
Meet George Washington	O	B	250+	Heilbroner, Joan	Random House
Meet Hillary Rodham Clinton	Q	B	250+	Spain, Valerie	Random House
Meet Jane Mt. Pleasant	H	B	183	Leveled Readers Science	Houghton Mifflin
Meet John F. Kennedy	Q	B	250+	White, Nancy Bean	Random House
Meet Johnny Appleseed	D	B	32	Independent Readers Social Studies	Houghton Mifflin
Meet Josefina	Q	HF	250+	The American Girls Collection	Pleasant Company
Meet Kirsten	Q	HF	250+	The American Girls Collection	Pleasant Company
Meet M & M	K	RF	250+	Ross, Pat	Penguin Group
Meet Martin Luther King, Jr.	R	B	250+	DeKay, James T.	Random House
Meet Me at the Water Hole	H	I	144	Storyteller-Night Crickets	Wright Group/McGraw Hill
Meet Messy Fred	I	F	250+	Popcorn	Sundance
Meet Molly	Q	HF	250+	The American Girls Collection	Pleasant Company
Meet Mr. Cricket	E	F	86	Carousel Readers	Pearson Learning Group
Meet My Family	C	RF	71	Early Connections	Benchmark Education
Meet My Mouse	H	RF	135	Little Celebrations	Pearson Learning Group
Meet Officer Jerry	H	I	173	Rosen Real Readers	Rosen Publishing Group
Meet Samantha	Q	HF	250+	The American Girls Collection	Pleasant Company
Meet Samuel Adams	P	B	447	Vocabulary Readers	Houghton Mifflin
Meet Some Tricksters!	J	I	301	Vocabulary Readers	Houghton Mifflin
Meet the Austins	W	RF	250+	L'Engle, Madeleine	Laurel-Leaf Books
Meet the Feet	J	I	189	Leveled Readers	Houghton Mifflin
Meet the Johnson Family	G	RF	52	Windows on Literacy	National Geographic
Meet the Lincoln Lions Band	L	RF	250+	Giff, Patricia Reilly	Bantam
Meet the Meerkats	L	I	250+	World Quest Adventures	World Quest Learning
*Meet the Molesons	L	F	250+	Bos, Burny	North-South Books
Meet the Octopus	K	I	250+	Bookshop	Mondo
Meet the Villarreals	M	B	387	Kratky, Lada Josefa	Hampton-Brown
Meet Thomas Jefferson	O	B	250+	Barrett, Marvin	Step-Up Books
Meet Tom Paxton	I	B	229	Little Celebrations	Pearson Learning Group
Meet William Joyce	I	B	207	Little Celebrations	Pearson Learning Group
Meet Yo-Yo Ma	R	B	1406	Leveled Readers	Houghton Mifflin
Meeting Sqauwky	N	I	250+	Books for Young Learners	Richard C. Owen
Meg and Jim's Sled Trip	I	RF	250+	Appleton-Smith, Laura	Flyleaf Publishing
Meg and Mog	J	F	236	Nicoll, Helen	Viking
Meg Mackintosh and The Case of the Curious Whale Watch	O	RF	250+	Landon, Lucinda	Secret Passage Press
Meg Mackintosh and The Case of the Missing Babe Ruth Baseball	O	RF	250+	Landon, Lucinda	Secret Passage Press
Meg Mackintosh and The Mystery at Camp Creepy	O	RF	250+	Landon, Lucinda	Secret Passage Press

* Collection of short stories

TITLE	LEVEL	GENRE	WORD COUNT	AUTHOR / SERIES	PUBLISHER / DISTRIBUTOR
Meg Mackintosh and The Mystery at the Medieval Castle	O	RF	250+	Landon, Lucinda	Secret Passage Press
Meg Mackintosh and The Mystery at the Soccer Match	O	RF	250+	Landon, Lucinda	Secret Passage Press
Meg Mackintosh and The Mystery in the Locked Library	O	RF	250+	Landon, Lucinda	Secret Passage Press
Megan in Ancient Greece	Q	HF	250+	Korman, Susan	Magic Attic
Megan's Balancing Act	Q	RF	250+	Korman, Susan	Magic Attic
Megan's Island	R	RF	250+	Roberts, Willo Davis	Aladdin
Meg's Cat	F	RF	117	Lighthouse	Rigby
Meg's Dearest Wish	Q	HF	250+	The Little Women Journals	Avon
Meg's Eggs	C	F	38	New Way Red	Steck-Vaughn
Meg's Mad Magnet	H	F	145	Supersonics	Rigby
Mei Fuh: Memories From China	P	B	250+	Schaeffer, Edith	Houghton Mifflin
Melting	F	I	69	Bookshop	Mondo
*Melting Snow Sculptures and Other Cases, The	O	RF	250+	Simon, Seymour	Avon
Memorial Day	L	I	250+	Frost, Helen	Red Brick Learning
Memories for Mom	P	RF	1517	Leveled Readers	Houghton Mifflin
Memories of Anne Frank	X	B	250+	Gold, Alison Leslie	Scholastic
Memories of Vietnam: War in the First Person	Z	HF	250+	Weiss, Ellen	Scholastic
Memory Boy	Z	F	250+	Weaver, Will	HarperCollins
Meow, What Now?	G	F	186	Seedlings	Continental Press
Mercury	N	I	250+	A True Book	Children's Press
Mercury	S	I	250+	Our Solar System	Compass Point Books
Mercy Otis Warren: A Woman of the Revolution	X	B	2210	Leveled Readers	Houghton Mifflin
Merlin and the Dragons	U	F	250+	Yolen, Jane	Penguin Group
Merlin: The Young Merlin Trilogy	V	TL	250+	Yolen, Jane	Scholastic
Mermaid Island	L	F	250+	Frith, Margaret	Grosset & Dunlap
Mermaids Don't Run Track	M	F	250+	Dadey, Debbie; Jones, Marcia Thornton	Scholastic
Merry Christmas, Amelia Bedelia	L	F	250+	Parish, Peggy	William Morrow
Merry-Go-Round	C	RF	66	Teacher's Choice Series	Pearson Learning Group
Merry-Go-Round, The	C	RF	45	Ready Readers	Pearson Learning Group
Merry-Go-Round, The	C	RF	62	Sunshine	Wright Group/McGraw Hill
Merry-Go-Round, The	C	RF	84	PM Story Books	Rigby
Mess Monster	G	F	179	Literacy 2000	Rigby
Mess, A	D	F	34	Ready Readers	Pearson Learning Group
Mess, The	D	RF	55	My First Reader	Grolier Press
Mess, The	B	RF	40	Sun Sprouts	ETA/Cuisenaire
Message to the World, A	S	I	813	Vocabulary Readers	Houghton Mifflin
Message, The	R	F	250+	Applegate, K. A.	Scholastic
Messages Without Words	Q	I	250+	Sunshine	Wright Group/McGraw Hill
Messenger	Y	F	250+	Lowry, Lois	Houghton Mifflin
Messy Bessey	I	RF	63	Rookie Readers	Children's Press
Messy Bessey's Closet	K	RF	92	Rookie Readers	Children's Press
Messy Bessey's Family Reunion	J	RF	190	McKissack, Patricia & Fredrick	Scholastic
Messy Bessey's Garden	I	RF	60	Rookie Readers	Children's Press
Messy Bessey's School Desk	J	RF	104	Rookie Readers	Children's Press
Messy Mark	F	RF	180	First Start	Troll Associates
Messy Meals	J	F	87	Franco, Betsy	Scholastic
Messy Monsters, The	G	F	167	Carousel Readers	Pearson Learning Group
Messy Moose	C	F	45	Little Books	Sadlier-Oxford
Messy Rooms, The	F	F	103	Lester the Lion Series	Pioneer Valley
Meteorite!: The Last Days of the Dinosaurs	W	I	250+	Norris, Richard	Steck-Vaughn

* Collection of short stories

TITLE	LEVEL	GENRE	WORD COUNT	AUTHOR / SERIES	PUBLISHER / DISTRIBUTOR
Meteorologists	M	I	250+	Community Helpers	Red Brick Learning
Meteors and Meteorites	P	I	250+	The Galaxy	Red Brick Learning
Meteors: The Truth Behind Shooting Stars	T	I	250+	Aronson, Billy	Franklin Watts
Metric Math	T	I	250+	Navigators Math Series	Benchmark Education
Metropolitan Cow	N	F	250+	Egan, Tim	Houghton Mifflin
Mexican Feast, A: The Foods and Recipes of Mexico	P	I	250+	Rosen Real Readers	Rosen Publishing Group
Mexican Holiday, A	C	I	24	The Candid Collection	Pearson Learning Group
Mexican War, 1846-1848, The	V	I	250+	Let Freedom Ring	Capstone Press
Mexico	O	I	250+	Many Cultures, One World	Capstone Press
Mexico	P	I	250+	Fact Finders	Capstone Press
Mexico	Q	I	250+	First Reports	Compass Point Books
Mexico	O	I	250+	Dahl, Michael	Red Brick Learning
Mexico	LB	I	22	Canizares, Susan; Chanko, Pamela	Scholastic
Mexico City Is Muy Grande	M	I	250+	Twig	Wright Group/McGraw Hill
Mexico's Smoking Mountains	W	I	1955	Leveled Readers	Houghton Mifflin
Mia Hamm, Journey of a Soccer Champion	S	B	1730	Leveled Readers	Houghton Mifflin
Mia Hamm: Soccer Star	Q	B	250+	Leveled Readers Language Support	Houghton Mifflin
Mia's Sun Hat	E	RF	32	Start to Read	School Zone
Mice	O	I	250+	Holmes, Kevin J.	Red Brick Learning
Mice	H	I	143	Literacy 2000	Rigby
Mice	J	I	250+	PM Animal Facts: Orange	Rigby
Mice and Max	G	F	169	Carousel Readers	Pearson Learning Group
Mice at Bat	I	F	250+	Oechsli, Kelly	HarperTrophy
Mice Have a Meeting, The	I	TL	250+	PM Plus Story Books	Rigby
Mice on Ice	H	F	51	Easy Phonics Readers	Teacher Created Materials
Mice on Ice	I	F	211	Sunshine	Wright Group/McGraw Hill
Mice on Ice	C	F	34	KinderReaders	Rigby
Michael and the Eggs	G	RF	154	Oxford Reading Tree	Oxford University Press
Michael in the Hospital	E	RF	91	Oxford Reading Tree	Oxford University Press
Michael Jordan	M	B	250+	Edwards, Nick	Scholastic
Michael Jordan	Q	B	250+	Lovitt, Chip	Scholastic
Michael Jordan: The Best Ever	T	B	250+	High Five Reading	Red Brick Learning
Michael's Picture	C	RF	33	Little Celebrations	Pearson Learning Group
Michelangelo	S	B	250+	Masterpieces: Artists and Their Works	Red Brick Learning
Michelangelo: His Life and Art	R	B	250+	Rosen Real Readers	Rosen Publishing Group
Michelle Kwan	N	B	250+	Biography	Benchmark Education
Michigan	S	I	250+	Land of Liberty	Red Brick Learning
Michigan	Q	I	250+	One Nation	Capstone Press
Michigan	R	I	250+	This Land Is Your Land	Compass Point Books
Mick and Max	G	RF	169	Carousel Readers	Pearson Learning Group
Mickey Maloney's Mail	M	RF	250+	Sails	Rigby
Mickey's Secret	K	RF	250+	Rigby Literacy	Rigby
Microscope	C	I	46	Story Box	Wright Group/McGraw Hill
Middle Ages, The	R	I	250+	Journey Through History	Barron's Educational
Middle Moffat, The	T	RF	250+	Estes, Eleanor	Language for Learning Assoc.
Middle of Nowhere, The	K	RF	250+	Rigby Literacy	Rigby
Midge in the Hospital	E	RF	91	Oxford Reading Tree	Oxford University Press
Midnight Circus, The	WB	F	N/A	Collington, Peter	Alfred A. Knopf
Midnight Fox, The	R	RF	250+	Byars, Betsy	Scholastic
Midnight Horse, The	V	F	250+	Fleischman, Sid	Bantam

* Collection of short stories

TITLE	LEVEL	GENRE	WORD COUNT	AUTHOR / SERIES	PUBLISHER / DISTRIBUTOR
Midnight Magic	U	F	250+	Avi	Scholastic
Midnight on the Moon	M	F	250+	Osborne, Mary Pope	Random House
Midnight Pig, The	M	F	250+	Action Packs	Rigby
Midnight Rescue	N	RF	250+	Literacy Tree	Rigby
Midwife's Apprentice, The	X	HF	250+	Cushman, Karen	HarperTrophy
Mieko and the Fifth Treasure	O	HF	250+	Coerr, Eleanor	Bantam
Mighty Ironclads and Other Amazements	U	I	2454	Independent Readers Social Studies	Houghton Mifflin
Mighty Machines	I	I	127	Windows on Literacy	National Geographic
Mighty Mammals	Q	I	250+	Explorers	Wright Group/McGraw Hill
Mighty Maya, The	U	I	250+	Leveled Readers Language Support	Houghton Mifflin
Mighty, The	V	RF	250+	Philbrick, Rodman	Scholastic
Migration, The	D	I	45	Wonder World	Wright Group/McGraw Hill
Miguel Hidalgo, Father of Mexican Independence	Q	B	1145	Leveled Readers Social Studies	Houghton Mifflin
Mike and Tony: Best Friends	G	RF	171	Ziefert, Harriet	Penguin Group
Mike Ghost's Delicious Rainbow	F	F	157	TOTTS	Tott Publications
Mike Swan, Sink or Swim	J	RF	250+	Heiligman, Deborah	Bantam
Mike's Bike	J	RF	250+	Supersonics	Rigby
Mike's Bike	E	RF	82	Dominie Phonics Readers	Pearson Learning Group
Mike's First Haircut	G	RF	136	First Start	Troll Associates
Mike's New Bike	F	RF	183	First Start	Troll Associates
Mile High, A	K	F	331	Book Bank	Wright Group/McGraw Hill
Miles on the Mississippi	M	I	337	Independent Readers Social Studies	Houghton Mifflin
Military Helicopters	K	I	106	Mighty Machines	Capstone Press
Milking	F	RF	67	Wonder World	Wright Group/McGraw Hill
Milkshake Man, The	L	F	250+	Cole, Sally	Wright Group/McGraw Hill
Milkweed	Y	HF	250+	Spinelli, Jerry	Random House
Mill on the Hill, The	I	F	187	Supersonics	Rigby
Millard Fillmore	U	B	250+	Profiles of the Presidents	Compass Point Books
Millennium Prophecies	Z	I	250+	Innes, Brian	Steck-Vaughn
Miller Who Tried to Please Everyone, The	K	TL	250+	Aesop's Fables	Pearson Learning Group
Milo and the Fire Engine Parade	J	RF	250+	Bookshop	Mondo
Milo and the Greatest Trick Ever!	J	RF	250+	Bookshop	Mondo
Milo's Great Invention	M	RF	250+	Pair-It Books	Steck-Vaughn
Milton Hershey: Chocolate King Town Builder	P	B	250+	Simon, Charnan	Children's Press
Milton the Early Riser	J	F	148	Kraus, Robert	Aladdin
Milwaukee Cows	E	F	79	Story Box	Wright Group/McGraw Hill
Mina's Spring of Colors	S	RF	250+	Gilmore, Rachna	Fitzhenry & Whiteside
Minerva's Dream	M	F	250+	Pair-It Books	Steck-Vaughn
Mine's the Best	G	RF	104	Bonsall, Crosby	HarperCollins
Ming Lo Moves the Mountain	J	F	250+	Lobel, Arnold	Scholastic
Minh's New Life	L	RF	250+	PM Plus Story Books	Rigby
Mini Mammals	R	I	250+	Explorers	Wright Group/McGraw Hill
Minibeasts	Q	I	250+	The News	Richard C. Owen
Minnesota	R	I	250+	This Land Is Your Land	Compass Point Books
Minnie and Moo Go to Paris	J	F	250+	Cazet, Denys	DK Publishing
Minpins, The	P	F	250+	Dahl, Roald	Penguin Group
Min's Plane Ride	B	RF	49	Bookshop	Mondo
Min-Yo and the Moon Dragon	N	TL	250+	Hillman, Elizabeth	OSI
Miracle at the Plate	M	RF	250+	Christopher, Matt	Little, Brown & Co.
Miracle Worker, The	Z	B	250+	Gibson, William	Bantam

* Collection of short stories

TITLE	LEVEL	GENRE	WORD COUNT	AUTHOR / SERIES	PUBLISHER / DISTRIBUTOR
Miracle's Boys	Z	RF	250+	Woodson, Jacqueline	Penguin Group
Miracles on Maple Hill	R	RF	250+	Sorensen, Virginia	Scholastic
Miranda and the Movies	U	HF	250+	Kendall, Jane	OSI
Mirandy and Brother Wind	R	F	250+	McKissack, Patricia	Alfred A. Knopf
Miriam Dives Into a Good Book	N	F	653	Leveled Readers	Houghton Mifflin
Mirounga's Pup	L	RF	250+	Books for Young Learners	Richard C. Owen
Mirror Magic	C	RF	20	Harry's Math Books	Outside the Box
Mirror, The	D	RF	112	Story Box	Wright Group/McGraw Hill
Mischief	M	RF	250+	Pacific Literacy	Pacific Learning
Miserable Mill, The	V	F	250+	Snicket, Lemony	Scholastic
Misfortune Cookie, The	N	F	250+	The Zack Files	Grosset & Dunlap
Misha Disappears	K	RF	250+	Literacy 2000	Rigby
Mishi-Na	I	F	217	Sunshine	Wright Group/McGraw Hill
Mishmash	N	RF	250+	Cone, Molly	Pocket Books
Miss Geeta's Hair	D	F	44	Joy Readers	Pearson Learning Group
Miss Geneva's Lantern	P	RF	250+	Bookshop	Mondo
Miss Hen's Feast	I	F	434	Leveled Readers	Houghton Mifflin
Miss McKenzie Had a Farm	J	F	515	Pair-It Books	Steck-Vaughn
Miss Mouse Gets Married	K	TL	250+	Folk Tales	Wright Group/McGraw Hill
Miss Muffett and the Spider	I	F	270	Ready Readers	Pearson Learning Group
Miss Nelson Has a Field Day	L	RF	250+	Allard, Harry	Scholastic
Miss Nelson is Missing	L	RF	598	Allard, Harry	Houghton Mifflin
Miss Piggy's Night Out	J	F	250+	Hunter, Sandra H.	Puffin Books
Miss Popple's Pets	A	RF	28	Literacy 2000	Rigby
Miss Rumphius	M	RF	250+	Cooney, Barbara	Penguin Group
Missing Fossil Mystery, The	L	RF	250+	Herman, Emily	Hyperion
Missing 'Gator of Gumbo Limbo, The	S	RF	250+	George, Jean Craighead	HarperTrophy
Missing May	W	RF	250+	Rylant, Cynthia	Bantam
Missing Necklace, The	H	F	231	Reading Unlimited	Pearson Learning Group
Missing Osprey Nest, The	Q	RF	250+	Ragged Island Mysteries	Wright Group/McGraw Hill
Missing Parrot, The	J	RF	491	Early Connections	Benchmark Education
Missing Pet Mystery, The	H	RF	174	Instant Readers	Harcourt School Publishers
Missing Pet, The	K	RF	618	Pair-It Books	Steck-Vaughn
Missing Suit, The	H	F	250+	Phonics and Friends	Hampton-Brown
Missing Tooth, The	J	RF	250+	Cole, Joanna	Random House
Missing Will, The	M	RF	250+	Schultz, Irene	Wright Group/McGraw Hill
Mission Control	N	I	250+	Explore Space	Red Brick Learning
Mississippi	R	I	250+	This Land Is Your Land	Compass Point Books
Mississippi Bridge	S	HF	250+	Taylor, Mildred	Bantam
Missouri	R	I	250+	This Land Is Your Land	Compass Point Books
Misty of Chincoteague	R	RF	250+	Henry, Marguerite	Aladdin
Misty Sleeps	E	RF	56	Books for Young Learners	Richard C. Owen
Misty's Mischief	H	F	61	Campbell, Rod	Viking
Misty's Twilight	R	RF	250+	Henry, Marguerite	Aladdin
Mitch and Amy	O	RF	250+	Cleary, Beverly	HarperCollins
Mitch to the Rescue	I	RF	302	PM Story Books-Orange	Rigby
Mitchell Is Moving	J	F	250+	Sharmat, Marjorie Weinman	Simon & Schuster
Mitt for Me, A	B	RF	34	First Stories	Pacific Learning
Mitten, The	M	TL	250+	Brett, Jan	Scholastic
Mix It Up	C	I	35	Twig	Wright Group/McGraw Hill
Mix It Up!	C	I	44	Leveled Readers Science	Houghton Mifflin
Mix It Up!	D	I	52	Rigby Focus	Rigby
Mix, Make, and Munch	J	I	245	Home Connection Collection	Rigby
Mixed-up Max	Q	F	250+	King-Smith, Dick	Troll Associates

* Collection of short stories

TITLE	LEVEL	GENRE	WORD COUNT	AUTHOR / SERIES	PUBLISHER / DISTRIBUTOR
Mixed-Up Mystery, A	T	I	1541	Independent Readers Science	Houghton Mifflin
Mixed-Up Wigs, The	I	F	199	Leveled Readers	Houghton Mifflin
Mixing Colors	B	I	15	Rigby Literacy	Rigby
Mixing Things	C	I	51	Leveled Readers Science	Houghton Mifflin
Miyu and the Cranes for Peace	Q	RF	949	Leveled Readers	Houghton Mifflin
Mmm . . . Very Nice	E	F	91	Home Connection Collection	Rigby
Moana's Island	J	RF	450	Sunshine	Wright Group/McGraw Hill
Moccasin Trail	W	RF	250+	McGraw, Eloise	Scholastic
Moccasins	LB	I	20	Twig	Wright Group/McGraw Hill
Model, The	B	I	18	Smart Starts	Rigby
Models	G	I	231	Yellow Umbrella Books	Red Brick Learning
Modern Times	R	I	250+	Journey Through History	Barron's Educational
Mog at the Zoo	L	F	250+	Nicoll, Helen	Penguin Group
Moggy the Mouser	J	F	250+	Voyages	SRA/McGraw Hill
Mog's Mumps	L	F	250+	Nicoll, Helen	Penguin Group
Moki	Q	HF	250+	Penny, Grace Jackson	Penguin Group
*Mollie Whuppie	K	TL	250+	New Way Orange	Steck-Vaughn
Molly Learns a Lesson	Q	HF	250+	The American Girls Collection	Pleasant Company
Molly Makes a Graph	G	RF	110	Seedlings	Continental Press
Molly Pitcher: Young Patriot	O	B	250+	Childhood of Famous Americans	Aladdin
Molly Saves the Day	Q	HF	250+	The American Girls Collection	Pleasant Company
Molly the Brave and Me	K	RF	250+	O'Connor, Jane	Random House
Molly's Bracelet	I	RF	250+	Voyages	SRA/McGraw Hill
Molly's Broccoli	I	RF	233	Ready Readers	Pearson Learning Group
Molly's Hard Bargain	I	RF	180	Instant Readers	Harcourt School Publishers
Molly's Mailbox	F	RF	122	Teacher's Choice Series	Pearson Learning Group
Molly's Pilgrim	M	RF	250+	Cohen, Barbara	Bantam
Molly's Surprise	Q	HF	250+	The American Girls Collection	Pleasant Company
Mom	A	I	24	PM Starters	Rigby
Mom Can Fix Anything	D	RF	74	Learn to Read	Creative Teaching Press
Mom Dresses Up	A	RF	46	Mom and Dad Series	Pioneer Valley
Mom Goes Shopping	A	RF	34	Mom and Dad Series	Pioneer Valley
Mom Is a Painter	B	I	34	Bebop Books	Lee & Low Books Inc.
Mom Likes Hats	A	RF	40	Mom and Dad Series	Pioneer Valley
Mom Named Dad, A	L	RF	250+	Rigby Literacy	Rigby
Mom Paints the House	H	RF	220	Foundations	Wright Group/McGraw Hill
Mom, You're Fired!	O	RF	250+	Robinson, Nancy K.	Scholastic
Mommy, Where Are You?	B	RF	64	Ziefert, Harriet; Boon, Emilie	Puffin Books
Momotaro	M	F	631	Sunshine	Wright Group/McGraw Hill
Moms	B	RF	34	Handprints B	Educator's Publishing Service
Moms and Dads	A	I	36	PM Starters	Rigby
Mom's Birthday	I	RF	229	Sunshine	Wright Group/McGraw Hill
Mom's Diet	I	RF	228	Sunshine	Wright Group/McGraw Hill
Mom's Getting Married	K	RF	376	Sunshine	Wright Group/McGraw Hill
Mom's Haircut	H	RF	99	Literacy 2000	Rigby
Mom's Hat	C	RF	39	Joy Readers	Pearson Learning Group
Mom's New Car	D	RF	116	Foundations	Wright Group/McGraw Hill
Mom's Secret	H	RF	143	Costain, Meredith	Scholastic
Mom's Shoes	E	RF	133	Handprints C, Set 2	Educator's Publishing Service
Mom's Stories	D	RF	32	Vocabulary Readers	Houghton Mifflin
Monarch Butterflies	G	I	56	Pebble Books	Capstone Press
Monarch Butterfly	I	I	28	Book Bank	Wright Group/McGraw Hill

* Collection of short stories

TITLE	LEVEL	GENRE	WORD COUNT	AUTHOR / SERIES	PUBLISHER / DISTRIBUTOR
Monarch Butterfly	N	I	250+	Life Cycles	Creative Teaching Press
Monarch Butterfly, The	I	I	152	Foundations	Wright Group/McGraw Hill
Monday Came	K	RF	250+	Voyages	SRA/McGraw Hill
Mondo and Gordo Weather the Storm	L	F	759	Early Connections	Benchmark Education
Monet	S	B	250+	Masterpieces: Artists and Their Works	Red Brick Learning
Monet	R	B	250+	Venezia, Mike	Children's Press
Money	M	I	250+	Early Connections	Benchmark Education
Money	J	I	250+	Twig	Wright Group/McGraw Hill
Money	M	I	250+	Spyglass Books	Compass Point Books
Money Boot, The	N	RF	250+	Russell, Ginny	Fitzhenry & Whiteside
Money in My Pocket	G	I	133	Twig	Wright Group/McGraw Hill
Money Math	H	I	247	Yellow Umbrella Books	Red Brick Learning
Money Riddles That Count	K	I	250+	Fetty, Margaret	Steck-Vaughn
Money Saving and Spending	I	I	174	Rosen Real Readers	Rosen Publishing Group
Money, Money, Money!	O	I	250+	Bookweb	Rigby
Mongols, The	S	I	250+	Journey Into Civilization	Chelsea House
Monica and the Summer Party	M	RF	250+	Sunflower	Intercultural Center for Research in Education
Monica goes to the Zoo	M	RF	250+	Sunflower	Intercultural Center for Research in Education
Monkey and Fire	J	F	372	Literacy 2000	Rigby
Monkey Bridge, The	D	F	66	Sunshine	Wright Group/McGraw Hill
Monkey Hop, The	C	F	26	Joy Readers	Pearson Learning Group
Monkey Island	V	RF	250+	Fox, Paula	Orchard Books
Monkey Moves	B	I	16	Pair-It Books	Steck-Vaughn
Monkey on the Roof	D	RF	92	PM Plus Story Books	Rigby
Monkey See, Monkey Do	E	F	89	Gave, Marc	Scholastic
Monkey Tricks	H	RF	328	PM Turquoise	Rigby
Monkey Tricks	E	F	81	Joy Readers	Pearson Learning Group
Monkeys	B	I	27	Canizares, Susan; Chanko, Pamela	Scholastic
Monkeys	G	I	27	Reading Unlimited	Pearson Learning Group
Monkeys & Apes	K	I	250+	PM Animal Facts: Turquoise	Rigby
Monkey's Friends	C	F	36	Literacy 2000	Rigby
Monsoon Civilizations	V	I	2591	Independent Readers Social Studies	Houghton Mifflin
Monster	Z	RF	250+	Myers, Walter Dean	HarperCollins
Monster	I	F	201	Read Alongs	Rigby
Monster and the Baby	D	F	48	Mueller, Virginia	Puffin Books
Monster at the Beach, The	E	RF	82	Storyteller-Moon Rising	Wright Group/McGraw Hill
Monster Bus	F	F	103	The Monster Bus Series	Pearson Learning Group
Monster Bus Goes on a Hot Air Balloon Trip	I	F	254	The Monster Bus Series	Pearson Learning Group
Monster Bus Goes to the Races	H	F	158	The Monster Bus Series	Pearson Learning Group
Monster Bus Goes to Yellowstone Park	I	F	259	The Monster Bus Series	Pearson Learning Group
Monster Can't Sleep	D	F	52	Mueller, Virginia	Puffin Books
Monster for Hire	M	F	250+	Wilson, Trevor	Mondo
Monster from Mercury, The	L	F	250+	Popcorn	Sundance
Monster from the Sea, The	K	TL	250+	Bank Street	Bantam
Monster is Coming, The	K	F	250+	Rigby Literacy	Rigby
Monster Manners	J	F	250+	Cole, Joanna	Scholastic
Monster Math School Time	G	F	120	Maccarone, Grace	Scholastic
Monster Meals	C	F	33	Literacy 2000	Rigby
Monster Money	H	F	130	Maccarone, Grace	Scholastic
Monster Mop	LB	F	8	Ready Readers	Pearson Learning Group

* Collection of short stories

TITLE	LEVEL	GENRE	WORD COUNT	AUTHOR / SERIES	PUBLISHER / DISTRIBUTOR
Monster Movie	K	F	250+	Cole, Joanna	Scholastic
Monster of Mirror Mountain, The	K	F	250+	Literacy 2000	Rigby
Monster of the Year	S	F	250+	Coville, Bruce	Pocket Books
Monster Party	A	F	20	Smart Starts	Rigby
Monster Party	A	F	20	Literacy 2000	Rigby
Monster Party	A	F	29	Bookshop	Mondo
Monster Rabbit Runs Amuck!	M	RF	250+	Giff, Patricia Reilly	Bantam
Monster Sandwich, A	C	F	36	Story Box	Wright Group/McGraw Hill
Monster Soup	LB	F	33	Rigby Literacy	Rigby
Monster Stew	F	F	117	Learn to Read	Creative Teaching Press
Monster Trucks	M	I	250+	Blazers	Capstone Press
Monster Under The Bed, The	K	F	250+	Ready Readers	Pearson Learning Group
Monster, Monster	C	F	38	Reading Corners	Pearson Learning Group
Monster, The	D	RF	29	Harry's Math Books	Outside the Box
Monster, The	C	RF	83	Sun Sprouts	ETA/Cuisenaire
Monsters	C	F	30	TOTTS	Tott Publications
Monsters Don't Scuba Dive	M	F	250+	Dadey, Debbie; Jones, Marcia Thornton	Scholastic
Monster's New Friend, The	K	F	250+	Rigby Literacy	Rigby
Monsters Next Door, The	L	RF	250+	Dadey, Debbie; Jones, Marcia Thornton	Scholastic
Monsters of the Deep	L	I	250+	Swartz, Stanley L.	Pearson Learning Group
Monsters of the Myth	T	I	522	Vocabulary Readers	Houghton Mifflin
Monster's Party, The	C	F	92	Story Box	Wright Group/McGraw Hill
Monster's Ring, The	R	F	250+	Coville, Bruce	Pocket Books
Monsters' Tea Party, The	E	F	129	Learn to Read	Creative Teaching Press
Monsters!	D	F	45	My First Reader	Grolier Press
Montana	R	I	250+	This Land Is Your Land	Compass Point Books
Months	H	I	135	The Calendar	Capstone Press
Monticello	T	I	250+	We The People	Compass Point Books
Monticello	V	I	250+	Cornerstones of Freedom	Children's Press
Monty, the Missing Cat	E	RF	100	Developing Books	Pioneer Valley
Moon	S	I	250+	Our Solar System	Compass Point Books
Moon	F	RF	38	Books for Young Learners	Richard C. Owen
Moon and the Mirror, The	M	TL	250+	Literacy 2000	Rigby
Moon Boy	J	F	250+	Bank Street	Bantam
Moon Bridge, The	W	HF	250+	Savin, Marcia	Scholastic
Moon Cake, The	E	RF	127	Joy Readers	Pearson Learning Group
Moon Journal	L	RF	250+	Rigby Literacy	Rigby
Moon Over Tennessee: A Boy's Civil War Journal	W	B	250+	Crist-Evans, Craig	Houghton Mifflin
Moon Stories	J	F	250+	Ready Readers	Pearson Learning Group
Moon Story	E	RF	157	Sunshine	Wright Group/McGraw Hill
Moon, The	U	I	250+	A First Book	Franklin Watts
Moon, The	K	I	250+	Pebble Books	Red Brick Learning
Moon, The	D	F	139	Joy Readers	Pearson Learning Group
Moon, The	L	I	139	Twig	Wright Group/McGraw Hill
Moon, The	D	I	51	Rigby Focus	Rigby
Moon, The	N	I	250+	Literacy 2000	Rigby
Moon, The	Q	I	250+	Eye on the Universe	Crabtree
Moonbeam Cow	K	TL	228	Books for Young Learners	Richard C. Owen
Moonhorse	M	F	250+	Osborne, Mary Pope	Alfred A. Knopf
Moonlight	D	RF	48	Literacy 2000	Rigby
Moonlight on the River	R	RF	250+	Kovacs, Deborah	Penguin Group
Moonlit Owl, You	I	RF	225	Cambridge Reading	Pearson Learning Group

* Collection of short stories

TITLE	LEVEL	GENRE	WORD COUNT	AUTHOR / SERIES	PUBLISHER / DISTRIBUTOR
Moonwalk: The First Trip to the Moon	O	I	250+	Donnelly, Judy	Random House
Moose Is Loose, A	F	F	120	Little Readers	Houghton Mifflin
Moose, The	R	I	250+	Hemstock, Annie	Red Brick Learning
Moose's Loose Tooth	G	F	142	Spinelle, Mary Louise	Kaeden Books
Moppet on the Run	J	RF	250+	PM Story Books	Rigby
More Adventures of the Great Brain	T	RF	250+	Fitzgerald, John D.	Yearling
More and More Clowns	D	F	249	Van Allen, Roach	SRA/McGraw Hill
More Monsters in School	N	RF	250+	Godfrey, M.	Fitzhenry & Whiteside
More or Less Fish Story	E	F	68	Wylie, Joanne & David	Children's Press
More Perfect than the Moon	R	HF	250+	MacLachlan, Patricia	HarperCollins
More Perfect Union: The Story of Our Constitution	S	I	250+	Maestro, Betsy & Giulio	William Morrow
More Places to Visit	L	I	238	Windows on Literacy	National Geographic
More Spaghetti I Say	G	F	340	Gelman, Rita	Scholastic
More Spaghetti!	I	RF	250+	PM Plus Story Books	Rigby
*More Stories from Grandma's Attic	O	RF	250+	Richardson, Arleta	Chariot Victor Publishing
*More Stories Huey Tells	N	RF	250+	Cameron, Ann	Alfred A. Knopf
*More Stories Julian Tells	N	RF	250+	Cameron, Ann	Random House
*More Tales of Amanda Pig	L	F	1939	Van Leeuwen, Jean	Penguin Group
*More Tales of Oliver Pig	L	F	250+	Van Leeuwen, Jean	Puffin Books
More Than One	I	F	238	Sunshine	Wright Group/McGraw Hill
*More! More! More!	M	TL	250+	Story Box	Wright Group/McGraw Hill
Morgan's Zoo	Q	F	250+	Howe, James	Aladdin
Morning Bath	J	F	250+	Sunshine	Wright Group/McGraw Hill
Morning Dance, The	K	RF	268	Jellybeans	Rigby
Morning Girl	S	HF	250+	Dorris, Michael	Hyperion
Morning Queen, The	J	F	250+	Sunshine	Wright Group/McGraw Hill
Morning Star	J	F	250+	Literacy 2000	Rigby
Morris and Boris at the Circus	J	F	250+	Wiseman, Bernard	HarperTrophy
Morris Goes to School	J	F	250+	Wiseman, Bernard	HarperTrophy
Morris the Moose	H	F	250+	Wiseman, Bernard	HarperTrophy
Morse and the Telegraph	N	B	524	Leveled Readers Science	Houghton Mifflin
Mosquito	C	I	46	Book Bank	Wright Group/McGraw Hill
Mosquito Buzzed, A	E	F	133	Little Readers	Houghton Mifflin
Mosquitoes	E	I	39	Pebble Books	Grolier Press
Mossflower	Z	F	250+	Jacques, Brian	Ace Books
Most Beautiful Child, The	M	TL	250+	Cambridge Reading	Pearson Learning Group
Most Beautiful Place in the World, The	O	RF	250+	Cameron, Ann	Alfred A. Knopf
Most Scary Ghost	H	F	355	Jellybeans	Rigby
Most Terrible Creature in the World, The	M	F	340	Pacific Literacy	Pacific Learning
Most Wonderful Doll in the World, The	O	RF	250+	McGinley, Phyllis	Scholastic
Mostly Michael	Q	RF	250+	Smith, Robert Kimmel	Bantam
Mother and Me	B	RF	48	Spinelle, Nancy Louise	Kaeden Books
Mother Bird	C	RF	75	PM Plus Story Books	Rigby
Mother Hen	G	F	205	Book Bank	Wright Group/McGraw Hill
Mother Hippopotamus	A	F	7	Foundations	Wright Group/McGraw Hill
Mother Hippopotamus Gets Wet	J	F	421	Foundations	Wright Group/McGraw Hill
Mother Hippopotamus Goes Canoeing	L	F	250+	Foundations	Wright Group/McGraw Hill
Mother Hippopotamus Goes Shopping	C	F	79	Foundations	Wright Group/McGraw Hill
Mother Hippopotamus's Dry Skin	I	F	201	Foundations	Wright Group/McGraw Hill
Mother Hippopotamus's Hiccups	I	F	162	Foundations	Wright Group/McGraw Hill
Mother Octopus	J	RF	119	Books for Young Learners	Richard C. Owen
Mother Sea Turtle	K	I	240	Foundations	Wright Group/McGraw Hill
Mother Sun's Rest Day	H	F	250+	Momentum Literacy Program	Troll Associates

* Collection of short stories

TITLE	LEVEL	GENRE	WORD COUNT	AUTHOR / SERIES	PUBLISHER / DISTRIBUTOR
Mother Teresa	M	B	250+	First Biographies	Red Brick Learning
Mother Tiger and Her Cubs	G	F	212	PM Plus Story Books	Rigby
Mothers	B	I	26	Pebble Books	Capstone Press
Mother's Day	F	I	128	Fiesta Holiday Series	Pearson Learning Group
Mother's Day	E	RF	118	PM Plus Story Books	Rigby
Mother's Helpers	K	RF	250+	Ready Readers	Pearson Learning Group
Moths	I	I	102	Bugs, Bugs, Bugs	Capstone Press
Moths	I	I	65	Pebble Books	Red Brick Learning
Motion	Q	I	250+	Simply Science	Compass Point Books
Motion	N	I	250+	Our Physical World	Capstone Press
Motion	I	I	155	Instant Readers	Harcourt School Publishers
Motion: Push and Pull, Fast and Slow	N	I	250+	Amazing Science	Picture Window Books
Motorbike Race, The	C	RF	48	Joy Readers	Pearson Learning Group
Motorcross Freestyle	M	I	250+	Blazers	Capstone Press
Motorcycle Photo, The	J	RF	250+	PM Plus Story Books	Rigby
Motorcycle Police	S	I	250+	Law Enforcement	Capstone Press
Mound Builders, The	P	I	426	Independent Readers Social Studies	Houghton Mifflin
Mound of the Dead: The City of Mohenjo-Daro	X	I	2018	Independent Readers Social Studies	Houghton Mifflin
Mount Rushmore	Q	I	250+	Let's See	Compass Point Books
Mount St. Helens	O	I	250+	Early Connections	Benchmark Education
Mount Vernon	V	I	250+	Cornerstones of Freedom	Children's Press
Mountain Bike Challenge, The	Q	I	250+	Morgan, Patrick	Pacific Learning
Mountain Bike Mania	O	RF	250+	Action Packs	Rigby
Mountain Gorillas	O	I	250+	Wonder World	Wright Group/McGraw Hill
Mountain Gorillas in Danger	N	I	250+	Soar To Success	Houghton Mifflin
Mountain Hike, The	F	RF	176	Developing Books, Set 2	Pioneer Valley
Mountain Lion, The	O	I	250+	Crewe, Sabrina	Steck-Vaughn
Mountain Man and the President, The	Q	B	250+	First Reports	Compass Point Books
Mountain Men of the West	S	I	250+	The Library of the Westward Expansion	Rosen Publishing Group
Mountains	L	I	250+	Early Connections	Benchmark Education
Mountains	Q	I	250+	First Reports	Compass Point Books
Mountains	S	I	250+	Weitzman, David	Steck-Vaughn
Mountains of Fire	M	I	153	Windows on Literacy	National Geographic
Mountains of Quilt, The	N	F	250+	Willard, Nancy	OSI
Mountains, Hills, and Cliffs	M	I	250+	PM Plus Nonfiction	Rigby
Mounted Police	S	I	250+	Law Enforcement	Capstone Press
Mouse	C	F	40	Story Box	Wright Group/McGraw Hill
Mouse and Owl	I	RF	250+	Start to Read	School Zone
Mouse and the Elephant, The	J	TL	250+	Little Readers	Houghton Mifflin
Mouse and the Motorcycle, The	O	F	250+	Cleary, Beverly	Avon Camelot
Mouse Around	WB	F	N/A	Collington, Peter	Alfred A. Knopf
Mouse Called Wolf, A	O	F	250+	King-Smith, Dick	Alfred A. Knopf
Mouse Deer and the Crocodiles, The	J	TL	250+	PM Plus Story Books	Rigby
Mouse Deer Escapes, The	J	TL	250+	PM Plus Story Books	Rigby
Mouse Finds a House	D	F	72	Start to Read	School Zone
Mouse in the Forest, The	I	I	211	Leveled Readers	Houghton Mifflin
Mouse Magic	O	RF	250+	Baglio, Ben M.	Scholastic
Mouse Manual	M	F	250+	Sails	Rigby
Mouse Monster	J	F	302	Jellybeans	Rigby
Mouse of Amherst, The	Q	F	250+	Spires, Elizabeth	Farrar, Straus and Giroux
Mouse Party!	M	F	250+	Little Celebrations	Pearson Learning Group

* Collection of short stories

TITLE	LEVEL	GENRE	WORD COUNT	AUTHOR / SERIES	PUBLISHER / DISTRIBUTOR
Mouse Rap, The	W	RF	250+	Myers, Walter Dean	HarperTrophy
*Mouse Soup	J	F	1350	Lobel, Arnold	HarperCollins
*Mouse Tales	J	F	1519	Lobel, Arnold	HarperCollins
Mouse Train	B	F	48	Story Box	Wright Group/McGraw Hill
Mouse Views	LB	RF	12	McMillan, Bruce	Holiday House
Mouse Who Wanted to Marry, The	J	F	250+	Bank Street	Bantam
Mouse, The	C	F	26	Pacific Literacy	Pacific Learning
Mouse's Baby Blanket	D	F	68	Brown, Beverly Swerdlow	Continental Press
Mouse's House	D	F	70	New Way Red	Steck-Vaughn
Mouse's Meadow	C	I	62	Independent Readers Science	Houghton Mifflin
Mousetrap	G	RF	49	Snowball, Diane	Scholastic
Move it	E	I	58	Wonder World	Wright Group/McGraw Hill
Move It!	L	I	268	Spyglass Books	Compass Point Books
Move Like Us!	H	RF	250+	Home Connection Collection	Rigby
Move Over!	E	F	118	Story Basket	Wright Group/McGraw Hill
Moves Make the Man, The	Z	RF	250+	Brooks, Bruce	HarperTrophy
Movie Magic	T	I	250+	Sunshine	Wright Group/McGraw Hill
Moving	B	I	56	Little Red Readers	Sundance
Moving Day	C	RF	28	Rigby Literacy	Rigby
Moving Day	G	RF	215	Momentum Literacy Program	Troll Associates
Moving Day	D	RF	90	Foundations	Wright Group/McGraw Hill
Moving Day	E	RF	110	Sunshine	Wright Group/McGraw Hill
Moving In	E	RF	82	Foundations	Wright Group/McGraw Hill
Moving Mama to Town	X	RF	250+	Young, Ronder Thomas	Bantam
Moving Things	M	I	250+	Sunshine	Wright Group/McGraw Hill
Moving to America	E	RF	81	Carousel Readers	Pearson Learning Group
Mr. and Mrs. Murphy and Bernard	K	F	250+	Little Celebrations	Pearson Learning Group
Mr. Ape	O	F	250+	King-Smith, Dick	Alfred A. Knopf
Mr. Beekman's Deli	H	F	96	Story Basket	Wright Group/McGraw Hill
Mr. Beep	M	F	250+	Read Alongs	Rigby
Mr. Bitter's Butter	H	F	231	Story Basket	Wright Group/McGraw Hill
Mr. Brown	C	RF	20	KinderReaders	Rigby
Mr. Bumbleticker	B	F	28	Foundations	Wright Group/McGraw Hill
Mr. Bumbleticker Goes Shopping	J	F	391	Foundations	Wright Group/McGraw Hill
Mr. Bumbleticker Goes to the Zoo	L	RF	250+	Foundations	Wright Group/McGraw Hill
Mr. Bumbleticker Likes to Cook	I	F	196	Foundations	Wright Group/McGraw Hill
Mr. Bumbleticker Likes to Fix Machines	I	F	142	Foundations	Wright Group/McGraw Hill
Mr. Bumbleticker's Apples	I	F	338	Foundations	Wright Group/McGraw Hill
Mr. Bumbleticker's Birthday	E	F	110	Foundations	Wright Group/McGraw Hill
Mr. Clutterbus	H	F	250+	Voyages	SRA/McGraw Hill
Mr. Crawford	E	RF	119	Foundations	Wright Group/McGraw Hill
Mr. Cricket Finds a Friend	G	F	134	Carousel Readers	Pearson Learning Group
Mr. Cricket Takes a Vacation	E	F	165	Carousel Readers	Pearson Learning Group
Mr. Cricket's New Home	F	F	121	Carousel Readers	Pearson Learning Group
Mr. Egg	E	F	22	Pair-It Books	Steck-Vaughn
Mr. Fahrenheit and Mr. Celsius	T	I	1330	Leveled Readers Science	Houghton Mifflin
Mr. Fin's Trip	E	F	130	Ready Readers	Pearson Learning Group
Mr. Fixit	H	RF	196	Sunshine	Wright Group/McGraw Hill
Mr. Fizzle, the Man Who Went "Boo!"	I	F	250+	Home Connection Collection	Rigby
Mr. Grump	D	F	73	Sunshine	Wright Group/McGraw Hill
Mr. Gumpy's Motor Car	L	RF	250+	Burningham, John	HarperCollins
Mr. Gumpy's Outing	L	RF	283	Burningham, John	Henry Holt & Co.
Mr. Hoot's Room	J	F	250+	The Wright Skills	Wright Group/McGraw Hill
Mr. Lincoln's Drummer	W	HF	250+	Wisler, G. Clifton	Penguin Group

* Collection of short stories

TITLE	LEVEL	GENRE	WORD COUNT	AUTHOR / SERIES	PUBLISHER / DISTRIBUTOR
Mr. Mancini's Rats	K	F	250+	Popcorn	Sundance
Mr. McCready's Cleaning Day	H	F	119	Shilling, Tracy	Scholastic
Mr. McGillicuddy's Clocks	M	RF	250+	Voyages	SRA/McGraw Hill
Mr. McGrah's New Car	H	F	119	Book Bank	Wright Group/McGraw Hill
Mr. Merton's Vacation	K	RF	250+	Sails	Rigby
Mr. Miller's Old Car	F	RF	108	Seedlings	Continental Press
Mr. Mulch's Magic Mixtures	L	F	250+	Cambridge Reading	Pearson Learning Group
Mr. Mysterious & Company	R	F	250+	Fleischman, Sid	Beech Tree Books
Mr. Noisy	D	F	90	Learn to Read	Creative Teaching Press
Mr. Noisy Builds a House	D	F	35	Learn to Read	Creative Teaching Press
Mr. Noisy Paints His House	E	F	159	Learn to Read	Creative Teaching Press
Mr. Noisy's Book of Patterns	G	F	47	Learn to Read	Creative Teaching Press
Mr. Noisy's Helpers	F	F	81	Learn to Read	Creative Teaching Press
Mr. Pepperpot's Pet	K	F	250+	Literacy 2000	Rigby
Mr. Popper's Penguins	Q	F	250+	Atwater, Richard & Florence	Dell
Mr. Potter's Pet	N	F	250+	King-Smith, Dick	Hyperion
*Mr. President: A Book of U.S. Presidents	S	B	250+	Sullivan, George	Scholastic
Mr. Putter & Tabby Row the Boat	J	RF	250+	Rylant, Cynthia	Harcourt Trade
Mr. Putter & Tabby Take the Train	J	RF	250+	Rylant, Cynthia	Harcourt Trade
Mr. Putter & Tabby Toot the Horn	J	RF	250+	Rylant, Cynthia	Harcourt Trade
Mr. Putter and Tabby Bake the Cake	J	RF	250+	Rylant, Cynthia	Harcourt Trade
Mr. Putter and Tabby Fly the Plane	J	RF	250+	Rylant, Cynthia	Harcourt Trade
Mr. Putter and Tabby Pick the Pears	J	RF	250+	Rylant, Cynthia	Harcourt Trade
Mr. Putter and Tabby Pour the Tea	J	RF	250+	Rylant, Cynthia	Harcourt Trade
Mr. Putter and Tabby Walk the Dog	J	RF	250+	Rylant, Cynthia	Harcourt Trade
Mr. Rabbit and the Moon	F	F	137	New Way Red	Steck-Vaughn
Mr. Revere and I	U	F	250+	Lawson, Robert	Little, Brown & Co.
Mr. Smarty Loves to Party	F	F	101	Storyteller-Moon Rising	Wright Group/McGraw Hill
Mr. Sun and Mr. Sea	L	F	506	Sunshine	Wright Group/McGraw Hill
Mr. Sun and Mr. Sea	I	F	202	Little Celebrations	Pearson Learning Group
Mr. Tucket	U	HF	250+	Paulsen, Gary	Bantam
Mr. Verdi's New Path	I	F	250+	Home Connection Collection	Rigby
Mr. Whisper	H	F	325	Sunshine	Wright Group/McGraw Hill
Mr. Wind	F	F	37	Literacy 2000	Rigby
Mr. Wink	E	F	86	Ready Readers	Pearson Learning Group
Mr. Wolf	D	F	48	Joy Readers	Pearson Learning Group
Mr. Wolf Leaves Town	H	TL	208	Alphakids	Sundance
Mr. Wolf Tries Again	H	TL	218	Alphakids	Sundance
Mr. Wumple's Travels	I	F	259	Read Alongs	Rigby
Mrs. Always Goes Shopping	M	RF	423	Sunshine	Wright Group/McGraw Hill
Mrs. Barnett's Birthday	I	RF	135	Sunshine	Wright Group/McGraw Hill
Mrs. Bold	F	RF	94	Literacy 2000	Rigby
Mrs. Brice's Mice	I	F	250+	Hoff, Syd	HarperTrophy
Mrs. Bubble's Baby	M	F	250+	Pacific Literacy	Pacific Learning
Mrs. Cheng's Surprise	G	RF	186	Leveled Readers	Houghton Mifflin
Mrs. Cook's Hats	LB	RF	31	Mader, Jan	Kaeden Books
Mrs. Frisby and the Rats of NIMH	V	F	250+	O'Brien, Robert C.	Aladdin
Mrs. Grindy's Shoes	I	F	211	Sunshine	Wright Group/McGraw Hill
Mrs. Honey's List	J	RF	250+	Voyages	SRA/McGraw Hill
Mrs. Huggins and Her Hen Hannah	K	F	250+	Dabcovich, Lydia	Dutton
Mrs. Jeepers' Batty Vacation	L	RF	250+	Dadey, Debbie; Jones, Marcia Thornton	Scholastic
Mrs. Jeepers in Outer Space	M	RF	250+	Dadey, Debbie; Jones, Marcia Thornton	Scholastic

* Collection of short stories

TITLE	LEVEL	GENRE	WORD COUNT	AUTHOR / SERIES	PUBLISHER / DISTRIBUTOR
Mrs. Keen	G	RF	88	City Stories	Rigby
Mrs. Lunch	LB	F	17	Joy Readers	Pearson Learning Group
Mrs. McNosh Hangs Up Her Wash	H	F	166	Little Celebrations	Pearson Learning Group
Mrs. Mog's Cats	F	F	124	Rigby Literacy	Rigby
Mrs. Muddle's Mud-Puddle	I	F	181	Sunshine	Wright Group/McGraw Hill
Mrs. Murphy's Bears	I	RF	188	Little Readers	Houghton Mifflin
Mrs. Murphy's Crows	H	RF	120	Books for Young Learners	Richard C. Owen
Mrs. Patches and Her Fudge	J	F	250+	The Wright Skills	Wright Group/McGraw Hill
*Mrs. Piggle-Wiggle	O	F	250+	MacDonald, Betty	Scholastic
*Mrs. Piggle-Wiggle's Farm	O	F	250+	MacDonald, Betty	Scholastic
*Mrs. Piggle-Wiggle's Magic	O	F	250+	MacDonald, Betty	Scholastic
Mrs. Pomelili's Wet Week	G	F	215	Book Bank	Wright Group/McGraw Hill
Mrs. Sato's Hens	D	F	51	Little Readers	Houghton Mifflin
Mrs. Sato's Hens	D	F	51	Little Celebrations	Pearson Learning Group
Mrs. Sheep's Garden	K	F	953	Kratky, Lada	Hampton-Brown
Mrs. Spider's Beautiful Web	H	F	250+	PM Story Books	Rigby
Mrs. Tuck's Little Tune	F	RF	195	Ready Readers	Pearson Learning Group
Mrs. Wishy Washy	E	F	102	Story Box	Wright Group/McGraw Hill
Mrs. Wishy-Washy's Tub	B	F	38	Story Box	Wright Group/McGraw Hill
Mt. St. Helens	S	I	1492	Independent Readers Science	Houghton Mifflin
Much Ado About Aldo	O	RF	250+	Hurwitz, Johanna	Penguin Group
Mud	B	RF	30	Science	Outside the Box
Mud	D	RF	68	Lewison, Wendy Cheyette	Random House
Mud Pie	C	RF	14	Literacy 2000	Rigby
Mud Pies	E	RF	143	Start to Read	School Zone
Mud Pies	C	RF	56	TOTTS	Tott Publications
Mud Pony, The	L	TL	764	Sunshine	Wright Group/McGraw Hill
Mud Pony, The	M	TL	250+	Reading Rainbow	Scholastic
Mud Puddles	C	RF	24	TOTTS	Tott Publications
Mud Walk	E	F	183	Story Box	Wright Group/McGraw Hill
Mud!	D	RF	68	Lewison, Wendy Cheyette	Scholastic
Mud, Mud, Mud	G	I	83	Windows on Literacy	National Geographic
Muddledy Fuddledy Mixed-Up Day, The	M	F	250+	Redhead, Janet Slater	Steck-Vaughn
Mudskipper	G	I	132	Twig	Wright Group/McGraw Hill
Mufaro's Beautiful Daughters: An African Tale	N	TL	250+	Steptoe, John	Scholastic
Muffin Is Trapped	J	RF	250+	PM Story Books	Rigby
Muffy and Fluffy	F	RF	155	First Start	Troll Associates
Muffy's Secret Admirer	M	RF	250+	Brown, Marc	Little, Brown & Co.
Muggie Maggie	O	RF	250+	Cleary, Beverly	Avon Camelot
Multi-Tasker, The	V	RF	3226	Leveled Readers	Houghton Mifflin
Mumbo Jumbo's Shoes	I	F	130	Book Bus	Creative Edge
Mummies	M	I	250+	All Aboard Reading	Grosset & Dunlap
Mummies and Their Mysteries	X	I	250+	Wilcox, Charlotte	Carolrhoda Books
Mummies Don't Coach Softball	M	F	250+	Dadey, Debbie; Jones, Marcia Thornton	Scholastic
Mummies in the Morning	M	F	250+	Osborne, Mary Pope	Random House
Mummies Made in Egypt	R	I	250+	Aliki	HarperCollins
Mummy's Curse, The	O	F	250+	SupaDoopers	Sundance
Mummy's Gold, The	L	F	250+	McMullan, Kate	Grosset & Dunlap
Mumps	D	RF	112	PM Story Books	Rigby
Mumps	D	RF	108	Carousel Readers	Pearson Learning Group
Munching Mark	G	RF	88	Tadpoles	Rigby
Munching Monster	I	F	261	Storyteller-Moon Rising	Wright Group/McGraw Hill
Mural, The	F	I	262	Visions	Wright Group/McGraw Hill

* Collection of short stories

TITLE	LEVEL	GENRE	WORD COUNT	AUTHOR / SERIES	PUBLISHER / DISTRIBUTOR
Mural, The	O	RF	801	Leveled Readers	Houghton Mifflin
Murals for Joy	N	RF	745	Leveled Readers	Houghton Mifflin
Muscles: Our Muscular System	T	I	250+	Simon, Seymour	HarperTrophy
Muscular System, The	K	I	131	Human Body Systems	Red Brick Learning
Museum, The	D	RF	41	Sunshine	Wright Group/McGraw Hill
Mushrooms and Other Fungi	P	I	250+	Sunshine	Wright Group/McGraw Hill
Mushrooms for Dinner	G	F	177	PM Story Books	Rigby
Music Counts	P	I	250+	Navigators Math Series	Benchmark Education
Music Machine, The	G	F	231	Sunshine	Wright Group/McGraw Hill
Music of Dolphins, The	V	RF	250+	Hesse, Karen	Scholastic
Music of Tito Puente, The	J	B	127	Vocabulary Readers	Houghton Mifflin
Music Students	E	RF	83	Dominie Phonics Reader	Pearson Learning Group
Mustangs	U	I	250+	Gillespie, Lorraine	Red Brick Learning
Mutt and the Lifeguards	M	RF	754	Sunshine	Wright Group/McGraw Hill
My Accident	C	RF	46	PM Starters	Rigby
My Apartment	LB	RF	20	Visions	Wright Group/McGraw Hill
My Apple Tree	D	I	48	Yellow Umbrella Books	Red Brick Learning
My Baby	D	F	64	Storyteller-First Snow	Wright Group/McGraw Hill
My Backpack	B	I	72	First Stories	Pacific Learning
My Backyard	LB	I	14	Little Books for Early Readers	University of Maine
My Balloon Man	C	I	56	First Stories	Pacific Learning
My Bean Plant	H	I	146	Windows on Literacy	National Geographic
My Bed	E	RF	65	Book Bus	Creative Edge
My Bed Is Soft	B	I	42	Windows on Literacy	National Geographic
My Best Friend	I	RF	147	Hutchins, Pat	Greenwillow
My Best Friend	C	RF	28	Little Celebrations	Pearson Learning Group
My Best Friend	C	RF	63	Carousel Readers	Pearson Learning Group
My Best Sandwich	D	RF	25	Hartley, Susan; Armstrong, Shane	Scholastic
My Big Box	D	RF	94	Voyages	SRA/McGraw Hill
My Big Brother	E	I	103	PM Nonfiction-Yellow	Rigby
My Big Rock	B	RF	42	Bebop Books	Lee & Low Books Inc.
My Big Surprise	H	F	139	Instant Readers	Harcourt School Publishers
My Big Wheel	C	RF	38	Visions	Wright Group/McGraw Hill
My Bike	D	I	42	Pacific Literacy	Pacific Learning
My Bike	D	I	38	Storyteller-First Snow	Wright Group/McGraw Hill
My Birthday Party	LB	RF	16	Little Readers	Houghton Mifflin
My Birthday Party	C	RF	38	Visions	Wright Group/McGraw Hill
My Birthday Surprise	G	RF	153	Foundations	Wright Group/McGraw Hill
My Black Cat	C	RF	52	Early Emergent	Pioneer Valley
My Boat	G	RF	133	Sunshine	Wright Group/McGraw Hill
My Body	D	I	250+	Sun Sprouts	ETA/Cuisenaire
My Body	M	I	250+	Schaefer, Lola M.	Benchmark Education
My Body	C	I	47	Discovery World	Rigby
My Body Works	E	I	131	Twig	Wright Group/McGraw Hill
My Book	C	RF	32	Sunshine	Wright Group/McGraw Hill
My Book	C	RF	63	PM Plus Story Books	Rigby
My Book	A	RF	17	Maris, Ron	Viking
My Box	WB	RF	N/A	Instant Readers	Harcourt School Publishers
My Box	A	RF	94	Smart Starts	Rigby
My Box	D	RF	94	Books for Young Learners	Richard C. Owen
My Breakfast	D	RF	54	Lighthouse	Rigby
My Brother	D	RF	51	Rise & Shine	Hampton-Brown
My Brother is a Superhero	S	RF	250+	Sheldon, Dyan	Candlewick Press
My Brother is a Visitor From Another Planet	S	RF	250+	Sheldon, Dyan	Candlewick Press

* Collection of short stories

TITLE	LEVEL	GENRE	WORD COUNT	AUTHOR / SERIES	PUBLISHER / DISTRIBUTOR
*My Brother Louis Measures Worms and Other Louis Stories	T	RF	250+	Robinson, Barbara	HarperTrophy
My Brother Sam is Dead	Y	HF	250+	Collier, James & Christopher	Scholastic
My Brother Wants to Be Like Me	D	RF	62	Mader, Jan	Kaeden Books
My Brother, Ant	J	RF	250+	Byars, Betsy	Viking
My Brother, My Sister, and I	V	HF	250+	Watkins, Yoko Kawashima	Aladdin
My Brother, Owen	I	RF	150	Book Bank	Wright Group/McGraw Hill
My Brother, the Brat	E	RF	62	Hello Reader	Scholastic
My Brother, the Knight	M	RF	250+	Social Studies Connects	The Kane Press
My Brother, the Spy	N	RF	250+	SupaDoopers	Sundance
My Brother's Motorcycle	D	RF	45	Visions	Wright Group/McGraw Hill
My Brown Bear Barney	H	RF	82	Butler, Dorothy	Morrow
My Brown Cow	D	I	62	Story Box	Wright Group/McGraw Hill
My Buddy	B	RF	32	First Stories	Pacific Learning
My Buddy, My Friend	D	RF	33	Visions	Wright Group/McGraw Hill
My Bug Box	E	RF	99	Books for Young Learners	Pacific Learning
My Busy Day	B	RF	41	Early Emergent	Pioneer Valley
My Calculator Book	E	RF	50	Gosset, Rachel; Ballinger, Margaret	Scholastic
My Camera	C	RF	41	Rigby Literacy	Rigby
My Cat	A	RF	28	Leveled Readers Science	Houghton Mifflin
My Cat	D	RF	40	Ready Readers	Pearson Learning Group
My Cat	A	I	37	Early Connections	Benchmark Education
My Cat	D	I	42	Sunshine	Wright Group/McGraw Hill
My Cat	A	RF	47	First Stories	Pacific Learning
My Cat	F	RF	42	My World	Steck-Vaughn
My Cat	A	RF	28	Leveled Readers	Houghton Mifflin
My Cat	B	RF	47	Lighthouse	Rigby
My Cat	H	I	79	Taylor, Judy	Macmillan
My Cat Muffin	C	RF	35	Gardner, Marjory	Scholastic
My Cat Sam	H	F	147	Supersonics	Rigby
My Cats	A	RF	41	Robinson, Eileen	Scholastic
*My Cat's Surprise	D	RF	71	New Way Blue	Steck-Vaughn
My Chair	B	RF	24	Pacific Literacy	Pacific Learning
My Circus Family	C	F	42	Bookshop	Mondo
My Circus Friend	C	F	42	Lake, Mary Dixon	Mondo
My City	C	I	99	Rigby Literacy	Rigby
My Class	LB	I	14	Stewart, Josie; Salem, Lynn	Continental Press
My Classroom	A	I	31	At School Series	Pioneer Valley
My Clock is Sick	D	F	45	Ready Readers	Pearson Learning Group
My Clothes	LB	I	12	Vocabulary Readers	Houghton Mifflin
My Clothes	B	RF	36	PM Plus Starters	Rigby
My Clothes	C	RF	86	Foundations	Wright Group/McGraw Hill
My Clothes	LB	RF	16	Carousel Earlybirds	Pearson Learning Group
My Color	B	I	22	Mann, Rachel	Scholastic
My Computer	F	I	76	Wonder World	Wright Group/McGraw Hill
My Cousin Jake	H	RF	123	City Stories	Rigby
My Dad	E	I	114	PM Nonfiction-Yellow	Rigby
My Dad	F	I	79	Talk About Books	Pearson Learning Group
My Dad and I	B	RF	52	Handprints B	Educator's Publishing Service
My Dad Cooks	C	RF	29	Carousel Readers	Pearson Learning Group
My Dad Has Asthma	I	I	138	Wonder World	Wright Group/McGraw Hill
My Dad Lost His Job	E	RF	76	Carousel Readers	Pearson Learning Group

* Collection of short stories

TITLE	LEVEL	GENRE	WORD COUNT	AUTHOR / SERIES	PUBLISHER / DISTRIBUTOR
My Dad's Truck	E	I	57	Costain, Merideth	Scholastic
My Daniel	T	HF	250+	Conrad, Pam	HarperTrophy
My Darling Kitten	WB	RF	N/A	Collington, Peter	Alfred A. Knopf
My Day	B	RF	24	Sunshine	Wright Group/McGraw Hill
My Day	C	RF	51	Barney, Mike	Kaeden Books
My Day	C	RF	44	Rise & Shine	Hampton-Brown
My Dog	C	I	46	Vocabulary Readers	Houghton Mifflin
My Dog	D	I	51	Sunshine	Wright Group/McGraw Hill
My Dog	G	RF	79	My World	Steck-Vaughn
My Dog	C	RF	79	Early Emergent	Pioneer Valley
My Dog	A	RF	72	Instant Readers	Harcourt School Publishers
My Dog	G	I	72	Taylor, Judy	Macmillan
My Dog	D	RF	38	Visions	Wright Group/McGraw Hill
My Dog and I	B	RF	55	Lighthouse	Rigby
*My Dog and Other Stories	I	RF	250+	Story Steps	Rigby
My Dog Ben	C	RF	19	Voyages	SRA/McGraw Hill
My Dog Fuzzy	B	RF	27	Books for Young Learners/ Emergent	Richard C. Owen
My Dog Rusty	G	RF	75	City Stories	Rigby
My Dog Talks	E	RF	250+	Herman, Gail	Scholastic
My Dog Willy	C	RF	71	Little Readers	Houghton Mifflin
My Dog, Miffy	D	RF	38	Visions	Wright Group/McGraw Hill
My Dog's the Best	F	RF	175	Calmenson, Stephanie	Scholastic
My Doll	A	F	32	Sun Sprouts	ETA/Cuisenaire
My Doll	E	RF	86	Yukish, Joe	Kaeden Books
My Dream	C	RF	34	Wildsmith, Brian	Oxford University Press
My Dream of Martin Luther King	R	I	250+	Ringgold, Faith	Crown
My Faces	E	RF	62	Rhythm 'N' Rhyme Readers	Pearson Learning Group
My Family	LB	I	12	Vocabulary Readers	Houghton Mifflin
My Family	B	RF	46	First Stories	Pacific Learning
My Family	B	RF	87	Carousel Earlybirds	Pearson Learning Group
My Family	A	RF	28	Sunshine	Wright Group/McGraw Hill
My Family	A	RF	28	Leveled Readers Social Studies	Houghton Mifflin
My Family	D	I	88	Leveled Readers	Houghton Mifflin
My Family	B	RF	31	Bebop Books	Lee & Low Books Inc.
My Family & the Wasps	N	F	250+	Parker, John	Pearson Learning Group
My Family Band	C	RF	50	Instant Readers	Harcourt School Publishers
My Family Has Fun	A	RF	28	Leveled Readers Emergent	Houghton Mifflin
My Family Keeps Fit	G	RF	98	Windows on Literacy	National Geographic
My Family Split Up	H	RF	85	City Kids	Rigby
My Family Tree	I	I	229	Windows on Literacy	National Geographic
My Family Tree	D	I	107	Story Steps	Rigby
My Farm	N	RF	250+	Lester, Alison	Houghton Mifflin
My Father	J	RF	194	Mayer, Laura	Scholastic
My Father The Mad Professor	P	F	250+	Action Packs	Rigby
My Father's Dragon	N	F	250+	Gannett, Ruth Stiles	Random House
My Favorite Bear	J	I	146	Books for Young Learners	Richard C. Owen
My Favorite Days	J	I	250+	Rigby Literacy	Rigby
My Favorite Foods	I	RF	100	Early Readers	Compass Point Books
My Feet	B	I	25	Twig	Wright Group/McGraw Hill
My Feet Are Just Right	I	I	220	Sunshine	Wright Group/McGraw Hill
My First Book About the Internet	M	I	250+	Cromwell, Sharon	Troll Associates
*My First Book of Biographies: Great Men and Women Every Child Should Know	P	B	250+	Marzollo, Jean	Scholastic

* Collection of short stories

TITLE	LEVEL	GENRE	WORD COUNT	AUTHOR / SERIES	PUBLISHER / DISTRIBUTOR
My First Business: Lemonade Stand	K	RF	548	Leveled Readers Social Studies	Houghton Mifflin
My First Snow	F	I	127	Independent Readers Science	Houghton Mifflin
My Fish	A	RF	24	Phonics and Friends	Hampton-Brown
My Fish Are Fine with Me	G	RF	78	City Stories	Rigby
My Fish Bowl	B	I	29	Foundations	Wright Group/McGraw Hill
My Fish Does Not Chirp	E	I	77	Ready Readers	Pearson Learning Group
My Fish Tank	J	I	238	Windows on Literacy	National Geographic
My Five Senses	C	I	36	Independent Readers Science	Houghton Mifflin
My Five Senses	F	I	42	Rosen Real Readers	Rosen Publishing Group
My Five Senses	F	I	142	Early Connections	Benchmark Education
My Five Senses	LB	I	5	Windows on Literacy	National Geographic
My Fort	LB	I	17	Little Books for Early Readers	University of Maine
My Friend	B	RF	41	Sunshine	Wright Group/McGraw Hill
My Friend	E	RF	95	Foundations	Wright Group/McGraw Hill
My Friend Alan	D	RF	65	Carousel Readers	Pearson Learning Group
My Friend and I	C	RF	78	Windows on Literacy	National Geographic
My Friend at School	C	RF	30	Visions	Wright Group/McGraw Hill
My Friend Goes Left	F	RF	72	Start to Read	School Zone
My Friend Jess	H	RF	124	Wonder World	Wright Group/McGraw Hill
My Friend the Monster	N	F	250+	Bulla, Clyde Robert	Harper & Row
My Friend Trent	H	RF	186	Foundations	Wright Group/McGraw Hill
My Friends	G	F	152	Gomi, Taro	Scholastic
My Friends	D	RF	58	Little Celebrations	Pearson Learning Group
My Frisbee	B	RF	31	Rigby Literacy	Rigby
My Garden	C	I	33	Rosen Real Readers	Rosen Publishing Group
My Garden	B	I	37	Ostrow, Jesse S.	Scholastic
My Global Address	G	I	84	Learn to Read	Creative Teaching Press
My Goldfish	G	I	239	Walker, Pamela	Scholastic
My Grandfather's Face	B	RF	27	Literacy 2000	Rigby
My Grandma	E	RF	67	Early Connections	Benchmark Education
My Grandma and Grandpa	E	I	130	PM Nonfiction	Rigby
My Grandma, the Rock Star	L	RF	250+	Rigby Literacy	Rigby
My Grandpa	F	I	75	Bookshop	Mondo
My Great Big Brother	F	RF	65	Book Bank	Wright Group/McGraw Hill
My Great-Aunt Arizona	N	RF	250+	Houston, Gloria	HarperCollins
My Green Thumb	K	F	351	Leveled Readers	Houghton Mifflin
My Gymnastics Class	F	I	33	iOpeners	Pearson Learning Group
My Hair	F	RF	124	Bookshop	Mondo
My Hamster, Van	E	RF	73	Ready Readers	Pearson Learning Group
My Hard-Boiled Egg	F	I	94	Windmill Books	Rigby
My Helicopter Ride	C	F	42	Foundations	Wright Group/McGraw Hill
My Hiroshima	T	HF	250+	Morimoto, Junko	Penguin Group
My Hobby	H	I	155	Rigby Focus	Rigby
My Holiday Diary	F	RF	95	Stepping Stones	Nelson/Michaels Assoc.
My Home	B	I	49	Science	Outside the Box
My Home	C	F	46	Story Box	Wright Group/McGraw Hill
My Home	C	RF	56	Sunshine	Wright Group/McGraw Hill
My Home	A	F	56	Smart Starts	Rigby
My Home	K	F	250+	Rhyme and Analogy	Oxford University Press
My Home is High	B	F	23	Literacy 2000	Rigby
My Home Is Just Right for Me	G	F	250+	Momentum Literacy Program	Troll Associates
My Horse	B	I	22	Bebop Books	Lee & Low Books Inc.
My House	B	I	25	Voyages	SRA/McGraw Hill
My House	F	RF	126	Literacy 2000	Rigby

* Collection of short stories

TITLE	LEVEL	GENRE	WORD COUNT	AUTHOR / SERIES	PUBLISHER / DISTRIBUTOR
My House	G	RF	43	Book Bunny Series	Creative Edge
My House	A	RF	40	Carousel Earlybirds	Pearson Learning Group
My House	F	RF	52	Cat on the Mat	Oxford University Press
My House	E	F	79	My First Reader	Grolier Press
My Kitchen	F	I	80	Rockwell, Harlow	Morrow
My Kite	C	RF	37	Williams, Deborah	Kaeden Books
My Letter	C	RF	51	Wonder World	Wright Group/McGraw Hill
My Life	K	RF	250+	Pistone, Paul	Scholastic
My Life as a Fifth-Grade Comedian	T	RF	250+	Levy, Elizabeth	HarperTrophy
My Life in a Town	C	I	24	Rosen Real Readers	Rosen Publishing Group
My Life in Dog Years	S	B	250+	Paulsen, Gary	Bantam
My Life in the Mountains	D	I	59	Rosen Real Readers	Rosen Publishing Group
My Life on an Island	C	I	43	Rosen Real Readers	Rosen Publishing Group
My Little Brother	C	RF	59	Windmill	Rigby
My Little Brother Ben	D	RF	35	Books for Young Learners	Richard C. Owen
My Little Cat	B	RF	57	PM Plus Starters	Rigby
My Little Dog	C	F	90	PM Starters	Rigby
My Little Mouse	C	I	32	Book Bank	Wright Group/McGraw Hill
My Little Sister	G	RF	143	Story Box	Wright Group/McGraw Hill
My Little Sister	D	RF	44	Joy Readers	Pearson Learning Group
My Little Sister	E	I	120	PM Nonfiction-Yellow	Rigby
My Little Sister	C	RF	36	First Stories	Pacific Learning
My Lost Top	E	RF	70	Ready Readers	Pearson Learning Group
My Louisiana Sky	T	RF	250+	Holt, Kimberly Willis	Random House
My Lucky Hat	J	F	250+	Bookshop	Mondo
My Lunch	C	RF	70	Early Emergent	Pioneer Valley
My Mama	C	RF	25	Visions	Wright Group/McGraw Hill
My Messy Room	D	RF	82	Packard, Mary	Scholastic
My Models	E	RF	143	Early Connections	Benchmark Education
My Mom	F	I	91	Talk About Books	Pearson Learning Group
My Mom	B	I	40	Little Books for Early Readers	University of Maine
My Mom and Dad	D	RF	86	Story Box	Wright Group/McGraw Hill
My Mom and Dad Take Care of Me	B	I	44	Windows on Literacy	National Geographic
My Mom and I	A	RF	42	Little Books for Early Readers	University of Maine
My Monster and Me	B	F	37	Ready Readers	Pearson Learning Group
My Monster Friends	F	F	94	Literacy 2000	Rigby
My Mother Got Married (And Other Disasters)	P	RF	250+	Park, Barbara	Random House
My Mysterious World	O	B	250+	Mahy, Margaret	Richard C. Owen
My Name Is America	Z	HF	250+	White, Ellen Emerson	Scholastic
My Name is Maria Isabel	N	RF	250+	Ada, Alma Flor	Aladdin
My Name is Not Angelica	V	HF	250+	O'Dell, Scott	Bantam
My Name is Yun Jim	N	RF	250+	Murphy, Catherine	Wright Group/McGraw Hill
My Native American School	F	RF	86	Gould, Carol	Kaeden Books
My Neighborhood	K	I	250+	Early Connections	Benchmark Education
My Neighborhood	J	RF	391	Leveled Readers	Houghton Mifflin
My Nest	C	I	42	Little Celebrations	Pearson Learning Group
My Nest Is Best	D	RF	92	Foundations	Wright Group/McGraw Hill
My New Boy	F	F	102	Step into Reading	Random House
My New House	C	RF	26	Reading Corners	Pearson Learning Group
My New Mom	K	RF	282	Sunshine	Wright Group/McGraw Hill
My New Pet	E	I	151	Sun Sprouts	ETA/Cuisenaire
My New Pet	F	RF	105	Little Readers	Houghton Mifflin
My New Quilt	H	I	170	Rigby Focus	Rigby
My New Rocket	D	F	128	Bookshop	Mondo

* Collection of short stories

TITLE	LEVEL	GENRE	WORD COUNT	AUTHOR / SERIES	PUBLISHER / DISTRIBUTOR
My Old Cat	E	RF	110	Foundations	Wright Group/McGraw Hill
My Old Cat and the Computer	F	RF	81	Foundations	Wright Group/McGraw Hill
My Old Gold Boat	G	F	51	Easy Phonics Readers	Teacher Created Materials
My Own Place	J	RF	250+	Voyages	SRA/McGraw Hill
My Own Two Feet	W	B	250+	Cleary, Beverly	Avon
My Painting	B	RF	31	First Stories	Pacific Learning
My Pal Al	E	RF	81	Real Kids Readers	Millbrook Press
My Party	C	I	35	The Candid Collection	Pearson Learning Group
My Pen Pal	K	RF	250+	Twig	Wright Group/McGraw Hill
My Pet	C	I	18	KinderReaders	Rigby
My Pet	D	RF	65	Salem, Lynn; Stewart, Josie	Continental Press
My Pet Bobby	E	F	150	Little Readers	Houghton Mifflin
My Picture	C	RF	37	Carousel Readers	Pearson Learning Group
My Picture	A	RF	23	Story Box	Wright Group/McGraw Hill
My Pigs	F	I	123	Miller, Heather	Scholastic
My Place	A	RF	34	Story Steps	Rigby
My Place	A	RF	28	Foundations	Wright Group/McGraw Hill
My Planet	A	I	28	Smart Starts	Rigby
My Plant	D	I	96	Rigby Literacy	Rigby
My Pony	C	RF	49	Rise & Shine	Hampton-Brown
My Pony Minnie	E	RF	59	Sunshine	Wright Group/McGraw Hill
My Prairie Summer	M	RF	250+	Pair-It Books	Steck-Vaughn
My Pumpkin	C	I	52	Teacher's Choice Series	Pearson Learning Group
My Pup	D	RF	65	Leveled Readers	Houghton Mifflin
My Puppy	B	RF	14	Sunshine	Wright Group/McGraw Hill
My Puppy	C	RF	33	Little Celebrations	Pearson Learning Group
My Red Rowboat	E	RF	89	Early Readers	Compass Point Books
My Red Scarf	F	I	120	Rigby Focus	Rigby
My Ride	C	RF	56	Foundations	Wright Group/McGraw Hill
My River	F	F	53	Halpern, Shari	Scholastic
My Rocket	A	F	28	KinderReaders	Rigby
My Rocks	C	RF	43	Early Connections	Benchmark Education
My Room	A	RF	15	Leveled Readers Emergent	Houghton Mifflin
My Room	A	RF	28	Carousel Earlybirds	Pearson Learning Group
My Room	LB	F	14	Ready Readers	Pearson Learning Group
My Room	A	RF	15	Twig	Wright Group/McGraw Hill
My Sand Castle	C	RF	44	PM Plus Starters	Rigby
My School	A	I	34	At School Series	Pioneer Valley
My School	B	I	34	Little Readers	Houghton Mifflin
My School	C	RF	40	TOTTS	Tott Publications
My School Day	LB	I	6	Windows on Literacy	National Geographic
My Scrapbook	K	I	312	Storyteller Nonfiction	Wright Group/McGraw Hill
My Secret Hiding Place	G	RF	155	First Start	Troll Associates
My Secret Place	G	RF	121	Wonder World	Wright Group/McGraw Hill
My Shadow	C	RF	42	Foundations	Wright Group/McGraw Hill
My Shadow	F	RF	116	Ready Readers	Pearson Learning Group
My Shadow	E	I	46	Pacific Literacy	Pacific Learning
My Shadow	A	RF	29	Book Bank	Wright Group/McGraw Hill
My Shadow	C	RF	35	Sunshine	Wright Group/McGraw Hill
My Shadow Clock	H	I	180	Sun Sprouts	ETA/Cuisenaire
My Shoes	B	RF	25	Rise & Shine	Hampton-Brown
My Side of the Mountain	U	RF	250+	George, Jean Craighead	Penguin Group
My Sister Annie	S	RF	250+	Dodds, Bill	Boyds Mills Press
My Sister Is My Friend	B	RF	32	Instant Readers	Harcourt School Publishers

* Collection of short stories

TITLE	LEVEL	GENRE	WORD COUNT	AUTHOR / SERIES	PUBLISHER / DISTRIBUTOR
My Sister Jess	I	RF	120	Supersonics	Rigby
My Sister June	H	RF	182	Ready Readers	Pearson Learning Group
My Sister the Witch	R	RF	250+	Conford, Ellen	Troll Associates
My Sister's Getting Married	K	RF	300	Foundations	Wright Group/McGraw Hill
My Skateboard	G	I	81	Sun Sprouts	ETA/Cuisenaire
My Skateboard	I	RF	81	City Kids	Rigby
My Skateboard	D	RF	89	Carousel Readers	Pearson Learning Group
My Skin	D	I	64	Wonder World	Wright Group/McGraw Hill
My Skin Looks After Me	G	I	82	Pacific Literacy	Pacific Learning
My Sloppy Tiger	I	F	211	Sunshine	Wright Group/McGraw Hill
My Sloppy Tiger Goes to School	J	F	217	Sunshine	Wright Group/McGraw Hill
My Son, the Time Traveler	N	F	250+	The Zack Files	Grosset & Dunlap
My Special Job	E	RF	110	Pacific Literacy	Pacific Learning
My Special Place	E	RF	116	Teacher's Choice Series	Pearson Learning Group
My Special Place	E	RF	33	Home Connection Collection	Rigby
My Stepmother	I	RF	121	City Stories	Rigby
My Story	A	RF	17	Wonder World	Wright Group/McGraw Hill
My Stuffed Animals	C	RF	50	Handprints B	Educator's Publishing Service
My Teacher	A	I	32	At School Series	Pioneer Valley
My Teacher Flunked the Planet	S	F	250+	Coville, Bruce	Pocket Books
My Teacher Fried My Brains	S	F	250+	Coville, Bruce	Pocket Books
My Teacher Glows in the Dark	S	F	250+	Coville, Bruce	Pocket Books
My Teacher Helps Me	C	RF	37	Visions	Wright Group/McGraw Hill
My Teacher Is an Alien	S	F	250+	Coville, Bruce	Pocket Books
My Teacher Turns into a Tyrannosaurus	O	F	250+	SupaDoopers	Sundance
My Teacher's Leaving	I	RF	154	City Kids	Rigby
My Three-Wheeler	C	RF	38	Visions	Wright Group/McGraw Hill
My Tiger Cat	E	F	76	Frankford, Marilyn	Kaeden Books
My Time Box	I	RF	225	Early Connections	Benchmark Education
My Tooth Is About to Fall Out	I	RF	173	Maccarone, Grace	Scholastic
My Tooth is Loose!	H	RF	250+	Silverman, Martin	Puffin Books
My Tower	A	RF	15	Windmill	Wright Group/McGraw Hill
My Tower	C	RF	61	PM Plus Story Books	Rigby
My Town	A	I	33	Early Connections	Benchmark Education
My Town at Work	M	I	250+	Windows on Literacy	National Geographic
My Town Used To Be Small	G	I	79	Windows on Literacy	National Geographic
My Toy Box Is Heavy	D	RF	99	Windows on Literacy	National Geographic
My Toys	A	RF	28	Little Books for Early Readers	University of Maine
My Treasure Garden	J	RF	134	Book Bank	Wright Group/McGraw Hill
My Turn Your Turn	D	RF	78	Book Bus	Creative Edge
My Twin!	C	RF	40	Ready Readers	Pearson Learning Group
My Two Families	K	RF	250+	PM Story Books-Silver	Rigby
My Two Homes	E	RF	69	Carousel Readers	Pearson Learning Group
My Uncle's Truck	C	RF	24	Visions	Wright Group/McGraw Hill
My Vacation	D	RF	60	Rigby Literacy	Rigby
My Very Hungry Pet	F	RF	334	Reading Corners	Pearson Learning Group
My Walk	WB	I	N/A	Windows on Literacy	National Geographic
My Walk Home	F	RF	71	Windows on Literacy	National Geographic
My Wartime Summers	V	HF	250+	Cutler, Jane	HarperCollins
My Weather Station	G	I	313	Leveled Readers Science	Houghton Mifflin
My Week	D	RF	137	Early Connections	Benchmark Education
My Weekly Chores	C	RF	44	Visions	Wright Group/McGraw Hill
My Weird Mother	M	RF	250+	SupaDoopers	Sundance

* Collection of short stories

TITLE	LEVEL	GENRE	WORD COUNT	AUTHOR / SERIES	PUBLISHER / DISTRIBUTOR
My Wild Woolly	F	F	87	Instant Readers	Harcourt Trade
My Wonderful Aunt, Story Five	M	F	493	Sunshine	Wright Group/McGraw Hill
My Wonderful Aunt, Story Four	M	F	436	Sunshine	Wright Group/McGraw Hill
My Wonderful Aunt, Story One	M	F	193	Sunshine	Wright Group/McGraw Hill
My Wonderful Aunt, Story Six	M	F	432	Sunshine	Wright Group/McGraw Hill
My Wonderful Aunt, Story Three	M	F	392	Sunshine	Wright Group/McGraw Hill
My Wonderful Aunt, Story Two	M	F	199	Sunshine	Wright Group/McGraw Hill
My Wonderful Chair	F	F	109	Windmill	Wright Group/McGraw Hill
My Writing Day	O	B	250+	Adler, David A.	Richard C. Owen
Mysteries of the Ancients	Z	I	250+	Innes, Brian	Steck-Vaughn
Mysteries of the Bermuda Triangle	Z	I	2348	Leveled Readers	Houghton Mifflin
Mysteries of the Deep	R	I	531	Vocabulary Readers	Houghton Mifflin
Mysteries of UFOs, The	Z	I	250+	Innes, Brian	Steck-Vaughn
Mysterious Giant Squid, The	Z	I	2415	Leveled Readers	Houghton Mifflin
*Mysterious Green Swimmer and Other Cases, The	O	RF	250+	Simon, Seymour	Avon
Mysterious Healing	Z	I	250+	Innes, Brian	Steck-Vaughn
Mysterious I.O.U., The	M	RF	250+	Schultz, Irene	Wright Group/McGraw Hill
Mysterious Ocean Highway: Benjamin Franklin and the Gulf Stream	T	B	250+	Heiligman, Deborah	Steck-Vaughn
*Mysterious Tracks and Other Cases, The	O	RF	250+	Simon, Seymour	Avon
Mystery at the Zoo	T	F	1733	Leveled Readers	Houghton Mifflin
Mystery Bay	P	RF	250+	Krueger, Carol	Rigby
Mystery Box,The	I	RF	326	New Way Orange	Steck-Vaughn
Mystery Coin	J	RF	379	Independent Readers Social Studies	Houghton Mifflin
Mystery Food	E	RF	62	Leveled Readers Science	Houghton Mifflin
Mystery in the Attic, The	L	RF	250+	Leveled Readers Language Support	Houghton Mifflin
Mystery in the Night Woods	M	F	250+	Peterson, John	Scholastic
Mystery Man, The	K	RF	250+	Rigby Literacy	Rigby
Mystery of Lighthouse Cave, The	P	RF	250+	Leveled Readers Language Support	Houghton Mifflin
Mystery of Magnets, The	P	I	250+	iOpeners	Pearson Learning Group
Mystery of Moody Manor, The	Q	F	250+	Ragged Island Mysteries	Wright Group/McGraw Hill
Mystery of Mrs. Kim, The	M	RF	250+	Rigby Literacy	Rigby
Mystery of Pony Hollow, The	N	F	250+	Hall, Lynn	Random House
Mystery of the Blue Box, The	N	I	841	Independent Readers Science	Houghton Mifflin
Mystery of the Blue Ring, The	L	RF	250+	Giff, Patricia Reilly	Bantam
Mystery of the Cupboard	R	F	250+	Banks, Lynne Reid	Avon Camelot
Mystery of the Dark Old House, The	M	F	250+	Schultz, Irene	Wright Group/McGraw Hill
Mystery of the Fire in the Sky	Q	RF	250+	Mystery Solvers	Troll Associates
Mystery of the Missing Dog, The	J	F	250+	Levy, Elizabeth	Scholastic
Mystery of the Missing Dog, The	M	RF	250+	Schultz, Irene	Wright Group/McGraw Hill
Mystery of the Missing Leopard, The	Q	F	250+	Leonhardt, Alice	Steck-Vaughn
Mystery of the Missing Malamute, The	M	RF	250+	Kleinhenz, Sydnie Meltzer	Wright Group/McGraw Hill
Mystery of the Missing Red Mitten, The	H	RF	246	Little Readers	Houghton Mifflin
Mystery of the Noises in the Attic, The	N	F	606	Leveled Readers	Houghton Mifflin
Mystery of the Phantom Pony, The	N	RF	250+	Stepping Stone	Random House
Mystery of the Pirate Ghost, The	L	F	250+	Hayes, Geoffrey	Random House
Mystery of the Stolen Bike, The	M	F	250+	Brown, Marc	Little, Brown & Co.
Mystery of the Talking Tail, The	M	F	250+	SupaDoopers	Sundance
Mystery of the Three Keys, The	M	RF	250+	Schultz, Irene	Wright Group/McGraw Hill
Mystery of the Tooth Gremlin	L	RF	250+	Graves, Bonnie	Hyperion

* Collection of short stories

TITLE	LEVEL	GENRE	WORD COUNT	AUTHOR / SERIES	PUBLISHER / DISTRIBUTOR
Mystery on October Road	O	RF	250+	Herzig, A. C.; Mali, Jane	Scholastic
Mystery Seeds	L	RF	250+	Reading Unlimited	Pearson Learning Group
*Mystery Stories	R	RF	250+	Higgins, James	Houghton Mifflin
Mystery Valley	P	SF	250+	Bookweb	Rigby
Myth or Mystery?	Q	F	250+	Literacy Tree	Rigby
Mythical Beasts	T	F	250+	Wildcats	Wright Group/McGraw Hill
Mythical Horse, The	T	I	250+	Sunshine	Wright Group/McGraw Hill
Mythmakers	T	I	250+	Wildcats	Wright Group/McGraw Hill
*Myths	S	TL	250+	Goodman, Ronald; Pierce, Robert; Wagner, Betty Jane	Houghton Mifflin
Nadia Comaneci	M	B	250+	Cole, Sally	Wright Group/McGraw Hill
Name for a Dog, A	I	RF	258	Windmill Books	Rigby
Name for Rabbit, A	H	F	94	Pacific Literacy	Pacific Learning
Name Garden, A	F	I	125	Sunshine	Wright Group/McGraw Hill
Name Is the Same, The	G	RF	115	Ready Readers	Pearson Learning Group
Name, The	H	RF	159	Voyages	SRA/McGraw Hill
Named, The	Z	F	250+	Curly, Marianne	Bloomsbury Children's Books
Names and Games	H	I	115	Literacy Tree	Rigby
Naming the Cat	L	RF	250+	Soar To Success	Houghton Mifflin
Nana Rescue, The	J	RF	250+	Voyages	SRA/McGraw Hill
Nana's in the Plum Tree	M	RF	250+	Pacific Literacy	Pacific Learning
Nana's Kitchen	J	RF	250+	Walton, Darwin McBeth	Steck-Vaughn
Nana's Orchard	F	RF	92	Gould, Carol	Kaeden Books
Nana's Place	I	RF	211	Gibson, Akimi; Meyer, K.	Scholastic
Nana's Sweet Potato Pie	E	RF	233	Visions	Wright Group/McGraw Hill
Nana's Tomatoes	M	RF	587	Leveled Readers Science	Houghton Mifflin
Nannies for Hire	M	RF	250+	Hest, Amy	William Morrow
Nanny Goat's Nap	C	F	96	Ready Readers	Pearson Learning Group
Nap Time	C	RF	24	KinderReaders	Rigby
Napping House, The	I	F	268	Wood, Don & Audrey	Harcourt Trade
Nasty, Stinky Sneakers	R	RF	250+	Bunting, Eve	HarperTrophy
Nat Turner: Rebellious Slave	T	B	250+	Let Freedom Ring	Capstone Press
Nat, Nan, and Pam	C	RF	30	Leveled Readers	Houghton Mifflin
Natalia and her Grandma	N	RF	250+	Sunflower	Intercultural Center for Research in Education
Natchez Under the Hill	T	HF	250+	Applegate, Stan	Peachtree
Nate the Great	K	RF	250+	Sharmat, Marjorie Weinman	Bantam
Nate the Great and Me	K	RF	250+	Sharmat, Marjorie Weinman	Random House
Nate the Great and the Boring Beach Bag	K	RF	250+	Sharmat, Marjorie Weinman	Bantam
Nate the Great and the Crunchy Christmas	K	RF	250+	Sharmat, Marjorie Weinman	Bantam
Nate the Great and the Fishy Prize	K	RF	250+	Sharmat, Marjorie Weinman	Bantam
Nate the Great and the Halloween Hunt	K	RF	250+	Sharmat, Marjorie Weinman	Bantam
Nate the Great and the Lost List	K	RF	250+	Sharmat, Marjorie Weinman	Bantam
Nate the Great and the Missing Key	K	RF	250+	Sharmat, Marjorie Weinman	Bantam
Nate the Great and the Mushy Valentine	K	RF	250+	Sharmat, Marjorie Weinman	Bantam
Nate the Great and the Musical Note	K	RF	250+	Sharmat, Marjorie Weinman	Bantam
Nate the Great and the Phony Clue	K	RF	250+	Sharmat, Marjorie Weinman	Bantam
Nate the Great and the Pillowcase	K	RF	250+	Sharmat, Marjorie Weinman	Bantam
Nate the Great and the Snowy Trail	K	RF	250+	Sharmat, Marjorie Weinman	Bantam
Nate the Great and the Sticky Case	K	RF	250+	Sharmat, Marjorie Weinman	Bantam
Nate the Great and the Stolen Base	K	RF	250+	Sharmat, Marjorie Weinman	Bantam
Nate the Great and the Tardy Tortoise	K	RF	250+	Sharmat, Marjorie Weinman	Bantam
Nate the Great Goes Down in the Dumps	K	RF	250+	Sharmat, Marjorie Weinman	Bantam

* Collection of short stories

| --- | --- | --- | --- | --- | --- |
Nate the Great Goes Undercover	K	RF	250+	Sharmat, Marjorie Weinman	Bantam
Nate the Great Saves the King of Sweden	K	RF	250+	Sharmat, Marjorie Weinman	Bantam
Nate the Great Stalks Stupidweed	K	RF	250+	Sharmat, Marjorie Weinman	Bantam
Nathan and Nicholas Alexander	K	F	250+	Delacre, Lulu	Scholastic
Nation of Nations, A	S	HF	1931	Leveled Readers Social Studies	Houghton Mifflin
National Anthem, The	N	I	250+	A True Book	Children's Press
National Parks	S	I	250+	iOpeners	Pearson Learning Group
National Velvet	X	RF	250+	Bagnold, Enid	Avon Books
Native American Art	O	I	250+	Motil, Rebecca	Scholastic
Native American Art from the Pueblos	P	I	250+	Rosen Real Readers	Rosen Publishing Group
Native American Baskets	L	I	195	Phonics Readers	Compass Point Books
Native American Foods and Recipes	O	I	250+	Rosen Real Readers	Rosen Publishing Group
*Native American Stories	Q	TL	250+	Bruchac, Joseph	Fulcrum Publishing
Native Americans	O	I	250+	Navigators Fiction Series	Benchmark Education
Native Americans	P	I	250+	Explorers	Wright Group/McGraw Hill
Natural History Museum, The	K	I	250+	Stepping Stones	Nelson/Michaels Assoc.
Nature Club, The	O	RF	755	Leveled Readers	Houghton Mifflin
Nature Hike	C	HF	32	Twig	Wright Group/McGraw Hill
Nature! Wild and Wonderful	O	B	250+	Pringle, Laurence	Richard C. Owen
Nature's Celebration	M	I	250+	Literacy 2000	Rigby
Nature's Fireworks: A Book About Lightning	M	I	250+	Amazing Science	Picture Window Books
Nature's Power	Q	I	250+	Hummer, Patricia K.	Steck-Vaughn
Naughty Ann, The	G	F	159	PM Story Books	Rigby
Naughty Happy Monkey	C	F	33	Joy Readers	Pearson Learning Group
Naughty Kitten!	LB	RF	18	Smart Starts	Rigby
Naughty Nancy Goes to School	WB	F	N/A	Goodall, John S.	Andre Deutsch
Naughty Patch	D	RF	74	Foundations	Wright Group/McGraw Hill
Navajo Code Talkers, The	U	I	2549	Independent Readers Social Studies	Houghton Mifflin
Navajo Longwalk	S	HF	250+	Armstrong, Nancy M.	Scholastic
Navajo, The	U	I	250+	The Heinle Reading Library	Thomson Learning
Near Death Experiences	X	I	250+	The Unexplained	Capstone Press
Nebraska	R	I	250+	This Land Is Your Land	Compass Point Books
Necklace of Raindrops and Other Stories, A	S	TL	250+	Aiken, Joan	Random House
Necklaces	B	RF	34	Phonics and Friends	Hampton-Brown
Ned	C	RF	30	Leveled Readers Language Support	Houghton Mifflin
Ned's Noise Machine	C	F	36	Rigby Literacy	Rigby
Needs and Wants	C	I	43	Early Connections	Benchmark Education
Negro Leagues of Baseball, The	V	I	3319	Leveled Readers Social Studies	Houghton Mifflin
Neighbor From Outer Space, The	N	F	250+	George, Maureen	Scholastic
Neighborhood Clubhouse, The	J	RF	474	Visions	Wright Group/McGraw Hill
Neighborhood Event, The	I	RF	309	Leveled Readers	Houghton Mifflin
Neighborhood Party, The	P	RF	250+	Leveled Readers Language Support	Houghton Mifflin
Neighborhood Party, The	C	RF	60	Pair-It Books	Steck-Vaughn
Neighborhood Picnic, The	G	I	157	Visions	Wright Group/McGraw Hill
Neil Armstrong	M	B	250+	Explore Space!	Capstone Press
Neil Armstrong: Young Flyer	O	B	250+	Childhood of Famous Americans	Aladdin
Nellie Bly	J	B	270	Leveled Readers Social Studies	Houghton Mifflin
Nellie McClung	X	B	250+	The Canadians	Fitzhenry & Whiteside
Nelson Gets a Fright	K	RF	387	PM Story Books	Rigby
Nelson is Kidnapped	M	RF	250+	PM Story Books-Silver	Rigby
Nelson Mandela	Q	B	250+	First Biographies	Steck-Vaughn

* Collection of short stories

TITLE	LEVEL	GENRE	WORD COUNT	AUTHOR / SERIES	PUBLISHER / DISTRIBUTOR
Nelson Mandela: "No Easy Walk to Freedom"	X	B	250+	Denenberg, Barry	Scholastic
Nelson Mandela: Freedom for South Africa	T	B	250+	Dell, Pamela	Children's Press
Nelson Mandela: South Africa's Silent Voice of Protest	X	B	250+	Hargrove, Jim	Children's Press
Nelson the Baby Elephant	J	RF	350	PM Turquoise	Rigby
Nemo and the Ship of Gold	O	I	250+	Leveled Readers Language Support	Houghton Mifflin
Neptune	S	I	250+	Our Solar System	Compass Point Books
Neptune	N	I	250+	A True Book	Children's Press
Nero Hawley's Fight for Freedom	Q	B	545	Vocabulary Readers	Houghton Mifflin
Nervous System, The	M	I	213	Human Body Systems	Red Brick Learning
Nervous System, The	N	I	250+	A True Book	Children's Press
Nest Full of Eggs, A	B	I	25	Pair-It Books	Steck-Vaughn
Nest on the Beach, The	H	RF	243	PM Plus Story Books	Rigby
Nest, The	C	F	34	Sunshine	Wright Group/McGraw Hill
Nest, The	C	F	32	Story Box	Wright Group/McGraw Hill
Nesting Place, The	K	HF	356	PM Turquoise	Rigby
Nestor	K	F	250+	Bookshop	Mondo
Nests	M	I	222	Vocabulary Readers	Houghton Mifflin
Nests	C	I	35	Wonder World	Wright Group/McGraw Hill
Nests	D	I	58	Literacy 2000	Rigby
Nests, Nests, Nests	C	I	42	Canizares, Susan; Reid, Mary	Scholastic
Netherlands	Q	I	250+	First Reports	Compass Point Books
Netherlands, The	O	I	250+	Dahl, Michael	Red Brick Learning
Nevada	R	I	250+	This Land Is Your Land	Compass Point Books
Never Be	D	RF	73	Salem, Lynn; Stewart, Josie	Continental Press
Never Bored on Boards	O	I	250+	Literacy 2000	Rigby
Never Cry Wolf	Z	B	250+	Mowat, Farley	Bantam
Never Hit a Ghost with a Baseball Bat	O	RF	250+	Clifford, Eth	Scholastic
Never Hitch a Ride With a Martian!	N	SF	250+	Clark, Tony	Pacific Learning
Never Say Never	G	F	225	Ready Readers	Pearson Learning Group
Never Say Quit	T	RF	250+	Wallace, Bill	Pocket Books
Never Snap at a Bubble	G	F	89	Giant Step Reader	Educational Insights
Never Trust a Cat Who Wears Earrings	N	F	250+	The Zack Files	Grosset & Dunlap
Never Turn Back: Father Serra's Mission	S	B	250+	Rawls, Jim	Steck-Vaughn
Never-Told Story, The	H	RF	138	Literacy Tree	Rigby
New and Old	B	I	46	Windows on Literacy	National Geographic
New at the Zoo	E	F	84	New Reader Series	Bungalo Books
New Baby	WB	RF	N/A	McCullu, Emily Arnold	Harper & Row
New Baby Calf, The	H	RF	240	Chase, Edith; Reid, Barbara	Scholastic
New Baby, The	E	RF	133	PM Story Books	Rigby
New Balloon, A	E	RF	36	Pacific Literacy	Pacific Learning
New Beginnings	J	RF	277	Books for Young Learners	Richard C. Owen
New Bike, The	F	RF	96	Start to Read	School Zone
New Bike, The	J	RF	526	Sunshine	Wright Group/McGraw Hill
New Boots	E	RF	127	PM Plus Story Books	Rigby
New Building, The	H	RF	78	Sunshine	Wright Group/McGraw Hill
New Butterfly, The	D	I	55	Sun Sprouts	ETA/Cuisenaire
New Car, The	K	RF	250+	Sunshine	Wright Group/McGraw Hill
New Cat, The	LB	F	29	Pacific Literacy	Pacific Learning
New Citizens	L	I	250+	Twig	Wright Group/McGraw Hill
New Clothes	F	RF	107	Windows on Literacy	National Geographic
New Club, The	I	RF	267	Leveled Readers	Houghton Mifflin
New Dog, A	D	RF	52	Oxford Reading Tree	Oxford University Press

* Collection of short stories

TITLE	LEVEL	GENRE	WORD COUNT	AUTHOR / SERIES	PUBLISHER / DISTRIBUTOR
New England's Whales	Q	I	856	Independent Readers Social Studies	Houghton Mifflin
New Forest, The	J	RF	250+	Talking Points	Pearson Learning Group
New Friends	E	RF	89	Leveled Readers Language Support	Houghton Mifflin
New Friends in a New Land: A Thanksgiving Story	N	I	250+	Stamper, Judith Bauer	Steck-Vaughn
New Girl, The	K	RF	250+	Pacific Literacy	Pacific Learning
New Glasses for Max	H	RF	239	PM Plus Story Books	Rigby
New Gym Shoes	F	RF	175	Yukish, Joe	Kaeden Books
New Hampshire	R	I	250+	This Land Is Your Land	Compass Point Books
New Hat, The	C	RF	37	Rigby Literacy	Rigby
New Highway, The	C	I	67	Foundations	Wright Group/McGraw Hill
New House for Mole and Mouse, A	G	F	223	Ziefert, Harriet	Penguin Group
New House, The	LB	F	15	Sunshine	Wright Group/McGraw Hill
New House, The	D	F	112	Bookshop	Mondo
New Jersey	Q	I	250+	Kummer, Patricia K.	Red Brick Learning
New Jersey	R	I	250+	This Land Is Your Land	Compass Point Books
New Kid in Town	N	RF	250+	Kroll, Stephen	Avon Camelot
New Kid, The	F	RF	124	Real Kid Readers	The Millbrook Press
*New Kids In Town	Y	B	250+	Bode, Janet	Scholastic
New Kind of Art, A	T	I	527	Vocabulary Readers	Houghton Mifflin
New Kind of Magic, The	P	F	250+	Szymanski, Lois	Avon Camelot
New Land, The: A First Year on the Prairie	M	I	250+	Reynolds, Marilynn	Orca Book Publishers
New Language, New Friends	Q	I	250+	iOpeners	Pearson Learning Group
New Light for the Lodge, A	L	F	250+	Smith, Ben	Wright Group/McGraw Hill
New Mexico	R	I	250+	This Land Is Your Land	Compass Point Books
New Mexico	S	I	250+	Thompson, Kathleen	Steck-Vaughn
New Nest, A	LB	I	14	Pair-It Books	Steck-Vaughn
New Nest, The	F	RF	207	Foundations	Wright Group/McGraw Hill
New Pants	B	F	20	Story Box	Wright Group/McGraw Hill
New Paper, Everyone!	G	I	53	Pacific Literacy	Pacific Learning
New Puppy, A	G	I	250+	Momentum Literacy Program	Troll Associates
New Road, The	D	I	49	Joy Readers	Pearson Learning Group
New School for Megan, A	J	RF	250+	PM Story Books	Rigby
New School, A	B	RF	24	Vocabulary Readers	Houghton Mifflin
New School, A	G	RF	137	Windows on Literacy	National Geographic
New School, The	J	RF	210	City Kids	Rigby
New Shoes	C	RF	29	Wonder World	Wright Group/McGraw Hill
New Sled, The	E	RF	85	Leveled Readers	Houghton Mifflin
New Sneakers	F	RF	34	Oxford Reading Tree	Oxford University Press
New Soccer Nets	G	RF	123	Early Connections	Benchmark Education
New Tricks	I	RF	250+	Voyages	SRA/McGraw Hill
New Year's Around the World	O	I	250+	Trumbore, Cindy	Pearson Learning Group
New York	S	I	250+	Thompson, Kathleen	Steck-Vaughn
New York	R	I	250+	This Land Is Your Land	Compass Point Books
New York	S	I	250+	Land of Liberty	Red Brick Learning
New York	T	I	250+	Hello U.S.A.	Lerner Publishing
New York	Q	I	250+	One Nation	Capstone Press
New York City	T	I	250+	Kent, Deborah	Children's Press
New York City Buildings	F	I	59	Books for Young Learners	Richard C. Owen
*Newbery Christmas, A: Fourteen Stories of Christmas by Newbery Award-Winning Authors	W	RF	250+	Greenberg, Martin H.; Waugh, Charles G.	Delacorte

TITLE	LEVEL	GENRE	WORD COUNT	AUTHOR / SERIES	PUBLISHER / DISTRIBUTOR
*Newbery Halloween, A: A Dozen Scary Stories by Newbery Award-Winning Authors	W	F	250+	Greenberg, Martin H.; Waugh, Charles G.	Delacorte
Newborn Animals	J	I	250+	Momentum Literacy Program	Troll Associates
Newf	N	TL	250+	Killilea, Marie	Putnam & Grosset
News Flash!	R	I	250+	Hill, Sharon	Pacific Learning
Newspaper Carriers	M	I	250+	Community Helpers	Red Brick Learning
Newspaper for Dad, A	G	RF	192	New Way Green	Steck-Vaughn
Newspaper Kids, The	Q	RF	250+	Phillips, Juanita	HarperCollins
Newspaper, The	G	RF	132	Twig	Wright Group/McGraw Hill
Newt	J	F	250+	Novak, Matt	HarperTrophy
Newton's Laws	Z	I	2853	Leveled Readers Science	Houghton Mifflin
Next Door	A	F	31	Rigby Literacy	Rigby
Next Spring an Oriole	N	HF	250+	Whelan, Gloria	Random House
Next Stop!	I	RF	250+	Ellis, Sarah	Fitzhenry & Whiteside
Next Stop, New York City!	O	RF	250+	Giff, Patricia Reilly	Bantam
Next Time I Will	K	RF	250+	Bank Street	Bantam
Nez Perce Tribe, The	P	I	250+	Lassieur, Allison	Red Brick Learning
Nez Perce, The	R	I	250+	First Reports	Compass Point Books
Niagra Falls	L	I	184	Rosen Real Readers	Rosen Publishing Group
Niagra Falls, The Power of Water	T	I	1840	Independent Readers Science	Houghton Mifflin
Nibble, Nibble, Jenny Archer	M	RF	250+	Conford, Ellen	Little, Brown & Co.
Nibbles	J	RF	250+	Cambridge Reading	Pearson Learning Group
Nibbly Mouse	E	F	116	Voyages	SRA/McGraw Hill
Nicaragua	O	I	250+	Countries of the World	Red Brick Learning
Nice Hit!: You Can Play Baseball	M	I	250+	Game Day	Picture Window Books
Nice New Neighbors	K	RF	250+	Brandenberg, Franz	Scholastic
Nicest Day, The	L	RF	400	Leveled Readers	Houghton Mifflin
Nick Goes Fishing	I	RF	123	Yukish, Joe	Kaeden Books
Nickels and Pennies	E	I	53	Williams, Deborah	Kaeden Books
Nicketty-Nacketty Noo-Noo-Noo	K	F	250+	Cowley, Joy	Mondo
Nick's Glasses	D	RF	51	Pacific Literacy	Pacific Learning
Nick's Pet	E	F	119	Teacher's Choice Series	Pearson Learning Group
Nicky Upstairs and Downstairs	G	F	179	Ziefert, Harriet	Penguin Group
Nicole Digs a Hole	G	RF	138	Start to Read	School Zone
Nicole Helps Grandma	B	I	35	Little Books for Early Readers	University of Maine
Nigeria	O	I	250+	Thoennes, Kristin	Red Brick Learning
Night	Z	B	250+	Wiesel, Elie	Bantam Books
Night and Day	E	I	112	Ready Readers	Pearson Learning Group
Night Animals	D	RF	56	Ready Readers	Pearson Learning Group
Night Birds on Nantucket	V	HF	250+	Aiken, Joan	Houghton Mifflin
Night Cat	L	I	250+	World Quest Adventures	World Quest Learning
Night Crossing, The	P	SF	250+	Bookweb	Rigby
Night Crossing, The	O	HF	250+	Ackerman, Karen	Alfred A. Knopf
Night Diving	H	I	101	Twig	Wright Group/McGraw Hill
Night Flyers, The	W	RF	250+	Jones, Elizabeth McDavid	Pleasant Company
Night in the Desert	D	I	69	Carousel Readers	Pearson Learning Group
Night Journey, The	T	HF	250+	Lasky, Kathryn	Puffin Books
Night Journeys	U	HF	250+	Avi	Avon
Night Light, The	K	RF	554	Leveled Readers	Houghton Mifflin
Night Lights	H	I	172	Independent Readers Science	Houghton Mifflin
Night Lights, A Cruise Around the Solar System	R	I	250+	Hill, David	Pacific Learning
Night Music	P	HF	250+	Voyages in Time	Wright Group/McGraw Hill
Night Noises	G	RF	104	Sunshine	Wright Group/McGraw Hill
Night Noises	G	RF	97	Storyteller-Moon Rising	Wright Group/McGraw Hill

* Collection of short stories

TITLE	LEVEL	GENRE	WORD COUNT	AUTHOR / SERIES	PUBLISHER / DISTRIBUTOR
Night of the Chupacabras	Y	RF	250+	Lee, Marie G.	Avon Camelot
Night of the Ninjas	M	F	250+	Osborne, Mary Pope	Random House
Night of the Twisters	U	RF	250+	Ruckman, Ivy	HarperTrophy
Night Out, The	M	RF	250+	Sails	Rigby
Night Owls, The	M	I	368	Wonder World	Wright Group/McGraw Hill
Night Quee's Blue Velvet Dress, The	Q	F	250+	Pair-It Books	Steck-Vaughn
Night Sky	LB	I	15	Twig	Wright Group/McGraw Hill
Night Sky, The	G	I	120	Windows on Literacy	National Geographic
Night Sky, The	G	RF	226	Ready Readers	Pearson Learning Group
Night Swimmers, The	S	RF	250+	Byars, Betsy	Dell
*Night Terrors, Stories of Shadow and Substance	Z	F	250+	Duncan, Lois	Aladdin
Night the Heads Came, The	Y	SF	250+	Sleator, William	Puffin Books
Night the Lights Went Out, The	H	RF	155	Little Readers	Houghton Mifflin
Night the White Deer Died, The	Z	HF	250+	Paulsen, Gary	Dell
Night Train, The	E	F	65	Story Box	Wright Group/McGraw Hill
Night Walk	E	RF	47	Prokopchak, Ann	Kaeden Books
Night Walk	F	RF	51	Books for Young Learners	Richard C. Owen
Night Walk, The	G	RF	91	Instant Readers	Harcourt School Publishers
Night Walk, The	L	RF	667	PM Story Books-Gold	Rigby
Night Without Stars, A	S	RF	250+	Howe, James	Aladdin
Nightingale, The	J	TL	563	Tales from Hans Andersen	Wright Group/McGraw Hill
Nightjohn	W	HF	250+	Paulsen, Gary	Bantam
Nightmare	M	RF	250+	Action Packs	Rigby
Nightmare Hill	F	RF	129	Developing Books, Set 1	Pioneer Valley
*Nightmare Hour: Time for Terror	W	F	250+	Stine, R. L.	HarperCollins
Nightmare Mountain	X	RF	250+	Kehret, Peg	Puffin Books
Nighttime	C	RF	25	Science	Outside the Box
Nighttime	C	RF	44	Story Box	Wright Group/McGraw Hill
Nighty-Nightmare	R	F	250+	Howe, James	Avon Camelot
Niki's Walk	WB	RF	N/A	Tanner, Jane	Curriculum Press
Nikki Giovanni	T	B	1729	Leveled Readers	Houghton Mifflin
Nikki Giovanni: A Special Poet	O	B	605	Leveled Readers	Houghton Mifflin
Niles Likes to Smile	F	RF	80	Little Books	Sadlier-Oxford
Nine Days of Camping, The	E	RF	254	Twig	Wright Group/McGraw Hill
Nine Lives of Adventure Cat, The	L	F	250+	Clymer, Susan	Scholastic
Nine Man Tree	Z	RF	250+	Peck, Robert Newton	Random House
Nine Men Chase a Hen	G	F	74	Start to Read	School Zone
*Nine True Dolphin Stories	M	I	250+	Davidson, Margaret	Scholastic
Ninjas Don't Bake Pumpkin Pies	M	RF	250+	Dadey, Debbie; Jones, Marcia Thornton	Scholastic
Ninjas, Piranhas, and Galileo	V	RF	250+	Smith, Greg Leitich	Little, Brown & Co.
Nishal's Box	I	F	250+	Cambridge Reading	Pearson Learning Group
Nissa's Place	Y	RF	250+	LaFaye, A.	Simon & Schuster
No Arm in Left Field	M	RF	250+	Christopher, Matt	Little, Brown & Co.
No Ball Games	I	F	250+	Rigby Literacy	Rigby
No Ball Games Here	H	RF	128	Ziefert, Harriet	Penguin Group
No Cookies Before Dinner	D	RF	138	Developing Books, Set 1	Pioneer Valley
No Copycats Allowed!	L	RF	250+	Graves, Bonnie	Hyperion
No Dinner for Sally	J	RF	340	Literacy 2000	Rigby
*No Dogs Allowed	O	RF	73	Cutler, Jane	Farrar, Straus and Giroux
No Dogs Allowed	F	RF	73	Books for Young Learners	Richard C. Owen
No Extras	F	RF	90	Literacy 2000	Rigby
No Fighting, No Biting!	K	RF	250+	Minarik, Else Holmelund	HarperTrophy

* Collection of short stories

TITLE	LEVEL	GENRE	WORD COUNT	AUTHOR / SERIES	PUBLISHER / DISTRIBUTOR
No Flying in the House	P	F	250+	Brock, Betty	HarperCollins
No Good in Art	I	RF	250+	Cohen, Miriam	Bantam
No Jumping On The Bed!	L	F	250+	Arnold, Tedd	Scholastic
No Laughing Matter	Q	RF	250+	Ragged Island Mysteries	Wright Group/McGraw Hill
No Luck	F	RF	120	Stewart, Josie; Salem, Lynn	Continental Press
No Mail for Mitchell	H	F	250+	Siracusa, Catherine	Random House
No Matter How You Play It	J	I	129	Instant Readers	Harcourt School Publishers
No Money? No Problem!	L	RF	250+	Social Studies Connects	The Kane Press
No More Lost and Found	J	I	137	Vocabulary Readers	Houghton Mifflin
No More Magic	R	SF	250+	Avi	Alfred A. Knopf
No More Monsters for Me!	J	F	250+	Parish, Peggy	HarperTrophy
No One Else Like Me	D	I	129	Early Connections	Benchmark Education
No One is Going to Nashville	O	RF	250+	Jukes, Mavis	Alfred A. Knopf
No One Likes Me	D	F	71	Sun Sprouts	ETA/Cuisenaire
No Pretty Pictures: A Child of War	Z	B	250+	Lobel, Anita	Greenwillow
No Promises in the Wind	Z	HF	250+	Hunt, Irene	Berkley Books
No Room For a Dog	N	RF	250+	Nichols, Joan Kane	Hearst
No Rules For Rex!	L	RF	250+	Social Studies Connects	The Kane Press
No Running!	H	RF	183	Lighthouse	Rigby
No Safe Place	P	SF	250+	Orbit Double Takes	Pacific Learning
No Singing Today	H	RF	250+	Bookshop	Mondo
No Tooth, No Quarter!	K	F	250+	Buller, Jon	Random House
No Trouble at All!	M	RF	250+	Literacy Tree	Rigby
No Way, Tooth Decay!	T	F	1186	Leveled Readers	Houghton Mifflin
No Way, Winky Blue!	N	F	4053	Jane, Pamela	Mondo
No, Bo!	D	RF	109	Handprints C, Set 1	Educator's Publishing Service
No, I Won't	E	F	174	Seedlings	Continental Press
No, No	D	F	91	Story Box	Wright Group/McGraw Hill
No, You Can't	D	RF	52	Sunshine	Wright Group/McGraw Hill
Noah's Ark	T	I	250+	Cambridge Reading	Pearson Learning Group
Noah's Ark	WB	F	N/A	Spier, Peter	Doubleday Books
*Nobel Prize Winners	T	B	250+	Hacker, Carlotta	Crabtree
Nobody Knew My Name	I	RF	276	Foundations	Wright Group/McGraw Hill
Nobody Listens to Andrew	I	F	250+	Little Readers	Houghton Mifflin
Nobody Owns the Sky: The Story of "Brave Bessie" Coleman	M	B	250+	Lindbergh, Reeve	Candlewick Press
Nobody's Family Is Going to Change	U	RF	250+	Fitzhugh, Louise	Farrar, Straus and Giroux
Noggin and Bobbin By the Sea	I	F	204	Little Celebrations	Pearson Learning Group
Noggin and Bobbin in the Garden	E	F	57	Little Celebrations	Pearson Learning Group
Noise	G	RF	138	Sunshine	Wright Group/McGraw Hill
Noise Festival, The	J	RF	250+	Sunshine	Wright Group/McGraw Hill
Noise in the Night	I	F	250+	Start to Read	School Zone
Noises	E	I	49	Literacy 2000	Rigby
Noises!!!	C	RF	98	Teacher's Choice Series	Pearson Learning Group
Noisy and Quiet	A	I	26	Vocabulary Readers	Houghton Mifflin
Noisy Breakfast	D	F	32	Blonder, Ellen	Scholastic
Noisy Nora	I	F	204	Wells, Rosemary	Scholastic
Noisy Toys	E	RF	77	Home Connection Collection	Rigby
Noonday Friends, The	R	RF	250+	Stolz, Mary	Scholastic
Nora Plays All Day	B	RF	42	Little Books	Sadlier-Oxford
Norma Jean, Jumping Bean	J	F	250+	Cole, Joanna	Random House
Norman Newman and the Werewolf of Walnut Street	Q	F	250+	Conford, Ellen	Troll Associates

* Collection of short stories

TITLE	LEVEL	GENRE	WORD COUNT	AUTHOR / SERIES	PUBLISHER / DISTRIBUTOR
Norman Rockwell	T	B	250+	Cohen, Joel H.	Grolier Publishing
North America	N	I	250+	Continents	Capstone Press
North America	Q	I	250+	Petersen, David	Grolier Publishing
North Carolina	T	I	250+	Hello U.S.A.	Lerner Publishing
North Carolina	T	I	250+	Fradin, Dennis Brindell	Children's Press
North Carolina	S	I	250+	Portrait of America	Steck-Vaughn
North Carolina	R	I	250+	This Land Is Your Land	Compass Point Books
North Dakota	R	I	250+	This Land Is Your Land	Compass Point Books
North Pole Walk	R	I	250+	Orbit Double Takes	Pacific Learning
North Star To Freedom	U	I	250+	Gorrell, Gena K.	Random House
Nory Ryan's Song	T	HF	250+	Giff, Patricia Reilly	Delacorte
Nose Book	E	I	111	Perkins, Al	Random House
Nose for Trouble, A	P	RF	250+	Wilson, Nancy Hope	Avon
Noses	C	RF	46	Science	Outside the Box
Noses	E	I	56	Literacy 2000	Rigby
Not Enough Cupcakes	I	F	292	Talking Point Series	Pearson Learning Group
Not Enough Water	D	RF	84	Armstrong, Shane; Hartley, Susan	Scholastic
*Not Guilty	X	B	250+	Sullivan, George	Scholastic
Not Me, Said the Monkey	G	F	118	West, Colin	Harper & Row
Not Now! Said the Cow	J	F	250+	Bank Street	Bantam
Not Now, Sam	F	RF	159	Early Connections	Benchmark Education
Not That I Care	V	RF	250+	Vail, Rachel	Scholastic
Not Too Many	G	RF	193	Sun Sprouts	ETA/Cuisenaire
Not Too Small at All	I	F	251	Seedlings	Continental Press
Not Too Small at All	H	RF	250+	Salem, Lynn	Continental Press
*Not Too Young and Other Stories	L	RF	250+	New Way Literature	Steck-Vaughn
Not Very Messy, Unless . . .	F	F	94	Seedlings	Continental Press
Not What It Seems	P	RF	250+	Wildcats	Wright Group/McGraw Hill
Not Yet!	D	RF	64	Reading Links	Steck-Vaughn
Not Yet, Nathan	G	RF	127	Cambridge Reading	Pearson Learning Group
Not Your Usual Goat	K	F	656	Leveled Readers	Houghton Mifflin
Notes from Mom	F	RF	99	Salem, Lynn; Stewart, Josie	Continental Press
Notes to Dad	F	RF	114	Stewart, Josie; Salem, Lynn	Continental Press
Nothing But The Truth	U	RF	250+	Avi	Hearst
Nothing But Trouble, Trouble, Trouble	Q	RF	250+	Hermes, Patricia	Scholastic
Nothing Ever Happens	F	F	49	City Stories	Rigby
Nothing in the Mailbox	F	RF	73	Books for Young Learners	Richard C. Owen
Nothing to Be Scared About	K	RF	343	Sunshine	Wright Group/McGraw Hill
Nothing's Fair in Fifth Grade	R	RF	250+	DeClements, Barthe	Scholastic
Not-Just-Anybody Family, The	P	RF	250+	Byars, Betsy	Dell
*Not-So-Dead Fish and Other Cases, The	O	RF	250+	Simon, Seymour	Avon
Not-So-Perfect Rosie	N	RF	250+	Giff, Patricia Reilly	Penguin Group
Not-So-Scary-Scarecrow, The	I	RF	166	Ready Readers	Pearson Learning Group
Noura Comes to Cleveland	L	RF	717	Leveled Readers Social Studies	Houghton Mifflin
Novio Boy	X	TL	250+	Soto, Gary	Harcourt Trade
Now and Long Ago	L	I	189	Phonics Readers	Compass Point Books
Now and Then	D	I	78	Windows on Literacy	National Geographic
Now I Am Five	I	RF	582	Sunshine	Wright Group/McGraw Hill
Now I Ride	D	I	63	Carousel Readers	Pearson Learning Group
Now Is Your Time! The African-American Struggle	Y	I	250+	Myers, Walter Dean	HarperCollins
Now It's Hot	C	I	49	Rigby Focus	Rigby
Now Listen, Stanley	K	F	250+	Literacy 2000	Rigby
Now We Can Go	C	RF	25	Jonas, Ann	Greenwillow

* Collection of short stories

TITLE	LEVEL	GENRE	WORD COUNT	AUTHOR / SERIES	PUBLISHER / DISTRIBUTOR
Now You See It, Now You Don't	M	I	204	Independent Readers Science	Houghton Mifflin
Now You See Me . . . Now You Don't	N	F	250+	The Zack Files	Grosset & Dunlap
Nowhere and Nothing	I	RF	143	Sunshine	Wright Group/McGraw Hill
Number Cruncher, The	L	F	250+	Sunshine	Wright Group/McGraw Hill
Number One	J	SF	170	Pacific Literacy	Pacific Learning
Number the Stars	U	HF	250+	Lowry, Lois	Bantam
Numbering All the Bones	Y	HF	250+	Rinaldi, Ann	Hyperion
Numbers	B	I	86	Canizares, Susan; Moreton, Daniel	Scholastic
Numbers All Around	B	I	40	Yellow Umbrella Books	Red Brick Learning
Numbers All Around	LB	I	12	Canizares, Susan; Chessen, Betsey	Scholastic
Numbers All around Me	G	F	140	Learn to Read	Creative Teaching Press
Numbers Are Everywhere	E	I	125	Early Connections	Benchmark Education
Numbers Are Everywhere	E	I	131	Twig	Wright Group/McGraw Hill
Numbers We Know	J	I	139	Spyglass Books	Compass Point Books
Numbers: Counting It Up	L	I	250+	Exploring Math	Capstone Press
Nurses	M	I	250+	Community Workers	Compass Point Books
Nurses	M	I	250+	Ready, Dee	Red Brick Learning
Nut Pie for Jud, A	D	I	46	Ready Readers	Pearson Learning Group
Oak Tree, An	I	I	141	Book Bus	Creative Edge
Oak Tree and Fir Tree	G	F	102	New Way Red	Steck-Vaughn
Oak Tree Controversy	N	RF	250+	Bookweb	Rigby
Oak Trees	F	I	132	Pebble Books	Capstone Press
Oatmeal	F	I	96	Wonder World	Wright Group/McGraw Hill
Obadiah	G	TL	105	Story Box	Wright Group/McGraw Hill
Obadiah the Bold	N	RF	250+	Turkle, Brinton	Penguin Group
Obee & Mungedeech	T	RF	250+	Martin, Trude	Aladdin
Observations of Emma Boyle, The	U	RF	2623	Leveled Readers	Houghton Mifflin
Obstacle Course, The	H	RF	211	Foundations	Wright Group/McGraw Hill
Obstacles in Our Way	L	RF	250+	Home Connection Collection	Rigby
Ocean Animals	J	I	204	Early Connections	Benchmark Education
Ocean by the Lake, The	N	I	250+	Little Celebrations	Pearson Learning Group
Ocean Detectives: Solving Mysteries of the Sea	W	I	250+	Cerullo, Mary	Steck-Vaughn
Ocean Facts	D	I	40	Rosen Real Readers	Rosen Publishing Group
Ocean Life	Q	I	250+	Explorers	Wright Group/McGraw Hill
Ocean Life: Tide Pool Creatures	Q	I	250+	Leonhardt, Alice	Steck-Vaughn
Ocean of Story, The: Fairy Tales From India	U	TL	250+	Ness, Caroline	Lothrop, Lee & Shepard
Ocean Tide Pool	P	I	250+	L'Hommedieu, Arthur John	Grolier Press
Ocean Tides	M	I	250+	Rosen Real Readers	Rosen Publishing Group
Ocean Waves	B	I	21	Twig	Wright Group/McGraw Hill
Ocean, The	H	I	139	Yellow Umbrella Books	Red Brick Learning
Oceanography	Q	I	2127	Independent Readers Social Studies	Houghton Mifflin
Oceans	Q	I	250+	The Wonders of our World	Crabtree
Oceans	Q	I	250+	First Reports	Compass Point Books
Oceans of Grass: The Prairie	O	I	707	Leveled Readers Social Studies	Houghton Mifflin
Oceans, Seas, and Coasts	M	I	250+	PM Plus Nonfiction	Rigby
Octopus Goes to School	C	F	42	Bordelon, Carolyn	Continental Press
Octopuses	J	I	94	Under the Sea	Capstone Press
Octopuses	G	I	47	Pebble Books	Capstone Press
Octopuses and Squids	O	I	328	Wonder World	Wright Group/McGraw Hill
Octopuses, Squid & Cuttlefish	L	I	231	Marine Life For Young Readers	Pearson Learning Group
Odd and Even Numbers	I	I	250+	Yellow Umbrella Books	Red Brick Learning
Odd Socks	G	RF	83	Literacy 2000	Rigby
*Oddballs	X	B	250+	Sleator, William	Puffin Books

* Collection of short stories

TITLE	LEVEL	GENRE	WORD COUNT	AUTHOR / SERIES	PUBLISHER / DISTRIBUTOR
*Odder Than Ever	Z	F	250+	Coville, Bruce	Harcourt Trade
*Oddly Enough	Z	F	250+	Coville, Bruce	Pocket Books
Odds on Oliver	P	RF	250+	Greene, Carol	Puffin Books
Odin's Wisdom	Z	TL	2644	Leveled Readers	Houghton Mifflin
Of Colors and Things	WB	I	N/A	Hoban, Tana	Scholastic
Of Mice and Men	Z	RF	250+	Steinbeck, John	Penguin Group
Of Nightingales That Weep	U	HF	250+	Paterson, Katherine	HarperCollins
Off and Running	S	RF	250+	Soto, Gary	Dell
Off the Map: The Journals of Lewis and Clark	U	I	250+	Roop, Peter & Connie	Walker & Company
Off to Grandma's House	D	RF	80	Little Celebrations	Pearson Learning Group
Off to School	C	RF	45	Story Steps	Rigby
Off To Sea: An Inside Look at a Research Cruise	T	I	250+	Kovacs, Deborah	Steck-Vaughn
Off To Squintum's/The Four Musicians	N	TL	1268	Collins, Gillian	Mondo
Off to the Library	C	RF	46	Seedlings	Continental Press
Off to the Shop	H	F	323	Storyteller-Night Crickets	Wright Group/McGraw Hill
Off to Work	B	RF	41	Literacy 2000	Rigby
Off We Go!	LB	RF	16	Pacific Literacy	Pacific Learning
Officially Interesting	Q	RF	1460	Leveled Readers	Houghton Mifflin
Ogden Nash: Playing with Words	U	B	1770	Leveled Readers	Houghton Mifflin
Ogs Discover Fire and Other Stuff, The	N	F	250+	Navigators Drama Series	Benchmark Education
Oh a Hunting We Will Go	E	TL	346	Langstaff, John	Macmillan
Oh Boy, Boston!	O	RF	250+	Giff, Patricia Reilly	Bantam
Oh Dear	F	F	109	Campbell, Rod	Macmillan
Oh No Otis!	E	F	45	Rookie Readers	Children's Press
Oh No!	E	RF	118	Bookshop	Mondo
Oh No!	E	F	118	Sun Sprouts	ETA/Cuisenaire
Oh No!	F	RF	122	Traditional Tales & More	Rigby
Oh, Brother	P	RF	250+	Wilson, Johnniece M.	Scholastic
Oh, Cats!	E	RF	93	Buck, Nola	HarperTrophy
Oh, Columbus!	K	F	250+	Literacy 2000	Rigby
Oh, Jump in a Sack	E	F	130	Story Box	Wright Group/McGraw Hill
Oh, No!	C	F	53	Joy Readers	Pearson Learning Group
Oh, No!	G	RF	128	Little Celebrations	Pearson Learning Group
Oh, No, Sherman	E	RF	66	Erickson, Betty	Continental Press
Oh, What a Daughter!	L	F	250+	Literacy 2000	Rigby
Ohio	S	I	250+	Thompson, Kathleen	Steck-Vaughn
Ohio	R	I	250+	This Land Is Your Land	Compass Point Books
Ohio	S	I	250+	Land of Liberty	Red Brick Learning
Ohio	Q	I	250+	One Nation	Capstone Press
Oil on Water	P	I	250+	Sails	Rigby
Oil Spill!	L	I	250+	Soar To Success	Houghton Mifflin
Oil Spills	P	I	250+	Rigby Focus	Rigby
Oil!	P	I	450	Independent Readers Social Studies	Houghton Mifflin
Oink Oink	LB	F	15	Geisert, Arthur	Houghton Mifflin
Ojibwa Indians, The	P	I	250+	Lund, Bill	Red Brick Learning
Ojibwa, The: Wild Rice Gatherers	R	I	250+	America's First Peoples	Capstone Press
Oklahoma	R	I	250+	This Land Is Your Land	Compass Point Books
Ola Shakes It Up	T	RF	250+	Hyppolite, Joanne	Random House
Ola's Wake	R	RF	250+	Stone, B. J.	Henry Holt & Co.
Old and New	G	I	54	Sun Sprouts	ETA/Cuisenaire
Old and New	C	I	50	Interaction	Rigby
Old and New	B	I	54	Early Connections	Benchmark Education
Old Bones	M	RF	848	Sunshine	Wright Group/McGraw Hill

* Collection of short stories

TITLE	LEVEL	GENRE	WORD COUNT	AUTHOR / SERIES	PUBLISHER / DISTRIBUTOR
Old Bumpy Alligator	E	F	69	Books for Young Learners	Richard C. Owen
Old Car, The	F	RF	135	Voyages	SRA/McGraw Hill
Old Cat, New Cat	G	RF	169	Wonder World	Wright Group/McGraw Hill
Old Devil Wind	J	F	250+	Martin, Jr., Bill	Harcourt Trade
Old Enough for Magic	L	F	250+	Pickett, A.	HarperTrophy
Old Friend, An	J	RF	250+	Sunshine	Wright Group/McGraw Hill
Old Friends	M	RF	345	Literacy 2000	Rigby
Old Friends, Near Friends	J	I	250+	Rigby Literacy	Rigby
Old Grizzly	H	F	185	Sunshine	Wright Group/McGraw Hill
Old Hat, New Hat	H	F	115	Berenstain, Stan & Jan	Random House
Old House, The	J	RF	375	Story Box	Wright Group/McGraw Hill
*Old Key, The	T	TL	250+	Literacy 2000	Rigby
Old King Cole	C	F	29	Seedlings	Continental Press
Old King Cole	E	TL	33	Jumbled Tumbled Tales & Rhymes	Rigby
Old MacDonald Had a Farm	J	TL	250+	Traditional Songs	Picture Window Books
Old MacDonald Had a Farm	F	TL	250+	PM Readalongs	Rigby
Old MacDonald Had a Farm	D	TL	103	Jones, Carol	Houghton Mifflin
Old MacDonald Had a Farm	D	TL	118	Rounds, Glen	Holiday House
Old MacDonald's Fun Time Farm	B	F	34	Instant Readers	Harcourt School Publishers
Old Malolo Had a Farm	H	F	250+	Sunshine	Wright Group/McGraw Hill
Old Man and the Bear, The	M	RF	250+	Hanel, Wolfram	North-South Books
Old Man's Mitten, The	I	TL	378	Bookshop	Mondo
Old Meadow, The	S	F	250+	Selden, George	Farrar, Straus and Giroux
Old Mother Hubbard	H	F	117	Literacy 2000	Rigby
Old Oak Tree, The	F	F	108	Little Celebrations	Pearson Learning Group
Old Recipe Book, The	L	F	250+	Smith, Ben	Wright Group/McGraw Hill
Old Red Rocking Chair, The	M	RF	250+	Root, Phyllis	Scholastic
Old Steam Train, The	F	RF	43	Literacy 2000	Rigby
Old Store, New Store	C	I	56	Leveled Readers Social Studies	Houghton Mifflin
Old Teeth, New Teeth	F	I	53	Wonder World	Wright Group/McGraw Hill
Old Toad, The	E	F	189	Phonics and Friends	Hampton-Brown
Old Tom and the Rogue	M	HF	250+	Wilson, Trevor	Pearson Learning Group
Old Train, The	F	RF	68	Books for Young Learners	Richard C. Owen
Old Tuatara	C	F	33	Pacific Literacy	Pacific Learning
Old Woman and Her Pig, The: An Old English Tale	K	TL	250+	Litzinger, Rosanne	OSI
Old Woman and the Pig, The	D	RF	68	Tiger Cub	Peguis
Old Woman in a Shoe, The	E	TL	38	Jumbled Tumbled Tales & Rhymes	Rigby
Old Woman Who Lived in a Shoe, The	D	F	56	Seedlings	Continental Press
Old Woman Who Lived in a Vinegar Bottle	M	TL	1161	Douglas, Ann	Mondo
Old Woman, The	H	F	69	Sunshine	Wright Group/McGraw Hill
Old Woman's Nose, The	K	F	250+	Sunshine	Wright Group/McGraw Hill
Old Yeller	V	RF	250+	Gipson, Fred	Scholastic
*Oliver and Amanda's Halloween	L	F	250+	Van Leeuwen, Jean	Puffin Books
*Oliver Pig at School	L	F	250+	Van Leeuwen, Jean	Puffin Books
*Oliver, Amanda, and Grandmother Pig	L	F	250+	Van Leeuwen, Jean	Puffin Books
Olive's Ocean	V	RF	250+	Henkes, Kevin	HarperCollins
Olympic Champions	S	I	250+	iOpeners	Pearson Learning Group
Olympic Dreams	O	RF	250+	Navigators Fiction Series	Benchmark Education
Olympic Softball Stars	R	I	577	Vocabulary Readers	Houghton Mifflin
Olympics and the Mini Olympics, The	N	I	250+	Mack, Rachel	Wright Group/McGraw Hill
Olympics, The	O	I	250+	Windows on Literacy	National Geographic
On a Boat	B	RF	20	Novek, Minda	Scholastic
On a Chair	C	F	30	Story Box	Wright Group/McGraw Hill

* Collection of short stories

TITLE	LEVEL	GENRE	WORD COUNT	AUTHOR / SERIES	PUBLISHER / DISTRIBUTOR
On a Cold, Cold Day	C	F	33	Tadpoles	Rigby
On a Dark and Scary Night	F	F	50	Shared Reading	Rigby
On a Hill	D	RF	53	Start to Read	School Zone
On a Map	D	I	60	Windows on Literacy	National Geographic
On a Walk	A	RF	5	Ready Readers	Pearson Learning Group
On All Kinds of Days	C	I	50	Yellow Umbrella Books	Red Brick Learning
On and Off	B	I	60	PM Plus Nonfiction	Rigby
On and Off the Road	M	I	250+	Wildcats	Wright Group/McGraw Hill
On Board the Santa Maria	T	I	2391	Independent Readers Social Studies	Houghton Mifflin
On Board The Titanic	T	I	250+	Tanaka, Shelley	Hyperion/Madison Press
On Christmas Eve	WB	RF	N/A	Collington, Peter	Alfred A. Knopf
On Earth	B	I	35	Leveled Readers Social Studies	Houghton Mifflin
On Fortune's Wheel	Z	F	250+	Voigt, Cynthia	Aladdin
On Friday the Giant	K	F	240	The Giant	Wright Group/McGraw Hill
On Guard	R	RF	250+	Napoli, Donna Jo	Puffin Books
On Monday the Giant	K	F	250+	The Giant	Wright Group/McGraw Hill
On My Honor	S	RF	250+	Bauer, Marion Dane	Bantam
On My Street	H	I	292	Visions	Wright Group/McGraw Hill
On My Way	N	B	250+	DePaola, Tomie	Penguin Group
On Our Farm	A	I	14	Bebop Books	Lee & Low Books Inc.
On Our Street	C	RF	52	Little Red Readers	Sundance
On Safari	N	I	250+	Windows on Literacy	National Geographic
On Safari	A	I	28	Smart Starts	Rigby
On Saturday	C	RF	44	Handprints B	Educator's Publishing Service
On Saturday	C	I	28	Little Red Readers	Sundance
On Site	S	I	250+	Pollock, John	Mondo
On Stage	E	I	94	Early Connections	Benchmark Education
On Sunday the Giant	K	F	250+	The Giant	Wright Group/McGraw Hill
On the Air	S	I	250+	Wonder World	Wright Group/McGraw Hill
On the Air	L	I	250+	Rigby Literacy	Rigby
On the Banks of Plum Creek	Q	HF	250+	Wilder, Laura Ingalls	HarperCollins
On the Banks of the Bayou	Q	HF	250+	MacBride, Roger Lea	HarperCollins
On the Beach	J	I	258	Leveled Readers	Houghton Mifflin
On the Beach	B	RF	28	Smart Starts	Rigby
On the Beams	N	I	328	Independent Readers Social Studies	Houghton Mifflin
On the bridge at Avignon	F	TL	250+	PM Readalongs	Rigby
On the Computer	D	I	67	Twig	Wright Group/McGraw Hill
On the Edge	S	I	250+	Action Packs	Rigby
On The Far Side Of The Mountain	V	RF	250+	George, Jean Craighead	Puffin Books
On the Farm	A	I	24	Vocabulary Readers	Houghton Mifflin
On the Farm	N	I	250+	iOpeners	Pearson Learning Group
On the Farm	C	I	18	Literacy 2000	Rigby
On the Farm	D	RF	18	Sun Sprouts	ETA/Cuisenaire
On the Go	C	RF	43	Learn to Read	Creative Teaching Press
On the Go	G	I	250+	Yellow Umbrella Books	Red Brick Learning
On the Ground	C	I	40	Sunshine	Wright Group/McGraw Hill
On the Job	F	RF	79	City Stories	Rigby
On the Line	B	RF	35	Teacher's Choice Series	Pearson Learning Group
On the List	N	F	250+	Sails	Rigby
On the Menu	N	F	250+	Sails	Rigby
On the Moon	H	I	77	Windows on Literacy	National Geographic

* Collection of short stories

TITLE	LEVEL	GENRE	WORD COUNT	AUTHOR / SERIES	PUBLISHER / DISTRIBUTOR
On the Move	S	I	250+	Sunshine	Wright Group/McGraw Hill
On the Move	D	I	26	Wonder World	Wright Group/McGraw Hill
On the Move	B	I	28	Windows on Literacy	National Geographic
On the Open Plains	J	I	250+	Momentum Literacy Program	Troll Associates
On the Right Track	N	I	250+	Home Connection Collection	Rigby
On the Road	C	I	47	Teacher's Choice Series	Pearson Learning Group
On the Rocks	A	I	42	Windows on Literacy	National Geographic
On the School Bus	F	RF	62	Little Readers	Houghton Mifflin
On the Silk Road: Ancient Baghdad	L	I	250+	Leveled Readers Language Support	Houghton Mifflin
On the Way Home	S	HF	250+	Wilder, Laura Ingalls	HarperCollins
On the Way to the Moon	O	F	250+	Gold, Becky	Pearson Learning Group
On the Weekend	WB	I	N/A	Windows on Literacy	National Geographic
On This Earth	D	I	71	Rise & Shine	Hampton-Brown
On Thursday the Giant	K	F	250+	The Giant	Wright Group/McGraw Hill
On Top of Concord Hill	Q	HF	250+	Wilkes, Maria D.	HarperCollins
On Top of Spaghetti	G	F	105	Little Celebrations	Pearson Learning Group
On Top of the World	Q	I	588	Vocabulary Readers	Houghton Mifflin
On Tuesday the Giant	K	F	250+	The Giant	Wright Group/McGraw Hill
On Vacation	D	I	88	Little Red Readers	Sundance
On Wednesday the Giant	K	F	250+	The Giant	Wright Group/McGraw Hill
On Wings of a Dragon	Y	F	250+	Taylor, Cora	Fitzhenry & Whiteside
On With the Show!	M	I	250+	Pair-It Books	Steck-Vaughn
Once I Was a Plum Tree	Q	RF	250+	Hurwitz, Johanna	Beech Tree Books
Once on this Island	S	HF	250+	Whelan, Gloria	HarperTrophy
Once Upon a Marigold	W	F	250+	Ferris, Jean	Harcourt Trade
Once upon a Rhyme	M	F	250+	Pacific Literacy	Pacific Learning
Once Upon a Story	M	I	227	Vocabulary Readers	Houghton Mifflin
Once Upon a Time	H	F	243	Ready Readers	Pearson Learning Group
Once Upon a Time	T	I	250+	Literacy 2000	Rigby
Once Upon a Time	O	B	250+	Bunting, Eve	Richard C. Owen
Once Upon a Time in Junior High	U	RF	250+	Norment, Lisa	Scholastic
Once When I Was Shipwrecked	L	F	250+	Literacy 2000	Rigby
One Blue Hen	F	F	108	Cambridge Reading	Pearson Learning Group
One and Only Special Me, The	E	RF	73	Learn to Read	Creative Teaching Press
One Bad Thing About Father, The	M	RF	250+	Monjo, F. N.	HarperTrophy
One Bear All Alone	H	F	107	Bucknall, Caroline	Dial Books
One Bee Got on the Bus	C	F	43	Ready Readers	Pearson Learning Group
One Bird	Y	RF	250+	Mori, Kyoko	Ballantine Books
One Bird Sat on the Fence	C	I	40	Wonder World	Wright Group/McGraw Hill
One Birthday, Two Traditions	D	RF	56	Independent Readers Social Studies	Houghton Mifflin
One Chick, One Egg	D	F	64	Step-By-Step Series	Pearson Learning Group
One Cold, Wet Night	D	F	134	Story Box	Wright Group/McGraw Hill
One Day	C	RF	48	Teacher's Choice Series	Pearson Learning Group
One Day in May	N	F	710	Leveled Readers	Houghton Mifflin
One Day in the Alpine Tundra	P	I	250+	George, Jean Craighead	HarperCollins
One Day in the Desert	P	I	250+	George, Jean Craighead	HarperCollins
One Day in the Tropical Rain Forest	S	I	250+	George, Jean Craighead	HarperTrophy
One Day in the Woods	P	I	250+	George, Jean Craighead	HarperTrophy
One Day, Two Stars	N	RF	250+	Leveled Readers Language Support	Houghton Mifflin
One Drop of Water and a Million More	K	I	156	Book Bank	Wright Group/McGraw Hill
One- Eyed Jake	M	F	547	Hutchins, Pat	Morrow

* Collection of short stories

TITLE	LEVEL	GENRE	WORD COUNT	AUTHOR / SERIES	PUBLISHER / DISTRIBUTOR
One Fat Summer	Y	RF	250+	Lipsyte, Robert	HarperCollins
One for You and One for Me	C	RF	27	Blaxland, Wendy	Scholastic
One for You and One for Me	I	I	354	Early Connections	Benchmark Education
One Frog, One Fly	C	F	26	Blaxland, Wendy	Scholastic
One Giant Leap	S	I	250+	Fraser, Mary Ann	Henry Holt & Co.
One Green Frog	H	I	215	Yellow Umbrella Books	Red Brick Learning
One Happy Classroom	D	RF	49	Rookie Readers	Children's Press
One Hot Summer Night	I	RF	126	Bookshop	Mondo
One Hundred Books	I	I	217	Story Box	Wright Group/McGraw Hill
One Hundred Hungry Ants	K	F	250+	Pinczes, Elinor	Houghton Mifflin
One Hundredth Thing about Caroline, The	R	RF	250+	Lowry, Lois	Bantam
One Hunter	LB	F	15	Hutchins, Pat	Greenwillow
One in the Middle Is the Green Kangaroo, The	M	RF	250+	Blume, Judy	Bantam
One Little Elephant	H	F	174	Sunshine	Wright Group/McGraw Hill
One Little Slip	C	F	33	Instant Readers	Harcourt School Publishers
One Lucky Summer	O	RF	250+	Kvasnosky, Laura McGee	Penguin Group
One Man Show	O	B	250+	Asch, Frank	Richard C. Owen
One Monday Morning	G	F	180	Shulevitz, Uri	Scribner
One More Child	D	RF	28	Harry's Math Books	Outside the Box
One More River	V	HF	250+	Banks, Lynne Reid	Avon Camelot
*One More River to Cross	X	B	250+	Haskins, Jim	Scholastic
One More Time	C	RF	45	Instant Readers	Harcourt School Publishers
One Night	I	RF	92	Carter, Jackie	Scholastic
One O'Clock Is Time for One Nap	D	RF	56	Harry's Math Books	Outside the Box
One Piece Missing	K	SF	250+	Rigby Literacy	Rigby
*One Potato, Tu	T	RF	250+	Pearson, Gayle	Scholastic
One Quiet Afternoon	I	F	155	Instant Readers	Harcourt School Publishers
One Racer	F	I	106	Leveled Readers Science	Houghton Mifflin
One Smart Chick	G	F	250	Rigby Literacy	Rigby
One Soccer Game	C	RF	29	Harry's Math Books	Outside the Box
One Sock, Two Socks	H	RF	179	Reading Corners	Pearson Learning Group
One Stormy Night	F	RF	165	Story Basket	Wright Group/McGraw Hill
One Sun in the Sky	E	RF	120	Windmill	Wright Group/McGraw Hill
One Thing I'm Good At	R	RF	250+	Williams, Karen Lynn	William Morrow
One Thousand Currant Buns	H	F	213	Sunshine	Wright Group/McGraw Hill
One Who Came Back, The	X	RF	250+	Mazzio, Joann	Houghton Mifflin
One, One Is the Sun	B	RF	42	Story Box	Wright Group/McGraw Hill
One, Two, Buckle My Shoe	D	TL	27	Instant Readers	Harcourt School Publishers
One, Two, Three, Four	D	F	89	Rise & Shine	Hampton-Brown
One, Two, Three, Four	LB	F	21	KinderReaders	Rigby
One-Eyed Cat	S	RF	250+	Fox, Paula	Bantam
One-Man Band	H	RF	144	Leveled Readers Science	Houghton Mifflin
Oni Wa Soto	M	TL	250+	Story Vines	Wright Group/McGraw Hill
Onion John	U	HF	250+	Krumgold, Joseph	Harper & Row
Onion Sundaes	L	RF	250+	Adler, David A.	Random House
Onion Tears	Q	RF	250+	Kidd, Diana	William Morrow
*On-Line Spaceman and Other Cases, The	O	RF	250+	Simon, Seymour	Avon
Only an Octopus	H	RF	236	Literacy 2000	Rigby
Only Earth and Sky Last Forever	Y	HF	250+	Benchley, Nathaniel	HarperCollins
Ontario	T	I	250+	Hello Canada	Fitzhenry & Whiteside
Oogly Gum Chasing Game, The	K	F	250+	Literacy 2000	Rigby
Oops!	D	F	62	Mayer, Mercer	Penguin Group
Oops! Why Did I Do That?	K	RF	416	Early Connections	Benchmark Education
Open Door Club, The	L	RF	570	Leveled Readers	Houghton Mifflin

* Collection of short stories

TITLE	LEVEL	GENRE	WORD COUNT	AUTHOR / SERIES	PUBLISHER / DISTRIBUTOR
Open It!	D	I	27	Pacific Literacy	Pacific Learning
Open Wide	G	I	189	Home Connection Collection	Rigby
Open Wide	C	F	56	Mitchell, Robin	Scholastic
Open Your Eyes, Sidney Miffet	H	RF	107	Seedlings	Continental Press
Open Your Mouth	F	F	201	Sunshine	Wright Group/McGraw Hill
Opening Night	M	RF	250+	Navigators Fiction Series	Benchmark Education
Opening Night	X	I	2265	Leveled Readers	Houghton Mifflin
Opposite of Pig, The	K	F	250+	Little Celebrations	Pearson Learning Group
Oprah Winfrey, A Voice for the People	U	B	250+	Brooks, Philip	Grolier Publishing
Optometrist, The	G	I	191	PM Nonfiction-Blue	Rigby
Orange: Seeing Orange All Around Us	K	I	250+	Colors	Capstone Press
Oranges for Orange Juice	F	I	25	Learn to Read	Creative Teaching Press
Orca Song	K	RF	250+	Armour	Scholastic
Orca Whales	F	I	85	Seedlings	Continental Press
Orca Whales	H	I	85	Salem, Lynn	Wright Group/McGraw Hill
*Orca's Family and More Northwest Coast Stories	P	TL	250+	Challenger, James Robert	Heritage House
Orchestra, The	C	F	33	Foundations	Wright Group/McGraw Hill
Ordinary Genius, The Story of Albert Einstein	U	B	250+	McPherson, Stephanie S.	The Lerner Group
Ordinary Miracles	Y	RF	250+	Tolan, Stephanie S.	Morrow
Oregon	R	I	250+	This Land Is Your Land	Compass Point Books
Oregon Trail, The	T	I	250+	The Heinle Reading Library	Thomson Learning
Oregon Trail, The	V	I	250+	Let Freedom Ring	Red Brick Learning
Oregon Trail, The	S	I	250+	The Library of the Westward Expansion	Rosen Publishing Group
Oregon Trail, The	T	I	250+	We The People	Compass Point Books
Oregon Trail, The	V	I	250+	Cornerstones of Freedom	Children's Press
Origami	L	I	250+	How-To Series	Benchmark Education
Original Adventures of Hank the Cowdog, The	Q	F	250+	Erickson, John R.	Gulf
Orphan of Ellis Island, The	S	HF	250+	Woodruff, Elvira	Scholastic
Orphan Train	K	RF	250+	The Wright Skills	Wright Group/McGraw Hill
Orphan Train Adventures: Caught in the Act	W	HF	250+	Nixon, Joan Lowery	Bantam
Orphan Train Adventures: Circle of Love	W	HF	250+	Nixon, Joan Lowery	Bantam
Orphan Train Adventures: Dangerous Promise, A	W	HF	250+	Nixon, Joan Lowery	Dell
Orphan Train Adventures: Family Apart, A	W	HF	250+	Nixon, Joan Lowery	Dell
Orphan Train Adventures: In the Face of Danger	W	HF	250+	Nixon, Joan Lowery	Dell
Orphan Train Adventures: Keeping Secrets	W	HF	250+	Nixon, Joan Lowery	Dell
Orphan Train Adventures: Place to Belong, A	W	HF	250+	Nixon, Joan Lowery	Dell
Orphan Train Children: Aggie's Home	Q	HF	250+	Nixon, Joan Lowery	Yearling
Orphan Train Journey	S	HF	1247	Leveled Readers	Houghton Mifflin
Orson Welles and The War of the Worlds	V	I	1917	Leveled Readers	Houghton Mifflin
Oscar & Tatiana	N	RF	250+	Literacy 2000	Rigby
Oscar Otter	J	F	250+	Benchley, Nathaniel	HarperTrophy
Oscar's Day	J	I	154	iOpeners	Pearson Learning Group
Osceola: Patriot and Warrior	T	B	250+	Jumper, Moses; Sonder, Ben	Steck-Vaughn
Osprey	M	I	250+	Cambridge Reading	Pearson Learning Group
Ostriches	M	I	250+	Sails	Rigby
Other Side of the Lake, The	L	F	250+	Little Celebrations	Pearson Learning Group
Other Side, The	G	F	182	Sun Sprouts	ETA/Cuisenaire
Others See Us	Z	F	250+	Sleator, William	Puffin Books
Otherwise Known As Sheila the Great	R	RF	250+	Blume, Judy	Bantam
Otis Spofford	O	RF	250+	Cleary, Beverly	Avon
Otter, Otter	C	I	39	Phonics and Friends	Hampton-Brown
Otto the Cat	I	F	250+	Herman, Gail	Grosset & Dunlap

* Collection of short stories

TITLE	LEVEL	GENRE	WORD COUNT	AUTHOR / SERIES	PUBLISHER / DISTRIBUTOR
Ouch!	L	RF	250+	Noonan, Diana	Pearson Learning Group
Ouch!	LB	RF	40	Literacy 2000	Rigby
Ouch!	B	I	40	Science	Outside the Box
Our "Current" World	T	I	250+	Navigators Social Studies Series	Benchmark Education
Our Adobe House	L	I	250+	Greetings	Rigby
Our American Flag	O	I	250+	McCloskey, Susan	Wright Group/McGraw Hill
Our Baby	J	RF	128	Foundations	Wright Group/McGraw Hill
Our Baby	B	RF	14	Literacy 2000	Rigby
Our Baby	E	I	90	PM Nonfiction-Yellow	Rigby
Our Baby	D	RF	70	Voyages	SRA/McGraw Hill
Our Bodies	J	I	250+	PM Plus Nonfiction	Rigby
Our Book of Maps	N	I	250+	Discovery World	Rigby
Our Busy Bodies	K	I	144	Home Connection Collection	Rigby
Our Camping Trip	E	RF	120	Lighthouse	Rigby
Our Car	C	RF	32	Sunshine	Wright Group/McGraw Hill
Our Car	G	I	94	Bookshop	Mondo
Our Cat	E	RF	99	Foundations	Wright Group/McGraw Hill
Our Changing Earth	R	I	250+	Belcher, Angie	Pacific Learning
Our Chore Chart	D	I	65	Storyteller-First Snow	Wright Group/McGraw Hill
Our Class Survey	F	I	128	Early Connections	Benchmark Education
Our Classroom	E	RF	53	Leveled Readers Social Studies	Houghton Mifflin
Our Clothes	J	I	250+	PM Plus Nonfiction	Rigby
Our Clubhouse	WB	I	N/A	Windows on Literacy	National Geographic
Our Dad	C	RF	41	Little Books for Early Readers	University of Maine
Our Dog Sam	B	RF	56	Literacy 2000	Rigby
Our Earth	F	I	53	Rosen Real Readers	Rosen Publishing Group
Our Earth	D	I	33	Discovery Links	Newbridge
Our Endangered Planet (Oceans)	W	I	250+	Hoff, Mary; Rodgers, Mary	Lerner Publishing
Our Eyes	I	I	869	Sunshine	Wright Group/McGraw Hill
Our Families	B	I	52	Leveled Readers Social Studies	Houghton Mifflin
Our Families	B	I	26	Rigby Literacy	Rigby
Our Farm	C	I	37	Rosen Real Readers	Rosen Publishing Group
Our Favorite Things To Do	F	I	241	Yellow Umbrella Books	Capstone Press
Our Favorites	G	I	217	Learn to Read	Creative Teaching Press
Our Flag	C	I	21	Leveled Readers Social Studies	Houghton Mifflin
Our Flag	I	I	93	Phonics Readers	Compass Point Books
Our Flag	M	HF	250+	Rothman, Cynthia	Scholastic
Our Four Walls	L	RF	422	Leveled Readers	Houghton Mifflin
Our Garage	F	RF	80	Urmston, Kathleen; Evans, Karen	Kaeden Books
Our Garden	B	I	16	Literacy 2000	Rigby
Our Goat	D	RF	27	Costain, Meredith	Scholastic
Our Government	M	I	250+	People, Spaces & Places	Rand McNally
Our Grandad	C	RF	30	Sunshine	Wright Group/McGraw Hill
Our Granny	C	RF	41	Sunshine	Wright Group/McGraw Hill
Our Home is the Pond	E	I	52	Independent Readers Science	Houghton Mifflin
Our House Had a Mouse	E	F	102	Worthington, Denise	Continental Press
Our House Is a Safe House	G	I	163	PM Plus Nonfiction	Rigby
Our Magazine Article	P	I	250+	Rigby Focus	Rigby
Our Mom	E	I	107	PM Nonfiction-Yellow	Rigby
Our Money	E	I	74	Leveled Readers Social Studies	Houghton Mifflin
Our Money	J	I	255	Early Connections	Benchmark Education
Our Moon	H	I	161	Early Connections	Benchmark Education
Our Mysterious Universe	Y	I	250+	iOpeners	Pearson Learning Group
Our National Holidays	Q	I	250+	Let's See	Compass Point Books

* Collection of short stories

TITLE	LEVEL	GENRE	WORD COUNT	AUTHOR / SERIES	PUBLISHER / DISTRIBUTOR
Our National Parks	Q	I	250+	Let's See	Compass Point Books
Our National Treasures	O	I	250+	Bookshop	Mondo
Our Natural Resources	M	I	1234	Leveled Readers Social Studies	Houghton Mifflin
Our New Baby	F	RF	59	City Stories	Rigby
Our New House	G	RF	68	PM Plus Nonfiction	Rigby
Our New Principal	K	RF	149	City Kids	Rigby
Our New Puppy	C	RF	29	Windows on Literacy	National Geographic
Our Old Friend, Bear	J	RF	250+	PM Story Books-Silver	Rigby
Our Only May Amelia	R	HF	250+	Holm, Jennifer	HarperCollins
Our Parents	G	I	142	PM Nonfiction-Blue	Rigby
Our Party	B	RF	40	Leveled Readers Social Studies	Houghton Mifflin
Our Planet	R	I	250+	Worldwise	Grolier Press
Our Playhouse	D	RF	46	Voyages	SRA/McGraw Hill
Our Polliwogs	I	RF	91	Books for Young Learners	Richard C. Owen
Our Pumpkin	B	I	29	Learn to Read	Creative Teaching Press
Our Rocket	B	I	28	Pacific Literacy	Pacific Learning
Our School	H	RF	98	City Kids	Rigby
Our School	C	I	46	Twig	Wright Group/McGraw Hill
Our School	H	RF	46	Well-Being Series	Dominie Press
Our Senses	K	I	179	Spyglass Books	Compass Point Books
Our Senses	D	I	39	Rise & Shine	Hampton-Brown
Our Senses	F	I	182	Discovery Links	Newbridge
Our Skeleton	I	I	105	Sunshine Books	Wright Group/McGraw Hill
Our Soccer Team	G	RF	139	Literacy Tree	Rigby
Our Star, the Sun	N	I	599	Leveled Readers Science	Houghton Mifflin
Our Street	C	RF	40	Sunshine	Wright Group/McGraw Hill
Our Sun	J	I	166	Early Connections	Benchmark Education
Our Sun	I	I	131	Rosen Real Readers	Rosen Publishing Group
Our Teacher	G	RF	168	Windows on Literacy	National Geographic
Our Teacher, Miss Pool	D	F	62	Pacific Literacy	Pacific Learning
Our Town	H	I	129	Windows on Literacy	National Geographic
Our Town	B	RF	37	Little Red Readers	Sundance
Our Town	G	RF	129	Well-Being Series	Pearson Learning Group
Our Town Mural	M	RF	660	Leveled Readers	Houghton Mifflin
Our Tree House	E	RF	144	Twig	Wright Group/McGraw Hill
Our Week	C	RF	37	Storyteller-First Snow	Wright Group/McGraw Hill
*Our World of Mysteries: Fascinating Facts About the Planet Earth	X	I	250+	Lord, Suzanne	Scholastic
Our World of Wonders	Q	I	250+	Canetti, Yanitzia	Steck-Vaughn
Out After Dark	H	RF	114	Book Bank	Wright Group/McGraw Hill
Out and About	Q	I	250+	Explorers	Wright Group/McGraw Hill
Out in Space	L	I	224	Spyglass Books	Compass Point Books
Out in the Big Wild World	K	F	430	Jellybeans	Rigby
Out in the Weather	B	I	56	PM Starters	Rigby
Out of Bounds	Z	HF	250+	Naidoo, Beverly	HarperCollins
Out of Darkness: The Story of Louis Braille	S	B	250+	Freedman, Russell	Houghton Mifflin
Out of Reach	G	RF	86	Literacy Tree	Rigby
Out of Sight	C	I	52	Rigby Literacy	Rigby
Out of the Dust	X	HF	250+	Hesse, Karen	Scholastic
Out the Door	E	RF	150	Rookie Readers	Children's Press
Outcast of Redwall, The	Z	F	250+	Jacques, Brian	Ace Books
Outdoor Adventures	W	I	250+	iOpeners	Pearson Learning Group
Outing, An	E	RF	68	Sunshine	Wright Group/McGraw Hill
Outrageously Alice	U	RF	250+	Naylor, Phyllis Reynolds	Aladdin

* Collection of short stories

TITLE	LEVEL	GENRE	WORD COUNT	AUTHOR / SERIES	PUBLISHER / DISTRIBUTOR
Outside and Inside	C	I	43	Twig	Wright Group/McGraw Hill
Outside and Inside Bats	Q	I	250+	Markle, Sandra	Simon & Schuster
Outside and Inside Kangaroos	Q	I	250+	Markle, Sandra	Atheneum
Outside and Inside Sharks	Q	I	250+	Markle, Sandra	Simon & Schuster
Outside and Inside Snakes	Q	I	250+	Markle, Sandra	Simon & Schuster
Outside and Inside Spiders	Q	I	250+	Markle, Sandra	Simon & Schuster
Outside Dog, The	K	RF	250+	Pomerantz, Charlotte	HarperTrophy
Outside the Window	B	I	31	Vocabulary Readers	Houghton Mifflin
Outside, Inside	D	RF	97	Teacher's Choice Series	Pearson Learning Group
Outsiders, The	Z	RF	250+	Hinton, S. E.	Penguin Group
Outwitting the Tiger	L	TL	250+	Voyages	SRA/McGraw Hill
Ovals: Seeing Ovals All Around Us	K	I	214	Shapes	Capstone Press
Over and Over	D	RF	39	Ray's Readers	Outside the Box
Over in the Meadow	F	TL	250+	PM Readalongs	Rigby
Over in the Meadow	F	F	228	Cambridge Reading	Pearson Learning Group
Over in the Meadow	G	F	242	Little Readers	Houghton Mifflin
Over Sea, Under Stone	X	F	250+	Cooper, Susan	Simon & Schuster
Over the Bridge	B	I	50	Little Red Readers	Sundance
Over the Marble Mountain	E	RF	92	Voyages	SRA/McGraw Hill
Over the Oregon Trail	D	I	131	Twig	Wright Group/McGraw Hill
Over Under in the Garden	WB	I	N/A	Schories, Pat	Farrar, Straus and Giroux
Overcoming Challenges: The Life of Charles F. Bolden, Jr.	Q	B	250+	Walton, Darwin McBeth	Steck-Vaughn
Over-Under	E	RF	29	Rookie Readers	Children's Press
Owl and the Pussy	K	TL	250+	PM Animal Facts: Gold	Rigby
Owl and the Pussy Cat	L	TL	215	Lear, Edward	Scholastic
*Owl At Home	J	F	1488	Lobel, Arnold	HarperCollins
Owl in the Office	Q	RF	250+	Baglio, Ben M.	Scholastic
Owl Moon	O	B	250+	Yolen, Jane	Scholastic
Owl, That's Who!, An	D	I	31	Rosen Real Readers	Rosen Publishing Group
Owl, That's Who, An	E	I	31	Rosen Real Readers	Rosen Publishing Group
Owlbert	K	RF	250+	Soar To Success	Houghton Mifflin
Owliver	H	F	106	Kraus, Robert	Simon & Schuster
Owls	M	I	250+	PM Animal Facts: Gold	Rigby
Owls	I	I	250+	Pebble Books	Red Brick Learning
Owls	R	I	250+	Kalman, Bobbie	Crabtree
Owls	O	I	250+	Holmes, Kevin J.	Red Brick Learning
Owls in the Family	P	F	250+	Mowat, Farley	Bantam
Owls in the Garden	L	RF	670	PM Gold	Rigby
Ox-Cart Man	K	HF	250+	Hall, Donald	Scholastic
P. J. Funnybunny Camps Out	I	F	250+	Sadler, Marilyn	Random House
P. W. Cracker Sees the World	Q	F	250+	Yoshizawa, Linda	Steck-Vaughn
P.S. Longer Letter Later	U	RF	250+	Danziger, Paula; Martin, Ann M.	Scholastic
Pablo Picasso	P	B	250+	Lowery, Linda	Lerner Publishing
Pack 109	J	RF	164	Thaler, Mike	Scholastic
Pack a Picnic	E	F	140	Learn to Read	Creative Teaching Press
Package, The	E	RF	35	Bauer, Roger	Kaeden Books
Packing	B	RF	37	Foundations	Wright Group/McGraw Hill
Packing My Bag	B	RF	52	PM Starters	Rigby
Paco's Garden	G	RF	118	Books for Young Learners	Richard C. Owen
Pagan's Crusade	Y	HF	250+	Jinks, Catherine	Candlewick Press
Pagemaster, The	P	F	250+	Horowitz, Jordan	Scholastic
Paint Brush Kid, The	M	RF	250+	Bulla, Clyde Robert	Random House
Paint the Sky	LB	F	14	Sunshine	Wright Group/McGraw Hill

* Collection of short stories

TITLE	LEVEL	GENRE	WORD COUNT	AUTHOR / SERIES	PUBLISHER / DISTRIBUTOR
Paintball	Q	I	250+	X-Sports	Capstone Press
Painter, The	C	RF	31	Ray's Readers	Outside the Box
Painters	A	I	23	Twig	Wright Group/McGraw Hill
Painting	C	RF	24	Story Box	Wright Group/McGraw Hill
Painting Day, The	H	RF	250+	Voyages	SRA/McGraw Hill
Painting Lesson, The	K	F	250+	Pacific Literacy	Pacific Learning
Painting Shapes	F	I	148	Early Connections	Benchmark Education
Pair of Babies, A	D	I	70	Early Connections	Benchmark Education
Pajama Party	M	RF	250+	Hest, Amy	William Morrow
Pajama Party, The	D	F	46	Sunshine	Wright Group/McGraw Hill
Pakistan	W	I	250+	Countries and Cultures	Capstone Press
Pal the Pony	G	RF	224	Herman, R. A.	Grosset & Dunlap
Palm Trees	H	I	123	Pebble Books	Capstone Press
Paloma's Party	L	I	250+	Little Celebrations	Pearson Learning Group
Pam & Sam at the Park	C	F	108	Carousel Earlybirds	Pearson Learning Group
Pam & Sam at the Zoo	C	F	84	Carousel Earlybirds	Pearson Learning Group
Pam & Sam Fly Over the City	C	F	80	Carousel Earlybirds	Pearson Learning Group
Pam & Sam on the Beach	C	F	94	Carousel Earlybirds	Pearson Learning Group
Pan Woman	P	RF	1145	Leveled Readers	Houghton Mifflin
Panama Canal, The	W	I	250+	Cornerstones of Freedom	Children's Press
Pancake, The	K	TL	250+	Lobel, Anita	Bantam
Pancakes	WB	RF	N/A	Rigby Literacy	Rigby
Pancakes	G	RF	181	Foundations	Wright Group/McGraw Hill
Pancakes for Breakfast	C	RF	108	Emergent	Pioneer Valley
Pancakes for Breakfast	WB	F	N/A	DePaola, Tomie	Doubleday Books
Pancakes for Breakfast	H	F	99	Books for Young Learners	Richard C. Owen
Pancakes for Supper	H	RF	96	Literacy 2000	Rigby
Pancakes!	F	F	106	Ready Readers	Pearson Learning Group
Pancakes, Crackers, and Pizza	C	RF	63	Rookie Readers	Children's Press
Panda Bear, The	D	I	28	Rosen Real Readers	Rosen Publishing Group
Panda, The	L	I	250+	Sunshine	Wright Group/McGraw Hill
Panda's Birthday Surprise	F	F	141	Seedlings	Continental Press
Pandas Have Cubs	M	I	250+	Animals and Their Young	Compass Point Books
Pandas in the Mountains	M	F	735	PM Gold	Rigby
Panda's Surprise	H	F	242	Little Readers	Houghton Mifflin
Pandora's Box	Q	RF	250+	Literacy 2000	Rigby
Pangaea	X	I	3186	Leveled Readers Science	Houghton Mifflin
Panning for Gold	O	RF	825	Leveled Readers Science	Houghton Mifflin
Pansies for Mom	G	I	56	Windows on Literacy	National Geographic
Papa Penguin's Surprise	F	RF	136	Seedlings	Continental Press
Papagayo the Mischief Maker	N	TL	250+	McDermott, Gerald	Harcourt Trade
Papa's Spaghetti	G	F	248	Literacy 2000	Rigby
Paper Bag Trail	E	RF	67	Schreiber, Anne; Doughty, A.	Scholastic
Paper Birds, The	K	RF	363	Foundations	Wright Group/McGraw Hill
Paper Crane, The	M	F	250+	Soar To Success	Houghton Mifflin
Paper Crunch	K	I	250+	Rigby Literacy	Rigby
Paper Patchwork	F	I	54	Pacific Literacy	Pacific Learning
Paper Route, The	K	RF	314	New Way Green	Steck-Vaughn
Paper Shapes	N	I	250+	Voyages	SRA/McGraw Hill
Paper Trail, The	I	RF	253	Windmill Books	Rigby
Parachutes	J	RF	145	Storyteller-Moon Rising	Wright Group/McGraw Hill
Parade in Valencia	K	RF	214	Leveled Readers Language Support	Houghton Mifflin
Parade, The	B	RF	67	PM Plus Starters	Rigby

TITLE	LEVEL	GENRE	WORD COUNT	AUTHOR / SERIES	PUBLISHER / DISTRIBUTOR
Parade, The	B	I	56	Leveled Readers Emergent	Houghton Mifflin
Parades!	C	I	24	Pair-It Books	Steck-Vaughn
Parakeet Girl, The	J	F	250+	Sadler, Marilyn	Random House
Parakeets	J	I	250+	PM Animal Facts: Orange	Rigby
Pardon? Said the Giraffe	F	F	123	West, Colin	Harper & Row
Parents	C	I	60	Pebble Books	Capstone Press
Parents' Night Fright	K	RF	250+	Levy, Elizabeth	Scholastic
Park Rangers	M	I	250+	Community Helpers	Red Brick Learning
Park Ranger's Day, A	H	I	195	Rosen Real Readers	Rosen Publishing Group
Park, The	G	RF	155	Windows on Literacy	National Geographic
Park's Quest	U	RF	250+	Paterson, Katherine	Puffin Books
Parrot Talk	K	RF	250+	Cambridge Reading	Pearson Learning Group
Parrotfish	G	I	51	Pebble Books	Capstone Press
Parrots	L	I	250+	Bridgestone Books	Capstone Press
Parrots	J	I	94	Pebble Books	Red Brick Learning
Part of the Sky, A	Z	HF	250+	Peck, Robert Newton	Random House
Partners	L	I	159	Home Connection Collection	Rigby
Parts Make Up a Whole	J	I	219	Early Connections	Benchmark Education
Parts of a Plant	K	I	164	Phonics Readers	Compass Point Books
Parts of a Whole	G	I	161	Early Connections	Benchmark Education
Parts of a Whole	M	I	250+	Yellow Umbrella Books	Capstone Press
Party Food	A	I	25	Rigby Focus	Rigby
Party for a Rabbit, A	C	F	70	Early Connections	Benchmark Education
Party for Brown Mouse, A	E	F	149	PM Plus Story Books	Rigby
Party Game, The	G	RF	115	Home Connection Collection	Rigby
Party Games	J	RF	399	Foundations	Wright Group/McGraw Hill
Party Hats	B	RF	72	PM Plus Starters	Rigby
Party Time	J	I	250+	Rigby Literacy	Rigby
Party Time at the Milky Way	I	F	160	Sunshine	Wright Group/McGraw Hill
Party, A	A	RF	28	Leveled Readers Emergent	Houghton Mifflin
Party, A	A	RF	14	Story Box	Wright Group/McGraw Hill
Party, The	F	RF	56	Book Bus	Creative Edge
Party, The	D	RF	26	Ready Readers	Pearson Learning Group
Paru Has a Bath	J	RF	242	Pacific Literacy	Pacific Learning
Parvana's Journey	W	RF	250+	Ellis, Deborah	Douglas & McIntyre
Pasquale's Gift	J	RF	250+	Voyages	SRA/McGraw Hill
Pass the Pasta, Please	D	I	63	Storyteller-Setting Sun	Wright Group/McGraw Hill
Pass the Present	C	F	86	Storyteller-First Snow	Wright Group/McGraw Hill
Passager: The Young Merlin Trilogy	V	F	250+	Yolen, Jane	Scholastic
Passing Poetry	R	RF	785	Leveled Readers	Houghton Mifflin
Passover	O	I	250+	Holidays and Festivals	Compass Point Books
Pasta	N	I	250+	Little Celebrations	Pearson Learning Group
Pat and Pea Soup	J	RF	187	Books for Young Learners	Richard C. Owen
Pat and Pig	B	F	34	Leveled Readers	Houghton Mifflin
Pat Mora, the Storyteller	L	B	278	Vocabulary Readers	Houghton Mifflin
Pat Mora: Two Languages, One Poet	P	B	769	Leveled Readers	Houghton Mifflin
Pat, Pat, Pat	B	RF	37	Book Bank	Wright Group/McGraw Hill
Patches	M	RF	250+	Szymanski, Lois	Avon Camelot
Patchwork Patterns	G	RF	64	Little Celebrations	Pearson Learning Group
Pathfinder: Mission to Mars	P	I	250+	Rigby Literacy	Rigby
Patrick and the Leprechaun	L	F	677	PM Gold	Rigby
Patrick Doyle is Full of Blarney	O	HF	250+	Armstrong, Jennifer	Random House
Pat's New Puppy	E	RF	88	Reading Unlimited	Pearson Learning Group
Pat's Perfect Pizza	C	RF	37	Ready Readers	Pearson Learning Group

* Collection of short stories

TITLE	LEVEL	GENRE	WORD COUNT	AUTHOR / SERIES	PUBLISHER / DISTRIBUTOR
Pat's Train	D	RF	22	KinderReaders	Rigby
Patterns	C	I	32	Berger, Samantha; Moreton, Daniel	Scholastic
Patterns	J	I	122	Spyglass Books	Compass Point Books
Patterns	E	I	57	Literacy 2000	Rigby
Patterns	C	I	35	Discovery Links	Newbridge
Patterns	C	I	57	Story Steps	Rigby
Patterns All Around	B	I	55	Early Connections	Benchmark Education
Patterns All around Me	E	I	181	Learn to Read	Creative Teaching Press
Patterns are Fun!	C	I	35	Story Steps	Rigby
Patterns: What Comes Next?	L	I	250+	Exploring Math	Capstone Press
Patty and Pop's Picnic	C	RF	57	Little Books	Sadlier-Oxford
Paul	F	I	54	Pacific Literacy	Pacific Learning
Paul and Lucy	J	RF	250+	Stepping Stones	Nelson/Michaels Assoc.
Paul Bunyan	J	TL	250+	Jumbled Tumbled Tales & Rhymes	Rigby
Paul Bunyan	N	TL	250+	Tall Tales	Compass Point Books
Paul Cezanne	R	B	250+	Venezia, Mike	Children's Press
Paul Gauguin	R	B	250+	Venezia, Mike	Children's Press
Paul Harvey's The Rest Of The Story	Z	I	250+	Harvey, Jr., Paul	Bantam
Paul Klee	R	B	250+	Venezia, Mike	Children's Press
Paul Laurence Dunbar, Poet	S	B	542	Vocabulary Readers	Houghton Mifflin
Paul Revere	V	B	250+	Cornerstones of Freedom	Children's Press
Paul Revere's Ride	S	HF	250+	Literacy 2000	Rigby
Paul Revere's Ride	T	I	250+	We The People	Compass Point Books
Paul the Artist	P	RF	1356	Leveled Readers	Houghton Mifflin
Paul the Pitcher	D	RF	86	Rookie Readers	Children's Press
Paulo the Pilot	F	F	131	Windmill Books	Rigby
Paul's Day at School	B	I	38	Little Books for Early Readers	University of Maine
Pawnee Nation, The	P	I	250+	Walters, Anna Lee	Red Brick Learning
Pawpaw patch	F	TL	174	PM Readalongs	Rigby
Paws and Claws and Other Stories	D	F	120	Story Steps	Rigby
Pea or the Flea?, The	F	RF	66	Start to Read	School Zone
Peace Ring, The	L	F	250+	Cambridge Reading	Pearson Learning Group
Peacefulness	L	I	250+	Character Education	Red Brick Learning
Peaches All the Time	J	I	149	Early Connections	Benchmark Education
Peaches the Pig	E	F	120	Little Readers	Houghton Mifflin
Peanut	Q	I	250+	Selsam, Millicent	William Morrow
Peanut Butter	E	RF	60	Little Celebrations	Pearson Learning Group
Peanut Butter and Jelly	E	RF	164	Little Readers	Houghton Mifflin
Peanut Butter and Jelly	G	F	156	Wescott, Nadine B.	Penguin Group
Peanut Butter Gang, The	K	F	250+	Siracusa, Catherine	Hyperion
Peanuts	J	F	250+	Sunshine	Wright Group/McGraw Hill
Peanuts	J	I	149	Windows on Literacy	National Geographic
Peanuts	K	I	250+	Rigby Literacy	Rigby
Pearl, The	Z	RF	250+	Steinbeck, John	Penguin Group
Peas and Potatoes: 1, 2, 3	B	RF	44	Pair-It Books	Steck-Vaughn
Peas in a Pod	F	F	173	Cambridge Reading	Pearson Learning Group
Pebbles	C	RF	30	Science	Outside the Box
Pecos Bill	N	TL	250+	Tall Tales	Compass Point Books
Pedal Power	C	I	22	Pacific Literacy	Pacific Learning
Pedal Power	J	I	226	Rigby Literacy	Rigby
Peddler's Caps, The	J	TL	250+	PM Story Books-Purple	Rigby
Pedro's Journal	Q	HF	250+	Conrad, Pam	Scholastic
Pee Wee Scouts	L	RF	250+	Delton, Judy	Yearling

TITLE	LEVEL	GENRE	WORD COUNT	AUTHOR / SERIES	PUBLISHER / DISTRIBUTOR
Pee Wee Scouts on First	L	RF	250+	Delton, Judy	Bantam
Pee Wee Scouts on Parade	L	RF	250+	Delton, Judy	Bantam
Pee Wee Scouts on Skis	L	RF	250+	Delton, Judy	Bantam
Pee Wee Scouts: A Big Box of Memories	L	RF	250+	Delton, Judy	Bantam
Pee Wee Scouts: A Pee Wee Christmas	L	RF	250+	Delton, Judy	Bantam
Pee Wee Scouts: Bad, Bad Bunnies	L	RF	250+	Delton, Judy	Bantam
Pee Wee Scouts: Blue Skies, French Fries	L	RF	250+	Delton, Judy	Bantam
Pee Wee Scouts: Bookworm Buddies	L	RF	250+	Delton, Judy	Bantam
Pee Wee Scouts: Camp Ghost Away	L	RF	250+	Delton, Judy	Bantam
Pee Wee Scouts: Computer Clues	L	RF	250+	Delton, Judy	Bantam
Pee Wee Scouts: Cookies and Crutches	L	RF	250+	Delton, Judy	Bantam
Pee Wee Scouts: Eggs with Legs	L	RF	250+	Delton, Judy	Bantam
Pee Wee Scouts: Fishy Wishes	L	RF	250+	Delton, Judy	Bantam
Pee Wee Scouts: Greedy Groundhogs	L	RF	250+	Delton, Judy	Bantam
Pee Wee Scouts: Grumpy Pumpkins	L	RF	250+	Delton, Judy	Bantam
Pee Wee Scouts: Halloween Helpers	L	RF	250+	Delton, Judy	Bantam
Pee Wee Scouts: Lights, Action, Land-Ho!	L	RF	250+	Delton, Judy	Bantam
Pee Wee Scouts: Lucky Dog Days	L	RF	250+	Delton, Judy	Bantam
Pee Wee Scouts: Moans and Groans and Dinosaur Bones	L	RF	250+	Delton, Judy	Bantam
Pee Wee Scouts: Molly for Mayor	L	RF	250+	Delton, Judy	Bantam
Pee Wee Scouts: Peanut-Butter Pilgrims	L	RF	250+	Delton, Judy	Bantam
Pee Wee Scouts: Pedal Power	L	RF	250+	Delton, Judy	Bantam
Pee Wee Scouts: Pee Wee Pool Party	L	RF	250+	Delton, Judy	Bantam
Pee Wee Scouts: Piles of Pets	L	RF	250+	Delton, Judy	Bantam
Pee Wee Scouts: Planet Pee Wee	L	RF	250+	Delton, Judy	Bantam
Pee Wee Scouts: Rosy Noses, Freezing Toes	L	RF	250+	Delton, Judy	Bantam
Pee Wee Scouts: Send in the Clowns	L	RF	250+	Delton, Judy	Bantam
Pee Wee Scouts: Sky Babies	L	RF	250+	Delton, Judy	Bantam
Pee Wee Scouts: Sonny's Secret	L	RF	250+	Delton, Judy	Bantam
Pee Wee Scouts: Spring Sprouts	L	RF	250+	Delton, Judy	Bantam
Pee Wee Scouts: Stage Frightened	L	RF	250+	Delton, Judy	Bantam
Pee Wee Scouts: Super Duper Pee Wee!	L	RF	250+	Delton, Judy	Bantam
Pee Wee Scouts: Teeny Weeny Zucchinis	L	RF	250+	Delton, Judy	Bantam
Pee Wee Scouts: That Mushy Stuff	L	RF	250+	Delton, Judy	Bantam
Pee Wee Scouts: The Pee Wee Jubilee	L	RF	250+	Delton, Judy	Bantam
Pee Wee Scouts: The Pooped Troop	L	RF	250+	Delton, Judy	Bantam
Pee Wee Scouts: Trash Bash	L	RF	250+	Delton, Judy	Bantam
Pee Wee Scouts: Tricks and Treats	L	RF	250+	Delton, Judy	Bantam
Pee Wee Scouts: Wild, Wild West	L	RF	250+	Delton, Judy	Bantam
Peek-a-boo at the Zoo	E	F	49	New Reader Series	Bungalo Books
Pele	H	B	36	Canizares, Susan; Berger, Samantha	Scholastic
Pen Pals	D	RF	92	Bookshop	Mondo
Pencil, The	B	I	97	PM Starters	Rigby
Penguin Chick, The	I	I	105	Windows on Literacy	National Geographic
Penguin Family, The	J	I	301	Leveled Readers	Houghton Mifflin
Penguin Pete	L	F	250+	Pfister, Marcus	North-South Books
Penguin Rescue	L	RF	250+	PM Story Books	Rigby
Penguin, The	O	I	250+	Crewe, Sabrina	Steck-Vaughn
Penguins	O	I	250+	First Reports	Compass Point Books
Penguins	O	I	250+	Woolley, M.; Pigdon, K.	Mondo
Penguins	O	I	250+	Holmes, Kevin J.	Red Brick Learning
Penguins	L	I	250+	Reed, Janet	Scholastic

* Collection of short stories

TITLE	LEVEL	GENRE	WORD COUNT	AUTHOR / SERIES	PUBLISHER / DISTRIBUTOR
Penguins	D	I	250+	Rosen Real Readers	Rosen Publishing Group
Penguins Are Waterbirds	K	I	250+	Bookshop	Mondo
Penguin's Chicks	D	I	38	Pacific Literacy	Pacific Learning
Penguins of the Galápagos	P	I	250+	Young Readers' Series	Barron's Educational
Penguins on Parade	O	F	250+	Little Celebrations	Pearson Learning Group
Pennsylvania	Q	I	250+	One Nation	Capstone Press
Pennsylvania	R	I	250+	This Land Is Your Land	Compass Point Books
Penny Candy	K	I	250+	Early Connections	Benchmark Education
Penny Changes the Day, A	J	RF	250+	Fetty, Margaret	Steck-Vaughn
People and Places	R	I	250+	Rigby Focus	Rigby
People and Places	H	I	240	Yellow Umbrella Books	Red Brick Learning
People Are Living Things	K	I	250+	Home Connection Collection	Rigby
People Are Working	E	I	71	Pacific Literacy	Pacific Learning
People at Work	J	I	250+	Momentum Literacy Program	Troll Associates
People Build Dams	F	I	46	Windows on Literacy	National Geographic
People Can Build	E	I	46	Sunshine	Wright Group/McGraw Hill
People Change the Land	H	I	222	Yellow Umbrella Books	Red Brick Learning
*People Could Fly, American Black Folktales	X	TL	250+	Hamilton, Virginia	Alfred A. Knopf
People Dance	E	I	46	Wonder World	Wright Group/McGraw Hill
People from the Past	R	I	250+	Explorers	Wright Group/McGraw Hill
People Go Up	A	I	18	Windows on Literacy	National Geographic
People in My Town	A	I	36	Rosen Real Readers	Rosen Publishing Group
People in the Rain Forest	O	I	250+	Pirotta, Saviour	Steck-Vaughn
People Live Here	F	I	42	Windows on Literacy	National Geographic
People Live in the Desert	J	I	163	Windows on Literacy	National Geographic
People of the Ice Age	K	I	286	Rigby Focus	Rigby
People on the Beach	F	RF	87	Carousel Readers	Pearson Learning Group
People on the Move	Q	I	250+	iOpeners	Pearson Learning Group
People Parts	B	I	42	Independent Readers Science	Houghton Mifflin
People Say Hello	C	I	37	Learn to Read	Creative Teaching Press
People Use Tools	A	I	24	Early Connections	Benchmark Education
People Who Help Us	D	I	62	Foundations	Wright Group/McGraw Hill
People Who Keep You Safe	C	I	84	Careers Series	Benchmark Education
People Who Lead Us	I	I	155	Windows on Literacy	National Geographic
People Who Save Animals	E	I	143	Careers Series	Benchmark Education
People Who Traveled with Lewis and Clark, The	N	B	555	Leveled Readers Social Studies	Houghton Mifflin
People Who Use Magnets at Work	H	I	148	Early Connections	Benchmark Education
People Work	G	I	232	Yellow Umbrella Books	Red Brick Learning
People Work at the Supermarket	E	I	77	Windows on Literacy	National Geographic
Pepper Goes to School	H	RF	125	Foundations	Wright Group/McGraw Hill
Pepper Sees Me	A	I	28	Little Books for Early Readers	University of Maine
Peppers	D	I	32	Rise & Shine	Hampton-Brown
Pepper's Adventure	H	RF	250+	PM Story Books	Rigby
Percival	I	RF	303	Literacy 2000	Rigby
Perfect Instrument, The	O	RF	786	Leveled Readers	Houghton Mifflin
Perfect Kite Weather	C	I	56	Vocabulary Readers	Houghton Mifflin
Perfect Paper	K	I	250+	Rigby Literacy	Rigby
Perfect Paper Planes	K	RF	250+	PM Plus Story Books	Rigby
Perfect Person, The	Q	SF	250+	Bookweb	Rigby
Perfect Pet, The	C	RF	30	Instant Readers	Harcourt School Publishers
Perfect Pony, A	O	RF	250+	Szymanski, Lois	Avon Camelot
Perfect Pretzels	L	I	232	Twig	Wright Group/McGraw Hill
Perfect the Pig	L	F	250+	Jeschke, Susan	Scholastic
Peril in the Bessledorf Parachute Factory	U	RF	250+	Naylor, Phyllis Reynolds	Atheneum

* Collection of short stories

TITLE	LEVEL	GENRE	WORD COUNT	AUTHOR / SERIES	PUBLISHER / DISTRIBUTOR
Perilous Road, The	U	HF	250+	Steele, William	Scholastic
Perlitas	I	RF	98	Books for Young Learners	Richard C. Owen
Perseus and Medusa	V	TL	250+	Leveled Readers Language Support	Houghton Mifflin
Person from Planet X, The	H	F	250+	Sunshine	Wright Group/McGraw Hill
Peru	O	I	250+	Thoennes, Kristin	Red Brick Learning
Pesky Paua, The	H	F	267	Book Bank	Wright Group/McGraw Hill
Pet Care	E	I	35	Chessen, Betsey	Scholastic
Pet Day	F	RF	92	Home Connection Collection	Rigby
Pet Day	G	RF	175	Instant Readers	Harcourt School Publishers
Pet Day	E	F	70	Sun Sprouts	ETA/Cuisenaire
Pet Day at School	E	I	103	Story Steps	Rigby
Pet Day at School	I	RF	198	City Kids	Rigby
Pet Dreams	K	F	410	Leveled Readers	Houghton Mifflin
Pet for Me, A	C	RF	73	Early Emergent	Pioneer Valley
Pet for Me, A	E	RF	152	Alphakids	Sundance
Pet for Pat, A	D	RF	45	Rookie Readers	Children's Press
Pet for Sol, A	N	F	619	Leveled Readers	Houghton Mifflin
Pet for You, A	K	I	531	Pair-It Books	Steck-Vaughn
Pet Parade	O	RF	250+	Giff, Patricia Reilly	Bantam
Pet Parade	C	F	33	Literacy 2000	Rigby
Pet Peeves	M	RF	250+	Social Studies Connects	The Kane Press
Pet Pictures	J	I	181	Vocabulary Readers	Houghton Mifflin
Pet Riddles and Jokes	I	F	154	Instant Readers	Harcourt School Publishers
Pet Shop	D	F	167	Story Box	Wright Group/McGraw Hill
Pet Shop, The	C	RF	32	Oxford Reading Tree	Oxford University Press
Pet Sitters Plus Five	L	RF	250+	Springstubb, Tricia	Scholastic
Pet Store, The	A	I	49	Bookshop	Mondo
Pet Tarantula, The	I	F	208	Storyteller Nonfiction	Wright Group/McGraw Hill
Pet That I Want, The	E	F	57	Packard, Mary	Scholastic
Pet Vet	N	I	250+	Pacific Literacy	Pacific Learning
Pet Your Pet	H	F	93	Early Reader	Compass Point Books
Pete Discovers Gravity	M	RF	947	Early Connections	Benchmark Education
Pete for President	M	RF	250+	Social Studies Connects	The Kane Press
Pete Little	G	F	222	PM Story Books	Rigby
Pete Paints a Picture	C	RF	87	Story Steps	Rigby
Pete the Parakeet	F	F	133	First Start	Troll Associates
Peter and the North Wind	L	TL	250+	Littledale, Freya	Scholastic
Peter and the Pennytree	G	F	119	First Start	Troll Associates
Peter and the Wolf	J	TL	250+	PM Plus Story Books	Rigby
Peter Pan	X	F	250+	Barrie, J. M.	Aladdin
Peter Piper	E	TL	32	Jumbled Tumbled Tales & Rhymes	Rigby
Peter Salem: Hero of the Revolution	T	B	1096	Independent Readers Social Studies	Houghton Mifflin
Peter Stuyvesant: New Amsterdam and the Origins of New York	W	B	250+	The Library of American Lives and Times	Rosen Publishing Group
Peter Tchaikovsky	Q	B	250+	Venezia, Mike	Children's Press
Peter the Pumpkin-Eater	M	RF	250+	Action Packs	Rigby
Peter's Chair	J	RF	250+	Keats, Ezra Jack	HarperTrophy
Peter's Dream	I	F	186	Start to Read	School Zone
Peter's Harvest	Q	RF	1085	Leveled Readers	Houghton Mifflin
Peter's Move	H	RF	224	Little Readers	Houghton Mifflin
Peter's Painting	F	F	147	Bookshop	Mondo
Pete's Bad Day	G	RF	164	Ready Readers	Pearson Learning Group

* Collection of short stories

TITLE	LEVEL	GENRE	WORD COUNT	AUTHOR / SERIES	PUBLISHER / DISTRIBUTOR
Pete's New Shoes	G	RF	91	Literacy 2000	Rigby
Pete's Peacock	F	RF	89	Dominie Phonics Reader	Pearson Learning Group
Pete's Story	L	F	250+	Literacy 2000	Rigby
Pete's Tickets	D	RF	65	Seedlings	Continental Press
Pets	B	I	31	Vocabulary Readers	Houghton Mifflin
Pets	J	F	90	Pacific Literacy	Pacific Learning
Pets	A	I	33	PM Starters	Rigby
Pets	F	RF	56	Literacy 2000	Rigby
Pets for the Twins	E	RF	101	Leveled Readers	Houghton Mifflin
Pets in a Jar: Collecting and Caring for Small Wild Animals	W	I	250+	Simon, Seymour	Penguin Group
Pets Lost-and-Found	L	I	250+	Rigby Literacy	Rigby
Pets Need People	M	I	250+	Literacy 2000	Rigby
Pets, The	C	RF	28	Learn to Read	Creative Teaching Press
Phan's Diary	N	RF	250+	PM Ruby	Rigby
Phantom Tollbooth, The	W	F	250+	Juster, Norton	Bantam
Phantoms Don't Drive Sports Cars	M	F	250+	Dadey, Debbie; Jones, Marcia Thornton	Scholastic
Pheasant and Kingfisher	L	TL	250+	Bookshop	Mondo
Pheasant Hunting	S	I	250+	The Great Outdoors	Red Brick Learning
Philip Hall Likes Me. I Reckon Maybe.	Y	RF	250+	Greene, Bette	Puffin Books
Philippa and the Dragon	G	F	137	Literacy 2000	Rigby
Philippines, The	O	I	250+	Davis, Lucile	Red Brick Learning
Phoebe The Spy	R	HF	250+	Griffin, Judith Berry	Scholastic
Phoenix Rising	W	RF	250+	Hesse, Karen	Penguin Group
Photo Book, The	C	RF	50	PM Story Books	Rigby
Photo Contest, The	O	RF	250+	Leveled Readers Language Support	Houghton Mifflin
Photo Time	C	RF	59	PM Plus Story Books	Rigby
Photograph, The	I	F	250+	Popcorn	Sundance
Photographic Memory	O	RF	250+	PM Ruby	Rigby
Photos, Photos	N	I	250+	Wildcats	Wright Group/McGraw Hill
Phyllis Wheatley: First African-American Poet	N	B	250+	Rookie Biographies	Children's Press
Piano Recital, The	K	RF	250+	Rigby Literacy	Rigby
Picasso	S	B	250+	Masterpieces: Artists and Their Works	Red Brick Learning
Picasso	R	B	250+	Venezia, Mike	Children's Press
Pick a Pet	C	RF	40	Little Celebrations	Pearson Learning Group
Pick a Pumpkin	I	F	250+	Leveled Readers Language Support	Houghton Mifflin
Pick Up Nick!	H	RF	219	Ready Readers	Pearson Learning Group
Picked for the Team	L	RF	709	PM Gold	Rigby
Picking a Pet	I	I	224	Sunshine	Wright Group/McGraw Hill
Picking Apples	E	RF	128	Developing Books	Pioneer Valley
Picking Apples	F	I	53	Pebble Books	Capstone Press
Picking Apples and Pumpkins	L	I	250+	Hutchings, Amy & Richard	Scholastic
Picking Up Papers	K	RF	161	City Kids	Rigby
Pickle Puss	L	RF	250+	Giff, Patricia Reilly	Bantam
Pickles Gets Lost	G	RF	154	Pickles the Dog Series	Pioneer Valley
Pickles Goes to School	E	RF	90	Pickles the Dog Series	Pioneer Valley
Pickles Helps Out	F	RF	160	Pickles the Dog Series	Pioneer Valley
Pickles in My Soup	F	F	88	Rookie Reader	Children's Press
Picky Prince, The	J	F	250+	Rigby Literacy	Rigby
Picnic	WB	RF	N/A	McCully, Emily Arnold	Harper & Row

TITLE	LEVEL	GENRE	WORD COUNT	AUTHOR / SERIES	PUBLISHER / DISTRIBUTOR
Picnic Boat, The	G	RF	210	PM Plus Story Books	Rigby
Picnic in the Sand, A	LB	RF	14	Ready Readers	Pearson Learning Group
Picnic in the Sky, The	D	F	80	Foundations	Wright Group/McGraw Hill
Picnic on the Sidewalk	F	RF	108	Seedlings	Continental Press
Picnic Tea	I	RF	224	Stepping Stones	Nelson/Michaels Assoc.
Picnic, The	C	RF	48	Teacher's Choice Series	Pearson Learning Group
Picnic, The	F	RF	122	Wonder World	Wright Group/McGraw Hill
Picnic, The	G	RF	151	Home Connection Collection	Rigby
Picnic, The	D	RF	96	Handprints C, Set 1	Educator's Publishing Service
Picnic, The	LB	RF	18	Book Bank	Wright Group/McGraw Hill
Picnic, The	LB	RF	48	First Stories	Pacific Learning
Picture Book of Abraham Lincoln, A	M	B	250+	Adler, David A.	Holiday House
Picture Book of Amelia Earhart, A	M	B	250+	Adler, David A.	Holiday House
Picture Book of Anne Frank, A	M	B	250+	Adler, David A.	Holiday House
Picture Book of Benjamin Franklin, A	M	B	250+	Adler, David A.	Holiday House
Picture Book of Christopher Columbus, A	M	B	250+	Adler, David A.	Holiday House
Picture Book of Davy Crockett, A	M	B	250+	Adler, David A.	Holiday House
Picture Book of Eleanor Roosevelt, A	M	B	250+	Adler, David A.	Holiday House
Picture Book of Florence Nightingale, A	M	B	250+	Adler, David A.	Holiday House
Picture Book of Frederick Douglass, A	M	B	250+	Adler, David A.	Holiday House
Picture Book of George Washington Carver, A	M	B	250+	Adler, David A.	Holiday House
Picture Book of George Washington, A	M	B	250+	Adler, David A.	Holiday House
Picture Book of Harriet Tubman, A	M	B	250+	Adler, David A.	Holiday House
Picture Book of Helen Keller, A	M	B	250+	Adler, David A.	Holiday House
Picture Book of Jackie Robinson, A	M	B	250+	Adler, David A.	Holiday House
Picture Book of Jesse Owens, A	N	B	250+	Adler, David A.	Holiday House
Picture Book of John F. Kennedy, A	N	B	250+	Adler, David A.	Holiday House
Picture Book of Louis Braille, A	M	B	250+	Adler, David A.	Holiday House
Picture Book of Martin Luther King, Jr., A	M	B	250+	Adler, David A.	Holiday House
Picture Book of Patrick Henry, A	M	B	250+	Adler, David A.	Holiday House
Picture Book of Paul Revere, A	M	B	250+	Adler, David A.	Holiday House
Picture Book of Robert E. Lee, A	N	B	250+	Adler, David A.	Holiday House
Picture Book of Rosa Parks, A	M	B	250+	Adler, David A.	Holiday House
Picture Book of Sacagawea, A	M	B	250+	Adler, David A.	Holiday House
Picture Book of Simon Bolivar, A	Q	B	250+	Adler, David A.	Bantam
Picture Book of Sitting Bull, A	M	B	250+	Adler, David A.	Holiday House
Picture Book of Sojourner Truth, A	M	B	250+	Adler, David A.	Holiday House
Picture Book of Thomas Alva Edison, A	M	B	250+	Adler, David A.	Holiday House
Picture Book of Thomas Jefferson, A	M	B	250+	Adler, David A.	Holiday House
Picture Book of Thurgood Marshall, A	M	B	250+	Adler, David A.	Holiday House
Picture for Harold's Room, A	H	F	550	Johnson, Crockett	HarperCollins
Picture of Freedom, A	T	HF	250+	McKissack, Patricia C.	Scholastic
Picture Perfect	Z	RF	250+	Alphin, Elaine Marie	Carolrhoda Books
Picture Tricks	I	I	250+	Phonics Readers Plus	Steck-Vaughn
Picture, A	C	I	58	Storyteller-First Snow	Wright Group/McGraw Hill
Pictures	E	RF	76	Teacher's Choice Series	Pearson Learning Group
Pictures of Hollis Woods	V	RF	250+	Giff, Patricia Reilly	Scholastic
Pictures to Words: The Origins of Writing	V	I	2032	Independent Readers Social Studies	Houghton Mifflin
Pie Day	H	F	250+	Phonics and Friends	Hampton-Brown
Pie Magic	N	F	250+	Cornell, Laura	Beech Tree Books
Pie Thief, A: a play	J	F	250+	Story Box	Wright Group/McGraw Hill
Pie, The	F	RF	117	Developing Books, Set 1	Pioneer Valley

* Collection of short stories

TITLE	LEVEL	GENRE	WORD COUNT	AUTHOR / SERIES	PUBLISHER / DISTRIBUTOR
Piece of Cake	I	I	250+	Home Connection Collection	Rigby
Pied Piper	L	TL	250+	Hunia, Fran	Ladybird Books
Pied Piper of Hamelin, The	K	TL	250+	Hautzig, Deborah	Random House
Pied Piper, The	M	TL	585	Sunshine	Wright Group/McGraw Hill
Pierre	K	RF	490	Sendak, Maurice	Scholastic
Pierre August Renoir	R	B	250+	Venezia, Mike	Children's Press
Pig That Learned to Jig, The	I	F	140	Wonder World	Wright Group/McGraw Hill
Pig William's Midnight Walk	H	F	354	Book Bank	Wright Group/McGraw Hill
Pigeon Feathers	M	TL	250+	Books for Young Learners	Richard C. Owen
Piggle	K	F	250+	Bonsall, Crosby	HarperCollins
Piglet in a Playpen	P	RF	250+	Daniels, Lucy	Barron's Educational
Piglet in a Playpen	Q	RF	250+	Baglio, Ben M.	Scholastic
Pigman & Me, The	Z	B	250+	Zindel, Paul	Dell
Pigman's Legacy, The	Z	RF	250+	Zindel, Paul	Harper & Row
Pignocchio	L	F	250+	Pair-It Books	Steck-Vaughn
Pigpen Party, The	I	F	186	Literacy Tree	Rigby
Pigs	C	F	29	Learn to Read	Creative Teaching Press
Pigs	D	I	54	Vocabulary Readers	Houghton Mifflin
Pigs	L	I	250+	PM Animal Facts: Purple	Rigby
Pigs at Odds	L	F	250+	Axelrod, Amy	Aladdin
Pigs Have Piglets	M	I	250+	Animals and Their Young	Compass Point Books
Pigs Might Fly	R	F	250+	King-Smith, Dick	Scholastic
Pigs on the Farm	G	I	72	Pebble Books	Capstone Press
Pigs Peek	C	F	28	Books for Young Learners	Richard C. Owen
Pig's Tall Hat	E	F	81	Leveled Readers Language Support	Houghton Mifflin
Pike River Phantom, The	R	F	250+	Wright, Betty	Scholastic
Pilar Speaks Up	T	RF	1354	Leveled Readers	Houghton Mifflin
Pile in Pete's Room, The	K	RF	745	Sunshine	Wright Group/McGraw Hill
Pilgrim Children Had Many Chores	F	I	47	Learn to Read	Creative Teaching Press
Pilgrim Voices: Our First Year in the New World	T	HF	250+	Roop, Connie & Peter	Walker & Company
Pilgrims of Plimouth, The	T	I	250+	Sewall, Marcia	Simon & Schuster
Pilgrims, The	R	I	250+	The Heinle Reading Library	Thomson Learning
Pilgrims, The	V	I	250+	Cornerstones of Freedom	Children's Press
Pillow Sale, The	B	F	26	KinderReaders	Rigby
Pilots	M	I	250+	Community Workers	Compass Point Books
Pinata Party	C	RF	31	Bebop Books	Lee & Low Books Inc.
Pinata Time	D	RF	71	Teacher's Choice Series	Pearson Learning Group
Pinballs, The	S	RF	250+	Byars, Betsy	HarperTrophy
Pine Hollow: Changing Leads	W	RF	250+	Bryant, Bonnie	Bantam
Pine Hollow: Conformation Faults	W	RF	250+	Bryant, Bonnie	Bantam
Pine Hollow: Reining In	W	RF	250+	Bryant, Bonnie	Bantam
Pine Hollow: The Long Ride	W	RF	250+	Bryant, Bonnie	Bantam
Pine Hollow: The Trail Home	W	RF	250+	Bryant, Bonnie	Bantam
Pine Trees	H	I	138	Pebble Books	Capstone Press
Pink Pig	B	RF	23	Ready Readers	Pearson Learning Group
Pink: Seeing Pink All around Us	L	I	250+	Colors	Capstone Press
Pinky and Rex	L	RF	250+	Howe, James	Simon & Schuster
Pinky and Rex and the Bully	L	RF	250+	Howe, James	Simon & Schuster
Pinky and Rex and the Double-Dad Weekend	L	RF	250+	Howe, James	Simon & Schuster
Pinky and Rex and the Mean Old Witch	L	RF	250+	Howe, James	Simon & Schuster
Pinky and Rex and the New Baby	L	RF	250+	Howe, James	Simon & Schuster
Pinky and Rex and the New Neighbors	L	RF	250+	Howe, James	Simon & Schuster
Pinky and Rex and the Perfect Pumpkin	L	RF	250+	Howe, James	Simon & Schuster

TITLE	LEVEL	GENRE	WORD COUNT	AUTHOR / SERIES	PUBLISHER / DISTRIBUTOR
Pinky and Rex and the School Play	L	RF	250+	Howe, James	Simon & Schuster
Pinky and Rex and the Spelling Bee	L	RF	250+	Howe, James	Simon & Schuster
Pinky and Rex Get Married	L	RF	250+	Howe, James	Simon & Schuster
Pinky and Rex Go to Camp	L	RF	250+	Howe, James	Aladdin
Pinocchio	J	TL	250+	Jumbled Tumbled Tales & Rhymes	Rigby
Pioneer Bear	L	F	250+	Sandin, Joan	Random House
Pioneer Cat	N	HF	250+	Hooks, William H.	Random House
Pioneer Families	L	I	250+	Rosen Real Readers	Rosen Publishing Group
Pioneer Girl, The Story of Laura Ingalls Wilder	R	B	250+	Anderson, William	HarperCollins
Pioneer Way, The	Q	I	250+	Kummer, Patricia K.	Steck-Vaughn
Pioneers	T	I	250+	Sandler, Martin W.	HarperTrophy
Pip and the Little Monkey	F	RF	112	Oxford Reading Tree	Oxford University Press
Pip at the Zoo	F	RF	70	Oxford Reading Tree	Oxford University Press
Pippa's Pet Pest	D	RF	35	Home Connection Collection	Rigby
Pippi Goes on Board	O	F	250+	Lindgren, Astrid	Puffin Books
Pippi in the South Seas	O	F	250+	Lindgren, Astrid	Puffin Books
Pippi Longstocking	O	F	250+	Lindgren, Astrid	Penguin Group
Pirate Feast, The	H	F	172	Story Basket	Wright Group/McGraw Hill
Pirate Pie	M	F	250+	Vaughan, Marcia	Pacific Learning
Pirate Traps	K	F	370	Story Box	Wright Group/McGraw Hill
Pirates Don't Wear Pink Sunglasses	M	F	250+	Dadey, Debbie; Jones, Marcia Thornton	Scholastic
Pirates Past Noon	M	F	250+	Osborne, Mary Pope	Scholastic
Pirate's Promise	N	RF	250+	Bulla, Clyde Robert	HarperTrophy
Pirate's Treasure, The	E	F	63	Joy Readers	Pearson Learning Group
Pita's Birthday	H	F	250+	Ready to Read	Pacific Learning
Pitching Trouble	N	RF	250+	Kroll, Stephen	Avon Camelot
Pitty Pitty Pat	C	F	45	Little Celebrations	Pearson Learning Group
Pizza for Dinner	H	RF	164	Literacy 2000	Rigby
Pizza for Everyone	K	I	251	Pair-It Books	Steck-Vaughn
Pizza Maker, The	D	RF	57	Harry's Math Books	Outside the Box
Pizza Parts	O	I	250+	Early Connections	Benchmark Education
Pizza Party!	F	RF	79	Maccarone, Grace	Scholastic
Pizza Pokey	I	F	280	Pair-It Books	Steck-Vaughn
Pizza, The	D	RF	100	Foundations	Wright Group/McGraw Hill
Place Called Heartbreak, A: A Story of Vietnam	U	I	250+	Myers, Walter Dean	Steck-Vaughn
Place for Nicholas, A	E	RF	82	Instant Readers	Harcourt Trade
Place in the Sun, A	U	HF	250+	Rubalcaba, Jill	Puffin Books
Place to Call Home, A	Y	RF	250+	Koller, Jackie French	Aladdin
Place To Hide, A	Y	B	250+	Petit, Jayne	Scholastic
Places	C	I	88	Little Red Readers	Sundance
Places I Like	B	I	49	Little Red Readers	Sundance
Places in the United States	J	I	200	Leveled Readers	Houghton Mifflin
Places to Visit	L	I	202	Windows on Literacy	National Geographic
Plain and Fancy	WB	I	N/A	Vocabulary Readers	Houghton Mifflin
Plain Girl	Q	RF	250+	Sorensen, Virginia	Harcourt Trade
Plan a Party	E	I	47	Vocabulary Readers	Houghton Mifflin
Plane Ride, The	F	I	68	Little Red Readers	Sundance
Plane Rides	G	I	160	Walker, Pamela	Scholastic
Planes, Trains, and More	E	I	43	iOpeners	Pearson Learning Group
Planet Boring	P	F	250+	Cook, Nathan	Pacific Learning
Planet Earth	L	I	197	Rigby Focus	Rigby
Planet of Junior Brown, The	Z	RF	250+	Hamilton, Virginia	Aladdin
Planet X	L	SF	250+	Popcorn	Sundance

* Collection of short stories

TITLE	LEVEL	GENRE	WORD COUNT	AUTHOR / SERIES	PUBLISHER / DISTRIBUTOR
Planets of Our Solar System	M	I	250+	Rigby Focus	Rigby
Planets, The	K	I	250+	Out In Space	Red Brick Learning
Planets, The	Q	I	101	Explorers	Wright Group/McGraw Hill
Planets, The	J	I	101	Wonder World	Wright Group/McGraw Hill
Planning a Birthday Party	N	I	250+	Bookshop	Mondo
Planning Dinner	H	RF	250+	Urmston, Kathleen; Evans, Karen	Kaeden Books
Plant and Animal Partners	M	I	587	Early Connections	Benchmark Education
Plant Blossoms	M	I	250+	Look Once Look Again	Creative Teaching Press
Plant Fruits and Seeds	M	I	250+	Look Once Look Again	Creative Teaching Press
Plant Kingdom, The	Q	I	250+	Explorers	Wright Group/McGraw Hill
Plant Leaves	N	I	250+	Look Once Look Again	Creative Teaching Press
Plant Packages: A Book About Seeds	M	I	250+	Growing Things	Picture Window Books
Plant Plumbing: A Book About Roots and Stems	M	I	250+	Growing Things	Picture Window Books
Plant Stems and Roots	N	I	250+	Look Once Look Again	Creative Teaching Press
Plant That Ate Dirty Socks Goes Up in Space	S	F	250+	McArthur, Nancy	Avon Camelot
Plant, The	A	I	32	Sun Sprouts	ETA/Cuisenaire
Planting a Garden	E	I	62	Ready Readers	Pearson Learning Group
Planting a Garden	D	I	48	Leveled Readers Language Support	Houghton Mifflin
Planting Beans and Beets	E	I	53	Leveled Readers	Houghton Mifflin
Plants	O	I	250+	Rigby Focus	Rigby
Plants	P	I	250+	Simply Science	Compass Point Books
Plants	J	I	162	Early Connections	Benchmark Education
Plants	B	I	51	Leveled Readers Science	Houghton Mifflin
Plants	I	I	250+	Momentum Literacy Program	Troll Associates
Plants and Animals live Here	F	I	54	Windows on Literacy	National Geographic
Plants and Flowers	M	I	250+	It's Science!	Children's Press
Plants and Seeds	I	I	148	Sunshine	Wright Group/McGraw Hill
Plants Grow From Seeds	I	I	109	Phonics Readers	Compass Point Books
Plants in the Park	B	I	35	Windows on Literacy	National Geographic
Plants of My Aunt	J	F	429	Jellybeans	Rigby
Plants of the Coral Reef	W	I	1832	Leveled Readers Science	Houghton Mifflin
Plants on My Plate	G	I	101	Windows on Literacy	National Geographic
Plants that Eat Animals	L	I	250+	Read-About Science	Children's Press
Platypus	P	I	1098	Short, Joan.; Green, J.; Bird, Bettina	Mondo
Play Ball	LB	RF	7	Bookshop	Mondo
Play Ball	LB	I	14	Twig	Wright Group/McGraw Hill
Play Ball!	D	RF	30	Books for Young Learners	Richard C. Owen
Play Ball!	F	RF	49	Instant Readers	Harcourt School Publishers
Play Ball!	R	I	250+	Explorers	Wright Group/McGraw Hill
Play Ball, Amelia Bedelia	L	F	250+	Parish, Peggy	Harper & Row
Play Ball, Kate	D	RF	39	Giant First Step	Troll Associates
Play Ball, Sherman	F	RF	88	Erickson, Betty	Continental Press
Play Dough	C	RF	63	Foundations	Wright Group/McGraw Hill
Play It Again Sam	I	RF	139	Literacy 2000	Rigby
Play It Safe!	G	I	92	Phonics Readers	Compass Point Books
Play, Bear	G	F	219	Sun Sprouts	ETA/Cuisenaire
Play, The	B	RF	33	First Stories	Pacific Learning
Play, The	L	RF	588	Leveled Readers	Houghton Mifflin
Play, The	B	RF	44	PM Starters	Rigby
Play, The	C	RF	23	Rigby Literacy	Rigby
Playful Platypus, The	C	F	35	Learn to Read	Creative Teaching Press
Playground Fun	D	I	127	Early Connections	Benchmark Education

* Collection of short stories

TITLE	LEVEL	GENRE	WORD COUNT	AUTHOR / SERIES	PUBLISHER / DISTRIBUTOR
Playground Opposites	B	I	21	Pair-It Books	Steck-Vaughn
Playground Play	B	RF	39	Handprints B	Educator's Publishing Service
Playground Problem Solvers	G	F	199	Learn to Read	Creative Teaching Press
Playground Science	R	I	250+	iOpeners	Pearson Learning Group
Playground, The	C	RF	108	Early Emergent	Pioneer Valley
Playground, The	A	I	16	Twig	Wright Group/McGraw Hill
Playhouse for Monster	C	F	34	Mueller, Virginia	Whitman
Playhouse, The	K	RF	197	Pacific Literacy	Pacific Learning
Playhouse, The	C	RF	34	Rigby Literacy	Rigby
Playing	B	RF	55	First Stories	Pacific Learning
Playing	A	I	39	PM Starters	Rigby
Playing Ball	E	RF	170	Handprints C, Set 2	Educator's Publishing Service
Playing Favorites	N	RF	250+	Kroll, Steven	Avon Camelot
Playing Games	F	RF	89	Phonics Readers	Pearson Learning Group
Playing in the Snow	C	RF	61	Early Emergent	Pioneer Valley
Playing It Safe	F	I	135	Early Connections	Benchmark Education
Playing Outside	C	RF	56	PM Plus Starters	Rigby
Playing Soccer	I	RF	123	Foundations	Wright Group/McGraw Hill
Playing Sports	B	I	24	Early Connections	Benchmark Education
Playing with Dad	F	RF	146	Foundations	Wright Group/McGraw Hill
Playing With Dough	D	I	94	PM Plus Nonfiction	Rigby
Playing with My Cat	C	RF	83	Early Emergent	Pioneer Valley
Playing with Words	S	I	250+	Action Packs	Rigby
Playing with Words	O	B	250+	Howe, James	Richard C. Owen
Playtime	C	F	66	Voyages	SRA/McGraw Hill
Please Don't Be Mine, Julie Valentine!	R	RF	250+	Strasser, Todd	Scholastic
Please, Do Not Drop Your Jelly Beans	I	RF	180	Storyteller-Night Crickets	Wright Group/McGraw Hill
Please, Miss	H	RF	90	Cambridge Reading	Pearson Learning Group
Please, Mom!	D	RF	92	Lighthouse	Rigby
Pleasing the Ghost	V	F	250+	Creech, Sharon	HarperCollins
Pledge of Allegiance, The	N	I	250+	American Symbols	Capstone Press
Plenty of Pets	F	RF	173	Instant Readers	Harcourt School Publishers
Plop!	C	F	30	Story Box	Wright Group/McGraw Hill
Plumbers	M	I	250+	Boraas, Tracey	Red Brick Learning
Pluto	S	I	250+	Our Solar System	Compass Point Books
Pluto	N	I	250+	A First Book	Franklin Watts
Pluto	N	I	250+	A True Book	Children's Press
Plymouth Colony, The	T	I	250+	We The People	Compass Point Books
Plymouth Partnership, A: Pilgrims and Native Americans	R	I	250+	The Library of the Pilgrims	Rosen Publishing Group
Plymouth: Surviving the First Winter	R	I	250+	The Library of the Pilgrims	Rosen Publishing Group
Pocahantas	Q	B	838	Independent Readers Social Studies	Houghton Mifflin
Pocahontas	M	B	250+	First Biographies	Red Brick Learning
Pocahontas: Daughter of a Chief	N	B	250+	Rookie Biographies	Children's Press
Pocahontas: Peacemaker and Friend to the Colonists	M	B	250+	Biographies	Picture Window Books
Pocahontas: The Life of an Indian Princess	M	B	250+	Rosen Real Readers	Rosen Publishing Group
Pocket for Corduroy, A	K	F	250+	Freeman, Don	Scholastic
Pocket Full of Acorns, A	L	RF	250+	Beames, Michael	Pearson Learning Group
Pocket Full of Seeds, A	V	HF	250+	Sachs, Marilyn	Scholastic

* Collection of short stories

TITLE	LEVEL	GENRE	WORD COUNT	AUTHOR / SERIES	PUBLISHER / DISTRIBUTOR
Pocketful of Goobers, A: Story of George Washington Carver	Q	B	250+	Mitchell, Barbara	Carolrhoda Books
Pockets	D	RF	32	Visions	Wright Group/McGraw Hill
Poem for Grandma, A	M	RF	250+	Leveled Readers Language Support	Houghton Mifflin
Poet from the Plains, A	N	B	353	Vocabulary Readers	Houghton Mifflin
Poetry of Basketball, The	P	RF	250+	Leveled Readers Language Support	Houghton Mifflin
Poison Evidence	Z	I	250+	Forensic Crime Solvers	Capstone Press
Polar Babies	F	I	115	Susan Ring	Random House
Polar Bear, The	S	I	250+	Hemstock, Annie	Red Brick Learning
Polar Bears	E	I	78	Vocabulary Readers	Houghton Mifflin
Polar Bears	F	I	77	Story Steps	Rigby
Polar Bears	K	I	276	Wonder World	Wright Group/McGraw Hill
Polar Bears	G	I	67	Windows on Literacy	National Geographic
Polar Bears	F	I	77	Pebble Books	Capstone Press
Polar Bears	N	I	250+	PM Animal Facts: Silver	Rigby
Polar Bears Past Bedtime	M	F	250+	Osborne, Mary Pope	Random House
Polar Bears: In Living Color	L	I	250+	Rigby Literacy	Rigby
Polar Regions	N	I	250+	Habitats of the World	Pearson Learning Group
Poles Apart	J	F	250+	Rigby Literacy	Rigby
Police Cars	J	I	125	Mighty Machines	Capstone Press
Police Cars	I	I	177	Pebble Books	Grolier Press
Police Cars	M	I	250+	Transportation	Compass Point Books
Police Files	N	RF	250+	Sails	Rigby
Police Officers	L	I	250+	Community Workers	Compass Point Books
Police Officers	M	I	250+	Ready, Dee	Red Brick Learning
Politeness	M	I	250+	Character Education	Red Brick Learning
Polka Dots!	F	I	102	Little Celebrations	Pearson Learning Group
Pollution	F	I	46	Wonder World	Wright Group/McGraw Hill
Polly's Shop	E	RF	130	Ready Readers	Pearson Learning Group
Pompeii . . . Buried Alive!	N	I	250+	Kunhardt, Edith	Random House
Ponce de Leon: Juan Ponce de Leon Searches for the Fountain of Youth	U	B	250+	Exploring the World	Compass Point Books
Pond for Tim, A	D	RF	62	Counters & Seekers	Steck-Vaughn
Pond Party	D	F	33	Little Celebrations	Pearson Learning Group
Pond Where Harriet Lives, The	H	TL	151	Story-Teller Night	Wright Group/McGraw Hill
Pond, A	A	I	14	Discovery Links	Newbridge
Pond, The	C	I	25	Books for Young Learners	Richard C. Owen
Pond, The	C	F	54	Joy Readers	Pearson Learning Group
Ponies at the Point	Q	RF	250+	Baglio, Ben M.	Scholastic
Pony Express, The	I	I	128	Independent Readers Social Studies	Houghton Mifflin
Pony Express, The	U	I	250+	We The People	Compass Point Books
Pony Express, The	V	I	250+	Cornerstones of Freedom	Children's Press
Pony For Jeremiah, A	R	HF	250+	Miller, Robert H.	Silver Burdett Press
Pony Named Shawney, A	P	RF	3075	Small, Mary	Mondo
Pony on the Porch	Q	RF	250+	Baglio, Ben M.	Scholastic
Pony Pals: A Pony for Keeps	O	RF	250+	Betancourt, Jeanne	Scholastic
Pony Pals: A Pony in Trouble	O	RF	250+	Betancourt, Jeanne	Scholastic
Pony Pals: Detective Pony	O	RF	250+	Betancourt, Jeanne	Scholastic
Pony Pals: Don't Hurt My Pony	O	RF	250+	Betancourt, Jeanne	Scholastic
Pony Pals: Give Me Back My Pony	O	RF	250+	Betancourt, Jeanne	Scholastic
Pony Pals: Good-bye Pony	O	RF	250+	Betancourt, Jeanne	Scholastic

* Collection of short stories

TITLE	LEVEL	GENRE	WORD COUNT	AUTHOR / SERIES	PUBLISHER / DISTRIBUTOR
Pony Pals: I Want a Pony	O	RF	250+	Betancourt, Jeanne	Scholastic
Pony Pals: Keep Out, Pony!	O	RF	250+	Betancourt, Jeanne	Scholastic
Pony Pals: Pony to the Rescue	O	RF	250+	Betancourt, Jeanne	Scholastic
Pony Pals: Pony-Sitters	O	RF	250+	Betancourt, Jeanne	Scholastic
Pony Pals: Runaway Pony	O	RF	250+	Betancourt, Jeanne	Scholastic
Pony Pals: The Blind Pony	O	RF	250+	Betancourt, Jeanne	Scholastic
Pony Pals: The Ghost Pony	O	RF	250+	Betancourt, Jeanne	Scholastic
Pony Pals: The Girl Who Hated Ponies	O	RF	250+	Betancourt, Jeanne	Scholastic
Pony Pals: The Lonely Pony	O	RF	250+	Betancourt, Jeanne	Scholastic
Pony Pals: The Wild Pony	O	RF	250+	Betancourt, Jeanne	Scholastic
Pony Pals: Too Many Ponies	O	RF	250+	Betancourt, Jeanne	Scholastic
Pony Parade	O	RF	250+	Baglio, Ben M.	Scholastic
Pony Tails: Jasmine and the Jumping Pony	P	RF	250+	Bryant, Bonnie	Bantam
Pony Tails: Jasmine's Christmas Ride	P	RF	250+	Bryant, Bonnie	Bantam
Pony Tails: May Takes the Lead	P	RF	250+	Bryant, Bonnie	Bantam
Pony Trouble	L	RF	250+	Gasque, Dale Blackwell	Hyperion
Pookie and Joe	K	F	250+	Literacy 2000	Rigby
Pool Boy	Y	RF	250+	Simmons, Michael	Roaring Book Press
Pool of Fire, The	V	F	250+	Christopher, John	Aladdin
Pool, The	D	RF	129	Handprints C, Set 1	Educator's Publishing Service
Poopsie Pomerantz Pick Up Your Feet	P	RF	250+	Giff, Patricia Reilly	Dell
Poor Girl, Rich Girl	T	RF	250+	Wilson, Johnniece Marshall	Language for Learning Assoc.
Poor Little Kittens	P	RF	1173	Leveled Readers	Houghton Mifflin
Poor Miss Dee!	I	RF	247	Story Box	Wright Group/McGraw Hill
Poor Old Polly	F	F	111	Story Box	Wright Group/McGraw Hill
Poor Panda	WB	F	N/A	Rigby Literacy	Rigby
Poor Polly Pig	F	F	57	Start to Read	School Zone
Poor Puppy!	B	RF	52	First Stories	Pacific Learning
Poor Sore Paw, The	I	F	244	Sunshine	Wright Group/McGraw Hill
Pop . . . Pop . . . Popcorn	C	I	40	Home Connection Collection	Rigby
POP Pops the Popcorn	E	RF	60	Ready Readers	Pearson Learning Group
Popcorn and Candy	I	I	161	Windows on Literacy	National Geographic
Popcorn Book, The	N	I	250+	DePaola, Tomie	Holiday House
Popcorn Book, The	K	I	208	Reading Unlimited	Pearson Learning Group
Popcorn Days & Buttermilk Nights	U	RF	250+	Paulsen, Gary	Penguin Group
Popcorn Fun	H	RF	217	PM Plus Story Books	Rigby
Popcorn Shop, The	J	RF	250+	Low, Alice	Scholastic
*Poppleton	J	F	250+	Rylant, Cynthia	Scholastic
*Poppleton and Friends	J	F	250+	Rylant, Cynthia	Blue Sky Press
*Poppleton Everyday	J	F	250+	Rylant, Cynthia	Scholastic
*Poppleton Forever	J	F	250+	Rylant, Cynthia	Scholastic
*Poppleton Has Fun	J	F	250+	Rylant, Cynthia	Scholastic
*Poppleton In Fall	J	F	250+	Rylant, Cynthia	Scholastic
*Poppleton in Spring	J	F	250+	Rylant, Cynthia	Scholastic
Poppy	S	F	250+	Avi	Avon
Poppy and Rye	S	F	250+	Avi	Avon
Poppy, The	K	I	152	Pacific Literacy	Pacific Learning
Poppy's Timeline	U	RF	1759	Leveled Readers	Houghton Mifflin
Pop's Truck	K	RF	250+	Voyages	SRA/McGraw Hill
Porcupine, A	D	I	49	Wonder World	Wright Group/McGraw Hill
Porcupine's Pajama Party	J	F	250+	Harshman, Terry Webb	HarperTrophy

* Collection of short stories

TITLE	LEVEL	GENRE	WORD COUNT	AUTHOR / SERIES	PUBLISHER / DISTRIBUTOR
Portia and the Math Problems	N	B	250+	Leveled Readers Language Support	Houghton Mifflin
Possum's Bare Tail	N	TL	770	Leveled Readers	Houghton Mifflin
Postcard Pest, The	M	RF	250+	Giff, Patricia Reilly	Bantam
Postcards From France	N	I	250+	Arnold, Helen	Steck-Vaughn
Postcards From Kenya	N	I	250+	Arnold, Helen	Steck-Vaughn
Postcards from Pop	H	RF	122	Literacy Tree	Rigby
Postcards From South Africa	N	I	250+	Dawson, Zoe	Steck-Vaughn
Postcards From Vietnam	N	I	250+	Allard, Denise	Steck-Vaughn
Postman Pete	J	RF	250+	Bookshop	Mondo
*Pot of Gold, A/Clever Farmer, The	L	TL	250+	Pacific Literacy	Pacific Learning
Pot of Gold, The	I	TL	266	Reading Unlimited	Pearson Learning Group
Pot of Stone Soup, A	L	TL	250+	Ready Readers	Pearson Learning Group
Potato	N	RF	250+	Peirce, Robin	Wright Group/McGraw Hill
Potato Chips	I	RF	101	City Kids	Rigby
Potato Harvest Time	A	I	33	Little Books for Early Readers	University of Maine
Potato Pride	P	RF	1000	Leveled Readers	Houghton Mifflin
Potato Printing	G	I	174	Sun Sprouts	ETA/Cuisenaire
Potato: A Tale From the Great Depression	L	HF	250+	Soar To Success	Houghton Mifflin
Potatoes	I	I	78	Windows on Literacy	National Geographic
Potatoes on Tuesday	C	F	28	Little Celebrations	Pearson Learning Group
Potatoes, Potatoes	H	I	91	Wonder World	Wright Group/McGraw Hill
Potter in Fiji, A	N	I	453	Wonder World	Wright Group/McGraw Hill
Pourquoi Tales	N	TL	523	Vocabulary Readers	Houghton Mifflin
Powder Puff Puzzle, The	L	RF	250+	Giff, Patricia Reilly	Bantam
Power Machines	N	I	250+	Robbins, Ken	Henry Holt & Co.
*Power of Light, The	V	TL	250+	Singer, Isaac Bashevis	Farrar, Straus and Giroux
Power of Nature, The	K	I	274	Early Connections	Benchmark Education
Power of Water, The	L	I	250+	Home Connection Collection	Rigby
Power of Wind, The	T	I	1983	Leveled Readers Science	Houghton Mifflin
Powerhouse, Inside a Nuclear Power Plant	Z	I	250+	Wilcox, Charlotte	Carolrhoda Books
Powers of Congress, The	W	I	250+	Cornerstones of Freedom	Children's Press
Powers of the Mind	Z	I	250+	Innes, Brian	Steck-Vaughn
Powhatan, The: A Confederacy of Native American Tribes	S	I	250+	American Indian Nations	Capstone Press
Powwow	F	I	29	Books for Young Learners	Richard C. Owen
Powwow Summer: A Family Celebrates the Circle of Life	S	I	250+	Rendon, Marcie R.	Carolrhoda Books
Practice Makes Perfect	D	RF	111	Teacher's Choice Series	Pearson Learning Group
Prairie Danger	T	HF	1722	Leveled Readers	Houghton Mifflin
Prairie Dogs	L	I	212	Twig	Wright Group/McGraw Hill
Prairie Dogs and Their Burrows	J	I	130	Pebble Plus	Capstone Press
Prairie School	Q	I	505	Vocabulary Readers	Houghton Mifflin
Prairie Songs	Q	HF	250+	Conrad, Pam	HarperTrophy
Prairie Town	F	I	62	Seedlings	Continental Press
Praying Mantis, The	D	I	46	Pacific Literacy	Pacific Learning
Praying Mantises	I	I	78	Insects	Red Brick Learning
Praying Mantises	H	I	96	Bugs, Bugs, Bugs!	Red Brick Learning
Preacher's Boy	T	RF	250+	Paterson, Katherine	Houghton Mifflin
Precious Stones	T	I	1331	Leveled Readers Science	Houghton Mifflin
Predators in the Rain Forest	O	I	250+	Pirotta, Saviour	Steck-Vaughn
Prehistoric Record Breakers	N	I	250+	Discovery World	Rigby
Prehistory to Egypt	R	I	250+	Journey Through History	Barron's Educational
Preparing for Lift-Off	Q	I	453	Vocabulary Readers	Houghton Mifflin

TITLE	LEVEL	GENRE	WORD COUNT	AUTHOR / SERIES	PUBLISHER / DISTRIBUTOR
Present for LaNita, A	L	RF	835	Leveled Readers Social Studies	Houghton Mifflin
Present From Aunt Skidoo, The	M	RF	250+	Literacy 2000	Rigby
Present, The	B	I	36	First Stories	Pacific Learning
Present, The	E	F	30	Literacy 2000	Rigby
Presents	D	F	43	Storyteller-First Snow	Wright Group/McGraw Hill
Presidency of the United States, The	V	I	250+	American Civics	Red Brick Learning
Presidency, The	Q	I	250+	Let's See	Compass Point Books
Presidency, The	N	I	250+	A True Book	Children's Press
Presidential Elections	W	I	250+	Cornerstones of Freedom	Children's Press
Presidents' Day	L	I	250+	Frost, Helen	Red Brick Learning
Press a Button	E	I	43	Windows on Literacy	National Geographic
Pretty Cool, For a Cat	Q	RF	1707	Leveled Readers	Houghton Mifflin
Pretty Good Magic	J	RF	250+	Dubowski, Cathy East & Mark	Random House
Prickles the Porcupine	K	RF	430	PM Plus Story Books	Rigby
Pride of Puerto Rico: The Life of Roberto Clemente	W	B	250+	Walker, Paul Robert	Harcourt Trade
Pride of the Rockets	N	RF	250+	Kroll, Stephen	Avon Camelot
Prince Among Donkeys, A	K	RF	250+	Rigby Literacy	Rigby
Prince Amos	R	RF	250+	Paulsen, Gary	Bantam
Prince William	Q	B	250+	Rand, Gloria	Henry Holt & Co.
Princess and the Castle, The	J	F	250+	Leonhardt, Alice	Steck-Vaughn
Princess and the Pea, The	I	TL	304	Traditional Tales	Pearson Learning Group
Princess and the Peas, The	K	TL	250+	Enrichment	Wright Group/McGraw Hill
Princess and the Wise Woman, The	K	TL	250+	Ready Readers	Pearson Learning Group
Princess Diaries, The	Z	RF	250+	Cabot, Meg	HarperTrophy
Princess Euphorbia	N	RF	250+	SupaDoopers	Sundance
Princess in Love	Z	RF	250+	Cabot, Meg	HarperTrophy
Princess Josie's Pets	L	RF	250+	Macdonald, Maryann	Hyperion
Princess Rosa's Winter	K	F	250+	Hindley, Judy	Wright Group/McGraw Hill
Princess Who Couldn't Cry, The	G	TL	300	Ready Readers	Pearson Learning Group
Princess Who Loved to Cook, The	M	F	250+	Cartwright, Pauline	Pearson Learning Group
Princess Who Wanted the Moon, The	M	F	250+	Lane, Sheila; Kemp, Marion	Wood Lock Educational
Princess, the Mud Pies, and the Dragon, The	I	TL	250+	Little Readers	Houghton Mifflin
Princesses Don't Wear Jeans	M	RF	250+	Bookshop	Mondo
Printing Machine, The	G	F	102	Literacy 2000	Rigby
Priscilla and the Dinosaurs	K	RF	340	Sunshine	Wright Group/McGraw Hill
Private Captain: A Story of Gettysburg	W	HF	250+	Crisp, Marty	Philomel Books
Private Notebook of Katie Roberts, Age 11, The	P	RF	250+	Hest, Amy	Candlewick Press
Prize for Purry, A	K	RF	250+	Literacy 2000	Rigby
Pro Stock Trucks	T	I	250+	The World's Fastest	Red Brick Learning
Probability	P	I	250+	Early Connections	Benchmark Education
Problems with My Pudding	N	I	950	Leveled Readers Science	Houghton Mifflin
Processed Food	F	I	54	Wonder World	Wright Group/McGraw Hill
Prohibition	X	I	2560	Independent Readers Social Studies	Houghton Mifflin
Project Apollo	N	I	250+	A True Book	Children's Press
Project Gemini	N	I	250+	A True Book	Children's Press
Project Mercury	N	I	250+	A True Book	Children's Press
Promise Me the Moon	V	RF	250+	Barnes, Joyce Annette	Penguin Group
Proof of Magic	Q	F	250+	Ragged Island Mysteries	Wright Group/McGraw Hill
Prophecy of the Stones, The	Z	F	250+	Bujor, Flavia	Hyperion
Protecting Sea Turtles	R	I	250+	Leveled Readers Language Support	Houghton Mifflin

* Collection of short stories

TITLE	LEVEL	GENRE	WORD COUNT	AUTHOR / SERIES	PUBLISHER / DISTRIBUTOR
Protecting Your Home: Book About Firefighters, A	H	I	89	Community Workers	Picture Window Books
Protectors, The	Y	RF	3223	Leveled Readers	Houghton Mifflin
Proud Taste For Scarlet And Miniver	W	F	250+	Konigsburg, E. L.	Dell
Prudence	N	I	250+	Raatma, Lucia	Red Brick Learning
PS, I Love You Gramps	O	RF	250+	Literacy Tree	Rigby
PT Boats	T	I	250+	Land and Sea	Capstone Press
Pterodactyl at the Airport	K	F	185	Wesley & the Dinosaurs	Wright Group/McGraw Hill
Pterosaur's Long Flight	I	HF	301	PM Story Books-Orange	Rigby
Public Library, The	K	I	250+	Stepping Stones	Nelson/Michaels Assoc.
Pudding Problems	N	RF	921	Leveled Readers Science	Houghton Mifflin
Pueblo	K	I	114	Leveled Readers Social Studies	Houghton Mifflin
Pueblo Indians, The	P	I	250+	Ross, Pamela	Red Brick Learning
Pueblo Ruins	Q	I	250+	Rigby Literacy	Rigby
Pueblo, The	R	I	250+	First Reports	Compass Point Books
Pueblo, The: Southwestern Potters	R	I	250+	America's First Peoples	Capstone Press
Puerto Rico	R	I	250+	This Land Is Your Land	Compass Point Books
Puffins	H	I	104	Seedlings	Continental Press
Pug and Chug	I	F	250+	Supersonics	Rigby
Pukeko Morning	G	I	148	Pacific Literacy	Pacific Learning
Pullman Strike, The	V	I	1541	Leveled Readers Social Studies	Houghton Mifflin
Pumpkin Grows, A	E	I	176	Bookshop	Mondo
Pumpkin House, The	J	F	250+	Literacy 2000	Rigby
Pumpkin That Kim Carved, The	H	RF	149	Little Readers	Houghton Mifflin
Pumpkin, The	E	I	56	Story Box	Wright Group/McGraw Hill
Pumpkins	M	I	250+	Ray, Mary Lyn	Harcourt Trade
Punchinello	F	TL	250+	PM Readalongs	Rigby
Puppet Play, A	C	I	54	Storyteller-First Snow	Wright Group/McGraw Hill
Puppet Show	F	RF	105	First Start	Troll Associates
Puppet Show, The	E	I	25	Literacy 2000	Rigby
Puppet Show, The	B	RF	25	Phonics and Friends	Hampton-Brown
Puppeteer's Apprentice, The	Z	HF	250+	Love, D. Anne	Simon & Schuster
Puppets	G	I	47	Canizares, Susan; Berger, Samantha	Scholastic
Puppets	P	I	250	Literacy Tree	Rigby
Puppets	J	I	250+	Little Celebrations	Pearson Learning Group
Puppets for a Play	D	I	45	Home Connection Collection	Rigby
Puppies in the Pantry	Q	RF	250+	Baglio, Ben M.	Scholastic
Puppies, Dogs, and Blue Northers	S	I	250+	Paulsen, Gary	Delacorte
Puppy at the Door	J	RF	250+	PM Plus Story Books	Rigby
Puppy Chase, The	I	RF	250+	Cambridge Reading	Pearson Learning Group
Puppy Love	N	RF	250+	Duffey, Betsy	Puffin Books
Puppy Play	D	RF	67	Emergent Books	Pioneer Valley
Puppy Puzzle	O	RF	250+	Baglio, Ben M.	Scholastic
Puppy Who Wanted a Boy, The	L	F	250+	Thayer, Jane	Scholastic
Puppy, The	B	RF	37	First Stories	Pacific Learning
Pure Dead Wicked	W	F	250+	Gliori, Debi	Random House
Purple Climbing Days	M	RF	250+	Giff, Patricia Reilly	Bantam
Purple Is Part of a Rainbow	E	RF	131	Rookie Readers	Children's Press
Purple Walrus and Other Perfect Pets	O	RF	250+	Wildcats	Wright Group/McGraw Hill
Purple: Seeing Purple All Around Us	K	I	250+	Colors	Capstone Press
Push and Pull	H	I	49	Yellow Umbrella Books	Red Brick Learning
Push and Pull	E	I	184	Pebble Books	Capstone Press
Push and Pull	G	I	49	iOpeners	Pearson Learning Group

*Collection of short stories

TITLE	LEVEL	GENRE	WORD COUNT	AUTHOR / SERIES	PUBLISHER / DISTRIBUTOR
Push It or Pull It?	F	RF	162	Instant Readers	Harcourt School Publishers
Push or Pull	L	I	316	Independent Readers Science	Houghton Mifflin
Push or Pull?	A	I	7	Discovery Links	Newbridge
Push or Pull?	J	I	154	Phonics Readers	Compass Point Books
Push or Pull?	C	I	73	Windows on Literacy	National Geographic
Push!	D	RF	21	Oxford Reading Tree	Oxford University Press
Pushcart War, The	Y	F	250+	Merrill, Jean	Bantam
Puss-in-Boots	K	TL	250+	PM Tales and Plays-Purple	Rigby
Pussy Cat	F	TL	143	Literacy 2000	Rigby
Pussy Cat, Pussy Cat	D	F	44	Seedlings	Continental Press
Put Me in the Zoo	H	B	250+	Lopshire, Robert	Random House
Putting on a Concert and The Television News	L	RF	250+	Voyages	SRA/McGraw Hill
Putting on a Play	Q	I	424	Vocabulary Readers	Houghton Mifflin
Puzzle, The	A	I	32	Sun Sprouts	ETA/Cuisenaire
Puzzle, The	B	RF	32	Smart Starts	Rigby
Puzzle,The	B	I	28	Storyteller Nonfiction	Wright Group/McGraw Hill
Pyjama Party, The	K	RF	250+	Cambridge Reading	Pearson Learning Group
Pyramid	X	I	250+	Macaulay, David	Scholastic
Pyramids in the Bush: A Book about Mallee Fowl	T	I	250+	Sunshine	Wright Group/McGraw Hill
Pyramids of Ancient Egypt, The	V	I	250+	Leveled Readers Language Support	Houghton Mifflin
Pyramids of Egypt, The	S	I	250+	Rosen Real Readers	Rosen Publishing Group
Pyramids of Giza, The	W	I	1718	Leveled Readers	Houghton Mifflin
Python Caught the Eagle, The	C	F	60	Voyages	SRA/McGraw Hill
Qillak	M	RF	250+	Jensen, Ned	Wright Group/McGraw Hill
Quack!	E	F	48	Ready Readers	Pearson Learning Group
Quack, Quack, Quack	D	F	97	Carousel Readers	Pearson Learning Group
Quack, Quack, Quack!	I	F	219	Sunshine	Wright Group/McGraw Hill
Quack, Said the Billy Goat	H	F	88	Causley, Charles	Harper & Row
Quackers, the Troublesome Duck	M	F	250+	Ellen, Leslie	Pearson Learning Group
Quake!	T	RF	250+	Cottonwood, Joe	Language for Learning Assoc.
Quarter Story, The	E	I	99	Williams, Deborah	Kaeden Books
Quarters for Everyone	S	RF	1798	Leveled Readers	Houghton Mifflin
Quarters Toss, The	P	RF	250+	Leveled Readers Language Support	Houghton Mifflin
Queen and the Dragon, The	I	F	243	New Way Green	Steck-Vaughn
Queen Eleanor: Independent Spirit in the Medieval World	X	B	250+	Brooks, Polly Schoyer	Houghton Mifflin
Queen Jelly Bean	J	F	250+	The Wright Skills	Wright Group/McGraw Hill
Queen Made a Quilt	D	RF	46	Ray's Readers	Outside the Box
Queen of Hearts, The	E	TL	26	Jumbled Tumbled Tales & Rhymes	Rigby
Queen of the Bean	N	RF	250+	Action Packs	Rigby
Queen of the Pool	N	RF	250+	PM Emerald	Rigby
Queen on a Quilt	C	F	26	Ready Readers	Pearson Learning Group
Queen's Parrot, The: A Play	J	TL	365	Literacy 2000	Rigby
Quest for California's Gold, The	S	I	250+	The Library of the Westward Expansion	Rosen Publishing Group
Quest For Medusa's Head, The	W	TL	1385	Leveled Readers	Houghton Mifflin
Questions and Answers About Forest Animals	P	I	250+	Chinery, Michael	Kingfisher
Questions and Answers About Freshwater Animals	P	I	250+	Chinery, Michael	Kingfisher
Questions, Questions, Questions	F	RF	190	Visions	Wright Group/McGraw Hill

* Collection of short stories

TITLE	LEVEL	GENRE	WORD COUNT	AUTHOR / SERIES	PUBLISHER / DISTRIBUTOR
Quick and Quiet	C	F	38	Phonics and Friends	Hampton-Brown
Quick Chick	J	F	250+	Hoban, Julia	Puffin Books
Quick Duck, The	H	F	165	Phonics Readers	Scholastic
Quick, Go Peek!	E	F	83	Little Celebrations	Pearson Learning Group
Quiet in the Library!	H	F	113	Sunshine	Wright Group/McGraw Hill
Quiet Morning for Mom, A	H	RF	169	Lighthouse	Rigby
Quiet TV Lunch, A	L	F	250+	Popcorn	Sundance
Quiet World, The	K	RF	250+	Voyages	SRA/McGraw Hill
Quilt for Kiri, A	K	RF	367	Pacific Literacy	Pacific Learning
Quilt for Kristy, A	J	RF	250+	The Wright Skills	Wright Group/McGraw Hill
Quilt Story, The	L	HF	250+	Johnston, Tony; DePaola, Tomie	Scholastic
Quilt with a Difference, A	N	I	250+	Pacific Literacy	Pacific Learning
Quilt, The	I	RF	165	Jonas, Ann	Morrow
Quilting in America	I	I	152	Vocabulary Readers	Houghton Mifflin
Quilts	C	RF	35	Foundations	Wright Group/McGraw Hill
Quilts	E	I	131	Twig	Wright Group/McGraw Hill
Quork Attack	L	F	250+	Rigby Literacy	Rigby
R is for Radish!	J	F	250+	Coxe, Molly	Random House
Rabbit and the Coyote, The	Q	F	979	Leveled Readers	Houghton Mifflin
Rabbit and Turtle Go to School	E	F	67	Instant Readers	Harcourt Trade
Rabbit Catches the Sun	M	F	621	Sunshine	Wright Group/McGraw Hill
Rabbit for You, A: Caring for your Rabbit	M	I	250+	Pet Care	Picture Window Books
Rabbit Makes Toast	K	F	250+	Popcorn	Sundance
Rabbit Race	O	RF	250+	Baglio, Ben M.	Scholastic
Rabbit Stew	L	F	250+	Literacy 2000	Rigby
Rabbit, The	H	RF	59	Burningham, John	Crowell
Rabbits	D	I	37	All About Pets	Red Brick Learning
Rabbits	N	I	250+	Literacy 2000	Rigby
Rabbits and Their Burrows	J	I	136	Animal Homes	Capstone Press
Rabbit's Birthday Kite	J	F	250+	Bank Street	Bantam
Rabbits' Ears	F	RF	179	PM Plus Story Books	Rigby
Rabbits Have Bunnies	M	I	250+	Animals and Their Young	Compass Point Books
Rabbits in Space	J	F	216	Talking Point Series	Pearson Learning Group
Rabbits on the Farm	I	I	103	Pebble Books	Red Brick Learning
Rabbit's Party	G	F	351	Bunting, Eve; Sloan-Childers, E.	Scholastic
Rabbit's Real Birthday	J	F	250+	Rigby Literacy	Rigby
Rabbit's Robber	L	F	250+	Popcorn	Sundance
Rabbit's Tail	K	TL	250+	Cambridge Reading	Pearson Learning Group
Rabbit's Tricks	I	F	250+	Robinson, Fay	Wright Group/McGraw Hill
Rabble Starkey	T	RF	250+	Lowry, Lois	Bantam
Raccoon on the Moon	I	RF	250+	Start to Read	School Zone
Raccoons	M	I	250+	PM Animal Facts: Gold	Rigby
Race Cars	M	I	250+	Transportation	Compass Point Books
Race Is On, The	D	F	45	New Way Red	Steck-Vaughn
Race of the River Runner	P	HF	540	Leveled Readers	Houghton Mifflin
Race to Green End, The	J	F	506	PM Turquoise	Rigby
Race to the Mountain, The	H	TL	174	Leveled Readers Language Support	Houghton Mifflin
Race to the Pole	R	I	250+	Windows on Literacy	National Geographic
Race, The	C	RF	25	Sunshine	Wright Group/McGraw Hill
Race, The	F	RF	145	Little Readers	Houghton Mifflin
Race, The	E	F	30	Little Celebrations	Pearson Learning Group
Race, The	B	RF	78	Leveled Readers Emergent	Houghton Mifflin
Race, The	I	F	451	New Way Green	Steck-Vaughn

TITLE	LEVEL	GENRE	WORD COUNT	AUTHOR / SERIES	PUBLISHER / DISTRIBUTOR
Race, The	B	RF	34	Windmill	Wright Group/McGraw Hill
Rachel Carson	J	B	279	Leveled Readers	Houghton Mifflin
Rachel Carson, Scientist and Writer	N	B	370	Independent Readers Social Studies	Houghton Mifflin
Rachel Carson: Friend of Nature	N	B	250+	Rookie Biographies	Children's Press
Rachel to the Rescue	O	RF	250+	SupaDoopers	Sundance
Racing Danger	Q	I	737	Leveled Readers	Houghton Mifflin
Racing with the Sun	Q	I	250+	Orbit Double Takes	Pacific Learning
Radar Jammers: The EA-6B Prowlers	R	I	250+	War Planes	Red Brick Learning
Radio	O	I	250+	Let's See	Compass Point Books
Radio Scare	T	I	250+	Leveled Readers Language Support	Houghton Mifflin
Ragbag	G	F	41	Supersonics	Rigby
Raging Dragon, The (Will to Conquer Series: Book 2)	Z	F	250+	Lamensdorf, Len	SeaScape Press
Ragweed	U	F	250+	Avi	Avon
Railroad Revolution	R	I	618	Vocabulary Readers	Houghton Mifflin
Railroad Toad	K	F	178	Schade, Susan	Random House
Rain	C	RF	34	Learn to Read	Creative Teaching Press
Rain	J	I	250+	Voyages	SRA/McGraw Hill
Rain	K	I	263	Pebble Books	Capstone Press
Rain	G	RF	68	Literacy 2000	Rigby
Rain	C	I	56	Kalan, Robert	Greenwillow
Rain	B	RF	52	Reading Corners	Pearson Learning Group
Rain	D	RF	45	Step-By-Step Series	Pearson Learning Group
Rain and the Sun, The	E	I	45	Wonder World	Wright Group/McGraw Hill
Rain Forest	R	I	250+	Worldwise	Grolier Press
Rain Forest Adventure	L	F	482	Pair-It Books	Steck-Vaughn
Rain Forest Animals	J	I	151	Phonics Readers	Compass Point Books
Rain Forest Plants	M	I	580	Lundberg, Linda	Harcourt School Publishers
Rain Forest Plants	I	I	151	Alphakids	Sundance
Rain Forest Tree, A	Q	I	250+	Kite, Lorien	Crabtree
Rain Forest, A	LB	I	18	Rigby Focus	Rigby
Rain Forest, The	Q	I	191	Action Packs	Rigby
Rain Forest, The	N	I	191	Windows on Literacy	National Geographic
Rain Forests	S	I	250+	The Heinle Reading Library	Thomson Learning
Rain Forests	Q	I	250+	First Reports	Compass Point Books
Rain Ghost, The	X	F	250+	Kilworth, Garry	Scholastic
Rain in the Hills	D	RF	41	Book Bank	Wright Group/McGraw Hill
Rain Is Not My Indian Name	Z	RF	250+	Smith, Cynthia Leitich	HarperCollins
Rain Is Water	E	I	82	PM Plus Nonfiction	Rigby
Rain or Shine	Q	I	250+	Explorers	Wright Group/McGraw Hill
Rain or Shine?	C	I	21	Twig	Wright Group/McGraw Hill
Rain Puddle	J	RF	250+	Holl, Adelaide	Morrow
Rain! Rain!	D	RF	29	Rookie Readers	Children's Press
Rain, Rain	E	RF	58	Pacific Literacy	Pacific Learning
Rain, Rain, and More Rain	H	RF	250+	Momentum Literacy Program	Troll Associates
Rain, Rivers, and Rain Again	M	I	250+	Sunshine	Wright Group/McGraw Hill
Rain, Snow, and Hail	J	I	250+	Discovery World	Rigby
Rain, The	G	RF	171	Foundations	Wright Group/McGraw Hill
Rain, The	C	RF	76	Leveled Readers Emergent	Houghton Mifflin
Rainbow Bird, A	LB	I	18	Pair-It Books	Steck-Vaughn
Rainbow of My Own	C	F	52	Freeman, Don	Penguin Group
Rainbow Parrot	I	TL	174	Literacy Tree	Rigby

* Collection of short stories

TITLE	LEVEL	GENRE	WORD COUNT	AUTHOR / SERIES	PUBLISHER / DISTRIBUTOR
*Rainbow People, The	V	F	250+	Yep, Lawrence	HarperTrophy
Rainbow Solution, The	N	RF	250+	Literacy 2000	Rigby
Rainbow Somewhere, A	G	RF	201	Ready Readers	Pearson Learning Group
Rainbow Wings	M	F	250+	Nevinski, Margaret	Wright Group/McGraw Hill
Rainbow, A	B	I	29	Rigby Focus	Rigby
Rainbows	L	I	250+	Rigby Literacy	Rigby
Rainbows All Around	M	RF	250+	Hardin, Suzanne	Pacific Learning
Rainbows and Moonbeams	I	RF	238	Sunshine	Wright Group/McGraw Hill
Rainbows of the Sea	L	I	250+	Thomas, Meredith	Mondo
Raindrop, A	C	RF	41	Teacher's Choice Series	Pearson Learning Group
Raindrops	B	I	34	Bookshop	Mondo
Raindrops	C	RF	66	Gay, Sandy	Scholastic
Rainy Day Alphabet Book	E	RF	82	Posner, Jackie; Wiener, Sara	Scholastic
Rainy Day Counting	B	I	30	Twig	Wright Group/McGraw Hill
Rainy Day Dream	WB	F	N/A	Chesworth, Michael	Farrar, Straus and Giroux
Rainy Day Solution, A	K	I	161	Vocabulary Readers	Houghton Mifflin
Rainy Day, A	D	RF	105	New Way Blue	Steck-Vaughn
Rainy Day, A	E	I	52	Pebble Books	Capstone Press
Rainy Day, Sunny Day	E	F	135	Early Connections	Benchmark Education
Rainy Days at School	H	RF	118	City Kids	Rigby
Rairarubia	S	F	250+	Adams, W. Royce	Lost Coast Press
Rally Car Race	J	RF	250+	PM Plus Story Books	Rigby
Ralph S. Mouse	O	F	250+	Cleary, Beverly	HarperTrophy
Ramona and Her Father	O	RF	250+	Cleary, Beverly	Avon
Ramona and Her Mother	O	RF	250+	Cleary, Beverly	Avon
Ramona Forever	O	RF	250+	Cleary, Beverly	Hearst
Ramona Quimby, Age 8	O	RF	250+	Cleary, Beverly	Hearst
Ramona the Brave	O	RF	250+	Cleary, Beverly	Hearst
Ramona the Pest	O	RF	250+	Cleary, Beverly	Avon
Rand and the Fox, The	H	TL	93	Cambridge Reading	Pearson Learning Group
Randy Moss	Y	B	250+	Sports Heroes	Red Brick Learning
Randy's Room	C	RF	32	Harry's Math Books	Outside the Box
Rap Party, The	H	RF	300	Foundations	Wright Group/McGraw Hill
Rapid Robert Roadrunner	H	F	125	Reese, Bob	Children's Press
Raptors: Hunters in the Sky	R	I	250+	Rauzon, Mark J.	Wright Group/McGraw Hill
Rapunzel	L	TL	250+	Literacy 2000	Rigby
Rascal	V	HF	250+	North, Sterling	Scholastic
Rascal	G	RF	108	Rigby Literacy	Rigby
Rashee and the Seven Elephants	M	RF	250+	Little Celebrations	Pearson Learning Group
Rat-a-tat-tat	E	F	107	Literacy 2000	Rigby
Rat's Funny Story	C	F	39	Story Box	Wright Group/McGraw Hill
*Rats on the Range and Other Stories	O	F	250+	Marshall, James	Penguin Group
*Rats on the Roof and Other Stories	O	F	250+	Marshall, James	Penguin Group
Rat's Tale, A	T	F	250+	Seidler, Tor	HarperTrophy
*Rats!	O	RF	250+	Cutler, Jane	Farrar, Straus and Giroux
Rats, Bats, and Black Puddings	K	F	714	Pacific Literacy	Pacific Learning
Rattlesnake Looks for Food, The	E	RF	105	Foundations	Wright Group/McGraw Hill
Ratty Tatty	H	F	181	Sunshine	Wright Group/McGraw Hill
*Raven's Call and More Northwest Coast Stories	P	TL	250+	Challenger, James Robert	Heritage House
Raven's Gift	L	F	160	Books For Young Learners	Richard C. Owen
Ray Ran	C	RF	34	Ray's Readers	Outside the Box
Rays	I	I	48	Pebble Books	Red Brick Learning
Reaching the Sky	C	RF	46	Sunshine	Wright Group/McGraw Hill
Reaction We Need, The	U	I	2708	Leveled Readers Science	Houghton Mifflin

* Collection of short stories

TITLE	LEVEL	GENRE	WORD COUNT	AUTHOR / SERIES	PUBLISHER / DISTRIBUTOR
Read to Your Bunny	F	F	38	Wells, Rosemary	Scholastic
Reading a Graph	F	I	251	Early Connections	Benchmark Education
Reading a Map	M	I	250+	Rosen Real Readers	Rosen Publishing Group
Reading Is Everywhere	D	RF	53	Sunshine	Wright Group/McGraw Hill
Reading Lesson, The	F	RF	78	Teacher's Choice Series	Pearson Learning Group
Reading Partners	A	I	48	At School Series	Pioneer Valley
Reading Robot, The	H	F	224	Sunshine	Wright Group/McGraw Hill
Reading Under the Covers	D	RF	25	Visions	Wright Group/McGraw Hill
Ready for School	C	RF	41	Teacher's Choice Series	Pearson Learning Group
Ready for School	E	RF	77	Windmill Books	Rigby
Ready Steady Jump	D	I	25	Pacific Literacy	Pacific Learning
Ready, Get Set, Go!	G	RF	137	First Set	Troll Associates
Ready, Set, Go	H	F	250+	Stadler, John	HarperTrophy
Ready, Set, Go!	D	I	26	Canizares, Susan; Chanko, Pamela	Scholastic
Ready, Set, Go!	K	RF	250+	Pacific Literacy	Pacific Learning
Ready, Set, Jump!	M	I	250+	Rigby Literacy	Rigby
Ready, Steady, Rhyme!	J	RF	250+	Rigby Literacy	Rigby
Real Facts About Rivers	I	I	159	Rosen Real Readers	Rosen Publishing Group
Real Princess, The	I	TL	193	Jumbled Tumbled Tales & Rhymes	Rigby
Real Team Soccer	R	RF	1207	Leveled Readers	Houghton Mifflin
Real Thief, The	U	F	250+	Steig, William	Farrar, Straus and Giroux
Real-Skin Rubber Monster Mask, The	H	F	104	Cohen, Miriam	Bantam
Reason to Run, A	Q	RF	250+	Leveled Readers Language Support	Houghton Mifflin
Rebecca and the Concert	I	RF	374	PM StoryBooks	Rigby
Rebus Bears, The	I	F	250+	Reit, Seymour	Bantam
Recess	A	I	27	At School Series	Pioneer Valley
Recess	B	RF	26	Teacher's Choice Series	Pearson Learning Group
Rectangles: Seeing Rectangles All Around Us	K	I	199	Shapes	Capstone Press
Recycle It!	G	I	118	Discovery Links	Newbridge
Recycle!	B	I	33	Leveled Readers Science	Houghton Mifflin
Recycling a Can	M	I	250+	Rosen Real Readers	Rosen Publishing Group
Recycling Dump	D	I	48	Little Celebrations	Pearson Learning Group
Red	E	F	71	Instant Readers	Harcourt School Publishers
Red and Blue and Yellow	D	I	100	PM Nonfiction-Red	Rigby
Red and Blue Mittens	M	RF	250+	Reading Unlimited	Pearson Learning Group
Red and I Visit the Vet	F	RF	196	Ready Readers	Pearson Learning Group
Red and the Big Bad Wolf	W	F	1357	Leveled Readers	Houghton Mifflin
Red Balloon, The	C	RF	34	Joy Readers	Pearson Learning Group
Red Box, The	H	RF	250+	Phonics Readers Plus	Steck-Vaughn
Red Cap	W	HF	250+	Wisler, G. Clifton	Penguin Group
Red Dog	U	RF	250+	Wallace, Bill	Simon & Schuster
*Red Doll and Other Stories, The	H	F	250+	New Way Literature	Steck-Vaughn
Red Egg and Ginger	M	RF	250+	Greetings	Rigby
Red Means Good Fortune: A Story of San Francisco's Chinatown	S	I	250+	Goldin, Barbara Diamond	Penguin Group
Red Midnight	Y	HF	250+	Mikaelsen, Ben	HarperTrophy
Red Nose Frost: A Traditional Tale From Russia	L	TL	250+	Rigby Literacy	Rigby
Red or Blue?	LB	RF	13	Ready Readers	Pearson Learning Group
Red Planet, The	S	I	250+	Orbit Double Takes	Pacific Learning
Red Puppy	C	RF	85	PM Plus Story Books	Rigby
Red Ribbon Rosie	M	RF	250+	Marzollo, Jean	Random House
*Red Riding Hood and the Flower in the Woods	L	TL	250+	New Way Literature	Steck-Vaughn
Red Rose, The	E	F	127	Story Box	Wright Group/McGraw Hill

* Collection of short stories

TITLE	LEVEL	GENRE	WORD COUNT	AUTHOR / SERIES	PUBLISHER / DISTRIBUTOR
Red Scarf Girl: Memoir of the Cultural Revolution	Z	B	250+	Jiang, Ji Li	HarperTrophy
Red Shoes, The	L	RF	250+	Sails	Rigby
Red Socks and Yellow Socks	G	F	155	Sunshine	Wright Group/McGraw Hill
Red Sox and the World Series, The	O	I	460	Vocabulary Readers	Houghton Mifflin
Red Squirrel Hides Some Nuts	E	RF	128	PM Plus Story Books	Rigby
Red Squirrel's Adventure	H	RF	223	PM Plus Story Books	Rigby
Red, White, and Blue	LB	I	21	Canizares, Susan; Chessen, Betsey	Scholastic
Red, White, and Blue	LB	I	21	Canizares, Susan; Chessen, Betsey	Scholastic
Red: Seeing Red All Around Us	L	I	250+	Colors	Capstone Press
Red-Tailed Hawk, The	L	RF	197	Books For Young Learners	Richard C. Owen
Reduce, Reuse, and Recycle	K	I	326	Early Connections	Benchmark Education
Redwall	Z	F	250+	Jacques, Brian	Avon
Redy to Ride	F	RF	103	City Stories	Rigby
Reefs	T	I	250+	iOpeners	Pearson Learning Group
Reflections	I	F	110	Jonas, Ann	Morrow
Refugees, The	P	RF	250+	Marriott, Janice	Pacific Learning
Regarding the Fountain: A Tale, in Letter, of Liars and Leaks	U	F	250+	Klise, Kate	Avon
Regina's Ride	P	RF	1017	Leveled Readers	Houghton Mifflin
Relationships of Living Things	R	I	250+	Atwater, Mary et al.	Macmillan/McGraw Hill
Rella's Wish	R	TL	1207	Leveled Readers	Houghton Mifflin
REM World	U	F	250+	Philbrick, Rodman	Scholastic
Remarkable Journey of Prince Jen, The	V	F	250+	Alexander, Lloyd	Bantam
Rembrandt	S	B	250+	Masterpieces: Artists and Their Works	Capstone Press
Remember Not To Forget: A Memory of the Holocaust	V	I	250+	Finkelstein, Norman H.	William Morrow
Remember the Ladies: The First Women's Rights Convention	U	I	250+	Johnston, Norma	Scholastic
Remembering the Big Quake	R	I	250+	Trussell-Cullen, Alan	Pacific Learning
Remnants	W	SF	250+	Applegate, K. A.	Scholastic
Rent a Third Grader	O	RF	250+	Hiller, B. B.	Scholastic
Report To the Principal's Office	U	RF	250+	Spinelli, Jerry	Scholastic
Reptiles	M	I	250+	First Facts	Capstone Press
Reptiles and Amphibians	L	I	250+	Rosen Real Readers	Rosen Publishing Group
Reptiles and Amphibians	R	I	250+	Explorers	Wright Group/McGraw Hill
Rescue Boats	J	I	124	Mighty Machines	Capstone Press
Rescue!	O	RF	250+	Wildcats	Wright Group/McGraw Hill
Rescue!	J	RF	250+	Lighthouse	Rigby
Rescue!	J	RF	250+	Sunshine	Wright Group/McGraw Hill
Rescue, The	L	RF	176	Pacific Literacy	Pacific Learning
Rescue, The	H	RF	155	PM Extensions-Green	Rigby
Rescuers, The	S	F	250+	Sharp, Margery	Dell
Rescuing Nelson	J	F	369	PM Turquoise	Rigby
Respect	L	I	250+	Character Education	Red Brick Learning
Respect	G	RF	163	Well-Being Series	Dominie Press
Respect the Winds	M	TL	250+	Reeder, Paul	Wright Group/McGraw Hill
Respiratory System, The	M	I	212	Human Body Systems	Red Brick Learning
Responsibility	L	I	250+	Character Education	Red Brick Learning
Restless Spirit	Z	B	250+	Partridge, Elizabeth	Penguin Group
Return of Rinaldo, the Sly Fox	M	TL	250+	Scheffler, Ursel	North-South Books
Return of the Great Brain, The	T	RF	250+	Fitzgerald, John D.	Dell
Return of the Home Run Kid	N	RF	250+	Christopher, Matt	Scholastic

TITLE	LEVEL	GENRE	WORD COUNT	AUTHOR / SERIES	PUBLISHER / DISTRIBUTOR
Return of the Third-Grade Ghosthunters, The	M	RF	250+	Maccarone, Grace	Scholastic
Return of Wild Whoopers, The	X	I	3122	Leveled Readers	Houghton Mifflin
Return to Howliday Inn	P	F	250+	Howe, James	Avon Camelot
Reuse and Recycle	I	I	118	Instant Readers	Harcourt School Publishers
Revenge of the Mummy	P	RF	250+	Parker, A. E.	Scholastic
Revolution!	V	HF	3239	Leveled Readers	Houghton Mifflin
Revolutionary Poet: A Story About Phillis Wheatley	Q	B	250+	Weidt, Maryann N.	Carolrhoda Books
Revolutionary War on Wednesday	M	F	250+	Osborne, Mary Pope	Random House
Rex Plays Fetch	J	RF	250+	PM Plus Story Books	Rigby
Rex to the Rescue	G	F	159	Sunshine	Wright Group/McGraw Hill
Rex's Dance	E	F	103	Little Readers	Houghton Mifflin
Rhinos	O	I	250+	Holmes, Kevin J.	Red Brick Learning
Rhode Island	R	I	250+	This Land Is Your Land	Compass Point Books
Rhyme Game, The	G	RF	159	Storyteller-Setting Sun	Wright Group/McGraw Hill
Rhymes	A	I	9	Ready Readers	Pearson Learning Group
Rhyming Riddles	H	I	240	Cambridge Reading	Pearson Learning Group
Rhythm and Shoes	N	I	250+	Pacific Literacy	Pacific Learning
Ribbit!	A	I	7	Little Celebrations	Pearson Learning Group
Ribbon, The	C	I	46	Rise & Shine	Hampton-Brown
Ribsy	O	RF	250+	Cleary, Beverly	Hearst
Rice	O	I	250+	Windows on Literacy	National Geographic
Rice	L	I	132	Literacy Tree	Rigby
Rice Cakes	H	F	332	Literacy 2000	Rigby
Richard M. Nixon	U	B	250+	Profiles of the Presidents	Compass Point Books
Riches from Nature	K	I	382	Early Connections	Benchmark Education
Richie the Greedy Mouse	I	F	179	Sunshine	Wright Group/McGraw Hill
Rick and Rosie	B	RF	28	Phonics and Friends	Hampton-Brown
Rick's Dream Adventure	K	F	250+	World Quest Adventures	World Quest Learning
Riddle Book	F	F	189	Reading Unlimited	Pearson Learning Group
Riddle of the Anasazi, The	Z	I	1637	Leveled Readers	Houghton Mifflin
Riddle of The Red Purse, The	L	RF	250+	Giff, Patricia Reilly	Bantam
Riddle of the Rosetta Stone, The	V	I	250+	Giblin, James Cross	HarperTrophy
Riddles	E	I	51	Literacy 2000	Rigby
Riddles of the Universe	S	I	250+	Bonallack, John	Pacific Learning
Ride in the Country, A	D	RF	83	Carousel Readers	Pearson Learning Group
Rides Are Fun	WB	I	N/A	Windows on Literacy	National Geographic
Riding	C	RF	67	Foundations	Wright Group/McGraw Hill
Riding	H	I	210	Wonder World	Wright Group/McGraw Hill
Riding Freedom	P	HF	250+	Ryan, Pam Munoz	Scholastic
Riding High	K	RF	529	PM Story Books	Rigby
Riding Out the Storm	S	RF	1426	Leveled Readers	Houghton Mifflin
Riding the Skateboard Ramps	K	RF	250+	PM Plus Story Books	Rigby
Riding the Steam Train	L	I	250+	Pacific Literacy	Pacific Learning
Riding to Craggy Rock	J	RF	386	PM Turquoise	Rigby
Riding with the Vaqueros	T	HF	1790	Leveled Readers	Houghton Mifflin
Rifle, The	T	HF	250+	Paulsen, Gary	Dell
Right at Home	K	I	250+	Spyglass Books	Compass Point Books
Right Fly, The	U	RF	1878	Leveled Readers	Houghton Mifflin
Right or Wrong?	O	RF	250+	Wildcats	Wright Group/McGraw Hill
Right Outside My Window	H	RF	121	Bookshop	Mondo
Right Pet, The	D	F	66	Leveled Readers	Houghton Mifflin
Right Place for Jupiter, The	K	RF	250+	PM Story Books-Silver	Rigby
Righteous Revenge of Artemis Bonner, The	U	RF	250+	Myers, Walter Dean	HarperTrophy

* Collection of short stories

TITLE	LEVEL	GENRE	WORD COUNT	AUTHOR / SERIES	PUBLISHER / DISTRIBUTOR
Rinaldo the Sly Fox	M	TL	250+	Scheffler, Ursel	North-South Books
Ring of Endless Light, A	W	F	250+	L'Engle, Madeleine	Dell
Ring of Fire, The	V	I	2580	Leveled Readers Social Studies	Houghton Mifflin
Ripeka's Carving	J	RF	250+	Literacy 2000	Rigby
*Rip-Roaring Russell	M	RF	250+	Hurwitz, Johanna	Penguin Group
Riptide	O	RF	250+	Weller, Frances Ward	Putnam & Grosset
Rise and Shine, Mariko-chan	K	RF	250+	Tomioka, Chiyoko	Scholastic
Rising Stars of the NBA	P	B	250+	Layden, Joe	Scholastic
Rising Up, Falling Down	L	I	205	Spyglass Books	Compass Point Books
Rita Moreno	K	B	250+	Leveled Readers Language Support	Houghton Mifflin
Rita Moreno: Shining Star	M	B	593	Leveled Readers	Houghton Mifflin
Rita Rolls	C	RF	36	Little Celebrations	Pearson Learning Group
River Apart, A	X	HF	250+	Sutherland, Robert	Fitzhenry & Whiteside
River Grows, The	E	I	70	Ready Readers	Pearson Learning Group
River Life	N	I	250+	Windows on Literacy	National Geographic
River of No Return	T	RF	1845	Leveled Readers	Houghton Mifflin
River Otter	I	I	208	Independent Readers Science	Houghton Mifflin
River Patrol Boats	T	I	250+	Land and Sea	Capstone Press
River Race	N	HF	250+	Leveled Readers Language Support	Houghton Mifflin
River Rafting Fun	J	RF	250+	PM Plus Story Books	Rigby
River Rapids Ride, The	J	RF	283	Sunshine	Wright Group/McGraw Hill
River Rats	O	RF	250+	Belcher, Angie	Pacific Learning
River Runners	M	RF	250+	Literacy Tree	Rigby
River Through the Ages	U	I	250+	Steele, Philip	Troll Associates
River, The	C	I	40	Science	Outside the Box
River, The	D	I	42	Foundations	Wright Group/McGraw Hill
River, The	R	RF	250+	Paulsen, Gary	Dell
Rivers in the Rain Forest	O	I	250+	Pirotta, Saviour	Steck-Vaughn
River's Journey, A	G	I	116	Rigby Focus	Rigby
River's Journey, The	N	I	221	Windows on Literacy	National Geographic
Rivers, Streams, and Lakes	M	I	250+	PM Plus Nonfiction	Rigby
Road Goes By, A	J	I	250+	Momentum Literacy Program	Troll Associates
Road Robber	I	F	250+	Sunshine	Wright Group/McGraw Hill
Road Through the Ages	U	I	250+	Steele, Philip	Troll Associates
Road to Memphis, The	X	HF	250+	Taylor, Mildred D.	Penguin Group
Road to Seneca Falls, The	R	B	250+	Swain, Gwenyth	Carolrhoda Books
Road Work Ahead	I	RF	207	Little Readers	Houghton Mifflin
Roads and Bridges	I	RF	253	Alphakids	Sundance
Roald Dahl's Revolting Rhymes	R	F	250+	Dahl, Roald	Puffin Books
Roanoke: The Lost Colony	T	I	250+	The Library of the Thirteen Colonies and The Lost Colony	Rosen Publishing Group
Roar Like a Tiger	E	RF	148	PM Plus Story Books	Rigby
Roaring Down the Rapids	O	RF	634	Leveled Readers	Houghton Mifflin
Robber Pig and the Ginger Bear	M	F	403	Read Alongs	Rigby
Robber Pig and the Green Eggs	M	F	250+	Read Alongs	Rigby
Robber, The	B	RF	25	Smart Starts	Rigby
Robber, The	M	RF	1255	Sunshine	Wright Group/McGraw Hill
Robbie Hood, Hurricane Hunter	S	B	1150	Independent Readers Science	Houghton Mifflin
Robby in the River	I	RF	250+	Lighthouse	Rigby
Robert and the Rocket	H	F	146	Waldron, Leesa	Scholastic
Robert E. Lee	U	B	250+	Let Freedom Ring	Red Brick Learning
Robert E. Lee	T	B	1940	Leveled Readers Social Studies	Houghton Mifflin

* Collection of short stories

TITLE	LEVEL	GENRE	WORD COUNT	AUTHOR / SERIES	PUBLISHER / DISTRIBUTOR
Robert Frost: New England Poet	R	B	250+	Leveled Readers Language Support	Houghton Mifflin
Robert Frost: The Journey of a Poet	U	B	963	Leveled Readers	Houghton Mifflin
Robert Goddard	K	B	250+	Schaefer, Lola M.	Red Brick Learning
Robert Makes a Graph	H	I	160	Coulton, Mia	Kaeden Books
Robert the Rose Horse	I	F	250+	Heilbroner, Joan	Random House
Roberto Clemente, Baseball Superstar	V	B	1776	Leveled Readers	Houghton Mifflin
Roberto Clemente: Baseball Superstar	N	B	250+	Rookie Biographies	Children's Press
Roberto's Smile	C	RF	43	Story Box	Wright Group/McGraw Hill
Robin Hood and the Silver Trophy	L	TL	250+	PM Tales and Plays-Silver	Rigby
Robin Hood Meets Little John	L	TL	250+	PM Story Books	Rigby
Robinson Crusoe	T	HF	250+	High-Fliers	Pacific Learning
Robinson Crusoe	P	TL	250+	Dolch, E. W.; Marguerite, P.	Scholastic
Robocat	K	F	295	Leveled Readers	Houghton Mifflin
Robocat Stops Crime!	J	F	323	Leveled Readers Language Support	Houghton Mifflin
Robot, The	A	F	18	Smart Starts	Rigby
Robot-a-cise	K	F	250+	Sunshine	Wright Group/McGraw Hill
Robots	S	I	250+	iOpeners	Pearson Learning Group
Rock	M	I	250+	First Facts	Capstone Press
Rock Climbing	Q	I	250+	Lund, Bill	Red Brick Learning
Rock Climbing	O	I	250+	Sunshine	Wright Group/McGraw Hill
Rock Garden, The	H	RF	139	Windmill Books	Rigby
Rock in the Road, The	J	F	457	Pacific Literacy	Pacific Learning
Rock Pools	I	I	250+	Momentum Literacy Program	Troll Associates
Rock Pools, The	B	I	49	PM Starters	Rigby
Rock Records	Y	I	250+	iOpeners	Pearson Learning Group
Rock-a-Bye Moon	H	F	107	Pair-It Books	Steck-Vaughn
Rocket Ship, The	I	RF	250+	PM Plus Story Books	Rigby
Rocket Surpise, A	L	RF	250+	Sunshine	Wright Group/McGraw Hill
Rocket, The	F	RF	41	City Stories	Rigby
Rockets	C	I	49	Little Celebrations	Pearson Learning Group
Rockin' Reptiles	L	F	250+	Calmenson, Stephanie & Cole	Beech Tree Books
Rocking and Rolling Along	I	RF	73	Evangeline Nicholas Collection	Wright Group/McGraw Hill
Rockity Rock	C	RF	36	KinderReaders	Rigby
Rocks	L	I	157	Early Connections	Benchmark Education
Rocks	N	I	250+	Simply Science	Compass Point Books
Rocks	D	I	49	Voyages	SRA/McGraw Hill
Rocks	B	I	33	Leveled Readers Science	Houghton Mifflin
Rocks	F	I	112	Discovery Links	Newbridge
Rocks	E	I	59	Science	Harcourt School Publishers
Rocks & Minerals	R	I	250+	The Wonders of our World	Crabtree
Rocks and Fossils	M	I	250+	Rosen Real Readers	Rosen Publishing Group
Rocks From Space	M	I	250+	Rigby Focus	Rigby
Rocks Rocks Rocks	E	I	76	Independent Readers Science	Houghton Mifflin
Rocks: Hard, Soft, Smooth, and Rough	N	I	250+	Amazing Science	Picture Window Books
Rocky Mountain Fur Trade, The	S	I	250+	The Library of the Westward Expansion	Rosen Publishing Group
Rodeo!	N	I	1186	Leveled Readers Social Studies	Houghton Mifflin
Rodney, the Surfing Duck	N	F	250+	SupaDoopers	Sundance
Rodzina	Y	HF	250+	Cushman, Karen	Clarion
Rogue Robot	P	F	250+	Bookweb	Rigby
Roll of Thunder, Hear My Cry	W	HF	250+	Taylor, Mildred D.	Penguin Group

* Collection of short stories

TITLE	LEVEL	GENRE	WORD COUNT	AUTHOR / SERIES	PUBLISHER / DISTRIBUTOR
Roll On, Columbia	R	I	826	Independent Readers Social Studies	Houghton Mifflin
Roll Out the Red Rug	E	F	68	Ready Readers	Pearson Learning Group
Roll Over	F	F	220	Gerstein, Mordicai	Crown
Roll Over!	C	F	201	Peek, Merle	Clarion
Roller Blades, The	F	RF	137	Foundations	Wright Group/McGraw Hill
Roller Coaster	C	RF	45	Joy Readers	Pearson Learning Group
Roller Coaster Ride	K	RF	484	PM Plus Story Books	Rigby
Roller Coaster Ride, The	G	RF	106	Carousel Readers	Pearson Learning Group
Roller Coaster, The	D	RF	115	Handprints C, Set 1	Educator's Publishing Service
Roller Coaster, The	B	F	34	KinderReaders	Rigby
Roller Coaster, The	I	RF	194	Sunshine	Wright Group/McGraw Hill
Roller Skates!	J	RF	250+	Calmenson, Stephanie	Scholastic
Rollerama	N	RF	250+	SupaDoopers	Sundance
Rollercoaster	K	RF	250+	Rigby Literacy	Rigby
Rollercoaster Science	N	I	250+	Rigby Literacy	Rigby
Rolling	C	I	46	Sun Sprouts	ETA/Cuisenaire
Rollo and Tweedy and the Ghost at Dougal Castle	K	F	250+	Allen, Laura Jean	HarperTrophy
*Roly-Poly	I	F	1227	Story Box	Wright Group/McGraw Hill
Romana Acosta Banuelos	K	B	218	Leveled Readers Social Studies	Houghton Mifflin
Ronald W. Reagan	U	B	250+	Profiles of the Presidents	Compass Point Books
Roof and a Door, A	D	I	93	PM Nonfiction-Red	Rigby
Room for One More	G	RF	132	City Stories	Rigby
Room for Pip	E	F	175	Bookshop	Mondo
Rooster and the Weather Vane, The	H	F	235	First Start	Troll Associates
Rooster's Gift, The	M	F	250+	Conrad, Pam	HarperCollins
Root Cellar, The	V	HF	250+	Lunn, Janet	Penguin Group
Rope Swing, The	E	RF	77	Oxford Reading Tree	Oxford University Press
Rosa and Fredo	M	F	250+	SupaDoopers	Sundance
Rosa at the Zoo	H	RF	135	Pacific Literacy	Pacific Learning
Rosa Parks	Q	B	250+	Photo-Illustrated Biographies	Red Brick Learning
Rosa Parks	M	B	250+	First Biographies	Red Brick Learning
Rosa Parks	P	B	250+	Greenfield, Eloise	HarperTrophy
Rosa Parks: My Story	U	B	250+	Parks, Rosa	Scholastic
Rosalyn Yalow	W	B	2138	Leveled Readers Science	Houghton Mifflin
Rosa's Tonsils	K	RF	337	Foundations	Wright Group/McGraw Hill
Rose	F	F	82	Wheeler, Cindy	Alfred A. Knopf
Rose Rest Home, The	K	RF	304	Sunshine	Wright Group/McGraw Hill
Roses for Anna	K	RF	250+	Rigby Literacy	Rigby
Roses for Renee	J	RF	395	Evangeline Nicholas Collection	Wright Group/McGraw Hill
Rosie at the Zoo	H	RF	135	Pacific Literacy	Pacific Learning
Rosie the Riveter	Z	I	250+	Colman, Penny	Crown
Rosie, the Nosy Goat	D	RF	56	Sunshine	Wright Group/McGraw Hill
Rosie: A Visiting Dog's Story	N	I	250+	Soar To Success	Houghton Mifflin
Rosie's Big City Ballet	N	RF	250+	Giff, Patricia Reilly	Penguin Group
Rosie's Button Box	G	RF	233	Stepping Stones	Nelson/Michaels Assoc.
Rosie's House	K	RF	250+	Literacy 2000	Rigby
Rosie's Nutcracker Dreams	N	RF	250+	Giff, Patricia Reilly	Penguin Group
Rosie's Party	E	F	111	Little Readers	Houghton Mifflin
Rosie's Pool	G	F	130	Little Readers	Houghton Mifflin
Rosie's Story	L	RF	250+	Bookshop	Mondo
Rosie's Walk	F	F	32	Hutchins, Pat	Macmillan

* Collection of short stories

TITLE	LEVEL	GENRE	WORD COUNT	AUTHOR / SERIES	PUBLISHER / DISTRIBUTOR
*Rotating Rollerblades and Other Cases, The	O	RF	250+	Simon, Seymour	Avon
Rotten Reggie	G	RF	232	TOTTS	Tott Publications
Rough Riders, The	W	B	250+	Cornerstones of Freedom	Children's Press
Rough-Face Girl, The	S	TL	250+	Martin, Rafe; Shannon, David	Scholastic
Round	C	I	40	Windmill Books	Rigby
Round and Round	C	RF	38	Story Box	Wright Group/McGraw Hill
Round and Round the Seasons Go	E	I	43	Learn to Read	Creative Teaching Press
Round and Round: The Story of Wheels	N	I	250+	Home Connection Collection	Rigby
Row Your Boat	C	F	18	Literacy 2000	Rigby
Row Your Boat	C	F	18	Literacy Tree	Rigby
Row, Row, Row Your Boat	J	RF	250+	Bank Street	Bantam
Roxy	WB	F	N/A	Ready to Read	Pacific Learning
Roy and the Parakeet	E	F	74	Oxford Reading Tree	Oxford University Press
Roy at the Fun Park	G	RF	111	Oxford Reading Tree	Oxford University Press
Roy G. Biv	D	F	68	Story Box	Wright Group/McGraw Hill
Royal Baby-Sitters, The	J	RF	435	Sunshine	Wright Group/McGraw Hill
Royal Dinner, The	H	F	250+	Literacy Tree	Rigby
Royal Drum, The	L	TL	250+	Bookshop	Mondo
Royal Family, The	LB	F	17	Stewart, Josie; Salem, Lynn	Continental Press
Royal Goose, The	H	F	198	Ready Readers	Pearson Learning Group
Royal Zookeeper, The	K	F	431	Early Connections	Benchmark Education
Rubber	M	I	250+	First Facts	Capstone Press
Rubber Duck	I	F	170	Early Readers	Compass Point Books
Rubber Inventor: The Story of Charles Goodyear	S	B	912	Independent Readers Science	Houghton Mifflin
Rubbery Arms and Baggy Bodies	O	I	250+	Sails	Rigby
Rube Goldberg's Silly Machines	R	B	438	Independent Readers Science	Houghton Mifflin
Ruby and the Smoke, The	Y	F	250+	Pullman, Phillip	Laurel-Leaf Books
Ruby Holler	V	RF	250+	Creech, Sharon	HarperCollins
Ruby the Copycat	K	RF	250+	Rathman, Peggy	Scholastic
Ruff and Me	C	RF	30	First Stories	Pacific Learning
Rug Weavers	J	RF	182	Leveled Readers Language Support	Houghton Mifflin
Rules	J	I	265	Early Connections	Benchmark Education
Rules for Pets	C	F	54	Joy Readers	Pearson Learning Group
Rules Help	C	I	69	Windows on Literacy	National Geographic
Rules of the Ride	P	RF	1023	Leveled Readers	Houghton Mifflin
Rumble, Rumble, Boom!	D	I	26	Pacific Literacy	Pacific Learning
Rummage Sale, The	E	RF	81	Oxford Reading Tree	Oxford University Press
Rumpelstiltskin	J	TL	940	Traditional Tales	Pearson Learning Group
Rumpelstiltskin	K	TL	250+	PM Tales and Plays-Gold	Rigby
Rumpelstiltskin	M	TL	250+	Once Upon a Time	Wright Group/McGraw Hill
Rumpelstiltskin	J	TL	250+	Jumbled Tumbled Tales & Rhymes	Rigby
Rumpelstiltskin	J	TL	250+	Bookshop	Mondo
Rumpelstiltskin	N	TL	250+	Zelinsky, Paul O.	Scholastic
Rum-Tum-Tum	E	F	62	Story Box	Wright Group/McGraw Hill
Run For It!	D	F	64	Rigby Literacy	Rigby
Run!	B	F	28	Sunshine	Wright Group/McGraw Hill
Run! Run!	C	F	64	Bookshop	Mondo
Run, Rabbit, Run!	D	RF	96	PM Plus Story Books	Rigby
Run, Run, Run	B	RF	19	Joy Readers	Pearson Learning Group
Runaround Rowdy	L	RF	250+	PM Story Books	Rigby
Runaway Ball, The	K	RF	250+	Rigby Literacy	Rigby
Runaway Hank	J	RF	250+	The Wright Skills	Wright Group/McGraw Hill
Runaway Monkey	B	F	39	Stewart, Josie; Salem, Lynn	Continental Press

* Collection of short stories

TITLE	LEVEL	GENRE	WORD COUNT	AUTHOR / SERIES	PUBLISHER / DISTRIBUTOR
Runaway Ralph	O	F	250+	Cleary, Beverly	Hearst
Runaway Sandy	E	RF	97	Leveled Readers	Houghton Mifflin
Runaway to Freedom: A Story of the Underground Railway	T	I	250+	Smucker, Barbara	HarperTrophy
Runaway Wheels, The	B	F	32	Pair-It Books	Steck-Vaughn
Running	C	RF	39	Foundations	Wright Group/McGraw Hill
Running	A	RF	31	Sun Sprouts	ETA/Cuisenaire
Running	F	RF	185	Visions	Wright Group/McGraw Hill
Running Out of Time	W	SF	250+	Haddix, Margaret Peterson	Simon & Schuster
Running Shoes, The	K	RF	519	PM Plus Story Books	Rigby
Rupert and the Griffin	Q	F	250+	Literacy 2000	Rigby
Rush, Rush, Rush	E	RF	52	Ready Readers	Pearson Learning Group
*Russell and Elisa	M	RF	250+	Hurwitz, Johanna	Penguin Group
*Russell Rides Again	M	RF	250+	Hurwitz, Johanna	Penguin Group
*Russell Sprouts	M	RF	250+	Hurwitz, Johanna	Penguin Group
Russia	Q	I	250+	First Reports	Compass Point Books
Russia	P	I	250+	Fact Finders	Capstone Press
Russia	O	I	250+	Thoennes, Kristin	Red Brick Learning
Rutherford B. Hayes	U	B	250+	Profiles of the Presidents	Compass Point Books
Ruthie's Perfect Poem	N	RF	744	Leveled Readers	Houghton Mifflin
Ryan's Dog Ringo	P	RF	250+	Literacy 2000	Rigby
Sable	O	RF	250+	Hesse, Karen	Henry Holt & Co.
Sacagawea	N	I	242	Leveled Readers	Houghton Mifflin
Sacagawea	P	B	250+	Photo-Illustrated Biographies	Red Brick Learning
Sacagawea's Journey	M	B	250+	Leveled Readers Language Support	Houghton Mifflin
Sacajawea	N	B	250+	Biography	Benchmark Education
Sacajawea	Y	B	250+	Bruchac, Joseph	Harcourt Trade
Sack Race, A	E	RF	106	New Way Blue	Steck-Vaughn
Sacks of Gold	I	F	263	Sunshine	Wright Group/McGraw Hill
Sad Monster	E	F	160	Handprints D, Set 1	Educator's Publishing Service
Sadako and the Thousand Paper Cranes	R	HF	250+	Coerr, Eleanor	Bantam
Sadie and the Snowman	L	RF	250+	Morgan, Allen	Scholastic
Sadie, Remember	L	HF	250+	Kline, Carol	Sundance
Safe at Work	D	I	99	Early Connections	Benchmark Education
Safe Harbor, A	K	I	167	Windows on Literacy	National Geographic
Safe Place, The	H	TL	147	Pacific Literacy	Pacific Learning
Safe Return	Q	RF	250+	Dexter, Catherine	Candlewick Press
Safety	C	I	35	Interaction	Rigby
Safety at the Playground	E	I	42	Rosen Real Readers	Rosen Publishing Group
Safety Counts	C	F	52	Learn to Read	Creative Teaching Press
Safety First	C	I	131	Twig	Wright Group/McGraw Hill
Safety on the School Bus	E	I	38	Rosen Real Readers	Rosen Publishing Group
Safety Signs	G	I	112	Early Connections	Benchmark Education
Saguaro	E	I	44	Books for Young Learners	Richard C. Owen
Sahara Special	S	RF	250+	Codell, Esme Raji	Hyperion
Sailing to a New Land	K	HF	250+	PM Plus Story Books	Rigby
Salad	A	F	36	Carousel Earlybirds	Pearson Learning Group
Salad Feast, A	D	RF	57	Little Readers	Houghton Mifflin
Salad Vegetables	A	I	27	Story Box	Wright Group/McGraw Hill
Salad Vegetables	LB	I	15	Foundations	Wright Group/McGraw Hill
Salamandastron	Z	F	250+	Jacques, Brian	Ace Books
Salamanders and Alligators	M	I	710	Leveled Readers Science	Houghton Mifflin

* Collection of short stories

TITLE	LEVEL	GENRE	WORD COUNT	AUTHOR / SERIES	PUBLISHER / DISTRIBUTOR
Salem Days: Life in a Colonial Seaport	T	I	250+	Adventures in Colonial America	Troll Associates
Salem Witch Trials, The	U	I	1093	Leveled Readers Social Studies	Houghton Mifflin
Sally and the Daisy	C	RF	60	PM Story Books	Rigby
Sally and the Elephant	C	I	45	Wonder World	Wright Group/McGraw Hill
Sally and the Sparrows	E	RF	151	PM Extensions-Yellow	Rigby
Sally Ride	H	B	77	Leveled Readers Social Studies	Houghton Mifflin
Sally Ride in Space	L	B	235	Vocabulary Readers	Houghton Mifflin
Sally Ride: Astronaut, Scientist, Teacher	M	B	250+	Biographies	Picture Window Books
Sally the Great	H	RF	250+	Home Connection Collection	Rigby
Sally's Beans	D	RF	123	PM Story Books	Rigby
Sally's Friends	F	RF	128	PM Story Books	Rigby
Sally's New Shoes	B	RF	58	PM Starters	Rigby
Sally's Picture	G	RF	125	Literacy 2000	Rigby
Sally's Red Bucket	E	RF	127	PM Story Books	Rigby
Sally's Spaceship	E	RF	86	Ready Readers	Pearson Learning Group
Sally's Surprise Garden	H	RF	148	Literacy Tree	Rigby
Salmon	N	I	250+	Bookshop	Mondo
Salmon Story, A	G	I	132	Twig	Wright Group/McGraw Hill
*Salmon's Journey and More Northwest Coast Stories	P	TL	250+	Challenger, James Robert	Heritage House
Salt	J	I	247	Rigby Focus	Rigby
Salty Dog	L	RF	250+	Rand, Gloria	Henry Holt & Co.
Sam	D	RF	87	Early Connections	Benchmark Education
Sam	C	RF	17	KinderReaders	Rigby
Sam and Bingo	C	RF	53	PM Plus Story Books	Rigby
Sam and Dasher	G	RF	53	Rookie Readers	Children's Press
Sam and Kim	O	I	250+	Pacific Literacy	Pacific Learning
Sam and the Firefly	J	F	250+	Eastman, Philip D.	Random House
Sam and the Lucky Money	N	RF	250+	Soar To Success	Houghton Mifflin
Sam and the Waves	D	RF	122	PM Plus Story Books	Rigby
Sam Goes to School	E	RF	131	PM Plus Story Books	Rigby
Sam Houston	N	B	248	Pebble Books	Capstone Press
Sam King and Little Bull	L	RF	250+	Wilson, Trevor	Pearson Learning Group
Sam Plays Paddle Ball	F	F	161	PM Plus Story Books	Rigby
Sam the Garbage Hound	G	F	53	Rookie Readers	Children's Press
Sam the Minuteman	J	HF	250+	Benchley, Nathaniel	HarperTrophy
Sam the Scarecrow	F	F	143	First Start	Troll Associates
Sam Who Never Forgets	K	F	281	Rice, Eve	Morrow
Sam Writes	D	RF	62	Book Bank	Wright Group/McGraw Hill
*Sam, Sam, and Other Stories	F	F	250+	Story Steps	Rigby
Samantha Saves the Day	Q	RF	250+	The American Girls Collection	Pleasant Company
Samantha's Surprise	Q	RF	250+	The American Girls Collection	Pleasant Company
Same But Different	I	RF	184	Sunshine	Wright Group/McGraw Hill
Same Stuff as Stars, The	V	RF	250+	Paterson, Katherine	Clarion
Same Team	C	I	44	The Candid Collection	Pearson Learning Group
Same, But Different, The	Q	RF	1205	Leveled Readers	Houghton Mifflin
Samir and Yonatan	Z	RF	250+	Carmi, Daniella	Scholastic
Sammy at the Farm	C	RF	83	Urmston, Kathleen; Evans, Karen	Kaeden Books
Sammy Gets a Ride	F	F	91	Evans, Karen; Urmston, Kathleen	Kaeden Books
Sammy Keyes and the Art of Deception	T	RF	250+	Van Draanen, Wendelin	Random House
Sammy Keyes and the Curse of Moustache Mary	T	RF	250+	Van Draanen, Wendelin	Random House
Sammy Keyes and the Hotel Thief	T	RF	250+	Van Draanen, Wendelin	Random House
Sammy Keyes and the Runaway Elf	T	RF	250+	Van Draanen, Wendelin	Random House

* Collection of short stories

TITLE	LEVEL	GENRE	WORD COUNT	AUTHOR / SERIES	PUBLISHER / DISTRIBUTOR
Sammy Keyes and the Sisters of Mercy	T	RF	250+	Van Draanen, Wendelin	Random House
Sammy Keyes and the Skeleton Man	T	RF	250+	Van Draanen, Wendelin	Random House
Sammy the Seal	H	F	250+	Hoff, Syd	HarperTrophy
Sammy's Hamburger Caper	I	F	250	Urmston, Kathleen	Kaeden Books
Sammy's Moving	F	F	166	Evans, Karen; Urmston, Kathleen	Kaeden Books
Sammy's Sneeze	D	RF	69	Home Connection Collection	Rigby
Sammy's Supper	I	RF	293	Reading Unlimited	Pearson Learning Group
Sam's Ball	D	RF	64	Lindgren, Barbro	Morrow
Sam's Balloon	C	RF	54	PM Plus Story Books	Rigby
Sam's Big Clean-up	K	RF	287	Windmill Books	Rigby
Sam's Big Day	H	RF	74	Cat on the Mat	Oxford University Press
Sam's Cap	E	RF	78	Dominie Phonics Reader	Pearson Learning Group
Sam's Cookie	D	RF	52	Lindgren, Barbro	Morrow
Sam's Dog	D	RF	52	Sun Sprouts	ETA/Cuisenaire
Sam's Glasses	M	RF	250+	Literacy 2000	Rigby
Sam's Haircut	H	RF	226	PM Plus Story Books	Rigby
Sam's Mask	E	RF	36	Pacific Literacy	Pacific Learning
Sam's Painting	F	RF	181	PM Plus Story Books	Rigby
Sam's Picnic	D	RF	104	PM Plus Story Books	Rigby
Sam's Race	C	RF	64	PM Plus Story Books	Rigby
Sam's Seasons	E	RF	143	Pair-It Books	Steck-Vaughn
Sam's Snacks	I	F	250+	Cambridge Reading	Pearson Learning Group
Sam's Solution	K	RF	250+	Literacy 2000	Rigby
Sam's Teddy Bear	D	RF	60	Lindgren, Barbro	Morrow
Sam's Wagon	D	RF	83	Lindgren, Barbro	Morrow
Samuel de Champlain in Canada	V	B	3002	Leveled Readers	Houghton Mifflin
Samuel de Champlain: Commander of New France	U	B	1694	Leveled Readers Social Studies	Houghton Mifflin
Samuel Eaton's Day: A Day in the Life of a Pilgrim Boy	Q	I	250+	Waters, Kate	Scholastic
Samuel's Choice	S	HF	250+	Berleth, Richard	Scholastic
Samuel's Sprout	F	RF	194	Little Celebrations	Pearson Learning Group
Samurai's Daughter, The	Q	TL	250+	San Souci, Robert D.	Penguin Group
San Domingo	R	I	250+	Henry, Marguerite	Scholastic
San Francisco Earthquake, The	Q	I	618	Vocabulary Readers	Houghton Mifflin
San Francisco Exploratorium, The	O	I	250+	Little Celebrations	Pearson Learning Group
San Francisco Shakes	U	I	2116	Independent Readers Science	Houghton Mifflin
San Francisco: Then and Now	P	I	476	Independent Readers Social Studies	Houghton Mifflin
Sand	M	I	250+	Windows on Literacy	National Geographic
Sand	E	RF	78	Giant Step Readers	Educational Insights
Sand	H	I	49	iOpeners	Pearson Learning Group
Sand	B	I	32	Voyages	SRA/McGraw Hill
Sand Castle Contest, The	E	RF	173	Pair-It Books	Steck-Vaughn
Sand Castles	G	RF	80	Wonder World	Wright Group/McGraw Hill
Sand On The Move: The Story of Dunes	U	I	250+	A First Book	Franklin Watts
Sand Picnic, The	E	RF	123	New Way White	Steck-Vaughn
Sandcastle, The	A	I	32	First Stories	Pacific Learning
Sandcastle, The	C	I	31	Sun Sprouts	ETA/Cuisenaire
Sandcastles	J	I	419	Leveled Readers Science	Houghton Mifflin
Sandman to the Rescue	T	RF	1758	Leveled Readers	Houghton Mifflin
Sandra Day O'Connor	O	I	318	Independent Readers Social Studies	Houghton Mifflin
Sandwich Hero, The	K	RF	250+	Literacy 2000	Rigby

TITLE	LEVEL	GENRE	WORD COUNT	AUTHOR / SERIES	PUBLISHER / DISTRIBUTOR
Sandwich Person, A	G	I	63	Wonder World	Wright Group/McGraw Hill
Sandwich, The	J	RF	250+	Story Box	Wright Group/McGraw Hill
Sandwich, The	C	RF	68	Carousel Earlybirds	Pearson Learning Group
Sandwiches	D	RF	64	New Way	Steck-Vaughn
Sandwiches, Sandwiches	D	RF	54	Pair-It Books	Steck-Vaughn
Sandy	C	F	32	Ready Readers	Pearson Learning Group
Sandy Runs Away	E	RF	102	Leveled Readers Language Support	Houghton Mifflin
Sandy's Suitcase	K	RF	250+	Edwards, Elsy	SRA/McGraw Hill
Santa Claus Doesn't Mop Floors	M	F	250+	Dadey, Debbie; Jones, Marcia Thornton	Scholastic
Santa Fe Trail, The	V	I	250+	Cornerstones of Freedom	Children's Press
Santa Fe Trail, The	T	I	250+	We The People	Compass Point Books
Sara Crewe	O	HF	250+	Burnett, Frances Hodgson	Scholastic
Sarah and the Barking Dog	I	RF	328	PM Story Books-Orange	Rigby
Sarah and Will	H	RF	251	Alphakids	Sundance
Sarah Bishop	X	HF	250+	O'Dell, Scott	Scholastic
Sarah Morton's Day: Day in the Life of a Pilgrim Girl, A	Q	B	250+	Waters, Kate	Scholastic
Sarah Snail	E	RF	55	Voyages	SRA/McGraw Hill
Sarah, Plain and Tall	R	HF	250+	MacLachlan, Patricia	HarperTrophy
Sarah's Seed	E	RF	107	Literacy Tree	Rigby
Sara's Lovely Songs	I	RF	250+	Ready Readers	Pearson Learning Group
Sarny: A Life Remembered	W	HF	250+	Paulsen, Gary	Delacorte
Satellites	O	I	250+	Let's See	Compass Point Books
Saturday Adventure, The	J	RF	250+	Rigby Literacy	Rigby
Saturday Club, The	K	RF	250+	Melton, Holly	Hampton-Brown
Saturday Morning	G	RF	180	Pacific Literacy	Pacific Learning
Saturday Morning Breakfast	E	RF	65	Teacher's Choice Series	Pearson Learning Group
Saturday Mornings	D	RF	63	Bookshop	Mondo
Saturday Sandwiches	I	RF	154	Evangeline Nicholas Collection	Wright Group/McGraw Hill
Saturn	N	I	250+	A First Book	Franklin Watts
Saturn	N	I	250+	A True Book	Children's Press
Saturn	S	I	250+	Our Solar System	Compass Point Books
Saturnalia	W	RF	250+	Fleischman, Paul	HarperCollins
Saul's Special Pet	J	F	250+	Leveled Readers Language Support	Houghton Mifflin
Save Our Earth	S	I	250+	iOpeners	Pearson Learning Group
Save our Tree	D	I	56	Leveled Readers Social Studies	Houghton Mifflin
Save Queen of Sheba	V	HF	250+	Moeri, Louise	Puffin Books
Save That Trash!	G	I	181	Ready Readers	Pearson Learning Group
Save the Everglades	R	I	250+	Stamper, Judith Bauer	Steck-Vaughn
Save the Manatee	N	I	250+	Friesinger, Alison	Random House
Save the Rain Forests	L	I	250+	Read-About Science	Children's Press
Save the Rain Forests	L	I	250+	Fowler, Allan	Scholastic
Save the River!	M	SF	250+	Pair-It Books	Steck-Vaughn
Save the Sea Turtles!	M	I	250+	Leonhardt, Alice	Steck-Vaughn
Saving America's Wild Horses	Q	I	494	Vocabulary Readers	Houghton Mifflin
Saving Hoppo	I	RF	250+	PM Plus Story Books	Rigby
Saving Money	O	I	250+	Let's See	Compass Point Books
Saving Money	M	I	250+	First Facts	Capstone Press
Saving Sea Turtles	S	I	1483	Leveled Readers	Houghton Mifflin
Saving the Park	N	RF	250+	Wilson, Sarah	Pacific Learning
Saving The Yellow Eye	P	I	250+	Darby, John	Pacific Learning

* Collection of short stories

TITLE	LEVEL	GENRE	WORD COUNT	AUTHOR / SERIES	PUBLISHER / DISTRIBUTOR
Saving Wild One	V	RF	2109	Leveled Readers	Houghton Mifflin
Say "Cheese"	L	RF	250+	Giff, Patricia Reilly	Bantam
Say "Hi" Up High	F	F	61	Early Readers	Compass Point Books
Say Cheese	J	I	169	Rigby Focus	Rigby
Say Cheese!	F	RF	128	Storyteller-Moon Rising	Wright Group/McGraw Hill
Say Good Night	G	RF	155	Ziefert, Harriet	Puffin Books
Say Good Night	G	F	59	Start to Read	School Zone
Say Hello!	A	RF	15	Rise & Shine	Hampton-Brown
Say Hola, Sarah	N	RF	250+	Giff, Patricia Reilly	Bantam
Say It, Sign It	G	RF	169	Epstein, Elaine	Scholastic
Say Yes	W	RF	250+	Couloumbis, Audrey	Putnam
Scaly Things	Q	I	250+	Explorers	Wright Group/McGraw Hill
Scare and Dare	H	RF	284	Alphakids	Sundance
Scare for Bear, A	F	F	182	Sun Sprouts	ETA/Cuisenaire
Scare in the City, A	N	RF	250+	Chanek, Sherilin	Hampton-Brown
Scarecrow, The	L	RF	250+	Pacific Literacy	Pacific Learning
Scarecrow, The	D	RF	97	Little Red Readers	Sundance
Scarecrow, The	C	F	31	Literacy 2000	Rigby
Scarecrows	D	I	39	Pebble Books	Capstone Press
Scarecrow's Friends	C	F	56	Start to Read	School Zone
Scared	D	RF	59	Twig	Wright Group/McGraw Hill
Scared at Night	H	RF	250+	Early Transitional, Set 2	Pioneer Valley
Scared Stiff	V	F	250+	Malcolm, Jahnna N.	Scholastic
Scaredy Bears	K	F	250+	Sunshine	Wright Group/McGraw Hill
Scaredy Cat	C	F	85	Learn to Read	Creative Teaching Press
Scaredy Cat	B	RF	29	Rigby Literacy	Rigby
Scaredy Cat Runs Away	D	F	57	Learn to Read	Creative Teaching Press
Scaredy Dog	K	RF	250+	Thomas, Jane Resh	Hyperion
Scare-Kid	K	F	250+	Literacy 2000	Rigby
Scary Day, The	N	RF	250+	Bennett, Jean	Pacific Learning
Scary Larry	G	F	62	Rookie Readers	Children's Press
Scary Monster	C	F	19	Eifrig, Kate	Kaeden Books
Scary Sharks	O	I	250+	Fearsome, Scary, and Creepy Animals	Enslow Publishers, Inc.
Scary Spiders!	J	RF	198	Sunshine	Wright Group/McGraw Hill
Scat! Said the Cat	D	F	33	Sunshine	Wright Group/McGraw Hill
Schernoff Discoveries, The	T	RF	250+	Paulsen, Gary	Dell
School	D	I	50	Berger, Samantha; Chanko, Pamela	Scholastic
School Bus	LB	RF	51	Crews, Donald	Morrow
School Bus Drivers	M	I	250+	Ready, Dee	Red Brick Learning
School Bus Ride, The	G	RF	160	Little Red Readers	Sundance
School Bus, The	E	RF	60	Sunshine	Wright Group/McGraw Hill
School Day!	A	RF	16	Cervantes, Jesus	Scholastic
School Days	U	I	250+	Literacy 2000	Rigby
School Days in 1700	Q	I	975	Independent Readers Social Studies	Houghton Mifflin
School Days Long Ago and Today	A	I	32	Leveled Readers Social Studies	Houghton Mifflin
School Fair, The	J	RF	250+	PM Plus Story Books	Rigby
School in Colonial America	K	I	250+	Welcome Books	Children's Press
School Is Closed	H	F	250+	Phonics Readers Plus	Steck-Vaughn
School Lunch	LB	RF	14	Ready Readers	Pearson Learning Group
School Mouse, The	P	F	250+	King-Smith, Dick	Hyperion
School Mural, The	L	RF	250+	Pair-It Books	Steck-Vaughn

TITLE	LEVEL	GENRE	WORD COUNT	AUTHOR / SERIES	PUBLISHER / DISTRIBUTOR
School Newspaper, The	O	I	250+	Sunshine	Wright Group/McGraw Hill
School Play, The	G	RF	103	City Stories	Rigby
School Principals	M	I	250+	Boraas, Tracey	Red Brick Learning
School Recyclers	L	RF	380	Leveled Readers Science	Houghton Mifflin
School Secretaries	M	I	250+	Community Helpers	Red Brick Learning
School Today and Long Ago	H	I	110	Windows on Literacy	National Geographic
School Vacation	J	RF	113	City Kids	Rigby
School, The	E	RF	27	Burningham, John	Crowell
Schools Around the World	E	I	78	Pair-It Books	Steck-Vaughn
School's Out	N	RF	250+	Hurwitz, Johanna	Scholastic
Schoolyard Mystery, The	L	RF	250+	Levy, Elizabeth	Scholastic
Science - Just Add Salt	L	I	250+	Markle, Sandra	Scholastic
Science Fair Surprise, The	Q	RF	250+	Burke, Melissa Blackwell	Steck-Vaughn
Science Outside	I	I	33	Canizares, Susan; Chessen, Betsey	Scholastic
Science Tools	E	I	52	Canizares, Susan; Chessen, Betsey	Scholastic
Scientist, The	G	I	195	Adventures in Reading	Pearson Learning Group
Scientists	I	I	56	Chanko, Pamela; Berger, Samantha	Scholastic
Scientists in Space	U	I	3502	Leveled Readers Science	Houghton Mifflin
Scissors	D	I	51	Storyteller-Setting Sun	Wright Group/McGraw Hill
Scit, Scat, Scaredy Cat!	F	F	59	Sunshine	Wright Group/McGraw Hill
Score!: You Can Play Soccer	M	I	250+	Game Day	Picture Window Books
Scoring Points	P	RF	250+	Leveled Readers Language Support	Houghton Mifflin
Scorpions	Z	RF	250+	Myers, Walter Dean	HarperTrophy
Scots Pine, The	M	I	250+	Cambridge Reading	Pearson Learning Group
Scrappers No Easy Out	Q	RF	250+	Hughes, Dean	Aladdin
Scrappers No Fear	Q	RF	250+	Hughes, Dean	Aladdin
Scratch My Back	D	F	66	Foundations	Wright Group/McGraw Hill
Screech!	D	RF	43	Literacy 2000	Rigby
Scribe of Ancient China, A	W	HF	2134	Leveled Readers	Houghton Mifflin
Scrubbing Machine, The	F	F	148	Story Box	Wright Group/McGraw Hill
Scruffy	K	RF	250+	Parish, Peggy	HarperTrophy
Scruffy	I	RF	250	Leveled Readers	Houghton Mifflin
Scruffy Messed It Up	G	RF	105	Literacy 2000	Rigby
Scrumptious Sundae	B	RF	18	Literacy 2000	Rigby
Scruncher Goes Wandering	M	RF	250+	Krailing, Tessa	Barron's Educational
Sculpture	L	I	250+	Little Celebrations	Pearson Learning Group
Sea and Land Animals	J	I	250+	Windows on Literacy	National Geographic
Sea Anemones	G	I	58	Pebble Books	Capstone Press
Sea Animals	B	I	46	Vocabulary Readers	Houghton Mifflin
Sea Animals	K	I	250+	Little Red Readers	Sundance
Sea Horses	J	I	90	Under the Sea	Capstone Press
Sea Horses	F	I	67	Pebble Books	Capstone Press
Sea Lights	L	I	128	Books for Young Learners	Richard C. Owen
Sea Monsters Don't Ride Motorcycles	M	RF	250+	Dadey, Debbie; Jones, Marcia Thornton	Scholastic
Sea of Animals, A	K	I	213	Spyglass Books	Compass Point Books
Sea Otter Goes Hunting	J	RF	250+	PM Plus Story Books	Rigby
Sea Otter Inlet	O	I	250+	Godkin, Celia	Fitzhenry & Whiteside
Sea Otter Rescue: The Aftermath of an Oil Spill	W	I	250+	Smith, Roland	Scholastic
Sea Otters	L	I	406	Storyteller Nonfiction	Wright Group/McGraw Hill
Sea Snakes	I	I	66	Pebble Books	Red Brick Learning
Sea Star	R	RF	250+	Henry, Marguerite	Aladdin

* Collection of short stories

TITLE	LEVEL	GENRE	WORD COUNT	AUTHOR / SERIES	PUBLISHER / DISTRIBUTOR
Sea Star, A	E	I	82	Ready Readers	Pearson Learning Group
Sea Stars	E	I	63	Pebble Books	Capstone Press
Sea Turtle Night	I	I	200	Ready Readers	Pearson Learning Group
Sea Turtles	J	I	118	Under the Sea	Capstone Press
Sea Turtles	L	I	553	Leveled Readers	Houghton Mifflin
Sea Turtles	K	I	296	Marine Life For Young Readers	Pearson Learning Group
Sea Turtles	G	I	50	Pebble Books	Red Brick Learning
Sea Turtles	J	I	118	Pebble Plus	Capstone Press
Sea Urchins	G	I	51	Pebble Books	Capstone Press
Sea Wall, The	K	I	251	Foundations	Wright Group/McGraw Hill
Sea Where I Swim, The	F	I	134	Voyages	SRA/McGraw Hill
Seabirds	S	I	250+	A First Book	Franklin Watts
Seagull Is Clever	E	RF	98	PM Story Books	Rigby
Seagull, The	C	F	78	Story Steps	Rigby
Seahorses	M	I	250+	Bookshop	Mondo
Seal	M	I	250+	Cambridge Reading	Pearson Learning Group
Seals	I	I	103	Under the Sea	Red Brick Learning
Seals	G	I	42	Pebble Books	Red Brick Learning
Seals and Sea Lions	N	I	250+	Cole, Sally	Wright Group/McGraw Hill
Seals of the World	J	I	251	Vocabulary Readers	Houghton Mifflin
Search and Discover	O	I	250+	Discovery Links	Newbridge
Search for Delicious, The	U	F	250+	Babbitt, Natalie	Farrar, Straus and Giroux
Search for Oil	V	I	3343	Leveled Readers Science	Houghton Mifflin
Search for the Lost Cave, The	M	F	250+	Schultz, Irene	Wright Group/McGraw Hill
Searching for Sea Lions	P	I	250+	Westerskov, Kim	Pacific Learning
Seashells	L	I	186	Marine Life For Young Readers	Pearson Learning Group
Season to Season	F	I	113	Pair-It Books	Steck-Vaughn
Seasons	A	I	29	Vocabulary Readers	Houghton Mifflin
Seasons	A	I	28	Leveled Readers Science	Houghton Mifflin
Seasons	N	I	250+	Simply Science	Compass Point Books
Seasons	N	I	250+	A True Book	Children's Press
Seasons	C	I	28	Discovery World	Rigby
Seasons	H	I	250+	Yellow Umbrella Books	Red Brick Learning
Seasons	H	I	119	Instant Readers	Harcourt School Publishers
Seasons and Weather	M	I	250+	PM Plus Nonfiction	Rigby
Seasons Project	H	I	218	Sun Sprouts	ETA/Cuisenaire
Seasons, The	D	I	84	Early Connections	Benchmark Education
Seasons, The	J	I	193	Phonics Readers	Compass Point Books
Seasons, The	C	RF	84	Rigby Focus	Rigby
Seat Belt Song, The	K	RF	505	PM Turquoise	Rigby
Seawall	O	RF	250+	PM Ruby	Rigby
Seaward	X	F	250+	Cooper, Susan	Simon & Schuster
Sebastian	G	F	162	Alphakids	Sundance
Second Birthday, A	L	I	250+	Greetings	Rigby
Second Chance	N	RF	250+	Kroll, Stephen	Avon Camelot
Second Grade - Friends Again!	M	RF	250+	Cohen, Miriam	Scholastic
Second Mrs. Giaconda, The	T	HF	250+	Konigsburg, E. L.	Language for Learning Assoc.
Second Story Sally	N	RF	250+	SupaDoopers	Sundance
Second-Grade Friends	M	RF	250+	Cohen, Miriam	Scholastic
Second-Grade Star	N	RF	250+	Alberts, Nancy	Scholastic
Secondhand Star	L	RF	250+	Macdonald, Maryann	Hyperion
Secret	G	RF	114	Instant Readers	Harcourt School Publishers
Secret at the Polk Street School, The	M	RF	250+	Giff, Patricia Reilly	Bantam

TITLE	LEVEL	GENRE	WORD COUNT	AUTHOR / SERIES	PUBLISHER / DISTRIBUTOR
Secret Cave, The	I	RF	250+	PM Plus Story Books	Rigby
Secret Code, The	G	RF	69	Rookie Readers	Children's Press
Secret Friend, The	E	RF	189	Little Readers	Houghton Mifflin
Secret Friend, The	E	RF	196	Little Celebrations	Pearson Learning Group
Secret Garden, The	U	RF	250+	Burnett, Frances H.	Scholastic
Secret Hideaway, The	K	RF	618	PM Gold	Rigby
Secret Land of the Past	N	F	250+	Schlein, Miriam	Scholastic
Secret Lives of Mr. and Mrs. Smith, The	K	F	395	Sunshine	Wright Group/McGraw Hill
Secret Message, The	E	RF	68	Literacy Tree	Rigby
Secret Notes	G	RF	214	Sun Sprouts	ETA/Cuisenaire
Secret of Bunratty Castle, The	Q	F	250+	Action Packs	Rigby
Secret of Foghorn Island, The	L	F	250+	Step into Reading	Random House
Secret of Kiribu Tapu Lagoon, The	S	I	250+	Literacy 2000	Rigby
Secret of NIMH, The	V	F	250+	O'Brien, Robert C.	Scholastic
Secret of Silk, The	K	I	234	Rigby Focus	Rigby
Secret of Spooky House, The	J	F	352	Sunshine	Wright Group/McGraw Hill
Secret of the Monster Book, The	M	F	250+	Schultz, Irene	Wright Group/McGraw Hill
Secret of the Old Oak Trunk, The	M	F	250+	Schultz, Irene	Wright Group/McGraw Hill
Secret of the Seal, The	P	RF	250+	Davis, Deborah	Alfred A. Knopf
Secret of the Silver Shoes, The	Q	F	250+	Massie, Elizabeth	Steck-Vaughn
Secret of the Song, The	M	F	250+	Schultz, Irene	Wright Group/McGraw Hill
Secret Secret Passage, The	P	RF	250+	Parker, A. E.	Scholastic
Secret Silver Lining, A	Q	RF	250+	Ragged Island Mysteries	Wright Group/McGraw Hill
Secret Soldier, The: The Story of Deborah Sampson	O	B	250+	McGovern, Ann	Scholastic
Secret Soup	E	RF	51	Literacy 2000	Rigby
Secret Valentine	G	F	223	First Start	Troll Associates
Secret Valley, The	O	HF	250+	Bulla, Clyde Robert	Scholastic
Secret, The	N	RF	250+	PM Emerald	Rigby
Secret, The: A Traditional Tale From Wales	K	TL	250+	Rigby Literacy	Rigby
Secrets in the Fire	Z	HF	250+	Mankell, Henning	Annick Press
Secrets of Rapa Nui, The	Z	I	2362	Leveled Readers	Houghton Mifflin
Secrets of the Desert	Q	I	250+	Literacy 2000	Rigby
Secrets of the Fun Park	O	I	250+	Home Connection Collection	Rigby
Secrets of the Rain Forest	O	I	250+	Myers, Edward	Pearson Learning Group
Sector 7	WB	F	N/A	Wiesner, David	Clarion
Security Guards	M	I	250+	Community Helpers	Red Brick Learning
See How It Grows	C	I	34	Learn to Read	Creative Teaching Press
See Me	WB	I	N/A	Vocabulary Readers	Houghton Mifflin
See Me Reading	D	RF	35	Ray's Readers	Outside the Box
See Our Show	C	RF	38	Rigby Focus	Rigby
See the Boats Go!	D	RF	42	Windows on Literacy	National Geographic
See the Ocean	B	RF	26	Science	Outside the Box
See the Seasons	B	I	16	Instant Readers	Harcourt School Publishers
See the Shapes	B	I	37	Rigby Focus	Rigby
See You in Second Grade	J	RF	250+	Cohen, Miriam	Bantam
See You Tomorrow, Charles	J	RF	250+	Cohen, Miriam	Bantam
Seed is a Promise, A	O	I	250+	Merrill, Claire	Scholastic
Seed Song, The	E	I	41	Learn to Read	Creative Teaching Press
Seed Surprise	E	RF	67	Seedlings	Continental Press
Seed, The	A	I	14	Wonder World	Wright Group/McGraw Hill
Seed, The	D	I	51	Sunshine	Wright Group/McGraw Hill
*Seedfolks	W	RF	250+	Fleishman, Paul	HarperTrophy
Seeds	B	I	30	Rise & Shine	Hampton-Brown

* Collection of short stories

TITLE	LEVEL	GENRE	WORD COUNT	AUTHOR / SERIES	PUBLISHER / DISTRIBUTOR
Seeds	K	I	250+	Sunshine	Wright Group/McGraw Hill
Seeds	J	I	210	Pebble Books	Capstone Press
Seeds Grow	I	I	90	Sunshine Books	Wright Group/McGraw Hill
Seeds Grow Into Plants	G	I	78	Windows on Literacy	National Geographic
Seeds, Seeds, Seeds	E	I	96	Sunshine	Wright Group/McGraw Hill
Seeing	K	I	149	Pebble Books	Capstone Press
Seeing Earth from Space	Y	I	250+	Lauber, Patricia	Scholastic
Seeing is Not Believing	U	I	250+	iOpeners	Pearson Learning Group
Seeing the Circle	O	B	250+	Bruchac, Joseph	Richard C. Owen
Seeing the School Doctor	K	RF	167	City Kids	Rigby
Seeing Things Up Close	F	I	72	Windows on Literacy	National Geographic
Seeing with Heat	R	I	436	Independent Readers Science	Houghton Mifflin
Seekers of Truth	U	B	250+	Real Lives	Troll Associates
Sees Behind Trees	T	HF	250+	Dorris, Michael	Language for Learning Assoc.
Seesaw, The	C	RF	100	Emergent	Pioneer Valley
Seesaw, The	C	F	46	Voyages	SRA/McGraw Hill
Selchie's Seed, The	W	F	250+	Oppenheim, Shulamith Levey	OSI
Selena Who Speaks in Silence	J	RF	311	Evangeline Nicholas Collection	Wright Group/McGraw Hill
Self-Discipline	N	I	250+	Raatma, Lucia	Red Brick Learning
Selfish Giant, The	L	F	250+	Literacy 2000	Rigby
Self-Respect	M	I	250+	Character Education	Red Brick Learning
Selu and Kana Ti	K	TL	250+	Folk Tales	Mondo
Seminole Indians, The	P	I	250+	Lund, Bill	Red Brick Learning
Seminole, The	R	I	250+	First Reports	Compass Point Books
Seminole, The: Patchworkers of the Everglades	R	I	250+	America's First Peoples	Capstone Press
Sending Messages	B	I	49	Wonder World	Wright Group/McGraw Hill
Sending Signals	H	I	163	Literacy Tree	Rigby
Senses	E	I	66	Voyages	SRA/McGraw Hill
Sequoyah	O	B	865	Leveled Readers Social Studies	Houghton Mifflin
Serena and Venus Williams	T	B	250+	Sports Heroes	Red Brick Learning
Serpent's Children, The	W	HF	250+	Yep, Laurence	HarperTrophy
Sets: Sorting into Groups	L	I	250+	Exploring Math	Capstone Press
Seven	H	RF	131	Early Connections	Benchmark Education
Seven Continents	L	I	202	Windows on Literacy	National Geographic
Seven Cool Cats	F	F	97	Seedlings	Continental Press
Seven Foolish Fishermen	K	TL	250+	PM Tales and Plays-Gold	Rigby
Seven Kisses in a Row	O	RF	250+	MacLachlan, Patricia	HarperCollins
Seven little ducks	F	TL	190	PM Readalongs	Rigby
Seven Little Monsters	H	F	55	Sendak, Maurice	HarperCollins
Seven Natural Wonders, The	Q	I	250+	Navigators Social Studies Series	Benchmark Education
Seven Stones of Sligo	O	TL	250+	PM Ruby	Rigby
*Seven Strange and Ghostly Tales	Y	F	250+	Jacques, Brian	Penguin Group
Seven Treasure Hunts, The	M	RF	250+	Byars, Betsy	HarperTrophy
Seventh Grade Weirdo	S	RF	250+	Wardlaw, Lee	Scholastic
Seventh Tower, The: The Fall	W	F	250+	Nix, Garth	Scholastic
Sewing Machine, The	Q	I	250+	Great Inventions	Capstone Press
Shabanu: Daughter of the Wind	Z	RF	250+	Staples, Suzanne Fisher	Random House
Shades of Gray	W	HF	250+	Reeder, Carolyn	Avon Camelot
Shadow Dance	D	RF	66	Little Celebrations	Pearson Learning Group
Shadow of a Bull	U	RF	250+	Wojciechowska, Maia	Simon & Schuster
Shadow of the Wolf	N	I	250+	Whelan, Gloria	Random House
Shadow Over Second	M	RF	250+	Christopher, Matt	Little, Brown & Co.
Shadow Play	WB	I	N/A	Windows on Literacy	National Geographic

* Collection of short stories

TITLE	LEVEL	GENRE	WORD COUNT	AUTHOR / SERIES	PUBLISHER / DISTRIBUTOR
Shadow Puppets	K	I	236	Rigby Focus	Rigby
Shadow Puppets	H	I	163	Alphakids	Sundance
Shadows	F	I	110	Independent Readers Science	Houghton Mifflin
Shadows	E	RF	190	Visions	Wright Group/McGraw Hill
Shadows	J	I	250+	Otto, Carolyn B.	Scholastic
Shadows	F	I	130	Wonder World	Wright Group/McGraw Hill
Shadows	D	RF	35	Literacy 2000	Rigby
*Shadows & Moonshine	V	TL	250+	Aiken, Joan	David R. Godine
*Shady Deal, The: Tales of Cleverness and Cunning	Q	TL	250+	Literacy 2000	Rigby
Shag Goes Fishing, The	E	RF	51	Ready to Read	Pacific Learning
Shaggy	C	RF	23	Windows on Literacy	National Geographic
Shaggy Sheep, The	J	RF	301	Wonders	Hampton-Brown
Shaji in New York	T	RF	1906	Leveled Readers	Houghton Mifflin
Shane	V	HF	250+	Schaefer, Jack	Random House
Shane and Ned	E	F	52	Windmill Books	Rigby
Shape in the Dark, The: A Story of Hadrian's Wall	Z	HF	2603	Leveled Readers	Houghton Mifflin
Shape Maker, The	A	RF	24	Harry's Math Books	Outside the Box
Shape of Things, The	K	I	124	Spyglass Books	Compass Point Books
Shape Story, A	D	RF	56	Seedlings	Continental Press
Shape Walk	C	RF	25	Little Celebrations	Pearson Learning Group
Shapes	C	I	30	Rise & Shine	Hampton-Brown
Shapes	A	I	24	Urmston, Kathleen; Evans, Karen	Kaeden Books
Shapes	B	I	40	Early Connections	Benchmark Education
Shapes	B	I	19	Discovery World	Rigby
Shapes	D	I	98	Carousel Readers	Pearson Learning Group
Shapes	C	I	31	Visions	Wright Group/McGraw Hill
Shapes at the Beach	D	I	46	Rosen Real Readers	Rosen Publishing Group
Shapes Everywhere	E	I	82	Early Connections	Benchmark Education
Shapes in My World	D	I	47	Visions	Wright Group/McGraw Hill
Shapes in the City	K	I	191	Twig	Wright Group/McGraw Hill
Shapes in the Sky: A Book About Clouds	M	I	250+	Amazing Science	Picture Window Books
Shapes of Water, The: Stories About Patterns and Shapes	N	I	250+	Shannan, Gillian	Pacific Learning
Shapes: Discovering Flats and Solids	L	I	250+	Exploring Math	Capstone Press
Shaping the Earth	L	I	233	Rigby Focus	Rigby
Share Bear	D	F	96	Sun Sprouts	ETA/Cuisenaire
Sharing	C	RF	24	Literacy 2000	Rigby
Sharing	C	RF	33	Harry's Math Books	Outside the Box
Sharing Danny's Dad	G	RF	89	Little Celebrations	Pearson Learning Group
Sharing Time	D	RF	113	Carousel Readers	Pearson Learning Group
Shark in a Sack	C	F	65	Sunshine	Wright Group/McGraw Hill
Shark in School	N	RF	250+	Giff, Patricia Reilly	Bantam
Shark Lady: The Adventures of Eugenie Clark	O	B	250+	McGovern, Ann	Scholastic
Shark!	L	I	479	Leveled Readers Science	Houghton Mifflin
Sharks	O	I	250+	First Reports	Compass Point Books
Sharks	H	I	155	Ready Readers	Pearson Learning Group
Sharks	G	I	42	Pebble Books	Red Brick Learning
Sharks	O	I	250+	Holmes, Kevin J.	Red Brick Learning
Sharks	M	I	250+	Gibbons, Gail	Holiday House
Sharks	L	I	238	Wonder World	Wright Group/McGraw Hill
Sharks	I	I	238	Pebble Plus	Capstone Press
Sharks	N	I	250+	Bookshop	Mondo

* Collection of short stories

TITLE	LEVEL	GENRE	WORD COUNT	AUTHOR / SERIES	PUBLISHER / DISTRIBUTOR
Sharks	T	I	250+	Simon, Seymour	HarperTrophy
Sharks and Rays	L	I	250+	Marine Life For Young Readers	Pearson Learning Group
Sharks and Rays	Q	I	250+	Explorers	Wright Group/McGraw Hill
Sharon the Shark	I	F	266	Supersonics	Rigby
Shawnee, The	R	I	250+	First Reports	Compass Point Books
She Said	C	RF	35	Ready Readers	Pearson Learning Group
Sheeba	L	F	250+	Noonan, Diana	Pearson Learning Group
Sheep	L	I	250+	PM Animal Facts: Purple	Rigby
Sheep Have Lambs	M	I	250+	Animals and Their Young	Compass Point Books
Sheep in a Jeep	G	F	83	Shaw, Nancy	Houghton Mifflin
Sheep on the Farm	G	I	66	Pebble Books	Capstone Press
Sheep Sheep Sheep	J	TL	250+	Redhead, Janet Slater	Steck-Vaughn
Sheepdog in the Snow	Q	RF	250+	Baglio, Ben M.	Scholastic
Sheepdog Max	F	F	171	Sun Sprouts	ETA/Cuisenaire
Sheep's Bell	C	RF	37	Ready Readers	Pearson Learning Group
Sheila Rae, the Brave	K	F	250+	Henkes, Kevin	Scholastic
Shelf Life	Y	RF	250+	Paulsen, Gary	Simon & Schuster
She'll Be Coming Around the Mountain	J	TL	250+	Traditional Songs	Picture Window Books
She'll Be Coming Around the Mountain	E	F	250+	Learn to Read	Creative Teaching Press
She'll Be Coming Around the Mountain	J	RF	250+	Bank Street	Bantam
Shell Shopping	F	RF	145	Ready Readers	Pearson Learning Group
Shell-Flower	S	I	1761	Leveled Readers	Houghton Mifflin
Shell-Flower and the Strangers	R	I	250+	Leveled Readers	Houghton Mifflin
Shells	B	I	39	Seedlings	Continental Press
Shells	A	I	34	Rigby Literacy	Rigby
Shelter	I	I	60	Canizares, Susan; Moreton, Daniel	Scholastic
Sheriffs and Deputy Sheriffs	S	I	250+	Law Enforcement	Capstone Press
Sherman Shoots . . .	B	RF	16	Ray's Readers	Outside the Box
Shh! We're Writing the Constitution	T	I	250+	Fritz, Jean	G.P. Putnam's Sons
SHHH	F	RF	66	Henkes, Kevin	Greenwillow
Shhhh!	G	F	68	Kline, Suzy	Whitman
Shiloh	R	RF	250+	Naylor, Phyllis Reynolds	Bantam
Shine Sun	F	RF	115	Rookie Readers	Children's Press
Shingo's Grandfather	K	RF	370	Sunshine	Wright Group/McGraw Hill
*Shining Blue Planet and Other Cases, The	O	RF	250+	Simon, Seymour	Avon
Shintaro's Umbrellas	I	RF	95	Books for Young Learners	Richard C. Owen
Ship in a Bottle, The	Q	RF	250+	Ragged Island Mysteries	Wright Group/McGraw Hill
Ships	L	I	275	Wonder World	Wright Group/McGraw Hill
Ships at Sea	K	I	250+	PM Plus	Rigby
Shipwreck Saturday	K	RF	250+	Cosby, Bill	Scholastic
Shipwrecked!	Q	F	250+	Bookweb	Rigby
Shoe	K	RF	250+	Rigby Literacy	Rigby
Shoe Grabber, The	I	F	260	Read Alongs	Rigby
Shoebag	P	F	250+	James, Mary	Scholastic
Shoemaker and the Elves, The	J	TL	250+	Sunshine	Wright Group/McGraw Hill
Shoes	B	RF	40	Little Readers	Houghton Mifflin
Shoes	F	I	73	Talk About Books	Pearson Learning Group
Shoes	D	I	150	Winthrop, Elizabeth	HarperTrophy
Shoes	A	RF	16	Little Celebrations	Pearson Learning Group
Shoes	D	F	79	Book Bank	Wright Group/McGraw Hill
Shoes	D	RF	150	Sun Sprouts	ETA/Cuisenaire
Shoes for Everyone: A Story About Jan Matzeliger	R	B	250+	Mitchell, Barbara	Carolrhoda Books
Shoes Through the Ages	Q	I	250+	Brill, Marlene Targ	Steck-Vaughn

TITLE	LEVEL	GENRE	WORD COUNT	AUTHOR / SERIES	PUBLISHER / DISTRIBUTOR
Shoeshine Girl	N	RF	250+	Bulla, Clyde Robert	HarperTrophy
Shonto Begay: His Life and Work	Y	B	2196	Leveled Readers	Houghton Mifflin
Shoo Fly	D	RF	76	Sun Sprouts	ETA/Cuisenaire
Shoo!	C	F	37	Sunshine	Wright Group/McGraw Hill
Shoo, Crow! Shoo!	F	F	41	Early Readers	Compass Point Books
Shoo, Fly	B	F	31	Science	Outside the Box
Shoo, Fly!	B	RF	24	Story Box	Wright Group/McGraw Hill
*Shoo, Shoo, Shoo!	H	F	239	Story Steps	Rigby
Shoot of Corn, A	L	RF	250+	Cambridge Reading	Pearson Learning Group
Shooting Star, The	M	RF	661	PM Gold	Rigby
Shooting Stars	R	RF	250+	Costello, Emily	Dell
Shopping	D	RF	44	Sunshine	Wright Group/McGraw Hill
Shopping	J	RF	250+	Sunshine	Wright Group/McGraw Hill
Shopping	D	RF	26	Literacy 2000	Rigby
Shopping	LB	RF	15	Sunshine	Wright Group/McGraw Hill
Shopping	E	RF	101	Storyteller-Setting Sun	Wright Group/McGraw Hill
Shopping	C	I	78	Little Red Readers	Sundance
Shopping	J	I	254	Leveled Readers	Houghton Mifflin
Shopping	C	I	41	Interaction	Rigby
Shopping	E	RF	170	Handprints C, Set 2	Educator's Publishing Service
Shopping	E	I	45	Read-More-Books	Pearson Learning Group
Shopping at the Mall	G	RF	145	Urmston, Kathleen; Evans, Karen	Kaeden Books
Shopping at the Supermarket	B	I	46	Foundations	Wright Group/McGraw Hill
Shopping Day	D	I	44	Vocabulary Readers	Houghton Mifflin
Shopping for School	C	RF	33	Visions	Wright Group/McGraw Hill
Shopping List, The	G	I	120	Windows on Literacy	National Geographic
Shopping Mall, The	B	I	44	PM Starters	Rigby
Shopping with a Crocodile	L	F	250+	Pacific Literacy	Pacific Learning
Shopping with Dad	C	RF	43	Home Connection Collection	Rigby
Shopping with Dad	C	RF	72	Windows on Literacy	National Geographic
Shortest Kid in the World	K	RF	250+	Bliss, Corinne Demas	Random House
Shortstop from Tokyo	M	RF	250+	Christopher, Matt	Little, Brown & Co.
Shorty	M	RF	250+	Literacy 2000	Rigby
Shots	I	RF	90	City Kids	Rigby
Should There Be Zoos?: A Persuasive Text	S	I	250+	Bookshop	Mondo
Should We Have Pets?: A Persuasive Text	N	I	250+	Bookshop	Mondo
Should You Ever?	I	F	69	Tiger Cub	Peguis
Shoveling Snow	F	RF	109	Cummings, Pat	Scholastic
Show and Tell	E	RF	214	Alphakids	Sundance
Show and Tell	K	RF	201	City Kids	Rigby
Show and Tell	G	RF	190	First Start	Troll Associates
Show and Tell	A	RF	32	Little Books	Sadlier-Oxford
Show and Tell	I	RF	201	Little Celebrations	Pearson Learning Group
Show and Tell	F	RF	111	Little Red Readers	Sundance
Show Me a Snake Hole	L	RF	250+	Frederick, Shirley	Hampton-Brown
Show Must Go On!, The	L	RF	586	Leveled Readers	Houghton Mifflin
Show of Hands, A	L	I	250+	Rigby Literacy	Rigby
Show Time at the Polk Street School	M	RF	250+	Giff, Patricia Reilly	Bantam
Show Us Your Wings	G	I	132	Yellow Umbrella Books	Red Brick Learning
Show-and-Tell	H	RF	205	Cambridge Reading	Pearson Learning Group
Show-and-Tell	J	RF	220	Foundations	Wright Group/McGraw Hill
Show-and-Tell Frog, The	J	F	250+	Oppenheim, Joanna	Bantam
Show-and-Tell War, The	N	RF	250+	Smith, Janice Lee	HarperTrophy

* Collection of short stories

TITLE	LEVEL	GENRE	WORD COUNT	AUTHOR / SERIES	PUBLISHER / DISTRIBUTOR
Shrewbettina Goes to Work	WB	F	N/A	Goodall, John	McElderry
Shush!	D	RF	29	Pacific Literacy	Pacific Learning
Shut the Door	D	RF	46	Visions	Wright Group/McGraw Hill
Shy People's Picnic, The	M	F	250+	Little Celebrations	Pearson Learning Group
Si Won's Victory	M	RF	250+	Little Celebrations	Pearson Learning Group
Sick Bear, The	D	RF	61	Joy Readers	Pearson Learning Group
Sick in Bed	F	RF	109	Little Red Readers	Sundance
Sid and Sam	E	RF	120	Buck, Nola	HarperTrophy
Sidetrack Sam	K	RF	250+	Literacy 2000	Rigby
Sidewalk Story	N	RF	250+	Mathis, Sharon Bell	Penguin Group
*Sideways Arithmetic from Wayside School	S	I	250+	Sachar, Louis	Scholastic
*Sideways Stories from Wayside School	P	F	250+	Sachar, Louis	Hearst
Sierra	Q	I	250+	Siebert, Diane	HarperCollins
Sieur de La Salle	Q	B	250+	Biographies-Great Explorers	Capstone Press
Sight, The	Z	F	250+	Clement-Davies, David	Penguin Group
Sign of the Beaver	T	HF	250+	Speare, Elizabeth George	Bantam
Sign of the Chrysanthemum, The	U	RF	250+	Paterson, Katherine	HarperTrophy
Signs	F	I	40	Canizares, Susan; Chanko, Pamela	Scholastic
Signs	LB	I	21	Yellow Umbrella Books	Red Brick Learning
Signs	C	I	35	Little Celebrations	Pearson Learning Group
Signs	E	I	131	Twig	Wright Group/McGraw Hill
Signs	B	I	24	Literacy 2000	Rigby
Signs	C	I	40	Carousel Earlybirds	Pearson Learning Group
Signs of Spring	H	F	250+	Bookshop	Mondo
Signs on the Way	F	I	106	Windows on Literacy	National Geographic
Silent Boy, The	Y	RF	250+	Lowry, Lois	Houghton Mifflin
Silent Hero, The	O	I	250+	Shea, George	Random House
Silent to the Bone	V	RF	250+	Konigsburg, E. L.	Atheneum
Silent World, A	L	RF	250+	Literacy 2000	Rigby
Silk Route, The	U	HF	250+	Major, John S.	HarperCollins
Silkworms	N	I	250+	Blackburn, Rachel	Wright Group/McGraw Hill
Silly Aunt Tilly	H	F	176	Instant Readers	Harcourt School Publishers
Silly Billys	H	F	250+	Sunshine	Wright Group/McGraw Hill
Silly Cat Tricks	D	F	83	Teacher's Choice Series	Pearson Learning Group
Silly Old Possum	C	RF	41	Story Box	Wright Group/McGraw Hill
Silly Supper, The	J	RF	250+	The Wright Skills	Wright Group/McGraw Hill
Silly Tilly's Valentine	K	F	250+	Hoban, Lillian	HarperTrophy
Silly Times with Two Silly Trolls	I	F	250+	Jewell, Nancy	HarperTrophy
Silly Willy	M	RF	250+	Bookshop	Mondo
Silly Willy and Silly Billy	J	F	221	Foundations	Wright Group/McGraw Hill
Silver	N	RF	250+	Whelan, Gloria	Random House
Silver and Prince	L	RF	250+	PM Story Books-Silver	Rigby
Silver Pony, The	WB	F	N/A	Ward, Lynd	Houghton Mifflin
Silverwing: How One Small Bat Became a Noble Hero	U	F	250+	Oppel, Kenneth	Simon & Schuster
Silvia's Soccer Game	F	RF	138	Ready Readers	Pearson Learning Group
Simon and the Aliens	N	SF	250+	SupaDoopers	Sundance
Simon Bolivar	W	B	1858	Leveled Readers Social Studies	Houghton Mifflin
Simon's Big Challenge	Q	RF	250+	Day, Mark	Steck-Vaughn
Simple Machines	M	I	250+	Rosen Real Readers	Rosen Publishing Group
Simple Machines	O	I	250+	Windows on Literacy	National Geographic
Simple Machines	L	I	250+	Early Connections	Benchmark Education
Simple Solution	I	RF	250+	Literacy Tree	Rigby
Simply Alice	V	RF	250+	Naylor, Phyllis Reynolds	Simon & Schuster

* Collection of short stories

TITLE	LEVEL	GENRE	WORD COUNT	AUTHOR / SERIES	PUBLISHER / DISTRIBUTOR
Simply Sam	E	RF	69	Voyages	SRA/McGraw Hill
Sing a Song	E	F	154	Story Box	Wright Group/McGraw Hill
Sing Down the Moon	T	HF	250+	O'Dell, Scott	Language for Learning Assoc.
Sing for Your Father, Su Phan	W	HF	250+	Pevsner, Stella; Tang, Fay	Bantam
*Sing to the Moon	K	F	2448	Story Box	Wright Group/McGraw Hill
*Singing Drum, The	T	TL	250+	Literacy 2000	Rigby
Singing Giant, The: A Play	H	F	250+	Rigby Literacy	Rigby
Singing Giant, The: A Story	H	F	250+	Rigby Literacy	Rigby
Singing Princess, The	K	F	250+	Rigby Literacy	Rigby
Single Shard, A	U	HF	250+	Park, Linda Sue	Clarion
Sing-Song Tree, The	L	I	250+	Sunshine	Wright Group/McGraw Hill
Sink or Float	F	I	91	Instant Readers	Harcourt School Publishers
Sink or Float?	E	I	112	Learn to Read	Creative Teaching Press
Sink or Float?	C	I	36	Independent Readers Science	Houghton Mifflin
Sione Went Fishing	I	RF	225	Sunshine	Wright Group/McGraw Hill
Sione's Talo	H	TL	164	Nelisi, Lino	Scholastic
Sioux Indians, The	P	I	250+	Lund, Bill	Red Brick Learning
Sioux, The	R	I	250+	First Reports	Compass Point Books
Sioux, The: Nomadic Buffalo Hunters	R	I	250+	America's First Peoples	Capstone Press
Sir Arthur	P	B	250+	Apte, Sunita	Scholastic
Sir Down, Dog	G	RF	192	Sun Sprouts	ETA/Cuisenaire
Sister	W	RF	250+	Greenfield, Eloise	HarperCollins
Sisters	B	I	28	Pebble Books	Capstone Press
Sisters	E	I	77	Talk About Books	Pearson Learning Group
Sit, Ned!	D	RF	67	Leveled Readers	Houghton Mifflin
Sit, Pig!	A	RF	20	Vocabulary Readers	Houghton Mifflin
Sit, Sam	F	RF	165	Early Connections	Benchmark Education
Sitting	E	F	46	Literacy 2000	Rigby
Sitting Bull	N	B	217	Pebble Books	Capstone Press
Six Cats	C	RF	50	Joy Readers	Pearson Learning Group
Six Empty Pockets	F	RF	85	Rookie Readers	Children's Press
Six Fine Fish	F	F	252	Ready Readers	Pearson Learning Group
Six Foolish Fishermen	L	TL	715	Elkin, Benjamin	Children's Press
Six Go By	C	F	24	Ready Readers	Pearson Learning Group
Six Legs	B	I	34	Harry's Math Books	Outside the Box
Six Little Chicks	F	F	227	Sun Sprouts	ETA/Cuisenaire
Six Pieces of Cake	C	RF	40	Harry's Math Books	Outside the Box
Six Things to Make	L	I	250+	Bookshop	Mondo
Six Voyages of Pleasant Fieldmouse, The	R	F	250+	Wahl, Jan	Tom Doherty
Six Wet Pets	B	F	31	Leveled Readers Language Support	Houghton Mifflin
*Sixteen Short Stories by Outstanding Writers	Z	RF	250+	Gallo, Donald R.	Dell
Sixth Grade Can Really Kill You	S	RF	250+	DeClements, Barthe	Scholastic
Sixth Grade Secrets	S	RF	250+	Sachar, Louis	Scholastic
Sixth-Grade Sleepover	R	RF	250+	Bunting, Eve	Scholastic
Size: Many Ways to Measure	L	I	250+	Exploring Math	Capstone Press
Sizes	C	I	32	Discovery World	Rigby
Skate Jam, The	P	RF	250+	Orbit Double Takes	Pacific Learning
Skateboard Bill	J	RF	79	Voyages	SRA/McGraw Hill
Skateboard Tough	M	RF	250+	Christopher, Matt	Little, Brown & Co.
Skateboarding	M	I	250+	Blazers	Capstone Press
Skateboarding	Q	I	250+	X-Sports	Capstone Press
Skateboarding	O	I	250+	PM Nonfiction-Emerald	Rigby

TITLE	LEVEL	GENRE	WORD COUNT	AUTHOR / SERIES	PUBLISHER / DISTRIBUTOR
Skateboarding	F	RF	147	Developing Books, Set 1	Pioneer Valley
Skateboarding Greats: Champs of the Ramps	R	I	250+	Skateboarding	Red Brick Learning
Skateboarding History: From the Backyard to the Big Time	R	I	250+	Skateboarding	Red Brick Learning
Skateboards: Designs and Equipment	R	I	250+	Skateboarding	Red Brick Learning
Skateparks: Grab Your Skateboard	R	I	250+	Skateboarding	Red Brick Learning
Skates for Luke	I	RF	346	PM Story Books-Orange	Rigby
Skates of Uncle Richard, The	P	RF	250+	Fenner, Carol	Random House
Skateway to Freedom	V	HF	250+	Alma, Ann	Orca Book Publishers
Skating	C	F	52	Story Box	Wright Group/McGraw Hill
Skating	B	F	35	Foundations	Wright Group/McGraw Hill
Skating at Rainbow Lake	J	RF	250+	PM Story Books-Silver	Rigby
Skating on Thin Ice	G	RF	130	First Start	Troll Associates
Skating to Fame	Q	I	524	Vocabulary Readers	Houghton Mifflin
Skating Trail, The	I	RF	250+	PM Plus Story Books	Rigby
Skating Whiz	E	RF	40	Visions	Wright Group/McGraw Hill
Skeletal System, The	K	I	166	Human Body Systems	Red Brick Learning
Skeleton On The Bus, The	J	F	250+	Literacy 2000	Rigby
Skeletons Don't Play Tubas	M	F	250+	Dadey, Debbie; Jones, Marcia Thornton	Scholastic
Skeletons Inside and Out	S	I	250+	iOpeners	Pearson Learning Group
Ski Lesson, The	H	I	155	Storyteller-Moon Rising	Wright Group/McGraw Hill
Ski School	LB	RF	34	Little Books for Early Readers	University of Maine
Skier, The	B	RF	48	PM Starters	Rigby
Skimper-Scamper	G	F	208	Instant Readers	Harcourt Trade
Skin	F	I	97	Literacy 2000	Rigby
Skin I'm In, The	W	RF	250+	Flake, Sharon G.	Hyperion
Skin, Skin	E	I	44	Wonder World	Wright Group/McGraw Hill
Skinny-Bones	P	RF	250+	Park, Barbara	Random House
Skip Count Song, The	F	I	84	Learn to Read	Creative Teaching Press
Skipper's Balloon	E	RF	62	Oxford Reading Tree	Oxford University Press
Skipper's Birthday	E	RF	64	Oxford Reading Tree	Oxford University Press
Skipper's Idea	E	RF	81	Oxford Reading Tree	Oxford University Press
Skipper's Laces	E	RF	66	Oxford Reading Tree	Oxford University Press
Skirt, The	N	RF	250+	Soto, Gary	Bantam
Skittles and Skullbones	J	F	250+	Supersonics	Rigby
Skunks	H	I	111	Seedlings	Continental Press
Skunks	M	I	250+	PM Animal Facts: Gold	Rigby
Sky	N	RF	506	Leveled Readers	Houghton Mifflin
Sky Changes	M	I	250+	PM Plus Nonfiction	Rigby
Sky Dogs	U	RF	250+	Yolen, Jane	OSI
Sky High	L	F	619	Pair-It Books	Steck-Vaughn
Sky Is Falling Down, The	D	TL	101	Joy Readers	Pearson Learning Group
Sky Is Falling, The	F	TL	186	Folk Tales	Pioneer Valley
Sky Is Falling, The	I	F	181	Storyteller-Setting Sun	Wright Group/McGraw Hill
Sky Rider	O	RF	250+	Belcher, Angie	Pacific Learning
Sky Time	F	F	366	Phonics and Friends	Hampton-Brown
Sky Watch	Q	I	250+	Explorers	Wright Group/McGraw Hill
SkyFire	J	F	250+	Asch, Frank	Scholastic
Skylark	R	HF	250+	MacLachlan, Patricia	HarperTrophy
Sky's the Limit, The	Q	RF	250+	Wildcats	Wright Group/McGraw Hill
Sky's the Limit, The	P	I	250+	Christiansen, Tony	Pacific Learning
SkyScraper, The	K	I	252	Little Red Readers	Sundance
Slake's Limbo	Y	RF	250+	Holman, Felice	Aladdin

TITLE	LEVEL	GENRE	WORD COUNT	AUTHOR / SERIES	PUBLISHER / DISTRIBUTOR
"Slam Dunk" Sanchez	G	RF	238	Sunshine	Wright Group/McGraw Hill
Slam Dunk Saturday	M	RF	250+	Marzollo, Jean	Random House
Slam!	W	RF	250+	Myers, Walter Dean	Scholastic
Slave Dancer, The	Y	HF	250+	Fox, Paula	Random House
Sled, The	D	RF	84	Leveled Readers Language Support	Houghton Mifflin
Sleep Tight	H	RF	163	Cambridge Reading	Pearson Learning Group
Sleepers, Wake	T	SF	250+	Jacobs, Paul Samuel	Language for Learning Assoc.
Sleeping	I	RF	114	Book Bank	Wright Group/McGraw Hill
Sleeping	E	I	43	Literacy 2000	Rigby
Sleeping Animals	H	I	194	Alphakids	Sundance
Sleeping Beauty	K	TL	250+	Enrichment	Wright Group/McGraw Hill
Sleeping Beauty, The	L	TL	250+	PM Tales and Plays-Silver	Rigby
Sleeping Out	D	RF	49	Story Box	Wright Group/McGraw Hill
Sleep-Over Mouse	D	F	63	My First Reader	Grolier Press
Sleepover, The	H	RF	297	Leveled Readers	Houghton Mifflin
Sleepy Bear	F	I	80	Literacy 2000	Rigby
Sleepy Bear	E	I	153	Foundations	Wright Group/McGraw Hill
Sleepy Dog	D	F	118	Ziefert, Harriet	Random House
Sleepy Polar Bear	H	F	97	Hiris, Monica	Kaeden Books
Sleepy Zoo	B	F	58	Sun Sprouts	ETA/Cuisenaire
Slice of Pizza, A	I	RF	175	Twig	Wright Group/McGraw Hill
Slides	D	I	58	Pacific Literacy	Pacific Learning
Slim Shorty and the Mules	L	RF	411	Reading Unlimited	Pearson Learning Group
Slip and Slide	K	I	215	Spyglass Books	Compass Point Books
Slippery Planet, The	L	F	250+	Cambridge Reading	Pearson Learning Group
Slippery Slope, The	V	F	250+	Snicket, Lemony	Scholastic
Slippery, Sloppery Spaghetti	H	RF	250+	Home Connection Collection	Rigby
Slither McCreep and His Brother, Joe	K	RF	250+	Johnston, Tony	OSI
Slithery Snakes and Unicorns	I	F	289	Sunshine	Wright Group/McGraw Hill
Sloppy Tiger and the Party	I	F	293	Sunshine	Wright Group/McGraw Hill
Sloppy Tiger Bedtime	I	F	320	Sunshine	Wright Group/McGraw Hill
Slow Poke Snail	G	RF	117	Instant Readers	Harcourt School Publishers
Sluefoot Sue's Wild Ride	T	F	1831	Leveled Readers	Houghton Mifflin
Slug and Bug	B	F	42	Leveled Readers Language Support	Houghton Mifflin
Slugs and Snails	P	I	250+	Mini Pets	Steck-Vaughn
Slugs and Snails	N	I	250+	Bookshop	Mondo
Slugs and Snails	H	I	132	Wonder World	Wright Group/McGraw Hill
Slumber Party Organizer, The	P	I	250+	Sunshine	Wright Group/McGraw Hill
Slump, The	N	RF	250+	Kroll, Stephen	Avon Camelot
Sly Fox and Little Red Hen	K	TL	250+	PM Tales and Plays-Purple	Rigby
Sly Fox and Red Hen	F	TL	314	Hunia, Fran	Ladybird Books
Small and Large	E	I	89	iOpeners	Pearson Learning Group
Small Baby Raccoon, A	G	RF	104	Ready Readers	Pearson Learning Group
Small Pig	I	F	250+	Lobel, Arnold	HarperTrophy
Small Rabbit Goes Visiting	H	F	445	Book Bank	Wright Group/McGraw Hill
Small Sailboat, A	I	RF	135	Books for Young Learners	Richard C. Owen
Small Treasures	F	RF	52	Gibson, Akimi	Scholastic
Small Wolf	J	HF	250+	Benchley, Nathaniel	HarperTrophy
Small World, A	H	RF	146	Sunshine	Wright Group/McGraw Hill
Smallest Cow in the World, The	K	RF	250+	Paterson, Katherine	HarperTrophy
Smallest Horses, The	J	RF	250+	PM Plus Story Books	Rigby

* Collection of short stories

TITLE	LEVEL	GENRE	WORD COUNT	AUTHOR / SERIES	PUBLISHER / DISTRIBUTOR
Smallest Tree, The	K	F	250+	Literacy 2000	Rigby
Smart Pigs	H	RF	102	Stewart, Josie	Continental Press
Smartest Bear and His Brother Oliver, The	N	F	250+	Bach, Alice	Bantam
Smartest Man in Ireland, The	S	F	250+	Hunter, Mollie	OSI
Smartest One in Class, The	H	RF	68	City Stories	Rigby
Smarty Pants	E	F	116	Story Box	Wright Group/McGraw Hill
Smasher	O	RF	250+	King-Smith, Dick	Random House
Smelling	I	I	111	Pebble Books	Red Brick Learning
Smelly Armor	J	F	282	Story Box	Wright Group/McGraw Hill
Smile	D	F	38	Read-Alongs	Rigby
Smile and Say "Cheetah"	I	RF	200	World Quest Adventures	World Quest Learning
Smile if You Like Circles	J	I	250+	Phonics Readers Plus	Steck-Vaughn
Smile! Said Dad	D	RF	66	Pacific Literacy	Pacific Learning
Smile, Baby!	F	RF	165	Little Readers	Houghton Mifflin
Smile, The	K	RF	253	Read Alongs	Rigby
Smile, The	D	RF	53	Pacific Literacy	Pacific Learning
Smiles	F	RF	366	Visions	Wright Group/McGraw Hill
Smiling Salad, A	C	RF	32	Pair-It Books	Steck-Vaughn
Smiling Stan, the Pedicab Man	E	RF	121	Joy Readers	Pearson Learning Group
Smith: John Smith and the Settlement of Jamestown	U	B	250+	Exploring the World	Compass Point Books
Smokey the Dragon	M	F	250+	Bennett, Jean	Pearson Learning Group
Smokie	E	RF	47	Carousel Readers	Pearson Learning Group
Smoky the Cow Horse	S	RF	250+	James, Will	Scholastic
Smooth or Rough?	D	I	49	Rigby Focus	Rigby
Smudge-Face: A Native American Cinderella Tale	M	TL	580	Leveled Readers	Houghton Mifflin
Snack for Roberto, A	D	RF	82	Early Emergent, Set 2	Pioneer Valley
Snack Time	G	RF	59	City Kids	Rigby
Snacks	D	RF	19	Joy Readers	Pearson Learning Group
Snaggle Doodles	M	RF	250+	Giff, Patricia Reilly	Bantam
Snail Girl	H	RF	250+	Momentum Literacy Program	Troll Associates
Snail Saves the Day	G	F	76	Stadler, John	HarperCollins
Snail That Snored, The	I	F	250+	Phonics Readers Plus	Steck-Vaughn
Snail Trail, The	I	F	243	Sunshine	Wright Group/McGraw Hill
Snails	O	I	67	Holmes, Kevin J.	Red Brick Learning
Snails	E	I	67	Foundations	Wright Group/McGraw Hill
Snails	A	I	40	First Stories	Pacific Learning
Snails and Slugs	E	I	54	Sun Sprouts	ETA/Cuisenaire
Snails in School	H	I	181	Discovery Links	Newbridge
Snake Alarm	M	RF	250+	Krailing, Tessa	Barron's Educational
Snake at the Lake	J	F	250+	The Wright Skills	Wright Group/McGraw Hill
Snake Goes Away	C	F	55	Rigby Literacy	Rigby
Snake Hunts for Lunch	E	RF	115	Hoenecke, Karen	Kaeden Books
Snake Slithers, A	H	I	82	Reading Unlimited	Pearson Learning Group
Snake!	M	RF	641	Sunshine	Wright Group/McGraw Hill
Snake, The	O	I	250+	Crewe, Sabrina	Steck-Vaughn
Snakebite	J	RF	271	Story Box	Wright Group/McGraw Hill
Snakes	O	I	250+	First Reports	Compass Point Books
Snakes	E	I	250+	Pebble Books	Capstone Press
Snakes	J	I	448	Sunshine	Wright Group/McGraw Hill
Snakes	LB	I	25	Twig	Wright Group/McGraw Hill
Snakes	E	I	37	Visions	Wright Group/McGraw Hill
Snakes	Q	I	250+	Explorers	Wright Group/McGraw Hill

* Collection of short stories

TITLE	LEVEL	GENRE	WORD COUNT	AUTHOR / SERIES	PUBLISHER / DISTRIBUTOR
Snakes	L	I	252	Wonder World	Wright Group/McGraw Hill
Snakes	I	I	208	Momentum Literacy Program	Troll Associates
Snakes	K	I	259	Foundations	Wright Group/McGraw Hill
Snakes and Lizards	I	I	205	Yellow Umbrella Books	Red Brick Learning
Snake's Dinner	E	F	156	Alphakids	Sundance
Snake's Sore Head	F	F	139	Storyteller-Moon Rising	Wright Group/McGraw Hill
Snakes!	L	I	250+	Recht Penner, Lucille	Random House
Snakes!: Deadly Predators or Harmless Pets?	S	I	250+	High Five Reading	Red Brick Learning
Snakes: Cold-Blooded Crawlers	M	I	250+	The Wild World of Animals	Red Brick Learning
Snap Likes Ginger Cookies	E	F	63	Gosset, Rachel	Scholastic
Snap!	B	F	31	Sunshine	Wright Group/McGraw Hill
Snap! Splash!	G	I	48	Pacific Literacy	Pacific Learning
Snap! Splat!	C	F	25	Sunshine	Wright Group/McGraw Hill
Snapshots	D	RF	20	Bebop Books	Lee & Low Books Inc.
Sneakers	K	I	388	Sunshine	Wright Group/McGraw Hill
Sneakers! Sneakers!	F	F	49	Little Celebrations	Pearson Learning Group
Sneezes	F	RF	36	Literacy 2000	Rigby
Snickers	I	RF	250+	Momentum Literacy Program	Troll Associates
Snick-Snack Sniffle-Nose	H	F	187	Supersonics	Rigby
Snip, Snap	I	F	250+	Sunshine	Wright Group/McGraw Hill
Snip-Snap, Clickety-Click	C	F	54	Little Celebrations	Pearson Learning Group
Snorkeling	I	RF	233	Leveled Readers Language Support	Houghton Mifflin
Snot Stew	P	F	250+	Wallace, Bill	Pocket Books
Snow	C	RF	47	Science	Outside the Box
Snow	E	I	28	Book Bank	Wright Group/McGraw Hill
Snow	A	I	11	Vocabulary Readers	Houghton Mifflin
Snow	D	I	21	Sunshine	Wright Group/McGraw Hill
Snow	B	I	29	Discovery Links	Newbridge
Snow	H	RF	217	Young Writers' World	Nelson/Michaels Assoc.
Snow	B	I	33	Hoenecke, Karen	Kaeden Books
Snow Bright and the Seven Sumos	M	F	250+	SupaDoopers	Sundance
Snow Bright and the Tooth Magician	M	F	250+	SupaDoopers	Sundance
Snow Cover	C	RF	29	Little Celebrations	Pearson Learning Group
Snow Daughter, The	L	TL	505	Sunshine	Wright Group/McGraw Hill
Snow Day	I	RF	250+	Bliss, Corinne Demas	Random House
Snow Goes To Town	L	F	250+	Literacy 2000	Rigby
Snow in the Kitchen	L	RF	250+	Cambridge Reading	Pearson Learning Group
Snow Is Cold	C	I	47	Little Readers	Houghton Mifflin
Snow Joe	D	RF	59	Rookie Readers	Children's Press
Snow on the Hill	H	RF	213	PM Extensions-Green	Rigby
Snow Treasure	R	HF	250+	McSwigan, Marie	Scholastic
Snow Walk	LB	RF	32	Reading Corners	Pearson Learning Group
Snow Walker, The	L	HF	250+	Wetterer, Margaret K. & Charles M.	Carolrhoda Books
Snow White and Rose Red	K	TL	250+	Hunia, Fran	Ladybird Books
Snow White and the Seven Dwarfs	I	TL	250+	Enrichment	Wright Group/McGraw Hill
Snow White and the Seven Dwarfs	K	TL	250+	PM Tales and Plays-Gold	Rigby
Snow, The	D	RF	36	Sunshine	Wright Group/McGraw Hill
Snow, The	G	RF	112	Burningham, John	Crowell
Snowball Fight	WB	RF	N/A	Rigby Literacy	Rigby
Snowball Fight!	D	RF	35	Wonder World	Wright Group/McGraw Hill
Snowball War, The	K	RF	250+	Chardiet, Bernice	Scholastic
Snowball, The	G	F	92	Armstrong, Jennifer	Random House

TITLE	LEVEL	GENRE	WORD COUNT	AUTHOR / SERIES	PUBLISHER / DISTRIBUTOR
Snowball, the White Mouse	G	RF	223	PM Plus Story Books	Rigby
Snowboarding	Q	I	250+	X-Sports	Capstone Press
Snowboarding	Q	I	250+	To the Extreme	Capstone Press
Snowboarding Diary	O	I	250+	PM Nonfiction-Emerald	Rigby
Snowboarding for Fun!	S	I	250+	Sports for Fun	Compass Point Books
Snowflakes	F	RF	80	Seedlings	Continental Press
Snowflakes	D	RF	49	Urmston, Kathleen; Evans, Karen	Kaeden Books
Snowman	C	RF	21	Sunshine	Wright Group/McGraw Hill
Snowman	A	RF	19	Story Box	Wright Group/McGraw Hill
Snowman	LB	RF	14	Smart Starts	Rigby
Snowman, A	C	I	59	Foundations	Wright Group/McGraw Hill
Snowman, The	B	I	32	Story Steps	Rigby
Snowman, The	E	RF	76	Oxford Reading Tree	Oxford University Press
Snowman, The	WB	F	N/A	Briggs, Raymond	Random House
Snowman, The	B	RF	76	Leveled Readers Emergent	Houghton Mifflin
Snowmobiling	S	I	250+	The Great Outdoors	Red Brick Learning
Snowshoe Thompson	K	HF	250+	Levinson, N. Smiler	HarperTrophy
Snowy Day, A	E	I	54	Pebble Books	Capstone Press
Snowy Day, The	J	RF	319	Keats, Ezra Jack	Scholastic
Snowy Gets a Wash	E	RF	181	PM Extensions-Yellow	Rigby
Snuggle Up	F	RF	125	Harrison, P.; Worthington, Denise	Continental Press
So Do I	D	RF	49	Teacher's Choice Series	Pearson Learning Group
So Far From the Bamboo Grove	V	HF	250+	Watkins, Yoko Kawashima	William Morrow
So Long Stinky Queen	M	RF	250+	First Flight	Fitzhenry & Whiteside
So Many Birthdays	I	RF	250+	Momentum Literacy Program	Troll Associates
So Many Circles	C	I	36	Yellow Umbrella Books	Red Brick Learning
So Many Snakes	I	I	152	Rosen Real Readers	Rosen Publishing Group
So Many Strawberries	E	RF	75	Books for Young Learners	Richard C. Owen
So Many Things to Do	A	RF	21	Home Connection Collection	Rigby
So Sleepy	D	RF	33	Books for Young Learners	Richard C. Owen
So That's What It Is!	F	I	133	Rigby Literacy	Rigby
So What?	I	RF	250+	Cohen, Miriam	Bantam
So You Want to Move a Building?	M	I	380	Pacific Literacy	Pacific Learning
So, So Sam	G	RF	107	TOTTS	Tott Publications
Soap Soup and Other Verses	K	TL	250+	Kuskin, Karla	HarperTrophy
Soap Story, A	H	RF	95	City Stories	Rigby
Soccer	M	I	250+	Little Celebrations	Pearson Learning Group
Soccer	E	I	78	Sun Sprouts	ETA/Cuisenaire
Soccer at the Park	F	RF	131	PM Extensions-Yellow	Rigby
Soccer Cousins	K	RF	250+	Marzollo, Jean	Scholastic
Soccer for Fun	S	I	250+	Sports for Fun	Compass Point Books
Soccer Fun!	N	RF	661	Leveled Readers	Houghton Mifflin
Soccer Game!	F	RF	63	Maccarone, Grace	Scholastic
Soccer Mania!	M	RF	250+	Tamar, Erika	Random House
Soccer Sam	M	RF	250+	Marzollo, Jean	Random House
Soccer Stars, Best Friend Face-off	R	RF	250+	Costello, Emily	Dell
*Sock Gobbler and Other Stories, The	M	F	250+	Learning Media	Pacific Learning
Socks	LB	RF	21	Smart Start	Rigby
Socks	D	RF	250+	Rigby Literacy	Rigby
Socks	B	RF	21	Ready Readers	Pearson Learning Group
Socks	O	RF	250+	Cleary, Beverly	Avon
Socks Off	H	RF	177	Alphakids	Sundance
Sod Houses on the Great Plains	N	I	250+	Rounds, Glen	Holiday House
Soddies	M	I	250+	Twig	Wright Group/McGraw Hill

* Collection of short stories

TITLE	LEVEL	GENRE	WORD COUNT	AUTHOR / SERIES	PUBLISHER / DISTRIBUTOR
Soil	K	I	381	Windows on Literacy	National Geographic
Soil	N	I	250+	Simply Science	Compass Point Books
Sojourner Truth	U	B	250+	Let Freedom Ring	Red Brick Learning
Sojourner Truth	P	B	250+	McLoone, Margo	Red Brick Learning
Sojourner Truth	L	B	250+	Pebble Books	Red Brick Learning
Sojourner Truth, Speaker for Equal Rights	O	B	374	Independent Readers Social Studies	Houghton Mifflin
Sojourner Truth: Ain't I a Woman?	V	B	250+	McKissack, Fredrick & Patricia	Scholastic
Solar Energy	V	I	2068	Leveled Readers Science	Houghton Mifflin
Solar Storms	R	I	250+	Rosen Real Readers	Rosen Publishing Group
Solar System, The	U	I	250+	The Heinle Reading Library	Thomson Learning
Solar System, The	P	I	250+	Bridgestone Books	Capstone Press
Solar System, The	N	I	250+	A True Book	Children's Press
Solar System, The	N	I	250+	Simply Science	Compass Point Books
Solar-Powered Sam	J	F	148	Books for Young Learners	Richard C. Owen
Soldier Boy	T	HF	250+	Burks, Brian	Harcourt Trade
Soldier's Heart	V	HF	250+	Paulsen, Gary	Random House
Solid or Not?	G	I	113	Early Connections	Benchmark Education
Solid, Liquid, Gas: What Is Matter?	R	I	250+	Rosen Real Readers	Rosen Publishing Group
Solids, Liquids, Gases	N	I	250+	Simply Science	Compass Point Books
Solitary Blue, A	W	RF	250+	Voigt, Cynthia	Scholastic
Solo Flyer	L	RF	605	PM Gold	Rigby
Solo Girl	M	RF	250+	Pinkey, Andrea Davis	Hyperion
Solve It!	K	RF	250+	Goldish, Meish	Scholastic
Somalia	O	I	250+	Countries of the World	Red Brick Learning
Some Days Are Like That	D	RF	69	Teacher's Choice Series	Pearson Learning Group
Some Dog!	O	RF	250+	PM Ruby	Rigby
Some Dogs Don't	B	F	29	Tiger Cub	Peguis
Some Friend	R	RF	250+	Warner, Sally	Alfred A. Knopf
Some Kids Are Blind	J	I	134	Understanding Differences	Red Brick Learning
Some Kids Are Deaf	J	I	158	Understanding Differences	Red Brick Learning
Some Kids Use Wheelchairs	I	I	123	Understanding Differences	Red Brick Learning
Some Kids Wear Leg Braces	J	I	144	Understanding Differences	Red Brick Learning
Some Machines are Enormous	J	I	250+	Bookshop	Mondo
*Some of the Kinder Planets	U	SF	250+	Wynne-Jones, Tim	Penguin Group
Some People	D	I	50	Reading Corners	Pearson Learning Group
Some Snakes	J	I	118	Voyages	SRA/McGraw Hill
Some Things Float	C	I	41	Windows on Literacy	National Geographic
Some Things Go Together	C	RF	133	Twig	Wright Group/McGraw Hill
Someday a Tree	P	RF	250+	Bunting, Eve	Clarion
Someday Cyril	N	RF	250+	Gershator, Phillis	Mondo
*Somehow Tenderness Survives: Stories of Southern Africa	Z	HF	250+	Rochman, Hazel	HarperTrophy
Someone is Following Pip Ramsey	N	RF	250+	Roy, Ron	Random House
Someone to Count On	T	RF	250+	Hermes, Patricia	Language for Learning Assoc.
Something Else	L	F	250+	Cave, Kathryn	Mondo
Something Everyone Needs	J	RF	250+	Ready Readers	Pearson Learning Group
Something for Everyone	R	RF	1371	Leveled Readers	Houghton Mifflin
*Something Is There and Other Stories	J	F	250+	Story Steps	Rigby
Something is Waiting	J	I	94	Literacy Tree	Rigby
Something Nasty	I	F	250+	Popcorn	Sundance
Something New	D	I	72	Little Celebrations	Pearson Learning Group
Something Noise, The	J	RF	276	Windmill Books	Rigby

* Collection of short stories

TITLE	LEVEL	GENRE	WORD COUNT	AUTHOR / SERIES	PUBLISHER / DISTRIBUTOR
Something Queer at the Ball Park	N	RF	250+	Levy, Elizabeth	Bantam
Something Queer at the Haunted School	N	RF	250+	Levy, Elizabeth	Bantam
Something Queer at the Lemonade Stand	N	RF	250+	Levy, Elizabeth	Bantam
Something Queer at the Library	N	RF	250+	Levy, Elizabeth	Bantam
Something Queer at the Scary Movie	N	RF	250+	Levy, Elizabeth	Hyperion
Something Queer in Outer Space	N	RF	250+	Levy, Elizabeth	Hyperion
Something Queer in the Cafeteria	N	RF	250+	Levy, Elizabeth	Hyperion
Something Queer in the Wild West	N	RF	250+	Levy, Elizabeth	Hyperion
Something Queer Is Going On	N	RF	250+	Levy, Elizabeth	Bantam
Something Queer on Vacation	N	RF	250+	Levy, Elizabeth	Bantam
Something Soft for Danny Bear	M	F	493	Literacy 2000	Rigby
Something Special For Miss Margery	J	F	250+	Voyages	SRA/McGraw Hill
Something to Munch	E	RF	58	Ready Readers	Pearson Learning Group
Something to Share	D	RF	98	Carousel Readers	Pearson Learning Group
Something Upstairs	T	RF	250+	Avi	Language for Learning Assoc.
Something Very Sorry	R	RF	250+	Bohlmeijer, Arno	Putnam & Grosset
Sometimes	B	RF	18	Literacy 2000	Rigby
Sometimes	C	RF	25	Wonder World	Wright Group/McGraw Hill
Sometimes . . .	F	RF	31	City Stories	Rigby
Sometimes . . .	B	RF	25	Home Connection Collection	Rigby
Sometimes I Feel Like a Storm Cloud	M	RF	250+	Bookshop	Mondo
Sometimes I Share	H	RF	108	Ziefert, Harriet	HarperCollins
Sometimes I'm Silly	C	RF	24	Visions	Wright Group/McGraw Hill
Sometimes Things Change	G	I	71	Rookie Readers	Children's Press
Somewhere	J	TL	93	Bookshop	Mondo
Somewhere in the Universe	I	I	167	Literacy Tree	Rigby
Son of the Mob	Z	RF	250+	Korman, Gordon	Hyperion
Song Lee and the Hamster Hunt	L	RF	250+	Kline, Suzy	Penguin Group
Song Lee and the Leech Man	L	RF	250+	Kline, Suzy	Penguin Group
Song Lee In Room 2B	L	RF	250+	Kline, Suzy	Penguin Group
Song of the Giraffe	O	RF	250+	Jacobs, Shannon K.	Little, Brown & Co.
Song of the Mantis, The	S	I	250+	Literacy 2000	Rigby
Song of the Stranger	T	RF	250+	Tung, Angela	Lowell House
Song of the Trees	R	HF	250+	Taylor, Mildred	Bantam
Songbird, The	B	F	39	Ray's Readers	Outside the Box
Sonic Quest	W	F	250+	Roberts, Katherine	Scholastic
Sons of Liberty	Y	RF	250+	Griffin, Adele	Hyperion
Sophie Hits Six	M	F	250+	King-Smith, Dick	Candlewick Press
Sophie in the Saddle	M	F	250+	King-Smith, Dick	Candlewick Press
Sophie Is Seven	M	F	250+	King-Smith, Dick	Candlewick Press
Sophie's Box	G	F	174	Cambridge Reading	Pearson Learning Group
Sophie's Chicken	H	RF	107	Tadpoles	Rigby
Sophie's Lucky	M	F	250+	King-Smith, Dick	Candlewick Press
Sophie's Singing Mother	J	RF	313	Jellybeans	Rigby
Sophie's Snail	M	F	250+	King-Smith, Dick	Candlewick Press
Sophie's Tom	M	F	250+	King-Smith, Dick	Candlewick Press
Sor Juana Inez de la Cruz	O	B	693	Leveled Readers Social Studies	Houghton Mifflin
Sorting My Money	J	I	209	Early Connections	Benchmark Education
SOS Titanic	V	HF	250+	Bunting, Eve	Harcourt Trade
Sound	N	I	250+	Windows on Literacy	National Geographic
Sound, Heat & Light: Energy at Work	L	I	250+	Berger, Melvin	Scholastic
Sound: Loud, Soft, High, and Low	M	I	250+	Amazing Science	Picture Window Books
Sounder	T	RF	250+	Armstrong, William	Scholastic

* Collection of short stories

TITLE	LEVEL	GENRE	WORD COUNT	AUTHOR / SERIES	PUBLISHER / DISTRIBUTOR
Sounds	J	I	200	Early Connections	Benchmark Education
Sounds	N	I	250+	Lighthouse	Rigby
Sounds All Around	A	I	28	Independent Readers Science	Houghton Mifflin
Sounds all Around	G	I	153	Discovery Links	Newbridge
Sounds All Around Us	K	I	168	Phonics Readers	Compass Point Books
Sounds Around Us, The	C	I	22	Rosen Real Readers	Rosen Publishing Group
Sounds in the Night	F	RF	126	Visions	Wright Group/McGraw Hill
Sounds of Music, The	G	I	140	Leveled Readers Science	Houghton Mifflin
Soup	I	F	250+	Sunshine	Wright Group/McGraw Hill
Soup	A	I	17	Little Celebrations	Pearson Learning Group
Soup	Q	RF	250+	Peck, Robert Newton	Bantam
Soup Can Telephone	I	I	190	Wonder World	Wright Group/McGraw Hill
Soup Fit for a King	J	RF	250+	Sunshine	Wright Group/McGraw Hill
Soup for Snail	E	F	61	Leveled Readers Language Support	Houghton Mifflin
South Africa	Q	I	250+	First Reports	Compass Point Books
South Africa	O	I	250+	Countries of the World	Red Brick Learning
South America	N	I	250+	Continents	Capstone Press
South Carolina	R	I	250+	This Land Is Your Land	Compass Point Books
South Dakota	R	I	250+	This Land Is Your Land	Compass Point Books
South Korea	O	I	250+	Davis, Lucile	Red Brick Learning
South Pole Bound	O	RF	788	Leveled Readers	Houghton Mifflin
Southern Sounds	S	I	2194	Independent Readers Social Studies	Houghton Mifflin
Souvenirs	K	RF	179	Literacy 2000	Rigby
Space	R	I	250+	Worldwise	Grolier Press
Space	H	I	100	Sunshine	Wright Group/McGraw Hill
Space Aliens in Our School	D	F	45	Joy Readers	Pearson Learning Group
Space Animals	P	I	474	Independent Readers Science	Houghton Mifflin
Space Ant Goes Home	F	F	194	Rigby Literacy	Rigby
Space Ark, The	B	SF	20	Sunshine	Wright Group/McGraw Hill
Space Cat	K	F	250+	Sails	Rigby
Space Commander: Eileen Collins	U	B	250+	Leveled Readers Language Support	Houghton Mifflin
Space Dog and Roy	L	F	250+	Standiford, Natalie	Random House
Space Dog and the Pet Show	L	F	250+	Standiford, Natalie	Random House
Space Dog in Trouble	L	F	250+	Standiford, Natalie	Random House
Space Dog the Hero	L	F	250+	Standiford, Natalie	Random House
Space Exploration	S	I	250+	Our Solar System	Compass Point Books
Space Journey	A	F	19	Sunshine	Wright Group/McGraw Hill
Space Junk	O	RF	250+	Wildcats	Wright Group/McGraw Hill
Space Math	R	I	250+	Rosen Real Readers	Rosen Publishing Group
Space Missions	N	I	250+	Explore Space!	Red Brick Learning
Space Quest	O	I	250+	Discovery World	Rigby
Space Race	J	F	213	Sunshine	Wright Group/McGraw Hill
Space Rock	L	F	250+	Buller, Jon	Random House
Space Rocks: A Look at Asteroids and Comets	M	I	250+	Rosen Real Readers	Rosen Publishing Group
Space Shuttle, The	D	I	45	Sunshine	Wright Group/McGraw Hill
Space Station	Q	I	250+	Orbit Double Takes	Pacific Learning
Space Station Orion	L	F	250+	Rigby Literacy	Rigby
*Space Station Plot and Other Cases, The	O	RF	250+	Simon, Seymour	Avon
Space Stations	O	I	250+	Ryan, Cheryl	Wright Group/McGraw Hill
Space Stations	N	I	250+	A True Book	Children's Press
Space Suits	N	I	250+	Explore Space	Red Brick Learning

* Collection of short stories

TITLE	LEVEL	GENRE	WORD COUNT	AUTHOR / SERIES	PUBLISHER / DISTRIBUTOR
Space Travel	U	I	250+	The Heinle Reading Library	Thomson Learning
Space Walks	M	I	250+	Explore Space	Red Brick Learning
Space Wardrobe	W	I	1501	Independent Readers Science	Houghton Mifflin
Spaceship	B	I	27	Hoenecke, Karen	Kaeden Books
Spaghetti Party, The	K	RF	250+	Bank Street	Bantam
Spaghetti! Spaghetti!	G	RF	85	Book Bank	Wright Group/McGraw Hill
Spanish Omelette	L	RF	250+	PM Story Books-Silver	Rigby
Spanish-American War, The	W	I	250+	Cornerstones of Freedom	Children's Press
Sparky's Bone	F	F	273	Ready Readers	Pearson Learning Group
Sparrows, The	F	I	60	Books for Young Learners	Richard C. Owen
Speak	Z	RF	250+	Anderson, Laurie Halse	Penguin Group
Speak Up!	F	F	194	Sunshine	Wright Group/McGraw Hill
Special Cake, The	K	RF	250+	Cambridge Reading	Pearson Learning Group
Special Clothes	J	RF	411	Leveled Readers	Houghton Mifflin
Special Delivery	B	F	54	Bookshop	Mondo
Special Effects	P	I	250+	Wildcats	Wright Group/McGraw Hill
Special Foods, Special Places	WB	I	N/A	Windows on Literacy	National Geographic
Special Friend, A	F	RF	80	Carousel Readers	Pearson Learning Group
Special Gifts	M	RF	250+	Rylant, Cynthia	Aladdin
Special Places	E	RF	96	Rigby Literacy	Rigby
Special Present, The	L	RF	250+	Cole, Sally	Wright Group/McGraw Hill
Special Ride, The	K	RF	647	PM Gold	Rigby
Special Stories	J	I	189	Vocabulary Readers	Houghton Mifflin
Special Things	G	RF	128	Literacy 2000	Rigby
Special Trip, A	O	RF	910	Leveled Readers Science	Houghton Mifflin
Specs	J	B	250+	Ready Set Read	Steck-Vaughn
Spectacular Stone Soup	L	RF	250+	Giff, Patricia Reilly	Yearling
Speech, The	P	RF	250+	Leveled Readers Language Support	Houghton Mifflin
Speeches on the Air	Z	I	2358	Leveled Readers	Houghton Mifflin
Speed Boat, The	C	RF	170	Sunshine	Wright Group/McGraw Hill
Speed Racer	F	RF	74	Leveled Readers Science	Houghton Mifflin
*Speeding Sleigh and Other Cases, The	O	RF	250+	Simon, Seymour	Avon
Speedy Bee	D	F	106	PM Plus Story Books	Rigby
*Speedy Pasta and Other Cases, The	O	RF	250+	Simon, Seymour	Avon
*Speedy Snake and Other Cases, The	O	RF	250+	Simon, Seymour	Avon
*Speedy Soapbox Car and Other Cases, The	O	RF	250+	Simon, Seymour	Avon
Spell Casters, Phoebe's Fortune	R	F	250+	Warriner, Holly	Aladdin
Spencer School Sleepover, The	M	RF	250+	Floyd, Lucy	Wright Group/McGraw Hill
Spending Money	O	I	250+	Let's See	Compass Point Books
Spending Money	L	I	250+	First Facts	Capstone Press
Spicy-Herby Day, A	G	RF	117	Evangeline Nicholas Collection	Wright Group/McGraw Hill
Spider	D	F	43	Sunshine	Wright Group/McGraw Hill
Spider and the King, The	L	TL	250+	Literacy 2000	Rigby
Spider Bank, The	L	I	250+	Story Steps	Rigby
Spider Boy	R	RF	250+	Fletcher, Ralph	Bantam
Spider Can't Fly	G	F	149	Book Bank	Wright Group/McGraw Hill
Spider in My Bedroom, A	K	RF	477	PM Plus Story Books	Rigby
Spider Kane and the Mystery at Jumbo Nightcrawler's	O	F	250+	Osborne, Mary Pope	Random House
Spider Kane and the Mystery Under the May-Apple	O	F	250+	Osborne, Mary Pope	Random House
Spider Legs	D	I	52	Twig	Wright Group/McGraw Hill
Spider Man	M	I	250+	Literacy 2000	Rigby

* Collection of short stories

TITLE	LEVEL	GENRE	WORD COUNT	AUTHOR / SERIES	PUBLISHER / DISTRIBUTOR
Spider Night	K	F	250+	Kunari, Anna	Hampton-Brown
Spider Relatives	Q	I	250+	Literacy 2000	Rigby
Spider Spins	D	F	36	Ray's Readers	Outside the Box
Spider, Spider	D	F	70	Sunshine	Wright Group/McGraw Hill
Spider, The	O	I	250+	Crewe, Sabrina	Steck-Vaughn
Spiders	N	I	250+	Minibeasts	Franklin Watts
Spiders	O	I	250+	Holmes, Kevin J.	Red Brick Learning
Spiders	E	I	75	Wonder World	Wright Group/McGraw Hill
Spiders	P	I	250+	Mini Pets	Steck-Vaughn
Spiders	E	I	53	Discovery Links	Newbridge
Spiders	M	I	250+	Bookshop	Mondo
Spiders	G	I	53	Pebble Plus	Red Brick Learning
Spiders and the Web	K	I	187	Animal Homes	Capstone Press
Spiders and Their Webs	I	I	162	Sunshine Books	Wright Group/McGraw Hill
Spiders Are Special Animals	J	I	166	Sunshine	Wright Group/McGraw Hill
Spiders Everywhere	D	F	36	Books for Young Learners	Richard C. Owen
Spiders in Space	I	F	242	Sunshine	Wright Group/McGraw Hill
Spiders Spin Silk	J	I	183	Windows on Literacy	National Geographic
Spider's Web	N	I	250+	Back, Christine	Silver Burdett Press
Spider's Web, A	L	I	323	Wonder World	Wright Group/McGraw Hill
Spiders!	J	I	185	Rosen Real Readers	Rosen Publishing Group
Spiders, Spiders Everywhere!	D	RF	80	Learn to Read	Creative Teaching Press
Spies on the Devil's Belt	W	HF	250+	Haynes, Betsy	Scholastic
Spike and the Concert	L	RF	250+	Cambridge Reading	Pearson Learning Group
Spinning Snake, A	F	RF	156	Sunshine	Wright Group/McGraw Hill
Spinning Top	I	I	182	Wonder World	Wright Group/McGraw Hill
Spirit of Hope	N	F	250+	Bookshop	Mondo
Spirit of St. Louis, The	V	I	250+	Cornerstones of Freedom	Children's Press
Spirit Quest	S	RF	250+	Sharpe, Susan	Scholastic
Splash	C	F	34	Foundations	Wright Group/McGraw Hill
Splash!	E	RF	85	Leveled Readers Language Support	Houghton Mifflin
Splash!	D	RF	63	New Way Red	Steck-Vaughn
Splash!	E	RF	85	Joy Readers	Pearson Learning Group
Splash!	A	I	35	Bebop Books	Lee & Low Books Inc.
Splash!	D	F	35	Sun Sprouts	ETA/Cuisenaire
Splashing Dad	C	RF	37	Early Emergent	Pioneer Valley
Splatter	N	RF	250+	Marriott, Janice	Pacific Learning
Splish Splash!	B	RF	28	Windmill	Wright Group/McGraw Hill
Splish! Splash!	D	F	45	Little Celebrations	Pearson Learning Group
Splish! Splash!: A Book About Rain	M	I	250+	Amazing Science	Picture Window Books
Splishy-Sploshy	E	F	127	Story Basket	Wright Group/McGraw Hill
Splosh	C	F	47	Story Box	Wright Group/McGraw Hill
Spoiled Rotten	L	RF	250+	DeClements, Barthe	Hyperion
Spooky Pet	B	RF	24	Smart Starts	Rigby
Spooky Riddles	I	TL	182	Brown, Marc	Random House
Spooky Swap Sound, The	G	F	179	Sunshine	Wright Group/McGraw Hill
Spooky Tail of Prewitt Peacock, The	M	F	250+	Peet, Bill	Houghton Mifflin
Sports Are Fun	B	I	21	Pair-It Books	Steck-Vaughn
Sports Around the World	I	I	192	Early Connections	Benchmark Education
Sports Bag	F	I	147	Sun Sprouts	ETA/Cuisenaire
Sports Bloopers	P	I	250+	Hollander, Phyllis & Zander	Scholastic
Sports Cars	M	I	250+	Blazers	Capstone Press
Sports Day	C	RF	24	Home Connection Collection	Rigby

* Collection of short stories

TITLE	LEVEL	GENRE	WORD COUNT	AUTHOR / SERIES	PUBLISHER / DISTRIBUTOR
Sports for All	Q	I	250+	Explorers	Wright Group/McGraw Hill
*Sports Hall of Fame	O	B	250+	Bookshop	Mondo
Sports Heroes	R	I	250+	PM Nonfiction-Ruby	Rigby
Sports Legends	O	B	250+	Navigators Fiction Series	Benchmark Education
Sports Matters: A Magazine for Kids	L	I	250+	Rigby Literacy	Rigby
Sports Mysteries: Case of the Basketball Video	P	RF	250+	Edwards, T. J.	Scholastic
Sports Mysteries: Case Of The Missing Pitcher	P	RF	250+	Edwards, T. J.	Scholastic
Sports of the First Americans	T	I	1590	Leveled Readers Social Studies	Houghton Mifflin
Sports on Wheels	R	I	250+	PM Nonfiction-Ruby	Rigby
Sports Skills	S	I	250+	Sunshine	Wright Group/McGraw Hill
Sports Technology	R	I	250+	PM Nonfiction-Ruby	Rigby
Sportsmanship	M	I	250+	Character Education	Red Brick Learning
Spot That Cat!	J	I	208	Story Box	Wright Group/McGraw Hill
Spots	E	RF	116	Real Kids Readers	Millbrook Press
Spots	LB	RF	27	Smart Starts	Rigby
Spots	C	I	41	Sunshine	Wright Group/McGraw Hill
Spots	B	F	31	Visions	Wright Group/McGraw Hill
Spots	E	RF	48	Literacy 2000	Rigby
Spots and Stripes	A	I	24	Rosen Real Readers	Rosen Publishing Group
Spot's Birthday Party	I	F	97	Hill, Eric	Putnam
Spot's First Christmas	J	RF	102	Hill, Eric	Putnam
Spot's First Walk	G	F	63	Hill, Eric	Putnam
Spots!	E	RF	55	Oxford Reading Tree	Oxford University Press
Spots, Feathers and Curly Tails	C	I	42	Tafuri, Nancy	Morrow
*Spotted Pony, The: A Collection of Hanukkah Stories	U	TL	250+	Kimmel, Eric A.	Holiday House
Spray-Paint Mystery, The	O	RF	250+	Medearis, Angela Shelf	Scholastic
Spreading the Word	Q	I	250+	Wildcats	Wright Group/McGraw Hill
Spring	C	I	47	Carousel Readers	Pearson Learning Group
Spring	E	I	58	Sunshine	Wright Group/McGraw Hill
Spring	I	I	142	Pebble Books	Capstone Press
Spring Fever!	T	F	250+	Lerangis, Peter	Language for Learning Assoc.
Spring Has Sprung	K	I	250+	Spyglass Books	Compass Point Books
Spring in the City	B	I	46	Leveled Readers Emergent	Houghton Mifflin
Spring in the City	M	F	46	Leveled Readers	Houghton Mifflin
Spring Pops Up	C	I	26	Instant Readers	Harcourt School Publishers
Spring Rain	A	I	24	Vocabulary Readers	Houghton Mifflin
Spring Snow	D	RF	48	Little Books for Early Readers	University of Maine
Spring, Summer, Fall, Winter	G	I	64	Windows on Literacy	National Geographic
Springs	F	I	142	Alphakids	Sundance
Springs	M	I	245	Books for Young Learners	Richard C. Owen
Springtime Rock and Roll, The	H	F	249	Literacy Tree	Rigby
Spy Down the Street, The	M	F	250+	Schultz, Irene	Wright Group/McGraw Hill
Spy in the Attic, The	M	RF	250+	Scheffler, Ursel	North-South Books
Spy Manual	M	I	250+	Sails	Rigby
Spy Maps	N	F	250+	Sails	Rigby
Spy on Third Base, The	M	RF	250+	Christopher, Matt	Little, Brown & Co.
Squanto and the First Thanksgiving	L	HF	250+	Celsi, Teresa	Steck-Vaughn
Squanto: Friend of the Pilgrims	O	B	250+	Bulla, Clyde Robert	Scholastic
Squares	B	I	27	Harry's Math Books	Outside the Box
Squares Everywhere	C	I	26	Discovery Links	Newbridge
Squares: Seeing Squares All Around Us	K	I	183	Shapes	Capstone Press
Squeaky Car, The	G	RF	200	New Way Green	Steck-Vaughn

* Collection of short stories

TITLE	LEVEL	GENRE	WORD COUNT	AUTHOR / SERIES	PUBLISHER / DISTRIBUTOR
Squeaky Clean	C	RF	29	Stewart, Josie	Continental Press
Squire Takes a Wife, A	J	F	250+	Ready Set Read	Steck-Vaughn
Squirrels	N	I	460	Storyteller Nonfiction	Wright Group/McGraw Hill
Squirrels	F	RF	109	Ready Readers	Pearson Learning Group
Squirrels	I	I	250+	Pebble Books	Red Brick Learning
Squirrels and Their Nests	J	I	130	Pebble Plus	Capstone Press
Squirrels in the School	Q	RF	250+	Baglio, Ben M.	Scholastic
Squirrels: Furry Scurriers	M	I	250+	The Wild World of Animals	Red Brick Learning
Ssh, Don't Wake the Baby	F	RF	135	Voyages	SRA/McGraw Hill
Sssh!	C	RF	49	Book Bank	Wright Group/McGraw Hill
St. Lawrence Seaway, The	O	I	371	Independent Readers Social Studies	Houghton Mifflin
St. Patrick's Day	P	I	250+	Let's See	Compass Point Books
Stables Are for Horses	I	I	66	Windmill	Wright Group/McGraw Hill
Stacey and the Haunted Masquerade	O	RF	250+	Martin, Ann M.	Scholastic
Stacey and the Missing Ring	O	RF	250+	Martin, Ann M.	Scholastic
Stacey and the Mystery at the Mall	O	RF	250+	Martin, Ann M.	Scholastic
Stacey and the Mystery Money	O	RF	250+	Martin, Ann M.	Scholastic
Stacy Says Good-Bye	L	RF	250+	Giff, Patricia Reilly	Bantam
Stage Fright	O	RF	250+	Orbit Double Takes	Pacific Learning
Stage Fright	N	RF	250+	Martin, Ann M.	Scholastic
Staircase to the Sky	E	RF	133	Visions	Wright Group/McGraw Hill
Stallion's Call, The	E	F	77	Salem, Lynn; Stewart, Josie	Continental Press
Stamps	G	I	58	Wonder World	Wright Group/McGraw Hill
Stan Packs	E	RF	84	Ready Readers	Pearson Learning Group
Stan the Hot Dog Man	K	RF	250+	Kessler, Ethel & Leonard	HarperTrophy
Stand Tall	U	RF	250+	Bauer, Joan	Penguin Group
Standing in the Light	T	RF	250+	Osborne, Mary Pope	Scholastic
*Standing Tall: The Stories of Ten Hispanic Americans	X	B	250+	Palacios, Argentina	Scholastic
Stanley	I	F	250+	Hoff, Syd	HarperTrophy
Stanley and the Magic Lamp	P	F	250+	Brown, Jeff	HarperTrophy
Star	M	RF	250+	Simon, Jo Ann	Random House
Star and Patches	K	RF	440	PM Plus Story Books	Rigby
Star Fisher, The	S	RF	250+	Yep, Lawrence	Scholastic
Star Gazing in Our Solar System	J	I	202	Independent Readers Science	Houghton Mifflin
Star Pictures	D	I	43	iOpeners	Pearson Learning Group
Star Pictures	K	I	96	Books for Young Learners	Richard C. Owen
Star Thief	P	RF	250+	Bilbrough, Norman	Pacific Learning
Starfish & Urchins	K	I	322	Marine Life For Young Readers	Pearson Learning Group
Starfishers to the Rescue	M	SF	250+	Dreyer, Ellen	Pearson Learning Group
Stargirl	V	RF	250+	Spinelli, Jerry	Alfred A. Knopf
Starring First Grade	J	RF	250+	Cohen, Miriam	Bantam
Starring Rosie	N	RF	250+	Giff, Patricia Reilly	Penguin Group
Stars	G	I	105	Sunshine	Wright Group/McGraw Hill
Stars	P	I	250+	The Galaxy	Red Brick Learning
Stars	N	I	250+	A True Book	Children's Press
Stars	H	I	181	Discovery Links	Newbridge
Stars	I	I	181	Yellow Umbrella Books	Red Brick Learning
Stars, The	K	I	102	Pebble Books	Red Brick Learning
Stars: Seeing Stars All Around Us	J	I	193	Shapes	Capstone Press
Starshine	H	F	224	Sunshine	Wright Group/McGraw Hill
Start and Stop	F	I	49	Pebble Books	Red Brick Learning

* Collection of short stories

TITLE	LEVEL	GENRE	WORD COUNT	AUTHOR / SERIES	PUBLISHER / DISTRIBUTOR
Start of the American Revolutionary War, The: Paul Revere Rides at Midnight	S	I	250+	Headlines from History	Rosen Publishing Group
Starting a Business	S	I	596	Vocabulary Readers	Houghton Mifflin
Starting a Rock Collection	T	I	250+	Independent Readers Science	Houghton Mifflin
Starting Points	Y	I	250+	iOpeners	Pearson Learning Group
Starting School	E	RF	97	Voyages	SRA/McGraw Hill
Statue of Liberty, The	V	I	250+	The Heinle Reading Library	Thomson Learning
Statue of Liberty, The	N	I	250+	American Symbols	Capstone Press
Statue of Liberty, The	Q	I	250+	Let's See	Compass Point Books
Statue of Liberty, The	J	I	250+	Penner, Lucille	Random House
Statue of Liberty, The	Q	I	250+	National Landmarks	Red Brick Learning
Statue of Liberty, The	N	I	250+	A True Book	Children's Press
Statues Across America	K	I	293	Vocabulary Readers	Houghton Mifflin
Stay Away from Simon!	O	RF	250+	Carrick, Carol	Clarion
Stay Cool	E	F	134	Start to Read	School Zone
Stay! Keeper's Story	U	F	250+	Lowry, Lois	Random House
Staying Healthy	W	I	250+	iOpeners	Pearson Learning Group
Staying Healthy	LB	I	7	Windows on Literacy	National Geographic
Staying Healthy: Eating Right	O	I	250+	McGinty, Alice B.	Franklin Watts
Staying Nine	O	RF	250+	Conrad, Pam	HarperTrophy
Staying Well	F	I	154	Early Connections	Benchmark Education
Staying with Grandma Norma	F	RF	168	Salem, Lynn; Stewart, Josie	Continental Press
Steal Away . . . to Freedom	Z	RF	250+	Armstrong, Jennifer	Scholastic
Stealing Freedom	U	HF	250+	Carbone, Lisa	Random House
Stealing Home: The Story of Jackie Robinson	V	B	250+	Denenberg, Barry	Scholastic
Steam Power	L	I	308	Rigby Focus	Rigby
Stella	E	RF	57	Storyteller-Moon Rising	Wright Group/McGraw Hill
Stems	K	I	231	Pebble Books	Capstone Press
Stephen Hawking	V	B	2515	Leveled Readers Science	Houghton Mifflin
Stepping Back in Time	W	RF	2045	Leveled Readers	Houghton Mifflin
Stepping Stones	C	F	42	Sunshine	Wright Group/McGraw Hill
Stepping Through Time	N	I	250+	Rigby Literacy	Rigby
Steps, The	T	RF	250+	Cohn, Rachel	Simon & Schuster
Sterkarm Handshake, The	Z	F	250+	Price, Susan	Scholastic
Steve's Room	G	RF	171	Ready Readers	Pearson Learning Group
Stew for Egor's Mom, A	G	F	162	Ready Readers	Pearson Learning Group
Stick to It!: The Story of Wilma Rudolph	M	B	250+	Spyglass Books	Compass Point Books
Sticks and Stones, Bobbie Bones	P	RF	250+	Roberts, Brenda C.	Scholastic
Sticky Stanley	F	F	97	First Start	Troll Associates
Still Standing	O	I	388	Independent Readers Science	Houghton Mifflin
Stingrays	I	I	126	Wonder World	Wright Group/McGraw Hill
Stitches	G	RF	250+	Ziefert, Harriet	Puffin Books
Stock Cars	T	I	250+	The World's Fastest	Red Brick Learning
Stomachs	N	I	250+	Sails	Rigby
Stone Fox	P	RF	250+	Gardiner, John Reynolds	HarperTrophy
Stone in My Hand, A	W	RF	250+	Clinton, Cathryn	Candlewick Press
Stone in the Road, A	L	TL	250+	Bookshop	Mondo
Stone Mouse, The	K	F	250+	Rigby Literacy	Rigby
Stone Soup	H	TL	250+	Rigby Literacy	Rigby
Stone Soup	J	TL	250+	PM Tales and Plays-Turquoise	Rigby
Stone Soup	J	TL	932	McGovern, Ann	Scholastic
*Stone Soup and Other Stories	L	TL	250+	New Way Literature	Steck-Vaughn
Stone Works	K	I	124	Wonder World	Wright Group/McGraw Hill
Stonehenge: Mystery Unsolved?	U	I	1754	Leveled Readers	Houghton Mifflin

* Collection of short stories

| --- | --- | --- | --- | --- | --- |
Stonehenge: Still a Mystery	T	I	250+	Leveled Readers Language Support	Houghton Mifflin
Stones in Water	X	RF	250+	Napoli, Donna Jo	Puffin Books
Stop	C	F	54	Story Box	Wright Group/McGraw Hill
Stop Knitting, Nina!	I	F	250+	Home Connection Collection	Rigby
Stop That	C	F	41	Ready Readers	Pearson Learning Group
Stop That Noise!	C	RF	21	Pacific Literacy	Pacific Learning
Stop That Noise!	A	F	21	KinderReaders	Rigby
Stop That Rabbit	G	F	168	First Start	Troll Associates
Stop the Car!	G	RF	179	Lighthouse	Rigby
Stop!	B	RF	90	PM Starters	Rigby
Stop!	C	RF	31	Wonder World	Wright Group/McGraw Hill
Stop!	A	RF	12	Ready Readers	Pearson Learning Group
*Stop! And Other Stories	E	F	161	Story Steps	Rigby
Stop, Look, and Listen	G	RF	102	Literacy Tree	Rigby
Stop, Look, and Listen	C	RF	71	Lighthouse	Rigby
Stop, Stop	M	F	250+	Hurd, Edith Thacher	HarperCollins
Stores	C	RF	66	Carousel Readers	Pearson Learning Group
Stories	C	RF	43	Learn to Read	Creative Teaching Press
*Stories for Children	V	TL	250+	Singer, Isaac Bashevis	Farrar, Straus and Giroux
*Stories From the Days of Christopher Columbus	U	HF	250+	Young, Richard; Young, Judy Dockery	August House
*Stories Huey Tells, The	N	RF	250+	Cameron, Ann	Alfred A. Knopf
Stories in Stone	M	I	250+	Pacific Literacy	Pacific Learning
Stories in Stone: The World of Animal Fossils	U	I	250+	A First Book	Franklin Watts
*Stories Julian Tells, The	N	RF	250+	Cameron, Ann	Alfred A. Knopf
*Stories of the North	Y	RF	250+	London, Jack	Scholastic
Storm at Coldwater Creek	M	HF	250+	Blackaby, Susan	Wright Group/McGraw Hill
Storm at Sea, A	R	HF	1145	Leveled Readers	Houghton Mifflin
Storm Book, The	P	I	250+	Zolotow, Charlotte	HarperCollins
Storm Chasers	L	RF	250+	Navigators Fiction Series	Benchmark Education
Storm in the Night	N	RF	250+	Stolz, Mary	HarperCollins
Storm on the Beach, A	I	RF	72	Book Bank	Wright Group/McGraw Hill
Storm!	E	I	49	Wonder World	Wright Group/McGraw Hill
Storm, The	E	RF	71	Foundations	Wright Group/McGraw Hill
Storm, The	E	RF	33	Literacy 2000	Rigby
Storm, The	G	RF	75	Books for Young Learners	Richard C. Owen
Storm, The	C	I	28	Voyages	SRA/McGraw Hill
Storm, The	B	I	19	Sunshine	Wright Group/McGraw Hill
Storm, The	C	RF	29	Story Box	Wright Group/McGraw Hill
Stormbreaker	Z	RF	250+	Horowitz, Anthony	Scholastic
Storms	N	I	250+	Windows on Literacy	National Geographic
Storms	N	I	250+	PM Plus Story Books	Rigby
Storms!	L	I	359	Pair-It Books	Steck-Vaughn
Stormy Weather	O	I	250+	Navigators Fiction Series	Benchmark Education
Stormy Weather	G	I	88	Twig	Wright Group/McGraw Hill
Stormy, Misty's Foal	R	RF	250+	Henry, Marguerite	Aladdin
Story Box, The	K	RF	592	Leveled Readers	Houghton Mifflin
Story of a Book, The	L	I	250+	Reeder, Paul	Wright Group/McGraw Hill
Story of Alexander Graham Bell, Inventor of the Telephone	O	B	250+	Davidson, Margaret	Scholastic
Story of Amy Johnson, The: Pioneering Woman Navigator	R	B	250+	Literacy 2000	Rigby
Story of Benjamin Franklin, Amazing American	O	B	250+	Davidson, Margaret	Scholastic

* Collection of short stories

TITLE	LEVEL	GENRE	WORD COUNT	AUTHOR / SERIES	PUBLISHER / DISTRIBUTOR
Story of Big Bess Call, The	M	TL	250+	Bovetz, Marcie	Wright Group/McGraw Hill
Story of Books, The	O	I	250+	Sunshine	Wright Group/McGraw Hill
Story of Bunker's Cove	R	I	250+	Leveled Readers Language Support	Houghton Mifflin
Story of Chicken Licken	I	TL	250+	Ormerod, Jan	Lothrop
Story of Corn, The	H	I	171	Ready Readers	Pearson Learning Group
Story of Doña Chila, The	P	B	250+	Moore, Eva	Scholastic
Story of George Washington Carver, The	Q	B	250+	Moore, Eva	Bantam
Story of Geronimo, The	T	B	250+	Cornerstones of Freedom	Children's Press
Story of Harriet Tubman, The: Conductor of the Underground Railroad	S	B	250+	McMullan, Kate	Scholastic
Story of Harriet Tubman, The: Freedom Train	T	B	250+	Sterling, Dorothy	Bantam
Story of High Street, The	WB	RF	N/A	Goodall, John S.	Andre Deutsch
Story of Hungbu and Nolbu, The	K	TL	250+	Bookshop	Mondo
Story of Jackie Robinson, The: Bravest Man in Baseball	O	B	250+	Davidson, Margaret	Scholastic
Story of Jeans, The	M	I	250+	Discovery World	Rigby
Story of Juan Bobo, The	D	TL	58	Leveled Readers Language Support	Houghton Mifflin
Story of Laura Ingalls Wilder, Pioneer Girl, The	Q	B	250+	Stine, Megan	Bantam
Story of Muhammad Ali: Heavyweight Champion of the World, The	S	B	250+	Denenberg, Barry	Dell
Story of My Life, The	X	B	250+	Keller, Helen	Bantam
Story of My Life, The	P	B	250+	Leveled Readers Language Support	Houghton Mifflin
Story of Oskar Schindler, The	Z	B	2470	Leveled Readers	Houghton Mifflin
Story of Pluto, The	S	I	2306	Leveled Readers Science	Houghton Mifflin
Story of Ruby Bridges, The	O	B	250+	Coles, Robert	Scholastic
Story of Running Water, The	J	TL	287	Cambridge Reading	Pearson Learning Group
Story of Sacagawea, The	O	B	250+	Rosen Real Readers	Rosen Publishing Group
Story of Small Fry, The	P	I	250+	Action Packs	Rigby
Story of Sue, The: T Rex	X	I	2391	Independent Readers Science	Houghton Mifflin
Story of the Mayflower Compact, The	T	I	250+	Cornerstones of Freedom	Children's Press
Story of the Mexican Jumping Bean, The	M	TL	250+	Story Vines	Wright Group/McGraw Hill
Story of The Persian Gulf War, The	W	I	250+	Cornerstones of Freedom	Children's Press
Story of the Pony Express, The	P	I	250+	Windows on Literacy	National Geographic
Story of The Sinking of the Battleship Maine, The	W	I	250+	Cornerstones of Freedom	Children's Press
Story of The Surrender at Yorktown, The	V	I	250+	Cornerstones of Freedom	Children's Press
Story of the White House, The	S	I	250+	Waters, Kate	Scholastic
Story of The Women's Movement, The	V	I	250+	Cornerstones of Freedom	Children's Press
Story of Thomas Alva Edison, Inventor, The	R	B	250+	Davidson, Margaret	Scholastic
Story of Walt Disney, Maker of Magical Worlds, The	O	B	250+	Selden, Bernice	Bantam
Story of Waltzing Matilda, The	V	I	2872	Independent Readers Social Studies	Houghton Mifflin
Story of William Tell, The	M	TL	250+	PM Story Books-Silver	Rigby
Story of You, The	M	I	482	Sunshine	Wright Group/McGraw Hill
Story Sticks	F	I	58	Instant Readers	Harcourt School Publishers
Story Teller's Story, A	O	B	250+	Martin, Rafe	Richard C. Owen
Story Time	C	RF	32	Ready Readers	Pearson Learning Group
Story, a Story, A: An African Tale	M	TL	250+	Haley, Gail E.	Aladdin
Storytellers	L	I	506	Storyteller Nonfiction	Wright Group/McGraw Hill
Storyteller's Beads, The	Y	RF	250+	Kurtz, Jane	Harcourt Trade

* Collection of short stories

TITLE	LEVEL	GENRE	WORD COUNT	AUTHOR / SERIES	PUBLISHER / DISTRIBUTOR
Storytelling Around the World	P	I	573	Vocabulary Readers	Houghton Mifflin
Stowaway	W	HF	250+	Hesse, Karen	Simon & Schuster
Straight From the Horses Mouth	P	I	250+	Sunshine	Wright Group/McGraw Hill
Straight Line Wonder, The	J	F	250+	Bookshop	Mondo
Strange Bird, A	P	F	1024	Leveled Readers	Houghton Mifflin
*Strange Clues and Other Cases, The	O	RF	250+	Simon, Seymour	Avon
Strange Creatures	N	SF	250+	Cartwright, Pauline	Pacific Learning
Strange Day in Mayville, A	L	TL	250+	Leveled Readers Language Support	Houghton Mifflin
Strange Jobs	Q	I	250+	Sunshine	Wright Group/McGraw Hill
Strange Life of Undersea Vents, The	W	I	2522	Leveled Readers	Houghton Mifflin
Strange Meetings	Q	F	250+	Literacy 2000	Rigby
*Strange Museum and Other Cases, The	O	RF	250+	Simon, Seymour	Avon
Strange Plants	O	I	250+	Windows on Literacy	National Geographic
Strange Plants	J	I	433	Leveled Readers Science	Houghton Mifflin
Strange Plants	E	I	30	Books for Young Learners	Richard C. Owen
Strange Rocks	U	I	2135	Leveled Readers Science	Houghton Mifflin
Strange Shoe, The	L	TL	250+	PM Tales and Plays-Silver	Rigby
Strange Things	L	RF	289	Books for Young Learners	Richard C. Owen
Stranger at the Window	U	RF	250+	Alcock, Vivien	Houghton Mifflin
Stranger Came Ashore, A	U	F	250+	Hunter, Mollie	HarperTrophy
Stranger's Gift, The	L	TL	250+	Literacy 2000	Rigby
Strawberries	C	I	37	Little Books for Early Readers	University of Maine
Strawberry Hill	Y	RF	250+	LaFaye, A.	Simon & Schuster
Strawberry Jam	E	RF	77	Oxford Reading Tree	Oxford University Press
Strawberry Picking	J	RF	250+	Cambridge Reading	Pearson Learning Group
Strawberry Pop And Soda Crackers	K	RF	396	Little Celebrations	Pearson Learning Group
Stray, The	R	RF	250+	King-Smith, Dick	Alfred A. Knopf
Streak, The	N	RF	250+	Kroll, Stephen	Avon Camelot
Stream, The	F	F	43	Voyages	SRA/McGraw Hill
Stream, The	C	RF	24	Science	Outside the Box
Street Action	O	I	250+	Wildcats	Wright Group/McGraw Hill
Street Musicians	J	RF	283	Sunshine	Wright Group/McGraw Hill
Street Skating: Grinds and Grabs	Q	I	250+	Skateboarding	Capstone Press
Streets of Gold	U	HF	1933	Leveled Readers	Houghton Mifflin
Strider	R	RF	250+	Cleary, Beverly	HarperCollins
Strike	O	I	250+	Pacific Literacy	Pacific Learning
Strike Fighters: The F/A-18E/F Super Hornets	R	I	250+	War Planes	Red Brick Learning
Strike Four!	H	RF	250+	Ziefert, Harriet	Puffin Books
Strike Me Down with a Stringbean	L	F	404	Read Alongs	Rigby
Strike Out!	M	RF	250+	Howard, Tristan	Scholastic
String Food	K	I	250+	Home Connection Collection	Rigby
String Performers	J	I	250+	Home Connection Collection	Rigby
Strings	C	I	53	Storyteller-First Snow	Wright Group/McGraw Hill
Strings, Ropes, and Cables	I	I	250+	Home Connection Collection	Rigby
Striped Ice Cream	N	RF	250+	Lexau, Joan M.	Scholastic
Stripes	LB	I	28	Twig	Wright Group/McGraw Hill
Strongest Animal, The	F	RF	58	Books for Young Learners	Richard C. Owen
Strongest One of All, The	H	TL	222	Instant Readers	Harcourt School Publishers
Stuart Little	R	F	250+	White, E. B.	HarperTrophy
Stubborn Goat, The	I	F	212	Alphakids	Sundance
Stuck at the End of the Ice Age	Z	I	1877	Leveled Readers	Houghton Mifflin
Stuck in Neutral	Z	RF	250+	Trueman, Terry	HarperCollins

TITLE	LEVEL	GENRE	WORD COUNT	AUTHOR / SERIES	PUBLISHER / DISTRIBUTOR
Stuck in the Ice	M	I	250+	Leveled Readers Language Support	Houghton Mifflin
Stuck in the Muck	E	F	139	Spinelle, Nancy Louise	Kaeden Books
Stuck in the Mud	E	RF	120	Lighthouse	Rigby
Stuck in the Tar Pits	W	I	250+	Independent Readers Science	Houghton Mifflin
Stuck on an Island	H	RF	181	Sunshine	Wright Group/McGraw Hill
Studying a Glacier	M	I	501	Leveled Readers Science	Houghton Mifflin
Studying the Past	T	I	512	Vocabulary Readers	Houghton Mifflin
Stump Hill	K	RF	627	Early Connections	Benchmark Education
Stumpy's Secret	P	RF	250+	Hager, Mandy	Pacific Learning
Stuyvesant, Peter: New Amsterdam and the Origins of New York	W	B	250+	Power Plus	Rosen Publishing Group
Sub, The	P	RF	250+	Peterson, P. J.	Puffin Books
Submarines	T	I	250+	Land and Sea	Capstone Press
Subtle Knife, The	Z	F	250+	Pullman, Philip	Ballantine Books
Subtraction Fun	K	I	250+	Yellow Umbrella Books	Capstone Press
Sue Likes Blue	G	RF	131	Start to Read	School Zone
Sugar Bush, The	K	I	250+	Greetings	Rigby
Sugar Cakes Cyril	M	RF	4022	Gershator, Phillis	Mondo
Sugar Snow	J	HF	250+	Wilder, Laura Ingalls	HarperCollins
Sugaring Season (Making Maple Syrup)	S	I	250+	Burns, Diane	Carolrhoda Books
Sugaring Time	S	I	250+	Lasky, Kathryn	Macmillan
Suki and the Case of the Lost Bunnies	K	RF	250+	Ready Readers	Pearson Learning Group
Sulky Simon	J	RF	246	Windmill Books	Rigby
Summer	I	I	178	Pebble Books	Capstone Press
Summer	E	I	73	Sunshine	Wright Group/McGraw Hill
Summer	B	RF	45	Leveled Readers Language Support	Houghton Mifflin
Summer at Cove Lake	G	RF	288	Ready Readers	Pearson Learning Group
Summer Camp	J	RF	182	City Kids	Rigby
Summer Day, A	C	I	74	Leveled Readers	Houghton Mifflin
Summer Fun	J	I	261	Spyglass Books	Compass Point Books
Summer Fun	E	RF	30	Literacy 2000	Rigby
Summer I Shrank My Grandmother, The	Q	F	250+	Woodruff, Elvira	Bantam
Summer in the South, A	Q	F	250+	Marshall, James	Houghton Mifflin
*Summer Life, A	Z	RF	250+	Soto, Gary	Bantam
Summer Mail	W	RF	3361	Leveled Readers	Houghton Mifflin
Summer of My German Soldier	Z	HF	250+	Greene, Bette	Dell
Summer of the Great-Grandmother, The	Z	B	250+	L'Engle, Madeleine	HarperCollins
Summer of the Swans, The	U	RF	250+	Byars, Betsy	Penguin Group
Summer Rays	V	RF	3077	Leveled Readers	Houghton Mifflin
Summer Sands	M	RF	839	Evangeline Nicholas Collection	Wright Group/McGraw Hill
Summer Switch	R	F	250+	Rodgers, Mary	HarperTrophy
Summer to Die, A	T	RF	250+	Lowry, Lois	Dell
Summer Trips	I	I	272	Visions	Wright Group/McGraw Hill
Summer Wheels	O	B	250+	Bunting, Eve	Harcourt Trade
Summertime in the Big Woods	J	HF	250+	Wilder, Laura Ingalls	HarperCollins
Sun	S	I	250+	Our Solar System	Compass Point Books
Sun	O	I	250+	Vogt, Gregory L.	Red Brick Learning
Sun & Spoon	R	RF	250+	Henkes, Kevin	Penguin Group
Sun Flower, A	B	RF	42	Foundations	Wright Group/McGraw Hill
Sun Power	P	I	250+	Rigby Focus	Rigby
Sun Power	G	I	79	Windows on Literacy	National Geographic
Sun Shines on Me, The	B	I	34	Science	Outside the Box

* Collection of short stories

TITLE	LEVEL	GENRE	WORD COUNT	AUTHOR / SERIES	PUBLISHER / DISTRIBUTOR
Sun Smile	I	F	250+	Story Box	Wright Group/McGraw Hill
Sun Up, Sun Down	H	I	148	Independent Readers Science	Houghton Mifflin
Sun, a Flower, A	LB	I	42	Foundations	Wright Group/McGraw Hill
Sun, Moon, Earth	E	I	53	Leveled Readers Science	Houghton Mifflin
Sun, Rain, and Snow	B	I	72	Leveled Readers Emergent	Houghton Mifflin
Sun, The	N	I	250+	Windows on Literacy	National Geographic
Sun, The	N	I	573	Leveled Readers Science	Houghton Mifflin
Sun, The	E	I	42	Discovery Links	Newbridge
Sun, The	J	I	219	Wonder World	Wright Group/McGraw Hill
Sun, The	B	I	32	Rigby Focus	Rigby
Sun, The	N	I	250+	Literacy 2000	Rigby
Sun, The	K	I	42	Pebble Books	Red Brick Learning
Sun, the Wind & Tashira, The	J	TL	371	Folk Tales	Mondo
Sun, the Wind, and the Rain, The	G	RF	170	PM Plus Nonfiction	Rigby
Sunburn	B	I	48	Prokopchak, Ann	Kaeden Books
Sunburn	J	RF	176	City Kids	Rigby
Sunday Horse	N	RF	250+	Literacy Tree	Rigby
Sunflower	N	I	250+	Life Cycles	Creative Teaching Press
Sunflower Seeds	D	I	48	Story Box	Wright Group/McGraw Hill
Sunflower That Went Flop, The	K	F	637	Story Box	Wright Group/McGraw Hill
Sunflowers	E	I	33	Books for Young Learners	Richard C. Owen
Sunflowers	D	I	35	Pebble Books	Capstone Press
Sunken Treasure	P	I	250+	Gibbons, Gail	Houghton Mifflin
Sunny Day, A	E	I	65	Pebble Books	Capstone Press
Sunny-Side Up	M	RF	250+	Giff, Patricia Reilly	Bantam
Sunrise	C	F	46	Literacy 2000	Rigby
Sun's Family of Planets, The	L	I	250+	Read-About Science	Children's Press
Sun's Magic, The	B	I	28	Seedlings	Continental Press
Sun's Strength, The: An Ancient Chinese Myth	W	TL	1972	Leveled Readers	Houghton Mifflin
Sunset of the Sabertooth	M	F	250+	Osborne, Mary Pope	Random House
Sunset Pond, The	I	RF	250+	Appleton-Smith, Laura	Flyleaf Publishing
Sunshine	WB	RF	N/A	Ormerod, Jan	Lothrop, Lee & Shepard
Sunshine	L	I	307	Pebble Books	Capstone Press
Sunshine Street	H	RF	110	Sunshine	Wright Group/McGraw Hill
Sunshine, Moonshine	E	RF	128	Armstrong, Jennifer	Random House
Sunshine, the Black Cat	G	RF	143	Carousel Readers	Pearson Learning Group
Sunshine: A Book About Sunlight	M	I	250+	Amazing Science	Picture Window Books
Super Amos	R	RF	250+	Paulsen, Gary	Bantam
Super Animals	F	I	149	Leveled Readers Science	Houghton Mifflin
Super Duper Sandwich, The	I	F	202	Books for Young Learners	Richard C. Owen
Super Hero	B	RF	33	Sunshine	Wright Group/McGraw Hill
Super Parrot	J	RF	250+	Real Reading	Steck-Vaughn
Super Pig's Adventures	E	F	133	New Way Blue	Steck-Vaughn
Super Sandwich	E	I	72	Little Red Readers	Sundance
Super Shopping	D	RF	41	Rigby Literacy	Rigby
Super Smile Shop, The	H	F	254	Story Basket	Wright Group/McGraw Hill
Super Space Stations	M	I	250+	Rosen Real Readers	Rosen Publishing Group
Super Supermarket Plan, The	J	RF	250+	Home Connection Collection	Rigby
Super Terrific Me!	D	RF	64	Early Learning Modules	Steck-Vaughn
Superbikes	T	I	250+	The World's Fastest	Red Brick Learning
Supercharged Infield	M	RF	250+	Christopher, Matt	Little, Brown & Co.
Super-Duper Sunflower Seeds, The	I	F	389	Book Bank	Wright Group/McGraw Hill
Superfudge	Q	RF	250+	Blume, Judy	Bantam
Superkids	H	F	165	Sunshine	Wright Group/McGraw Hill

* Collection of short stories

TITLE	LEVEL	GENRE	WORD COUNT	AUTHOR / SERIES	PUBLISHER / DISTRIBUTOR
Supermarket Chase, The	K	RF	438	Sunshine	Wright Group/McGraw Hill
Supermarket Managers	M	I	250+	Community Helpers	Red Brick Learning
Supermarket, The	K	I	255	Pebble Books	Capstone Press
Supernova	N	RF	250+	PM Ruby	Rigby
Superstars	I	F	252	Sunshine	Wright Group/McGraw Hill
Super-tuned!	N	RF	250+	PM Emerald	Rigby
Supper for Cal	H	RF	189	Leveled Readers	Houghton Mifflin
Supreme Court of the United States, The	W	I	250+	American Civics	Red Brick Learning
Supreme Court, The	N	I	250+	A True Book	Children's Press
Surf Carnival, The	K	RF	434	PM Story Books	Rigby
Surfer, The	D	RF	40	Wonder World	Wright Group/McGraw Hill
Surfing the Information Highway	H	I	137	Wonder World	Wright Group/McGraw Hill
Surf's Up	P	RF	250+	Wildcats	Wright Group/McGraw Hill
Surprise Box, The	I	RF	250+	Voyages	SRA/McGraw Hill
Surprise Cake	C	F	32	Literacy 2000	Rigby
Surprise Dinner, The	L	RF	680	PM Gold	Rigby
Surprise Feast, The	O	I	250+	Rigby Focus	Rigby
Surprise for Mom	E	RF	101	Urmston, Kathleen; Evans, Karen	Kaeden Books
Surprise for Zack, A	I	RF	250+	PM Plus Story Books	Rigby
Surprise from the Sky	I	F	295	Windmill Books	Rigby
Surprise Invitation, The	J	RF	250+	PM Plus Story Books	Rigby
Surprise Party	K	I	333	Hutchins, Pat	Macmillan
Surprise Party, The	I	F	192	New Way Green	Steck-Vaughn
Surprise Party, The	J	RF	250+	Prager, Annabelle	Random House
Surprise Pet, A	C	F	54	Leveled Readers Language Support	Houghton Mifflin
Surprise Snow, The	K	RF	545	Leveled Readers	Houghton Mifflin
*Surprise Visit, The	G	F	250+	New Way Blue	Steck-Vaughn
Surprise!	I	RF	168	Little Celebrations	Pearson Learning Group
Surprise!	D	F	28	Story Steps	Rigby
Surprise!	D	RF	28	My First Reader	Grolier Press
Surprise, The	H	F	124	Literacy 2000	Rigby
Surprise, The	A	F	14	Story Box	Wright Group/McGraw Hill
Surprising Myself	O	B	250+	Fritz, Jean	Richard C. Owen
Surprising Swimmers: Nature's Most Amazing Animals	R	I	250+	Fredericks, Anthony D.	NorthWord Press
Surrender at Appomattox, The	U	I	1530	Leveled Readers Social Studies	Houghton Mifflin
Surrender at Yorktown	S	I	600	Leveled Readers Social Studies	Houghton Mifflin
Surrender at Yorktown	P	I	250+	Leveled Readers	Houghton Mifflin
Survival Animal Adaptations	V	I	250+	iOpeners	Pearson Learning Group
Survival in the Storm	X	HF	250+	Janke, Katelan	Scholastic
Survival of Fish, The	M	I	946	Science	Wright Group/McGraw Hill
Survival!: Cave In	S	HF	250+	Duey, Kathleen; Bale, Karen A.	Simon & Schuster
Survival!: Fire	R	HF	250+	Duey, Kathleen; Bale, Karen A.	Aladdin
Survive!	Q	RF	250+	Wildcats	Wright Group/McGraw Hill
Survivors in the Frozen North	L	RF	250+	PM Plus Story Books	Rigby
Susan B. Anthony	N	B	237	Pebble Books	Capstone Press
Susan B. Anthony	P	B	250+	Davis, Lucile	Red Brick Learning
Susan B. Anthony, Fighter for Women's Rights	N	I	381	Independent Readers Social Studies	Houghton Mifflin
Susan B. Anthony: Champion of Women's Rights	R	B	250+	Monsell, Helen Albee	Simon & Schuster
Susanna of the Alamo	T	B	250+	Jakes, John	Language for Learning Assoc.

TITLE	LEVEL	GENRE	WORD COUNT	AUTHOR / SERIES	PUBLISHER / DISTRIBUTOR
Susie Goes Shopping	F	F	194	First Start	Troll Associates
Swamp Hen	F	I	59	Pacific Literacy	Pacific Learning
Swamp Monsters	K	F	250+	Christian, Mary Blount	Puffin Books
Swamp of the Hideous Zombies	M	F	250+	Hayes, Geoffrey	Random House
Swan Family, The	F	RF	172	PM Plus Story Books	Rigby
Swans	D	I	53	Joy Readers	Pearson Learning Group
Swat it!	D	F	46	Bauer, Roger	Kaeden Books
SWAT Teams	S	I	250+	Law Enforcement	Capstone Press
Sweet Clara and the Freedom Quilt	S	HF	250+	Hopkinson, Deborah	Scholastic
Sweet Memories Still	Q	RF	250+	Kinsey-Warnock, Natalie	Bantam
Sweet or Sour?	I	I	177	Sunshine	Wright Group/McGraw Hill
Sweet Potato Pie	E	RF	72	Rockwell, Anne	Random House
Sweet to Eat	I	RF	105	Pacific Literacy	Pacific Learning
Sweetest Present, The	E	F	80	Leveled Readers	Houghton Mifflin
Swiftly Tilting Planet, A	V	F	250+	L'Engle, Madeleine	Bantam
Swimming	C	RF	65	Carousel Readers	Pearson Learning Group
Swimming Across the Pool	J	RF	250+	PM Plus Story Books	Rigby
Swimming for Fun	S	I	250+	Sports for Fun	Compass Point Books
Swimming Lessons	W	RF	2005	Leveled Readers	Houghton Mifflin
Swimming Lessons	I	I	200	Storyteller Nonfiction	Wright Group/McGraw Hill
Swimming Pool, The	C	RF	29	Visions	Wright Group/McGraw Hill
Swimming With a Dragon	H	RF	230	PM Plus Story Books	Rigby
Swing	A	RF	18	Story Box	Wright Group/McGraw Hill
Swing, Swing, Swing	C	F	93	Tuchman, G.; Dieterichs, S.	Scholastic
Switcharound	R	RF	250+	Lowry, Lois	Random House
Switzerland	O	I	250+	Countries of the World	Red Brick Learning
Swoop!	I	RF	250+	PM Plus Story Books	Rigby
Sword in the Stone, The	J	TL	250+	Maccarone, Grace	Scholastic
*Sword of the Samurai: Adventure Stories From Japan	S	HF	250+	Kimmel, Eric A.	HarperCollins
Sydney - Where Biscuits Go Surfing	R	RF	250+	Coy, Michael	Scholastic
Sylvia Earle, First Lady of the Sea	G	B	98	Independent Readers Science	Houghton Mifflin
Symmetry in Our World	O	I	250+	Early Connections	Benchmark Education
T. J.'s Tree	G	RF	77	Literacy 2000	Rigby
Tabby	WB	RF	N/A	Aliki	HarperCollins
Tabby in the Tree	F	RF	200	PM Story Books	Rigby
Table for Two	L	TL	250+	Little Celebrations	Pearson Learning Group
Tadpole Diary	O	I	250+	Literacy Tree	Rigby
Tails	I	I	170	Sunshine	Wright Group/McGraw Hill
Tails	E	I	59	Discovery Links	Newbridge
Tails	D	I	52	Wonder World	Wright Group/McGraw Hill
Tails	B	I	42	Book Bank	Wright Group/McGraw Hill
Tails	E	I	59	Bookshop	Mondo
Tails	F	I	47	Literacy 2000	Rigby
Tails and Claws	C	I	65	Wonder World	Wright Group/McGraw Hill
Tails Can Tell	I	I	346	Wonder World	Wright Group/McGraw Hill
Take a Bite	C	F	19	Little Celebrations	Pearson Learning Group
Take a Bow, Jody	D	RF	78	Eaton, Audrey; Kennedy, Jane	Continental Press
Take a Chance	X	RF	2464	Leveled Readers	Houghton Mifflin
Take a Guess	C	F	45	Little Celebrations	Pearson Learning Group
Take a Guess: A Look At Estimation	K	I	164	Spyglass Books	Compass Point Books
Take A Look	N	I	250+	Wildcats	Wright Group/McGraw Hill
Take a Look at My Family	F	RF	155	Phonics and Friends	Hampton-Brown
Take Care of Our Earth	M	I	250+	Pair-It Books	Steck-Vaughn

TITLE	LEVEL	GENRE	WORD COUNT	AUTHOR / SERIES	PUBLISHER / DISTRIBUTOR
Take the Subway	F	I	111	Vocabulary Readers	Houghton Mifflin
Takeaway!	G	F	40	Book Bus	Creative Edge
Taken by the Wind	M	RF	250+	Wahman, Joe	Wright Group/McGraw Hill
Taking Care of a Hamster	D	I	65	Leveled Readers Science	Houghton Mifflin
Taking Care of Baby	G	I	159	Discovery Links	Newbridge
Taking Care of Farm Animals	WB	I	N/A	Windows on Literacy	National Geographic
Taking Care of Our World	H	I	137	Rosen Real Readers	Rosen Publishing Group
Taking Care of Our World	E	I	137	Visions	Wright Group/McGraw Hill
Taking Care of Ourselves	J	I	250+	PM Plus Nonfiction	Rigby
Taking Care of Pets	B	I	55	Yellow Umbrella Books	Red Brick Learning
Taking Care of Rosie	E	RF	61	Salem, Lynn; Stewart, Josie	Continental Press
Taking Care of Terrific	S	RF	250+	Lowry, Lois	Dell
Taking Care of Yoki	R	RF	250+	Campbell, Barbara	HarperTrophy
Taking Jason to Grandma's	F	RF	118	Book Bank	Wright Group/McGraw Hill
Taking Liberty	X	HF	250+	Rinaldi, Ann	Simon & Schuster
Taking Our Photo	E	RF	132	Voyages	SRA/McGraw Hill
Taking Photographs	M	I	788	Early Connections	Benchmark Education
Taking Pictures	E	RF	137	Alphakids	Sundance
Taking Sides	S	RF	250+	Soto, Gary	Harcourt Trade
Taking to the Air	Q	I	250+	Literacy Tree	Rigby
Taking You Places: Book About Bus Drivers, A	H	I	127	Community Workers	Picture Window Books
Tale of Cowboy	A	RF	31	Reading Unlimited	Pearson Learning Group
Tale of Cowboy Roy, The	H	F	185	Ready Readers	Pearson Learning Group
Tale of Despereaux, The	U	F	250+	DiCamillo, Kate	Candlewick Press
Tale of Peter Rabbit, The	L	TL	250+	Potter, Beatrix	Scholastic
Tale of the Christmas Mouse	H	F	97	First Start	Troll Associates
Tale of the Golden Goose, The	L	TL	250+	Behr, Alexandra	Hampton-Brown
Tale of the Turnip, The	I	TL	250+	PM Traditional Tales-Orange	Rigby
Tale of Veruschka Babuschka, The	M	TL	250+	Literacy 2000	Rigby
Talent Contest, The	K	RF	250+	PM Story Books-Silver	Rigby
Talent Night at School	F	RF	102	Little Red Readers	Sundance
Talented Alex	O	RF	772	Leveled Readers	Houghton Mifflin
*Tales from the Homeplace: Adventures of a Texas Farm Girl	S	RF	250+	Burandt, Harriet; Dale, Shelley	Bantam
*Tales from the Underground Railroad	S	HF	250+	Connell, Kate	Steck-Vaughn
Tales Mummies Tell	W	I	250+	Lauber, Patricia	Scholastic
Tales of a Fourth Grade Nothing	Q	RF	250+	Blume, Judy	Bantam
*Tales of Amanda Pig	L	F	250+	Van Leeuwen, Jean	Puffin Books
Tales of Olga da Polga, The	P	F	250+	Bond, Michael	Houghton Mifflin
*Tales of Oliver Pig	L	F	250+	Van Leeuwen, Jean	Puffin Books
Tales of Real Escape	X	B	250+	Dowswell, Paul	Scholastic
Talk About a Family	O	RF	250+	Greenfield, Eloise	HarperTrophy
Talk! Talk! Talk!	N	I	50	Little Celebrations	Pearson Learning Group
Talk, Talk, Talk	C	RF	56	Literacy 2000	Rigby
Talking Earth, The	U	RF	250+	George, Jean Craighead	HarperTrophy
Talking to Faith Ringgold	S	B	250+	Ringgold, Faith; Freeman, Linda; Roucher, Nancy	Crown
Talking to Our Friends	F	I	138	Rigby Focus	Rigby
Talking Yam, The	I	F	340	Little Readers	Houghton Mifflin
Tall Stories About Snakes	G	I	141	Voyages	SRA/McGraw Hill
*Tall Tale and Other Cases, The	O	RF	250+	Simon, Seymour	Avon
Tall Tale of John Henry, The	N	TL	250+	Neufeld, David	Scholastic
Tall Tale to Tell, A	O	I	860	Independent Readers Social Studies	Houghton Mifflin

* Collection of short stories

TITLE	LEVEL	GENRE	WORD COUNT	AUTHOR / SERIES	PUBLISHER / DISTRIBUTOR
Tall Tales	O	TL	615	Vocabulary Readers	Houghton Mifflin
Tall Tales	O	RF	250+	PM Emerald	Rigby
Tall Tales	I	RF	139	Literacy Tree	Rigby
Tall Things	D	I	83	PM Nonfiction-Red	Rigby
Tall Tony	K	RF	383	Leveled Readers	Houghton Mifflin
Taller and Smaller	D	F	29	Sun Sprouts	ETA/Cuisenaire
Taller Than Molly	C	F	43	Harry's Math Books	Outside the Box
Tallest Boy in the Class, The	J	RF	396	Leveled Readers Language Support	Houghton Mifflin
Tallest Sunflower, The	I	I	250+	Counters & Seekers	Steck-Vaughn
Tame and Wild	L	I	306	Spyglass Books	Compass Point Books
Tamika and the Wisdom Rings	O	RF	250+	Yarbrough, Camille	Random House
Tangerine	U	RF	250+	Bloor, Edward	Scholastic
Tangled Threads: A Hmong Girl's Story	Z	RF	250+	Shea, Pegi Deitz	Clarion
Tania's Tooth	I	RF	131	Sunshine	Wright Group/McGraw Hill
Tanya On Track	U	RF	1978	Leveled Readers	Houghton Mifflin
Tar Beach	P	HF	250+	Ringgold, Faith	Crown
Tarantula	K	I	144	Alphakids	Sundance
Tarantula in My Purse, The	U	B	250+	George, Jean Craighead	HarperCollins
Tarantulas	K	I	97	Pebble Books	Red Brick Learning
Tarantulas are Spiders	F	I	39	Bookshop	Mondo
Tasmanian Devils	R	I	250+	Morris, Rod	Pacific Learning
Tasmanian Devils	M	I	250+	PM Animal Facts: Gold	Rigby
Taste of America	T	I	250+	iOpeners	Pearson Learning Group
Taste of Blackberries, A	S	RF	250+	Smith, Doris Buchanan	Scholastic
Taste of Salt: The Story of Modern Haiti	W	I	250+	Temple, Frances	HarperTrophy
Taste Sensation	E	I	115	Visions	Wright Group/McGraw Hill
Tasting	I	I	141	Pebble Books	Red Brick Learning
Tasty Bug, A	D	I	50	Little Celebrations	Pearson Learning Group
Tattercoat and the Magical Flute, A Cinderella Tale from England	M	TL	692	Leveled Readers Language Support	Houghton Mifflin
Tattercoat, A Cinderella Tale from England	N	TL	250+	Leveled Readers	Houghton Mifflin
Taxi, The	C	F	45	Joy Readers	Pearson Learning Group
T-Ball	D	RF	35	Visions	Wright Group/McGraw Hill
Tchin the Storyteller	N	B	269	Vocabulary Readers	Houghton Mifflin
Tea	K	I	267	Wonder World	Wright Group/McGraw Hill
Tea Overboard! The Boston Tea Party	V	I	1753	Leveled Readers	Houghton Mifflin
Tea Party	C	RF	38	Carousel Readers	Pearson Learning Group
Tea Party, The	C	F	76	Storyteller-First Snow	Wright Group/McGraw Hill
Teach Us, Amelia Bedelia	L	F	250+	Parish, Peggy	Scholastic
Teacher Talk	H	RF	68	City Stories	Rigby
Teacher, The	G	I	155	PM Nonfiction-Blue	Rigby
Teachers	L	I	250+	Community Workers	Compass Point Books
Teachers	M	I	250+	Deedrick, Tami	Red Brick Learning
Teachers at Our School	I	RF	115	City Kids	Rigby
Teacher's Pet	O	RF	250+	Hurwitz, Johanna	Scholastic
Teacher's Pet	L	F	250+	Dicks, Terrance	Scholastic
Team of Two, A	P	I	566	Vocabulary Readers	Houghton Mifflin
Team Player, The	S	RF	1115	Leveled Readers	Houghton Mifflin
Team Players	Q	I	555	Vocabulary Readers	Houghton Mifflin
Team Sports	B	I	23	Twig	Wright Group/McGraw Hill
Teamwork	F	I	148	Yellow Umbrella Books	Capstone Press
Tears of a Tiger	Z	RF	250+	Draper, Sharon M.	Simon & Schuster
Teasing Dad	F	RF	158	PM Extensions-Blue	Rigby

* Collection of short stories

TITLE	LEVEL	GENRE	WORD COUNT	AUTHOR / SERIES	PUBLISHER / DISTRIBUTOR
Teasing Mom	H	RF	239	PM Plus Story Books	Rigby
Technology Today	J	I	166	Early Connections	Benchmark Education
Tecumseh	V	B	250+	Cornerstones of Freedom	Children's Press
Tecumseh: Shawnee Leader	T	B	250+	Let Freedom Ring	Capstone Press
Tedd & Huggly	C	F	47	Canizares, Susan; Berger, Samantha	Scholastic
Teddy Bear for Sale	G	F	152	Herman, Gail	Scholastic
Teddy Bear, Teddy Bear	E	F	38	Tiger Cub	Peguis
Teddy Bears	I	I	180	Purkis, Sallie	Nelson/Michaels Assoc.
Teddy Bears Cure a Cold	K	F	240	Gretz, Susanna	Scholastic
Teddy Bear's Picnic	D	F	66	PM Plus Story Books	Rigby
Ted's Letter	E	RF	76	Dominie Phonics Reader	Pearson Learning Group
Ted's Red Ball	G	F	131	Supersonics	Rigby
Ted's Red Sled	D	RF	69	Ready Readers	Pearson Learning Group
Tee-Ball	C	RF	53	Little Celebrations	Pearson Learning Group
Teeny Tiny	H	TL	250+	Rigby Literacy	Rigby
Teeny Tiny	I	TL	250+	Bennett, Jill	Putnam
Teeny Tiny Taste, A	H	RF	112	City Stories	Rigby
Teeny Tiny Tina	C	F	34	Literacy 2000	Rigby
Teeny Tiny Woman, The	J	TL	369	Seuling, Barbara	Scholastic
Teeny Tiny Woman, The	F	TL	250+	O'Connor, Jane	Random House
Teeny-Tiny Woman, The	H	TL	231	Ziefert, Harriet	Puffin Books
Teeter-Totter, The	C	TL	35	Joy Readers	Pearson Learning Group
Teeth	N	I	250+	Rigby Literacy	Rigby
Teeth	C	I	26	Wonder World	Wright Group/McGraw Hill
Teeth	K	I	470	Sunshine	Wright Group/McGraw Hill
Teeth	D	I	71	Story Box	Wright Group/McGraw Hill
Telephone, The: A Great Invention	J	I	165	Leveled Readers Social Studies	Houghton Mifflin
Telephones	O	I	250+	Let's See	Compass Point Books
Television	O	I	250+	Let's See	Compass Point Books
Television Drama	Q	RF	250+	Literacy 2000	Rigby
Television, The	Q	I	250+	Great Inventions	Capstone Press
Tell It to a Friend	K	I	250+	Home Connection Collection	Rigby
Tell Me A Story	J	RF	236	Voyages	SRA/McGraw Hill
Tell Me a Story	O	B	250+	London, Jonathan	Richard C. Owen
Tell Me a Story, Grandpa	L	RF	250+	Little Celebrations	Pearson Learning Group
Tell Me About Turtles	D	I	31	Rosen Real Readers	Rosen Publishing Group
Tell Me No Lies	Q	RF	250+	Ragged Island Mysteries	Wright Group/McGraw Hill
Tell Me Why Planes Have Wings	O	I	250+	Whiz Kids	Franklin Watts
Tell Them We Remember	Y	I	250+	Bachrach, Susan D.	Little, Brown & Co.
Telling Stories Through Art	N	I	250+	Reimer, Luther	Wright Group/McGraw Hill
Telling Time Through the Ages	Q	I	250+	Navigators Social Studies Series	Benchmark Education
Tell-tale	H	RF	250+	Story Box	Wright Group/McGraw Hill
Temperature	M	I	250+	First Facts	Capstone Press
Temperature: Heating Up and Cooling Down	M	I	250+	Amazing Science	Picture Window Books
Ten Apples Up on Top	J	F	250+	LaSieg, Theo	Random House
Ten Bears in My Bed	G	F	252	Mack, Stan	Pantheon
Ten Cats Have Hats: A Counting Book	E	F	89	Marzollo, Jean	Scholastic
Ten Crazy Caterpillars	C	F	40	Voyages	SRA/McGraw Hill
Ten Easy Tips for Staying Safe	L	I	250+	Rosen Real Readers	Rosen Publishing Group
Ten Happy Elephants	I	F	201	Sunshine	Wright Group/McGraw Hill
Ten Little Bears	G	F	211	Reading Unlimited	Pearson Learning Group
Ten Little Caterpillars	F	F	102	Literacy 2000	Rigby
Ten Little Garden Snails	H	F	101	PM Story Books	Rigby

* Collection of short stories

TITLE	LEVEL	GENRE	WORD COUNT	AUTHOR / SERIES	PUBLISHER / DISTRIBUTOR
Ten Little Men	E	F	38	Literacy 2000	Rigby
Ten Loopy Caterpillars	I	F	191	Jellybeans	Rigby
Ten Minutes Till Bedtime	LB	RF	16	Rathmann, Peggy	Putnam
Ten O'Clock Club, The	N	F	250+	York, Carol Beach	Scholastic
Ten Sleepy Sheep	G	F	65	Keller, Holly	Greenwillow
Ten Traveling Tigers	H	F	165	Little Readers	Houghton Mifflin
*Ten True Animal Rescues	O	I	250+	Betancourt, Jeanne	Scholastic
Ten Yellow Buses	H	RF	146	Twig	Wright Group/McGraw Hill
Ten, Nine, Eight	H	RF	59	Bang, Molly	Scholastic
Tenement Writer, The: An Immigrant's Story	T	I	250+	Sonder, Ben	Steck-Vaughn
Ten-Gallon Hat, The	K	F	250+	Voyages	SRA/McGraw Hill
Tennessee	R	I	250+	This Land Is Your Land	Compass Point Books
Tennessee Summer	R	RF	2198	Leveled Readers	Houghton Mifflin
Tennessee Tornado, The: Wilma Rudolph	T	B	2097	Leveled Readers	Houghton Mifflin
Ten-Second Race, The	F	F	102	Learn to Read	Creative Teaching Press
Tent, The	V	RF	250+	Paulsen, Gary	Bantam
Tents	I	RF	175	Reading Unlimited	Pearson Learning Group
Termites	I	RF	130	Books for Young Learners	Richard C. Owen
Termites	I	I	72	Pebble Books	Red Brick Learning
Terrible Armadillo	I	F	229	Jellybeans	Rigby
Terrible Fright, A	K	TL	291	Story Box	Wright Group/McGraw Hill
*Terrible Test Mark and Other Cases, The	O	RF	250+	Simon, Seymour	Avon
Terrible Tiger	G	F	124	Rigby Literacy	Rigby
*Terrible Tiger and Sleeping Beauty	L	TL	250+	New Way Literature	Steck-Vaughn
Terrible Tiger, The	G	F	140	Sunshine	Wright Group/McGraw Hill
Terrible Twos	E	RF	86	Tadpoles	Rigby
Terrific Shoes	C	RF	19	Ready Readers	Pearson Learning Group
Terrific Trees	K	I	250+	Rigby Literacy	Rigby
Terror In the Towers	O	B	250+	Kerson, Adrian	Random House
Tess and Paddy	J	RF	242	Sunshine	Wright Group/McGraw Hill
Tess and the Cat	D	RF	81	Sun Sprouts	ETA/Cuisenaire
Texas	S	I	250+	Land of Liberty	Red Brick Learning
Texas	Q	I	250+	One Nation	Capstone Press
Texas	R	I	250+	This Land Is Your Land	Compass Point Books
Thailand	O	I	250+	Thoennes, Kristin	Red Brick Learning
Thank You	J	I	250+	Ready to Read	Pearson Learning Group
Thank You!	D	I	41	Chessen, Betsey; Chanko, Pamela	Scholastic
Thank You, Amelia Bedelia	L	F	250+	Little Readers	Houghton Mifflin
Thank You, Jackie Robinson	P	B	250+	Cohen, Barbara	Scholastic
Thank You, Nicky!	F	F	119	Ziefert, Harriet	Penguin Group
Thank You, Sandra Cisneros	N	RF	250+	Leveled Readers	Houghton Mifflin
Thanks to Sandra Cisneros	O	RF	940	Leveled Readers Language Support	Houghton Mifflin
Thanksgiving	O	I	250+	Holidays and Festivals	Compass Point Books
Thanksgiving	J	I	95	Pebble Books	Capstone Press
Thanksgiving	P	I	250+	Let's See	Compass Point Books
Thanksgiving	E	I	95	Fiesta Holiday Series	Pearson Learning Group
Thanksgiving	B	F	40	First Stories	Pacific Learning
Thanksgiving	F	F	75	Urmston, Kathleen; Evans, Karen	Kaeden Books
Thanksgiving Day	L	I	132	National Holidays	Red Brick Learning
Thanksgiving: Why We Celebrate It the Way We Do	P	I	250+	Hintz, Martin & Kate	Red Brick Learning
Thao Kham, the Pebble Shooter	M	TL	250+	Story Vines	Wright Group/McGraw Hill
That Cat!	G	RF	146	Ready Readers	Pearson Learning Group

* Collection of short stories

TITLE	LEVEL	GENRE	WORD COUNT	AUTHOR / SERIES	PUBLISHER / DISTRIBUTOR
That Dog!	G	RF	213	Foundations	Wright Group/McGraw Hill
That Fat Hat	K	F	250+	Barkan, Joanne	Scholastic
That Fly	C	F	26	Ready Readers	Pearson Learning Group
That Looks Different!	K	I	227	Windows on Literacy	National Geographic
That Old House	K	F	250+	Rigby Literacy	Rigby
That Pig Can't Do a Thing	F	F	83	Ready Readers	Pearson Learning Group
That Wild Berries Should Grow	U	HF	250+	Whelan, Gloria	Books for Young Readers
*That's a Laugh: Four Funny Fables	M	TL	250+	Literacy 2000	Rigby
That's Dangerous	D	F	71	Voyages	SRA/McGraw Hill
That's Determination!	L	RF	250+	Rigby Literacy	Rigby
That's Fair, Bear	H	F	250+	Sun Sprouts	ETA/Cuisenaire
That's HOT!	L	I	250+	Spyglass Books	Compass Point Books
That's Mine	LB	RF	15	Rigby Literacy	Rigby
That's Not All	G	F	105	Start to Read	School Zone
That's Not My Hobby!	J	RF	250+	Rigby Literacy	Rigby
That's Not Our Dog	I	RF	250+	PM Plus Story Books	Rigby
That's Really Weird!	K	F	129	Read Alongs	Rigby
Theft in Time, A: Timedetectors II	V	HF	250+	Action Packs	Rigby
Then & Now	C	I	60	Berger, Samantha; Moreton, Daniel	Scholastic
Then Again, Maybe I Won't	T	RF	250+	Blume, Judy	Language for Learning Assoc.
Then and Now	J	I	250+	Discovery World	Rigby
Then and Now	H	I	250+	iOpeners	Pearson Learning Group
Then and Now	J	RF	250+	Early Connections	Benchmark Education
Theodore	D	F	35	Ray's Readers	Outside the Box
Theodore Roosevelt	U	B	250+	Profiles of the Presidents	Compass Point Books
Theodore Roosevelt	N	B	208	Pebble Books	Capstone Press
Theodore Roosevelt: Friend of Nature	P	B	756	Leveled Readers	Houghton Mifflin
Therapy Dogs to the Rescue	L	I	250+	Rigby Literacy	Rigby
There are Mice in Our School	I	RF	95	City Kids	Rigby
There Are No Polar Bears Down There	G	I	48	Voyages	SRA/McGraw Hill
There Are Spots On . . .	LB	I	14	Little Books for Early Readers	University of Maine
There Is a Planet	C	I	52	Sunshine	Wright Group/McGraw Hill
There Is a Town	D	RF	116	Heiman, Gail	Random House
There Is No Water	J	RF	250+	Home Connection Collection	Rigby
There Stood Our Dog	I	F	250+	Voyages	SRA/McGraw Hill
There Was a Crooked Man	E	F	40	Sunshine	Wright Group/McGraw Hill
There Was a Mouse	D	RF	77	Books for Young Learners	Richard C. Owen
There's A Boy In The Girls' Bathroom	Q	RF	250+	Sachar, Louis	Alfred A. Knopf
*There's a Carrot in My Ear and Other Noodle Tails	J	TL	250+	Schwartz, Alvin	HarperTrophy
There's a Dinosaur!	L	I	250+	Stone, Evelyn	Hampton-Brown
There's a Dog in the Yard	I	I	119	City Kids	Rigby
There's a Frog in My Sleeping Bag	R	RF	250+	Clymer, Susan	Scholastic
There's a Hamster in My Lunchbox	R	RF	250+	Clymer, Susan	Scholastic
There's a Hippopotamus Under My Bed	J	RF	250+	Thaler, Mike	Avon
There's a Monster in the Tree	E	F	250+	Learn to Read	Creative Teaching Press
There's a Mouse in the House	B	F	42	Bookshop	Mondo
There's a Nightmare in My Closet	I	F	153	Mayer, Mercer	Penguin Group
There's a Rainbow in the River	L	RF	250+	Home Connection Collection	Rigby
There's a Ship Outside My Window	O	RF	250+	PM Ruby	Rigby
There's a Tarantula in My Homework	R	RF	250+	Clymer, Susan	Scholastic
There's an Alligator Under My Bed	J	RF	250+	Mayer, Mercer	Penguin Group

* Collection of short stories

TITLE	LEVEL	GENRE	WORD COUNT	AUTHOR / SERIES	PUBLISHER / DISTRIBUTOR
There's an Owl in the Shower	Q	RF	250+	George, Jean Craighead	HarperCollins
There's No One Like Me!	D	I	80	Sunshine	Wright Group/McGraw Hill
There's No Place Like Home	R	I	250+	Hill, David	Pacific Learning
There's Something in My Attic	J	RF	258	Mayer, Mercer	Penguin Group
These Lands Are Ours: Tecumseh's Fight For the Old Northwest	T	B	250+	Connell, Kate	Steck-Vaughn
These Legs	C	I	42	Foundations	Wright Group/McGraw Hill
These Old Rags	M	RF	352	Evangeline Nicholas Collection	Wright Group/McGraw Hill
Theseus and the Minotaur	W	I	250+	World Mythology	Capstone Press
They All Ran Away	C	F	82	Lighthouse	Rigby
They Call Me . . .	D	I	31	The Candid Collection	Pearson Learning Group
They Came From Center Field	R	RF	250+	Gutman, Dan	Scholastic
They Changed the World	R	I	250+	iOpeners	Pearson Learning Group
*They Led The Way: 14 American Women	O	B	250+	Johnston, Johanna	Scholastic
They Shall Be Heard: Susan B. Anthony & Elizabeth Cady Stanton	T	B	250+	Connell, Kate	Steck-Vaughn
They Survived Mount St. Helens!	O	I	250+	Stine, Megan	Random House
They Worked Together	O	I	250+	iOpeners	Pearson Learning Group
*Thief in the Village, A	V	RF	250+	Berry, James	Puffin Books
Thief Lord, The	V	F	250+	Funke, Cornelia	Scholastic
Thief of Hearts	V	RF	250+	Yep, Laurence	HarperCollins
Thing in the Log, The	H	RF	81	Reading Unlimited	Pearson Learning Group
Things Birds Eat, The	C	I	38	Chessen, Betsey	Scholastic
Things Can Change	B	I	27	Leveled Readers Science	Houghton Mifflin
Things Change	M	I	569	Bourne, Phyllis Montenegro	Hampton-Brown
Things Don't Change Much	L	RF	250+	Home Connection Collection	Rigby
Things I Can Do	B	I	36	Little Readers	Houghton Mifflin
Things I Can Do	B	I	36	Little Red Readers	Sundance
Things I Do for Fun	B	I	36	Little Red Readers	Sundance
Things I Do with My Friends	B	I	35	Little Red Readers	Sundance
Things I Like	C	I	39	Little Readers	Houghton Mifflin
Things I Like	C	RF	42	Carousel Earlybirds	Pearson Learning Group
Things I Like	D	F	42	Browne, Anthony	Random House
Things I Like to Do	C	RF	58	Foundations	Wright Group/McGraw Hill
Things I Like to Do	C	RF	63	Carousel Earlybirds	Pearson Learning Group
Things I See	A	I	28	Leveled Readers Emergent	Houghton Mifflin
Things Not Seen	V	F	250+	Clements, Andrew	Scholastic
Things on Wheels	C	I	69	Little Red Readers	Sundance
Things People Do for Fun	H	I	124	Foundations	Wright Group/McGraw Hill
Things That Drag Behind	D	I	42	Teacher's Choice Series	Pearson Learning Group
Things That Go: A Traveling Alphabet	L	I	250+	Reit, Seymour	Bantam
Things That Help Me	C	I	18	Pacific Literacy	Pacific Learning
Things That Melt	G	I	84	Leveled Readers Science	Houghton Mifflin
Things That Protect You	D	RF	51	Foundations	Wright Group/McGraw Hill
Things to Read	LB	I	18	Little Books for Early Readers	University of Maine
Things to See in Maine	LB	I	14	Little Books for Early Readers	University of Maine
Things With Wings	J	I	267	Storyteller Nonfiction	Wright Group/McGraw Hill
Think Like a Scientist	Q	I	250+	Burke, Melissa Blackwell	Steck-Vaughn
Think, Think, Think: Learning About Your Brain	M	I	250+	Amazing Body	Picture Window Books
Thinking About Ants	L	I	250+	Bookshop	Mondo
Third Grade Bullies	N	RF	250+	Levy, Elizabeth	Hyperion
Third Grade Stars	P	RF	250+	Ransom, Candice	Troll Associates
Thirteen	R	RF	250+	Ransom, Candice	Scholastic
This and That	D	RF	22	Home Connection Collection	Rigby

* Collection of short stories

TITLE	LEVEL	GENRE	WORD COUNT	AUTHOR / SERIES	PUBLISHER / DISTRIBUTOR
This Can't Be Happening at Macdonald Hall	S	RF	250+	Korman, Gordon	Scholastic
This Farm	C	I	39	Yellow Umbrella Books	Red Brick Learning
This Food Grows Here	A	I	16	Windows on Literacy	National Geographic
This Game	B	I	63	Carousel Earlybirds	Pearson Learning Group
This Gecko	E	I	57	Twig	Wright Group/McGraw Hill
This Hat	D	RF	52	Little Celebrations	Pearson Learning Group
This Is an Island	D	RF	46	Windows on Literacy	National Geographic
This Is Lobstering	A	I	27	Little Books for Early Readers	University of Maine
This Is Me	E	RF	70	Rigby Literacy	Rigby
This Is Me	B	I	70	Sun Sprouts	ETA/Cuisenaire
This Is My Family	D	I	36	Read-More Books	Pearson Learning Group
This Is My Friend	C	RF	77	Foundations	Wright Group/McGraw Hill
This Is My Home	C	F	51	Joy Readers	Pearson Learning Group
This Is My House	L	I	250+	Dorros, Arthur	Scholastic
This Is My Street	I	RF	229	Windows on Literacy	National Geographic
This Is the Bear	I	F	211	Hayes, Sarah & Craig	Harper & Row
This is the House That Bjorn	I	RF	172	Tiger Cub	Peguis
This Is the Place for Me	I	F	250+	Cole, Joanna	Scholastic
This Is the Plate	D	RF	28	Little Celebrations	Pearson Learning Group
This is the Register	F	RF	81	Cambridge Reading	Pearson Learning Group
This Is the Seed	I	F	171	Little Celebrations	Pearson Learning Group
This Is the Seed	D	RF	115	Seedlings	Continental Press
This Is the Way	F	RF	200	Learn to Read	Creative Teaching Press
This is Water	B	I	24	Bookshop	Mondo
This Little Pig	D	F	43	Seedlings	Continental Press
This Little Seed	E	I	58	Rigby Focus	Rigby
This Mouth	D	I	64	Wonder World	Wright Group/McGraw Hill
This Old Car	H	RF	79	Voyages	SRA/McGraw Hill
This One Can Run	B	I	34	Science	Outside the Box
This Piece or That Piece?	E	F	88	Leveled Readers	Houghton Mifflin
This Place is Dry	R	I	250+	Cobb, Vicki	Walker & Company
This Place is Wet	R	I	250+	Cobb, Vicki	Walker & Company
This Room Is a Mess!	I	RF	250+	Ready Readers	Pearson Learning Group
This Tail Belongs to . . .	B	I	24	Science	Outside the Box
This Tall	B	RF	41	Foundations	Wright Group/McGraw Hill
Thomas Alva Edison: Great Inventor	Q	B	250+	Levinson, Nancy Smiler	Scholastic
Thomas Edison	K	I	145	Windows on Literacy	National Geographic
Thomas Edison	P	B	250+	Linder, Greg	Red Brick Learning
Thomas Edison and the Light Bulb	Q	I	619	Independent Readers Science	Houghton Mifflin
Thomas Had a Temper	F	RF	139	Alphakids	Sundance
Thomas Jefferson	N	I	157	Independent Readers Social Studies	Houghton Mifflin
Thomas Jefferson	U	B	250+	Profiles of the Presidents	Compass Point Books
Thomas Jefferson: Author, Inventor, President	N	B	250+	Rookie Biographies	Children's Press
Thomas Jefferson: Man with a Vision	U	B	250+	Crisman, Ruth	Scholastic
Those Amazingly Useful Ears	O	I	250+	Frederick, Shirley	Hampton-Brown
Those Tricky Animals	M	I	250+	Literacy Tree	Rigby
Thoughts, Pictures, and Words	O	B	250+	Kuskin, Karla	Richard C. Owen
Three Bears, The	D	F	101	Lighthouse	Rigby
Three Bears, The	G	TL	344	Folk Tales	Pioneer Valley
Three Bears, The	K	TL	873	Galdone, Paul	Clarion
Three Bears, The	I	TL	250+	Tiger Cub	Peguis
Three Billy Goats Gruff	I	TL	250+	Sunshine	Wright Group/McGraw Hill
Three Billy Goats Gruff	I	TL	536	Traditional Tales	Pearson Learning Group

TITLE	LEVEL	GENRE	WORD COUNT	AUTHOR / SERIES	PUBLISHER / DISTRIBUTOR
Three Billy Goats Gruff, The	I	F	250+	Southgate, Vera	Ladybird Books
Three Billy Goats Gruff, The	F	TL	250+	Folk Tales	Pioneer Valley
Three Billy Goats Gruff, The	G	TL	140	Little Readers	Houghton Mifflin
Three Billy Goats Gruff, The	I	TL	450	PM Traditional Tales-Orange	Rigby
Three Billy Goats Gruff, The	K	TL	478	Stevens, Janet	Harcourt School Publishers
Three Billy Goats Gruff, The	K	TL	250+	Asbjornsen, P. C.; Moe, J. E.	Harcourt School Publishers
Three Billy Goats Gruff, The	H	TL	250+	New Way Green	Steck-Vaughn
Three Billy Goats Gruff, The	I	TL	250+	Literacy Tree	Rigby
Three Billy Goats Gruff, The	I	TL	549	Brown, Marcia	Harcourt School Publishers
Three Blind Mice Mystery, The	L	F	250+	Krensky, Stephen	Bantam
*Three By the Sea	J	RF	250+	Marshall, Edward	Puffin Books
Three Cheers for Hippo	G	F	90	Stadler, John	HarperCollins
Three Days on a River in a Red Canoe	K	I	250+	Williams, Vera B.	Scholastic
Three Ducks Went Wandering	K	F	250+	Roy, Ron	Clarion
Three Goats, The	F	TL	128	Storyteller-Setting Sun	Wright Group/McGraw Hill
Three Investigators, The Mystery of the Fiery Eye	Y	RF	250+	Arthur, Robert	Random House
Three Jars Full	F	I	89	Rigby Focus	Rigby
Three Kinds of Bears	Q	I	3256	Leveled Readers Science	Houghton Mifflin
Three Kittens	G	F	116	Ginsburg, Mirra	Crown
Three Little Ducks	E	F	102	Story Box	Wright Group/McGraw Hill
Three Little Kittens	H	TL	164	Ready Readers	Pearson Learning Group
Three Little Monkeys	E	F	36	Sunshine	Wright Group/McGraw Hill
Three Little Pigs	H	TL	39	Hunia, Fran	Ladybird Books
Three Little Pigs	L	TL	250+	Once Upon a Time	Wright Group/McGraw Hill
Three Little Pigs	L	TL	919	Galdone, Paul	Houghton Mifflin
Three Little Pigs	C	TL	39	Sunshine	Wright Group/McGraw Hill
Three Little Pigs and One Big Pig	E	TL	123	Ready Readers	Pearson Learning Group
Three Little Pigs Wise Up and The Princess, the Prince, and the Vegetables, The	M	F	250+	Navigators Fiction Series	Benchmark Education
Three Little Pigs, The	G	TL	250+	We Both Read	Treasure Bay
Three Little Pigs, The	H	TL	346	Reading Corners	Pearson Learning Group
Three Little Pigs, The	I	TL	523	PM Traditional Tales-Orange	Rigby
Three Little Pigs, The	H	TL	392	New Way Blue	Steck-Vaughn
Three Little Pigs, The	L	TL	250+	Marshall, James	Scholastic
Three Little Pigs, The	G	TL	250+	Little Readers	Houghton Mifflin
Three Little Pigs, The	I	TL	250+	Literacy 2000	Rigby
Three Little Pigs, The	F	TL	274	Alphakids	Sundance
Three Little Pigs, The	H	TL	276+	Reading Unlimited	Pearson Learning Group
Three Little Pigs, The	I	TL	568	Traditional Tales	Pearson Learning Group
Three Little Pigs, The	I	TL	250+	Ziefert, Harriet	Puffin Books
Three Little Pigs, The	D	TL	99	Folk Tales	Pioneer Valley
Three Little Witches	G	F	189	First Start	Troll Associates
Three Lives to Live	T	F	250+	Lindbergh, Anne	Little, Brown & Co.
Three Magicians, The	K	F	250+	Literacy 2000	Rigby
Three Muddy Monkeys	F	F	180	Foundations	Wright Group/McGraw Hill
Three Ships for Columbus	N	I	250+	Stories of America	Steck-Vaughn
Three Sillies, The	L	F	250+	Literacy 2000	Rigby
Three Silly Cowboys, The	H	F	213	Ready Readers	Pearson Learning Group
Three Silly Monkeys	E	F	150	Foundations	Wright Group/McGraw Hill
Three Silly Monkeys Go Fishing	I	F	163	Foundations	Wright Group/McGraw Hill
Three Smart Pals	L	RF	250+	Rocklin, Joanne	Scholastic
*Three Stories You Can Read to Your Cat	K	F	250+	Miller, Sara Swan	Houghton Mifflin
*Three Stories You Can Read to Your Dog	K	F	250+	Miller, Sara Swan	Houghton Mifflin

* Collection of short stories

TITLE	LEVEL	GENRE	WORD COUNT	AUTHOR / SERIES	PUBLISHER / DISTRIBUTOR
Three Twentieth-Century Dictators	Y	I	250+	Navigators Biography Series	Benchmark Education
*Three Up a Tree	J	RF	250+	Marshall, James	Puffin Books
Three White Sheep	B	F	20	Ready Readers	Pearson Learning Group
Three Wishes	L	F	250+	Popcorn	Sundance
Three Wishes	H	TL	250+	Ready Readers	Pearson Learning Group
Three Wishes, The	K	TL	501	Sunshine	Wright Group/McGraw Hill
Three Wishes, The	L	TL	250+	Bookshop	Mondo
*Three Wishes, The	O	TL	250+	Literacy 2000	Rigby
Three-Legged Race, The	H	RF	202	Windmill Books	Rigby
Threw and Through	K	F	255	Sunshine	Wright Group/McGraw Hill
Thrills at the Fair	J	RF	250+	The Wright Skills	Wright Group/McGraw Hill
Through Grandpa's Eyes	P	RF	250+	MacLachlan, Patricia	HarperTrophy
Through the Cell Wall	Z	I	2080	Independent Readers Science	Houghton Mifflin
Through the Day	C	I	76	Rigby Literacy	Rigby
Through the Eyes of Your Ancestors: A Step-by-Step Guide to Uncovering Your Family's History	V	I	250+	Taylor, Maureen	Houghton Mifflin
Through the Garden Door	M	F	250+	Reeves, Barbara	Pearson Learning Group
Through the Medicine Cabinet	N	F	250+	The Zack Files	Grosset & Dunlap
Throw-Away Pets	N	RF	250+	Duffey, Betsy	Puffin Books
*Throwing Shadows	T	RF	250+	Konigsburg, E. L.	Language for Learning Assoc.
Thumbelina	K	TL	807	Tales from Hans Andersen	Wright Group/McGraw Hill
Thumbprint Critters	D	I	27	Little Celebrations	Pearson Learning Group
Thumpety-Rah!	G	F	98	Sunshine	Wright Group/McGraw Hill
Thump-Thump: Learning About Your Heart	M	I	250+	Amazing Body	Picture Window Books
Thunder and Lightning	K	I	250+	Pfeffer, Wendy	Scholastic
Thunder At Gettysburg	S	I	250+	Gauch, Patricia Lee	Bantam
Thunder Rolling in the Mountains	U	HF	250+	O'Dell, Scott; Hall, Elizabeth	Bantam
Thunder Valley	T	RF	250+	Paulsen, Gary	Bantam
Thunderstorm is Coming!, A	I	I	130	Vocabulary Readers	Houghton Mifflin
Thunderstorms	N	I	250+	A True Book	Children's Press
Thurgood Marshall	P	B	250+	Photo-Illustrated Biographies	Red Brick Learning
Thurgood Marshall	L	B	250+	Pebble Books	Red Brick Learning
Thurgood Marshall and Civil Rights	V	I	2540	Independent Readers Social Studies	Houghton Mifflin
Thurgood Marshall: First Black Supreme Court Justice	N	B	250+	Rookie Biographies	Children's Press
Tick Tock World Clocks	F	I	43	iOpeners	Pearson Learning Group
Ticket to Canada	U	RF	1904	Leveled Readers	Houghton Mifflin
Tickle-Bugs, The	J	F	250+	Literacy 2000	Rigby
Tick-Tock	C	RF	53	Story Box	Wright Group/McGraw Hill
Tic-Tac-Toe Three in a Row	H	RF	132	Stamper, Judith Bauer	Scholastic
Tides	I	I	210	Wonder World	Wright Group/McGraw Hill
Tidy Titch	I	RF	231	Hutchins, Pat	Morrow
Ties That Bind, Ties That Break	X	HF	250+	Namioka, Lensey	Delacorte
Tiger & the Mad Millionaire, The	L	F	250+	Voyages	SRA/McGraw Hill
Tiger Dave	G	F	33	Books for Young Learners	Richard C. Owen
Tiger Dreams	J	RF	193	Cambridge Reading	Pearson Learning Group
Tiger Eyes	W	RF	250+	Blume, Judy	Bantam
Tiger Hunt	J	RF	250+	Rigby Literacy	Rigby
Tiger Is a Scaredy Cat	F	F	220	Phillips, Joan	Random House
Tiger Rising, The	T	RF	250+	DiCamillo, Kate	Candlewick Press
Tiger Runs Away	G	RF	213	PM Extensions-Blue	Rigby
Tiger Tales	O	F	250+	Little Celebrations	Pearson Learning Group

* Collection of short stories

TITLE	LEVEL	GENRE	WORD COUNT	AUTHOR / SERIES	PUBLISHER / DISTRIBUTOR
Tiger Woods	N	B	250+	Biography	Benchmark Education
Tiger Woods: An American Master	R	B	250+	Edwards, Nicholas	Scholastic
Tiger Woods: Unbeatable!	X	B	2056	Leveled Readers	Houghton Mifflin
Tiger, the Man, and the Jackal, The	K	F	520	Leveled Readers	Houghton Mifflin
Tiger, Tiger	C	F	55	PM Story Books	Rigby
Tigers at Twilight	M	F	250+	Osborne, Mary Pope	Random House
Tiger's Clock	C	F	28	Learn to Read	Creative Teaching Press
Tiger's Promise, Based on a Folktale from India, The	J	TL	250+	Leveled Readers Language Support	Houghton Mifflin
Tiger's Tummy Ache	I	TL	220	Ready Readers	Pearson Learning Group
Tigers, Elephants, and Giraffes	A	I	18	Vocabulary Readers	Houghton Mifflin
Tigers: Striped Stalkers	M	I	250+	The Wild World of Animals	Red Brick Learning
Tight End	M	RF	250+	Christopher, Matt	Little, Brown & Co.
Tikki Tikki Tembo	N	TL	250+	Mosel, Arlene	Scholastic
Till's Christmas	R	RF	250+	Thacker, Nola	Scholastic
Tiltawhirl John	U	RF	250+	Paulsen, Gary	Penguin Group
Timber Box, The	M	TL	250+	Enrichment	Wright Group/McGraw Hill
Time Apart, A	T	RF	250+	Stanley, Diane	William Morrow
Time Benders	T	SF	250+	Paulsen, Gary	Bantam
Time Capsule, The	M	SF	257	Book Bank	Wright Group/McGraw Hill
Time Flies	R	I	250+	Literacy 2000	Rigby
Time Flies	WB	F	N/A	Rohmann, Eric	Crown
Time for a Bath	D	RF	60	Mader, Jan	Kaeden Books
Time for a Change	C	RF	31	Pacific Literacy	Pacific Learning
Time for a Family	K	I	108	Literacy Tree	Rigby
Time for a Party	F	I	111	Discovery World	Rigby
Time for Andrew	S	F	250+	Hahn, Mary	Avon Camelot
Time for Bed	C	RF	28	Smart Starts	Rigby
Time for Bed	B	RF	28	Science	Outside the Box
Time for Bed	C	RF	27	Rosen Real Readers	Rosen Publishing Group
Time for Bed, Little Bear	I	F	303	Story Basket	Wright Group/McGraw Hill
Time for Dinner	LB	F	15	Smart Starts	Rigby
Time for Dinner	B	I	38	PM Starters	Rigby
Time for Lunch	B	RF	28	Ready Readers	Pearson Learning Group
Time for Play	D	RF	85	PM Plus Nonfiction	Rigby
Time for Sale	Q	F	250+	Literacy 2000	Rigby
Time for School	A	I	32	At School Series	Pioneer Valley
Time for Sleep!	D	F	62	Sunshine	Wright Group/McGraw Hill
Time for Soup!	LB	I	12	Vocabulary Readers	Houghton Mifflin
Time for Tacos	B	RF	26	Bebop Books	Lee & Low Books Inc.
Time for Tea	B	RF	20	Phonics and Friends	Hampton-Brown
Time Line of the American Revolution, A	R	I	250+	Rosen Real Readers	Rosen Publishing Group
*Time Machine and Other Cases, The	O	RF	250+	Simon, Seymour	Avon
Time Machine, The	Z	SF	250+	Wells, H. G.	Scholastic
Time of Angels, A	W	F	250+	Hesse, Karen	Hyperion
Time Song, The	G	I	99	Learn to Read	Creative Teaching Press
Time to Celebrate!	M	I	250+	iOpeners	Pearson Learning Group
Time to Eat	LB	I	3	Windows on Literacy	National Geographic
Time to Estimate	L	I	250+	Yellow Umbrella Books	Capstone Press
Time to Sleep	C	I	52	Independent Readers Science	Houghton Mifflin
Time to Tell Time	L	I	116	Spyglass Books	Compass Point Books
Time Warp Kids: Summer Reading is Killing Me!	P	F	250+	Scieszka, Jon	Puffin Books
Time Warp Trio: 2095	P	SF	250+	Scieszka, Jon	Penguin Group

* Collection of short stories

TITLE	LEVEL	GENRE	WORD COUNT	AUTHOR / SERIES	PUBLISHER / DISTRIBUTOR
Time Warp Trio: Good, the Bad, and the Goofy, The	P	SF	250+	Scieszka, Jon	Penguin Group
Time Warp Trio: Knights of the Kitchen Table, The	P	F	250+	Scieszka, Jon	Penguin Group
Time Warp Trio: Not-So-Jolly Roger, The	P	F	250+	Scieszka, Jon	Penguin Group
Time Warp Trio: Tut Tut	P	F	250+	Scieszka, Jon	Penguin Group
Time Warp Trio: Your Mother Was a Neanderthal	P	F	250+	Scieszka, Jon	Penguin Group
Timedetectors	N	SF	250+	SupaDoopers	Sundance
Timedetectors	V	SF	250+	Literacy 2000	Rigby
Timeline of Electricity	S	I	948	Leveled Readers Science	Houghton Mifflin
Time's Up!	L	F	250+	Sunshine	Wright Group/McGraw Hill
Timmy	E	RF	54	Literacy 2000	Rigby
Timmy Tries	C	RF	22	Little Celebrations	Pearson Learning Group
Timothy Whuffenpuffen-Whippersnapper	S	F	250+	Literacy 2000	Rigby
Timothy's Five-City Tour	M	F	250+	Pair-It Books	Steck-Vaughn
Tim's Bedtime	J	F	250+	Supersonics	Rigby
Tim's Favorite Toy	F	RF	202	PM Extensions-Blue	Rigby
Tim's Paintings	A	RF	33	Smart Starts	Rigby
Tim's Pig	B	F	41	Leveled Readers	Houghton Mifflin
Tim's Pig Eats	B	F	39	Leveled Readers Language Support	Houghton Mifflin
Tim's Pumpkin	I	RF	250+	Home Connection Collection	Rigby
Tin Can Man, The	E	RF	105	Real Kids Readers	Millbrook Press
Tin Lizzy	M	RF	425	Windmill Books	Rigby
Tin Treasures	J	I	250+	Greetings	Rigby
Tina's Taxi	F	RF	83	Franco, Betsy	Scholastic
Tiny and the Big Wave	F	RF	163	PM Extensions-Yellow	Rigby
Tiny Christmas Elf, The	G	F	173	First Start	Troll Associates
Tiny Creatures	J	I	250+	Discovery World	Rigby
Tiny Dinosaurs	L	RF	250+	PM Story Books	Rigby
Tiny Little Woman, The	D	F	74	Joy Readers	Pearson Learning Group
Tiny Woman's Coat, The	H	F	147	Sunshine	Wright Group/McGraw Hill
Tippu	K	F	250+	Soar To Success	Houghton Mifflin
Tiptoe Round the Corner	H	F	96	Voyages	SRA/McGraw Hill
Tires	F	RF	180	Foundations	Wright Group/McGraw Hill
Titanic	S	HF	250+	Duey, Kathleen; Bale, Karen A.	Simon & Schuster
Titanic Crossing	R	HF	250+	Williams, Barbara	Scholastic
Titanic Sinks!, The	T	I	250+	Conklin, Thomas	Random House
Titanic, The	V	I	250+	Cornerstones of Freedom	Children's Press
Titanic, The: Lost . . . and Found	N	I	250+	Donnelly, Judy	Random House
Titch	G	RF	121	Hutchins, Pat	Penguin Group
Tittle-Tattle Goose	E	F	117	Story Box	Wright Group/McGraw Hill
To Be a Slave	Z	I	250+	Lester, Julius	Dial Books
To Fly with the Swallows: A Story of Old California	S	I	250+	deRuiz, Dana Catharine	Steck-Vaughn
To JJ From CC	P	RF	250+	Literacy 2000	Rigby
To Kill a Mockingbird	Z	HF	250+	Lee, Harper	Warner Books
To Market, to Market	I	TL	393	Story Box	Wright Group/McGraw Hill
To New York	D	RF	32	Story Box	Wright Group/McGraw Hill
To School	A	F	22	Sunshine	Wright Group/McGraw Hill
To Tell the Truth, A Native American Cinderella Tale	L	TL	250+	Leveled Readers Language Support	Houghton Mifflin
To the Beach	D	RF	43	Urmston, Kathleen; Evans, Karen	Kaeden Books

TITLE	LEVEL	GENRE	WORD COUNT	AUTHOR / SERIES	PUBLISHER / DISTRIBUTOR
To the Moon and Beyond	S	I	250+	Lott, Linda	Wright Group/McGraw Hill
To the Ocean	C	I	26	Twig	Wright Group/McGraw Hill
To the Top of Mount Everest	T	I	2432	Leveled Readers Science	Houghton Mifflin
To the Top!: Climbing the World's Highest Mountain	N	B	250+	Kramer, Sydelle	Random House
To Town	F	F	148	Story Box	Wright Group/McGraw Hill
To Work	C	RF	43	Sunshine	Wright Group/McGraw Hill
Toad for Tuesday, A	O	F	250+	Erickson, Russell E.	Beech Tree Books
Toad Takes Off	I	F	216	Schade, Susan; Buller, John	Random House
Toast	C	RF	82	First Stories	Pacific Learning
Toast for Mom	I	RF	250+	Ready Readers	Pearson Learning Group
Toby and B. J.	I	F	307	PM Story Books-Orange	Rigby
Toby and the Accident	J	F	329	PM StoryBooks	Rigby
Toby and the Big Red Van	I	F	291	PM Story Books-Orange	Rigby
Toby and the Big Tree	I	F	298	PM Story Books-Orange	Rigby
Toby at Stony Bay	J	F	494	PM Story Books	Rigby
Toby Tomato	D	F	54	Little Celebrations	Pearson Learning Group
Today	I	RF	151	Early Connections	Benchmark Education
Today I Got Yelled At	J	RF	174	City Kids	Rigby
Today is Monday	E	TL	103	Instant Readers	Harcourt School Publishers
Today's Weather Is . . . A Book of Experiments	O	I	250+	Bookshop	Mondo
Toenails	E	I	83	Voyages	SRA/McGraw Hill
Toes	L	I	250+	Sunshine	Wright Group/McGraw Hill
Together	C	RF	37	Sunshine	Wright Group/McGraw Hill
Toilet Paper Tigers, The	Q	RF	250+	Korman, Gordon	Bantam
Tolerance	L	I	250+	Character Education	Red Brick Learning
Toliver's Secret	T	HF	250+	Brady, Esther Wood	Alfred A. Knopf
Tom and His Tractor	C	RF	27	Cat on the Mat	Oxford University Press
Tom Edison's Bright Idea	N	B	250+	Keller, Jack	Steck-Vaughn
Tom Gets Fit	D	RF	150	New Way Red	Steck-Vaughn
Tom Is Brave	D	RF	57	PM Story Books	Rigby
Tom Sawyer	J	B	250+	Jumbled Tumbled Tales & Rhymes	Rigby
Tom the TV Cat	J	F	250+	Heilbroner, Joan	Random House
*Tom, Babette & Simon	T	F	250+	Avi	Avon
Tom, the Dragon	M	F	522	New Way Orange	Steck-Vaughn
Tomato Picking Day	L	I	250+	Pipher, Tom	Wright Group/McGraw Hill
Tomato Rose	I	RF	250+	Phonics Readers Plus	Steck-Vaughn
Tomatoes	M	I	250+	Cole, Sally	Wright Group/McGraw Hill
Tomatoes and Bricks	E	RF	126	Windmill	Wright Group/McGraw Hill
Tomb of Nebamun, The	S	I	250+	Cambridge Reading	Pearson Learning Group
Tomie dePaola	L	B	196	First Biographies	Red Brick Learning
Tommy Snake's Problem	H	F	328	TOTTS	Tott Publications
Tommy Thompson's Ship of Gold	P	I	685	Leveled Readers	Houghton Mifflin
Tommy's Treasure	I	RF	232	Literacy 2000	Rigby
Tommy's Tummy Ache	C	F	20	Literacy 2000	Rigby
Tomorrow's Wizard	R	F	250+	MacLachlan, Patricia	Scholastic
Tom's Box	I	F	250+	Cambridge Reading	Pearson Learning Group
Tom's Friend	M	RF	250+	Voyages	SRA/McGraw Hill
Tom's Midnight Garden	V	F	250+	Pearce, Philippa	HarperTrophy
Tom's Ride	G	RF	185	PM Plus Story Books	Rigby
Tom's Rubber Band	E	RF	82	Sunshine	Wright Group/McGraw Hill
Tom's Trousers	G	RF	173	Storyteller-Night Crickets	Wright Group/McGraw Hill
Tom-Ti-Ra and the Mysterious Noise	B	F	26	Book Bus	Creative Edge
Tongue Twister Prize, The	J	RF	331	Little Books	Sadlier-Oxford

* Collection of short stories

TITLE	LEVEL	GENRE	WORD COUNT	AUTHOR / SERIES	PUBLISHER / DISTRIBUTOR
Tongues Are for Tasting, Licking, Tricking	L	I	250+	Literacy 2000	Rigby
Tonight on the Titanic	M	F	250+	Osborne, Mary Pope	Random House
Toning The Sweep	Y	RF	250+	Johnson, Angela	Scholastic
Tony and the Butterfly	J	RF	250+	Literacy Tree	Rigby
Tony Hawk: Skateboarding Legend	Q	I	250+	Skateboarding	Capstone Press
Too Big for Me	D	F	70	Story Box	Wright Group/McGraw Hill
Too Busy for Pets!	J	RF	472	Sunshine	Wright Group/McGraw Hill
Too Fast	A	F	36	Reading Corners	Pearson Learning Group
Too High!	D	RF	66	Ready Readers	Pearson Learning Group
Too Hot to Handle	M	RF	250+	Christopher, Matt	Little, Brown & Co.
Too Hot!	C	RF	39	Lighthouse	Rigby
Too Late!	G	F	226	Foundations	Wright Group/McGraw Hill
Too Little	E	RF	119	Foundations	Wright Group/McGraw Hill
Too Little	D	RF	83	Sun Sprouts	ETA/Cuisenaire
Too Many Animals	G	F	111	Alphakids	Sundance
Too Many Babas	K	TL	250+	Croll, Carolyn	HarperTrophy
Too Many Babas	K	TL	250+	Little Readers	Houghton Mifflin
Too Many Balloons	D	RF	182	Rookie Readers	Children's Press
*Too Many Bones	G	F	125	New Way Blue	Steck-Vaughn
Too Many Cars	LB	RF	15	Hartley, Susan; Armstrong, Shane	Scholastic
Too Many Clothes	C	RF	24	Literacy 2000	Rigby
Too Many Mice	J	F	250+	Bank Street	Bantam
Too Many Nuts	H	RF	132	Books for Young Learners	Richard C. Owen
Too Many Puppies	J	RF	250+	Brewster, Patience	Scholastic
Too Many Rabbits	J	RF	250+	Parish, Peggy	Bantam
Too Many Steps	J	RF	424	Foundations	Wright Group/McGraw Hill
Too Many Tamales	M	RF	250+	Soto, Gary	Putnam & Grosset
Too Much	B	RF	27	Teacher's Choice Series	Pearson Learning Group
Too Much Ketchup	D	F	30	Ready Readers	Pearson Learning Group
Too Much Magic	R	F	250+	Sterman, Betsy & Samuel	HarperTrophy
Too Much Noise	J	TL	250+	McGovern, Ann	Scholastic
Too Much Noise	H	TL	340	Literacy 2000	Rigby
*Too Much Talk and Other Stories	J	TL	250+	New Way Literature	Steck-Vaughn
Too Much Trouble for Grandpa	K	F	250+	Lewis, Rob	Mondo
Too Much Trouble for Grandpa	J	F	250+	Sokoloff, Myka-Lynne	Sadlier-Oxford
Too Small Jill	J	RF	306	Little Books	Sadlier-Oxford
Too Soon to Say Goodbye	S	RF	250+	Kent, Deborah	Scholastic
Tool Box, The	H	RF	144	Rockwell, Anne	Macmillan
Tools and Gadgets	T	I	250+	Historic Communities	Crabtree
Tools Can Help Us See	G	I	107	Windows on Literacy	National Geographic
Tools Measure Weather	I	I	145	Windows on Literacy	National Geographic
Tools Scientists Use	K	I	184	Windows on Literacy	National Geographic
Tools to Use	D	I	42	Little Red Readers	Sundance
Toot! Toot!	LB	F	21	Joy Readers	Pearson Learning Group
Toot, Toot	C	I	47	Wildsmith, Brian	Oxford University Press
Tooter Pepperday	L	RF	250+	Spinelli, Jerry	Random House
Tooth Fairy, The	D	F	57	My First Reader	Grolier Press
Tooth Fairy, The	WB	F	N/A	Collington, Peter	Wright Group/McGraw Hill
Tooth Race, The	I	RF	250+	Little Readers	Houghton Mifflin
Toothbrush Tale	G	F	117	New Way Blue	Steck-Vaughn
Toothpaste Millionaire, The	T	RF	250+	Merrill, Jean	Houghton Mifflin
Toothwalkers	N	I	250+	Sails	Rigby
Too-Tight Shoes	I	RF	170	Evangeline Nicholas Collection	Wright Group/McGraw Hill
Top Cat	O	I	250+	Byars, Betsy	Penguin Group

* Collection of short stories

TITLE	LEVEL	GENRE	WORD COUNT	AUTHOR / SERIES	PUBLISHER / DISTRIBUTOR
Top Cat	K	F	250+	Story Steps	Rigby
*Top Ten Shakespeare Stories	Z	HF	250+	Terry, Deary	Scholastic
Torn Thread	W	HF	250+	Isaacs, Anne	Scholastic
Tornado	O	I	250+	Byars, Betsy	HarperTrophy
Tornado	E	I	37	Spinelle, Nancy Louise	Kaeden Books
Tornado Chasers	T	RF	1520	Independent Readers Science	Houghton Mifflin
Tornado Tony	H	RF	182	Well-Being Series	Pearson Learning Group
Tornado!	R	RF	1470	Leveled Readers Social Studies	Houghton Mifflin
Tornado, The	L	RF	250+	PM Story Books	Rigby
Tornadoes!	N	I	250+	Hopping, Lorraine Jean	Scholastic
Tortillas	E	RF	71	Gonzalez-Jensen, Margarita	Scholastic
Tortoise and the Hare, The	H	TL	148	Cambridge Reading	Pearson Learning Group
*Tortoise Shell and Other African Stories, The	N	TL	250+	Smith, Geof	Scholastic
Tossed Salad	C	I	28	Twig	Wright Group/McGraw Hill
Total Eclipse of the Sun	W	I	250+	Independent Readers Science	Houghton Mifflin
Totara Tree, The	M	RF	391	Book Bank	Wright Group/McGraw Hill
Totem Poles	L	I	246	Twig	Wright Group/McGraw Hill
Totem Poles	D	I	46	Leveled Readers Social Studies	Houghton Mifflin
Totem Poles of North America	D	I	42	Leveled Readers Social Studies	Houghton Mifflin
Touch	C	I	39	Twig	Wright Group/McGraw Hill
*Touch of Gold and Other Stories, The	M	TL	250+	Lane, Sheila; Kemp, Marion	Wood Lock Educational
Touch of Sepia, A	M	RF	250+	Voyages	SRA/McGraw Hill
Touch the Earth	L	RF	250+	Bookshop	Mondo
Touchdown for Tommy	M	RF	250+	Christopher, Matt	Little, Brown & Co.
Touchdown!: You Can Play Football	M	I	250+	Game Day	Picture Window Books
Touching	J	I	142	Pebble Books	Capstone Press
Touching Spirit Bear	Y	F	250+	Mikaelsen, Ben	HarperCollins
Tournament Trouble	R	RF	250+	Costello, Emily	Dell
Tower, The	P	SF	250+	Orbit Double Takes	Pacific Learning
Towers	M	I	250+	Rigby Literacy	Rigby
Town in Trouble, A	P	F	1019	Leveled Readers	Houghton Mifflin
Town Mouse and Country Mouse	K	TL	250+	PM Tales and Plays-Purple	Rigby
Town Mouse and Country Mouse, The	I	TL	172	Aesop	Wright Group/McGraw Hill
Toy Box, A	LB	I	19	Literacy 2000	Rigby
Toy Box, The	LB	RF	14	Ready Readers	Pearson Learning Group
Toy Box, The	B	RF	49	Sun Sprouts	ETA/Cuisenaire
Toy Box, The	B	I	49	PM Plus Starters	Rigby
Toy Farm, The	I	RF	311	PM Story Books-Orange	Rigby
Toy Maker, The	B	RF	31	Ray's Readers	Outside the Box
Toy Models	A	I	40	Early Connections	Benchmark Education
Toy Shop, The	L	RF	250+	Book Project	Sundance
Toy Store, The	B	RF	55	Leveled Readers Emergent	Houghton Mifflin
Toy Tooth, The	I	RF	250+	Rigby Literacy	Rigby
Toy Town	C	I	36	Home Connection Collection	Rigby
Toy Trouble	H	F	250+	Bookshop	Mondo
Toymil and the Bear	I	RF	233	Story Box	Wright Group/McGraw Hill
Toys	E	I	76	Talk About Books	Pearson Learning Group
Toys	D	RF	106	Tiger Cub	Peguis
Toys	C	I	41	Windows on Literacy	National Geographic
Toys	B	RF	37	Foundations	Wright Group/McGraw Hill
Toys and Play	F	RF	194	PM Plus Nonfiction	Rigby
Toys Can Move	LB	I	7	Windows on Literacy	National Geographic
Toys Long Ago	D	I	54	Yellow Umbrella Books	Red Brick Learning
Toys' Party, The	F	F	48	Oxford Reading Tree	Oxford University Press

* Collection of short stories

TITLE	LEVEL	GENRE	WORD COUNT	AUTHOR / SERIES	PUBLISHER / DISTRIBUTOR
Toys with Wheels	C	I	41	Home Connection Collection	Rigby
Toytown Fire Engine, The	D	F	105	PM Plus Story Books	Rigby
Toytown Helicopter, The	D	F	97	PM Plus Story Books	Rigby
Toytown Race Car, The	F	F	188	PM Plus Story Books	Rigby
Toytown Rescue, The	D	F	100	PM Plus Story Books	Rigby
Tracey and the Sun	M	F	250+	Sails	Rigby
Tracing the Anasazi	P	I	830	Independent Readers Social Studies	Houghton Mifflin
Tracker	T	RF	250+	Paulsen, Gary	Scholastic
Tracks	L	I	250+	Voyages	SRA/McGraw Hill
Tracks	C	I	25	Sunshine	Wright Group/McGraw Hill
Tracks	C	I	49	Twig	Wright Group/McGraw Hill
Tracks in the Sand	L	I	250+	Sunshine	Wright Group/McGraw Hill
Tracks in the Sand	I	I	125	Levin, Amy	Scholastic
Tractor Trailers	N	I	250+	Schaefer, Lola M.	Red Brick Learning
Tractors	M	I	250+	Transportation	Compass Point Books
Tradition of the Harvest, The	P	RF	250+	Leveled Readers Language Support	Houghton Mifflin
Traffic	A	I	30	Lighthouse	Rigby
Traffic Jam	F	RF	55	City Stories	Rigby
Traffic Jam	LB	RF	18	Voyages	SRA/McGraw Hill
Traffic Jam	E	RF	133	Harper, Leslie	Kaeden Books
Traffic Jam	D	RF	18	Little Red Readers	Sundance
Traffic Jam, The	A	RF	33	Handprints B	Educator's Publishing Service
Traffic Light Sandwich	H	I	87	Wonder World	Wright Group/McGraw Hill
Trail Home, The	S	RF	2004	Leveled Readers	Houghton Mifflin
Trail of Tears, 1838, The	V	I	250+	Let Freedom Ring	Capstone Press
Trailblazers!	O	RF	250+	Action Packs	Rigby
Train Ride	C	RF	15	Bebop Books	Lee & Low Books Inc.
Train Ride Story, The	I	F	189	Sunshine	Wright Group/McGraw Hill
Train Ride, The	C	F	29	Literacy 2000	Rigby
Train that Ran Away	I	F	32	Jellybeans	Rigby
Train Time	L	I	250+	Baehr, Lisa	Hampton-Brown
Train to the West?	O	I	279	Vocabulary Readers	Houghton Mifflin
Train Wreck	S	HF	250+	Duey, Kathleen; Bale, Karen A.	Simon & Schuster
Train, The	C	RF	27	Visions	Wright Group/McGraw Hill
Training a Police Dog	G	I	103	Vocabulary Readers	Houghton Mifflin
Training for Space	T	I	508	Vocabulary Readers	Houghton Mifflin
Training for the Olympics	T	I	1381	Independent Readers Science	Houghton Mifflin
Training My Dog	L	I	917	Leveled Readers Science	Houghton Mifflin
Trains	Q	I	250+	Literacy 2000	Rigby
Trains	T	I	250+	The World's Fastest	Red Brick Learning
Trains on the Rails	K	I	250+	PM Plus	Rigby
Traitor: The Case of Benedict Arnold	X	B	250+	Fritz, Jean	Putnam & Grosset
Transcontinental Railroad, The	V	I	250+	Cornerstones of Freedom	Children's Press
Transcontinental Railroad, The	S	I	250+	The Library of the Westward Expansion	Rosen Publishing Group
Transforming Trash	S	I	250+	Quinn, Pat	Pacific Learning
Transportation Museum, The	C	I	79	Little Red Readers	Sundance
Transportation Through Time	Q	I	250+	Rigby Focus	Rigby
Transportation Time Line, A	P	I	250+	Discovery World	Rigby
Transportation Yesterday and Today	M	I	659	Relf, Coco	Harcourt School Publishers
Trapped By a Teacher	Q	RF	250+	Action Packs	Rigby

* Collection of short stories

TITLE	LEVEL	GENRE	WORD COUNT	AUTHOR / SERIES	PUBLISHER / DISTRIBUTOR
Trapped!	L	RF	250+	New Way Literature	Steck-Vaughn
Trapped!	O	RF	250+	SupaDoopers	Sundance
Trash	H	F	130	Sunshine	Wright Group/McGraw Hill
Trash Can Band, The	J	RF	252	Little Books	Sadlier-Oxford
Travel Money, U.S.A.	I	I	245	Early Connections	Benchmark Education
Travel Smart	P	I	250+	iOpeners	Pearson Learning Group
Travelers and Traders	Q	I	250+	Explorers	Wright Group/McGraw Hill
Traveling	C	F	86	Foundations	Wright Group/McGraw Hill
Traveling Across Australia	O	I	250+	Windows on Literacy	National Geographic
Traveling by Train	O	I	485	Leveled Readers Social Studies	Houghton Mifflin
Traveling Guitar, The	O	RF	674	Leveled Readers	Houghton Mifflin
Traveling Ted's Postcards	C	F	161	Little Celebrations	Pearson Learning Group
Travels of Alvar Nunez Cebeza de Vaca, The	X	B	3751	Leveled Readers Social Studies	Houghton Mifflin
Travels of Marco Polo, The	T	I	250+	Explorers & Exploration	Steck-Vaughn
Travels with Rainie Marie	S	B	250+	Martin, Patricia	Hyperion
Treasure Cave, The	L	F	250+	Cambridge Reading	Pearson Learning Group
Treasure Hunt	O	I	250+	Early Connections	Benchmark Education
Treasure Hunt	LB	F	14	Smart Starts	Rigby
Treasure Hunting	M	RF	250+	Literacy 2000	Rigby
Treasure in the Attic	G	RF	153	Seedlings	Continental Press
Treasure Island	Z	F	250+	Stevenson, Robert Lewis	Scholastic
Treasure Island, A	F	RF	177	PM Plus Story Books	Rigby
Treasure Map, The	B	F	32	Harry's Math Books	Outside the Box
Treasure of Alpheus Winterborn, The	S	F	250+	Bellairs, John	Penguin Group
Treasure of El Patrón, The	T	RF	250+	Paulsen, Gary	Bantam
Treasure of the Lost Lagoon, The	K	F	250+	Hayes, Geoffrey	Random House
Treasure on Fraser Street, The	K	RF	250+	Home Connection Collection	Rigby
Treasure!	J	RF	250+	Phonics Readers Plus	Steck-Vaughn
Treasures	L	RF	263	Books for Young Learners	Richard C. Owen
Treasures in the Dust	U	HF	250+	Porter, Tracey	HarperTrophy
*Treasury of Pirate Stories, A	S	F	250+	Bradman, Tony	Kingfisher
Treat, The	E	F	96	Leveled Readers Language Support	Houghton Mifflin
Tree Branch, The	WB	RF	N/A	Instant Readers	Harcourt School Publishers
Tree by Leaf	V	F	250+	Voigt, Cynthia	Simon & Schuster
Tree Can Be, A	E	I	74	Nayer, Judy	Scholastic
Tree Falls Down, A	M	F	250+	Orbit Double Takes	Pacific Learning
Tree Fell Over the River, A	C	RF	72	Little Red Readers	Sundance
Tree for all Seasons, A	B	I	24	Independent Readers Science	Houghton Mifflin
Tree Fort, The	H	RF	160	Early Transitional, Set 2	Pioneer Valley
Tree Frogs	J	I	87	Pebble Books	Red Brick Learning
Tree Horse, A	H	RF	220	PM Plus Story Books	Rigby
Tree House Fun	G	RF	165	First Start	Troll Associates
Tree House, The	B	RF	32	Sunshine	Wright Group/McGraw Hill
Tree House, The	E	RF	25	Brown, Roberta; Carey, Sue	Scholastic
Tree House, The	B	F	30	Story Box	Wright Group/McGraw Hill
Tree is a Home, A	H	I	203	Learn to Read	Creative Teaching Press
Tree Is a Home, A	I	I	135	Pacific Literacy	Pacific Learning
Tree Is My Home, A	G	RF	114	Leveled Readers Science	Houghton Mifflin
Tree of Birds	J	F	250+	Leveled Readers Language Support	Houghton Mifflin
Tree Stump, The	B	TL	34	Little Celebrations	Pearson Learning Group
Tree, The	F	RF	101	Sunshine	Wright Group/McGraw Hill
Tree, The	G	I	94	Alphakids	Sundance

* Collection of short stories

TITLE	LEVEL	GENRE	WORD COUNT	AUTHOR / SERIES	PUBLISHER / DISTRIBUTOR
Tree, the Trunk, and the Tuba, The	Q	RF	250+	Literacy 2000	Rigby
Treehouse	D	I	43	Hoenecke, Karen	Kaeden Books
Treehouse Club, The	N	RF	250+	Navigators Fiction Series	Benchmark Education
Treehouse Club, The	F	RF	158	Home Connection Collection	Rigby
Trees	A	I	28	Twig	Wright Group/McGraw Hill
Trees	H	I	28	Sun Sprouts	ETA/Cuisenaire
Trees	L	I	158	Bookshop	Mondo
Trees	K	I	388	Early Connections	Benchmark Education
Trees	J	I	124	Literacy 2000	Rigby
Trees	H	I	194	Momentum Literacy Program	Troll Associates
Trees and Leaves	S	I	250+	Nature Club	Troll Associates
Trees and Leaves	F	I	33	iOpeners	Pearson Learning Group
Trees and Plants in the Rain Forest	O	I	250+	Pirotta, Saviour	Steck-Vaughn
Trees Are Special	I	I	85	Sunshine	Wright Group/McGraw Hill
Trees Are Terrific!	G	I	123	Yellow Umbrella Books	Red Brick Learning
Trees Belong To Everyone	L	I	250+	Literacy 2000	Rigby
Tree's Life, A	J	I	102	Windows on Literacy	National Geographic
Trek, The	I	RF	158	Jonas, Ann	Greenwillow
Trevor from Trinidad	Q	RF	1685	Leveled Readers	Houghton Mifflin
Trevor's New Home	O	RF	250+	Leveled Readers Language Support	Houghton Mifflin
Triangles	I	I	178	Shapes	Red Brick Learning
Triathlon	Q	I	250+	Lund, Bill	Red Brick Learning
Triceratops and the Crocodiles, The	I	HF	250+	PM Plus Story Books	Rigby
Triceratops on the Farm	L	F	208	Wesley & the Dinosaurs	Wright Group/McGraw Hill
Trick or Treat Halloween	F	RF	131	First Start	Troll Associates
Trick, The	F	RF	65	New Way Red	Steck-Vaughn
Tricking the Tiger	J	TL	250+	PM Plus Story Books	Rigby
Tricking Tracy	F	RF	125	Tadpoles	Rigby
Tricks	I	I	218	Sun Sprouts	ETA/Cuisenaire
Trickster Ghost, The	O	F	250+	Showell, E.	Scholastic
Tricksters	M	RF	250+	SupaDoopers	Sundance
Tricksters, The	D	F	49	Ray's Readers	Outside the Box
Tricky Insects and Other Fun Creatures	K	I	250+	Spyglass Books	Compass Point Books
Tricky Sticky Problem, The	H	RF	71	Pacific Literacy	Pacific Learning
Triffic the Extraordinary Pig	R	F	250+	King-Smith, Dick	Bantam
Trilobites	K	I	141	Books for Young Learners	Richard C. Owen
Trip Across the Country, A	C	RF	47	Independent Readers Social Studies	Houghton Mifflin
Trip Around the Gulf of Mexico, A	M	I	250+	People, Spaces & Places	Rand McNally
Trip into Space, A	I	I	129	Little Red Readers	Sundance
Trip into Space, A	H	I	79	Story Steps	Rigby
Trip on the Erie Canal, A	L	RF	260	Independent Readers Social Studies	Houghton Mifflin
Trip Through Our Solar System, A	L	I	250+	Rosen Real Readers	Rosen Publishing Group
Trip Through the Airport, A	L	I	250+	Rigby Literacy	Rigby
Trip to a Pond	B	RF	33	Leveled Readers Science	Houghton Mifflin
Trip to Freedom	M	B	250+	Greetings	Rigby
Trip to Japan, A	M	I	250+	Rosen Real Readers	Rosen Publishing Group
Trip to the Aquarium, A	LB	RF	18	Kloes, Carol	Kaeden Books
Trip to the Beach, A	E	I	44	iOpeners	Pearson Learning Group
Trip to the City, A	E	F	119	Bookshop	Mondo
Trip to the Dentist, A	I	I	196	Rosen Real Readers	Rosen Publishing Group
Trip to the Doctor, A	B	I	36	Windows on Literacy	National Geographic

TITLE	LEVEL	GENRE	WORD COUNT	AUTHOR / SERIES	PUBLISHER / DISTRIBUTOR
Trip to the Fire Station	K	I	182	Rosen Real Readers	Rosen Publishing Group
Trip to the Park, The	H	RF	277	Foundations	Wright Group/McGraw Hill
Trip to the Post Office, A	I	I	191	Rosen Real Readers	Rosen Publishing Group
Trip to the Station, A	I	I	241	Rosen Real Readers	Rosen Publishing Group
Trip to the Video Store, A	H	RF	203	Foundations	Wright Group/McGraw Hill
Trip to the Zoo, A	F	I	93	Independent Readers Science	Houghton Mifflin
Trip to the Zoo, A	C	RF	78	Carousel Readers	Pearson Learning Group
Trip to the Zoo, A	F	I	112	Rosen Real Readers	Rosen Publishing Group
Trip, The	E	F	108	Ready Readers	Pearson Learning Group
Triplet Trouble and the Bicycle Race	L	RF	250+	Dadey, Debbie; Jones, Marcia Thornton	Scholastic
Triplet Trouble and the Class Trip	L	RF	250+	Dadey, Debbie; Jones, Marcia Thornton	Scholastic
Triplet Trouble and the Cookie Contest	L	RF	250+	Dadey, Debbie; Jones, Marcia Thornton	Scholastic
Triplet Trouble and the Field Day Disaster	L	RF	250+	Dadey, Debbie; Jones, Marcia Thornton	Scholastic
Triplet Trouble and the Pizza Party	L	RF	250+	Dadey, Debbie; Jones, Marcia Thornton	Scholastic
Triplet Trouble and the Red Heart Race	L	RF	250+	Dadey, Debbie; Jones, Marcia Thornton	Scholastic
Triplet Trouble and the Runaway Reindeer	L	RF	250+	Dadey, Debbie; Jones, Marcia Thornton	Scholastic
Triplet Trouble and the Talent Show Mess	L	RF	250+	Dadey, Debbie; Jones, Marcia Thornton	Scholastic
Trixie	L	RF	250+	Voyages	SRA/McGraw Hill
Trixie and the Cyber Pet	M	F	250+	Krailing, Tessa	Barron's Educational
Trixie's Summer	J	RF	250+	PM Plus Story Books	Rigby
Trog	J	F	432	Sunshine	Wright Group/McGraw Hill
Trojan Horse, The	N	I	250+	Literacy 2000	Rigby
Trojan Horse, The: How the Greeks Won the War	N	HF	250+	Little, Emily	Random House
Troll Tricks	H	TL	250+	Phonics Readers	Scholastic
Trolley Ride	A	I	16	Vocabulary Readers	Houghton Mifflin
Trolley Ride, The	C	F	87	Tadpoles	Rigby
Trolls Don't Ride Roller Coasters	M	F	250+	Dadey, Debbie; Jones, Marcia Thornton	Scholastic
Troop of Little Dinosaurs, A	J	HF	250+	PM Story Books	Rigby
Tropical Rainforests	N	I	250+	Habitats of the World	Pearson Learning Group
Troquois, The: Longhouse Builders	R	I	250+	America's First Peoples	Capstone Press
Trouble	E	RF	113	Teacher's Choice Series	Pearson Learning Group
Trouble Dolls	P	F	250+	Buffett, Jimmy; Savannah, Jane	Harcourt School Publishers
Trouble in the Ark	J	F	119	Rose, Gerald	Oxford University Press
Trouble in the Sandbox	J	RF	318	Foundations	Wright Group/McGraw Hill
Trouble River	S	HF	250+	Byars, Betsy	Scholastic
Trouble with Buster, The	N	RF	250+	Lorimer, Janet	Scholastic
Trouble with Heathrow, The	I	RF	173	Sunshine	Wright Group/McGraw Hill
Trouble with Herbert, The	L	F	1830	Eyles, Heather	Mondo
Trouble with Oatmeal, The	O	RF	250+	PM Emerald	Rigby
Trouble with Parents, The	N	RF	250+	SupaDoopers	Sundance
Trouble with Patrick, The	O	RF	250+	Action Packs	Rigby
Trouble with Tuck, The	R	RF	250+	Taylor, Theodore	Avon
Troublemaker	M	RF	250+	SupaDoopers	Sundance
Troubles with Bubbles	E	F	89	New Reader Series	Bungalo Books

* Collection of short stories

TITLE	LEVEL	GENRE	WORD COUNT	AUTHOR / SERIES	PUBLISHER / DISTRIBUTOR
Troubling a Star	V	F	250+	L'Engle, Madeleine	Dell
Trout Summer	T	RF	250+	Conly, Jane Leslie	Scholastic
Truck Is Stuck, The	B	RF	23	Ready Readers	Pearson Learning Group
Truck Parade, The	K	RF	483	PM Plus Story Books	Rigby
Truck Stop, The	LB	RF	25	Kloes, Carol	Kaeden Books
Trucker	P	RF	250+	Beale, Fleur	Pacific Learning
Trucks	C	I	27	Pebble Books	Capstone Press
Trucks	I	I	38	Literacy 2000	Rigby
Trucks	C	I	38	Literacy 2000	Rigby
Trucks	E	I	196	Foundations	Wright Group/McGraw Hill
Trucks	A	I	35	Little Books for Early Readers	University of Maine
Trucks	C	I	24	Twig	Wright Group/McGraw Hill
Trucks	A	RF	56	Bookshop	Mondo
Trucks	T	I	250+	The World's Fastest	Red Brick Learning
Trucks on the Road	K	I	250+	PM Plus	Rigby
Truckster	F	F	194	Instant Readers	Harcourt School Publishers
True Confessions	S	RF	250+	Tashjian, Janet	Scholastic
True Confessions of Charlotte Doyle, The	V	HF	250+	Avi	Avon
True Cortez, A	P	RF	685	Leveled Readers	Houghton Mifflin
True Crimes and How They Were Solved	Z	I	250+	Larsen, Anita	Scholastic
True or False?	G	I	119	Ready Readers	Pearson Learning Group
True Stories about Abraham Lincoln	O	B	250+	Gross, Ruth Belov	Scholastic
True Story of Balto, The	L	I	250+	Standiford, Natalie	Random House
True Story of the Three Little Pigs, The	Q	TL	250+	Scieszka, Jon	Scholastic
*True-Life Treasure Hunts	N	I	250+	Donnelly, Judy	Random House
Truman's Aunt Farm	K	F	250+	Soar To Success	Houghton Mifflin
Trumpet of the Swan, The	R	F	250+	White, E. B.	Scholastic
Trumpeter of Krakow, The	Z	HF	250+	Kelly, Eric P.	Aladdin
Truth About the Moon, The	M	TL	250+	Bess, Clayton	Houghton Mifflin
Try Again, Emma	I	RF	250+	Lighthouse	Rigby
Try Again, Hannah	G	RF	228	PM Extensions-Green	Rigby
Try It	D	RF	49	Reading Corners	Pearson Learning Group
Try It!	T	I	250+	iOpeners	Pearson Learning Group
Try This!	I	I	250+	Rigby Literacy	Rigby
Try to Be a Brave Girl, Sarah	F	RF	102	Windmill	Wright Group/McGraw Hill
T-Shirt Triplets, The	L	RF	344	Literacy 2000	Rigby
T-Shirts	F	RF	112	Pacific Literacy	Pacific Learning
Tsunami	Z	I	2393	Leveled Readers	Houghton Mifflin
Tsunami!	Q	I	784	Independent Readers Science	Houghton Mifflin
Tuba Lessons	WB	RF	N/A	Bartlett, T. C.; Monique, Felix	Harcourt School Publishers
Tubes in My Ears: My Trip to the Hospital	K	I	250+	Bookshop	Mondo
Tuck Everlasting	V	F	250+	Babbitt, Natalie	Farrar, Straus and Giroux
Tucker Finds Adventure	J	F	250+	Fletcher, Rusty	Pearson Learning Group
Tucket's Gold	U	HF	250+	Paulsen, Gary	Bantam
Tucket's Ride	U	HF	250+	Paulsen, Gary	Bantam
Tuesday	WB	F	N/A	Wiesner, David	Clarion
Tug of War	I	TL	250+	Folk Tales	Wright Group/McGraw Hill
Tug of War, The	G	F	194	Story Steps	Rigby
Tugboats	O	I	250+	Schaefer, Lola M.	Red Brick Learning
Tulips for Dad	J	RF	250+	Cambridge Reading	Pearson Learning Group
Tummy Ache	J	RF	104	Sunshine	Wright Group/McGraw Hill
Tundra	Q	I	250+	First Reports	Compass Point Books
Tunnels	L	I	262	Windows on Literacy	National Geographic
Tupac Shakur	Z	B	250+	Rock Music Library	Capstone Press

TITLE	LEVEL	GENRE	WORD COUNT	AUTHOR / SERIES	PUBLISHER / DISTRIBUTOR
Turkey That Ate My Father, The	Q	F	250+	Marney, Dean	Scholastic
Turkey Trouble	M	RF	250+	Giff, Patricia Reilly	Bantam
Turkey: Between Europe and Asia	Y	I	3597	Leveled Readers Social Studies	Houghton Mifflin
Turkeys on the Farm	I	I	94	Pebble Books	Red Brick Learning
Turkeys' Side of It, The	N	RF	250+	Smith, Janice Lee	HarperTrophy
Turn Homeward, Hannalee	T	HF	250+	Beatty, Patricia	William Morrow
Turn It Down!	U	I	250+	iOpeners	Pearson Learning Group
Turn on a Faucet	L	I	238	Windows on Literacy	National Geographic
Turn Up the Radio	R	I	795	Independent Readers Social Studies	Houghton Mifflin
Turnip, The	F	TL	250+	Ziefert, Harriet	Puffin Books
Turtle Flies South	K	F	250+	Literacy 2000	Rigby
Turtle Nest	H	I	85	Books for Young Learners	Richard C. Owen
Turtle Talk	I	I	217	Storyteller-Setting Sun	Wright Group/McGraw Hill
Turtle Trouble	E	RF	157	Seedlings	Continental Press
Turtle, The	D	I	68	Foundations	Wright Group/McGraw Hill
Turtles	S	I	250+	A First Book	Franklin Watts
Turtles	E	I	250+	Pebble Books	Capstone Press
Turtle's Big Race	J	TL	250+	Pair-It Books	Steck-Vaughn
Turtle's Small Pond	J	TL	572	Leveled Readers	Houghton Mifflin
Turtles Take Their Time	L	I	250+	Read-About Science	Children's Press
Tutankhamen's Gift	R	I	250+	Sabuda, Robert	Simon & Schuster
Tut's Mummy: Lost and Found	P	I	250+	Donnelly, Judy	Random House
Tuttle's Shell	K	F	250+	Bookshop	Mondo
TV Kid, The	R	RF	250+	Byars, Betsy	Puffin Books
TV Reporters	M	I	250+	Boraas, Tracey	Red Brick Learning
TV Time-Out	M	RF	250+	Blackaby, Susan	Wright Group/McGraw Hill
Tweedle-De-Dee Tumbleweed	G	F	103	Reese, Bob	Children's Press
Twelve Dancing Princesses	M	I	250+	Enrichment	Wright Group/McGraw Hill
Twenty-One Balloons, The	V	SF	250+	DuBois, William	Scholastic
Twiddle Twins' Haunted House, The	L	F	1141	Goldsmith, Howard	Mondo
Twiddle Twins' Music Box Mystery, The	L	F	250+	Goldsmith, Howard	Mondo
Twiddle Twins' Single Footprint Mystery, The	L	F	250+	Goldsmith, Howard	Mondo
Twilight In Grace Falls	W	RF	250+	Honeycutt, Natalie	Avon
Twinkie Squad, The	S	RF	250+	Korman, Gordon	Scholastic
Twins	H	I	113	Vocabulary Readers	Houghton Mifflin
Twins, The	H	RF	250+	Early Transitional, Set 1	Pioneer Valley
Twisters	M	I	250+	Early Connections	Benchmark Education
Twisters and Other Terrible Storms	R	I	250+	Osborne, Will; Osborne, Mary Pope	Random House
Twisters and Other Wind Storms	P	I	250+	Wildcats	Wright Group/McGraw Hill
Twisting Up a Storm	R	I	250+	Duksta, Cheryl	Pacific Learning
Twits, The	S	F	250+	Dahl, Roald	Penguin Group
Two	E	RF	84	Carousel Readers	Pearson Learning Group
Two	A	I	17	Little Celebrations	Pearson Learning Group
Two Baby Elephants	I	F	240	Lighthouse	Rigby
Two Baskets	E	RF	181	Bookshop	Mondo
Two Bear Cubs	H	F	89	Jonas, Ann	Morrow
Two by Two	G	TL	88	Cambridge Reading	Pearson Learning Group
Two Can Do It!	C	RF	32	Canizares, Susan; Chessen, Betsey	Scholastic
Two Cold Ears	O	B	560	Leveled Readers	Houghton Mifflin
Two Crazy Pigs	I	F	250+	Nagel, Karen Berman	Scholastic
Two Eyes, A Nose, and a Mouth	I	I	169	Grobel Intrater, Roberta	Scholastic
Two Eyes, Two Ears	D	I	83	PM Nonfiction-Red	Rigby

* Collection of short stories

TITLE	LEVEL	GENRE	WORD COUNT	AUTHOR / SERIES	PUBLISHER / DISTRIBUTOR
Two Feet	F	RF	129	Pescoe, Gwen	Educational Insights
Two Foolish Cats, The	K	F	250+	Literacy 2000	Rigby
Two Hungry Hippos	M	I	250+	Adams, Alison	Benchmark Education
Two Is a Pair	E	I	78	Teacher's Choice Series	Pearson Learning Group
Two Languages	K	I	202	Vocabulary Readers	Houghton Mifflin
Two Little Birds	D	RF	60	Story Steps	Rigby
Two Little Chicks	C	F	32	KinderReaders	Rigby
Two Little Dogs	E	F	74	Story Box	Wright Group/McGraw Hill
Two Little Ducks Get Lost	F	F	178	PM Plus Story Books	Rigby
Two Little Goldfish	I	RF	344	PM Story Books-Orange	Rigby
Two Little Mice, The	I	F	163	Literacy 2000	Rigby
Two More	LB	F	16	Voyages	SRA/McGraw Hill
Two Ogres, The	F	F	116	Joy Readers	Pearson Learning Group
Two Plus One Goes A.P.E.	L	RF	250+	Springstubb, Tricia	Scholastic
Two Plus Two	E	RF	44	Teacher's Choice Series	Pearson Learning Group
Two Points	B	RF	40	Kennedy, Jane.; Eaton, Audrey	Continental Press
Two Red Tugs	L	F	547	PM Story Books	Rigby
Two Runaways, The	M	RF	250+	Schultz, Irene	Wright Group/McGraw Hill
*Two Silly Trolls	J	F	250+	Jewell, Nancy	HarperTrophy
Two Stupid Cats	G	F	140	Sunshine	Wright Group/McGraw Hill
Two Tickets to Freedom: The True Story of Ellen and William Craft	S	HF	250+	Freedman, Florence	Scholastic
Two Traditions of Dance	P	I	382	Vocabulary Readers	Houghton Mifflin
*Two Tricky Tales	L	TL	250+	Pacific Literacy	Pacific Learning
Two Turtles	LB	RF	13	Ready Readers	Pearson Learning Group
Two Yellow Eyes	F	F	211	Sun Sprouts	ETA/Cuisenaire
Two-Part Invention	Z	B	250+	L'Engle, Madeleine	HarperCollins
Two-Star Day	O	RF	446	Leveled Readers	Houghton Mifflin
Tyler Toad and Thunder	M	F	250+	Crowe, Robert	Dutton
Tyler's Train	C	RF	42	Little Celebrations	Pearson Learning Group
Types of Trees	D	I	29	Vocabulary Readers	Houghton Mifflin
Tyrannosaurus Rex	M	I	250+	Prehistoric Creatures Then and Now	Steck-Vaughn
Tyrannosaurus Rex	M	I	250+	Discovering Dinosaurs	Capstone Press
Tyrannosaurus Rex	O	I	250+	True Books	Children's Press
Tyrannosaurus the Terrible	L	F	182	Wesley & the Dinosaurs	Wright Group/McGraw Hill
Ty's One-man Band	L	RF	250+	Walter, Mildred Pitts	Scholastic
U.S. Airforce, The	N	I	250+	The U.S. Armed Forces	Capstone Press
U.S. Army, The	N	I	250+	The U.S. Armed Forces	Capstone Press
U.S. Congress, The	Q	I	250+	Let's See	Compass Point Books
U.S. Constitution, The	T	I	250+	We The People	Compass Point Books
U.S. Marine Corps, The	N	I	250+	The U.S. Armed Forces	Capstone Press
U.S. Navy, The	N	I	250+	The U.S. Armed Forces	Capstone Press
U.S. Supreme Court, The	Q	I	250+	Let's See	Compass Point Books
UFOs	X	I	250+	The Unexplained	Capstone Press
Ugly Duckling, The	I	TL	250+	Literacy 2000	Rigby
Ugly Duckling, The	J	TL	452	PM Tales and Plays-Turquoise	Rigby
Ugly Duckling, The	J	TL	558	Tales from Hans Andersen	Wright Group/McGraw Hill
Ugly Mug	P	RF	250+	Joseph, Vivienne	Pacific Learning
Uh-Oh!	D	RF	62	Rigby Literacy	Rigby
Uh-Oh! Said the Crow	J	F	250+	Oppenheim, Joanna	Bantam
Ultimate Field Trip 1: Adventures in the Amazon Rain Forest	S	I	250+	Goodman, Susan E.	Simon & Schuster
Ulysses S. Grant	U	B	250+	Profiles of the Presidents	Compass Point Books

* Collection of short stories

TITLE	LEVEL	GENRE	WORD COUNT	AUTHOR / SERIES	PUBLISHER / DISTRIBUTOR
Ulysses S. Grant	U	B	250+	Let Freedom Ring	Red Brick Learning
Umbrella	C	F	73	Story Box	Wright Group/McGraw Hill
Umbrellas	L	I	430	Sunshine	Wright Group/McGraw Hill
Unbelievable Johnny Appleseed, The	N	B	250+	Leveled Readers Language Support	Houghton Mifflin
Unbelievable!	K	SF	250+	Shulman, Lisa	Hampton-Brown
Unclaimed Treasures	X	RF	250+	MacLachlan, Patricia	HarperTrophy
Uncle Buncle's House	C	RF	56	Sunshine	Wright Group/McGraw Hill
Uncle Carlos's Barbecue	H	RF	207	Foundations	Wright Group/McGraw Hill
Uncle Elephant	J	F	1784	Lobel, Arnold	HarperCollins
Uncle Elephant and Uncle Tiger	D	TL	77	Joy Readers	Pearson Learning Group
Uncle Jim	G	RF	127	Windmill Books	Rigby
Uncle Joe	H	F	149	Pacific Literacy	Pacific Learning
Uncle Tease	N	RF	250+	Literacy Tree	Rigby
Uncle Timi's Sleep	G	RF	102	Pacific Literacy	Pacific Learning
Uncles	D	I	36	Pebble Books	Capstone Press
Uncle's Bakery	H	RF	81	Early Reader	Compass Point Books
Uncle's Clever Tricks	D	RF	61	Joy Readers	Pearson Learning Group
Under a Full Moon	D	F	65	Leveled Readers	Houghton Mifflin
Under a Microscope	H	I	254	Sunshine	Wright Group/McGraw Hill
Under My Bed	C	F	49	Little Celebrations	Pearson Learning Group
Under My Bed	D	F	49	Literacy 2000	Rigby
Under My Nose	O	B	250+	Ehlert, Lois	Richard C. Owen
Under My Sombrero	F	F	79	Books for Young Learners	Richard C. Owen
Under the Bed	A	RF	28	Smart Starts	Rigby
Under the Big Top	E	I	103	Twig	Wright Group/McGraw Hill
Under the Blood-Red Sun	W	HF	250+	Salisbury, Graham	Bantam
Under the Bright Lights	R	I	466	Vocabulary Readers	Houghton Mifflin
Under the City	K	I	206	Sunshine	Wright Group/McGraw Hill
Under the Ground	Q	I	250+	Wildcats	Wright Group/McGraw Hill
Under the Ground	C	I	42	Foundations	Wright Group/McGraw Hill
Under the Ground	K	I	250+	Pluckrose, Henry	Franklin Watts
Under the Ground	P	I	250+	Literacy 2000	Rigby
Under the Ocean	T	I	614	Vocabulary Readers	Houghton Mifflin
Under the Old Oak Tree	G	F	205	Seedlings	Continental Press
Under the Royal Palms	V	B	250+	Ada, Alma Flor	Scholastic
Under the Sky	C	I	44	Learn to Read	Creative Teaching Press
Under the Umbrella	C	RF	60	Phonics and Friends	Hampton-Brown
Under Water	A	I	35	Twig	Wright Group/McGraw Hill
Under Wraps	U	I	250+	Goldish, Meish	Scholastic
Undercover Tailback	O	RF	250+	Christopher, Matt	Scholastic
Underfoot	N	I	250+	Look Once Look Again	Creative Teaching Press
Underground	C	I	31	Twig	Wright Group/McGraw Hill
Underground Railroad, The	V	I	250+	Bial, Raymond	Houghton Mifflin
Underground Railroad, The	V	I	250+	Cornerstones of Freedom	Children's Press
Underground Railroad, The	N	I	250+	Twig	Wright Group/McGraw Hill
Underground Rescue	W	RF	2180	Leveled Readers	Houghton Mifflin
Understanding Newton's Laws	Y	I	2888	Leveled Readers Science	Houghton Mifflin
Understudies	P	RF	250+	Bookweb	Rigby
Underwater	I	I	100	Start to Read	School Zone
Underwater Animals	Q	I	250+	Explorers	Wright Group/McGraw Hill
Underwater Journey	F	I	60	Sunshine	Wright Group/McGraw Hill
Underwater with Jacques Cousteau	L	B	633	Leveled Readers Science	Houghton Mifflin

* Collection of short stories

TITLE	LEVEL	GENRE	WORD COUNT	AUTHOR / SERIES	PUBLISHER / DISTRIBUTOR
Undying Glory: The Story of the Massachusetts 54th Regiment	U	HF	250+	Cox, Clinton	Scholastic
Unexpected Hero, An	W	RF	2407	Leveled Readers	Houghton Mifflin
Unexpected Treasure	Q	RF	250+	Ragged Island Mysteries	Wright Group/McGraw Hill
Unhappy Troll, The	D	F	47	Ray's Readers	Outside the Box
Unicorns Don't Give Sleigh Rides	M	F	250+	Dadey, Debbie; Jones, Marcia Thornton	Scholastic
United Nations, The	R	I	250+	Rigby Focus	Rigby
United States Constitution, The	V	I	250+	Let Freedom Ring	Red Brick Learning
United States Holocaust Memorial Museum, The	W	I	250+	Cornerstones of Freedom	Children's Press
United States Marshals Service	S	I	250+	Law Enforcement	Capstone Press
*Universal Solvent and Other Cases, The	O	RF	250+	Simon, Seymour	Avon
Universe, The	Q	I	250+	Pair-It-Books	Steck-Vaughn
Unsinkable Madame C. J. Walker, The	Y	B	3573	Leveled Readers	Houghton Mifflin
Until We Got Princess	E	RF	94	Bookshop	Mondo
Unusual Coin, The	O	F	951	Leveled Readers	Houghton Mifflin
Unusual Machines	J	I	229	Little Red Readers	Sundance
Unusual Show, An	H	F	63	Blonder, Ellen	Scholastic
Unusual Spiders	N	I	250+	Jensen, Ned	Wright Group/McGraw Hill
Up and Away	Q	I	250+	Explorers	Wright Group/McGraw Hill
Up and Away!: Taking a Flight	N	RF	250+	Bookshop	Mondo
Up and Down	C	I	81	PM Plus Nonfiction	Rigby
Up and Down	C	RF	68	Rigby Literacy	Rigby
Up and Down	D	RF	99	New Way Red	Steck-Vaughn
Up and Down	B	I	25	Little Books for Early Readers	University of Maine
Up and Down	C	RF	92	Handprints C, Set 1	Educator's Publishing Service
Up and Down	E	RF	79	Storyteller-Setting Sun	Wright Group/McGraw Hill
Up and Up	WB	RF	N/A	Hughes, Shirley	Lothrop, Lee & Shepard
Up Close	G	I	123	Discovery Links	Newbridge
Up High in the Mountains	N	RF	250+	Wildcats	Wright Group/McGraw Hill
Up in a Tree	C	RF	47	Sunshine	Wright Group/McGraw Hill
Up in the Air	P	I	250+	Wildcats	Wright Group/McGraw Hill
Up in the Sky	B	I	56	PM Plus Starters	Rigby
Up the Amazon	Q	I	250+	Windows on Literacy	National Geographic
Up the Haystack	H	RF	251	Bookshop	Mondo
Up the Tree	D	RF	41	New Way Red	Steck-Vaughn
Up the Tree	B	RF	38	First Stories	Pacific Learning
Up They Go	B	RF	30	Ready Readers	Pearson Learning Group
Up Went Edmond	D	F	26	Pacific Literacy	Pacific Learning
Up Went the Goat	C	F	38	Start to Read	School Zone
Up, Down, and All Around	D	I	44	Windows on Literacy	National Geographic
Up, Up, and Away	B	I	40	Lighthouse	Rigby
Up, Up, and Away	M	I	250+	Twig	Wright Group/McGraw Hill
Up, Up, and Away: The Story of Amelia Earhart	F	B	42	Canizares, Susan; Chanko, Pamela	Scholastic
Ups and Downs of Carl Davis III, The	T	RF	250+	Guy, Rosa	Language for Learning Assoc.
Upside-Down Elephant, The	K	RF	396	Leveled Readers	Houghton Mifflin
Upside-Down Reader, The	L	F	250+	Gruber, Wolfram	North-South Books
Upstate Autumn	R	RF	1676	Leveled Readers	Houghton Mifflin
Uranus	O	I	250+	Vogt, Gregory L.	Red Brick Learning
Uranus	S	I	250+	Our Solar System	Compass Point Books
Uranus	N	I	250+	A True Book	Children's Press
Urban Wildlife	R	I	1212	Leveled Readers	Houghton Mifflin

* Collection of short stories

TITLE	LEVEL	GENRE	WORD COUNT	AUTHOR / SERIES	PUBLISHER / DISTRIBUTOR
Us and Uncle Fraud	S	RF	250+	Lowry, Lois	Houghton Mifflin
Usborne Book of Inventors, The	W	B	250+	Reid, Struan; Fara, Patricia	Scholastic
Usborne Book of Inventors, The: From Davinci to Biro	X	B	250+	Reid, Struan; Fara, Patricia	Scholastic
Use Your Beak!	F	RF	106	Erickson, Betty	Continental Press
Using a Beak	M	I	250+	Sails	Rigby
Using a Microscope	H	I	182	Rigby Focus	Rigby
Using a Tail	M	I	250+	Sails	Rigby
Using Magnets	F	I	160	Early Connections	Benchmark Education
Using Nature's Gifts	K	I	250+	People, Spaces & Places	Rand McNally
Using Numbers at Work	C	I	75	Early Connections	Benchmark Education
Using Rocks	K	I	167	Windows on Literacy	National Geographic
Using the Library	L	I	291	Wonder World	Wright Group/McGraw Hill
Using the River	M	I	250+	Rigby Literacy	Rigby
Using Tools	C	I	30	Discovery Links	Newbridge
Using Tools at Work	E	I	118	Early Connections	Benchmark Education
Using Wheels	G	I	115	Little Red Readers	Sundance
Using Your Safety Senses	K	I	413	Leveled Readers Science	Houghton Mifflin
Using Your Senses at School	F	I	37	Windows on Literacy	National Geographic
Utah	R	I	250+	This Land Is Your Land	Compass Point Books
Utes, The	P	I	250+	Native Peoples	Red Brick Learning
V is for Vest	C	I	35	Learn to Read	Creative Teaching Press
Vacation Journal, A	M	B	250+	Discovery World	Rigby
Vacation Under the Volcano	M	F	250+	Osborne, Mary Pope	Random House
Vacation, The	C	RF	94	Emergent	Pioneer Valley
Vacations	B	RF	22	Smart Starts	Rigby
Vagabond Crabs	J	I	117	Literacy 2000	Rigby
Valentine Star, The	M	RF	250+	Giff, Patricia Reilly	Bantam
Valentine's Checkup	C	RF	45	Little Books	Sadlier-Oxford
Valentine's Day	O	I	250+	Holidays and Festivals	Compass Point Books
Valentine's Day	E	I	132	Fiesta Holiday Series	Pearson Learning Group
Valentine's Day	P	I	250+	Let's See	Compass Point Books
Valentine's Day	J	I	132	Pebble Books	Capstone Press
Valentine's Day	C	F	49	Story Box	Wright Group/McGraw Hill
Vampire Trouble	L	F	250+	Dadey, Debbie; Jones, Marcia Thornton	Scholastic
Vampire Who Came For Christmas, The	Q	F	250+	Regan, Diane Curtis	Bantam
Vampires Don't Wear Polka Dots	M	F	250+	Dadey, Debbie; Jones, Marcia Thornton	Scholastic
Van Gogh	S	B	250+	Masterpieces: Artists and Their Works	Red Brick Learning
Van Gogh Cafe, The	S	RF	250+	Rylant, Cynthia	Harcourt School Publishers
Van, The	B	RF	48	Phonics and Friends	Hampton-Brown
Vanished!: The Mysterious Disappearance of Amelia Earhart	P	B	250+	Kulling, Monica	Random House
Vegetable Group, The	G	I	88	Pebble Books	Capstone Press
Vegetable Soup	A	I	24	Vocabulary Readers	Houghton Mifflin
Vegetable Soup	E	F	67	Leveled Readers	Houghton Mifflin
Vegetable Soup	G	RF	84	Morris, Ann	Scholastic
Vegetables	LB	I	7	Windows on Literacy	National Geographic
Vegetables and How They Grow	F	I	86	Rosen Real Readers	Rosen Publishing Group
Vehicles for Fun and Sports	K	I	439	PM Plus	Rigby
Vehicles in the Air	K	I	436	PM Plus	Rigby
Velveteen Rabbit, The	Q	F	250+	Williams, Margery	Hearst

* Collection of short stories

TITLE	LEVEL	GENRE	WORD COUNT	AUTHOR / SERIES	PUBLISHER / DISTRIBUTOR
Venus	W	I	250+	World Mythology	Capstone Press
Venus	N	I	250+	A True Book	Children's Press
Venus	S	I	250+	Our Solar System	Compass Point Books
Venus	Q	I	250+	Vogt, Gregory L.	The Millbrook Press
Vermont	R	I	250+	This Land Is Your Land	Compass Point Books
Vert Skating: Mastering the Ramp	Q	I	250+	Skateboarding	Capstone Press
Very Best Fish, The	N	RF	250+	Leveled Readers Language Support	Houghton Mifflin
Very Big	D	I	49	Ready Readers	Pearson Learning Group
Very Big Potato, The	H	RF	250+	Cherrington, Janelle	Scholastic
Very Busy Spider, The	I	F	263	Carle, Eric	Philomel Books
Very Funny Act, A	H	RF	181	Home Connection Collection	Rigby
Very Greedy Dog, The	H	TL	228	Aesop's Fables	Pearson Learning Group
Very Happy Birthday, A	M	RF	1017	Jellybeans	Rigby
Very Hungry Caterpillar, The	J	F	237	Carle, Eric	Philomel Books
Very Special Kwanzaa, A	O	I	250+	Chocolate, Deborah M. Newton	Scholastic
Very Strange Dollhouse, A	L	F	250+	Dussling, Jennifer	Grosset & Dunlap
Very Strong Baby, The	E	F	74	Joy Readers	Pearson Learning Group
Very Thin Cat of Alloway Road, The	L	RF	250+	Literacy 2000	Rigby
Veterans Day	L	I	96	National Holidays	Red Brick Learning
Veterans Day	K	I	250+	Cotton, Jaqueline S.	Scholastic
Veterans Day	N	I	250+	Leveled Readers Social Studies	Houghton Mifflin
Veterans' Day	N	I	555	Leveled Readers Social Studies	Houghton Mifflin
Veterinarians	M	I	250+	Community Workers	Compass Point Books
Veterinarians	L	I	250+	Ready, Dee	Red Brick Learning
Vibrations	H	I	38	Pebble Books	Red Brick Learning
Vicar of Nibbleswick, The	O	RF	250+	Dahl, Roald	Puffin Books
Vicky the High Jumper	K	I	250+	Literacy 2000	Rigby
Vicky's Box	J	F	412	Cambridge Reading	Pearson Learning Group
Victor and the Computer Cat	F	RF	92	Oxford Reading Tree	Oxford University Press
Victor and the Kite	F	F	84	Oxford Reading Tree	Oxford University Press
Victor and the Martian	H	F	109	Oxford Reading Tree	Oxford University Press
Victor and the Sail-cart	H	F	94	Oxford Reading Tree	Oxford University Press
Victor Makes a TV	H	F	85	Reading Unlimited	Pearson Learning Group
Victor Sews	P	RF	1323	Leveled Readers	Houghton Mifflin
Victor Takes a Sewing Class	N	RF	250+	Leveled Readers Language Support	Houghton Mifflin
Victor the Champion	G	F	102	Oxford Reading Tree	Oxford University Press
Victor the Hero	H	F	103	Oxford Reading Tree	Oxford University Press
Video Game	F	RF	109	Alphakids	Sundance
Vietnam	Q	I	250+	First Reports	Compass Point Books
Vietnam	O	I	250+	Dahl, Michael	Red Brick Learning
Vietnam Veterans Memorial, The	Q	I	250+	National Landmarks	Red Brick Learning
Vietnam Women's Memorial, The	W	I	250+	Cornerstones of Freedom	Children's Press
View from Above, A	M	I	250+	Rigby Literacy	Rigby
View from Saturday, The	U	F	250+	Konigsburg, E. L.	Atheneum
Viking Ships at Sunrise	M	F	250+	Osborne, Mary Pope	Random House
Vikings, The	S	I	250+	Journey Into Civilization	Chelsea House
Vile Village, The	V	F	250+	Snicket, Lemony	Scholastic
Village by the Sea, The	U	RF	250+	Fox, Paula	Bantam
Virginia	R	I	250+	This Land Is Your Land	Compass Point Books
Virtual Fred	O	SF	250+	Courtney, Vincent	Random House
Visit to a Museum	N	I	306	Leveled Readers Social Studies	Houghton Mifflin
Visit to a Pueblo, A	K	I	129	Vocabulary Readers	Houghton Mifflin

* Collection of short stories

TITLE	LEVEL	GENRE	WORD COUNT	AUTHOR / SERIES	PUBLISHER / DISTRIBUTOR
Visit to Cousin Boris	I	F	250+	Popcorn	Sundance
Visit to the Airport, A	H	I	105	Pebble Plus	Red Brick Learning
Visit to the Apple Orchards, A	H	I	114	Pebble Plus	Red Brick Learning
Visit to the City, A	D	I	54	Vocabulary Readers	Houghton Mifflin
Visit to the Dentist's Office, A	H	I	116	Pebble Plus	Red Brick Learning
Visit to the Doctor, A	A	I	28	Little Books for Early Readers	University of Maine
Visit to the Library, A	E	I	109	Foundations	Wright Group/McGraw Hill
Visit to the Police Station, A	I	I	115	Pebble Plus	Capstone Press
Visit to the Statue of Liberty, A	G	I	77	Independent Readers Social Studies	Houghton Mifflin
Visit to Vancouver Island, A	O	RF	1261	Leveled Readers Social Studies	Houghton Mifflin
Visiting a Village	T	I	250+	Kalman, Bobbie	Scholastic
Visiting Grandma and Grandpa	G	RF	136	Carousel Readers	Pearson Learning Group
Visiting the Eagle Hotel	M	I	250+	Rigby Literacy	Rigby
Visiting the Police Station	I	I	200	Rosen Real Readers	Rosen Publishing Group
Visiting the Vet	H	I	140	Sun Sprouts	ETA/Cuisenaire
Visiting the Vet	H	I	259	Foundations	Wright Group/McGraw Hill
Visitor, The	I	F	250+	Popcorn	Sundance
Visitors	E	RF	46	Literacy 2000	Rigby
Viva Mexico	L	I	432	Leveled Readers Social Studies	Houghton Mifflin
Viva México!: A Story of Benito Juárez and Cinco de Mayo	Q	B	250+	Stories of America	Steck-Vaughn
Voice of the People, The: American Democracy in Action	V	I	250+	Maestro, Betsy & Giulio	William Morrow
Voice of the Pioneer: Carrie Chapman Catt	R	B	1916	Leveled Readers Social Studies	Houghton Mifflin
Volcano	C	I	44	Science	Outside the Box
Volcano	U	I	250+	Lauber, Patricia	Scholastic
Volcano Goddess Will See You Now, The	N	F	250+	The Zack Files	Grosset & Dunlap
Volcano Woman	M	TL	250+	Cambridge Reading	Pearson Learning Group
Volcanoes	Q	I	250+	Windows on Literacy	National Geographic
Volcanoes	N	I	250+	Early Connections	Benchmark Education
Volcanoes	Q	I	250+	Worldwise	Grolier Press
Volcanoes	N	I	250+	A True Book	Children's Press
Volcanoes	V	I	250+	iOpeners	Pearson Learning Group
Volcanoes	L	I	250+	Sunshine	Wright Group/McGraw Hill
Volcanoes	Q	I	250+	Explorers	Wright Group/McGraw Hill
Volcanoes and Earthquakes	T	I	250+	Lauber, Patricia	Language for Learning Assoc.
Volcanoes and Geysers	O	I	250+	PM Plus Story Books	Rigby
Volcanoes Around the World	O	I	380	Vocabulary Readers	Houghton Mifflin
Volcanoes National Park	S	I	1396	Leveled Readers Science	Houghton Mifflin
Voting and Elections	Q	I	250+	Let's See	Compass Point Books
Voyage Across the Pacific	S	I	1250	Leveled Readers	Houghton Mifflin
Voyage of Mae Jemison, The	H	B	46	Canizares, Susan; Berger, Samantha	Scholastic
Voyage of Patience Goodspeed, The	U	HF	250+	Frederick, Heather Vogel	Simon & Schuster
Voyage of the Clowns, The	J	F	250+	The Wright Skills	Wright Group/McGraw Hill
Voyage of the Fram, The	R	I	611	Vocabulary Readers	Houghton Mifflin
Voyage of the Frog, The	S	RF	250+	Paulsen, Gary	Bantam
Voyage to Antartica	T	I	2505	Leveled Readers Science	Houghton Mifflin
Voyage, The	M	F	250+	Pair-It Books	Steck-Vaughn
Voyager: An Adventure Through Space	Q	I	250+	Gustafson, John	Scholastic
Vroom!	G	F	167	Rigby Literacy	Rigby
Vulpes The Red Fox	T	F	250+	George, Jean Craighead	Puffin Books

* Collection of short stories

TITLE	LEVEL	GENRE	WORD COUNT	AUTHOR / SERIES	PUBLISHER / DISTRIBUTOR
Vultures on Vacation	C	F	36	Ready Readers	Pearson Learning Group
W.E.B. DuBois and the Fight for a Just Society	R	B	904	Leveled Readers Social Studies	Houghton Mifflin
Wacky Jacks	L	RF	250+	Adler, David A.	Random House
Wacky Plant Cycles	O	I	250+	Bookshop	Mondo
Wacky Wheels	N	I	250+	Pacific Literacy	Pacific Learning
Wagon Ride, The	E	RF	115	Teacher's Choice Series	Pearson Learning Group
Wagon Wheels	K	HF	250+	Brenner, Barbara	HarperTrophy
Wagon, The	H	RF	78	Reading Unlimited	Pearson Learning Group
Wainscott Weasel, The	T	F	250+	Seidler, Tor	HarperCollins
Wait for Me	C	RF	75	Little Books	Sadlier-Oxford
Wait for Me	D	RF	185	Visions	Wright Group/McGraw Hill
Wait for Your Turn!	H	RF	141	Teacher's Choice Series	Pearson Learning Group
Wait Skates	G	RF	58	Rookie Readers	Children's Press
Wait Till Helen Comes	U	F	250+	Hahn, Mary Downing	Houghton Mifflin
Wait Until Next Year	V	RF	2226	Leveled Readers	Houghton Mifflin
Waiting	G	RF	59	Literacy 2000	Rigby
Waiting	A	RF	28	Story Box	Wright Group/McGraw Hill
Waiting	E	RF	75	Voyages	SRA/McGraw Hill
Waiting for a Frog	G	RF	124	Coats, Glenn	Kaeden Books
Waiting for Granny	F	RF	179	Leveled Readers Language Support	Houghton Mifflin
Waiting for the Rain	J	RF	307	Foundations	Wright Group/McGraw Hill
Waiting in Line	F	RF	74	City Stories	Rigby
Wake Me in Spring	J	F	301	Preller, James	Scholastic
Wake Up Ginger	C	F	70	Bookshop	Mondo
Wake Up Mom!	C	RF	94	Sunshine	Wright Group/McGraw Hill
Wake Up!	C	F	62	Story Steps	Rigby
Wake Up, Dad	C	RF	67	PM Story Books	Rigby
Wake Up, Emily, It's Mother's Day	M	RF	250+	Giff, Patricia Reilly	Yearling
Wake Up, Scooterville	K	RF	250+	Stamper, Judith Bauer	Scholastic
Wake Up, Sleepyheads!	F	RF	35	Little Books	Sadlier-Oxford
Wake Up, Sun!	E	F	250+	Harrison, David	Random House
Wake Up, Wake Up!	D	F	110	Wildsmith, Brian & Rebecca	Scholastic
Wake Up, Young Soldier	R	I	864	Independent Readers Social Studies	Houghton Mifflin
Wake-Up, Baby!	J	F	209	Oppenheim, Joanna	Bantam
Walk for Pickles, A	D	RF	82	Pickles the Dog Series	Pioneer Valley
Walk in My Woods, A	D	I	83	Independent Readers Science	Houghton Mifflin
*Walk in My World, A	Y	RF	250+	Mazer, Anne	Persea Books
Walk in the Rain, A	B	RF	28	Pair-It Books	Steck-Vaughn
Walk in the Woods, A	F	F	212	Leveled Readers	Houghton Mifflin
Walk Through a Rainforest, A: Life in the Ituri Forest of Zaire	V	RF	250+	Creech, Sharon	HarperCollins
Walk Through History on the Freedom Trail	Q	I	828	Leveled Readers Social Studies	Houghton Mifflin
Walk Two Moons	W	RF	250+	Creech, Sharon	HarperCollins
Walk With Grandpa, A	L	RF	388	Read Alongs	Rigby
Walk with John Muir, A	U	B	2237	Independent Readers Social Studies	Houghton Mifflin
Walk, Ride, Run	D	RF	116	PM Plus Story Books	Rigby
Walk, The	B	RF	29	Early Emergent	Pioneer Valley
Walk, The	G	RF	129	Reading Unlimited	Pearson Learning Group
Walkathon, The	K	RF	250+	PM Story Books-Silver	Rigby
Walker's Crossing	X	RF	250+	Naylor, Phyllis Reynolds	Aladdin
Walking	M	I	250+	Literacy 2000	Rigby

* Collection of short stories

TITLE	LEVEL	GENRE	WORD COUNT	AUTHOR / SERIES	PUBLISHER / DISTRIBUTOR
Walking by the Rio	K	RF	118	Books for Young Learners	Richard C. Owen
Walking For Freedom: The Montgomery Bus Boycott	R	I	250+	Kelso, Richard	Steck-Vaughn
Walking Home Alone	J	RF	327	Books for Young Learners	Richard C. Owen
Walking in the Autumn	H	I	206	PM Nonfiction-Green	Rigby
Walking in the Jungle	E	RF	113	Little Red Readers	Sundance
Walking in the Spring	H	I	168	PM Nonfiction-Green	Rigby
Walking in the Summer	H	I	233	PM Nonfiction-Green	Rigby
Walking in the Winter	H	I	251	PM Nonfiction-Green	Rigby
Walking on the Moon	N	I	250+	Explore Space	Red Brick Learning
Walking the Choctaw Road	Y	TL	250+	Tingle, Tim	Cinco Puntos Press
Walking the Dog	D	RF	69	Sun Sprouts	ETA/Cuisenaire
Walking the Dogs	H	RF	80	City Stories	Rigby
Walking the Road to Freedom: A Story About Sojourner Truth	Q	B	250+	Ferris, Jeri	Dell
Walking to School	C	RF	38	Voyages	SRA/McGraw Hill
Walking Up Walls	I	I	140	Windows on Literacy	National Geographic
Walking, Walking	C	I	32	Twig	Wright Group/McGraw Hill
Walkingsticks	I	I	89	Bugs, Bugs, Bugs	Capstone Press
Walkingsticks	I	I	83	Pebble Books	Red Brick Learning
Wall of Names, A: The Story of the Vietnam Veterans Memorial	P	I	250+	Donnelly, Judy	Random House
Wall, The	P	HF	250+	Bunting, Eve	Clarion
Walls of the World	X	I	250+	iOpeners	Pearson Learning Group
Walruses	I	I	55	Pebble Books	Red Brick Learning
Walt Disney's World	G	I	96	Leveled Readers Social Studies	Houghton Mifflin
Walter and the Inventor's Garden	L	F	250+	Pacific Literacy	Pacific Learning
Walter Hottle Bottle	L	RF	250+	Voyages	SRA/McGraw Hill
Walter the Warlock	M	F	250+	Hautzig, Deborah	Random House
Walter's Worries	L	F	250+	Pacific Literacy	Pacific Learning
Wampanoag, The: The People of the First Light	S	I	250+	American Indian Nations	Capstone Press
Wanderer, The	V	RF	250+	Creech, Sharon	HarperCollins
Wanted . . . Mud Blossom	P	RF	250+	Byars, Betsy	Dell
Wanted Dead or Alive: The True Story of Harriet Tubman	P	B	250+	McGovern, Ann	Scholastic
War Comes to Willy Freeman	U	HF	250+	Collier, James & Christopher	Dell
*War Dog Heroes: True Stories of Dog Courage in Wartime	S	I	250+	Sanderson, Jeannette	Scholastic
War of 1812, The	V	I	250+	Let Freedom Ring	Capstone Press
War of 1812, The	S	I	250+	A First Book	Franklin Watts
War of the Worlds, The	Z	SF	250+	Wells, H. G.	Tom Doherty
War Shirt, The	M	RF	250+	Greetings	Rigby
War With Grandpa, The	S	RF	250+	Smith, Robert Kimmel	Bantam
Warm Clothes	C	I	51	Pebble Books	Capstone Press
Warming Up! Cooling Off!	I	I	553	Sunshine	Wright Group/McGraw Hill
Warning: Volcano!: The Story of Mount St. Helens	O	I	250+	Rosen Real Readers	Rosen Publishing Group
Warren G. Harding	U	B	250+	Profiles of the Presidents	Compass Point Books
Warthogs	O	I	250+	Holmes, Kevin J.	Red Brick Learning
Warton and the King of the Skies	O	F	250+	Erickson, Russell E.	Houghton Mifflin
Wash Day	A	RF	35	Voyages	SRA/McGraw Hill
Washing	E	RF	150	Foundations	Wright Group/McGraw Hill
Washing Our Dog	H	RF	120	Alphakids	Sundance
Washing the Dog	G	I	84	Little Red Readers	Sundance

* Collection of short stories

TITLE	LEVEL	GENRE	WORD COUNT	AUTHOR / SERIES	PUBLISHER / DISTRIBUTOR
Washing the Dog	G	I	84	Little Readers	Houghton Mifflin
Washing the Elephant	B	F	35	Lighthouse	Rigby
Washington	R	I	250+	This Land Is Your Land	Compass Point Books
Washington Monument, The	Q	I	250+	National Landmarks	Red Brick Learning
Washington, D.C.	R	I	250+	This Land Is Your Land	Compass Point Books
Washington, D.C.	L	I	163	Rosen Real Readers	Rosen Publishing Group
Washington, D.C.	K	I	187	Windows on Literacy	National Geographic
Wasps	I	I	59	Pebble Books	Red Brick Learning
Waste Not: Time to Recycle	K	I	250+	Spyglass Books	Compass Point Books
Waste of Space, A	M	RF	250+	SupaDoopers	Sundance
Watch by the Sea, The	L	RF	250+	Cambridge Reading	Pearson Learning Group
Watch It Grow	K	I	243	Spyglass Books	Compass Point Books
Watch Me	E	RF	151	Handprints C, Set 2	Educator's Publishing Service
Watch Me Zoom	C	RF	45	Windmill Books	Rigby
Watch Out	B	F	44	Bookshop	Mondo
Watch Out!	C	F	27	Literacy 2000	Rigby
Watch Out, Man-Eating Snake	L	RF	250+	Giff, Patricia Reilly	Bantam
Watch the Sky	D	I	41	Windows on Literacy	National Geographic
Watcher, The	Z	RF	250+	Howe, James	Simon & Schuster
Watchers: I.D.	V	SF	250+	Lerangis, Peter	Scholastic
Watchers: Island	V	SF	250+	Lerangis, Peter	Scholastic
Watchers: Lab 6	V	SF	250+	Lerangis, Peter	Scholastic
Watchers: Last Stop	V	SF	250+	Lerangis, Peter	Scholastic
Watchers: Rewind	V	SF	250+	Lerangis, Peter	Scholastic
Watchers: War	V	SF	250+	Lerangis, Peter	Scholastic
Watching Every Drop	M	I	250+	Home Connection Collection	Rigby
Watching Josh	Q	RF	250+	Ragged Island Mysteries	Wright Group/McGraw Hill
Watching the Game	G	RF	210	Momentum Literacy Program	Troll Associates
Watching the Weather	G	I	142	Discovery Links	Newbridge
Watching the Whales	L	RF	267	Foundations	Wright Group/McGraw Hill
Watching TV	E	RF	89	Foundations	Wright Group/McGraw Hill
Watching TV	B	RF	18	Sunshine	Wright Group/McGraw Hill
Water	A	HF	21	Yellow Umbrella Books	Red Brick Learning
Water	C	RF	20	Carousel Readers	Pearson Learning Group
Water	J	I	250+	Momentum Literacy Program	Troll Associates
Water	J	I	164	Windows on Literacy	National Geographic
Water	B	RF	33	Sunshine	Wright Group/McGraw Hill
Water	N	I	250+	Simply Science	Compass Point Books
Water	B	I	36	Science	Outside the Box
Water	H	I	94	Wonder World	Wright Group/McGraw Hill
Water	E	I	99	Early Connections	Benchmark Education
Water	B	I	28	Literacy 2000	Rigby
Water	B	I	24	Little Celebrations	Pearson Learning Group
Water All Around	C	I	26	Leveled Readers Science	Houghton Mifflin
Water and Wind	N	I	250+	PM Plus Story Books	Rigby
Water as a Gas	L	I	127	Pebble Books	Capstone Press
Water as a Liquid	I	I	141	Pebble Books	Red Brick Learning
Water as a Solid	J	I	113	Pebble Books	Red Brick Learning
Water at Work	K	I	159	Instant Readers	Harcourt School Publishers
Water Boatman, The	F	I	44	Pacific Literacy	Pacific Learning
Water Buffalo Days	P	B	250+	Huynh, Quong Nhuong	HarperTrophy
Water Bugs	I	I	76	Pebble Books	Red Brick Learning
Water Can Be . . .	B	I	17	Science	Outside the Box

TITLE	LEVEL	GENRE	WORD COUNT	AUTHOR / SERIES	PUBLISHER / DISTRIBUTOR
Water Can Change	K	I	138	Windows on Literacy	National Geographic
Water Changes	C	I	36	Discovery Links	Newbridge
Water Changes	D	I	25	Instant Readers	Harcourt School Publishers
Water Cycle, The	L	I	146	Pebble Books	Capstone Press
Water Cycle, The	J	I	250+	Yellow Umbrella Books	Capstone Press
Water Falling	D	I	41	Literacy 2000	Rigby
Water Fight, The	E	RF	64	Oxford Reading Tree	Oxford University Press
Water for the World	M	I	250+	Home Connection Collection	Rigby
Water Goes Up! Water Goes Down!	K	I	299	Early Connections	Benchmark Education
*Water Lilies and Other Stories	L	TL	250+	New Way Literature	Steck-Vaughn
Water Monsters	Z	I	250+	Innes, Brian	Steck-Vaughn
Water Power	J	I	86	Windows on Literacy	National Geographic
Water Wise	N	I	250+	iOpeners	Pearson Learning Group
Water! Water!	F	I	186	Story Basket	Wright Group/McGraw Hill
Water! Water!	C	I	33	Sunshine	Wright Group/McGraw Hill
Water, Ice, and Steam	J	I	143	Rosen Real Readers	Rosen Publishing Group
Water, Ice, and Steam	I	I	150	Rosen Real Readers	Rosen Publishing Group
Water, Land, and Air	H	I	76	Windows on Literacy	National Geographic
Water, Water	B	I	48	Rigby Literacy	Rigby
Water, Water Everywhere	F	RF	61	Books for Young Learners	Richard C. Owen
Water, Water Everywhere!	C	I	27	Leveled Readers Science	Houghton Mifflin
Water: A Natural Resource	P	I	250+	Rigby Focus	Rigby
Water: Liquid, Solid, Gas	M	I	240	Twig	Wright Group/McGraw Hill
Water: Up, Down, and All Around	M	I	250+	Amazing Science	Picture Window Books
Waterfalls, Glaciers, and Avalanches	M	I	250+	PM Plus Nonfiction	Rigby
Waterhole	K	I	149	Planet Earth	Rigby
Waterhole, The	L	F	250+	Sunshine	Wright Group/McGraw Hill
Watermelon	J	I	61	Books for Young Learners	Richard C. Owen
Watermelon	E	I	81	Rise & Shine	Hampton-Brown
Watermelon for Lunch	G	F	196	Leveled Readers	Houghton Mifflin
Watermelon, The	D	RF	80	Joy Readers	Pearson Learning Group
Watermelons	WB	I	N/A	Windows on Literacy	National Geographic
Water's Journey	G	I	114	Instant Readers	Harcourt School Publishers
Watership Down	Y	F	250+	Adams, Richard	Avon
Waterstone, The	X	F	250+	Rupp, Rebecca	Candlewick Press
Watsons Go to Birmingham - 1963, The	U	HF	250+	Curtis, Christopher Paul	Bantam
Waves	E	F	70	Voyages	SRA/McGraw Hill
Waves and Rays	Y	I	2452	Independent Readers Science	Houghton Mifflin
Waves: The Changing Surface of the Sea	J	I	204	Wonder World	Wright Group/McGraw Hill
Waving Sheep, The	H	F	252	PM Story Books	Rigby
Wax Man, The	I	TL	250+	Loya, Olga	Scholastic
Wax Museum	L	I	250+	Cook, Donald	Grosset & Dunlap
Way Down South	F	F	109	Learn to Read	Creative Teaching Press
Way I Go to School, The	B	I	53	PM Starters	Rigby
Way Things Were, The	D	I	39	iOpeners	Pearson Learning Group
Way to Go	E	RF	138	Bookshop	Mondo
Way West, The: Journal of a Pioneer Woman	R	B	250+	Knight, Amelia Stewart	Simon & Schuster
Wayne's Box	E	F	114	Cambridge Reading	Pearson Learning Group
Ways to Go	D	RF	37	Early Readers	Compass Point Books
*Wayside School Gets a Little Stranger	P	F	250+	Sachar, Louis	Avon Camelot
*Wayside School is Falling Down	P	F	250+	Sachar, Louis	Avon
We All Play Sports	C	I	26	Pacific Literacy	Pacific Learning
We All Scream For Ice Cream	I	I	219	Early Connections	Benchmark Education
We Are a Big Family	A	RF	28	Leveled Readers Emergent	Houghton Mifflin

* Collection of short stories

TITLE	LEVEL	GENRE	WORD COUNT	AUTHOR / SERIES	PUBLISHER / DISTRIBUTOR
We Are All Alike	M	I	250+	Schaefer, Lola M.	Benchmark Education
We Are Best Friends	H	RF	629	Aliki	Morrow
We Are Firefighters	I	I	67	Vocabulary Readers	Houghton Mifflin
We Are Painting	A	RF	38	Alexander, Francie	Scholastic
We Are Playing	B	RF	19	Rigby Literacy	Rigby
We Are Singing	B	RF	26	Ready Readers	Pearson Learning Group
We Are Twins	A	I	24	Little Books for Early Readers	University of Maine
We Can	A	F	21	KinderReaders	Rigby
We Can Do It!	LB	RF	19	Rigby Focus	Rigby
We Can Eat the Plants	C	RF	38	Learn to Read	Creative Teaching Press
We Can Make Graphs	D	I	58	Learn to Read	Creative Teaching Press
We Can Make Pizza	A	I	30	Little Books for Early Readers	University of Maine
We Can Play	E	RF	58	TOTTS	Tott Publications
We Can Recycle	I	I	231	Independent Readers Science	Houghton Mifflin
We Can Recycle	B	I	28	Leveled Readers Science	Houghton Mifflin
We Can Run	C	RF	77	PM Starters	Rigby
We Can Share at School	B	RF	35	Learn to Read	Creative Teaching Press
We Can Share It	H	F	140	Little Celebrations	Pearson Learning Group
We Care for Our School	I	I	134	Wonder World	Wright Group/McGraw Hill
We Clean Up!	D	RF	35	Home Connection Collection	Rigby
We Dance	C	I	30	Pacific Literacy	Pacific Learning
We Dress Up	B	RF	56	PM Plus Starters	Rigby
We Eat Rice	C	RF	46	Bebop Books	Lee & Low Books Inc.
We Get Squished!	B	F	31	First Stories	Pacific Learning
We Go Out	A	I	41	PM Starters	Rigby
We Go to Grandma's House	C	I	63	Windows on Literacy	National Geographic
We Go to School	B	RF	27	Carousel Earlybirds	Pearson Learning Group
We Honor America	H	I	132	Rosen Real Readers	Rosen Publishing Group
We Just Moved!	I	F	250+	Krensky, Stephen	Scholastic
We Like	C	RF	42	Foundations	Wright Group/McGraw Hill
We Like Fish	D	I	109	PM Starters	Rigby
We Like Fruit	B	RF	33	Lee, Millen	Scholastic
We Like Pie!	A	RF	28	Leveled Readers Emergent	Houghton Mifflin
We Like Summer!	C	RF	41	Blevins, Wiley	Scholastic
We Like the Sun	C	RF	30	Pair-It Books	Steck-Vaughn
We Like to Graph	C	I	48	Coulton, Mia	Kaeden Books
We Like to Play	C	RF	70	Tarlow, Ellen	Scholastic
We Like to Play!	A	I	28	Leveled Readers Emergent	Houghton Mifflin
We Live Here	B	RF	25	Salzman, Gabriel	Scholastic
We Love Recess	C	I	63	Fiesta Series	Pearson Learning Group
We Love the Farm	C	RF	54	Lighthouse	Rigby
We Make Cookies	E	RF	48	Pair-It Books	Steck-Vaughn
We Make Music	D	F	44	Literacy 2000	Rigby
We Make Pizza	C	RF	37	Carousel Readers	Pearson Learning Group
We Need Zoo Keepers	H	I	72	Helpers in Our Community	Red Brick Learning
We Need Auto Mechanics	I	I	79	Pebble Books	Red Brick Learning
We Need Child Care Workers	E	I	58	Helpers in Our community	Red Brick Learning
We Need Construction Workers	I	I	59	Helpers in Our Community	Red Brick Learning
We Need Custodians	E	I	33	Pebble Books	Capstone Press
We Need Dentists	H	I	54	Pebble Books	Red Brick Learning
We Need Doctors	H	I	42	Pebble Books	Red Brick Learning
We Need Farmers	H	I	45	Pebble Books	Red Brick Learning
We Need Fire Fighters	G	I	64	Pebble Books	Red Brick Learning
We Need Garbage Collectors	I	I	77	Helpers in Our Community	Red Brick Learning

* Collection of short stories

TITLE	LEVEL	GENRE	WORD COUNT	AUTHOR / SERIES	PUBLISHER / DISTRIBUTOR
We Need Insects	N	I	250+	iOpeners	Pearson Learning Group
We Need Librarians	I	I	78	Pebble Books	Red Brick Learning
We Need Mail Carriers	G	I	61	Pebble Books	Red Brick Learning
We Need Nurses	H	I	65	Pebble Books	Red Brick Learning
We Need Pharmacists	I	I	81	Pebble Books	Red Brick Learning
We Need Plumbers	I	I	107	Pebble Books	Red Brick Learning
We Need Police Officers	G	I	59	Pebble Books	Red Brick Learning
We Need Principals	E	I	53	Pebble Books	Capstone Press
We Need School Bus Drivers	G	I	112	Pebble Books	Capstone Press
We Need Teachers	E	I	53	Pebble Books	Capstone Press
We Need Trees	C	I	33	Hoenecke, Karen	Kaeden Books
We Need Veterinarians	G	I	48	Pebble Books	Red Brick Learning
We Need Water	I	I	99	Pebble Books	Red Brick Learning
We Need Water	D	I	26	Science	Outside the Box
We Play Music	A	RF	20	Bebop Books	Lee & Low Books Inc.
We Play Together	A	RF	22	Blevins, Wiley	Scholastic
We Read	A	I	20	Blevins, Wiley	Scholastic
We Remember the Holocaust	Y	I	250+	Adler, David A.	Henry Holt & Co.
We Ride	B	I	40	Carousel Earlybirds	Pearson Learning Group
We Ride!	A	I	31	Vocabulary Readers	Houghton Mifflin
We Scream for Ice Cream	K	RF	250+	Chardiet, Bernice; Maccarone, Grace	Scholastic
We Shall Not Be Moved	Z	I	250+	Dash, Joan	Scholastic
We Ski	B	I	35	Storyteller-First Snow	Wright Group/McGraw Hill
We Use Numbers	J	I	298	Early Connections	Benchmark Education
We Use Water	C	I	48	Early Connections	Benchmark Education
We Use Water	B	I	42	Windows on Literacy	National Geographic
We Want Jobs!: A Story of the Great Depression	R	I	250+	Norrell, Robert J.	Steck-Vaughn
We Want That	F	RF	158	Visions	Wright Group/McGraw Hill
We Want Watermelon	B	RF	49	Phonics and Friends	Hampton-Brown
We Went Flying	C	RF	40	Carousel Earlybirds	Pearson Learning Group
We Went to the Zoo	B	I	32	Little Red Readers	Sundance
We Were There, Too!: Young People in U.S. History	Y	B	250+	Hoose, Phillip	Farrar, Straus and Giroux
We Wrote to Grandma	H	RF	239	Momentum Literacy Program	Troll Associates
Weather	N	I	250+	Simply Science	Compass Point Books
Weather	LB	I	14	Smart Starts	Rigby
Weather	N	I	250+	Literacy 2000	Rigby
Weather	O	I	250+	Fleisher, Julian	Scholastic
Weather	E	I	138	Early Connections	Benchmark Education
Weather	C	I	54	Chanko, Pamela; Moreton, Daniel	Scholastic
Weather Alert!	N	I	314	Independent Readers Social Studies	Houghton Mifflin
Weather Chart, The	B	I	24	Sunshine	Wright Group/McGraw Hill
Weather Days	A	I	24	Vocabulary Readers	Houghton Mifflin
Weather Drum, The	M	TL	250+	Cambridge Reading	Pearson Learning Group
Weather Forecast, The	I	F	272	Story Box	Wright Group/McGraw Hill
Weather in the City	C	I	68	Windows on Literacy	National Geographic
Weather Report, The	E	I	119	Rosen Real Readers	Rosen Publishing Group
Weather Today	H	RF	129	Windows on Literacy	National Geographic
Weather Watch	N	I	624	Wonders!	Hampton-Brown
Weather Watcher, The	K	I	245	Spyglass Books	Compass Point Books
Weather Watching	L	I	339	Rigby Focus	Rigby
Weather Watching	Q	I	250+	Explorers	Wright Group/McGraw Hill

* Collection of short stories

TITLE	LEVEL	GENRE	WORD COUNT	AUTHOR / SERIES	PUBLISHER / DISTRIBUTOR
Weather Wise	L	I	250+	Spyglass Books	Compass Point Books
Weather Words and What They Mean	R	I	250+	Gibbons, Gail	Scholastic
Weathering the Storm	W	RF	2125	Leveled Readers	Houghton Mifflin
Weaver's Gift, The	K	RF	269	Leveled Readers	Houghton Mifflin
*Weaving Contest, The	O	TL	250+	Literacy 2000	Rigby
Wedding Day Disaster	M	RF	250+	SupaDoopers	Sundance
Wedding, The	J	RF	250+	Sunshine	Wright Group/McGraw Hill
Wedding, The	F	RF	50	Literacy 2000	Rigby
Wee Whopper	H	F	181	Windmill Books	Rigby
Wee Willie Winkie	D	RF	34	Seedlings	Continental Press
Weedy Sea Dragons	G	I	106	Seedlings	Continental Press
Week in the Woods, A	T	RF	250+	Clements, Andrew	Simon & Schuster
Week of Surprises, A	F	RF	138	Leveled Readers Language Support	Houghton Mifflin
Week of the Jellyhoppers, The	R	F	250+	Literacy 2000	Rigby
Week with Aunt Bea, A	D	RF	62	Bookshop	Mondo
Week, A	H	I	115	The Calendar	Capstone Press
Weight Lifting	Q	I	250+	Lund, Bill	Red Brick Learning
Weird Walkers	R	I	250+	Fredericks, Anthony D.	NorthWord Press
Welcome Home	L	I	250+	Early Connections	Benchmark Education
Welcome to Brazil	M	I	250+	Spyglass Books	Compass Point Books
Welcome to Canada	M	I	250+	Spyglass Books	Compass Point Books
Welcome to Hong Kong!	J	I	174	Vocabulary Readers	Houghton Mifflin
Welcome to Japan	M	I	250+	Spyglass Books	Compass Point Books
Welcome to Kenya	M	I	250+	Spyglass Books	Compass Point Books
Welcome to Mexico	M	TL	250+	Spyglass Books	Compass Point Books
Welcome to Our School	G	RF	101	Leveled Readers Social Studies	Houghton Mifflin
Welcome to Russia	M	I	250+	Spyglass Books	Compass Point Books
Welcome to the Bakery	J	I	122	Vocabulary Readers	Houghton Mifflin
Welcome to the White House	F	I	106	Independent Readers Social Studies	Houghton Mifflin
Welcome to the Zigzag Zoo	B	F	42	Phonics and Friends	Hampton-Brown
Welcome, Wilma	O	F	667	Leveled Readers	Houghton Mifflin
Well Done, Sam	I	RF	250+	Cambridge Reading	Pearson Learning Group
*Well I Never	K	F	2517	Story Box	Wright Group/McGraw Hill
We'll Never Forget You, Roberto Clemente	Q	B	250+	Engel, Trudie	Scholastic
Well, The	T	HF	250+	Taylor, Mildred D.	Puffin Books
Well-fed Bear,The	E	F	35	Literacy 2000	Rigby
Welsh Lamb, A	L	RF	250+	Cambridge Reading	Pearson Learning Group
We're a Team!	H	RF	100	City Stories	Rigby
We're Going Camping	J	I	111	Windows on Literacy	National Geographic
We're Going on a Bear Hunt	I	TL	363	Rosen, Michael	Macmillan
We're Going on a Picnic	H	RF	250+	Cambridge Reading	Pearson Learning Group
We're in Big Trouble, Black Board Bear	I	F	250+	Alexander, Martha	Dial Books
We're Just Looking	E	RF	115	Seedlings	Continental Press
We're Off to Thunder Mountain	L	RF	250+	Bookshop	Mondo
Werewolf Chronicles, The	T	F	250+	Philbrick, Rodman; Harnett, Lynn	Scholastic
Werewolves Don't Go To Summer Camp	M	F	250+	Dadey, Debbie; Jones, Marcia Thornton	Scholastic
West Side Kids: Don't Call Me Slob-o	R	RF	250+	Orgel, Doris	Hyperion
West Side Kids: The Big Idea	R	RF	250+	Schecter, Ellen	Hyperion
West Side Kids: The Pet Sitters	R	RF	250+	Schecter, Ellen	Hyperion
West Virginia	R	I	250+	This Land Is Your Land	Compass Point Books
West Virginia: Facts and Symbols	O	I	250+	Feeney, Kathy	Red Brick Learning

* Collection of short stories

TITLE	LEVEL	GENRE	WORD COUNT	AUTHOR / SERIES	PUBLISHER / DISTRIBUTOR
Westing Game, The	V	RF	250+	Raskin, Ellen	Penguin Group
Wet Day at School, A	J	RF	130	Sunshine	Wright Group/McGraw Hill
Wet Grass	H	RF	188	Story Box	Wright Group/McGraw Hill
Wet Paint	E	F	92	Storyteller-Setting Sun	Wright Group/McGraw Hill
Wet Weather Camping	J	RF	250+	PM Plus Story Books	Rigby
Wetland Home, A	Q	I	250+	Sunshine	Wright Group/McGraw Hill
Wetlands	Q	I	250+	First Reports	Compass Point Books
Wetlands	K	I	175	Rigby Focus	Rigby
Whale Is Not A Fish, A: And Other Animal Mix-ups	P	I	250+	Berger, Melvin	Scholastic
Whale Music	N	RF	771	Leveled Readers	Houghton Mifflin
Whale Tales	N	I	250+	Westerskov, Kim	Pacific Learning
Whale Watch	B	I	27	Ready Readers	Pearson Learning Group
Whale Watchers, The	E	F	63	Windmill Books	Rigby
Whale Watching	J	I	250+	Pacific Literacy	Pacific Learning
Whale! Nantucket Whaling Days	S	I	2363	Independent Readers Social Studies	Houghton Mifflin
Whale, The	O	I	250+	Crewe, Sabrina	Steck-Vaughn
Whales	O	I	250+	Simon, Seymour	Houghton Mifflin
Whales	O	I	250+	Soar To Success	Houghton Mifflin
Whales	N	I	250+	PM Animal Facts: Silver	Rigby
Whales	I	I	45	Pebble Plus	Capstone Press
Whales	I	I	45	Pebble Books	Red Brick Learning
Whales	O	I	250+	Holmes, Kevin J.	Red Brick Learning
Whales	O	I	250+	Bookshop	Mondo
Whales	M	I	333	Wonder World	Wright Group/McGraw Hill
Whales	G	I	150	Foundations	Wright Group/McGraw Hill
Whales - The Gentle Giants	L	I	250+	Milton, Joyce	Random House
Whales in the Ocean	D	I	35	Rosen Real Readers	Rosen Publishing Group
Whales on the Move	N	I	250+	Little Celebrations	Pearson Learning Group
Whales' Song, The	N	I	250+	Sheldon, Dyan	Penguin Group
Whale's Year, The	J	I	212	Lighthouse	Rigby
Whales: Giants of the Deep	M	I	250+	The Wild World of Animals	Red Brick Learning
What a Bad Dog!	D	RF	52	Oxford Reading Tree	Oxford University Press
What a Birthday!	G	RF	138	Leveled Readers Language Support	Houghton Mifflin
What a Catch!	G	RF	118	Instant Readers	Harcourt School Publishers
What a Day!	K	RF	621	Miranda, Anne	Hampton-Brown
What a Dog!	F	RF	134	First Start	Troll Associates
What a Dog!	H	RF	223	Story Basket	Wright Group/McGraw Hill
What a Funny Thing to Do	K	RF	236	Stepping Stones	Nelson/Michaels Assoc.
What a Great Idea!	L	RF	250+	Home Connection Collection	Rigby
What a Haircut!	J	RF	250+	Voyages	SRA/McGraw Hill
What a Hamster Needs	C	I	46	Leveled Readers Science	Houghton Mifflin
What a Job!	M	I	250+	Rigby Literacy	Rigby
What a Load of Garbage	L	I	250+	Lighthouse	Rigby
*What a Mess!	G	RF	124	New Way Blue	Steck-Vaughn
What a Mess!	LB	RF	14	Smart Starts	Rigby
What a Mess!	C	RF	79	Bookshop	Mondo
What a Mess!	C	RF	51	Story Box	Wright Group/McGraw Hill
What a Noise!	I	RF	165	Pacific Literacy	Pacific Learning
What a Pant!	S	I	250+	Sunshine	Wright Group/McGraw Hill
What a School	F	RF	100	Salem, Lynn; Stewart, Josie	Continental Press
What a Shower!	B	RF	23	Instant Readers	Harcourt School Publishers

* Collection of short stories

TITLE	LEVEL	GENRE	WORD COUNT	AUTHOR / SERIES	PUBLISHER / DISTRIBUTOR
What a Spelling Test!	I	F	123	City Stories	Rigby
What a Street!	B	RF	28	Bebop Books	Lee & Low Books Inc.
What a Tale!	C	RF	38	Wildsmith, Brian	Oxford University Press
What a Trip, Amber Brown	L	RF	250+	Danziger, Paula	Puffin Books
What a Waste	H	I	180	Sun Sprouts	ETA/Cuisenaire
What a Week!	C	RF	64	Rigby Literacy	Rigby
What a Week!	C	RF	36	Home Connection Collection	Rigby
What a Wonderful Idea	O	RF	1059	Leveled Readers	Houghton Mifflin
What a Year	N	RF	250+	DePaola, Tomie	Penguin Group
What About Bennie?	H	RF	124	Literacy Tree	Rigby
What Am I Going to Be?	H	RF	111	Storyteller-Moon Rising	Wright Group/McGraw Hill
What Am I Made Of?	N	I	250+	Bennett, David	Scholastic
What Am I?	D	I	51	Story Steps	Rigby
What Am I?	C	I	51	Williams, Deborah	Kaeden Books
What Am I?	G	I	124	Sunshine	Wright Group/McGraw Hill
What Am I?	F	I	100	Sun Sprouts	ETA/Cuisenaire
What Am I?	LB	RF	16	Just Beginning	Modern Curriculum
What Am I?	I	I	100	Foundations	Wright Group/McGraw Hill
What Am I?	B	RF	50	Handprints B	Educator's Publishing Service
What Ancient Astronomers Knew	U	I	2852	Leveled Readers Science	Houghton Mifflin
What Angela Needs	K	RF	250+	Voyages	SRA/McGraw Hill
What Animal Lives Here?	H	I	250+	Woolley, M.; Pigdon, K.	Mondo
What Animals Do You See?	C	I	50	Read-More Books	Pearson Learning Group
What Animals Eat	E	I	75	Little Red Readers	Sundance
What Are Caves?	K	I	108	Pebble Books	Red Brick Learning
What Are Deserts?	K	I	105	Pebble Books	Capstone Press
What Are Forests?	K	I	114	Pebble Books	Capstone Press
What Are Friends For?	C	I	33	Rosen Real Readers	Rosen Publishing Group
What are Inclined Planes?	M	I	70	Pebble Books	Red Brick Learning
What Are Lakes?	K	I	92	Pebble Books	Red Brick Learning
What are Levers?	M	I	66	Pebble Books	Red Brick Learning
What Are Mountains?	K	I	70	Pebble Books	Capstone Press
What Are My Chances?	J	I	393	Early Connections	Benchmark Education
What Are Oceans?	K	I	97	Pebble Books	Capstone Press
What are Pulleys?	M	I	88	Pebble Books	Red Brick Learning
What Are Purple Elephants Good For?	H	F	136	Reading Corners	Pearson Learning Group
What Are Rivers?	K	I	111	Pebble Books	Red Brick Learning
What are Screws?	M	I	65	Pebble Books	Red Brick Learning
What Are Volcanoes?	K	I	108	Pebble Books	Red Brick Learning
What Are We Doing?	A	F	21	KinderReaders	Rigby
What are Wedges?	M	I	60	Pebble Books	Red Brick Learning
What are Wheels and Axles?	M	I	70	Pebble Books	Red Brick Learning
What Are You Called?	C	I	66	Voyages	SRA/McGraw Hill
What Are You Doing?	D	RF	101	Foundations	Wright Group/McGraw Hill
What Are You Figuring Now?	P	B	250+	Ferris, Jeri	Scholastic
What Are You Going to Buy?	F	F	180	Read Alongs	Rigby
What Are You?	A	F	27	Literacy 2000	Rigby
What Bear Cubs Like to Do	I	I	83	Little Books	Sadlier-Oxford
What Bears Like	A	I	21	Cherrington, Janelle	Scholastic
What Blows in the Wind?	A	RF	36	Science	Outside the Box
What Came Out of My Bean?	H	RF	158	Book Bank	Wright Group/McGraw Hill
What Can a Diver See?	D	I	44	Windows on Literacy	National Geographic
What Can Change?	G	I	96	Discovery Links	Newbridge

TITLE	LEVEL	GENRE	WORD COUNT	AUTHOR / SERIES	PUBLISHER / DISTRIBUTOR
What Can Float?	B	I	27	Ready Readers	Pearson Learning Group
What Can Float?	C	I	32	Windmill Books	Rigby
What Can Fly?	B	I	29	Discovery Links	Newbridge
What Can Fly?	C	I	33	Joy Readers	Pearson Learning Group
What Can Fly?	B	I	28	Literacy 2000	Rigby
What Can Go Fast?	B	I	37	Little Red Readers	Sundance
What Can Hurt?	C	I	30	Windmill Books	Rigby
What Can I Buy?	F	RF	156	Moriarty, Julie	Scholastic
What Can I Buy?	C	I	33	Rosen Real Readers	Rosen Publishing Group
What Can I Do Today?	A	I	20	Windows on Literacy	National Geographic
What Can I Do?	H	I	250+	Greetings	Rigby
What Can I Do?	C	I	42	Read-More Books	Pearson Learning Group
What Can I Do?	C	I	42	Foundations	Wright Group/McGraw Hill
What Can I Read?	A	RF	28	Carousel Earlybirds	Pearson Learning Group
What Can I See?	C	I	42	Foundations	Wright Group/McGraw Hill
What Can It Be?	N	I	250+	Schaefer, Lola M.	Benchmark Education
What Can It Be?	F	I	113	Storyteller-First Snow	Wright Group/McGraw Hill
What Can Jigarees Do?	A	F	22	Story Box	Wright Group/McGraw Hill
What Can Jump?	A	I	32	Windmill Books	Rigby
What Can She Do?	A	I	21	Little Books for Early Readers	University of Maine
What Can Sing?	D	I	65	Sun Sprouts	ETA/Cuisenaire
What Can Swim?	B	I	30	Windmill Books	Rigby
What Can This Animal Do?	B	I	28	Foundations	Wright Group/McGraw Hill
What Can We Do Today?	G	RF	146	Carousel Readers	Pearson Learning Group
What Can We Do?	J	RF	439	Leveled Readers Social Studies	Houghton Mifflin
What Can We Smell?	C	I	44	Windmill Books	Rigby
What Can You Be?	C	I	166	Tiger Cub	Peguis
What Can You Do with a Ball of String?	G	RF	250+	Home Connection Collection	Rigby
What Can You Do with an Elephant House?	R	I	250+	Gaynor, Miriam; Goodwin, A.	Pacific Learning
What Can You Do?	A	I	18	Vocabulary Readers	Houghton Mifflin
What Can You Do?	C	I	59	Tiger Cub	Peguis
What Can You Hear?	D	I	80	Tiger Cub	Peguis
What Can You Make?	B	I	22	Ready Readers	Pearson Learning Group
What Can You Measure With a Lollipop?	H	I	159	Early Connections	Benchmark Education
What Can You See?	C	I	43	Vocabulary Readers	Houghton Mifflin
What Can You See?	C	I	25	Literacy 2000	Rigby
What Can You See?	C	RF	31	Rigby Literacy	Rigby
What Can You See?	B	I	31	Tiger Cub	Peguis
What Can You Taste?	B	I	45	Windmill Books	Rigby
What Cat Is That?	J	RF	250+	Real Reading	Steck-Vaughn
What Causes Forest Fires?	N	I	868	Leveled Readers Science	Houghton Mifflin
What Changes Our Earth?	K	I	273	People, Places & Spaces	Rand McNally
What Color Is the Sky?	F	I	74	Windows on Literacy	National Geographic
What Comes First?	C	I	56	Bookshop	Mondo
What Comes from a Cow?	G	I	85	Sunshine	Wright Group/McGraw Hill
What Comes from Eggs?	B	I	74	Bookshop	Mondo
What Comes in Threes?	C	F	41	Learn to Read	Creative Teaching Press
What Comes in Twos?	D	I	125	Early Connections	Benchmark Education
What Comes Next?	J	I	250+	Early Connections	Benchmark Education
What Comes Out at Night?	B	I	48	Little Red Readers	Sundance
What Computers Do	I	I	186	Yellow Umbrella Books	Red Brick Learning
What Could I Be?	C	RF	64	Foundations	Wright Group/McGraw Hill
What Could it Be?	B	RF	19	Instant Readers	Harcourt School Publishers
What Daddies Do Best	F	F	113	Numeroff, Laura Joffe	Simon & Schuster

* Collection of short stories

TITLE	LEVEL	GENRE	WORD COUNT	AUTHOR / SERIES	PUBLISHER / DISTRIBUTOR
What Did Ben Want?	A	RF	28	Smart Starts	Rigby
What Did I Forget?	D	RF	43	Teacher's Choice Series	Pearson Learning Group
What Did I Use?	C	I	65	Discovery World	Rigby
What Did Kim Catch?	C	RF	48	Literacy 2000	Rigby
What Did They Drive?	D	RF	73	Windows on Literacy	National Geographic
What Did They Want?	C	RF	28	Smart Starts	Rigby
What Did You Bring?	B	I	23	Ready Readers	Pearson Learning Group
What Did You Eat Today?	L	F	250+	Literacy Tree	Rigby
What Did You Lose, Santa?	WB	F	N/A	Amoss, Berthe	Harper & Row
What Dinah Saw	M	F	250+	Lighthouse	Rigby
What Dinosaurs Ate	F	I	44	Planet Earth	Rigby
What Do Animals Do?	E	I	29	Little Red Readers	Sundance
What Do Artists Use?	F	I	31	Canizares, Susan; Berger, Samantha	Scholastic
*What Do Fish Have To Do With Anything?	W	RF	250+	Avi	Candlewick Press
What Do I See in the Garden?	F	I	108	Wonder World	Wright Group/McGraw Hill
What Do I See?	B	I	28	Twig	Wright Group/McGraw Hill
What Do I Wear?	J	I	40	Leveled Readers Social Studies	Houghton Mifflin
What Do Insects Do?	A	I	24	Canizares, Susan; Chanko, Pamela	Scholastic
What Do Pets Need?	E	I	67	Windows on Literacy	National Geographic
What Do Pets Need?	E	I	106	Early Connections	Benchmark Education
What Do Scientists Do?	B	I	24	Twig	Wright Group/McGraw Hill
What Do Scientists Do?	H	I	79	Discovery Links	Newbridge
What Do We Have to Get?	E	RF	117	Ready Readers	Pearson Learning Group
What Do We Have?	C	F	28	Step-By-Step Series	Pearson Learning Group
What Do You Do?	G	F	125	Little Celebrations	Pearson Learning Group
What Do You Do?	E	I	162	Tiger Cub	Peguis
What Do You Have?	C	I	165	Tiger Cub	Peguis
What Do You Have?	C	I	88	Windmill Books	Rigby
What Do You Hear When Cows Sing?	J	F	250+	Maestro, Marco & Giulio	HarperTrophy
What Do You Hear?	D	I	60	Windmill Books	Rigby
What Do You Know About Dolphins?	J	I	137	Windows on Literacy	National Geographic
What Do You Like to Eat?	D	I	99	Foundations	Wright Group/McGraw Hill
What Do You Like to Wear?	D	I	50	Read-More Books	Pearson Learning Group
What Do You Like?	B	I	52	Little Books for Early Readers	University of Maine
What Do You Like?	B	RF	52	Storyteller	Wright Group/McGraw Hill
What Do You Play	A	I	25	Science	Outside the Box
What Do You See at the Pet Store?	C	I	27	Read-More Books	Pearson Learning Group
What Do You See by the Sea?	A	I	14	Little Books	Sadlier-Oxford
What Do You See?	F	F	89	Learn to Read	Creative Teaching Press
What Do You See?	A	RF	71	Phonics and Friends	Hampton-Brown
What Do You See?	E	I	71	Science	Harcourt School Publishers
What Do You See?	B	I	20	Carousel Readers	Pearson Learning Group
What Do You See?	C	I	35	Windmill Books	Rigby
What Do You Think?	O	I	250+	Wildcats	Wright Group/McGraw Hill
What Do You Touch?	C	I	50	Windmill Books	Rigby
What Do You Want That For?	E	RF	149	Lighthouse	Rigby
What Does a Firefighter Do?	G	I	136	Yellow Umbrella Books	Red Brick Learning
What Does a Garden Need?	G	I	118	Discovery Links	Newbridge
What Does a Governor Do?	L	I	288	Independent Readers Social Studies	Houghton Mifflin
What Does an Electrician Do?	T	I	1322	Independent Readers Science	Houghton Mifflin
What Does Greedy Cat Like?	C	RF	35	Pacific Literacy	Pacific Learning
What Does It Do?	J	I	198	Ready Set Read	Steck-Vaughn

* Collection of short stories

Organized Alphabetically by Book Title   **339**

TITLE	LEVEL	GENRE	WORD COUNT	AUTHOR / SERIES	PUBLISHER / DISTRIBUTOR
What Does Lucy Like?	A	RF	11	Little Books	Sadlier-Oxford
What Else?	I	RF	154	Sunshine	Wright Group/McGraw Hill
What Every Girl (except me) Knows	V	RF	250+	Baskin, Nora Raleigh	Little, Brown & Co.
What Feels Cold?	B	I	30	Windmill Books	Rigby
What Feels Hot?	A	I	28	Windmill Books	Rigby
What Feels Sticky?	B	I	26	Windmill Books	Rigby
What Fell Out?	D	RF	32	Carousel Readers	Pearson Learning Group
What Floats?	D	I	46	Sun Sprouts	ETA/Cuisenaire
What Floats?	C	I	16	Twig	Wright Group/McGraw Hill
What Floats? What Sinks?	J	I	185	Early Connections	Benchmark Education
What Fun!	F	F	250+	Sun Sprouts	ETA/Cuisenaire
What Game Shall We Play?	H	F	306	Hutchins, Pat	Sundance
What Gives You Goose Bumps?	H	RF	140	Home Connection Collection	Rigby
What Goes Around and Around?	B	I	46	Windmill Books	Rigby
What Goes in the Bathtub?	C	RF	31	Literacy 2000	Rigby
What Goes into a Salad?	C	RF	22	Home Connection Collection	Rigby
What Goes Together?	A	I	28	Leveled Readers Science	Houghton Mifflin
What Goes Up and Down?	C	I	40	Windmill Books	Rigby
What Goes Up High?	A	I	38	Windmill Books	Rigby
What Goes Up?	B	I	42	Rigby Literacy	Rigby
What Grows From a Tree?	I	I	250+	Yellow Umbrella Books	Red Brick Learning
What Grows Here?	C	I	37	Windows on Literacy	National Geographic
What Grows on Trees?	E	I	49	Start to Read	School Zone
What Grows There	P	I	448	Independent Readers Social Studies	Houghton Mifflin
What Grows?	B	I	21	Rigby Focus	Rigby
What Hangs from the Tree?	C	I	42	Questions & Answers	Pearson Learning Group
What Happened at the Boston Tea Party?	Q	I	250+	Rosen Real Readers	Rosen Publishing Group
What Happened to Aunt Cordelia	J	RF	250+	Voyages	SRA/McGraw Hill
What Happened?	G	I	60	Learn to Read	Creative Teaching Press
What Happens at the Bank?	K	I	388	Leveled Readers Social Studies	Houghton Mifflin
What Happens When You Recycle?	K	I	215	Discovery World	Rigby
What Has Changed?	A	I	18	Windows on Literacy	National Geographic
What Has Spots?	B	I	33	Literacy 2000	Rigby
What Has Stripes?	C	I	25	Ballinger, Margaret	Scholastic
What Has Wheels?	A	I	28	Hoenecke, Karen	Kaeden Books
What Has Wings?	H	RF	250+	Momentum Literacy Program	Troll Associates
What Hatches?	J	I	250+	Yellow Umbrella Books	Capstone Press
What Hearts	S	RF	250+	Brooks, Bruce	Language for Learning Assoc.
What Helps a Bird to Fly?	F	I	95	Birds Series	Pearson Learning Group
What I Left on My Plate	C	RF	54	Teacher's Choice Series	Pearson Learning Group
What I Like at School	C	I	64	Little Red Readers	Sundance
What I Like to Wear	D	I	93	Home Connection Collection	Rigby
What I Wear	D	RF	76	Sun Sprouts	ETA/Cuisenaire
What I Would Do	I	RF	173	Read Alongs	Rigby
What I'd Like to Be	F	I	112	Little Red Readers	Sundance
What If . . .	E	RF	57	Teacher's Choice Series	Pearson Learning Group
What if You Get Lost	D	I	40	Rosen Real Readers	Rosen Publishing Group
What If?	C	F	41	Little Celebrations	Pearson Learning Group
What in the World is the World Wide Web?	S	I	250+	Quinn, Pat	Pacific Learning
What Is a Bird?	H	I	71	Pebble Books	Red Brick Learning
What Is a Family?	J	I	250+	Spyglass Books	Compass Point Books
What Is a Fish?	H	I	77	Pebble Books	Red Brick Learning

* Collection of short stories

TITLE	LEVEL	GENRE	WORD COUNT	AUTHOR / SERIES	PUBLISHER / DISTRIBUTOR
What Is a Fly?	M	I	561	Sunshine	Wright Group/McGraw Hill
What Is a Food Chain?	G	I	71	Instant Readers	Harcourt School Publishers
What Is a Government?	W	I	250+	iOpeners	Pearson Learning Group
What Is a Huggles?	B	F	41	Sunshine	Wright Group/McGraw Hill
What is a Mammal?	F	I	102	Rosen Real Readers	Rosen Publishing Group
What Is a Mammal?	I	I	70	Pebble Books	Red Brick Learning
What is a Map?	H	I	250+	Yellow Umbrella Books	Red Brick Learning
What is a Mountain?	I	I	231	Rosen Real Readers	Rosen Publishing Group
What Is a Park?	H	I	138	Discovery World	Rigby
What Is a Park?	J	I	230	People, Places & Spaces	Rand McNally
What Is a Poem?	G	I	69	Vocabulary Readers	Houghton Mifflin
What Is a Rainbow?	H	I	115	Rosen Real Readers	Rosen Publishing Group
What is a Reptile?	M	I	183	Now I Know	Troll Associates
What Is a Reptile?	I	I	67	Pebble Books	Red Brick Learning
What Is an Amphibian?	K	I	85	Pebble Books	Red Brick Learning
What is an Elephant?	H	TL	165	Story Box	Wright Group/McGraw Hill
What Is an Insect?	A	I	36	Yellow Umbrella Books	Red Brick Learning
What Is an Insect?	H	I	57	Pebble Books	Red Brick Learning
What Is at the Top?	E	F	197	Ready Readers	Pearson Learning Group
What Is Bat?	G	F	136	Literacy 2000	Rigby
What is Being Moved?	WB	RF	N/A	Windows on Literacy	National Geographic
What Is Big?	D	RF	72	Armstrong, Shane; Hartley, Susan	Scholastic
What Is Blue?	C	I	31	Carousel Earlybirds	Pearson Learning Group
What is Congress?	P	I	628	Leveled Readers Social Studies	Houghton Mifflin
What Is Delicious?	C	I	25	Windmill Books	Rigby
What Is Enormous?	B	I	33	Windmill Books	Rigby
What Is Fast?	A	I	30	Windmill Books	Rigby
What Is Fierce?	B	I	32	Windmill Books	Rigby
What Is Fun?	C	I	34	Windmill Books	Rigby
What Is Green?	B	I	30	Carousel Earlybirds	Pearson Learning Group
What Is He Looking For?	A	F	42	KinderReaders	Rigby
What Is in Space?	B	I	35	Yellow Umbrella Books	Red Brick Learning
What Is in Space?	C	I	41	Science	Wright Group/McGraw Hill
What is in the Box?	D	RF	51	Instant Readers	Harcourt School Publishers
What Is in the Closet?	E	F	107	Story Box	Wright Group/McGraw Hill
What Is in the Sky?	J	I	174	Phonics Readers	Compass Point Books
What Is in the Sky?	B	I	32	Rosen Real Readers	Rosen Publishing Group
What Is It Called?	D	RF	48	Reading Unlimited	Pearson Learning Group
What Is It Made Of?	J	I	250+	Independent Readers Science	Houghton Mifflin
What Is It?	E	I	69	Storyteller-First Snow	Wright Group/McGraw Hill
What Is It?	F	I	135	Foundations	Wright Group/McGraw Hill
What Is It?	G	I	69	iOpeners	Pearson Learning Group
What Is It?	B	F	35	Rigby Literacy	Rigby
What Is Little?	LB	I	22	Rise & Shine	Hampton-Brown
What Is Matter?	L	I	250+	Schaefer, Lola M.	Benchmark Education
What Is Money?	M	I	250+	First Facts	Capstone Press
What Is Noisy?	B	I	31	Windmill Books	Rigby
What Is Old?	C	I	32	Windmill Books	Rigby
What Is Red?	B	I	27	Carousel Earlybirds	Pearson Learning Group
What Is Red?	B	I	30	Literacy 2000	Rigby
What Is Scary?	B	I	31	Windmill Books	Rigby
What Is Slippery?	C	I	26	Windmill Books	Rigby
What Is Slow?	C	I	29	Windmill Books	Rigby
What Is Soft?	C	I	30	Windmill Books	Rigby

* Collection of short stories

TITLE	LEVEL	GENRE	WORD COUNT	AUTHOR / SERIES	PUBLISHER / DISTRIBUTOR
What Is Tall?	B	I	30	Windmill Books	Rigby
What Is That?	C	I	61	Ready Readers	Pearson Learning Group
What Is That? Said the Cat	F	F	118	Maccarone, Grace	Scholastic
What Is the Media?	T	I	2493	Independent Readers Social Studies	Houghton Mifflin
What Is the U.S. Constitution?	R	I	250+	Rosen Real Readers	Rosen Publishing Group
What Is the Weather Today?	B	I	49	Leveled Readers Science	Houghton Mifflin
What Is the Weather Today?	H	I	250+	Momentum Literacy Program	Troll Associates
What Is This Skeleton?	C	I	48	Science	Wright Group/McGraw Hill
What Is This?	A	I	29	KinderReaders	Rigby
What Is This?	A	I	25	Little Books for Early Readers	University of Maine
What Is This?	C	I	28	Ready Readers	Pearson Learning Group
What Is This?	A	I	25	Tiger Cub	Peguis
What Is Under the Hat?	B	F	29	Ready Readers	Pearson Learning Group
What Is White?	B	I	26	Carousel Earlybirds	Pearson Learning Group
What Is Yellow?	B	I	26	Carousel Earlybirds	Pearson Learning Group
What Is Young?	C	I	31	Windmill Books	Rigby
What Jamie Saw	T	RF	250+	Coman, Carolyn	Penguin Group
What Jessie Really Likes	C	RF	59	Lighthouse	Rigby
What Joe Hamster Finds	J	F	250+	Sunshine	Wright Group/McGraw Hill
What Joy Found	L	RF	250+	Ready Readers	Pearson Learning Group
What Keeps Them Warm?	L	I	156	Pacific Literacy	Pacific Learning
What Kind of Animals?	D	I	37	Leveled Readers Science	Houghton Mifflin
What Kind of Babysitter Is This?	L	RF	250+	Johnson, Dolores	Scholastic
What Kind of Dog Am I?	C	I	21	Twig	Wright Group/McGraw Hill
What Kind of Sound?	B	I	25	Yellow Umbrella Books	Red Brick Learning
What Lays Eggs?	I	I	216	Momentum Literacy Program	Troll Associates
What Lays Eggs?	D	I	56	Storyteller Nonfiction	Wright Group/McGraw Hill
What Lives in a Swamp?	B	I	36	Windows on Literacy	National Geographic
What Lives in a Tide Pool?	J	I	187	Windows on Literacy	National Geographic
What Lives on a Prairie?	N	I	250+	Rosen Real Readers	Rosen Publishing Group
What Made Teddalik Laugh	M	TL	250+	Folk Tales	Wright Group/McGraw Hill
What Made This?	B	I	21	Science	Outside the Box
What Magnets Can Do	K	I	250+	Fowler, Allan	Scholastic
What Makes a Bird a Bird?	O	I	250+	Garelick, May	Mondo
What Makes a Garden Grow?	E	I	83	Independent Readers Science	Houghton Mifflin
What Makes a Shadow?	B	I	27	Leveled Readers Science	Houghton Mifflin
What Makes a Tiger Hard to See?	I	I	253	Windows on Literacy	National Geographic
What Makes It Go?	C	I	29	iOpeners	Pearson Learning Group
What Makes Light?	F	I	119	Sunshine	Wright Group/McGraw Hill
What Makes Me Healthy?	H	I	132	Windows on Literacy	National Geographic
What Makes Ten?	D	I	34	Yellow Umbrella Books	Red Brick Learning
What Mommies Do Best	F	F	113	Numeroff, Laura Joffe	Simon & Schuster
What My Dog Knows	L	RF	866	Leveled Readers Science	Houghton Mifflin
What Mynah Bird Saw	F	TL	90	Sunshine	Wright Group/McGraw Hill
What Next, Baby Bear?	L	F	313	Murphy, Jill	Dial Books
What Next?	F	F	277	Story Basket	Wright Group/McGraw Hill
What on Earth?	I	F	133	Sunshine	Wright Group/McGraw Hill
What People Do	E	I	113	Early Connections	Benchmark Education
What People Do	H	I	148	Little Red Readers	Sundance
What People Wore During the American Revolution	T	I	250+	Clothing, Costumes and Uniforms Throughout American History	Rosen Publishing Group
What People Wore During the Westward Expansion	T	I	250+	Clothing, Costumes and Uniforms Throughout American History	Rosen Publishing Group

* Collection of short stories

TITLE	LEVEL	GENRE	WORD COUNT	AUTHOR / SERIES	PUBLISHER / DISTRIBUTOR
What People Wore in Colonial America	T	I	250+	Clothing, Costumes and Uniforms Throughout American History	Rosen Publishing Group
What People Wore in Early America	T	I	250+	Clothing, Costumes and Uniforms Throughout American History	Rosen Publishing Group
What Plant Is This?	C	I	22	Windows on Literacy	National Geographic
What Plants and Animals Need	K	I	200	Phonics Readers	Compass Point Books
What Plays Music?	C	I	36	Questions & Answers	Pearson Learning Group
What Pushes? What Pulls?	I	I	141	Early Connections	Benchmark Education
What Rhymes With . . .	A	I	9	Ready Readers	Pearson Learning Group
What Rhymes With Cat?	LB	F	4	Ready Readers	Pearson Learning Group
What Season Is it?	F	I	79	Leveled Readers Social Studies	Houghton Mifflin
What Season Is This?	C	I	24	Wonder World	Wright Group/McGraw Hill
What Shall I Do?	M	RF	584	Sunshine	Wright Group/McGraw Hill
What Shall I Wear?	E	I	58	Book Bank	Wright Group/McGraw Hill
"What Shall Workers Do?"	W	I	2287	Independent Readers Social Studies	Houghton Mifflin
What Should I Wear?	C	RF	70	Lighthouse	Rigby
What Should We Wear?	F	I	50	iOpeners	Pearson Learning Group
What Smells Good?	C	I	26	Windmill Books	Rigby
What the Dinosaurs Saw	I	I	123	Schlein, Miriam	Scholastic
What the King Likes	B	F	32	Sun Sprouts	ETA/Cuisenaire
What Things Go Together	LB	RF	26	Literacy 2000	Rigby
What Time Is It?	D	I	43	Learn to Read	Creative Teaching Press
What Time Is It?	B	RF	48	Instant Readers	Harcourt School Publishers
What Time Is It?	D	RF	65	Moriarty, Julie	Scholastic
What Time Is It?	B	I	48	Rosen Real Readers	Rosen Publishing Group
What Time Is It?	E	RF	136	Teacher's Choice Series	Pearson Learning Group
What Time Is It?	W	I	35	iOpeners	Pearson Learning Group
What to Wear?	D	RF	42	Harry's Math Books	Outside the Box
What Tommy Did	E	RF	125	Literacy 2000	Rigby
What Was That?	E	RF	66	Leveled Readers	Houghton Mifflin
What Was This?	F	I	53	Wonder World	Wright Group/McGraw Hill
What We Do at School	A	F	31	Bookshop	Mondo
What We Like	B	RF	43	Early Connections	Benchmark Education
What We Like	D	RF	71	Little Red Readers	Sundance
What Were Castles For?	R	I	250+	Usborne Starting Point History	EDC Publishing
What Will Float?	G	I	224	Sunshine Books	Wright Group/McGraw Hill
What Will I Be?	D	I	104	Early Connections	Benchmark Education
What Will the Weather Be?	H	I	207	Rigby Literacy	Rigby
What Will You Pack?	B	RF	35	Ready Readers	Pearson Learning Group
What Would Joey Do?	T	RF	250+	Gantos, Jack	Farrar, Straus and Giroux
What Would the Zoo Do?	D	F	59	Salem, Lynn	Continental Press
What Would You Do?	M	I	392	Vocabulary Readers	Houghton Mifflin
What Would You Do?	G	RF	160	Sunshine	Wright Group/McGraw Hill
What Would You Like?	D	F	52	Sunshine	Wright Group/McGraw Hill
What You See Is What You Get	I	F	192	McLenighan, Valjean	Modern Curriculum
Whatcha Got?	M	RF	250+	Social Studies Connects	The Kane Press
Whatever Am I Going to Do Now?	M	RF	250+	Little Celebrations	Pearson Learning Group
Whatever Will These Become?	H	I	47	Literacy Tree	Rigby
Whatever Will These Become?	E	I	47	Literacy 2000	Rigby
What's Alike?	WB	I	N/A	Windows on Literacy	National Geographic
What's Alive?	D	I	53	Discovery Links	Newbridge
What's Around the Corner?	H	RF	90	Literacy Tree	Rigby
What's Behind This Door?	B	I	43	Twig	Wright Group/McGraw Hill

* Collection of short stories

TITLE	LEVEL	GENRE	WORD COUNT	AUTHOR / SERIES	PUBLISHER / DISTRIBUTOR
What's Best for Red?	K	RF	444	Eggers, Casey	Hampton-Brown
What's Black and White and Moos?	E	I	78	Twig	Wright Group/McGraw Hill
What's Cooking, Jenny Archer?	M	RF	250+	Conford, Ellen	Little, Brown & Co.
What's Cooking?	H	RF	287	Bookshop	Mondo
What's Cooking?	Q	I	250+	Cartwright, Pauline	Pacific Learning
What's for Dinner	Q	I	250+	Sunshine	Wright Group/McGraw Hill
What's for Dinner, Dad?	K	RF	459	Sunshine	Wright Group/McGraw Hill
What's for Dinner?	B	I	35	Hoenecke, Karen	Kaeden Books
What's for Dinner?	E	RF	112	Seedlings	Continental Press
What's for Lunch	E	F	91	New Way Red	Steck-Vaughn
What's for Lunch?	B	F	36	Story Box	Wright Group/McGraw Hill
What's for Lunch?	H	F	169	Ready Readers	Pearson Learning Group
What's for Lunch?	D	I	49	Rise & Shine	Hampton-Brown
What's For Lunch?	A	I	30	Vocabulary Readers	Houghton Mifflin
What's for Lunch?	C	F	48	Carle, Eric	Scholastic
What's Going On?	C	RF	21	Learn to Read	Creative Teaching Press
What's Happening?: A Book of Explanations	Q	I	250+	Bookshop	Mondo
What's in a Park?	G	I	46	Chessen, Betsey; Chanko, Pamela	Scholastic
What's in Here?	E	I	122	Sun Sprouts	ETA/Cuisenaire
What's In My Pocket	F	I	72	Learn to Read	Creative Teaching Press
What's in the Bag?	E	HF	98	Visions	Wright Group/McGraw Hill
What's in the Box?	B	I	24	Rigby Literacy	Rigby
What's in the Woods?	J	RF	250+	The Wright Skills	Wright Group/McGraw Hill
What's in This Egg?	A	F	16	Sunshine	Wright Group/McGraw Hill
What's Inside?	K	I	238	Wonder World	Wright Group/McGraw Hill
What's Inside?	H	I	138	Windows on Literacy	National Geographic
What's Inside?	E	I	37	Sunshine	Wright Group/McGraw Hill
What's Inside?	LB	RF	47	Hoenecke, Karen	Kaeden Books
What's Inside?	G	I	50	Foundations	Wright Group/McGraw Hill
What's It For?	D	I	47	Visions	Wright Group/McGraw Hill
What's It Like to Be a Fish?	L	I	250+	Little Readers	Houghton Mifflin
What's Living at Your Place?	Q	I	250+	Chapman, Bruce	Pacific Learning
What's Missing?	D	RF	102	Spinelle, Nancy Louise	Kaeden Books
What's Missing?	K	I	252	Book Bank	Wright Group/McGraw Hill
What's My Job?	B	I	25	Windows on Literacy	National Geographic
What's New at the Zoo?	H	F	151	Instant Readers	Harcourt School Publishers
What's on My Farm?	B	RF	38	Rise & Shine	Hampton-Brown
What's on the Road?	B	I	34	Windows on Literacy	National Geographic
What's on the Ships?	G	I	170	Windows on Literacy	National Geographic
What's On the Truck?	I	I	137	Windows on Literacy	National Geographic
What's on Your T-Shirt?	C	RF	64	Carousel Readers	Pearson Learning Group
What's Round?	A	I	14	Discovery Links	Newbridge
What's That Noise?	B	RF	23	Science	Outside the Box
What's That Smell?	H	RF	56	Pacific Literacy	Pacific Learning
What's That?	B	RF	33	Sunshine	Wright Group/McGraw Hill
What's That?	I	F	250+	Popcorn	Sundance
What's That?	C	RF	27	Carousel Earlybirds	Pearson Learning Group
What's That?	C	F	28	The Book Project	Sundance
What's the Address?	L	I	186	iOpeners	Pearson Learning Group
What's the Big Idea, Ben Franklin?	O	B	250+	Fritz, Jean	Scholastic
What's the Matter with Herbie Jones?	N	RF	250+	Kline, Suzy	Penguin Group
What's the Matter, Kelly Beans?	N	RF	250+	Enderle, Judith R.; Tessler, S. G.	Candlewick Press
What's the Time	F	RF	74	Cambridge Reading	Pearson Learning Group
What's the Time Mr. Wolf?	C	F	49	Windmill	Wright Group/McGraw Hill

* Collection of short stories

TITLE	LEVEL	GENRE	WORD COUNT	AUTHOR / SERIES	PUBLISHER / DISTRIBUTOR
What's the Weather Like Today?	D	I	119	Learn to Read	Creative Teaching Press
What's the Weather?	B	RF	21	Cali, Jennifer	Scholastic
What's This Matter?	F	I	88	Independent Readers Science	Houghton Mifflin
What's This Spider Doing?	E	I	89	Story Steps	Rigby
What's This?	N	I	250+	Literacy 2000	Rigby
What's Under My Bed?	C	RF	18	Visions	Wright Group/McGraw Hill
What's Under the Ocean	H	I	108	Now I Know	Troll Associates
What's Underneath?	K	I	200	Discovery World	Rigby
What's Up?	B	I	26	Pacific Literacy	Pacific Learning
What's Up?	E	RF	26	Instant Readers	Harcourt School Publishers
What's Your Story?	WB	RF	N/A	Voyages	SRA/McGraw Hill
What's Zero?	I	I	250+	Yellow Umbrella Books	Red Brick Learning
Wheat	D	I	52	Canizares, Susan; Chanko, Pamela	Scholastic
Wheel, The	C	RF	102	Joy Readers	Pearson Learning Group
Wheelbarrow Garden, The	H	RF	231	PM Plus Story Books	Rigby
Wheels	D	I	69	Cobb, Annie	Random House
Wheels	C	I	29	Discovery Links	Newbridge
Wheels	D	I	49	Rise & Shine	Hampton-Brown
Wheels	C	I	27	Literacy 2000	Rigby
Wheels	E	RF	62	Nayer, Judy	Scholastic
Wheels	D	RF	27	Voyages	SRA/McGraw Hill
Wheels	C	I	39	Sunshine	Wright Group/McGraw Hill
Wheels	D	I	33	Windows on Literacy	National Geographic
Wheels	D	I	33	Sun Sprouts	ETA/Cuisenaire
Wheels on the Bus	I	TL	362	Kovalski, Mary Ann	Little, Brown & Co.
Wheels on the Bus, The	J	TL	250+	Traditional Songs	Picture Window Books
When a Storm Comes	J	I	172	Windows on Literacy	National Geographic
When Bob Woke Up Late	G	RF	139	Ready Readers	Pearson Learning Group
When Children Worked	N	I	292	Independent Readers Social Studies	Houghton Mifflin
When Dad Came Home	F	RF	46	Literacy 2000	Rigby
When Dad Got Lost	F	RF	113	City Stories	Rigby
When Dad Went Fishing	H	RF	250+	Cambridge Reading	Pearson Learning Group
When Dad Went to Daycare	H	RF	211	Sunshine	Wright Group/McGraw Hill
When Do Cars Stop?	C	I	62	Questions & Answers	Pearson Learning Group
When Do You Feel	F	I	132	Twig	Wright Group/McGraw Hill
When Goldilocks Went to the House of the Bears	E	TL	165	Tiger Cub	Peguis
When Goldilocks Went to the House of the Bears	F	TL	156	Bookshop	Mondo
When I Broke the Office Window	L	RF	257	City Kids	Rigby
When I First Came to This Land	K	TL	250+	Ziefert, Harriet	Scholastic
When I Forgot	N	RF	250+	Marriott, Janice	Pacific Learning
When I Get Bigger	K	RF	205	Mayer, Mercer	Donovan
When I Go See Gram	G	RF	123	Ready Readers	Pearson Learning Group
When I Go to Grandma's House	M	RF	199	Cleary, Brian	Kaeden Books
When I Grow Up	B	RF	58	Lighthouse	Rigby
When I Grow Up	F	RF	63	Rhythm 'N' Rhyme Readers	Pearson Learning Group
When I Grow Up	C	RF	38	Rise & Shine	Hampton-Brown
When I Look Up	B	RF	55	Foundations	Wright Group/McGraw Hill
When I Play	C	RF	31	Literacy 2000	Rigby
When I Pretend	C	RF	40	Literacy 2000	Rigby
When I Turned Six	I	HF	150	Voyages	SRA/McGraw Hill

* Collection of short stories

TITLE	LEVEL	GENRE	WORD COUNT	AUTHOR / SERIES	PUBLISHER / DISTRIBUTOR
When I Visit My Cousin	E	I	67	Independent Readers Social Studies	Houghton Mifflin
When I Was Sick	F	RF	53	Literacy 2000	Rigby
*When I Was Young and Wild Bill's Secret Wish	P	RF	250+	Miggs, W. B.	Pacific Learning
*When I Was Your Age: Original Stories About Growing Up (Vol. 1)	W	B	250+	Ehrlich, Amy (Ed.)	Candlewick Press
When I'm Older	F	RF	156	Literacy 2000	Rigby
When It Rains	C	RF	39	Foundations	Wright Group/McGraw Hill
When It Rains	F	I	106	Frankford, Marilyn	Kaeden Books
When It Rains	E	RF	36	Voyages	SRA/McGraw Hill
When It Rains . . .	C	I	37	Teacher's Choice Series	Pearson Learning Group
When It Snowed	C	RF	33	Home Connection Collection	Rigby
When Itchy Witchy Sneezes	C	F	39	Sunshine	Wright Group/McGraw Hill
When Johnny Went Marching: Young Americans Fight the Civil War	Y	I	250+	Wisler, B. Clifton	HarperCollins
When Jose Hits That Ball	G	RF	45	Pacific Literacy	Pacific Learning
When Justice Failed: The Fred Korematsu Story	U	B	250+	Chin, Steven A.	Steck-Vaughn
When Lana Was Absent	F	RF	78	Tadpoles	Rigby
When Lincoln Was a Boy	E	I	132	Twig	Wright Group/McGraw Hill
When Mr. Quinn Snored	C	F	31	Little Books	Sadlier-Oxford
When My Dad Came to School	M	RF	230	City Kids	Rigby
When Plague Strikes	Z	I	250+	Giblin, James Cross	HarperCollins
When Robins Sing	H	I	238	Twig	Wright Group/McGraw Hill
When Sophie Gets Angry - Really, Really Angry . . .	K	RF	166	Bang, Molly	Scholastic
When Spring Comes	D	I	23	Windows on Literacy	National Geographic
When the Beginning Began: Stories About God, the Creatures, and Us	U	TL	250+	Lester, Julius	OSI
When the Circus Came to Town	R	RF	250+	Horvath, Polly	Sunburst
When the Circus Comes to Town	A	I	40	Little Red Readers	Sundance
When the Cookernup Store Burned Down	K	F	250+	Sunshine	Wright Group/McGraw Hill
When the Earth Was Bare	P	TL	250+	Voyages	SRA/McGraw Hill
*When the Giants Came to Town	L	F	250+	Leonard, Marcia	Scholastic
When the King Rides By	J	F	247	Bookshop	Mondo
When the Moon Was Blue	I	F	174	Literacy 2000	Rigby
When the Rain Comes	C	I	54	Windows on Literacy	National Geographic
When the Sun Goes Down	G	I	109	Wonder World	Wright Group/McGraw Hill
When the Tide Goes Out	D	I	74	Story Steps	Rigby
When the Toy Shop Shuts	WB	F	N/A	The Book Project	Sundance
When the Tripods Came	V	F	250+	Christopher, John	Aladdin
When The Truck Got Stuck!	M	RF	250+	Cowley, Joy	Pacific Learning
When the TV Broke	H	RF	209	Ziefert, Harriet	Puffin Books
When the Volcano Erupted	J	F	262	PM Turquoise	Rigby
When the Water Closes Over My Head	R	RF	250+	Napoli, Donna	Puffin Books
When the Wind Blows	G	I	107	Rigby Focus	Rigby
When They Were Little Like Me	E	I	70	Leveled Readers Social Studies	Houghton Mifflin
When Tony Got Lost at the Zoo	L	RF	122	City Kids	Rigby
When We Are Big	E	RF	123	Ready Readers	Pearson Learning Group
When Will I Read?	I	RF	250+	Cohen, Miriam	Bantam
When Will We Be Sisters?	K	RF	250+	Kroll, Virginia	Scholastic
When You Were a Baby	G	RF	104	Jonas, Ann	Morrow
When Zachary Beaver Came to Town	Y	RF	250+	Holt, Kimberly Willis	Dell Yearling
Where and Why?	C	RF	28	Learn to Read	Creative Teaching Press
Where Are My Socks?	D	RF	42	Pacific Literacy	Pacific Learning

* Collection of short stories

TITLE	LEVEL	GENRE	WORD COUNT	AUTHOR / SERIES	PUBLISHER / DISTRIBUTOR
Where Are the Babies?	B	I	8	PM Starters	Rigby
Where Are the Bears?	K	F	250+	Winters, Kay	Bantam
Where Are the Car Keys?	B	RF	36	Windmill	Wright Group/McGraw Hill
Where Are The Dinosaurs?	B	I	60	Bookshop	Mondo
Where Are the Eggs?	F	I	152	Discovery Links	Newbridge
Where Are the Seeds?	D	I	67	Wonder World	Wright Group/McGraw Hill
Where Are the Sunhats?	D	RF	130	PM Story Books	Rigby
Where Are the Wolves?	R	I	250+	Motil, Rebecca	Scholastic
Where Are They Going?	C	I	38	Windows on Literacy	National Geographic
Where Are They Going?	C	F	42	Story Box	Wright Group/McGraw Hill
Where Are They?	D	RF	98	Rigby Literacy	Rigby
Where Are They?	B	I	98	Rosen Real Readers	Rosen Publishing Group
Where Are They?	C	RF	24	Humphrey, Kiesha	Scholastic
Where Are We?	B	RF	72	Early Emergent	Pioneer Valley
Where Are You Going, Aja Rose?	D	RF	100	Sunshine	Wright Group/McGraw Hill
Where Are You Going, Little Mouse?	H	F	148	Kraus, Robert	Greenwillow
Where Are You Going?	D	RF	66	Learn to Read	Creative Teaching Press
Where Are You Going?	B	F	42	KinderReaders	Rigby
Where Babies Play	C	F	36	Instant Readers	Harcourt School Publishers
Where Can a Hippo Hide?	D	F	41	Ready Readers	Pearson Learning Group
Where Can I Play?	C	RF	45	Windows on Literacy	National Geographic
Where Can I Write?	C	RF	42	Early Emergent	Pioneer Valley
Where Can It Be?	E	RF	83	Jonas, Ann	Morrow
Where Can Kitty Sleep?	B	RF	15	Windmill	Wright Group/McGraw Hill
Where Can Pussy Sleep?	B	RF	15	Windmill	Wright Group/McGraw Hill
Where Can Teddy Go?	E	RF	141	Foundations	Wright Group/McGraw Hill
Where Can We Go from Here?	F	I	54	Spinelle, Nancy Louise	Kaeden Books
Where Can We Put an Elephant?	B	F	48	Windmill	Wright Group/McGraw Hill
Where Did All the Water Go?	F	I	139	PM Plus Nonfiction	Rigby
Where Did It Go?	F	F	216	Learn to Read	Creative Teaching Press
Where Did the Maya Go?	P	F	250+	Action Packs	Rigby
Where Did They Go?	D	RF	102	Teacher's Choice Series	Pearson Learning Group
Where Dinosaurs Walked	K	I	189	Phonics Readers	Compass Point Books
Where Do Animals Live	F	I	187	Bookshop	Mondo
Where Do Birds Live?	C	I	57	Chessen, Betsey	Scholastic
Where Do Bugs Live?	D	I	33	Pair-It Books	Steck-Vaughn
Where Do I Live?	C	I	29	Visions	Wright Group/McGraw Hill
Where Do Monsters Live?	C	F	56	Learn to Read	Creative Teaching Press
Where Do Plants Grow?	D	I	28	iOpeners	Pearson Learning Group
Where Do Puddles Go?	J	I	250+	Rookie Read-About Science	Children's Press
Where Do the Puddles Go?	L	I	170	Windows on Literacy	National Geographic
Where Do They Go?	D	RF	66	Rigby Literacy	Rigby
Where Do They Live?	C	I	45	Ready Readers	Pearson Learning Group
Where Do We Go?	B	RF	22	Ready Readers	Pearson Learning Group
Where Do You Live?	N	I	250+	People, Places & Spaces	Rand McNally
Where Do You Live?	C	I	68	Tiger Cub	Peguis
Where Do You Live?	L	I	250+	Twig	Wright Group/McGraw Hill
Where Do You Live?	I	I	68	Windows on Literacy	National Geographic
Where Do You Play?	D	I	131	Twig	Wright Group/McGraw Hill
Where Do You Think You're Going, Christopher Columbus?	S	B	250+	Fritz, Jean	Putnam & Grosset
Where Does a Leopard Hide?	C	I	108	Foundations	Wright Group/McGraw Hill
Where Does All the Garbage Go?	K	I	250+	Twig	Wright Group/McGraw Hill
Where Does Breakfast Come From?	E	I	56	iOpeners	Pearson Learning Group

* Collection of short stories

TITLE	LEVEL	GENRE	WORD COUNT	AUTHOR / SERIES	PUBLISHER / DISTRIBUTOR
Where Does Breakfast Come From?	H	I	170	Discovery World	Rigby
Where Does Energy Come From?	J	I	245	Leveled Readers Social Studies	Houghton Mifflin
Where Does Food Come From?	I	I	169	PM Plus Nonfiction	Rigby
Where Does Food Grow?	D	I	43	Blevins, Wiley	Scholastic
Where Does Garbage Go?	K	I	250+	Soar To Success	Houghton Mifflin
Where Does It Go?	C	I	61	Questions & Answers	Pearson Learning Group
Where Does It Park?	C	I	51	Canizares, Susan	Scholastic
Where Does Rain Come From?	N	I	250+	Rosen Real Readers	Rosen Publishing Group
Where Does the Butterfly Go When It Rains?	K	RF	250+	Bookshop	Mondo
Where Does the Garbage Go?	M	I	250+	Soar To Success	Houghton Mifflin
Where Does the Rabbit Hop?	E	I	71	Ready Readers	Pearson Learning Group
Where Does the Teacher Sleep?	C	F	50	Gibson, Kathleen	Continental Press
Where Does the Water Go?	L	I	189	Windows on Literacy	National Geographic
Where Does the Wind Go?	M	I	95	Bookshop	Mondo
Where I Live	B	RF	36	Carousel Earlybirds	Pearson Learning Group
Where I Live	C	RF	35	Pacific Literacy	Pacific Learning
Where in the World is the Perfect Family?	P	RF	250+	Hest, Amy	Penguin Group
Where is Blackbeard's Ship?	O	I	286	Vocabulary Readers	Houghton Mifflin
Where Is Curly?	D	F	69	Rigby Literacy	Rigby
Where Is Daniel?	E	RF	135	Carousel Readers	Pearson Learning Group
Where Is Eric?	C	RF	29	Rigby Literacy	Rigby
Where Is Gabby?	B	RF	21	Early Emergent	Pioneer Valley
Where Is Hannah?	D	RF	141	PM Extensions-Red	Rigby
Where Is Happy Monkey?	C	F	46	Joy Readers	Pearson Learning Group
Where Is It Going?	A	I	20	Windows on Literacy	National Geographic
Where Is It Safe to Play?	D	I	103	PM Plus Nonfiction	Rigby
Where is it?	D	RF	250+	Book Bus	Creative Edge
Where Is It?	B	RF	21	Ready Readers	Pearson Learning Group
Where Is It?	D	RF	32	Rookie Readers	Children's Press
Where Is It?	F	I	32	Tiger Cub	Peguis
Where Is Jake?	E	RF	35	My First Reader	Grolier Press
Where Is Kate's Skate?	D	RF	46	KinderReaders	Rigby
Where Is Lunch?	B	F	25	Pacific Literacy	Pacific Learning
Where Is Marco?	C	F	75	Bookshop	Mondo
Where Is Max?	C	F	54	Sun Sprouts	ETA/Cuisenaire
Where Is Miss Pool?	D	RF	55	Pacific Literacy	Pacific Learning
Where Is My Ball?	B	F	24	The Book Project	Sundance
Where Is My Bone?	C	F	42	Sunshine	Wright Group/McGraw Hill
Where Is My Cat?	D	RF	102	Handprints C, Set 1	Educator's Publishing Service
Where Is My Caterpillar?	H	F	277	Wonder World	Wright Group/McGraw Hill
Where Is My Grandma?	C	RF	74	Foundations	Wright Group/McGraw Hill
Where Is My Pencil?	C	RF	34	Little Celebrations	Pearson Learning Group
Where Is My Pet?	A	RF	34	Smart Start	Rigby
Where Is My Puppy?	B	RF	33	Bebop Books	Lee & Low Books Inc.
Where is my Spider?	H	RF	225	Story Box	Wright Group/McGraw Hill
Where Is My Teacher?	B	I	43	Little Books for Early Readers	University of Maine
Where Is Nancy?	E	RF	56	Literacy 2000	Rigby
Where Is She?	A	I	35	Little Books for Early Readers	University of Maine
Where Is Skunk?	D	F	65	Story Box	Wright Group/McGraw Hill
Where Is Teddy's Head?	A	RF	27	Windmill	Wright Group/McGraw Hill
Where Is the Bear?	K	F	250+	Nims, Bonnie	Whitman
Where Is the Cat?	C	I	28	Read-More Books	Pearson Learning Group
Where is the Crab?	C	I	30	Vocabulary Readers	Houghton Mifflin

* Collection of short stories

TITLE	LEVEL	GENRE	WORD COUNT	AUTHOR / SERIES	PUBLISHER / DISTRIBUTOR
Where is the Dog?	A	I	18	Vocabulary Readers	Houghton Mifflin
Where Is the Milk?	D	RF	87	Foundations	Wright Group/McGraw Hill
Where Is the Queen?	H	F	109	Ready Readers	Pearson Learning Group
Where Is the School Bus?	D	RF	40	Carousel Readers	Pearson Learning Group
Where Is the Snake?	C	F	60	The Book Project	Sundance
Where is the Sun?	D	I	70	Leveled Readers Science	Houghton Mifflin
Where Is Water?	C	I	36	Twig	Wright Group/McGraw Hill
Where is White Rabbit?	K	RF	250+	Pacific Literacy	Pacific Learning
Where Is Your Home?	I	I	126	Phonics Readers	Compass Point Books
Where Is Zig?	D	F	63	Leveled Readers	Houghton Mifflin
Where Jeans Come From	K	I	250+	Ready Readers	Pearson Learning Group
Where People Live	J	RF	259	Early Connections	Benchmark Education
*Where the Flame Trees Bloom	U	B	250+	Ada, Alma Flor	Simon & Schuster
Where the Ground Meets the Sky	Y	HF	250+	Davies, Jacqueline	Marshall Cavendish
Where the Lilies Bloom	Y	RF	250+	Cleavers, Vera & Bill	HarperTrophy
Where the Red Fern Grows	X	RF	250+	Rawls, Wilson	Bantam
Where the River Runs: A Portrait of a Refugee Family	W	B	250+	Graff, Nancy Price	Scholastic
Where the Wild Things Are	J	F	339	Sendak, Maurice	Harper & Row
Where There Was Smoke	M	I	250+	Martinucci, Suzanne	Scholastic
Where to Buy It	B	I	45	Rosen Real Readers	Rosen Publishing Group
Where to Look for a Dinosaur	O	F	250+	Most, Bernard	OSI
Where Was Atlantis?	Z	I	250+	Innes, Brian	Steck-Vaughn
Where Was Patrick Henry on the 29th of May?	R	B	250+	Fritz, Jean	Scholastic
Where We Live	C	I	34	Vocabulary Readers	Houghton Mifflin
Where Will I Sit?	F	RF	78	Teacher's Choice Series	Pearson Learning Group
Where Will You Sleep Tonight?	C	I	77	Foundations	Wright Group/McGraw Hill
Where's Al?	D	F	49	Barton, Byron	Houghton Mifflin
Where's Baby Tom?	D	RF	91	Book Bank	Wright Group/McGraw Hill
Where's Bear?	C	F	41	Windmill	Wright Group/McGraw Hill
Where's Cupcake?	D	RF	71	Little Readers	Houghton Mifflin
Where's Henry?	F	RF	112	Home Connection Collection	Rigby
Where's Little Mole?	C	F	43	Little Celebrations	Pearson Learning Group
Where's Lulu?	I	RF	250+	Hooks, William H.	Bantam
Where's My Backpack?	C	RF	27	Little Celebrations	Pearson Learning Group
Where's My Daddy?	F	F	87	Watanabe, Shigeo	Putnam
Where's My Snack?	I	RF	250+	Sunshine	Wright Group/McGraw Hill
Where's My Yellow Yo-Yo?	B	RF	36	Phonics and Friends	Hampton-Brown
Where's Spot?	E	F	65	Hill, Eric	Putnam
Where's Sylvester's Bed?	F	RF	78	Wonder World	Wright Group/McGraw Hill
Where's the Baby?	E	RF	139	Alphakids	Sundance
Where's the Bus?	L	F	250+	Sunshine	Wright Group/McGraw Hill
Where's the Dog?	B	RF	36	Windmill Books	Rigby
Where's the Egg Cup?	B	RF	25	Windmill	Wright Group/McGraw Hill
Where's the Fish?	B	F	39	Gomi, Taro	Morrow
Where's the Frog?	D	I	46	Discovery Links	Newbridge
Where's the Halloween Treat?	C	RF	102	Ziefert, Harriet	Penguin Group
Where's the Puppy?	D	RF	70	Dwight, Laura	Checkerboard
Where's the Snow?	G	RF	142	Erickson, Betty	Continental Press
Where's Tim?	C	F	38	Sunshine	Wright Group/McGraw Hill
Where's Tony?	J	RF	114	City Kids	Rigby
Where's Your Tooth?	C	RF	53	Learn to Read	Creative Teaching Press
Which Animal Is That?	I	I	250+	Momentum Literacy Program	Troll Associates
Which Animal?	B	I	14	Foundations	Wright Group/McGraw Hill

* Collection of short stories

TITLE	LEVEL	GENRE	WORD COUNT	AUTHOR / SERIES	PUBLISHER / DISTRIBUTOR
Which Clothes Do You Wear?	C	I	49	Foundations	Wright Group/McGraw Hill
Which Comes First?	J	I	250+	Voyages	SRA/McGraw Hill
Which Egg Is Mine?	D	F	65	Rise & Shine	Hampton-Brown
Which Hat Today?	E	RF	94	Gosset, Rachel; Ballinger, Margaret	Scholastic
Which Holiday Is It?	I	I	110	Phonics Readers	Compass Point Books
Which Insects Live Here?	J	I	129	Rigby Literacy	Rigby
Which Is Heavier?	D	I	51	Questions & Answers	Pearson Learning Group
Which Juice Would You Like?	C	F	28	Step-By-Step Series	Pearson Learning Group
Which One Does Not Belong?	B	I	20	Windows on Literacy	National Geographic
Which One Is Which?	G	I	187	Sunshine	Wright Group/McGraw Hill
Which Toys?	D	I	40	Home Connection Collection	Rigby
Which Way Home?	C	RF	26	Little Celebrations	Pearson Learning Group
Which Way, Jack?	O	F	250+	Action Packs	Rigby
Which Way, Wendy	M	RF	250+	Social Studies Connects	The Kane Press
Which Witch?	S	F	250+	Ibbotson, Eva	Puffin Books
Whipping Boy, The	R	F	250+	Fleischman, Sid	Troll Associates
Whiskers	C	I	32	Wonder World	Wright Group/McGraw Hill
Whisper and Shout	C	I	92	Twig	Wright Group/McGraw Hill
Whistle for Willie	L	RF	380	Keats, Ezra Jack	Penguin Group
Whistle Like a Bird	D	RF	53	Pair-It Books	Steck-Vaughn
Whistle Tooth, The	H	RF	188	Storyteller-Night Crickets	Wright Group/McGraw Hill
Whistler's Hollow	T	HF	250+	Dadey, Debbie	Bloomsbury Children's Books
White Bird	N	RF	250+	Bulla, Clyde Robert	Random House
White Dragon: Anna Allen in the Face of Danger	R	I	1253	Leveled Readers	Houghton Mifflin
White Elephants	L	RF	250+	Sunshine	Wright Group/McGraw Hill
White Elephants and Yellow Jackets	O	I	250+	Action Packs	Rigby
White Fang	Y	RF	250+	London, Jack	Scholastic
White Horse, The	K	F	250+	Literacy 2000	Rigby
White House, The	N	I	250+	American Symbols	Capstone Press
White House, The	V	I	250+	Cornerstones of Freedom	Children's Press
White House, The	Q	I	250+	Let's See	Compass Point Books
White Mountain, The	V	F	250+	Christopher, John	Aladdin
White Paw, Black Paw	C	F	41	KinderReaders	Rigby
White Wednesday	H	RF	321	Literacy 2000	Rigby
White: Seeing White All Around Us	L	I	250+	Colors	Capstone Press
Whiteout	N	RF	1029	Leveled Readers	Houghton Mifflin
White-Tailed Deer, The	R	I	250+	Zwaschka, Michael	Red Brick Learning
Whizz! Click!	L	RF	285	Pacific Literacy	Pacific Learning
Who Am I ?	D	I	81	Rise & Shine	Hampton-Brown
Who Am I?	B	F	32	The Book Project	Sundance
Who Am I?	E	I	64	Christensen, Nancy	Scholastic
Who Are We?	C	RF	30	Home Connection Collection	Rigby
Who Are You?	C	RF	55	Book Bank	Wright Group/McGraw Hill
Who Ate the Broccoli?	E	F	42	Little Readers	Houghton Mifflin
Who Ate the Pizza?	C	RF	59	Foundations	Wright Group/McGraw Hill
Who Builds?	I	I	97	Yellow Umbrella Books	Red Brick Learning
Who Came By Here?	C	RF	31	Rise & Shine	Hampton-Brown
Who Came Out?	F	F	45	Ready Readers	Pearson Learning Group
Who Can Be a Hero?	A	I	41	Leveled Readers Social Studies	Houghton Mifflin
Who Can Fix the Computer?	G	RF	178	Handprints D, Set 1	Educator's Publishing Service
Who Can Hop?	C	I	35	Questions & Answers	Pearson Learning Group

* Collection of short stories

TITLE	LEVEL	GENRE	WORD COUNT	AUTHOR / SERIES	PUBLISHER / DISTRIBUTOR
Who Can Play?	B	RF	26	Sun Sprouts	ETA/Cuisenaire
Who Can Read?	C	RF	72	Handprints C, Set 1	Educator's Publishing Service
Who Can See the Camel?	C	RF	70	Story Box	Wright Group/McGraw Hill
Who Can?	B	RF	35	Bookshop	Mondo
Who Cleans the Museum?	I	RF	85	Books for Young Learners	Richard C. Owen
Who Cried for Pie?	D	F	86	First Start	Troll Associates
Who Eats What?	N	I	697	Leveled Readers Science	Houghton Mifflin
Who Fed the Chickens?	C	F	14	Little Celebrations	Pearson Learning Group
Who Goes Out on Halloween?	G	RF	163	Alexander, Sue	Bantam
Who Grows Up in the Desert?: A Book About Desert Animals and Their Offspring	L	I	250+	Who Grows Up Here?	Picture Window Books
Who Grows Up in the Forest?: A Book About Forest Animals and Their Offspring	L	I	250+	Who Grows Up Here?	Picture Window Books
Who Grows Up in the Ocean?: A Book About Ocean Animals and Their Offspring	L	I	250+	Who Grows Up Here?	Picture Window Books
Who Grows Up in the Rain Forest?: A Book About Rain Forest Animals and Their Offspring	L	I	250+	Who Grows Up Here?	Picture Window Books
Who Grows Up in the Snow?: A Book About Polar Animals and Their Offspring	L	I	250+	Who Grows Up Here?	Picture Window Books
Who Grows Up on the Farm?: A Book About Farm Animals and Their Offspring	K	I	250+	Who Grows Up Here?	Picture Window Books
Who Has a Tail?	G	I	186	Ready Readers	Pearson Learning Group
Who Has Wings?	C	I	30	Questions & Answers	Pearson Learning Group
Who Hid?	B	RF	25	Leber, Nancy	Scholastic
Who is a Friend?	F	I	191	Yellow Umbrella Books	Capstone Press
Who Is Carrie?	W	HF	250+	Collier, James & Christopher	Bantam
Who Is Coming?	E	RF	28	Rookie Readers	Children's Press
Who Is Ready?	C	RF	36	Ready Readers	Pearson Learning Group
Who is Taller?	F	I	163	Sun Sprouts	ETA/Cuisenaire
Who Is Taller?	C	RF	26	Learn to Read	Creative Teaching Press
Who Is the Robot?	C	RF	67	Pacific Literacy	Pacific Learning
Who Is the Tallest?	F	I	91	Alphakids	Sundance
Who Is the Tallest?	D	RF	46	Sunshine	Wright Group/McGraw Hill
Who Is Who?	D	RF	115	Rookie Readers	Children's Press
Who Keeps Us Safe?	B	I	28	Yellow Umbrella Books	Red Brick Learning
Who Killed Mr. Boddy?	P	RF	250+	Parker, A. E.	Scholastic
Who Lays Eggs?	G	I	132	Twig	Wright Group/McGraw Hill
Who Likes Ice Cream?	A	F	15	Literacy 2000	Rigby
Who Likes It Hot?	K	F	250+	Bookshop	Mondo
Who Likes the Cold?	A	I	29	Twig	Wright Group/McGraw Hill
Who Likes the Night?	G	RF	250+	Phonics and Friends	Hampton-Brown
Who Likes to Swim?	D	I	100	Teacher's Choice Series	Pearson Learning Group
Who Likes Water?	B	F	35	KinderReaders	Rigby
Who Lives at the Zoo?	LB	I	11	Windows on Literacy	National Geographic
Who Lives Here?	C	I	62	Learn to Read	Creative Teaching Press
Who Lives Here?	I	I	230	Little Readers	Houghton Mifflin
Who Lives Here?	C	I	42	Questions & Answers	Pearson Learning Group
Who Lives Here?	C	I	28	Story Box	Wright Group/McGraw Hill
Who Lives Here?	F	I	185	Storyteller Nonfiction	Wright Group/McGraw Hill
Who Lives Here?	B	I	43	Windows on Literacy	National Geographic
Who Lives Here?	F	I	100	Leveled Readers Science	Houghton Mifflin
Who Lives in a Tree?	B	I	46	Canizares, Susan; Moreton, Daniel	Scholastic
Who Lives in a Tree?	C	I	43	Discovery Links	Newbridge

TITLE	LEVEL	GENRE	WORD COUNT	AUTHOR / SERIES	PUBLISHER / DISTRIBUTOR
Who Lives in the Arctic?	B	I	48	Canizares, Susan; Chanko, Pamela	Scholastic
Who Lives in the Sea?	B	I	69	Bookshop	Mondo
Who Lives in the Woods?	F	I	110	Pair-It Books	Steck-Vaughn
Who Lives in this Hole?	C	I	25	Twig	Wright Group/McGraw Hill
Who Lives on a Farm?	B	I	36	Story Steps	Rigby
Who Looks After Me?	M	I	250+	Literacy 2000	Rigby
Who Looks After Me?	B	I	20	Windows on Literacy	National Geographic
Who Looks After Our World?	E	I	45	Home Connection Collection	Rigby
Who Loves Getting Wet?	I	F	204	Sunshine	Wright Group/McGraw Hill
Who Made That?	C	RF	31	Ready Readers	Pearson Learning Group
Who Made These Tracks?	B	I	24	Literacy 2000	Rigby
Who Made These Tracks?	D	I	45	Teacher's Choice Series	Pearson Learning Group
Who Makes the Rules?	M	I	250+	Schafer, Lola M.	Benchmark Education
Who Needs Math?	K	RF	349	Story Box	Wright Group/McGraw Hill
Who Needs Teeth?	I	I	116	Phonics Readers	Compass Point Books
Who Passed Through?	K	RF	380	Leveled Readers	Houghton Mifflin
Who Pushed Humpty?	K	TL	250+	Literacy 2000	Rigby
Who Put That Hair in My Toothbrush?	V	RF	250+	Spinelli, Jerry	Little, Brown & Co.
Who Reads?	B	I	25	Teacher's Choice Series	Pearson Learning Group
Who Really Killed Cock Robin?	U	RF	250+	George, Jean Craighead	HarperTrophy
Who Rides the Bus?	C	RF	19	Little Celebrations	Pearson Learning Group
Who Sank the Boat?	K	F	219	Allen, Pamela	Coward
Who Says?	D	F	36	My First Reader	Grolier Press
Who Says?	C	I	49	Twig	Wright Group/McGraw Hill
Who Shot the President?: The Death of John F. Kennedy	P	I	250+	Donnelly, Judy	Random House
Who Spilled the Beans?	E	F	87	Story Basket	Wright Group/McGraw Hill
Who Stole the Fish?	H	F	250+	Cambridge Reading	Pearson Learning Group
Who Stole the Tiger's Eye?	Q	F	250+	Sunshine	Wright Group/McGraw Hill
Who Stole the Wizard of Oz?	P	RF	250+	Avi	Alfred A. Knopf
Who the Man	X	RF	250+	Lynch, Chris	HarperCollins
Who Took Our Cake?	E	RF	98	Rigby Focus	Rigby
Who Took the Cake?	C	RF	32	First Stories	Pacific Learning
Who Took the Cookies from the Cookie Jar?	D	F	81	Learn to Read	Creative Teaching Press
Who Took the Farmer's Hat?	I	F	340	Nodset, Joan	Scholastic
Who Uses These Tools?	B	I	23	Twig	Wright Group/McGraw Hill
Who Wants a Ride?	I	RF	214	Bernard, Robin	Scholastic
Who Wants Arthur?	J	F	250+	Leveled Readers Language Support	Houghton Mifflin
Who Wants One?	I	F	212	Serfozo, Mary	Macmillan
Who Wants to Live in My House?	D	RF	60	Book Bank	Wright Group/McGraw Hill
Who Wants to See the Doctor?	F	I	116	Adventures in Reading	Pearson Learning Group
Who Was Betsy Ross?	M	B	250+	Rosen Real Readers	Rosen Publishing Group
Who Was Marjorie Harris Carr?	O	B	597	Leveled Readers Science	Houghton Mifflin
Who Was Paul Revere?	M	B	250+	Rosen Real Readers	Rosen Publishing Group
Who Was Poor Richard? Colonials to Remember	V	I	2615	Independent Readers Social Studies	Houghton Mifflin
Who Wears This Hat?	H	I	139	Windows on Literacy	National Geographic
Who Wears This Hat?	B	I	42	Windmill	Wright Group/McGraw Hill
Who Were the First People?	R	I	250+	Usborne Starting Point History	EDC Publishing
Who Were the Romans?	R	I	250+	Usborne Starting Point History	EDC Publishing
Who Were the Vikings?	R	I	250+	Usborne Starting Point History	EDC Publishing
Who Will Be My Friends?	F	RF	205	Hoff, Syd	HarperTrophy
Who Will Be My Mother?	E	F	156	Story Box	Wright Group/McGraw Hill

* Collection of short stories

TITLE	LEVEL	GENRE	WORD COUNT	AUTHOR / SERIES	PUBLISHER / DISTRIBUTOR
Who Will Help Me?	C	RF	53	Home Connection Collection	Rigby
Who Will Help?	B	RF	20	Carousel Readers	Pearson Learning Group
Who Will Help?	D	TL	93	Learn to Read	Creative Teaching Press
Who Will Help?	F	RF	74	New Way Red	Steck-Vaughn
Who Will Look Out for Danny?	S	RF	250+	Action Packs	Rigby
Who Will Use This?	H	I	154	Rigby Literacy	Rigby
Who Will Win the Race?	D	RF	53	Sunshine	Wright Group/McGraw Hill
Who Works at the Beach?	G	I	102	Windows on Literacy	National Geographic
Who Works at the Zoo?	D	I	31	Windows on Literacy	National Geographic
Who Works Here?	D	I	57	Questions & Answers	Pearson Learning Group
Who?	E	F	46	Storyteller-Setting Sun	Wright Group/McGraw Hill
Who'll Hold the Baby?	F	RF	181	Voyages	SRA/McGraw Hill
Whoops	I	F	250+	Supersonics	Rigby
Whoops!	E	RF	49	Little Celebrations	Pearson Learning Group
Whoops! It Works!	O	I	250+	Lopez, Orlando	Pearson Learning Group
Who's a Pest?	J	F	250+	Bonsall, Crosby	HarperTrophy
Who's Afraid of Shadows?	I	RF	219	Talking Point Series	Pearson Learning Group
Who's Afraid of the Big, Bad Bully?	K	RF	250+	Slater, Teddy	Scholastic
Who's Afraid of the Dark?	I	RF	250+	Bonsall, Crosby	HarperTrophy
Who's Afraid?	I	RF	165	Reading Unlimited	Pearson Learning Group
Who's at School?	A	I	36	Rosen Real Readers	Rosen Publishing Group
Who's Behind the Door at My House?	G	RF	184	Salmon, Michael	Steck-Vaughn
Who's Behind the Door at My School?	G	RF	187	Salmon, Michael	Steck-Vaughn
Who's Coming for a Ride?	B	F	25	Literacy 2000	Rigby
Who's Going to Lick the Bowl?	C	RF	18	Story Box	Wright Group/McGraw Hill
Who's Hiding There?	I	RF	242	Pair-It Books	Steck-Vaughn
Who's Hiding?	D	I	51	Learn to Read	Creative Teaching Press
Who's in Love with Arthur?	M	F	250+	Brown, Marc	Little, Brown & Co.
Who's in the Jungle?	F	I	116	Ready Readers	Pearson Learning Group
Who's in the Nest?	E	F	75	Start to Read	School Zone
Who's in the Shed?	I	F	202	Literacy Tree	Rigby
Who's Looking After the Baby?	H	RF	127	Foundations	Wright Group/McGraw Hill
Who's That Stepping on Plymouth Rock?	R	I	250+	Fritz, Jean	Putnam & Grosset
Who's There?	B	F	49	Bookshop	Mondo
Who's There?	E	F	92	Story Box	Wright Group/McGraw Hill
Whose Birthday Is It Today?	C	RF	50	Book Bank	Wright Group/McGraw Hill
Whose Bones?	B	I	28	Fernandez, Queta	Scholastic
Whose Ears Are These?: A Look at Aminal Ears - Short, Flat, and Floppy	M	I	250+	Whose Is It? Science	Picture Window Books
Whose Egg Is This?	E	F	99	Story Steps	Rigby
Whose Eggs Are These?	E	RF	125	Sunshine	Wright Group/McGraw Hill
Whose Eyes Are These?: A Look at Animal Eyes - Big, Round, and Narrow	M	I	250+	Whose Is It? Science	Picture Window Books
Whose Feet Are These? A Look at Hooves, Paws, and Claws	M	I	250+	Whose Is It? Science	Picture Window Books
Whose Footprints?	D	I	125	Lighthouse	Rigby
Whose Forest Is It?	C	RF	45	Learn to Read	Creative Teaching Press
Whose Legs Are These?: A Look at Animal Legs - Kicking, Running, and Hopping	M	I	250+	Whose Is It? Science	Picture Window Books
Whose List Is This?	C	F	14	Little Celebrations	Pearson Learning Group
Whose Mouse Are You?	H	F	98	Kraus, Robert	Macmillan
Whose Mouth Is This?: A Look at Bills, Suckers, and Tubes	M	I	250+	Whose Is It? Science	Picture Window Books

TITLE	LEVEL	GENRE	WORD COUNT	AUTHOR / SERIES	PUBLISHER / DISTRIBUTOR
Whose Nose Is This?: A Look at Beaks, Snouts, and Trunks	M	I	250+	Whose Is It? Science	Picture Window Books
Whose Shoes?	D	I	84	Twig	Wright Group/McGraw Hill
Whose Shoes?	K	RF	250+	Sunshine	Wright Group/McGraw Hill
Whose Side Are You On?	Q	RF	250+	Moore, Emily	Bantam
Whose Side Are You On?	K	TL	250+	Cisco, Cheyenne	Sadlier-Oxford
Whose Skin Is This?: A Look at Animal Skin - Scaly, Furry, and Prickly	M	I	250+	Whose Is It? Science	Picture Window Books
Whose Tail Is This?: A Look at Tails - Swishing, Wiggling, and Rattling	M	I	250+	Whose Is It? Science	Picture Window Books
Whose Tracks?	B	I	14	Little Celebrations	Pearson Learning Group
Whose Way Today?	M	RF	683	Leveled Readers	Houghton Mifflin
Why Bear Sleeps All Winter	L	TL	647	Leveled Readers	Houghton Mifflin
Why Bears Have Short Tails, A Norwegian Tale	Q	F	1093	Leveled Readers	Houghton Mifflin
Why Can't I Fly?	G	F	449	Gelman, Rita	Scholastic
Why Cats Wash After Dinner	I	TL	128	Pacific Literacy	Pacific Learning
Why Coyote Howls at Night	Q	TL	250+	Moore, Emily	Farrar, Straus and Giroux
Why Coyote Howls at Night	K	TL	274	Little Books	Sadlier-Oxford
Why Crocodiles Live in Rivers	J	TL	415	Sunshine	Wright Group/McGraw Hill
Why Cry?	I	I	121	Sunshine	Wright Group/McGraw Hill
Why Did They Come?	N	I	157	Windows on Literacy	National Geographic
Why do Elephants Wear Hats	J	F	115	O'Toole, Mary	Pearson Learning Group
Why Do I Feel Safe?	D	I	61	Questions & Answers	Pearson Learning Group
Why Do I Need to Know When?	G	RF	198	Visions	Wright Group/McGraw Hill
Why Do Worms Come Up When It Rains?	I	I	202	Seedlings	Continental Press
Why Does It Work?	Y	I	2160	Independent Readers Science	Houghton Mifflin
Why Don't You Get a Horse, Sam Adams?	R	B	250+	Fritz, Jean	G.P. Putnam's Sons
Why Elephants Have Long Noses	G	TL	175	Literacy 2000	Rigby
Why I Like Laura	G	RF	193	Phonics and Friends	Hampton-Brown
Why Mosquitoes Buzz in People's Ears	N	TL	250+	Aardema, Verna	Scholastic
Why Not?	G	RF	167	Voyages	SRA/McGraw Hill
Why People Move	K	I	250+	People, Places & Spaces	Rand McNally
Why Polar Bears Like Snow . . . and Flamingos Don't	O	I	250+	Navigators Fiction Series	Benchmark Education
Why Rabbits Have Long Ears	L	TL	250+	Literacy 2000	Rigby
Why Rabbit's Tail Is Short	G	TL	296	Leveled Readers	Houghton Mifflin
Why the Bear's Tail is Short	J	TL	431	Sunshine	Wright Group/McGraw Hill
Why the Kangaroo Hops	K	I	391	Sunshine	Wright Group/McGraw Hill
Why the Leopard Has Spots	L	I	250+	Pair-It Books	Steck-Vaughn
Why the Ocean Is Salty	Q	I	250+	Leonhardt, Alice	Steck-Vaughn
Why the Rooster Crows at Sunrise	K	TL	250+	Sunshine	Wright Group/McGraw Hill
Why The Sea Is Salty	L	TL	250+	Literacy 2000	Rigby
Why There Are Shooting Stars	K	TL	362	Pacific Literacy	Pacific Learning
Why We Measure	K	I	178	Spyglass Books	Compass Point Books
Why Write?	D	I	47	Moreton, Daniel; Berger, Samantha	Scholastic
Why?	D	I	68	Twig	Wright Group/McGraw Hill
Wibble Wobble, Albatross!	H	I	101	Pacific Literacy	Pacific Learning
Wibble-Wobble	H	RF	263	Storyteller-Night Crickets	Wright Group/McGraw Hill
Wicked Pirates, The	I	F	226	Sunshine	Wright Group/McGraw Hill
Wide Window, The	V	F	250+	Snicket, Lemony	Scholastic
Wide-mouthed Frog, The	E	F	121	Literacy 2000	Rigby
Wig for Pig, A	D	F	52	Leveled Readers	Houghton Mifflin
Wiggle and Giggle	H	RF	163	Cambridge Reading	Pearson Learning Group

* Collection of short stories

TITLE	LEVEL	GENRE	WORD COUNT	AUTHOR / SERIES	PUBLISHER / DISTRIBUTOR
Wigglebottom	G	RF	134	Cambridge Reading	Pearson Learning Group
Wiggly Worm	G	F	115	Literacy 2000	Rigby
Wiggly, Jiggly, Joggly, Tooth, A	E	RF	61	Little Celebrations	Pearson Learning Group
Wiggly-Jiggly Line, The	I	F	128	Book Bank	Wright Group/McGraw Hill
Wilamina and the Weather Conditions	M	F	250+	Reimer, Luther	Wright Group/McGraw Hill
Wilbert Took a Walk	H	F	216	Ready Readers	Pearson Learning Group
*Wilbur's Wild Ride	E	RF	164	Story Steps	Rigby
Wild Adaptations	P	I	924	Independent Readers Science	Houghton Mifflin
Wild and Wooly Mammoths	P	I	250+	Aliki	HarperCollins
Wild Babies	O	I	250+	Simon, Seymour	HarperCollins
Wild Baby Animals	N	I	250+	Little Celebrations	Pearson Learning Group
Wild Bear	A	I	21	Pacific Literacy	Pacific Learning
*Wild Bird and Other Stories of Adventure	O	RF	250+	Belcher, Angie	Pacific Learning
Wild Cat Guide, The	M	I	250+	Lighthouse	Rigby
Wild Cats	Q	I	250+	Leonhardt, Alice	Steck-Vaughn
Wild Crayons	J	F	270	Story Box	Wright Group/McGraw Hill
Wild Culpepper Cruise, The	O	RF	250+	Paulsen, Gary	Bantam
Wild Horses	R	I	250+	Action Packs	Rigby
Wild Swans, The	L	TL	754	Tales from Hans Andersen	Wright Group/McGraw Hill
Wild Weather	V	I	2411	Leveled Readers Science	Houghton Mifflin
Wild Weather	K	I	187	Rigby Focus	Rigby
Wild Weather, Tall Tales	M	F	321	Vocabulary Readers	Houghton Mifflin
Wild Wet Wellington Wind	I	RF	104	Pacific Literacy	Pacific Learning
Wild Wicked Winifred and Horrible Hank	L	F	250+	Popcorn	Sundance
Wild Wicked Winifred and the Pirates	L	F	250+	Popcorn	Sundance
Wild Wicked Winifred and the Sea Serpent	L	F	250+	Popcorn	Sundance
Wild Wicked Winifred and the Treasure Map	L	F	250+	Popcorn	Sundance
Wild Willie and King Kyle Detectives	N	F	250+	Joosse, Barbara M.	Bantam
Wild Wind, The	H	F	246	Story Box	Wright Group/McGraw Hill
Wild, Wild Wolves	M	I	250+	Milton, Joyce	Random House
Wild, Wooly Child, The	J	F	315	Read Alongs	Rigby
Wilde Street Club and Molly, The	M	RF	965	Sunshine	Wright Group/McGraw Hill
Wilde Street Club and the Duck Man, The	M	RF	1057	Sunshine	Wright Group/McGraw Hill
Wilderness Road, 1775, The	V	I	250+	Let Freedom Ring	Capstone Press
Wildfires	N	I	250+	A True Book	Children's Press
Wildlife	J	I	145	Independent Readers Social Studies	Houghton Mifflin
Wildlife	J	I	250+	Independent Readers Science	Houghton Mifflin
Wildlife Helpers	G	I	132	Twig	Wright Group/McGraw Hill
Wildlife Photographer Frank Greenway	T	I	250+	iOpeners	Pearson Learning Group
Wilfrid Laurier	X	B	250+	The Canadians	Fitzhenry & Whiteside
Will It Rain on the Parade?	H	RF	102	Wonder World	Wright Group/McGraw Hill
Will Power	I	RF	250+	Rigby Literacy	Rigby
Will Rogers	O	B	250+	Schott, Jane A.	Carolrhoda Books
Will You Play With Me?	D	RF	84	Book Bus	Creative Edge
Will You Play with Us?	D	RF	62	Bookshop	Mondo
Will You Play?	D	F	96	Sun Sprouts	ETA/Cuisenaire
William Bradford and Plymouth: A Colony Grows	R	I	250+	The Library of the Pilgrims	Rosen Publishing Group
William Henry Harrison	U	B	250+	Profiles of the Presidents	Compass Point Books
William Howard Taft	U	B	250+	Profiles of the Presidents	Compass Point Books
William Jefferson Clinton	U	B	250+	Profiles of the Presidents	Compass Point Books
William McKinley	U	B	250+	Profiles of the Presidents	Compass Point Books

* Collection of short stories

TITLE	LEVEL	GENRE	WORD COUNT	AUTHOR / SERIES	PUBLISHER / DISTRIBUTOR
William Penn	V	I	2200	Independent Readers Social Studies	Houghton Mifflin
William Problem, The	S	RF	250+	Baker, Barbara	Puffin Books
William Tell	I	TL	127	Jumbled Tumbled Tales & Rhymes	Rigby
William, Where Are You?	F	F	239	Gerstein, Mordicai	Crown
William's Journal	N	HF	250+	Early Connections	Benchmark Education
William's Skateboard	G	RF	100	Windmill	Wright Group/McGraw Hill
William's Wheelchair Race	J	RF	279	Sunshine	Wright Group/McGraw Hill
Williamsburg	V	I	250+	Cornerstones of Freedom	Children's Press
Williamsburg	U	I	250+	We The People	Compass Point Books
Willie the Slowpoke	G	F	125	First Start	Troll Associates
Willie's Wonderful Pet	I	RF	315	Cebulash, Mel	Scholastic
Williwaw!	V	RF	250+	Bodett, Tom	Alfred A. Knopf
Willow Pattern, The	P	TL	250+	Action Packs	Rigby
Willy the Helper	D	RF	79	Little Readers	Houghton Mifflin
Willy the Wizard	C	F	42	Learn to Read	Creative Teaching Press
Willy's Hats	E	RF	65	Stewart, Josie.; Salem, Lynn	Continental Press
Wilma Mankiller	P	B	250+	Lowery, Linda	Carolrhoda Books
Wilma's Wagon	D	RF	48	Ready Readers	Pearson Learning Group
Wind	E	RF	89	Ready to Read	Pearson Learning Group
Wind and Storms	K	I	868	Sunshine	Wright Group/McGraw Hill
Wind and Sun	I	TL	238	Sunshine	Wright Group/McGraw Hill
Wind and Sun	G	TL	170	Literacy 2000	Rigby
*Wind and the Sun and Other Stories, The	J	F	250+	New Way Orange	Steck-Vaughn
Wind and the Sun, The	K	TL	399	Leveled Readers	Houghton Mifflin
Wind and the Sun, The: An Aesop Fable	G	TL	234	Rigby Literacy	Rigby
Wind And Water: Two Great Powers	U	I	2567	Independent Readers Social Studies	Houghton Mifflin
Wind Blew, The	J	RF	169	Hutchins, Pat	Puffin Books
Wind Blows Strong, The	E	RF	114	Sunshine	Wright Group/McGraw Hill
Wind Blows, The	C	RF	38	Learn to Read	Creative Teaching Press
Wind Eagle, The	K	RF	370	Wonders	Hampton-Brown
Wind in the Door, A	V	F	250+	L'Engle, Madeleine	Bantam
Wind Power	J	I	103	Pacific Literacy	Pacific Learning
Wind Power	I	I	116	Windows on Literacy	National Geographic
Wind Surfing	D	RF	224	Sunshine	Wright Group/McGraw Hill
Wind That Would Not Blow, The	M	TL	250+	Kunari, Anna	Hampton-Brown
Wind, The	K	I	179	Spyglass Books	Compass Point Books
Wind, The	E	I	36	Discovery Links	Newbridge
Wind, The	E	I	64	Pacific Literacy	Pacific Learning
Wind, The	F	I	84	Voyages	SRA/McGraw Hill
Wind, The	D	RF	34	Wonder World	Wright Group/McGraw Hill
Wind, Water and Ice	R	I	1829	Independent Readers Science	Houghton Mifflin
Windmills	S	I	783	Independent Readers Science	Houghton Mifflin
Window, The	V	RF	250+	Ingold, Jeanette	Harcourt Trade
Windy Day, A	E	I	53	Pebble Books	Capstone Press
Windy Ways	G	I	97	Independent Readers Science	Houghton Mifflin
Wing High, Goofah	Q	RF	250+	Literacy 2000	Rigby
Winged Cat, The: A Tale of Ancient Egypt	U	TL	250+	Lattimore, Deborah Nourse	HarperCollins
Winging It	U	I	250+	iOpeners	Pearson Learning Group
Wingman	O	F	250+	Pinkwater, Daniel	Bantam
Wingman on Ice	M	RF	250+	Christopher, Matt	Little, Brown & Co.
Wings	W	TL	250+	Yolen, Jane; Nolan, Dennis	OSI
Wings	A	I	24	Rigby Literacy	Rigby

* Collection of short stories

TITLE	LEVEL	GENRE	WORD COUNT	AUTHOR / SERIES	PUBLISHER / DISTRIBUTOR
Wings	LB	I	14	KinderReaders	Rigby
Wings	Q	F	250+	Brittain, Bill	HarperTrophy
Wings for a Day	T	F	1842	Leveled Readers	Houghton Mifflin
Winklepoo the Wicked	M	F	1614	Sunshine	Wright Group/McGraw Hill
Winslow Homer, American Painter	N	I	348	Independent Readers Social Studies	Houghton Mifflin
Winter	E	I	56	Discovery Links	Newbridge
Winter	H	I	172	Storyteller-Setting Sun	Wright Group/McGraw Hill
Winter	C	I	49	Carousel Readers	Pearson Learning Group
Winter	C	I	54	Foundations	Wright Group/McGraw Hill
Winter	I	I	240	Pebble Books	Capstone Press
Winter Days in the Big Woods	J	HF	250+	Wilder, Laura Ingalls	HarperCollins
Winter Fun	LB	RF	13	Teacher's Choice Series	Pearson Learning Group
Winter in Alaska	O	I	347	Vocabulary Readers	Houghton Mifflin
Winter Is Here	D	I	55	Weinberger, Kimberly	Scholastic
Winter Is Here	E	I	24	Windows on Literacy	National Geographic
Winter on the Farm	J	HF	250+	Wilder, Laura Ingalls	HarperCollins
Winter on the Ice	L	F	506	PM Plus Story Books	Rigby
Winter Recess	D	RF	87	Emergent Books	Pioneer Valley
Winter Room, The	U	RF	250+	Paulsen, Gary	Bantam
Winter Sleeps	F	RF	158	Reading Corners	Pearson Learning Group
Winter Solstice, The	Q	I	250+	Jackson, Ellen	Millbrook Press
Winter Survival	O	I	250+	Literacy Tree	Rigby
Winter Wind, The	H	F	250+	Momentum Literacy Program	Troll Associates
Winter Woollies	K	I	289	Storyteller Nonfiction	Wright Group/McGraw Hill
Winterdance: The Fine Madness of Running the Iditarod	W	B	250+	Paulsen, Gary	Harcourt Trade
Winter's Song	H	RF	233	Ready Readers	Pearson Learning Group
Wired World: A Short History of the Internet	U	I	1527	Leveled Readers Social Studies	Houghton Mifflin
Wisconsin	R	I	250+	This Land Is Your Land	Compass Point Books
Wise Old Turtle, The	K	TL	250+	World Quest Adventures	World Quest Learning
*Wish Fish, The	P	TL	250+	Action Packs	Rigby
Wish Giver, The	T	F	250+	Brittain, Bill	HarperTrophy
Wish on a Unicorn	T	RF	250+	Hesse, Karen	Penguin Group
Wishes Don't Come True	M	RF	250+	Bookshop	Mondo
Wishing for a Horse	D	RF	105	Carousel Readers	Pearson Learning Group
Wishing for Fishing	H	RF	250+	Phonics Readers Plus	Steck-Vaughn
Wishy-Washy Day	E	F	65	Story Basket	Wright Group/McGraw Hill
Witch Hunt: It Happened in Salem Village	Q	I	250+	Krensky, Stephen	Random House
Witch of Blackbird Pond, The	W	HF	250+	Speare, Elizabeth George	Bantam
*Witch of Fourth Street, The	S	HF	250+	Levoy, Myron	Language for Learning Assoc.
Witchcraft of Salem Village, The	U	I	250+	Jackson, Shirley	Random House
Witches Don't Do Backflips	M	F	250+	Dadey, Debbie; Jones, Marcia Thornton	Scholastic
Witches of Worm, The	V	F	250+	Snyder, Zilpha K.	Random House
Witches, The	R	F	250+	Dahl, Roald	Penguin Group
Witch's Cat	P	F	250+	Chew, Ruth	Scholastic
Witch's Haircut, The	G	F	135	Windmill	Wright Group/McGraw Hill
With a Dance and a Roar	P	I	663	Leveled Readers	Houghton Mifflin
With My Mom and Dad	C	I	63	Early Connections	Benchmark Education
Wiz	D	F	76	Voyages	SRA/McGraw Hill
Wizard and the Rainbow, The	K	F	250+	Sunshine	Wright Group/McGraw Hill
Wizard and Wart at Sea	J	F	250+	Smith, Janice Lee	HarperTrophy

TITLE	LEVEL	GENRE	WORD COUNT	AUTHOR / SERIES	PUBLISHER / DISTRIBUTOR
Wizard Came to Visit, A	K	F	250+	Sunshine	Wright Group/McGraw Hill
Wizard of Earthsea, A	Z	F	250+	LeGuin, Ursula K.	Bantam
Wizard of Oz, The	U	F	250+	Baum, L. Frank	Scholastic
Wizard of Oz, The	L	TL	903	Hunia, Fran	Ladybird Books
Wizards Don't Need Computers	M	F	250+	Dadey, Debbie; Jones, Marcia Thornton	Scholastic
Wobbly Tooth, The	F	RF	74	Oxford Reading Tree	Oxford University Press
Wobbly Tooth, The	D	RF	102	Literacy 2000	Rigby
Wole Soyinka	X	B	1951	Leveled Readers Social Studies	Houghton Mifflin
Wolf and the Old Woman, The	I	TL	250+	Voyages	SRA/McGraw Hill
Wolf and the Seven Little Kids	L	TL	250+	Hunia, Fran	Ladybird Books
Wolf and the Seven Little Kids, The	J	TL	254	Literacy Tree	Rigby
Wolf Song	J	RF	130	Books for Young Learners	Richard C. Owen
Wolf Talk	H	I	159	Instant Readers	Harcourt School Publishers
Wolf Who Cried Boy, The	M	F	250+	Hartman, Bob	Scholastic
Wolf, The	S	I	250+	Dahl, Michael	Red Brick Learning
Wolfgang Amadeus Mozart: Musical Genius	N	B	250+	Rookie Biographies	Children's Press
Wolfman Sam	O	RF	250+	Levy, Elizabeth	HarperTrophy
Wolfmen Don't Hula Dance	M	RF	250+	Dadey, Debbie; Jones, Marcia Thornton	Scholastic
Wolf's Cake	I	F	250+	Sunshine	Wright Group/McGraw Hill
Wolf's Chicken Stew, The	J	F	250+	Leveled Readers Language Support	Houghton Mifflin
Wolf's First Deer	M	RF	434	Book Bank	Wright Group/McGraw Hill
Wolves	E	I	68	Seedlings	Continental Press
Wolves	N	I	250+	PM Animal Facts: Silver	Rigby
Wolves	F	I	132	Twig	Wright Group/McGraw Hill
Wolves	I	I	188	Pair-It Books	Steck-Vaughn
Wolves	Q	I	250+	Literacy 2000	Rigby
Wolves	U	I	250+	The Untamed World	Steck-Vaughn
Wolves Have Pups	M	I	250+	Animals and Their Young	Compass Point Books
Wolves of Willoughby Chase, The	V	HF	250+	Aiken, Joan	Bantam
*Woman Hollering Creek	Z	RF	250+	Cisneros, Sandra	Random House
Woman Who Flummoxed the Fairies, The	O	TL	250+	Forest, Heather	Harcourt Trade
Women at Work	G	I	112	Foundations	Wright Group/McGraw Hill
Women in the Vietnam War	U	I	848	Independent Readers Social Studies	Houghton Mifflin
Women Inventors	P	I	996	Leveled Readers Science	Houghton Mifflin
*Women Inventors	O	B	250+	Blashfield, Jean	Red Brick Learning
Women of Valor	U	B	250+	Real Lives	Troll Associates
Women Pioneers in Medicine	T	I	2664	Independent Readers Science	Houghton Mifflin
Women Pioneers of Medicine	R	B	2018	Leveled Readers Science	Houghton Mifflin
Women Suffrage Movement, 1848-1920, The	V	I	250+	Let Freedom Ring	Capstone Press
Women Who Shaped the West	V	B	250+	Cornerstones of Freedom	Children's Press
Women Writers: Voices from the 1800s	T	I	2535	Independent Readers Social Studies	Houghton Mifflin
Women's Voting Rights	V	I	250+	Cornerstones of Freedom	Children's Press
Wonder Kid Meets the Evil Lunch Snatcher	M	RF	250+	Duncan, Lois	Little, Brown & Co.
Wonder of Bald Eagles, The	M	I	250+	Soar To Success	Houghton Mifflin
Wonder of Wolves, The	M	I	250+	Soar To Success	Houghton Mifflin
Wonderful Alexander and the Catwings	N	F	250+	LeGuin, Ursula	Scholastic
Wonderful Ears	I	I	1017	Science	Wright Group/McGraw Hill
Wonderful Eyes	M	I	1070	Science	Wright Group/McGraw Hill

* Collection of short stories

TITLE	LEVEL	GENRE	WORD COUNT	AUTHOR / SERIES	PUBLISHER / DISTRIBUTOR
Wonderful Sky Boat, The: And Other Native American Tales of the Southeast	S	TL	250+	Curry, Jane Louise	Simon & Schuster
*Wonderful Story of Henry Sugar, The: And Six More	U	F	250+	Dahl, Roald	Penguin Group
Wonderful Things	F	RF	98	Early Readers	Compass Point Books
Wonders of the World	N	I	250+	Sunshine	Wright Group/McGraw Hill
Wood	B	I	26	Twig	Wright Group/McGraw Hill
Wood	E	I	48	Windows on Literacy	National Geographic
Wood and Other Materials	G	I	97	Discovery World	Rigby
Wood Frog	O	I	250+	Life Cycles	Creative Teaching Press
Wood Stork Swamp	N	RF	250+	Orbit Double Takes	Pacific Learning
Woodcutter and the Bear, The: A Play	M	TL	250+	Rigby Literacy	Rigby
Woodlanders Begin, The	M	F	250+	Schultz, Irene	Wright Group/McGraw Hill
Woodpeckers	I	I	85	Pebble Books	Red Brick Learning
Woodrow Wilson	U	B	250+	Profiles of the Presidents	Compass Point Books
Woods, Irons, and Greens	R	I	250+	Wildcats	Wright Group/McGraw Hill
Woodsong	T	B	250+	Paulsen, Gary	Dell
Woody Guthrie	I	B	199	Leveled Readers Social Studies	Houghton Mifflin
Woof!	C	F	40	Literacy 2000	Rigby
Wool	F	I	91	Sunshine	Wright Group/McGraw Hill
Wool Keeps Me Warm	K	I	214	Windows on Literacy	National Geographic
Woolly Sally	I	RF	147	Pacific Literacy	Pacific Learning
Woolly, Woolly	E	F	136	Literacy 2000	Rigby
Woosh!	E	RF	124	Story Box	Wright Group/McGraw Hill
Word Machine, The	D	F	33	Sunshine	Wright Group/McGraw Hill
Wordful Child, A	O	B	250+	Lyon, George Ella	Richard C. Owen
Words	U	RF	250+	Paulsen, Gary	Penguin Group
Words	M	I	578	Pacific Literacy	Pacific Learning
Words are Everywhere	E	I	46	Literacy 2000	Rigby
Words By Heart	U	HF	250+	Sebestyen, Ouida	Bantam Doubleday Dell
Words of Stone	V	RF	250+	Henkes, Kevin	Penguin Group
Wordsong	K	RF	192	Bobber Books	Wright Group/McGraw Hill
Work	C	RF	65	TOTTS	Tott Publications
Work Helicopter, The	I	F	250+	PM Plus Story Books	Rigby
Work of Leonardo Da Vinci, The	T	I	1810	Leveled Readers Science	Houghton Mifflin
Work Vehicles	J	I	245	Windows on Literacy	National Geographic
Work We Do, The	K	I	250+	Spyglass Books	Compass Point Books
Workers	LB	F	16	KinderReaders	Rigby
Worker's Tools, A	F	I	93	Discovery World	Rigby
Working	C	I	174	Instant Readers	Harcourt School Publishers
Working	G	I	174	Yellow Umbrella Books	Red Brick Learning
Working at Home	B	I	28	Little Red Readers	Sundance
Working Cotton	N	RF	250+	Williams, Sherley Anne	Harcourt Trade
Working for Dad	D	RF	31	Visions	Wright Group/McGraw Hill
Working on Water	L	I	250+	Home Connection Collection	Rigby
Working Together	G	I	50	Yellow Umbrella Books	Red Brick Learning
Working Together	C	I	50	Early Connections	Benchmark Education
Working Together	I	I	222	Rigby Focus	Rigby
Working with Animals	I	I	250+	Home Connection Collection	Rigby
Working with Metal	L	I	299	Rigby Focus	Rigby
World Around Us, The	C	I	29	Little Red Readers	Sundance
World in a Supermarket, The	LB	I	24	Learn to Read	Creative Teaching Press
World in Grandfather's Hands, The	V	RF	250+	Strete, Craig Kee	Clarion

* Collection of short stories

TITLE	LEVEL	GENRE	WORD COUNT	AUTHOR / SERIES	PUBLISHER / DISTRIBUTOR
World in Your Kitchen, The	L	I	347	Independent Readers Social Studies	Houghton Mifflin
World of Birds, A	B	I	49	Bookshop	Mondo
World of Dogs, The	Q	I	250+	Pair-It Books	Steck-Vaughn
World of Fun, A	G	I	176	Instant Readers	Harcourt School Publishers
World of Games, A	P	RF	676	Leveled Readers	Houghton Mifflin
World of Imagination, A	R	I	250+	Literacy 2000	Rigby
World of Kites, A	M	I	272	Vocabulary Readers	Houghton Mifflin
World of Snow, A	M	RF	250+	Livorse, Kay	Houghton Mifflin
World Worth Keeping, A	V	I	250+	Sunshine	Wright Group/McGraw Hill
World's Best Dog-Walker, The	Q	RF	250+	Zollman, Pam	Steck-Vaughn
World's Biggest Baby, The	H	I	239	Ready Readers	Pearson Learning Group
World's Greatest Juggler, The	E	F	105	Little Readers	Houghton Mifflin
World's Greatest Toe Show, The	M	RF	250+	Lamb, Nancy; Singer, Muff	Troll Associates
World's Largest Plants, The: A Book About Trees	M	I	250+	Growing Things	Picture Window Books
Worm Rap	H	F	251	Alphakids	Sundance
Worm Work	P	I	250+	Sails	Rigby
Worm, The	C	F	38	Sun Sprouts	ETA/Cuisenaire
Worms	D	F	39	Literacy 2000	Rigby
Worms	P	I	250+	Mini Pets	Steck-Vaughn
Worms for Breakfast	I	TL	250+	Little Readers	Houghton Mifflin
Worm's Home, A	K	I	281	Independent Readers Science	Houghton Mifflin
Worms, Wonderful Worms	L	I	250+	Voyages	SRA/McGraw Hill
Worrisome Wombat, The	M	F	250+	Voyages	SRA/McGraw Hill
Worst Show-and-Tell Ever, The	J	SF	250+	Walsh, Rita	Troll Associates
Worst Witch at Sea, The	P	F	250+	Murphy, Jill	Candlewick Press
Worst Witch Strikes Again, The	P	F	250+	Murphy, Jill	Candlewick Press
Worst Witch, The	P	F	250+	Murphy, Jill	Puffin Books
Would You Like to Fly?	C	F	52	Twig	Wright Group/McGraw Hill
Wow!	D	F	145	Bookshop	Mondo
Wow! Look at This!	B	I	34	Science	Outside the Box
Wow! What a Week!	J	RF	364	Wonders	Hampton-Brown
Wreck Trek	S	I	250+	Belcher, Angie	Pacific Learning
Wrestling Sturbridge	Z	RF	250+	Wallace, Rich	Random House
Wright Brothers at Kitty Hawk, The	K	B	250+	Schaefer, Lola M.	Red Brick Learning
Wright Brothers, First Flyers, The	V	I	2700	Independent Readers Science	Houghton Mifflin
Wright Brothers, The	U	B	250+	Sobol, Donald J.	Scholastic
Wright Brothers, The	Y	B	250+	Freedman, Russell	Holiday House
Wright Brothers, The	M	B	250+	Biography	Benchmark Education
Wringer	U	RF	250+	Spinelli, Jerry	HarperTrophy
Wrinkle in Time, A	W	F	250+	L'Engle, Madeleine	Bantam Doubleday Dell
Wrinkles	C	I	32	Literacy 2000	Rigby
Write It Down!	U	I	250+	iOpeners	Pearson Learning Group
Write Up a Storm with the Polk Street School	M	RF	250+	Giff, Patricia Reilly	Bantam
Writer of the Plains: A Story about Willa Cather	Q	B	250+	Streissguth, Tom	Carolrhoda Books
Writer's Work, A	N	I	481	Wonder World	Wright Group/McGraw Hill
Writing Bug, The	O	B	250+	Hopkins, Lee Bennett	Richard C. Owen
Writing Places	E	I	30	Chanko, Pamela	Scholastic
Wrong Way Around Magic	N	F	250+	Chew, Ruth	Scholastic
Wrong Way Reggie	J	RF	304	Little Celebrations	Pearson Learning Group
Wrong-Way Rabbit, The	J	F	304	Slater, Teddy	Scholastic
Wyoming	R	I	250+	This Land Is Your Land	Compass Point Books
Wyoming: Facts and Symbols	O	I	250+	Dubois, Muriel L.	Red Brick Learning
X Marks the Spot	N	I	250+	Home Connection Collection	Rigby

* Collection of short stories

TITLE	LEVEL	GENRE	WORD COUNT	AUTHOR / SERIES	PUBLISHER / DISTRIBUTOR
X Ray, The	C	RF	48	Learn to Read	Creative Teaching Press
X-Games, The: Skateboarding's Greatest Event	Q	I	250+	Skateboarding	Capstone Press
X-rays	X	I	3158	Leveled Readers Science	Houghton Mifflin
X-Rays	O	I	250+	Voyages	SRA/McGraw Hill
Xuanzang, Chinese Hero	W	B	3100	Leveled Readers Social Studies	Houghton Mifflin
Yabby Tale, A	N	RF	250+	Sunshine	Wright Group/McGraw Hill
Yahoo for You	E	RF	137	Early Readers	Compass Point Books
Yakkity-Yak	C	F	49	Learn to Read	Creative Teaching Press
Yang the Eldest and His Odd Jobs	P	RF	250+	Namioka, Lensey	Bantam
Yang the Second and Her Secret Admirer	P	RF	250+	Namioka, Lensey	Bantam
Yang the Third and Her Impossible Family	P	RF	250+	Namioka, Lensey	Bantam
Yang the Youngest and His Terrible Ear	P	RF	250+	Namioka, Lensey	Bantam
Yao's Wild Ride	Q	HF	250+	Leveled Readers Language Support	Houghton Mifflin
Yard Sale, The	I	RF	250+	Little Readers	Houghton Mifflin
Yard Sale, The	K	RF	250+	Windows on Literacy	National Geographic
Yasmin and the Flood	F	RF	81	Oxford Reading Tree	Oxford University Press
Yasmin's Box	G	F	170	Cambridge Reading	Pearson Learning Group
Year Down Yonder, A	V	RF	250+	Peck, Richard	Penguin Group
Year in Antartica, A	R	I	250+	iOpeners	Pearson Learning Group
Year Mom Won the Pennant, The	M	RF	250+	Christopher, Matt	Little, Brown & Co.
Year of Impossible Goodbyes	W	HF	250+	Choi, Sook Nyui	Yearling
Year of the Panda, The	N	RF	250+	Soar To Success	Houghton Mifflin
Year of the Sawdust Man, The	Y	RF	250+	LaFaye, A.	Simon & Schuster
Year with Mother Bear, A	I	I	164	Storyteller Nonfiction	Wright Group/McGraw Hill
Year, A	H	I	137	The Calendar	Capstone Press
Yearling, The	X	RF	250+	Rawlings, Marjorie Kinnan	Simon & Schuster
Yellow	B	I	32	Literacy 2000	Rigby
Yellow Ball	LB	RF	18	Bang, Molly	Morrow
Yellow Overalls	L	F	250+	Literacy 2000	Rigby
Yellow Yarn Mystery, The	B	F	61	Little Books	Sadlier-Oxford
Yellow: Seeing Yellow All Around Us	K	I	250+	Colors	Capstone Press
Yellowstone 1988: Summer of Fire	W	I	250+	Lauber, Patricia	Scholastic
Yellowstone, Our First National Park	R	I	1288	Leveled Readers Social Studies	Houghton Mifflin
Yellowstone: Our First National Park	N	I	250+	Rosen Real Readers	Rosen Publishing Group
Yes Ma'am	H	RF	125	Story Box	Wright Group/McGraw Hill
Yes, I Can	C	RF	30	Teacher's Choice Series	Pearson Learning Group
Yes, I Can!	D	F	45	Ready Readers	Pearson Learning Group
Yes, It Does	D	I	91	Teacher's Choice Series	Pearson Learning Group
Yikes! Grandma's a Teenager	N	F	250+	The Zack Files	Grosset & Dunlap
Yippy-Day-Yippy-Doo!	E	RF	117	Sunshine	Wright Group/McGraw Hill
Yo Ho! Yo Ho!	I	F	164	Voyages	SRA/McGraw Hill
Yoga Class	B	RF	28	Bebop Books	Lee & Low Books Inc.
Yolonda's Genius	V	RF	250+	Fenner, Carol	Aladdin
Yonder	M	RF	250+	Johnston, Tony	Penguin Group
Yoo Hoo, Moon!	I	F	250+	Blocksma, Mary	Bantam
Yoshiko's Surprise	E	RF	81	Seedlings	Continental Press
You	C	I	20	Carousel Earlybirds	Pearson Learning Group
You and Your Teeth	I	I	1009	Sunshine	Wright Group/McGraw Hill
You Are Much Too Small	J	F	250+	Bank Street	Bantam
You Are Special	K	I	250+	Sunshine	Wright Group/McGraw Hill
*You Be The Detective	Q	RF	250+	Miller, Marvin	Scholastic
*You Be The Detective II	Q	RF	250+	Miller, Marvin	Scholastic
*You Be The Jury	Q	I	250+	Miller, Marvin	Scholastic

* Collection of short stories

TITLE	LEVEL	GENRE	WORD COUNT	AUTHOR / SERIES	PUBLISHER / DISTRIBUTOR
*You Be The Jury: Courtroom V	Q	I	250+	Miller, Marvin	Bantam
You Can Always Tell Cathy from Caitlin	K	RF	583	Sunshine	Wright Group/McGraw Hill
You Can Canoe!: A Book of Sporting Activities	O	I	250+	Literacy Tree	Rigby
You Can Cook	M	I	250+	Woo, Lornette	Steck-Vaughn
You Can Do It	F	F	176	Sun Sprouts	ETA/Cuisenaire
You Can Make a Memory Scrapbook	J	I	179	How-To Series	Benchmark Education
You Can Make a Pom-pom	G	I	39	Windows on Literacy	National Geographic
You Can Make a Timer	F	I	124	How-To Series	Benchmark Education
You Can Make Skittles	G	I	128	Sunshine	Wright Group/McGraw Hill
You Can Recycle!	K	I	219	Rigby Focus	Rigby
You Can't Catch Me	J	F	250+	Oppenheim, Joanne	Houghton Mifflin
You Can't Catch Me!	D	RF	89	Lighthouse	Rigby
You Can't Catch Me!	I	F	244	Cambridge Reading	Pearson Learning Group
You Can't Eat Your Chicken Pox, Amber Brown	N	RF	250+	Danziger, Paula	Scholastic
You Did It!	G	RF	246	Sunshine	Wright Group/McGraw Hill
You Do Ride Well	H	RF	165	Windmill Books	Rigby
You Don't Look Like Your Mother	L	F	250+	Bookshop	Mondo
You Look Funny	G	RF	180	First Start	Troll Associates
You Might Fall	H	RF	180	Stepping Stones	Nelson/Michaels Assoc.
You Should Try That with a Rhino	E	F	123	Home Connection Collection	Rigby
You Shouldn't Have to Say Good-bye	T	RF	250+	Hermes, Patricia	Scholastic
You Want Women to Vote, Lizzie Stanton?	W	B	250+	Fritz, Jean	Penguin Group
You'll Roar	H	F	73	Instant Readers	Harcourt School Publishers
You'll Soon Grow into Them Titch	H	RF	191	Hutchins, Pat	Morrow
Young Arthur Ashe: Brave Champion	L	B	250+	First-Start Biography	Troll Associates
Young Cam Jansen and the Ice Skate Mystery	J	RF	250+	Adler, David A.	Puffin Books
Young Cam Jansen and the Lost Tooth	J	RF	250+	Adler, David A.	Puffin Books
Young Cam Jansen and the Missing Cookie	J	RF	250+	Adler, David A.	Puffin Books
Young Clara Barton: Battlefield Nurse	L	B	250+	First-Start Biography	Troll Associates
Young Davy Crockett: Frontier Fighter	L	B	250+	First-Start Biography	Troll Associates
Young Geographers	O	I	250+	People, Spaces & Places	Rand McNally
Young Helen Keller: Woman of Courage	L	B	250+	First-Start Biography	Troll Associates
Young Jackie Robinson: Baseball Hero	L	B	250+	First-Start Biography	Troll Associates
Young Jim Thorpe: All-American Athlete	L	B	250+	First-Start Biography	Troll Associates
Young Joan	X	HF	250+	Dana, Barbara	HarperTrophy
Young Land Lords, The	X	RF	250+	Myers, Walter Dean	Penguin Group
Young Martin's Promise	N	B	250+	Stories of America	Steck-Vaughn
Young Mozart	O	B	250+	Isadora, Rachel	Penguin Group
Young Orville and Wilbur Wright: First to Fly	L	B	250+	First-Start Biography	Troll Associates
Young Reggie Jackson: Hall of Fame Champion	L	B	250+	First-Start Biography	Troll Associates
Young Rosa Parks: Civil Rights Heroine	L	B	250+	First-Start Biography	Troll Associates
Young Squanto: The First Thanksgiving	L	B	250+	First-Start Biography	Troll Associates
Young Thurgood Marshall: Fighter for Equality	L	B	250+	First-Start Biography	Troll Associates
Young Tom Edison: Great Inventor	L	B	250+	First-Start Biography	Troll Associates
Young Wolf's First Hunt	M	RF	250+	Shefelman, Janice	Random House
Youngest Giraffe, The	I	RF	250+	PM Plus Story Books	Rigby
Youngest in the Family	F	RF	144	Visions	Wright Group/McGraw Hill
Your Body	J	I	208	Early Connections	Benchmark Education
Your Bones	P	I	250+	Your Body	Red Brick Learning
Your Brain	P	I	250+	Your Body	Red Brick Learning
Your Heart	L	I	250+	Early Connections	Benchmark Education
Your Heart	P	I	250+	Your Body	Red Brick Learning
Your Heart and Blood	M	I	250+	Rigby Focus	Rigby
Your Lungs	P	I	250+	Your Body	Red Brick Learning

* Collection of short stories

TITLE	LEVEL	GENRE	WORD COUNT	AUTHOR / SERIES	PUBLISHER / DISTRIBUTOR
Your Move, J. P.!	R	RF	250+	Lowry, Lois	Random House
Your Muscles	P	I	250+	Your Body	Red Brick Learning
Your Nervous System	M	I	366	Early Connections	Benchmark Education
Your Senses	H	I	138	Pebble Books	Red Brick Learning
Your Stomach	P	I	250+	Your Body	Red Brick Learning
Your Teeth	J	I	131	Pebble Books	Capstone Press
You're My Nikki	M	RF	250+	Eisenberg, Phyllis Rose	Penguin Group
You're Out	N	RF	250+	Kroll, Stephen	Avon Camelot
You're So Clever	H	RF	188	Voyages	SRA/McGraw Hill
You've Got Cheetah-Mail	M	I	250+	World Quest Adventures	World Quest Learning
Yo-Yo a Go-Go	F	RF	177	Rigby Literacy	Rigby
Yo-Yo Ma: Musical Superstar	Q	B	250+	Leveled Readers Language Support	Houghton Mifflin
Yo-Yo Tricks	P	I	250+	Games Around the World	Compass Point Books
Yo-yos	G	RF	62	City Kids	Rigby
Yo-Yo's	O	I	250+	PM Nonfiction-Emerald	Rigby
Yuck Soup	B	F	25	Sunshine	Wright Group/McGraw Hill
Yuck!	K	F	250+	Leveled Readers Language Support	Houghton Mifflin
Yukadoos	I	F	121	Jellybeans	Rigby
Yum and Yuk	I	F	125	Story Box	Wright Group/McGraw Hill
Yum! Yum!	D	F	84	Bookshop	Mondo
Yummy Lunch, A	B	RF	22	Early Emergent	Pioneer Valley
Yummy, Tum, Tee	C	F	51	Little Celebrations	Pearson Learning Group
Yummy, Yummy	F	F	115	Grey, Judith	Troll Associates
Zachary and the Pony Express	P	HF	250+	Leveled Readers Language Support	Houghton Mifflin
Zachary Taylor	U	B	250+	Profiles of the Presidents	Compass Point Books
Zacharys' Plans, The	O	F	250+	Sails	Rigby
Zachary's Ride	R	HF	1780	Leveled Readers	Houghton Mifflin
Zack and Nate	H	RF	250+	Early Emergent, Set 2	Pioneer Valley
Zack's Alligator	K	F	250+	Mozelle, Shirley	HarperTrophy
Zack's Alligator	K	F	250+	Little Readers	Houghton Mifflin
Zack's Alligator Goes to School	K	F	250+	Mozelle, Shirley	HarperTrophy
Zack's Halloween Costume	D	RF	103	Early Emergent, Set 3	Pioneer Valley
Zack's House	D	RF	114	Early Emergent, Set 2	Pioneer Valley
Zack's Moving Day Surprise	F	RF	122	Developing Books, Set 3	Pioneer Valley
Zala Runs for Her Life	J	F	250+	PM Story Books-Purple	Rigby
Zap!	G	F	83	Seedlings	Continental Press
Zap! I'm a Mind Reader	N	SF	250+	The Zack Files	Grosset & Dunlap
Zebras	N	I	250+	Meadows, Graham; Vial, Claire	Pearson Learning Group
Zebras	H	I	78	Seedlings	Continental Press
Zebras	O	I	250+	Holmes, Kevin J.	Red Brick Learning
Zebra's Yellow Van	C	F	31	Ready Readers	Pearson Learning Group
Zeely	R	RF	250+	Hamilton, Virginia	Macmillan
Zeke Takes a Bath	J	F	532	Leveled Readers	Houghton Mifflin
Zemti	L	TL	250+	Books for Young Learners	Richard C. Owen
Zeros and Ones	S	I	250+	Wildcats	Wright Group/McGraw Hill
Zero's Slider	M	RF	250+	Christopher, Matt	Little, Brown & Co.
Zeus	W	I	250+	World Mythology	Capstone Press
Ziggy and the Cat	E	RF	72	Windmill Books	Rigby
Zigzag Movement	F	I	50	Pebble Books	Red Brick Learning
Zinnia, The	B	RF	34	Ray's Readers	Outside the Box

* Collection of short stories

TITLE	LEVEL	GENRE	WORD COUNT	AUTHOR / SERIES	PUBLISHER / DISTRIBUTOR
Zip Me Up	E	RF	171	Handprints C, Set 2	Educator's Publishing Service
Zippers	C	RF	21	Books for Young Learners	Richard C. Owen
Zipping, Zapping, Zooming Bats	N	I	250+	Soar To Success	Houghton Mifflin
Zip-Zip, Rattle-Bang!	E	F	141	Story Basket	Wright Group/McGraw Hill
Zithers	G	RF	55	Little Celebrations	Pearson Learning Group
Zlata's Diary	X	B	250+	Filipovic, Zlata	Puffin Books
Zoe at the Fancy Dress Ball	J	RF	250+	Literacy 2000	Rigby
Zoe's Birthday Presents	D	RF	83	Emergent	Pioneer Valley
Zombies Don't Play Soccer	M	F	250+	Dadey, Debbie; Jones, Marcia Thornton	Scholastic
Zomo the Rabbit: A Trickster Tale from West Africa	M	TL	250+	McDermott, Gerald	Harcourt Trade
Zoo Babies	F	I	51	Little Celebrations	Pearson Learning Group
Zoo Food	C	I	58	Reading Corners	Pearson Learning Group
Zoo in Willy's Bed, The	E	RF	81	Gorman, Kate Sturnman	Continental Press
Zoo Keepers	M	I	250+	Deedrick, Tami	Red Brick Learning
Zoo Map	G	I	96	Windows on Literacy	National Geographic
Zoo Overnight	L	RF	250+	Pacific Literacy	Pacific Learning
Zoo Party, A	H	RF	134	Book Bank	Wright Group/McGraw Hill
Zoo, A	LB	I	14	Literacy 2000	Rigby
Zoo, The	C	RF	33	Carousel Readers	Pearson Learning Group
Zoo, The	B	I	32	Handprints B	Educator's Publishing Service
Zoo, The	B	I	31	Wonder World	Wright Group/McGraw Hill
Zookeepers Sleepers, The	E	F	76	New Reader Series	Bungalo Books
Zoo-Looking	G	RF	149	Bookshop	Mondo
Zoom! Zoom!	C	F	43	Joy Readers	Pearson Learning Group
Zooman Sam	P	RF	250+	Lowry, Lois	Houghton Mifflin
Zoomers, The	A	F	28	Kinderstarters	Rigby
Zoos Back to Nature?	W	I	250+	iOpeners	Pearson Learning Group
Zulu Dog	V	RF	250+	Ferreira, Anton	Farrar, Straus and Giroux
Zuni, The	R	I	250+	First Reports	Compass Point Books
Zunid	J	RF	250+	Stepping Stones	Nelson/Michaels Assoc.

* Collection of short stories

Book List

(ORGANIZED BY LEVEL)

TITLE	LEVEL	GENRE	WORD COUNT	AUTHOR / SERIES	PUBLISHER / DISTRIBUTOR
Ah-Choo	WB	F	N/A	Mayer, Mercer	Dial Books
Angel and the Soldier Boy, The	WB	F	N/A	Collington, Peter	Alfred A. Knopf
Anno's USA	WB	I	N/A	Mitsumaso, Anna	Philomel Books
Apple Bird, The	WB	F	N/A	Wildsmith, Brian	Oxford University Press
Baby Bear's Ride	WB	F	N/A	Ready Readers	Pearson Learning Group
Balloons	WB	RF	N/A	Rigby Literacy	Rigby
Ben's Dream	WB	F	N/A	Van Allsburg, Chris	Houghton Mifflin
Best Friends	WB	RF	N/A	Books for Young Learners	Richard C. Owen
Big and Little	WB	I	N/A	Vocabulary Readers	Houghton Mifflin
Bobbie and the Kite	WB	RF	N/A	Rigby Literacy	Rigby
Boy, a Dog, and a Frog, A	WB	F	N/A	Mayer, Mercer	Dial Books
Carl Goes Shopping	WB	F	N/A	Day, Alexandra	Green Tiger Press
Carl Goes to Daycare	WB	F	N/A	Day, Alexandra	Green Tiger Press
Carl's Afternoon in the Park	WB	F	N/A	Day, Alexandra	Green Tiger Press
Carl's Birthday	WB	F	N/A	Day, Alexandra	Green Tiger Press
Changes	WB	I	N/A	Book Bank	Wright Group/McGraw Hill
Changes, Changes	WB	I	N/A	Hutchins, Pat	Aladdin
Circus, The	WB	I	N/A	Carle, Eric	HarperCollins
Clown	WB	I	N/A	Blake, Quentin	Henry Holt & Co.
Count and See	WB	I	N/A	Hoban, Tana	Macmillan
Curly and the Cherries	WB	RF	N/A	Rigby Literacy	Rigby
Deep in the Forest	WB	TL	N/A	Turkle, Brinton	Dutton
Dog's Life, A	WB	I	N/A	Windows on Literacy	National Geographic
First Snow	WB	RF	N/A	McCully, Emily Arnold	Harper & Row
Free Fall	WB	F	N/A	Wiesner, David	Lothrop, Lee & Shepard
Frog Goes to Dinner	WB	F	N/A	Mayer, Mercer	Dial Books
Frog on His Own	WB	F	N/A	Mayer, Mercer	Dial Books
Getting Ready	WB	I	N/A	Windows on Literacy	National Geographic
Gift, The	WB	RF	N/A	Prater, J.	Wright Group/McGraw Hill
Good Dog, Carl	WB	F	N/A	Day, Alexandra	Green Tiger Press
Good Dog, Carl	WB	RF	N/A	Day, Alexandra	Simon & Schuster
Grey Lady and the Strawberry Snatcher, The	WB	F	N/A	Bang, Molly	Aladdin
Have Numbers, Will Travel	WB	I	N/A	Gosset, Rachel	Scholastic
Have You Seen My Duckling?	WB	F	N/A	Tafuri, Nancy	Greenwillow
House	WB	I	N/A	Felix, Monique	Stewart, Tabori & Chang
Hunter and the Animals, The	WB	RF	N/A	DePaola, Tomie	Holiday House
I Can't Find It!	WB	RF	N/A	Rigby Literacy	Rigby
I Like Being Outdoors	WB	I	N/A	Windows on Literacy	National Geographic
I Take Care of My Dog	WB	RF	N/A	Rigby Literacy	Rigby
In the Garden	WB	I	N/A	Windows on Literacy	National Geographic
In the Woods	WB	I	N/A	Christini, Ermanno; Puricelli, Luigi	Scholastic
Inside-Outside Book of London, The	WB	I	N/A	Monro, Roxie	Dutton
Inside-Outside Book of Washington, DC	WB	I	N/A	Monro, Roxie	Dutton
Is It Red? Is It Yellow? Is It Blue?	WB	F	N/A	Hoban, Tana	Greenwillow
It's Dinner Time	WB	I	N/A	Windows on Literacy	National Geographic
Jungle Walk	WB	RF	N/A	Tafuri, Nancy	Greenwillow
Just in Passing	WB	RF	N/A	Bonners, Susan	Lothrop, Lee & Shepard
Keeping Clean	WB	I	N/A	Windows on Literacy	National Geographic
Leap Frog	WB	RF	N/A	Ready to Read	Pacific Learning

* Collection of short stories

TITLE	LEVEL	GENRE	WORD COUNT	AUTHOR / SERIES	PUBLISHER / DISTRIBUTOR
Little Pickle	WB	F	N/A	Collington, Peter	Dutton
Little Red Riding Hood	WB	TL	N/A	Goodall, John	McElderry
Little Turtle	WB	RF	N/A	Books for Young Learners	Richard C. Owen
Look What I Can Do	WB	F	N/A	Aruego, Jose	Macmillan
Midnight Circus, The	WB	F	N/A	Collington, Peter	Alfred A. Knopf
Mouse Around	WB	F	N/A	Collington, Peter	Alfred A. Knopf
My Box	WB	RF	N/A	Instant Readers	Harcourt School Publishers
My Darling Kitten	WB	RF	N/A	Collington, Peter	Alfred A. Knopf
My Walk	WB	I	N/A	Windows on Literacy	National Geographic
Naughty Nancy Goes to School	WB	F	N/A	Goodall, John S.	Andre Deutsch
New Baby	WB	RF	N/A	McCullu, Emily Arnold	Harper & Row
Niki's Walk	WB	RF	N/A	Tanner, Jane	Curriculum Press
Noah's Ark	WB	F	N/A	Spier, Peter	Doubleday Books
Of Colors and Things	WB	I	N/A	Hoban, Tana	Scholastic
On Christmas Eve	WB	RF	N/A	Collington, Peter	Alfred A. Knopf
On the Weekend	WB	I	N/A	Windows on Literacy	National Geographic
Our Clubhouse	WB	I	N/A	Windows on Literacy	National Geographic
Over Under in the Garden	WB	I	N/A	Schories, Pat	Farrar, Straus and Giroux
Pancakes	WB	RF	N/A	Rigby Literacy	Rigby
Pancakes for Breakfast	WB	F	N/A	DePaola, Tomie	Doubleday Books
Picnic	WB	RF	N/A	McCully, Emily Arnold	Harper & Row
Plain and Fancy	WB	I	N/A	Vocabulary Readers	Houghton Mifflin
Poor Panda	WB	F	N/A	Rigby Literacy	Rigby
Rainy Day Dream	WB	F	N/A	Chesworth, Michael	Farrar, Straus and Giroux
Rides Are Fun	WB	I	N/A	Windows on Literacy	National Geographic
Roxy	WB	F	N/A	Ready to Read	Pacific Learning
Sector 7	WB	F	N/A	Wiesner, David	Clarion
See Me	WB	I	N/A	Vocabulary Readers	Houghton Mifflin
Shadow Play	WB	I	N/A	Windows on Literacy	National Geographic
Shrewbettina Goes to Work	WB	F	N/A	Goodall, John	McElderry
Silver Pony, The	WB	F	N/A	Ward, Lynd	Houghton Mifflin
Snowball Fight	WB	RF	N/A	Rigby Literacy	Rigby
Snowman, The	WB	F	N/A	Briggs, Raymond	Random House
Special Foods, Special Places	WB	I	N/A	Windows on Literacy	National Geographic
Story of High Street, The	WB	RF	N/A	Goodall, John S.	Andre Deutsch
Sunshine	WB	RF	N/A	Ormerod, Jan	Lothrop, Lee & Shepard
Tabby	WB	RF	N/A	Aliki	HarperCollins
Taking Care of Farm Animals	WB	I	N/A	Windows on Literacy	National Geographic
Time Flies	WB	F	N/A	Rohmann, Eric	Crown
Tooth Fairy, The	WB	F	N/A	Collington, Peter	Wright Group/McGraw Hill
Tree Branch, The	WB	RF	N/A	Instant Readers	Harcourt School Publishers
Tuba Lessons	WB	RF	N/A	Bartlett, T. C.; Monique, Felix	Harcourt School Publishers
Tuesday	WB	F	N/A	Wiesner, David	Clarion
Up and Up	WB	RF	N/A	Hughes, Shirley	Lothrop, Lee & Shepard
Watermelons	WB	I	N/A	Windows on Literacy	National Geographic
What Did You Lose, Santa?	WB	F	N/A	Amoss, Berthe	Harper & Row
What is Being Moved?	WB	RF	N/A	Windows on Literacy	National Geographic
What's Alike?	WB	I	N/A	Windows on Literacy	National Geographic
What's Your Story?	WB	RF	N/A	Voyages	SRA/McGraw Hill
When the Toy Shop Shuts	WB	F	N/A	The Book Project	Sundance
1, 2, Kangaroo	LB	F	54	Reading Corners	Pearson Learning Group
10 Cats	LB	RF	13	Leveled Readers Language Support	Houghton Mifflin
All Over Me!	LB	RF	24	Pair-It Books	Steck-Vaughn

* Collection of short stories

TITLE	LEVEL	GENRE	WORD COUNT	AUTHOR / SERIES	PUBLISHER / DISTRIBUTOR
Alligators All Around	LB	F	59	Sendak, Maurice	HarperCollins
Animal Sculpture	LB	I	24	Canizares, Susan; Chanko, Pamela	Scholastic
Animals	LB	I	14	Instant Readers	Harcourt School Publishers
Apples	LB	I	23	Berger, Samantha; Chessen, Betsey	Scholastic
Aquarium, The	LB	I	24	KinderReaders	Rigby
Aquarium, The	LB	I	18	Kloes, Carol	Kaeden Books
At School	LB	I	12	Rise & Shine	Hampton-Brown
At the Beach	LB	RF	15	Rigby Literacy	Rigby
At the Fair	LB	I	14	Little Books for Early Readers	University of Maine
At the Playground	LB	I	8	Windows on Literacy	National Geographic
At the Playground	LB	I	25	Visions	Wright Group/McGraw Hill
At the Store	LB	I	14	Visions	Wright Group/McGraw Hill
At the Truckstop	LB	RF	25	Kloes, Carol	Kaeden Books
Babies on the Move	LB	I	30	Canizares, Susan; Moreton, Daniel	Scholastic
Baby Gets Dressed	LB	RF	16	Sunshine	Wright Group/McGraw Hill
Baby Says	LB	RF	26	Steptoe, John	Morrow
Baking a Cake	LB	I	7	Windows on Literacy	National Geographic
Balloons, The	LB	RF	19	Sunshine	Wright Group/McGraw Hill
Barbecue, The	LB	RF	14	Sunshine	Wright Group/McGraw Hill
Bath, The	LB	RF	14	Ready Readers	Pearson Learning Group
Bear, The	LB	I	17	Carousel Earlybirds	Pearson Learning Group
Big and Little	LB	I	24	KinderReaders	Rigby
Big and Little	LB	I	59	Berger, Samantha; Chanko, Pamela	Scholastic
Bike Parade, The	LB	RF	16	Literacy 2000	Rigby
Bike, The	LB	I	14	Twig	Wright Group/McGraw Hill
Birds	LB	I	12	Vocabulary Readers	Houghton Mifflin
Birthday Cake, The	LB	F	22	Sunshine	Wright Group/McGraw Hill
Birthday Party, The	LB	I	16	Rise & Shine	Hampton-Brown
Boat, The	LB	RF	14	Pacific Literacy	Pacific Learning
Building with Blocks	LB	RF	20	Sunshine	Wright Group/McGraw Hill
Busy Bees	LB	RF	12	Voyages	SRA/McGraw Hill
Busy Bird	LB	F	14	Pacific Literacy	Pacific Learning
Buttons Buttons	LB	I	26	Learn to Read	Creative Teaching Press
Buzzing Bees	LB	RF	69	Mathtales	Mimosa
Carmen's Colors	LB	RF	14	Bebop Books	Lee & Low Books Inc.
Chocolate Chip Cookies	LB	I	12	Preiss, Leah Palmer	Henry Holt & Co.
Chop, Simmer, Season	LB	I	21	Brandenburg, Alexa	OSI
Christmas	LB	I	16	Smart Start	Rigby
Church	LB	I	17	Visions	Wright Group/McGraw Hill
Circus, The	LB	I	31	Literacy 2000	Rigby
City Lights	LB	RF	16	Visions	Wright Group/McGraw Hill
Closer and Closer	LB	I	13	Twig	Wright Group/McGraw Hill
Clown Face	LB	RF	14	Twig	Wright Group/McGraw Hill
Clown, The	LB	I	29	Urmston, Kathleen; Evans, Karen	Kaeden Books
Clown, The	LB	I	13	Smart Starts	Rigby
Clown, The	LB	I	31	First Stories	Pacific Learning
Colors	LB	I	6	Vocabulary Readers	Houghton Mifflin
Colors	LB	I	9	Leveled Readers Language Support	Houghton Mifflin
Colors in the City	LB	I	61	Urmston, Kathleen; Evans, Karen	Kaeden Books
Colours	LB	I	8	Pienkowski, Jan	Penguin Group
Cookies	LB	I	15	Twig	Wright Group/McGraw Hill

* Collection of short stories

TITLE	LEVEL	GENRE	WORD COUNT	AUTHOR / SERIES	PUBLISHER / DISTRIBUTOR
Count the Animals	LB	I	10	Windows on Literacy	National Geographic
Curly and His Friends	LB	RF	15	Rigby Literacy	Rigby
Detective Max	LB	RF	32	Pair-It Books	Steck-Vaughn
Dinner!	LB	RF	19	Sunshine	Wright Group/McGraw Hill
Dog Day!, A	LB	RF	21	Smart Starts	Rigby
Dozen Eggs, A	LB	RF	14	Harry's Math Books	Outside the Box
Dressing Up	LB	RF	12	Sunshine	Wright Group/McGraw Hill
Eggshell Garden, The	LB	RF	14	Sunshine	Wright Group/McGraw Hill
Face Sandwich, The	LB	RF	16	Sunshine	Wright Group/McGraw Hill
Fall Harvest	LB	I	16	Little Books for Early Readers	University of Maine
Families	LB	I	8	Windows on Literacy	National Geographic
Farm, The	LB	I	14	Literacy 2000	Rigby
Farm, The	LB	I	14	Smart Starts	Rigby
Farm, The	LB	I	14	Ready Readers	Pearson Learning Group
Feelings	LB	I	12	Canizares, Susan	Scholastic
Feet!	LB	I	28	Ray's Readers	Outside the Box
First Day of School	LB	RF	16	Visions	Wright Group/McGraw Hill
First Things	LB	RF	18	Home Connection Collection	Rigby
Fish Colors	LB	I	6	Vocabulary Readers	Houghton Mifflin
Flower Box, The	LB	I	14	Twig	Wright Group/McGraw Hill
Flowers for Grandma	LB	RF	8	Windows on Literacy	National Geographic
For Breakfast	LB	I	22	Visions	Wright Group/McGraw Hill
Fruit Salad	LB	I	7	Windows on Literacy	National Geographic
Fruit Salad	LB	I	15	Literacy 2000	Rigby
Garden Birthday	LB	F	15	Instant Readers	Harcourt School Publishers
Garden, The	LB	I	14	Instant Readers	Harcourt School Publishers
Getting Dressed	LB	RF	16	Sunshine	Wright Group/McGraw Hill
Giant, The	LB	F	20	Joy Readers	Pearson Learning Group
Going to School	LB	RF	21	Smart Starts	Rigby
Going to the Beach	LB	RF	30	Pacific Literacy	Pacific Learning
Goodnight Bobbie	LB	RF	15	Rigby Literacy	Rigby
Goodnight, Gorilla	LB	F	25	Rothmann, Peggy	Putnam
Hannah's Halloween	LB	I	14	Little Books for Early Readers	University of Maine
Happy Birthday, Estela!	LB	RF	30	Pacific Literacy	Pacific Learning
Hat, The	LB	F	12	Ready Readers	Pearson Learning Group
Hats	LB	I	46	Williams, Deborah	Kaeden Books
Heads and Tails	LB	I	29	Windmill Books	Rigby
Helicopter Over Hawaii	LB	I	21	Twig	Wright Group/McGraw Hill
Help! Help!	LB	RF	14	Joy Readers	Pearson Learning Group
Here Comes the Cat	LB	RF	24	Asch, Frank	Scholastic
House Book, The	LB	I	17	Windows on Literacy	National Geographic
House Cleaning	LB	RF	19	Book Bank	Wright Group/McGraw Hill
House for a Mouse, A	LB	F	21	Pacific Literacy	Pacific Learning
How Does It Feel?	LB	I	11	Windows on Literacy	National Geographic
How Many Bugs in a Box?	LB	F	126	Carter, David	Simon & Schuster
Huggles Breakfast	LB	F	14	Sunshine	Wright Group/McGraw Hill
Huggles Can Juggle	LB	F	15	Sunshine	Wright Group/McGraw Hill
Huggles Goes Away	LB	F	14	Sunshine	Wright Group/McGraw Hill
Hungry Fox, The	LB	I	12	Rigby Literacy	Rigby
I Like Fruit	LB	RF	18	Visions	Wright Group/McGraw Hill
I Like Shapes	LB	RF	21	Armstrong, Shane	Scholastic
I Read Signs	LB	I	12	Hoban, Tana	Greenwillow
I Read Symbols	LB	I	14	Hoban, Tana	Greenwillow
I Walk and Read	LB	I	16	Hoban, Tana	Greenwillow

* Collection of short stories

TITLE	LEVEL	GENRE	WORD COUNT	AUTHOR / SERIES	PUBLISHER / DISTRIBUTOR
I Want My Own Room!	LB	RF	25	Visions	Wright Group/McGraw Hill
In My Backyard	LB	RF	18	Visions	Wright Group/McGraw Hill
In the City	LB	RF	22	Home Connection Collection	Rigby
In the Mountains	LB	I	14	Twig	Wright Group/McGraw Hill
It Can Fly	LB	I	8	Windows on Literacy	National Geographic
Joe Joe	LB	RF	22	Montezinos, Nina	McElderry
Juggling	LB	RF	15	Rigby Literacy	Rigby
Legs	LB	I	21	Twig	Wright Group/McGraw Hill
Let's Build a Tower	LB	RF	15	Literacy 2000	Rigby
Letter, The	LB	RF	15	Twig	Wright Group/McGraw Hill
Lights at Night	LB	I	33	Pacific Literacy	Pacific Learning
Little House	LB	F	14	Ready Readers	Pearson Learning Group
Lobstering	LB	I	14	Little Books for Early Readers	University of Maine
Look at Me	LB	I	13	Windows on Literacy	National Geographic
Look at Me	LB	I	17	Little Books for Early Readers	University of Maine
Look! Snow!	LB	RF	14	Montezinos, Nina	McElderry
Looking for Halloween	LB	RF	49	Urmston, Kathleen; Evans, Karen	Kaeden Books
Love Is	LB	RF	11	Visions	Wright Group/McGraw Hill
Magic!	LB	RF	23	Twig	Wright Group/McGraw Hill
Making Movies	LB	I	43	Sunshine	Wright Group/McGraw Hill
Marching Band	LB	RF	35	Urmston, Kathleen; Evans, Karen	Kaeden Books
Mexico	LB	I	22	Canizares, Susan; Chanko, Pamela	Scholastic
Moccasins	LB	I	20	Twig	Wright Group/McGraw Hill
Monster Mop	LB	F	8	Ready Readers	Pearson Learning Group
Monster Soup	LB	F	33	Rigby Literacy	Rigby
Mouse Views	LB	RF	12	McMillan, Bruce	Holiday House
Mrs. Cook's Hats	LB	RF	31	Mader, Jan	Kaeden Books
Mrs. Lunch	LB	F	17	Joy Readers	Pearson Learning Group
My Apartment	LB	RF	20	Visions	Wright Group/McGraw Hill
My Backyard	LB	I	14	Little Books for Early Readers	University of Maine
My Birthday Party	LB	RF	16	Little Readers	Houghton Mifflin
My Class	LB	I	14	Stewart, Josie; Salem, Lynn	Continental Press
My Clothes	LB	I	12	Vocabulary Readers	Houghton Mifflin
My Clothes	LB	RF	16	Carousel Earlybirds	Pearson Learning Group
My Family	LB	I	12	Vocabulary Readers	Houghton Mifflin
My Five Senses	LB	I	5	Windows on Literacy	National Geographic
My Fort	LB	I	17	Little Books for Early Readers	University of Maine
My Room	LB	F	14	Ready Readers	Pearson Learning Group
My School Day	LB	I	6	Windows on Literacy	National Geographic
Naughty Kitten!	LB	RF	18	Smart Starts	Rigby
New Cat, The	LB	F	29	Pacific Literacy	Pacific Learning
New House, The	LB	F	15	Sunshine	Wright Group/McGraw Hill
New Nest, A	LB	I	14	Pair-It Books	Steck-Vaughn
Night Sky	LB	I	15	Twig	Wright Group/McGraw Hill
Numbers All Around	LB	I	12	Canizares, Susan; Chessen, Betsey	Scholastic
Off We Go!	LB	RF	16	Pacific Literacy	Pacific Learning
Oink Oink	LB	F	15	Geisert, Arthur	Houghton Mifflin
One Hunter	LB	F	15	Hutchins, Pat	Greenwillow
One, Two, Three, Four	LB	F	21	KinderReaders	Rigby
Ouch!	LB	RF	40	Literacy 2000	Rigby
Paint the Sky	LB	F	14	Sunshine	Wright Group/McGraw Hill
Picnic in the Sand, A	LB	RF	14	Ready Readers	Pearson Learning Group
Picnic, The	LB	RF	18	Book Bank	Wright Group/McGraw Hill
Picnic, The	LB	RF	48	First Stories	Pacific Learning

* Collection of short stories

TITLE	LEVEL	GENRE	WORD COUNT	AUTHOR / SERIES	PUBLISHER / DISTRIBUTOR
Play Ball	LB	RF	7	Bookshop	Mondo
Play Ball	LB	I	14	Twig	Wright Group/McGraw Hill
Rain Forest, A	LB	I	18	Rigby Focus	Rigby
Rainbow Bird, A	LB	I	18	Pair-It Books	Steck-Vaughn
Red or Blue?	LB	RF	13	Ready Readers	Pearson Learning Group
Red, White, and Blue	LB	I	21	Canizares, Susan; Chessen, Betsey	Scholastic
Red, White, and Blue	LB	I	21	Canizares, Susan; Chessen, Betsey	Scholastic
Royal Family, The	LB	F	17	Stewart, Josie; Salem, Lynn	Continental Press
Salad Vegetables	LB	I	15	Foundations	Wright Group/McGraw Hill
School Bus	LB	RF	51	Crews, Donald	Morrow
School Lunch	LB	RF	14	Ready Readers	Pearson Learning Group
Shopping	LB	RF	15	Sunshine	Wright Group/McGraw Hill
Signs	LB	I	21	Yellow Umbrella Books	Red Brick Learning
Ski School	LB	RF	34	Little Books for Early Readers	University of Maine
Snakes	LB	I	25	Twig	Wright Group/McGraw Hill
Snow Walk	LB	RF	32	Reading Corners	Pearson Learning Group
Snowman	LB	RF	14	Smart Starts	Rigby
Socks	LB	RF	21	Smart Start	Rigby
Spots	LB	RF	27	Smart Starts	Rigby
Staying Healthy	LB	I	7	Windows on Literacy	National Geographic
Stripes	LB	I	28	Twig	Wright Group/McGraw Hill
Sun, a Flower, A	LB	I	42	Foundations	Wright Group/McGraw Hill
Ten Minutes Till Bedtime	LB	RF	16	Rathmann, Peggy	Putnam
That's Mine	LB	RF	15	Rigby Literacy	Rigby
There Are Spots On . . .	LB	I	14	Little Books for Early Readers	University of Maine
Things to Read	LB	I	18	Little Books for Early Readers	University of Maine
Things to See in Maine	LB	I	14	Little Books for Early Readers	University of Maine
Time for Dinner	LB	F	15	Smart Starts	Rigby
Time for Soup!	LB	I	12	Vocabulary Readers	Houghton Mifflin
Time to Eat	LB	I	3	Windows on Literacy	National Geographic
Too Many Cars	LB	RF	15	Hartley, Susan; Armstrong, Shane	Scholastic
Toot! Toot!	LB	F	21	Joy Readers	Pearson Learning Group
Toy Box, A	LB	I	19	Literacy 2000	Rigby
Toy Box, The	LB	RF	14	Ready Readers	Pearson Learning Group
Toys Can Move	LB	I	7	Windows on Literacy	National Geographic
Traffic Jam	LB	RF	18	Voyages	SRA/McGraw Hill
Treasure Hunt	LB	F	14	Smart Starts	Rigby
Trip to the Aquarium, A	LB	RF	18	Kloes, Carol	Kaeden Books
Truck Stop, The	LB	RF	25	Kloes, Carol	Kaeden Books
Two More	LB	F	16	Voyages	SRA/McGraw Hill
Two Turtles	LB	RF	13	Ready Readers	Pearson Learning Group
Vegetables	LB	I	7	Windows on Literacy	National Geographic
We Can Do It!	LB	RF	19	Rigby Focus	Rigby
Weather	LB	I	14	Smart Starts	Rigby
What a Mess!	LB	RF	14	Smart Starts	Rigby
What Am I?	LB	RF	16	Just Beginning	Modern Curriculum
What Is Little?	LB	I	22	Rise & Shine	Hampton-Brown
What Rhymes With Cat?	LB	F	4	Ready Readers	Pearson Learning Group
What Things Go Together	LB	RF	26	Literacy 2000	Rigby
What's Inside?	LB	RF	47	Hoenecke, Karen	Kaeden Books
Who Lives at the Zoo?	LB	I	11	Windows on Literacy	National Geographic
Wings	LB	I	14	KinderReaders	Rigby
Winter Fun	LB	RF	13	Teacher's Choice Series	Pearson Learning Group
Workers	LB	F	16	KinderReaders	Rigby

* Collection of short stories

TITLE	LEVEL	GENRE	WORD COUNT	AUTHOR / SERIES	PUBLISHER / DISTRIBUTOR
World in a Supermarket, The	LB	I	24	Learn to Read	Creative Teaching Press
Yellow Ball	LB	RF	18	Bang, Molly	Morrow
Zoo, A	LB	I	14	Literacy 2000	Rigby
Amazing Race, The	A	RF	28	Smart Starts	Rigby
Animals	A	I	28	Smart Starts	Rigby
Animals That Work	A	I	14	Foundations	Wright Group/McGraw Hill
At School	A	I	28	Little Books for Early Readers	University of Maine
At the Ocean	A	I	29	Little Books for Early Readers	University of Maine
At the Pool	A	I	29	Vocabulary Readers	Houghton Mifflin
Autumn Leaves	A	I	17	Pebble Books	Capstone Press
Baby	A	RF	29	Instant Readers	Harcourt School Publishers
Baby	A	I	28	Little Books for Early Readers	University of Maine
Baby	A	I	24	PM Plus Starters	Rigby
Baby Animals	A	I	24	Vocabulary Readers	Houghton Mifflin
Baby Bear's Toys	A	F	35	Phonics and Friends	Hampton-Brown
Baby Chimp	A	RF	14	Twig	Wright Group/McGraw Hill
Balloon Ride	A	F	32	Early Connections	Benchmark Education
Be Quiet	A	RF	25	Literacy 2000	Rigby
Beach, The	A	I	16	Little Celebrations	Pearson Learning Group
Bear's Ball	A	F	32	Sun Sprouts	ETA/Cuisenaire
Bennie	A	RF	29	Ray's Readers	Outside the Box
Big Chase, The	A	F	14	Foundations	Wright Group/McGraw Hill
Big Things	A	I	33	PM Starters	Rigby
Birthday Party, The	A	RF	15	Sunshine	Wright Group/McGraw Hill
Birthday, The	A	I	23	Little Books for Early Readers	University of Maine
Blueberries from Maine	A	RF	28	Little Books for Early Readers	University of Maine
Boat, The	A	RF	28	Sunshine	Wright Group/McGraw Hill
Bouquet, The	A	RF	38	Carousel Earlybirds	Pearson Learning Group
Box, The	A	RF	31	First Stories	Pacific Learning
Brenda's Birthday	A	RF	18	Story Box	Wright Group/McGraw Hill
Bunny's Recess	A	I	35	Little Books for Early Readers	University of Maine
Busy Dad	A	RF	24	Mom and Dad Series	Pioneer Valley
Can I Have a Pet?	A	RF	36	Bebop Books	Lee & Low Books Inc.
Car Ride, The	A	RF	41	Little Red Readers	Sundance
Cars	A	I	18	Pebble Books	Capstone Press
Cat on the Move	A	F	30	Phonics and Friends	Hampton-Brown
Cat, The	A	I	42	Little Books for Early Readers	University of Maine
Cat, The	A	I	28	Leveled Readers Science	Houghton Mifflin
Cats	A	I	24	Vocabulary Readers	Houghton Mifflin
Chick's Walk	A	F	14	Story Box	Wright Group/McGraw Hill
Chinese Kites	A	I	15	Twig	Wright Group/McGraw Hill
Circus Clown, The	A	RF	31	Literacy 2000	Rigby
Circus Train, The	A	F	48	Little Red Readers	Sundance
Cleaning Up	A	I	26	Early Connections	Benchmark Education
Clouds	A	RF	47	Bookshop	Mondo
Coats	A	I	32	Ray's Readers	Outside the Box
Colors	A	I	9	Little Red Readers	Sundance
Come and Have Fun	A	F	49	KinderReaders	Rigby
Come On Up	A	F	16	KinderReaders	Rigby
Costume Party	A	RF	32	Joy Readers	Pearson Learning Group
Count with Me	A	I	49	Little Books	Sadlier-Oxford
Craft Makers	A	I	24	Early Connections	Benchmark Education
Crash	A	RF	29	First Stories	Pacific Learning
Crazy Cats	A	I	42	Little Books for Early Readers	University of Maine

* Collection of short stories

TITLE	LEVEL	GENRE	WORD COUNT	AUTHOR / SERIES	PUBLISHER / DISTRIBUTOR
Dad	A	I	24	PM Starters	Rigby
Dad Goes to School	A	RF	43	Mom and Dad Series	Pioneer Valley
Dad's Turkey Sandwich	A	RF	26	Mom and Dad Series	Pioneer Valley
Day at School, A	A	I	21	Leveled Readers Emergent	Houghton Mifflin
Dig, Dig	A	RF	12	Cat on the Mat	Oxford University Press
Dinner	A	F	21	KinderReaders	Rigby
Dinosaur, The	A	F	14	Sunshine	Wright Group/McGraw Hill
Do You Like My Pet?	A	F	35	Phonics and Friends	Hampton-Brown
Do You Want to be My Friend?	A	F	8	Carle, Eric	Penguin Group
Dog School	A	RF	11	TOTTS	Tott Publications
Don't Splash Me!	A	RF	24	Windmill	Wright Group/McGraw Hill
Down to Town	A	F	26	Sunshine	Wright Group/McGraw Hill
Dressing Up	A	F	32	PM Starters	Rigby
Dressing Up	A	RF	12	Jellybeans	Rigby
Eating	A	RF	29	Foundations	Wright Group/McGraw Hill
Eating Apples	A	I	17	Pebble Books	Capstone Press
Elena Makes Tortillas	A	I	18	Pacific Literacy	Pacific Learning
Escalator, The	A	RF	23	Story Box	Wright Group/McGraw Hill
Every Morning	A	I	30	Twig	Wright Group/McGraw Hill
Everyone Wears Wool	A	I	21	Pair-It Books	Steck-Vaughn
Fair, The	A	RF	40	First Stories	Pacific Learning
Fall	A	I	22	Little Books for Early Readers	University of Maine
Farm Animals	A	I	24	Vocabulary Readers	Houghton Mifflin
Farm Animals	A	I	28		Belle Rivers Readers
Farm, A	A	I	28	Little Books for Early Readers	University of Maine
Farm, The	A	I	42	Little Readers	Houghton Mifflin
Farm, The	A	I	28	Little Books for Early Readers	University of Maine
Feeding	A	I	40	Sun Sprouts	ETA/Cuisenaire
Feelings	A	I	24	Windows on Literacy	National Geographic
Feet	A	I	14	Foundations	Wright Group/McGraw Hill
First Day of School, The	A	RF	28	Bookshop	Mondo
Flowers	A	I	27	Bookshop	Mondo
Flowers	A	I	27	Hoenecke, Karen	Kaeden Books
Friend for Me, A	A	I	48	First Stories	Pacific Learning
Friends	A	I	21	Leveled Readers Emergent	Houghton Mifflin
Frogs	A	I	13	Twig	Wright Group/McGraw Hill
Fruit	A	I	28	Leveled Readers Emergent	Houghton Mifflin
Fruit Salad	A	I	37	Sun Sprouts	ETA/Cuisenaire
Fun With Friends	A	RF	21	Bookshop	Mondo
Games	A	F	28	KinderReaders	Rigby
Garden, A	A	I	40	Foundations	Wright Group/McGraw Hill
Getting Home	A	I	24	Windows on Literacy	National Geographic
Ghost, The	A	RF	26	Story Box	Wright Group/McGraw Hill
Go Sea It!	A	I	16	Little Celebrations	Pearson Learning Group
Go, Go, Go	A	RF	17	Story Box	Wright Group/McGraw Hill
Go, Go, Go	A	I	23	Little Books for Early Readers	University of Maine
Going on Vacation	A	I	40	PM Plus Starters	Rigby
Going Out	A	F	42	KinderReaders	Rigby
Going to School	A	RF	28	Leveled Readers Emergent	Houghton Mifflin
Gotcha Box, The	A	RF	30	Story Box	Wright Group/McGraw Hill
Guess How Many I Have	A	I	24	Early Connections	Benchmark Education
Hair	A	RF	32	Carousel Earlybirds	Pearson Learning Group
Happy Birthday, Brother!	A	I	24	Vocabulary Readers	Houghton Mifflin
Have a Cookout	A	RF	21	Little Books for Early Readers	University of Maine

* Collection of short stories

TITLE	LEVEL	GENRE	WORD COUNT	AUTHOR / SERIES	PUBLISHER / DISTRIBUTOR
Helen's Job	A	RF	24	Phonics and Friends	Hampton-Brown
Here Is Hen	A	F	21	Leveled Readers Language Support	Houghton Mifflin
Hide and Seek	A	F	38	Smart Starts	Rigby
Hiding	A	F	28	KinderReaders	Rigby
House, A	A	I	32	PM Starters One	Rigby
How I Move	A	RF	21	Leveled Readers Science	Houghton Mifflin
How Many Animals?	A	I	25	Vocabulary Readers	Houghton Mifflin
How to Make a Mudpie	A	I	32	Learn to Read	Creative Teaching Press
How to Make a Salad	A	I	12	Vocabulary Readers	Houghton Mifflin
I Am	A	RF	21	Klein, Adria	Scholastic
I Am . . .	A	RF	20	Sunshine	Wright Group/McGraw Hill
I Am Jumping	A	RF	24	Sun Sprouts	ETA/Cuisenaire
I Am Running	A	I	24	PM Plus Starters	Rigby
I Am Thankful	A	RF	42	Carousel Earlybirds	Pearson Learning Group
I Am Water	A	I	25	Independent Readers Science	Houghton Mifflin
I Can	A	RF	21	Carousel Earlybirds	Pearson Learning Group
I Can Change Things!	A	RF	29	Leveled Readers Science	Houghton Mifflin
I Can Draw	A	I	33	Sun Sprouts	ETA/Cuisenaire
I Can Hear	A	RF	32	TOTTS	Tott Publications
I Can Move!	A	I	18	Vocabulary Readers	Houghton Mifflin
I Can Paint	A	RF	35	Book Bank	Wright Group/McGraw Hill
I Can Push	A	RF	29	Bookshop	Mondo
I Can Read	A	I	35	Learn to Read	Creative Teaching Press
I Can Read	A	RF	35	Pacific Literacy	Pacific Learning
I Can Ride	A	I	66	Sun Sprouts	ETA/Cuisenaire
I Can See	A	I	35	Independent Readers Science	Houghton Mifflin
I Can See	A	F	40	Carousel Earlybirds	Pearson Learning Group
I Can Write	A	RF	40	Learn to Read	Pacific Learning
I Feel Sick	A	RF	15	Science	Outside the Box
I Hear!	A	I	33	Early Connections	Benchmark Education
I Help My Dad	A	I	24	Windows on Literacy	National Geographic
I Like	A	RF	24	Sunshine	Wright Group/McGraw Hill
I Like Apples	A	RF	12	Windows on Literacy	National Geographic
I Like Balloons	A	RF	27	Reading Corners	Pearson Learning Group
I Like Bikes	A	I	24	Sun Sprouts	ETA/Cuisenaire
I Like Me	A	RF	31	Visions	Wright Group/McGraw Hill
I Like to Eat	A	RF	41	Reading Corners	Pearson Learning Group
I Like to Paint	A	RF	29	Reading Corners	Pearson Learning Group
I Like to Read	A	RF	44	Early Emergent	Pioneer Valley
I Paint	A	I	22	Literacy 2000	Rigby
I Paint	A	RF	22	Bookshop	Mondo
I Read	A	RF	38	Reading Corners	Pearson Learning Group
I See	A	I	32	Early Connections	Benchmark Education
I See	A	I	32	Sun Sprouts	ETA/Cuisenaire
I See Bugs	A	I	30	Blevins, Wiley	Scholastic
I See Patterns	A	I	42	Learn to Read	Creative Teaching Press
I See Spring!	A	I	18	Vocabulary Readers	Houghton Mifflin
I Spy	A	RF	31	Lighthouse	Rigby
In My Pocket	A	I	28	Sun Sprouts	ETA/Cuisenaire
In My School	A	I	27	Little Books for Early Readers	University of Maine
In Our Classroom	A	I	33	PM Plus Starters	Rigby
In the Garden	A	I	32	PM Plus Starters	Rigby
In the Shopping Cart	A	I	24	PM Starters	Rigby

* Collection of short stories

TITLE	LEVEL	GENRE	WORD COUNT	AUTHOR / SERIES	PUBLISHER / DISTRIBUTOR
In the Supermarket	A	RF	24	Smart Starts	Rigby
In the Teacup	A	F	35	KinderReaders	Rigby
Inside School	A	I	35	Little Books for Early Readers	University of Maine
Iron Horse, The	A	F	21	Smart Starts	Rigby
It's Spring	A	I	24	Vocabulary Readers	Houghton Mifflin
It's Time!	A	I	24	Early Connections	Benchmark Education
Jake	A	I	35	Little Books for Early Readers	University of Maine
James Is Hiding	A	RF	24	Windmill	Wright Group/McGraw Hill
Jobs Around Town	A	I	31	Leveled Readers Social Studies	Houghton Mifflin
Jordan Is Hiding	A	RF	24	Little Books for Early Readers	University of Maine
Kitten, The	A	RF	40	Sun Sprouts	ETA/Cuisenaire
Let's Go	A	RF	32	Reading Corners	Pearson Learning Group
Let's Go!	A	I	30	Vocabulary Readers	Houghton Mifflin
Life on a Farm	A	I	24	Early Connections	Benchmark Education
Little Bears	A	I	37	Bookshop	Mondo
Little Brother	A	RF	14	Sunshine	Wright Group/McGraw Hill
Little Lion, The	A	I	29	Phonics and Friends	Hampton-Brown
Little Monkeys	A	I	21	Windows on Literacy	National Geographic
Little Things	A	I	33	PM Starters	Rigby
Log Hotel, The	A	F	22	Little Celebrations	Pearson Learning Group
Look	A	F	20	Sunshine	Wright Group/McGraw Hill
Look at Conor	A	RF	27	Little Books for Early Readers	University of Maine
Look at Me!	A	F	27	KinderReaders	Rigby
Look at Me!	A	RF	27	Leveled Readers Emergent	Houghton Mifflin
Look at the Garden	A	I	43	Windmill Books	Rigby
Look at the Lizard	A	I	33	Bookshop	Mondo
Look Closer	A	I	21	Ready Readers	Pearson Learning Group
Lost	A	RF	29	TOTTS	Tott Publications
Lunch at the Zoo	A	RF	32	Bookshop	Mondo
Magnet Fishing Game	A	I	28	How-To Series	Benchmark Education
Make It!	A	RF	21	Phonics and Friends	Hampton-Brown
Making a Garden	A	RF	28	Foundations	Wright Group/McGraw Hill
Max Comes Home	A	RF	24	First Stories	Pacific Learning
Me	A	I	24	PM Starters	Rigby
Miss Popple's Pets	A	RF	28	Literacy 2000	Rigby
Mom	A	I	24	PM Starters	Rigby
Mom Dresses Up	A	RF	46	Mom and Dad Series	Pioneer Valley
Mom Goes Shopping	A	RF	34	Mom and Dad Series	Pioneer Valley
Mom Likes Hats	A	RF	40	Mom and Dad Series	Pioneer Valley
Moms and Dads	A	I	36	PM Starters	Rigby
Monster Party	A	F	20	Smart Starts	Rigby
Monster Party	A	F	20	Literacy 2000	Rigby
Monster Party	A	F	29	Bookshop	Mondo
Mother Hippopotamus	A	F	7	Foundations	Wright Group/McGraw Hill
My Book	A	RF	17	Maris, Ron	Viking
My Box	A	RF	94	Smart Starts	Rigby
My Cat	A	RF	28	Leveled Readers	Houghton Mifflin
My Cat	A	RF	28	Leveled Readers Science	Houghton Mifflin
My Cat	A	RF	47	First Stories	Pacific Learning
My Cat	A	I	37	Early Connections	Benchmark Education
My Cats	A	RF	41	Robinson, Eileen	Scholastic
My Classroom	A	I	31	At School Series	Pioneer Valley
My Dog	A	RF	72	Instant Readers	Harcourt School Publishers
My Doll	A	F	32	Sun Sprouts	ETA/Cuisenaire

* Collection of short stories

TITLE	LEVEL	GENRE	WORD COUNT	AUTHOR / SERIES	PUBLISHER / DISTRIBUTOR
My Family	A	RF	28	Leveled Readers Social Studies	Houghton Mifflin
My Family	A	RF	28	Sunshine	Wright Group/McGraw Hill
My Family Has Fun	A	RF	28	Leveled Readers Emergent	Houghton Mifflin
My Fish	A	RF	24	Phonics and Friends	Hampton-Brown
My Home	A	F	56	Smart Starts	Rigby
My House	A	RF	40	Carousel Earlybirds	Pearson Learning Group
My Mom and I	A	RF	42	Little Books for Early Readers	University of Maine
My Picture	A	RF	23	Story Box	Wright Group/McGraw Hill
My Place	A	RF	28	Foundations	Wright Group/McGraw Hill
My Place	A	RF	34	Story Steps	Rigby
My Planet	A	I	28	Smart Starts	Rigby
My Rocket	A	F	28	KinderReaders	Rigby
My Room	A	RF	28	Carousel Earlybirds	Pearson Learning Group
My Room	A	RF	15	Twig	Wright Group/McGraw Hill
My Room	A	RF	15	Leveled Readers Emergent	Houghton Mifflin
My School	A	I	34	At School Series	Pioneer Valley
My Shadow	A	RF	29	Book Bank	Wright Group/McGraw Hill
My Story	A	RF	17	Wonder World	Wright Group/McGraw Hill
My Teacher	A	I	32	At School Series	Pioneer Valley
My Tower	A	RF	15	Windmill	Wright Group/McGraw Hill
My Town	A	I	33	Early Connections	Benchmark Education
My Toys	A	RF	28	Little Books for Early Readers	University of Maine
Next Door	A	F	31	Rigby Literacy	Rigby
Noisy and Quiet	A	I	26	Vocabulary Readers	Houghton Mifflin
On a Walk	A	RF	5	Ready Readers	Pearson Learning Group
On Our Farm	A	I	14	Bebop Books	Lee & Low Books Inc.
On Safari	A	I	28	Smart Starts	Rigby
On the Farm	A	I	24	Vocabulary Readers	Houghton Mifflin
On the Rocks	A	I	42	Windows on Literacy	National Geographic
Painters	A	I	23	Twig	Wright Group/McGraw Hill
Party Food	A	I	25	Rigby Focus	Rigby
Party, A	A	RF	14	Story Box	Wright Group/McGraw Hill
Party, A	A	RF	28	Leveled Readers Emergent	Houghton Mifflin
People Go Up	A	I	18	Windows on Literacy	National Geographic
People in My Town	A	I	36	Rosen Real Readers	Rosen Publishing Group
People Use Tools	A	I	24	Early Connections	Benchmark Education
Pepper Sees Me	A	I	28	Little Books for Early Readers	University of Maine
Pet Store, The	A	I	49	Bookshop	Mondo
Pets	A	I	33	PM Starters	Rigby
Plant, The	A	I	32	Sun Sprouts	ETA/Cuisenaire
Playground, The	A	I	16	Twig	Wright Group/McGraw Hill
Playing	A	I	39	PM Starters	Rigby
Pond, A	A	I	14	Discovery Links	Newbridge
Potato Harvest Time	A	I	33	Little Books for Early Readers	University of Maine
Push or Pull?	A	I	7	Discovery Links	Newbridge
Puzzle, The	A	I	32	Sun Sprouts	ETA/Cuisenaire
Reading Partners	A	I	48	At School Series	Pioneer Valley
Recess	A	I	27	At School Series	Pioneer Valley
Rhymes	A	I	9	Ready Readers	Pearson Learning Group
Ribbit!	A	I	7	Little Celebrations	Pearson Learning Group
Robot, The	A	F	18	Smart Starts	Rigby
Running	A	RF	31	Sun Sprouts	ETA/Cuisenaire
Salad	A	F	36	Carousel Earlybirds	Pearson Learning Group
Salad Vegetables	A	I	27	Story Box	Wright Group/McGraw Hill

* Collection of short stories

TITLE	LEVEL	GENRE	WORD COUNT	AUTHOR / SERIES	PUBLISHER / DISTRIBUTOR
Sandcastle, The	A	I	32	First Stories	Pacific Learning
Say Hello!	A	RF	15	Rise & Shine	Hampton-Brown
School Day!	A	RF	16	Cervantes, Jesus	Scholastic
School Days Long Ago and Today	A	I	32	Leveled Readers Social Studies	Houghton Mifflin
Seasons	A	I	29	Vocabulary Readers	Houghton Mifflin
Seasons	A	I	28	Leveled Readers Science	Houghton Mifflin
Seed, The	A	I	14	Wonder World	Wright Group/McGraw Hill
Shape Maker, The	A	RF	24	Harry's Math Books	Outside the Box
Shapes	A	I	24	Urmston, Kathleen; Evans, Karen	Kaeden Books
Shells	A	I	34	Rigby Literacy	Rigby
Shoes	A	RF	16	Little Celebrations	Pearson Learning Group
Show and Tell	A	RF	32	Little Books	Sadlier-Oxford
Sit, Pig!	A	RF	20	Vocabulary Readers	Houghton Mifflin
Snails	A	I	40	First Stories	Pacific Learning
Snow	A	I	11	Vocabulary Readers	Houghton Mifflin
Snowman	A	RF	19	Story Box	Wright Group/McGraw Hill
So Many Things to Do	A	RF	21	Home Connection Collection	Rigby
Sounds All Around	A	I	28	Independent Readers Science	Houghton Mifflin
Soup	A	I	17	Little Celebrations	Pearson Learning Group
Space Journey	A	F	19	Sunshine	Wright Group/McGraw Hill
Splash!	A	I	35	Bebop Books	Lee & Low Books Inc.
Spots and Stripes	A	I	24	Rosen Real Readers	Rosen Publishing Group
Spring Rain	A	I	24	Vocabulary Readers	Houghton Mifflin
Stop That Noise!	A	F	21	KinderReaders	Rigby
Stop!	A	RF	12	Ready Readers	Pearson Learning Group
Surprise, The	A	F	14	Story Box	Wright Group/McGraw Hill
Swing	A	RF	18	Story Box	Wright Group/McGraw Hill
Tale of Cowboy	A	RF	31	Reading Unlimited	Pearson Learning Group
Things I See	A	I	28	Leveled Readers Emergent	Houghton Mifflin
This Food Grows Here	A	I	16	Windows on Literacy	National Geographic
This Is Lobstering	A	I	27	Little Books for Early Readers	University of Maine
Tigers, Elephants, and Giraffes	A	I	18	Vocabulary Readers	Houghton Mifflin
Time for School	A	I	32	At School Series	Pioneer Valley
Tim's Paintings	A	RF	33	Smart Starts	Rigby
To School	A	F	22	Sunshine	Wright Group/McGraw Hill
Too Fast	A	F	36	Reading Corners	Pearson Learning Group
Toy Models	A	I	40	Early Connections	Benchmark Education
Traffic	A	I	30	Lighthouse	Rigby
Traffic Jam, The	A	RF	33	Handprints B	Educator's Publishing Service
Trees	A	I	28	Twig	Wright Group/McGraw Hill
Trolley Ride	A	I	16	Vocabulary Readers	Houghton Mifflin
Trucks	A	I	35	Little Books for Early Readers	University of Maine
Trucks	A	RF	56	Bookshop	Mondo
Two	A	I	17	Little Celebrations	Pearson Learning Group
Under the Bed	A	RF	28	Smart Starts	Rigby
Under Water	A	I	35	Twig	Wright Group/McGraw Hill
Vegetable Soup	A	I	24	Vocabulary Readers	Houghton Mifflin
Visit to the Doctor, A	A	I	28	Little Books for Early Readers	University of Maine
Waiting	A	RF	28	Story Box	Wright Group/McGraw Hill
Wash Day	A	RF	35	Voyages	SRA/McGraw Hill
Water	A	HF	21	Yellow Umbrella Books	Red Brick Learning
We Are a Big Family	A	RF	28	Leveled Readers Emergent	Houghton Mifflin
We Are Painting	A	RF	38	Alexander, Francie	Scholastic

* Collection of short stories

TITLE	LEVEL	GENRE	WORD COUNT	AUTHOR / SERIES	PUBLISHER / DISTRIBUTOR
We Are Twins	A	I	24	Little Books for Early Readers	University of Maine
We Can	A	F	21	KinderReaders	Rigby
We Can Make Pizza	A	I	30	Little Books for Early Readers	University of Maine
We Go Out	A	I	41	PM Starters	Rigby
We Like Pie!	A	RF	28	Leveled Readers Emergent	Houghton Mifflin
We Like to Play!	A	I	28	Leveled Readers Emergent	Houghton Mifflin
We Play Music	A	RF	20	Bebop Books	Lee & Low Books Inc.
We Play Together	A	RF	22	Blevins, Wiley	Scholastic
We Read	A	I	20	Blevins, Wiley	Scholastic
We Ride!	A	I	31	Vocabulary Readers	Houghton Mifflin
Weather Days	A	I	24	Vocabulary Readers	Houghton Mifflin
What Are We Doing?	A	F	21	KinderReaders	Rigby
What Are You?	A	F	27	Literacy 2000	Rigby
What Bears Like	A	I	21	Cherrington, Janelle	Scholastic
What Blows in the Wind?	A	RF	36	Science	Outside the Box
What Can I Do Today?	A	I	20	Windows on Literacy	National Geographic
What Can I Read?	A	RF	28	Carousel Earlybirds	Pearson Learning Group
What Can Jigarees Do?	A	F	22	Story Box	Wright Group/McGraw Hill
What Can Jump?	A	I	32	Windmill Books	Rigby
What Can She Do?	A	I	21	Little Books for Early Readers	University of Maine
What Can You Do?	A	I	18	Vocabulary Readers	Houghton Mifflin
What Did Ben Want?	A	RF	28	Smart Starts	Rigby
What Do Insects Do?	A	I	24	Canizares, Susan; Chanko, Pamela	Scholastic
What Do You Play	A	I	25	Science	Outside the Box
What Do You See by the Sea?	A	I	14	Little Books	Sadlier-Oxford
What Do You See?	A	RF	71	Phonics and Friends	Hampton-Brown
What Does Lucy Like?	A	RF	11	Little Books	Sadlier-Oxford
What Feels Hot?	A	I	28	Windmill Books	Rigby
What Goes Together?	A	I	28	Leveled Readers Science	Houghton Mifflin
What Goes Up High?	A	I	38	Windmill Books	Rigby
What Has Changed?	A	I	18	Windows on Literacy	National Geographic
What Has Wheels?	A	I	28	Hoenecke, Karen	Kaeden Books
What Is an Insect?	A	I	36	Yellow Umbrella Books	Red Brick Learning
What Is Fast?	A	I	30	Windmill Books	Rigby
What Is He Looking For?	A	F	42	KinderReaders	Rigby
What Is This?	A	I	25	Little Books for Early Readers	University of Maine
What Is This?	A	I	25	Tiger Cub	Peguis
What Is This?	A	I	29	KinderReaders	Rigby
What Rhymes With . . .	A	I	9	Ready Readers	Pearson Learning Group
What We Do at School	A	F	31	Bookshop	Mondo
What's For Lunch?	A	I	30	Vocabulary Readers	Houghton Mifflin
What's in This Egg?	A	F	16	Sunshine	Wright Group/McGraw Hill
What's Round?	A	I	14	Discovery Links	Newbridge
When the Circus Comes to Town	A	I	40	Little Red Readers	Sundance
Where Is It Going?	A	I	20	Windows on Literacy	National Geographic
Where Is My Pet?	A	RF	34	Smart Start	Rigby
Where Is She?	A	I	35	Little Books for Early Readers	University of Maine
Where Is Teddy's Head?	A	RF	27	Windmill	Wright Group/McGraw Hill
Where is the Dog?	A	I	18	Vocabulary Readers	Houghton Mifflin
Who Can Be a Hero?	A	I	41	Leveled Readers Social Studies	Houghton Mifflin
Who Likes Ice Cream?	A	F	15	Literacy 2000	Rigby
Who Likes the Cold?	A	I	29	Twig	Wright Group/McGraw Hill
Who's at School?	A	I	36	Rosen Real Readers	Rosen Publishing Group
Wild Bear	A	I	21	Pacific Literacy	Pacific Learning

* Collection of short stories

TITLE	LEVEL	GENRE	WORD COUNT	AUTHOR / SERIES	PUBLISHER / DISTRIBUTOR
Wings	A	I	24	Rigby Literacy	Rigby
Zoomers, The	A	F	28	Kinderstarters	Rigby
1, 2, 3 in the Box	B	RF	23	Tarlow, Ellen	Scholastic
100 Days	B	RF	16	Bebop Books	Lee & Low Books Inc.
7 Uses for Air	B	I	46	Independent Readers Science	Houghton Mifflin
Airplane, The	B	RF	21	Sunshine	Wright Group/McGraw Hill
All Dressed Up	B	RF	38	Visions	Wright Group/McGraw Hill
All Fall Down	B	F	23	Instant Readers	Harcourt School Publishers
All Kinds of Things	B	I	24	Pacific Literacy	Pacific Learning
All of Me	B	RF	25	Literacy 2000	Rigby
All Wet!	B	I	28	Ready Readers	Pearson Learning Group
Animal Babies	B	I	114	Little Red Readers	Sundance
Animal Habitats	B	I	73	Little Celebrations	Pearson Learning Group
Animal Habitats	B	I	73	Little Red Readers	Sundance
Animal Homes	B	I	48	Little Red Readers	Sundance
Animal Homes	B	I	48	Early Connections	Benchmark Education
Animal Hospital, The	B	I	24	Windows on Literacy	National Geographic
Animal Legs	B	I	37	Discovery World	Rigby
Animal Walk, The	B	RF	39	Rigby Literacy	Rigby
Animals Hiding	B	I	61	Bookshop	Mondo
Animals Sleeping	B	RF	61	Bookshop	Mondo
Animals Went to Bed, The	B	F	32	Smart Starts	Rigby
Ants	B	I	16	Discovery Links	Newbridge
Ants Love Picnics, Too	B	F	27	Literacy 2000	Rigby
Apple Picking	B	RF	44	Bookshop	Mondo
Are You Afraid of . . .?	B	I	18	Little Celebrations	Pearson Learning Group
Around and Around	B	I	72	PM Plus Nonfiction	Rigby
Astronaut	B	I	22	Hoenecke, Karen	Kaeden Books
Astronaut, The	B	RF	30	Sunshine	Wright Group/McGraw Hill
At Home and at School	B	I	32	Leveled Readers Social Studies	Houghton Mifflin
At My School	B	I	43	Little Books for Early Readers	University of Maine
At School	B	I	29	Vocabulary Readers	Houghton Mifflin
At School	B	I	23	Sunshine	Wright Group/McGraw Hill
At the Airport	B	I	42	Leveled Readers Social Studies	Houghton Mifflin
At the Beach	B	I	74	Leveled Readers Emergent	Houghton Mifflin
At the Beach	B	I	30	Discovery Links	Newbridge
At the Museum	B	RF	28	Ready Readers	Pearson Learning Group
At the Playground	B	I	54	Little Books for Early Readers	University of Maine
At the Pond	B	RF	51	Leveled Readers Science	Houghton Mifflin
At the Store	B	I	21	Read-More Books	Pearson Learning Group
At the Wildlife Park	B	I	34	Little Red Readers	Sundance
At the Zoo	B	I	40	PM Starters	Rigby
At the Zoo	B	I	40	Early Connections	Benchmark Education
At the Zoo	B	RF	54	Little Readers	Houghton Mifflin
At the Zoo	B	I	40	Leveled Readers Emergent	Houghton Mifflin
At the Zoo	B	RF	29	Kloes, Carol	Kaeden Books
At Work	B	I	54	Independent Readers Social Studies	Houghton Mifflin
At Work	B	I	29	Bookshop	Mondo
Baby Animals	B	I	44	Reading Corners	Pearson Learning Group
Baby Animals	B	I	89	Rigby Literacy	Rigby
Ball Game	B	RF	16	Literacy 2000	Rigby
Ball Games	B	RF	44	PM Starters	Rigby
Balloons	B	I	55	Early Emergent	Pioneer Valley

* Collection of short stories

TITLE	LEVEL	GENRE	WORD COUNT	AUTHOR / SERIES	PUBLISHER / DISTRIBUTOR
Balloons	B	RF	57	PM Plus Starters	Rigby
Bare Feet	B	RF	40	Visions	Wright Group/McGraw Hill
Barn Dance, The	B	RF	46	Leveled Readers Emergent	Houghton Mifflin
Baseball	B	RF	14	Sunshine	Wright Group/McGraw Hill
Basket Full of Surprises, A	B	RF	43	Little Books	Sadlier-Oxford
Basketball	B	I	20	Wonder World	Wright Group/McGraw Hill
Bath Time	B	I	44	Bebop Books	Lee & Low Books Inc.
Bath, The	B	RF	28	Smart Starts	Rigby
Be Quiet	B	RF	25	Smart Starts	Rigby
Beans	B	I	35	Pebble Books	Capstone Press
Bear Needs a Place to Climb, A	B	I	49	Independent Readers Science	Houghton Mifflin
Bears	B	I	59	Storyteller Nonfiction	Wright Group/McGraw Hill
Beautiful Flowers	B	I	28	Wonder World	Wright Group/McGraw Hill
Because I'm Little	B	RF	51	Home Connection Collection	Rigby
Bedtime Fun	B	RF	46	Bebop Books	Lee & Low Books Inc.
Bees Buzzed, The	B	RF	41	Science	Outside the Box
Before I Go to School	B	I	71	Storyteller-First Snow	Wright Group/McGraw Hill
Ben's Red Car	B	RF	49	PM Starters	Rigby
Best Friends	B	I	28	Bebop Books	Lee & Low Books Inc.
Big and Little	B	I	68	PM Plus Starters	Rigby
Big and Little	B	F	40	Carousel Earlybirds	Pearson Learning Group
Big and Little	B	RF	21	Foundations	Wright Group/McGraw Hill
Big and Little	B	I	38	Rigby Literacy	Rigby
Big Cat, Little Cat	B	I	61	Rigby Focus	Rigby
Big Mammals	B	I	42	Little Red Readers	Sundance
Big or Little?	B	I	35	Bebop Books	Lee & Low Books Inc.
Big or Small?	B	I	30	Yellow Umbrella Books	Red Brick Learning
Big Sea Animals	B	I	79	PM Plus Starters	Rigby
Big, Big Box, A	B	RF	35	Ready Readers	Pearson Learning Group
Bird Talk: Kok, Kok	B	F	42	Little Celebrations	Pearson Learning Group
Birds	B	I	18	Rigby Focus	Rigby
Birthday Bug, The	B	RF	53	Story Steps	Rigby
Bobbie and the Monster	B	RF	24	Rigby Literacy	Rigby
Books	B	RF	29	Sunshine	Wright Group/McGraw Hill
Books	B	I	21	Smart Starts	Rigby
Bootscooting	B	I	38	First Stories	Pacific Learning
Breakfast at the Farm	B	RF	56	Bookshop	Mondo
Bridge, The	B	F	32	Story Box	Wright Group/McGraw Hill
Brothers	B	I	36	Pebble Books	Capstone Press
Bubble Gum	B	RF	21	Carousel Readers	Pearson Learning Group
Buffy	B	F	28	Literacy 2000	Rigby
Bug Watching	B	I	25	Twig	Wright Group/McGraw Hill
Bundle Up!	B	RF	35	Science	Outside the Box
Bunny Opposites	B	F	14	Pair-It Books	Steck-Vaughn
Camping	B	RF	19	Literacy 2000	Rigby
Can You Do This?	B	F	20	The Book Project	Sundance
Can You Find It?	B	I	34	Ready Readers	Pearson Learning Group
Carrots	B	I	51	Pebble Books	Capstone Press
Cars	B	I	30	Little Readers	Houghton Mifflin
Cat and Dog	B	RF	41	Leveled Readers	Houghton Mifflin
Cat and Mouse	B	F	75	PM Starters	Rigby
Cat Called, The	B	F	18	Ray's Readers	Outside the Box
Cat Came Back, The	B	TL	22	Ready Readers	Pearson Learning Group
Cat on the Mat	B	F	37	Wildsmith, Brian	Oxford University Press

* Collection of short stories

TITLE	LEVEL	GENRE	WORD COUNT	AUTHOR / SERIES	PUBLISHER / DISTRIBUTOR
Catching	B	I	35	Teacher's Choice Series	Pearson Learning Group
Cat's Day, A	B	I	23	Twig	Wright Group/McGraw Hill
Cats, Cats, Cats	B	I	14	Pair-It Books	Steck-Vaughn
Changing Colors	B	I	16	Pair-It Books	Steck-Vaughn
Chicken Soup	B	I	38	Fitros, Pamela	Kaeden Books
Chickens	B	I	24	Pebble Books	Capstone Press
Chocolate Cake, The	B	RF	23	Story Box	Wright Group/McGraw Hill
Chocolate Chip Cookies	B	I	32	Ready Readers	Pearson Learning Group
Circus	B	I	20	Twig	Wright Group/McGraw Hill
City and the Country, The	B	I	48	Leveled Readers Emergent	Houghton Mifflin
City Bus, The	B	RF	21	Visions	Wright Group/McGraw Hill
Clap Your Hands!	B	I	22	Pair-It Books	Steck-Vaughn
Clean Up Your Room	B	RF	35	Visions	Wright Group/McGraw Hill
Climbing	B	I	48	PM Starters	Rigby
Clock Watch	B	I	76	Early Connections	Benchmark Education
Clouds	B	RF	42	Voyages	SRA/McGraw Hill
Cold and Hot	B	RF	24	Bebop Books	Lee & Low Books Inc.
Colors	B	I	38	Science	Outside the Box
Colors at the Zoo	B	I	59	Little Books	Sadlier-Oxford
Come and Play	B	F	104	Bookshop	Mondo
Come and Play	B	F	34	Interaction	Rigby
Come In!	B	F	20	The Book Project	Sundance
Come On!	B	RF	22	Sunshine	Wright Group/McGraw Hill
Costume Party, The	B	RF	15	Sunshine	Wright Group/McGraw Hill
Counting One to Five	B	I	64	Early Connections	Benchmark Education
Creepy Crawlies	B	RF	38	Carousel Earlybirds	Pearson Learning Group
Curly Finds a Home	B	F	30	Rigby Literacy	Rigby
Cutting Our Food	B	I	40	Early Connections	Benchmark Education
Dad	B	RF	21	Little Readers	Houghton Mifflin
Dan Gets Dressed	B	RF	42	Story Box	Wright Group/McGraw Hill
Dancing Shoes	B	F	23	Literacy 2000	Rigby
Day at the Fair, A	B	RF	42	Bebop Books	Lee & Low Books Inc.
Dear Santa	B	F	50	Literacy 2000	Rigby
Different Seasons	B	I	37	Leveled Readers Science	Houghton Mifflin
Dinosaur	B	I	17	Science	Outside the Box
Dinosaur Dance, The	B	F	52	Little Books	Sadlier-Oxford
Dinosaur Party	B	F	27	Smart Starts	Rigby
Diver, The	B	RF	30	Sunshine	Wright Group/McGraw Hill
Do You Like Grapes?	B	RF	31	Science	Outside the Box
Dog	B	RF	37	Pacific Literacy	Pacific Learning
Dogs	B	RF	27	Levin, Amy	Scholastic
Don't Wake the Baby	B	RF	18	Literacy 2000	Rigby
Dreaming	B	RF	23	Smart Starts	Rigby
Dressing Up	B	RF	25	Smart Starts	Rigby
Eat It, Print It	B	I	70	Rigby Literacy	Rigby
Eating Breakfast	B	I	18	Rosen Real Readers	Rosen Publishing Group
Edmond Went Splash	B	F	69	First Stories	Pacific Learning
Eggs!	B	RF	28	Ready Readers	Pearson Learning Group
Everybody Wears Braids	B	RF	30	Bebop Books	Lee & Low Books Inc.
Faces	B	RF	27	Sunshine	Wright Group/McGraw Hill
Fall	B	I	12	Discovery Links	Newbridge
Families	B	I	49	Interaction	Rigby
Family Counts	B	RF	19	Rise & Shine	Hampton-Brown
Family Picnic	B	RF	18	Bebop Books	Lee & Low Books Inc.

* Collection of short stories

TITLE	LEVEL	GENRE	WORD COUNT	AUTHOR / SERIES	PUBLISHER / DISTRIBUTOR
Family Time	B	I	16	Pair-It Books	Steck-Vaughn
Family Work and Fun	B	I	38	Little Red Readers	Sundance
Farley Frog	B	F	33	Pair-It Books	Steck-Vaughn
Farm, The	B	I	79	Leveled Readers Emergent	Houghton Mifflin
Farm, The	B	I	21	Sunshine	Wright Group/McGraw Hill
Fast and Faster	B	I	24	Windows on Literacy	National Geographic
Fathers	B	I	26	Pebble Books	Capstone Press
Fence, The	B	F	44	Bookshop	Mondo
Festival, the	B	I	37	Windows on Literacy	National Geographic
Finger Puppet, The	B	RF	18	Sunshine	Wright Group/McGraw Hill
Fish Picture, A	B	RF	58	First Stories	Pacific Learning
Fish Print	B	I	25	Bebop Books	Lee & Low Books Inc.
Fishing	B	I	41	Little Books for Early Readers	University of Maine
Flags Everywhere!	B	I	25	Independent Readers Social Studies	Houghton Mifflin
Flowers Have Colors	B	I	29	Cherrington, Janelle	Scholastic
Fly High	B	RF	24	Visions	Wright Group/McGraw Hill
Flying and Floating	B	I	64	Little Red Readers	Sundance
Follow the Leader	B	RF	15	Windmill	Wright Group/McGraw Hill
Follow the Leader	B	RF	32	Independent Readers Social Studies	Houghton Mifflin
Food to Eat	B	I	29	Little Readers	Houghton Mifflin
Football	B	I	28	Visions	Wright Group/McGraw Hill
For My Birthday	B	RF	48	Lighthouse	Rigby
Fourth of July, The	B	I	17	Windows on Literacy	National Geographic
Friends	B	RF	36	Little Readers	Houghton Mifflin
Friends	B	I	21	Rigby Literacy	Rigby
Frightened	B	F	42	Story Box	Wright Group/McGraw Hill
From Sheep to Sweater	B	I	28	Tarlow, Ellen	Scholastic
Fruit	B	I	20	Rise & Shine	Hampton-Brown
Fruit Salad	B	I	24	Early Emergent	Pioneer Valley
Fruit Trees	B	I	24	Visions	Wright Group/McGraw Hill
Fun with Friends	B	RF	18	Rise & Shine	Hampton-Brown
Fun with Hats	B	F	38	Bookshop	Mondo
Furry	B	I	19	Little Celebrations	Pearson Learning Group
Gabby Visits Buster	B	RF	39	Early Emergent	Pioneer Valley
Games	B	I	28	Berger, Samantha; Moreton, Daniel	Scholastic
Garden Colors	B	F	15	Pair-It Books	Steck-Vaughn
Garden, The	B	RF	63	Leveled Readers Emergent	Houghton Mifflin
Getting Dressed	B	RF	40	Carousel Earlybirds	Pearson Learning Group
Getting Ready	B	I	29	Little Books for Early Readers	University of Maine
Getting There	B	I	36	Wonder World	Wright Group/McGraw Hill
Giant's Breakfast, The	B	F	42	Literacy 2000	Rigby
Giant's Day Out, The	B	F	26	Smart Starts	Rigby
Gifts for Everyone	B	F	35	Rigby Literacy	Rigby
Gifts, The	B	RF	34	Story Box	Wright Group/McGraw Hill
Give Me a Hug	B	RF	28	Sunshine	Wright Group/McGraw Hill
Go Teddy!	B	I	27	Windows on Literacy	National Geographic
Go-carts, The	B	RF	46	PM Starters	Rigby
Going Fishing	B	F	22	Ready Readers	Pearson Learning Group
Going for a Ride	B	RF	40	Little Books for Early Readers	University of Maine
Going for a Ride	B	I	67	Leveled Readers Emergent	Houghton Mifflin
Going in the Car	B	RF	24	Sunshine	Wright Group/McGraw Hill

* Collection of short stories

TITLE	LEVEL	GENRE	WORD COUNT	AUTHOR / SERIES	PUBLISHER / DISTRIBUTOR
Going Out	B	RF	48	PM Plus Starters	Rigby
Going Places	B	F	49	First Stories	Pacific Learning
Going Shopping	B	RF	31	Rigby Literacy	Rigby
Going Up and Down	B	RF	51	Early Emergent	Pioneer Valley
Going Up?	B	F	26	Little Celebrations	Pearson Learning Group
Good Girl	B	F	18	Ready Readers	Pearson Learning Group
Good to Eat	B	I	31	Twig	Wright Group/McGraw Hill
Gorilla Games	B	F	27	Phonics and Friends	Hampton-Brown
Great Enormous Hamburger, The	B	F	36	Sunshine	Wright Group/McGraw Hill
Green Grass	B	F	26	Story Box	Wright Group/McGraw Hill
Growing	B	I	23	Windmill	Wright Group/McGraw Hill
Hair	B	I	37	Foundations	Wright Group/McGraw Hill
Halloween	B	RF	44	Story Box	Wright Group/McGraw Hill
Hands	B	I	15	Twig	Wright Group/McGraw Hill
Hands, Hands, Hands	B	RF	17	Little Celebrations	Pearson Learning Group
Happy Holidays	B	I	27	Teacher's Choice Series	Pearson Learning Group
Hard at Work	B	RF	66	Early Emergent	Pioneer Valley
Harry's Hat	B	RF	45	Little Books	Sadlier-Oxford
Hats Around the World	B	I	59	Charlesworth, Liza	Scholastic
Have You Seen My Cat?	B	F	93	Carle, Eric	Putnam
Having Fun	B	RF	35	Early Emergent	Pioneer Valley
Headache, The	B	RF	20	Oxford Reading Tree	Oxford University Press
Hello Flower	B	RF	20	Bebop Books	Lee & Low Books Inc.
Hello Goodbye	B	F	29	Literacy 2000	Rigby
Here Comes the Bus	B	RF	21	Bebop Books	Lee & Low Books Inc.
Here Comes the Parade!	B	RF	32	Pair-It Books	Steck-Vaughn
Here I Am!	B	RF	36	First Stories	Pacific Learning
Here Is . . .	B	I	49	Carousel Earlybirds	Pearson Learning Group
Here Is a Box	B	I	91	Rigby Literacy	Rigby
Here's Skipper	B	RF	28	Salem, Lynn; Stewart, Josie	Continental Press
Hide and Seek	B	RF	38	Literacy 2000	Rigby
Homes	B	I	63	Bookshop	Mondo
Homes for People	B	I	40	Early Connections	Benchmark Education
Honk!	B	F	36	Bookshop	Mondo
Houses	B	I	64	Rigby Literacy	Rigby
How Can You Fix It?	B	I	56	Rigby Literacy	Rigby
How Many Fish?	B	F	30	Gosset, Rachel; Ballinger, Margaret	Scholastic
How Many Jelly Beans	B	RF	61	Phonics and Friends	Hampton-Brown
How Many Legs?	B	I	19	Windmill	Wright Group/McGraw Hill
How Many Monkeys?	B	F	16	Pair-It Books	Steck-Vaughn
How to Make a Hen House	B	I	25	Ready Readers	Pearson Learning Group
How to Make a Wind Sock	B	F	20	Tarlow, Ellen	Scholastic
How's the Weather	B	I	29	Learn to Read	Creative Teaching Press
I Am	B	RF	32	Seedlings	Continental Press
I Am	B	RF	32	Little Readers	Houghton Mifflin
I Am a Star	B	RF	32	Little Readers	Houghton Mifflin
I Am Frightened	B	RF	41	Story Box	Wright Group/McGraw Hill
I Am Going	B	RF	31	Sun Sprouts	ETA/Cuisenaire
I Can	B	RF	21	New Way	Steck-Vaughn
I Can	B	RF	54	Little Readers	Houghton Mifflin
I Can	B	RF	40	Ready Readers	Pearson Learning Group
I Can Fly	B	F	21	Sunshine	Wright Group/McGraw Hill
I Can Hop. Can You?	B	I	41	Independent Readers Science	Houghton Mifflin

TITLE	LEVEL	GENRE	WORD COUNT	AUTHOR / SERIES	PUBLISHER / DISTRIBUTOR
I Can Make Music	B	I	41	Little Red Readers	Sundance
I Can Make You Red	B	F	43	The Book Project	Sundance
I Can Move!	B	I	39	Leveled Readers Science	Houghton Mifflin
I Can Play	B	RF	32	Handprints B	Educator's Publishing Service
I Can See	B	RF	36	Rigby Focus	Rigby
I Can Write, Can You?	B	RF	30	Stewart, Josie; Salem, Lynn	Continental Press
I Could Be	B	RF	40	Visions	Wright Group/McGraw Hill
I Get Tired	B	RF	37	Carousel Earlybirds	Pearson Learning Group
I Go, Go, Go	B	F	21	Sunshine	Wright Group/McGraw Hill
I Have a Pet	B	RF	35	Reading Corners	Pearson Learning Group
I Like	B	RF	53	Early Connections	Benchmark Education
I Like Green	B	F	28	The Book Project	Sundance
I Like Rice	B	I	36	First Stories	Pacific Learning
I Like to Help	B	RF	46	Little Books for Early Readers	University of Maine
I Like to Read	B	RF	49	Little Books for Early Readers	University of Maine
I Love Camping	B	RF	34	Early Emergent	Pioneer Valley
I Love My Family	B	RF	31	Sunshine	Wright Group/McGraw Hill
I Love My Family	B	RF	34	Foundations	Wright Group/McGraw Hill
I Run	B	RF	22	Carousel Earlybirds	Pearson Learning Group
I See	B	F	29	Bookshop	Mondo
I See Colors	B	I	23	Learn to Read	Creative Teaching Press
I See Colors	B	RF	50	Little Readers	Houghton Mifflin
I See Fish	B	I	45	Curry, Don L.	Scholastic
I See Shapes	B	I	37	Learn to Read	Creative Teaching Press
I See Tails!	B	I	42	Rise & Shine	Hampton-Brown
I Spy	B	RF	30	Story Steps	Rigby
I Want a Red Ball	B	F	29	The Book Project	Sundance
I Want to Be...	B	F	46	The Book Project	Sundance
I Wash	B	RF	33	First Stories	Pacific Learning
I Write	B	RF	40	Little Books for Early Readers	University of Maine
Ice-Cream Stick	B	RF	35	Story Box	Wright Group/McGraw Hill
Iggy Iguana's Trip	B	F	43	Phonics and Friends	Hampton-Brown
I'm Hungry	B	I	25	Fitros, Pamela	Kaeden Books
I'm Red	B	F	25	The Book Project	Sundance
In My Garden	B	RF	35	Bookshop	Mondo
In My Pocket	B	RF	34	Instant Readers	Harcourt School Publishers
In My Toolbox	B	I	36	Foundations	Wright Group/McGraw Hill
In Spring	B	I	34	Science	Outside the Box
In Spring	B	I	15	Discovery Links	Newbridge
In the Air	B	I	20	Sunshine	Wright Group/McGraw Hill
In the Bathroom	B	RF	24	Smart Starts	Rigby
In the Box	B	F	64	The Book Project	Sundance
In the Car	B	RF	32	First Stories	Pacific Learning
In the Country, In the City	B	I	71	Rigby Literacy	Rigby
In the Forest	B	I	38	Science	Outside the Box
In the Mirror	B	RF	26	Story Box	Wright Group/McGraw Hill
In the Rain	B	F	19	Ready Readers	Pearson Learning Group
In the Sea	B	I	41	Little Red Readers	Sundance
In the Sky	B	I	42	Little Red Readers	Sundance
In the Tree	B	I	36	Windows on Literacy	National Geographic
In the Tree	B	RF	48	Leveled Readers Emergent	Houghton Mifflin
In the Woods	B	F	25	Gibson, Akimi	Scholastic
In the Woods	B	I	48	Bookshop	Mondo

* Collection of short stories

TITLE	LEVEL	GENRE	WORD COUNT	AUTHOR / SERIES	PUBLISHER / DISTRIBUTOR
It's About Time	B	I	39	Twig	Wright Group/McGraw Hill
It's My Bread	B	F	43	Pacific Literacy	Pacific Learning
Jack-in-the-Box	B	RF	34	Literacy 2000	Rigby
Jack-O-Lantern	B	I	37	Twig	Wright Group/McGraw Hill
Jake Can Play	B	RF	42	Little Books for Early Readers	University of Maine
Jan Can Juggle	B	RF	25	Ready Readers	Pearson Learning Group
Joan's Garden	B	F	34	Sun Sprouts	ETA/Cuisenaire
Jobs	B	I	29	Bookshop	Mondo
Jump Rope	B	RF	18	Bebop Books	Lee & Low Books Inc.
Jump, Jump, Kangaroo	B	F	31	Story Box	Wright Group/McGraw Hill
Jumpers	B	F	21	Sunshine	Wright Group/McGraw Hill
Jungle Spots	B	F	28	Little Celebrations	Pearson Learning Group
Just Look at You	B	RF	16	Sunshine	Wright Group/McGraw Hill
Keep Out!	B	RF	19	Ready Readers	Pearson Learning Group
Keys	B	I	31	Ready Readers	Pearson Learning Group
King's Birthday, The	B	F	35	Ray's Readers	Outside the Box
Kites	B	F	41	Phonics and Friends	Hampton-Brown
Kittens	B	RF	33	Curry, Don L.	Scholastic
Laundromat, The	B	RF	25	Visions	Wright Group/McGraw Hill
Legs	B	F	15	Gosset, Rachel; Ballinger, Margaret	Scholastic
Lester's Bedtime	B	F	39	Lester the Lion Series	Pioneer Valley
Let's Go	B	I	81	Early Connections	Benchmark Education
Let's Look Outside	B	I	38	Early Connections	Benchmark Education
Let's Move!	B	RF	29	Ready Readers	Pearson Learning Group
Let's Play	B	RF	40	Little Books for Early Readers	University of Maine
Let's Pretend	B	RF	40	Home Connection Collection	Rigby
Little Kittens	B	F	27	Ready Readers	Pearson Learning Group
Little Red Hen, The	B	TL	87	Windmill	Wright Group/McGraw Hill
Little Red Hen, The	B	TL	96	Folk Tales	Pioneer Valley
Little Seed, A	B	I	18	Smart Starts	Rigby
Living or Nonliving	B	I	27	Instant Readers	Harcourt School Publishers
Locked Out!	B	RF	15	Twig	Wright Group/McGraw Hill
Long, Long Tail, The	B	F	33	Sunshine	Wright Group/McGraw Hill
Look at Kyle	B	I	46	Little Books for Early Readers	University of Maine
Look at Me	B	RF	48	PM Starters	Rigby
Look at Me!	B	RF	35	Lighthouse	Rigby
Look at Pickles	B	RF	90	Pickles the Dog Series	Pioneer Valley
Look at the Animals	B	I	64	Early Connections	Benchmark Education
Look at the House	B	F	53	PM Plus Starters	Rigby
Look at the Ocean, A	B	I	50	Little Books for Early Readers	University of Maine
Look at the Tree	B	I	22	Windows on Literacy	National Geographic
Look at This	B	I	57	Carousel Earlybirds	Pearson Learning Group
Look Down!	B	I	51	Early Connections	Benchmark Education
Look Out!	B	F	15	Literacy 2000	Rigby
Look Out, Dan!	B	F	34	Story Box	Wright Group/McGraw Hill
Look What I Found!	B	RF	29	Science	Outside the Box
Look What I Found!	B	RF	29	Lighthouse	Rigby
Look! Now Look!	B	I	9	Rigby Literacy	Rigby
Looking Down	B	RF	64	First Stories	Pacific Learning
Loose Tooth	B	RF	51	Bebop Books	Lee & Low Books Inc.
Lost!	B	RF	18	Smart Starts	Rigby
Lots and Lots of Stairs	B	RF	33	Little Books for Early Readers	University of Maine
Lots of Things	B	RF	23	Reading Corners	Pearson Learning Group

* Collection of short stories

TITLE	LEVEL	GENRE	WORD COUNT	AUTHOR / SERIES	PUBLISHER / DISTRIBUTOR
Lots of Toys	B	I	47	Carousel Earlybirds	Pearson Learning Group
Loud Sounds, Quiet Sounds	B	I	26	Rosen Real Readers/Red	Rosen Publishing Group
Lunch at the Zoo	B	RF	64	Blaxland, Wendy; Brimage, C.	Scholastic
Lunchtime at the Zoo	B	RF	53	First Stories	Pacific Learning
Magnets	B	I	28	Seedlings	Continental Press
Major Jump	B	F	21	Sunshine	Wright Group/McGraw Hill
Making a Bird	B	I	32	PM Plus Nonfiction	Rigby
Making a Dinosaur	B	I	32	PM Plus Nonfiction	Rigby
Making a Rabbit	B	I	32	PM Plus Nonfiction	Rigby
Making Mountains	B	I	35	Gosset, Rachel; Ballinger, Margaret	Scholastic
Making Pictures	B	RF	48	Foundations	Wright Group/McGraw Hill
Max Jumps	B	F	37	Sun Sprouts	ETA/Cuisenaire
Max's Box	B	RF	43	Little Celebrations	Pearson Learning Group
Mess, The	B	RF	40	Sun Sprouts	ETA/Cuisenaire
Min's Plane Ride	B	RF	49	Bookshop	Mondo
Mitt for Me, A	B	RF	34	First Stories	Pacific Learning
Mixing Colors	B	I	15	Rigby Literacy	Rigby
Model, The	B	I	18	Smart Starts	Rigby
Mom Is a Painter	B	I	34	Bebop Books	Lee & Low Books Inc.
Mommy, Where Are You?	B	RF	64	Ziefert, Harriet; Boon, Emilie	Puffin Books
Moms	B	RF	34	Handprints B	Educator's Publishing Service
Monkey Moves	B	I	16	Pair-It Books	Steck-Vaughn
Monkeys	B	I	27	Canizares, Susan; Chanko, Pamela	Scholastic
Mother and Me	B	RF	48	Spinelle, Nancy Louise	Kaeden Books
Mothers	B	I	26	Pebble Books	Capstone Press
Mouse Train	B	F	48	Story Box	Wright Group/McGraw Hill
Moving	B	I	56	Little Red Readers	Sundance
Mr. Bumbleticker	B	F	28	Foundations	Wright Group/McGraw Hill
Mrs. Wishy-Washy's Tub	B	F	38	Story Box	Wright Group/McGraw Hill
Mud	B	RF	30	Science	Outside the Box
My Backpack	B	I	72	First Stories	Pacific Learning
My Bed Is Soft	B	I	42	Windows on Literacy	National Geographic
My Big Rock	B	RF	42	Bebop Books	Lee & Low Books Inc.
My Buddy	B	RF	32	First Stories	Pacific Learning
My Busy Day	B	RF	41	Early Emergent	Pioneer Valley
My Cat	B	RF	47	Lighthouse	Rigby
My Chair	B	RF	24	Pacific Literacy	Pacific Learning
My Clothes	B	RF	36	PM Plus Starters	Rigby
My Color	B	I	22	Mann, Rachel	Scholastic
My Dad and I	B	RF	52	Handprints B	Educator's Publishing Service
My Day	B	RF	24	Sunshine	Wright Group/McGraw Hill
My Dog and I	B	RF	55	Lighthouse	Rigby
My Dog Fuzzy	B	RF	27	Books for Young Learners/Emergent	Richard C. Owen
My Family	B	RF	46	First Stories	Pacific Learning
My Family	B	RF	31	Bebop Books	Lee & Low Books Inc.
My Family	B	RF	87	Carousel Earlybirds	Pearson Learning Group
My Feet	B	I	25	Twig	Wright Group/McGraw Hill
My Fish Bowl	B	I	29	Foundations	Wright Group/McGraw Hill
My Friend	B	RF	41	Sunshine	Wright Group/McGraw Hill
My Frisbee	B	RF	31	Rigby Literacy	Rigby

* Collection of short stories

TITLE	LEVEL	GENRE	WORD COUNT	AUTHOR / SERIES	PUBLISHER / DISTRIBUTOR
My Garden	B	I	37	Ostrow, Jesse S.	Scholastic
My Grandfather's Face	B	RF	27	Literacy 2000	Rigby
My Home	B	I	49	Science	Outside the Box
My Home is High	B	F	23	Literacy 2000	Rigby
My Horse	B	I	22	Bebop Books	Lee & Low Books Inc.
My House	B	I	25	Voyages	SRA/McGraw Hill
My Little Cat	B	RF	57	PM Plus Starters	Rigby
My Mom	B	I	40	Little Books for Early Readers	University of Maine
My Mom and Dad Take Care of Me	B	I	44	Windows on Literacy	National Geographic
My Monster and Me	B	F	37	Ready Readers	Pearson Learning Group
My Painting	B	RF	31	First Stories	Pacific Learning
My Puppy	B	RF	14	Sunshine	Wright Group/McGraw Hill
My School	B	I	34	Little Readers	Houghton Mifflin
My Shoes	B	RF	25	Rise & Shine	Hampton-Brown
My Sister Is My Friend	B	RF	32	Instant Readers	Harcourt School Publishers
Necklaces	B	RF	34	Phonics and Friends	Hampton-Brown
Nest Full of Eggs, A	B	I	25	Pair-It Books	Steck-Vaughn
New and Old	B	I	46	Windows on Literacy	National Geographic
New Pants	B	F	20	Story Box	Wright Group/McGraw Hill
New School, A	B	RF	24	Vocabulary Readers	Houghton Mifflin
Nicole Helps Grandma	B	I	35	Little Books for Early Readers	University of Maine
Nora Plays All Day	B	RF	42	Little Books	Sadlier-Oxford
Numbers	B	I	86	Canizares, Susan; Moreton, Daniel	Scholastic
Numbers All Around	B	I	40	Yellow Umbrella Books	Red Brick Learning
Ocean Waves	B	I	21	Twig	Wright Group/McGraw Hill
Off to Work	B	RF	41	Literacy 2000	Rigby
Old and New	B	I	54	Early Connections	Benchmark Education
Old MacDonald's Fun Time Farm	B	F	34	Instant Readers	Harcourt School Publishers
On a Boat	B	RF	20	Novek, Minda	Scholastic
On and Off	B	I	60	PM Plus Nonfiction	Rigby
On Earth	B	I	35	Leveled Readers Social Studies	Houghton Mifflin
On the Beach	B	RF	28	Smart Starts	Rigby
On the Line	B	RF	35	Teacher's Choice Series	Pearson Learning Group
On the Move	B	I	28	Windows on Literacy	National Geographic
One, One Is the Sun	B	RF	42	Story Box	Wright Group/McGraw Hill
Ouch!	B	I	40	Science	Outside the Box
Our Baby	B	RF	14	Literacy 2000	Rigby
Our Dog Sam	B	RF	56	Literacy 2000	Rigby
Our Families	B	I	52	Leveled Readers Social Studies	Houghton Mifflin
Our Families	B	I	26	Rigby Literacy	Rigby
Our Garden	B	I	16	Literacy 2000	Rigby
Our Party	B	RF	40	Leveled Readers Social Studies	Houghton Mifflin
Our Pumpkin	B	I	29	Learn to Read	Creative Teaching Press
Our Rocket	B	I	28	Pacific Literacy	Pacific Learning
Our Town	B	RF	37	Little Red Readers	Sundance
Out in the Weather	B	I	56	PM Starters	Rigby
Outside the Window	B	I	31	Vocabulary Readers	Houghton Mifflin
Over the Bridge	B	I	50	Little Red Readers	Sundance
Packing	B	RF	37	Foundations	Wright Group/McGraw Hill
Packing My Bag	B	RF	52	PM Starters	Rigby
Parade, The	B	RF	67	PM Plus Starters	Rigby
Parade, The	B	I	56	Leveled Readers Emergent	Houghton Mifflin
Party Hats	B	RF	72	PM Plus Starters	Rigby
Pat and Pig	B	F	34	Leveled Readers	Houghton Mifflin

* Collection of short stories

TITLE	LEVEL	GENRE	WORD COUNT	AUTHOR / SERIES	PUBLISHER / DISTRIBUTOR
Pat, Pat, Pat	B	RF	37	Book Bank	Wright Group/McGraw Hill
Patterns All Around	B	I	55	Early Connections	Benchmark Education
Paul's Day at School	B	I	38	Little Books for Early Readers	University of Maine
Peas and Potatoes: 1, 2, 3	B	RF	44	Pair-It Books	Steck-Vaughn
Pencil, The	B	I	97	PM Starters	Rigby
People Parts	B	I	42	Independent Readers Science	Houghton Mifflin
Pets	B	I	31	Vocabulary Readers	Houghton Mifflin
Pillow Sale, The	B	F	26	KinderReaders	Rigby
Pink Pig	B	RF	23	Ready Readers	Pearson Learning Group
Places I Like	B	I	49	Little Red Readers	Sundance
Plants	B	I	51	Leveled Readers Science	Houghton Mifflin
Plants in the Park	B	I	35	Windows on Literacy	National Geographic
Play, The	B	RF	33	First Stories	Pacific Learning
Play, The	B	RF	44	PM Starters	Rigby
Playground Opposites	B	I	21	Pair-It Books	Steck-Vaughn
Playground Play	B	RF	39	Handprints B	Educator's Publishing Service
Playing	B	RF	55	First Stories	Pacific Learning
Playing Sports	B	I	24	Early Connections	Benchmark Education
Poor Puppy!	B	RF	52	First Stories	Pacific Learning
Present, The	B	I	36	First Stories	Pacific Learning
Puppet Show, The	B	RF	25	Phonics and Friends	Hampton-Brown
Puppy, The	B	RF	37	First Stories	Pacific Learning
Puzzle, The	B	RF	32	Smart Starts	Rigby
Puzzle, The	B	I	28	Storyteller Nonfiction	Wright Group/McGraw Hill
Race, The	B	RF	78	Leveled Readers Emergent	Houghton Mifflin
Race, The	B	RF	34	Windmill	Wright Group/McGraw Hill
Rain	B	RF	52	Reading Corners	Pearson Learning Group
Rainbow, A	B	I	29	Rigby Focus	Rigby
Raindrops	B	I	34	Bookshop	Mondo
Rainy Day Counting	B	I	30	Twig	Wright Group/McGraw Hill
Recess	B	RF	26	Teacher's Choice Series	Pearson Learning Group
Recycle!	B	I	33	Leveled Readers Science	Houghton Mifflin
Rick and Rosie	B	RF	28	Phonics and Friends	Hampton-Brown
Robber, The	B	RF	25	Smart Starts	Rigby
Rock Pools, The	B	I	49	PM Starters	Rigby
Rocks	B	I	33	Leveled Readers Science	Houghton Mifflin
Roller Coaster, The	B	F	34	KinderReaders	Rigby
Run!	B	F	28	Sunshine	Wright Group/McGraw Hill
Run, Run, Run	B	RF	19	Joy Readers	Pearson Learning Group
Runaway Monkey	B	F	39	Stewart, Josie; Salem, Lynn	Continental Press
Runaway Wheels, The	B	F	32	Pair-It Books	Steck-Vaughn
Sally's New Shoes	B	RF	58	PM Starters	Rigby
Sand	B	I	32	Voyages	SRA/McGraw Hill
Scaredy Cat	B	RF	29	Rigby Literacy	Rigby
Scrumptious Sundae	B	RF	18	Literacy 2000	Rigby
Sea Animals	B	I	46	Vocabulary Readers	Houghton Mifflin
See the Ocean	B	RF	26	Science	Outside the Box
See the Seasons	B	I	16	Instant Readers	Harcourt School Publishers
See the Shapes	B	I	37	Rigby Focus	Rigby
Seeds	B	I	30	Rise & Shine	Hampton-Brown
Sending Messages	B	I	49	Wonder World	Wright Group/McGraw Hill
Shapes	B	I	19	Discovery World	Rigby
Shapes	B	I	40	Early Connections	Benchmark Education

* Collection of short stories

TITLE	LEVEL	GENRE	WORD COUNT	AUTHOR / SERIES	PUBLISHER / DISTRIBUTOR
Shells	B	I	39	Seedlings	Continental Press
Sherman Shoots . . .	B	RF	16	Ray's Readers	Outside the Box
Shoes	B	RF	40	Little Readers	Houghton Mifflin
Shoo, Fly	B	F	31	Science	Outside the Box
Shoo, Fly!	B	RF	24	Story Box	Wright Group/McGraw Hill
Shopping at the Supermarket	B	I	46	Foundations	Wright Group/McGraw Hill
Shopping Mall, The	B	I	44	PM Starters	Rigby
Signs	B	I	24	Literacy 2000	Rigby
Sisters	B	I	28	Pebble Books	Capstone Press
Six Legs	B	I	34	Harry's Math Books	Outside the Box
Six Wet Pets	B	F	31	Leveled Readers Language Support	Houghton Mifflin
Skating	B	F	35	Foundations	Wright Group/McGraw Hill
Skier, The	B	RF	48	PM Starters	Rigby
Sleepy Zoo	B	F	58	Sun Sprouts	ETA/Cuisenaire
Slug and Bug	B	F	42	Leveled Readers Language Support	Houghton Mifflin
Snap!	B	F	31	Sunshine	Wright Group/McGraw Hill
Snow	B	I	33	Hoenecke, Karen	Kaeden Books
Snow	B	I	29	Discovery Links	Newbridge
Snowman, The	B	I	32	Story Steps	Rigby
Snowman, The	B	RF	76	Leveled Readers Emergent	Houghton Mifflin
Socks	B	RF	21	Ready Readers	Pearson Learning Group
Some Dogs Don't	B	F	29	Tiger Cub	Peguis
Sometimes	B	RF	18	Literacy 2000	Rigby
Sometimes . . .	B	RF	25	Home Connection Collection	Rigby
Songbird, The	B	F	39	Ray's Readers	Outside the Box
Space Ark, The	B	SF	20	Sunshine	Wright Group/McGraw Hill
Spaceship	B	I	27	Hoenecke, Karen	Kaeden Books
Special Delivery	B	F	54	Bookshop	Mondo
Splish Splash!	B	RF	28	Windmill	Wright Group/McGraw Hill
Spooky Pet	B	RF	24	Smart Starts	Rigby
Sports Are Fun	B	I	21	Pair-It Books	Steck-Vaughn
Spots	B	F	31	Visions	Wright Group/McGraw Hill
Spring in the City	B	I	46	Leveled Readers Emergent	Houghton Mifflin
Squares	B	I	27	Harry's Math Books	Outside the Box
Stop!	B	RF	90	PM Starters	Rigby
Storm, The	B	I	19	Sunshine	Wright Group/McGraw Hill
Summer	B	RF	45	Leveled Readers Language Support	Houghton Mifflin
Sun Flower, A	B	RF	42	Foundations	Wright Group/McGraw Hill
Sun Shines on Me, The	B	I	34	Science	Outside the Box
Sun, Rain, and Snow	B	I	72	Leveled Readers Emergent	Houghton Mifflin
Sun, The	B	I	32	Rigby Focus	Rigby
Sunburn	B	I	48	Prokopchak, Ann	Kaeden Books
Sun's Magic, The	B	I	28	Seedlings	Continental Press
Super Hero	B	RF	33	Sunshine	Wright Group/McGraw Hill
Tails	B	I	42	Book Bank	Wright Group/McGraw Hill
Taking Care of Pets	B	I	55	Yellow Umbrella Books	Red Brick Learning
Team Sports	B	I	23	Twig	Wright Group/McGraw Hill
Thanksgiving	B	F	40	First Stories	Pacific Learning
There's a Mouse in the House	B	F	42	Bookshop	Mondo
Things Can Change	B	I	27	Leveled Readers Science	Houghton Mifflin
Things I Can Do	B	I	36	Little Red Readers	Sundance

TITLE	LEVEL	GENRE	WORD COUNT	AUTHOR / SERIES	PUBLISHER / DISTRIBUTOR
Things I Can Do	B	I	36	Little Readers	Houghton Mifflin
Things I Do for Fun	B	I	36	Little Red Readers	Sundance
Things I Do with My Friends	B	I	35	Little Red Readers	Sundance
This Game	B	I	63	Carousel Earlybirds	Pearson Learning Group
This Is Me	B	I	70	Sun Sprouts	ETA/Cuisenaire
This is Water	B	I	24	Bookshop	Mondo
This One Can Run	B	I	34	Science	Outside the Box
This Tail Belongs to . . .	B	I	24	Science	Outside the Box
This Tall	B	RF	41	Foundations	Wright Group/McGraw Hill
Three White Sheep	B	F	20	Ready Readers	Pearson Learning Group
Time for Bed	B	RF	28	Science	Outside the Box
Time for Dinner	B	I	38	PM Starters	Rigby
Time for Lunch	B	RF	28	Ready Readers	Pearson Learning Group
Time for Tacos	B	RF	26	Bebop Books	Lee & Low Books Inc.
Time for Tea	B	RF	20	Phonics and Friends	Hampton-Brown
Tim's Pig	B	F	41	Leveled Readers	Houghton Mifflin
Tim's Pig Eats	B	F	39	Leveled Readers Language Support	Houghton Mifflin
Tom-Ti-Ra and the Mysterious Noise	B	F	26	Book Bus	Creative Edge
Too Much	B	RF	27	Teacher's Choice Series	Pearson Learning Group
Toy Box, The	B	RF	49	Sun Sprouts	ETA/Cuisenaire
Toy Box, The	B	I	49	PM Plus Starters	Rigby
Toy Maker, The	B	RF	31	Ray's Readers	Outside the Box
Toy Store, The	B	RF	55	Leveled Readers Emergent	Houghton Mifflin
Toys	B	RF	37	Foundations	Wright Group/McGraw Hill
Treasure Map, The	B	F	32	Harry's Math Books	Outside the Box
Tree for all Seasons, A	B	I	24	Independent Readers Science	Houghton Mifflin
Tree House, The	B	RF	32	Sunshine	Wright Group/McGraw Hill
Tree House, The	B	F	30	Story Box	Wright Group/McGraw Hill
Tree Stump, The	B	TL	34	Little Celebrations	Pearson Learning Group
Trip to a Pond	B	RF	33	Leveled Readers Science	Houghton Mifflin
Trip to the Doctor, A	B	I	36	Windows on Literacy	National Geographic
Truck Is Stuck, The	B	RF	23	Ready Readers	Pearson Learning Group
Two Points	B	RF	40	Kennedy, Jane.; Eaton, Audrey	Continental Press
Up and Down	B	I	25	Little Books for Early Readers	University of Maine
Up in the Sky	B	I	56	PM Plus Starters	Rigby
Up the Tree	B	RF	38	First Stories	Pacific Learning
Up They Go	B	RF	30	Ready Readers	Pearson Learning Group
Up, Up, and Away	B	I	40	Lighthouse	Rigby
Vacations	B	RF	22	Smart Starts	Rigby
Van, The	B	RF	48	Phonics and Friends	Hampton-Brown
Walk in the Rain, A	B	RF	28	Pair-It Books	Steck-Vaughn
Walk, The	B	RF	29	Early Emergent	Pioneer Valley
Washing the Elephant	B	F	35	Lighthouse	Rigby
Watch Out	B	F	44	Bookshop	Mondo
Watching TV	B	RF	18	Sunshine	Wright Group/McGraw Hill
Water	B	I	28	Literacy 2000	Rigby
Water	B	I	24	Little Celebrations	Pearson Learning Group
Water	B	I	36	Science	Outside the Box
Water	B	RF	33	Sunshine	Wright Group/McGraw Hill
Water Can Be . . .	B	I	17	Science	Outside the Box
Water, Water	B	I	48	Rigby Literacy	Rigby
Way I Go to School, The	B	I	53	PM Starters	Rigby
We Are Playing	B	RF	19	Rigby Literacy	Rigby

* Collection of short stories

TITLE	LEVEL	GENRE	WORD COUNT	AUTHOR / SERIES	PUBLISHER / DISTRIBUTOR
We Are Singing	B	RF	26	Ready Readers	Pearson Learning Group
We Can Recycle	B	I	28	Leveled Readers Science	Houghton Mifflin
We Can Share at School	B	RF	35	Learn to Read	Creative Teaching Press
We Dress Up	B	RF	56	PM Plus Starters	Rigby
We Get Squished!	B	F	31	First Stories	Pacific Learning
We Go to School	B	RF	27	Carousel Earlybirds	Pearson Learning Group
We Like Fruit	B	RF	33	Lee, Millen	Scholastic
We Live Here	B	RF	25	Salzman, Gabriel	Scholastic
We Ride	B	I	40	Carousel Earlybirds	Pearson Learning Group
We Ski	B	I	35	Storyteller-First Snow	Wright Group/McGraw Hill
We Use Water	B	I	42	Windows on Literacy	National Geographic
We Want Watermelon	B	RF	49	Phonics and Friends	Hampton-Brown
We Went to the Zoo	B	I	32	Little Red Readers	Sundance
Weather Chart, The	B	I	24	Sunshine	Wright Group/McGraw Hill
Welcome to the Zigzag Zoo	B	F	42	Phonics and Friends	Hampton-Brown
Whale Watch	B	I	27	Ready Readers	Pearson Learning Group
What a Shower!	B	RF	23	Instant Readers	Harcourt School Publishers
What a Street!	B	RF	28	Bebop Books	Lee & Low Books Inc.
What Am I?	B	RF	50	Handprints B	Educator's Publishing Service
What Can Float?	B	I	27	Ready Readers	Pearson Learning Group
What Can Fly?	B	I	28	Literacy 2000	Rigby
What Can Fly?	B	I	29	Discovery Links	Newbridge
What Can Go Fast?	B	I	37	Little Red Readers	Sundance
What Can Swim?	B	I	30	Windmill Books	Rigby
What Can This Animal Do?	B	I	28	Foundations	Wright Group/McGraw Hill
What Can You Make?	B	I	22	Ready Readers	Pearson Learning Group
What Can You See?	B	I	31	Tiger Cub	Peguis
What Can You Taste?	B	I	45	Windmill Books	Rigby
What Comes from Eggs?	B	I	74	Bookshop	Mondo
What Comes Out at Night?	B	I	48	Little Red Readers	Sundance
What Could it Be?	B	RF	19	Instant Readers	Harcourt School Publishers
What Did You Bring?	B	I	23	Ready Readers	Pearson Learning Group
What Do I See?	B	I	28	Twig	Wright Group/McGraw Hill
What Do Scientists Do?	B	I	24	Twig	Wright Group/McGraw Hill
What Do You Like?	B	I	52	Little Books for Early Readers	University of Maine
What Do You Like?	B	RF	52	Storyteller	Wright Group/McGraw Hill
What Do You See?	B	I	20	Carousel Readers	Pearson Learning Group
What Feels Cold?	B	I	30	Windmill Books	Rigby
What Feels Sticky?	B	I	26	Windmill Books	Rigby
What Goes Around and Around?	B	I	46	Windmill Books	Rigby
What Goes Up?	B	I	42	Rigby Literacy	Rigby
What Grows?	B	I	21	Rigby Focus	Rigby
What Has Spots?	B	I	33	Literacy 2000	Rigby
What Is a Huggles?	B	F	41	Sunshine	Wright Group/McGraw Hill
What Is Enormous?	B	I	33	Windmill Books	Rigby
What Is Fierce?	B	I	32	Windmill Books	Rigby
What Is Green?	B	I	30	Carousel Earlybirds	Pearson Learning Group
What Is in Space?	B	I	35	Yellow Umbrella Books	Red Brick Learning
What Is in the Sky?	B	I	32	Rosen Real Readers	Rosen Publishing Group
What Is It?	B	F	35	Rigby Literacy	Rigby
What Is Noisy?	B	I	31	Windmill Books	Rigby
What Is Red?	B	I	27	Carousel Earlybirds	Pearson Learning Group
What Is Red?	B	I	30	Literacy 2000	Rigby

* Collection of short stories

TITLE	LEVEL	GENRE	WORD COUNT	AUTHOR / SERIES	PUBLISHER / DISTRIBUTOR
What Is Scary?	B	I	31	Windmill Books	Rigby
What Is Tall?	B	I	30	Windmill Books	Rigby
What Is the Weather Today?	B	I	49	Leveled Readers Science	Houghton Mifflin
What Is Under the Hat?	B	F	29	Ready Readers	Pearson Learning Group
What Is White?	B	I	26	Carousel Earlybirds	Pearson Learning Group
What Is Yellow?	B	I	26	Carousel Earlybirds	Pearson Learning Group
What Kind of Sound?	B	I	25	Yellow Umbrella Books	Red Brick Learning
What Lives in a Swamp?	B	I	36	Windows on Literacy	National Geographic
What Made This?	B	I	21	Science	Outside the Box
What Makes a Shadow?	B	I	27	Leveled Readers Science	Houghton Mifflin
What the King Likes	B	F	32	Sun Sprouts	ETA/Cuisenaire
What Time Is It?	B	RF	48	Instant Readers	Harcourt School Publishers
What Time Is It?	B	I	48	Rosen Real Readers	Rosen Publishing Group
What We Like	B	RF	43	Early Connections	Benchmark Education
What Will You Pack?	B	RF	35	Ready Readers	Pearson Learning Group
What's Behind This Door?	B	I	43	Twig	Wright Group/McGraw Hill
What's for Dinner?	B	I	35	Hoenecke, Karen	Kaeden Books
What's for Lunch?	B	F	36	Story Box	Wright Group/McGraw Hill
What's in the Box?	B	I	24	Rigby Literacy	Rigby
What's My Job?	B	I	25	Windows on Literacy	National Geographic
What's on My Farm?	B	RF	38	Rise & Shine	Hampton-Brown
What's on the Road?	B	I	34	Windows on Literacy	National Geographic
What's That Noise?	B	RF	23	Science	Outside the Box
What's That?	B	RF	33	Sunshine	Wright Group/McGraw Hill
What's the Weather?	B	RF	21	Cali, Jennifer	Scholastic
What's Up?	B	I	26	Pacific Literacy	Pacific Learning
When I Grow Up	B	RF	58	Lighthouse	Rigby
When I Look Up	B	RF	55	Foundations	Wright Group/McGraw Hill
Where Are the Babies?	B	I	8	PM Starters	Rigby
Where Are the Car Keys?	B	RF	36	Windmill	Wright Group/McGraw Hill
Where Are The Dinosaurs?	B	I	60	Bookshop	Mondo
Where Are They?	B	I	98	Rosen Real Readers	Rosen Publishing Group
Where Are We?	B	RF	72	Early Emergent	Pioneer Valley
Where Are You Going?	B	F	42	KinderReaders	Rigby
Where Can Kitty Sleep?	B	RF	15	Windmill	Wright Group/McGraw Hill
Where Can Pussy Sleep?	B	RF	15	Windmill	Wright Group/McGraw Hill
Where Can We Put an Elephant?	B	F	48	Windmill	Wright Group/McGraw Hill
Where Do We Go?	B	RF	22	Ready Readers	Pearson Learning Group
Where I Live	B	RF	36	Carousel Earlybirds	Pearson Learning Group
Where Is Gabby?	B	RF	21	Early Emergent	Pioneer Valley
Where Is It?	B	RF	21	Ready Readers	Pearson Learning Group
Where Is Lunch?	B	F	25	Pacific Literacy	Pacific Learning
Where Is My Ball?	B	F	24	The Book Project	Sundance
Where Is My Puppy?	B	RF	33	Bebop Books	Lee & Low Books Inc.
Where Is My Teacher?	B	I	43	Little Books for Early Readers	University of Maine
Where to Buy It	B	I	45	Rosen Real Readers	Rosen Publishing Group
Where's My Yellow Yo-Yo?	B	RF	36	Phonics and Friends	Hampton-Brown
Where's the Dog?	B	RF	36	Windmill Books	Rigby
Where's the Egg Cup?	B	RF	25	Windmill	Wright Group/McGraw Hill
Where's the Fish?	B	F	39	Gomi, Taro	Morrow
Which Animal?	B	I	14	Foundations	Wright Group/McGraw Hill
Which One Does Not Belong?	B	I	20	Windows on Literacy	National Geographic
Who Am I?	B	F	32	The Book Project	Sundance
Who Can Play?	B	RF	26	Sun Sprouts	ETA/Cuisenaire

* Collection of short stories

TITLE	LEVEL	GENRE	WORD COUNT	AUTHOR / SERIES	PUBLISHER / DISTRIBUTOR
Who Can?	B	RF	35	Bookshop	Mondo
Who Hid?	B	RF	25	Leber, Nancy	Scholastic
Who Keeps Us Safe?	B	I	28	Yellow Umbrella Books	Red Brick Learning
Who Likes Water?	B	F	35	KinderReaders	Rigby
Who Lives Here?	B	I	43	Windows on Literacy	National Geographic
Who Lives in a Tree?	B	I	46	Canizares, Susan; Moreton, Daniel	Scholastic
Who Lives in the Arctic?	B	I	48	Canizares, Susan; Chanko, Pamela	Scholastic
Who Lives in the Sea?	B	I	69	Bookshop	Mondo
Who Lives on a Farm?	B	I	36	Story Steps	Rigby
Who Looks After Me?	B	I	20	Windows on Literacy	National Geographic
Who Made These Tracks?	B	I	24	Literacy 2000	Rigby
Who Reads?	B	I	25	Teacher's Choice Series	Pearson Learning Group
Who Uses These Tools?	B	I	23	Twig	Wright Group/McGraw Hill
Who Wears This Hat?	B	I	42	Windmill	Wright Group/McGraw Hill
Who Will Help?	B	RF	20	Carousel Readers	Pearson Learning Group
Who's Coming for a Ride?	B	F	25	Literacy 2000	Rigby
Who's There?	B	F	49	Bookshop	Mondo
Whose Bones?	B	I	28	Fernandez, Queta	Scholastic
Whose Tracks?	B	I	14	Little Celebrations	Pearson Learning Group
Wood	B	I	26	Twig	Wright Group/McGraw Hill
Working at Home	B	I	28	Little Red Readers	Sundance
World of Birds, A	B	I	49	Bookshop	Mondo
Wow! Look at This!	B	I	34	Science	Outside the Box
Yellow	B	I	32	Literacy 2000	Rigby
Yellow Yarn Mystery, The	B	F	61	Little Books	Sadlier-Oxford
Yoga Class	B	RF	28	Bebop Books	Lee & Low Books Inc.
Yuck Soup	B	F	25	Sunshine	Wright Group/McGraw Hill
Yummy Lunch, A	B	RF	22	Early Emergent	Pioneer Valley
Zinnia, The	B	RF	34	Ray's Readers	Outside the Box
Zoo, The	B	I	31	Wonder World	Wright Group/McGraw Hill
Zoo, The	B	I	32	Handprints B	Educator's Publishing Service
Across the Seasons	C	I	75	Early Connections	Benchmark Education
All About Dinosaurs	C	I	34	Teacher's Choice Series	Pearson Learning Group
All Fall Down	C	F	72	Wildsmith, Brian	Oxford University Press
All Through the Week with Cat and Dog	C	F	91	Learn to Read	Creative Teaching Press
Alley Cat	C	RF	30	Books for Young Learners	Richard C. Owen
Along Comes Jake	C	RF	86	Sunshine	Wright Group/McGraw Hill
Alphabet Race, The	C	F	7	Visions	Wright Group/McGraw Hill
Am I Ready Now?	C	RF	41	Visions	Wright Group/McGraw Hill
Amazing Magnets	C	I	53	Twig	Wright Group/McGraw Hill
Animal Sounds	C	I	21	Visions	Wright Group/McGraw Hill
Animal Stretches	C	RF	35	Little Celebrations	Pearson Learning Group
Animals at Night	C	I	35	Windows on Literacy	National Geographic
Animals Eat	C	I	27	We Do Too Series	Pearson Learning Group
Animals Have Babies	C	I	42	We Do Too Series	Pearson Learning Group
Animals Have Homes	C	I	31	We Do Too Series	Pearson Learning Group
Animals Hide and Seek	C	I	56	Twig	Wright Group/McGraw Hill
Animals I Like to Feed	C	I	38	Little Red Readers	Sundance
Animals in the Rain Forest	C	I	33	Vocabulary Readers	Houghton Mifflin
Animals in Winter	C	I	42	Rosen Real Readers	Rosen Publishing Group
Animals Keep Warm	C	I	25	We Do Too Series	Pearson Learning Group
Animals Make Noises	C	I	19	We Do Too Series	Pearson Learning Group
Animals Play	C	I	27	We Do Too Series	Pearson Learning Group

TITLE	LEVEL	GENRE	WORD COUNT	AUTHOR / SERIES	PUBLISHER / DISTRIBUTOR
Anna's Sandwich	C	RF	33	Windmill Books	Rigby
Ants Everywhere	C	RF	24	Visions	Wright Group/McGraw Hill
Ants on a Picnic	C	F	35	Joy Readers	Pearson Learning Group
Apple Star, The	C	RF	33	First Stories	Pacific Learning
Apples	C	I	45	Williams, Deborah	Kaeden Books
Asleep	C	RF	26	Joy Readers	Pearson Learning Group
Astronaut Adventure	C	F	41	Phonics and Friends	Hampton-Brown
At Christmas	C	RF	26	Visions	Wright Group/McGraw Hill
At the Beach	C	I	74	Sun Sprouts	ETA/Cuisenaire
At the Fair	C	RF	58	Rise & Shine	Hampton-Brown
At the Farm	C	I	52	Little Red Readers	Sundance
At the Ice Cream Shop	C	I	35	Vocabulary Readers	Houghton Mifflin
At the Lake	C	RF	23	KinderReaders	Rigby
At the Library	C	I	69	PM Starters	Rigby
At the Ocean	C	RF	26	Early Emergent	Pioneer Valley
At the Park	C	I	40	Harry's Math Books	Outside the Box
At the Park	C	I	32	Bebop Books	Lee & Low Books Inc.
At the Playground	C	I	86	Little Red Readers	Sundance
At the Pool	C	I	64	Foundations	Wright Group/McGraw Hill
At the Supermarket	C	I	60	Little Red Readers	Sundance
At the Supermarket	C	RF	60	Little Readers	Houghton Mifflin
At the Toy Store	C	I	35	PM Plus Nonfiction	Rigby
At the Zoo	C	I	73	Little Red Readers	Sundance
At Work	C	I	29	Geist, Ellen	Scholastic
Awww	C	RF	35	Little Celebrations	Pearson Learning Group
Baby Animals at Home	C	I	64	Twig	Wright Group/McGraw Hill
Baby Animals Learn	C	I	52	Chanko, Pamela; Berger, Samantha	Scholastic
Baby Can Ride	C	I	67	Leveled Readers Emergent	Houghton Mifflin
Baby Food	C	RF	21	Dunn, Tansy	Scholastic
Baby in the Cart	C	RF	84	Foundations	Wright Group/McGraw Hill
Baby Lamb's First Drink	C	F	64	PM Story Books	Rigby
Baby Owls, The	C	RF	90	PM Extensions-Red	Rigby
Baby Wakes Up	C	RF	50	PM Plus Story Books	Rigby
Bags, Cans, Pots, and Pans	C	RF	56	Ready Readers	Pearson Learning Group
*Bake a Cake and other stories	C	RF	94	Story Steps	Rigby
Baking Day	C	F	35	Windmill Books	Rigby
Balancing	C	I	46	Twig	Wright Group/McGraw Hill
Ball, The	C	RF	40	KinderReaders	Rigby
Balls	C	I	33	Windows on Literacy	National Geographic
Banana Shake	C	RF	44	Book Bank	Wright Group/McGraw Hill
Band, The	C	RF	31	Voyages	SRA/McGraw Hill
Band, The	C	I	33	Sun Sprouts	ETA/Cuisenaire
Barn Dance	C	F	47	Story Box	Wright Group/McGraw Hill
Barnyard Baseball	C	F	19	Pair-It Books	Steck-Vaughn
Basketball	C	RF	23	Visions	Wright Group/McGraw Hill
Bath Time	C	I	23	Wonder World	Wright Group/McGraw Hill
Bats, The	C	I	21	Twig	Wright Group/McGraw Hill
Batter Up	C	I	8	Bebop Books	Lee & Low Books Inc.
Batter Up!	C	RF	39	Bookshop	Mondo
Bay Run, The	C	RF	80	Foundations	Wright Group/McGraw Hill
Be a Clown	C	I	29	The Candid Collection	Pearson Learning Group
Beads	C	I	16	Instant Readers	Harcourt School Publishers
Bear Eats Fish, A	C	I	44	Windows on Literacy	National Geographic

* Collection of short stories

TITLE	LEVEL	GENRE	WORD COUNT	AUTHOR / SERIES	PUBLISHER / DISTRIBUTOR
Beds	C	I	44	Interaction	Rigby
Bedtime	C	RF	23	Books for Young Learners	Richard C. Owen
Bedtime	C	RF	83	PM Plus Story Books	Rigby
Bedtime for Bear	C	F	12	Instant Readers	Harcourt School Publishers
Bee, The	C	RF	26	Story Box	Wright Group/McGraw Hill
Beetles	C	I	36	Science	Outside the Box
Being Friends	C	I	21	Rosen Real Readers	Rosen Publishing Group
Bella's Birthday	C	RF	59	Bella and Rosie Series	Pioneer Valley
Ben and the Cold	C	RF	76	Sun Sprouts	ETA/Cuisenaire
Ben Runs	C	RF	66	Sun Sprouts	ETA/Cuisenaire
Ben the Bold	C	RF	71	Literacy 2000	Rigby
Ben's Banana	C	F	60	Foundations	Wright Group/McGraw Hill
Ben's Bath	C	RF	56	Sun Sprouts	ETA/Cuisenaire
Ben's Colors	C	RF	75	Sun Sprouts	ETA/Cuisenaire
Ben's Pets	C	RF	30	Ready Readers	Pearson Learning Group
Best Friends	C	RF	34	Windows on Literacy	National Geographic
Best Friends	C	I	43	Rosen Real Readers	Rosen Publishing Group
Best Place, The	C	F	77	Leveled Readers	Houghton Mifflin
Best Place, The	C	RF	61	Literacy 2000	Rigby
Bicycle, The	C	F	29	Story Box	Wright Group/McGraw Hill
Big and Little	C	I	66	Little Readers	Houghton Mifflin
Big and Little	C	I	56	Early Connections	Benchmark Education
Big and Little	C	I	36	Sunshine	Wright Group/McGraw Hill
Big Barn, The	C	RF	81	Teacher's Choice Series	Pearson Learning Group
Big Boo Bird, The	C	F	66	Joy Readers	Pearson Learning Group
Big Enough	C	RF	49	Visions	Wright Group/McGraw Hill
Big Fish, The	C	RF	82	Early Emergent	Pioneer Valley
Big Hill, The	C	F	55	PM Plus Story Books	Rigby
Big Kick, The	C	RF	67	PM Story Books	Rigby
Big Long Animal Song	C	F	29	Little Celebrations	Pearson Learning Group
Big Sister	C	RF	44	Visions	Wright Group/McGraw Hill
Big Snowball Fight	C	RF	15	Bebop Books	Lee & Low Books Inc.
Big, Bigger, Biggest	C	I	31	Windows on Literacy	National Geographic
Big, Small, or Just Right?	C	F	40	Leveled Readers Language Support	Houghton Mifflin
Bigger and Bigger	C	I	49	Twig	Wright Group/McGraw Hill
B-I-N-G-O	C	RF	41	Tiger Cub	Peguis
Bird Feeder, The	C	I	31	Storyteller-First Snow	Wright Group/McGraw Hill
Bird Feeder, The	C	RF	40	Sun Sprouts	ETA/Cuisenaire
Bird Has Feathers, A	C	I	27	Science	Outside the Box
Bird's Bad Day	C	F	36	Instant Readers	Harcourt School Publishers
Birthday Cake for Ben, A	C	RF	59	PM Extensions-Red	Rigby
Birthday Candles	C	RF	52	Carousel Readers	Pearson Learning Group
Birthday Party, A	C	RF	47	Early Emergent	Pioneer Valley
Birthday, A	C	F	39	New Way	Steck-Vaughn
Birthday, The	C	RF	30	Harry's Math Books	Outside the Box
Birthdays	C	RF	59	Foundations	Wright Group/McGraw Hill
Black and White	C	I	32	Voyages	SRA/McGraw Hill
Blocks	C	RF	60	Early Emergent	Pioneer Valley
Blue Day	C	RF	35	Literacy 2000	Rigby
Bo and Peter	C	RF	44	Franco, Betsy	Scholastic
Bo Peep's Sheep	C	TL	39	Pair-It Books	Steck-Vaughn
Boats	C	I	100	Pebble Books	Capstone Press
Bobbie and the Parade	C	RF	49	Rigby Literacy	Rigby

* Collection of short stories

TITLE	LEVEL	GENRE	WORD COUNT	AUTHOR / SERIES	PUBLISHER / DISTRIBUTOR
Bones	C	I	56	Rigby Literacy	Rigby
Books	C	RF	21	Beginning Literacy	Scholastic
Boots	C	RF	57	Schreiber, Anne; Doughty, Arbo	Scholastic
Boots for Toots	C	F	41	Pacific Literacy	Pacific Learning
Boss	C	F	48	Foundations	Wright Group/McGraw Hill
Bottles, Boxes, and Bins	C	I	36	Twig	Wright Group/McGraw Hill
Box, The	C	RF	30	Leveled Readers Language Support	Houghton Mifflin
Breakfast	C	RF	35	Foundations	Wright Group/McGraw Hill
Breakfast	C	I	37	Little Books for Early Readers	University of Maine
Breakfast for Pickles	C	RF	62	Pickles the Dog Series	Pioneer Valley
Breakfast in Bed	C	RF	10	Voyages	SRA/McGraw Hill
Breakfast with John	C	RF	29	Books for Young Learners	Richard C. Owen
Breathing Under Water	C	I	39	Sunshine	Wright Group/McGraw Hill
Brown Bear, Brown Bear	C	F	185	Martin, Bill	Henry Holt & Co.
Brownie	C	RF	38	Hooker, Karen	Continental Press
Bubbles	C	RF	31	Sunshine	Wright Group/McGraw Hill
Bubbles	C	RF	33	Literacy 2000	Rigby
Bubbles	C	I	34	Discovery Links	Newbridge
Bubbles Everywhere	C	I	41	Twig	Wright Group/McGraw Hill
Buckle My Shoe	C	RF	31	Sunshine	Wright Group/McGraw Hill
Bugs!	C	F	32	Rookie Readers	Children's Press
Buildings	C	I	61	Chessen, Betsey; Chanko, Pamela	Scholastic
Bump!	C	F	12	KinderReaders	Rigby
Bumper Cars, The	C	RF	94	PM Extensions-Red	Rigby
Bus Ride, The	C	F	175	Reading Unlimited	Pearson Learning Group
Bus Ride, The	C	F	164	Little Celebrations	Pearson Learning Group
Bus, The	C	I	46	Twig	Wright Group/McGraw Hill
Buster	C	I	36	Twig	Wright Group/McGraw Hill
Busy Mosquito, The	C	F	112	Foundations	Wright Group/McGraw Hill
Busy People	C	RF	40	Little Celebrations	Pearson Learning Group
Butterflies	C	I	16	Instant Readers	Harcourt School Publishers
Butterfly, The	C	I	21	Science	Outside the Box
Buttons	C	RF	81	First Stories	Pacific Learning
Buzzing Flies	C	RF	45	Sunshine	Wright Group/McGraw Hill
Cactus Town	C	RF	43	Sunshine	Wright Group/McGraw Hill
Cake, The	C	I	40	Sun Sprouts	ETA/Cuisenaire
Call 911	C	I	22	Twig	Wright Group/McGraw Hill
Camping	C	RF	49	Foundations	Wright Group/McGraw Hill
Can I Have a Lick?	C	RF	69	Carousel Readers	Pearson Learning Group
Can I Play?	C	F	30	The Book Project	Sundance
Can We Go?	C	RF	25	Cherrington, Janelle	Scholastic
Can You Fly?	C	I	51	Foundations	Wright Group/McGraw Hill
Can You Read a Map?	C	F	38	Learn to Read	Creative Teaching Press
Can You See Me?	C	I	48	Foundations	Wright Group/McGraw Hill
Can You See the Eggs?	C	I	87	PM Starters	Rigby
Caring	C	I	47	Interaction	Rigby
Caring for Our Pets	C	I	74	Early Connections	Benchmark Education
Carrot, The	C	F	48	Leveled Readers Language Support	Houghton Mifflin
Cars	C	I	30	Little Readers	Houghton Mifflin
Cat and Dog	C	F	71	Learn to Read	Creative Teaching Press
Cat Prints	C	RF	25	Pair-It Books	Steck-Vaughn
Cat, The	C	RF	23	Smart Starts	Rigby

* Collection of short stories

TITLE	LEVEL	GENRE	WORD COUNT	AUTHOR / SERIES	PUBLISHER / DISTRIBUTOR
Cats	C	I	45	Williams, Deborah	Kaeden Books
Cave, The	C	RF	67	Book Bank	Wright Group/McGraw Hill
Chalk Talk	C	I	69	Storyteller-First Snow	Wright Group/McGraw Hill
Champions	C	I	13	Twig	Wright Group/McGraw Hill
Charles	C	RF	48	Learn to Read	Creative Teaching Press
Cheese, Please?	C	RF	62	Story Steps	Rigby
Chew, Chew, Chew	C	RF	24	Literacy 2000	Rigby
Chicken and Egg Chores	C	RF	27	Little Books for Early Readers	University of Maine
Chicken for Dinner	C	RF	27	Story Box	Wright Group/McGraw Hill
Children	C	I	45	Pebble Books	Capstone Press
Child's Day, A	C	RF	34	Sunshine	Wright Group/McGraw Hill
City Life	C	I	32	Rosen Real Readers	Rosen Publishing Group
City Senses	C	I	85	Twig	Wright Group/McGraw Hill
Clay Today!	C	RF	37	Learn to Read	Creative Teaching Press
Cleaning Day	C	RF	26	Bebop Books	Lee & Low Books Inc.
Clever Happy Monkey	C	F	28	Joy Readers	Pearson Learning Group
Climbing	C	F	34	Literacy 2000	Rigby
Clothes	C	I	25	Interaction	Rigby
Clouds	C	RF	44	Science	Outside the Box
Clouds	C	I	67	Handprints C, Set 1	Educator's Publishing Service
Clown and Elephant	C	F	38	Story Box	Wright Group/McGraw Hill
Cocoons and Cases	C	I	59	Rigby Literacy	Rigby
Come and Play, Cats!	C	RF	45	Early Emergent	Pioneer Valley
Come Play With Me	C	F	36	Little Readers	Houghton Mifflin
Come to My House	C	F	56	Joy Readers	Pearson Learning Group
Come with Me	C	RF	25	Story Box	Wright Group/McGraw Hill
Cool Off	C	RF	37	Bookshop	Mondo
Copycat	C	F	54	Story Box	Wright Group/McGraw Hill
Costume Party	C	RF	64	Early Connections	Benchmark Education
Costumes	C	I	36	Pebble Books	Capstone Press
Costumes	C	RF	23	Oxford Reading Tree	Oxford University Press
Counting Seeds	C	I	63	Early Connections	Benchmark Education
Courtney's Twos	C	RF	30	Harry's Math Books	Outside the Box
Cowboy, The	C	RF	35	Step-By-Step Series	Pearson Learning Group
Crawl, Caterpillar, Crawl!	C	RF	24	Pair-It Books	Steck-Vaughn
Cross-Country Race	C	RF	33	Windmill Books	Rigby
Crossing the Creek	C	F	35	Learn to Read	Creative Teaching Press
Curly Is Hungry	C	F	41	Rigby Literacy	Rigby
Dad and I	C	RF	59	Rise & Shine	Hampton-Brown
Dan the Flying Man	C	F	60	Story Box	Wright Group/McGraw Hill
Dance, The	C	F	35	Learn to Read	Creative Teaching Press
Dancing	C	RF	38	Visions	Wright Group/McGraw Hill
Danger	C	RF	66	Story Box	Wright Group/McGraw Hill
Danny and the Four Seasons	C	RF	55	Coulter, Mia	Maryruth Books
Day at School, A	C	RF	38	Sunshine	Wright Group/McGraw Hill
Day with My Dad, A	C	RF	88	Fiesta Series	Pearson Learning Group
Day with Your Dog, A	C	I	32	Rosen Real Readers	Rosen Publishing Group
Desert Day	C	I	23	Twig	Wright Group/McGraw Hill
Desert, The	C	I	34	Carousel Readers	Pearson Learning Group
Dig	C	F	20	KinderReaders	Rigby
Divers, The	C	I	25	Wonder World	Wright Group/McGraw Hill
Dogs Learn Every Day	C	I	38	Vocabulary Readers	Houghton Mifflin
Don't Leave Anything Behind!	C	RF	26	Literacy 2000	Rigby

* Collection of short stories

TITLE	LEVEL	GENRE	WORD COUNT	AUTHOR / SERIES	PUBLISHER / DISTRIBUTOR
Down the Hill	C	RF	94	New Way Red	Steck-Vaughn
Down the Hill	C	RF	32	KinderReaders	Rigby
Dragon, The	C	F	130	Sunshine	Wright Group/McGraw Hill
Dragon's Dream	C	F	34	Learn to Read	Creative Teaching Press
Dream Horse	C	F	47	Pair-It Books	Steck-Vaughn
Dressing Up	C	RF	31	Literacy 2000	Rigby
Dressing-up Box, The	C	RF	61	Book Bank	Wright Group/McGraw Hill
Early in the Morning	C	RF	56	Windows on Literacy	National Geographic
Ears	C	I	37	Rise & Shine	Hampton-Brown
Eating Out	C	RF	31	Sunshine	Wright Group/McGraw Hill
Eek! Look at This!	C	I	66	Rigby Literacy	Rigby
Egg, The	C	F	48	Joy Readers	Pearson Learning Group
Eggs	C	I	30	Windows on Literacy	National Geographic
Elephant Walk	C	F	44	Sunshine	Wright Group/McGraw Hill
Elephant Walk	C	RF	50	Rigby Literacy	Rigby
Elephants	C	F	224	Phonics and Friends	Hampton-Brown
Elephant's Trunk, An	C	F	31	Little Celebrations	Pearson Learning Group
Emily's Babysitter	C	RF	67	Emergent	Pioneer Valley
End, The	C	RF	106	Tiger Cub	Peguis
Enormous Egg, The	C	F	52	Learn to Read	Creative Teaching Press
Every Monday	C	F	52	Pair-It Books	Steck-Vaughn
Everyone Eats	C	I	44	Discovery Links	Newbridge
Eyes	C	I	64	Wonder World	Wright Group/McGraw Hill
Families	C	I	32	Rosen Real Readers	Rosen Publishing Group
Family Bike Ride	C	RF	55	Handprints C, Set 1	Educator's Publishing Service
Family of Five, A	C	F	26	Pair-It Books	Steck-Vaughn
Family Pets	C	I	37	Pebble Books	Capstone Press
Farm Concert, The	C	F	74	Story Box	Wright Group/McGraw Hill
Farm in Spring, The	C	I	69	PM Starters	Rigby
Farmer Brown's Garden	C	F	48	Windmill Books	Rigby
Fast Athletes	C	I	104	Careers Series	Benchmark Education
Fast, Faster, Fastest	C	I	66	Twig	Wright Group/McGraw Hill
Feeding the Baby	C	I	51	Home Connection Collection	Rigby
Feeding Time	C	RF	55	Carousel Readers	Pearson Learning Group
Felix, the Very Hungry Fish	C	F	32	Little Books	Sadlier-Oxford
Ferry, The	C	RF	27	Sunshine	Wright Group/McGraw Hill
Fiesta Time	C	I	28	Little Celebrations	Pearson Learning Group
Filbert the Fly	C	F	28	Literacy 2000	Rigby
Find It	C	RF	63	Carousel Earlybirds	Pearson Learning Group
Fingerprint Family	C	I	24	Rigby Literacy	Rigby
Fireworks	C	RF	29	Joy Readers	Pearson Learning Group
First and Last	C	I	44	Teacher's Choice Series	Pearson Learning Group
Fish and the Cat, The	C	F	91	Sun Sprouts	ETA/Cuisenaire
Fish Bowl, The	C	I	48	Sun Sprouts	ETA/Cuisenaire
Fish Stew for Supper	C	I	56	First Stories	Pacific Learning
Fishing	C	RF	15	Instant Readers	Harcourt School Publishers
Fishing	C	RF	35	Story Box	Wright Group/McGraw Hill
Fishing	C	RF	63	PM Starters	Rigby
Fishing	C	I	35	KinderReaders	Rigby
Fishy Story, A	C	F	102	Pair-It Books	Steck-Vaughn
Fitness	C	F	60	Foundations	Wright Group/McGraw Hill
Five Senses, The	C	I	53	Rigby Focus	Rigby
Flat Hat, The	C	I	24	KinderReaders	Rigby

* Collection of short stories

TITLE	LEVEL	GENRE	WORD COUNT	AUTHOR / SERIES	PUBLISHER / DISTRIBUTOR
Flight Deck	C	I	30	Wonder World	Wright Group/McGraw Hill
Floating	C	I	29	Little Blue Readers	Sundance
Flower Girl, The	C	RF	90	PM Extensions-Red	Rigby
Flying	C	F	26	Story Box	Wright Group/McGraw Hill
Flying	C	I	49	Crews, Donald	Mulberry Books
Folk Dancer	C	I	36	The Candid Collection	Pearson Learning Group
Follow the Leader	C	RF	62	First Stories	Pacific Learning
Footprints	C	I	69	Rigby Focus	Rigby
Four Ice Creams	C	RF	61	PM Starters	Rigby
Four Seasons, The	C	RF	20	Learn to Read	Creative Teaching Press
Fox on the Box, The	C	RF	36	Little Readers	Houghton Mifflin
Fox on the Box, The	C	RF	36	Start to Read	School Zone
Fox, The	C	RF	24	Books for Young Learners	Richard C. Owen
Friends Share	C	I	34	Vocabulary Readers	Houghton Mifflin
Frogs	C	I	34	Pair-It Books	Steck-Vaughn
Frogs	C	F	36	Joy Readers	Pearson Learning Group
Frogs Can Jump	C	I	41	Book Bank	Wright Group/McGraw Hill
Fun and Games, Then and Now	C	I	42	Independent Readers Social Studies	Houghton Mifflin
Fun at School	C	RF	50	Foundations	Wright Group/McGraw Hill
Fun Food	C	I	29	Home Connection Collection	Rigby
Fun on the Slide	C	RF	37	Early Emergent	Pioneer Valley
Fun with Mo and Toots	C	F	41	Pacific Literacy	Pacific Learning
Fun with Simple Machines	C	RF	28	Tarlow, Ellen	Scholastic
Gabby Is Hungry	C	RF	78	Emergent	Pioneer Valley
Games	C	RF	69	Berger, Samantha; Moreton, Daniel	Scholastic
Garbage	C	I	51	Wonder World	Wright Group/McGraw Hill
Getting Fit	C	I	15	Wonder World	Wright Group/McGraw Hill
Getting Ready for School	C	I	109	Little Red Readers	Sundance
Getting Ready for the Ball	C	F	27	Literacy 2000	Rigby
Giant and the Boy, The	C	F	44	Sunshine	Wright Group/McGraw Hill
Giant's Pizza, The	C	RF	28	Joy Readers	Pearson Learning Group
Giant's Rice, The	C	F	28	Joy Readers	Pearson Learning Group
Giant-Size Hamburger, A	C	F	38	Wonder World	Wright Group/McGraw Hill
Giddy Up	C	RF	49	Cat on the Mat	Oxford University Press
Gillian's Nines	C	RF	29	Harry's Math Books	Outside the Box
Glitter Trouble	C	RF	32	Learn to Read	Creative Teaching Press
Goat, The	C	RF	17	KinderReaders	Rigby
Going Fishing	C	RF	30	Visions	Wright Group/McGraw Hill
Going for a Ride	C	RF	52	Early Emergent	Pioneer Valley
Going Places	C	I	32	Rosen Real Readers	Rosen Publishing Group
Going to Grandpa's	C	RF	37	Frankford, Marilyn	Kaeden Books
Going to School	C	I	30	Windows on Literacy	National Geographic
Going to School	C	I	43	Story Box	Wright Group/McGraw Hill
Going to School	C	I	50	Sunshine	Wright Group/McGraw Hill
Going to the Beach	C	RF	75	Carousel Readers	Pearson Learning Group
Going to the Park	C	RF	41	Home Connection Collection	Rigby
Going to the Park with Grandaddy	C	RF	30	Visions	Wright Group/McGraw Hill
Goldilocks	C	TL	19	Tarlow, Ellen	Scholastic
Goldilocks and the Three Bears	C	TL	54	Little Books	Sadlier-Oxford
Good Dog	C	RF	43	Sun Sprouts	ETA/Cuisenaire
Good Home, A	C	F	77	Leveled Readers Language Support	Houghton Mifflin

* Collection of short stories

TITLE	LEVEL	GENRE	WORD COUNT	AUTHOR / SERIES	PUBLISHER / DISTRIBUTOR
Good Morning!	C	F	51	Science	Outside the Box
Good Old Mom	C	RF	34	Oxford Reading Tree	Oxford University Press
Good-bye, Zoo	C	RF	48	Ready Readers	Pearson Learning Group
Grab Bag, The	C	RF	85	PM Plus Story Books	Rigby
Grab It!	C	RF	45	Leveled Readers Language Support	Houghton Mifflin
Grandfathers	C	I	41	Pebble Books	Capstone Press
Grandmother and I	C	RF	53	Home Connection Collection	Rigby
Grandmother Is Tired	C	RF	31	Joy Readers	Pearson Learning Group
Grandmothers	C	I	50	Pebble Books	Capstone Press
Grandpa	C	RF	61	Rigby Literacy	Rigby
Grandpa and I	C	RF	40	Home Connection Collection	Rigby
Grandpa's Visit	C	RF	38	Vocabulary Readers	Houghton Mifflin
Gregory's Dog	C	RF	23	Cat on the Mat	Oxford University Press
Growing	C	I	42	Story Steps	Rigby
Growing a Plant	C	I	43	Early Connections	Benchmark Education
Growing Up Is Fun	C	I	87	The Candid Collection	Pearson Learning Group
Grumpy Grizzly	C	RF	40	Learn to Read	Creative Teaching Press
Guess What the Moon Saw?	C	RF	38	Home Connection Collection	Rigby
Guess What the Sun Saw?	C	RF	36	Home Connection Collection	Rigby
Guinea Pigs	C	I	34	Sun Sprouts	ETA/Cuisenaire
Hair	C	I	60	Sun Sprouts	ETA/Cuisenaire
Hair	C	RF	35	Little Celebrations	Pearson Learning Group
Halloween	C	RF	87	Handprints C, Set 1	Educator's Publishing Service
Halloween Mask for Monster	C	F	38	Mueller, Virginia	Whitman
Hands	C	RF	39	Literacy 2000	Rigby
Hands at Work	C	I	50	Windows on Literacy	National Geographic
Happy 100th Day!	C	RF	35	Little Celebrations	Pearson Learning Group
Happy Birthday	C	F	26	Instant Readers	Harcourt School Publishers
Happy Birthday!	C	RF	28	Literacy 2000	Rigby
Happy Birthday, Frog	C	F	87	Story Box	Wright Group/McGraw Hill
Happy Face, Sad Face	C	I	77	Foundations	Wright Group/McGraw Hill
Happy Monkey in the Shed	C	F	30	Joy Readers	Pearson Learning Group
Hat Trick	C	RF	38	Literacy 2000	Rigby
Hats	C	RF	43	Little Readers	Houghton Mifflin
Hats	C	RF	35	Joy Readers	Pearson Learning Group
Hats	C	I	27	Twig	Wright Group/McGraw Hill
Hats!	C	F	28	Learn to Read	Creative Teaching Press
Have You Seen?	C	RF	38	Literacy 2000	Rigby
Heat and Eat!	C	I	79	Independent Readers Science	Houghton Mifflin
Hedgehog Is Hungry	C	RF	48	PM Story Books	Rigby
Hello	C	F	63	Story Box	Wright Group/McGraw Hill
Hello Puppet	C	I	26	Voyages	SRA/McGraw Hill
Hello, Friend	C	F	39	Instant Readers	Harcourt School Publishers
Help Me!	C	F	55	New Way Red	Steck-Vaughn
Help!	C	RF	57	Rigby Literacy	Rigby
Help!	C	I	57	Reading Corners	Pearson Learning Group
"Help!" Said Jed	C	TL	35	Instant Readers	Harcourt School Publishers
Helping Dad	C	RF	34	Sunshine	Wright Group/McGraw Hill
Here Comes the Rain!	C	I	47	Little Books	Sadlier-Oxford
Here Is a Carrot	C	I	96	Foundations	Wright Group/McGraw Hill
Here Is a Seed	C	RF	23	Science	Outside the Box
Here's a House	C	I	45	Windmill	Wright Group/McGraw Hill

* Collection of short stories

TITLE	LEVEL	GENRE	WORD COUNT	AUTHOR / SERIES	PUBLISHER / DISTRIBUTOR
Here's What I Made	C	RF	38	Literacy 2000	Rigby
Hey Coach!	C	RF	37	TOTTS	Tott Publications
Hey There, Bear!	C	F	39	Little Celebrations	Pearson Learning Group
Hickory, Dickory Pizza Clock	C	F	92	Little Celebrations	Pearson Learning Group
Hide!	C	F	81	Sun Sprouts	ETA/Cuisenaire
Hide-and-Go-Seek	C	F	66	First Stories	Pacific Learning
Hike at Day Camp, The	C	RF	32	Visions	Wright Group/McGraw Hill
Homes	C	I	69	Storyteller Nonfiction	Wright Group/McGraw Hill
Homes Around the World	C	I	73	Early Connections	Benchmark Education
Hop and Stop	C	RF	35	Books for Young Learners	Richard C. Owen
Hot and Cold	C	I	47	Windows on Literacy	National Geographic
Hot Dogs (Sausages)	C	RF	84	PM Story Books	Rigby
Hot Potato and Cold Potato	C	I	77	Foundations	Wright Group/McGraw Hill
Hot Sidewalks	C	RF	28	Visions	Wright Group/McGraw Hill
House	C	I	47	Little Celebrations	Pearson Learning Group
House for Me, A	C	I	71	Twig	Wright Group/McGraw Hill
Houses	C	I	35	Little Celebrations	Pearson Learning Group
Houses	C	RF	38	Windmill	Wright Group/McGraw Hill
Houses	C	I	64	Story Box	Wright Group/McGraw Hill
How Many Frogs?	C	I	44	Leveled Readers Language Support	Houghton Mifflin
How Many Kittens?	C	I	37	Twig	Wright Group/McGraw Hill
How Many Legs?	C	F	47	Science	Outside the Box
How Many?	C	I	45	Learn to Read	Creative Teaching Press
How to Make a Hot Dog	C	I	48	Story Box	Wright Group/McGraw Hill
How to Make a Sandwich	C	I	27	Visions	Wright Group/McGraw Hill
How to Make Can Stilts	C	I	28	Story Box	Wright Group/McGraw Hill
How to Make Snack Mix	C	I	47	Oppenlander, Meredith	Kaeden Books
Hug Is Warm, A	C	F	60	Sunshine	Wright Group/McGraw Hill
Humpity-Bump!	C	F	36	Little Celebrations	Pearson Learning Group
Humpty Dumpty	C	F	42	Seedlings	Continental Press
Hungry Bear	C	F	22	Smart Starts	Rigby
Hungry Goat, The	C	F	33	Rise & Shine	Hampton-Brown
Hungry Hedgehog	C	F	79	Story Steps	Rigby
Hungry Kitten	C	F	50	Teacher's Choice Series	Pearson Learning Group
I Am a Bookworm	C	F	32	Sunshine	Wright Group/McGraw Hill
I Am a Dentist	C	I	20	Read-More Books	Pearson Learning Group
I Am an Artist	C	I	30	Rosen Real Readers	Rosen Publishing Group
I Am Busy	C	RF	43	Windows on Literacy	National Geographic
I Am Special	C	RF	38	Learn to Read	Creative Teaching Press
I Can	C	RF	27	Visions	Wright Group/McGraw Hill
I Can Dig	C	I	45	Can You Do This?	SRA/McGraw Hill
I Can Do Anything!	C	RF	21	Sunshine	Wright Group/McGraw Hill
I Can Do It Myself	C	RF	37	Literacy 2000	Rigby
I Can Do Many Things	C	RF	43	Carousel Readers	Pearson Learning Group
I Can Draw	C	RF	37	Learn to Read	Creative Teaching Press
I Can Draw	C	RF	75	Carousel Earlybirds	Pearson Learning Group
I Can Eat	C	I	51	Can You Do This?	SRA/McGraw Hill
I Can Fly	C	F	68	Lighthouse	Rigby
I Can Jump	C	F	40	Sunshine	Wright Group/McGraw Hill
I Can Paint a Picture	C	I	26	Rosen Real Readers	Rosen Publishing Group
I Can Play	C	I	45	Can You Do This?	SRA/McGraw Hill
I Can Read	C	RF	38	Teacher's Choice Series	Pearson Learning Group
I Can Read Anything	C	F	42	Sunshine	Wright Group/McGraw Hill

* Collection of short stories

TITLE	LEVEL	GENRE	WORD COUNT	AUTHOR / SERIES	PUBLISHER / DISTRIBUTOR
I Can Ride	C	I	66	Can You Do This?	SRA/McGraw Hill
I Can Take Care of the Earth	C	I	72	Independent Readers Science	Houghton Mifflin
I Can Taste	C	I	31	Teacher's Choice Series	Pearson Learning Group
I Can Wash	C	RF	66	Carousel Earlybirds	Pearson Learning Group
I Can't See	C	RF	36	Little Celebrations	Pearson Learning Group
I Climb	C	I	57	This Is the Way I Go	SRA/McGraw Hill
I Crawl	C	I	56	This Is the Way I Go	SRA/McGraw Hill
I Dress Up Like Mama	C	RF	35	Visions	Wright Group/McGraw Hill
I Eat Leaves	C	I	47	Bookshop	Mondo
I Feel Cold	C	RF	57	Home Connection Collection	Rigby
I Feel Hot	C	RF	58	Home Connection Collection	Rigby
I Fly	C	I	57	This Is the Way I Go	SRA/McGraw Hill
I Found a Can	C	I	33	Twig	Wright Group/McGraw Hill
I Get Ready for School	C	RF	37	Visions	Wright Group/McGraw Hill
I Grow Too!	C	I	30	Start to Read	School Zone
I Have a Watch!	C	RF	60	Williams, Deborah	Kaeden Books
I Have Shoes	C	RF	24	Visions	Wright Group/McGraw Hill
I Jump	C	I	56	This Is the Way I Go	SRA/McGraw Hill
I Like	C	RF	24	Literacy 2000	Rigby
I Like Dogs	C	RF	35	Rigby Literacy	Rigby
I Like Green	C	RF	47	Literacy 2000	Rigby
I Like Painting	C	RF	42	Little Red Readers	Sundance
I Like to Count	C	RF	40	Ready Readers	Pearson Learning Group
I Like to Eat	C	RF	56	Sunshine	Wright Group/McGraw Hill
I Like to Find Things	C	I	40	Sunshine	Wright Group/McGraw Hill
I Like to Jump	C	F	50	Rigby Literacy	Rigby
I Like to Play	C	RF	50	Carousel Readers	Pearson Learning Group
I Like to Ride	C	RF	72	Little Readers	Houghton Mifflin
I Like to Write	C	RF	62	Carousel Readers	Pearson Learning Group
I Live on a Farm	C	I	42	Read-More Books	Pearson Learning Group
I Love a Parade	C	I	38	Yellow Umbrella Books	Red Brick Learning
I Love Bugs	C	RF	40	Bookshop	Mondo
I Love Ladybugs	C	RF	68	Van Allen, Roach	Wright Group/McGraw Hill
I Love Music	C	RF	41	Carousel Readers	Pearson Learning Group
I Make Clay Pots	C	I	29	Bebop Books	Lee & Low Books Inc.
I Need . . .	C	RF	23	Ray's Readers	Outside the Box
I Picked a Flower	C	RF	33	Science	Outside the Box
I Play Soccer	C	RF	31	Bebop Books	Lee & Low Books Inc.
I Remember	C	RF	26	Literacy 2000	Rigby
I Run	C	I	56	This Is the Way I Go	SRA/McGraw Hill
I See	C	RF	29	Teacher's Choice Series	Pearson Learning Group
I See Flags	C	I	31	Blevins, Wiley	Scholastic
I See Monkeys	C	RF	39	Williams, Deborah	Kaeden Books
I See Patterns	C	I	43	Yellow Umbrella Books	Red Brick Learning
I See You	C	I	56	Twig	Wright Group/McGraw Hill
I Spy	C	RF	29	Literacy Tree	Rigby
I Swim	C	I	57	This Is the Way I Go	SRA/McGraw Hill
I Thought I Couldn't	C	RF	40	Visions	Wright Group/McGraw Hill
I Want a Pet	C	RF	46	Start to Read	School Zone
I Want a Pet	C	RF	46	Little Readers	Houghton Mifflin
I Want Ice Cream	C	RF	18	Story Box	Wright Group/McGraw Hill
I Went to the Beach	C	RF	25	Books for Young Learners	Richard C. Owen
I Went Walking	C	RF	105	Williams, Sue	Harcourt Trade
I Wonder	C	RF	49	Little Celebrations	Pearson Learning Group

* Collection of short stories

TITLE	LEVEL	GENRE	WORD COUNT	AUTHOR / SERIES	PUBLISHER / DISTRIBUTOR
I Write	C	RF	19	Sunshine	Wright Group/McGraw Hill
Ice Cream	C	RF	49	Sunshine	Wright Group/McGraw Hill
If You Meet a Dragon	C	F	31	Story Box	Wright Group/McGraw Hill
I'm Bigger Than You!	C	F	48	Sunshine	Wright Group/McGraw Hill
I'm Hungry	C	RF	37	Visions	Wright Group/McGraw Hill
I'm Not, I'm Not	C	RF	19	Windmill	Wright Group/McGraw Hill
In My Bed	C	RF	57	Literacy 2000	Rigby
In My Garden	C	RF	36	Carousel Readers	Pearson Learning Group
In My Room	C	F	44	Literacy 2000	Rigby
In Nonna's Kitchen	C	I	32	Home Connection Collection	Rigby
In Ravi's Fort	C	RF	78	Lighthouse	Rigby
In the Arctic	C	I	43	Science	Outside the Box
In the Box	C	RF	64	Leveled Readers Emergent	Houghton Mifflin
In the Box	C	RF	33	Phonics and Friends	Hampton-Brown
In the City	C	RF	50	Rise & Shine	Hampton-Brown
In the City	C	RF	45	Pasternac, Susana	Scholastic
In the Dark Forest	C	I	24	Pacific Literacy	Pacific Learning
In the Forest	C	RF	42	Twig	Wright Group/McGraw Hill
In the Forest	C	F	71	Schiller, Melissa	Scholastic
In the Kitchen	C	I	16	Canizares, Susan; Chessen, Betsey	Scholastic
In the Sea	C	I	41	Sunshine	Wright Group/McGraw Hill
In the Toy Shop	C	F	29	The Book Project	Sundance
In the Van	C	RF	55	Leveled Readers	Houghton Mifflin
In Went Goldilocks	C	TL	30	Literacy 2000	Rigby
Insect and Spider	C	F	50	Science	Outside the Box
Is It Alive?	C	RF	26	Learn to Read	Creative Teaching Press
Is it almost ready?	C	RF	53	Book Bus	Creative Edge
Is It Hot? Is It Not?	C	I	30	Phonics Readers	Compass Point Books
Is It Metal?	C	I	19	Rigby Focus	Rigby
Is It Time?	C	RF	52	Campbell, J. G.	Scholastic
Is This a Monster?	C	F	93	Bookshop	Mondo
Itch! Itch!	C	RF	76	Bookshop	Mondo
It's Football Time	C	RF	24	Geddes, Diana	Kaeden Books
It's Melting	C	RF	16	Learn to Read	Creative Teaching Press
It's Raining!	C	I	32	Pair-It Books	Steck-Vaughn
It's Too Loud	C	I	53	Independent Readers Science	Houghton Mifflin
I've Lost My Boot	C	RF	18	Windmill	Wright Group/McGraw Hill
J: My Name Is Jess	C	RF	61	Little Books	Sadlier-Oxford
Jack and Billy	C	RF	50	PM Plus Story Books	Rigby
Jackets	C	RF	42	Joy Readers	Pearson Learning Group
Jack's Birthday	C	RF	89	PM Plus Story Books	Rigby
Jack's Pack	C	I	22	KinderReaders	Rigby
Jake's Map	C	RF	63	Leveled Readers Language Support	Houghton Mifflin
Jan's New Fan	C	RF	34	KinderReaders	Rigby
Jill Jumps	C	F	35	Ray's Readers	Outside the Box
Jobs at Home	C	I	35	Leveled Readers Language Support	Houghton Mifflin
Jobs Up High	C	I	62	Early Connections	Benchmark Education
Joshua James Likes Trucks	C	RF	50	Rookie Readers	Children's Press
Juicy Peach	C	RF	18	Bebop Books	Lee & Low Books Inc.
July 4th	C	RF	20	Instant Readers	Harcourt School Publishers
Jump and Thump!	C	RF	18	Home Connection Collection	Rigby
Jump, Frog	C	F	33	Stewart, Josie; Salem, Lynn	Continental Press

* Collection of short stories

TITLE	LEVEL	GENRE	WORD COUNT	AUTHOR / SERIES	PUBLISHER / DISTRIBUTOR
Jumping Shoes	C	RF	34	Joy Readers	Pearson Learning Group
Junk Box, The	C	RF	54	Windmill Books	Rigby
Just Add Water	C	I	41	Discovery World	Rigby
Just Like Grandpa	C	RF	49	Little Celebrations	Pearson Learning Group
Just Like You!	C	F	28	Instant Readers	Harcourt School Publishers
Just Me	C	RF	51	Literacy 2000	Rigby
Just Right!	C	F	75	Leveled Readers	Houghton Mifflin
Kay's Birthday	C	RF	26	KinderReaders	Rigby
Keeping Baby Animals Safe	C	I	56	Little Books	Sadlier-Oxford
Keeping Cool	C	I	18	Pacific Literacy	Pacific Learning
King's Ring, The	C	F	38	KinderReaders	Rigby
Kink the Mink	C	F	18	KinderReaders	Rigby
Kip and Tip	C	I	24	KinderReaders	Rigby
Kites	C	RF	42	Ling, Bettina	Scholastic
Kites	C	RF	41	Joy Readers	Pearson Learning Group
Kitten Chased a Fly	C	RF	57	Windmill	Wright Group/McGraw Hill
Kittens	C	RF	22	Literacy 2000	Rigby
Kitty and the Birds	C	F	64	PM Story Books	Rigby
Kitty Cat	C	RF	57	PM Plus Story Books	Rigby
Knock, Knock	C	F	56	Little Celebrations	Pearson Learning Group
Laundry Day	C	RF	28	Bebop Books	Lee & Low Books Inc.
Lazy Pig, The	C	F	78	PM Story Books	Rigby
Leaves	C	I	29	Hoenecke, Karen	Kaeden Books
Leaves, Fruits, Seeds, and Roots	C	I	26	Pacific Literacy	Pacific Learning
Legs, Legs, Legs	C	I	36	Wonder World	Wright Group/McGraw Hill
Let's Celebrate	C	I	33	Rise & Shine	Hampton-Brown
Let's Go	C	RF	30	Windmill	Wright Group/McGraw Hill
Let's Go Shopping	C	I	34	Rise & Shine	Hampton-Brown
Let's Have a Swim	C	F	74	Sunshine	Wright Group/McGraw Hill
Let's Paint	C	RF	51	Rise & Shine	Hampton-Brown
Let's Play Ball	C	F	68	New Way Red	Steck-Vaughn
Let's Pretend	C	RF	82	PM Plus Story Books	Rigby
Levi Sings	C	RF	29	Teacher's Choice Series	Pearson Learning Group
Library, The	C	RF	33	Carousel Readers	Pearson Learning Group
Light	C	I	30	Twig	Wright Group/McGraw Hill
Lights Go On	C	I	45	Windows on Literacy	National Geographic
Lin's Backpack	C	RF	49	Little Celebrations	Pearson Learning Group
Little and Big	C	I	57	Little Red Readers	Sundance
Little Bike, The	C	F	29	Joy Readers	Pearson Learning Group
Little Bo-Peep	C	F	48	Seedlings	Continental Press
Little Brother	C	RF	31	Story Box	Wright Group/McGraw Hill
Little Chimp	C	F	50	PM Plus Story Books	Rigby
Little Chimp and Big Chimp	C	RF	66	PM Plus Story Books	Rigby
Little Cousins' Visit, The	C	RF	123	Emergent	Pioneer Valley
Little Fish	C	F	192	Tiger Cub	Peguis
Little Hearts	C	RF	44	Story Box	Wright Group/McGraw Hill
Little Lady, The	C	RF	37	Ray's Readers	Outside the Box
Little Mouse	C	F	59	Handprints B	Educator's Publishing Service
Little Pig	C	F	63	Story Box	Wright Group/McGraw Hill
Little Sister	C	RF	40	Mitchell, Robin	Scholastic
Little Snowman, The	C	RF	59	PM Extensions-Red	Rigby
Living Things	C	I	57	Independent Readers Science	Houghton Mifflin
Living Things	C	I	43	Leveled Readers Science	Houghton Mifflin

* Collection of short stories

TITLE	LEVEL	GENRE	WORD COUNT	AUTHOR / SERIES	PUBLISHER / DISTRIBUTOR
Living Things Need Water	C	I	26	Windows on Literacy	National Geographic
Lizard on a Stick	C	RF	38	Wonder World	Wright Group/McGraw Hill
Log, The	C	RF	29	New Way Red	Steck-Vaughn
Look Again	C	I	47	Bookshop	Mondo
Look at Danny	C	RF	39	Coulter, Mia	Macmillan
Look at Me	C	RF	62	Early Connections	Benchmark Education
Look at My Weaving	C	I	69	First Stories	Pacific Learning
Look at This Mess!	C	RF	50	First Stories	Pacific Learning
Look Out the Window	C	RF	67	Story Steps	Rigby
Look Out, Fish!	C	F	65	Lighthouse	Rigby
Look!	C	RF	43	Little Celebrations	Pearson Learning Group
Look! Bugs!	C	I	32	Seedlings	Continental Press
Looking After a Dog	C	I	58	Sun Sprouts	ETA/Cuisenaire
Looking at Plants	C	I	44	Leveled Readers Science	Houghton Mifflin
Looking Down	C	RF	70	PM Starters	Rigby
Looking for Eggs	C	RF	47	Windmill Books	Rigby
Looks Like Rain!	C	RF	24	Science	Outside the Box
Lost	C	RF	38	Story Box	Wright Group/McGraw Hill
Lost!	C	RF	57	Harry's Math Books	Outside the Box
Lots of Dogs	C	I	68	Teacher's Choice Series	Pearson Learning Group
Lots of Dolls!	C	I	61	The Candid Collection	Pearson Learning Group
Lunch	C	RF	42	Harry's Math Books	Outside the Box
Lunch Orders	C	RF	18	Tadpoles	Rigby
Lunch Time	C	RF	69	Carousel Readers	Pearson Learning Group
Machines	C	I	36	Little Celebrations	Pearson Learning Group
Mae-Nerd	C	F	44	Teacher's Choice Series	Pearson Learning Group
Magic Food	C	F	26	Smart Starts	Rigby
Magic Machine, The	C	F	163	Sunshine	Wright Group/McGraw Hill
Magnets	C	I	55	Early Connections	Benchmark Education
Magnifying Glass, The	C	I	45	Foundations	Wright Group/McGraw Hill
Mail Came Today, The	C	RF	35	Carousel Readers	Pearson Learning Group
Make a Drum	C	I	29	Early Connections	Benchmark Education
Make a Pinata	C	I	16	Little Celebrations	Pearson Learning Group
Make a Turkey	C	I	14	Bebop Books	Lee & Low Books Inc.
Making a Hat	C	I	24	Windows on Literacy	National Geographic
Making a House	C	I	89	Early Connections	Benchmark Education
Making Music	C	I	35	Wonder World	Wright Group/McGraw Hill
Making Patterns	C	I	30	Twig	Wright Group/McGraw Hill
Making Soup	C	RF	77	Leveled Readers Emergent	Houghton Mifflin
Mama Hen, Come Quick	C	F	35	Ready Readers	Pearson Learning Group
Manners Please	C	RF	27	Pair-It-Books	Steck-Vaughn
Masks	C	I	41	Pebble Books	Capstone Press
Max Gets Ready	C	RF	48	Rigby Literacy	Rigby
Me	C	RF	41	Reading Corners	Pearson Learning Group
Me (boy)	C	I	34	Tonon, Terry	Kaeden Books
Me (girl)	C	I	34	Tonon, Terry	Kaeden Books
Me and My Pup	C	RF	34	Leveled Readers Language Support	Houghton Mifflin
Mean Giant, The	C	F	69	Sun Sprouts	ETA/Cuisenaire
Measure It	C	I	56	Twig	Wright Group/McGraw Hill
Meet My Family	C	RF	71	Early Connections	Benchmark Education
Meg's Eggs	C	F	38	New Way Red	Steck-Vaughn
Merry-Go-Round	C	RF	66	Teacher's Choice Series	Pearson Learning Group
Merry-Go-Round, The	C	RF	62	Sunshine	Wright Group/McGraw Hill

* Collection of short stories

TITLE	LEVEL	GENRE	WORD COUNT	AUTHOR / SERIES	PUBLISHER / DISTRIBUTOR
Merry-Go-Round, The	C	RF	45	Ready Readers	Pearson Learning Group
Merry-Go-Round, The	C	RF	84	PM Story Books	Rigby
Messy Moose	C	F	45	Little Books	Sadlier-Oxford
Mexican Holiday, A	C	I	24	The Candid Collection	Pearson Learning Group
Mice on Ice	C	F	34	KinderReaders	Rigby
Michael's Picture	C	RF	33	Little Celebrations	Pearson Learning Group
Microscope	C	I	46	Story Box	Wright Group/McGraw Hill
Mirror Magic	C	RF	20	Harry's Math Books	Outside the Box
Mix It Up	C	I	35	Twig	Wright Group/McGraw Hill
Mix It Up!	C	I	44	Leveled Readers Science	Houghton Mifflin
Mixing Things	C	I	51	Leveled Readers Science	Houghton Mifflin
Mom's Hat	C	RF	39	Joy Readers	Pearson Learning Group
Monkey Hop, The	C	F	26	Joy Readers	Pearson Learning Group
Monkey's Friends	C	F	36	Literacy 2000	Rigby
Monster Meals	C	F	33	Literacy 2000	Rigby
Monster Sandwich, A	C	F	36	Story Box	Wright Group/McGraw Hill
Monster, Monster	C	F	38	Reading Corners	Pearson Learning Group
Monster, The	C	RF	83	Sun Sprouts	ETA/Cuisenaire
Monsters	C	F	30	TOTTS	Tott Publications
Monster's Party, The	C	F	92	Story Box	Wright Group/McGraw Hill
Mosquito	C	I	46	Book Bank	Wright Group/McGraw Hill
Mother Bird	C	RF	75	PM Plus Story Books	Rigby
Mother Hippopotamus Goes Shopping	C	F	79	Foundations	Wright Group/McGraw Hill
Motorbike Race, The	C	RF	48	Joy Readers	Pearson Learning Group
Mouse	C	F	40	Story Box	Wright Group/McGraw Hill
Mouse, The	C	F	26	Pacific Literacy	Pacific Learning
Mouse's Meadow	C	I	62	Independent Readers Science	Houghton Mifflin
Moving Day	C	RF	28	Rigby Literacy	Rigby
Mr. Brown	C	RF	20	KinderReaders	Rigby
Mud Pie	C	RF	14	Literacy 2000	Rigby
Mud Pies	C	RF	56	TOTTS	Tott Publications
Mud Puddles	C	RF	24	TOTTS	Tott Publications
My Accident	C	RF	46	PM Starters	Rigby
My Balloon Man	C	I	56	First Stories	Pacific Learning
My Best Friend	C	RF	63	Carousel Readers	Pearson Learning Group
My Best Friend	C	RF	28	Little Celebrations	Pearson Learning Group
My Big Wheel	C	RF	38	Visions	Wright Group/McGraw Hill
My Birthday Party	C	RF	38	Visions	Wright Group/McGraw Hill
My Black Cat	C	RF	52	Early Emergent	Pioneer Valley
My Body	C	I	47	Discovery World	Rigby
My Book	C	RF	32	Sunshine	Wright Group/McGraw Hill
My Book	C	RF	63	PM Plus Story Books	Rigby
My Camera	C	RF	41	Rigby Literacy	Rigby
My Cat Muffin	C	RF	35	Gardner, Marjory	Scholastic
My Circus Family	C	F	42	Bookshop	Mondo
My Circus Friend	C	F	42	Lake, Mary Dixon	Mondo
My City	C	I	99	Rigby Literacy	Rigby
My Clothes	C	RF	86	Foundations	Wright Group/McGraw Hill
My Dad Cooks	C	RF	29	Carousel Readers	Pearson Learning Group
My Day	C	RF	44	Rise & Shine	Hampton-Brown
My Day	C	RF	51	Barney, Mike	Kaeden Books
My Dog	C	I	46	Vocabulary Readers	Houghton Mifflin
My Dog	C	RF	79	Early Emergent	Pioneer Valley
My Dog Ben	C	RF	19	Voyages	SRA/McGraw Hill

* Collection of short stories

TITLE	LEVEL	GENRE	WORD COUNT	AUTHOR / SERIES	PUBLISHER / DISTRIBUTOR
My Dog Willy	C	RF	71	Little Readers	Houghton Mifflin
My Dream	C	RF	34	Wildsmith, Brian	Oxford University Press
My Family Band	C	RF	50	Instant Readers	Harcourt School Publishers
My Five Senses	C	I	36	Independent Readers Science	Houghton Mifflin
My Friend and I	C	RF	78	Windows on Literacy	National Geographic
My Friend at School	C	RF	30	Visions	Wright Group/McGraw Hill
My Garden	C	I	33	Rosen Real Readers	Rosen Publishing Group
My Helicopter Ride	C	F	42	Foundations	Wright Group/McGraw Hill
My Home	C	RF	56	Sunshine	Wright Group/McGraw Hill
My Home	C	F	46	Story Box	Wright Group/McGraw Hill
My Kite	C	RF	37	Williams, Deborah	Kaeden Books
My Letter	C	RF	51	Wonder World	Wright Group/McGraw Hill
My Life in a Town	C	I	24	Rosen Real Readers	Rosen Publishing Group
My Life on an Island	C	I	43	Rosen Real Readers	Rosen Publishing Group
My Little Brother	C	RF	59	Windmill	Rigby
My Little Dog	C	F	90	PM Starters	Rigby
My Little Mouse	C	I	32	Book Bank	Wright Group/McGraw Hill
My Little Sister	C	RF	36	First Stories	Pacific Learning
My Lunch	C	RF	70	Early Emergent	Pioneer Valley
My Mama	C	RF	25	Visions	Wright Group/McGraw Hill
My Nest	C	I	42	Little Celebrations	Pearson Learning Group
My New House	C	RF	26	Reading Corners	Pearson Learning Group
My Party	C	I	35	The Candid Collection	Pearson Learning Group
My Pet	C	I	18	KinderReaders	Rigby
My Picture	C	RF	37	Carousel Readers	Pearson Learning Group
My Pony	C	RF	49	Rise & Shine	Hampton-Brown
My Pumpkin	C	I	52	Teacher's Choice Series	Pearson Learning Group
My Puppy	C	RF	33	Little Celebrations	Pearson Learning Group
My Ride	C	RF	56	Foundations	Wright Group/McGraw Hill
My Rocks	C	RF	43	Early Connections	Benchmark Education
My Sand Castle	C	RF	44	PM Plus Starters	Rigby
My School	C	RF	40	TOTTS	Tott Publications
My Shadow	C	RF	35	Sunshine	Wright Group/McGraw Hill
My Shadow	C	RF	42	Foundations	Wright Group/McGraw Hill
My Stuffed Animals	C	RF	50	Handprints B	Educator's Publishing Service
My Teacher Helps Me	C	RF	37	Visions	Wright Group/McGraw Hill
My Three-Wheeler	C	RF	38	Visions	Wright Group/McGraw Hill
My Tower	C	RF	61	PM Plus Story Books	Rigby
My Twin!	C	RF	40	Ready Readers	Pearson Learning Group
My Uncle's Truck	C	RF	24	Visions	Wright Group/McGraw Hill
My Weekly Chores	C	RF	44	Visions	Wright Group/McGraw Hill
Nanny Goat's Nap	C	F	96	Ready Readers	Pearson Learning Group
Nap Time	C	RF	24	KinderReaders	Rigby
Nat, Nan, and Pam	C	RF	30	Leveled Readers	Houghton Mifflin
Nature Hike	C	HF	32	Twig	Wright Group/McGraw Hill
Naughty Happy Monkey	C	F	33	Joy Readers	Pearson Learning Group
Ned	C	RF	30	Leveled Readers Language Support	Houghton Mifflin
Ned's Noise Machine	C	F	36	Rigby Literacy	Rigby
Needs and Wants	C	I	43	Early Connections	Benchmark Education
Neighborhood Party, The	C	RF	60	Pair-It Books	Steck-Vaughn
Nest, The	C	F	34	Sunshine	Wright Group/McGraw Hill
Nest, The	C	F	32	Story Box	Wright Group/McGraw Hill

* Collection of short stories

TITLE	LEVEL	GENRE	WORD COUNT	AUTHOR / SERIES	PUBLISHER / DISTRIBUTOR
Nests	C	I	35	Wonder World	Wright Group/McGraw Hill
Nests, Nests, Nests	C	I	42	Canizares, Susan; Reid, Mary	Scholastic
New Hat, The	C	RF	37	Rigby Literacy	Rigby
New Highway, The	C	I	67	Foundations	Wright Group/McGraw Hill
New Shoes	C	RF	29	Wonder World	Wright Group/McGraw Hill
Nighttime	C	RF	25	Science	Outside the Box
Nighttime	C	RF	44	Story Box	Wright Group/McGraw Hill
Noises!!!	C	RF	98	Teacher's Choice Series	Pearson Learning Group
Noses	C	RF	46	Science	Outside the Box
Now It's Hot	C	I	49	Rigby Focus	Rigby
Now We Can Go	C	RF	25	Jonas, Ann	Greenwillow
Octopus Goes to School	C	F	42	Bordelon, Carolyn	Continental Press
Off to School	C	RF	45	Story Steps	Rigby
Off to the Library	C	RF	46	Seedlings	Continental Press
Oh, No!	C	F	53	Joy Readers	Pearson Learning Group
Old and New	C	I	50	Interaction	Rigby
Old King Cole	C	F	29	Seedlings	Continental Press
Old Store, New Store	C	I	56	Leveled Readers Social Studies	Houghton Mifflin
Old Tuatara	C	F	33	Pacific Literacy	Pacific Learning
On a Chair	C	F	30	Story Box	Wright Group/McGraw Hill
On a Cold, Cold Day	C	F	33	Tadpoles	Rigby
On All Kinds of Days	C	I	50	Yellow Umbrella Books	Red Brick Learning
On Our Street	C	RF	52	Little Red Readers	Sundance
On Saturday	C	RF	44	Handprints B	Educator's Publishing Service
On Saturday	C	I	28	Little Red Readers	Sundance
On the Farm	C	I	18	Literacy 2000	Rigby
On the Go	C	RF	43	Learn to Read	Creative Teaching Press
On the Ground	C	I	40	Sunshine	Wright Group/McGraw Hill
On the Road	C	I	47	Teacher's Choice Series	Pearson Learning Group
One Bee Got on the Bus	C	F	43	Ready Readers	Pearson Learning Group
One Bird Sat on the Fence	C	I	40	Wonder World	Wright Group/McGraw Hill
One Day	C	RF	48	Teacher's Choice Series	Pearson Learning Group
One for You and One for Me	C	RF	27	Blaxland, Wendy	Scholastic
One Frog, One Fly	C	F	26	Blaxland, Wendy	Scholastic
One Little Slip	C	F	33	Instant Readers	Harcourt School Publishers
One More Time	C	RF	45	Instant Readers	Harcourt School Publishers
One Soccer Game	C	RF	29	Harry's Math Books	Outside the Box
Open Wide	C	F	56	Mitchell, Robin	Scholastic
Orchestra, The	C	F	33	Foundations	Wright Group/McGraw Hill
Otter, Otter	C	I	39	Phonics and Friends	Hampton-Brown
Our Car	C	RF	32	Sunshine	Wright Group/McGraw Hill
Our Dad	C	RF	41	Little Books for Early Readers	University of Maine
Our Farm	C	I	37	Rosen Real Readers	Rosen Publishing Group
Our Flag	C	I	21	Leveled Readers Social Studies	Houghton Mifflin
Our Grandad	C	RF	30	Sunshine	Wright Group/McGraw Hill
Our Granny	C	RF	41	Sunshine	Wright Group/McGraw Hill
Our New Puppy	C	RF	29	Windows on Literacy	National Geographic
Our School	C	I	46	Twig	Wright Group/McGraw Hill
Our Street	C	RF	40	Sunshine	Wright Group/McGraw Hill
Our Week	C	RF	37	Storyteller-First Snow	Wright Group/McGraw Hill
Out of Sight	C	I	52	Rigby Literacy	Rigby
Outside and Inside	C	I	43	Twig	Wright Group/McGraw Hill
Painter, The	C	RF	31	Ray's Readers	Outside the Box

* Collection of short stories

TITLE	LEVEL	GENRE	WORD COUNT	AUTHOR / SERIES	PUBLISHER / DISTRIBUTOR
Painting	C	RF	24	Story Box	Wright Group/McGraw Hill
Pam & Sam at the Park	C	F	108	Carousel Earlybirds	Pearson Learning Group
Pam & Sam at the Zoo	C	F	84	Carousel Earlybirds	Pearson Learning Group
Pam & Sam Fly Over the City	C	F	80	Carousel Earlybirds	Pearson Learning Group
Pam & Sam on the Beach	C	F	94	Carousel Earlybirds	Pearson Learning Group
Pancakes for Breakfast	C	RF	108	Emergent	Pioneer Valley
Pancakes, Crackers, and Pizza	C	RF	63	Rookie Readers	Children's Press
Parades!	C	I	24	Pair-It Books	Steck-Vaughn
Parents	C	I	60	Pebble Books	Capstone Press
Party for a Rabbit, A	C	F	70	Early Connections	Benchmark Education
Pass the Present	C	F	86	Storyteller-First Snow	Wright Group/McGraw Hill
Pat's Perfect Pizza	C	RF	37	Ready Readers	Pearson Learning Group
Patterns	C	I	32	Berger, Samantha; Moreton, Daniel	Scholastic
Patterns	C	I	35	Discovery Links	Newbridge
Patterns	C	I	57	Story Steps	Rigby
Patterns are Fun!	C	I	35	Story Steps	Rigby
Patty and Pop's Picnic	C	RF	57	Little Books	Sadlier-Oxford
Pebbles	C	RF	30	Science	Outside the Box
Pedal Power	C	I	22	Pacific Literacy	Pacific Learning
People Say Hello	C	I	37	Learn to Read	Creative Teaching Press
People Who Keep You Safe	C	I	84	Careers Series	Benchmark Education
Perfect Kite Weather	C	I	56	Vocabulary Readers	Houghton Mifflin
Perfect Pet, The	C	RF	30	Instant Readers	Harcourt School Publishers
Pet for Me, A	C	RF	73	Early Emergent	Pioneer Valley
Pet Parade	C	F	33	Literacy 2000	Rigby
Pet Shop, The	C	RF	32	Oxford Reading Tree	Oxford University Press
Pete Paints a Picture	C	RF	87	Story Steps	Rigby
Pets, The	C	RF	28	Learn to Read	Creative Teaching Press
Photo Book, The	C	RF	50	PM Story Books	Rigby
Photo Time	C	RF	59	PM Plus Story Books	Rigby
Pick a Pet	C	RF	40	Little Celebrations	Pearson Learning Group
Picnic, The	C	RF	48	Teacher's Choice Series	Pearson Learning Group
Picture, A	C	I	58	Storyteller-First Snow	Wright Group/McGraw Hill
Pigs	C	F	29	Learn to Read	Creative Teaching Press
Pigs Peek	C	F	28	Books for Young Learners	Richard C. Owen
Pinata Party	C	RF	31	Bebop Books	Lee & Low Books Inc.
Pitty Pitty Pat	C	F	45	Little Celebrations	Pearson Learning Group
Places	C	I	88	Little Red Readers	Sundance
Play Dough	C	RF	63	Foundations	Wright Group/McGraw Hill
Play, The	C	RF	23	Rigby Literacy	Rigby
Playful Platypus, The	C	F	35	Learn to Read	Creative Teaching Press
Playground, The	C	RF	108	Early Emergent	Pioneer Valley
Playhouse for Monster	C	F	34	Mueller, Virginia	Whitman
Playhouse, The	C	RF	34	Rigby Literacy	Rigby
Playing in the Snow	C	RF	61	Early Emergent	Pioneer Valley
Playing Outside	C	RF	56	PM Plus Starters	Rigby
Playing with My Cat	C	RF	83	Early Emergent	Pioneer Valley
Playtime	C	F	66	Voyages	SRA/McGraw Hill
Plop!	C	F	30	Story Box	Wright Group/McGraw Hill
Pond, The	C	I	25	Books for Young Learners	Richard C. Owen
Pond, The	C	F	54	Joy Readers	Pearson Learning Group
Pop . . . Pop . . . Popcorn	C	I	40	Home Connection Collection	Rigby
Potatoes on Tuesday	C	F	28	Little Celebrations	Pearson Learning Group

* Collection of short stories

TITLE	LEVEL	GENRE	WORD COUNT	AUTHOR / SERIES	PUBLISHER / DISTRIBUTOR
Puppet Play, A	C	I	54	Storyteller-First Snow	Wright Group/McGraw Hill
Push or Pull?	C	I	73	Windows on Literacy	National Geographic
Python Caught the Eagle, The	C	F	60	Voyages	SRA/McGraw Hill
Queen on a Quilt	C	F	26	Ready Readers	Pearson Learning Group
Quick and Quiet	C	F	38	Phonics and Friends	Hampton-Brown
Quilts	C	RF	35	Foundations	Wright Group/McGraw Hill
Race, The	C	RF	25	Sunshine	Wright Group/McGraw Hill
Rain	C	RF	34	Learn to Read	Creative Teaching Press
Rain	C	I	56	Kalan, Robert	Greenwillow
Rain or Shine?	C	I	21	Twig	Wright Group/McGraw Hill
Rain, The	C	RF	76	Leveled Readers Emergent	Houghton Mifflin
Rainbow of My Own	C	F	52	Freeman, Don	Penguin Group
Raindrop, A	C	RF	41	Teacher's Choice Series	Pearson Learning Group
Raindrops	C	RF	66	Gay, Sandy	Scholastic
Randy's Room	C	RF	32	Harry's Math Books	Outside the Box
Rat's Funny Story	C	F	39	Story Box	Wright Group/McGraw Hill
Ray Ran	C	RF	34	Ray's Readers	Outside the Box
Reaching the Sky	C	RF	46	Sunshine	Wright Group/McGraw Hill
Ready for School	C	RF	41	Teacher's Choice Series	Pearson Learning Group
Red Balloon, The	C	RF	34	Joy Readers	Pearson Learning Group
Red Puppy	C	RF	85	PM Plus Story Books	Rigby
Ribbon, The	C	I	46	Rise & Shine	Hampton-Brown
Riding	C	RF	67	Foundations	Wright Group/McGraw Hill
Rita Rolls	C	RF	36	Little Celebrations	Pearson Learning Group
River, The	C	I	40	Science	Outside the Box
Roberto's Smile	C	RF	43	Story Box	Wright Group/McGraw Hill
Rockets	C	I	49	Little Celebrations	Pearson Learning Group
Rockity Rock	C	RF	36	KinderReaders	Rigby
Roll Over!	C	F	201	Peek, Merle	Clarion
Roller Coaster	C	RF	45	Joy Readers	Pearson Learning Group
Rolling	C	I	46	Sun Sprouts	ETA/Cuisenaire
Round	C	I	40	Windmill Books	Rigby
Round and Round	C	RF	38	Story Box	Wright Group/McGraw Hill
Row Your Boat	C	F	18	Literacy Tree	Rigby
Row Your Boat	C	F	18	Literacy 2000	Rigby
Ruff and Me	C	RF	30	First Stories	Pacific Learning
Rules for Pets	C	F	54	Joy Readers	Pearson Learning Group
Rules Help	C	I	69	Windows on Literacy	National Geographic
Run! Run!	C	F	64	Bookshop	Mondo
Running	C	RF	39	Foundations	Wright Group/McGraw Hill
Safety	C	I	35	Interaction	Rigby
Safety Counts	C	F	52	Learn to Read	Creative Teaching Press
Safety First	C	I	131	Twig	Wright Group/McGraw Hill
Sally and the Daisy	C	RF	60	PM Story Books	Rigby
Sally and the Elephant	C	I	45	Wonder World	Wright Group/McGraw Hill
Sam	C	RF	17	KinderReaders	Rigby
Sam and Bingo	C	RF	53	PM Plus Story Books	Rigby
Same Team	C	I	44	The Candid Collection	Pearson Learning Group
Sammy at the Farm	C	RF	83	Urmston, Kathleen; Evans, Karen	Kaeden Books
Sam's Balloon	C	RF	54	PM Plus Story Books	Rigby
Sam's Race	C	RF	64	PM Plus Story Books	Rigby
Sandcastle, The	C	I	31	Sun Sprouts	ETA/Cuisenaire
Sandwich, The	C	RF	68	Carousel Earlybirds	Pearson Learning Group
Sandy	C	F	32	Ready Readers	Pearson Learning Group

* Collection of short stories

TITLE	LEVEL	GENRE	WORD COUNT	AUTHOR / SERIES	PUBLISHER / DISTRIBUTOR
Scarecrow, The	C	F	31	Literacy 2000	Rigby
Scarecrow's Friends	C	F	56	Start to Read	School Zone
Scaredy Cat	C	F	85	Learn to Read	Creative Teaching Press
Scary Monster	C	F	19	Eifrig, Kate	Kaeden Books
Seagull, The	C	F	78	Story Steps	Rigby
Seasons	C	I	28	Discovery World	Rigby
Seasons, The	C	RF	84	Rigby Focus	Rigby
See How It Grows	C	I	34	Learn to Read	Creative Teaching Press
See Our Show	C	RF	38	Rigby Focus	Rigby
Seesaw, The	C	RF	100	Emergent	Pioneer Valley
Seesaw, The	C	F	46	Voyages	SRA/McGraw Hill
Shaggy	C	RF	23	Windows on Literacy	National Geographic
Shape Walk	C	RF	25	Little Celebrations	Pearson Learning Group
Shapes	C	I	30	Rise & Shine	Hampton-Brown
Shapes	C	I	31	Visions	Wright Group/McGraw Hill
Sharing	C	RF	24	Literacy 2000	Rigby
Sharing	C	RF	33	Harry's Math Books	Outside the Box
Shark in a Sack	C	F	65	Sunshine	Wright Group/McGraw Hill
She Said	C	RF	35	Ready Readers	Pearson Learning Group
Sheep's Bell	C	RF	37	Ready Readers	Pearson Learning Group
Shoo!	C	F	37	Sunshine	Wright Group/McGraw Hill
Shopping	C	I	41	Interaction	Rigby
Shopping	C	I	78	Little Red Readers	Sundance
Shopping for School	C	RF	33	Visions	Wright Group/McGraw Hill
Shopping with Dad	C	RF	72	Windows on Literacy	National Geographic
Shopping with Dad	C	RF	43	Home Connection Collection	Rigby
Signs	C	I	40	Carousel Earlybirds	Pearson Learning Group
Signs	C	I	35	Little Celebrations	Pearson Learning Group
Silly Old Possum	C	RF	41	Story Box	Wright Group/McGraw Hill
Sink or Float?	C	I	36	Independent Readers Science	Houghton Mifflin
Six Cats	C	RF	50	Joy Readers	Pearson Learning Group
Six Go By	C	F	24	Ready Readers	Pearson Learning Group
Six Pieces of Cake	C	RF	40	Harry's Math Books	Outside the Box
Sizes	C	I	32	Discovery World	Rigby
Skating	C	F	52	Story Box	Wright Group/McGraw Hill
Smiling Salad, A	C	RF	32	Pair-It Books	Steck-Vaughn
Snake Goes Away	C	F	55	Rigby Literacy	Rigby
Snap! Splat!	C	F	25	Sunshine	Wright Group/McGraw Hill
Snip-Snap, Clickety-Click	C	F	54	Little Celebrations	Pearson Learning Group
Snow	C	RF	47	Science	Outside the Box
Snow Cover	C	RF	29	Little Celebrations	Pearson Learning Group
Snow Is Cold	C	I	47	Little Readers	Houghton Mifflin
Snowman	C	RF	21	Sunshine	Wright Group/McGraw Hill
Snowman, A	C	I	59	Foundations	Wright Group/McGraw Hill
So Many Circles	C	I	36	Yellow Umbrella Books	Red Brick Learning
Some Things Float	C	I	41	Windows on Literacy	National Geographic
Some Things Go Together	C	RF	133	Twig	Wright Group/McGraw Hill
Sometimes	C	RF	25	Wonder World	Wright Group/McGraw Hill
Sometimes I'm Silly	C	RF	24	Visions	Wright Group/McGraw Hill
Sounds Around Us, The	C	I	22	Rosen Real Readers	Rosen Publishing Group
Speed Boat, The	C	RF	170	Sunshine	Wright Group/McGraw Hill
Splash	C	F	34	Foundations	Wright Group/McGraw Hill
Splashing Dad	C	RF	37	Early Emergent	Pioneer Valley
Splosh	C	F	47	Story Box	Wright Group/McGraw Hill

* Collection of short stories

TITLE	LEVEL	GENRE	WORD COUNT	AUTHOR / SERIES	PUBLISHER / DISTRIBUTOR
Sports Day	C	RF	24	Home Connection Collection	Rigby
Spots	C	I	41	Sunshine	Wright Group/McGraw Hill
Spots, Feathers and Curly Tails	C	I	42	Tafuri, Nancy	Morrow
Spring	C	I	47	Carousel Readers	Pearson Learning Group
Spring Pops Up	C	I	26	Instant Readers	Harcourt School Publishers
Squares Everywhere	C	I	26	Discovery Links	Newbridge
Squeaky Clean	C	RF	29	Stewart, Josie	Continental Press
Sssh!	C	RF	49	Book Bank	Wright Group/McGraw Hill
Stepping Stones	C	F	42	Sunshine	Wright Group/McGraw Hill
Stop	C	F	54	Story Box	Wright Group/McGraw Hill
Stop That	C	F	41	Ready Readers	Pearson Learning Group
Stop That Noise!	C	RF	21	Pacific Literacy	Pacific Learning
Stop!	C	RF	31	Wonder World	Wright Group/McGraw Hill
Stop, Look, and Listen	C	RF	71	Lighthouse	Rigby
Stores	C	RF	66	Carousel Readers	Pearson Learning Group
Stories	C	RF	43	Learn to Read	Creative Teaching Press
Storm, The	C	RF	29	Story Box	Wright Group/McGraw Hill
Storm, The	C	I	28	Voyages	SRA/McGraw Hill
Story Time	C	RF	32	Ready Readers	Pearson Learning Group
Strawberries	C	I	37	Little Books for Early Readers	University of Maine
Stream, The	C	RF	24	Science	Outside the Box
Strings	C	I	53	Storyteller-First Snow	Wright Group/McGraw Hill
Summer Day, A	C	I	74	Leveled Readers	Houghton Mifflin
Sunrise	C	F	46	Literacy 2000	Rigby
Surprise Cake	C	F	32	Literacy 2000	Rigby
Surprise Pet, A	C	F	54	Leveled Readers Language Support	Houghton Mifflin
Swimming	C	RF	65	Carousel Readers	Pearson Learning Group
Swimming Pool, The	C	RF	29	Visions	Wright Group/McGraw Hill
Swing, Swing, Swing	C	F	93	Tuchman, G.; Dieterichs, S.	Scholastic
Tails and Claws	C	I	65	Wonder World	Wright Group/McGraw Hill
Take a Bite	C	F	19	Little Celebrations	Pearson Learning Group
Take a Guess	C	F	45	Little Celebrations	Pearson Learning Group
Talk, Talk, Talk	C	RF	56	Literacy 2000	Rigby
Taller Than Molly	C	F	43	Harry's Math Books	Outside the Box
Taxi, The	C	F	45	Joy Readers	Pearson Learning Group
Tea Party	C	RF	38	Carousel Readers	Pearson Learning Group
Tea Party, The	C	F	76	Storyteller-First Snow	Wright Group/McGraw Hill
Tedd & Huggly	C	F	47	Canizares, Susan; Berger, Samantha	Scholastic
Tee-Ball	C	RF	53	Little Celebrations	Pearson Learning Group
Teeny Tiny Tina	C	F	34	Literacy 2000	Rigby
Teeter-Totter, The	C	TL	35	Joy Readers	Pearson Learning Group
Teeth	C	I	26	Wonder World	Wright Group/McGraw Hill
Ten Crazy Caterpillars	C	F	40	Voyages	SRA/McGraw Hill
Terrific Shoes	C	RF	19	Ready Readers	Pearson Learning Group
That Fly	C	F	26	Ready Readers	Pearson Learning Group
Then & Now	C	I	60	Berger, Samantha; Moreton, Daniel	Scholastic
There Is a Planet	C	I	52	Sunshine	Wright Group/McGraw Hill
These Legs	C	I	42	Foundations	Wright Group/McGraw Hill
They All Ran Away	C	F	82	Lighthouse	Rigby
Things Birds Eat, The	C	I	38	Chessen, Betsey	Scholastic
Things I Like	C	I	39	Little Readers	Houghton Mifflin

* Collection of short stories

TITLE	LEVEL	GENRE	WORD COUNT	AUTHOR / SERIES	PUBLISHER / DISTRIBUTOR
Things I Like	C	RF	42	Carousel Earlybirds	Pearson Learning Group
Things I Like to Do	C	RF	63	Carousel Earlybirds	Pearson Learning Group
Things I Like to Do	C	RF	58	Foundations	Wright Group/McGraw Hill
Things on Wheels	C	I	69	Little Red Readers	Sundance
Things That Help Me	C	I	18	Pacific Literacy	Pacific Learning
This Farm	C	I	39	Yellow Umbrella Books	Red Brick Learning
This Is My Friend	C	RF	77	Foundations	Wright Group/McGraw Hill
This Is My Home	C	F	51	Joy Readers	Pearson Learning Group
Three Little Pigs	C	TL	39	Sunshine	Wright Group/McGraw Hill
Through the Day	C	I	76	Rigby Literacy	Rigby
Tick-Tock	C	RF	53	Story Box	Wright Group/McGraw Hill
Tiger, Tiger	C	F	55	PM Story Books	Rigby
Tiger's Clock	C	F	28	Learn to Read	Creative Teaching Press
Time for a Change	C	RF	31	Pacific Literacy	Pacific Learning
Time for Bed	C	RF	27	Rosen Real Readers	Rosen Publishing Group
Time for Bed	C	RF	28	Smart Starts	Rigby
Time to Sleep	C	I	52	Independent Readers Science	Houghton Mifflin
Timmy Tries	C	RF	22	Little Celebrations	Pearson Learning Group
To the Ocean	C	I	26	Twig	Wright Group/McGraw Hill
To Work	C	RF	43	Sunshine	Wright Group/McGraw Hill
Toast	C	RF	82	First Stories	Pacific Learning
Together	C	RF	37	Sunshine	Wright Group/McGraw Hill
Tom and His Tractor	C	RF	27	Cat on the Mat	Oxford University Press
Tommy's Tummy Ache	C	F	20	Literacy 2000	Rigby
Too Hot!	C	RF	39	Lighthouse	Rigby
Too Many Clothes	C	RF	24	Literacy 2000	Rigby
Toot, Toot	C	I	47	Wildsmith, Brian	Oxford University Press
Tossed Salad	C	I	28	Twig	Wright Group/McGraw Hill
Touch	C	I	39	Twig	Wright Group/McGraw Hill
Toy Town	C	I	36	Home Connection Collection	Rigby
Toys	C	I	41	Windows on Literacy	National Geographic
Toys with Wheels	C	I	41	Home Connection Collection	Rigby
Tracks	C	I	49	Twig	Wright Group/McGraw Hill
Tracks	C	I	25	Sunshine	Wright Group/McGraw Hill
Train Ride	C	RF	15	Bebop Books	Lee & Low Books Inc.
Train Ride, The	C	F	29	Literacy 2000	Rigby
Train, The	C	RF	27	Visions	Wright Group/McGraw Hill
Transportation Museum, The	C	I	79	Little Red Readers	Sundance
Traveling	C	F	86	Foundations	Wright Group/McGraw Hill
Traveling Ted's Postcards	C	F	161	Little Celebrations	Pearson Learning Group
Tree Fell Over the River, A	C	RF	72	Little Red Readers	Sundance
Trip Across the Country, A	C	RF	47	Independent Readers Social Studies	Houghton Mifflin
Trip to the Zoo, A	C	RF	78	Carousel Readers	Pearson Learning Group
Trolley Ride, The	C	F	87	Tadpoles	Rigby
Trucks	C	I	38	Literacy 2000	Rigby
Trucks	C	I	27	Pebble Books	Capstone Press
Trucks	C	I	24	Twig	Wright Group/McGraw Hill
Two Can Do It!	C	RF	32	Canizares, Susan; Chessen, Betsey	Scholastic
Two Little Chicks	C	F	32	KinderReaders	Rigby
Tyler's Train	C	RF	42	Little Celebrations	Pearson Learning Group
Umbrella	C	F	73	Story Box	Wright Group/McGraw Hill
Uncle Buncle's House	C	RF	56	Sunshine	Wright Group/McGraw Hill
Under My Bed	C	F	49	Little Celebrations	Pearson Learning Group

* Collection of short stories

TITLE	LEVEL	GENRE	WORD COUNT	AUTHOR / SERIES	PUBLISHER / DISTRIBUTOR
Under the Ground	C	I	42	Foundations	Wright Group/McGraw Hill
Under the Sky	C	I	44	Learn to Read	Creative Teaching Press
Under the Umbrella	C	RF	60	Phonics and Friends	Hampton-Brown
Underground	C	I	31	Twig	Wright Group/McGraw Hill
Up and Down	C	RF	68	Rigby Literacy	Rigby
Up and Down	C	I	81	PM Plus Nonfiction	Rigby
Up and Down	C	RF	92	Handprints C, Set 1	Educator's Publishing Service
Up in a Tree	C	RF	47	Sunshine	Wright Group/McGraw Hill
Up Went the Goat	C	F	38	Start to Read	School Zone
Using Numbers at Work	C	I	75	Early Connections	Benchmark Education
Using Tools	C	I	30	Discovery Links	Newbridge
V is for Vest	C	I	35	Learn to Read	Creative Teaching Press
Vacation, The	C	RF	94	Emergent	Pioneer Valley
Valentine's Checkup	C	RF	45	Little Books	Sadlier-Oxford
Valentine's Day	C	F	49	Story Box	Wright Group/McGraw Hill
Volcano	C	I	44	Science	Outside the Box
Vultures on Vacation	C	F	36	Ready Readers	Pearson Learning Group
Wait for Me	C	RF	75	Little Books	Sadlier-Oxford
Wake Up Ginger	C	F	70	Bookshop	Mondo
Wake Up Mom!	C	RF	94	Sunshine	Wright Group/McGraw Hill
Wake Up!	C	F	62	Story Steps	Rigby
Wake Up, Dad	C	RF	67	PM Story Books	Rigby
Walking to School	C	RF	38	Voyages	SRA/McGraw Hill
Walking, Walking	C	I	32	Twig	Wright Group/McGraw Hill
Warm Clothes	C	I	51	Pebble Books	Capstone Press
Watch Me Zoom	C	RF	45	Windmill Books	Rigby
Watch Out!	C	F	27	Literacy 2000	Rigby
Water	C	RF	20	Carousel Readers	Pearson Learning Group
Water All Around	C	I	26	Leveled Readers Science	Houghton Mifflin
Water Changes	C	I	36	Discovery Links	Newbridge
Water! Water!	C	I	33	Sunshine	Wright Group/McGraw Hill
Water, Water Everywhere!	C	I	27	Leveled Readers Science	Houghton Mifflin
We All Play Sports	C	I	26	Pacific Literacy	Pacific Learning
We Can Eat the Plants	C	RF	38	Learn to Read	Creative Teaching Press
We Can Run	C	RF	77	PM Starters	Rigby
We Dance	C	I	30	Pacific Literacy	Pacific Learning
We Eat Rice	C	RF	46	Bebop Books	Lee & Low Books Inc.
We Go to Grandma's House	C	I	63	Windows on Literacy	National Geographic
We Like	C	RF	42	Foundations	Wright Group/McGraw Hill
We Like Summer!	C	RF	41	Blevins, Wiley	Scholastic
We Like the Sun	C	RF	30	Pair-It Books	Steck-Vaughn
We Like to Graph	C	I	48	Coulton, Mia	Kaeden Books
We Like to Play	C	RF	70	Tarlow, Ellen	Scholastic
We Love Recess	C	I	63	Fiesta Series	Pearson Learning Group
We Love the Farm	C	RF	54	Lighthouse	Rigby
We Make Pizza	C	RF	37	Carousel Readers	Pearson Learning Group
We Need Trees	C	I	33	Hoenecke, Karen	Kaeden Books
We Use Water	C	I	48	Early Connections	Benchmark Education
We Went Flying	C	RF	40	Carousel Earlybirds	Pearson Learning Group
Weather	C	I	54	Chanko, Pamela; Moreton, Daniel	Scholastic
Weather in the City	C	I	68	Windows on Literacy	National Geographic
What a Hamster Needs	C	I	46	Leveled Readers Science	Houghton Mifflin
What a Mess!	C	RF	51	Story Box	Wright Group/McGraw Hill

* Collection of short stories

TITLE	LEVEL	GENRE	WORD COUNT	AUTHOR / SERIES	PUBLISHER / DISTRIBUTOR
What a Mess!	C	RF	79	Bookshop	Mondo
What a Tale!	C	RF	38	Wildsmith, Brian	Oxford University Press
What a Week!	C	RF	36	Home Connection Collection	Rigby
What a Week!	C	RF	64	Rigby Literacy	Rigby
What Am I?	C	I	51	Williams, Deborah	Kaeden Books
What Animals Do You See?	C	I	50	Read-More Books	Pearson Learning Group
What Are Friends For?	C	I	33	Rosen Real Readers	Rosen Publishing Group
What Are You Called?	C	I	66	Voyages	SRA/McGraw Hill
What Can Float?	C	I	32	Windmill Books	Rigby
What Can Fly?	C	I	33	Joy Readers	Pearson Learning Group
What Can Hurt?	C	I	30	Windmill Books	Rigby
What Can I Buy?	C	I	33	Rosen Real Readers	Rosen Publishing Group
What Can I Do?	C	I	42	Read-More Books	Pearson Learning Group
What Can I Do?	C	I	42	Foundations	Wright Group/McGraw Hill
What Can I See?	C	I	42	Foundations	Wright Group/McGraw Hill
What Can We Smell?	C	I	44	Windmill Books	Rigby
What Can You Be?	C	I	166	Tiger Cub	Peguis
What Can You Do?	C	I	59	Tiger Cub	Peguis
What Can You See?	C	I	43	Vocabulary Readers	Houghton Mifflin
What Can You See?	C	I	25	Literacy 2000	Rigby
What Can You See?	C	RF	31	Rigby Literacy	Rigby
What Comes First?	C	I	56	Bookshop	Mondo
What Comes in Threes?	C	F	41	Learn to Read	Creative Teaching Press
What Could I Be?	C	RF	64	Foundations	Wright Group/McGraw Hill
What Did I Use?	C	I	65	Discovery World	Rigby
What Did Kim Catch?	C	RF	48	Literacy 2000	Rigby
What Did They Want?	C	RF	28	Smart Starts	Rigby
What Do We Have?	C	F	28	Step-By-Step Series	Pearson Learning Group
What Do You Have?	C	I	165	Tiger Cub	Peguis
What Do You Have?	C	I	88	Windmill Books	Rigby
What Do You See at the Pet Store?	C	I	27	Read-More Books	Pearson Learning Group
What Do You See?	C	I	35	Windmill Books	Rigby
What Do You Touch?	C	I	50	Windmill Books	Rigby
What Does Greedy Cat Like?	C	RF	35	Pacific Literacy	Pacific Learning
What Floats?	C	I	16	Twig	Wright Group/McGraw Hill
What Goes in the Bathtub?	C	RF	31	Literacy 2000	Rigby
What Goes into a Salad?	C	RF	22	Home Connection Collection	Rigby
What Goes Up and Down?	C	I	40	Windmill Books	Rigby
What Grows Here?	C	I	37	Windows on Literacy	National Geographic
What Hangs from the Tree?	C	I	42	Questions & Answers	Pearson Learning Group
What Has Stripes?	C	I	25	Ballinger, Margaret	Scholastic
What I Left on My Plate	C	RF	54	Teacher's Choice Series	Pearson Learning Group
What I Like at School	C	I	64	Little Red Readers	Sundance
What If?	C	F	41	Little Celebrations	Pearson Learning Group
What Is Blue?	C	I	31	Carousel Earlybirds	Pearson Learning Group
What Is Delicious?	C	I	25	Windmill Books	Rigby
What Is Fun?	C	I	34	Windmill Books	Rigby
What Is in Space?	C	I	41	Science	Wright Group/McGraw Hill
What Is Old?	C	I	32	Windmill Books	Rigby
What Is Slippery?	C	I	26	Windmill Books	Rigby
What Is Slow?	C	I	29	Windmill Books	Rigby
What Is Soft?	C	I	30	Windmill Books	Rigby
What Is That?	C	I	61	Ready Readers	Pearson Learning Group
What Is This Skeleton?	C	I	48	Science	Wright Group/McGraw Hill

TITLE	LEVEL	GENRE	WORD COUNT	AUTHOR / SERIES	PUBLISHER / DISTRIBUTOR
What Is This?	C	I	28	Ready Readers	Pearson Learning Group
What Is Young?	C	I	31	Windmill Books	Rigby
What Jessie Really Likes	C	RF	59	Lighthouse	Rigby
What Kind of Dog Am I?	C	I	21	Twig	Wright Group/McGraw Hill
What Makes It Go?	C	I	29	iOpeners	Pearson Learning Group
What Plant Is This?	C	I	22	Windows on Literacy	National Geographic
What Plays Music?	C	I	36	Questions & Answers	Pearson Learning Group
What Season Is This?	C	I	24	Wonder World	Wright Group/McGraw Hill
What Should I Wear?	C	RF	70	Lighthouse	Rigby
What Smells Good?	C	I	26	Windmill Books	Rigby
What's for Lunch?	C	F	48	Carle, Eric	Scholastic
What's Going On?	C	RF	21	Learn to Read	Creative Teaching Press
What's on Your T-Shirt?	C	RF	64	Carousel Readers	Pearson Learning Group
What's That?	C	F	28	The Book Project	Sundance
What's That?	C	RF	27	Carousel Earlybirds	Pearson Learning Group
What's the Time Mr. Wolf?	C	F	49	Windmill	Wright Group/McGraw Hill
What's Under My Bed?	C	RF	18	Visions	Wright Group/McGraw Hill
Wheel, The	C	RF	102	Joy Readers	Pearson Learning Group
Wheels	C	I	27	Literacy 2000	Rigby
Wheels	C	I	39	Sunshine	Wright Group/McGraw Hill
Wheels	C	I	29	Discovery Links	Newbridge
When Do Cars Stop?	C	I	62	Questions & Answers	Pearson Learning Group
When I Grow Up	C	RF	38	Rise & Shine	Hampton-Brown
When I Play	C	RF	31	Literacy 2000	Rigby
When I Pretend	C	RF	40	Literacy 2000	Rigby
When It Rains	C	RF	39	Foundations	Wright Group/McGraw Hill
When It Rains . . .	C	I	37	Teacher's Choice Series	Pearson Learning Group
When It Snowed	C	RF	33	Home Connection Collection	Rigby
When Itchy Witchy Sneezes	C	F	39	Sunshine	Wright Group/McGraw Hill
When Mr. Quinn Snored	C	F	31	Little Books	Sadlier-Oxford
When the Rain Comes	C	I	54	Windows on Literacy	National Geographic
Where and Why?	C	RF	28	Learn to Read	Creative Teaching Press
Where Are They Going?	C	F	42	Story Box	Wright Group/McGraw Hill
Where Are They Going?	C	I	38	Windows on Literacy	National Geographic
Where Are They?	C	RF	24	Humphrey, Kiesha	Scholastic
Where Babies Play	C	F	36	Instant Readers	Harcourt School Publishers
Where Can I Play?	C	RF	45	Windows on Literacy	National Geographic
Where Can I Write?	C	RF	42	Early Emergent	Pioneer Valley
Where Do Birds Live?	C	I	57	Chessen, Betsey	Scholastic
Where Do I Live?	C	I	29	Visions	Wright Group/McGraw Hill
Where Do Monsters Live?	C	F	56	Learn to Read	Creative Teaching Press
Where Do They Live?	C	I	45	Ready Readers	Pearson Learning Group
Where Do You Live?	C	I	68	Tiger Cub	Peguis
Where Does a Leopard Hide?	C	I	108	Foundations	Wright Group/McGraw Hill
Where Does It Go?	C	I	61	Questions & Answers	Pearson Learning Group
Where Does It Park?	C	I	51	Canizares, Susan	Scholastic
Where Does the Teacher Sleep?	C	F	50	Gibson, Kathleen	Continental Press
Where I Live	C	RF	35	Pacific Literacy	Pacific Learning
Where Is Eric?	C	RF	29	Rigby Literacy	Rigby
Where Is Happy Monkey?	C	F	46	Joy Readers	Pearson Learning Group
Where Is Marco?	C	F	75	Bookshop	Mondo
Where Is Max?	C	F	54	Sun Sprouts	ETA/Cuisenaire
Where Is My Bone?	C	F	42	Sunshine	Wright Group/McGraw Hill
Where Is My Grandma?	C	RF	74	Foundations	Wright Group/McGraw Hill

* Collection of short stories

TITLE	LEVEL	GENRE	WORD COUNT	AUTHOR / SERIES	PUBLISHER / DISTRIBUTOR
Where Is My Pencil?	C	RF	34	Little Celebrations	Pearson Learning Group
Where Is the Cat?	C	I	28	Read-More Books	Pearson Learning Group
Where is the Crab?	C	I	30	Vocabulary Readers	Houghton Mifflin
Where Is the Snake?	C	F	60	The Book Project	Sundance
Where Is Water?	C	I	36	Twig	Wright Group/McGraw Hill
Where We Live	C	I	34	Vocabulary Readers	Houghton Mifflin
Where Will You Sleep Tonight?	C	I	77	Foundations	Wright Group/McGraw Hill
Where's Bear?	C	F	41	Windmill	Wright Group/McGraw Hill
Where's Little Mole?	C	F	43	Little Celebrations	Pearson Learning Group
Where's My Backpack?	C	RF	27	Little Celebrations	Pearson Learning Group
Where's the Halloween Treat?	C	RF	102	Ziefert, Harriet	Penguin Group
Where's Tim?	C	F	38	Sunshine	Wright Group/McGraw Hill
Where's Your Tooth?	C	RF	53	Learn to Read	Creative Teaching Press
Which Clothes Do You Wear?	C	I	49	Foundations	Wright Group/McGraw Hill
Which Juice Would You Like?	C	F	28	Step-By-Step Series	Pearson Learning Group
Which Way Home?	C	RF	26	Little Celebrations	Pearson Learning Group
Whiskers	C	I	32	Wonder World	Wright Group/McGraw Hill
Whisper and Shout	C	I	92	Twig	Wright Group/McGraw Hill
White Paw, Black Paw	C	F	41	KinderReaders	Rigby
Who Are We?	C	RF	30	Home Connection Collection	Rigby
Who Are You?	C	RF	55	Book Bank	Wright Group/McGraw Hill
Who Ate the Pizza?	C	RF	59	Foundations	Wright Group/McGraw Hill
Who Came By Here?	C	RF	31	Rise & Shine	Hampton-Brown
Who Can Hop?	C	I	35	Questions & Answers	Pearson Learning Group
Who Can Read?	C	RF	72	Handprints C, Set 1	Educator's Publishing Service
Who Can See the Camel?	C	RF	70	Story Box	Wright Group/McGraw Hill
Who Fed the Chickens?	C	F	14	Little Celebrations	Pearson Learning Group
Who Has Wings?	C	I	30	Questions & Answers	Pearson Learning Group
Who Is Ready?	C	RF	36	Ready Readers	Pearson Learning Group
Who Is Taller?	C	RF	26	Learn to Read	Creative Teaching Press
Who Is the Robot?	C	RF	67	Pacific Literacy	Pacific Learning
Who Lives Here?	C	I	28	Story Box	Wright Group/McGraw Hill
Who Lives Here?	C	I	62	Learn to Read	Creative Teaching Press
Who Lives Here?	C	I	42	Questions & Answers	Pearson Learning Group
Who Lives in a Tree?	C	I	43	Discovery Links	Newbridge
Who Lives in this Hole?	C	I	25	Twig	Wright Group/McGraw Hill
Who Made That?	C	RF	31	Ready Readers	Pearson Learning Group
Who Rides the Bus?	C	RF	19	Little Celebrations	Pearson Learning Group
Who Says?	C	I	49	Twig	Wright Group/McGraw Hill
Who Took the Cake?	C	RF	32	First Stories	Pacific Learning
Who Will Help Me?	C	RF	53	Home Connection Collection	Rigby
Who's Going to Lick the Bowl?	C	RF	18	Story Box	Wright Group/McGraw Hill
Whose Birthday Is It Today?	C	RF	50	Book Bank	Wright Group/McGraw Hill
Whose Forest Is It?	C	RF	45	Learn to Read	Creative Teaching Press
Whose List Is This?	C	F	14	Little Celebrations	Pearson Learning Group
Willy the Wizard	C	F	42	Learn to Read	Creative Teaching Press
Wind Blows, The	C	RF	38	Learn to Read	Creative Teaching Press
Winter	C	I	49	Carousel Readers	Pearson Learning Group
Winter	C	I	54	Foundations	Wright Group/McGraw Hill
With My Mom and Dad	C	I	63	Early Connections	Benchmark Education
Woof!	C	F	40	Literacy 2000	Rigby
Work	C	RF	65	TOTTS	Tott Publications
Working	C	I	174	Instant Readers	Harcourt School Publishers

* Collection of short stories

TITLE	LEVEL	GENRE	WORD COUNT	AUTHOR / SERIES	PUBLISHER / DISTRIBUTOR
Working Together	C	I	50	Early Connections	Benchmark Education
World Around Us, The	C	I	29	Little Red Readers	Sundance
Worm, The	C	F	38	Sun Sprouts	ETA/Cuisenaire
Would You Like to Fly?	C	F	52	Twig	Wright Group/McGraw Hill
Wrinkles	C	I	32	Literacy 2000	Rigby
X Ray, The	C	RF	48	Learn to Read	Creative Teaching Press
Yakkity-Yak	C	F	49	Learn to Read	Creative Teaching Press
Yes, I Can	C	RF	30	Teacher's Choice Series	Pearson Learning Group
You	C	I	20	Carousel Earlybirds	Pearson Learning Group
Yummy, Tum, Tee	C	F	51	Little Celebrations	Pearson Learning Group
Zebra's Yellow Van	C	F	31	Ready Readers	Pearson Learning Group
Zippers	C	RF	21	Books for Young Learners	Richard C. Owen
Zoo Food	C	I	58	Reading Corners	Pearson Learning Group
Zoo, The	C	RF	33	Carousel Readers	Pearson Learning Group
Zoom! Zoom!	C	F	43	Joy Readers	Pearson Learning Group
Accidents	D	RF	35	Visions	Wright Group/McGraw Hill
Add the Animals	D	I	74	Early Connections	Benchmark Education
After School	D	I	58	Sunshine	Wright Group/McGraw Hill
All Join In	D	F	38	Literacy 2000	Rigby
All Kinds of Fish	D	F	37	Instant Readers	Harcourt School Publishers
All Kinds of Food	D	RF	72	Carousel Readers	Pearson Learning Group
All Kinds of Food	D	I	72	Learn to Read	Creative Teaching Press
All Pull Together	D	F	69	Home Connection Collection	Rigby
Amy Goes to School	D	RF	89	Literacy Tree	Rigby
Animal Crackers	D	F	194	Bookshop	Mondo
Animal Homes	D	I	53	Instant Readers	Harcourt School Publishers
Animal Noises	D	I	56	Little Red Readers	Sundance
Animal Shapes	D	I	14	Wildsmith, Brian	Oxford University Press
Animal Tracks	D	I	152	Wonder World	Wright Group/McGraw Hill
Animals	D	I	70	Foundations	Wright Group/McGraw Hill
Animals at the Mall	D	F	39	Teacher's Choice Series	Pearson Learning Group
Animals Hide	D	I	55	Discovery Links	Newbridge
Animals in the Desert	D	I	31	Carousel Readers	Pearson Learning Group
Anna's Big Day	D	RF	73	Sun Sprouts	ETA/Cuisenaire
Ant, The	D	F	48	Ray's Readers	Outside the Box
Apple Floats, An	D	I	35	Science	Outside the Box
Apple Trees	D	I	62	Pebble Books	Capstone Press
Are You There?	D	F	81	Sun Sprouts	ETA/Cuisenaire
As Fast as a Fox	D	RF	69	Ready Readers	Pearson Learning Group
At Grandma's House	D	RF	66	Teacher's Choice Series	Pearson Learning Group
At Last!	D	RF	41	Rigby Literacy	Rigby
At Night	D	RF	21	Literacy Tree	Rigby
At the Fair	D	I	116	Little Red Readers	Sundance
At the Fair	D	RF	175	Sunshine	Wright Group/McGraw Hill
At the Horse Show	D	I	24	Books for Young Learners	Richard C. Owen
At the Park	D	I	91	Little Red Readers	Sundance
At the Park	D	I	37	Hoenecke, Karen	Kaeden Books
At the Park	D	RF	74	Teacher's Choice Series	Pearson Learning Group
At the Supermarket	D	I	29	Read-More Books	Pearson Learning Group
At the Toyshop	D	RF	41	Home Connection Collection	Rigby
At the Vet	D	RF	83	Leveled Readers	Houghton Mifflin
At the Water Hole	D	I	70	Little Red Readers	Sundance
At the Zoo	D	RF	116	Predictable Storybooks	SRA/McGraw Hill
At the Zoo	D	RF	37	Little Celebrations	Pearson Learning Group

* Collection of short stories

TITLE	LEVEL	GENRE	WORD COUNT	AUTHOR / SERIES	PUBLISHER / DISTRIBUTOR
Auntie Maria and the Cat	D	RF	215	Sunshine	Wright Group/McGraw Hill
Aunts	D	I	49	Pebble Books	Capstone Press
Babies	D	I	42	Canizares, Susan; Chanko, Pamela	Scholastic
Baby Animals	D	I	78	Foundations	Wright Group/McGraw Hill
Baby Animals	D	I	41	Discovery Links	Newbridge
Baby Birds	D	I	37	Windows on Literacy	National Geographic
Baby Birds	D	I	51	Pebble Books	Capstone Press
Baby Elephant Gets Lost	D	F	90	Foundations	Wright Group/McGraw Hill
Baby Hippo	D	RF	117	PM Extensions-Yellow	Rigby
Baby Panda	D	RF	97	PM Plus Story Books	Rigby
Baby Shark, The	D	I	49	Windows on Literacy	National Geographic
Baby's Birthday	D	RF	53	Literacy 2000	Rigby
Bad Day, The	D	RF	93	Teacher's Choice Series	Pearson Learning Group
Baked Potatoes	D	RF	73	Book Bank	Wright Group/McGraw Hill
Baking	D	I	27	Harry's Math Books	Outside the Box
Ball Bounced, The	D	F	33	Tafuri, Nancy	Morrow
Ball Game, A	D	I	72	Carousel Readers	Pearson Learning Group
Ballerina Girl	D	RF	77	My First Reader	Grolier Press
Balloon, The	D	F	64	Carousel Readers	Pearson Learning Group
Balloons!	D	F	56	Storyteller-First Snow	Wright Group/McGraw Hill
Banana Monster, The	D	F	54	Joy Readers	Pearson Learning Group
Barney Bear Gets Dressed	D	F	38	Learn to Read	Creative Teaching Press
Bath for a Beagle	D	RF	102	First Start	Troll Associates
Bats at Bat	D	F	36	Pair-It Books	Steck-Vaughn
Bats, Bats, Bats	D	I	29	Rosen Real Readers	Rosen Publishing Group
Beach, The	D	RF	38	Book Bank	Wright Group/McGraw Hill
Beak Book, The	D	I	48	Chanko, Pamela	Scholastic
Bear Escape, The	D	F	42	Pair-It Books	Steck-Vaughn
Bear Lived in a Cave, A	D	I	102	Little Red Readers	Sundance
Bears	D	F	56	Joy Readers	Pearson Learning Group
Bears in the Night	D	F	108	Berenstain, Stan & Jan	Random House
Bears on Wheels	D	F	89	Berenstain, Stan & Jan	Random House
Bears' Picnic, The	D	F	61	Story Box	Wright Group/McGraw Hill
Bears, Bears Everywhere	D	F	52	Rookie Readers	Children's Press
Bears, Bears, Bears	D	RF	76	Step-By-Step Series	Pearson Learning Group
Beat This	D	RF	79	Ready Readers	Pearson Learning Group
Beep, Beep, Beep	D	F	86	Foundations	Wright Group/McGraw Hill
Beetles	D	I	39	Pebble Books	Capstone Press
Bella and Rosie Play Hide and Seek	D	RF	118	Bella and Rosie Series	Pioneer Valley
Ben's Fun Box	D	RF	63	New Way Red	Steck-Vaughn
Ben's Teddy Bear	D	RF	68	PM Story Books	Rigby
Ben's Treasure Hunt	D	RF	72	PM Story Books	Rigby
Best Friends	D	RF	15	Instant Readers	Harcourt School Publishers
Best Friends	D	RF	68	Little Readers	Houghton Mifflin
Best Places, The	D	RF	68	Ready Readers	Pearson Learning Group
Big and Green	D	I	12	Wonder World	Wright Group/McGraw Hill
Big and Little	D	F	92	Joy Readers	Pearson Learning Group
Big Box, The	D	F	81	Leveled Readers	Houghton Mifflin
Big Bradley	D	F	30	Ray's Readers	Outside the Box
Big Cat, The	D	RF	41	Ready Readers	Pearson Learning Group
BIG Elephants	D	I	41	Rosen Real Readers	Rosen Publishing Group
Big Hill, The	D	F	19	Story Box	Wright Group/McGraw Hill
Big Sneeze, The	D	F	112	Foundations	Wright Group/McGraw Hill
Big Tug	D	F	80	Leveled Readers	Houghton Mifflin

* Collection of short stories

TITLE	LEVEL	GENRE	WORD COUNT	AUTHOR / SERIES	PUBLISHER / DISTRIBUTOR
Big, Hit, The	D	RF	120	PM Plus Story Books	Rigby
Bigger Than? Smaller Than?	D	I	123	Early Connections	Benchmark Education
Bike Ride, The	D	RF	100	Emergent	Pioneer Valley
Bike Ride, The	D	RF	72	Leveled Readers Language Support	Houghton Mifflin
Bike Trip, The	D	RF	60	Leveled Readers	Houghton Mifflin
Bill and Ted at the Store	D	F	50	Joy Readers	Pearson Learning Group
Bill of Rights, The	D	I	364	Independent Readers Social Studies	Houghton Mifflin
Billy Can Count	D	RF	122	PM Plus Story Books	Rigby
Billy Is Hiding	D	RF	97	PM Plus Story Books	Rigby
Bingo	D	TL	179	PM Readalongs	Rigby
Bingo's Ice-Cream Cone	D	RF	88	PM Plus Story Books	Rigby
Bird Feeder, The	D	I	55	Coulton, Mia	Kaeden Books
Birds	D	I	39	All About Pets	Red Brick Learning
Birds Need Trees	D	I	63	Teacher's Choice Series	Pearson Learning Group
Birthday Balloons	D	F	104	Rigby Literacy	Rigby
Birthday Bear	D	F	91	Sun Sprouts	ETA/Cuisenaire
Birthday Cake	D	RF	27	Literacy 2000	Rigby
Black and White	D	I	77	Storyteller Nonfiction	Wright Group/McGraw Hill
Blackberries	D	F	107	PM Story Books	Rigby
Blow, Wind, Blow!	D	RF	114	Story Steps	Rigby
Blue Bug and the Bullies	D	F	18	Poulet, Virginia	Children's Press
Blue Bug Goes to School	D	F	57	Poulet, Virginia	Children's Press
Blue Bug's Vegetable Garden	D	F	27	Poulet, Virginia	Children's Press
Blueberry Muffins	D	RF	191	Story Box	Wright Group/McGraw Hill
Boat Trip, The	D	F	70	Carousel Earlybirds	Pearson Learning Group
Boats	D	I	57	Twig	Wright Group/McGraw Hill
Boats, Boats, Boats	D	I	44	My First Reader	Grolier Press
Bobbie and the Baby	D	RF	62	Rigby Literacy	Rigby
Boogie-Woogie Man, The	D	F	101	Story Box	Wright Group/McGraw Hill
Boom Boom Bay!	D	RF	130	Phonics and Friends	Hampton-Brown
Boots for the King	D	F	93	Sun Sprouts	ETA/Cuisenaire
Boring Day, The	D	RF	81	Emergent Books	Pioneer Valley
Bossy and Wag	D	F	63	Sun Sprouts	ETA/Cuisenaire
Boxes of Fun	D	RF	95	Story Steps	Rigby
Boys and Girls	D	RF	62	Williams, Deborah	Kaeden Books
Braids	D	RF	24	Visions	Wright Group/McGraw Hill
Bread	D	RF	69	Sunshine	Wright Group/McGraw Hill
Bread for the Ducks	D	RF	109	PM Plus Story Books	Rigby
Breakfast	D	RF	23	Voyages	SRA/McGraw Hill
Breakfast on the Farm	D	I	73	Storyteller Nonfiction	Wright Group/McGraw Hill
Bricks, Wood, and Stones	D	I	54	Windows on Literacy	National Geographic
Bridges	D	RF	62	Seedlings	Continental Press
Bridges	D	I	49	Canizares, Susan; Moreton, Daniel	Scholastic
Brushing Well	D	I	42	Pebble Books	Capstone Press
Bulldozer, The	D	I	48	Sunshine	Wright Group/McGraw Hill
Bumble Bee	D	I	53	Pacific Literacy	Pacific Learning
Bump, Bump, Bump	D	RF	51	Cat on the Mat	Oxford University Press
Bunny, Bunny	D	F	40	My First Reader	Grolier Press
Busy Week, A	D	RF	49	Pair-It Books	Steck-Vaughn
But Granny Did!	D	RF	58	Voyages	SRA/McGraw Hill
By the Tree	D	RF	75	Ready Readers	Pearson Learning Group
Cake for Mom, A	D	RF	63	Home Connection Collection	Rigby

* Collection of short stories

TITLE	LEVEL	GENRE	WORD COUNT	AUTHOR / SERIES	PUBLISHER / DISTRIBUTOR
Camping	D	RF	64	Hooker, Karen	Kaeden Books
Can a Cow Hop?	D	I	40	Ready Readers	Pearson Learning Group
Can You Find the Pattern?	D	I	113	Visions	Wright Group/McGraw Hill
Can't You See We're Reading?	D	RF	71	Stepping Stones	Nelson/Michaels Assoc.
Car Followed Us, A	D	RF	54	Books for Young Learners	Richard C. Owen
Carry-Out Food	D	RF	56	Tadpoles	Rigby
Cat and the King, The	D	F	30	Literacy 2000	Rigby
Cat at School?, A	D	RF	58	Independent Readers Social Studies	Houghton Mifflin
Cat Tails	D	I	40	Books for Young Learners	Richard C. Owen
Cat That Sat, The	D	RF	66	Start to Read	School Zone
Cat Traps	D	F	93	Coxe, Molly	Random House
Cat Who Loved Red, The	D	F	63	Salem, Lynn; Stewart, Josie	Continental Press
Cats	D	I	43	All About Pets	Red Brick Learning
Chick and the Duckling, The	D	F	112	Ginsburg, Mirra	Macmillan
Chickens	D	I	23	Books for Young Learners	Richard C. Owen
Chickens Are Here!, The	D	I	50	Vocabulary Readers	Houghton Mifflin
Chicks Don't Say Quack	D	F	86	Sun Sprouts	ETA/Cuisenaire
Chinese New Year	D	I	33	Pacific Literacy	Pacific Learning
Chores	D	RF	50	Windows on Literacy	National Geographic
Circus, The	D	RF	42	Wonder World	Wright Group/McGraw Hill
City Mouse and Country Mouse	D	TL	87	Learn to Read	Creative Teaching Press
City Noises	D	RF	37	Instant Readers	Harcourt School Publishers
Cleaning Teeth	D	I	37	Wonder World	Wright Group/McGraw Hill
Clever Fox	D	RF	114	PM Plus Story Books	Rigby
Clever Little Bird	D	F	73	Storyteller-Setting Sun	Wright Group/McGraw Hill
Closet in the Hall, The	D	F	84	Wonder World	Wright Group/McGraw Hill
Clothes	D	RF	63	Voyages	SRA/McGraw Hill
Clouds	D	RF	40	Costain, Meredith	Scholastic
Clown in the Well, The	D	F	140	Story Box	Wright Group/McGraw Hill
Come and Play	D	F	104	Story Steps	Rigby
Come and Play, Sarah!	D	RF	49	Sunshine	Wright Group/McGraw Hill
Come On, Mom	D	RF	56	New Way	Steck-Vaughn
Come Play With Me	D	RF	69	Leveled Readers	Houghton Mifflin
Come to My Party	D	RF	84	Windows on Literacy	National Geographic
Communities	D	I	42	Pebble Books	Capstone Press
Computer Game, The	D	RF	75	Rigby Literacy	Rigby
Cookies	D	RF	18	Little Celebrations	Pearson Learning Group
Cooling Off	D	RF	104	Reading Corners	Pearson Learning Group
Counting Around Town	D	RF	84	Early Connections	Benchmark Education
Cousins	D	I	41	Pebble Books	Capstone Press
Crabs on a Rock	D	RF	77	Sun Sprouts	ETA/Cuisenaire
Cracker Jack, The	D	F	25	Sunshine	Wright Group/McGraw Hill
Crickets	D	I	48	Pebble Books	Capstone Press
Crickets on the Go	D	F	56	Little Celebrations	Pearson Learning Group
Daddy Works Out	D	RF	39	Visions	Wright Group/McGraw Hill
Dad's Garden	D	RF	25	Literacy 2000	Rigby
Dancing	D	I	27	Canizares, Susan; Chessen, Betsey	Scholastic
Danny's Dollars	D	RF	88	Reading Corners	Pearson Learning Group
Danny's Five Senses	D	RF	52	Coulter, Mia	Maryruth Books
Day and Night	D	I	102	Twig	Wright Group/McGraw Hill
Definitely, Positively, Absolutely NO!	D	F	147	Story Basket	Wright Group/McGraw Hill
Dilly Duck and Dally Duck	D	F	139	PM Plus Story Books	Rigby
Dinosaur Times	D	RF	43	Sunshine	Wright Group/McGraw Hill

* Collection of short stories

TITLE	LEVEL	GENRE	WORD COUNT	AUTHOR / SERIES	PUBLISHER / DISTRIBUTOR
Dinosaurs Galore	D	F	34	Eaton, Audrey; Kennedy, Jane	Continental Press
Dirty Larry	D	RF	53	Rookie Readers	Children's Press
Do You Remember When?	D	RF	198	Visions	Wright Group/McGraw Hill
Doctor Boondoggle	D	F	51	Story Box	Wright Group/McGraw Hill
Doctor Foster	D	F	68	Seedlings	Continental Press
Does a Penguin Have Fur?	D	RF	74	Rigby Literacy	Rigby
Dog Called Mischief, A	D	RF	42	Cat on the Mat	Oxford University Press
Dog Went for a Walk	D	RF	51	Voyages	SRA/McGraw Hill
Dogs	D	I	44	All About Pets	Red Brick Learning
Don't Be Late	D	F	111	Gibson, Akimi	Scholastic
Dress Up	D	RF	80	Carousel Readers	Pearson Learning Group
Drum, The	D	TL	117	Instant Readers	Harcourt School Publishers
Ducks	D	F	94	Story Box	Wright Group/McGraw Hill
Early in the Morning	D	RF	55	Rise & Shine	Hampton-Brown
Eat Your Broccoli	D	RF	72	Books for Young Learners	Richard C. Owen
Ebenezer and the Sneeze	D	RF	77	Story Box	Wright Group/McGraw Hill
Eek!	D	F	103	Lester the Lion Series	Pioneer Valley
Eggs for Breakfast	D	I	126	PM Nonfiction-Red	Rigby
Eight Friends in All	D	RF	64	Ready Readers	Pearson Learning Group
Elephant's Trunk, An	D	I	49	Windows on Literacy	National Geographic
Elevator	D	F	90	Story Box	Wright Group/McGraw Hill
Everyday Math	D	I	102	Early Connections	Benchmark Education
Fables	D	I	40	Vocabulary Readers	Houghton Mifflin
Fabulous Fruits	D	I	121	Fiesta Series	Pearson Learning Group
Face in the Dark, The	D	RF	64	Storyteller-Setting Sun	Wright Group/McGraw Hill
Faces	D	I	250+	Little Celebrations	Pearson Learning Group
Faces of Mount Rushmore	D	I	36	Leveled Readers Social Studies	Houghton Mifflin
Fall Colors	D	I	23	Windows on Literacy	National Geographic
Families	D	I	60	Pebble Books	Capstone Press
Family Names	D	RF	36	Visions	Wright Group/McGraw Hill
Family Soccer	D	RF	55	Geddes, Diana	Kaeden Books
Fantail, Fantail	D	F	67	Pacific Literacy	Pacific Learning
Farm Chores	D	RF	35	Early Emergent, Set 4	Pioneer Valley
Farm Day	D	F	36	Little Celebrations	Pearson Learning Group
Farm Work	D	F	80	Early Connections	Benchmark Education
Fast Machines	D	RF	146	Foundations	Wright Group/McGraw Hill
Fast-Draw Freddie	D	F	50	Rookie Readers	Children's Press
Father Bear Goes Fishing	D	F	98	PM Story Books	Rigby
Feeding Time at the Zoo	D	RF	73	Windmill Books	Rigby
Feelings	D	RF	39	Rise & Shine	Hampton-Brown
Feet	D	RF	18	Story Box	Wright Group/McGraw Hill
Festival, The	D	I	146	Fiesta Series	Pearson Learning Group
First Day of School	D	RF	60	Carousel Readers	Pearson Learning Group
First in Line	D	RF	77	Teacher's Choice Series	Pearson Learning Group
Fish	D	I	34	All About Pets	Red Brick Learning
Fish	D	I	58	Sun Sprouts	ETA/Cuisenaire
Fish	D	I	58	Wonder World	Wright Group/McGraw Hill
Fishing	D	RF	48	Yukish, Joe	Kaeden Books
Fishy Color Story	D	F	142	Wylie, Joanne & David	Children's Press
Five Ducks	D	RF	89	Joy Readers	Pearson Learning Group
Five Little Monsters	D	F	146	Learn to Read	Creative Teaching Press
Five Senses	D	RF	101	Sun Sprouts	ETA/Cuisenaire
Fly, The	D	F	78	Story Steps	Rigby
Follow the Leader	D	RF	75	Teacher's Choice Series	Pearson Learning Group

* Collection of short stories

TITLE	LEVEL	GENRE	WORD COUNT	AUTHOR / SERIES	PUBLISHER / DISTRIBUTOR
Follow the Sun	D	RF	60	Leveled Readers Science	Houghton Mifflin
Food from Plants	D	RF	66	Rigby Literacy	Rigby
Food from the Farm	D	RF	78	Home Connection Collection	Rigby
Footprints in the Snow	D	RF	39	Benjamin, Cynthia	Scholastic
Fox's Box	D	I	72	Dominie Phonics Reader	Pearson Learning Group
Fred Said	D	RF	35	Sunshine	Wright Group/McGraw Hill
Freddie the Frog	D	F	132	First Start	Troll Associates
Friends	D	I	60	Sun Sprouts	ETA/Cuisenaire
Friends	D	I	134	Fiesta Series	Pearson Learning Group
Friends Go Together	D	RF	36	Pair-It Books	Steck-Vaughn
Friendship Salad	D	RF	42	Instant Readers	Harcourt School Publishers
Frito Jumps In	D	RF	34	Step-By-Step Series	Pearson Learning Group
Frog and the Fly, The	D	F	33	Cat on the Mat	Oxford University Press
Frogs	D	I	28	Pebble Books	Capstone Press
Frogs on a Log	D	F	75	Teacher's Choice Series	Pearson Learning Group
From Bud to Blossom	D	I	40	Pebble Books	Capstone Press
From Egg to Robin	D	I	31	Canizares, Susan; Chessen, Betsey	Scholastic
From the Farm to the Table	D	I	26	Rosen Real Readers	Rosen Publishing Group
Fruit Salad	D	I	18	Hoenecke, Karen	Kaeden Books
Fruit Salad	D	I	37	Wonder World	Wright Group/McGraw Hill
Fun	D	RF	45	Yannone, Deborah	Kaeden Books
Fun and Food to Eat	D	F	68	Leveled Readers Language Support	Houghton Mifflin
Fun in the Snow	D	I	76	Leveled Readers	Houghton Mifflin
Fun with Magnets	D	I	38	Rosen Real Readers	Rosen Publishing Group
Fun, Fun, Fun	D	I	71	Leveled Readers	Houghton Mifflin
Funny Faces and Funny Places	D	I	45	Ready Readers	Pearson Learning Group
Fur	D	RF	32	Mark, Jan	Harper & Row
Fussy Wolf	D	F	60	Sun Sprouts	ETA/Cuisenaire
Garage Sale, The	D	RF	44	Harry's Math Books	Outside the Box
Gardening	D	RF	77	Foundations	Wright Group/McGraw Hill
Geoffrey the Dinosaur	D	F	36	Sunshine	Wright Group/McGraw Hill
Ghosts' Secret, The	D	F	79	TOTTS	Tott Publications
Ginger	D	RF	43	Parker, Ant	Mondo
Gingerbread Men, The	D	I	37	Sunshine	Wright Group/McGraw Hill
Glasses	D	RF	19	Visions	Wright Group/McGraw Hill
Go to Bed!	D	RF	45	Joy Readers	Pearson Learning Group
Go!	D	RF	44	Little Readers	Houghton Mifflin
Gobble, Gobble, Gone	D	F	58	Little Celebrations	Pearson Learning Group
Going Here and There	D	RF	124	Early Connections	Benchmark Education
Going Out	D	RF	94	Foundations	Wright Group/McGraw Hill
Going Shopping	D	RF	92	Carousel Readers	Pearson Learning Group
Going to the Pool	D	RF	55	Pair-It Books	Steck-Vaughn
Going to the Vet	D	I	46	Sunshine	Wright Group/McGraw Hill
Going to Town With Mom and Dad	D	RF	85	Early Connections	Benchmark Education
Good Bad Cat, The	D	RF	65	Little Readers	Houghton Mifflin
Good Bad Cat, The	D	RF	65	Start to Read	School Zone
Good for You	D	F	44	Sunshine	Wright Group/McGraw Hill
Good Night Sky	D	RF	32	Seedlings	Continental Press
Good Night!	D	F	73	Leveled Readers Language Support	Houghton Mifflin
Good Night, Little Bug	D	F	54	Ready Readers	Pearson Learning Group
Good Night, Little Kitten	D	F	78	My First Reader	Grolier Press
Good-Bye, Fox	D	F	27	Instant Readers	Harcourt School Publishers

* Collection of short stories

TITLE	LEVEL	GENRE	WORD COUNT	AUTHOR / SERIES	PUBLISHER / DISTRIBUTOR
Good-Bye, Lucy	D	RF	60	Sunshine	Wright Group/McGraw Hill
Goodnight	D	RF	83	Voyages	SRA/McGraw Hill
Goodnight!	D	RF	61	Joy Readers	Pearson Learning Group
Goose Chase	D	F	43	Ready Readers	Pearson Learning Group
Gram's Hat	D	RF	76	Leveled Readers	Houghton Mifflin
Grandma and Me	D	I	68	Sun Sprouts	ETA/Cuisenaire
Grandma's Letter	D	RF	67	Foundations	Wright Group/McGraw Hill
Grandpa and Me	D	I	36	Sun Sprouts	ETA/Cuisenaire
Grass Is for Goats	D	RF	84	Joy Readers	Pearson Learning Group
Gravity	D	I	33	Wonder World	Wright Group/McGraw Hill
Greedy Cat Is Hungry	D	RF	103	Pacific Literacy	Pacific Learning
Green Means Go	D	I	25	Yellow Umbrella Books	Red Brick Learning
Green Snake, The	D	I	131	Twig	Wright Group/McGraw Hill
Green, Green	D	RF	114	Little Readers	Houghton Mifflin
Grocery Shopping	D	RF	34	Yannone, Deborah	Kaeden Books
Gulp!	D	F	103	Story Box	Wright Group/McGraw Hill
Haddie's Caps	D	F	90	Ready Readers	Pearson Learning Group
Haircut, The	D	RF	27	Hartley, Susan; Armstrong, Shane	Scholastic
Halloween	D	RF	32	Visions	Wright Group/McGraw Hill
Hamsters	D	I	39	All About Pets	Red Brick Learning
Happy Monkey's Peanuts	D	F	63	Joy Readers	Pearson Learning Group
Harry's Hats	D	F	49	Teacher's Choice Series	Pearson Learning Group
Have You Got Everything, Colin?	D	RF	72	Rigby Literacy	Rigby
Have You Seen Joe?	D	RF	57	Home Connection Collection	Rigby
Having Fun	D	I	78	Windows on Literacy	National Geographic
Hello Chick!	D	I	54	Leveled Readers Language Support	Houghton Mifflin
Hello, Dad!	D	RF	16	Pacific Literacy	Pacific Learning
Hello, Little Chick!	D	I	56	Leveled Readers	Houghton Mifflin
Help Me	D	RF	107	Emergent	Pioneer Valley
Helping	D	RF	79	Joy Readers	Pearson Learning Group
Helping My Dad	D	RF	90	Teacher's Choice Series	Pearson Learning Group
Helping You	D	I	53	Interaction	Rigby
Henry and the Helicopter	D	RF	58	Literacy 2000	Rigby
Here Comes Little Chimp	D	F	69	PM Plus Story Books	Rigby
Here We Go Round the Mulberry Bush	D	RF	187	Little Readers	Houghton Mifflin
Hey Diddle Diddle	D	F	53	Seedlings	Continental Press
Hey, Diddle, Diddle!	D	TL	30	Sunshine	Wright Group/McGraw Hill
Hi Dog	D	RF	137	Ready Readers	Pearson Learning Group
Hickory Dickory Dock	D	F	20	Instant Readers	Harcourt School Publishers
Hide and Seek	D	RF	108	PM Extensions-Red	Rigby
Hide and Seek	D	F	63	Brown, Roberta; Carey, Sue	Scholastic
Hide and Seek	D	RF	49	New Way Red	Steck-Vaughn
Hide and Seek	D	RF	49	Start to Read	School Zone
Hogboggit, The	D	RF	65	Pacific Literacy	Pacific Learning
Hoiho's Chicks	D	I	38	Pacific Literacy	Pacific Learning
Home at Last	D	F	94	Sun Sprouts	ETA/Cuisenaire
Home for Little Teddy, A	D	F	153	PM Extensions-Red	Rigby
Home, A	D	I	40	Instant Readers	Harcourt School Publishers
Homes	D	I	42	Rise & Shine	Hampton-Brown
Homes Around the World	D	I	192	iOpeners	Pearson Learning Group
Honey Bees	D	I	41	Pebble Books	Capstone Press
Hoofprints	D	RF	62	Teacher's Choice Series	Pearson Learning Group
Hooray for Snow	D	RF	15	Voyages	SRA/McGraw Hill

* Collection of short stories

TITLE	LEVEL	GENRE	WORD COUNT	AUTHOR / SERIES	PUBLISHER / DISTRIBUTOR
Hope Not	D	RF	83	Salem, Lynn; Stewart, Josie	Continental Press
Horace	D	F	56	Story Box	Wright Group/McGraw Hill
Horrible Big Black Bug, The	D	RF	50	Tadpoles	Rigby
Horse Feathers	D	I	41	Pair-It Books	Steck-Vaughn
Horses	D	I	43	All About Pets	Red Brick Learning
How Are We the Same?	D	I	100	Teacher's Choice Series	Pearson Learning Group
How Can I Help?	D	I	65	Questions & Answers	Pearson Learning Group
How Do I Feel?	D	I	64	Questions & Answers	Pearson Learning Group
How Has It Changed?	D	I	103	Rigby Literacy	Rigby
How Long Do Animals Live?	D	I	65	Pacific Literacy	Pacific Learning
How Machines Help	D	I	143	Sunshine	Wright Group/McGraw Hill
How Many Can Play?	D	I	46	Canizares, Susan; Chessen, Betsey	Scholastic
How Many Legs?	D	I	74	Bookshop	Mondo
How Many Pets?	D	RF	37	Bookshop	Mondo
How to Make a Bird Feeder	D	I	80	Rigby Literacy	Rigby
How Will I Get to Grandma's House?	D	F	103	Blevins, Wiley	Scholastic
Huge Carrot, The	D	F	50	Leveled Readers	Houghton Mifflin
Humpty Dumpty	D	F	28	Instant Readers	Harcourt School Publishers
Humpty Dumpty	D	TL	27	Peppe, Rodney	Penguin Group
Humpty Dumpty	D	TL	26	Jumbled Tumbled Tales & Rhymes	Rigby
Hungry Goat, The	D	F	30	Ray's Readers	Outside the Box
Hungry Kitten, The	D	F	95	PM Story Books	Rigby
Hurricane	D	RF	36	Joy Readers	Pearson Learning Group
Hurry Up	D	RF	49	Voyages	SRA/McGraw Hill
I Am	D	RF	27	Rookie Readers	Children's Press
I Am a Fireman	D	I	45	Read-More Books	Pearson Learning Group
I Am a Train Driver	D	I	32	Read-More Books	Pearson Learning Group
I Am an Explorer	D	RF	32	Rookie Readers	Children's Press
I Can Build a House	D	I	52	Watanabe, Shiego	Viking
I Can Do It!	D	RF	74	Early Learning Modules	Steck-Vaughn
I Can Help	D	RF	65	Teacher's Choice Series	Pearson Learning Group
I Can See You	D	RF	66	Sun Sprouts	ETA/Cuisenaire
I Can Swim	D	RF	61	Ready Readers	Pearson Learning Group
I Can Use a Computer	D	RF	52	Teacher's Choice Series	Pearson Learning Group
I Can't Sleep	D	F	71	Learn to Read	Creative Teaching Press
I Could Be	D	RF	71	Sun Sprouts	ETA/Cuisenaire
I Do Not Like Peas	D	RF	32	Visions	Wright Group/McGraw Hill
I Go to Gymnastics	D	I	58	Sun Sprouts	ETA/Cuisenaire
I Like Books	D	F	168	Browne, Anthony	Random House
I Like My Picture!	D	RF	160	Teacher's Choice Series	Pearson Learning Group
I Like Worms!	D	F	213	Sunshine	Wright Group/McGraw Hill
I Live in a House	D	I	51	Read-More Books	Pearson Learning Group
I Live in an Apartment	D	I	41	Read-More Books	Pearson Learning Group
I Love Chickens	D	F	67	Story Box	Wright Group/McGraw Hill
I Love Fishing	D	RF	37	Rookie Readers	Children's Press
I Love Mud and Mud Loves Me	D	RF	121	Stephens, Vicki	Scholastic
I Love My Grandma	D	RF	36	Rise & Shine	Hampton-Brown
I Meowed	D	RF	58	Books for Young Learners	Richard C. Owen
I Want to be a Ballerina	D	RF	66	Teacher's Choice Series	Pearson Learning Group
I Wish I Had a Dinosaur	D	F	46	Little Celebrations	Pearson Learning Group
I Work at Night	D	RF	49	Windows on Literacy	National Geographic
Ice Is . . . Whee!	D	RF	59	Rookie Readers	Children's Press
If Germs Were Purple	D	F	53	Carousel Readers	Pearson Learning Group
I'll Run Away	D	RF	53	Home Connection Collection	Rigby

* Collection of short stories

TITLE	LEVEL	GENRE	WORD COUNT	AUTHOR / SERIES	PUBLISHER / DISTRIBUTOR
I'm a Little Seed	D	F	30	Pair-It Books	Steck-Vaughn
I'm Brave	D	RF	51	Sunshine	Wright Group/McGraw Hill
I'm Hungry	D	RF	84	Tuer, Judy	Scholastic
In My Desert	D	I	24	Little Celebrations	Pearson Learning Group
In My Family	D	RF	61	Windows on Literacy	National Geographic
In My Room	D	RF	58	Seedlings	Continental Press
In Summer	D	I	36	Discovery Links	Newbridge
In the Barn	D	I	38	Vocabulary Readers	Houghton Mifflin
In the Box	D	I	36	Sun Sprouts	ETA/Cuisenaire
In the Chicken Coop	D	I	56	Twig	Wright Group/McGraw Hill
In the Country	D	I	54	Vocabulary Readers	Houghton Mifflin
In the Country	D	RF	21	Home Connection Collection	Rigby
In the Desert	D	I	62	Sunshine	Wright Group/McGraw Hill
In the Desert	D	I	51	Pacific Literacy	Pacific Learning
In the Garden	D	I	90	Literacy 2000	Rigby
In the Park	D	RF	65	Foundations	Wright Group/McGraw Hill
In the Yard	D	RF	88	Rigby Literacy	Rigby
International Day	D	I	47	Home Connection Collection	Rigby
Is a Dollar Enough?	D	RF	75	Visions	Wright Group/McGraw Hill
Is it Rough? Is it Smooth?	D	I	45	Rosen Real Readers	Rosen Publishing Group
Island, The	D	RF	24	Wildsmith, Brian	Oxford University Press
It Didn't Frighten Me	D	F	250+	Bookshop	Mondo
It Sounds Like Music	D	I	56	Pair-It Books	Steck-Vaughn
It's a Party	D	I	24	Berger, Samantha; Moreton, Daniel	Scholastic
It's Game Day	D	RF	65	Salem, Lynn; Stewart, Josie	Continental Press
It's Hot	D	RF	54	Ready Readers	Pearson Learning Group
Jack	D	TL	11	Jumbled Tumbled Tales & Rhymes	Rigby
Jack and Jill	D	F	40	Seedlings	Continental Press
Jack and Jill	D	TL	25	Jumbled Tumbled Tales & Rhymes	Rigby
Jack-O-Lanterns	D	I	47	Pebble Books	Capstone Press
Jake Makes a Map	D	RF	55	Leveled Readers	Houghton Mifflin
Jenny in Bed	D	RF	76	Lighthouse	Rigby
Jimmy	D	RF	83	Foundations	Wright Group/McGraw Hill
Jo and the Spider	D	RF	78	Sun Sprouts	ETA/Cuisenaire
Job for You, A	D	I	56	Independent Readers Social Studies	Houghton Mifflin
Jobs	D	I	71	Leveled Readers	Houghton Mifflin
Jolly Roger, the Pirate	D	F	138	PM Extensions-Yellow	Rigby
Julia's Lists	D	RF	47	Little Celebrations	Pearson Learning Group
Jump Right In	D	RF	50	Ready Readers	Pearson Learning Group
Jumprope	D	RF	31	Visions	Wright Group/McGraw Hill
Jungle Parade: A Singing Game	D	F	105	Little Celebrations	Pearson Learning Group
Just Like Dad	D	RF	44	Hiris, Monica	Kaeden Books
Just Like Me!	D	RF	62	Sunshine	Wright Group/McGraw Hill
Just Like My Grandpa	D	RF	48	Rise & Shine	Hampton-Brown
Kangaroo in the Kitchen	D	F	72	Ready Readers	Pearson Learning Group
Karina	D	RF	40	Step-By-Step Series	Pearson Learning Group
Keep the Beat	D	RF	48	Little Celebrations	Pearson Learning Group
Keeping Cool	D	I	18	Foundations	Wright Group/McGraw Hill
Kenji's Haircut	D	RF	105	Lighthouse	Rigby
Kevin Counts	D	RF	83	Seedlings	Continental Press
Kindergarten	D	RF	118	Carousel Readers	Pearson Learning Group
King's Surprise, The	D	F	54	Stewart, Josie; Salem, Lynn	Continental Press

* Collection of short stories

TITLE	LEVEL	GENRE	WORD COUNT	AUTHOR / SERIES	PUBLISHER / DISTRIBUTOR
Kite, The	D	RF	59	My First Reader	Grolier Press
Kitten Is a Baby Cat, A	D	I	64	Blevins, Wiley	Scholastic
Kitty Cat and Fat Cat	D	F	98	PM Plus Story Books	Rigby
Kitty Cat and the Fish	D	F	73	PM Plus Story Books	Rigby
Know Your Birthday Manners	D	F	38	Instant Readers	Harcourt School Publishers
Koala Bears	D	I	37	Rosen Real Readers	Rosen Publishing Group
Ladybugs	D	I	42	Pebble Books	Capstone Press
Late One Night	D	RF	97	Mader, Jan	Kaeden Books
Later	D	RF	106	Teacher's Choice Series	Pearson Learning Group
Laundromat, The	D	RF	25	Sunshine	Wright Group/McGraw Hill
Lazy Mary	D	RF	191	Story Box	Wright Group/McGraw Hill
Learning About Clouds	D	I	18	Rosen Real Readers	Rosen Publishing Group
Learning About Leaves	D	I	37	Rosen Real Readers	Rosen Publishing Group
Legs	D	I	21	Literacy 2000	Rigby
Lemon Tree, The	D	RF	28	Harry's Math Books	Outside the Box
Let's Be Friends	D	I	23	Pair-It Books	Steck-Vaughn
Let's Grab It!	D	RF	60	Leveled Readers	Houghton Mifflin
Let's Measure It!	D	F	100	Learn to Read	Creative Teaching Press
Let's Play Today	D	RF	68	Leveled Readers Language Support	Houghton Mifflin
Library, The	D	RF	96	Emergent	Pioneer Valley
Like Me	D	RF	20	Book Bank	Wright Group/McGraw Hill
Listen	D	RF	35	Visions	Wright Group/McGraw Hill
Little Bear	D	F	77	My First Reader	Grolier Press
Little Boy Blue	D	TL	32	Sunshine	Wright Group/McGraw Hill
Little Chimp Runs Away	D	F	104	PM Plus Story Books	Rigby
Little Hen, The	D	F	107	Ready Readers	Pearson Learning Group
Little Jack Horner	D	TL	29	Jumbled Tumbled Tales & Rhymes	Rigby
Little Meanie's Lunch	D	F	90	Story Box	Wright Group/McGraw Hill
Little Miss Muffet	D	RF	59	Seedlings	Continental Press
Little Miss Muffet	D	TL	26	Jumbled Tumbled Tales & Rhymes	Rigby
Little Panda, The	D	I	40	Windows on Literacy	National Geographic
Little Rabbit Is Sad	D	F	97	Williams, Deborah	Kaeden Books
Living on the Farm	D	I	155	Early Connections	Benchmark Education
Lizard Loses His Tail	D	RF	54	PM Story Books	Rigby
Lock the Gate!	D	RF	41	Leveled Readers	Houghton Mifflin
Long Ago	D	I	105	Early Connections	Benchmark Education
Long Ago and Today	D	I	72	Learn to Read	Creative Teaching Press
Longest Noodle in the World, The	D	F	66	Joy Readers	Pearson Learning Group
Look at Me	D	RF	67	Carousel Readers	Pearson Learning Group
Look for Me	D	RF	71	Story Box	Wright Group/McGraw Hill
Look in Mom's Purse	D	RF	60	Carousel Readers	Pearson Learning Group
Look into Space, A	D	I	71	Discovery World	Rigby
Look Out!	D	F	53	Sunshine	Wright Group/McGraw Hill
Look Up, Look Down	D	I	165	PM Nonfiction-Red	Rigby
Look, Bear	D	F	51	Sun Sprouts	ETA/Cuisenaire
Looking After Grandpa	D	RF	91	Foundations	Wright Group/McGraw Hill
Looking for Birds	D	I	74	Leveled Readers	Houghton Mifflin
Looking for Frogs	D	I	50	Leveled Readers	Houghton Mifflin
Looking for Numbers	D	I	91	Early Connections	Benchmark Education
Lost and Found	D	RF	64	Carousel Readers	Pearson Learning Group
*Lost and Found	D	RF	55	New Way Red	Steck-Vaughn
Lost Glove, The	D	RF	105	Foundations	Wright Group/McGraw Hill
Lost in the Fog	D	F	59	Ready Readers	Pearson Learning Group

* Collection of short stories

TITLE	LEVEL	GENRE	WORD COUNT	AUTHOR / SERIES	PUBLISHER / DISTRIBUTOR
Lost in the Woods	D	RF	120	Bella and Rosie Series	Pioneer Valley
Lost!	D	RF	57	Harry's Math Books	Outside the Box
Lump in My Bed, A	D	RF	48	Book Bank	Wright Group/McGraw Hill
Lumpy Rug	D	RF	86	Dominie Phonics Reader	Pearson Learning Group
Lunchtime	D	RF	82	Rigby Literacy	Rigby
Lyla and the New Piano	D	F	85	Lester the Lion Series	Pioneer Valley
Magnet, The	D	I	115	Sun Sprouts	ETA/Cuisenaire
Make A Bird Feeder	D	I	62	How-To Series	Benchmark Education
Make a Valentine	D	RF	33	Bookshop	Mondo
Make It Spin	D	I	18	Pacific Literacy	Pacific Learning
Making a Cat and a Mouse	D	I	121	PM Plus Nonfiction	Rigby
Making a Memory	D	I	53	Ballinger, Margaret	Scholastic
Making Pancakes	D	RF	39	Carousel Readers	Pearson Learning Group
Making Things	D	RF	64	Foundations	Wright Group/McGraw Hill
Malawi: Keeper of the Trees	D	I	250+	Little Celebrations	Pearson Learning Group
Mama and Kit Go Away	D	F	84	Leveled Readers	Houghton Mifflin
Mama Goes to School	D	RF	47	Visions	Wright Group/McGraw Hill
Many Friends, Many Languages	D	I	98	Fiesta Series	Pearson Learning Group
March Along with Me	D	F	56	Literacy 2000	Rigby
March, March, Marching	D	RF	60	Teacher's Choice Series	Pearson Learning Group
Market, The	D	RF	48	Joy Readers	Pearson Learning Group
Markets	D	I	44	Chanko, Pamela; Berger, Samantha	Scholastic
Mary Wore Her Red Dress	D	F	170	Peek, Merle	Clarion
Mary, Mary	D	TL	21	Jumbled Tumbled Tales & Rhymes	Rigby
Matt Drives the Car	D	RF	136	Early Emergent, Set 3	Pioneer Valley
Max in a Tree	D	F	86	Sun Sprouts	ETA/Cuisenaire
Maybe I'll Be	D	F	49	Carousel Readers	Pearson Learning Group
Me Too!	D	F	70	Sunshine	Wright Group/McGraw Hill
Meat Pies	D	I	21	Bebop Books	Lee & Low Books Inc.
Meet a Community Helper	D	RF	41	Independent Readers Social Studies	Houghton Mifflin
Meet Johnny Appleseed	D	B	32	Independent Readers Social Studies	Houghton Mifflin
Mess, A	D	F	34	Ready Readers	Pearson Learning Group
Mess, The	D	RF	55	My First Reader	Grolier Press
Migration, The	D	I	45	Wonder World	Wright Group/McGraw Hill
Mirror, The	D	RF	112	Story Box	Wright Group/McGraw Hill
Miss Geeta's Hair	D	F	44	Joy Readers	Pearson Learning Group
Mix It Up!	D	I	52	Rigby Focus	Rigby
Mom Can Fix Anything	D	RF	74	Learn to Read	Creative Teaching Press
Mom's New Car	D	RF	116	Foundations	Wright Group/McGraw Hill
Mom's Stories	D	RF	32	Vocabulary Readers	Houghton Mifflin
Monkey Bridge, The	D	F	66	Sunshine	Wright Group/McGraw Hill
Monkey on the Roof	D	RF	92	PM Plus Story Books	Rigby
Monster and the Baby	D	F	48	Mueller, Virginia	Puffin Books
Monster Can't Sleep	D	F	52	Mueller, Virginia	Puffin Books
Monster, The	D	RF	29	Harry's Math Books	Outside the Box
Monsters!	D	F	45	My First Reader	Grolier Press
Moon, The	D	I	51	Rigby Focus	Rigby
Moon, The	D	F	139	Joy Readers	Pearson Learning Group
Moonlight	D	RF	48	Literacy 2000	Rigby
More and More Clowns	D	F	249	Van Allen, Roach	SRA/McGraw Hill
Mouse Finds a House	D	F	72	Start to Read	School Zone

* Collection of short stories

TITLE	LEVEL	GENRE	WORD COUNT	AUTHOR / SERIES	PUBLISHER / DISTRIBUTOR
Mouse's Baby Blanket	D	F	68	Brown, Beverly Swerdlow	Continental Press
Mouse's House	D	F	70	New Way Red	Steck-Vaughn
Moving Day	D	RF	90	Foundations	Wright Group/McGraw Hill
Mr. Grump	D	F	73	Sunshine	Wright Group/McGraw Hill
Mr. Noisy	D	F	90	Learn to Read	Creative Teaching Press
Mr. Noisy Builds a House	D	F	35	Learn to Read	Creative Teaching Press
Mr. Wolf	D	F	48	Joy Readers	Pearson Learning Group
Mrs. Sato's Hens	D	F	51	Little Celebrations	Pearson Learning Group
Mrs. Sato's Hens	D	F	51	Little Readers	Houghton Mifflin
Mud	D	RF	68	Lewison, Wendy Cheyette	Random House
Mud!	D	RF	68	Lewison, Wendy Cheyette	Scholastic
Mumps	D	RF	112	PM Story Books	Rigby
Mumps	D	RF	108	Carousel Readers	Pearson Learning Group
Museum, The	D	RF	41	Sunshine	Wright Group/McGraw Hill
My Apple Tree	D	I	48	Yellow Umbrella Books	Red Brick Learning
My Baby	D	F	64	Storyteller-First Snow	Wright Group/McGraw Hill
My Best Sandwich	D	RF	25	Hartley, Susan; Armstrong, Shane	Scholastic
My Big Box	D	RF	94	Voyages	SRA/McGraw Hill
My Bike	D	I	42	Pacific Literacy	Pacific Learning
My Bike	D	I	38	Storyteller-First Snow	Wright Group/McGraw Hill
My Body	D	I	250+	Sun Sprouts	ETA/Cuisenaire
My Box	D	RF	94	Books for Young Learners	Richard C. Owen
My Breakfast	D	RF	54	Lighthouse	Rigby
My Brother	D	RF	51	Rise & Shine	Hampton-Brown
My Brother Wants to Be Like Me	D	RF	62	Mader, Jan	Kaeden Books
My Brother's Motorcycle	D	RF	45	Visions	Wright Group/McGraw Hill
My Brown Cow	D	I	62	Story Box	Wright Group/McGraw Hill
My Buddy, My Friend	D	RF	33	Visions	Wright Group/McGraw Hill
My Cat	D	I	42	Sunshine	Wright Group/McGraw Hill
My Cat	D	RF	40	Ready Readers	Pearson Learning Group
*My Cat's Surprise	D	RF	71	New Way Blue	Steck-Vaughn
My Clock is Sick	D	F	45	Ready Readers	Pearson Learning Group
My Dog	D	I	51	Sunshine	Wright Group/McGraw Hill
My Dog	D	RF	38	Visions	Wright Group/McGraw Hill
My Dog, Miffy	D	RF	38	Visions	Wright Group/McGraw Hill
My Family	D	I	88	Leveled Readers	Houghton Mifflin
My Family Tree	D	I	107	Story Steps	Rigby
My Friend Alan	D	RF	65	Carousel Readers	Pearson Learning Group
My Friends	D	RF	58	Little Celebrations	Pearson Learning Group
My Life in the Mountains	D	I	59	Rosen Real Readers	Rosen Publishing Group
My Little Brother Ben	D	RF	35	Books for Young Learners	Richard C. Owen
My Little Sister	D	RF	44	Joy Readers	Pearson Learning Group
My Messy Room	D	RF	82	Packard, Mary	Scholastic
My Mom and Dad	D	RF	86	Story Box	Wright Group/McGraw Hill
My Nest Is Best	D	RF	92	Foundations	Wright Group/McGraw Hill
My New Rocket	D	F	128	Bookshop	Mondo
My Pet	D	RF	65	Salem, Lynn; Stewart, Josie	Continental Press
My Plant	D	I	96	Rigby Literacy	Rigby
My Pup	D	RF	65	Leveled Readers	Houghton Mifflin
My Skateboard	D	RF	89	Carousel Readers	Pearson Learning Group
My Skin	D	I	64	Wonder World	Wright Group/McGraw Hill
My Toy Box Is Heavy	D	RF	99	Windows on Literacy	National Geographic
My Turn Your Turn	D	RF	78	Book Bus	Creative Edge
My Vacation	D	RF	60	Rigby Literacy	Rigby

* Collection of short stories

TITLE	LEVEL	GENRE	WORD COUNT	AUTHOR / SERIES	PUBLISHER / DISTRIBUTOR
My Week	D	RF	137	Early Connections	Benchmark Education
Naughty Patch	D	RF	74	Foundations	Wright Group/McGraw Hill
Nests	D	I	58	Literacy 2000	Rigby
Never Be	D	RF	73	Salem, Lynn; Stewart, Josie	Continental Press
New Butterfly, The	D	I	55	Sun Sprouts	ETA/Cuisenaire
New Dog, A	D	RF	52	Oxford Reading Tree	Oxford University Press
New House, The	D	F	112	Bookshop	Mondo
New Road, The	D	I	49	Joy Readers	Pearson Learning Group
Nick's Glasses	D	RF	51	Pacific Literacy	Pacific Learning
Night Animals	D	RF	56	Ready Readers	Pearson Learning Group
Night in the Desert	D	I	69	Carousel Readers	Pearson Learning Group
No Cookies Before Dinner	D	RF	138	Developing Books, Set 1	Pioneer Valley
No One Else Like Me	D	I	129	Early Connections	Benchmark Education
No One Likes Me	D	F	71	Sun Sprouts	ETA/Cuisenaire
No, Bo!	D	RF	109	Handprints C, Set 1	Educator's Publishing Service
No, No	D	F	91	Story Box	Wright Group/McGraw Hill
No, You Can't	D	RF	52	Sunshine	Wright Group/McGraw Hill
Noisy Breakfast	D	F	32	Blonder, Ellen	Scholastic
Not Enough Water	D	RF	84	Armstrong, Shane; Hartley, Susan	Scholastic
Not Yet!	D	RF	64	Reading Links	Steck-Vaughn
Now and Then	D	I	78	Windows on Literacy	National Geographic
Now I Ride	D	I	63	Carousel Readers	Pearson Learning Group
Nut Pie for Jud, A	D	I	46	Ready Readers	Pearson Learning Group
Ocean Facts	D	I	40	Rosen Real Readers	Rosen Publishing Group
Off to Grandma's House	D	RF	80	Little Celebrations	Pearson Learning Group
Old MacDonald Had a Farm	D	TL	103	Jones, Carol	Houghton Mifflin
Old MacDonald Had a Farm	D	TL	118	Rounds, Glen	Holiday House
Old Woman and the Pig, The	D	RF	68	Tiger Cub	Peguis
Old Woman Who Lived in a Shoe, The	D	F	56	Seedlings	Continental Press
On a Hill	D	RF	53	Start to Read	School Zone
On a Map	D	I	60	Windows on Literacy	National Geographic
On the Computer	D	I	67	Twig	Wright Group/McGraw Hill
On the Farm	D	RF	18	Sun Sprouts	ETA/Cuisenaire
On the Move	D	I	26	Wonder World	Wright Group/McGraw Hill
On This Earth	D	I	71	Rise & Shine	Hampton-Brown
On Vacation	D	I	88	Little Red Readers	Sundance
One Birthday, Two Traditions	D	RF	56	Independent Readers Social Studies	Houghton Mifflin
One Chick, One Egg	D	F	64	Step-By-Step Series	Pearson Learning Group
One Cold, Wet Night	D	F	134	Story Box	Wright Group/McGraw Hill
One Happy Classroom	D	RF	49	Rookie Readers	Children's Press
One More Child	D	RF	28	Harry's Math Books	Outside the Box
One O'Clock Is Time for One Nap	D	RF	56	Harry's Math Books	Outside the Box
One, Two, Buckle My Shoe	D	TL	27	Instant Readers	Harcourt School Publishers
One, Two, Three, Four	D	F	89	Rise & Shine	Hampton-Brown
Oops!	D	F	62	Mayer, Mercer	Penguin Group
Open It!	D	I	27	Pacific Literacy	Pacific Learning
Our Baby	D	RF	70	Voyages	SRA/McGraw Hill
Our Chore Chart	D	I	65	Storyteller-First Snow	Wright Group/McGraw Hill
Our Earth	D	I	33	Discovery Links	Newbridge
Our Goat	D	RF	27	Costain, Meredith	Scholastic
Our Playhouse	D	RF	46	Voyages	SRA/McGraw Hill
Our Senses	D	I	39	Rise & Shine	Hampton-Brown

* Collection of short stories

TITLE	LEVEL	GENRE	WORD COUNT	AUTHOR / SERIES	PUBLISHER / DISTRIBUTOR
Our Teacher, Miss Pool	D	F	62	Pacific Literacy	Pacific Learning
Outside, Inside	D	RF	97	Teacher's Choice Series	Pearson Learning Group
Over and Over	D	RF	39	Ray's Readers	Outside the Box
Over the Oregon Trail	D	I	131	Twig	Wright Group/McGraw Hill
Owl, That's Who!, An	D	I	31	Rosen Real Readers	Rosen Publishing Group
Pair of Babies, A	D	I	70	Early Connections	Benchmark Education
Pajama Party, The	D	F	46	Sunshine	Wright Group/McGraw Hill
Panda Bear, The	D	I	28	Rosen Real Readers	Rosen Publishing Group
Party, The	D	RF	26	Ready Readers	Pearson Learning Group
Pass the Pasta, Please	D	I	63	Storyteller-Setting Sun	Wright Group/McGraw Hill
Pat's Train	D	RF	22	KinderReaders	Rigby
Paul the Pitcher	D	RF	86	Rookie Readers	Children's Press
Paws and Claws and Other Stories	D	F	120	Story Steps	Rigby
Pen Pals	D	RF	92	Bookshop	Mondo
Penguins	D	I	250+	Rosen Real Readers	Rosen Publishing Group
Penguin's Chicks	D	I	38	Pacific Literacy	Pacific Learning
People Who Help Us	D	I	62	Foundations	Wright Group/McGraw Hill
Peppers	D	I	32	Rise & Shine	Hampton-Brown
Pet for Pat, A	D	RF	45	Rookie Readers	Children's Press
Pet Shop	D	F	167	Story Box	Wright Group/McGraw Hill
Pete's Tickets	D	RF	65	Seedlings	Continental Press
Picnic in the Sky, The	D	F	80	Foundations	Wright Group/McGraw Hill
Picnic, The	D	RF	96	Handprints C, Set 1	Educator's Publishing Service
Pigs	D	I	54	Vocabulary Readers	Houghton Mifflin
Pinata Time	D	RF	71	Teacher's Choice Series	Pearson Learning Group
Pippa's Pet Pest	D	RF	35	Home Connection Collection	Rigby
Pizza Maker, The	D	RF	57	Harry's Math Books	Outside the Box
Pizza, The	D	RF	100	Foundations	Wright Group/McGraw Hill
Planting a Garden	D	I	48	Leveled Readers Language Support	Houghton Mifflin
Play Ball!	D	RF	30	Books for Young Learners	Richard C. Owen
Play Ball, Kate	D	RF	39	Giant First Step	Troll Associates
Playground Fun	D	I	127	Early Connections	Benchmark Education
Playing With Dough	D	I	94	PM Plus Nonfiction	Rigby
Please, Mom!	D	RF	92	Lighthouse	Rigby
Pockets	D	RF	32	Visions	Wright Group/McGraw Hill
Pond for Tim, A	D	RF	62	Counters & Seekers	Steck-Vaughn
Pond Party	D	F	33	Little Celebrations	Pearson Learning Group
Pool, The	D	RF	129	Handprints C, Set 1	Educator's Publishing Service
Porcupine, A	D	I	49	Wonder World	Wright Group/McGraw Hill
Practice Makes Perfect	D	RF	111	Teacher's Choice Series	Pearson Learning Group
Praying Mantis, The	D	I	46	Pacific Literacy	Pacific Learning
Presents	D	F	43	Storyteller-First Snow	Wright Group/McGraw Hill
Puppets for a Play	D	I	45	Home Connection Collection	Rigby
Puppy Play	D	RF	67	Emergent Books	Pioneer Valley
Push!	D	RF	21	Oxford Reading Tree	Oxford University Press
Pussy Cat, Pussy Cat	D	F	44	Seedlings	Continental Press
Quack, Quack, Quack	D	F	97	Carousel Readers	Pearson Learning Group
Queen Made a Quilt	D	RF	46	Ray's Readers	Outside the Box
Rabbits	D	I	37	All About Pets	Red Brick Learning
Race Is On, The	D	F	45	New Way Red	Steck-Vaughn
Rain	D	RF	45	Step-By-Step Series	Pearson Learning Group

* Collection of short stories

TITLE	LEVEL	GENRE	WORD COUNT	AUTHOR / SERIES	PUBLISHER / DISTRIBUTOR
Rain in the Hills	D	RF	41	Book Bank	Wright Group/McGraw Hill
Rain! Rain!	D	RF	29	Rookie Readers	Children's Press
Rainy Day, A	D	RF	105	New Way Blue	Steck-Vaughn
Reading Is Everywhere	D	RF	53	Sunshine	Wright Group/McGraw Hill
Reading Under the Covers	D	RF	25	Visions	Wright Group/McGraw Hill
Ready Steady Jump	D	I	25	Pacific Literacy	Pacific Learning
Ready, Set, Go!	D	I	26	Canizares, Susan; Chanko, Pamela	Scholastic
Recycling Dump	D	I	48	Little Celebrations	Pearson Learning Group
Red and Blue and Yellow	D	I	100	PM Nonfiction-Red	Rigby
Ride in the Country, A	D	RF	83	Carousel Readers	Pearson Learning Group
Right Pet, The	D	F	66	Leveled Readers	Houghton Mifflin
River, The	D	I	42	Foundations	Wright Group/McGraw Hill
Rocks	D	I	49	Voyages	SRA/McGraw Hill
Roller Coaster, The	D	RF	115	Handprints C, Set 1	Educator's Publishing Service
Roof and a Door, A	D	I	93	PM Nonfiction-Red	Rigby
Rosie, the Nosy Goat	D	RF	56	Sunshine	Wright Group/McGraw Hill
Roy G. Biv	D	F	68	Story Box	Wright Group/McGraw Hill
Rumble, Rumble, Boom!	D	I	26	Pacific Literacy	Pacific Learning
Run For It!	D	F	64	Rigby Literacy	Rigby
Run, Rabbit, Run!	D	RF	96	PM Plus Story Books	Rigby
Safe at Work	D	I	99	Early Connections	Benchmark Education
Salad Feast, A	D	RF	57	Little Readers	Houghton Mifflin
Sally's Beans	D	RF	123	PM Story Books	Rigby
Sam	D	RF	87	Early Connections	Benchmark Education
Sam and the Waves	D	RF	122	PM Plus Story Books	Rigby
Sam Writes	D	RF	62	Book Bank	Wright Group/McGraw Hill
Sammy's Sneeze	D	RF	69	Home Connection Collection	Rigby
Sam's Ball	D	RF	64	Lindgren, Barbro	Morrow
Sam's Cookie	D	RF	52	Lindgren, Barbro	Morrow
Sam's Dog	D	RF	52	Sun Sprouts	ETA/Cuisenaire
Sam's Picnic	D	RF	104	PM Plus Story Books	Rigby
Sam's Teddy Bear	D	RF	60	Lindgren, Barbro	Morrow
Sam's Wagon	D	RF	83	Lindgren, Barbro	Morrow
Sandwiches	D	RF	64	New Way	Steck-Vaughn
Sandwiches, Sandwiches	D	RF	54	Pair-It Books	Steck-Vaughn
Saturday Mornings	D	RF	63	Bookshop	Mondo
Save our Tree	D	I	56	Leveled Readers Social Studies	Houghton Mifflin
Scarecrow, The	D	RF	97	Little Red Readers	Sundance
Scarecrows	D	I	39	Pebble Books	Capstone Press
Scared	D	RF	59	Twig	Wright Group/McGraw Hill
Scaredy Cat Runs Away	D	F	57	Learn to Read	Creative Teaching Press
Scat! Said the Cat	D	F	33	Sunshine	Wright Group/McGraw Hill
School	D	I	50	Berger, Samantha; Chanko, Pamela	Scholastic
Scissors	D	I	51	Storyteller-Setting Sun	Wright Group/McGraw Hill
Scratch My Back	D	F	66	Foundations	Wright Group/McGraw Hill
Screech!	D	RF	43	Literacy 2000	Rigby
Seasons, The	D	I	84	Early Connections	Benchmark Education
See Me Reading	D	RF	35	Ray's Readers	Outside the Box
See the Boats Go!	D	RF	42	Windows on Literacy	National Geographic
Seed, The	D	I	51	Sunshine	Wright Group/McGraw Hill
Shadow Dance	D	RF	66	Little Celebrations	Pearson Learning Group
Shadows	D	RF	35	Literacy 2000	Rigby

* Collection of short stories

TITLE	LEVEL	GENRE	WORD COUNT	AUTHOR / SERIES	PUBLISHER / DISTRIBUTOR
Shape Story, A	D	RF	56	Seedlings	Continental Press
Shapes	D	I	98	Carousel Readers	Pearson Learning Group
Shapes at the Beach	D	I	46	Rosen Real Readers	Rosen Publishing Group
Shapes in My World	D	I	47	Visions	Wright Group/McGraw Hill
Share Bear	D	F	96	Sun Sprouts	ETA/Cuisenaire
Sharing Time	D	RF	113	Carousel Readers	Pearson Learning Group
Shoes	D	F	79	Book Bank	Wright Group/McGraw Hill
Shoes	D	RF	150	Sun Sprouts	ETA/Cuisenaire
Shoes	D	I	150	Winthrop, Elizabeth	HarperTrophy
Shoo Fly	D	RF	76	Sun Sprouts	ETA/Cuisenaire
Shopping	D	RF	44	Sunshine	Wright Group/McGraw Hill
Shopping	D	RF	26	Literacy 2000	Rigby
Shopping Day	D	I	44	Vocabulary Readers	Houghton Mifflin
Shush!	D	RF	29	Pacific Literacy	Pacific Learning
Shut the Door	D	RF	46	Visions	Wright Group/McGraw Hill
Sick Bear, The	D	RF	61	Joy Readers	Pearson Learning Group
Silly Cat Tricks	D	F	83	Teacher's Choice Series	Pearson Learning Group
Sit, Ned!	D	RF	67	Leveled Readers	Houghton Mifflin
Sky Is Falling Down, The	D	TL	101	Joy Readers	Pearson Learning Group
Sled, The	D	RF	84	Leveled Readers Language Support	Houghton Mifflin
Sleeping Out	D	RF	49	Story Box	Wright Group/McGraw Hill
Sleep-Over Mouse	D	F	63	My First Reader	Grolier Press
Sleepy Dog	D	F	118	Ziefert, Harriet	Random House
Slides	D	I	58	Pacific Literacy	Pacific Learning
Smile	D	F	38	Read-Alongs	Rigby
Smile! Said Dad	D	RF	66	Pacific Literacy	Pacific Learning
Smile, The	D	RF	53	Pacific Literacy	Pacific Learning
Smooth or Rough?	D	I	49	Rigby Focus	Rigby
Snack for Roberto, A	D	RF	82	Early Emergent, Set 2	Pioneer Valley
Snacks	D	RF	19	Joy Readers	Pearson Learning Group
Snapshots	D	RF	20	Bebop Books	Lee & Low Books Inc.
Snow	D	I	21	Sunshine	Wright Group/McGraw Hill
Snow Joe	D	RF	59	Rookie Readers	Children's Press
Snow, The	D	RF	36	Sunshine	Wright Group/McGraw Hill
Snowball Fight!	D	RF	35	Wonder World	Wright Group/McGraw Hill
Snowflakes	D	RF	49	Urmston, Kathleen; Evans, Karen	Kaeden Books
So Do I	D	RF	49	Teacher's Choice Series	Pearson Learning Group
So Sleepy	D	RF	33	Books for Young Learners	Richard C. Owen
Socks	D	RF	250+	Rigby Literacy	Rigby
Some Days Are Like That	D	RF	69	Teacher's Choice Series	Pearson Learning Group
Some People	D	I	50	Reading Corners	Pearson Learning Group
Something New	D	I	72	Little Celebrations	Pearson Learning Group
Something to Share	D	RF	98	Carousel Readers	Pearson Learning Group
Space Aliens in Our School	D	F	45	Joy Readers	Pearson Learning Group
Space Shuttle, The	D	I	45	Sunshine	Wright Group/McGraw Hill
Speedy Bee	D	F	106	PM Plus Story Books	Rigby
Spider	D	F	43	Sunshine	Wright Group/McGraw Hill
Spider Legs	D	I	52	Twig	Wright Group/McGraw Hill
Spider Spins	D	F	36	Ray's Readers	Outside the Box
Spider, Spider	D	F	70	Sunshine	Wright Group/McGraw Hill
Spiders Everywhere	D	F	36	Books for Young Learners	Richard C. Owen
Spiders, Spiders Everywhere!	D	RF	80	Learn to Read	Creative Teaching Press
Splash!	D	RF	63	New Way Red	Steck-Vaughn

* Collection of short stories

TITLE	LEVEL	GENRE	WORD COUNT	AUTHOR / SERIES	PUBLISHER / DISTRIBUTOR
Splash!	D	F	35	Sun Sprouts	ETA/Cuisenaire
Splish! Splash!	D	F	45	Little Celebrations	Pearson Learning Group
Spring Snow	D	RF	48	Little Books for Early Readers	University of Maine
Star Pictures	D	I	43	iOpeners	Pearson Learning Group
Story of Juan Bobo, The	D	TL	58	Leveled Readers Language Support	Houghton Mifflin
Sunflower Seeds	D	I	48	Story Box	Wright Group/McGraw Hill
Sunflowers	D	I	35	Pebble Books	Capstone Press
Super Shopping	D	RF	41	Rigby Literacy	Rigby
Super Terrific Me!	D	RF	64	Early Learning Modules	Steck-Vaughn
Surfer, The	D	RF	40	Wonder World	Wright Group/McGraw Hill
Surprise!	D	F	28	Story Steps	Rigby
Surprise!	D	RF	28	My First Reader	Grolier Press
Swans	D	I	53	Joy Readers	Pearson Learning Group
Swat it!	D	F	46	Bauer, Roger	Kaeden Books
Tails	D	I	52	Wonder World	Wright Group/McGraw Hill
Take a Bow, Jody	D	RF	78	Eaton, Audrey; Kennedy, Jane	Continental Press
Taking Care of a Hamster	D	I	65	Leveled Readers Science	Houghton Mifflin
Tall Things	D	I	83	PM Nonfiction-Red	Rigby
Taller and Smaller	D	F	29	Sun Sprouts	ETA/Cuisenaire
Tasty Bug, A	D	I	50	Little Celebrations	Pearson Learning Group
T-Ball	D	RF	35	Visions	Wright Group/McGraw Hill
Teddy Bear's Picnic	D	F	66	PM Plus Story Books	Rigby
Ted's Red Sled	D	RF	69	Ready Readers	Pearson Learning Group
Teeth	D	I	71	Story Box	Wright Group/McGraw Hill
Tell Me About Turtles	D	I	31	Rosen Real Readers	Rosen Publishing Group
Tess and the Cat	D	RF	81	Sun Sprouts	ETA/Cuisenaire
Thank You!	D	I	41	Chessen, Betsey; Chanko, Pamela	Scholastic
That's Dangerous	D	F	71	Voyages	SRA/McGraw Hill
Theodore	D	F	35	Ray's Readers	Outside the Box
There Is a Town	D	RF	116	Heiman, Gail	Random House
There Was a Mouse	D	RF	77	Books for Young Learners	Richard C. Owen
There's No One Like Me!	D	I	80	Sunshine	Wright Group/McGraw Hill
They Call Me . . .	D	I	31	The Candid Collection	Pearson Learning Group
Things I Like	D	F	42	Browne, Anthony	Random House
Things That Drag Behind	D	I	42	Teacher's Choice Series	Pearson Learning Group
Things That Protect You	D	RF	51	Foundations	Wright Group/McGraw Hill
This and That	D	RF	22	Home Connection Collection	Rigby
This Hat	D	RF	52	Little Celebrations	Pearson Learning Group
This Is an Island	D	RF	46	Windows on Literacy	National Geographic
This Is My Family	D	I	36	Read-More Books	Pearson Learning Group
This Is the Plate	D	RF	28	Little Celebrations	Pearson Learning Group
This Is the Seed	D	RF	115	Seedlings	Continental Press
This Little Pig	D	F	43	Seedlings	Continental Press
This Mouth	D	I	64	Wonder World	Wright Group/McGraw Hill
Three Bears, The	D	F	101	Lighthouse	Rigby
Three Little Pigs, The	D	TL	99	Folk Tales	Pioneer Valley
Thumbprint Critters	D	I	27	Little Celebrations	Pearson Learning Group
Time for a Bath	D	RF	60	Mader, Jan	Kaeden Books
Time for Play	D	RF	85	PM Plus Nonfiction	Rigby
Time for Sleep!	D	F	62	Sunshine	Wright Group/McGraw Hill
Tiny Little Woman, The	D	F	74	Joy Readers	Pearson Learning Group
To New York	D	RF	32	Story Box	Wright Group/McGraw Hill
To the Beach	D	RF	43	Urmston, Kathleen; Evans, Karen	Kaeden Books

* Collection of short stories

TITLE	LEVEL	GENRE	WORD COUNT	AUTHOR / SERIES	PUBLISHER / DISTRIBUTOR
Toby Tomato	D	F	54	Little Celebrations	Pearson Learning Group
Tom Gets Fit	D	RF	150	New Way Red	Steck-Vaughn
Tom Is Brave	D	RF	57	PM Story Books	Rigby
Too Big for Me	D	F	70	Story Box	Wright Group/McGraw Hill
Too High!	D	RF	66	Ready Readers	Pearson Learning Group
Too Little	D	RF	83	Sun Sprouts	ETA/Cuisenaire
Too Many Balloons	D	RF	182	Rookie Readers	Children's Press
Too Much Ketchup	D	F	30	Ready Readers	Pearson Learning Group
Tools to Use	D	I	42	Little Red Readers	Sundance
Tooth Fairy, The	D	F	57	My First Reader	Grolier Press
Totem Poles	D	I	46	Leveled Readers Social Studies	Houghton Mifflin
Totem Poles of North America	D	I	42	Leveled Readers Social Studies	Houghton Mifflin
Toys	D	RF	106	Tiger Cub	Peguis
Toys Long Ago	D	I	54	Yellow Umbrella Books	Red Brick Learning
Toytown Fire Engine, The	D	F	105	PM Plus Story Books	Rigby
Toytown Helicopter, The	D	F	97	PM Plus Story Books	Rigby
Toytown Rescue, The	D	F	100	PM Plus Story Books	Rigby
Traffic Jam	D	RF	18	Little Red Readers	Sundance
Treehouse	D	I	43	Hoenecke, Karen	Kaeden Books
Tricksters, The	D	F	49	Ray's Readers	Outside the Box
Try It	D	RF	49	Reading Corners	Pearson Learning Group
Turtle, The	D	I	68	Foundations	Wright Group/McGraw Hill
Two Eyes, Two Ears	D	I	83	PM Nonfiction-Red	Rigby
Two Little Birds	D	RF	60	Story Steps	Rigby
Types of Trees	D	I	29	Vocabulary Readers	Houghton Mifflin
Uh-Oh!	D	RF	62	Rigby Literacy	Rigby
Uncle Elephant and Uncle Tiger	D	TL	77	Joy Readers	Pearson Learning Group
Uncles	D	I	36	Pebble Books	Capstone Press
Uncle's Clever Tricks	D	RF	61	Joy Readers	Pearson Learning Group
Under a Full Moon	D	F	65	Leveled Readers	Houghton Mifflin
Under My Bed	D	F	49	Literacy 2000	Rigby
Unhappy Troll, The	D	F	47	Ray's Readers	Outside the Box
Up and Down	D	RF	99	New Way Red	Steck-Vaughn
Up the Tree	D	RF	41	New Way Red	Steck-Vaughn
Up Went Edmond	D	F	26	Pacific Literacy	Pacific Learning
Up, Down, and All Around	D	I	44	Windows on Literacy	National Geographic
Very Big	D	I	49	Ready Readers	Pearson Learning Group
Visit to the City, A	D	I	54	Vocabulary Readers	Houghton Mifflin
Wait for Me	D	RF	185	Visions	Wright Group/McGraw Hill
Wake Up, Wake Up!	D	F	110	Wildsmith, Brian & Rebecca	Scholastic
Walk for Pickles, A	D	RF	82	Pickles the Dog Series	Pioneer Valley
Walk in My Woods, A	D	I	83	Independent Readers Science	Houghton Mifflin
Walk, Ride, Run	D	RF	116	PM Plus Story Books	Rigby
Walking the Dog	D	RF	69	Sun Sprouts	ETA/Cuisenaire
Watch the Sky	D	I	41	Windows on Literacy	National Geographic
Water Changes	D	I	25	Instant Readers	Harcourt School Publishers
Water Falling	D	I	41	Literacy 2000	Rigby
Watermelon, The	D	RF	80	Joy Readers	Pearson Learning Group
Way Things Were, The	D	I	39	iOpeners	Pearson Learning Group
Ways to Go	D	RF	37	Early Readers	Compass Point Books
We Can Make Graphs	D	I	58	Learn to Read	Creative Teaching Press
We Clean Up!	D	RF	35	Home Connection Collection	Rigby
We Like Fish	D	I	109	PM Starters	Rigby
We Make Music	D	F	44	Literacy 2000	Rigby

* Collection of short stories

TITLE	LEVEL	GENRE	WORD COUNT	AUTHOR / SERIES	PUBLISHER / DISTRIBUTOR
We Need Water	D	I	26	Science	Outside the Box
Wee Willie Winkie	D	RF	34	Seedlings	Continental Press
Week with Aunt Bea, A	D	RF	62	Bookshop	Mondo
Whales in the Ocean	D	I	35	Rosen Real Readers	Rosen Publishing Group
What a Bad Dog!	D	RF	52	Oxford Reading Tree	Oxford University Press
What Am I?	D	I	51	Story Steps	Rigby
What Are You Doing?	D	RF	101	Foundations	Wright Group/McGraw Hill
What Can a Diver See?	D	I	44	Windows on Literacy	National Geographic
What Can Sing?	D	I	65	Sun Sprouts	ETA/Cuisenaire
What Can You Hear?	D	I	80	Tiger Cub	Peguis
What Comes in Twos?	D	I	125	Early Connections	Benchmark Education
What Did I Forget?	D	RF	43	Teacher's Choice Series	Pearson Learning Group
What Did They Drive?	D	RF	73	Windows on Literacy	National Geographic
What Do You Hear?	D	I	60	Windmill Books	Rigby
What Do You Like to Eat?	D	I	99	Foundations	Wright Group/McGraw Hill
What Do You Like to Wear?	D	I	50	Read-More Books	Pearson Learning Group
What Fell Out?	D	RF	32	Carousel Readers	Pearson Learning Group
What Floats?	D	I	46	Sun Sprouts	ETA/Cuisenaire
What I Like to Wear	D	I	93	Home Connection Collection	Rigby
What I Wear	D	RF	76	Sun Sprouts	ETA/Cuisenaire
What if You Get Lost	D	I	40	Rosen Real Readers	Rosen Publishing Group
What Is Big?	D	RF	72	Armstrong, Shane; Hartley, Susan	Scholastic
What is in the Box?	D	RF	51	Instant Readers	Harcourt School Publishers
What Is It Called?	D	RF	48	Reading Unlimited	Pearson Learning Group
What Kind of Animals?	D	I	37	Leveled Readers Science	Houghton Mifflin
What Lays Eggs?	D	I	56	Storyteller Nonfiction	Wright Group/McGraw Hill
What Makes Ten?	D	I	34	Yellow Umbrella Books	Red Brick Learning
What Time Is It?	D	RF	65	Moriarty, Julie	Scholastic
What Time Is It?	D	I	43	Learn to Read	Creative Teaching Press
What to Wear?	D	RF	42	Harry's Math Books	Outside the Box
What We Like	D	RF	71	Little Red Readers	Sundance
What Will I Be?	D	I	104	Early Connections	Benchmark Education
What Would the Zoo Do?	D	F	59	Salem, Lynn	Continental Press
What Would You Like?	D	F	52	Sunshine	Wright Group/McGraw Hill
What's Alive?	D	I	53	Discovery Links	Newbridge
What's for Lunch?	D	I	49	Rise & Shine	Hampton-Brown
What's It For?	D	I	47	Visions	Wright Group/McGraw Hill
What's Missing?	D	RF	102	Spinelle, Nancy Louise	Kaeden Books
What's the Weather Like Today?	D	I	119	Learn to Read	Creative Teaching Press
Wheat	D	I	52	Canizares, Susan; Chanko, Pamela	Scholastic
Wheels	D	I	69	Cobb, Annie	Random House
Wheels	D	RF	27	Voyages	SRA/McGraw Hill
Wheels	D	I	33	Windows on Literacy	National Geographic
Wheels	D	I	49	Rise & Shine	Hampton-Brown
Wheels	D	I	33	Sun Sprouts	ETA/Cuisenaire
When Spring Comes	D	I	23	Windows on Literacy	National Geographic
When the Tide Goes Out	D	I	74	Story Steps	Rigby
Where Are My Socks?	D	RF	42	Pacific Literacy	Pacific Learning
Where Are the Seeds?	D	I	67	Wonder World	Wright Group/McGraw Hill
Where Are the Sunhats?	D	RF	130	PM Story Books	Rigby
Where Are They?	D	RF	98	Rigby Literacy	Rigby
Where Are You Going, Aja Rose?	D	RF	100	Sunshine	Wright Group/McGraw Hill
Where Are You Going?	D	RF	66	Learn to Read	Creative Teaching Press
Where Can a Hippo Hide?	D	F	41	Ready Readers	Pearson Learning Group

* Collection of short stories

TITLE	LEVEL	GENRE	WORD COUNT	AUTHOR / SERIES	PUBLISHER / DISTRIBUTOR
Where Did They Go?	D	RF	102	Teacher's Choice Series	Pearson Learning Group
Where Do Bugs Live?	D	I	33	Pair-It Books	Steck-Vaughn
Where Do Plants Grow?	D	I	28	iOpeners	Pearson Learning Group
Where Do They Go?	D	RF	66	Rigby Literacy	Rigby
Where Do You Play?	D	I	131	Twig	Wright Group/McGraw Hill
Where Does Food Grow?	D	I	43	Blevins, Wiley	Scholastic
Where Is Curly?	D	F	69	Rigby Literacy	Rigby
Where Is Hannah?	D	RF	141	PM Extensions-Red	Rigby
Where Is It Safe to Play?	D	I	103	PM Plus Nonfiction	Rigby
Where is it?	D	RF	250+	Book Bus	Creative Edge
Where Is It?	D	RF	32	Rookie Readers	Children's Press
Where Is Kate's Skate?	D	RF	46	KinderReaders	Rigby
Where Is Miss Pool?	D	RF	55	Pacific Literacy	Pacific Learning
Where Is My Cat?	D	RF	102	Handprints C, Set 1	Educator's Publishing Service
Where Is Skunk?	D	F	65	Story Box	Wright Group/McGraw Hill
Where Is the Milk?	D	RF	87	Foundations	Wright Group/McGraw Hill
Where Is the School Bus?	D	RF	40	Carousel Readers	Pearson Learning Group
Where is the Sun?	D	I	70	Leveled Readers Science	Houghton Mifflin
Where Is Zig?	D	F	63	Leveled Readers	Houghton Mifflin
Where's Al?	D	F	49	Barton, Byron	Houghton Mifflin
Where's Baby Tom?	D	RF	91	Book Bank	Wright Group/McGraw Hill
Where's Cupcake?	D	RF	71	Little Readers	Houghton Mifflin
Where's the Frog?	D	I	46	Discovery Links	Newbridge
Where's the Puppy?	D	RF	70	Dwight, Laura	Checkerboard
Which Egg Is Mine?	D	F	65	Rise & Shine	Hampton-Brown
Which Is Heavier?	D	I	51	Questions & Answers	Pearson Learning Group
Which Toys?	D	I	40	Home Connection Collection	Rigby
Whistle Like a Bird	D	RF	53	Pair-It Books	Steck-Vaughn
Who Am I ?	D	I	81	Rise & Shine	Hampton-Brown
Who Cried for Pie?	D	F	86	First Start	Troll Associates
Who Is the Tallest?	D	RF	46	Sunshine	Wright Group/McGraw Hill
Who Is Who?	D	RF	115	Rookie Readers	Children's Press
Who Likes to Swim?	D	I	100	Teacher's Choice Series	Pearson Learning Group
Who Made These Tracks?	D	I	45	Teacher's Choice Series	Pearson Learning Group
Who Says?	D	F	36	My First Reader	Grolier Press
Who Took the Cookies from the Cookie Jar?	D	F	81	Learn to Read	Creative Teaching Press
Who Wants to Live in My House?	D	RF	60	Book Bank	Wright Group/McGraw Hill
Who Will Help?	D	TL	93	Learn to Read	Creative Teaching Press
Who Will Win the Race?	D	RF	53	Sunshine	Wright Group/McGraw Hill
Who Works at the Zoo?	D	I	31	Windows on Literacy	National Geographic
Who Works Here?	D	I	57	Questions & Answers	Pearson Learning Group
Who's Hiding?	D	I	51	Learn to Read	Creative Teaching Press
Whose Footprints?	D	I	125	Lighthouse	Rigby
Whose Shoes?	D	I	84	Twig	Wright Group/McGraw Hill
Why Do I Feel Safe?	D	I	61	Questions & Answers	Pearson Learning Group
Why Write?	D	I	47	Moreton, Daniel; Berger, Samantha	Scholastic
Why?	D	I	68	Twig	Wright Group/McGraw Hill
Wig for Pig, A	D	F	52	Leveled Readers	Houghton Mifflin
Will You Play With Me?	D	RF	84	Book Bus	Creative Edge
Will You Play with Us?	D	RF	62	Bookshop	Mondo
Will You Play?	D	F	96	Sun Sprouts	ETA/Cuisenaire
Willy the Helper	D	RF	79	Little Readers	Houghton Mifflin

TITLE	LEVEL	GENRE	WORD COUNT	AUTHOR / SERIES	PUBLISHER / DISTRIBUTOR
Wilma's Wagon	D	RF	48	Ready Readers	Pearson Learning Group
Wind Surfing	D	RF	224	Sunshine	Wright Group/McGraw Hill
Wind, The	D	RF	34	Wonder World	Wright Group/McGraw Hill
Winter Is Here	D	I	55	Weinberger, Kimberly	Scholastic
Winter Recess	D	RF	87	Emergent Books	Pioneer Valley
Wishing for a Horse	D	RF	105	Carousel Readers	Pearson Learning Group
Wiz	D	F	76	Voyages	SRA/McGraw Hill
Wobbly Tooth, The	D	RF	102	Literacy 2000	Rigby
Word Machine, The	D	F	33	Sunshine	Wright Group/McGraw Hill
Working for Dad	D	RF	31	Visions	Wright Group/McGraw Hill
Worms	D	F	39	Literacy 2000	Rigby
Wow!	D	F	145	Bookshop	Mondo
Yes, I Can!	D	F	45	Ready Readers	Pearson Learning Group
Yes, It Does	D	I	91	Teacher's Choice Series	Pearson Learning Group
You Can't Catch Me!	D	RF	89	Lighthouse	Rigby
Yum! Yum!	D	F	84	Bookshop	Mondo
Zack's Halloween Costume	D	RF	103	Early Emergent, Set 3	Pioneer Valley
Zack's House	D	RF	114	Early Emergent, Set 2	Pioneer Valley
Zoe's Birthday Presents	D	RF	83	Emergent	Pioneer Valley
1 Is for One	E	F	82	Bookshop	Mondo
100 Years Ago	E	I	119	Learn to Read	Creative Teaching Press
20 Pennies	E	RF	212	Teacher's Choice Series	Pearson Learning Group
ABC Who's Got Me?	E	F	40	Instant Readers	Harcourt School Publishers
Absolutely Not!	E	F	199	Story Steps	Rigby
A-Counting We Will Go	E	RF	191	Learn to Read	Creative Teaching Press
After Goldilocks	E	F	44	Instant Readers	Harcourt School Publishers
Alien at the Zoo	E	F	85	Sunshine	Wright Group/McGraw Hill
All About Apples	E	I	35	Rosen Real Readers	Rosen Publishing Group
All Around Our Country	E	I	112	Hutchins, Jeannie	Scholastic
All By Myself	E	RF	105	Foundations	Wright Group/McGraw Hill
All By Myself	E	F	157	Mayer, Mercer	Golden
All I Did	E	RF	83	Instant Readers	Harcourt School Publishers
All Kinds of Books	E	I	77	Canizares, Susan; Chessen, Betsey	Scholastic
All Kinds of Wheels	E	I	76	Pair-It Books	Steck-Vaughn
All Night Long	E	RF	65	Visions	Wright Group/McGraw Hill
All Over the World	E	RF	82	Jones, D.	Continental Press
Angry Old Woman, The	E	F	126	Adventures in Reading	Pearson Learning Group
Animal Babies	E	I	114	Rookie Readers	Children's Press
Animal Coverings	E	I	153	Early Connections	Benchmark Education
Animal Moms and Dads	E	I	121	Tarlow, Ellen	Scholastic
Animal Pals	E	I	111	Cherrington, Janelle	Scholastic
Animal Worlds	E	I	94	Early Connections	Benchmark Education
Animals and Their Babies	E	I	166	Early Connections	Benchmark Education
Animals in the Fall	E	I	34	Pebble Books	Capstone Press
Animals Love the Fair	E	F	43	Literacy 2000	Rigby
Ant, The	E	F	97	Ready Readers	Pearson Learning Group
Ants	E	I	50	Pebble Books	Capstone Press
Ants, Ants, Ants	E	I	131	Sunshine	Wright Group/McGraw Hill
Apple Farm, The	E	RF	95	Ready Readers	Pearson Learning Group
Apple Pie Family, The	E	RF	72	Pair-It Books	Steck-Vaughn
Apples and More Apples	E	I	97	Pair-It Books	Steck-Vaughn
Are You the New Principal?	E	RF	120	Teacher's Choice Series	Pearson Learning Group
Around and About	E	RF	209	Sun Sprouts	ETA/Cuisenaire
Around My School	E	I	60	Exploring History & Geography	Rigby

* Collection of short stories

TITLE	LEVEL	GENRE	WORD COUNT	AUTHOR / SERIES	PUBLISHER / DISTRIBUTOR
Around the Neighborhood	E	I	74	Pair-It Books	Steck-Vaughn
At Grandma's House	E	RF	118	Handprints D, Set 1	Educator's Publishing Service
At the Beach	E	RF	43	Literacy 2000	Rigby
At the Beach	E	RF	85	Oxford Reading Tree	Oxford University Press
At the Car Wash	E	RF	143	Visions	Wright Group/McGraw Hill
At the Park	E	RF	29	Oxford Reading Tree	Oxford University Press
At the Pond	E	I	55	Vocabulary Readers	Houghton Mifflin
At the Seaside	E	RF	85	Oxford Reading Tree	Oxford University Press
At the Track	E	RF	122	Ready Readers	Pearson Learning Group
At the Zoo	E	I	54	Vocabulary Readers	Houghton Mifflin
Baby Animals	E	I	109	Rigby Focus	Rigby
Baby Bear Goes Fishing	E	F	112	PM Story Books	Rigby
Baby, The	E	RF	60	Burningham, John	Crowell
Baby's Dinner	E	RF	26	Literacy 2000	Rigby
Baby-Sitter, The	E	RF	69	Oxford Reading Tree	Oxford University Press
Back and Forth	E	I	54	Pebble Books	Capstone Press
Bad Dream, The	E	RF	88	Teacher's Choice Series	Pearson Learning Group
Bad Hair Day	E	RF	113	Teacher's Choice Series	Pearson Learning Group
Ball Game, The	E	RF	45	Packard, David	Scholastic
Baseball Fun	E	RF	51	Geddes, Diana	Kaeden Books
Bath for Patches, A	E	RF	89	Carousel Readers	Pearson Learning Group
Bats, Bats, Bats	E	I	33	Pair-It Books	Steck-Vaughn
Bear Facts	E	I	41	Pair-It Books	Steck-Vaughn
Bears, Bears, Bears	E	F	250+	Story Steps	Rigby
Bears, Bears, Everywhere	E	F	67	Learn to Read	Creative Teaching Press
Beautiful Bugs	E	I	70	Fleming, Maria	Scholastic
Beaver Tale, A	E	I	228	Twig	Wright Group/McGraw Hill
Bed Rest	E	I	34	Rhythm 'N' Rhyme Readers	Pearson Learning Group
Behind the Rocks	E	RF	50	Wonder World	Wright Group/McGraw Hill
Ben Ate It	E	RF	130	Teacher's Choice Series	Pearson Learning Group
Ben Lost a Tooth	E	I	31	iOpeners	Pearson Learning Group
Benny's Baby Brother	E	RF	89	Start to Read	School Zone
Ben's Dad	E	RF	102	PM Story Books	Rigby
Best Birthday Mole Ever Had, The	E	F	252	Ready Readers	Pearson Learning Group
Best Friends	E	RF	31	Fitros, Pamela	Kaeden Books
Beth's Bed	E	RF	81	Supersonics	Rigby
Between the Tides	E	I	52	Wonder World	Wright Group/McGraw Hill
Biff's Aeroplane	E	RF	64	Oxford Reading Tree	Oxford University Press
Big and Little Dinosaurs	E	I	50	Planet Earth	Rigby
Big Ben	E	RF	100	Real Kids Readers	Millbrook Press
Big Egg	E	F	103	Coxe, Molly	Random House
Big Friend, Little Friend	E	RF	56	Greenfield, Eloise	Houghton Mifflin
Big Hole, The	E	RF	150	Developing Books	Pioneer Valley
Big Pig, Little Pig	E	F	54	Little Celebrations	Pearson Learning Group
Big Rocks, Little Rocks	E	I	180	Early Connections	Benchmark Education
Big Seed, The	E	RF	83	New Way	Steck-Vaughn
Big Snow, The	E	RF	150	Developing Books	Pioneer Valley
Big Toe, The	E	F	123	Story Box	Wright Group/McGraw Hill
Big Yellow Castle, The	E	RF	135	PM Plus Story Books	Rigby
Big, Brown Box, The	E	RF	93	Voyages	SRA/McGraw Hill
Biggest Sandwich Ever, The	E	F	87	Pair-It Books	Steck-Vaughn
Bike That Spike Likes, The	E	RF	91	Ready Readers	Pearson Learning Group
Bill's Baby	E	RF	41	Tadpoles	Rigby

TITLE	LEVEL	GENRE	WORD COUNT	AUTHOR / SERIES	PUBLISHER / DISTRIBUTOR
Bill's Trip	E	RF	77	Dominie Phonics Reader	Pearson Learning Group
Bingo's Birthday	E	RF	116	PM Plus Story Books	Rigby
Bird Flies By, A	E	I	87	Windows on Literacy	National Geographic
Bird on the Bus, A	E	RF	115	Leveled Readers	Houghton Mifflin
Birthday Celebrations	E	I	111	Early Connections	Benchmark Education
Birthday Present, The	E	F	86	Leveled Readers Language Support	Houghton Mifflin
Black Bears	E	I	50	Pebble Books	Capstone Press
Black Kitten, The	E	RF	115	Handprints C, Set 2	Educator's Publishing Service
Blanket, The	E	RF	65	Burningham, John	Crowell
Blue Bug's Book of Colors	E	F	49	Poulet, Virginia	Children's Press
Bobbie's Airplane	E	RF	64	Oxford Reading Tree	Oxford University Press
Bobby's Zoo	E	RF	54	Rookie Readers	Children's Press
Boogly, The	E	F	61	Literacy 2000	Rigby
Boo-Hoo	E	F	149	Story Box	Wright Group/McGraw Hill
Book Week	E	RF	71	Oxford Reading Tree	Oxford University Press
Boots and Shoes	E	F	68	Cooper, Anne	Kaeden Books
Bottle Garden, A	E	I	52	Wonder World	Wright Group/McGraw Hill
Box Can Be Many Things, A	E	RF	51	Rookie Readers	Children's Press
Boxes	E	F	103	Foundations	Wright Group/McGraw Hill
Boxes, Boxes, Boxes	E	RF	63	Stewart, Josie; Salem, Lynn	Continental Press
Brave Father Mouse	E	RF	92	PM Story Books	Rigby
Brothers	E	I	65	Talk About Books	Pearson Learning Group
Brown Bears	E	I	45	Pebble Books	Capstone Press
Bruno's Birthday	E	RF	32	Literacy 2000	Rigby
Brushes	E	I	109	Rigby Literacy	Rigby
Bubble Gum Can Be Trouble	E	RF	147	Visions	Wright Group/McGraw Hill
Bumble Bees	E	I	56	Pebble Books	Capstone Press
Burrows	E	I	51	Storyteller-Setting Sun	Wright Group/McGraw Hill
Buster McCluster	E	F	71	Wonder World	Wright Group/McGraw Hill
Buster McCluster has Chicken Pox	E	RF	77	Wonder World	Wright Group/McGraw Hill
Buster the Balloon	E	F	70	Mathtales	Mimosa
Busy Street	E	RF	67	Tadpoles	Rigby
Butch, the Outdoor Cat	E	RF	65	Carousel Readers	Pearson Learning Group
Butterflies	E	I	41	Pebble Books	Capstone Press
Buzz Is Part of a Bee, A	E	RF	56	Rookie Readers	Children's Press
By Myself or with My Friends	E	RF	200	Learn to Read	Creative Teaching Press
By the Stream	E	RF	73	Oxford Reading Tree	Oxford University Press
Cake, The	E	RF	250+	Story Steps	Rigby
Calico Cat's Rainbow	E	F	78	Charles, Donald	Children's Press
Camping	E	RF	264	Sunshine	Wright Group/McGraw Hill
Camping Out	E	RF	141	Visions	Wright Group/McGraw Hill
Camping Trip, The	E	RF	71	Leveled Readers Language Support	Houghton Mifflin
Castle	E	I	37	Exploring History & Geography	Rigby
Cat Games	E	F	229	Ziefert, Harriet	Puffin Books
Catch It, Marvin	E	RF	61	Windmill Books	Rigby
Catch That Frog	E	F	131	Reading Unlimited	Pearson Learning Group
Catherine the Counter	E	RF	86	Sunshine	Wright Group/McGraw Hill
Cecil the Caterpillar	E	F	130	Lighthouse	Rigby
Celebrating Mother's Day: Mom's Memory Box	E	F	100	Learn to Read	Creative Teaching Press
Charlie's Black Hen	E	RF	89	Seedlings	Continental Press
Charlie's P.E. Gear	E	RF	102	Lighthouse	Rigby

* Collection of short stories

TITLE	LEVEL	GENRE	WORD COUNT	AUTHOR / SERIES	PUBLISHER / DISTRIBUTOR
Chen's Christmas Tree	E	RF	166	Developing Books	Pioneer Valley
Chicken and the Egg, The	E	I	68	Sun Sprouts	ETA/Cuisenaire
Chicken Feed	E	RF	67	Joy Readers	Pearson Learning Group
Chicken Little	E	TL	107	Sunshine	Wright Group/McGraw Hill
Chocolate, Chocolate, Chocolate	E	RF	106	Visions	Wright Group/McGraw Hill
Chook, Chook	E	RF	42	Sunshine	Wright Group/McGraw Hill
Choosing a Puppy	E	RF	158	PM Extensions-Yellow	Rigby
Christmas Shopping	E	RF	48	Literacy 2000	Rigby
Cinco de Mayo	E	I	120	Fiesta Holiday Series	Pearson Learning Group
Cinderella Dressed in Yellow	E	F	81	Learn to Read	Creative Teaching Press
Circular Movement	E	I	43	Pebble Books	Capstone Press
City Cat and the Country Cat, The	E	F	152	Ready Readers	Pearson Learning Group
City Life and Country Life	E	F	66	Moriarty, Julie	Scholastic
City Scenes	E	RF	24	Pacific Literacy	Pacific Learning
City Storm	E	I	180	Twig	Wright Group/McGraw Hill
Click	E	RF	41	Books for Young Learners	Richard C. Owen
Clifford Can	E	F	55	Blevins, Wiley	Scholastic
Close Your Eyes	E	RF	131	Foundations	Wright Group/McGraw Hill
Cold Day, A	E	I	71	Pebble Books	Capstone Press
Collections	E	RF	54	Ballinger, Margaret; Gosset, Rachel	Scholastic
Colorful Ghost, The	E	F	135	TOTTS	Tott Publications
Colors of Horses	E	I	49	Brand, Mona	Kaeden Books
Communities	E	I	59	Wonder World	Wright Group/McGraw Hill
Cookies to Share	E	RF	45	Pair-It Books	Steck-Vaughn
Cooking Thanksgiving Dinner	E	RF	126	Early Emergent	Pioneer Valley
Cook-Out, The	E	RF	78	Oxford Reading Tree	Oxford University Press
Cool in the Summer	E	I	63	Windows on Literacy	National Geographic
Costume Parade, The	E	RF	57	Learn to Read	Creative Teaching Press
Covers	E	RF	30	Little Celebrations	Pearson Learning Group
Crabs	E	I	46	Pebble Books	Capstone Press
Creepy Caterpillar	E	F	118	Little Readers	Houghton Mifflin
Crocodile and a Whale, A	E	RF	127	PM Plus Story Books	Rigby
Cupcakes	E	F	68	Leveled Readers	Houghton Mifflin
Curious Cat	E	F	95	Little Celebrations	Pearson Learning Group
Curly to the Rescue	E	F	107	Rigby Literacy	Rigby
Custard	E	RF	82	Wonder World	Wright Group/McGraw Hill
Dad and Beth Clean Up	E	RF	113	Book Bus	Creative Edge
Dad's Bathtime	E	RF	114	Literacy Tree	Rigby
Dad's Bike	E	RF	52	Literacy 2000	Rigby
Dalmations	E	I	70	Seedlings	Continental Press
Dan and Dan	E	RF	96	Real Kids Readers	Millbrook Press
Dan Goes Home	E	F	153	Story Basket	Wright Group/McGraw Hill
Dancing	E	I	42	Instant Readers	Harcourt School Publishers
Dancing Dinosaurs	E	F	45	Little Celebrations	Pearson Learning Group
Dandelion, The	E	RF	99	Sunshine	Wright Group/McGraw Hill
Daniel's Basketball Team	E	RF	80	Carousel Readers	Pearson Learning Group
Danny and Abby Are Friends	E	RF	109	Coulter, Mia	Maryruth Books
Danny Gets Fit	E	RF	177	Coulter, Mia	Maryruth Books
Danny's New Toy	E	RF	70	Coulter, Mia	Maryruth Books
Day Shopping, A	E	RF	157	Foundations	Wright Group/McGraw Hill
Days at the Beach	E	I	85	Sun Sprouts	ETA/Cuisenaire
Days of Adventure	E	F	47	Bookshop	Mondo
Deep in the Woods	E	RF	164	Carousel Readers	Pearson Learning Group

* Collection of short stories

TITLE	LEVEL	GENRE	WORD COUNT	AUTHOR / SERIES	PUBLISHER / DISTRIBUTOR
Desert Friends	E	I	48	Ray's Readers	Outside the Box
Designs	E	I	15	Little Celebrations	Pearson Learning Group
Detective Dog and the Search for Cat	E	F	142	Learn to Read	Creative Teaching Press
Diana Made Dinner	E	RF	81	Carousel Readers	Pearson Learning Group
Diddle Diddle Dumpling	E	F	54	Seedlings	Continental Press
Dinosaur Fun Facts	E	I	84	Pair-It Books	Steck-Vaughn
Dinosaurs	E	I	37	Instant Readers	Harcourt School Publishers
Dinosaurs Dance	E	F	17	Rookie Readers	Children's Press
Dishy-Washy	E	F	92	Story Basket	Wright Group/McGraw Hill
Dizzy Lizzy	E	RF	37	Literacy 2000	Rigby
Do Ladybugs Go to School?	E	F	75	Visions	Wright Group/McGraw Hill
Dog and the Bone, The	E	TL	67	Leveled Readers	Houghton Mifflin
Don't Be Silly	E	F	76	Teacher's Choice Series	Pearson Learning Group
Don't Forget	E	RF	80	Literacy Tree	Rigby
Don't Panic!	E	RF	122	Book Bank	Wright Group/McGraw Hill
Don't Talk to Strangers	E	I	157	Rosen Real Readers	Rosen Publishing Group
Don't You Laugh at Me!	E	F	167	Sunshine	Wright Group/McGraw Hill
Double Dutch	E	RF	191	Visions	Wright Group/McGraw Hill
Down at the River	E	RF	51	Pacific Literacy	Pacific Learning
Down By the Bay	E	RF	121	Little Celebrations	Pearson Learning Group
Down By the Stream	E	I	97	Independent Readers Science	Houghton Mifflin
Down on the Farm	E	F	244	Learn to Read	Creative Teaching Press
Down the Street	E	RF	66	Little Celebrations	Pearson Learning Group
Down the Well	E	F	200	Sun Sprouts	ETA/Cuisenaire
Downtown Lost & Found	E	F	55	New Reader Series	Bungalo Books
Dragon!	E	F	68	Wonder World	Wright Group/McGraw Hill
Dragonflies	E	I	39	Pebble Books	Capstone Press
Drawbridge	E	I	29	Books for Young Learners	Richard C. Owen
Dreams	E	RF	93	Book Bank	Wright Group/McGraw Hill
Dressed-Up Sammy	E	F	91	Urmston, Kathleen; Evans, Karen	Kaeden Books
Duck, Duck, Goose!	E	F	92	My First Reader	Grolier Press
Ear Book	E	I	119	Perkins, Al	Random House
Ears	E	I	74	Rigby Literacy	Rigby
Earthquake	E	RF	40	Wonder World	Wright Group/McGraw Hill
Easter	E	I	112	Fiesta Holiday Series	Pearson Learning Group
Eat Your Peas, Louise	E	RF	83	Rookie Readers	Children's Press
Elephant Play	E	F	35	Sun Sprouts	ETA/Cuisenaire
Elephants Are Coming, The	E	F	138	Little Readers	Houghton Mifflin
Elephant's Trunk, The	E	I	60	Seedlings	Continental Press
Engelbert's Exercises	E	F	23	Little Celebrations	Pearson Learning Group
Engines	E	I	81	Sunshine	Wright Group/McGraw Hill
Every Bird Has a Beak	E	I	49	Birds Series	Pearson Learning Group
Every Bird Has Feathers	E	I	50	Birds Series	Pearson Learning Group
Every Bird has Two Feet	E	I	46	Birds Series	Pearson Learning Group
Every Day But Sunday	E	RF	83	Home Connection Collection	Rigby
Every Mother Bird Builds a Nest	E	I	62	Birds Series	Pearson Learning Group
Everyone Says Sh-h-h!	E	RF	93	Rigby Literacy	Rigby
Excuses, Excuses	E	RF	104	Tadpoles	Rigby
Eyes are Everywhere	E	I	131	Ready Readers	Pearson Learning Group
Fall	E	I	73	Sunshine	Wright Group/McGraw Hill
Fall Harvest	E	I	39	Pebble Books	Capstone Press
Families Share	E	RF	72	Learn to Read	Creative Teaching Press
Family, The	E	RF	55	Sunshine	Wright Group/McGraw Hill
Famous Feet	E	F	34	Instant Readers	Harcourt School Publishers

* Collection of short stories

TITLE	LEVEL	GENRE	WORD COUNT	AUTHOR / SERIES	PUBLISHER / DISTRIBUTOR
Fans and Umbrellas	E	TL	107	Joy Readers	Pearson Learning Group
Fantastic Cake, The	E	RF	169	Story Box	Wright Group/McGraw Hill
Farm Alarm	E	F	103	Early Connections	Benchmark Education
Farmer and the Skunk	E	F	139	Tiger Cub	Peguis
Farmer in the Dell	E	F	114	Parkinson, Kathy	Whitman
Farmer Mike	E	RF	52	Leveled Readers	Houghton Mifflin
Farmer Upsy-Daisy	E	F	129	Start to Read	School Zone
Fast Food	E	RF	112	Foundations	Wright Group/McGraw Hill
Fastest Gazelle, The	E	RF	146	Literacy 2000	Rigby
Feast, The	E	F	58	Leveled Readers	Houghton Mifflin
Find a Caterpillar	E	I	102	Book Bank	Wright Group/McGraw Hill
FInd the Prize	E	RF	39	Independent Readers Social Studies	Houghton Mifflin
Fire and Water	E	TL	127	Story Box	Wright Group/McGraw Hill
Fire! Fire!	E	RF	164	PM Story Books	Rigby
Firefighters	E	RF	250+	Bookshop	Mondo
Fireflies	E	I	57	Vocabulary Readers	Houghton Mifflin
Fireflies	E	I	49	Pebble Books	Capstone Press
Fishing	E	RF	47	Wonder World	Wright Group/McGraw Hill
Fishing Contest, The	E	RF	84	Literacy Tree	Rigby
Five Little Dinosaurs	E	F	113	Ready Readers	Pearson Learning Group
Five Little Monkeys Going to the Zoo	E	F	201	Valerie Cutteridge's First Grade	Continental Press
Five Little Monkeys Jumping on the Bed	E	TL	200	Christelow, Eileen	Houghton Mifflin
Five Little Monsters Went to School	E	F	65	Learn to Read	Creative Teaching Press
Fix It, Fox	E	F	62	Ready Readers	Pearson Learning Group
Fizz and Splutter	E	F	92	Story Box	Wright Group/McGraw Hill
Floppy's Bath	E	F	55	Oxford Reading Tree	Oxford University Press
Flowers for Mom	E	RF	88	Carousel Readers	Pearson Learning Group
Fluffy Chicks	E	RF	50	Book Bank	Wright Group/McGraw Hill
Food for Healthy Teeth	E	I	40	Pebble Books	Capstone Press
Foot Book	E	F	108	Seuss, Dr.	Random House
Forgetful Fred	E	RF	78	Tadpoles	Rigby
Four Seasons, The	E	I	154	Early Connections	Benchmark Education
Four Very Big Beans	E	RF	79	Instant Readers	Harcourt School Publishers
Free to Fly	E	RF	96	Gibson, Kathleen	Continental Press
Fresh Fall Leaves	E	RF	50	Franco, Betsy	Scholastic
Friend for Little White Rabbit	E	F	113	PM Story Books	Rigby
Frog's Day	E	F	101	Instant Readers	Harcourt School Publishers
Frog's Lunch	E	F	89	Lillegard, Dee	Scholastic
From Blossom to Fruit	E	I	44	Pebble Books	Capstone Press
From the Air	E	I	107	Wonder World	Wright Group/McGraw Hill
From the Skyscraper	E	I	82	Windows on Literacy	National Geographic
Fruit Facts	E	I	198	Rosen Real Readers	Rosen Publishing Group
Fun at the Beach	E	RF	88	Rigby Focus	Rigby
Fun Place to Eat, A	E	RF	90	Ready Readers	Pearson Learning Group
Funny Fish Story	E	F	152	Rookie Readers	Children's Press
Funny Man, A	E	F	244	Jensen, Patricia	Scholastic
Fuzz, Feathers, Fur	E	I	131	Twig	Wright Group/McGraw Hill
George Washington	E	B	69	Independent Readers Social Studies	Houghton Mifflin
George's Show and Tell	E	RF	133	Early Emergent	Pioneer Valley
Get Lost Becka!	E	RF	102	Start to Read	School Zone
Get the Ball, Slim	E	RF	94	Real Kids Readers	Millbrook Press
Getting Ready for School	E	RF	109	Foundations	Wright Group/McGraw Hill

* Collection of short stories

TITLE	LEVEL	GENRE	WORD COUNT	AUTHOR / SERIES	PUBLISHER / DISTRIBUTOR
Giggle Box, The	E	F	176	Story Box	Wright Group/McGraw Hill
Gingerbread Man, The	E	F	79	Instant Readers	Harcourt School Publishers
Giraffe Made Her Laugh, The	E	F	70	Learn to Read	Creative Teaching Press
Glenda the Lion	E	F	88	Ready Readers	Pearson Learning Group
Gloves	E	RF	103	Story Box	Wright Group/McGraw Hill
Go Back to Sleep	E	RF	74	Literacy 2000	Rigby
Go Dog Go	E	F	250+	Eastman, Philip D.	Random House
Go-cart, The	E	RF	47	Oxford Reading Tree	Oxford University Press
Going Fishing	E	RF	26	Literacy 2000	Rigby
Going to Lucy's House	E	RF	151	Sunshine	Wright Group/McGraw Hill
Going to the Beach	E	I	30	Little Red Readers	Sundance
Goldilocks and the Three Bears	E	TL	184	Hunia, Fran	Ladybird Books
Good Boy, Andrew!	E	RF	85	Literacy 2000	Rigby
*Good Catch!, A	E	RF	191	New Way Red	Steck-Vaughn
Good Choices for Cat and Dog	E	F	97	Learn to Read	Creative Teaching Press
Good Morning, Who's Snoring?	E	F	127	Story Steps	Rigby
Good Night	E	RF	114	Start to Read	School Zone
Good-bye Perky	E	RF	54	Twig	Wright Group/McGraw Hill
Grandmother	E	RF	60	Joy Readers	Pearson Learning Group
Grandpa	E	RF	70	Sunshine	Wright Group/McGraw Hill
Grandpa Knits Hats	E	RF	55	Wonder World	Wright Group/McGraw Hill
Grandpa's Boat	E	RF	108	Developing Books	Pioneer Valley
Grandpa's Train	E	RF	69	Early Emergent, Set 3	Pioneer Valley
Granny's Visit	E	RF	144	Leveled Readers Language Support	Houghton Mifflin
Great Car Race, The	E	F	162	Carousel Readers	Pearson Learning Group
Greedy Cat's Breakfast	E	F	53	Story Basket	Wright Group/McGraw Hill
Green Footprints	E	RF	42	Literacy 2000	Rigby
Green Green Green	E	F	218	Instant Readers	Harcourt School Publishers
Grow, Seed, Grow	E	I	36	Discovery Links	Newbridge
Grumpy Elephant	E	F	100	Story Box	Wright Group/McGraw Hill
Guess What Kind of Ball	E	RF	219	Urmston, Kathleen; Evans, Karen	Kaeden Books
Guess What!	E	RF	28	Literacy 2000	Rigby
Guess What?	E	RF	120	Foundations	Wright Group/McGraw Hill
Guinea Pigs	E	I	250+	Pebble Books	Capstone Press
Gum on the Drum, The	E	F	41	Start to Read	School Zone
Halloween	E	I	128	Fiesta Holiday Series	Pearson Learning Group
Halloween Danny	E	F	51	Coulter, Mia	Maryruth Books
Happy Egg	E	F	210	Kraus, Robert	Scholastic
Hats!	E	RF	59	Early Readers	Compass Point Books
Haunted House, The	E	F	77	Story Box	Wright Group/McGraw Hill
Have You Seen the Tooth Fairy?	E	RF	187	Visions	Wright Group/McGraw Hill
Healthy Visit, A	E	I	44	New Way Red	Steck-Vaughn
Heat all Around	E	I	120	Leveled Readers Science	Houghton Mifflin
Heat Changes Things	E	I	46	Windows on Literacy	National Geographic
Hello, Hello, Hello	E	RF	56	Sunshine	Wright Group/McGraw Hill
Helping Mom and Dad	E	RF	121	Learn to Read	Creative Teaching Press
Hen Can, A	E	F	159	Tiger Cub	Peguis
Henry	E	RF	77	Books for Young Learners	Richard C. Owen
Henry's Busy Day	E	F	112	Campbell, Rod	Penguin Group
Here Come the Shapes	E	F	118	PM Plus Story Books	Rigby
Here Comes Annette!	E	RF	143	Voyages	SRA/McGraw Hill
Hermit Crab	E	I	111	PM Story Books	Rigby
Hi Clouds	E	F	142	Rookie Reader	Children's Press

* Collection of short stories

TITLE	LEVEL	GENRE	WORD COUNT	AUTHOR / SERIES	PUBLISHER / DISTRIBUTOR
Hide and Seek	E	F	60	Instant Readers	Harcourt School Publishers
Hide and Seek	E	F	228	Sun Sprouts	ETA/Cuisenaire
Hi-De-Hi	E	F	110	Little Celebrations	Pearson Learning Group
Hiding	E	I	97	Foundations	Wright Group/McGraw Hill
Home Run, The	E	RF	92	Teacher's Choice Series	Pearson Learning Group
Home Sweet Home	E	I	172	Roffey, Maureen	Bodley
Honey Bees and Hives	E	I	58	Pebble Books	Capstone Press
Honey Hunt	E	RF	63	Sunshine	Wright Group/McGraw Hill
Honey, My Rabbit	E	RF	56	Voyages	SRA/McGraw Hill
Hop, Skip, Run	E	RF	109	Real Kids Readers	Millbrook Press
Horses	E	I	131	Pebble Books	Capstone Press
Hot Day, A	E	I	61	Pebble Books	Capstone Press
Hot Rod Harry	E	RF	66	Rookie Readers	Children's Press
How 100 Dandelions Grew	E	I	173	Instant Readers	Harcourt School Publishers
How Can I Help?	E	RF	73	Learn to Read	Creative Teaching Press
How Dog Lost His Bone	E	TL	100	Leveled Readers Language Support	Houghton Mifflin
How Flowers Grow	E	I	68	Rosen Real Readers	Rosen Publishing Group
How Many Ants?	E	RF	35	Rookie Readers	Children's Press
How Many Hot Dogs?	E	I	115	Story Box	Wright Group/McGraw Hill
How Many Legs?	E	I	104	Early Connections	Benchmark Education
How Many Seeds?	E	I	42	Pair-It Books	Steck-Vaughn
How Many?	E	I	147	Early Connections	Benchmark Education
How to Grow a Plant	E	I	172	Visions	Wright Group/McGraw Hill
How to Make a Sun Hat	E	I	87	Home Connection Collection	Rigby
Howie Has a Stomachache	E	F	100	Moore, Johnny R.	Continental Press
Humpback Whales	E	I	48	Pair-It Books	Steck-Vaughn
Hungry Farmer, The	E	RF	149	Learn to Read	Creative Teaching Press
Hungry Fox, The	E	F	158	Early Connections	Benchmark Education
Hungry Happy Monkey	E	F	77	Joy Readers	Pearson Learning Group
Hungry Horse	E	RF	35	Literacy 2000	Rigby
Hurry Squirrel!	E	RF	72	Start to Read	School Zone
I Am a Drummer	E	I	32	iOpeners	Pearson Learning Group
I Am a Photographer	E	I	32	Read-More Books	Pearson Learning Group
I Am Cold	E	RF	136	Foundations	Wright Group/McGraw Hill
I Am Hot	E	RF	123	Foundations	Wright Group/McGraw Hill
I Am King!	E	F	57	My First Reader	Grolier Press
I Can Be Anything	E	RF	242	Pair-It Books	Steck-Vaughn
I Can Do It Myself	E	RF	150	Visions	Wright Group/McGraw Hill
I Can Find	E	I	131	Teacher's Choice Series	Pearson Learning Group
I Can Play Tangram	E	I	99	Pacific Literacy	Pacific Learning
I Can See	E	RF	38	Cervantes, Jesus	Scholastic
I Can Squeak	E	RF	154	Windmill	Wright Group/McGraw Hill
I Can't Open It!	E	F	76	Rigby Literacy	Rigby
I Did It!	E	RF	213	Handprints D, Set 1	Educator's Publishing Service
I Got a Goldfish	E	F	92	Ready Readers	Pearson Learning Group
I Have a Home	E	RF	79	Sunshine	Wright Group/McGraw Hill
I Know Karate	E	RF	62	Packard, Mary	Scholastic
I Like It When . . .	E	RF	82	Ready Set Read	Steck-Vaughn
I Like Mess	E	RF	74	Real Kids Readers	Millbrook Press
I Love Camping	E	RF	83	Carousel Readers	Pearson Learning Group
I Love Cats	E	RF	116	Rookie Readers	Children's Press
I Love You	E	F	121	Teacher's Choice Series	Pearson Learning Group

* Collection of short stories

TITLE	LEVEL	GENRE	WORD COUNT	AUTHOR / SERIES	PUBLISHER / DISTRIBUTOR
I Saw a Dinosaur	E	F	98	Book Bus	Creative Edge
I Smell Smoke!	E	RF	49	Sunshine	Wright Group/McGraw Hill
I Was Just About To Go To Bed	E	RF	107	Instant Readers	Harcourt School Publishers
I Wonder Why	E	RF	73	Foundations	Wright Group/McGraw Hill
If Horses Could Talk!	E	RF	32	Teacher's Choice Series	Pearson Learning Group
If I Were You	E	RF	77	Wildsmith, Brian	Oxford University Press
I'll Be a Pirate	E	F	53	Eifrig, Kate	Kaeden Books
I'm Telling	E	RF	71	Teacher's Choice Series	Pearson Learning Group
In a Dark, Dark Wood	E	F	81	Story Box	Wright Group/McGraw Hill
In a Dark, Dark Wood	E	TL	168	Carter, David	Simon & Schuster Trade
In a Painting	E	I	52	Canizares, Susan; Moreton, Daniel	Scholastic
In a Town	E	RF	47	Little Celebrations	Pearson Learning Group
In My Pocket	E	RF	195	Carousel Readers	Pearson Learning Group
In The Garden	E	I	N/A	Sun Sprouts	ETA/Cuisenaire
In the Rain Forest	E	I	57	Twig	Wright Group/McGraw Hill
Inside or Outside?	E	RF	57	Literacy 2000	Rigby
Inside Story, The	E	RF	43	Teacher's Choice Series	Pearson Learning Group
Inside, Outside, Upside Down	E	F	118	Berenstain, Stan & Jan	Random House
Is It Floating?	E	I	146	Sunshine	Wright Group/McGraw Hill
Is the Spaghetti Ready?	E	F	80	New Reader Series	Bungalo Books
Is Tomorrow My Birthday?	E	RF	87	Blaxland, Wendy	Scholastic
It Could Be Worse	E	F	108	Home Connection Collection	Rigby
It Looked Like Split Milk	E	RF	172	Shaw, Charles	Harper & Row
It Starts as a Seed	E	I	36	Rosen Real Readers	Rosen Publishing Group
It's Broken	E	RF	88	Dominie Phonics Reader	Pearson Learning Group
It's Noisy at Night	E	RF	80	Wonder World	Wright Group/McGraw Hill
It's Raining	E	I	86	Teacher's Choice Series	Pearson Learning Group
It's Time for Bed	E	RF	126	Visions	Wright Group/McGraw Hill
It's Time to Get Up	E	RF	143	Visions	Wright Group/McGraw Hill
Jack and Jill	E	TL	51	Sunshine	Wright Group/McGraw Hill
Jack's New Skates	E	RF	148	Developing Books	Pioneer Valley
Jan and the Jacket	E	RF	74	Oxford Reading Tree	Oxford University Press
Jane Goodall	E	B	183	Leveled Readers Science	Houghton Mifflin
Jane Goodall: Living With Chimpanzees	E	B	162	Leveled Readers Science	Houghton Mifflin
Jenny's Garden	E	RF	45	Leveled Readers Science	Houghton Mifflin
Jess in the Snow	E	RF	109	Handprints C, Set 2	Educator's Publishing Service
Jigaree, The	E	F	128	Story Box	Wright Group/McGraw Hill
Jimmy's Goal	E	RF	159	Foundations	Wright Group/McGraw Hill
Jobs	E	F	112	Benger, Wendy	Kaeden Books
Jobs: Making and Helping	E	I	63	Windows on Literacy	National Geographic
Jock Jerome	E	F	99	Voyages	SRA/McGraw Hill
Joe and the BMX Bike	E	RF	91	Oxford Reading Tree	Oxford University Press
Joe's Father	E	RF	138	Book Bank	Wright Group/McGraw Hill
Jolly Jumping Jelly Beans	E	F	121	Sunshine	Wright Group/McGraw Hill
Jolly Roger and the Treasure	E	F	129	PM Plus Story Books	Rigby
Juan Bobo	E	TL	55	Leveled Readers	Houghton Mifflin
Jumble Sale, The	E	RF	81	Oxford Reading Tree	Oxford University Press
Jumbo	E	RF	133	PM Plus Story Books	Rigby
Jumper	E	RF	125	Literacy Tree	Rigby
Just a Seed	E	I	74	Blaxland, Wendy	Scholastic
Just Like Grandpa	E	RF	81	Literacy 2000	Rigby
Just Like Me	E	RF	138	Rookie Readers	Children's Press
Just Like Us	E	RF	55	Ready Readers	Pearson Learning Group

* Collection of short stories

TITLE	LEVEL	GENRE	WORD COUNT	AUTHOR / SERIES	PUBLISHER / DISTRIBUTOR
Just Right for the Night	E	RF	69	Voyages	SRA/McGraw Hill
Katie's Caterpillar	E	RF	149	PM Plus Story Books	Rigby
Katydids	E	I	20	Books for Young Learners	Richard C. Owen
Keeping Fit!	E	F	36	Little Celebrations	Pearson Learning Group
King's Slippers, The	E	F	107	Sun Sprouts	ETA/Cuisenaire
Kipper's Birthday	E	RF	64	Oxford Reading Tree	Oxford University Press
Kitchen Tools	E	I	104	Foundations	Wright Group/McGraw Hill
Kite Dance	E	RF	65	Danforth, Audrey	Continental Press
Kitty Cat Plays Inside	E	F	134	PM Plus Story Books	Rigby
Knock, Knock	E	RF	96	Leveled Readers	Houghton Mifflin
Koalas	E	I	36	Literacy 2000	Rigby
Larry and the Cookie	E	RF	56	Rookie Readers	Children's Press
Leaf Boats, The	E	RF	132	PM Plus Story Books	Rigby
Learning About Rain	E	I	26	Rosen Real Readers	Rosen Publishing Group
Learning About Sand	E	I	42	Rosen Real Readers	Rosen Publishing Group
Lend a Hand	E	I	26	iOpeners	Pearson Learning Group
Let's Eat	E	RF	63	Teacher's Choice Series	Pearson Learning Group
Let's Go Camping	E	I	44	Vocabulary Readers	Houghton Mifflin
Let's Go Marching	E	RF	94	Ready Readers	Pearson Learning Group
Let's Go to a Museum	E	RF	181	Blevins, Wiley	Scholastic
Let's Play Basketball	E	RF	46	Geddes, Diana	Kaeden Books
Let's Take Care of the Earth	E	I	121	Learn to Read	Creative Teaching Press
Let's Visit the Moon	E	F	130	Instant Readers	Harcourt School Publishers
Life in the City	E	RF	184	Handprints D, Set 1	Educator's Publishing Service
Life of a Butterfly, The	E	I	46	Vocabulary Readers	Houghton Mifflin
Life of a Lion, The	E	I	28	Rosen Real Readers	Rosen Publishing Group
Like My Daddy	E	RF	129	Visions	Wright Group/McGraw Hill
Lion and the Mouse	E	TL	87	Herman, Gail	Random House
Lion and the Mouse, The	E	SF	91	Cambridge Reading	Pearson Learning Group
Lion's Dinner, The	E	F	111	Rigby Literacy	Rigby
Little Bird	E	TL	42	Sunshine	Wright Group/McGraw Hill
Little Boy and the Balloon Man	E	F	16	Tiger Cub	Peguis
Little Bulldozer	E	F	170	PM Story Books	Rigby
Little Chicks Sing, The	E	F	52	Instant Readers	Harcourt School Publishers
Little Chimp and Baby Chimp	E	F	184	PM Plus Story Books	Rigby
Little Frog's Monster Story	E	F	144	Ready Readers	Pearson Learning Group
Little Green Man Visits a Farm, The	E	F	183	Learn to Read	Creative Teaching Press
Little Monkey Is Stuck	E	F	251	Foundations	Wright Group/McGraw Hill
Little Princess	E	F	99	Seedlings	Continental Press
Little Red Riding Hood	E	TL	140	Bookshop	Mondo
Little Tommy Tucker	E	TL	30	Jumbled Tumbled Tales & Rhymes	Rigby
Little White Hen, The	E	F	159	PM Plus Story Books	Rigby
Little Zoot	E	F	33	Little Celebrations	Pearson Learning Group
Lizard	E	RF	80	Foundations	Wright Group/McGraw Hill
Lonely Bull, The	E	F	116	Pacific Literacy	Pacific Learning
Long Walk, A	E	I	131	Twig	Wright Group/McGraw Hill
Look Here!	E	RF	67	Wonder World	Wright Group/McGraw Hill
Look Out for Bingo	E	RF	138	PM Plus Story Books	Rigby
Look Up	E	I	44	Little Celebrations	Pearson Learning Group
Look What I Can Read!	E	RF	49	Instant Readers	Harcourt School Publishers
Look, Listen, and Learn	E	I	49	Canizares, Susan; Chanko, Pamela	Scholastic
Looking After Baby	E	I	143	Storyteller Nonfiction	Wright Group/McGraw Hill
Looking at Baby Animals	E	I	54	Teacher's Choice Series	Pearson Learning Group

* Collection of short stories

TITLE	LEVEL	GENRE	WORD COUNT	AUTHOR / SERIES	PUBLISHER / DISTRIBUTOR
Looking at Cities	E	I	30	iOpeners	Pearson Learning Group
Looking Down	E	I	130	Early Connections	Benchmark Education
Lost	E	RF	29	Sun Sprouts	ETA/Cuisenaire
Lost	E	RF	82	Literacy Tree	Rigby
Lost Cat!	E	RF	156	Bookshop	Mondo
Lost Mother, The	E	RF	112	Alphakids	Sundance
Lucky Duck, The	E	F	73	Ready Readers	Pearson Learning Group
Lucky Goes to Dog School	E	RF	127	PM Story Books	Rigby
Lucy's Box	E	F	108	Cambridge Reading	Pearson Learning Group
Lunch at the Pond	E	F	146	Foundations	Wright Group/McGraw Hill
Machines	E	I	44	Twig	Wright Group/McGraw Hill
Magic Money Box, The	E	I	71	Learn to Read	Creative Teaching Press
Magic Wand, The	E	F	100	Start to Read	School Zone
Magnets	E	I	52	Discovery Links	Newbridge
Mail Myself to You	E	RF	60	Little Celebrations	Pearson Learning Group
Make a Monster	E	I	31	Windows on Literacy	National Geographic
Make a Necklace	E	I	106	How-To Series	Benchmark Education
Make a Plan of Your Classroom	E	I	94	How-To Series	Benchmark Education
Make a Safety Puppet	E	I	107	How-To Series	Benchmark Education
Make a Worm Farm	E	I	98	Sun Sprouts	ETA/Cuisenaire
Make It Move!	E	I	29	Canizares, Susan; Chessen, Betsey	Scholastic
Making a Caterpillar	E	I	115	PM Plus Nonfiction	Rigby
Making Oatmeal	E	I	38	Interaction	Rigby
Making Raisins	E	I	35	Windows on Literacy	National Geographic
Mango Tree, The	E	F	163	Sun Sprouts	ETA/Cuisenaire
Maps, Maps, Maps	E	I	47	Rosen Real Readers	Rosen Publishing Group
Maria Goes to School	E	RF	174	Foundations	Wright Group/McGraw Hill
Maria Tallchief	E	B	48	Independent Readers Social Studies	Houghton Mifflin
Marketplace, The	E	RF	58	Visions	Wright Group/McGraw Hill
Martian Goo	E	F	65	Salem, Lynn; Stewart, Josie	Continental Press
Marvin's Manners	E	RF	32	Pair-It Books	Steck-Vaughn
Mask, The	E	I	45	Pair-It Books	Steck-Vaughn
Masks	E	I	62	Wonder World	Wright Group/McGraw Hill
Matthew the Magician	E	RF	116	Learn to Read	Creative Teaching Press
Max and the Clouds	E	F	211	Sun Sprouts	ETA/Cuisenaire
Max and the Little Plant	E	RF	134	PM Plus Story Books	Rigby
Max Goes Fishing	E	RF	147	PM Plus Story Books	Rigby
Max on a Hill	E	F	80	Sun Sprouts	ETA/Cuisenaire
Max on Ice	E	F	219	Sun Sprouts	ETA/Cuisenaire
Max Rides His Bike	E	RF	143	PM Plus Story Books	Rigby
May I Stay Home Today?	E	RF	73	Tadpoles	Rigby
Meanies Came to School, The	E	F	135	Story Basket	Wright Group/McGraw Hill
Meanies' Trick, The	E	F	93	Story Box	Wright Group/McGraw Hill
Measuring Time	E	I	217	Early Connections	Benchmark Education
Measuring Weather	E	I	99	Independent Readers Science	Houghton Mifflin
Meet an Author: Laura Kvasnosky	E	B	54	Sunshine	Wright Group/McGraw Hill
Meet Mr. Cricket	E	F	86	Carousel Readers	Pearson Learning Group
Mia's Sun Hat	E	RF	32	Start to Read	School Zone
Michael in the Hospital	E	RF	91	Oxford Reading Tree	Oxford University Press
Midge in the Hospital	E	RF	91	Oxford Reading Tree	Oxford University Press
Mike's Bike	E	RF	82	Dominie Phonics Readers	Pearson Learning Group
Milwaukee Cows	E	F	79	Story Box	Wright Group/McGraw Hill
Misty Sleeps	E	RF	56	Books for Young Learners	Richard C. Owen

* Collection of short stories

TITLE	LEVEL	GENRE	WORD COUNT	AUTHOR / SERIES	PUBLISHER / DISTRIBUTOR
Mmm . . . Very Nice	E	F	91	Home Connection Collection	Rigby
Mom's Shoes	E	RF	133	Handprints C, Set 2	Educator's Publishing Service
Monkey See, Monkey Do	E	F	89	Gave, Marc	Scholastic
Monkey Tricks	E	F	81	Joy Readers	Pearson Learning Group
Monster at the Beach, The	E	RF	82	Storyteller-Moon Rising	Wright Group/McGraw Hill
Monsters' Tea Party, The	E	F	129	Learn to Read	Creative Teaching Press
Monty, the Missing Cat	E	RF	100	Developing Books	Pioneer Valley
Moon Cake, The	E	RF	127	Joy Readers	Pearson Learning Group
Moon Story	E	RF	157	Sunshine	Wright Group/McGraw Hill
More or Less Fish Story	E	F	68	Wylie, Joanne & David	Children's Press
Mosquito Buzzed, A	E	F	133	Little Readers	Houghton Mifflin
Mosquitoes	E	I	39	Pebble Books	Grolier Press
Mother's Day	E	RF	118	PM Plus Story Books	Rigby
Move it	E	I	58	Wonder World	Wright Group/McGraw Hill
Move Over!	E	F	118	Story Basket	Wright Group/McGraw Hill
Moving Day	E	RF	110	Sunshine	Wright Group/McGraw Hill
Moving In	E	RF	82	Foundations	Wright Group/McGraw Hill
Moving to America	E	RF	81	Carousel Readers	Pearson Learning Group
Mr. Bumbleticker's Birthday	E	F	110	Foundations	Wright Group/McGraw Hill
Mr. Crawford	E	RF	119	Foundations	Wright Group/McGraw Hill
Mr. Cricket Takes a Vacation	E	F	165	Carousel Readers	Pearson Learning Group
Mr. Egg	E	F	22	Pair-It Books	Steck-Vaughn
Mr. Fin's Trip	E	F	130	Ready Readers	Pearson Learning Group
Mr. Noisy Paints His House	E	F	159	Learn to Read	Creative Teaching Press
Mr. Wink	E	F	86	Ready Readers	Pearson Learning Group
Mrs. Wishy Washy	E	F	102	Story Box	Wright Group/McGraw Hill
Mud Pies	E	RF	143	Start to Read	School Zone
Mud Walk	E	F	183	Story Box	Wright Group/McGraw Hill
Music Students	E	RF	83	Dominie Phonics Reader	Pearson Learning Group
My Bed	E	RF	65	Book Bus	Creative Edge
My Big Brother	E	I	103	PM Nonfiction-Yellow	Rigby
My Body Works	E	I	131	Twig	Wright Group/McGraw Hill
My Brother, the Brat	E	RF	62	Hello Reader	Scholastic
My Bug Box	E	RF	99	Books for Young Learners	Pacific Learning
My Calculator Book	E	RF	50	Gosset, Rachel; Ballinger, Margaret	Scholastic
My Dad	E	I	114	PM Nonfiction-Yellow	Rigby
My Dad Lost His Job	E	RF	76	Carousel Readers	Pearson Learning Group
My Dad's Truck	E	I	57	Costain, Merideth	Scholastic
My Dog Talks	E	RF	250+	Herman, Gail	Scholastic
My Doll	E	RF	86	Yukish, Joe	Kaeden Books
My Faces	E	RF	62	Rhythm 'N' Rhyme Readers	Pearson Learning Group
My Fish Does Not Chirp	E	I	77	Ready Readers	Pearson Learning Group
My Friend	E	RF	95	Foundations	Wright Group/McGraw Hill
My Grandma	E	RF	67	Early Connections	Benchmark Education
My Grandma and Grandpa	E	I	130	PM Nonfiction	Rigby
My Hamster, Van	E	RF	73	Ready Readers	Pearson Learning Group
My House	E	F	79	My First Reader	Grolier Press
My Little Sister	E	I	120	PM Nonfiction-Yellow	Rigby
My Lost Top	E	RF	70	Ready Readers	Pearson Learning Group
My Models	E	RF	143	Early Connections	Benchmark Education
My New Pet	E	I	151	Sun Sprouts	ETA/Cuisenaire
My Old Cat	E	RF	110	Foundations	Wright Group/McGraw Hill

* Collection of short stories

TITLE	LEVEL	GENRE	WORD COUNT	AUTHOR / SERIES	PUBLISHER / DISTRIBUTOR
My Pal Al	E	RF	81	Real Kids Readers	Millbrook Press
My Pet Bobby	E	F	150	Little Readers	Houghton Mifflin
My Pony Minnie	E	RF	59	Sunshine	Wright Group/McGraw Hill
My Red Rowboat	E	RF	89	Early Readers	Compass Point Books
My Shadow	E	I	46	Pacific Literacy	Pacific Learning
My Special Job	E	RF	110	Pacific Literacy	Pacific Learning
My Special Place	E	RF	33	Home Connection Collection	Rigby
My Special Place	E	RF	116	Teacher's Choice Series	Pearson Learning Group
My Tiger Cat	E	F	76	Frankford, Marilyn	Kaeden Books
My Two Homes	E	RF	69	Carousel Readers	Pearson Learning Group
Mystery Food	E	RF	62	Leveled Readers Science	Houghton Mifflin
Nana's Sweet Potato Pie	E	RF	233	Visions	Wright Group/McGraw Hill
New at the Zoo	E	F	84	New Reader Series	Bungalo Books
New Baby, The	E	RF	133	PM Story Books	Rigby
New Balloon, A	E	RF	36	Pacific Literacy	Pacific Learning
New Boots	E	RF	127	PM Plus Story Books	Rigby
New Friends	E	RF	89	Leveled Readers Language Support	Houghton Mifflin
New Sled, The	E	RF	85	Leveled Readers	Houghton Mifflin
Nibbly Mouse	E	F	116	Voyages	SRA/McGraw Hill
Nickels and Pennies	E	I	53	Williams, Deborah	Kaeden Books
Nick's Pet	E	F	119	Teacher's Choice Series	Pearson Learning Group
Night and Day	E	I	112	Ready Readers	Pearson Learning Group
Night Train, The	E	F	65	Story Box	Wright Group/McGraw Hill
Night Walk	E	RF	47	Prokopchak, Ann	Kaeden Books
Nine Days of Camping, The	E	RF	254	Twig	Wright Group/McGraw Hill
No, I Won't	E	F	174	Seedlings	Continental Press
Noggin and Bobbin in the Garden	E	F	57	Little Celebrations	Pearson Learning Group
Noises	E	I	49	Literacy 2000	Rigby
Noisy Toys	E	RF	77	Home Connection Collection	Rigby
Nose Book	E	I	111	Perkins, Al	Random House
Noses	E	I	56	Literacy 2000	Rigby
Numbers Are Everywhere	E	I	125	Early Connections	Benchmark Education
Numbers Are Everywhere	E	I	131	Twig	Wright Group/McGraw Hill
Oh a Hunting We Will Go	E	TL	346	Langstaff, John	Macmillan
Oh No Otis!	E	F	45	Rookie Readers	Children's Press
Oh No!	E	F	118	Sun Sprouts	ETA/Cuisenaire
Oh No!	E	RF	118	Bookshop	Mondo
Oh, Cats!	E	RF	93	Buck, Nola	HarperTrophy
Oh, Jump in a Sack	E	F	130	Story Box	Wright Group/McGraw Hill
Oh, No, Sherman	E	RF	66	Erickson, Betty	Continental Press
Old Bumpy Alligator	E	F	69	Books for Young Learners	Richard C. Owen
Old King Cole	E	TL	33	Jumbled Tumbled Tales & Rhymes	Rigby
Old Toad, The	E	F	189	Phonics and Friends	Hampton-Brown
Old Woman in a Shoe, The	E	TL	38	Jumbled Tumbled Tales & Rhymes	Rigby
On Stage	E	I	94	Early Connections	Benchmark Education
One and Only Special Me, The	E	RF	73	Learn to Read	Creative Teaching Press
One Sun in the Sky	E	RF	120	Windmill	Wright Group/McGraw Hill
Our Baby	E	I	90	PM Nonfiction-Yellow	Rigby
Our Camping Trip	E	RF	120	Lighthouse	Rigby
Our Cat	E	RF	99	Foundations	Wright Group/McGraw Hill
Our Classroom	E	RF	53	Leveled Readers Social Studies	Houghton Mifflin
Our Home is the Pond	E	I	52	Independent Readers Science	Houghton Mifflin
Our House Had a Mouse	E	F	102	Worthington, Denise	Continental Press

* Collection of short stories

TITLE	LEVEL	GENRE	WORD COUNT	AUTHOR / SERIES	PUBLISHER / DISTRIBUTOR
Our Mom	E	I	107	PM Nonfiction-Yellow	Rigby
Our Money	E	I	74	Leveled Readers Social Studies	Houghton Mifflin
Our Tree House	E	RF	144	Twig	Wright Group/McGraw Hill
Out the Door	E	RF	150	Rookie Readers	Children's Press
Outing, An	E	RF	68	Sunshine	Wright Group/McGraw Hill
Over the Marble Mountain	E	RF	92	Voyages	SRA/McGraw Hill
Over-Under	E	RF	29	Rookie Readers	Children's Press
Owl, That's Who, An	E	I	31	Rosen Real Readers	Rosen Publishing Group
Pack a Picnic	E	F	140	Learn to Read	Creative Teaching Press
Package, The	E	RF	35	Bauer, Roger	Kaeden Books
Paper Bag Trail	E	RF	67	Schreiber, Anne; Doughty, A.	Scholastic
Party for Brown Mouse, A	E	F	149	PM Plus Story Books	Rigby
Pat's New Puppy	E	RF	88	Reading Unlimited	Pearson Learning Group
Patterns	E	I	57	Literacy 2000	Rigby
Patterns All around Me	E	I	181	Learn to Read	Creative Teaching Press
Peaches the Pig	E	F	120	Little Readers	Houghton Mifflin
Peanut Butter	E	RF	60	Little Celebrations	Pearson Learning Group
Peanut Butter and Jelly	E	RF	164	Little Readers	Houghton Mifflin
Peek-a-boo at the Zoo	E	F	49	New Reader Series	Bungalo Books
People Are Working	E	I	71	Pacific Literacy	Pacific Learning
People Can Build	E	I	46	Sunshine	Wright Group/McGraw Hill
People Dance	E	I	46	Wonder World	Wright Group/McGraw Hill
People Who Save Animals	E	I	143	Careers Series	Benchmark Education
People Work at the Supermarket	E	I	77	Windows on Literacy	National Geographic
Pet Care	E	I	35	Chessen, Betsey	Scholastic
Pet Day	E	F	70	Sun Sprouts	ETA/Cuisenaire
Pet Day at School	E	I	103	Story Steps	Rigby
Pet for Me, A	E	RF	152	Alphakids	Sundance
Pet That I Want, The	E	F	57	Packard, Mary	Scholastic
Peter Piper	E	TL	32	Jumbled Tumbled Tales & Rhymes	Rigby
Pets for the Twins	E	RF	101	Leveled Readers	Houghton Mifflin
Picking Apples	E	RF	128	Developing Books	Pioneer Valley
Pickles Goes to School	E	RF	90	Pickles the Dog Series	Pioneer Valley
Pictures	E	RF	76	Teacher's Choice Series	Pearson Learning Group
Pig's Tall Hat	E	F	81	Leveled Readers Language Support	Houghton Mifflin
Pirate's Treasure, The	E	F	63	Joy Readers	Pearson Learning Group
Place for Nicholas, A	E	RF	82	Instant Readers	Harcourt Trade
Plan a Party	E	I	47	Vocabulary Readers	Houghton Mifflin
Planes, Trains, and More	E	I	43	iOpeners	Pearson Learning Group
Planting a Garden	E	I	62	Ready Readers	Pearson Learning Group
Planting Beans and Beets	E	I	53	Leveled Readers	Houghton Mifflin
Playing Ball	E	RF	170	Handprints C, Set 2	Educator's Publishing Service
Polar Bears	E	I	78	Vocabulary Readers	Houghton Mifflin
Polly's Shop	E	RF	130	Ready Readers	Pearson Learning Group
POP Pops the Popcorn	E	RF	60	Ready Readers	Pearson Learning Group
Present, The	E	F	30	Literacy 2000	Rigby
Press a Button	E	I	43	Windows on Literacy	National Geographic
Pumpkin Grows, A	E	I	176	Bookshop	Mondo
Pumpkin, The	E	I	56	Story Box	Wright Group/McGraw Hill
Puppet Show, The	E	I	25	Literacy 2000	Rigby
Purple Is Part of a Rainbow	E	RF	131	Rookie Readers	Children's Press
Push and Pull	E	I	184	Pebble Books	Capstone Press

* Collection of short stories

TITLE	LEVEL	GENRE	WORD COUNT	AUTHOR / SERIES	PUBLISHER / DISTRIBUTOR
Quack!	E	F	48	Ready Readers	Pearson Learning Group
Quarter Story, The	E	I	99	Williams, Deborah	Kaeden Books
Queen of Hearts, The	E	TL	26	Jumbled Tumbled Tales & Rhymes	Rigby
Quick, Go Peek!	E	F	83	Little Celebrations	Pearson Learning Group
Quilts	E	I	131	Twig	Wright Group/McGraw Hill
Rabbit and Turtle Go to School	E	F	67	Instant Readers	Harcourt Trade
Race, The	E	F	30	Little Celebrations	Pearson Learning Group
Rain and the Sun, The	E	I	45	Wonder World	Wright Group/McGraw Hill
Rain Is Water	E	I	82	PM Plus Nonfiction	Rigby
Rain, Rain	E	RF	58	Pacific Literacy	Pacific Learning
Rainy Day Alphabet Book	E	RF	82	Posner, Jackie; Wiener, Sara	Scholastic
Rainy Day, A	E	I	52	Pebble Books	Capstone Press
Rainy Day, Sunny Day	E	F	135	Early Connections	Benchmark Education
Rat-a-tat-tat	E	F	107	Literacy 2000	Rigby
Rattlesnake Looks for Food, The	E	RF	105	Foundations	Wright Group/McGraw Hill
Ready for School	E	RF	77	Windmill Books	Rigby
Red	E	F	71	Instant Readers	Harcourt School Publishers
Red Rose, The	E	F	127	Story Box	Wright Group/McGraw Hill
Red Squirrel Hides Some Nuts	E	RF	128	PM Plus Story Books	Rigby
Rex's Dance	E	F	103	Little Readers	Houghton Mifflin
Riddles	E	I	51	Literacy 2000	Rigby
River Grows, The	E	I	70	Ready Readers	Pearson Learning Group
Roar Like a Tiger	E	RF	148	PM Plus Story Books	Rigby
Rocks	E	I	59	Science	Harcourt School Publishers
Rocks Rocks Rocks	E	I	76	Independent Readers Science	Houghton Mifflin
Roll Out the Red Rug	E	F	68	Ready Readers	Pearson Learning Group
Room for Pip	E	F	175	Bookshop	Mondo
Rope Swing, The	E	RF	77	Oxford Reading Tree	Oxford University Press
Rosie's Party	E	F	111	Little Readers	Houghton Mifflin
Round and Round the Seasons Go	E	I	43	Learn to Read	Creative Teaching Press
Roy and the Parakeet	E	F	74	Oxford Reading Tree	Oxford University Press
Rummage Sale, The	E	RF	81	Oxford Reading Tree	Oxford University Press
Rum-Tum-Tum	E	F	62	Story Box	Wright Group/McGraw Hill
Runaway Sandy	E	RF	97	Leveled Readers	Houghton Mifflin
Rush, Rush, Rush	E	RF	52	Ready Readers	Pearson Learning Group
Sack Race, A	E	RF	106	New Way Blue	Steck-Vaughn
Sad Monster	E	F	160	Handprints D, Set 1	Educator's Publishing Service
Safety at the Playground	E	I	42	Rosen Real Readers	Rosen Publishing Group
Safety on the School Bus	E	I	38	Rosen Real Readers	Rosen Publishing Group
Saguaro	E	I	44	Books for Young Learners	Richard C. Owen
Sally and the Sparrows	E	RF	151	PM Extensions-Yellow	Rigby
Sally's Red Bucket	E	RF	127	PM Story Books	Rigby
Sally's Spaceship	E	RF	86	Ready Readers	Pearson Learning Group
Sam Goes to School	E	RF	131	PM Plus Story Books	Rigby
Sam's Cap	E	RF	78	Dominie Phonics Reader	Pearson Learning Group
Sam's Mask	E	RF	36	Pacific Literacy	Pacific Learning
Sam's Seasons	E	RF	143	Pair-It Books	Steck-Vaughn
Sand	E	RF	78	Giant Step Readers	Educational Insights
Sand Castle Contest, The	E	RF	173	Pair-It Books	Steck-Vaughn
Sand Picnic, The	E	RF	123	New Way White	Steck-Vaughn
Sandy Runs Away	E	RF	102	Leveled Readers Language Support	Houghton Mifflin
Sarah Snail	E	RF	55	Voyages	SRA/McGraw Hill

* Collection of short stories

TITLE	LEVEL	GENRE	WORD COUNT	AUTHOR / SERIES	PUBLISHER / DISTRIBUTOR
Sarah's Seed	E	RF	107	Literacy Tree	Rigby
Saturday Morning Breakfast	E	RF	65	Teacher's Choice Series	Pearson Learning Group
School Bus, The	E	RF	60	Sunshine	Wright Group/McGraw Hill
School, The	E	RF	27	Burningham, John	Crowell
Schools Around the World	E	I	78	Pair-It Books	Steck-Vaughn
Science Tools	E	I	52	Canizares, Susan; Chessen, Betsey	Scholastic
Sea Star, A	E	I	82	Ready Readers	Pearson Learning Group
Sea Stars	E	I	63	Pebble Books	Capstone Press
Seagull Is Clever	E	RF	98	PM Story Books	Rigby
Secret Friend, The	E	RF	189	Little Readers	Houghton Mifflin
Secret Friend, The	E	RF	196	Little Celebrations	Pearson Learning Group
Secret Message, The	E	RF	68	Literacy Tree	Rigby
Secret Soup	E	RF	51	Literacy 2000	Rigby
Seed Song, The	E	I	41	Learn to Read	Creative Teaching Press
Seed Surprise	E	RF	67	Seedlings	Continental Press
Seeds, Seeds, Seeds	E	I	96	Sunshine	Wright Group/McGraw Hill
Senses	E	I	66	Voyages	SRA/McGraw Hill
Shadows	E	RF	190	Visions	Wright Group/McGraw Hill
Shag Goes Fishing, The	E	RF	51	Ready to Read	Pacific Learning
Shane and Ned	E	F	52	Windmill Books	Rigby
Shapes Everywhere	E	I	82	Early Connections	Benchmark Education
She'll Be Coming Around the Mountain	E	F	250+	Learn to Read	Creative Teaching Press
Shopping	E	RF	170	Handprints C, Set 2	Educator's Publishing Service
Shopping	E	RF	101	Storyteller-Setting Sun	Wright Group/McGraw Hill
Shopping	E	I	45	Read-More-Books	Pearson Learning Group
Show and Tell	E	RF	214	Alphakids	Sundance
Sid and Sam	E	RF	120	Buck, Nola	HarperTrophy
Signs	E	I	131	Twig	Wright Group/McGraw Hill
Simply Sam	E	RF	69	Voyages	SRA/McGraw Hill
Sing a Song	E	F	154	Story Box	Wright Group/McGraw Hill
Sink or Float?	E	I	112	Learn to Read	Creative Teaching Press
Sisters	E	I	77	Talk About Books	Pearson Learning Group
Sitting	E	F	46	Literacy 2000	Rigby
Skating Whiz	E	RF	40	Visions	Wright Group/McGraw Hill
Skin, Skin	E	I	44	Wonder World	Wright Group/McGraw Hill
Skipper's Balloon	E	RF	62	Oxford Reading Tree	Oxford University Press
Skipper's Birthday	E	RF	64	Oxford Reading Tree	Oxford University Press
Skipper's Idea	E	RF	81	Oxford Reading Tree	Oxford University Press
Skipper's Laces	E	RF	66	Oxford Reading Tree	Oxford University Press
Sleeping	E	I	43	Literacy 2000	Rigby
Sleepy Bear	E	I	153	Foundations	Wright Group/McGraw Hill
Small and Large	E	I	89	iOpeners	Pearson Learning Group
Smarty Pants	E	F	116	Story Box	Wright Group/McGraw Hill
Smiling Stan, the Pedicab Man	E	RF	121	Joy Readers	Pearson Learning Group
Smokie	E	RF	47	Carousel Readers	Pearson Learning Group
Snails	E	I	67	Foundations	Wright Group/McGraw Hill
Snails and Slugs	E	I	54	Sun Sprouts	ETA/Cuisenaire
Snake Hunts for Lunch	E	RF	115	Hoenecke, Karen	Kaeden Books
Snakes	E	I	37	Visions	Wright Group/McGraw Hill
Snakes	E	I	250+	Pebble Books	Capstone Press
Snake's Dinner	E	F	156	Alphakids	Sundance
Snap Likes Ginger Cookies	E	F	63	Gosset, Rachel	Scholastic
Snow	E	I	28	Book Bank	Wright Group/McGraw Hill

* Collection of short stories

TITLE	LEVEL	GENRE	WORD COUNT	AUTHOR / SERIES	PUBLISHER / DISTRIBUTOR
Snowman, The	E	RF	76	Oxford Reading Tree	Oxford University Press
Snowy Day, A	E	I	54	Pebble Books	Capstone Press
Snowy Gets a Wash	E	RF	181	PM Extensions-Yellow	Rigby
So Many Strawberries	E	RF	75	Books for Young Learners	Richard C. Owen
Soccer	E	I	78	Sun Sprouts	ETA/Cuisenaire
Something to Munch	E	RF	58	Ready Readers	Pearson Learning Group
Soup for Snail	E	F	61	Leveled Readers Language Support	Houghton Mifflin
Special Places	E	RF	96	Rigby Literacy	Rigby
Spiders	E	I	75	Wonder World	Wright Group/McGraw Hill
Spiders	E	I	53	Discovery Links	Newbridge
Splash!	E	RF	85	Joy Readers	Pearson Learning Group
Splash!	E	RF	85	Leveled Readers Language Support	Houghton Mifflin
Splishy-Sploshy	E	F	127	Story Basket	Wright Group/McGraw Hill
Spots	E	RF	116	Real Kids Readers	Millbrook Press
Spots	E	RF	48	Literacy 2000	Rigby
Spots!	E	RF	55	Oxford Reading Tree	Oxford University Press
Spring	E	I	58	Sunshine	Wright Group/McGraw Hill
Staircase to the Sky	E	RF	133	Visions	Wright Group/McGraw Hill
Stallion's Call, The	E	F	77	Salem, Lynn; Stewart, Josie	Continental Press
Stan Packs	E	RF	84	Ready Readers	Pearson Learning Group
Starting School	E	RF	97	Voyages	SRA/McGraw Hill
Stay Cool	E	F	134	Start to Read	School Zone
Stella	E	RF	57	Storyteller-Moon Rising	Wright Group/McGraw Hill
*Stop! And Other Stories	E	F	161	Story Steps	Rigby
Storm!	E	I	49	Wonder World	Wright Group/McGraw Hill
Storm, The	E	RF	71	Foundations	Wright Group/McGraw Hill
Storm, The	E	RF	33	Literacy 2000	Rigby
Strange Plants	E	I	30	Books for Young Learners	Richard C. Owen
Strawberry Jam	E	RF	77	Oxford Reading Tree	Oxford University Press
Stuck in the Muck	E	F	139	Spinelle, Nancy Louise	Kaeden Books
Stuck in the Mud	E	RF	120	Lighthouse	Rigby
Summer	E	I	73	Sunshine	Wright Group/McGraw Hill
Summer Fun	E	RF	30	Literacy 2000	Rigby
Sun, Moon, Earth	E	I	53	Leveled Readers Science	Houghton Mifflin
Sun, The	E	I	42	Discovery Links	Newbridge
Sunflowers	E	I	33	Books for Young Learners	Richard C. Owen
Sunny Day, A	E	I	65	Pebble Books	Capstone Press
Sunshine, Moonshine	E	RF	128	Armstrong, Jennifer	Random House
Super Pig's Adventures	E	F	133	New Way Blue	Steck-Vaughn
Super Sandwich	E	I	72	Little Red Readers	Sundance
Surprise for Mom	E	RF	101	Urmston, Kathleen; Evans, Karen	Kaeden Books
Sweet Potato Pie	E	RF	72	Rockwell, Anne	Random House
Sweetest Present, The	E	F	80	Leveled Readers	Houghton Mifflin
Tails	E	I	59	Bookshop	Mondo
Tails	E	I	59	Discovery Links	Newbridge
Taking Care of Our World	E	I	137	Visions	Wright Group/McGraw Hill
Taking Care of Rosie	E	RF	61	Salem, Lynn; Stewart, Josie	Continental Press
Taking Our Photo	E	RF	132	Voyages	SRA/McGraw Hill
Taking Pictures	E	RF	137	Alphakids	Sundance
Taste Sensation	E	I	115	Visions	Wright Group/McGraw Hill
Teddy Bear, Teddy Bear	E	F	38	Tiger Cub	Peguis
Ted's Letter	E	RF	76	Dominie Phonics Reader	Pearson Learning Group

* Collection of short stories

TITLE	LEVEL	GENRE	WORD COUNT	AUTHOR / SERIES	PUBLISHER / DISTRIBUTOR
Ten Cats Have Hats: A Counting Book	E	F	89	Marzollo, Jean	Scholastic
Ten Little Men	E	F	38	Literacy 2000	Rigby
Terrible Twos	E	RF	86	Tadpoles	Rigby
Thanksgiving	E	I	95	Fiesta Holiday Series	Pearson Learning Group
There Was a Crooked Man	E	F	40	Sunshine	Wright Group/McGraw Hill
There's a Monster in the Tree	E	F	250+	Learn to Read	Creative Teaching Press
This Gecko	E	I	57	Twig	Wright Group/McGraw Hill
This Is Me	E	RF	70	Rigby Literacy	Rigby
This Little Seed	E	I	58	Rigby Focus	Rigby
This Piece or That Piece?	E	F	88	Leveled Readers	Houghton Mifflin
Three Little Ducks	E	F	102	Story Box	Wright Group/McGraw Hill
Three Little Monkeys	E	F	36	Sunshine	Wright Group/McGraw Hill
Three Little Pigs and One Big Pig	E	TL	123	Ready Readers	Pearson Learning Group
Three Silly Monkeys	E	F	150	Foundations	Wright Group/McGraw Hill
Timmy	E	RF	54	Literacy 2000	Rigby
Tin Can Man, The	E	RF	105	Real Kids Readers	Millbrook Press
Tittle-Tattle Goose	E	F	117	Story Box	Wright Group/McGraw Hill
Today is Monday	E	TL	103	Instant Readers	Harcourt School Publishers
Toenails	E	I	83	Voyages	SRA/McGraw Hill
Tomatoes and Bricks	E	RF	126	Windmill	Wright Group/McGraw Hill
Tom's Rubber Band	E	RF	82	Sunshine	Wright Group/McGraw Hill
Too Little	E	RF	119	Foundations	Wright Group/McGraw Hill
Tornado	E	I	37	Spinelle, Nancy Louise	Kaeden Books
Tortillas	E	RF	71	Gonzalez-Jensen, Margarita	Scholastic
Toys	E	I	76	Talk About Books	Pearson Learning Group
Traffic Jam	E	RF	133	Harper, Leslie	Kaeden Books
Treat, The	E	F	96	Leveled Readers Language Support	Houghton Mifflin
Tree Can Be, A	E	I	74	Nayer, Judy	Scholastic
Tree House, The	E	RF	25	Brown, Roberta; Carey, Sue	Scholastic
Trip to the Beach, A	E	I	44	iOpeners	Pearson Learning Group
Trip to the City, A	E	F	119	Bookshop	Mondo
Trip, The	E	F	108	Ready Readers	Pearson Learning Group
Trouble	E	RF	113	Teacher's Choice Series	Pearson Learning Group
Troubles with Bubbles	E	F	89	New Reader Series	Bungalo Books
Trucks	E	I	196	Foundations	Wright Group/McGraw Hill
Turtle Trouble	E	RF	157	Seedlings	Continental Press
Turtles	E	I	250+	Pebble Books	Capstone Press
Two	E	RF	84	Carousel Readers	Pearson Learning Group
Two Baskets	E	RF	181	Bookshop	Mondo
Two Is a Pair	E	I	78	Teacher's Choice Series	Pearson Learning Group
Two Little Dogs	E	F	74	Story Box	Wright Group/McGraw Hill
Two Plus Two	E	RF	44	Teacher's Choice Series	Pearson Learning Group
Under the Big Top	E	I	103	Twig	Wright Group/McGraw Hill
Until We Got Princess	E	RF	94	Bookshop	Mondo
Up and Down	E	RF	79	Storyteller-Setting Sun	Wright Group/McGraw Hill
Using Tools at Work	E	I	118	Early Connections	Benchmark Education
Valentine's Day	E	I	132	Fiesta Holiday Series	Pearson Learning Group
Vegetable Soup	E	F	67	Leveled Readers	Houghton Mifflin
Very Strong Baby, The	E	F	74	Joy Readers	Pearson Learning Group
Visit to the Library, A	E	I	109	Foundations	Wright Group/McGraw Hill
Visitors	E	RF	46	Literacy 2000	Rigby
Wagon Ride, The	E	RF	115	Teacher's Choice Series	Pearson Learning Group
Waiting	E	RF	75	Voyages	SRA/McGraw Hill

* Collection of short stories

TITLE	LEVEL	GENRE	WORD COUNT	AUTHOR / SERIES	PUBLISHER / DISTRIBUTOR
Wake Up, Sun!	E	F	250+	Harrison, David	Random House
Walking in the Jungle	E	RF	113	Little Red Readers	Sundance
Washing	E	RF	150	Foundations	Wright Group/McGraw Hill
Watch Me	E	RF	151	Handprints C, Set 2	Educator's Publishing Service
Watching TV	E	RF	89	Foundations	Wright Group/McGraw Hill
Water	E	I	99	Early Connections	Benchmark Education
Water Fight, The	E	RF	64	Oxford Reading Tree	Oxford University Press
Watermelon	E	I	81	Rise & Shine	Hampton-Brown
Waves	E	F	70	Voyages	SRA/McGraw Hill
Way to Go	E	RF	138	Bookshop	Mondo
Wayne's Box	E	F	114	Cambridge Reading	Pearson Learning Group
We Can Play	E	RF	58	TOTTS	Tott Publications
We Make Cookies	E	RF	48	Pair-It Books	Steck-Vaughn
We Need Child Care Workers	E	I	58	Helpers in Our community	Red Brick Learning
We Need Custodians	E	I	33	Pebble Books	Capstone Press
We Need Principals	E	I	53	Pebble Books	Capstone Press
We Need Teachers	E	I	53	Pebble Books	Capstone Press
Weather	E	I	138	Early Connections	Benchmark Education
Weather Report, The	E	I	119	Rosen Real Readers	Rosen Publishing Group
Well-fed Bear, The	E	F	35	Literacy 2000	Rigby
We're Just Looking	E	RF	115	Seedlings	Continental Press
Wet Paint	E	F	92	Storyteller-Setting Sun	Wright Group/McGraw Hill
Whale Watchers, The	E	F	63	Windmill Books	Rigby
What Animals Eat	E	I	75	Little Red Readers	Sundance
What Do Animals Do?	E	I	29	Little Red Readers	Sundance
What Do Pets Need?	E	I	106	Early Connections	Benchmark Education
What Do Pets Need?	E	I	67	Windows on Literacy	National Geographic
What Do We Have to Get?	E	RF	117	Ready Readers	Pearson Learning Group
What Do You Do?	E	I	162	Tiger Cub	Peguis
What Do You See?	E	I	71	Science	Harcourt School Publishers
What Do You Want That For?	E	RF	149	Lighthouse	Rigby
What Grows on Trees?	E	I	49	Start to Read	School Zone
What If . . .	E	RF	57	Teacher's Choice Series	Pearson Learning Group
What Is at the Top?	E	F	197	Ready Readers	Pearson Learning Group
What Is in the Closet?	E	F	107	Story Box	Wright Group/McGraw Hill
What Is It?	E	I	69	Storyteller-First Snow	Wright Group/McGraw Hill
What Makes a Garden Grow?	E	I	83	Independent Readers Science	Houghton Mifflin
What People Do	E	I	113	Early Connections	Benchmark Education
What Shall I Wear?	E	I	58	Book Bank	Wright Group/McGraw Hill
What Time Is It?	E	RF	136	Teacher's Choice Series	Pearson Learning Group
What Tommy Did	E	RF	125	Literacy 2000	Rigby
What Was That?	E	RF	66	Leveled Readers	Houghton Mifflin
Whatever Will These Become?	E	I	47	Literacy 2000	Rigby
What's Black and White and Moos?	E	I	78	Twig	Wright Group/McGraw Hill
What's for Dinner?	E	RF	112	Seedlings	Continental Press
What's for Lunch	E	F	91	New Way Red	Steck-Vaughn
What's in Here?	E	I	122	Sun Sprouts	ETA/Cuisenaire
What's in the Bag?	E	HF	98	Visions	Wright Group/McGraw Hill
What's Inside?	E	I	37	Sunshine	Wright Group/McGraw Hill
What's This Spider Doing?	E	I	89	Story Steps	Rigby
What's Up?	E	RF	26	Instant Readers	Harcourt School Publishers
Wheels	E	RF	62	Nayer, Judy	Scholastic

* Collection of short stories

TITLE	LEVEL	GENRE	WORD COUNT	AUTHOR / SERIES	PUBLISHER / DISTRIBUTOR
When Goldilocks Went to the House of the Bears	E	TL	165	Tiger Cub	Peguis
When I Visit My Cousin	E	I	67	Independent Readers Social Studies	Houghton Mifflin
When It Rains	E	RF	36	Voyages	SRA/McGraw Hill
When Lincoln Was a Boy	E	I	132	Twig	Wright Group/McGraw Hill
When They Were Little Like Me	E	I	70	Leveled Readers Social Studies	Houghton Mifflin
When We Are Big	E	RF	123	Ready Readers	Pearson Learning Group
Where Can It Be?	E	RF	83	Jonas, Ann	Morrow
Where Can Teddy Go?	E	RF	141	Foundations	Wright Group/McGraw Hill
Where Does Breakfast Come From?	E	I	56	iOpeners	Pearson Learning Group
Where Does the Rabbit Hop?	E	I	71	Ready Readers	Pearson Learning Group
Where Is Daniel?	E	RF	135	Carousel Readers	Pearson Learning Group
Where Is Jake?	E	RF	35	My First Reader	Grolier Press
Where Is Nancy?	E	RF	56	Literacy 2000	Rigby
Where's Spot?	E	F	65	Hill, Eric	Putnam
Where's the Baby?	E	RF	139	Alphakids	Sundance
Which Hat Today?	E	RF	94	Gosset, Rachel; Ballinger, Margaret	Scholastic
Who Am I?	E	I	64	Christensen, Nancy	Scholastic
Who Ate the Broccoli?	E	F	42	Little Readers	Houghton Mifflin
Who Is Coming?	E	RF	28	Rookie Readers	Children's Press
Who Looks After Our World?	E	I	45	Home Connection Collection	Rigby
Who Spilled the Beans?	E	F	87	Story Basket	Wright Group/McGraw Hill
Who Took Our Cake?	E	RF	98	Rigby Focus	Rigby
Who Will Be My Mother?	E	F	156	Story Box	Wright Group/McGraw Hill
Who?	E	F	46	Storyteller-Setting Sun	Wright Group/McGraw Hill
Whoops!	E	RF	49	Little Celebrations	Pearson Learning Group
Who's in the Nest?	E	F	75	Start to Read	School Zone
Who's There?	E	F	92	Story Box	Wright Group/McGraw Hill
Whose Egg Is This?	E	F	99	Story Steps	Rigby
Whose Eggs Are These?	E	RF	125	Sunshine	Wright Group/McGraw Hill
Wide-mouthed Frog, The	E	F	121	Literacy 2000	Rigby
Wiggly, Jiggly, Joggly, Tooth, A	E	RF	61	Little Celebrations	Pearson Learning Group
*Wilbur's Wild Ride	E	RF	164	Story Steps	Rigby
Willy's Hats	E	RF	65	Stewart, Josie.; Salem, Lynn	Continental Press
Wind	E	RF	89	Ready to Read	Pearson Learning Group
Wind Blows Strong, The	E	RF	114	Sunshine	Wright Group/McGraw Hill
Wind, The	E	I	64	Pacific Literacy	Pacific Learning
Wind, The	E	I	36	Discovery Links	Newbridge
Windy Day, A	E	I	53	Pebble Books	Capstone Press
Winter	E	I	56	Discovery Links	Newbridge
Winter Is Here	E	I	24	Windows on Literacy	National Geographic
Wishy-Washy Day	E	F	65	Story Basket	Wright Group/McGraw Hill
Wolves	E	I	68	Seedlings	Continental Press
Wood	E	I	48	Windows on Literacy	National Geographic
Woolly, Woolly	E	F	136	Literacy 2000	Rigby
Woosh!	E	RF	124	Story Box	Wright Group/McGraw Hill
Words are Everywhere	E	I	46	Literacy 2000	Rigby
World's Greatest Juggler, The	E	F	105	Little Readers	Houghton Mifflin
Writing Places	E	I	30	Chanko, Pamela	Scholastic
Yahoo for You	E	RF	137	Early Readers	Compass Point Books
Yippy-Day-Yippy-Doo!	E	RF	117	Sunshine	Wright Group/McGraw Hill
Yoshiko's Surprise	E	RF	81	Seedlings	Continental Press

* Collection of short stories

TITLE	LEVEL	GENRE	WORD COUNT	AUTHOR / SERIES	PUBLISHER / DISTRIBUTOR
You Should Try That with a Rhino	E	F	123	Home Connection Collection	Rigby
Ziggy and the Cat	E	RF	72	Windmill Books	Rigby
Zip Me Up	E	RF	171	Handprints C, Set 2	Educator's Publishing Service
Zip-Zip, Rattle-Bang!	E	F	141	Story Basket	Wright Group/McGraw Hill
Zoo in Willy's Bed, The	E	RF	81	Gorman, Kate Sturnman	Continental Press
Zookeepers Sleepers, The	E	F	76	New Reader Series	Bungalo Books
Above and Below	F	I	128	Sunshine	Wright Group/McGraw Hill
Across the Stream	F	F	94	Ginsburg, Mirra	Morrow
Ah, Treasure	F	F	19	Voyages	SRA/McGraw Hill
Airplanes	F	I	60	Pebble Books	Capstone Press
Alexander Ant Cools Off	F	F	76	Little Books	Sadlier-Oxford
Alfred	F	RF	54	Voyages	SRA/McGraw Hill
Alien Vacation	F	F	105	Instant Readers	Harcourt School Publishers
All Through the Year	F	I	261	Visions	Wright Group/McGraw Hill
Alma Flor Ada, Storyteller	F	B	75	Leveled Readers Language Support	Houghton Mifflin
Amy Loves the Snow	F	RF	127	Hoban, Julia	Scholastic
Amy Loves the Sun	F	RF	122	Hoban, Julia	Scholastic
Amy Loves the Wind	F	RF	116	Hoban, Julia	Scholastic
Animal Babies	F	I	131	Twig	Wright Group/McGraw Hill
Animal Patterns	F	I	130	Yellow Umbrella Books	Capstone Press
Animals at the Zoo	F	I	158	First Start	Troll Associates
Are We There Yet?	F	RF	127	Teacher's Choice Series	Pearson Learning Group
Are You a Ladybug?	F	I	116	Sunshine	Wright Group/McGraw Hill
Are You My Mommy?	F	F	112	Dijs, Carla	Simon & Schuster
Are You There, Bear?	F	F	42	Maris, Ron	Greenwillow
Artist, The	F	F	83	Books for Young Learners	Richard C. Owen
Ask Nicely	F	F	110	Literacy 2000	Rigby
Astronauts, The	F	F	112	Foundations	Wright Group/McGraw Hill
At Home Around the World	F	I	82	Rosen Real Readers	Rosen Publishing Group
At the Barbershop	F	RF	179	Visions	Wright Group/McGraw Hill
At the Library	F	F	31	Little Celebrations	Pearson Learning Group
At the Park	F	I	30	Yellow Umbrella Books	Capstone Press
At the Park	F	RF	163	Early Connections	Benchmark Education
At the Pool	F	RF	87	Oxford Reading Tree	Oxford University Press
Baby Bear Climbs a Tree	F	F	147	PM Plus Story Books	Rigby
Baby Bear's Hiding Place	F	F	187	PM Plus Story Books	Rigby
Baby Bear's Present	F	F	206	PM Story Books	Rigby
Baby Elephant's Sneeze	F	F	78	Foundations	Wright Group/McGraw Hill
Baking Bread	F	I	70	Windows on Literacy	National Geographic
Ballyhoo!	F	F	124	Story Basket	Wright Group/McGraw Hill
Bandages	F	F	139	Moskowitz, Ellen	Kaeden Books
Bang	F	F	55	Literacy 2000	Rigby
Barnaby Bullfrog	F	F	121	Seedlings	Continental Press
Barnyard Song	F	TL	196	PM Readalongs	Rigby
Be Careful, Matthew!	F	RF	80	Sunshine	Wright Group/McGraw Hill
Beach House, The	F	RF	164	PM Plus Story Books	Rigby
Bear Hunt	F	RF	146	Lighthouse	Rigby
Beep, Beep	F	F	51	Start to Read	School Zone
Ben at the Theme Park	F	RF	214	Sun Sprouts	ETA/Cuisenaire
Ben's New Trick	F	RF	219	Ready Readers	Pearson Learning Group
Best Cake, The	F	RF	162	PM Story Books	Rigby
Best Children in the World, The	F	F	148	Story Box	Wright Group/McGraw Hill

* Collection of short stories

TITLE	LEVEL	GENRE	WORD COUNT	AUTHOR / SERIES	PUBLISHER / DISTRIBUTOR
Best Class Trip, The	F	RF	214	Leveled Readers	Houghton Mifflin
Best Friends	F	HF	127	Learn to Read	Creative Teaching Press
Best Thing About Food, The	F	I	132	Twig	Wright Group/McGraw Hill
Betsy the Babysitter	F	RF	115	First Start	Troll Associates
Big Bird's Copycat Day	F	F	232	Lerner, Sharon	Random House
Big Black Bears	F	I	43	Rosen Real Readers	Rosen Publishing Group
Bigger or Smaller?	F	I	112	Sunshine	Wright Group/McGraw Hill
Biggest Cake in the World, The	F	F	120	Pacific Literacy	Pacific Learning
Bikes	F	I	133	Discovery Links	Newbridge
Billie's Book	F	I	110	Sunshine	Wright Group/McGraw Hill
Billy at School	F	RF	163	PM Plus Story Books	Rigby
Billy Goats Gruff	F	TL	381	Hunia, Fran	Ladybird Books
Bingo Goes to School	F	RF	171	PM Plus Story Books	Rigby
Bird Eggs	F	I	50	Pebble Books	Capstone Press
Bird Families	F	I	60	Pebble Books	Capstone Press
Bird Nests	F	I	78	Pebble Books	Capstone Press
Birds	F	I	54	Birds Series	Pearson Learning Group
Birds	F	I	68	Windows on Literacy	National Geographic
Birds	F	I	50	Literacy 2000	Rigby
Birthday Balloons	F	RF	182	PM Extensions-Blue	Rigby
Birthday Bird, The	F	RF	82	Books for Young Learners	Richard C. Owen
Birthday in the Woods, A	F	F	199	Salem, Lynn; Stewart, Josie	Continental Press
Birthday Presents	F	RF	162	PM Plus Story Books	Rigby
Biscuit	F	RF	132	Capucilli, Alyssa Satin	HarperTrophy
Biscuit Finds a Friend	F	RF	114	Capucilli, Alyssa Satin	HarperTrophy
Blast Off!	F	I	95	Ready Readers	Pearson Learning Group
Blue Bug Goes to the Library	F	F	59	Poulet, Virginia	Children's Press
Bobbie and the Play	F	RF	164	Rigby Literacy	Rigby
Bobbie Goes on Vacation	F	RF	240	Rigby Literacy	Rigby
Bobbie's New Coat	F	RF	189	Rigby Literacy	Rigby
Bossy Bettina	F	RF	97	Literacy 2000	Rigby
Brandon's New School	F	RF	163	Developing Books, Set 3	Pioneer Valley
Bread, Bread, Bread	F	I	95	Morris, Ann	Scholastic
Brown Cow Frowned, The	F	F	102	Seedlings	Continental Press
Brown Mouse Gets Some Corn	F	F	158	PM Plus Story Books	Rigby
Brown Mouse Plays a Trick	F	F	155	PM Plus Story Books	Rigby
Brutus Learns to Fetch	F	RF	155	Little Red Readers	Sundance
Buddies	F	F	177	Instant Readers	Harcourt School Publishers
Bug Party	F	I	131	Twig	Wright Group/McGraw Hill
Bug, a Bear, and a Boy, A	F	F	250+	McPhail, David	Scholastic
*Bugs And Other Stories	F	RF	250+	Story Steps	Rigby
Bugs for Breakfast	F	F	158	PM Plus Story Books	Rigby
Building Things	F	I	24	Sunshine	Wright Group/McGraw Hill
Buildings	F	I	85	Leveled Readers Science	Houghton Mifflin
Buildings on My Street	F	RF	109	Foundations	Wright Group/McGraw Hill
Bull's-eye!	F	RF	87	Oxford Reading Tree	Oxford University Press
Bully Bear	F	F	139	Rigby Literacy	Rigby
Bumble Bear	F	F	89	Start to Read	School Zone
Bump	F	I	217	Sun Sprouts	ETA/Cuisenaire
Bumpity, Bumpity, Bump	F	RF	62	Parker, Carol	Continental Press
Bus Ride, The	F	RF	99	Storyteller-Setting Sun	Wright Group/McGraw Hill
Buttercup Moon	F	RF	61	Book Bank	Wright Group/McGraw Hill
Butterfly and Me, The	F	RF	41	Reading Links	Steck-Vaughn
Butterfly Colors	F	I	52	Pebble Books	Capstone Press

* Collection of short stories

TITLE	LEVEL	GENRE	WORD COUNT	AUTHOR / SERIES	PUBLISHER / DISTRIBUTOR
Butterfly Eggs	F	I	57	Pebble Books	Capstone Press
Calico Cat at the Zoo	F	F	88	Charles, Donald	Children's Press
Calico the Cat	F	F	82	Charles, Donald	Children's Press
Camel Ben	F	RF	32	Books for Young Learners	Richard C. Owen
Camping	F	RF	71	Leveled Readers	Houghton Mifflin
Camping Outside	F	RF	95	Book Bank	Wright Group/McGraw Hill
Can I Help?	F	F	250	Janovitz, Marilyn	North-South Books
Car Accident, The	F	RF	161	Foundations	Wright Group/McGraw Hill
Carnival, The	F	RF	82	Oxford Reading Tree	Oxford University Press
Carrots, Peas, and Beans	F	RF	142	Sunshine	Wright Group/McGraw Hill
Cars	F	I	72	Rockwell, Anne	Dutton
Cars!	F	I	56	Independent Readers Social Studies	Houghton Mifflin
Cat and Dog at School	F	F	101	Learn to Read	Creative Teaching Press
Cat and Dog: The Super Snack	F	F	161	Learn to Read	Creative Teaching Press
Cat Chat	F	F	85	Ready Readers	Pearson Learning Group
Cat Goes Fiddle-i-fee	F	TL	333	Galdone, Paul	Houghton Mifflin
Cat in the Tree, A	F	F	79	Oxford Reading Tree	Oxford University Press
Caterpillars	F	I	54	Pebble Books	Capstone Press
Caterpillar's Adventure	F	F	69	Story Box	Wright Group/McGraw Hill
Cats and Kittens	F	I	44	Reading Unlimited	Pearson Learning Group
Cats Everywhere	F	RF	51	Books for Young Learners	Richard C. Owen
Cat's Party	F	F	39	Sunshine	Wright Group/McGraw Hill
Celebrating Father's Day: Father's Day is for Special People	F	RF	115	Learn to Read	Creative Teaching Press
Celebrating Thanksgiving: Giving Thanks	F	I	145	Learn to Read	Creative Teaching Press
Celebrating Valentine's Day: My Special Valentines	F	RF	137	Learn to Read	Creative Teaching Press
Chad and the Big Egg	F	F	204	Leveled Readers	Houghton Mifflin
Changing Schools	F	RF	53	City Stories	Rigby
Chase, The	F	F	85	Oxford Reading Tree	Oxford University Press
Chickens on the Farm	F	I	68	Vocabulary Readers	Houghton Mifflin
Children at Play	F	I	101	Little Red Readers	Sundance
Chinese New Year	F	I	79	Vocabulary Readers	Houghton Mifflin
Chloe the Chameleon	F	F	250+	Warren, Celia	Scholastic
Christmas	F	I	106	Fiesta Holiday Series	Pearson Learning Group
Christmas Tree, The	F	RF	163	PM StoryBooks	Rigby
Chug the Tractor	F	F	203	PM Story Books	Rigby
Class Teddy Bear	F	RF	106	Windows on Literacy	National Geographic
Clay Art	F	I	62	Chanko, Pamela; Chessen, Betsey	Scholastic
Clean-Up Time	F	RF	226	Handprints D, Set 1	Educator's Publishing Service
Cliff Can't Come	F	RF	276	Leveled Readers	Houghton Mifflin
Clothes	F	I	103	Talk About Books	Pearson Learning Group
Clown Around	F	F	67	Early Readers	Compass Point Books
Cluck! Quack! Moo!	F	RF	209	Sun Sprouts	ETA/Cuisenaire
Cock-A-Doodle-Do	F	RF	160	Brandenberg, Franz	Greenwillow
Cold Day, The	F	RF	80	Oxford Reading Tree	Oxford University Press
Colors	F	I	198	Foundations	Wright Group/McGraw Hill
Colors of My Day, The	F	I	147	Learn to Read	Creative Teaching Press
Come for a Swim!	F	RF	129	Sunshine	Wright Group/McGraw Hill
Come to My House!	F	RF	131	Sunshine	Wright Group/McGraw Hill
Cookie's Week	F	RF	84	Ward, Cindy	Putnam
Cooking Pot, The	F	F	132	Sunshine	Wright Group/McGraw Hill

* Collection of short stories

TITLE	LEVEL	GENRE	WORD COUNT	AUTHOR / SERIES	PUBLISHER / DISTRIBUTOR
Counting My Collections	F	I	126	Early Connections	Benchmark Education
Counting Stars	F	I	144	Early Connections	Benchmark Education
Creepy Crawlies	F	I	35	Voyages	SRA/McGraw Hill
Curlylocks and the Three Bears: A Play	F	TL	194	Rigby Literacy	Rigby
Dad Didn't Mind at All	F	RF	134	Literacy 2000	Rigby
Dad's Headache	F	RF	86	Sunshine	Wright Group/McGraw Hill
Dad's New Path	F	RF	218	Foundations	Wright Group/McGraw Hill
Dad's Shirt	F	RF	38	Joy Readers	Pearson Learning Group
Dancing Fly, The	F	F	108	Sunshine	Wright Group/McGraw Hill
Daniel	F	RF	161	Literacy 2000	Rigby
Danny and Bee's Safety Rules	F	RF	106	Coulter, Mia	Maryruth Books
Danny Looks for Abby	F	RF	120	Coulter, Mia	Maryruth Books
Danny's Groundhog Day	F	RF	126	Coulter, Mia	Maryruth Books
Dark Night, Sleepy Night	F	I	123	Ziefert, Harriet	Puffin Books
Dark, Dark Tale, A	F	F	115	Brown, Ruth	Penguin Group
Darryl the Doorman	F	RF	85	City Stories	Rigby
David Wiggles	F	RF	54	City Stories	Rigby
Day with Paramedics, A	F	I	147	Kottke, Jan	Scholastic
Dear Zoo	F	F	115	Campbell, Rod	Macmillan
Dinner by Five	F	RF	215	Ready Readers	Pearson Learning Group
Dinosaur Fan, The	F	F	125	Windmill Books	Rigby
Dinosaur, The	F	F	131	Joy Readers	Pearson Learning Group
Dinosaurs	F	I	115	Maccarone, Grace	Scholastic
Dinosaurs Dancing	F	F	115	Learn to Read	Creative Teaching Press
Dive In!	F	RF	133	Ready Readers	Pearson Learning Group
Do Animals Live in Plants?	F	I	56	Instant Readers	Harcourt School Publishers
Do Not Open This Book!	F	F	134	Story Basket	Wright Group/McGraw Hill
Does a Kangaroo Have a Mother Too?	F	I	214	Carle, Eric	Scholastic
Dog and Cat	F	RF	62	My First Reader	Grolier Press
Dog Named Honey, A	F	I	46	iOpeners	Pearson Learning Group
Dog Show, The	F	I	131	Foundations	Wright Group/McGraw Hill
Dogs	F	I	116	Foundations	Wright Group/McGraw Hill
Dogs at School	F	F	94	Books for Young Learners	Richard C. Owen
Doing Jobs Together	F	RF	194	Early Connections	Benchmark Education
Don't Let the Cat Out!	F	RF	109	Independent Readers Social Studies	Houghton Mifflin
Don't Throw It Away!	F	I	90	Wonder World	Wright Group/McGraw Hill
Down at the Billabong	F	RF	93	Voyages	SRA/McGraw Hill
Down by the Swamp	F	RF	50	Little Celebrations	Pearson Learning Group
Dozen Dogs, A	F	F	228	Ziefert, Harriet	Random House
*Dragon Hunt, The	F	F	53	New Way Red	Steck-Vaughn
Dragon's Lunch	F	F	85	Ready Readers	Pearson Learning Group
Dream, The	F	RF	54	Oxford Reading Tree	Oxford University Press
Duck with the Broken Wing, The	F	RF	189	PM Extensions-Blue	Rigby
Elephant Tricks	F	F	147	Sun Sprouts	ETA/Cuisenaire
Emily Can't Sleep	F	RF	124	Early Emergent, Set 2	Pioneer Valley
Eve Shops	F	RF	146	Ready Readers	Pearson Learning Group
Every Cat	F	RF	91	Instant Readers	Harcourt School Publishers
Everyday Patterns	F	I	110	Early Connections	Benchmark Education
Explorer, The	F	RF	73	City Stories	Rigby
Families	F	I	159	Yellow Umbrella Books	Capstone Press
Families	F	I	132	Twig	Wright Group/McGraw Hill
Family on Lake Street, The	F	RF	159	Teacher's Choice Series	Pearson Learning Group
Family Photos	F	RF	106	Literacy 2000	Rigby

* Collection of short stories

TITLE	LEVEL	GENRE	WORD COUNT	AUTHOR / SERIES	PUBLISHER / DISTRIBUTOR
Farmer Didn't Wake Up, The	F	F	185	Learn to Read	Creative Teaching Press
farmer in the dell, The	F	TL	159	PM Readalongs	Rigby
Farms	F	RF	102	Sunshine	Wright Group/McGraw Hill
Farms	F	I	153	Foundations	Wright Group/McGraw Hill
Feeling Angry	F	I	70	Emotions	Red Brick Learning
Feeling Happy	F	I	57	Emotions	Red Brick Learning
Feeling Sad	F	I	62	Emotions	Red Brick Learning
Feeling Scared	F	I	62	Emotions	Red Brick Learning
Festivals	F	I	40	Berger, Samantha; Chanko, Pamela	Scholastic
Find the Wild Animal	F	I	108	Foley, Cate	Scholastic
Find Yourself a Friend	F	RF	261	Visions	Wright Group/McGraw Hill
Finding a Wooly Mammoth	F	I	120	Independent Readers Science	Houghton Mifflin
Fire on Toytown Hill, The	F	F	166	PM Plus Story Books	Rigby
Firefighter Wears a Helmet, A	F	I	79	Windows on Literacy	National Geographic
Firehouse Sal	F	RF	52	Rookie Readers	Children's Press
First Aid	F	I	44	Canizares, Susan; Chanko, Pamela	Scholastic
Fishy Alphabet Story	F	F	126	Wylie, Joanne & David	Children's Press
Five Little Monkeys	F	F	81	Bookshop	Mondo
Flies	F	I	56	Pebble Books	Capstone Press
Floppy the Hero	F	F	74	Oxford Reading Tree	Oxford University Press
Fly, Butterfly	F	I	49	Discovery Links	Newbridge
Flying High	F	RF	250+	Predictable Storybooks	SRA/McGraw Hill
Food Comes From Farms	F	I	75	Windows on Literacy	National Geographic
Food for You	F	I	85	Leveled Readers Science	Houghton Mifflin
Foolish Goose	F	F	141	Start To Read	School Zone
Fourth of July, The	F	I	153	Ready Readers	Pearson Learning Group
Freddie's Spaghetti	F	RF	250+	Doyle, Charlotte	Random House
Friendly Snowman	F	F	144	Joyce, William	Scholastic
Friendly Snowman	F	F	134	First Start	Troll Associates
Friends	F	RF	57	Bookshop	Mondo
From Seed to Pumpkin	F	I	148	Kottke, Jan	Scholastic
Gecko's Story	F	F	61	Books for Young Learners	Richard C. Owen
Get Lost!	F	RF	219	Foundations	Wright Group/McGraw Hill
Getting Around	F	I	182	Chessen, Betsey; Moreton, Daniel	Scholastic
Giants	F	F	52	Blaxland, Wendy	Scholastic
Gingerbread Boy	F	TL	137	New Way Red	Steck-Vaughn
Gingerbread Man, The	F	TL	180	Little Readers	Houghton Mifflin
Gobble! Gobble! Munch!	F	F	64	Rhythm 'N' Rhyme Readers	Pearson Learning Group
Going Fishing	F	F	240	Leveled Readers	Houghton Mifflin
Going Fishing	F	RF	26	Voyages	SRA/McGraw Hill
Going for a Walk	F	RF	82	DeRegniers, Beatrice Schenk	Harper & Row
Going Shopping	F	RF	99	Leveled Readers Social Studies	Houghton Mifflin
Going Shopping	F	I	112	Bookshop	Mondo
Going to School	F	I	171	Foundations	Wright Group/McGraw Hill
Going to the Dentist	F	I	122	Pebble Books	Capstone Press
Going to the Doctor	F	RF	101	City Stories	Rigby
Goldilocks Comes Back	F	TL	134	Pair-It Books	Steck-Vaughn
Good Food	F	I	78	Leveled Readers Science	Houghton Mifflin
Good Night, City Lights	F	RF	74	City Stories	Rigby
Good Night, Little Brother	F	RF	69	Literacy 2000	Rigby
Grandma and the Pirate	F	RF	105	Lloyd, David	Crown
Grandma's Memories	F	RF	102	Literacy 2000	Rigby
Grandma's Present	F	RF	191	Foundations	Wright Group/McGraw Hill

* Collection of short stories

TITLE	LEVEL	GENRE	WORD COUNT	AUTHOR / SERIES	PUBLISHER / DISTRIBUTOR
Grandpa Snored	F	RF	51	Literacy 2000	Rigby
Grandpa's Candy Store	F	RF	65	Books for Young Learners	Richard C. Owen
Grandpa's Clues	F	RF	198	Rigby Literacy	Rigby
Grandpa's Cookies	F	F	193	Little Readers	Houghton Mifflin
Grasshoppers	F	I	50	Pebble Books	Capstone Press
Great Attitude, A	F	B	196	Learn to Read	Creative Teaching Press
Great White Sharks	F	I	98	Pair-It Books	Steck-Vaughn
Green Bananas	F	F	49	Tadpoles	Rigby
Green Eyes	F	RF	111	Literacy 2000	Rigby
Gregory's Garden	F	RF	70	Cat on the Mat	Oxford University Press
Growing Up, Up, Up Book	F	RF	120	First Start	Troll Associates
Grumbles, Growls, and Roars	F	I	133	Twig	Wright Group/McGraw Hill
Grump, The	F	RF	73	Literacy 2000	Rigby
Guess Who's Coming to Dinner?	F	RF	130	Literacy 2000	Rigby
Habitat Is Where We Live, A	F	I	132	Twig	Wright Group/McGraw Hill
Halloween Parade	F	RF	101	Ziefert, Harriet	Puffin Books
Hands, Hands, Hands	F	I	85	Bookshop	Mondo
Happy Jack	F	F	99	First Start	Troll Associates
Harry Goes to Day Camp	F	F	250+	Ziefert, James	Puffin Books
Harry Goes to Fun Land	F	F	166	Ziefert, Harriet	Puffin Books
Harry's House	F	RF	83	Medearis, Angela; Keeter, Susan	Scholastic
Hats	F	I	114	Wonder World	Wright Group/McGraw Hill
Hats	F	I	88	Talk About Books	Pearson Learning Group
Have You Ever Found a Beetle?	F	I	94	Voyages	SRA/McGraw Hill
Have You Seen the Crocodile?	F	F	150	West, Colin	Harper & Row
Hawks	F	RF	87	Seedlings	Continental Press
Hay Making	F	I	62	Wonder World	Wright Group/McGraw Hill
Hello!	F	I	17	Chessen, Betsey; Bergen, Samantha	Scholastic
Hello, Doctor	F	RF	44	Rookie Reader	Children's Press
Helping	F	RF	103	Well-Being Series	Pearson Learning Group
Helping	F	RF	79	Bookshop	Mondo
Henry	F	F	141	Instant Readers	Harcourt School Publishers
Henry Runs Away	F	RF	150	Books for Young Learners	Richard C. Owen
Here Comes a Bus	F	F	171	Ziefert, Harriet	Penguin Group
Here Comes Everyone	F	RF	78	Cambridge Reading	Pearson Learning Group
Here we go round the mulberry bush	F	TL	208	PM Readalongs	Rigby
Herman the Helper Lends a Hand	F	F	198	Kraus, Robert	Windmill
Hole in the Hedge, The	F	F	188	Sunshine	Wright Group/McGraw Hill
Hole Is A Great Home, A	F	RF	236	Phonics and Friends	Hampton-Brown
Homework	F	RF	57	City Stories	Rigby
Honey Bees and Honey	F	I	57	Pebble Books	Capstone Press
Honey for Baby Bear	F	F	200	PM Story Books	Rigby
Hooray for Snail	F	F	102	Stadler, John	HarperCollins
Horses	F	I	131	Twig	Wright Group/McGraw Hill
Horse's Hiccups	F	F	83	Storyteller-Moon Rising	Wright Group/McGraw Hill
Hot Sunny Days	F	I	122	PM Plus Nonfiction	Rigby
House for Little Red	F	RF	78	Just Beginning	Modern Curriculum
House in the Tree, The	F	RF	202	PM Story Books	Rigby
House on the Hill, The	F	F	189	PM Plus Story Books	Rigby
How Animals Hide	F	I	98	Wonder World	Wright Group/McGraw Hill
How Big Is Big?	F	I	158	Ziefert, Harriet	Puffin Books
How Do You Say Hello to A Ghost?	F	F	149	Tiger Cub	Peguis
How Far Will I Fly?	F	RF	94	Oyama, Sachi	Scholastic

* Collection of short stories

TITLE	LEVEL	GENRE	WORD COUNT	AUTHOR / SERIES	PUBLISHER / DISTRIBUTOR
How I Go	F	I	138	Early Connections	Benchmark Education
How Many Ducks?	F	F	88	Chapman, Cindy	Scholastic
How Spiders Live	F	I	145	Sunshine	Wright Group/McGraw Hill
Hug Bug	F	F	65	Start to Read	School Zone
Huggly, Snuggly Pets	F	RF	142	Giant Step Readers	Educational Insights
Humpback Whales	F	I	72	Ready Readers	Pearson Learning Group
Hungry Giant, The	F	F	183	Story Box	Wright Group/McGraw Hill
Hungry Giant's Lunch, The	F	F	140	Story Box	Wright Group/McGraw Hill
Hungry Turtle	F	I	173	Handprints D, Set 1	Educator's Publishing Service
Hup Pups	F	F	89	Supersonics	Rigby
Huzzard Buzzard	F	F	112	Reese, Bob	Children's Press
I Can Fly	F	F	107	Carousel Readers	Pearson Learning Group
I Can See My Shadow	F	I	55	Windows on Literacy	National Geographic
I Can Spell Dinosaur	F	RF	82	Predictable Storybooks	SRA/McGraw Hill
I Can!	F	I	131	Twig	Wright Group/McGraw Hill
I Don't Like Peas	F	RF	89	Start to Read	School Zone
I Have a New Baby Brother	F	F	163	Learn to Read	Creative Teaching Press
I Have Another Language	F	RF	92	Instant Readers	Harcourt School Publishers
I Know That Tune!	F	RF	201	Foundations	Wright Group/McGraw Hill
I Listen	F	RF	84	Windows on Literacy	National Geographic
I Need a Book	F	RF	113	Sunshine	Wright Group/McGraw Hill
I Need a Rest	F	RF	119	Home Connection Collection	Rigby
I Need to Clean My Room	F	RF	157	Learn to Read	Creative Teaching Press
I Saw a Sign	F	RF	100	Literacy Tree	Rigby
I Want a Dog	F	RF	192	Sun Sprouts	ETA/Cuisenaire
I Want to Be a Clown	F	RF	82	Start to Read	School Zone
I Went to Visit a Friend One Day	F	F	111	Voyages	SRA/McGraw Hill
I Wonder	F	RF	67	Sunshine	Wright Group/McGraw Hill
I Wonder Why?	F	I	95	Wonder World	Wright Group/McGraw Hill
If Animals Came to School	F	F	125	Learn to Read	Creative Teaching Press
If I Had an Elephant	F	F	90	Teacher's Choice Series	Pearson Learning Group
If You Miss Your Bus	F	F	160	Leveled Readers	Houghton Mifflin
If You Were a Bat	F	F	78	Instant Readers	Harcourt School Publishers
I'm Glad I'm Me	F	RF	147	Windmill Books	Rigby
I'm King of the Castle	F	F	184	Watanabe, Shigeo	Philomel Books
I'm Looking for My Hat	F	RF	89	Book Bank	Wright Group/McGraw Hill
In My Bucket	F	RF	94	Carousel Readers	Pearson Learning Group
In Our Classroom	F	I	89	Windows on Literacy	National Geographic
In Our Country	F	I	63	Canizares, Susan; Moreton, Daniel	Scholastic
In the Park	F	I	96	Literacy 2000	Rigby
In the Yard	F	RF	40	Early Readers	Compass Point Books
In-Line Skates, The	F	RF	137	Foundations	Wright Group/McGraw Hill
Interruptions	F	F	81	Bookshop	Mondo
Is Anyone Home?	F	RF	65	Maris, Ron	Greenwillow
Is Jim In?	F	RF	106	Supersonics	Rigby
Is This You?	F	RF	250+	Krauss, Ruth	Scholastic
Is Your Pail Full?	F	RF	162	Mishica, Clare	Continental Press
It Is Raining	F	I	56	PM Plus Nonfiction	Rigby
It Started As a Seed	F	I	126	Learn to Read	Creative Teaching Press
It Would Be Fun!	F	F	203	Start to Read	School Zone
Itchy, Itchy Chicken Pox	F	RF	131	Maccarone, Grace	Scholastic
It's Alright to Cry	F	RF	138	Teacher's Choice Series	Pearson Learning Group
It's Not Fair	F	RF	51	Tadpoles	Rigby

* Collection of short stories

TITLE	LEVEL	GENRE	WORD COUNT	AUTHOR / SERIES	PUBLISHER / DISTRIBUTOR
It's Taco Time	F	I	56	Teacher's Choice Series	Pearson Learning Group
Jace, Mace, and the Big Race	F	RF	124	Start to Read	School Zone
Jackie's New Friend	F	I	168	O'Connor, C. M.	Continental Press
Jacks and More Jacks	F	F	79	Little Celebrations	Pearson Learning Group
Jacob's Day	F	RF	51	Windows on Literacy	National Geographic
Jane's Car	F	RF	121	PM Story Books	Rigby
Jasper	F	RF	107	Books for Young Learners	Richard C. Owen
Jeremy's Cake	F	RF	97	Storyteller-Moon Rising	Wright Group/McGraw Hill
Jessica's Dress-Ups	F	RF	130	Voyages	SRA/McGraw Hill
Jimmy's Birthday Balloon	F	RF	95	Foundations	Wright Group/McGraw Hill
Jip the Pirate	F	F	142	New Way Blue	Steck-Vaughn
Joan's Hat	F	F	174	Sun Sprouts	ETA/Cuisenaire
Joe and the Mouse	F	RF	138	Oxford Reading Tree	Oxford University Press
Jog, Frog, Jog	F	F	72	Start to Read	School Zone
Johnny Lion's Rubber Boots	F	F	80	Hurd, Edith Thacher	HarperCollins
Just Like Daddy	F	F	93	Asch, Frank	Simon & Schuster
Just Like Me	F	RF	86	First Start	Troll Associates
Just-Right House, The	F	F	201	Leveled Readers	Houghton Mifflin
Katie Couldn't	F	RF	176	Rookie Readers	Children's Press
Kickball	F	RF	148	Handprints D, Set 1	Educator's Publishing Service
King Who Loved to Dance, The	F	F	82	Instant Readers	Harcourt School Publishers
King's Job	F	F	155	Handprints C, Set 2	Educator's Publishing Service
Kitty Cat and the Paint Can	F	F	165	PM Plus Story Books	Rigby
Koalas	F	I	45	Pebble Books	Capstone Press
Lady with the Alligator Purse	F	F	218	Wescott, Nadine Bernard	Little, Brown & Co.
Late for Soccer (Football)	F	RF	185	PM Story Books	Rigby
Leaf Rain	F	RF	82	Book Bank	Wright Group/McGraw Hill
Leafy Sea Dragons	F	I	183	Sun Sprouts	ETA/Cuisenaire
Learning About Snow	F	I	42	Rosen Real Readers	Rosen Publishing Group
Leave It to Beavers	F	RF	102	Leveled Readers Science	Houghton Mifflin
Lemonade	F	F	140	Learn to Read	Creative Teaching Press
Let's Brush Our Teeth	F	I	78	Rosen Real Readers	Rosen Publishing Group
Let's Draw!	F	I	21	Rosen Real Readers	Rosen Publishing Group
Let's Get a Pet	F	RF	22	Jellybeans	Rigby
Let's Go Downtown	F	RF	85	City Stories	Rigby
Let's Go to a Fair	F	I	139	Welcome Books	Children's Press
Let's Wash Up	F	I	69	Rosen Real Readers	Rosen Publishing Group
Lightning Liz	F	F	41	Rookie Readers	Children's Press
Lili's Breakfast	F	RF	156	Storyteller-Setting Sun	Wright Group/McGraw Hill
Ling's New Friend	F	RF	164	Sun Sprouts	ETA/Cuisenaire
*Lion and the Mouse, The	F	TL	115	New Way Red	Steck-Vaughn
Lion and the Rabbit, The	F	TL	99	PM Story Books	Rigby
Lion's Lunch	F	F	201	Lighthouse	Rigby
Lion's Tail, The	F	F	147	Reading Unlimited	Pearson Learning Group
Little Bulldozer Helps Again	F	F	197	PM Extensions-Blue	Rigby
Little Car	F	F	181	Sunshine	Wright Group/McGraw Hill
Little Chimp and the Bees	F	F	160	PM Plus Story Books	Rigby
Little Green Frog	F	F	121	Learn to Read	Creative Teaching Press
Little Miss Muffet	F	TL	146	Literacy 2000	Rigby
Little Overcoat, The	F	TL	237	Bookshop	Mondo
Little Yellow Chicken's House, The	F	F	287	Story Basket	Wright Group/McGraw Hill
Look at Me	F	RF	104	Literacy 2000	Rigby

* Collection of short stories

TITLE	LEVEL	GENRE	WORD COUNT	AUTHOR / SERIES	PUBLISHER / DISTRIBUTOR
Look Down Low	F	I	66	Early Readers	Compass Point Books
Look for Me	F	I	208	Little Readers	Houghton Mifflin
Look! I Can Read!	F	RF	124	Hood, Susan	Grosset & Dunlap
Looking for a Letter	F	RF	223	New Way Green	Steck-Vaughn
Lost at the Fun Park	F	RF	192	PM Extensions-Blue	Rigby
Lost Socks	F	RF	159	PM Plus Story Books	Rigby
Lots of Balloons	F	RF	72	Early Readers	Compass Point Books
Lucky Day for Little Dinosaur, A	F	HF	135	PM Extensions-Yellow	Rigby
Lucky We Have a Station Wagon	F	RF	259	Foundations	Wright Group/McGraw Hill
Lucy's Sore Knee	F	RF	93	Windmill	Wright Group/McGraw Hill
Lunch	F	RF	156	Urmston, Kathleen; Evans, Karen	Kaeden Books
Lunch with Cat and Dog	F	F	122	Learn to Read	Creative Teaching Press
Lunchroom, The	F	RF	80	City Stories	Rigby
Lydia and the Letters	F	RF	84	Oxford Reading Tree	Oxford University Press
Lydia and the Present	F	RF	77	Oxford Reading Tree	Oxford University Press
Made with Glass	F	I	106	Cherrington, Janelle	Scholastic
Magnets	F	I	79	Sunshine	Wright Group/McGraw Hill
Magpie's Baking Day	F	F	132	PM Story Books	Rigby
Mai Li's Surprise	F	RF	63	Books for Young Learners	Richard C. Owen
Main Street	F	I	87	Leveled Readers Social Studies	Houghton Mifflin
Make a House	F	I	41	iOpeners	Pearson Learning Group
Make A Kite	F	I	49	Story Steps	Rigby
Make a Lei	F	I	39	Pacific Literacy	Pacific Learning
Make a Salad Face	F	I	82	Voyages	SRA/McGraw Hill
Making Breakfast	F	I	59	Windows on Literacy	National Geographic
Making It Go?	F	I	106	Independent Readers Science	Houghton Mifflin
Malcolm Magpie	F	I	126	Storyteller-Setting Sun	Wright Group/McGraw Hill
Map Book, The	F	I	144	Sunshine	Wright Group/McGraw Hill
Maple Trees	F	I	118	Pebble Books	Capstone Press
Maria's House	F	RF	138	Seedlings	Continental Press
Marks in the Sand	F	I	121	Windows on Literacy	National Geographic
Marmalade's Nap	F	F	57	Wheeler, Cindy	Alfred A. Knopf
Marmalade's Snowy Day	F	F	61	Wheeler, Cindy	Alfred A. Knopf
Marvella and the Moon	F	F	250+	Bookshop	Mondo
Marvelous Mammals	F	I	99	Independent Readers Science	Houghton Mifflin
Marvelous Me	F	F	29	Literacy 2000	Rigby
Math Is Everywhere	F	I	95	Sunshine	Wright Group/McGraw Hill
Max is a Star!	F	RF	160	Leveled Readers Language Support	Houghton Mifflin
Me and My Dog	F	RF	115	Sunshine	Wright Group/McGraw Hill
Meanies	F	F	158	Story Box	Wright Group/McGraw Hill
Meg's Cat	F	RF	117	Lighthouse	Rigby
Melting	F	I	69	Bookshop	Mondo
Messy Mark	F	RF	180	First Start	Troll Associates
Messy Rooms, The	F	F	103	Lester the Lion Series	Pioneer Valley
Mike Ghost's Delicious Rainbow	F	F	157	TOTTS	Tott Publications
Mike's New Bike	F	RF	183	First Start	Troll Associates
Milking	F	RF	67	Wonder World	Wright Group/McGraw Hill
Molly's Mailbox	F	RF	122	Teacher's Choice Series	Pearson Learning Group
Monster Bus	F	F	103	The Monster Bus Series	Pearson Learning Group
Monster Stew	F	F	117	Learn to Read	Creative Teaching Press
Moon	F	RF	38	Books for Young Learners	Richard C. Owen
Moose Is Loose, A	F	F	120	Little Readers	Houghton Mifflin
Mother's Day	F	I	128	Fiesta Holiday Series	Pearson Learning Group

* Collection of short stories

TITLE	LEVEL	GENRE	WORD COUNT	AUTHOR / SERIES	PUBLISHER / DISTRIBUTOR
Mountain Hike, The	F	RF	176	Developing Books, Set 2	Pioneer Valley
Mr. Cricket's New Home	F	F	121	Carousel Readers	Pearson Learning Group
Mr. Miller's Old Car	F	RF	108	Seedlings	Continental Press
Mr. Noisy's Helpers	F	F	81	Learn to Read	Creative Teaching Press
Mr. Rabbit and the Moon	F	F	137	New Way Red	Steck-Vaughn
Mr. Smarty Loves to Party	F	F	101	Storyteller-Moon Rising	Wright Group/McGraw Hill
Mr. Wind	F	F	37	Literacy 2000	Rigby
Mrs. Bold	F	RF	94	Literacy 2000	Rigby
Mrs. Mog's Cats	F	F	124	Rigby Literacy	Rigby
Mrs. Tuck's Little Tune	F	RF	195	Ready Readers	Pearson Learning Group
Muffy and Fluffy	F	RF	155	First Start	Troll Associates
Mural, The	F	I	262	Visions	Wright Group/McGraw Hill
My Cat	F	RF	42	My World	Steck-Vaughn
My Computer	F	I	76	Wonder World	Wright Group/McGraw Hill
My Dad	F	I	79	Talk About Books	Pearson Learning Group
My Dog's the Best	F	RF	175	Calmenson, Stephanie	Scholastic
My First Snow	F	I	127	Independent Readers Science	Houghton Mifflin
My Five Senses	F	I	142	Early Connections	Benchmark Education
My Five Senses	F	I	42	Rosen Real Readers	Rosen Publishing Group
My Friend Goes Left	F	RF	72	Start to Read	School Zone
My Grandpa	F	I	75	Bookshop	Mondo
My Great Big Brother	F	RF	65	Book Bank	Wright Group/McGraw Hill
My Gymnastics Class	F	I	33	iOpeners	Pearson Learning Group
My Hair	F	RF	124	Bookshop	Mondo
My Hard-Boiled Egg	F	I	94	Windmill Books	Rigby
My Holiday Diary	F	RF	95	Stepping Stones	Nelson/Michaels Assoc.
My House	F	RF	52	Cat on the Mat	Oxford University Press
My House	F	RF	126	Literacy 2000	Rigby
My Kitchen	F	I	80	Rockwell, Harlow	Morrow
My Mom	F	I	91	Talk About Books	Pearson Learning Group
My Monster Friends	F	F	94	Literacy 2000	Rigby
My Native American School	F	RF	86	Gould, Carol	Kaeden Books
My New Boy	F	F	102	Step into Reading	Random House
My New Pet	F	RF	105	Little Readers	Houghton Mifflin
My Old Cat and the Computer	F	RF	81	Foundations	Wright Group/McGraw Hill
My Pigs	F	I	123	Miller, Heather	Scholastic
My Red Scarf	F	I	120	Rigby Focus	Rigby
My River	F	F	53	Halpern, Shari	Scholastic
My Shadow	F	RF	116	Ready Readers	Pearson Learning Group
My Very Hungry Pet	F	RF	334	Reading Corners	Pearson Learning Group
My Walk Home	F	RF	71	Windows on Literacy	National Geographic
My Wild Woolly	F	F	87	Instant Readers	Harcourt Trade
My Wonderful Chair	F	F	109	Windmill	Wright Group/McGraw Hill
Name Garden, A	F	I	125	Sunshine	Wright Group/McGraw Hill
Nana's Orchard	F	RF	92	Gould, Carol	Kaeden Books
New Bike, The	F	RF	96	Start to Read	School Zone
New Clothes	F	RF	107	Windows on Literacy	National Geographic
New Gym Shoes	F	RF	175	Yukish, Joe	Kaeden Books
New Kid, The	F	RF	124	Real Kid Readers	The Millbrook Press
New Nest, The	F	RF	207	Foundations	Wright Group/McGraw Hill
New Sneakers	F	RF	34	Oxford Reading Tree	Oxford University Press
New York City Buildings	F	I	59	Books for Young Learners	Richard C. Owen
Night Walk	F	RF	51	Books for Young Learners	Richard C. Owen
Nightmare Hill	F	RF	129	Developing Books, Set 1	Pioneer Valley

* Collection of short stories

TITLE	LEVEL	GENRE	WORD COUNT	AUTHOR / SERIES	PUBLISHER / DISTRIBUTOR
Niles Likes to Smile	F	RF	80	Little Books	Sadlier-Oxford
No Dogs Allowed	F	RF	73	Books for Young Learners	Richard C. Owen
No Extras	F	RF	90	Literacy 2000	Rigby
No Luck	F	RF	120	Stewart, Josie; Salem, Lynn	Continental Press
Not Now, Sam	F	RF	159	Early Connections	Benchmark Education
Not Very Messy, Unless . . .	F	F	94	Seedlings	Continental Press
Notes from Mom	F	RF	99	Salem, Lynn; Stewart, Josie	Continental Press
Notes to Dad	F	RF	114	Stewart, Josie; Salem, Lynn	Continental Press
Nothing Ever Happens	F	F	49	City Stories	Rigby
Nothing in the Mailbox	F	RF	73	Books for Young Learners	Richard C. Owen
Oak Trees	F	I	132	Pebble Books	Capstone Press
Oatmeal	F	I	96	Wonder World	Wright Group/McGraw Hill
Oh Dear	F	F	109	Campbell, Rod	Macmillan
Oh No!	F	RF	122	Traditional Tales & More	Rigby
Old Car, The	F	RF	135	Voyages	SRA/McGraw Hill
Old MacDonald Had a Farm	F	TL	250+	PM Readalongs	Rigby
Old Oak Tree, The	F	F	108	Little Celebrations	Pearson Learning Group
Old Steam Train, The	F	RF	43	Literacy 2000	Rigby
Old Teeth, New Teeth	F	I	53	Wonder World	Wright Group/McGraw Hill
Old Train, The	F	RF	68	Books for Young Learners	Richard C. Owen
On a Dark and Scary Night	F	F	50	Shared Reading	Rigby
On the bridge at Avignon	F	TL	250+	PM Readalongs	Rigby
On the Job	F	RF	79	City Stories	Rigby
On the School Bus	F	RF	62	Little Readers	Houghton Mifflin
One Blue Hen	F	F	108	Cambridge Reading	Pearson Learning Group
One Racer	F	I	106	Leveled Readers Science	Houghton Mifflin
One Stormy Night	F	RF	165	Story Basket	Wright Group/McGraw Hill
Open Your Mouth	F	F	201	Sunshine	Wright Group/McGraw Hill
Oranges for Orange Juice	F	I	25	Learn to Read	Creative Teaching Press
Orca Whales	F	I	85	Seedlings	Continental Press
Our Class Survey	F	I	128	Early Connections	Benchmark Education
Our Earth	F	I	53	Rosen Real Readers	Rosen Publishing Group
Our Favorite Things To Do	F	I	241	Yellow Umbrella Books	Capstone Press
Our Garage	F	RF	80	Urmston, Kathleen; Evans, Karen	Kaeden Books
Our New Baby	F	RF	59	City Stories	Rigby
Our Senses	F	I	182	Discovery Links	Newbridge
Over in the Meadow	F	F	228	Cambridge Reading	Pearson Learning Group
Over in the Meadow	F	TL	250+	PM Readalongs	Rigby
Painting Shapes	F	I	148	Early Connections	Benchmark Education
Pancakes!	F	F	106	Ready Readers	Pearson Learning Group
Panda's Birthday Surprise	F	F	141	Seedlings	Continental Press
Papa Penguin's Surprise	F	RF	136	Seedlings	Continental Press
Paper Patchwork	F	I	54	Pacific Literacy	Pacific Learning
Pardon? Said the Giraffe	F	F	123	West, Colin	Harper & Row
Party, The	F	RF	56	Book Bus	Creative Edge
Paul	F	I	54	Pacific Literacy	Pacific Learning
Paulo the Pilot	F	F	131	Windmill Books	Rigby
Pawpaw patch	F	TL	174	PM Readalongs	Rigby
Pea or the Flea?, The	F	RF	66	Start to Read	School Zone
Peas in a Pod	F	F	173	Cambridge Reading	Pearson Learning Group
People Build Dams	F	I	46	Windows on Literacy	National Geographic
People Live Here	F	I	42	Windows on Literacy	National Geographic
People on the Beach	F	RF	87	Carousel Readers	Pearson Learning Group
Pet Day	F	RF	92	Home Connection Collection	Rigby

* Collection of short stories

TITLE	LEVEL	GENRE	WORD COUNT	AUTHOR / SERIES	PUBLISHER / DISTRIBUTOR
Pete the Parakeet	F	F	133	First Start	Troll Associates
Peter's Painting	F	F	147	Bookshop	Mondo
Pete's Peacock	F	RF	89	Dominie Phonics Reader	Pearson Learning Group
Pets	F	RF	56	Literacy 2000	Rigby
Picking Apples	F	I	53	Pebble Books	Capstone Press
Pickles Helps Out	F	RF	160	Pickles the Dog Series	Pioneer Valley
Pickles in My Soup	F	F	88	Rookie Reader	Children's Press
Picnic on the Sidewalk	F	RF	108	Seedlings	Continental Press
Picnic, The	F	RF	122	Wonder World	Wright Group/McGraw Hill
Pie, The	F	RF	117	Developing Books, Set 1	Pioneer Valley
Pilgrim Children Had Many Chores	F	I	47	Learn to Read	Creative Teaching Press
Pip and the Little Monkey	F	RF	112	Oxford Reading Tree	Oxford University Press
Pip at the Zoo	F	RF	70	Oxford Reading Tree	Oxford University Press
Pizza Party!	F	RF	79	Maccarone, Grace	Scholastic
Plane Ride, The	F	I	68	Little Red Readers	Sundance
Plants and Animals live Here	F	I	54	Windows on Literacy	National Geographic
Play Ball!	F	RF	49	Instant Readers	Harcourt School Publishers
Play Ball, Sherman	F	RF	88	Erickson, Betty	Continental Press
Playing Games	F	RF	89	Phonics Readers	Pearson Learning Group
Playing It Safe	F	I	135	Early Connections	Benchmark Education
Playing with Dad	F	RF	146	Foundations	Wright Group/McGraw Hill
Plenty of Pets	F	RF	173	Instant Readers	Harcourt School Publishers
Polar Babies	F	I	115	Susan Ring	Random House
Polar Bears	F	I	77	Pebble Books	Capstone Press
Polar Bears	F	I	77	Story Steps	Rigby
Polka Dots!	F	I	102	Little Celebrations	Pearson Learning Group
Pollution	F	I	46	Wonder World	Wright Group/McGraw Hill
Poor Old Polly	F	F	111	Story Box	Wright Group/McGraw Hill
Poor Polly Pig	F	F	57	Start to Read	School Zone
Powwow	F	I	29	Books for Young Learners	Richard C. Owen
Prairie Town	F	I	62	Seedlings	Continental Press
Processed Food	F	I	54	Wonder World	Wright Group/McGraw Hill
Punchinello	F	TL	250+	PM Readalongs	Rigby
Puppet Show	F	RF	105	First Start	Troll Associates
Push It or Pull It?	F	RF	162	Instant Readers	Harcourt School Publishers
Pussy Cat	F	TL	143	Literacy 2000	Rigby
Questions, Questions, Questions	F	RF	190	Visions	Wright Group/McGraw Hill
Rabbits' Ears	F	RF	179	PM Plus Story Books	Rigby
Race, The	F	RF	145	Little Readers	Houghton Mifflin
Read to Your Bunny	F	F	38	Wells, Rosemary	Scholastic
Reading a Graph	F	I	251	Early Connections	Benchmark Education
Reading Lesson, The	F	RF	78	Teacher's Choice Series	Pearson Learning Group
Red and I Visit the Vet	F	RF	196	Ready Readers	Pearson Learning Group
Redy to Ride	F	RF	103	City Stories	Rigby
Riddle Book	F	F	189	Reading Unlimited	Pearson Learning Group
Rocket, The	F	RF	41	City Stories	Rigby
Rocks	F	I	112	Discovery Links	Newbridge
Roll Over	F	F	220	Gerstein, Mordicai	Crown
Roller Blades, The	F	RF	137	Foundations	Wright Group/McGraw Hill
Rose	F	F	82	Wheeler, Cindy	Alfred A. Knopf
Rosie's Walk	F	F	32	Hutchins, Pat	Macmillan
Running	F	RF	185	Visions	Wright Group/McGraw Hill
Sally's Friends	F	RF	128	PM Story Books	Rigby
Sam Plays Paddle Ball	F	F	161	PM Plus Story Books	Rigby

* Collection of short stories

TITLE	LEVEL	GENRE	WORD COUNT	AUTHOR / SERIES	PUBLISHER / DISTRIBUTOR
Sam the Scarecrow	F	F	143	First Start	Troll Associates
*Sam, Sam, and Other Stories	F	F	250+	Story Steps	Rigby
Sammy Gets a Ride	F	F	91	Evans, Karen; Urmston, Kathleen	Kaeden Books
Sammy's Moving	F	F	166	Evans, Karen; Urmston, Kathleen	Kaeden Books
Sam's Painting	F	RF	181	PM Plus Story Books	Rigby
Samuel's Sprout	F	RF	194	Little Celebrations	Pearson Learning Group
Say "Hi" Up High	F	F	61	Early Readers	Compass Point Books
Say Cheese!	F	RF	128	Storyteller-Moon Rising	Wright Group/McGraw Hill
Scare for Bear, A	F	F	182	Sun Sprouts	ETA/Cuisenaire
Scit, Scat, Scaredy Cat!	F	F	59	Sunshine	Wright Group/McGraw Hill
Scrubbing Machine, The	F	F	148	Story Box	Wright Group/McGraw Hill
Sea Horses	F	I	67	Pebble Books	Capstone Press
Sea Where I Swim, The	F	I	134	Voyages	SRA/McGraw Hill
Season to Season	F	I	113	Pair-It Books	Steck-Vaughn
Seeing Things Up Close	F	I	72	Windows on Literacy	National Geographic
Seven Cool Cats	F	F	97	Seedlings	Continental Press
Seven little ducks	F	TL	190	PM Readalongs	Rigby
Shadows	F	I	110	Independent Readers Science	Houghton Mifflin
Shadows	F	I	130	Wonder World	Wright Group/McGraw Hill
Sheepdog Max	F	F	171	Sun Sprouts	ETA/Cuisenaire
Shell Shopping	F	RF	145	Ready Readers	Pearson Learning Group
SHHH	F	RF	66	Henkes, Kevin	Greenwillow
Shine Sun	F	RF	115	Rookie Readers	Children's Press
Shoes	F	I	73	Talk About Books	Pearson Learning Group
Shoo, Crow! Shoo!	F	F	41	Early Readers	Compass Point Books
Shoveling Snow	F	RF	109	Cummings, Pat	Scholastic
Show and Tell	F	RF	111	Little Red Readers	Sundance
Sick in Bed	F	RF	109	Little Red Readers	Sundance
Signs	F	I	40	Canizares, Susan; Chanko, Pamela	Scholastic
Signs on the Way	F	I	106	Windows on Literacy	National Geographic
Silvia's Soccer Game	F	RF	138	Ready Readers	Pearson Learning Group
Sink or Float	F	I	91	Instant Readers	Harcourt School Publishers
Sit, Sam	F	RF	165	Early Connections	Benchmark Education
Six Empty Pockets	F	RF	85	Rookie Readers	Children's Press
Six Fine Fish	F	F	252	Ready Readers	Pearson Learning Group
Six Little Chicks	F	F	227	Sun Sprouts	ETA/Cuisenaire
Skateboarding	F	RF	147	Developing Books, Set 1	Pioneer Valley
Skin	F	I	97	Literacy 2000	Rigby
Skip Count Song, The	F	I	84	Learn to Read	Creative Teaching Press
Sky Is Falling, The	F	TL	186	Folk Tales	Pioneer Valley
Sky Time	F	F	366	Phonics and Friends	Hampton-Brown
Sleepy Bear	F	I	80	Literacy 2000	Rigby
Sly Fox and Red Hen	F	TL	314	Hunia, Fran	Ladybird Books
Small Treasures	F	RF	52	Gibson, Akimi	Scholastic
Smile, Baby!	F	RF	165	Little Readers	Houghton Mifflin
Smiles	F	RF	366	Visions	Wright Group/McGraw Hill
Snake's Sore Head	F	F	139	Storyteller-Moon Rising	Wright Group/McGraw Hill
Sneakers! Sneakers!	F	F	49	Little Celebrations	Pearson Learning Group
Sneezes	F	RF	36	Literacy 2000	Rigby
Snowflakes	F	RF	80	Seedlings	Continental Press
Snuggle Up	F	RF	125	Harrison, P.; Worthington, Denise	Continental Press
So That's What It Is!	F	I	133	Rigby Literacy	Rigby
Soccer at the Park	F	RF	131	PM Extensions-Yellow	Rigby
Soccer Game!	F	RF	63	Maccarone, Grace	Scholastic

* Collection of short stories

TITLE	LEVEL	GENRE	WORD COUNT	AUTHOR / SERIES	PUBLISHER / DISTRIBUTOR
Sometimes . . .	F	RF	31	City Stories	Rigby
Sounds in the Night	F	RF	126	Visions	Wright Group/McGraw Hill
Space Ant Goes Home	F	F	194	Rigby Literacy	Rigby
Sparky's Bone	F	F	273	Ready Readers	Pearson Learning Group
Sparrows, The	F	I	60	Books for Young Learners	Richard C. Owen
Speak Up!	F	F	194	Sunshine	Wright Group/McGraw Hill
Special Friend, A	F	RF	80	Carousel Readers	Pearson Learning Group
Speed Racer	F	RF	74	Leveled Readers Science	Houghton Mifflin
Spinning Snake, A	F	RF	156	Sunshine	Wright Group/McGraw Hill
Sports Bag	F	I	147	Sun Sprouts	ETA/Cuisenaire
Springs	F	I	142	Alphakids	Sundance
Squirrels	F	RF	109	Ready Readers	Pearson Learning Group
Ssh, Don't Wake the Baby	F	RF	135	Voyages	SRA/McGraw Hill
Start and Stop	F	I	49	Pebble Books	Red Brick Learning
Staying Well	F	I	154	Early Connections	Benchmark Education
Staying with Grandma Norma	F	RF	168	Salem, Lynn; Stewart, Josie	Continental Press
Sticky Stanley	F	F	97	First Start	Troll Associates
Story Sticks	F	I	58	Instant Readers	Harcourt School Publishers
Stream, The	F	F	43	Voyages	SRA/McGraw Hill
Strongest Animal, The	F	RF	58	Books for Young Learners	Richard C. Owen
Super Animals	F	I	149	Leveled Readers Science	Houghton Mifflin
Susie Goes Shopping	F	F	194	First Start	Troll Associates
Swamp Hen	F	I	59	Pacific Literacy	Pacific Learning
Swan Family, The	F	RF	172	PM Plus Story Books	Rigby
Tabby in the Tree	F	RF	200	PM Story Books	Rigby
Tails	F	I	47	Literacy 2000	Rigby
Take a Look at My Family	F	RF	155	Phonics and Friends	Hampton-Brown
Take the Subway	F	I	111	Vocabulary Readers	Houghton Mifflin
Taking Jason to Grandma's	F	RF	118	Book Bank	Wright Group/McGraw Hill
Talent Night at School	F	RF	102	Little Red Readers	Sundance
Talking to Our Friends	F	I	138	Rigby Focus	Rigby
Tarantulas are Spiders	F	I	39	Bookshop	Mondo
Teamwork	F	I	148	Yellow Umbrella Books	Capstone Press
Teasing Dad	F	RF	158	PM Extensions-Blue	Rigby
Teeny Tiny Woman, The	F	TL	250+	O'Connor, Jane	Random House
Ten Little Caterpillars	F	F	102	Literacy 2000	Rigby
Ten-Second Race, The	F	F	102	Learn to Read	Creative Teaching Press
Thank You, Nicky!	F	F	119	Ziefert, Harriet	Penguin Group
Thanksgiving	F	F	75	Urmston, Kathleen; Evans, Karen	Kaeden Books
That Pig Can't Do a Thing	F	F	83	Ready Readers	Pearson Learning Group
This is the Register	F	RF	81	Cambridge Reading	Pearson Learning Group
This Is the Way	F	RF	200	Learn to Read	Creative Teaching Press
Thomas Had a Temper	F	RF	139	Alphakids	Sundance
Three Billy Goats Gruff, The	F	TL	250+	Folk Tales	Pioneer Valley
Three Goats, The	F	TL	128	Storyteller-Setting Sun	Wright Group/McGraw Hill
Three Jars Full	F	I	89	Rigby Focus	Rigby
Three Little Pigs, The	F	TL	274	Alphakids	Sundance
Three Muddy Monkeys	F	F	180	Foundations	Wright Group/McGraw Hill
Tick Tock World Clocks	F	I	43	iOpeners	Pearson Learning Group
Tiger Is a Scaredy Cat	F	F	220	Phillips, Joan	Random House
Time for a Party	F	I	111	Discovery World	Rigby
Tim's Favorite Toy	F	RF	202	PM Extensions-Blue	Rigby
Tina's Taxi	F	RF	83	Franco, Betsy	Scholastic
Tiny and the Big Wave	F	RF	163	PM Extensions-Yellow	Rigby

* Collection of short stories

TITLE	LEVEL	GENRE	WORD COUNT	AUTHOR / SERIES	PUBLISHER / DISTRIBUTOR
Tires	F	RF	180	Foundations	Wright Group/McGraw Hill
To Town	F	F	148	Story Box	Wright Group/McGraw Hill
Toys and Play	F	RF	194	PM Plus Nonfiction	Rigby
Toys' Party, The	F	F	48	Oxford Reading Tree	Oxford University Press
Toytown Race Car, The	F	F	188	PM Plus Story Books	Rigby
Traffic Jam	F	RF	55	City Stories	Rigby
Treasure Island, A	F	RF	177	PM Plus Story Books	Rigby
Tree, The	F	RF	101	Sunshine	Wright Group/McGraw Hill
Treehouse Club, The	F	RF	158	Home Connection Collection	Rigby
Trees and Leaves	F	I	33	iOpeners	Pearson Learning Group
Trick or Treat Halloween	F	RF	131	First Start	Troll Associates
Trick, The	F	RF	65	New Way Red	Steck-Vaughn
Tricking Tracy	F	RF	125	Tadpoles	Rigby
Trip to the Zoo, A	F	I	93	Independent Readers Science	Houghton Mifflin
Trip to the Zoo, A	F	I	112	Rosen Real Readers	Rosen Publishing Group
Truckster	F	F	194	Instant Readers	Harcourt School Publishers
Try to Be a Brave Girl, Sarah	F	RF	102	Windmill	Wright Group/McGraw Hill
T-Shirts	F	RF	112	Pacific Literacy	Pacific Learning
Turnip, The	F	TL	250+	Ziefert, Harriet	Puffin Books
Two Feet	F	RF	129	Pescoe, Gwen	Educational Insights
Two Little Ducks Get Lost	F	F	178	PM Plus Story Books	Rigby
Two Ogres, The	F	F	116	Joy Readers	Pearson Learning Group
Two Yellow Eyes	F	F	211	Sun Sprouts	ETA/Cuisenaire
Under My Sombrero	F	F	79	Books for Young Learners	Richard C. Owen
Underwater Journey	F	I	60	Sunshine	Wright Group/McGraw Hill
Up, Up, and Away: The Story of Amelia Earhart	F	B	42	Canizares, Susan; Chanko, Pamela	Scholastic
Use Your Beak!	F	RF	106	Erickson, Betty	Continental Press
Using Magnets	F	I	160	Early Connections	Benchmark Education
Using Your Senses at School	F	I	37	Windows on Literacy	National Geographic
Vegetables and How They Grow	F	I	86	Rosen Real Readers	Rosen Publishing Group
Victor and the Computer Cat	F	RF	92	Oxford Reading Tree	Oxford University Press
Victor and the Kite	F	F	84	Oxford Reading Tree	Oxford University Press
Video Game	F	RF	109	Alphakids	Sundance
Waiting for Granny	F	RF	179	Leveled Readers Language Support	Houghton Mifflin
Waiting in Line	F	RF	74	City Stories	Rigby
Wake Up, Sleepyheads!	F	RF	35	Little Books	Sadlier-Oxford
Walk in the Woods, A	F	F	212	Leveled Readers	Houghton Mifflin
Water Boatman, The	F	I	44	Pacific Literacy	Pacific Learning
Water! Water!	F	I	186	Story Basket	Wright Group/McGraw Hill
Water, Water Everywhere	F	RF	61	Books for Young Learners	Richard C. Owen
Way Down South	F	F	109	Learn to Read	Creative Teaching Press
We Want That	F	RF	158	Visions	Wright Group/McGraw Hill
Wedding, The	F	RF	50	Literacy 2000	Rigby
Week of Surprises, A	F	RF	138	Leveled Readers Language Support	Houghton Mifflin
Welcome to the White House	F	I	106	Independent Readers Social Studies	Houghton Mifflin
What a Dog!	F	RF	134	First Start	Troll Associates
What a School	F	RF	100	Salem, Lynn; Stewart, Josie	Continental Press
What Am I?	F	I	100	Sun Sprouts	ETA/Cuisenaire
What Are You Going to Buy?	F	F	180	Read Alongs	Rigby
What Can I Buy?	F	RF	156	Moriarty, Julie	Scholastic
What Can It Be?	F	I	113	Storyteller-First Snow	Wright Group/McGraw Hill

* Collection of short stories

TITLE	LEVEL	GENRE	WORD COUNT	AUTHOR / SERIES	PUBLISHER / DISTRIBUTOR
What Color Is the Sky?	F	I	74	Windows on Literacy	National Geographic
What Daddies Do Best	F	F	113	Numeroff, Laura Joffe	Simon & Schuster
What Dinosaurs Ate	F	I	44	Planet Earth	Rigby
What Do Artists Use?	F	I	31	Canizares, Susan; Berger, Samantha	Scholastic
What Do I See in the Garden?	F	I	108	Wonder World	Wright Group/McGraw Hill
What Do You See?	F	F	89	Learn to Read	Creative Teaching Press
What Fun!	F	F	250+	Sun Sprouts	ETA/Cuisenaire
What Helps a Bird to Fly?	F	I	95	Birds Series	Pearson Learning Group
What I'd Like to Be	F	I	112	Little Red Readers	Sundance
What is a Mammal?	F	I	102	Rosen Real Readers	Rosen Publishing Group
What Is It?	F	I	135	Foundations	Wright Group/McGraw Hill
What Is That? Said the Cat	F	F	118	Maccarone, Grace	Scholastic
What Makes Light?	F	I	119	Sunshine	Wright Group/McGraw Hill
What Mommies Do Best	F	F	113	Numeroff, Laura Joffe	Simon & Schuster
What Mynah Bird Saw	F	TL	90	Sunshine	Wright Group/McGraw Hill
What Next?	F	F	277	Story Basket	Wright Group/McGraw Hill
What Season Is it?	F	I	79	Leveled Readers Social Studies	Houghton Mifflin
What Should We Wear?	F	I	50	iOpeners	Pearson Learning Group
What Was This?	F	I	53	Wonder World	Wright Group/McGraw Hill
What's In My Pocket	F	I	72	Learn to Read	Creative Teaching Press
What's the Time	F	RF	74	Cambridge Reading	Pearson Learning Group
What's This Matter?	F	I	88	Independent Readers Science	Houghton Mifflin
When Dad Came Home	F	RF	46	Literacy 2000	Rigby
When Dad Got Lost	F	RF	113	City Stories	Rigby
When Do You Feel	F	I	132	Twig	Wright Group/McGraw Hill
When Goldilocks Went to the House of the Bears	F	TL	156	Bookshop	Mondo
When I Grow Up	F	RF	63	Rhythm 'N' Rhyme Readers	Pearson Learning Group
When I Was Sick	F	RF	53	Literacy 2000	Rigby
When I'm Older	F	RF	156	Literacy 2000	Rigby
When It Rains	F	I	106	Frankford, Marilyn	Kaeden Books
When Lana Was Absent	F	RF	78	Tadpoles	Rigby
Where Are the Eggs?	F	I	152	Discovery Links	Newbridge
Where Can We Go from Here?	F	I	54	Spinelle, Nancy Louise	Kaeden Books
Where Did All the Water Go?	F	I	139	PM Plus Nonfiction	Rigby
Where Did It Go?	F	F	216	Learn to Read	Creative Teaching Press
Where Do Animals Live	F	I	187	Bookshop	Mondo
Where Is It?	F	I	32	Tiger Cub	Peguis
Where Will I Sit?	F	RF	78	Teacher's Choice Series	Pearson Learning Group
Where's Henry?	F	RF	112	Home Connection Collection	Rigby
Where's My Daddy?	F	F	87	Watanabe, Shigeo	Putnam
Where's Sylvester's Bed?	F	RF	78	Wonder World	Wright Group/McGraw Hill
Who Came Out?	F	F	45	Ready Readers	Pearson Learning Group
Who is a Friend?	F	I	191	Yellow Umbrella Books	Capstone Press
Who is Taller?	F	I	163	Sun Sprouts	ETA/Cuisenaire
Who Is the Tallest?	F	I	91	Alphakids	Sundance
Who Lives Here?	F	I	100	Leveled Readers Science	Houghton Mifflin
Who Lives Here?	F	I	185	Storyteller Nonfiction	Wright Group/McGraw Hill
Who Lives in the Woods?	F	I	110	Pair-It Books	Steck-Vaughn
Who Wants to See the Doctor?	F	I	116	Adventures in Reading	Pearson Learning Group
Who Will Be My Friends?	F	RF	205	Hoff, Syd	HarperTrophy
Who Will Help?	F	RF	74	New Way Red	Steck-Vaughn
Who'll Hold the Baby?	F	RF	181	Voyages	SRA/McGraw Hill

* Collection of short stories

TITLE	LEVEL	GENRE	WORD COUNT	AUTHOR / SERIES	PUBLISHER / DISTRIBUTOR
Who's in the Jungle?	F	I	116	Ready Readers	Pearson Learning Group
William, Where Are You?	F	F	239	Gerstein, Mordicai	Crown
Wind, The	F	I	84	Voyages	SRA/McGraw Hill
Winter Sleeps	F	RF	158	Reading Corners	Pearson Learning Group
Wobbly Tooth, The	F	RF	74	Oxford Reading Tree	Oxford University Press
Wolves	F	I	132	Twig	Wright Group/McGraw Hill
Wonderful Things	F	RF	98	Early Readers	Compass Point Books
Wool	F	I	91	Sunshine	Wright Group/McGraw Hill
Worker's Tools, A	F	I	93	Discovery World	Rigby
Yasmin and the Flood	F	RF	81	Oxford Reading Tree	Oxford University Press
You Can Do It	F	F	176	Sun Sprouts	ETA/Cuisenaire
You Can Make a Timer	F	I	124	How-To Series	Benchmark Education
Youngest in the Family	F	RF	144	Visions	Wright Group/McGraw Hill
Yo-Yo a Go-Go	F	RF	177	Rigby Literacy	Rigby
Yummy, Yummy	F	F	115	Grey, Judith	Troll Associates
Zack's Moving Day Surprise	F	RF	122	Developing Books, Set 3	Pioneer Valley
Zigzag Movement	F	I	50	Pebble Books	Red Brick Learning
Zoo Babies	F	I	51	Little Celebrations	Pearson Learning Group
Adding It Up at the Zoo	G	I	250+	Yellow Umbrella Books	Red Brick Learning
Addition Annie	G	RF	30	Rookie Readers	Children's Press
After the Flood	G	RF	210	PM Extensions-Green	Rigby
All About You	G	I	250+	Anholt, Catherine & Laurence	Scholastic
All Kinds of Farms	G	I	146	Yellow Umbrella Books	Red Brick Learning
All Kinds of Rocks	G	RF	136	Instant Readers	Harcourt School Publishers
All Mixed Up	G	F	105	Little Books	Sadlier-Oxford
Alligator Shoes	G	F	122	Dorros, Arthur	Dutton
Alma Flor Ada: From a Family of Storytellers	G	B	75	Leveled Readers	Houghton Mifflin
Along Came Greedy Cat	G	F	166	Pacific Literacy	Pacific Learning
Amanda's Bear	G	F	154	Reading Corners	Pearson Learning Group
Amazing Fish, The	G	TL	167	Pair-It Books	Steck-Vaughn
Amazing Popple Seed, The	G	F	113	Read Alongs	Rigby
Angus Thought He Was Big	G	F	58	Giant Step Readers	Educational Insights
Animal Homes	G	I	193	PM Plus Nonfiction	Rigby
Animal Hospital	G	RF	193	Sunshine	Wright Group/McGraw Hill
Animal Inventions	G	I	80	Sunshine	Wright Group/McGraw Hill
Animal Skeletons	G	I	91	Alphakids	Sundance
Animals from Long Ago	G	I	141	Discovery Links	Newbridge
Answer the Phone, Fiona!	G	RF	119	Lighthouse	Rigby
*Ant and the Dove, The	G	TL	173	New Way Blue	Steck-Vaughn
Ants	G	I	94	Wonder World	Wright Group/McGraw Hill
Ants and the Grasshoppers, The	G	TL	144	New Way Blue	Steck-Vaughn
Apple Thief, The	G	F	62	Voyages	SRA/McGraw Hill
Apple Tree	G	RF	198	Literacy Tree	Rigby
Apple Tree Apple Tree	G	RF	340	Blocksma, Mary	Children's Press
Apron Annie in the Garden	G	RF	153	Learn to Read	Creative Teaching Press
Apron Annie's Pies	G	RF	167	Learn to Read	Creative Teaching Press
Artist in the Woods	G	F	228	Seedlings	Continental Press
At My Grandfather's	G	RF	63	City Stories	Rigby
At School	G	I	250+	Yellow Umbrella Books	Red Brick Learning
At the Game	G	F	85	City Stories	Rigby
At the Playground	G	I	151	Discovery Links	Newbridge
Aunt Jessie	G	RF	114	Literacy 2000	Rigby
Aunt Louisa Is Coming for Lunch	G	RF	118	Windmill Books	Rigby
Autumn Leaves	G	RF	84	Voyages	SRA/McGraw Hill

* Collection of short stories

TITLE	LEVEL	GENRE	WORD COUNT	AUTHOR / SERIES	PUBLISHER / DISTRIBUTOR
Awful Waffles	G	F	296	Williams, D. H.	Continental Press
Baby Elephant's New Bike	G	F	187	Foundations	Wright Group/McGraw Hill
Backyard Zoo	G	I	167	Ready Readers	Pearson Learning Group
Bad Boy, Billy	G	RF	129	Cambridge Reading	Pearson Learning Group
Balcony Garden	G	I	258	Storyteller Nonfiction	Wright Group/McGraw Hill
Barnaby's New House, The	G	RF	135	Literacy 2000	Rigby
Barnyard Math with Farmer Fred	G	RF	139	Learn to Read	Creative Teaching Press
Batter Up	G	RF	183	Adventures in Reading	Pearson Learning Group
Batteries	G	I	105	Early Connections	Benchmark Education
Beaks	G	I	125	Discovery Links	Newbridge
Bears and the Magpie, The	G	F	205	PM Plus Story Books	Rigby
Before the Fridge	G	I	88	Seedlings	Continental Press
Benny's School Trip	G	RF	217	Pair-It Books	Steck-Vaughn
Best Hats, The	G	RF	201	PM Plus Story Books	Rigby
Best Present, The	G	RF	146	Rigby Literacy	Rigby
Big Crocodile, The	G	F	61	Little Celebrations	Pearson Learning Group
Big Fat Worm, The	G	F	250+	Van Laan, Nancy	Random House
Big Mix-Up, The	G	F	70	City Stories	Rigby
Big Red Fire Engine	G	F	158	First Start	Troll Associates
Big Roundup, The	G	I	121	Wonder World	Wright Group/McGraw Hill
Big, Fat, Wide Mouth	G	F	183	Story Box	Wright Group/McGraw Hill
Bikes	G	RF	156	Foundations	Wright Group/McGraw Hill
Billy's Box	G	F	207	Cambridge Reading	Pearson Learning Group
Birthday Cake, The	G	RF	107	Rigby Focus	Rigby
Black Swan's Breakfast	G	RF	147	Book Bank	Wright Group/McGraw Hill
Blackbird's Nest	G	RF	71	Pacific Literacy	Pacific Learning
Blue Lollipops	G	RF	250	Stepping Stones	Nelson/Michaels Assoc.
Blue Sue	G	F	121	Ready Readers	Pearson Learning Group
BMX Billy	G	RF	93	Literacy 2000	Rigby
Boats	G	I	84	Rockwell, Anne	Penguin Group
Boris Bad Enough	G	F	167	Kraus, Robert	Simon & Schuster
Bot's Bits	G	F	99	Supersonics	Rigby
Braids for Naya	G	RF	89	City Stories	Rigby
Brave Triceratops	G	F	178	PM Story Books	Rigby
Breakfast in Bed	G	RF	36	Tadpoles	Rigby
Breakfast Time	G	F	250+	Bookshop	Mondo
Broken Flower Pot, The	G	RF	203	PM Plus Story Books	Rigby
Broken Window	G	RF	136	New Way Blue	Steck-Vaughn
Buffy's Tricks	G	RF	97	Literacy 2000	Rigby
Building a House	G	I	197	PM Plus Nonfiction	Rigby
Building Shapes	G	I	30	Canizares, Susan; Berger, Samantha	Scholastic
Bus Stop, The	G	RF	110	Hellen, Nancy	Orchard Books
Butterflies in My Garden	G	RF	177	Bookshop	Mondo
Buzz Said the Bee	G	F	62	Lewison, Wendy	Scholastic
Buzzzzzz Said the Bee	G	F	147	Hello Reader	Scholastic
Calico Cat at School	G	F	86	Charles, Donald	Children's Press
Calico Cat Meets Bookworm	G	F	90	Charles, Donald	Children's Press
Candlelight	G	RF	231	PM Story Books	Rigby
Captain B's Boat	G	F	158	Sunshine	Wright Group/McGraw Hill
Car Wash, The	G	I	98	Windows on Literacy	National Geographic
Caring for Our Lizard	G	I	133	Learn to Read	Creative Teaching Press
Carla's Breakfast	G	RF	225	Harper, Leslie	Kaeden Books
Carla's Ribbons	G	RF	212	Harper, Leslie	Kaeden Books

* Collection of short stories

TITLE	LEVEL	GENRE	WORD COUNT	AUTHOR / SERIES	PUBLISHER / DISTRIBUTOR
Carrot Seed, The	G	F	101	Krauss, Ruth	Harper & Row
Case of the Furry Thing, The	G	RF	267	Ready Readers	Pearson Learning Group
Cat and Dog Go Shopping	G	F	127	Learn to Read	Creative Teaching Press
Cat and Dog Make the Best, Biggest, Most Wonderful Cheese Sandwich	G	F	250+	Learn to Read	Creative Teaching Press
Cat That Broke the Rules, The	G	F	192	Ready Readers	Pearson Learning Group
Cat's Trip	G	F	158	Ready Readers	Pearson Learning Group
Cats, Cats, Cats	G	RF	217	Story Basket	Wright Group/McGraw Hill
Caves	G	I	79	Seedlings	Continental Press
Celebrations	G	I	37	Berger, Samantha; Moreton, Daniel	Scholastic
Celebrations	G	I	107	Storyteller-Moon Rising	Wright Group/McGraw Hill
Cement Tent	G	F	358	First Start	Troll Associates
Changing Caterpillar, The	G	I	56	Books for Young Learners	Richard C. Owen
Changing Weather	G	I	145	Early Connections	Benchmark Education
Charlie Strong and his favourite song	G	RF	120	Breakthrough	Longman/Bow
Cheetahs	G	RF	140	Seedlings	Continental Press
Chickens	G	I	105	Bookshop	Mondo
Chickens on the Farm	G	I	59	Pebble Books	Capstone Press
Chickens On Vacation	G	F	169	Seedlings	Continental Press
Christmas Santa Almost Missed, The	G	F	158	First Start	Troll Associates
Christmas Surprise	G	RF	145	First Start	Troll Associates
Circus Fun	G	RF	219	Momentum Literacy Program	Troll Associates
City Animals	G	RF	102	Higgins, Malcom	Houghton Mifflin
City Buildings	G	I	133	Discovery Links	Newbridge
City Garden, A	G	RF	77	City Stories	Rigby
City Shapes	G	I	177	Yellow Umbrella Books	Red Brick Learning
City Sights	G	I	250+	Phonics and Friends	Hampton-Brown
City Sounds	G	RF	142	Marzollo, Jean	Scholastic
Class Rules	G	RF	143	Windows on Literacy	National Geographic
Clever Brown Mouse	G	F	199	PM Plus Story Books	Rigby
Clever Penguins, The	G	I	174	PM Story Books	Rigby
Click!	G	RF	250+	Foundations	Wright Group/McGraw Hill
Coat Full of Bubbles, A	G	F	72	Books for Young Learners	Richard C. Owen
Collecting Things Is Fun!	G	RF	134	Learn to Read	Creative Teaching Press
Color It My Way	G	RF	123	Story Steps	Rigby
Come and See!	G	RF	134	Foundations	Wright Group/McGraw Hill
Come On, Tim	G	RF	198	PM Story Books	Rigby
Coo Coo Caroo	G	F	57	Books for Young Learners	Richard C. Owen
Cookie Jar, The	G	RF	106	Sunshine	Wright Group/McGraw Hill
Cooking at School	G	RF	68	City Kids	Rigby
Cooking Dinner	G	I	86	Windows on Literacy	National Geographic
Cool School, A	G	RF	138	City Stories	Rigby
Corals	G	I	51	Pebble Books	Capstone Press
Count Your Chickens	G	I	123	Yellow Umbrella Books	Red Brick Learning
Countdown	G	F	70	Literacy Tree	Rigby
Counting Money	G	I	122	Early Connections	Benchmark Education
Country Family	G	RF	262	Instant Readers	Harcourt School Publishers
Cows in the Garden	G	F	163	PM Story Books	Rigby
Cows on the Farm	G	I	56	Pebble Books	Capstone Press
Crafts	G	I	50	Chessen, Betsey; Chanko, Pamela	Scholastic
Crayola Counting Book, The	G	I	102	Learn to Read	Creative Teaching Press
Crazy Quilt, The	G	RF	148	Little Readers	Houghton Mifflin
Crazy Quilt, The	G	F	148	Little Celebrations	Pearson Learning Group

* Collection of short stories

TITLE	LEVEL	GENRE	WORD COUNT	AUTHOR / SERIES	PUBLISHER / DISTRIBUTOR
Critter Race	G	F	118	Reese, Bob	Children's Press
Crossing the Street	G	RF	142	City Stories	Rigby
Crunchy Munchy	G	F	189	Bookshop	Mondo
Cutting Machines	G	I	132	Sunshine Books	Wright Group/McGraw Hill
Dances We Do, The	G	I	131	Twig	Wright Group/McGraw Hill
Dan's Box	G	F	105	Cambridge Reading	Pearson Learning Group
Dark and Stormy Night, A	G	F	160	Little Red Readers	Sundance
Day and Night	G	I	115	Discovery Links	Newbridge
Day Buzzy Stopped Being Busy, The	G	F	147	First Start	Troll Associates
Day I Had to Play with My Sister, The	G	RF	139	Bonsall, Crosby	HarperCollins
Day in Japan, A	G	I	54	Moreton, Daniel; Berger, Samantha	Scholastic
Dee and Me	G	RF	189	Ready Readers	Pearson Learning Group
Deep Sea, The	G	I	152	Ready Readers	Pearson Learning Group
Deer and the Crocodile, The	G	F	178	Literacy 2000	Rigby
Dentist, The	G	I	201	PM Nonfiction-Blue	Rigby
Desert Dance	G	RF	184	Little Celebrations	Pearson Learning Group
Did You Know?	G	I	22	Learn to Read	Creative Teaching Press
Did you say, "Fire"?	G	F	158	Pacific Literacy	Pacific Learning
Different Tune, A	G	F	86	Start to Read	School Zone
Dinosaur Hunt, The	G	RF	155	Rigby Literacy	Rigby
Dinosaur Hunt, The	G	F	131	Windmill Books	Rigby
Dinosaur in Trouble	G	F	121	First Start	Troll Associates
Dinosaur Show and Tell	G	RF	212	Pair-It Books	Steck-Vaughn
Dinosaurs, Dinosaurs	G	I	96	Barton, Byron	HarperCollins
Diving	G	RF	164	Story Box	Wright Group/McGraw Hill
Do We Need It? Do We Want It?	G	I	111	Early Connections	Benchmark Education
Doctor, The	G	I	179	PM Nonfiction-Blue	Rigby
Dog, The	G	RF	56	Burningham, John	Crowell
Donkey in the Lion's Skin, The	G	TL	213	PM Plus Story Books	Rigby
Donkey in the Lion's Skin, The	G	TL	56	Aesop	Wright Group/McGraw Hill
Don't Cut Down This Tree	G	F	129	Voyages	SRA/McGraw Hill
Don't Tell!	G	RF	82	Little Books	Sadlier-Oxford
Down By the Sea	G	RF	173	PM Plus Story Books	Rigby
Dozen Dizzy Dogs, A	G	F	157	Bank Street	Bantam
Dr. Green	G	RF	141	Little Readers	Houghton Mifflin
Dragonflies	G	I	53	Books for Young Learners	Richard C. Owen
Dragonflies Are Super Bugs	G	I	101	Seedlings	Continental Press
Dream Around the World	G	F	138	Instant Readers	Harcourt School Publishers
Dreams	G	RF	98	Sunshine	Wright Group/McGraw Hill
Dry and Snug and Warm	G	RF	64	Book Bank	Wright Group/McGraw Hill
Duck Pond, The	G	RF	276	Leveled Readers	Houghton Mifflin
Each Peach, Pear, Plum	G	TL	115	Ahlberg, Allan & Janet	Penguin Group
Eagle Flies High, An	G	I	142	Ready Readers	Pearson Learning Group
Earth and Moon	G	I	250	Sunshine	Wright Group/McGraw Hill
Easter Bunny's Lost Egg	G	F	174	First Start	Troll Associates
Eat Up!	G	RF	95	Sunshine	Wright Group/McGraw Hill
Elephant and Envelope	G	F	158	Start to Read	School Zone
Ellen Ochoa	G	B	250+	Welcome Books	Children's Press
Every Shape and Size	G	I	97	Wonder World	Wright Group/McGraw Hill
Everybody Says	G	RF	70	Rookie Readers	Children's Press
Everyone Eats Bread	G	I	139	Yellow Umbrella Books	Red Brick Learning
Everyone Uses Math	G	I	211	Yellow Umbrella Books	Red Brick Learning
Fabulous Principal Pie, The	G	F	250+	Start to Read	School Zone

* Collection of short stories

TITLE	LEVEL	GENRE	WORD COUNT	AUTHOR / SERIES	PUBLISHER / DISTRIBUTOR
Face Painting	G	RF	90	Wonder World	Wright Group/McGraw Hill
Family Reunion	G	RF	243	Visions	Wright Group/McGraw Hill
Family Tree, The	G	F	213	Ready Readers	Pearson Learning Group
Far Away Moon	G	I	80	Pacific Literacy	Pacific Learning
Farmer Had a Pig, A	G	TL	149	Tiger Cub	Peguis
Fat Cat Sat on the Mat, The	G	F	250+	Karlin, Nurit	HarperTrophy
First Art Class, The	G	RF	250+	Leveled Readers Language Support	Houghton Mifflin
Fishing	G	RF	180	Foundations	Wright Group/McGraw Hill
Five Little Monkeys	G	F	160	Cambridge Reading	Pearson Learning Group
Five Little Speckled Frogs	G	RF	180	Tiger Cub	Peguis
Five Silly Fishermen	G	TL	250+	Edwards, Roberta	Random House
Flip Flop	G	RF	70	Books for Young Learners	Richard C. Owen
Footprints	G	RF	96	Literacy Tree	Rigby
Four Getters and Arf, The	G	F	123	Little Celebrations	Pearson Learning Group
Fourth of July, The	G	I	120	Fiesta Holiday Series	Pearson Learning Group
Fox and the Grapes, The	G	TL	60	Jumbled Tumbled Tales & Rhymes	Rigby
Freddie the Frog	G	F	250+	Supersonics	Rigby
Freeze Tag	G	RF	112	City Stories	Rigby
Friend for Max, A	G	RF	228	PM Plus Story Books	Rigby
Friend, A	G	RF	57	Literacy 2000	Rigby
Friends	G	RF	250+	Well-Being Series	Pearson Learning Group
Friends	G	RF	195	Reading Unlimited	Pearson Learning Group
Frogs	G	I	100	Storyteller-First Snow	Wright Group/McGraw Hill
From Here to There	G	I	179	Yellow Umbrella Books	Red Brick Learning
Fun at the Amusement Park	G	RF	176	Frankford, Marilyn	Kaeden Books
Fun in the Mud	G	RF	182	Foundations	Wright Group/McGraw Hill
Gabby and the Christmas Tree	G	F	113	Developing Books, Set 2	Pioneer Valley
Gabby Runs Away	G	RF	223	Developing Books, Set 1	Pioneer Valley
Garden, The	G	RF	21	Hoenecke, Karen	Kaeden Books
George's Story	G	RF	133	Developing Books	Pioneer Valley
Getting Glasses	G	I	82	Wonder World	Wright Group/McGraw Hill
Getting the Mail	G	RF	213	Voyages	SRA/McGraw Hill
Giant Gingerbread Man, The	G	TL	248	Alphakids	Sundance
Giant Pandas	G	I	72	Pebble Books	Capstone Press
Gift of Crayons, A	G	RF	226	Leveled Readers Language Support	Houghton Mifflin
Gingerbread Boy, The	G	TL	250+	Ziefert, Harriet	Puffin Books
Gingerbread Man, The	G	TL	139	Cambridge Reading	Pearson Learning Group
Glass	G	I	112	Rigby Focus	Rigby
Goat Who Wouldn't Come Home, The	G	F	184	Seedlings	Continental Press
Going Fishing	G	RF	117	Cambridge Reading	Pearson Learning Group
Going to the Symphony	G	I	132	Twig	Wright Group/McGraw Hill
Goldilocks	G	TL	244	Sunshine	Wright Group/McGraw Hill
Goldilocks and the Three Bears	G	TL	265	Storyteller Nonfiction	Wright Group/McGraw Hill
Goldilocks and the Three Bears	G	TL	250+	Literacy Tree	Rigby
*Gone Fishing	G	RF	180	Long, Erlene	Houghton Mifflin
Good Morning Isabel	G	RF	143	Literacy 2000	Rigby
Good Place to Live, A	G	I	97	Windows on Literacy	National Geographic
Goodnight Peter	G	RF	107	Windmill	Wright Group/McGraw Hill
Goose That Laid the Golden Egg, The	G	TL	73	Aesop	Wright Group/McGraw Hill
Grandma's Bicycle	G	RF	74	Read Alongs	Rigby
Grandpa, Grandpa	G	RF	122	Story Box	Wright Group/McGraw Hill
Grandpa's Garden Shed	G	I	68	Windows on Literacy	National Geographic

* Collection of short stories

TITLE	LEVEL	GENRE	WORD COUNT	AUTHOR / SERIES	PUBLISHER / DISTRIBUTOR
Grandpa's Lemonade	G	RF	138	Storyteller Nonfiction	Wright Group/McGraw Hill
Great Bug Hunt, The	G	RF	96	Rookie Readers	Children's Press
Great Day	G	RF	161	Alphakids	Sundance
Great Race, The	G	F	250+	McPhail, David	Scholastic
Great-Grandpa	G	RF	130	Voyages	SRA/McGraw Hill
Greedy Cat	G	F	166	Pacific Literacy	Pacific Learning
Greedy Gray Octopus, The	G	F	195	Tadpoles	Rigby
Gregor the Grumblesome Giant	G	F	212	Literacy 2000	Rigby
Grilled Cheese Sandwich	G	I	61	Windows on Literacy	National Geographic
Growing a Plant	G	I	115	Discovery World	Rigby
Growing Tomatoes	G	I	87	Alphakids	Sundance
Grumputer, The	G	F	235	Story Basket	Wright Group/McGraw Hill
Guard the House, Sam!	G	RF	46	Rookie Readers	Children's Press
Hairdresser, The	G	I	164	PM Nonfiction-Blue	Rigby
Hairy Bear	G	F	109	Story Box	Wright Group/McGraw Hill
Hairy Harry	G	I	92	Windows on Literacy	National Geographic
Hamlet the Hamster	G	RF	189	Breakthrough	Longman/Bow
Hand Me Downs, The	G	RF	156	Little Readers	Houghton Mifflin
Hannah's Hiccups	G	RF	196	Home Connection Collection	Rigby
Hansel and Gretel	G	TL	451	Hunia, Fran	Ladybird Books
Happy Birthday	G	RF	130	First Start	Troll Associates
Happy Mother's Day!	G	RF	101	Teacher's Choice Series	Pearson Learning Group
Harold's Flyaway Kite	G	F	166	First Start	Troll Associates
Harry Gets Ready for School	G	F	170	Ziefert, Harriet	Puffin Books
Harry Takes a Bath	G	F	132	Ziefert, Harriet	Puffin Books
Hay for Ambrosia	G	I	86	Pacific Literacy	Pacific Learning
Heat Changes Things	G	I	101	Instant Readers	Harcourt School Publishers
Here Comes Winter	G	RF	134	First Start	Troll Associates
Hermit Crab, The	G	RF	119	Sunshine	Wright Group/McGraw Hill
Hide, Spider!	G	F	179	Momentum Literacy Program	Troll Associates
Hippo Pot and Hippo Tot	G	F	88	Supersonics	Rigby
Hippo's Hiccups	G	F	208	Literacy 2000	Rigby
Hockey Practice	G	RF	134	Geddes, Diana	Kaeden Books
Home for a Dog, A	G	RF	146	Book Bus	Creative Edge
Home for a Puppy	G	RF	194	First Start	Troll Associates
Honey Bees and Flowers	G	I	67	Pebble Books	Capstone Press
Horrible Urktar of Or, The	G	F	143	Sunshine	Wright Group/McGraw Hill
House Hunting	G	RF	223	PM Story Books	Rigby
Houses	G	I	51	Learn to Read	Creative Teaching Press
Houses and Homes	G	RF	250+	PM Plus Poetry	Rigby
How Animals Move	G	I	132	Discovery Links	Newbridge
How Do Frogs Grow?	G	I	42	Discovery Links	Newbridge
How Do You Make a Bubble?	G	RF	250+	Hooks, William H.	Bantam
How Have I Grown	G	RF	235	Reid, Mary	Scholastic
How the Chick Tricked the Fox	G	F	167	Ready Readers	Pearson Learning Group
How the Sky Got Its Stars	G	TL	208	Instant Readers	Harcourt School Publishers
How to Clean a Dinosaur	G	F	208	Windmill Books	Rigby
How to Make a Card	G	I	69	Urmston, Kathleen; Evans, Karen	Kaeden Books
How to Make a Lion Mask	G	I	133	Instant Readers	Harcourt School Publishers
Hullabaloo at the Zoo	G	F	172	Lighthouse	Rigby
Hungry Animals	G	I	127	Little Readers	Houghton Mifflin
Hungry Chickens, The	G	F	107	Literacy Tree	Rigby
Hungry Giant's Birthday Cake, The	G	F	241	Story Basket	Wright Group/McGraw Hill
Hungry Giant's Soup, The	G	F	42	Story Basket	Wright Group/McGraw Hill

* Collection of short stories

TITLE	LEVEL	GENRE	WORD COUNT	AUTHOR / SERIES	PUBLISHER / DISTRIBUTOR
Hunt for Clues, A	G	RF	157	Ready Readers	Pearson Learning Group
I Am Generous	G	I	89	Pebble Books	Capstone Press
I Am Planet Earth	G	I	124	Marzollo, Jean	Scholastic
I Am Polite	G	I	76	Pebble Books	Capstone Press
I Can Breathe Underwater	G	RF	44	Windows on Literacy	National Geographic
I Can Do It, I Really Can	G	RF	195	Teacher's Choice Series	Pearson Learning Group
I Can Talk with My Hands	G	RF	146	Learn to Read	Creative Teaching Press
I Don't Think It's Fair	G	RF	147	Teacher's Choice Series	Pearson Learning Group
I Have a Question, Grandma	G	RF	124	Literacy 2000	Rigby
I Like Cheese	G	I	105	Welcome Books	Children's Press
I Saw a Dinosaur	G	F	55	Literacy 2000	Rigby
I Shop with My Daddy	G	RF	131	Maccarone, Grace	Scholastic
I Wish I Was Sick Too	G	RF	94	Brandenburg, Franz	Morrow
If a Tree Could Talk	G	F	62	Learn to Read	Creative Teaching Press
If We Could Do What the Animals Do	G	F	188	Learn to Read	Creative Teaching Press
I'll Make You a Card	G	RF	180	Early Readers	Compass Point Books
I'm a Caterpillar	G	I	169	Marzollo, Jean	Scholastic
I'm a Seed	G	F	181	Marzollo, Jean	Scholastic
I'm King of the Mountain	G	F	285	Pacific Literacy	Pacific Learning
In a Muddle	G	RF	93	Voyages	SRA/McGraw Hill
In My Head	G	RF	74	Voyages	SRA/McGraw Hill
In Search of Something Delicious	G	F	202	Seedlings	Continental Press
In the Forest	G	RF	95	Voyages	SRA/McGraw Hill
In the Hen House	G	RF	82	Oppenlander, Meredith	Kaeden Books
In the Woods	G	I	304	Reading Corners	Pearson Learning Group
In Times Long Ago	G	I	196	Learn to Read	Creative Teaching Press
Insects	G	I	107	Rigby Focus	Rigby
Insects That Bother Us	G	I	87	Foundations	Wright Group/McGraw Hill
Is it a Fruit?	G	I	101	Rigby Literacy	Rigby
Is It Time Yet?	G	RF	162	Foundations	Wright Group/McGraw Hill
It Started As an Egg	G	I	179	Learn to Read	Creative Teaching Press
It's a Bit Tricky	G	RF	250+	Home Connection Collection	Rigby
Jack and Billy and Rose	G	RF	179	PM Plus Story Books	Rigby
Jack DePert at the Supermarket	G	RF	188	Wonder World	Wright Group/McGraw Hill
Jason's Bus Ride	G	F	117	Ziefert, Harriet	Penguin Group
Jeb's Barn	G	RF	86	Little Celebrations	Pearson Learning Group
Jessie's Flower	G	F	132	Read Alongs	Rigby
Jim's Visit to Kim	G	RF	149	Ready Readers	Pearson Learning Group
Joe Makes a House	G	RF	174	PM Plus Story Books	Rigby
Joe's Blue Shoes	G	RF	130	Books for Young Learners	Richard C. Owen
Joey	G	RF	243	PM Extensions-Green	Rigby
Jon Sleeps On	G	RF	147	Little Red Readers	Sundance
Jordan's Soccer Ball	G	RF	210	PM Plus Story Books	Rigby
Jordan's Zoo	G	RF	90	City Stories	Rigby
Jungle Frogs	G	F	195	PM Plus Story Books	Rigby
Jungle Tiger Cat	G	F	120	Frankford, Marilyn	Kaeden Books
Just Enough	G	RF	107	Salem, Lynn; Stewart, Josie	Continental Press
Just for You	G	F	160	Mayer, Mercer	Donovan
Just Graph It!	G	I	156	Learn to Read	Creative Teaching Press
Just Like Me	G	RF	108	Learn to Read	Creative Teaching Press
Just My Luck	G	RF	136	Literacy 2000	Rigby
Just Right!	G	RF	105	Sunshine	Wright Group/McGraw Hill
Katie Did It	G	RF	105	Rookie Readers	Children's Press
Kittens	G	I	107	Discovery Links	Newbridge

* Collection of short stories

TITLE	LEVEL	GENRE	WORD COUNT	AUTHOR / SERIES	PUBLISHER / DISTRIBUTOR
Kitzikuba	G	F	198	Story Basket	Wright Group/McGraw Hill
"Ladies and Gentlemen"	G	RF	120	Early Readers	Compass Point Books
Ladybugs	G	I	250+	Pebble Plus	Red Brick Learning
Lake, The	G	I	53	Windows on Literacy	National Geographic
Last Game, The	G	RF	89	Start to Read	School Zone
Later, Rover	G	RF	200	Ziefert, Harriet	Puffin Books
Laughing Cake, The	G	F	89	Reading Corners	Pearson Learning Group
Left, Right	G	RF	182	Sunshine	Wright Group/McGraw Hill
Lemonade Stand, The	G	RF	148	City Stories	Rigby
Let's All Dance!	G	I	148	Vocabulary Readers	Houghton Mifflin
Let's Bake	G	I	195	Discovery Links	Newbridge
Let's Make Something New	G	I	116	Discovery Links	Newbridge
Lid, The	G	RF	111	Books for Young Learners	Richard C. Owen
Lift Off!	G	I	121	Pair-It Books	Steck-Vaughn
Light and Shadow	G	I	138	Discovery Links	Newbridge
Lion and the Mouse, The	G	TL	125	PM Story Books	Rigby
Lion and the Mouse, The	G	TL	250	Traditional Tales & More	Rigby
Lion and The Mouse, The	G	TL	250	Literacy 2000	Rigby
Lisa's Ices	G	RF	106	City Stories	Rigby
Listen to Me	G	RF	47	Rookie Readers	Children's Press
Little Danny Dinosaur	G	F	195	First Start	Troll Associates
Little Elephant	G	F	192	New Way Blue	Steck-Vaughn
Little Ghost Goes to School	G	F	210	TOTTS	Tott Publications
Little Ghost's Baby Brother	G	F	221	TOTTS	Tott Publications
Little Ghost's Vacation	G	F	118	TOTTS	Tott Publications
Little Number Stories: Addition	G	I	154	Learn to Read	Creative Teaching Press
Little Number Stories: Subtraction	G	I	133	Learn to Read	Creative Teaching Press
Little Panda	G	F	143	Books for Young Learners	Richard C. Owen
Little Red Hen, The	G	TL	250+	Cambridge Reading	Pearson Learning Group
Little Red Hen, The	G	TL	250+	Ziefert, Harriet	Puffin Books
Little Red Hen, The	G	TL	256	Storyteller-Moon Rising	Wright Group/McGraw Hill
Little Red Pig, The	G	F	214	Ready Readers	Pearson Learning Group
Little Red Riding Hood	G	TL	140	Sun Sprouts	ETA/Cuisenaire
Little Red Riding Hood	G	TL	140	Folk Tales	Pioneer Valley
Living Things	G	I	151	Rosen Real Readers	Rosen Publishing Group
Loading the Airplane	G	RF	140	Windows on Literacy	National Geographic
Locked Out	G	RF	15	PM Story Books	Rigby
Lollipop	G	F	59	Watson, Wendy	Crowell
Look and See	G	I	208	Learn to Read	Creative Teaching Press
Look in the Garden	G	RF	208	PM Plus Story Books	Rigby
Look What You Can Make!	G	I	203	Story Steps	Rigby
Looking after Suzie	G	RF	209	Well-Being Series	Dominie Press
Looking at Shapes	G	I	235	Yellow Umbrella Books	Red Brick Learning
Lost and Found	G	F	55	Instant Readers	Harcourt School Publishers
Lost Keys, The	G	RF	223	PM Plus Story Books	Rigby
Lots of Caps	G	F	205	New Way Blue	Steck-Vaughn
Louis Braille	G	B	132	Independent Readers Science	Houghton Mifflin
Lunch in Space	G	RF	156	Instant Readers	Harcourt School Publishers
Lydia and Her Cat	G	RF	77	Oxford Reading Tree	Oxford University Press
Lydia and Her Garden	G	RF	88	Oxford Reading Tree	Oxford University Press
Lydia and Her Kitten	G	RF	77	Oxford Reading Tree	Oxford University Press
Lydia and the Ducks	G	RF	87	Oxford Reading Tree	Oxford University Press
Lydia at the Shops	G	RF	72	Oxford Reading Tree	Oxford University Press
Magnets	G	I	71	Phonics Readers	Compass Point Books

* Collection of short stories

TITLE	LEVEL	GENRE	WORD COUNT	AUTHOR / SERIES	PUBLISHER / DISTRIBUTOR
Make a Glider	G	I	57	Storyteller-Setting Sun	Wright Group/McGraw Hill
Make a Rainbow Fish	G	I	139	Sun Sprouts	ETA/Cuisenaire
Making a Cake	G	I	125	Little Red Readers	Sundance
Making a Toy House	G	I	132	PM Plus Nonfiction	Rigby
Making Pictures	G	I	132	Vocabulary Readers	Houghton Mifflin
Manatees	G	I	73	Pebble Books	Red Brick Learning
Maps	G	I	99	Learn to Read	Creative Teaching Press
Maps	G	I	142	Early Connections	Benchmark Education
Math at the Store	G	I	127	Amato, William	Scholastic
Max and Jake	G	RF	212	PM Plus Story Books	Rigby
Max and the Birdhouse	G	RF	190	PM Plus Story Books	Rigby
Max the Pet Show Star	G	RF	175	Leveled Readers	Houghton Mifflin
Me Too!	G	F	200	Bookshop	Mondo
Measurement Mysteries	G	I	124	Learn to Read	Creative Teaching Press
Meet the Johnson Family	G	RF	52	Windows on Literacy	National Geographic
Meow, What Now?	G	F	186	Seedlings	Continental Press
Mess Monster	G	F	179	Literacy 2000	Rigby
Messy Monsters, The	G	F	167	Carousel Readers	Pearson Learning Group
Mice and Max	G	F	169	Carousel Readers	Pearson Learning Group
Michael and the Eggs	G	RF	154	Oxford Reading Tree	Oxford University Press
Mick and Max	G	RF	169	Carousel Readers	Pearson Learning Group
Mike and Tony: Best Friends	G	RF	171	Ziefert, Harriet	Penguin Group
Mike's First Haircut	G	RF	136	First Start	Troll Associates
Mine's the Best	G	RF	104	Bonsall, Crosby	HarperCollins
Models	G	I	231	Yellow Umbrella Books	Red Brick Learning
Molly Makes a Graph	G	RF	110	Seedlings	Continental Press
Monarch Butterflies	G	I	56	Pebble Books	Capstone Press
Money in My Pocket	G	I	133	Twig	Wright Group/McGraw Hill
Monkeys	G	I	27	Reading Unlimited	Pearson Learning Group
Monster Math School Time	G	F	120	Maccarone, Grace	Scholastic
Moose's Loose Tooth	G	F	142	Spinelle, Mary Louise	Kaeden Books
More Spaghetti I Say	G	F	340	Gelman, Rita	Scholastic
Mother Hen	G	F	205	Book Bank	Wright Group/McGraw Hill
Mother Tiger and Her Cubs	G	F	212	PM Plus Story Books	Rigby
Mousetrap	G	RF	49	Snowball, Diane	Scholastic
Moving Day	G	RF	215	Momentum Literacy Program	Troll Associates
Mr. Cricket Finds a Friend	G	F	134	Carousel Readers	Pearson Learning Group
Mr. Noisy's Book of Patterns	G	F	47	Learn to Read	Creative Teaching Press
Mrs. Cheng's Surprise	G	RF	186	Leveled Readers	Houghton Mifflin
Mrs. Keen	G	RF	88	City Stories	Rigby
Mrs. Pomelili's Wet Week	G	F	215	Book Bank	Wright Group/McGraw Hill
Mud, Mud, Mud	G	I	83	Windows on Literacy	National Geographic
Mudskipper	G	I	132	Twig	Wright Group/McGraw Hill
Munching Mark	G	RF	88	Tadpoles	Rigby
Mushrooms for Dinner	G	F	177	PM Story Books	Rigby
Music Machine, The	G	F	231	Sunshine	Wright Group/McGraw Hill
My Birthday Surprise	G	RF	153	Foundations	Wright Group/McGraw Hill
My Boat	G	RF	133	Sunshine	Wright Group/McGraw Hill
My Dog	G	RF	79	My World	Steck-Vaughn
My Dog	G	I	72	Taylor, Judy	Macmillan
My Dog Rusty	G	RF	75	City Stories	Rigby
My Family Keeps Fit	G	RF	98	Windows on Literacy	National Geographic
My Fish Are Fine with Me	G	RF	78	City Stories	Rigby
My Friends	G	F	152	Gomi, Taro	Scholastic

* Collection of short stories

TITLE	LEVEL	GENRE	WORD COUNT	AUTHOR / SERIES	PUBLISHER / DISTRIBUTOR
My Global Address	G	I	84	Learn to Read	Creative Teaching Press
My Goldfish	G	I	239	Walker, Pamela	Scholastic
My Home Is Just Right for Me	G	F	250+	Momentum Literacy Program	Troll Associates
My House	G	RF	43	Book Bunny Series	Creative Edge
My Little Sister	G	RF	143	Story Box	Wright Group/McGraw Hill
My Old Gold Boat	G	F	51	Easy Phonics Readers	Teacher Created Materials
My Secret Hiding Place	G	RF	155	First Start	Troll Associates
My Secret Place	G	RF	121	Wonder World	Wright Group/McGraw Hill
My Skateboard	G	I	81	Sun Sprouts	ETA/Cuisenaire
My Skin Looks After Me	G	I	82	Pacific Literacy	Pacific Learning
My Town Used To Be Small	G	I	79	Windows on Literacy	National Geographic
My Weather Station	G	I	313	Leveled Readers Science	Houghton Mifflin
Name Is the Same, The	G	RF	115	Ready Readers	Pearson Learning Group
Naughty Ann, The	G	F	159	PM Story Books	Rigby
Neighborhood Picnic, The	G	I	157	Visions	Wright Group/McGraw Hill
Never Say Never	G	F	225	Ready Readers	Pearson Learning Group
Never Snap at a Bubble	G	F	89	Giant Step Reader	Educational Insights
New House for Mole and Mouse, A	G	F	223	Ziefert, Harriet	Penguin Group
New Paper, Everyone!	G	I	53	Pacific Literacy	Pacific Learning
New Puppy, A	G	I	250+	Momentum Literacy Program	Troll Associates
New School, A	G	RF	137	Windows on Literacy	National Geographic
New Soccer Nets	G	RF	123	Early Connections	Benchmark Education
Newspaper for Dad, A	G	RF	192	New Way Green	Steck-Vaughn
Newspaper, The	G	RF	132	Twig	Wright Group/McGraw Hill
Nicky Upstairs and Downstairs	G	F	179	Ziefert, Harriet	Penguin Group
Nicole Digs a Hole	G	RF	138	Start to Read	School Zone
Night Noises	G	RF	104	Sunshine	Wright Group/McGraw Hill
Night Noises	G	RF	97	Storyteller-Moon Rising	Wright Group/McGraw Hill
Night Sky, The	G	I	120	Windows on Literacy	National Geographic
Night Sky, The	G	RF	226	Ready Readers	Pearson Learning Group
Night Walk, The	G	RF	91	Instant Readers	Harcourt School Publishers
Nine Men Chase a Hen	G	F	74	Start to Read	School Zone
Noise	G	RF	138	Sunshine	Wright Group/McGraw Hill
Not Me, Said the Monkey	G	F	118	West, Colin	Harper & Row
Not Too Many	G	RF	193	Sun Sprouts	ETA/Cuisenaire
Not Yet, Nathan	G	RF	127	Cambridge Reading	Pearson Learning Group
Numbers All around Me	G	F	140	Learn to Read	Creative Teaching Press
Oak Tree and Fir Tree	G	F	102	New Way Red	Steck-Vaughn
Obadiah	G	TL	105	Story Box	Wright Group/McGraw Hill
Octopuses	G	I	47	Pebble Books	Capstone Press
Odd Socks	G	RF	83	Literacy 2000	Rigby
Oh, No!	G	RF	128	Little Celebrations	Pearson Learning Group
Old and New	G	I	54	Sun Sprouts	ETA/Cuisenaire
Old Cat, New Cat	G	RF	169	Wonder World	Wright Group/McGraw Hill
On the Go	G	I	250+	Yellow Umbrella Books	Red Brick Learning
On Top of Spaghetti	G	F	105	Little Celebrations	Pearson Learning Group
One Monday Morning	G	F	180	Shulevitz, Uri	Scribner
One Smart Chick	G	F	250	Rigby Literacy	Rigby
Open Wide	G	I	189	Home Connection Collection	Rigby
Optometrist, The	G	I	191	PM Nonfiction-Blue	Rigby
Other Side, The	G	F	182	Sun Sprouts	ETA/Cuisenaire
Our Car	G	I	94	Bookshop	Mondo
Our Favorites	G	I	217	Learn to Read	Creative Teaching Press
Our House Is a Safe House	G	I	163	PM Plus Nonfiction	Rigby

* Collection of short stories

TITLE	LEVEL	GENRE	WORD COUNT	AUTHOR / SERIES	PUBLISHER / DISTRIBUTOR
Our New House	G	RF	68	PM Plus Nonfiction	Rigby
Our Parents	G	I	142	PM Nonfiction-Blue	Rigby
Our Soccer Team	G	RF	139	Literacy Tree	Rigby
Our Teacher	G	RF	168	Windows on Literacy	National Geographic
Our Town	G	RF	129	Well-Being Series	Pearson Learning Group
Out of Reach	G	RF	86	Literacy Tree	Rigby
Over in the Meadow	G	F	242	Little Readers	Houghton Mifflin
Paco's Garden	G	RF	118	Books for Young Learners	Richard C. Owen
Pal the Pony	G	RF	224	Herman, R. A.	Grosset & Dunlap
Pancakes	G	RF	181	Foundations	Wright Group/McGraw Hill
Pansies for Mom	G	I	56	Windows on Literacy	National Geographic
Papa's Spaghetti	G	F	248	Literacy 2000	Rigby
Park, The	G	RF	155	Windows on Literacy	National Geographic
Parrotfish	G	I	51	Pebble Books	Capstone Press
Parts of a Whole	G	I	161	Early Connections	Benchmark Education
Party Game, The	G	RF	115	Home Connection Collection	Rigby
Patchwork Patterns	G	RF	64	Little Celebrations	Pearson Learning Group
Peanut Butter and Jelly	G	F	156	Wescott, Nadine B.	Penguin Group
People Work	G	I	232	Yellow Umbrella Books	Red Brick Learning
Pet Day	G	RF	175	Instant Readers	Harcourt School Publishers
Pete Little	G	F	222	PM Story Books	Rigby
Peter and the Pennytree	G	F	119	First Start	Troll Associates
Pete's Bad Day	G	RF	164	Ready Readers	Pearson Learning Group
Pete's New Shoes	G	RF	91	Literacy 2000	Rigby
Philippa and the Dragon	G	F	137	Literacy 2000	Rigby
Pickles Gets Lost	G	RF	154	Pickles the Dog Series	Pioneer Valley
Picnic Boat, The	G	RF	210	PM Plus Story Books	Rigby
Picnic, The	G	RF	151	Home Connection Collection	Rigby
Pigs on the Farm	G	I	72	Pebble Books	Capstone Press
Plane Rides	G	I	160	Walker, Pamela	Scholastic
Plants on My Plate	G	I	101	Windows on Literacy	National Geographic
Play It Safe!	G	I	92	Phonics Readers	Compass Point Books
Play, Bear	G	F	219	Sun Sprouts	ETA/Cuisenaire
Playground Problem Solvers	G	F	199	Learn to Read	Creative Teaching Press
Polar Bears	G	I	67	Windows on Literacy	National Geographic
Potato Printing	G	I	174	Sun Sprouts	ETA/Cuisenaire
Princess Who Couldn't Cry, The	G	TL	300	Ready Readers	Pearson Learning Group
Printing Machine, The	G	F	102	Literacy 2000	Rigby
Pukeko Morning	G	I	148	Pacific Literacy	Pacific Learning
Puppets	G	I	47	Canizares, Susan; Berger, Samantha	Scholastic
Push and Pull	G	I	49	iOpeners	Pearson Learning Group
Rabbit's Party	G	F	351	Bunting, Eve; Sloan-Childers, E.	Scholastic
Ragbag	G	F	41	Supersonics	Rigby
Rain	G	RF	68	Literacy 2000	Rigby
Rain, The	G	RF	171	Foundations	Wright Group/McGraw Hill
Rainbow Somewhere, A	G	RF	201	Ready Readers	Pearson Learning Group
Rascal	G	RF	108	Rigby Literacy	Rigby
Ready, Get Set, Go!	G	RF	137	First Set	Troll Associates
Recycle It!	G	I	118	Discovery Links	Newbridge
Red Socks and Yellow Socks	G	F	155	Sunshine	Wright Group/McGraw Hill
Respect	G	RF	163	Well-Being Series	Dominie Press
Rex to the Rescue	G	F	159	Sunshine	Wright Group/McGraw Hill
Rhyme Game, The	G	RF	159	Storyteller-Setting Sun	Wright Group/McGraw Hill

* Collection of short stories

TITLE	LEVEL	GENRE	WORD COUNT	AUTHOR / SERIES	PUBLISHER / DISTRIBUTOR
River's Journey, A	G	I	116	Rigby Focus	Rigby
Roller Coaster Ride, The	G	RF	106	Carousel Readers	Pearson Learning Group
Room for One More	G	RF	132	City Stories	Rigby
Rosie's Button Box	G	RF	233	Stepping Stones	Nelson/Michaels Assoc.
Rosie's Pool	G	F	130	Little Readers	Houghton Mifflin
Rotten Reggie	G	RF	232	TOTTS	Tott Publications
Roy at the Fun Park	G	RF	111	Oxford Reading Tree	Oxford University Press
Safety Signs	G	I	112	Early Connections	Benchmark Education
Sally's Picture	G	RF	125	Literacy 2000	Rigby
Salmon Story, A	G	I	132	Twig	Wright Group/McGraw Hill
Sam and Dasher	G	RF	53	Rookie Readers	Children's Press
Sam the Garbage Hound	G	F	53	Rookie Readers	Children's Press
Sand Castles	G	RF	80	Wonder World	Wright Group/McGraw Hill
Sandwich Person, A	G	I	63	Wonder World	Wright Group/McGraw Hill
Saturday Morning	G	RF	180	Pacific Literacy	Pacific Learning
Save That Trash!	G	I	181	Ready Readers	Pearson Learning Group
Say Good Night	G	F	59	Start to Read	School Zone
Say Good Night	G	RF	155	Ziefert, Harriet	Puffin Books
Say It, Sign It	G	RF	169	Epstein, Elaine	Scholastic
Scary Larry	G	F	62	Rookie Readers	Children's Press
School Bus Ride, The	G	RF	160	Little Red Readers	Sundance
School Play, The	G	RF	103	City Stories	Rigby
Scientist, The	G	I	195	Adventures in Reading	Pearson Learning Group
Scruffy Messed It Up	G	RF	105	Literacy 2000	Rigby
Sea Anemones	G	I	58	Pebble Books	Capstone Press
Sea Turtles	G	I	50	Pebble Books	Red Brick Learning
Sea Urchins	G	I	51	Pebble Books	Capstone Press
Seals	G	I	42	Pebble Books	Red Brick Learning
Sebastian	G	F	162	Alphakids	Sundance
Secret	G	RF	114	Instant Readers	Harcourt School Publishers
Secret Code, The	G	RF	69	Rookie Readers	Children's Press
Secret Notes	G	RF	214	Sun Sprouts	ETA/Cuisenaire
Secret Valentine	G	F	223	First Start	Troll Associates
Seeds Grow Into Plants	G	I	78	Windows on Literacy	National Geographic
Sharing Danny's Dad	G	RF	89	Little Celebrations	Pearson Learning Group
Sharks	G	I	42	Pebble Books	Red Brick Learning
Sheep in a Jeep	G	F	83	Shaw, Nancy	Houghton Mifflin
Sheep on the Farm	G	I	66	Pebble Books	Capstone Press
Shhhh!	G	F	68	Kline, Suzy	Whitman
Shopping at the Mall	G	RF	145	Urmston, Kathleen; Evans, Karen	Kaeden Books
Shopping List, The	G	I	120	Windows on Literacy	National Geographic
Show and Tell	G	RF	190	First Start	Troll Associates
Show Us Your Wings	G	I	132	Yellow Umbrella Books	Red Brick Learning
Sir Down, Dog	G	RF	192	Sun Sprouts	ETA/Cuisenaire
Skating on Thin Ice	G	RF	130	First Start	Troll Associates
Skimper-Scamper	G	F	208	Instant Readers	Harcourt Trade
"Slam Dunk" Sanchez	G	RF	238	Sunshine	Wright Group/McGraw Hill
Slow Poke Snail	G	RF	117	Instant Readers	Harcourt School Publishers
Small Baby Raccoon, A	G	RF	104	Ready Readers	Pearson Learning Group
Snack Time	G	RF	59	City Kids	Rigby
Snail Saves the Day	G	F	76	Stadler, John	HarperCollins
Snap! Splash!	G	I	48	Pacific Literacy	Pacific Learning
Snow, The	G	RF	112	Burningham, John	Crowell
Snowball, The	G	F	92	Armstrong, Jennifer	Random House

* Collection of short stories

TITLE	LEVEL	GENRE	WORD COUNT	AUTHOR / SERIES	PUBLISHER / DISTRIBUTOR
Snowball, the White Mouse	G	RF	223	PM Plus Story Books	Rigby
So, So Sam	G	RF	107	TOTTS	Tott Publications
Solid or Not?	G	I	113	Early Connections	Benchmark Education
Sometimes Things Change	G	I	71	Rookie Readers	Children's Press
Sophie's Box	G	F	174	Cambridge Reading	Pearson Learning Group
Sounds all Around	G	I	153	Discovery Links	Newbridge
Sounds of Music, The	G	I	140	Leveled Readers Science	Houghton Mifflin
Spaghetti! Spaghetti!	G	RF	85	Book Bank	Wright Group/McGraw Hill
Special Things	G	RF	128	Literacy 2000	Rigby
Spicy-Herby Day, A	G	RF	117	Evangeline Nicholas Collection	Wright Group/McGraw Hill
Spider Can't Fly	G	F	149	Book Bank	Wright Group/McGraw Hill
Spiders	G	I	53	Pebble Plus	Red Brick Learning
Spooky Swap Sound, The	G	F	179	Sunshine	Wright Group/McGraw Hill
Spot's First Walk	G	F	63	Hill, Eric	Putnam
Spring, Summer, Fall, Winter	G	I	64	Windows on Literacy	National Geographic
Squeaky Car, The	G	RF	200	New Way Green	Steck-Vaughn
Stamps	G	I	58	Wonder World	Wright Group/McGraw Hill
Stars	G	I	105	Sunshine	Wright Group/McGraw Hill
Steve's Room	G	RF	171	Ready Readers	Pearson Learning Group
Stew for Egor's Mom, A	G	F	162	Ready Readers	Pearson Learning Group
Stitches	G	RF	250+	Ziefert, Harriet	Puffin Books
Stop That Rabbit	G	F	168	First Start	Troll Associates
Stop the Car!	G	RF	179	Lighthouse	Rigby
Stop, Look, and Listen	G	RF	102	Literacy Tree	Rigby
Storm, The	G	RF	75	Books for Young Learners	Richard C. Owen
Stormy Weather	G	I	88	Twig	Wright Group/McGraw Hill
Sue Likes Blue	G	RF	131	Start to Read	School Zone
Summer at Cove Lake	G	RF	288	Ready Readers	Pearson Learning Group
Sun Power	G	I	79	Windows on Literacy	National Geographic
Sun, the Wind, and the Rain, The	G	RF	170	PM Plus Nonfiction	Rigby
Sunshine, the Black Cat	G	RF	143	Carousel Readers	Pearson Learning Group
*Surprise Visit, The	G	F	250+	New Way Blue	Steck-Vaughn
Sylvia Earle, First Lady of the Sea	G	B	98	Independent Readers Science	Houghton Mifflin
T. J.'s Tree	G	RF	77	Literacy 2000	Rigby
Takeaway!	G	F	40	Book Bus	Creative Edge
Taking Care of Baby	G	I	159	Discovery Links	Newbridge
Tall Stories About Snakes	G	I	141	Voyages	SRA/McGraw Hill
Teacher, The	G	I	155	PM Nonfiction-Blue	Rigby
Teddy Bear for Sale	G	F	152	Herman, Gail	Scholastic
Ted's Red Ball	G	F	131	Supersonics	Rigby
Ten Bears in My Bed	G	F	252	Mack, Stan	Pantheon
Ten Little Bears	G	F	211	Reading Unlimited	Pearson Learning Group
Ten Sleepy Sheep	G	F	65	Keller, Holly	Greenwillow
Terrible Tiger	G	F	124	Rigby Literacy	Rigby
Terrible Tiger, The	G	F	140	Sunshine	Wright Group/McGraw Hill
That Cat!	G	RF	146	Ready Readers	Pearson Learning Group
That Dog!	G	RF	213	Foundations	Wright Group/McGraw Hill
That's Not All	G	F	105	Start to Read	School Zone
There Are No Polar Bears Down There	G	I	48	Voyages	SRA/McGraw Hill
Things That Melt	G	I	84	Leveled Readers Science	Houghton Mifflin
Three Bears, The	G	TL	344	Folk Tales	Pioneer Valley
Three Billy Goats Gruff, The	G	TL	140	Little Readers	Houghton Mifflin
Three Cheers for Hippo	G	F	90	Stadler, John	HarperCollins
Three Kittens	G	F	116	Ginsburg, Mirra	Crown

* Collection of short stories

TITLE	LEVEL	GENRE	WORD COUNT	AUTHOR / SERIES	PUBLISHER / DISTRIBUTOR
Three Little Pigs, The	G	TL	250+	We Both Read	Treasure Bay
Three Little Pigs, The	G	TL	250+	Little Readers	Houghton Mifflin
Three Little Witches	G	F	189	First Start	Troll Associates
Thumpety-Rah!	G	F	98	Sunshine	Wright Group/McGraw Hill
Tiger Dave	G	F	33	Books for Young Learners	Richard C. Owen
Tiger Runs Away	G	RF	213	PM Extensions-Blue	Rigby
Time Song, The	G	I	99	Learn to Read	Creative Teaching Press
Tiny Christmas Elf, The	G	F	173	First Start	Troll Associates
Titch	G	RF	121	Hutchins, Pat	Penguin Group
Tom's Ride	G	RF	185	PM Plus Story Books	Rigby
Tom's Trousers	G	RF	173	Storyteller-Night Crickets	Wright Group/McGraw Hill
Too Late!	G	F	226	Foundations	Wright Group/McGraw Hill
Too Many Animals	G	F	111	Alphakids	Sundance
*Too Many Bones	G	F	125	New Way Blue	Steck-Vaughn
Tools Can Help Us See	G	I	107	Windows on Literacy	National Geographic
Toothbrush Tale	G	F	117	New Way Blue	Steck-Vaughn
Training a Police Dog	G	I	103	Vocabulary Readers	Houghton Mifflin
Treasure in the Attic	G	RF	153	Seedlings	Continental Press
Tree House Fun	G	RF	165	First Start	Troll Associates
Tree Is My Home, A	G	RF	114	Leveled Readers Science	Houghton Mifflin
Tree, The	G	I	94	Alphakids	Sundance
Trees Are Terrific!	G	I	123	Yellow Umbrella Books	Red Brick Learning
True or False?	G	I	119	Ready Readers	Pearson Learning Group
Try Again, Hannah	G	RF	228	PM Extensions-Green	Rigby
Tug of War, The	G	F	194	Story Steps	Rigby
Tweedle-De-Dee Tumbleweed	G	F	103	Reese, Bob	Children's Press
Two by Two	G	TL	88	Cambridge Reading	Pearson Learning Group
Two Stupid Cats	G	F	140	Sunshine	Wright Group/McGraw Hill
Uncle Jim	G	RF	127	Windmill Books	Rigby
Uncle Timi's Sleep	G	RF	102	Pacific Literacy	Pacific Learning
Under the Old Oak Tree	G	F	205	Seedlings	Continental Press
Up Close	G	I	123	Discovery Links	Newbridge
Using Wheels	G	I	115	Little Red Readers	Sundance
Vegetable Group, The	G	I	88	Pebble Books	Capstone Press
Vegetable Soup	G	RF	84	Morris, Ann	Scholastic
Victor the Champion	G	F	102	Oxford Reading Tree	Oxford University Press
Visit to the Statue of Liberty, A	G	I	77	Independent Readers Social Studies	Houghton Mifflin
Visiting Grandma and Grandpa	G	RF	136	Carousel Readers	Pearson Learning Group
Vroom!	G	F	167	Rigby Literacy	Rigby
Wait Skates	G	RF	58	Rookie Readers	Children's Press
Waiting	G	RF	59	Literacy 2000	Rigby
Waiting for a Frog	G	RF	124	Coats, Glenn	Kaeden Books
Walk, The	G	RF	129	Reading Unlimited	Pearson Learning Group
Walt Disney's World	G	I	96	Leveled Readers Social Studies	Houghton Mifflin
Washing the Dog	G	I	84	Little Red Readers	Sundance
Washing the Dog	G	I	84	Little Readers	Houghton Mifflin
Watching the Game	G	RF	210	Momentum Literacy Program	Troll Associates
Watching the Weather	G	I	142	Discovery Links	Newbridge
Watermelon for Lunch	G	F	196	Leveled Readers	Houghton Mifflin
Water's Journey	G	I	114	Instant Readers	Harcourt School Publishers
We Need Fire Fighters	G	I	64	Pebble Books	Red Brick Learning
We Need Mail Carriers	G	I	61	Pebble Books	Red Brick Learning
We Need Police Officers	G	I	59	Pebble Books	Red Brick Learning

* Collection of short stories

TITLE	LEVEL	GENRE	WORD COUNT	AUTHOR / SERIES	PUBLISHER / DISTRIBUTOR
We Need School Bus Drivers	G	I	112	Pebble Books	Capstone Press
We Need Veterinarians	G	I	48	Pebble Books	Red Brick Learning
Weedy Sea Dragons	G	I	106	Seedlings	Continental Press
Welcome to Our School	G	RF	101	Leveled Readers Social Studies	Houghton Mifflin
Whales	G	I	150	Foundations	Wright Group/McGraw Hill
What a Birthday!	G	RF	138	Leveled Readers Language Support	Houghton Mifflin
What a Catch!	G	RF	118	Instant Readers	Harcourt School Publishers
*What a Mess!	G	RF	124	New Way Blue	Steck-Vaughn
What Am I?	G	I	124	Sunshine	Wright Group/McGraw Hill
What Can Change?	G	I	96	Discovery Links	Newbridge
What Can We Do Today?	G	RF	146	Carousel Readers	Pearson Learning Group
What Can You Do with a Ball of String?	G	RF	250+	Home Connection Collection	Rigby
What Comes from a Cow?	G	I	85	Sunshine	Wright Group/McGraw Hill
What Do You Do?	G	F	125	Little Celebrations	Pearson Learning Group
What Does a Firefighter Do?	G	I	136	Yellow Umbrella Books	Red Brick Learning
What Does a Garden Need?	G	I	118	Discovery Links	Newbridge
What Happened?	G	I	60	Learn to Read	Creative Teaching Press
What Is a Food Chain?	G	I	71	Instant Readers	Harcourt School Publishers
What Is a Poem?	G	I	69	Vocabulary Readers	Houghton Mifflin
What Is Bat?	G	F	136	Literacy 2000	Rigby
What Is It?	G	I	69	iOpeners	Pearson Learning Group
What Will Float?	G	I	224	Sunshine Books	Wright Group/McGraw Hill
What Would You Do?	G	RF	160	Sunshine	Wright Group/McGraw Hill
What's in a Park?	G	I	46	Chessen, Betsey; Chanko, Pamela	Scholastic
What's Inside?	G	I	50	Foundations	Wright Group/McGraw Hill
What's on the Ships?	G	I	170	Windows on Literacy	National Geographic
When Bob Woke Up Late	G	RF	139	Ready Readers	Pearson Learning Group
When I Go See Gram	G	RF	123	Ready Readers	Pearson Learning Group
When Jose Hits That Ball	G	RF	45	Pacific Literacy	Pacific Learning
When the Sun Goes Down	G	I	109	Wonder World	Wright Group/McGraw Hill
When the Wind Blows	G	I	107	Rigby Focus	Rigby
When You Were a Baby	G	RF	104	Jonas, Ann	Morrow
Where's the Snow?	G	RF	142	Erickson, Betty	Continental Press
Which One Is Which?	G	I	187	Sunshine	Wright Group/McGraw Hill
Who Can Fix the Computer?	G	RF	178	Handprints D, Set 1	Educator's Publishing Service
Who Goes Out on Halloween?	G	RF	163	Alexander, Sue	Bantam
Who Has a Tail?	G	I	186	Ready Readers	Pearson Learning Group
Who Lays Eggs?	G	I	132	Twig	Wright Group/McGraw Hill
Who Likes the Night?	G	RF	250+	Phonics and Friends	Hampton-Brown
Who Works at the Beach?	G	I	102	Windows on Literacy	National Geographic
Who's Behind the Door at My House?	G	RF	184	Salmon, Michael	Steck-Vaughn
Who's Behind the Door at My School?	G	RF	187	Salmon, Michael	Steck-Vaughn
Why Can't I Fly?	G	F	449	Gelman, Rita	Scholastic
Why Do I Need to Know When?	G	RF	198	Visions	Wright Group/McGraw Hill
Why Elephants Have Long Noses	G	TL	175	Literacy 2000	Rigby
Why I Like Laura	G	RF	193	Phonics and Friends	Hampton-Brown
Why Not?	G	RF	167	Voyages	SRA/McGraw Hill
Why Rabbit's Tail Is Short	G	TL	296	Leveled Readers	Houghton Mifflin
Wigglebottom	G	RF	134	Cambridge Reading	Pearson Learning Group
Wiggly Worm	G	F	115	Literacy 2000	Rigby
Wildlife Helpers	G	I	132	Twig	Wright Group/McGraw Hill
William's Skateboard	G	RF	100	Windmill	Wright Group/McGraw Hill

* Collection of short stories

TITLE	LEVEL	GENRE	WORD COUNT	AUTHOR / SERIES	PUBLISHER / DISTRIBUTOR
Willie the Slowpoke	G	F	125	First Start	Troll Associates
Wind and Sun	G	TL	170	Literacy 2000	Rigby
Wind and the Sun, The: An Aesop Fable	G	TL	234	Rigby Literacy	Rigby
Windy Ways	G	I	97	Independent Readers Science	Houghton Mifflin
Witch's Haircut, The	G	F	135	Windmill	Wright Group/McGraw Hill
Women at Work	G	I	112	Foundations	Wright Group/McGraw Hill
Wood and Other Materials	G	I	97	Discovery World	Rigby
Working	G	I	174	Yellow Umbrella Books	Red Brick Learning
Working Together	G	I	50	Yellow Umbrella Books	Red Brick Learning
World of Fun, A	G	I	176	Instant Readers	Harcourt School Publishers
Yasmin's Box	G	F	170	Cambridge Reading	Pearson Learning Group
You Can Make a Pom-pom	G	I	39	Windows on Literacy	National Geographic
You Can Make Skittles	G	I	128	Sunshine	Wright Group/McGraw Hill
You Did It!	G	RF	246	Sunshine	Wright Group/McGraw Hill
You Look Funny	G	RF	180	First Start	Troll Associates
Yo-yos	G	RF	62	City Kids	Rigby
Zap!	G	F	83	Seedlings	Continental Press
Zithers	G	RF	55	Little Celebrations	Pearson Learning Group
Zoo Map	G	I	96	Windows on Literacy	National Geographic
Zoo-Looking	G	RF	149	Bookshop	Mondo
100 Years Ago	H	I	135	Twig	Wright Group/McGraw Hill
ABC I Like Me!	H	F	136	Carlson, Nancy	Puffin Books
Accident, The	H	RF	313	Foundations	Wright Group/McGraw Hill
After School	H	RF	199	Foundations	Wright Group/McGraw Hill
Agua, Agua, Agua	H	TL	94	Little Celebrations	Pearson Learning Group
Aki's Special Gift	H	RF	240	Leveled Readers Language Support	Houghton Mifflin
Alien, The	H	F	177	Windmill Books	Rigby
Aliens on the Lawn	H	F	175	Windmill Books	Rigby
Ali's Story	H	RF	236	Sunshine	Wright Group/McGraw Hill
All About Ants	H	I	214	Rosen Real Readers	Rosen Publishing Group
All by Myself	H	RF	215	Cambridge Reading	Pearson Learning Group
All Dressed Up	H	RF	137	Voyages	SRA/McGraw Hill
Alone and Together	H	RF	292	Early Connections	Benchmark Education
Alphabet Game, The	H	F	272	Story Basket	Wright Group/McGraw Hill
And the Teacher Got Mad	H	RF	109	City Kids	Rigby
And the Teacher Smiled	H	RF	86	City Kids	Rigby
Andi's Wool	H	I	107	Books for Young Learners	Richard C. Owen
Andy (That's my Name)	H	F	104	DePaola, Tomie	Aladdin
Animal Shapes	H	I	133	Rigby Focus	Rigby
Animal Tricks	H	F	102	Wildsmith, Brian	Merrimak
Animals Build	H	I	129	Discovery Links	Newbridge
Animals Live Everywhere	H	I	250+	Phonics and Friends	Hampton-Brown
Annabel	H	RF	251	Story Basket	Wright Group/McGraw Hill
Ants	H	I	94	Pebble Plus	Red Brick Learning
Ants	H	I	250+	Sunshine	Wright Group/McGraw Hill
Art Class, The	H	RF	240	Leveled Readers	Houghton Mifflin
At the Ballpark	H	RF	105	Sunshine	Wright Group/McGraw Hill
At the Post Office	H	RF	100	City Stories	Rigby
At the Science Center	H	I	158	Discovery Links	Newbridge
Australia	H	I	27	Chessen, Betsey; Chanko, Pamela	Scholastic
Awful Mess, The	H	RF	58	Rockwell, Anne	Four Winds
Baby at Our House, The	H	RF	93	Foundations	Wright Group/McGraw Hill
Babysitter, The	H	RF	243	PM Extensions-Green	Rigby

TITLE	LEVEL	GENRE	WORD COUNT	AUTHOR / SERIES	PUBLISHER / DISTRIBUTOR
Barney Bear, World Traveler	H	F	65	Learn to Read	Creative Teaching Press
Barry and Bennie	H	F	251	Little Celebrations	Pearson Learning Group
Beach Creatures	H	I	231	Pair-It Books	Steck-Vaughn
Bear's Tale, The	H	TL	155	Books for Young Learners	Richard C. Owen
Becoming a Butterfly	H	I	83	Rosen Real Readers	Rosen Publishing Group
Bee My Valentine!	H	RF	250+	Cohen, Miriam	Bantam
Bees on Trees	H	F	250+	Sunshine	Wright Group/McGraw Hill
Bella Is a Bad Dog	H	RF	132	Bella and Rosie Series	Pioneer Valley
Ben's Tooth	H	RF	197	PM Story Books	Rigby
Better Look, A	H	I	106	Windows on Literacy	National Geographic
Big Box, The	H	RF	183	New Way Green	Steck-Vaughn
Big Chief of the Neverwoz, The	H	F	250+	Little Celebrations	Pearson Learning Group
Big Family, The	H	RF	250+	Sunshine	Wright Group/McGraw Hill
Big Game, The	H	RF	69	Pacific Literacy	Pacific Learning
Big Race, The	H	RF	250+	Home Connection Collection	School Zone
Big Red Apple, The	H	F	250+	Momentum Literacy Program	Troll Associates
Big Surprise, The	H	RF	123	Pacific Literacy	Pacific Learning
Big, Big Trucks	H	I	162	School Zone	School Zone
Bird Table, The	H	RF	166	Book Bank	Wright Group/McGraw Hill
Birds on Stage	H	F	153	Romay, Saturnino	Scholastic
Birthday Book	H	RF	93	Storybox	Wright Group/McGraw Hill
Birthday Cake, The	H	F	201	Story Box	Wright Group/McGraw Hill
Birthday Surprise	H	RF	265	Leveled Readers	Houghton Mifflin
Birthday Surprise, A	H	RF	157	Developing Books, Set 2	Pioneer Valley
Black-and-White Ruffed Lemurs	H	I	94	Seedlings	Continental Press
Block Party, The	H	I	127	Learn to Read	Creative Teaching Press
Blue Jay, The	H	RF	173	Little Readers	Houghton Mifflin
Blue Kangaroo, The	H	F	361	Leveled Readers	Houghton Mifflin
Bogle's Card	H	F	244	Sunshine	Wright Group/McGraw Hill
Bonnie on the Beach	H	RF	198	Little Readers	Houghton Mifflin
Book Club, The	H	RF	247	Leveled Readers Language Support	Houghton Mifflin
Boxes	H	F	153	Literacy 2000	Rigby
Boy and the Lion, The	H	TL	166	Aesop	Wright Group/McGraw Hill
Boy Who Cried Wolf, The	H	TL	324	Sunshine	Wright Group/McGraw Hill
Bozo	H	RF	94	Wonder World	Wright Group/McGraw Hill
Brooke and Her Crayons	H	RF	283	Leveled Readers	Houghton Mifflin
Bubble Gum	H	RF	66	City Kids	Rigby
Building a House	H	I	83	Barton, Byron	Morrow
But I Knew Better	H	RF	242	Home Connection Collection	Rigby
Buzz, Buzz, Buzz	H	F	162	Barton, Byron	Macmillan
Cake That Mack Ate, The	H	TL	189	Robart, Rose; Kovalski, Maryann	Little, Brown & Co.
Camouflage	H	I	154	Sunshine	Wright Group/McGraw Hill
Can I Play Outside?	H	RF	121	Literacy 2000	Rigby
Canada	H	I	68	Canizares, Susan; Berger, Samantha	Scholastic
Candy, the Old Car	H	F	234	PM Plus Story Books	Rigby
Captain Cat	H	F	250+	Hoff, Syd	HarperTrophy
Caring for Earth	H	I	80	Windows on Literacy	National Geographic
Carrot Soup	H	TL	142	Literacy Tree	Rigby
Cat on the Roof	H	RF	250+	Story Box	Wright Group/McGraw Hill
Cat Whispers	H	RF	250+	Rigby Literacy	Rigby
Cats and Mice	H	F	51	Gelman, Rita	Scholastic
Cats on the Farm	H	I	71	Pebble Books	Red Brick Learning

* Collection of short stories

TITLE	LEVEL	GENRE	WORD COUNT	AUTHOR / SERIES	PUBLISHER / DISTRIBUTOR
Caught in the Storm	H	RF	250+	Home Connection Collection	Rigby
Celebrating Patriotic Holidays: Honoring America	H	I	175	Learn to Read	Creative Teaching Press
Celebrating President's Day	H	I	181	Learn to Read	Creative Teaching Press
Chano	H	RF	124	Literacy 2000	Rigby
Chicken Licken	H	TL	233	Supersonics	Rigby
Chicken Pox	H	RF	220	Little Readers	Houghton Mifflin
Chili Pepper Pinata, The	H	RF	257	Story Box	Wright Group/McGraw Hill
Choose Me!	H	F	204	Reading Corners	Pearson Learning Group
Class Calender	H	I	81	Windows on Literacy	National Geographic
Classroom Caterpillars, The	H	RF	216	PM Plus Story Books	Rigby
Clean House for Mole and Mouse, A	H	F	201	Ziefert, Harriet	Scholastic
Cleaning Up the Park	H	I	153	Home Connection Collection	Rigby
Clean-Up Day	H	RF	179	Instant Readers	Harcourt School Publishers
Clever Tortoise, The	H	TL	202	Cambridge Reading	Pearson Learning Group
Clever, Crow, The	H	TL	223	PM Plus Story Books	Rigby
Clock That Couldn't Tell Time, The	H	F	310	Carousel Readers	Pearson Learning Group
Clouds	H	I	132	Twig	Wright Group/McGraw Hill
Clouds	H	I	108	Sunshine	Wright Group/McGraw Hill
Coco's Bell	H	RF	224	PM Plus Story Books	Rigby
Colin Powell, American Leader	H	B	77	Leveled Readers Social Studies	Houghton Mifflin
Come Out and Play Little Mouse	H	F	198	Kraus, Robert	Morrow
Come! Sit! Speak!	H	RF	57	Rookie Readers	Children's Press
Coral Reef, The	H	I	186	Discovery Links	Newbridge
Corn: From Table to Table	H	I	171	Discovery Links	Newbridge
Count!	H	RF	70	Fleming, Denise	Scholastic
Cow in the Garden and Other Stories, The	H	F	158	New Way Literature	Steck-Vaughn
Cow Up a Tree	H	F	215	Read Alongs	Rigby
Crab at the Bottom of the Sea, The	H	TL	141	Literacy 2000	Rigby
Crickets	H	I	89	Pebble Plus	Red Brick Learning
Cross-Country Race, The	H	RF	246	PM Story Books	Rigby
Dad Cooks Breakfast	H	RF	195	Windmill Books	Rigby
Dairy Group, The	H	I	97	Pebble Books	Red Brick Learning
Dandelions and Other Stories	H	F	250+	Story Steps	Rigby
Danny and the Dinosaur Go to Camp	H	F	250+	Hoff, Syd	HarperTrophy
Dan's Old Van	H	F	145	Supersonics	Rigby
Daughter of the Sun	H	RF	210	Storyteller-Night Crickets	Wright Group/McGraw Hill
Davy Crockett and the Wild Cat	H	F	148	Instant Readers	Harcourt School Publishers
Day at the Races, A	H	RF	85	Bauer, Roger	Kaeden Books
Day the Sky Fell Down, The	H	F	226	Lighthouse	Rigby
Day with Firefighters, A	H	I	171	Welcome Books	Children's Press
Day, A	H	I	134	The Calendar	Capstone Press
Dear Mabel!	H	RF	138	Little Celebrations	Pearson Learning Group
Dear Tom	H	RF	153	Wonder World	Wright Group/McGraw Hill
Debra's Dog	H	F	157	Tadpoles	Rigby
Deb's Secret Wish and Other Stories	H	F	250+	New Way Literature	Steck-Vaughn
Delivering Your Mail: Book About Mail Carriers, A	H	I	120	Community Workers	Picture Window Books
Digging to China	H	F	108	Books for Young Learners	Richard C. Owen
Dinosaurs	H	I	117	Sunshine	Wright Group/McGraw Hill
Dippy Dinner Drippers, The	H	F	181	Sunshine	Wright Group/McGraw Hill
Do That, Do This!	H	RF	151	Supersonics	Rigby
Doctor Has the Flu, The	H	RF	106	Ready Readers	Pearson Learning Group
Dog for Mrs. Muddle Mud-Puddle, A	H	F	194	Story Box	Wright Group/McGraw Hill

* Collection of short stories

TITLE	LEVEL	GENRE	WORD COUNT	AUTHOR / SERIES	PUBLISHER / DISTRIBUTOR
Doing My Job	H	I	188	Early Connections	Benchmark Education
Dolly's Car	H	RF	192	Handprints C, Set 2	Educator's Publishing Service
Donkey Work	H	I	129	Wonder World	Wright Group/McGraw Hill
Do-Whacky-Do	H	F	249	Read Alongs	Rigby
Dragon's Coming After You, The	H	F	156	Voyages	SRA/McGraw Hill
Dream in the Wishing Well	H	F	250+	Van Allen, Roach	SRA/McGraw Hill
Dress-Up Corner, The	H	RF	68	City Kids	Rigby
Drinking Water	H	I	79	Pebble Books	Red Brick Learning
Driving Mom Crazy	H	RF	131	City Stories	Rigby
Drummers, The	H	RF	80	Gould, Carol	Kaeden Books
Duck and Hen	H	F	193	Sunshine	Wright Group/McGraw Hill
Duke the Mule	H	F	59	Easy Phonics Readers	Teacher Created Materials
Dumpsideary Jelly	H	RF	250+	Momentum Literacy Program	Troll Associates
Earth, The	H	I	112	Windows on Literacy	National Geographic
Earthworm, The	H	I	157	Wonder World	Wright Group/McGraw Hill
Eating Right	H	I	151	Pebble Books	Red Brick Learning
Eating Well	H	I	124	Yellow Umbrella Books	Red Brick Learning
Election Day	H	RF	250+	McNamara, Margaret	Aladdin
Elephant in Trouble	H	F	98	First Start	Troll Associates
Ella's Time Line	H	RF	101	Windows on Literacy	National Geographic
Emma's Problem	H	RF	190	Literacy 2000	Rigby
Engelbert the Hero	H	F	113	Little Celebrations	Pearson Learning Group
Enormous Turnip, The	H	TL	431	Hunia, Fran	Ladybird Books
Enormous Watermelon, The	H	TL	304	Traditional Tales & More	Rigby
Eric's Birthday	H	RF	77	City Stories	Rigby
Erik and the Three Goats	H	F	257	Ready Readers	Pearson Learning Group
Everyone is Reading	H	RF	225	Cambridge Reading	Pearson Learning Group
Everywhere You Look	H	I	191	Sunshine	Wright Group/McGraw Hill
Exploring a Park	H	I	65	Vocabulary Readers	Houghton Mifflin
Families	H	I	160	Early Connections	Benchmark Education
Fancy Dress Parade, The	H	RF	171	Stepping Stones	Nelson/Michaels Assoc.
Fantastic Pumpkin, The	H	F	216	Rigby Literacy	Rigby
Farmyard Fiasco, A	H	F	186	Book Bank	Wright Group/McGraw Hill
Fast, Not Last	H	F	233	Sunshine	Wright Group/McGraw Hill
Faster! Faster!	H	F	285	Leveled Readers	Houghton Mifflin
Father Bear's Surprise	H	RF	224	PM Extensions-Green	Rigby
Fawn in the Forest, The	H	RF	227	PM Plus Story Books	Rigby
Feeding the Lambs	H	RF	61	PM Plus Nonfiction	Rigby
Feet	H	F	76	Book Bank	Wright Group/McGraw Hill
Fern and Burt	H	F	250+	Ready Readers	Pearson Learning Group
Finding Out About the Past	H	I	155	Windows on Literacy	National Geographic
First Day Back at School	H	RF	132	City Kids	Rigby
Five Beans	H	I	197	Sun Sprouts	ETA/Cuisenaire
Flip's Trick	H	RF	134	Ready Readers	Pearson Learning Group
Floating and Sinking	H	I	168	Sunshine	Wright Group/McGraw Hill
Flood	H	RF	170	Story Box	Wright Group/McGraw Hill
Flood, The	H	RF	237	PM Story Books	Rigby
Flying Fish, The	H	RF	215	PM Extensions-Green	Rigby
Follow My Leader	H	RF	96	Cambridge Reading	Pearson Learning Group
Food From Another Country	H	I	91	Windows on Literacy	National Geographic
Food Is Fun	H	RF	250+	PM Plus Poetry	Rigby
Football Fever	H	RF	51	Pacific Literacy	Pacific Learning
Footprints	H	RF	96	Book Bus	Creative Edge

* Collection of short stories

TITLE	LEVEL	GENRE	WORD COUNT	AUTHOR / SERIES	PUBLISHER / DISTRIBUTOR
Four Cheerful Chipmunks	H	F	250+	Phonics and Friends	Hampton-Brown
Fox and Crow, The	H	TL	201	Alphakids	Sundance
Fox and the Stork	H	F	149	New Way Blue	Steck-Vaughn
Fox Who Foxed, The	H	F	212	PM Story Books	Rigby
Francisco's Collection	H	RF	250+	Pacific Literacy	Pacific Learning
Freddy Frog's Note	H	F	253	Ready Readers	Pearson Learning Group
Frog Has a Sticky Tongue, A	H	I	176	Windows on Literacy	National Geographic
From Sky to Sea	H	I	40	Pacific Literacy	Pacific Learning
Fruit Pops	H	I	89	Windows on Literacy	National Geographic
Fun at Camp	H	RF	178	First Start	Troll Associates
Fun in the Snow	H	RF	132	Bella and Rosie Series	Pioneer Valley
Fun With Plaster	H	I	150	Rigby Focus	Rigby
Fur, Feathers, Scales, Skin	H	I	173	Discovery Links	Newbridge
George at the Zoo	H	F	250+	Voyages	SRA/McGraw Hill
George Shrinks	H	F	114	Joyce, William	Scholastic
Get Ready to Race	H	F	98	Instant Readers	Harcourt School Publishers
Getting Around	H	I	211	Momentum Literacy Program	Troll Associates
Giant and the Frippit, The	H	F	250+	Rigby Literacy	Rigby
Giant in the Bed, The	H	F	253	New Way Green	Steck-Vaughn
Giant's Boy, The	H	F	89	Sunshine	Wright Group/McGraw Hill
Giant's Cake, The	H	F	162	Literacy 2000	Rigby
Giant's Job, The	H	F	180	Stewart, Josie; Salem, Lynn	Continental Press
Gifts for Dad	H	RF	178	Urmston, Kathleen; Evans, Karen	Kaeden Books
Gigantic George	H	F	224	Little Celebrations	Pearson Learning Group
Gingerbread Man, The	H	TL	197	Sunshine	Wright Group/McGraw Hill
Gingerbread Man, The	H	TL	250+	Literacy 2000	Rigby
Giraffe's Sad Tale (With a Happy Ending)	H	F	250+	Alma Flor Ada	Hampton-Brown
Goal!	H	RF	232	Lighthouse	Rigby
Goat in the Chile Patch, The	H	TL	250+	Kratky, Lada Josefa	Hampton-Brown
Goggly Gookers	H	F	100	Story Basket	Wright Group/McGraw Hill
Going to School	H	RF	250	Cambridge Reading	Pearson Learning Group
Going to the Hospital	H	RF	335	Foundations	Wright Group/McGraw Hill
Golden Lasso, The	H	F	250+	Home Connection Collection	Rigby
Goldilocks and the Three Bears	H	TL	250+	Traditional Tales & More	Rigby
Goldilocks and The Three Bears	H	TL	250+	PM Tales and Plays-Turquoise	Rigby
Gonna Bird, The	H	F	209	Storyteller-Night Crickets	Wright Group/McGraw Hill
Good Idea, A	H	RF	250+	Leveled Readers Language Support	Houghton Mifflin
Good Manners	H	RF	222	Well-Being Series	Dominie Press
Good Morning, Monday	H	RF	77	Keenan, Sheila	Scholastic
Good Sports	H	I	206	Foundations	Wright Group/McGraw Hill
Good to Eat	H	I	152	Rigby Focus	Rigby
Good-bye Summer, Hello Fall	H	I	169	Ready Readers	Pearson Learning Group
Goodnight Goodnight	H	F	185	Literacy Tree	Rigby
Goodnight Moon	H	F	130	Brown, Margaret Wise	HarperCollins
Gorillas	H	I	185	Seedlings	Continental Press
Grain Group, The	H	I	108	Pebble Books	Red Brick Learning
Grandma's Cane	H	RF	250+	Story Box	Wright Group/McGraw Hill
Grandma's Stick	H	RF	250+	Story Box	Wright Group/McGraw Hill
Grandpa, Grandma, and the Tractor	H	RF	220	Ready Readers	Pearson Learning Group
Grandparents Are Fun!	H	I	216	Leveled Readers Language Support	Houghton Mifflin
Granny Bundle's Boring Walk	H	RF	250+	Stepping Stones	Nelson/Michaels Assoc.
Granny's Teeth	H	RF	169	Cambridge Reading	Pearson Learning Group

* Collection of short stories

TITLE	LEVEL	GENRE	WORD COUNT	AUTHOR / SERIES	PUBLISHER / DISTRIBUTOR
Grasshoppers	H	I	84	Pebble Plus	Red Brick Learning
Great Big Enormous Turnip, The	H	TL	250+	Tolstoi, Aleksei; Nikolaevich, Graf	Watts
Great Big Enormous Turnip, The	H	TL	317	Reading Unlimited	Pearson Learning Group
Great Invention, The	H	RF	108	City Stories	Rigby
Greedy Dog, The	H	F	148	New Way Blue	Steck-Vaughn
Green Grass Grows All Around, The	H	TL	144	Instant Readers	Harcourt School Publishers
Green Plants	H	RF	213	Foundations	Wright Group/McGraw Hill
Grow a Plant Inch by Inch	H	I	142	Rosen Real Readers	Rosen Publishing Group
Guide Dogs	H	I	107	Rosen Real Readers	Rosen Publishing Group
Hamburger	H	RF	49	City Kids	Rigby
Handy Dragon, A	H	F	159	Literacy 2000	Rigby
Happy Birthday, Danny and the Dinosaur	H	F	250+	Little Readers	Houghton Mifflin
Happy Birthday, Danny and the Dinosaur!	H	F	250+	Hoff, Syd	HarperTrophy
Happy Faces	H	RF	210	Reading Unlimited	Pearson Learning Group
Happy Pets, Healthy Pets	H	I	98	Spyglass Books	Compass Point Books
Harvest Time	H	I	184	Yellow Umbrella Books	Red Brick Learning
Hatching Chickens at School	H	RF	94	City Kids	Rigby
Hats for the Carnival	H	RF	231	Lighthouse	Rigby
Help for Rosie	H	RF	165	Bella and Rosie Series	Pioneer Valley
Help Me	H	TL	196	Story Box	Wright Group/McGraw Hill
Help!	H	RF	82	Giant Step Readers	Educational Insights
Helping You Heal	H	I	145	Community Workers	Picture Window Books
Helping You Learn: Book About Teachers, A	H	I	147	Community Workers	Picture Window Books
Henny Penny	H	TL	292	New Way Green	Steck-Vaughn
Henry's Tricks	H	RF	162	Books for Young Learners	Richard C. Owen
Here are My Hands	H	I	127	Bobber Book	SRA/McGraw Hill
Herman's Tooth	H	F	210	Foundations	Wright Group/McGraw Hill
Hiccups Would Not Stop, The	H	F	177	Ready Readers	Pearson Learning Group
Hide & Seek	H	I	138	Wonder World	Wright Group/McGraw Hill
Hide and Seek	H	RF	215	Foundations	Wright Group/McGraw Hill
Hide-and-Seek	H	F	250+	Momentum Literacy Program	Troll Associates
Hide-and-Seek	H	F	546	Leveled Readers	Houghton Mifflin
Hiking with Dad	H	RF	189	Wonder World	Wright Group/McGraw Hill
Hippo in June's Tub, A	H	F	85	Little Books	Sadlier-Oxford
Hippos	H	I	117	Story Steps	Rigby
Hobnob the Troll	H	F	165	Supersonics	Rigby
Hobson Family Vacation, The	H	RF	250+	Momentum Literacy Program	Troll Associates
Home for Mindy, A	H	I	250+	Rigby Literacy	Rigby
Horrible Thing with Hairy Feet	H	TL	208	Read Alongs	Rigby
Hospital Party, The	H	RF	237	PM Plus Story Books	Rigby
Hot Surprise, A	H	RF	162	Rigby Literacy	Rigby
House for Hickory, A	H	F	174	Bookshop	Mondo
How Bat Learned to Fly	H	TL	168	Storyteller-Night Crickets	Wright Group/McGraw Hill
How Big? How Much?	H	I	134	Hutchins, Jeannie	Scholastic
How Can We See in the Dark?	H	I	157	Sunshine	Wright Group/McGraw Hill
How Do I Put It On?	H	I	168	Watanabe, Shiego	Penguin Group
How Does My Garden Grow?	H	I	73	Windows on Literacy	National Geographic
How Does Your Salad Grow?	H	I	136	Alexander, Francie	Scholastic
How Things Move	H	I	214	Yellow Umbrella Books	Red Brick Learning
How to Make a Crocodile	H	F	62	Little Books	Sadlier-Oxford
How to Make a Mud Pie	H	RF	127	Little Readers	Houghton Mifflin
How to Make Sock Puppets	H	I	229	Bookshop	Mondo
How Turtle Got His Tail	H	F	248	Rigby Literacy	Rigby
How We Make Music	H	I	104	Rosen Real Readers	Rosen Publishing Group

TITLE	LEVEL	GENRE	WORD COUNT	AUTHOR / SERIES	PUBLISHER / DISTRIBUTOR
I Am Patriotic	H	I	76	Pebble Books	Red Brick Learning
I Am Tolerant	H	I	132	Pebble Books	Red Brick Learning
I Can't Wait to Read	H	RF	185	Adventures in Reading	Pearson Learning Group
I Don't Care	H	F	250+	Reading Friends	Pearson Learning Group
I Don't Care!	H	RF	250	TOTTS	Tott Publications
I Fixed Breakfast	H	RF	176	Teacher's Choice Series	Pearson Learning Group
I Know an Old Lady	H	F	82	Readalong Rhythms	Wright Group/McGraw Hill
I Try to Be a Good Person	H	RF	192	Learn to Read	Creative Teaching Press
I Was Walking Down the Road	H	F	299	Barchas, Sarah	Scholastic
Ice Fishing	H	I	140	Ready Readers	Pearson Learning Group
If	H	F	83	Sunshine	Wright Group/McGraw Hill
If I Had an Alligator	H	F	214	Mayer, Mercer	Dial Books
If I Were a Penguin	H	RF	159	Goeneil, Heidi	Little, Brown & Co.
If You Like Strawberries, Don't Read this Book	H	RF	101	Literacy 2000	Rigby
I'm a Good Reader	H	RF	188	Carousel Readers	Pearson Learning Group
I'm an Astronaut	H	F	162	Voyages	SRA/McGraw Hill
I'm Glad to Say	H	RF	165	Sunshine	Wright Group/McGraw Hill
I'm Sick Today	H	RF	150	Carousel Readers	Pearson Learning Group
In Grandma's Garden	H	RF	244	Sunshine	Wright Group/McGraw Hill
In My Bag	H	RF	237	Windows on Literacy	National Geographic
In the Afternoon	H	I	156	PM Nonfiction-Green	Rigby
In the Backyard	H	F	197	Little Celebrations	Pearson Learning Group
In the Bank	H	I	140	Independent Readers Social Studies	Houghton Mifflin
In the Morning	H	I	218	PM Nonfiction-Green	Rigby
Is That a Bear?	H	RF	225	Sunshine	Wright Group/McGraw Hill
Island Picnic, The	H	RF	236	PM Story Books	Rigby
It Must Be Clay	H	I	173	Independent Readers Science	Houghton Mifflin
It Takes Time to Grow	H	RF	57	Sunshine	Wright Group/McGraw Hill
Italy	H	I	34	Canizares, Susan; Chessen, Betsey	Scholastic
It's a Gift	H	I	156	Lighthouse	Rigby
It's a Good Thing That There Are Insects	H	I	250+	Fowler, Allan	Scholastic
It's a Zoo!	H	RF	100	City Stories	Rigby
It's Cold Where I Live	H	RF	98	Windows on Literacy	National Geographic
It's George!	H	RF	250+	Cohen, Miriam	Bantam
It's Magic	H	F	204	Start to Read	School Zone
It's Spring!	H	F	124	Berger, Samantha; Chanko, Pamela	Scholastic
It's Time!	H	I	175	Yellow Umbrella Books	Red Brick Learning
I've Got New Sneakers	H	RF	111	City Kids	Rigby
Jack and the Beanstalk	H	TL	170	Sunshine	Wright Group/McGraw Hill
Jack Plays the Violin	H	RF	250+	Schultz, Jessica	Scholastic
Jake's First Word	H	RF	204	Books for Young Learners	Richard C. Owen
Jane Mt. Pleasant	H	B	134	Leveled Readers Science	Houghton Mifflin
Jasmine's Duck	H	RF	207	Lighthouse	Rigby
Jellybean Tree, The	H	F	231	Sunshine	Wright Group/McGraw Hill
Jenny Lives on Hunter Street	H	RF	141	Book Bank	Wright Group/McGraw Hill
Jim's Trumpet	H	RF	304	Sunshine	Wright Group/McGraw Hill
Jobs For Dogs	H	I	188	Rigby Focus	Rigby
Joey's Rowboat	H	RF	83	Little Books	Sadlier-Oxford
Joke Book, The	H	I	143	Vocabulary Readers	Houghton Mifflin
Joke, The	H	F	186	Little Readers	Houghton Mifflin
Jokers	H	F	190	Breakthrough	Longman/Bow
Juan	H	RF	77	City Kids	Rigby

TITLE	LEVEL	GENRE	WORD COUNT	AUTHOR / SERIES	PUBLISHER / DISTRIBUTOR
Jumbaroo, The	H	F	173	Story Basket	Wright Group/McGraw Hill
Jump and Swim	H	RF	293	Leveled Readers	Houghton Mifflin
Jump in the Pool, A	H	RF	243	Leveled Readers Language Support	Houghton Mifflin
Jump Rope, The	H	RF	241	PM Plus Story Books	Rigby
Just Me and My Babysitter	H	F	182	Mayer, Mercer	Donovan
Just Me and My Dad	H	F	161	Mayer, Mercer	Donovan
Just Me and My Puppy	H	F	190	Mayer, Mercer	Donovan
Just This Once	H	F	252	Sunshine	Wright Group/McGraw Hill
Kangaroo from Wooloomooloo	H	F	254	Jellybeans	Rigby
Katie's Butterfly	H	RF	222	PM Plus Story Books	Rigby
Kenny's Big Present	H	RF	181	Leveled Readers	Houghton Mifflin
Kick-a-Lot Shoes, The	H	F	433	Story Box	Wright Group/McGraw Hill
Kiss for Little Bear, A	H	F	250+	Minarik, Else H.	HarperTrophy
Kit Finds a Mitt	H	RF	198	Leveled Readers	Houghton Mifflin
Kite That Flew Away, The	H	RF	279	Ready Readers	Pearson Learning Group
Korka the Mighty Elf	H	F	250+	Rigby Literacy	Rigby
Leafcutter Ant, The	H	I	77	Vocabulary Readers	Houghton Mifflin
Learning New Things	H	RF	156	Foundations	Wright Group/McGraw Hill
Lesson, The	H	RF	133	Cummings, Pat	Scholastic
Lester's Song	H	F	250+	Lester the Lion Series	Pioneer Valley
Let's Go Camping and Other Stories	H	F	250+	New Way Literature	Steck-Vaughn
Let's Look at Leopards	H	I	155	Rosen Real Readers	Rosen Publishing Group
Let's Take a Trip	H	F	178	Leveled Readers	Houghton Mifflin
Let's Take the Bus	H	RF	250+	Real Reading	Steck-Vaughn
Letters for Mr. James	H	RF	203	Sunshine	Wright Group/McGraw Hill
Lift the Sky Up	H	RF	133	Little Celebrations	Pearson Learning Group
Lift the Sky Up	H	RF	133	Little Readers	Houghton Mifflin
Lilly-Lolly-Little-Legs	H	RF	129	Literacy 2000	Rigby
Little Book of Street Rods, The	H	I	79	Books for Young Learners	Richard C. Owen
Little Brown House	H	RF	266	Jellybeans	Rigby
Little Chimp and the Termites	H	F	192	PM Plus Story Books	Rigby
Little Green Dandelion, A	H	RF	191	Books for Young Learners	Richard C. Owen
Little Kid	H	F	169	Literacy 2000	Rigby
Little Puffer Fish	H	F	133	Books for Young Learners	Richard C. Owen
Little Rabbit Who Wanted Red Wings, The	H	F	364	Seedlings	Continental Press
Little Red Bus, The	H	RF	222	PM Story Books	Rigby
Little Red Hen	H	TL	255	New Way Green	Steck-Vaughn
Little Red Hen, The	H	TL	375	Traditional Tales	Pearson Learning Group
Little Red Riding Hood	H	TL	250+	Hunia, Fran	Ladybird Books
Living Things Need Food	H	I	66	Windows on Literacy	National Geographic
Locked In	H	RF	228	PM Plus Story Books	Rigby
Lola and Miss Kitty	H	RF	250+	Little Readers	Houghton Mifflin
Lollipop Please, A	H	RF	73	Literacy 2000	Rigby
Look at the Calendar, A	H	I	139	Rosen Real Readers	Rosen Publishing Group
Look at the Stars	H	I	144	Rigby Focus	Rigby
Look-Alike Animals	H	I	130	Bernard, Robin	Scholastic
Looking for Angus	H	F	99	Ready Readers	Pearson Learning Group
Looking for Bears	H	RF	80	Books for Young Learners	Richard C. Owen
Loose Tooth, The	H	RF	112	Breakthrough	Longman/Bow
Lottie Goat & Donny Goat	H	F	145	Ready Readers	Pearson Learning Group
Luke's Adventures	H	F	98	City Stories	Rigby
Lunchbox, The	H	RF	90	Pacific Literacy	Pacific Learning
Machines at Work	H	I	101	Little Red Readers	Sundance

* Collection of short stories

TITLE	LEVEL	GENRE	WORD COUNT	AUTHOR / SERIES	PUBLISHER / DISTRIBUTOR
Maggie Moves Away	H	RF	327	Adventures in Reading	Pearson Learning Group
Make a "Talking" Card	H	I	165	Sunshine	Wright Group/McGraw Hill
Make a Dinosaur	H	I	208	Sun Sprouts	ETA/Cuisenaire
Make an Animal Mobile	H	I	116	How-to Series	Benchmark Education
Making a Mural	H	I	128	Vocabulary Readers	Houghton Mifflin
Making a Plate	H	I	183	Ready Readers	Pearson Learning Group
Making Money	H	I	129	Rosen Real Readers	Rosen Publishing Group
Making Music	H	RF	71	Early Reader	Compass Point Books
Making Paper	H	I	128	Rigby Focus	Rigby
Making Shapes	H	I	206	Early Connections	Benchmark Education
Making Tortillas	H	I	104	Windows on Literacy	National Geographic
Mama Cut My Hair	H	RF	134	Books for Young Learners	Richard C. Owen
Mammals	H	I	134	Yellow Umbrella Books	Red Brick Learning
Man in the Moon, The	H	I	173	Pair-It-Books	Steck-Vaughn
Maps Show Us the Way	H	I	94	Rosen Real Readers	Rosen Publishing Group
Mardi Gras	H	I	84	Vocabulary Readers	Houghton Mifflin
Me and My Shadow	H	F	247	Momentum Literacy Program	Troll Associates
Measure the Motion	H	I	146	Leveled Readers Science	Houghton Mifflin
Measuring Motion	H	I	113	Leveled Readers Science	Houghton Mifflin
Meat and Protein Group, The	H	I	117	Pebble Books	Red Brick Learning
Meet Jane Mt. Pleasant	H	B	183	Leveled Readers Science	Houghton Mifflin
Meet Me at the Water Hole	H	I	144	Storyteller-Night Crickets	Wright Group/McGraw Hill
Meet My Mouse	H	RF	135	Little Celebrations	Pearson Learning Group
Meet Officer Jerry	H	I	173	Rosen Real Readers	Rosen Publishing Group
Meg's Mad Magnet	H	F	145	Supersonics	Rigby
Mice	H	I	143	Literacy 2000	Rigby
Mice on Ice	H	F	51	Easy Phonics Readers	Teacher Created Materials
Missing Necklace, The	H	F	231	Reading Unlimited	Pearson Learning Group
Missing Pet Mystery, The	H	RF	174	Instant Readers	Harcourt School Publishers
Missing Suit, The	H	F	250+	Phonics and Friends	Hampton-Brown
Misty's Mischief	H	F	61	Campbell, Rod	Viking
Mom Paints the House	H	RF	220	Foundations	Wright Group/McGraw Hill
Mom's Haircut	H	RF	99	Literacy 2000	Rigby
Mom's Secret	H	RF	143	Costain, Meredith	Scholastic
Money Math	H	I	247	Yellow Umbrella Books	Red Brick Learning
Monkey Tricks	H	RF	328	PM Turquoise	Rigby
Monster Bus Goes to the Races	H	F	158	The Monster Bus Series	Pearson Learning Group
Monster Money	H	F	130	Maccarone, Grace	Scholastic
Months	H	I	135	The Calendar	Capstone Press
Morris the Moose	H	F	250+	Wiseman, Bernard	HarperTrophy
Most Scary Ghost	H	F	355	Jellybeans	Rigby
Mother Sun's Rest Day	H	F	250+	Momentum Literacy Program	Troll Associates
Move Like Us!	H	RF	250+	Home Connection Collection	Rigby
Mr. Beekman's Deli	H	F	96	Story Basket	Wright Group/McGraw Hill
Mr. Bitter's Butter	H	F	231	Story Basket	Wright Group/McGraw Hill
Mr. Clutterbus	H	F	250+	Voyages	SRA/McGraw Hill
Mr. Fixit	H	RF	196	Sunshine	Wright Group/McGraw Hill
Mr. McCready's Cleaning Day	H	F	119	Shilling, Tracy	Scholastic
Mr. McGrah's New Car	H	F	119	Book Bank	Wright Group/McGraw Hill
Mr. Whisper	H	F	325	Sunshine	Wright Group/McGraw Hill
Mr. Wolf Leaves Town	H	TL	208	Alphakids	Sundance
Mr. Wolf Tries Again	H	TL	218	Alphakids	Sundance
Mrs. McNosh Hangs Up Her Wash	H	F	166	Little Celebrations	Pearson Learning Group
Mrs. Murphy's Crows	H	RF	120	Books for Young Learners	Richard C. Owen

* Collection of short stories

TITLE	LEVEL	GENRE	WORD COUNT	AUTHOR / SERIES	PUBLISHER / DISTRIBUTOR
Mrs. Spider's Beautiful Web	H	F	250+	PM Story Books	Rigby
My Bean Plant	H	I	146	Windows on Literacy	National Geographic
My Big Surprise	H	F	139	Instant Readers	Harcourt School Publishers
My Brown Bear Barney	H	RF	82	Butler, Dorothy	Morrow
My Cat	H	I	79	Taylor, Judy	Macmillan
My Cat Sam	H	F	147	Supersonics	Rigby
My Cousin Jake	H	RF	123	City Stories	Rigby
My Family Split Up	H	RF	85	City Kids	Rigby
My Friend Jess	H	RF	124	Wonder World	Wright Group/McGraw Hill
My Friend Trent	H	RF	186	Foundations	Wright Group/McGraw Hill
My Hobby	H	I	155	Rigby Focus	Rigby
My New Quilt	H	I	170	Rigby Focus	Rigby
My Shadow Clock	H	I	180	Sun Sprouts	ETA/Cuisenaire
My Sister June	H	RF	182	Ready Readers	Pearson Learning Group
My Tooth is Loose!	H	RF	250+	Silverman, Martin	Puffin Books
Mystery of the Missing Red Mitten, The	H	RF	246	Little Readers	Houghton Mifflin
Name for Rabbit, A	H	F	94	Pacific Literacy	Pacific Learning
Name, The	H	RF	159	Voyages	SRA/McGraw Hill
Names and Games	H	I	115	Literacy Tree	Rigby
Nest on the Beach, The	H	RF	243	PM Plus Story Books	Rigby
Never-Told Story, The	H	RF	138	Literacy Tree	Rigby
New Baby Calf, The	H	RF	240	Chase, Edith; Reid, Barbara	Scholastic
New Building, The	H	RF	78	Sunshine	Wright Group/McGraw Hill
New Glasses for Max	H	RF	239	PM Plus Story Books	Rigby
Night Diving	H	I	101	Twig	Wright Group/McGraw Hill
Night Lights	H	I	172	Independent Readers Science	Houghton Mifflin
Night the Lights Went Out, The	H	RF	155	Little Readers	Houghton Mifflin
No Ball Games Here	H	RF	128	Ziefert, Harriet	Penguin Group
No Mail for Mitchell	H	F	250+	Siracusa, Catherine	Random House
No Running!	H	RF	183	Lighthouse	Rigby
No Singing Today	H	RF	250+	Bookshop	Mondo
Not Too Small at All	H	RF	250+	Salem, Lynn	Continental Press
Obstacle Course, The	H	RF	211	Foundations	Wright Group/McGraw Hill
Ocean, The	H	I	139	Yellow Umbrella Books	Red Brick Learning
Off to the Shop	H	F	323	Storyteller-Night Crickets	Wright Group/McGraw Hill
Old Grizzly	H	F	185	Sunshine	Wright Group/McGraw Hill
Old Hat, New Hat	H	F	115	Berenstain, Stan & Jan	Random House
Old Malolo Had a Farm	H	F	250+	Sunshine	Wright Group/McGraw Hill
Old Mother Hubbard	H	F	117	Literacy 2000	Rigby
Old Woman, The	H	F	69	Sunshine	Wright Group/McGraw Hill
On My Street	H	I	292	Visions	Wright Group/McGraw Hill
On the Moon	H	I	77	Windows on Literacy	National Geographic
Once Upon a Time	H	F	243	Ready Readers	Pearson Learning Group
One Bear All Alone	H	F	107	Bucknall, Caroline	Dial Books
One Green Frog	H	I	215	Yellow Umbrella Books	Red Brick Learning
One Little Elephant	H	F	174	Sunshine	Wright Group/McGraw Hill
One Sock, Two Socks	H	RF	179	Reading Corners	Pearson Learning Group
One Thousand Currant Buns	H	F	213	Sunshine	Wright Group/McGraw Hill
One-Man Band	H	RF	144	Leveled Readers Science	Houghton Mifflin
Only an Octopus	H	RF	236	Literacy 2000	Rigby
Open Your Eyes, Sidney Miffet	H	RF	107	Seedlings	Continental Press
Orca Whales	H	I	85	Salem, Lynn	Wright Group/McGraw Hill
Our Moon	H	I	161	Early Connections	Benchmark Education
Our School	H	RF	46	Well-Being Series	Dominie Press

* Collection of short stories

TITLE	LEVEL	GENRE	WORD COUNT	AUTHOR / SERIES	PUBLISHER / DISTRIBUTOR
Our School	H	RF	98	City Kids	Rigby
Our Town	H	I	129	Windows on Literacy	National Geographic
Out After Dark	H	RF	114	Book Bank	Wright Group/McGraw Hill
Owliver	H	F	106	Kraus, Robert	Simon & Schuster
Painting Day, The	H	RF	250+	Voyages	SRA/McGraw Hill
Palm Trees	H	I	123	Pebble Books	Capstone Press
Pancakes for Breakfast	H	F	99	Books for Young Learners	Richard C. Owen
Pancakes for Supper	H	RF	96	Literacy 2000	Rigby
Panda's Surprise	H	F	242	Little Readers	Houghton Mifflin
Park Ranger's Day, A	H	I	195	Rosen Real Readers	Rosen Publishing Group
Pele	H	B	36	Canizares, Susan; Berger, Samantha	Scholastic
People and Places	H	I	240	Yellow Umbrella Books	Red Brick Learning
People Change the Land	H	I	222	Yellow Umbrella Books	Red Brick Learning
People Who Use Magnets at Work	H	I	148	Early Connections	Benchmark Education
Pepper Goes to School	H	RF	125	Foundations	Wright Group/McGraw Hill
Pepper's Adventure	H	RF	250+	PM Story Books	Rigby
Person from Planet X, The	H	F	250+	Sunshine	Wright Group/McGraw Hill
Pesky Paua, The	H	F	267	Book Bank	Wright Group/McGraw Hill
Pet Your Pet	H	F	93	Early Reader	Compass Point Books
Peter's Move	H	RF	224	Little Readers	Houghton Mifflin
Pick Up Nick!	H	RF	219	Ready Readers	Pearson Learning Group
Picture for Harold's Room, A	H	F	550	Johnson, Crockett	HarperCollins
Pie Day	H	F	250+	Phonics and Friends	Hampton-Brown
Pig William's Midnight Walk	H	F	354	Book Bank	Wright Group/McGraw Hill
Pine Trees	H	I	138	Pebble Books	Capstone Press
Pirate Feast, The	H	F	172	Story Basket	Wright Group/McGraw Hill
Pita's Birthday	H	F	250+	Ready to Read	Pacific Learning
Pizza for Dinner	H	RF	164	Literacy 2000	Rigby
Planning Dinner	H	RF	250+	Urmston, Kathleen; Evans, Karen	Kaeden Books
Please, Miss	H	RF	90	Cambridge Reading	Pearson Learning Group
Pond Where Harriet Lives, The	H	TL	151	Story-Teller Night	Wright Group/McGraw Hill
Popcorn Fun	H	RF	217	PM Plus Story Books	Rigby
Postcards from Pop	H	RF	122	Literacy Tree	Rigby
Potatoes, Potatoes	H	I	91	Wonder World	Wright Group/McGraw Hill
Praying Mantises	H	I	96	Bugs, Bugs, Bugs!	Red Brick Learning
Protecting Your Home: Book About Firefighters, A	H	I	89	Community Workers	Picture Window Books
Puffins	H	I	104	Seedlings	Continental Press
Pumpkin That Kim Carved, The	H	RF	149	Little Readers	Houghton Mifflin
Push and Pull	H	I	49	Yellow Umbrella Books	Red Brick Learning
Put Me in the Zoo	H	B	250+	Lopshire, Robert	Random House
Quack, Said the Billy Goat	H	F	88	Causley, Charles	Harper & Row
Quick Duck, The	H	F	165	Phonics Readers	Scholastic
Quiet in the Library!	H	F	113	Sunshine	Wright Group/McGraw Hill
Quiet Morning for Mom, A	H	RF	169	Lighthouse	Rigby
Rabbit, The	H	RF	59	Burningham, John	Crowell
Race to the Mountain, The	H	TL	174	Leveled Readers Language Support	Houghton Mifflin
Rain, Rain, and More Rain	H	RF	250+	Momentum Literacy Program	Troll Associates
Rainy Days at School	H	RF	118	City Kids	Rigby
Rand and the Fox, The	H	TL	93	Cambridge Reading	Pearson Learning Group
Rap Party, The	H	RF	300	Foundations	Wright Group/McGraw Hill
Rapid Robert Roadrunner	H	F	125	Reese, Bob	Children's Press

* Collection of short stories

TITLE	LEVEL	GENRE	WORD COUNT	AUTHOR / SERIES	PUBLISHER / DISTRIBUTOR
Ratty Tatty	H	F	181	Sunshine	Wright Group/McGraw Hill
Reading Robot, The	H	F	224	Sunshine	Wright Group/McGraw Hill
Ready, Set, Go	H	F	250+	Stadler, John	HarperTrophy
Real-Skin Rubber Monster Mask, The	H	F	104	Cohen, Miriam	Bantam
Red Box, The	H	RF	250+	Phonics Readers Plus	Steck-Vaughn
*Red Doll and Other Stories, The	H	F	250+	New Way Literature	Steck-Vaughn
Red Squirrel's Adventure	H	RF	223	PM Plus Story Books	Rigby
Rescue, The	H	RF	155	PM Extensions-Green	Rigby
Rhyming Riddles	H	I	240	Cambridge Reading	Pearson Learning Group
Rice Cakes	H	F	332	Literacy 2000	Rigby
Riding	H	I	210	Wonder World	Wright Group/McGraw Hill
Right Outside My Window	H	RF	121	Bookshop	Mondo
Robert and the Rocket	H	F	146	Waldron, Leesa	Scholastic
Robert Makes a Graph	H	I	160	Coulton, Mia	Kaeden Books
Rock Garden, The	H	RF	139	Windmill Books	Rigby
Rock-a-Bye Moon	H	F	107	Pair-It Books	Steck-Vaughn
Rooster and the Weather Vane, The	H	F	235	First Start	Troll Associates
Rosa at the Zoo	H	RF	135	Pacific Literacy	Pacific Learning
Rosie at the Zoo	H	RF	135	Pacific Literacy	Pacific Learning
Royal Dinner, The	H	F	250+	Literacy Tree	Rigby
Royal Goose, The	H	F	198	Ready Readers	Pearson Learning Group
Safe Place, The	H	TL	147	Pacific Literacy	Pacific Learning
Sally Ride	H	B	77	Leveled Readers Social Studies	Houghton Mifflin
Sally the Great	H	RF	250+	Home Connection Collection	Rigby
Sally's Surprise Garden	H	RF	148	Literacy Tree	Rigby
Sammy the Seal	H	F	250+	Hoff, Syd	HarperTrophy
Sam's Big Day	H	RF	74	Cat on the Mat	Oxford University Press
Sam's Haircut	H	RF	226	PM Plus Story Books	Rigby
Sand	H	I	49	iOpeners	Pearson Learning Group
Sarah and Will	H	RF	251	Alphakids	Sundance
Scare and Dare	H	RF	284	Alphakids	Sundance
Scared at Night	H	RF	250+	Early Transitional, Set 2	Pioneer Valley
School Is Closed	H	F	250+	Phonics Readers Plus	Steck-Vaughn
School Today and Long Ago	H	I	110	Windows on Literacy	National Geographic
Seasons	H	I	250+	Yellow Umbrella Books	Red Brick Learning
Seasons	H	I	119	Instant Readers	Harcourt School Publishers
Seasons Project	H	I	218	Sun Sprouts	ETA/Cuisenaire
Sending Signals	H	I	163	Literacy Tree	Rigby
Seven	H	RF	131	Early Connections	Benchmark Education
Seven Little Monsters	H	F	55	Sendak, Maurice	HarperCollins
Shadow Puppets	H	I	163	Alphakids	Sundance
Sharks	H	I	155	Ready Readers	Pearson Learning Group
*Shoo, Shoo, Shoo!	H	F	239	Story Steps	Rigby
Show-and-Tell	H	RF	205	Cambridge Reading	Pearson Learning Group
Signs of Spring	H	F	250+	Bookshop	Mondo
Silly Aunt Tilly	H	F	176	Instant Readers	Harcourt School Publishers
Silly Billys	H	F	250+	Sunshine	Wright Group/McGraw Hill
Singing Giant, The: A Play	H	F	250+	Rigby Literacy	Rigby
Singing Giant, The: A Story	H	F	250+	Rigby Literacy	Rigby
Sione's Talo	H	TL	164	Nelisi, Lino	Scholastic
Ski Lesson, The	H	I	155	Storyteller-Moon Rising	Wright Group/McGraw Hill
Skunks	H	I	111	Seedlings	Continental Press
Sleep Tight	H	RF	163	Cambridge Reading	Pearson Learning Group
Sleeping Animals	H	I	194	Alphakids	Sundance

* Collection of short stories

TITLE	LEVEL	GENRE	WORD COUNT	AUTHOR / SERIES	PUBLISHER / DISTRIBUTOR
Sleepover, The	H	RF	297	Leveled Readers	Houghton Mifflin
Sleepy Polar Bear	H	F	97	Hiris, Monica	Kaeden Books
Slippery, Sloppery Spaghetti	H	RF	250+	Home Connection Collection	Rigby
Slugs and Snails	H	I	132	Wonder World	Wright Group/McGraw Hill
Small Rabbit Goes Visiting	H	F	445	Book Bank	Wright Group/McGraw Hill
Small World, A	H	RF	146	Sunshine	Wright Group/McGraw Hill
Smart Pigs	H	RF	102	Stewart, Josie	Continental Press
Smartest One in Class, The	H	RF	68	City Stories	Rigby
Snail Girl	H	RF	250+	Momentum Literacy Program	Troll Associates
Snails in School	H	I	181	Discovery Links	Newbridge
Snake Slithers, A	H	I	82	Reading Unlimited	Pearson Learning Group
Snick-Snack Sniffle-Nose	H	F	187	Supersonics	Rigby
Snow	H	RF	217	Young Writers' World	Nelson/Michaels Assoc.
Snow on the Hill	H	RF	213	PM Extensions-Green	Rigby
Soap Story, A	H	RF	95	City Stories	Rigby
Socks Off	H	RF	177	Alphakids	Sundance
Sometimes I Share	H	RF	108	Ziefert, Harriet	HarperCollins
Sophie's Chicken	H	RF	107	Tadpoles	Rigby
Space	H	I	100	Sunshine	Wright Group/McGraw Hill
Springtime Rock and Roll, The	H	F	249	Literacy Tree	Rigby
Stars	H	I	181	Discovery Links	Newbridge
Starshine	H	F	224	Sunshine	Wright Group/McGraw Hill
Stone Soup	H	TL	250+	Rigby Literacy	Rigby
Story of Corn, The	H	I	171	Ready Readers	Pearson Learning Group
Strike Four!	H	RF	250+	Ziefert, Harriet	Puffin Books
Strongest One of All, The	H	TL	222	Instant Readers	Harcourt School Publishers
Stuck on an Island	H	RF	181	Sunshine	Wright Group/McGraw Hill
Sun Up, Sun Down	H	I	148	Independent Readers Science	Houghton Mifflin
Sunshine Street	H	RF	110	Sunshine	Wright Group/McGraw Hill
Super Smile Shop, The	H	F	254	Story Basket	Wright Group/McGraw Hill
Superkids	H	F	165	Sunshine	Wright Group/McGraw Hill
Supper for Cal	H	RF	189	Leveled Readers	Houghton Mifflin
Surfing the Information Highway	H	I	137	Wonder World	Wright Group/McGraw Hill
Surprise, The	H	F	124	Literacy 2000	Rigby
Swimming With a Dragon	H	RF	230	PM Plus Story Books	Rigby
Taking Care of Our World	H	I	137	Rosen Real Readers	Rosen Publishing Group
Taking You Places: Book About Bus Drivers, A	H	I	127	Community Workers	Picture Window Books
Tale of Cowboy Roy, The	H	F	185	Ready Readers	Pearson Learning Group
Tale of the Christmas Mouse	H	F	97	First Start	Troll Associates
Teacher Talk	H	RF	68	City Stories	Rigby
Teasing Mom	H	RF	239	PM Plus Story Books	Rigby
Teeny Tiny	H	TL	250+	Rigby Literacy	Rigby
Teeny Tiny Taste, A	H	RF	112	City Stories	Rigby
Teeny-Tiny Woman, The	H	TL	231	Ziefert, Harriet	Puffin Books
Tell-tale	H	RF	250+	Story Box	Wright Group/McGraw Hill
Ten Little Garden Snails	H	F	101	PM Story Books	Rigby
Ten Traveling Tigers	H	F	165	Little Readers	Houghton Mifflin
Ten Yellow Buses	H	RF	146	Twig	Wright Group/McGraw Hill
Ten, Nine, Eight	H	RF	59	Bang, Molly	Scholastic
That's Fair, Bear	H	F	250+	Sun Sprouts	ETA/Cuisenaire
Then and Now	H	I	250+	iOpeners	Pearson Learning Group
Thing in the Log, The	H	RF	81	Reading Unlimited	Pearson Learning Group
Things People Do for Fun	H	I	124	Foundations	Wright Group/McGraw Hill
This Old Car	H	RF	79	Voyages	SRA/McGraw Hill

* Collection of short stories

TITLE	LEVEL	GENRE	WORD COUNT	AUTHOR / SERIES	PUBLISHER / DISTRIBUTOR
Three Billy Goats Gruff, The	H	TL	250+	New Way Green	Steck-Vaughn
Three Little Kittens	H	TL	164	Ready Readers	Pearson Learning Group
Three Little Pigs	H	TL	39	Hunia, Fran	Ladybird Books
Three Little Pigs, The	H	TL	392	New Way Blue	Steck-Vaughn
Three Little Pigs, The	H	TL	276+	Reading Unlimited	Pearson Learning Group
Three Little Pigs, The	H	TL	346	Reading Corners	Pearson Learning Group
Three Silly Cowboys, The	H	F	213	Ready Readers	Pearson Learning Group
Three Wishes	H	TL	250+	Ready Readers	Pearson Learning Group
Three-Legged Race, The	H	RF	202	Windmill Books	Rigby
Tic-Tac-Toe Three in a Row	H	RF	132	Stamper, Judith Bauer	Scholastic
Tiny Woman's Coat, The	H	F	147	Sunshine	Wright Group/McGraw Hill
Tiptoe Round the Corner	H	F	96	Voyages	SRA/McGraw Hill
Tommy Snake's Problem	H	F	328	TOTTS	Tott Publications
Too Many Nuts	H	RF	132	Books for Young Learners	Richard C. Owen
Too Much Noise	H	TL	340	Literacy 2000	Rigby
Tool Box, The	H	RF	144	Rockwell, Anne	Macmillan
Tornado Tony	H	RF	182	Well-Being Series	Pearson Learning Group
Tortoise and the Hare,The	H	TL	148	Cambridge Reading	Pearson Learning Group
Toy Trouble	H	F	250+	Bookshop	Mondo
Traffic Light Sandwich	H	I	87	Wonder World	Wright Group/McGraw Hill
Trash	H	F	130	Sunshine	Wright Group/McGraw Hill
Tree Fort, The	H	RF	160	Early Transitional, Set 2	Pioneer Valley
Tree Horse, A	H	RF	220	PM Plus Story Books	Rigby
Tree is a Home, A	H	I	203	Learn to Read	Creative Teaching Press
Trees	H	I	28	Sun Sprouts	ETA/Cuisenaire
Trees	H	I	194	Momentum Literacy Program	Troll Associates
Tricky Sticky Problem, The	H	RF	71	Pacific Literacy	Pacific Learning
Trip into Space, A	H	I	79	Story Steps	Rigby
Trip to the Park, The	H	RF	277	Foundations	Wright Group/McGraw Hill
Trip to the Video Store, A	H	RF	203	Foundations	Wright Group/McGraw Hill
Troll Tricks	H	TL	250+	Phonics Readers	Scholastic
Turtle Nest	H	I	85	Books for Young Learners	Richard C. Owen
Twins	H	I	113	Vocabulary Readers	Houghton Mifflin
Twins, The	H	RF	250+	Early Transitional, Set 1	Pioneer Valley
Two Bear Cubs	H	F	89	Jonas, Ann	Morrow
Uncle Carlos's Barbecue	H	RF	207	Foundations	Wright Group/McGraw Hill
Uncle Joe	H	F	149	Pacific Literacy	Pacific Learning
Uncle's Bakery	H	RF	81	Early Reader	Compass Point Books
Under a Microscope	H	I	254	Sunshine	Wright Group/McGraw Hill
Unusual Show, An	H	F	63	Blonder, Ellen	Scholastic
Up the Haystack	H	RF	251	Bookshop	Mondo
Using a Microscope	H	I	182	Rigby Focus	Rigby
Very Big Potato, The	H	RF	250+	Cherrington, Janelle	Scholastic
Very Funny Act, A	H	RF	181	Home Connection Collection	Rigby
Very Greedy Dog, The	H	TL	228	Aesop's Fables	Pearson Learning Group
Vibrations	H	I	38	Pebble Books	Red Brick Learning
Victor and the Martian	H	F	109	Oxford Reading Tree	Oxford University Press
Victor and the Sail-cart	H	F	94	Oxford Reading Tree	Oxford University Press
Victor Makes a TV	H	F	85	Reading Unlimited	Pearson Learning Group
Victor the Hero	H	F	103	Oxford Reading Tree	Oxford University Press
Visit to the Airport, A	H	I	105	Pebble Plus	Red Brick Learning
Visit to the Apple Orchards, A	H	I	114	Pebble Plus	Red Brick Learning
Visit to the Dentist's Office, A	H	I	116	Pebble Plus	Red Brick Learning
Visiting the Vet	H	I	140	Sun Sprouts	ETA/Cuisenaire

* Collection of short stories

TITLE	LEVEL	GENRE	WORD COUNT	AUTHOR / SERIES	PUBLISHER / DISTRIBUTOR
Visiting the Vet	H	I	259	Foundations	Wright Group/McGraw Hill
Voyage of Mae Jemison, The	H	B	46	Canizares, Susan; Berger, Samantha	Scholastic
Wagon, The	H	RF	78	Reading Unlimited	Pearson Learning Group
Wait for Your Turn!	H	RF	141	Teacher's Choice Series	Pearson Learning Group
Walking in the Autumn	H	I	206	PM Nonfiction-Green	Rigby
Walking in the Spring	H	I	168	PM Nonfiction-Green	Rigby
Walking in the Summer	H	I	233	PM Nonfiction-Green	Rigby
Walking in the Winter	H	I	251	PM Nonfiction-Green	Rigby
Walking the Dogs	H	RF	80	City Stories	Rigby
Washing Our Dog	H	RF	120	Alphakids	Sundance
Water	H	I	94	Wonder World	Wright Group/McGraw Hill
Water, Land, and Air	H	I	76	Windows on Literacy	National Geographic
Waving Sheep, The	H	F	252	PM Story Books	Rigby
We Are Best Friends	H	RF	629	Aliki	Morrow
We Can Share It	H	F	140	Little Celebrations	Pearson Learning Group
We Honor America	H	I	132	Rosen Real Readers	Rosen Publishing Group
We Need Zoo Keepers	H	I	72	Helpers in Our Community	Red Brick Learning
We Need Dentists	H	I	54	Pebble Books	Red Brick Learning
We Need Doctors	H	I	42	Pebble Books	Red Brick Learning
We Need Farmers	H	I	45	Pebble Books	Red Brick Learning
We Need Nurses	H	I	65	Pebble Books	Red Brick Learning
We Wrote to Grandma	H	RF	239	Momentum Literacy Program	Troll Associates
Weather Today	H	RF	129	Windows on Literacy	National Geographic
Wee Whopper	H	F	181	Windmill Books	Rigby
Week, A	H	I	115	The Calendar	Capstone Press
We're a Team!	H	RF	100	City Stories	Rigby
We're Going on a Picnic	H	RF	250+	Cambridge Reading	Pearson Learning Group
Wet Grass	H	RF	188	Story Box	Wright Group/McGraw Hill
What a Dog!	H	RF	223	Story Basket	Wright Group/McGraw Hill
What a Waste	H	I	180	Sun Sprouts	ETA/Cuisenaire
What About Bennie?	H	RF	124	Literacy Tree	Rigby
What Am I Going to Be?	H	RF	111	Storyteller-Moon Rising	Wright Group/McGraw Hill
What Animal Lives Here?	H	I	250+	Woolley, M.; Pigdon, K.	Mondo
What Are Purple Elephants Good For?	H	F	136	Reading Corners	Pearson Learning Group
What Came Out of My Bean?	H	RF	158	Book Bank	Wright Group/McGraw Hill
What Can I Do?	H	I	250+	Greetings	Rigby
What Can You Measure With a Lollipop?	H	I	159	Early Connections	Benchmark Education
What Do Scientists Do?	H	I	79	Discovery Links	Newbridge
What Game Shall We Play?	H	F	306	Hutchins, Pat	Sundance
What Gives You Goose Bumps?	H	RF	140	Home Connection Collection	Rigby
What Has Wings?	H	RF	250+	Momentum Literacy Program	Troll Associates
What Is a Bird?	H	I	71	Pebble Books	Red Brick Learning
What Is a Fish?	H	I	77	Pebble Books	Red Brick Learning
What is a Map?	H	I	250+	Yellow Umbrella Books	Red Brick Learning
What Is a Park?	H	I	138	Discovery World	Rigby
What Is a Rainbow?	H	I	115	Rosen Real Readers	Rosen Publishing Group
What is an Elephant?	H	TL	165	Story Box	Wright Group/McGraw Hill
What Is an Insect?	H	I	57	Pebble Books	Red Brick Learning
What Is the Weather Today?	H	I	250+	Momentum Literacy Program	Troll Associates
What Makes Me Healthy?	H	I	132	Windows on Literacy	National Geographic
What People Do	H	I	148	Little Red Readers	Sundance
What Will the Weather Be?	H	I	207	Rigby Literacy	Rigby
Whatever Will These Become?	H	I	47	Literacy Tree	Rigby

* Collection of short stories

TITLE	LEVEL	GENRE	WORD COUNT	AUTHOR / SERIES	PUBLISHER / DISTRIBUTOR
What's Around the Corner?	H	RF	90	Literacy Tree	Rigby
What's Cooking?	H	RF	287	Bookshop	Mondo
What's for Lunch?	H	F	169	Ready Readers	Pearson Learning Group
What's Inside?	H	I	138	Windows on Literacy	National Geographic
What's New at the Zoo?	H	F	151	Instant Readers	Harcourt School Publishers
What's That Smell?	H	RF	56	Pacific Literacy	Pacific Learning
What's Under the Ocean	H	I	108	Now I Know	Troll Associates
Wheelbarrow Garden, The	H	RF	231	PM Plus Story Books	Rigby
When Dad Went Fishing	H	RF	250+	Cambridge Reading	Pearson Learning Group
When Dad Went to Daycare	H	RF	211	Sunshine	Wright Group/McGraw Hill
When Robins Sing	H	I	238	Twig	Wright Group/McGraw Hill
When the TV Broke	H	RF	209	Ziefert, Harriet	Puffin Books
Where Are You Going, Little Mouse?	H	F	148	Kraus, Robert	Greenwillow
Where Does Breakfast Come From?	H	I	170	Discovery World	Rigby
Where Is My Caterpillar?	H	F	277	Wonder World	Wright Group/McGraw Hill
Where is my Spider?	H	RF	225	Story Box	Wright Group/McGraw Hill
Where Is the Queen?	H	F	109	Ready Readers	Pearson Learning Group
Whistle Tooth, The	H	RF	188	Storyteller-Night Crickets	Wright Group/McGraw Hill
White Wednesday	H	RF	321	Literacy 2000	Rigby
Who Stole the Fish?	H	F	250+	Cambridge Reading	Pearson Learning Group
Who Wears This Hat?	H	I	139	Windows on Literacy	National Geographic
Who Will Use This?	H	I	154	Rigby Literacy	Rigby
Who's Looking After the Baby?	H	RF	127	Foundations	Wright Group/McGraw Hill
Whose Mouse Are You?	H	F	98	Kraus, Robert	Macmillan
Wibble Wobble, Albatross!	H	I	101	Pacific Literacy	Pacific Learning
Wibble-Wobble	H	RF	263	Storyteller-Night Crickets	Wright Group/McGraw Hill
Wiggle and Giggle	H	RF	163	Cambridge Reading	Pearson Learning Group
Wilbert Took a Walk	H	F	216	Ready Readers	Pearson Learning Group
Wild Wind, The	H	F	246	Story Box	Wright Group/McGraw Hill
Will It Rain on the Parade?	H	RF	102	Wonder World	Wright Group/McGraw Hill
Winter	H	I	172	Storyteller-Setting Sun	Wright Group/McGraw Hill
Winter Wind, The	H	F	250+	Momentum Literacy Program	Troll Associates
Winter's Song	H	RF	233	Ready Readers	Pearson Learning Group
Wishing for Fishing	H	RF	250+	Phonics Readers Plus	Steck-Vaughn
Wolf Talk	H	I	159	Instant Readers	Harcourt School Publishers
World's Biggest Baby, The	H	I	239	Ready Readers	Pearson Learning Group
Worm Rap	H	F	251	Alphakids	Sundance
Year, A	H	I	137	The Calendar	Capstone Press
Yes Ma'am	H	RF	125	Story Box	Wright Group/McGraw Hill
You Do Ride Well	H	RF	165	Windmill Books	Rigby
You Might Fall	H	RF	180	Stepping Stones	Nelson/Michaels Assoc.
You'll Roar	H	F	73	Instant Readers	Harcourt School Publishers
You'll Soon Grow into Them Titch	H	RF	191	Hutchins, Pat	Morrow
Your Senses	H	I	138	Pebble Books	Red Brick Learning
You're So Clever	H	RF	188	Voyages	SRA/McGraw Hill
Zack and Nate	H	RF	250+	Early Emergent, Set 2	Pioneer Valley
Zebras	H	I	78	Seedlings	Continental Press
Zoo Party, A	H	RF	134	Book Bank	Wright Group/McGraw Hill
2 of Everything	I	RF	217	Talking Point Series	Pearson Learning Group
3-2-1 Blast-Off	I	RF	291	Talking Point Series	Pearson Learning Group
7 Facts About the Weather	I	I	231	Leveled Readers Science	Houghton Mifflin
About 100 Years Ago	I	I	250+	Yellow Umbrella Books	Red Brick Learning
Adding Arctic Animals	I	I	120	Yellow Umbrella Books	Red Brick Learning
Airport	I	I	116	Barton, Byron	HarperCollins

* Collection of short stories

TITLE	LEVEL	GENRE	WORD COUNT	AUTHOR / SERIES	PUBLISHER / DISTRIBUTOR
Albert the Albatross	I	F	191	Hoff, Syd	HarperCollins
All Kinds of Eyes	I	I	128	Pacific Literacy	Pacific Learning
All Tutus Should Be Pink	I	RF	243	Brownrigg, Sheri	Scholastic
Amazing Earthworm, The	I	I	169	Leveled Readers Language Support	Houghton Mifflin
Ambulance	I	I	116	Pebble Books	Capstone Press
Anansi's Narrow Waist	I	TL	157	Little Celebrations	Pearson Learning Group
And Billy Went Out to Play	I	RF	227	Bookshop	Mondo
Angelina Trueheart and the Fox	I	RF	228	Voyages	SRA/McGraw Hill
Angus and the Cat	I	F	250+	Flack, Marjorie	Viking
Animal Actions	I	I	190	Home Connection Collection	Rigby
Animal Armor	I	I	155	Windows on Literacy	National Geographic
Animal Builders	I	I	148	Little Celebrations	Pearson Learning Group
Animal Ears	I	I	250+	Yellow Umbrella Books	Red Brick Learning
Animal Feet	I	I	166	Rigby Literacy	Rigby
Animal Fibers	I	I	440	Science	Wright Group/McGraw Hill
Animal Groups	I	I	265	Early Connections	Benchmark Education
Animal Messengers	I	I	116	Discovery Links	Newbridge
Animal Neighbors	I	I	250	Vocabulary Readers	Houghton Mifflin
Animals at Night	I	I	215	First Start	Troll Associates
Animals at School	I	I	250+	Early Transitional, Set 1	Pioneer Valley
Animals Grow	I	I	152	Wonder World	Wright Group/McGraw Hill
Anna's Tree	I	RF	213	Windmill Books	Rigby
Ant and the Dove, The	I	TL	250+	PM Plus Story Books	Rigby
Ant and the Grasshopper, The	I	TL	231	Aesop's Fables	Pearson Learning Group
Ant and the Grasshopper, The: A Play	I	TL	250+	Literacy Tree	Rigby
Apple Tree	I	RF	110	Book Bank	Wright Group/McGraw Hill
Apples and Pumpkins	I	RF	185	Rockwell, Ann	Scholastic
April Who? April Fools	I	RF	197	Sunshine	Wright Group/McGraw Hill
Arctic Journey	I	I	198	Sunshine	Wright Group/McGraw Hill
Are They Look-Alikes?	I	I	194	Independent Readers Science	Houghton Mifflin
Are You My Mother?	I	F	250+	Eastman, Philip D.	Random House
Armando Asked, "Why?"	I	RF	250+	Ready Set Read	Steck-Vaughn
Astronauts	I	I	118	Phonics Readers	Compass Point Books
Astronauts	I	I	171	Wonder World	Wright Group/McGraw Hill
At the Lake	I	RF	176	Books for Young Learners	Richard C. Owen
At the Pet Store	I	I	177	Foundations	Wright Group/McGraw Hill
Atul's Christmas Hamster	I	I	250+	Cambridge Reading	Pearson Learning Group
Away Went the Hat	I	F	260	New Way Green	Steck-Vaughn
Baby Brother, The	I	RF	131	Voyages	SRA/McGraw Hill
Baby Monkey	I	F	250+	Reading Unlimited	Pearson Learning Group
Baby Writer	I	RF	182	Stepping Stones	Nelson/Michaels Assoc.
Backstage	I	I	250+	Twig	Wright Group/McGraw Hill
Balloons	I	I	211	Independent Readers Science	Houghton Mifflin
Barney's Horse	I	HF	250+	Hoff, Syd	HarperTrophy
Baron: Rescue Dog	I	RF	120	Books for Young Learners	Richard C. Owen
Baseball Game, The	I	F	211	Foundations	Wright Group/McGraw Hill
Basketball	I	I	159	Ready Readers	Pearson Learning Group
Bats	I	I	162	Phonics Readers	Compass Point Books
Bean Bag That Mom Made, The	I	RF	270	Tadpoles	Rigby
Bear's Bicycle, The	I	F	185	McLeod, Emilie	Little, Brown & Co.
Bears, Bears, Bears	I	F	250+	Little Readers	Houghton Mifflin
Because a Little Bug Went Ka-Choo	I	F	250+	Stone, Rosetta	Random House
Because Daddy Did My Hair	I	RF	214	Teacher's Choice Series	Pearson Learning Group

* Collection of short stories

TITLE	LEVEL	GENRE	WORD COUNT	AUTHOR / SERIES	PUBLISHER / DISTRIBUTOR
Ben and the Bear	I	F	250+	Riddell, Chris	Harper & Row
Ben Franklin's Fire Company	I	I	147	Leveled Readers Language Support	Houghton Mifflin
Benji's Pup	I	RF	439	Evangeline Nicholas Collection	Wright Group/McGraw Hill
Benny Bakes a Cake	I	RF	250+	Rice, Eve	Greenwillow
Bertie the Bear	I	F	250+	Allen, Pamela	Coward
Best Birthday Gift Ever, The	I	RF	249	Talking Point Series	Pearson Learning Group
Best Book for Terry Lee, The	I	RF	250+	Literacy Tree	Rigby
Best Car For Us, The	I	I	161	Windows on Literacy	National Geographic
Best Guess, The	I	RF	241	Foundations	Wright Group/McGraw Hill
Big Bad Rex	I	I	176	Erickson, Betty	Continental Press
Big Bad Wolf, The	I	RF	250+	PM Plus Story Books	Rigby
Big Bed, The	I	RF	346	Pacific Literacy	Pacific Learning
Big Dog, Little Dog	I	F	265	Eastman, Philip D.	Random House
Big Hungry Bear, The	I	F	148	Wood, Don & Audrey	Scholastic
Big Hush, The	I	RF	281	Story Box	Wright Group/McGraw Hill
Big Laugh, The	I	F	152	Sunshine	Wright Group/McGraw Hill
Big or Little?	I	RF	250+	Stinson, Kathy	Pearson Learning Group
Big Red Tomatoes	I	I	168	Windows on Literacy	National Geographic
Big Tease, The	I	RF	250+	Story Box	Wright Group/McGraw Hill
Big Tennis Match, A	I	I	122	Vocabulary Readers	Houghton Mifflin
Bigger Burger, A	I	RF	253	Story Box	Wright Group/McGraw Hill
Biggest Fish, The	I	RF	254	PM Story Books-Orange	Rigby
Bike For Alex, A	I	RF	250+	PM Plus Story Books	Rigby
Bike Lesson	I	F	250+	Berenstain, Stan & Jan	Random House
Bill	I	RF	166	Sunshine	Wright Group/McGraw Hill
Bird Barn, The	I	I	241	Foundations	Wright Group/McGraw Hill
Bird Beaks	I	I	180	Wonder World	Wright Group/McGraw Hill
Bird Race	I	TL	195	Leveled Readers	Houghton Mifflin
Bird Song	I	F	99	Storyteller-Night Crickets	Wright Group/McGraw Hill
Bird That Could Think, The	I	F	250+	PM Plus Story Books	Rigby
Birds, Bees, and Sailing Ships	I	F	243	Sunshine	Wright Group/McGraw Hill
Birthday Dog	I	RF	250+	Sunshine	Wright Group/McGraw Hill
Birthdays	I	I	147	Sunshine	Wright Group/McGraw Hill
Blossom's Babies	I	F	250+	Book Bus	Creative Edge
Blue Mittens, The	I	RF	250+	Mann, Rachel	Scholastic
Boards and More	I	RF	250+	Phonics Readers Plus	Steck-Vaughn
Body Parts Work Together	I	I	119	Instant Readers	Harcourt School Publishers
Boggywooga	I	F	274	Sunshine	Wright Group/McGraw Hill
Bogle's Feet	I	F	280	Sunshine	Wright Group/McGraw Hill
Bookstore Cat	I	RF	207	Little Readers	Houghton Mifflin
Boring Old Bed	I	RF	211	Sunshine	Wright Group/McGraw Hill
Boss For A Day	I	RF	250+	DePaola, Tomie	Grosset & Dunlap
Boy and the Wolf, The	I	TL	200	Book Bank	Wright Group/McGraw Hill
Boy Who Tried to Hide, The	I	TL	219	Storyteller-Night Crickets	Wright Group/McGraw Hill
Brave Little Mouse	I	F	249	Story Steps	Rigby
Breakfast for Bears	I	F	477	Leveled Readers	Houghton Mifflin
Broken Plate, The	I	RF	198	Foundations	Wright Group/McGraw Hill
Brownie Math	I	I	206	Rosen Real Readers	Rosen Publishing Group
Bubbles	I	RF	236	Leveled Readers Science	Houghton Mifflin
Buggy Riddles	I	F	221	Little Books	Sadlier-Oxford
Build Your Own Weather Station	I	I	250	Leveled Readers Science	Houghton Mifflin
Bulldozers	I	I	94	Pebble Plus	Capstone Press
Bumble Bees	I	I	123	Bugs, Bugs, Bugs	Capstone Press

* Collection of short stories

TITLE	LEVEL	GENRE	WORD COUNT	AUTHOR / SERIES	PUBLISHER / DISTRIBUTOR
Bun, The	I	TL	421	Storyteller-Moon Rising	Wright Group/McGraw Hill
Bunny Hop, The	I	F	250+	Slater, Teddy	Scholastic
Bunny Magic	I	RF	176	Books for Young Learners	Richard C. Owen
Busy Beavers, The	I	RF	362	PM Story Books-Orange	Rigby
Butterflies	I	I	94	Bugs, Bugs, Bugs	Capstone Press
Cabbage Caterpillar	I	F	221	Sunshine	Wright Group/McGraw Hill
Careful Crocodile, The	I	HF	271	PM Story Books-Orange	Rigby
Caring For Your Pets	I	I	175	Community Workers	Picture Window Books
Carla Gets a Pet	I	RF	250+	Ready Readers	Pearson Learning Group
Carla's Wheels	I	RF	200	Story Box	Wright Group/McGraw Hill
Carnivals Around the World	I	I	116	Lighthouse	Rigby
Cat and the Mice, The	I	F	526	Book Bank	Wright Group/McGraw Hill
Cat Came Back, The	I	TL	250+	Little Celebrations	Pearson Learning Group
Cat with No Tail, The	I	TL	137	Books for Young Learners	Richard C. Owen
Cats	I	I	137	Wonder World	Wright Group/McGraw Hill
Cat's Surprise Party	I	F	376	Leveled Readers	Houghton Mifflin
Cat's Whiskers, A	I	I	250+	Windows on Literacy	National Geographic
Celia and Ali	I	RF	137	Leveled Readers Language Support	Houghton Mifflin
Champ	I	RF	274	Story Box	Wright Group/McGraw Hill
Changes in Seasons	I	I	250+	Phonics Readers Plus	Steck-Vaughn
Changing Land, The	I	I	64	Pacific Literacy	Pacific Learning
Changing Shape	I	I	143	Rigby Literacy	Rigby
Charlie Needs a Cloak	I	HF	187	DePaola, Tomie	Prentice-Hall
Cherokee Little People, The: A Native American Tale	I	TL	250+	Rigby Literacy	Rigby
Chicken Licken	I	TL	346	Sunshine	Wright Group/McGraw Hill
Chicken Little	I	TL	250+	PM Traditional Tales-Orange	Rigby
Cinderella	I	TL	580	Traditional Tales	Pearson Learning Group
Circus Book, The	I	I	250+	Reading Unlimited	Pearson Learning Group
City Park, A	I	RF	59	Leveled Readers	Houghton Mifflin
Clap for the Show	I	RF	250+	Phonics and Friends	Hampton-Brown
Class Play with Ms. Vanilla, A	I	RF	234	Ehrlich, Fred	Puffin Books
Clay Creatures	I	I	213	Rigby Literacy	Rigby
Clean and Healthy	I	I	199	Rosen Real Readers	Rosen Publishing Group
Clean Beaches	I	I	155	Early Connections	Benchmark Education
Clean Out the Fridge, Fred	I	F	250+	Popcorn	Sundance
Cleaning My Room	I	I	189	Early Connections	Benchmark Education
Closet Under the Stairs, The	I	RF	214	Story Box	Wright Group/McGraw Hill
Clouds	I	I	249	Pebble Books	Capstone Press
Clucky	I	F	250+	PM Plus Story Books	Rigby
Clyde Klutter's Room	I	F	146	Sunshine	Wright Group/McGraw Hill
Cockroaches	I	I	60	Pebble Books	Red Brick Learning
Collecting Cones	I	I	127	Wonder World	Wright Group/McGraw Hill
Color of His Own, A	I	F	239	Lionni, Leo	Scholastic
Come and Have Fun	I	F	250+	Hurd, Edith Thacher	HarperCollins
Come Meet Some Seals	I	I	118	Little Books	Sadlier-Oxford
Communities	I	I	42	Yellow Umbrella Books	Red Brick Learning
Community Jobs	I	I	207	Early Connections	Benchmark Education
Computer Buttons	I	F	250+	Sunshine	Wright Group/McGraw Hill
Cooking Spaghetti	I	RF	150	City Kids	Rigby
Coral Reef, A	I	I	153	Rigby Focus	Rigby
Cowboy Jake	I	RF	174	Sunshine	Wright Group/McGraw Hill
Coyote Plants a Peach Tree	I	TL	233	Books for Young Learners	Richard C. Owen

* Collection of short stories

TITLE	LEVEL	GENRE	WORD COUNT	AUTHOR / SERIES	PUBLISHER / DISTRIBUTOR
Crabbing Time	I	RF	75	Books for Young Learners	Richard C. Owen
Crow and the Pitcher, The	I	TL	265	Aesop's Fables	Pearson Learning Group
Dad and the Mosquito	I	RF	246	Sunshine	Wright Group/McGraw Hill
Dalmatians	I	RF	70	Salem, Lynn	Continental Press
Dancin' Down	I	RF	193	Evangeline Nicholas Collection	Wright Group/McGraw Hill
Dancing Dragon, The	I	F	236	Bookshop	Mondo
Day at Rainbow Lake, A	I	I	250+	Phonics Readers Plus	Steck-Vaughn
Day I Tore My Shorts, The	I	RF	209	City Kids	Rigby
Day of the Dead, The	I	RF	250+	Greetings	Rigby
Day the Gorilla Came to School, The	I	RF	293	Sunshine	Wright Group/McGraw Hill
Definitely Different	I	RF	102	Voyages	SRA/McGraw Hill
Desert Animals	I	I	134	Spyglass Books	Compass Point Books
Different Faces from Different Places	I	I	148	Twig	Wright Group/McGraw Hill
Dig In	I	I	96	iOpeners	Pearson Learning Group
Digby	I	RF	250+	Little Readers	Houghton Mifflin
Dinosaur Chase, The	I	HF	240	PM Story Books-Orange	Rigby
Dinosaur Discovery	I	I	250+	Story Steps	Rigby
Dinosaur Who Lived in My Backyard, The	I	F	250+	Hennessy, Brendan G.	Scholastic
Dinosaurs & Other Reptiles	I	I	123	Planet Earth	Rigby
Dog From Outer Space, The	I	SF	250+	Lighthouse	Rigby
Dog School	I	RF	224	Story Steps	Rigby
Dogs	I	I	116	Hutchins, Pat	Wright Group/McGraw Hill
Dogs Love to Play Ball	I	F	159	Books for Young Learners	Richard C. Owen
Dogs on the Farm	I	I	85	Pebble Books	Red Brick Learning
Dog's Party	I	F	628	Leveled Readers	Houghton Mifflin
Dolphins	I	I	250+	Pebble Plus	Capstone Press
Dolphins	I	I	44	Pebble Books	Red Brick Learning
Don't Eat the Stick	I	F	250+	Sunshine	Wright Group/McGraw Hill
Don't Interrupt!	I	RF	225	Windmill Books	Rigby
Don't Let Ted Have Bubble Gum!	I	RF	250+	Phonics Readers Plus	Steck-Vaughn
Don't Stomp on That Bug	I	I	250+	Rigby Literacy	Rigby
Don't Throw Your Spinach	I	RF	155	Story Box	Wright Group/McGraw Hill
Don't Touch	I	RF	250+	Kline, Suzy	Penguin Group
Down by the Pond	I	I	118	Story Box	Wright Group/McGraw Hill
Down in the Woods	I	F	155	Storyteller-Moon Rising	Wright Group/McGraw Hill
Dragon	I	F	161	Pacific Literacy	Pacific Learning
Dragon Gets By	I	F	250+	Pilkey, Dave	Orchard Books
Dragon, The	I	F	250+	Story Box	Wright Group/McGraw Hill
*Dragonfly Dreams and Other Dreams	I	F	250+	Story Steps	Rigby
Dragon's Fat Cat	I	F	250+	Pilkey, Dave	Orchard Books
Dragon's Halloween	I	F	250+	Pilkey, Dave	Orchard Books
Dragon's Merry Christmas	I	F	250+	Pilkey, Dave	Orchard Books
Drat That Cat!	I	F	250+	Cambridge Reading	Pearson Learning Group
Dream Team, The	I	RF	250+	Lighthouse	Rigby
Dressing Up	I	RF	222	Stepping Stones	Nelson/Michaels Assoc.
Ducks on the Farm	I	I	91	Pebble Books	Red Brick Learning
Ducks on the Run	I	RF	250+	PM Plus Story Books	Rigby
Dump Trucks	I	I	119	Pebble Plus	Capstone Press
Eat Up, Gemma	I	RF	463	Hayes, Sarah	Sundance
Eating Lunch at School	I	RF	170	City Kids	Rigby
Eency Weency Spider	I	F	250+	Bank Street	Bantam
Elephant for the Holidays, An	I	F	118	Sunshine	Wright Group/McGraw Hill
Elephants	I	I	224	Foundations	Wright Group/McGraw Hill
Emily Loved Yellow	I	RF	99	Sunshine	Wright Group/McGraw Hill

* Collection of short stories

TITLE	LEVEL	GENRE	WORD COUNT	AUTHOR / SERIES	PUBLISHER / DISTRIBUTOR
Everyone Is a Scientist	I	I	197	Yellow Umbrella Books	Red Brick Learning
Exploring Space	I	I	250+	Sunshine Books	Wright Group/McGraw Hill
Families and Feasts	I	I	196	PM Plus Nonfiction	Rigby
Farm, The	I	I	228	Pebble Books	Capstone Press
Farmer and His Two Lazy Sons, The	I	TL	250+	Aesop's Fables	Pearson Learning Group
Fasi Sings and Fasi's Fish	I	RF	204	Pacific Literacy	Pacific Learning
Fast Food for Butterflies	I	I	170	Storyteller-Moon Rising	Wright Group/McGraw Hill
Fat Cat	I	TL	250+	Kent, Jack	Scholastic
Fat Cat Tompkin	I	F	196	Voyages	SRA/McGraw Hill
Fat Pig, The	I	TL	250+	Tiger Cub	Peguis
Father Bear Comes Home	I	F	331	Minarik, Else H.	HarperCollins
Fats, Oils, and Sweets	I	I	190	The Food Guide Pyramid	Capstone Press
Feathers and Flight	I	I	790	Sunshine	Wright Group/McGraw Hill
Feed Me! An Aesop Fable	I	TL	250+	Bank Street	Bantam
Fern's Purple Birthday	I	F	250+	Phonics Readers Plus	Steck-Vaughn
Fibers from Plants	I	I	392	Sunshine	Wright Group/McGraw Hill
Fight on the Hill, The	I	F	336	Read Alongs	Rigby
Finger Puppets, Finger Plays	I	I	268	Storyteller-Night Crickets	Wright Group/McGraw Hill
Fire at the Zoo, A	I	F	229	Sunshine	Wright Group/McGraw Hill
Fire Boats	I	I	188	Pebble Books	Capstone Press
Fire Engines	I	I	184	Pebble Books	Capstone Press
Fish from the Rainbow	I	F	239	Sunshine	Wright Group/McGraw Hill
Fishy Scales	I	F	107	Mathtales	Mimosa
Five Funny Uncles	I	RF	269	Story Box	Wright Group/McGraw Hill
Fix It	I	F	171	McPhail, David	Penguin Group
Flag For All, A	I	RF	250+	Rookie Choices	Children's Press
Flip, Flap, Flop	I	F	252	Sunshine	Wright Group/McGraw Hill
Flood, The	I	I	138	Wonder World	Wright Group/McGraw Hill
Fly Away Home	I	I	250+	Wonder World	Wright Group/McGraw Hill
Flyers	I	RF	250+	Rigby Literacy	Rigby
Flying Football, The	I	RF	250+	Cambridge Reading	Pearson Learning Group
Flying Saucer	I	RF	250+	Phonics Readers Plus	Steck-Vaughn
Follow Me!	I	F	250+	Ziefert, Harriet	Puffin Books
Follow the Applachian Trail	I	I	129	Leveled Readers Social Studies	Houghton Mifflin
Food Around the World	I	I	298	Early Connections	Benchmark Education
Food for Thought	I	I	250+	Yellow Umbrella Books	Red Brick Learning
Food Trappers	I	I	165	Wonder World	Wright Group/McGraw Hill
Fourth of July, The	I	I	153	Rosen Real Readers	Rosen Publishing Group
Fox and the Crow, The	I	TL	250+	Aesop's Fables	Pearson Learning Group
Fox Lives Here, A	I	I	160	Ready Readers	Pearson Learning Group
Fred Fixes a Faucet	I	F	250+	Popcorn	Sundance
Fred Goes Shopping	I	F	250+	Popcorn	Sundance
Fred Joins the Band	I	F	250+	Popcorn	Sundance
Fred's Big Lunch	I	F	250+	Popcorn	Sundance
Fred's Cold	I	F	250+	Popcorn	Sundance
Fred's Little Snack	I	F	250+	Popcorn	Sundance
Fred's Polka-Dot Sock	I	F	250+	Popcorn	Sundance
Fred's Weekend	I	F	250+	Popcorn	Sundance
Friend for Dragon, A	I	F	250+	Pilkey, Dave	Orchard Books
Friend for Kate, A	I	RF	250+	Cambridge Reading	Pearson Learning Group
Friendly Crocodile, The	I	F	218	Hiris, Monica	Kaeden Books
Friends	I	I	313	Early Connections	Benchmark Education
Friends Forever	I	TL	250+	Ready Readers	Pearson Learning Group
Friends Online	I	RF	318	Leveled Readers	Houghton Mifflin

* Collection of short stories

TITLE	LEVEL	GENRE	WORD COUNT	AUTHOR / SERIES	PUBLISHER / DISTRIBUTOR
Frog or Toad?	I	I	241	Ready Readers	Pearson Learning Group
Frog Prince, The	I	TL	250+	Jumbled Tumbled Tales & Rhymes	Rigby
Frog Prince, The	I	TL	572	Traditional Tales	Pearson Learning Group
Froggy Tale, A	I	F	250+	Literacy 2000	Rigby
From Acorn to Oak Tree	I	I	199	Welcome Books	Children's Press
From Field to Florist	I	I	142	Windows on Literacy	National Geographic
Fun Things to Make and Do	I	I	250+	Discovery World	Rigby
Funny Talk and More	I	F	250+	Bookshop	Mondo
Gardens on Green Street, The	I	RF	174	TOTTS	Tott Publications
Geese on the Farm	I	I	69	On the Farm	Red Brick Learning
Geraldine's Big Snow	I	RF	250+	Keller, Holly	Scholastic
Get-Up Machine, The	I	F	115	Sunshine	Wright Group/McGraw Hill
Ghost and the Sausage, The	I	F	250+	Story Box	Wright Group/McGraw Hill
Giant Bugs Were Real!	I	I	54	Seedlings	Continental Press
Giant Pandas: Gifts from China	I	I	250+	Rookie Read-About Science	Children's Press
Giant -Sized Day, A	I	F	245	Ready Readers	Pearson Learning Group
Giant's Stew, The	I	F	259	Sunshine	Wright Group/McGraw Hill
Giddyoocha	I	F	297	Story Box	Wright Group/McGraw Hill
Ginger	I	RF	232	Little Readers	Houghton Mifflin
Gingerbread Man	I	TL	250+	Hunia, Fran	Ladybird Books
Gingerbread Man, The	I	TL	180	Rose, Rita	Scholastic
Gingerbread Man, The	I	TL	544	Traditional Tales	Pearson Learning Group
Gingerbread Man, The	I	TL	250+	Tiger Cub	Peguis
Go Away Dog	I	RF	250+	Nodset, Joan	HarperCollins
Goats in the Turnip Field, The	I	TL	250+	PM Plus Story Books	Rigby
Goats on the Farm	I	I	67	Pebble Books	Red Brick Learning
Goha and His Donkey	I	F	114	Books for Young Learners	Richard C. Owen
Going Fishing	I	I	161	Windows on Literacy	National Geographic
Going Fishing	I	RF	250+	Momentum Literacy Program	Troll Associates
Going on a Field Trip	I	RF	288	Visions	Wright Group/McGraw Hill
Going to a Football Game	I	RF	131	City Kids	Rigby
Going to Grandma's	I	RF	250+	Read by Reading	Scholastic
Goldilocks	I	TL	250+	Jumbled Tumbled Tales & Rhymes	Rigby
Good Knee for a Cat, A	I	RF	205	Pacific Literacy	Pacific Learning
Good Luck Elephant	I	F	171	Sunshine	Wright Group/McGraw Hill
Good News	I	TL	250+	Brenner, Barbara	Bantam
Goodbye Gabby	I	RF	400	Early Transitional, Set 1	Pioneer Valley
Goodness Gracious	I	I	190	Literacy 2000	Rigby
Goodnight, Owl	I	F	181	Hutchins, Pat	Aladdin
Goodnight, Owl!	I	F	196	Hutchins, Pat	Macmillan
Gorillas	I	I	185	Stewart, Josie	Continental Press
Gracie's Cat	I	RF	250+	Cambridge Reading	Pearson Learning Group
Graffiti	I	RF	168	Sunshine	Wright Group/McGraw Hill
Grandfather's Mask	I	RF	245	Leveled Readers Language Support	Houghton Mifflin
Grandma Carol's Plant	I	RF	250+	Home Connection Collection	Rigby
Grandma J	I	RF	170	Instant Readers	Harcourt School Publishers
Grandma Moves In	I	RF	250+	Greetings	Rigby
Grandparents Are Great	I	I	257	Leveled Readers	Houghton Mifflin
Grandpa's Special Present	I	RF	286	Foundations	Wright Group/McGraw Hill
Great Pumpkin, The	I	F	239	Sunshine	Wright Group/McGraw Hill
Great Snakes!	I	I	161	Robinson, Fay	Scholastic
Green Dragon, The	I	F	131	Sunshine	Wright Group/McGraw Hill
Gregory, the Mean Dragon	I	F	250+	Phonics and Friends	Hampton-Brown

* Collection of short stories

TITLE	LEVEL	GENRE	WORD COUNT	AUTHOR / SERIES	PUBLISHER / DISTRIBUTOR
Griffin, the School Cat	I	RF	160	Sunshine	Wright Group/McGraw Hill
Grizzly and the Bumble-Bee	I	F	183	Sunshine	Wright Group/McGraw Hill
Grizzwold	I	F	250+	Hoff, Syd	HarperTrophy
Growing Older	I	I	216	Early Connections	Benchmark Education
Growing Radishes and Carrots	I	I	125	Bookshop	Mondo
Gruff Brothers, The	I	TL	250+	Hooks, William H.	Bantam
Guess What Today Is?	I	F	250+	Popcorn	Sundance
Guinea Pig Grass	I	RF	140	Literacy 2000	Rigby
Gumby Shop, The	I	F	359	Read Alongs	Rigby
Hannah	I	RF	250+	Stepping Stones	Nelson/Michaels Assoc.
Hanna's Butterfly	I	RF	158	Start to Read	School Zone
Hanukkah Party, The	I	RF	250+	Early Transitional, Set 1	Pioneer Valley
Happy and Sad	I	F	232	Sunshine	Wright Group/McGraw Hill
Happy Birthday, Duckling	I	I	154	Literacy Tree	Rigby
Happy Birthday, Sam	I	RF	213	Hutchins, Pat	Greenwillow
Happy Birthday, Sam!	I	RF	258	Leveled Readers	Houghton Mifflin
Happy Café, The	I	RF	238	Story Box	Wright Group/McGraw Hill
Happy Endings	I	F	213	Sunshine	Wright Group/McGraw Hill
Hare's Big Tug-of-War	I	TL	207	Instant Readers	Harcourt School Publishers
Hattie and the Fox	I	TL	321	Fox, Mem	Bradbury/Trumpet
Having My Hair Washed	I	RF	171	City Kids	Rigby
Healthy Food	I	I	162	PM Plus Nonfiction	Rigby
Heat	I	I	203	Early Connections	Benchmark Education
Hedgehog Day	I	I	121	Seedlings	Continental Press
Hello, Cat: You Need a Hat	I	F	250+	Gelman, Rita	Scholastic
Hello, First Grade	I	RF	250+	Ryder, Joanne	Troll Associates
Hen, The Rooster, and the Bean, The	I	TL	250+	Kratky, Lada Josefa	Hampton-Brown
Henny Penny	I	TL	582	Galdone, Paul	Clarion
Henny Penny	I	TL	250+	Zimmerman, H. Werner	Scholastic
Henry's New Friend	I	RF	250+	Leveled Readers Language Support	Houghton Mifflin
Here Comes the Strikeout	I	RF	250+	Little Readers	Houghton Mifflin
Herman Henry's Dog	I	F	250+	Little Readers	Houghton Mifflin
Hiccups	I	F	250+	Bookshop	Mondo
Hiccups for Elephant	I	F	250+	Preller, James	Scholastic
Hiccups for Hippo	I	F	100	Sunshine	Wright Group/McGraw Hill
Hide and Seek	I	I	250+	Phonics and Friends	Hampton-Brown
Hide-and-Seek All Week	I	RF	250+	DePaola, Tomie	Grosset & Dunlap
Hiding in Plain Sight	I	I	173	Instant Readers	Harcourt School Publishers
Hoketichee and the Manatee	I	RF	113	Books for Young Learners	Richard C. Owen
Hole in Harry's Pocket, The	I	RF	250+	Little Readers	Houghton Mifflin
Holidays at Our Home	I	RF	88	Leveled Readers Social Studies	Houghton Mifflin
Homes	I	I	244	Yellow Umbrella Books	Red Brick Learning
Homes Around the World	I	I	192	Rigby Focus	Rigby
Horns, Scales, Claws, and Tales	I	I	208	Story Steps	Rigby
*Horse and the Donkey, The	I	F	382	New Way Green	Steck-Vaughn
Horses on the Farm	I	I	120	Pebble Books	Red Brick Learning
Hot Dogs	I	RF	196	City Kids	Rigby
House that Jack Built, The	I	TL	201	Cat on the Mat	Oxford University Press
Houses	I	I	103	Windows on Literacy	National Geographic
How a Frog Grows	I	I	136	Phonics Readers	Compass Point Books
How Ants Live	I	I	159	Sunshine	Wright Group/McGraw Hill
How Are Magnets Used?	I	I	166	Windows on Literacy	National Geographic
How Birds Live	I	I	1090	Sunshine	Wright Group/McGraw Hill

TITLE	LEVEL	GENRE	WORD COUNT	AUTHOR / SERIES	PUBLISHER / DISTRIBUTOR
How Do Animals Stay Alive?	I	I	193	Early Connections	Benchmark Education
How Do Fish Live?	I	I	1242	Sunshine	Wright Group/McGraw Hill
How Does a Plant Grow?	I	I	115	Instant Readers	Harcourt School Publishers
How Flies Live	I	I	448	Sunshine	Wright Group/McGraw Hill
How Many Are Left?	I	I	225	Early Connections	Benchmark Education
How My Pet Grew	I	RF	235	Leveled Readers Science	Houghton Mifflin
How Owl Changed His Hoot	I	TL	227	Sunshine	Wright Group/McGraw Hill
How the Mouse Got Brown Teeth	I	F	250+	Bookshop	Mondo
How to Ride a Giraffe	I	F	191	Little Readers	Houghton Mifflin
Humongous Cat, The	I	F	250+	Sunshine	Wright Group/McGraw Hill
Hundred Hugs, A	I	F	229	Sunshine	Wright Group/McGraw Hill
Hungry Monster	I	F	241	Story Box	Wright Group/McGraw Hill
Hungry Sea Star, The	I	I	69	Books for Young Learners	Richard C. Owen
Hungry, Hungry Jack	I	RF	173	Lighthouse	Rigby
Hut in the Old Tree, The	I	RF	250+	PM Plus Story Books	Rigby
I Am a Star	I	I	195	Marzollo, Jean	Scholastic
I Bought My Lunch Today	I	I	90	City Kids	Rigby
I Can Do It	I	RF	200	Bookshop	Mondo
I Did That!	I	RF	250+	Momentum Literacy Program	Troll Associates
I Have a Paper Route	I	I	90	City Kids	Rigby
I Know That!	I	I	99	Sunshine	Wright Group/McGraw Hill
I Live in an Apartment Building	I	I	111	City Kids	Rigby
I Love Cats	I	RF	104	Bookshop	Mondo
I Ride the Waves	I	RF	61	Books for Young Learners	Richard C. Owen
I Spy a Fly	I	I	132	Wonder World	Wright Group/McGraw Hill
I Want to Be an Astronaut	I	RF	79	Barton, Byron	HarperCollins
I Want to Go Camping	I	RF	407	Leveled Readers	Houghton Mifflin
I Write for the Newspaper	I	I	145	Rosen Real Readers	Rosen Publishing Group
Ice	I	I	92	Windows on Literacy	National Geographic
Ice-Cream Factory, The	I	I	250+	Rigby Literacy	Rigby
If I Were an Ant	I	F	51	Rookie Readers	Children's Press
In My Garden	I	I	250+	Momentum Literacy Program	Troll Associates
In the Middle of the Night	I	RF	250+	Sunshine	Wright Group/McGraw Hill
Independence Hall	I	I	77	Leveled Readers	Houghton Mifflin
Invisible	I	F	111	Read Alongs	Rigby
Is the Wise Owl Wise?	I	F	250+	Rigby Literacy	Rigby
Is This My Dinner?	I	F	162	Black/Fry	Whitman
It Is Halloween!	I	RF	250+	Appleton-Smith, Laura	Flyleaf Publishing
It's Not Easy Being a Bunny	I	F	250+	Sadler, Marilyn	Random House
It's Not the Same	I	RF	250+	Sunshine	Wright Group/McGraw Hill
Jack & the Beanstalk	I	TL	250+	Literacy 2000	Rigby
Jack and Chug	I	F	337	PM Story Books-Orange	Rigby
Jack and the Beanstalk	I	TL	250+	Literacy 2000	Rigby
Jack in the Box	I	F	250+	Storybox	Wright Group/McGraw Hill
Jack's Boat	I	I	172	Windows on Literacy	National Geographic
Jackson's Monster	I	F	250+	Little Readers	Houghton Mifflin
Jamall's City Garden	I	I	250+	Rigby Literacy	Rigby
Jeff's Magnets	I	I	168	Instant Readers	Harcourt School Publishers
Jellyfish	I	I	58	Pebble Books	Red Brick Learning
Jennifer Pockets	I	RF	205	Book Bank	Wright Group/McGraw Hill
Jen's Best Gift Ever	I	RF	250+	Appleton-Smith, Laura	Flyleaf Publishing
Jessica in the Dark	I	RF	362	PM Story Books-Orange	Rigby
Jim Meets the Thing	I	F	250+	Cohen, Miriam	Bantam
Job for Giant Jim, A	I	RF	298	Sunshine	Wright Group/McGraw Hill

* Collection of short stories

TITLE	LEVEL	GENRE	WORD COUNT	AUTHOR / SERIES	PUBLISHER / DISTRIBUTOR
Jobs	I	I	112	Canizares, Susan; Chessen, Betsey	Scholastic
Joe's Pizza Parlor	I	RF	113	City Stories	Rigby
Jordan at the Big Game	I	RF	250+	PM Plus Story Books	Rigby
Josie Cleans Up	I	RF	213	Little Readers	Houghton Mifflin
Jump, Jump, Jump	I	F	236	Sunshine	Wright Group/McGraw Hill
Juno Loves Barney	I	RF	249	Voyages	SRA/McGraw Hill
Just a Mess	I	F	206	Mayer, Mercer	Donovan
Just Grandma and Me	I	F	186	Mayer, Mercer	Donovan
Just Like Everyone Else	I	RF	250+	Kuskin, Karla	HarperCollins
Just One Fish Would Do	I	RF	250+	Home Connection Collection	Rigby
Just One Guinea Pig	I	RF	339	PM Story Books-Orange	Rigby
Keeping Water Clean	I	I	117	Pebble Books	Red Brick Learning
Keeping You Healthy	I	I	185	Community Workers	Picture Window Books
Keeping You Safe: Book About Police Officers, A	I	I	112	Community Workers	Picture Window Books
Kids at Our School	I	RF	107	City Kids	Rigby
Kind Child, The	I	RF	250+	Hechinger, Nancy	Scholastic
King's Pudding, The	I	F	214	Literacy Tree	Rigby
Kite and the Butterflies, The	I	F	364	Book Bank	Wright Group/McGraw Hill
Kite That Got Away, The	I	RF	250+	PM Plus Story Books	Rigby
Knobby Knuckles, Knobby Knees	I	F	236	Sunshine	Wright Group/McGraw Hill
Laughing Hyena	I	F	250+	Lighthouse	Rigby
Lazy Fox	I	F	268	Leveled Readers	Houghton Mifflin
Learning About the Library	I	I	164	Rosen Real Readers	Rosen Publishing Group
Learning to Swim	I	RF	234	My World	Steck-Vaughn
Leaves	I	I	250+	Momentum Literacy Program	Troll Associates
Leo the Late Bloomer	I	F	164	Kraus, Robert	Simon & Schuster
Lester's Haircut	I	F	250+	Lester the Lion Series	Pioneer Valley
*Let Me In	I	TL	1814	Story Box	Wright Group/McGraw Hill
Let's Go Rock Climbing!	I	I	128	Vocabulary Readers	Houghton Mifflin
Let's Go to the Bank	I	I	233	Rosen Real Readers	Rosen Publishing Group
Let's Go to the Supermarket	I	I	198	Rosen Real Readers	Rosen Publishing Group
Let's Look at Rocks	I	I	186	Yellow Umbrella Books	Red Brick Learning
Let's Make Butter	I	I	224	Yellow Umbrella Books	Red Brick Learning
Liar, Liar Pants on Fire	I	RF	250+	Cohen, Miriam	Bantam
Licken Chicken	I	TL	250+	Tiger Cub	Peguis
Lid, The	I	F	111	Books for Young Learners	Richard C. Owen
Life in the Mangroves	I	I	172	Home Connection Collection	Rigby
Lift-Off!	I	SF	141	Pacific Literacy	Pacific Learning
Lighthouse Children, The	I	F	250+	Hoff, Syd	HarperTrophy
Lillian the Librarian	I	RF	315	Seedlings	Continental Press
Lion and the Mouse, The	I	TL	499	Aesop's Fables	Pearson Learning Group
Lion Roars, The	I	RF	270	Ready Readers	Pearson Learning Group
Lion Talk	I	I	216	Storyteller-Night Crickets	Wright Group/McGraw Hill
Lions and the Water Buffaloes, The	I	RF	250+	PM Plus Story Books	Rigby
Little Blue Horse, The	I	RF	250+	PM Plus Story Books	Rigby
Little Chick's Friend Duckling	I	F	572	Kwitz, Mary Deball	HarperTrophy
Little Critters	I	RF	127	Books for Young Learners	Richard C. Owen
Little Fish that Got Away	I	F	250+	Cook, Bernadine	Scholastic
Little Girl and Her Beetle, The	I	TL	250+	Literacy 2000	Rigby
Little House, The	I	TL	391	Pacific Literacy	Pacific Learning
Little Monkey	I	F	250+	Alphakids	Sundance
Little Mouse's Trail Tale	I	F	250+	Bookshop	Mondo
Little Puppy Rap	I	F	211	Sunshine	Wright Group/McGraw Hill
Little Red and the Wolf	I	TL	316	Pair-It Books	Steck-Vaughn

* Collection of short stories

TITLE	LEVEL	GENRE	WORD COUNT	AUTHOR / SERIES	PUBLISHER / DISTRIBUTOR
Little Red Hen	I	TL	250+	Hunia, Fran	Ladybird Books
Little Red Hen, The	I	TL	250+	PM Traditional Tales Orange	Rigby
Little Red Hen, The	I	TL	250+	Literacy 2000	Rigby
Little Red Hen, The	I	TL	226	Sunshine	Wright Group/McGraw Hill
Little Red Riding Hood	I	TL	250+	Jumbled Tumbled Tales & Rhymes	Rigby
Little Tuppen	I	TL	250+	Galdone, Paul	Houghton Mifflin
Little Work Plane, The	I	F	250+	PM Plus Story Books	Rigby
Little Yellow Chicken, The	I	F	322	Sunshine	Wright Group/McGraw Hill
Lizzie's Lunch	I	-F	118	Literacy Tree	Rigby
Lobster Fishing at Dawn	I	I	194	Ready Readers	Pearson Learning Group
Long and Short	I	F	228	Sunshine	Wright Group/McGraw Hill
Look Out!	I	RF	250+	PM Plus Story Books	Rigby
Look, We Can Fly Too	I	F	250+	Phonics Readers Plus	Steck-Vaughn
Look-Alike Animals	I	I	130	Bernard, Robin	Scholastic
Looking at Ants	I	I	250+	Yellow Umbrella Books	Red Brick Learning
Looking at Our World	I	I	188	Early Connections	Benchmark Education
Looking for a New House	I	RF	250+	Windows on Literacy	National Geographic
Looking for Luke	I	RF	250+	Sunshine	Wright Group/McGraw Hill
Lost in the Forest	I	HF	298	PM Story Books-Orange	Rigby
Lost in the Museum	I	RF	250+	Cohen, Miriam	Bantam
Lost Sheep, The	I	F	219	Little Readers	Houghton Mifflin
Lot Happened Today, A	I	RF	193	Ready Readers	Pearson Learning Group
Lunch Bunch, The	I	I	169	Storyteller-Moon Rising	Wright Group/McGraw Hill
Machines Make Fun Rides	I	I	182	Windows on Literacy	National Geographic
Machines That Fly	I	I	111	Windows on Literacy	National Geographic
Maggie's Pets	I	RF	250+	Early Transitional, Set 1	Pioneer Valley
Magic Pear Tree, The	I	TL	207	Little Celebrations	Pearson Learning Group
Magic Porridge Pot, The	I	TL	321	New Way Orange	Steck-Vaughn
Magic Store, The	I	RF	203	Sunshine	Wright Group/McGraw Hill
Magician's House, A	I	F	214	Sunshine	Wright Group/McGraw Hill
Magician's Lunch	I	F	272	Jellybeans	Rigby
Magnet Time	I	I	212	Independent Readers Science	Houghton Mifflin
Make a Boat That Floats	I	I	126	Book Bank	Wright Group/McGraw Hill
Make a Pinata	I	I	152	Windows on Literacy	National Geographic
Make Dinosaur Eggs	I	I	188	Sunshine	Wright Group/McGraw Hill
Make Mini Movies	I	I	309	Sunshine	Wright Group/McGraw Hill
Make Your Own Party	I	I	314	Sunshine	Wright Group/McGraw Hill
Making Caterpillars and Butterflies	I	I	162	Literacy 2000	Rigby
Making Concrete	I	I	136	Alphakids	Sundance
Making Money	I	I	129	Yellow Umbrella Books	Red Brick Learning
Making Party Food	I	I	221	PM Plus Nonfiction	Rigby
Man, the Boy, and the Donkey, The	I	TL	234	Story Box	Wright Group/McGraw Hill
Manners of a Pig, The	I	F	250+	Bookshop	Mondo
Many Kinds of Birds	I	I	290	Leveled Readers	Houghton Mifflin
Many Ways to 100	I	I	250+	Yellow Umbrella Books	Red Brick Learning
Marco Saves Grandpa	I	RF	232	Foundations	Wright Group/McGraw Hill
Maria	I	RF	72	City Kids	Rigby
Mark's Monster	I	F	250+	Reading Unlimited	Pearson Learning Group
Matsumura's Ice Sculpture	I	I	94	iOpeners	Pearson Learning Group
Maui and the Sun	I	TL	267	Story Box	Wright Group/McGraw Hill
McBungle's African Safari	I	F	336	Traditional Tales & More	Rigby
Meet Firefighter Jen	I	I	250+	Rosen Real Readers	Rosen Publishing Group
Meet Messy Fred	I	F	250+	Popcorn	Sundance
Meet Tom Paxton	I	B	229	Little Celebrations	Pearson Learning Group

* Collection of short stories

TITLE	LEVEL	GENRE	WORD COUNT	AUTHOR / SERIES	PUBLISHER / DISTRIBUTOR
Meet William Joyce	I	B	207	Little Celebrations	Pearson Learning Group
Meg and Jim's Sled Trip	I	RF	250+	Appleton-Smith, Laura	Flyleaf Publishing
Messy Bessey	I	RF	63	Rookie Readers	Children's Press
Messy Bessey's Garden	I	RF	60	Rookie Readers	Children's Press
Mice at Bat	I	F	250+	Oechsli, Kelly	HarperTrophy
Mice Have a Meeting, The	I	TL	250+	PM Plus Story Books	Rigby
Mice on Ice	I	F	211	Sunshine	Wright Group/McGraw Hill
Mighty Machines	I	I	127	Windows on Literacy	National Geographic
Mill on the Hill, The	I	F	187	Supersonics	Rigby
Mishi-Na	I	F	217	Sunshine	Wright Group/McGraw Hill
Miss Hen's Feast	I	F	434	Leveled Readers	Houghton Mifflin
Miss Muffett and the Spider	I	F	270	Ready Readers	Pearson Learning Group
Mitch to the Rescue	I	RF	302	PM Story Books-Orange	Rigby
Mixed-Up Wigs, The	I	F	199	Leveled Readers	Houghton Mifflin
Molly's Bracelet	I	RF	250+	Voyages	SRA/McGraw Hill
Molly's Broccoli	I	RF	233	Ready Readers	Pearson Learning Group
Molly's Hard Bargain	I	RF	180	Instant Readers	Harcourt School Publishers
Mom's Birthday	I	RF	229	Sunshine	Wright Group/McGraw Hill
Mom's Diet	I	RF	228	Sunshine	Wright Group/McGraw Hill
Monarch Butterfly	I	I	28	Book Bank	Wright Group/McGraw Hill
Monarch Butterfly, The	I	I	152	Foundations	Wright Group/McGraw Hill
Money Saving and Spending	I	I	174	Rosen Real Readers	Rosen Publishing Group
Monster	I	F	201	Read Alongs	Rigby
Monster Bus Goes on a Hot Air Balloon Trip	I	F	254	The Monster Bus Series	Pearson Learning Group
Monster Bus Goes to Yellowstone Park	I	F	259	The Monster Bus Series	Pearson Learning Group
Moonlit Owl, You	I	RF	225	Cambridge Reading	Pearson Learning Group
More Spaghetti!	I	RF	250+	PM Plus Story Books	Rigby
More Than One	I	F	238	Sunshine	Wright Group/McGraw Hill
Mother Hippopotamus's Dry Skin	I	F	201	Foundations	Wright Group/McGraw Hill
Mother Hippopotamus's Hiccups	I	F	162	Foundations	Wright Group/McGraw Hill
Moths	I	I	102	Bugs, Bugs, Bugs	Capstone Press
Moths	I	I	65	Pebble Books	Red Brick Learning
Motion	I	I	155	Instant Readers	Harcourt School Publishers
Mouse and Owl	I	RF	250+	Start to Read	School Zone
Mouse in the Forest, The	I	I	211	Leveled Readers	Houghton Mifflin
Mr. Bumbleticker Likes to Cook	I	F	196	Foundations	Wright Group/McGraw Hill
Mr. Bumbleticker Likes to Fix Machines	I	F	142	Foundations	Wright Group/McGraw Hill
Mr. Bumbleticker's Apples	I	F	338	Foundations	Wright Group/McGraw Hill
Mr. Fizzle, the Man Who Went "Boo!"	I	F	250+	Home Connection Collection	Rigby
Mr. Sun and Mr. Sea	I	F	202	Little Celebrations	Pearson Learning Group
Mr. Verdi's New Path	I	F	250+	Home Connection Collection	Rigby
Mr. Wumple's Travels	I	F	259	Read Alongs	Rigby
Mrs. Barnett's Birthday	I	RF	135	Sunshine	Wright Group/McGraw Hill
Mrs. Brice's Mice	I	F	250+	Hoff, Syd	HarperTrophy
Mrs. Grindy's Shoes	I	F	211	Sunshine	Wright Group/McGraw Hill
Mrs. Muddle's Mud-Puddle	I	F	181	Sunshine	Wright Group/McGraw Hill
Mrs. Murphy's Bears	I	RF	188	Little Readers	Houghton Mifflin
Mumbo Jumbo's Shoes	I	F	130	Book Bus	Creative Edge
Munching Monster	I	F	261	Storyteller-Moon Rising	Wright Group/McGraw Hill
My Best Friend	I	RF	147	Hutchins, Pat	Greenwillow
My Brother, Owen	I	RF	150	Book Bank	Wright Group/McGraw Hill
My Dad Has Asthma	I	I	138	Wonder World	Wright Group/McGraw Hill
*My Dog and Other Stories	I	RF	250+	Story Steps	Rigby
My Family Tree	I	I	229	Windows on Literacy	National Geographic

* Collection of short stories

TITLE	LEVEL	GENRE	WORD COUNT	AUTHOR / SERIES	PUBLISHER / DISTRIBUTOR
My Favorite Foods	I	RF	100	Early Readers	Compass Point Books
My Feet Are Just Right	I	I	220	Sunshine	Wright Group/McGraw Hill
My Sister Jess	I	RF	120	Supersonics	Rigby
My Skateboard	I	RF	81	City Kids	Rigby
My Sloppy Tiger	I	F	211	Sunshine	Wright Group/McGraw Hill
My Stepmother	I	RF	121	City Stories	Rigby
My Teacher's Leaving	I	RF	154	City Kids	Rigby
My Time Box	I	RF	225	Early Connections	Benchmark Education
My Tooth Is About to Fall Out	I	RF	173	Maccarone, Grace	Scholastic
Mystery Box,The	I	RF	326	New Way Orange	Steck-Vaughn
Name for a Dog, A	I	RF	258	Windmill Books	Rigby
Nana's Place	I	RF	211	Gibson, Akimi; Meyer, K.	Scholastic
Napping House, The	I	F	268	Wood, Don & Audrey	Harcourt Trade
Neighborhood Event, The	I	RF	309	Leveled Readers	Houghton Mifflin
New Club, The	I	RF	267	Leveled Readers	Houghton Mifflin
New Tricks	I	RF	250+	Voyages	SRA/McGraw Hill
Next Stop!	I	RF	250+	Ellis, Sarah	Fitzhenry & Whiteside
Nick Goes Fishing	I	RF	123	Yukish, Joe	Kaeden Books
Nishal's Box	I	F	250+	Cambridge Reading	Pearson Learning Group
No Ball Games	I	F	250+	Rigby Literacy	Rigby
No Good in Art	I	RF	250+	Cohen, Miriam	Bantam
Nobody Knew My Name	I	RF	276	Foundations	Wright Group/McGraw Hill
Nobody Listens to Andrew	I	F	250+	Little Readers	Houghton Mifflin
Noggin and Bobbin By the Sea	I	F	204	Little Celebrations	Pearson Learning Group
Noise in the Night	I	F	250+	Start to Read	School Zone
Noisy Nora	I	F	204	Wells, Rosemary	Scholastic
Not Enough Cupcakes	I	F	292	Talking Point Series	Pearson Learning Group
Not Too Small at All	I	F	251	Seedlings	Continental Press
Not-So-Scary-Scarecrow, The	I	RF	166	Ready Readers	Pearson Learning Group
Now I Am Five	I	RF	582	Sunshine	Wright Group/McGraw Hill
Nowhere and Nothing	I	RF	143	Sunshine	Wright Group/McGraw Hill
Oak Tree, An	I	I	141	Book Bus	Creative Edge
Odd and Even Numbers	I	I	250+	Yellow Umbrella Books	Red Brick Learning
Old Man's Mitten, The	I	TL	378	Bookshop	Mondo
One for You and One for Me	I	I	354	Early Connections	Benchmark Education
One Hot Summer Night	I	RF	126	Bookshop	Mondo
One Hundred Books	I	I	217	Story Box	Wright Group/McGraw Hill
One Night	I	RF	92	Carter, Jackie	Scholastic
One Quiet Afternoon	I	F	155	Instant Readers	Harcourt School Publishers
Otto the Cat	I	F	250+	Herman, Gail	Grosset & Dunlap
Our Eyes	I	I	869	Sunshine	Wright Group/McGraw Hill
Our Flag	I	I	93	Phonics Readers	Compass Point Books
Our Polliwogs	I	RF	91	Books for Young Learners	Richard C. Owen
Our Skeleton	I	I	105	Sunshine Books	Wright Group/McGraw Hill
Our Sun	I	I	131	Rosen Real Readers	Rosen Publishing Group
Owls	I	I	250+	Pebble Books	Red Brick Learning
P. J. Funnybunny Camps Out	I	F	250+	Sadler, Marilyn	Random House
Paper Trail, The	I	RF	253	Windmill Books	Rigby
Party Time at the Milky Way	I	F	160	Sunshine	Wright Group/McGraw Hill
Penguin Chick, The	I	I	105	Windows on Literacy	National Geographic
People Who Lead Us	I	I	155	Windows on Literacy	National Geographic
Percival	I	RF	303	Literacy 2000	Rigby
Perlitas	I	RF	98	Books for Young Learners	Richard C. Owen
Pet Day at School	I	RF	198	City Kids	Rigby

* Collection of short stories

TITLE	LEVEL	GENRE	WORD COUNT	AUTHOR / SERIES	PUBLISHER / DISTRIBUTOR
Pet Riddles and Jokes	I	F	154	Instant Readers	Harcourt School Publishers
Pet Tarantula, The	I	F	208	Storyteller Nonfiction	Wright Group/McGraw Hill
Peter's Dream	I	F	186	Start to Read	School Zone
Photograph, The	I	F	250+	Popcorn	Sundance
Pick a Pumpkin	I	F	250+	Leveled Readers Language Support	Houghton Mifflin
Picking a Pet	I	I	224	Sunshine	Wright Group/McGraw Hill
Picnic Tea	I	RF	224	Stepping Stones	Nelson/Michaels Assoc.
Picture Tricks	I	I	250+	Phonics Readers Plus	Steck-Vaughn
Piece of Cake	I	I	250+	Home Connection Collection	Rigby
Pig That Learned to Jig, The	I	F	140	Wonder World	Wright Group/McGraw Hill
Pigpen Party, The	I	F	186	Literacy Tree	Rigby
Pizza Pokey	I	F	280	Pair-It Books	Steck-Vaughn
Plants	I	I	250+	Momentum Literacy Program	Troll Associates
Plants and Seeds	I	I	148	Sunshine	Wright Group/McGraw Hill
Plants Grow From Seeds	I	I	109	Phonics Readers	Compass Point Books
Play It Again Sam	I	RF	139	Literacy 2000	Rigby
Playing Soccer	I	RF	123	Foundations	Wright Group/McGraw Hill
Please, Do Not Drop Your Jelly Beans	I	RF	180	Storyteller-Night Crickets	Wright Group/McGraw Hill
Police Cars	I	I	177	Pebble Books	Grolier Press
Pony Express, The	I	I	128	Independent Readers Social Studies	Houghton Mifflin
Poor Miss Dee!	I	RF	247	Story Box	Wright Group/McGraw Hill
Poor Sore Paw, The	I	F	244	Sunshine	Wright Group/McGraw Hill
Popcorn and Candy	I	I	161	Windows on Literacy	National Geographic
Pot of Gold, The	I	TL	266	Reading Unlimited	Pearson Learning Group
Potato Chips	I	RF	101	City Kids	Rigby
Potatoes	I	I	78	Windows on Literacy	National Geographic
Praying Mantises	I	I	78	Insects	Red Brick Learning
Princess and the Pea, The	I	TL	304	Traditional Tales	Pearson Learning Group
Princess, the Mud Pies, and the Dragon, The	I	TL	250+	Little Readers	Houghton Mifflin
Pterosaur's Long Flight	I	HF	301	PM Story Books-Orange	Rigby
Pug and Chug	I	F	250+	Supersonics	Rigby
Puppy Chase, The	I	RF	250+	Cambridge Reading	Pearson Learning Group
Quack, Quack, Quack!	I	F	219	Sunshine	Wright Group/McGraw Hill
Queen and the Dragon, The	I	F	243	New Way Green	Steck-Vaughn
Quilt, The	I	RF	165	Jonas, Ann	Morrow
Quilting in America	I	I	152	Vocabulary Readers	Houghton Mifflin
Rabbits on the Farm	I	I	103	Pebble Books	Red Brick Learning
Rabbit's Tricks	I	F	250+	Robinson, Fay	Wright Group/McGraw Hill
Raccoon on the Moon	I	RF	250+	Start to Read	School Zone
Race, The	I	F	451	New Way Green	Steck-Vaughn
Rain Forest Plants	I	I	151	Alphakids	Sundance
Rainbow Parrot	I	TL	174	Literacy Tree	Rigby
Rainbows and Moonbeams	I	RF	238	Sunshine	Wright Group/McGraw Hill
Rays	I	I	48	Pebble Books	Red Brick Learning
Real Facts About Rivers	I	I	159	Rosen Real Readers	Rosen Publishing Group
Real Princess, The	I	TL	193	Jumbled Tumbled Tales & Rhymes	Rigby
Rebecca and the Concert	I	RF	374	PM StoryBooks	Rigby
Rebus Bears, The	I	F	250+	Reit, Seymour	Bantam
Reflections	I	F	110	Jonas, Ann	Morrow
Reuse and Recycle	I	I	118	Instant Readers	Harcourt School Publishers
Richie the Greedy Mouse	I	F	179	Sunshine	Wright Group/McGraw Hill
River Otter	I	I	208	Independent Readers Science	Houghton Mifflin

* Collection of short stories

TITLE	LEVEL	GENRE	WORD COUNT	AUTHOR / SERIES	PUBLISHER / DISTRIBUTOR
Road Robber	I	F	250+	Sunshine	Wright Group/McGraw Hill
Road Work Ahead	I	RF	207	Little Readers	Houghton Mifflin
Roads and Bridges	I	RF	253	Alphakids	Sundance
Robby in the River	I	RF	250+	Lighthouse	Rigby
Robert the Rose Horse	I	F	250+	Heilbroner, Joan	Random House
Rock Pools	I	I	250+	Momentum Literacy Program	Troll Associates
Rocket Ship, The	I	RF	250+	PM Plus Story Books	Rigby
Rocking and Rolling Along	I	RF	73	Evangeline Nicholas Collection	Wright Group/McGraw Hill
Roller Coaster, The	I	RF	194	Sunshine	Wright Group/McGraw Hill
*Roly-Poly	I	F	1227	Story Box	Wright Group/McGraw Hill
Rubber Duck	I	F	170	Early Readers	Compass Point Books
Sacks of Gold	I	F	263	Sunshine	Wright Group/McGraw Hill
Same But Different	I	RF	184	Sunshine	Wright Group/McGraw Hill
Sammy's Hamburger Caper	I	F	250	Urmston, Kathleen	Kaeden Books
Sammy's Supper	I	RF	293	Reading Unlimited	Pearson Learning Group
Sam's Snacks	I	F	250+	Cambridge Reading	Pearson Learning Group
Sarah and the Barking Dog	I	RF	328	PM Story Books-Orange	Rigby
Sara's Lovely Songs	I	RF	250+	Ready Readers	Pearson Learning Group
Saturday Sandwiches	I	RF	154	Evangeline Nicholas Collection	Wright Group/McGraw Hill
Saving Hoppo	I	RF	250+	PM Plus Story Books	Rigby
Science Outside	I	I	33	Canizares, Susan; Chessen, Betsey	Scholastic
Scientists	I	I	56	Chanko, Pamela; Berger, Samantha	Scholastic
Scruffy	I	RF	250	Leveled Readers	Houghton Mifflin
Sea Snakes	I	I	66	Pebble Books	Red Brick Learning
Sea Turtle Night	I	I	200	Ready Readers	Pearson Learning Group
Seals	I	I	103	Under the Sea	Red Brick Learning
Secret Cave, The	I	RF	250+	PM Plus Story Books	Rigby
Seeds Grow	I	I	90	Sunshine Books	Wright Group/McGraw Hill
Sharks	I	I	238	Pebble Plus	Capstone Press
Sharon the Shark	I	F	266	Supersonics	Rigby
Shelter	I	I	60	Canizares, Susan; Moreton, Daniel	Scholastic
Shintaro's Umbrellas	I	RF	95	Books for Young Learners	Richard C. Owen
Shoe Grabber, The	I	F	260	Read Alongs	Rigby
Shots	I	RF	90	City Kids	Rigby
Should You Ever?	I	F	69	Tiger Cub	Peguis
Show and Tell	I	RF	201	Little Celebrations	Pearson Learning Group
Silly Times with Two Silly Trolls	I	F	250+	Jewell, Nancy	HarperTrophy
Simple Solution	I	RF	250+	Literacy Tree	Rigby
Sione Went Fishing	I	RF	225	Sunshine	Wright Group/McGraw Hill
Skates for Luke	I	RF	346	PM Story Books-Orange	Rigby
Skating Trail, The	I	RF	250+	PM Plus Story Books	Rigby
Sky Is Falling, The	I	F	181	Storyteller-Setting Sun	Wright Group/McGraw Hill
Sleeping	I	RF	114	Book Bank	Wright Group/McGraw Hill
Slice of Pizza, A	I	RF	175	Twig	Wright Group/McGraw Hill
Slithery Snakes and Unicorns	I	F	289	Sunshine	Wright Group/McGraw Hill
Sloppy Tiger and the Party	I	F	293	Sunshine	Wright Group/McGraw Hill
Sloppy Tiger Bedtime	I	F	320	Sunshine	Wright Group/McGraw Hill
Small Pig	I	F	250+	Lobel, Arnold	HarperTrophy
Small Sailboat, A	I	RF	135	Books for Young Learners	Richard C. Owen
Smelling	I	I	111	Pebble Books	Red Brick Learning
Smile and Say "Cheetah"	I	RF	200	World Quest Adventures	World Quest Learning
Snail That Snored, The	I	F	250+	Phonics Readers Plus	Steck-Vaughn
Snail Trail, The	I	F	243	Sunshine	Wright Group/McGraw Hill

* Collection of short stories

TITLE	LEVEL	GENRE	WORD COUNT	AUTHOR / SERIES	PUBLISHER / DISTRIBUTOR
Snakes	I	I	208	Momentum Literacy Program	Troll Associates
Snakes and Lizards	I	I	205	Yellow Umbrella Books	Red Brick Learning
Snickers	I	RF	250+	Momentum Literacy Program	Troll Associates
Snip, Snap	I	F	250+	Sunshine	Wright Group/McGraw Hill
Snorkeling	I	RF	233	Leveled Readers Language Support	Houghton Mifflin
Snow Day	I	RF	250+	Bliss, Corinne Demas	Random House
Snow White and the Seven Dwarfs	I	TL	250+	Enrichment	Wright Group/McGraw Hill
So Many Birthdays	I	RF	250+	Momentum Literacy Program	Troll Associates
So Many Snakes	I	I	152	Rosen Real Readers	Rosen Publishing Group
So What?	I	RF	250+	Cohen, Miriam	Bantam
Some Kids Use Wheelchairs	I	I	123	Understanding Differences	Red Brick Learning
Something Nasty	I	F	250+	Popcorn	Sundance
Somewhere in the Universe	I	I	167	Literacy Tree	Rigby
Soup	I	F	250+	Sunshine	Wright Group/McGraw Hill
Soup Can Telephone	I	I	190	Wonder World	Wright Group/McGraw Hill
Spiders and Their Webs	I	I	162	Sunshine Books	Wright Group/McGraw Hill
Spiders in Space	I	F	242	Sunshine	Wright Group/McGraw Hill
Spinning Top	I	I	182	Wonder World	Wright Group/McGraw Hill
Spooky Riddles	I	TL	182	Brown, Marc	Random House
Sports Around the World	I	I	192	Early Connections	Benchmark Education
Spot's Birthday Party	I	F	97	Hill, Eric	Putnam
Spring	I	I	142	Pebble Books	Capstone Press
Squirrels	I	I	250+	Pebble Books	Red Brick Learning
Stables Are for Horses	I	I	66	Windmill	Wright Group/McGraw Hill
Stanley	I	F	250+	Hoff, Syd	HarperTrophy
Stars	I	I	181	Yellow Umbrella Books	Red Brick Learning
Stingrays	I	I	126	Wonder World	Wright Group/McGraw Hill
Stop Knitting, Nina!	I	F	250+	Home Connection Collection	Rigby
Storm on the Beach, A	I	RF	72	Book Bank	Wright Group/McGraw Hill
Story of Chicken Licken	I	TL	250+	Ormerod, Jan	Lothrop
Strings, Ropes, and Cables	I	I	250+	Home Connection Collection	Rigby
Stubborn Goat, The	I	F	212	Alphakids	Sundance
Summer	I	I	178	Pebble Books	Capstone Press
Summer Trips	I	I	272	Visions	Wright Group/McGraw Hill
Sun Smile	I	F	250+	Story Box	Wright Group/McGraw Hill
Sunset Pond, The	I	RF	250+	Appleton-Smith, Laura	Flyleaf Publishing
Super Duper Sandwich, The	I	F	202	Books for Young Learners	Richard C. Owen
Super-Duper Sunflower Seeds, The	I	F	389	Book Bank	Wright Group/McGraw Hill
Superstars	I	F	252	Sunshine	Wright Group/McGraw Hill
Surprise Box, The	I	RF	250+	Voyages	SRA/McGraw Hill
Surprise for Zack, A	I	RF	250+	PM Plus Story Books	Rigby
Surprise from the Sky	I	F	295	Windmill Books	Rigby
Surprise Party, The	I	F	192	New Way Green	Steck-Vaughn
Surprise!	I	RF	168	Little Celebrations	Pearson Learning Group
Sweet or Sour?	I	I	177	Sunshine	Wright Group/McGraw Hill
Sweet to Eat	I	RF	105	Pacific Literacy	Pacific Learning
Swimming Lessons	I	I	200	Storyteller Nonfiction	Wright Group/McGraw Hill
Swoop!	I	RF	250+	PM Plus Story Books	Rigby
Tails	I	I	170	Sunshine	Wright Group/McGraw Hill
Tails Can Tell	I	I	346	Wonder World	Wright Group/McGraw Hill
Tale of the Turnip, The	I	TL	250+	PM Traditional Tales-Orange	Rigby
Talking Yam, The	I	F	340	Little Readers	Houghton Mifflin
Tall Tales	I	RF	139	Literacy Tree	Rigby

TITLE	LEVEL	GENRE	WORD COUNT	AUTHOR / SERIES	PUBLISHER / DISTRIBUTOR
Tallest Sunflower, The	I	I	250+	Counters & Seekers	Steck-Vaughn
Tania's Tooth	I	RF	131	Sunshine	Wright Group/McGraw Hill
Tasting	I	I	141	Pebble Books	Red Brick Learning
Teachers at Our School	I	RF	115	City Kids	Rigby
Teddy Bears	I	I	180	Purkis, Sallie	Nelson/Michaels Assoc.
Teeny Tiny	I	TL	250+	Bennett, Jill	Putnam
Ten Happy Elephants	I	F	201	Sunshine	Wright Group/McGraw Hill
Ten Loopy Caterpillars	I	F	191	Jellybeans	Rigby
Tents	I	RF	175	Reading Unlimited	Pearson Learning Group
Termites	I	I	72	Pebble Books	Red Brick Learning
Termites	I	RF	130	Books for Young Learners	Richard C. Owen
Terrible Armadillo	I	F	229	Jellybeans	Rigby
That's Not Our Dog	I	RF	250+	PM Plus Story Books	Rigby
There are Mice in Our School	I	RF	95	City Kids	Rigby
There Stood Our Dog	I	F	250+	Voyages	SRA/McGraw Hill
There's a Dog in the Yard	I	I	119	City Kids	Rigby
There's a Nightmare in My Closet	I	F	153	Mayer, Mercer	Penguin Group
This Is My Street	I	RF	229	Windows on Literacy	National Geographic
This Is the Bear	I	F	211	Hayes, Sarah & Craig	Harper & Row
This is the House That Bjorn	I	RF	172	Tiger Cub	Peguis
This Is the Place for Me	I	F	250+	Cole, Joanna	Scholastic
This Is the Seed	I	F	171	Little Celebrations	Pearson Learning Group
This Room Is a Mess!	I	RF	250+	Ready Readers	Pearson Learning Group
Three Bears, The	I	TL	250+	Tiger Cub	Peguis
Three Billy Goats Gruff	I	TL	536	Traditional Tales	Pearson Learning Group
Three Billy Goats Gruff	I	TL	250+	Sunshine	Wright Group/McGraw Hill
Three Billy Goats Gruff, The	I	F	250+	Southgate, Vera	Ladybird Books
Three Billy Goats Gruff, The	I	TL	549	Brown, Marcia	Harcourt School Publishers
Three Billy Goats Gruff, The	I	TL	250+	Literacy Tree	Rigby
Three Billy Goats Gruff, The	I	TL	450	PM Traditional Tales-Orange	Rigby
Three Little Pigs, The	I	TL	250+	Ziefert, Harriet	Puffin Books
Three Little Pigs, The	I	TL	568	Traditional Tales	Pearson Learning Group
Three Little Pigs, The	I	TL	523	PM Traditional Tales-Orange	Rigby
Three Little Pigs, The	I	TL	250+	Literacy 2000	Rigby
Three Silly Monkeys Go Fishing	I	F	163	Foundations	Wright Group/McGraw Hill
Thunderstorm is Coming!, A	I	I	130	Vocabulary Readers	Houghton Mifflin
Tides	I	I	210	Wonder World	Wright Group/McGraw Hill
Tidy Titch	I	RF	231	Hutchins, Pat	Morrow
Tiger's Tummy Ache	I	TL	220	Ready Readers	Pearson Learning Group
Time for Bed, Little Bear	I	F	303	Story Basket	Wright Group/McGraw Hill
Tim's Pumpkin	I	RF	250+	Home Connection Collection	Rigby
To Market, to Market	I	TL	393	Story Box	Wright Group/McGraw Hill
Toad Takes Off	I	F	216	Schade, Susan; Buller, John	Random House
Toast for Mom	I	RF	250+	Ready Readers	Pearson Learning Group
Toby and B. J.	I	F	307	PM Story Books-Orange	Rigby
Toby and the Big Red Van	I	F	291	PM Story Books-Orange	Rigby
Toby and the Big Tree	I	F	298	PM Story Books-Orange	Rigby
Today	I	RF	151	Early Connections	Benchmark Education
Tomato Rose	I	RF	250+	Phonics Readers Plus	Steck-Vaughn
Tommy's Treasure	I	RF	232	Literacy 2000	Rigby
Tom's Box	I	F	250+	Cambridge Reading	Pearson Learning Group
Tools Measure Weather	I	I	145	Windows on Literacy	National Geographic
Tooth Race, The	I	RF	250+	Little Readers	Houghton Mifflin
Too-Tight Shoes	I	RF	170	Evangeline Nicholas Collection	Wright Group/McGraw Hill

* Collection of short stories

TITLE	LEVEL	GENRE	WORD COUNT	AUTHOR / SERIES	PUBLISHER / DISTRIBUTOR
Town Mouse and Country Mouse, The	I	TL	172	Aesop	Wright Group/McGraw Hill
Toy Farm, The	I	RF	311	PM Story Books-Orange	Rigby
Toy Tooth, The	I	RF	250+	Rigby Literacy	Rigby
Toymil and the Bear	I	RF	233	Story Box	Wright Group/McGraw Hill
Tracks in the Sand	I	I	125	Levin, Amy	Scholastic
Train Ride Story, The	I	F	189	Sunshine	Wright Group/McGraw Hill
Train that Ran Away	I	F	32	Jellybeans	Rigby
Travel Money, U.S.A.	I	I	245	Early Connections	Benchmark Education
Tree Is a Home, A	I	I	135	Pacific Literacy	Pacific Learning
Trees Are Special	I	I	85	Sunshine	Wright Group/McGraw Hill
Trek, The	I	RF	158	Jonas, Ann	Greenwillow
Triangles	I	I	178	Shapes	Red Brick Learning
Triceratops and the Crocodiles, The	I	HF	250+	PM Plus Story Books	Rigby
Tricks	I	I	218	Sun Sprouts	ETA/Cuisenaire
Trip into Space, A	I	I	129	Little Red Readers	Sundance
Trip to the Dentist, A	I	I	196	Rosen Real Readers	Rosen Publishing Group
Trip to the Post Office, A	I	I	191	Rosen Real Readers	Rosen Publishing Group
Trip to the Station, A	I	I	241	Rosen Real Readers	Rosen Publishing Group
Trouble with Heathrow, The	I	RF	173	Sunshine	Wright Group/McGraw Hill
Trucks	I	I	38	Literacy 2000	Rigby
Try Again, Emma	I	RF	250+	Lighthouse	Rigby
Try This!	I	I	250+	Rigby Literacy	Rigby
Tug of War	I	TL	250+	Folk Tales	Wright Group/McGraw Hill
Turkeys on the Farm	I	I	94	Pebble Books	Red Brick Learning
Turtle Talk	I	I	217	Storyteller-Setting Sun	Wright Group/McGraw Hill
Two Baby Elephants	I	F	240	Lighthouse	Rigby
Two Crazy Pigs	I	F	250+	Nagel, Karen Berman	Scholastic
Two Eyes, A Nose, and a Mouth	I	I	169	Grobel Intrater, Roberta	Scholastic
Two Little Goldfish	I	RF	344	PM Story Books-Orange	Rigby
Two Little Mice, The	I	F	163	Literacy 2000	Rigby
Ugly Duckling, The	I	TL	250+	Literacy 2000	Rigby
Underwater	I	I	100	Start to Read	School Zone
Very Busy Spider, The	I	F	263	Carle, Eric	Philomel Books
Visit to Cousin Boris	I	F	250+	Popcorn	Sundance
Visit to the Police Station, A	I	I	115	Pebble Plus	Capstone Press
Visiting the Police Station	I	I	200	Rosen Real Readers	Rosen Publishing Group
Visitor, The	I	F	250+	Popcorn	Sundance
Walking Up Walls	I	I	140	Windows on Literacy	National Geographic
Walkingsticks	I	I	89	Bugs, Bugs, Bugs	Capstone Press
Walkingsticks	I	I	83	Pebble Books	Red Brick Learning
Walruses	I	I	55	Pebble Books	Red Brick Learning
Warming Up! Cooling Off!	I	I	553	Sunshine	Wright Group/McGraw Hill
Wasps	I	I	59	Pebble Books	Red Brick Learning
Water as a Liquid	I	I	141	Pebble Books	Red Brick Learning
Water Bugs	I	I	76	Pebble Books	Red Brick Learning
Water, Ice, and Steam	I	I	150	Rosen Real Readers	Rosen Publishing Group
Wax Man, The	I	TL	250+	Loya, Olga	Scholastic
We All Scream For Ice Cream	I	I	219	Early Connections	Benchmark Education
We Are Firefighters	I	I	67	Vocabulary Readers	Houghton Mifflin
We Can Recycle	I	I	231	Independent Readers Science	Houghton Mifflin
We Care for Our School	I	I	134	Wonder World	Wright Group/McGraw Hill
We Just Moved!	I	F	250+	Krensky, Stephen	Scholastic
We Need Auto Mechanics	I	I	79	Pebble Books	Red Brick Learning
We Need Construction Workers	I	I	59	Helpers in Our Community	Red Brick Learning

* Collection of short stories

TITLE	LEVEL	GENRE	WORD COUNT	AUTHOR / SERIES	PUBLISHER / DISTRIBUTOR
We Need Garbage Collectors	I	I	77	Helpers in Our Community	Red Brick Learning
We Need Librarians	I	I	78	Pebble Books	Red Brick Learning
We Need Pharmacists	I	I	81	Pebble Books	Red Brick Learning
We Need Plumbers	I	I	107	Pebble Books	Red Brick Learning
We Need Water	I	I	99	Pebble Books	Red Brick Learning
Weather Forecast, The	I	F	272	Story Box	Wright Group/McGraw Hill
Well Done, Sam	I	RF	250+	Cambridge Reading	Pearson Learning Group
We're Going on a Bear Hunt	I	TL	363	Rosen, Michael	Macmillan
We're in Big Trouble, Black Board Bear	I	F	250+	Alexander, Martha	Dial Books
Whales	I	I	45	Pebble Books	Red Brick Learning
Whales	I	I	45	Pebble Plus	Capstone Press
What a Noise!	I	RF	165	Pacific Literacy	Pacific Learning
What a Spelling Test!	I	F	123	City Stories	Rigby
What Am I?	I	I	100	Foundations	Wright Group/McGraw Hill
What Bear Cubs Like to Do	I	I	83	Little Books	Sadlier-Oxford
What Computers Do	I	I	186	Yellow Umbrella Books	Red Brick Learning
What Else?	I	RF	154	Sunshine	Wright Group/McGraw Hill
What Grows From a Tree?	I	I	250+	Yellow Umbrella Books	Red Brick Learning
What I Would Do	I	RF	173	Read Alongs	Rigby
What Is a Mammal?	I	I	70	Pebble Books	Red Brick Learning
What is a Mountain?	I	I	231	Rosen Real Readers	Rosen Publishing Group
What Is a Reptile?	I	I	67	Pebble Books	Red Brick Learning
What Lays Eggs?	I	I	216	Momentum Literacy Program	Troll Associates
What Makes a Tiger Hard to See?	I	I	253	Windows on Literacy	National Geographic
What on Earth?	I	F	133	Sunshine	Wright Group/McGraw Hill
What Pushes? What Pulls?	I	I	141	Early Connections	Benchmark Education
What the Dinosaurs Saw	I	I	123	Schlein, Miriam	Scholastic
What You See Is What You Get	I	F	192	McLenighan, Valjean	Modern Curriculum
What's On the Truck?	I	I	137	Windows on Literacy	National Geographic
What's That?	I	F	250+	Popcorn	Sundance
What's Zero?	I	I	250+	Yellow Umbrella Books	Red Brick Learning
Wheels on the Bus	I	TL	362	Kovalski, Mary Ann	Little, Brown & Co.
When I Turned Six	I	HF	150	Voyages	SRA/McGraw Hill
When the Moon Was Blue	I	F	174	Literacy 2000	Rigby
When Will I Read?	I	RF	250+	Cohen, Miriam	Bantam
Where Do You Live?	I	I	68	Windows on Literacy	National Geographic
Where Does Food Come From?	I	I	169	PM Plus Nonfiction	Rigby
Where Is Your Home?	I	I	126	Phonics Readers	Compass Point Books
Where's Lulu?	I	RF	250+	Hooks, William H.	Bantam
Where's My Snack?	I	RF	250+	Sunshine	Wright Group/McGraw Hill
Which Animal Is That?	I	I	250+	Momentum Literacy Program	Troll Associates
Which Holiday Is It?	I	TL	110	Phonics Readers	Compass Point Books
Who Builds?	I	I	97	Yellow Umbrella Books	Red Brick Learning
Who Cleans the Museum?	I	RF	85	Books for Young Learners	Richard C. Owen
Who Lives Here?	I	I	230	Little Readers	Houghton Mifflin
Who Loves Getting Wet?	I	F	204	Sunshine	Wright Group/McGraw Hill
Who Needs Teeth?	I	I	116	Phonics Readers	Compass Point Books
Who Took the Farmer's Hat?	I	F	340	Nodset, Joan	Scholastic
Who Wants a Ride?	I	RF	214	Bernard, Robin	Scholastic
Who Wants One?	I	F	212	Serfozo, Mary	Macmillan
Whoops	I	F	250+	Supersonics	Rigby
Who's Afraid of Shadows?	I	RF	219	Talking Point Series	Pearson Learning Group
Who's Afraid of the Dark?	I	RF	250+	Bonsall, Crosby	HarperTrophy
Who's Afraid?	I	RF	165	Reading Unlimited	Pearson Learning Group

* Collection of short stories

TITLE	LEVEL	GENRE	WORD COUNT	AUTHOR / SERIES	PUBLISHER / DISTRIBUTOR
Who's Hiding There?	I	RF	242	Pair-It Books	Steck-Vaughn
Who's in the Shed?	I	F	202	Literacy Tree	Rigby
Why Cats Wash After Dinner	I	TL	128	Pacific Literacy	Pacific Learning
Why Cry?	I	I	121	Sunshine	Wright Group/McGraw Hill
Why Do Worms Come Up When It Rains?	I	I	202	Seedlings	Continental Press
Wicked Pirates, The	I	F	226	Sunshine	Wright Group/McGraw Hill
Wiggly-Jiggly Line, The	I	F	128	Book Bank	Wright Group/McGraw Hill
Wild Wet Wellington Wind	I	RF	104	Pacific Literacy	Pacific Learning
Will Power	I	RF	250+	Rigby Literacy	Rigby
William Tell	I	TL	127	Jumbled Tumbled Tales & Rhymes	Rigby
Willie's Wonderful Pet	I	RF	315	Cebulash, Mel	Scholastic
Wind and Sun	I	TL	238	Sunshine	Wright Group/McGraw Hill
Wind Power	I	I	116	Windows on Literacy	National Geographic
Winter	I	I	240	Pebble Books	Capstone Press
Wolf and the Old Woman, The	I	TL	250+	Voyages	SRA/McGraw Hill
Wolf's Cake	I	F	250+	Sunshine	Wright Group/McGraw Hill
Wolves	I	I	188	Pair-It Books	Steck-Vaughn
Wonderful Ears	I	I	1017	Science	Wright Group/McGraw Hill
Woodpeckers	I	I	85	Pebble Books	Red Brick Learning
Woody Guthrie	I	B	199	Leveled Readers Social Studies	Houghton Mifflin
Woolly Sally	I	RF	147	Pacific Literacy	Pacific Learning
Work Helicopter, The	I	F	250+	PM Plus Story Books	Rigby
Working Together	I	I	222	Rigby Focus	Rigby
Working with Animals	I	I	250+	Home Connection Collection	Rigby
Worms for Breakfast	I	TL	250+	Little Readers	Houghton Mifflin
Yard Sale, The	I	RF	250+	Little Readers	Houghton Mifflin
Year with Mother Bear, A	I	I	164	Storyteller Nonfiction	Wright Group/McGraw Hill
Yo Ho! Yo Ho!	I	F	164	Voyages	SRA/McGraw Hill
Yoo Hoo, Moon!	I	F	250+	Blocksma, Mary	Bantam
You and Your Teeth	I	I	1009	Sunshine	Wright Group/McGraw Hill
You Can't Catch Me!	I	F	244	Cambridge Reading	Pearson Learning Group
Youngest Giraffe, The	I	RF	250+	PM Plus Story Books	Rigby
Yukadoos	I	F	121	Jellybeans	Rigby
Yum and Yuk	I	F	125	Story Box	Wright Group/McGraw Hill
7 Ways to Get Energy	J	I	193	Independent Readers Science	Houghton Mifflin
Add It Up	J	RF	311	Story Box	Wright Group/McGraw Hill
Addie Meets Max	J	RF	250+	Robins, Joan	Harper & Row
Addie's Bad Day	J	RF	566	Robins, Joan	HarperTrophy
Adventures of Snail at School	J	F	250+	Stadler, John	HarperTrophy
Ah Liang's Gift	J	RF	352	Sunshine	Wright Group/McGraw Hill
Ah-choo!	J	RF	291	Samuels, Aurora	Sadlier-Oxford
Aladdin & the Magic Lamp	J	TL	851	Traditional Tales	Pearson Learning Group
Alison Wendlebury	J	RF	250+	Literacy 2000	Rigby
All About Bats	J	I	250+	Ready Readers	Modern Curriculum
All About Me!	J	RF	250+	Pacific Literacy	Pacific Learning
All Kinds of People: What Makes Us Different	J	I	250+	Spyglass Books	Compass Point Books
Amazing Egg, The	J	I	220	Spyglass Books	Compass Point Books
Amazing Eggs	J	I	250+	Discovery World	Rigby
Amazing Maze, The	J	RF	334	Foundations	Wright Group/McGraw Hill
Ambulances	J	I	119	Mighty Machines	Capstone Press
And I Mean it Stanley	J	RF	184	Bonsall, Crosby	HarperCollins
Animal Senses	J	I	224	Spyglass Books	Compass Point Books
Animal Wrestlers, The	J	TL	338	Cambridge Reading	Pearson Learning Group
Animals of Alaska	J	I	147	Rosen Real Readers	Rosen Publishing Group

* Collection of short stories

TITLE	LEVEL	GENRE	WORD COUNT	AUTHOR / SERIES	PUBLISHER / DISTRIBUTOR
Annie's Pet	J	RF	250+	Bank Street	Bantam
Ant and the Grasshopper, The	J	TL	250+	PM Plus Story Books	Rigby
Ant and the Grasshopper, The	J	TL	250+	Story Steps	Rigby
Ant City	J	RF	393	PM Turquoise	Rigby
Ants and Grasshoppers, The	J	F	250+	The Wright Skills	Wright Group/McGraw Hill
Ants and Their Nests	J	I	150	Animal Homes	Capstone Press
Ants Go Marching, The	J	TL	250+	Traditional Songs	Picture Window Books
Apple Tree, The	J	I	160	Sunshine	Wright Group/McGraw Hill
Apples!	J	RF	503	Cambridge Reading	Pearson Learning Group
Art Around the World	J	I	239	Early Connections	Benchmark Education
Ask Mr. Bear	J	F	613	Flack, Marjorie	Macmillan
Astronauts in Space	J	I	135	Windows on Literacy	National Geographic
At the Doctor	J	I	250+	Story Starter	Wright Group/McGraw Hill
Aunt Eater Loves a Mystery	J	F	250+	Cushman, Doug	HarperTrophy
Aunt Eater's Mystery Christmas	J	F	250+	Cushman, Doug	HarperTrophy
Aunt Eater's Mystery Vacation	J	F	250+	Cushman, Doug	HarperTrophy
Author on My Street, The	J	RF	260	Books for Young Learners	Richard C. Owen
Backhoes	J	I	118	Pebble Plus	Capstone Press
Barnaby's Birthday	J	RF	214	Voyages	SRA/McGraw Hill
Baseball Ballerina	J	RF	250+	Cristaldi, Kathryn	Random House
Baseball Birthday Party, The	J	RF	250+	Prager, Annabelle	Random House
Be a Good Friend!	J	I	250+	Spyglass Books	Compass Point Books
Be a Good Sport!	J	I	250+	Spyglass Books	Compass Point Books
Be Safe on Your Bike	J	I	250+	Rosen Real Readers	Rosen Publishing Group
Beaks and Feet	J	I	234	Alphakids	Sundance
Bear and the Bees, The	J	TL	250+	PM Plus Story Books	Rigby
Bear Shadow	J	F	489	Asch, Frank	Simon & Schuster
Bears and Their Dens	J	I	131	Animal Homes	Capstone Press
Bears are Curious	J	I	250+	Milton, Joyce	Random House
Bear's Bargain	J	F	250+	Asch, Frank	Scholastic
Bear's Year, A	J	I	213	Phonics Readers	Compass Point Books
Beatrix Potter	J	B	135	iOpeners	Pearson Learning Group
Beautiful Pig	J	F	423	Read Alongs	Rigby
Beavers and Their Lodges	J	I	121	Pebble Plus	Capstone Press
Bees and Their Hives	J	I	112	Animal Homes	Capstone Press
Ben Franklin: Scientist	J	I	266	Leveled Readers Science	Houghton Mifflin
Bend, Stretch, and Leap	J	RF	250+	PM Plus Story Books	Rigby
Best Boat, The	J	I	690	Leveled Readers Science	Houghton Mifflin
Best Job for Scooter, The	J	RF	580	Leveled Readers	Houghton Mifflin
Best Little Monkeys in the World, The	J	F	250+	Standiford, Natalie	Random House
Best Nest	J	F	250+	Eastman, Philip D.	Random House
Best Pet, The	J	RF	250+	Lighthouse	Rigby
Better Than TV	J	RF	250+	Miller, Sara Swan	Bantam
Big Green Caterpillar, The	J	RF	161	Literacy 2000	Rigby
Big Mama and Grandma Ghana	J	RF	250+	Medearis, A. Shelf	Scholastic
Big Max	J	F	250+	Platt, Kin	HarperTrophy
Big Snow, The	J	I	150	Early Connections	Benchmark Education
Big, Bad Cook, The	J	TL	250+	Literacy Tree	Rigby
Billy Magee's New Car	J	RF	391	Foundations	Wright Group/McGraw Hill
Biography of Faith Ringgold, A	J	B	132	Vocabulary Readers	Houghton Mifflin
Bird Lady, The	J	I	250+	Story Steps	Rigby
Bird Watching	J	RF	475	PM Plus Story Books	Rigby
Birds and Their Nests	J	I	175	Animal Homes	Capstone Press
Birds' Nests	J	I	111	Wonder World	Wright Group/McGraw Hill

* Collection of short stories

TITLE	LEVEL	GENRE	WORD COUNT	AUTHOR / SERIES	PUBLISHER / DISTRIBUTOR
Bird's-Eye View	J	RF	393	PM Turquoise	Rigby
Blackboard Bear	J	F	117	Alexander, Martha	Penguin Group
Blood	J	I	241	Twig	Wright Group/McGraw Hill
Blossom	J	F	225	Voyages	SRA/McGraw Hill
Boa Constrictors	J	I	250+	Rain Forest Animals	Red Brick Learning
Bones	J	I	182	Rigby Focus	Rigby
Bootlace Soup	J	TL	250+	Voyages	SRA/McGraw Hill
Boring Old Bed	J	F	250+	Lighthouse	Rigby
Boy Who Cried Wolf, The	J	TL	460	Aesop's Fables	Pearson Learning Group
Boy Who Cried Wolf, The	J	TL	140	Littledale, Freya	Scholastic
Brave Little Tailor, The	J	TL	250+	PM Tales and Plays Turquoise	Rigby
Breakfast Around the World	J	I	101	Twig	Wright Group/McGraw Hill
Bring Me Your Horses	J	I	250+	Phonics and Friends	Hampton-Brown
Bringing the Rain to Kapiti Plain	J	TL	739	Aardema, Verna	Scholastic
Broken Bones	J	I	250+	Sunshine Books	Wright Group/McGraw Hill
Budgie's Dream	J	F	250+	Story Starter	Wright Group/McGraw Hill
Bush Bunyip, The	J	F	250+	Bookshop	Mondo
Busy Baby	J	RF	250+	Sunshine	Wright Group/McGraw Hill
Buzby	J	F	250+	Hoban, Julia	HarperTrophy
Cabin in the Hills, The	J	RF	349	PM Turquoise	Rigby
Camp Big Paw	J	RF	250+	Cushman, Doug	HarperTrophy
Can You See An Insect?	J	I	171	Windows on Literacy	National Geographic
Captain Bluefin's Underwater Ride	J	I	250+	Phonics Readers Plus	Steck-Vaughn
Carla's Corner	J	RF	646	Leveled Readers	Houghton Mifflin
Carmen's Star Party	J	RF	250+	Phonics and Friends	Hampton-Brown
Carrots Don't Talk!	J	F	250+	Ready Readers	Pearson Learning Group
Case of the Missing Snacks, The	J	RF	454	Sunshine	Wright Group/McGraw Hill
Cat and Rat Fall Out	J	TL	250+	Lighthouse	Rigby
Cat Concert	J	F	250+	Literacy 2000	Rigby
Cat in the Hat	J	F	250+	Seuss, Dr.	Random House
Catch the Cookie	J	F	250+	Little Celebrations	Pearson Learning Group
Cats	J	I	250+	PM Animal Facts: Orange	Rigby
*Cats and Other Stories	J	F	250+	Story Steps	Rigby
Celebrating Chanukah: Eight Nights	J	I	188	Learn to Read	Creative Teaching Press
Celebrating Chinese New Year: Nick's New Year	J	I	142	Learn to Read	Creative Teaching Press
Celebrating Christmas: Christmas Decorations	J	I	165	Learn to Read	Creative Teaching Press
Celebrating Cinco de Mayo: Fiesta Time!	J	I	41	Learn to Read	Creative Teaching Press
Celebrating Easter: The Easter Egg Hunt	J	I	166	Learn to Read	Creative Teaching Press
Celebrating Martin Luther King, Jr. Day: Dreaming of Change	J	I	152	Learn to Read	Creative Teaching Press
Celebrations Around the World	J	I	205	Early Connections	Benchmark Education
Cells	J	I	96	Wonder World	Wright Group/McGraw Hill
Changes Around Us	J	I	176	Instant Readers	Harcourt School Publishers
Charlie Best	J	F	250+	Voyages	SRA/McGraw Hill
Chicken in the Middle of the Road	J	RF	250+	Bookshop	Mondo
Children of Sierra Leone, The	J	I	142	Books For Young Learners	Richard C. Owen
Chili for Lindy	J	RF	250+	Leveled Readers Language Support	Houghton Mifflin
Chinese New Year, The	J	TL	250+	Troughton, Joanna	Pearson Learning Group
Chocolate Cake, The	J	RF	250+	PM Plus Story Books	Rigby
Chocolate-Chip Muffins	J	RF	204	Sunshine	Wright Group/McGraw Hill
Christmas	J	I	106	Pebble Books	Capstone Press
Christmas in the Big Woods	J	HF	250+	Wilder, Laura Ingalls	HarperCollins

TITLE	LEVEL	GENRE	WORD COUNT	AUTHOR / SERIES	PUBLISHER / DISTRIBUTOR
Christy's First Dive	J	RF	250+	Leveled Readers Language Support	Houghton Mifflin
Cicadas	J	I	87	Pebble Books	Red Brick Learning
Cinderella	J	TL	250+	Jumbled Tumbled Tales & Rhymes	Rigby
City Mouse-Country Mouse	J	TL	198	Wallner, John	Scholastic
Class Play, The	J	RF	250+	Little Readers	Houghton Mifflin
Clay Things, Play Things	J	I	250+	Phonics Readers	Scholastic
Clocks and More Clocks	J	RF	374	Hutchins, Pat	Scholastic
Clothes Around the World	J	I	214	Vocabulary Readers	Houghton Mifflin
Clouds	J	I	204	Independent Readers Science	Houghton Mifflin
Clouds	J	I	40	Early Connections	Benchmark Education
Clown Fish	J	I	123	Pebble Plus	Capstone Press
Coconut Lunches	J	RF	564	Sunshine	Wright Group/McGraw Hill
Collecting Badges	J	I	250+	Stepping Stones	Nelson/Michaels Assoc.
Collecting Shapes	J	I	250+	Stepping Stones	Nelson/Michaels Assoc.
Collections	J	RF	250+	Voyages	SRA/McGraw Hill
Color Wizard, The	J	F	250+	Bank Street	Bantam
Come Back, Pip!	J	RF	355	PM Plus Story Books	Rigby
Costume Party, The	J	RF	145	City Kids	Rigby
Could It Be?	J	RF	250+	Bank Street	Bantam
Countdown: a play	J	F	250+	Story Box	Wright Group/McGraw Hill
Counting Many Ways	J	I	250+	Yellow Umbrella Books	Capstone Press
Country Fair	J	HF	250+	Wilder, Laura Ingalls	HarperCollins
Cousin Kira	J	RF	250+	Sunshine	Wright Group/McGraw Hill
Cubby's Gum	J	F	250+	Ready Readers	Pearson Learning Group
Cupboard Full of Summer, A	J	RF	234	Pacific Literacy	Pacific Learning
Curious George Rides a Bike	J	F	250+	Rey, Margaret	Scholastic
Cynthia Rylant, Author	J	B	137	Vocabulary Readers	Houghton Mifflin
Dad's Surprise	J	RF	202	Foundations	Wright Group/McGraw Hill
Daisy	J	RF	250+	Stepping Stones	Nelson/Michaels Assoc.
Dan the Dunce	J	TL	539	Tales from Hans Andersen	Wright Group/McGraw Hill
Dance at Grandpa's	J	HF	250+	Wilder, Laura Ingalls	HarperCollins
Dancing to the River	J	TL	250+	Cambridge Reading	Pearson Learning Group
Danger in the Parking Lot	J	RF	250+	PM Plus Story Books	Rigby
Danny and the Dinosaur	J	F	250+	Hoff, Syd	Scholastic
Day I Lost My Bus Pass, The	J	RF	131	City Kids	Rigby
Day With a Mail Carrier, A	J	I	187	Welcome Books	Children's Press
Day With a Mechanic, A	J	I	147	Welcome Books	Children's Press
Deer in the Wood, The	J	HF	250+	Wilder, Laura Ingalls	HarperCollins
*Detective Dinosaur	J	F	250+	Skofield, James	HarperTrophy
Difficult Day, The	J	RF	304	Read Alongs	Rigby
Dinosaur Zoo, The	J	F	250+	Literacy Tree	Rigby
Dinosaur's Cold, The	J	F	244	Literacy 2000	Rigby
Ditching School	J	RF	128	City Kids	Rigby
Dog Family, The	J	I	250+	Story Steps	Rigby
Dogs	J	I	250+	PM Animal Facts: Orange	Rigby
Dogs Are My Favorite Things	J	RF	246	Bookshop	Mondo
Dogs at Work	J	I	250+	Little Readers	Houghton Mifflin
Dogstar	J	F	250+	Literacy 2000	Rigby
Dolly Madison, First Lady	J	B	250+	Leveled Readers Social Studies	Houghton Mifflin
Dolphins	J	I	111	Wonder World	Wright Group/McGraw Hill
Donkey's Tale, The	J	TL	250+	Bank Street	Bantam
Don't Be My Valentine: A Classroom Mystery	J	RF	250+	Lexau, Joan M.	HarperTrophy
Don't Eat Too Much Turkey	J	TL	250+	Cohen, Miriam	Bantam

* Collection of short stories

TITLE	LEVEL	GENRE	WORD COUNT	AUTHOR / SERIES	PUBLISHER / DISTRIBUTOR
Don't Worry	J	RF	339	Literacy 2000	Rigby
Doorbell Rang, The	J	RF	283	Hutchins, Pat	Greenwillow
Dragon Who Had the Measles, The	J	F	250+	Literacy 2000	Rigby
Dragon with a Cold	J	F	250+	Sunshine	Wright Group/McGraw Hill
Dragon's Scales, The	J	F	250+	Albee, Sarah	Random House
Drummer Hoff	J	TL	173	Emberly, Barbara	Prentice-Hall
Duck Goes to the Farm	J	F	373	Leveled Readers	Houghton Mifflin
Early Bird's Alarm Clock, The	J	F	250+	Daniel, Claire	Steck-Vaughn
Earthmovers	J	I	121	Pebble Plus	Capstone Press
Earth's Land and Water	J	I	234	Yellow Umbrella Books	Capstone Press
Earthworms	J	I	185	Leveled Readers	Houghton Mifflin
Eat Your Vegetables	J	I	157	iOpeners	Pearson Learning Group
Educating Arthur	J	F	250+	Soar To Success	Houghton Mifflin
Egg To Chick	J	I	250+	Selsam, Millicent E.	HarperTrophy
Eggs, Eggs, Eggs	J	I	188	Wonder World	Wright Group/McGraw Hill
Elaine	J	B	250+	Stepping Stones	Nelson/Michaels Assoc.
Elephant and the Bad Baby, The	J	F	250+	Hayes, Sarah	Sundance
Elephant in the House, An	J	F	546	Read Alongs	Rigby
Elephant Rescue	J	RF	250+	Leveled Readers Language Support	Houghton Mifflin
Elves and the Shoemaker, The	J	TL	300	PM Tales and Plays-Turquoise	Rigby
Emil	J	RF	250+	Stepping Stones	Nelson/Michaels Assoc.
Emilio and the River	J	RF	403	Sunshine	Wright Group/McGraw Hill
Emperor's New Clothes, The	J	TL	250+	Rigby Literacy	Rigby
Emperor's New Clothes, The	J	TL	571	Tales from Hans Andersen	Wright Group/McGraw Hill
Emu Who Wanted to Be a Horse, The	J	F	250+	Voyages	SRA/McGraw Hill
Encyclopedia of Tiny Creatures	J	I	250+	Discovery World	Rigby
Endless Puzzle, The	J	RF	416	Leveled Readers	Houghton Mifflin
Eva the Beekeeper	J	I	250+	iOpeners	Pearson Learning Group
Everybody Eats Bread	J	I	241	Literacy 2000	Rigby
Everyday Machines	J	I	188	Rigby Focus	Rigby
Facts About Forest Fires	J	I	250+	Rosen Real Readers	Rosen Publishing Group
Fair Day	J	RF	184	City Kids	Rigby
Fall Leaves	J	I	222	Leveled Readers	Houghton Mifflin
Families	J	F	184	Storyteller-Night Crickets	Wright Group/McGraw Hill
Family of Beavers, A	J	RF	141	Books for Young Learners	Richard C. Owen
Family Table, The	J	RF	274	Leveled Readers Language Support	Houghton Mifflin
Fantastic Washing Machine	J	F	250+	Sunshine	Wright Group/McGraw Hill
Farmer Boy Birthday, A	J	HF	250+	Wilder, Laura Ingalls	HarperCollins
Farmer Brown and Dapple Gray	J	RF	166	Books for Young Learners	Richard C. Owen
Farmer Joe's Hot Day	J	F	406	Richards, Nancy W.	Scholastic
Fascinating Faces	J	I	99	Literacy Tree	Rigby
*Fast and Funny	J	RF	1499	Story Box	Wright Group/McGraw Hill
Feeling Funny	J	F	250+	Sunshine	Wright Group/McGraw Hill
Feisty Old Woman Who Lived in the Cozy Cave	J	F	301	Foundations	Wright Group/McGraw Hill
Fins, Wings, and Legs	J	I	250+	iOpeners	Pearson Learning Group
Fire Cat, The	J	F	250+	Averill, Esther	HarperTrophy
Fire Station, The	J	I	237	Pebble Books	Capstone Press
Fire Trucks	J	I	127	Mighty Machines	Capstone Press
First Fire Company, The	J	I	182	Leveled Readers	Houghton Mifflin
First Flight	J	RF	250+	PM Plus Story Books	Rigby
First Grade Takes a Test	J	RF	250+	Cohen, Miriam	Bantam
Fizzkid the Inventor	J	F	250+	Rigby Literacy	Rigby

* Collection of short stories

TITLE	LEVEL	GENRE	WORD COUNT	AUTHOR / SERIES	PUBLISHER / DISTRIBUTOR
Flashlights	J	I	250+	Sunshine Books	Wright Group/McGraw Hill
Floating and Sinking	J	I	221	Alphakids	Sundance
Floating and Sinking	J	I	168	Bookshop	Mondo
Flora, a Friend for the Animals	J	RF	337	Sunshine	Wright Group/McGraw Hill
Florence Griffith-Joyner: Olympic Runner	J	B	184	Leveled Readers Language Support	Houghton Mifflin
Forgetful Fran	J	RF	250+	Sunshine	Wright Group/McGraw Hill
Fossil Hunters, The	J	I	207	Instant Readers	Harcourt School Publishers
*Four on the Shore	J	F	250+	Marshall, Edward	Puffin Books
*Fox All Week	J	F	250+	Marshall, Edward	Puffin Books
*Fox and His Friends	J	F	250+	Marshall, Edward	Puffin Books
Fox and the Crow, The	J	F	240	Instant Readers	Harcourt School Publishers
Fox and the Crow, The	J	TL	250+	PM Plus Story Books	Rigby
Fox and the Goat, The	J	TL	365	Aesop's Fables	Pearson Learning Group
*Fox at School	J	F	250+	Marshall, Edward	Puffin Books
*Fox Be Nimble	J	F	250+	Marshall, James	Puffin Books
Fox Fables	J	F	250+	Sunshine	Wright Group/McGraw Hill
*Fox In Love	J	F	250+	Marshall, Edward	Puffin Books
*Fox on Stage	J	F	250+	Marshall, James	Puffin Books
Fox on the Job	J	F	250+	Marshall, James	Puffin Books
*Fox on Wheels	J	F	250+	Marshall, Edward	Puffin Books
*Fox Outfoxed	J	F	250+	Marshall, James	Puffin Books
Foxes and Their Dens	J	I	146	Pebble Plus	Capstone Press
Fraidy Cats	J	F	250+	Krensky, Stephen	Scholastic
Frank The Fish Gets His Wish	J	F	250+	Appleton-Smith, Laura	Flyleaf Publishing
Froggy Learns to Swim	J	F	250+	London, Jonathan	Scholastic
From Farm to Store	J	I	181	Phonics Readers	Compass Point Books
From Hive to Home	J	I	200	Windows on Literacy	National Geographic
From Rocks to Sand: The Story of a Beach	J	I	224	Wonder World	Wright Group/McGraw Hill
From the Earth	J	I	186	Discovery Links	Newbridge
Funny Bones	J	F	250+	Ahlberg, Allan & Janet	Viking
Gallo and Zorro	J	F	369	Literacy 2000	Rigby
Games We Play	J	I	250+	PM Plus Nonfiction	Rigby
Garden Tools	J	I	165	Spyglass Books	Compass Point Books
Get Set and Go	J	F	250+	Real Reading	Steck-Vaughn
Get the Message	J	I	110	iOpeners	Pearson Learning Group
*Ghosts!: Ghostly Tales from Folklore	J	TL	250+	Schwartz, Alvin	HarperTrophy
Giant Balloons	J	I	185	Rigby Focus	Rigby
Giant Grass	J	I	250+	Story Steps	Rigby
Giant in the Forest, A	J	F	250+	Reading Unlimited	Pearson Learning Group
Giant Jumperee, The: A Play	J	F	250+	Rigby Literacy	Rigby
*Giant Soup	J	F	419	Pacific Literacy	Pacific Learning
Gift for Yoshi, A	J	RF	282	Leveled Readers	Houghton Mifflin
Gingerbread Man, The	J	TL	535	Traditional Tales & More	Rigby
Gizmos' Party, The	J	F	250+	Rigby Literacy	Rigby
Gizmos' Trip, The	J	F	250+	Rigby Literacy	Rigby
Going Swimming	J	RF	210	City Kids	Rigby
Going to the Bank	J	I	317	Foundations	Wright Group/McGraw Hill
Going to the City	J	I	250+	People, Spaces & Places	Rand McNally
Going to the Hairdresser	J	I	227	Foundations	Wright Group/McGraw Hill
Going to Town	J	HF	250+	Wilder, Laura Ingalls	HarperCollins
Going West	J	HF	250+	Wilder, Laura Ingalls	HarperCollins
Golden Dragon	J	F	250+	Supersonics	Rigby
Goldfish	J	I	250+	PM Animal Facts: Orange	Rigby

* Collection of short stories

TITLE	LEVEL	GENRE	WORD COUNT	AUTHOR / SERIES	PUBLISHER / DISTRIBUTOR
Good Dessert, A	J	F	250+	Leveled Readers Language Support	Houghton Mifflin
Goose Who Acted Like a Cow, The	J	F	250+	Phonics & Friends	Hampton-Brown
Gorillas	J	I	250+	Pebble Books	Red Brick Learning
Grandma's Pictures of The Past	J	RF	250+	Home Connection Collection	Rigby
*Grandpa at the Beach	J	F	250+	Lewis, Rob	Mondo
*Grandpa Comes To Stay	J	F	1083	Lewis, Rob	Mondo
Grandpa's Birthday	J	RF	250+	Literacy 2000	Rigby
Granny and the Desperadoes	J	RF	250+	Parish, Peggy	Simon & Schuster
Great Day for Up	J	F	180	Seuss, Dr.	Random House
Great Great Grandfather's Railroad	J	HF	250+	Sunshine Books	Wright Group/McGraw Hill
Great Inventor, A: An Wang	J	B	207	Leveled Readers Social Studies	Houghton Mifflin
Great Snake Escape, The	J	F	250+	Coxe, Molly	HarperTrophy
Great, Big, Giant Turnip, The	J	TL	610	Early Connections	Benchmark Education
Greedy King, The	J	RF	250+	Lighthouse	Rigby
Green Dragons, The	J	RF	250+	PM Story Books	Rigby
Green Eggs and Ham	J	F	250+	Seuss, Dr.	Random House
Growing Sprouts and Eva's Sprout Diary	J	RF	250+	Voyages	SRA/McGraw Hill
Grown-ups Say the Silliest Things	J	F	250+	Lighthouse	Rigby
Guinea Pigs	J	I	250+	PM Animal Facts: Orange	Rigby
Gus and Grandpa	J	RF	250+	Mills, Claudia	Sunburst
Ha-Ha Party, The	J	RF	250	Sunshine	Wright Group/McGraw Hill
Hailstorm, The	J	RF	386	PM Turquoise	Rigby
Hair Party, The	J	RF	250+	Literacy 2000	Rigby
Halloween	J	I	32	Pebble Books	Capstone Press
Hand, Hand, Fingers, Thumb	J	F	250+	Perkins, Al	Random House
Hannah and Her Dad	J	RF	250+	Voyages	SRA/McGraw Hill
Hard Workers	J	I	186	Phonics Readers	Compass Point Books
Hare and the Tortoise, The	J	TL	587	Aesop's Fables	Pearson Learning Group
Harry and the Lady Next Door	J	F	250+	Zion, Gene	HarperTrophy
Harvest Time	J	I	228	Spyglass Books	Compass Point Books
Hatupatu and the Birdwoman	J	F	250+	Story Box	Wright Group/McGraw Hill
Having a Haircut	J	RF	298	City Kids	Rigby
He Bear, She Bear	J	F	250+	Berenstain, Stan & Jan	Random House
Hearing	J	I	107	Pebble Books	Capstone Press
Hedgehog Bakes a Cake	J	F	250+	Bank Street	Bantam
Helga's Secret	J	RF	250+	Rigby Literacy	Rigby
Help! I'm Stuck!	J	F	250+	Little Celebrations	Pearson Learning Group
Helpful Becky	J	RF	250+	Phonics Readers Plus	Steck-Vaughn
Henry and Mudge and Annie's Good Move	J	RF	250+	Rylant, Cynthia	Aladdin
Henry and Mudge and the Bedtime Thumps	J	RF	250+	Rylant, Cynthia	Aladdin
Henry and Mudge and the Best Day of All	J	RF	250+	Rylant, Cynthia	Aladdin
Henry and Mudge and the Careful Cousin	J	RF	250+	Rylant, Cynthia	Aladdin
Henry and Mudge and the Forever Sea	J	RF	250+	Rylant, Cynthia	Aladdin
Henry and Mudge and the Happy Cat	J	RF	250+	Rylant, Cynthia	Aladdin
Henry and Mudge and the Long Weekend	J	RF	250+	Rylant, Cynthia	Aladdin
Henry and Mudge and the Sneaky Crackers	J	RF	250+	Rylant, Cynthia	Aladdin
Henry and Mudge and the Snowman Plan	J	RF	250+	Rylant, Cynthia	Aladdin
Henry and Mudge and the Starry Night	J	RF	250+	Rylant, Cynthia	Aladdin
Henry and Mudge and the Wild Wind	J	RF	250+	Rylant, Cynthia	Aladdin
Henry and Mudge Get the Cold Shivers	J	RF	250+	Rylant, Cynthia	Aladdin
Henry and Mudge in Puddle Trouble	J	RF	250+	Rylant, Cynthia	Aladdin
Henry and Mudge in the Family Trees	J	RF	250+	Rylant, Cynthia	Aladdin
Henry and Mudge in the Green Time	J	RF	250+	Rylant, Cynthia	Aladdin

* Collection of short stories

TITLE	LEVEL	GENRE	WORD COUNT	AUTHOR / SERIES	PUBLISHER / DISTRIBUTOR
Henry and Mudge in the Sparkle Days	J	RF	250+	Rylant, Cynthia	Aladdin
Henry and Mudge Take the Big Test	J	RF	250+	Rylant, Cynthia	Aladdin
Henry and Mudge Under the Yellow Moon	J	RF	250+	Rylant, Cynthia	Aladdin
Henry and Mudge: The First Book	J	RF	250+	Rylant, Cynthia	Aladdin
Here Comes Kate!	J	RF	250+	Real Reading	Steck-Vaughn
Herman the Helper	J	F	94	Kraus, Robert	Simon & Schuster
Hermie the Crab	J	RF	250+	PM Plus Story Books	Rigby
*Hide-and-Seek with Grandpa	J	F	250+	Lewis, Rob	Mondo
Hiding Places	J	I	250+	Storyteller-Night Crickets	Wright Group/McGraw Hill
Hippopotamus Ate the Teacher, A	J	F	250+	Thaler, Mike	Avon
His Majesty the King	J	F	250+	Little Celebrations	Pearson Learning Group
Holidays	J	I	191	Windows on Literacy	National Geographic
Home for Star and Patches, A	J	RF	250+	PM Plus Story Books	Rigby
Hooray for Midsommar!	J	RF	250+	Greetings	Rigby
Hop on Pop	J	F	250+	Seuss, Dr.	Random House
Horatio Whale	J	F	165	Book Bus	Creative Edge
Horse and the Bell, The	J	TL	250+	PM Plus Story Books	Rigby
Horse in Harry's Room, The	J	F	425	Hoff, Syd	HarperCollins
House that Jack Built, The	J	TL	250+	Peppe, Rodney	Delacorte
House That Jack's Friends Built, The	J	RF	254	Pair-It Books	Steck-Vaughn
House that Stood on Booker Hill, The	J	RF	250+	Ready Readers	Pearson Learning Group
How Big Is It?	J	RF	250+	Lighthouse	Rigby
How Do Seeds Travel?	J	I	179	Windows on Literacy	National Geographic
How Does My Bike Work?	J	I	127	Windows on Literacy	National Geographic
How Does Sound Travel?	J	I	148	Instant Readers	Harcourt School Publishers
How Grandmother Spider Got the Sun	J	TL	115	Little Readers	Houghton Mifflin
How Lizard Lost His Colors	J	TL	197	Literacy Tree	Rigby
How To Cook Scones	J	I	250+	Bookshop	Mondo
How To Make Salsa	J	I	192	Bookshop	Mondo
How Turtle Raced Beaver	J	TL	182	Literacy 2000	Rigby
I Am a Rock	J	I	250+	Marzollo, Jean	Scholastic
I Can Read with My Eyes Shut	J	F	250+	Seuss, Dr.	Random House
I Have Feelings!	J	F	250+	Book Shop	Mondo
I Like Shopping	J	RF	287	Sunshine	Wright Group/McGraw Hill
I Love to Sneeze	J	F	250+	Bank Street	Bantam
I Play Soccer	J	RF	97	City Kids	Rigby
I Saw the Boston Tea Party	J	HF	273	Independent Readers Social Studies	Houghton Mifflin
I Saw You in the Bathtub	J	TL	250+	Schwartz, Alvin	HarperTrophy
I Was at the Zoo	J	I	250+	Literacy Tree	Rigby
I Was So Mad	J	RF	232	Mayer, Mercer	Donovan
I Went to the Movies	J	RF	120	City Kids	Rigby
Ice Cream for You	J	I	214	Windows on Literacy	National Geographic
If Dogs Ruled the World	J	F	250+	McNulty, Faith	Scholastic
Imagine That	J	F	250+	Story Box	Wright Group/McGraw Hill
Imran and the Watch	J	RF	415	Cambridge Reading	Pearson Learning Group
*In a Dark, Dark Room	J	TL	250+	Schwartz, Alvin	HarperTrophy
In the Barrio	J	RF	130	Ada, Alma Flor	Scholastic
In the City of Rome	J	TL	250+	Literacy 2000	Rigby
In the Land of the Polar Bear	J	RF	250+	Robinson, F. R.	Steck-Vaughn
Insect-Eaters	J	I	213	Rigby Focus	Rigby
Insects	J	I	171	MacLulich, Carolyn	Scholastic
Into Space	J	I	250+	Momentum Literacy Program	Troll Associates
Invisible Spy, The	J	F	227	Foundations	Wright Group/McGraw Hill

* Collection of short stories

TITLE	LEVEL	GENRE	WORD COUNT	AUTHOR / SERIES	PUBLISHER / DISTRIBUTOR
It's Fun to Exercise	J	I	250+	Rosen Real Readers	Rosen Publishing Group
It's Snowing!	J	I	193	Find Out Readers	Continental Press
I've Been Working on the Railroad	J	TL	250+	Traditional Songs	Picture Window Books
Jaguars	J	I	78	Pebble Books	Red Brick Learning
Jake and the Copycats	J	RF	250+	Rocklin, Joanne	Bantam
Jake Greenthumb	J	F	250+	Bookshop	Mondo
Jamberry	J	F	111	Degen, Bruce	Harper & Row
Jellyfish	J	I	95	Pebble Plus	Capstone Press
Jets and the Rockets, The	J	RF	250+	PM Plus Story Books	Rigby
Jillian Jiggs	J	RF	250+	Gilman, Phoebe	Scholastic
Jimmy Lee Did It	J	RF	250+	Cummings, Pat	Lothrop
Jimmy Parker's New Job	J	RF	250+	Voyages	SRA/McGraw Hill
Johnny Lion's Book	J	F	250+	Hurd, Edith Thacher	HarperCollins
Jojo and the Robot	J	F	250+	Sunshine	Wright Group/McGraw Hill
Jonathan Buys a Present	J	RF	353	PM Story Books-Turquoise	Rigby
Jordan's Catch	J	RF	250+	PM Story Books	Rigby
Jumping Jack	J	F	250+	Rigby Literacy	Rigby
Just for Fun	J	F	250+	Literacy 2000	Rigby
Just Hanging Around	J	I	223	Storyteller-Night Crickets	Wright Group/McGraw Hill
*Just Like Me	J	F	2154	Story Box	Wright Group/McGraw Hill
Just Us Women	J	RF	250+	Caines, Jeannette	Scholastic
Kayaking at Blue Lake	J	RF	250+	PM Plus Story Books	Rigby
Keeping Score	J	I	240	Early Connections	Benchmark Education
Keeping Time	J	I	231	Early Connections	Benchmark Education
Kenny and the Little Kickers	J	F	250+	Mareollo, Claudio	Scholastic
Kermit and Robin's Scary Story	J	F	250+	Muntean, Michaela	Puffin Books
Kerplunk!	J	I	250	Spyglass Books	Compass Point Books
Kick, Pass, and Run	J	RF	250+	Kessler, Leonard	HarperTrophy
King Glitter and the Stars	J	F	318	Talking Point Series	Pearson Learning Group
King Midas and the Golden Touch	J	TL	250+	Traditional Tales	Pearson Learning Group
King of the Birds, The	J	F	250+	Rigby Literacy	Rigby
King of the Sky	J	RF	250+	Foundations	Wright Group/McGraw Hill
King Who Could Knit, The	J	F	250+	The Wright Skills	Wright Group/McGraw Hill
Kitchen Rules	J	I	153	Windows on Literacy	National Geographic
Knit, Knit, Knit, Knit	J	F	250+	Literacy 2000	Rigby
Krakus and the Dragon: A Polish Folktale	J	TL	250+	Leveled Readers Language Support	Houghton Mifflin
Kwasi: A Storysong	J	RF	250+	Greetings	Rigby
Lad Who Went to the North Wind, The	J	F	250+	Bookshop	Mondo
Lady Liberty	J	I	229	Twig	Wright Group/McGraw Hill
Last One In Is a Rotten Egg	J	RF	250+	Kessler, Leonard	HarperTrophy
Let's Be Enemies	J	RF	250+	Sendak, Maurice	Harper & Row
Let's Make a Kite	J	I	250+	Book Shop	Mondo
Let's Make Music	J	I	220	iOpeners	Pearson Learning Group
Library Day	J	F	250+	Sunshine	Wright Group/McGraw Hill
License Plates	J	RF	411	PM Turquoise	Rigby
Life Cycle of a Butterfly, The	J	I	211	Pebble Books	Red Brick Learning
Life Cycle of a Cat, The	J	I	108	Pebble Books	Red Brick Learning
Life Cycle of a Chicken, The	J	I	214	Pebble Books	Red Brick Learning
Life Cycle of a Dog, The	J	I	110	Pebble Books	Red Brick Learning
Life Cycle of a Frog, The	J	I	218	Pebble Books	Red Brick Learning
Life Cycle of a Whale, The	J	I	209	Pebble Books	Red Brick Learning
Life in the City	J	I	307	Early Connections	Benchmark Education
Life of a Bean, The	J	I	201	Independent Readers Science	Houghton Mifflin

TITLE	LEVEL	GENRE	WORD COUNT	AUTHOR / SERIES	PUBLISHER / DISTRIBUTOR
Light	J	I	150	Early Connections	Benchmark Education
Light	J	I	250+	Momentum Literacy Program	Troll Associates
Lion and the Mouse, The	J	TL	325	Little Books	Sadlier-Oxford
Lion and the Mouse, The	J	TL	285	Sunshine	Wright Group/McGraw Hill
Lion in the Night, The	J	F	250+	Momentum Literacy Program	Troll Associates
Little Adventure, A	J	RF	250+	PM Story Books-Silver	Rigby
Little Ant, The: A Folktale From New Mexico	J	TL	250+	Costigan, Shirleyann	Hampton-Brown
Little Bear	J	F	1664	Minarik, Else H.	HarperCollins
Little Bear's Friend	J	F	250+	Minarik, Else H.	HarperTrophy
Little Bear's Visit	J	F	250+	Minarik, Else H.	HarperTrophy
Little Black: A Pony	J	RF	250+	Farley, Walter	Random House
Little Blue and Little Yellow	J	F	250+	Lionni, Leo	Scholastic
Little Brother's Haircut	J	RF	250+	Story Box	Wright Group/McGraw Hill
Little Dinosaur Escapes	J	HF	389	PM Turquoise	Rigby
Little Dutch Boy, The	J	TL	250+	Jumbled Tumbled Tales & Rhymes	Rigby
Little Fireman	J	RF	250+	Brown, Margaret Wise	HarperCollins
Little Frog, Big Pond	J	F	250+	The Wright Skills	Wright Group/McGraw Hill
Little Frogs of Puerto Rico, The	J	RF	143	Books for Young Learners	Richard C. Owen
Little Gorilla	J	F	167	Bornstein, Ruth	Clarion
Little House Birthday, A	J	HF	250+	Wilder, Laura Ingalls	HarperCollins
Little Prairie House, A	J	HF	250+	Wilder, Laura Ingalls	HarperCollins
Little Red Riding Hood	J	TL	250+	PM Tales and Plays-Turquoise	Rigby
Living and Growing	J	I	250+	PM Plus Nonfiction	Rigby
Living With Others	J	I	250+	PM Plus Nonfiction	Rigby
Lizard's Grandmother	J	F	336	Sunshine	Wright Group/McGraw Hill
Log Hotel	J	RF	261	Schreiber, Anne	Scholastic
Lonely Dragon, The	J	F	250+	Momentum Literacy Program	Troll Associates
Look Inside	J	I	168	Storyteller Nonfiction	Wright Group/McGraw Hill
Look Out For Your Tail	J	F	250+	Literacy 2000	Rigby
Looking For Patterns	J	I	160	Early Connections	Benchmark Education
Machines	J	I	44	Sunshine Books	Wright Group/McGraw Hill
Magic Fish, The	J	TL	250+	Rylant, Cynthia	Scholastic
Magnets	J	I	259	Windows on Literacy	National Geographic
Mai's Big Surprise	J	RF	250+	The Wright Skills	Wright Group/McGraw Hill
Make a Bottle Orchestra	J	I	250	Sunshine	Wright Group/McGraw Hill
Make a Guitar	J	I	540	Sunshine	Wright Group/McGraw Hill
Make a Paper Airplane	J	I	158	How-To Series	Benchmark Education
Make a Tune	J	I	246	Kratky, Lada	Hampton-Brown
Make an Island	J	I	199	How-To Series	Benchmark Education
Make Masks for a Play	J	I	540	Sunshine	Wright Group/McGraw Hill
Making a Marionette	J	I	250+	Early Connections	Benchmark Education
Making Art	J	I	250+	Rosen Real Readers	Rosen Publishing Group
Making Collages	J	I	250+	Bookshop	Mondo
Making Friends	J	RF	214	Foundations	Wright Group/McGraw Hill
Making Ice Cream	J	I	176	How-To Series	Benchmark Education
Mama's Llamas	J	F	159	Books for Young Learners	Richard C. Owen
Marble Patch, The	J	RF	250+	PM Story Books	Rigby
March for Freedom	J	I	132	Twig	Wright Group/McGraw Hill
Marigold and Grandma On The Town	J	F	250+	Calmenson, Stephanie	HarperTrophy
Market Day for Mrs. Wordy	J	RF	177	Sunshine	Wright Group/McGraw Hill
Marvin One Too Many	J	RF	250+	Paterson, Katherine	HarperCollins
Matthew Likes to Read	J	RF	144	Pacific Literacy	Pacific Learning
Matthew's Tantrum	J	RF	250+	Literacy 2000	Rigby
Max	J	RF	234	Isadora, Rachel	Macmillan

* Collection of short stories

TITLE	LEVEL	GENRE	WORD COUNT	AUTHOR / SERIES	PUBLISHER / DISTRIBUTOR
Meet Some Tricksters!	J	I	301	Vocabulary Readers	Houghton Mifflin
Meet the Feet	J	I	189	Leveled Readers	Houghton Mifflin
Meg and Mog	J	F	236	Nicoll, Helen	Viking
Messy Bessey's Family Reunion	J	RF	190	McKissack, Patricia & Fredrick	Scholastic
Messy Bessey's School Desk	J	RF	104	Rookie Readers	Children's Press
Messy Meals	J	F	87	Franco, Betsy	Scholastic
Mice	J	I	250+	PM Animal Facts: Orange	Rigby
Mike Swan, Sink or Swim	J	RF	250+	Heiligman, Deborah	Bantam
Mike's Bike	J	RF	250+	Supersonics	Rigby
Milo and the Fire Engine Parade	J	RF	250+	Bookshop	Mondo
Milo and the Greatest Trick Ever!	J	RF	250+	Bookshop	Mondo
Milton the Early Riser	J	F	148	Kraus, Robert	Aladdin
Ming Lo Moves the Mountain	J	F	250+	Lobel, Arnold	Scholastic
Minnie and Moo Go to Paris	J	F	250+	Cazet, Denys	DK Publishing
Miss McKenzie Had a Farm	J	F	515	Pair-It Books	Steck-Vaughn
Miss Piggy's Night Out	J	F	250+	Hunter, Sandra H.	Puffin Books
Missing Parrot, The	J	RF	491	Early Connections	Benchmark Education
Missing Tooth, The	J	RF	250+	Cole, Joanna	Random House
Mitchell Is Moving	J	F	250+	Sharmat, Marjorie Weinman	Simon & Schuster
Mix, Make, and Munch	J	I	245	Home Connection Collection	Rigby
Moana's Island	J	RF	450	Sunshine	Wright Group/McGraw Hill
Moggy the Mouser	J	F	250+	Voyages	SRA/McGraw Hill
Money	J	I	250+	Twig	Wright Group/McGraw Hill
Monkey and Fire	J	F	372	Literacy 2000	Rigby
Monster Manners	J	F	250+	Cole, Joanna	Scholastic
Moon Boy	J	F	250+	Bank Street	Bantam
Moon Stories	J	F	250+	Ready Readers	Pearson Learning Group
Moppet on the Run	J	RF	250+	PM Story Books	Rigby
Morning Bath	J	F	250+	Sunshine	Wright Group/McGraw Hill
Morning Queen, The	J	F	250+	Sunshine	Wright Group/McGraw Hill
Morning Star	J	F	250+	Literacy 2000	Rigby
Morris and Boris at the Circus	J	F	250+	Wiseman, Bernard	HarperTrophy
Morris Goes to School	J	F	250+	Wiseman, Bernard	HarperTrophy
Mother Hippopotamus Gets Wet	J	F	421	Foundations	Wright Group/McGraw Hill
Mother Octopus	J	RF	119	Books for Young Learners	Richard C. Owen
Motorcycle Photo, The	J	RF	250+	PM Plus Story Books	Rigby
Mouse and the Elephant, The	J	TL	250+	Little Readers	Houghton Mifflin
Mouse Deer and the Crocodiles, The	J	TL	250+	PM Plus Story Books	Rigby
Mouse Deer Escapes, The	J	TL	250+	PM Plus Story Books	Rigby
Mouse Monster	J	F	302	Jellybeans	Rigby
*Mouse Soup	J	F	1350	Lobel, Arnold	HarperCollins
*Mouse Tales	J	F	1519	Lobel, Arnold	HarperCollins
Mouse Who Wanted to Marry, The	J	F	250+	Bank Street	Bantam
Mr. Bumbleticker Goes Shopping	J	F	391	Foundations	Wright Group/McGraw Hill
Mr. Hoot's Room	J	F	250+	The Wright Skills	Wright Group/McGraw Hill
Mr. Putter & Tabby Row the Boat	J	RF	250+	Rylant, Cynthia	Harcourt Trade
Mr. Putter & Tabby Take the Train	J	RF	250+	Rylant, Cynthia	Harcourt Trade
Mr. Putter & Tabby Toot the Horn	J	RF	250+	Rylant, Cynthia	Harcourt Trade
Mr. Putter and Tabby Bake the Cake	J	RF	250+	Rylant, Cynthia	Harcourt Trade
Mr. Putter and Tabby Fly the Plane	J	RF	250+	Rylant, Cynthia	Harcourt Trade
Mr. Putter and Tabby Pick the Pears	J	RF	250+	Rylant, Cynthia	Harcourt Trade
Mr. Putter and Tabby Pour the Tea	J	RF	250+	Rylant, Cynthia	Harcourt Trade
Mr. Putter and Tabby Walk the Dog	J	RF	250+	Rylant, Cynthia	Harcourt Trade
Mrs. Honey's List	J	RF	250+	Voyages	SRA/McGraw Hill

* Collection of short stories

TITLE	LEVEL	GENRE	WORD COUNT	AUTHOR / SERIES	PUBLISHER / DISTRIBUTOR
Mrs. Patches and Her Fudge	J	F	250+	The Wright Skills	Wright Group/McGraw Hill
Muffin Is Trapped	J	RF	250+	PM Story Books	Rigby
Music of Tito Puente, The	J	B	127	Vocabulary Readers	Houghton Mifflin
My Brother, Ant	J	RF	250+	Byars, Betsy	Viking
My Father	J	RF	194	Mayer, Laura	Scholastic
My Favorite Bear	J	I	146	Books for Young Learners	Richard C. Owen
My Favorite Days	J	I	250+	Rigby Literacy	Rigby
My Fish Tank	J	I	238	Windows on Literacy	National Geographic
My Lucky Hat	J	F	250+	Bookshop	Mondo
My Neighborhood	J	RF	391	Leveled Readers	Houghton Mifflin
My Own Place	J	RF	250+	Voyages	SRA/McGraw Hill
My Sloppy Tiger Goes to School	J	F	217	Sunshine	Wright Group/McGraw Hill
My Treasure Garden	J	RF	134	Book Bank	Wright Group/McGraw Hill
Mystery Coin	J	RF	379	Independent Readers Social Studies	Houghton Mifflin
Mystery of the Missing Dog, The	J	F	250+	Levy, Elizabeth	Scholastic
Nana Rescue, The	J	RF	250+	Voyages	SRA/McGraw Hill
Nana's Kitchen	J	RF	250+	Walton, Darwin McBeth	Steck-Vaughn
Neighborhood Clubhouse, The	J	RF	474	Visions	Wright Group/McGraw Hill
Nellie Bly	J	B	270	Leveled Readers Social Studies	Houghton Mifflin
Nelson the Baby Elephant	J	RF	350	PM Turquoise	Rigby
New Beginnings	J	RF	277	Books for Young Learners	Richard C. Owen
New Bike, The	J	RF	526	Sunshine	Wright Group/McGraw Hill
New Forest, The	J	RF	250+	Talking Points	Pearson Learning Group
New School for Megan, A	J	RF	250+	PM Story Books	Rigby
New School, The	J	RF	210	City Kids	Rigby
Newborn Animals	J	I	250+	Momentum Literacy Program	Troll Associates
Newt	J	F	250+	Novak, Matt	HarperTrophy
Nibbles	J	RF	250+	Cambridge Reading	Pearson Learning Group
Nightingale, The	J	TL	563	Tales from Hans Andersen	Wright Group/McGraw Hill
No Dinner for Sally	J	RF	340	Literacy 2000	Rigby
No Matter How You Play It	J	I	129	Instant Readers	Harcourt School Publishers
No More Lost and Found	J	I	137	Vocabulary Readers	Houghton Mifflin
No More Monsters for Me!	J	F	250+	Parish, Peggy	HarperTrophy
Noise Festival, The	J	RF	250+	Sunshine	Wright Group/McGraw Hill
Norma Jean, Jumping Bean	J	F	250+	Cole, Joanna	Random House
Not Now! Said the Cow	J	F	250+	Bank Street	Bantam
Number One	J	SF	170	Pacific Literacy	Pacific Learning
Numbers We Know	J	I	139	Spyglass Books	Compass Point Books
Ocean Animals	J	I	204	Early Connections	Benchmark Education
Octopuses	J	I	94	Under the Sea	Capstone Press
Old Devil Wind	J	F	250+	Martin, Jr., Bill	Harcourt Trade
Old Friend, An	J	RF	250+	Sunshine	Wright Group/McGraw Hill
Old Friends, Near Friends	J	I	250+	Rigby Literacy	Rigby
Old House, The	J	RF	375	Story Box	Wright Group/McGraw Hill
Old MacDonald Had a Farm	J	TL	250+	Traditional Songs	Picture Window Books
On the Beach	J	I	258	Leveled Readers	Houghton Mifflin
On the Open Plains	J	I	250+	Momentum Literacy Program	Troll Associates
Oscar Otter	J	F	250+	Benchley, Nathaniel	HarperTrophy
Oscar's Day	J	I	154	iOpeners	Pearson Learning Group
Our Baby	J	RF	128	Foundations	Wright Group/McGraw Hill
Our Bodies	J	I	250+	PM Plus Nonfiction	Rigby
Our Clothes	J	I	250+	PM Plus Nonfiction	Rigby
Our Money	J	I	255	Early Connections	Benchmark Education

* Collection of short stories

TITLE	LEVEL	GENRE	WORD COUNT	AUTHOR / SERIES	PUBLISHER / DISTRIBUTOR
Our Old Friend, Bear	J	RF	250+	PM Story Books-Silver	Rigby
Our Sun	J	I	166	Early Connections	Benchmark Education
*Owl At Home	J	F	1488	Lobel, Arnold	HarperCollins
Pack 109	J	RF	164	Thaler, Mike	Scholastic
Parachutes	J	RF	145	Storyteller-Moon Rising	Wright Group/McGraw Hill
Parakeet Girl, The	J	F	250+	Sadler, Marilyn	Random House
Parakeets	J	I	250+	PM Animal Facts: Orange	Rigby
Parrots	J	I	94	Pebble Books	Red Brick Learning
Parts Make Up a Whole	J	I	219	Early Connections	Benchmark Education
Party Games	J	RF	399	Foundations	Wright Group/McGraw Hill
Party Time	J	I	250+	Rigby Literacy	Rigby
Paru Has a Bath	J	RF	242	Pacific Literacy	Pacific Learning
Pasquale's Gift	J	RF	250+	Voyages	SRA/McGraw Hill
Pat and Pea Soup	J	RF	187	Books for Young Learners	Richard C. Owen
Patterns	J	I	122	Spyglass Books	Compass Point Books
Paul and Lucy	J	RF	250+	Stepping Stones	Nelson/Michaels Assoc.
Paul Bunyan	J	TL	250+	Jumbled Tumbled Tales & Rhymes	Rigby
Peaches All the Time	J	I	149	Early Connections	Benchmark Education
Peanuts	J	F	250+	Sunshine	Wright Group/McGraw Hill
Peanuts	J	I	149	Windows on Literacy	National Geographic
Pedal Power	J	I	226	Rigby Literacy	Rigby
Peddler's Caps, The	J	TL	250+	PM Story Books-Purple	Rigby
Penguin Family, The	J	I	301	Leveled Readers	Houghton Mifflin
Penny Changes the Day, A	J	RF	250+	Fetty, Margaret	Steck-Vaughn
People at Work	J	I	250+	Momentum Literacy Program	Troll Associates
People Live in the Desert	J	I	163	Windows on Literacy	National Geographic
Pet Pictures	J	I	181	Vocabulary Readers	Houghton Mifflin
Peter and the Wolf	J	TL	250+	PM Plus Story Books	Rigby
Peter's Chair	J	RF	250+	Keats, Ezra Jack	HarperTrophy
Pets	J	F	90	Pacific Literacy	Pacific Learning
Picky Prince, The	J	F	250+	Rigby Literacy	Rigby
Pie Thief, A: a play	J	F	250+	Story Box	Wright Group/McGraw Hill
Pinocchio	J	TL	250+	Jumbled Tumbled Tales & Rhymes	Rigby
Places in the United States	J	I	200	Leveled Readers	Houghton Mifflin
Planets, The	J	I	101	Wonder World	Wright Group/McGraw Hill
Plants	J	I	162	Early Connections	Benchmark Education
Plants of My Aunt	J	F	429	Jellybeans	Rigby
Poles Apart	J	F	250+	Rigby Literacy	Rigby
Police Cars	J	I	125	Mighty Machines	Capstone Press
Popcorn Shop, The	J	RF	250+	Low, Alice	Scholastic
*Poppleton	J	F	250+	Rylant, Cynthia	Scholastic
*Poppleton and Friends	J	F	250+	Rylant, Cynthia	Blue Sky Press
*Poppleton Everyday	J	F	250+	Rylant, Cynthia	Scholastic
*Poppleton Forever	J	F	250+	Rylant, Cynthia	Scholastic
*Poppleton Has Fun	J	F	250+	Rylant, Cynthia	Scholastic
*Poppleton In Fall	J	F	250+	Rylant, Cynthia	Scholastic
*Poppleton in Spring	J	F	250+	Rylant, Cynthia	Scholastic
Porcupine's Pajama Party	J	F	250+	Harshman, Terry Webb	HarperTrophy
Postman Pete	J	RF	250+	Bookshop	Mondo
Prairie Dogs and Their Burrows	J	I	130	Pebble Plus	Capstone Press
Pretty Good Magic	J	RF	250+	Dubowski, Cathy East & Mark	Random House
Princess and the Castle, The	J	F	250+	Leonhardt, Alice	Steck-Vaughn
Pumpkin House, The	J	F	250+	Literacy 2000	Rigby
Puppets	J	I	250+	Little Celebrations	Pearson Learning Group

* Collection of short stories

TITLE	LEVEL	GENRE	WORD COUNT	AUTHOR / SERIES	PUBLISHER / DISTRIBUTOR
Puppy at the Door	J	RF	250+	PM Plus Story Books	Rigby
Push or Pull?	J	I	154	Phonics Readers	Compass Point Books
Queen Jelly Bean	J	F	250+	The Wright Skills	Wright Group/McGraw Hill
Queen's Parrot, The: A Play	J	TL	365	Literacy 2000	Rigby
Quick Chick	J	F	250+	Hoban, Julia	Puffin Books
Quilt for Kristy, A	J	RF	250+	The Wright Skills	Wright Group/McGraw Hill
R is for Radish!	J	F	250+	Coxe, Molly	Random House
Rabbits and Their Burrows	J	I	136	Animal Homes	Capstone Press
Rabbit's Birthday Kite	J	F	250+	Bank Street	Bantam
Rabbits in Space	J	F	216	Talking Point Series	Pearson Learning Group
Rabbit's Real Birthday	J	F	250+	Rigby Literacy	Rigby
Race to Green End, The	J	F	506	PM Turquoise	Rigby
Rachel Carson	J	B	279	Leveled Readers	Houghton Mifflin
Rain	J	I	250+	Voyages	SRA/McGraw Hill
Rain Forest Animals	J	I	151	Phonics Readers	Compass Point Books
Rain Puddle	J	RF	250+	Holl, Adelaide	Morrow
Rain, Snow, and Hail	J	I	250+	Discovery World	Rigby
Rally Car Race	J	RF	250+	PM Plus Story Books	Rigby
Ready, Steady, Rhyme!	J	RF	250+	Rigby Literacy	Rigby
Rescue Boats	J	I	124	Mighty Machines	Capstone Press
Rescue!	J	RF	250+	Sunshine	Wright Group/McGraw Hill
Rescue!	J	RF	250+	Lighthouse	Rigby
Rescuing Nelson	J	F	369	PM Turquoise	Rigby
Rex Plays Fetch	J	RF	250+	PM Plus Story Books	Rigby
Riding to Craggy Rock	J	RF	386	PM Turquoise	Rigby
Ripeka's Carving	J	RF	250+	Literacy 2000	Rigby
River Rafting Fun	J	RF	250+	PM Plus Story Books	Rigby
River Rapids Ride, The	J	RF	283	Sunshine	Wright Group/McGraw Hill
Road Goes By, A	J	I	250+	Momentum Literacy Program	Troll Associates
Robocat Stops Crime!	J	F	323	Leveled Readers Language Support	Houghton Mifflin
Rock in the Road, The	J	F	457	Pacific Literacy	Pacific Learning
Roller Skates!	J	RF	250+	Calmenson, Stephanie	Scholastic
Roses for Renee	J	RF	395	Evangeline Nicholas Collection	Wright Group/McGraw Hill
Row, Row, Row Your Boat	J	RF	250+	Bank Street	Bantam
Royal Baby-Sitters, The	J	RF	435	Sunshine	Wright Group/McGraw Hill
Rug Weavers	J	RF	182	Leveled Readers Language Support	Houghton Mifflin
Rules	J	I	265	Early Connections	Benchmark Education
Rumpelstiltskin	J	TL	250+	Bookshop	Mondo
Rumpelstiltskin	J	TL	250+	Jumbled Tumbled Tales & Rhymes	Rigby
Rumpelstiltskin	J	TL	940	Traditional Tales	Pearson Learning Group
Runaway Hank	J	RF	250+	The Wright Skills	Wright Group/McGraw Hill
Salt	J	I	247	Rigby Focus	Rigby
Sam and the Firefly	J	F	250+	Eastman, Philip D.	Random House
Sam the Minuteman	J	HF	250+	Benchley, Nathaniel	HarperTrophy
Sandcastles	J	I	419	Leveled Readers Science	Houghton Mifflin
Sandwich, The	J	RF	250+	Story Box	Wright Group/McGraw Hill
Saturday Adventure, The	J	RF	250+	Rigby Literacy	Rigby
Saul's Special Pet	J	F	250+	Leveled Readers Language Support	Houghton Mifflin
Say Cheese	J	I	169	Rigby Focus	Rigby
Scary Spiders!	J	RF	198	Sunshine	Wright Group/McGraw Hill
School Fair, The	J	RF	250+	PM Plus Story Books	Rigby

* Collection of short stories

TITLE	LEVEL	GENRE	WORD COUNT	AUTHOR / SERIES	PUBLISHER / DISTRIBUTOR
School Vacation	J	RF	113	City Kids	Rigby
Sea and Land Animals	J	I	250+	Windows on Literacy	National Geographic
Sea Horses	J	I	90	Under the Sea	Capstone Press
Sea Otter Goes Hunting	J	RF	250+	PM Plus Story Books	Rigby
Sea Turtles	J	I	118	Under the Sea	Capstone Press
Sea Turtles	J	I	118	Pebble Plus	Capstone Press
Seals of the World	J	I	251	Vocabulary Readers	Houghton Mifflin
Seasons, The	J	I	193	Phonics Readers	Compass Point Books
Secret of Spooky House, The	J	F	352	Sunshine	Wright Group/McGraw Hill
See You in Second Grade	J	RF	250+	Cohen, Miriam	Bantam
See You Tomorrow, Charles	J	RF	250+	Cohen, Miriam	Bantam
Seeds	J	I	210	Pebble Books	Capstone Press
Selena Who Speaks in Silence	J	RF	311	Evangeline Nicholas Collection	Wright Group/McGraw Hill
Shadows	J	I	250+	Otto, Carolyn B.	Scholastic
Shaggy Sheep, The	J	RF	301	Wonders	Hampton-Brown
Sheep Sheep Sheep	J	TL	250+	Redhead, Janet Slater	Steck-Vaughn
She'll Be Coming Around the Mountain	J	TL	250+	Traditional Songs	Picture Window Books
She'll Be Coming Around the Mountain	J	RF	250+	Bank Street	Bantam
Shoemaker and the Elves, The	J	TL	250+	Sunshine	Wright Group/McGraw Hill
Shopping	J	RF	250+	Sunshine	Wright Group/McGraw Hill
Shopping	J	I	254	Leveled Readers	Houghton Mifflin
Show-and-Tell	J	RF	220	Foundations	Wright Group/McGraw Hill
Show-and-Tell Frog, The	J	F	250+	Oppenheim, Joanna	Bantam
Silly Supper, The	J	RF	250+	The Wright Skills	Wright Group/McGraw Hill
Silly Willy and Silly Billy	J	F	221	Foundations	Wright Group/McGraw Hill
Skateboard Bill	J	RF	79	Voyages	SRA/McGraw Hill
Skating at Rainbow Lake	J	RF	250+	PM Story Books-Silver	Rigby
Skeleton On The Bus, The	J	F	250+	Literacy 2000	Rigby
Skittles and Skullbones	J	F	250+	Supersonics	Rigby
SkyFire	J	F	250+	Asch, Frank	Scholastic
Small Wolf	J	HF	250+	Benchley, Nathaniel	HarperTrophy
Smallest Horses, The	J	RF	250+	PM Plus Story Books	Rigby
Smelly Armor	J	F	282	Story Box	Wright Group/McGraw Hill
Smile if You Like Circles	J	I	250+	Phonics Readers Plus	Steck-Vaughn
Snake at the Lake	J	F	250+	The Wright Skills	Wright Group/McGraw Hill
Snakebite	J	RF	271	Story Box	Wright Group/McGraw Hill
Snakes	J	I	448	Sunshine	Wright Group/McGraw Hill
Snowy Day, The	J	RF	319	Keats, Ezra Jack	Scholastic
Solar-Powered Sam	J	F	148	Books for Young Learners	Richard C. Owen
Some Kids Are Blind	J	I	134	Understanding Differences	Red Brick Learning
Some Kids Are Deaf	J	I	158	Understanding Differences	Red Brick Learning
Some Kids Wear Leg Braces	J	I	144	Understanding Differences	Red Brick Learning
Some Machines are Enormous	J	I	250+	Bookshop	Mondo
Some Snakes	J	I	118	Voyages	SRA/McGraw Hill
Something Everyone Needs	J	RF	250+	Ready Readers	Pearson Learning Group
*Something Is There and Other Stories	J	F	250+	Story Steps	Rigby
Something is Waiting	J	I	94	Literacy Tree	Rigby
Something Noise, The	J	RF	276	Windmill Books	Rigby
Something Special For Miss Margery	J	F	250+	Voyages	SRA/McGraw Hill
Somewhere	J	TL	93	Bookshop	Mondo
Sophie's Singing Mother	J	RF	313	Jellybeans	Rigby
Sorting My Money	J	I	209	Early Connections	Benchmark Education
Sounds	J	I	200	Early Connections	Benchmark Education
Soup Fit for a King	J	RF	250+	Sunshine	Wright Group/McGraw Hill

* Collection of short stories

TITLE	LEVEL	GENRE	WORD COUNT	AUTHOR / SERIES	PUBLISHER / DISTRIBUTOR
Space Race	J	F	213	Sunshine	Wright Group/McGraw Hill
Special Clothes	J	RF	411	Leveled Readers	Houghton Mifflin
Special Stories	J	I	189	Vocabulary Readers	Houghton Mifflin
Specs	J	B	250+	Ready Set Read	Steck-Vaughn
Spiders Are Special Animals	J	I	166	Sunshine	Wright Group/McGraw Hill
Spiders Spin Silk	J	I	183	Windows on Literacy	National Geographic
Spiders!	J	I	185	Rosen Real Readers	Rosen Publishing Group
Spot That Cat!	J	I	208	Story Box	Wright Group/McGraw Hill
Spot's First Christmas	J	RF	102	Hill, Eric	Putnam
Squire Takes a Wife, A	J	F	250+	Ready Set Read	Steck-Vaughn
Squirrels and Their Nests	J	I	130	Pebble Plus	Capstone Press
Star Gazing in Our Solar System	J	I	202	Independent Readers Science	Houghton Mifflin
Starring First Grade	J	RF	250+	Cohen, Miriam	Bantam
Stars: Seeing Stars All Around Us	J	I	193	Shapes	Capstone Press
Statue of Liberty, The	J	I	250+	Penner, Lucille	Random House
Stone Soup	J	TL	932	McGovern, Ann	Scholastic
Stone Soup	J	TL	250+	PM Tales and Plays-Turquoise	Rigby
Story of Running Water, The	J	TL	287	Cambridge Reading	Pearson Learning Group
Straight Line Wonder, The	J	F	250+	Bookshop	Mondo
Strange Plants	J	I	433	Leveled Readers Science	Houghton Mifflin
Strawberry Picking	J	RF	250+	Cambridge Reading	Pearson Learning Group
Street Musicians	J	RF	283	Sunshine	Wright Group/McGraw Hill
String Performers	J	I	250+	Home Connection Collection	Rigby
Sugar Snow	J	HF	250+	Wilder, Laura Ingalls	HarperCollins
Sulky Simon	J	RF	246	Windmill Books	Rigby
Summer Camp	J	RF	182	City Kids	Rigby
Summer Fun	J	I	261	Spyglass Books	Compass Point Books
Summertime in the Big Woods	J	HF	250+	Wilder, Laura Ingalls	HarperCollins
Sun, The	J	I	219	Wonder World	Wright Group/McGraw Hill
Sun, the Wind & Tashira, The	J	TL	371	Folk Tales	Mondo
Sunburn	J	RF	176	City Kids	Rigby
Super Parrot	J	RF	250+	Real Reading	Steck-Vaughn
Super Supermarket Plan, The	J	RF	250+	Home Connection Collection	Rigby
Surprise Invitation, The	J	RF	250+	PM Plus Story Books	Rigby
Surprise Party, The	J	RF	250+	Prager, Annabelle	Random House
Swimming Across the Pool	J	RF	250+	PM Plus Story Books	Rigby
Sword in the Stone, The	J	TL	250+	Maccarone, Grace	Scholastic
Taking Care of Ourselves	J	I	250+	PM Plus Nonfiction	Rigby
Tallest Boy in the Class, The	J	RF	396	Leveled Readers Language Support	Houghton Mifflin
Technology Today	J	I	166	Early Connections	Benchmark Education
Teeny Tiny Woman, The	J	TL	369	Seuling, Barbara	Scholastic
Telephone, The: A Great Invention	J	I	165	Leveled Readers Social Studies	Houghton Mifflin
Tell Me A Story	J	RF	236	Voyages	SRA/McGraw Hill
Ten Apples Up on Top	J	F	250+	LaSieg, Theo	Random House
Tess and Paddy	J	RF	242	Sunshine	Wright Group/McGraw Hill
Thank You	J	I	250+	Ready to Read	Pearson Learning Group
Thanksgiving	J	I	95	Pebble Books	Capstone Press
That's Not My Hobby!	J	RF	250+	Rigby Literacy	Rigby
Then and Now	J	RF	250+	Early Connections	Benchmark Education
Then and Now	J	I	250+	Discovery World	Rigby
There Is No Water	J	RF	250+	Home Connection Collection	Rigby
*There's a Carrot in My Ear and Other Noodle Tails	J	TL	250+	Schwartz, Alvin	HarperTrophy

* Collection of short stories

TITLE	LEVEL	GENRE	WORD COUNT	AUTHOR / SERIES	PUBLISHER / DISTRIBUTOR
There's a Hippopotamus Under My Bed	J	RF	250+	Thaler, Mike	Avon
There's an Alligator Under My Bed	J	RF	250+	Mayer, Mercer	Penguin Group
There's Something in My Attic	J	RF	258	Mayer, Mercer	Penguin Group
Things With Wings	J	I	267	Storyteller Nonfiction	Wright Group/McGraw Hill
*Three By the Sea	J	RF	250+	Marshall, Edward	Puffin Books
*Three Up a Tree	J	RF	250+	Marshall, James	Puffin Books
Thrills at the Fair	J	RF	250+	The Wright Skills	Wright Group/McGraw Hill
Tickle-Bugs, The	J	F	250+	Literacy 2000	Rigby
Tiger Dreams	J	RF	193	Cambridge Reading	Pearson Learning Group
Tiger Hunt	J	RF	250+	Rigby Literacy	Rigby
Tiger's Promise, Based on a Folktale from India, The	J	TL	250+	Leveled Readers Language Support	Houghton Mifflin
Tim's Bedtime	J	F	250+	Supersonics	Rigby
Tin Treasures	J	I	250+	Greetings	Rigby
Tiny Creatures	J	I	250+	Discovery World	Rigby
Toby and the Accident	J	F	329	PM StoryBooks	Rigby
Toby at Stony Bay	J	F	494	PM Story Books	Rigby
Today I Got Yelled At	J	RF	174	City Kids	Rigby
Tom Sawyer	J	B	250+	Jumbled Tumbled Tales & Rhymes	Rigby
Tom the TV Cat	J	F	250+	Heilbroner, Joan	Random House
Tongue Twister Prize, The	J	RF	331	Little Books	Sadlier-Oxford
Tony and the Butterfly	J	RF	250+	Literacy Tree	Rigby
Too Busy for Pets!	J	RF	472	Sunshine	Wright Group/McGraw Hill
Too Many Mice	J	F	250+	Bank Street	Bantam
Too Many Puppies	J	RF	250+	Brewster, Patience	Scholastic
Too Many Rabbits	J	RF	250+	Parish, Peggy	Bantam
Too Many Steps	J	RF	424	Foundations	Wright Group/McGraw Hill
Too Much Noise	J	TL	250+	McGovern, Ann	Scholastic
*Too Much Talk and Other Stories	J	TL	250+	New Way Literature	Steck-Vaughn
Too Much Trouble for Grandpa	J	F	250+	Sokoloff, Myka-Lynne	Sadlier-Oxford
Too Small Jill	J	RF	306	Little Books	Sadlier-Oxford
Touching	J	I	142	Pebble Books	Capstone Press
Trash Can Band, The	J	RF	252	Little Books	Sadlier-Oxford
Treasure!	J	RF	250+	Phonics Readers Plus	Steck-Vaughn
Tree Frogs	J	I	87	Pebble Books	Red Brick Learning
Tree of Birds	J	F	250+	Leveled Readers Language Support	Houghton Mifflin
Trees	J	I	124	Literacy 2000	Rigby
Tree's Life, A	J	I	102	Windows on Literacy	National Geographic
Tricking the Tiger	J	TL	250+	PM Plus Story Books	Rigby
Trixie's Summer	J	RF	250+	PM Plus Story Books	Rigby
Trog	J	F	432	Sunshine	Wright Group/McGraw Hill
Troop of Little Dinosaurs, A	J	HF	250+	PM Story Books	Rigby
Trouble in the Ark	J	F	119	Rose, Gerald	Oxford University Press
Trouble in the Sandbox	J	RF	318	Foundations	Wright Group/McGraw Hill
Tucker Finds Adventure	J	F	250+	Fletcher, Rusty	Pearson Learning Group
Tulips for Dad	J	RF	250+	Cambridge Reading	Pearson Learning Group
Tummy Ache	J	RF	104	Sunshine	Wright Group/McGraw Hill
Turtle's Big Race	J	TL	250+	Pair-It Books	Steck-Vaughn
Turtle's Small Pond	J	TL	572	Leveled Readers	Houghton Mifflin
*Two Silly Trolls	J	F	250+	Jewell, Nancy	HarperTrophy
Ugly Duckling, The	J	TL	558	Tales from Hans Andersen	Wright Group/McGraw Hill
Ugly Duckling, The	J	TL	452	PM Tales and Plays-Turquoise	Rigby
Uh-Oh! Said the Crow	J	F	250+	Oppenheim, Joanna	Bantam

* Collection of short stories

TITLE	LEVEL	GENRE	WORD COUNT	AUTHOR / SERIES	PUBLISHER / DISTRIBUTOR
Uncle Elephant	J	F	1784	Lobel, Arnold	HarperCollins
Unusual Machines	J	I	229	Little Red Readers	Sundance
Vagabond Crabs	J	I	117	Literacy 2000	Rigby
Valentine's Day	J	I	132	Pebble Books	Capstone Press
Very Hungry Caterpillar, The	J	F	237	Carle, Eric	Philomel Books
Vicky's Box	J	F	412	Cambridge Reading	Pearson Learning Group
Voyage of the Clowns, The	J	F	250+	The Wright Skills	Wright Group/McGraw Hill
Waiting for the Rain	J	RF	307	Foundations	Wright Group/McGraw Hill
Wake Me in Spring	J	F	301	Preller, James	Scholastic
Wake-Up, Baby!	J	F	209	Oppenheim, Joanna	Bantam
Walking Home Alone	J	RF	327	Books for Young Learners	Richard C. Owen
Water	J	I	250+	Momentum Literacy Program	Troll Associates
Water	J	I	164	Windows on Literacy	National Geographic
Water as a Solid	J	I	113	Pebble Books	Red Brick Learning
Water Cycle, The	J	I	250+	Yellow Umbrella Books	Capstone Press
Water Power	J	I	86	Windows on Literacy	National Geographic
Water, Ice, and Steam	J	I	143	Rosen Real Readers	Rosen Publishing Group
Watermelon	J	I	61	Books for Young Learners	Richard C. Owen
Waves: The Changing Surface of the Sea	J	I	204	Wonder World	Wright Group/McGraw Hill
We Use Numbers	J	I	298	Early Connections	Benchmark Education
Wedding, The	J	RF	250+	Sunshine	Wright Group/McGraw Hill
Welcome to Hong Kong!	J	I	174	Vocabulary Readers	Houghton Mifflin
Welcome to the Bakery	J	I	122	Vocabulary Readers	Houghton Mifflin
We're Going Camping	J	I	111	Windows on Literacy	National Geographic
Wet Day at School, A	J	RF	130	Sunshine	Wright Group/McGraw Hill
Wet Weather Camping	J	RF	250+	PM Plus Story Books	Rigby
Whale Watching	J	I	250+	Pacific Literacy	Pacific Learning
Whale's Year, The	J	I	212	Lighthouse	Rigby
What a Haircut!	J	RF	250+	Voyages	SRA/McGraw Hill
What Are My Chances?	J	I	393	Early Connections	Benchmark Education
What Can We Do?	J	RF	439	Leveled Readers Social Studies	Houghton Mifflin
What Cat Is That?	J	RF	250+	Real Reading	Steck-Vaughn
What Comes Next?	J	I	250+	Early Connections	Benchmark Education
What Do I Wear?	J	I	40	Leveled Readers Social Studies	Houghton Mifflin
What Do You Hear When Cows Sing?	J	F	250+	Maestro, Marco & Giulio	HarperTrophy
What Do You Know About Dolphins?	J	I	137	Windows on Literacy	National Geographic
What Does It Do?	J	I	198	Ready Set Read	Steck-Vaughn
What Floats? What Sinks?	J	I	185	Early Connections	Benchmark Education
What Happened to Aunt Cordelia	J	RF	250+	Voyages	SRA/McGraw Hill
What Hatches?	J	I	250+	Yellow Umbrella Books	Capstone Press
What Is a Family?	J	I	250+	Spyglass Books	Compass Point Books
What Is a Park?	J	I	230	People, Places & Spaces	Rand McNally
What Is in the Sky?	J	I	174	Phonics Readers	Compass Point Books
What Is It Made Of?	J	I	250+	Independent Readers Science	Houghton Mifflin
What Joe Hamster Finds	J	F	250+	Sunshine	Wright Group/McGraw Hill
What Lives in a Tide Pool?	J	I	187	Windows on Literacy	National Geographic
What's in the Woods?	J	RF	250+	The Wright Skills	Wright Group/McGraw Hill
Wheels on the Bus, The	J	TL	250+	Traditional Songs	Picture Window Books
When a Storm Comes	J	I	172	Windows on Literacy	National Geographic
When the King Rides By	J	F	247	Bookshop	Mondo
When the Volcano Erupted	J	F	262	PM Turquoise	Rigby
Where Do Puddles Go?	J	I	250+	Rookie Read-About Science	Children's Press
Where Does Energy Come From?	J	I	245	Leveled Readers Social Studies	Houghton Mifflin
Where People Live	J	RF	259	Early Connections	Benchmark Education

* Collection of short stories

TITLE	LEVEL	GENRE	WORD COUNT	AUTHOR / SERIES	PUBLISHER / DISTRIBUTOR
Where the Wild Things Are	J	F	339	Sendak, Maurice	Harper & Row
Where's Tony?	J	RF	114	City Kids	Rigby
Which Comes First?	J	I	250+	Voyages	SRA/McGraw Hill
Which Insects Live Here?	J	I	129	Rigby Literacy	Rigby
Who Wants Arthur?	J	F	250+	Leveled Readers Language Support	Houghton Mifflin
Who's a Pest?	J	F	250+	Bonsall, Crosby	HarperTrophy
Why Crocodiles Live in Rivers	J	TL	415	Sunshine	Wright Group/McGraw Hill
Why do Elephants Wear Hats	J	F	115	O'Toole, Mary	Pearson Learning Group
Why the Bear's Tail is Short	J	TL	431	Sunshine	Wright Group/McGraw Hill
Wild Crayons	J	F	270	Story Box	Wright Group/McGraw Hill
Wild, Wooly Child, The	J	F	315	Read Alongs	Rigby
Wildlife	J	I	250+	Independent Readers Science	Houghton Mifflin
Wildlife	J	I	145	Independent Readers Social Studies	Houghton Mifflin
William's Wheelchair Race	J	RF	279	Sunshine	Wright Group/McGraw Hill
*Wind and the Sun and Other Stories, The	J	F	250+	New Way Orange	Steck-Vaughn
Wind Blew, The	J	RF	169	Hutchins, Pat	Puffin Books
Wind Power	J	I	103	Pacific Literacy	Pacific Learning
Winter Days in the Big Woods	J	HF	250+	Wilder, Laura Ingalls	HarperCollins
Winter on the Farm	J	HF	250+	Wilder, Laura Ingalls	HarperCollins
Wizard and Wart at Sea	J	F	250+	Smith, Janice Lee	HarperTrophy
Wolf and the Seven Little Kids, The	J	TL	254	Literacy Tree	Rigby
Wolf Song	J	RF	130	Books for Young Learners	Richard C. Owen
Wolf's Chicken Stew, The	J	F	250+	Leveled Readers Language Support	Houghton Mifflin
Work Vehicles	J	I	245	Windows on Literacy	National Geographic
Worst Show-and-Tell Ever, The	J	SF	250+	Walsh, Rita	Troll Associates
Wow! What a Week!	J	RF	364	Wonders	Hampton-Brown
Wrong Way Reggie	J	RF	304	Little Celebrations	Pearson Learning Group
Wrong-Way Rabbit, The	J	F	304	Slater, Teddy	Scholastic
You Are Much Too Small	J	F	250+	Bank Street	Bantam
You Can Make a Memory Scrapbook	J	I	179	How-To Series	Benchmark Education
You Can't Catch Me	J	F	250+	Oppenheim, Joanne	Houghton Mifflin
Young Cam Jansen and the Ice Skate Mystery	J	RF	250+	Adler, David A.	Puffin Books
Young Cam Jansen and the Lost Tooth	J	RF	250+	Adler, David A.	Puffin Books
Young Cam Jansen and the Missing Cookie	J	RF	250+	Adler, David A.	Puffin Books
Your Body	J	I	208	Early Connections	Benchmark Education
Your Teeth	J	I	131	Pebble Books	Capstone Press
Zala Runs for Her Life	J	F	250+	PM Story Books-Purple	Rigby
Zeke Takes a Bath	J	F	532	Leveled Readers	Houghton Mifflin
Zoe at the Fancy Dress Ball	J	RF	250+	Literacy 2000	Rigby
Zunid	J	RF	250+	Stepping Stones	Nelson/Michaels Assoc.
15 Facts about Snakes	K	I	347	Rigby Focus	Rigby
Adios, Coyote	K	F	250+	Rigby Literacy	Rigby
Aircraft Carriers	K	I	124	Mighty Machines	Capstone Press
Alison's Puppy	K	RF	250+	Bauer, Marion Dane	Hyperion
Alison's Wings	K	RF	250+	Bauer, Marion Dane	Hyperion
All About Things People Do	K	I	250+	Rice, Melanie & Chris	Scholastic
Allen Say, Writer and Artist	K	B	219	Leveled Readers Social Studies	Houghton Mifflin
Allie's Basketball Dream	K	RF	250+	Soar To Success	Houghton Mifflin
Allie's Basketball Dream	K	RF	250+	Barber, Barbara E.; Ligasan, Darryl	Scholastic
Alligator Mouse and Other Disasters	K	F	250+	Voyages	SRA/McGraw Hill

TITLE	LEVEL	GENRE	WORD COUNT	AUTHOR / SERIES	PUBLISHER / DISTRIBUTOR
*Alligator Tails and Crocodile Cakes	K	F	250+	Moon, Nicola	Wright Group/McGraw Hill
Amalia and the Grasshopper	K	RF	392	Tello, Jerry; Krupinski, Loretta	Scholastic
Amazing Hands	K	I	250+	Rigby Literacy	Rigby
America's Birthplace: Independence Hall	K	RF	249	Leveled Readers Social Studies	Houghton Mifflin
Amy's Water Wings	K	F	250+	Lighthouse	Rigby
And Grandpa Sat on Friday	K	RF	250+	Voyages	SRA/McGraw Hill
Animal Band, The	K	TL	250+	PM Tales and Plays-Purple	Rigby
Animal Homes	K	I	193	Pair-It Books	Steck-Vaughn
Animals and Their Teeth	K	I	510	Sunshine	Wright Group/McGraw Hill
Animals' Eyes and Ears	K	I	411	Early Connections	Benchmark Education
Animals on the Move	K	I	145	Planet Earth	Rigby
Anthony's Unhappy Birthday	K	RF	560	Leveled Readers	Houghton Mifflin
Antonia Novello: Doctor for the Nation	K	B	204	Independent Readers Science	Houghton Mifflin
Anyone Can have a Pet	K	RF	503	PM Plus Story Books	Rigby
Anywhere Everywhere Bus, The	K	F	250+	Home Connection Collection	Rigby
Apple Pie Tree, The	K	I	250+	Zoe Hall	Scholastic
Are We Hurting the Earth?	K	I	363	Early Connections	Benchmark Education
Arguments	K	F	398	Read Alongs	Rigby
Arky, the Dinosaur With Feathers	K	HF	529	PM Plus Story Books	Rigby
Around-the-World Lunch, The	K	RF	250+	Canetti, Yanitzia	Steck-Vaughn
Arthur's Baby	K	F	250+	Brown, Marc	Scholastic
Arthur's Back to School Day	K	F	250+	Hoban, Lillian	HarperTrophy
Arthur's Camp-Out	K	F	250+	Hoban, Lillian	HarperTrophy
Arthur's Christmas Cookies	K	F	250+	Hoban, Lillian	HarperTrophy
Arthur's Eyes	K	F	250+	Brown, Marc	Scholastic
Arthur's Funny Money	K	F	250+	Hoban, Lillian	HarperTrophy
Arthur's Great Big Valentine	K	F	250+	Hoban, Lillian	HarperTrophy
Arthur's Honey Bear	K	F	250+	Hoban, Lillian	HarperCollins
Arthur's Loose Tooth	K	F	250+	Hoban, Lillian	HarperCollins
Arthur's Pen Pal	K	F	250+	Hoban, Lillian	HarperCollins
Arthur's Prize Reader	K	F	250+	Hoban, Lillian	HarperTrophy
Ashes for Gold	K	TL	250+	Folk Tales	Mondo
At the Water Hole	K	I	236	Foundations	Wright Group/McGraw Hill
Baba Yaga	K	TL	250+	Literacy 2000	Rigby
Baby Sister for Frances, A	K	F	250+	Hoban, Lillian	Scholastic
Bacon Saturday Mornings	K	RF	365	Books for Young Learners	Richard C. Owen
Baked Beans	K	I	221	Lighthouse	Rigby
Bargain For Frances, A	K	F	250+	Hoban, Russell	HarperTrophy
Barn Party	K	F	250+	O'Brien, Claire	Wright Group/McGraw Hill
Barney's Lovely Lunch	K	RF	330	Windmill Books	Rigby
Barrel of Gold, A	K	F	251	Story Box	Wright Group/McGraw Hill
Bat Bones and Spider Stew	K	RF	250+	Poploff, Michelle	Bantam
Bath Day for Brutus	K	RF	347	Little Red Readers	Sundance
Be Ready at Eight	K	F	250+	Parish, Peggy	Simon & Schuster
Beanbag	K	RF	250+	Literacy 2000	Rigby
Bear at the Beach	K	F	250+	Carmichael, Clay	North-South Books
Bear For Miguel, A	K	RF	250+	Alphin, Elaine Marie	HarperTrophy
Bear Goes to Town	K	F	250+	Browne, Anthony	Doubleday Books
Bear, The: An American Folk Song	K	F	250+	Bookshop	Mondo
Beauty and the Beast	K	TL	250+	PM Tales and Plays-Gold	Rigby
Beauty and the Beast	K	TL	250+	Sunshine	Wright Group/McGraw Hill
Beavers Beware!	K	I	250+	Bank Street	Bantam
Bedtime at Aunt Carmen's	K	RF	250	Ready Readers	Pearson Learning Group
Bedtime for Frances	K	F	250+	Hoban, Russell	Scholastic

* Collection of short stories

TITLE	LEVEL	GENRE	WORD COUNT	AUTHOR / SERIES	PUBLISHER / DISTRIBUTOR
Bedtime Story, A	K	RF	250+	Bookshop	Mondo
Bee's Home, A	K	I	127	Salem, Lynn	Continental Press
Benjamin Banneker: An American Scientist	K	B	374	Leveled Readers Science	Houghton Mifflin
Bessie Coleman: Queen of the Sky	K	B	229	Sunshine	Wright Group/McGraw Hill
Best Birthday Present, The	K	RF	250+	Literacy 2000	Rigby
Best Dog in the Whole World, The	K	RF	250+	Sunshine	Wright Group/McGraw Hill
Best Friends for Frances	K	F	250+	Hoban, Russell	HarperTrophy
Best Part, The	K	RF	250+	PM Story Books-Silver	Rigby
Best Ranger, The	K	RF	396	Leveled Readers	Houghton Mifflin
Best Teacher in the World, The	K	RF	250+	Chardiet, Bernice	Scholastic
Best Way to Play, The	K	I	250+	Cosby, Bill	Scholastic
Big Balloon Race, The	K	RF	250+	Coerr, Eleanor	HarperTrophy
Big Catch, The	K	RF	250+	Literacy 2000	Rigby
Big Fish Little Fish	K	TL	250+	Folk Tales	Wright Group/McGraw Hill
Big Prize, The	K	F	401	Adventures in Reading	Pearson Learning Group
Big Sneeze, The	K	F	131	Brown, Ruth	Lothrop
Biggest Bear in the Woods, The	K	F	250+	Little Celebrations	Pearson Learning Group
Biggest Pool of All, The	K	RF	250+	Sunshine	Wright Group/McGraw Hill
Big-Hearted Monkey and the Crocodile, The	K	TL	250+	World Quest Adventures	World Quest Learning
Big-Hearted Monkey and the Lion, The	K	TL	250+	World Quest Adventures	World Quest Learning
Bike for Brad, A	K	RF	510	PM Story Books	Rigby
Bird's-Eye View, A	K	I	250+	People, Spaces & Places	Rand McNally
Birthday Bike for Brimhall, A	K	RF	250+	Delton, Judy	Bantam
Birthday for Frances, A	K	F	250+	Hoban, Russell	Scholastic
Birthdays	K	I	59	Purkis, Sallie	Nelson/Michaels Assoc.
Blair's Deer	K	RF	250+	Phonics and Friends	Hampton-Brown
Blanche Bruce of Mississippi	K	B	413	Leveled Readers Social Studies	Houghton Mifflin
Blind Men and the Elephant, The	K	TL	250+	Backstein, Karen	Scholastic
Body Numbers	K	I	250+	Discovery World	Rigby
Bones for Lunch	K	F	221	Sunshine	Wright Group/McGraw Hill
Bony-Legs	K	F	250+	Cole, Joanna	Scholastic
Bootsie Barker Ballerina	K	F	250+	Bottner, Barbara	HarperTrophy
Box of Butterflies, A	K	RF	250+	Leveled Readers Language Support	Houghton Mifflin
Boy and His Donkey, A	K	F	250+	Literacy 2000	Rigby
Boy Named Boomer, A	K	B	250+	Esiason, Boomer	Scholastic
Boy Who Cried Wolf, The	K	TL	250+	PM Tales and Plays-Purple	Rigby
Brave Ben	K	RF	162	Literacy 2000	Rigby
Bread and Jam for Frances	K	F	250+	Hoban, Russell	Scholastic
Bremen-Town Musicians, The	K	TL	741	Gross, Ruth Belov	Scholastic
Brenda's Private Swing	K	RF	250+	Chardiet, Bernice; Maccarone, Grace	Scholastic
Brown Bear Figures it Out!	K	F	250+	Phonics and Friends	Hampton-Brown
Brown Bears	K	I	250+	PM Animal Facts: Turquoise	Rigby
Bubbling Crocodile	K	F	250+	Pacific Literacy	Pacific Learning
Buffalo Bill and the Pony Express	K	B	250+	Coerr, Eleanor	HarperTrophy
Bug Bus, The	K	F	250+	Sunshine	Wright Group/McGraw Hill
Building Lady Liberty	K	I	450	Leveled Readers Social Studies	Houghton Mifflin
Building the Railroad	K	I	250+	Twig	Wright Group/McGraw Hill
Bull in a China Shop, A	K	F	250+	Literacy 2000	Rigby
Bulldog George	K	RF	250+	Voyages	SRA/McGraw Hill
Bunny Runs Away	K	F	250+	Chardiet, Bernice; Maccarone, Grace	Scholastic
Bunrakkit	K	F	250+	Sunshine	Wright Group/McGraw Hill

* Collection of short stories

TITLE	LEVEL	GENRE	WORD COUNT	AUTHOR / SERIES	PUBLISHER / DISTRIBUTOR
Burps, Boogers, and Bad Breath	K	I	246	Spyglass Books	Compass Point Books
Bushfire in the Koala Reserve	K	RF	250+	PM Plus Story Books	Rigby
Busy Beavers	K	RF	80	Dabcovich, Lydia	Scholastic
Busy Bees	K	I	177	Rosen Real Readers	Rosen Publishing Group
Busy Guy, A	K	RF	72	Rookie Readers	Children's Press
Butterfly Day	K	RF	250+	Pacific Literacy	Pacific Learning
Butterfly's Life, A	K	I	250+	Burke, Melissa Blackwell	Steck-Vaughn
Button Soup	K	RF	250+	Bank Street	Bantam
Cabbage Princess, The	K	TL	250+	Literacy 2000	Rigby
Cactuses	K	I	237	Windows on Literacy	National Geographic
Call Mr. Vasquez, He'll Fix It!	K	I	250+	Our Neighborhood	Children's Press
Camel Called Bump-Along, A	K	F	373	Evangeline Nicholas Collection	Wright Group/McGraw Hill
Camouflage	K	I	202	Rigby Focus	Rigby
Camp Knock Knock	K	RF	250+	Duffey, Betsy	Bantam
Camp Knock Knock Mystery, The	K	RF	250+	Duffey, Betsy	Bantam
Camping with Claudine	K	RF	250+	Literacy 2000	Rigby
Can You Guess?	K	I	196	Yellow Umbrella Books	Capstone Press
Caps for Sale	K	F	675	Slobodkina, Esphyr	Harper & Row
Captain Bumble	K	F	510	Story Box	Wright Group/McGraw Hill
Captain Orinocos Onion	K	RF	250+	Voyages	SRA/McGraw Hill
Cardboard Box, A	K	TL	250+	Ready to Read	Pacific Learning
Carl's High Jump	K	RF	250+	PM Plus Story Books	Rigby
Carnival Horse, The	K	RF	499	PM Plus Story Books	Rigby
Case of the Cat's Meow, The	K	RF	250+	Bonsall, Crosby	HarperTrophy
Case of the Double Cross, The	K	RF	250+	Bonsall, Crosby	HarperTrophy
Case of the Dumb Bells, The	K	RF	250+	Bonsall, Crosby	HarperTrophy
Case of the Hungry Stranger, The	K	RF	1358	Bonsall, Crosby	HarperTrophy
Case of the Scaredy Cats, The	K	RF	250+	Bonsall, Crosby	HarperTrophy
Case of the Two Masked Robbers, The	K	F	250+	Hoban, Lillian	HarperTrophy
Cats' Burglar, The	K	F	250+	Parish, Peggy	Hearst
Cats of the Night	K	RF	379	Book Bank	Wright Group/McGraw Hill
Catten, The	K	F	769	Jellybeans	Rigby
Celia	K	RF	182	Leveled Readers	Houghton Mifflin
Change for Zoe, A	K	RF	250+	Home Connection Collection	Rigby
Chaos in the Kitchen	K	F	250+	Home Connection Collection	Rigby
Charlie the Bridesmaid	K	RF	250+	Rigby Literacy	Rigby
Cheerful King, The	K	F	351	Little Books	Sadlier-Oxford
Chicago Winds	K	I	173	Evangeline Nicholas Collection	Wright Group/McGraw Hill
Chickens Aren't the Only Ones	K	I	250+	Heller, Ruth	Scholastic
Chick-in-a-Box	K	RF	250+	Voyages	SRA/McGraw Hill
Children as Young Scientists	K	I	393	Early Connections	Benchmark Education
Chipmunk at Hollow Tree Lane	K	F	250+	Sherrow, Victoria	Scholastic
Chip's Dad	K	RF	250+	Rigby Literacy	Rigby
Choice for Sarah, A	K	RF	250+	PM Plus Story Books	Rigby
Cinderella	K	TL	250+	PM Tales and Plays-Gold	Rigby
Cinderella	K	TL	250+	Once Upon a Time	Wright Group/McGraw Hill
Clara and the Bookwagon	K	RF	250+	Levinson, Nancy Smiler	HarperTrophy
Clever Bird	K	F	250+	Little Celebrations	Pearson Learning Group
Clever Hamburger	K	F	560	Jellybeans	Rigby
Clever Mr. Brown	K	F	397	Story Box	Wright Group/McGraw Hill
Clifford, the Big Red Dog	K	F	241	Bridwell, Norman	Scholastic
Clifford, The Firehouse Dog	K	F	250+	Bridwell, Norman	Scholastic
Clifford, the Small Red Puppy	K	F	499	Bridwell, Norman	Scholastic
Clifford's First Halloween	K	F	250+	Bridwell, Norman	Scholastic

* Collection of short stories

TITLE	LEVEL	GENRE	WORD COUNT	AUTHOR / SERIES	PUBLISHER / DISTRIBUTOR
Clouds, Rain, and Fog	K	I	488	Sunshine	Wright Group/McGraw Hill
Clubhouse, The	K	RF	659	PM Gold	Rigby
Colin Powell	K	B	250+	Welcome Books	Children's Press
Collecting Leaves	K	I	250+	Stepping Stones	Nelson/Michaels Assoc.
Colonial Families	K	I	250+	Rosen Real Readers	Rosen Publishing Group
Come Here Spinner!	K	F	250+	Foundations	Wright Group/McGraw Hill
Come On Down	K	I	250+	World Quest Adventures	World Quest Learning
Commander Toad and the Big Black Hole	K	F	250+	Yolen, Jane	Putnam & Grosset
Commander Toad and the Dis-Asteroid	K	F	250+	Yolen, Jane	Putnam & Grosset
Commander Toad and the Intergalactic Spy	K	F	250+	Yolen, Jane	Putnam & Grosset
Commander Toad and the Planet of the Grapes	K	F	250+	Yolen, Jane	Putnam & Grosset
Commander Toad and the Space Pirates	K	F	250+	Yolen, Jane	Putnam & Grosset
Commander Toad And The Voyage Home	K	F	250+	Yolen, Jane	Putnam & Grosset
Commander Toad in Space	K	F	250+	Yolen, Jane	Scholastic
Computers Are for Everyone	K	I	464	Sunshine	Wright Group/McGraw Hill
Concert Night	K	RF	250+	Literacy 2000	Rigby
Concrete	K	I	123	Books for Young Learners	Richard C. Owen
Concrete Mixers	K	I	110	Pebble Books	Capstone Press
Contest, The	K	RF	250+	PM Plus Story Books	Rigby
Cooking Contest, The	K	RF	904	Early Connections	Benchmark Education
Cool Customs	K	I	250+	Spyglass Books	Compass Point Books
Cool Tools	K	I	250+	Spyglass Books	Compass Point Books
Cooped Up	K	RF	250+	Pacific Literacy	Pacific Learning
Coral	K	I	250+	Marine Life For Young Readers	Pearson Learning Group
Corals	K	I	133	Under the Sea	Capstone Press
Corduroy	K	F	250+	Freeman, Don	Scholastic
Corn	K	I	221	Windows on Literacy	National Geographic
Corn Husk Doll, The	K	RF	250+	Schiller, Melissa	Scholastic
Cotton Comes From Plants	K	I	161	Windows on Literacy	National Geographic
Count on Your Body	K	I	250+	Rigby Literacy	Rigby
Counting Insects	K	I	230	Early Connections	Benchmark Education
Cranes	K	I	105	Pebble Books	Capstone Press
Crocodile Lake	K	F	322	Pacific Literacy	Pacific Learning
Crosby Crocodile's Disguise	K	F	250+	LIteracy 2000	Rigby
Cunning Creatures	K	I	250+	Home Connection Collection	Rigby
Cutting and Sticking	K	RF	250+	Cambridge Reading	Pearson Learning Group
Dabble Duck	K	RF	250+	Ellis, Anne Leo	HarperTrophy
Dabbling in Dough	K	I	250+	Book Bank	Wright Group/McGraw Hill
Daniel's Dog	K	RF	250+	Bogart, Jo Allen	Scholastic
Daniel's Duck	K	RF	250+	Bulla, Clyde Robert	HarperTrophy
Darcy and Gran Don't Like Babies	K	RF	250+	Cutler, Jane	Scholastic
Dash, the Young Meerkat	K	RF	250+	PM Plus Story Books	Rigby
Day in the Life of a Garbage Collector, A	K	I	250+	First Facts	Capstone Press
Day in Town, A	K	RF	206	Story Box	Wright Group/McGraw Hill
Day Jimmy's Boa Ate the Wash, The	K	F	250+	Noble, Trinka H.	Scholastic
Day with Emily Emeryboard	K	F	250+	Foundations	Wright Group/McGraw Hill
*Days With Frog and Toad	K	F	250+	Lobel, Arnold	HarperTrophy
Dede and the Dinosaur	K	F	232	Cumpiano, Ina	Hampton-Brown
Desert Animals	K	I	195	Rosen Real Readers	Rosen Publishing Group
Desert Life	K	I	129	Independent Readers Science	Houghton Mifflin
Desert Machine, The	K	I	202	Sunshine	Wright Group/McGraw Hill
Desert Rain	K	I	214	Windows on Literacy	National Geographic
Deserts	K	I	212	Early Connections	Benchmark Education
Different Homes Around the World	K	I	200	Rigby Literacy	Rigby

TITLE	LEVEL	GENRE	WORD COUNT	AUTHOR / SERIES	PUBLISHER / DISTRIBUTOR
*Digby and Kate	K	F	250+	Baker, Barbara	Puffin Easy-to-Read
Dinosaur Days	K	RF	250+	Ready Readers	Pearson Learning Group
Dinosaur Detectives	K	F	250+	Pacific Literacy	Pacific Learning
Dinosaur on the Motorway	K	F	231	Wesley and the Dinosaurs	Wright Group/McGraw Hill
Dinosaur Time	K	I	250+	Parish, Peggy	HarperTrophy
Dinosaurs	K	I	193	Bookshop	Mondo
Dinosaurs on the Motorway	K	F	250+	Wesley & the Dinosaurs	Wright Group/McGraw Hill
Dipplidocus in the Garden, A	K	F	210	Wesley and the Dinosaurs	Wright Group/McGraw Hill
Discovering Dinosaurs	K	I	211	Spyglass Books	Compass Point Books
Dive, The	K	RF	488	Leveled Readers	Houghton Mifflin
Do You Like Cats?	K	I	250+	Bank Street	Bantam
Doctor's Office, The	K	I	272	Pebble Books	Capstone Press
Dog Called Bear, A	K	RF	438	PM Story Books	Rigby
Dog Show, The	K	RF	250+	Cambridge Reading	Pearson Learning Group
Dollar, The	K	RF	169	Books for Young Learners	Richard C. Owen
Dolphin on the Wall, The	K	RF	250+	PM Story Books-Silver	Rigby
Dolphins	K	I	111	Bookshop	Mondo
Donald's Garden	K	RF	250+	Reading Unlimited	Pearson Learning Group
Don't Touch It, Lily	K	F	250+	Popcorn	Sundance
Douglas Florian	K	B	250+	Leveled Readers Language Support	Houghton Mifflin
Dragon Feet	K	F	153	Books For Young Learners	Richard C. Owen
Dragon Who Came to Dinner, The	K	F	250+	The Wright Skills	Wright Group/McGraw Hill
Dragon's Birthday, The	K	F	250+	Literacy 2000	Rigby
Earthworms	K	I	212	Rigby Focus	Rigby
Eat Right, Feel Good	K	I	250+	Rosen Real Readers	Rosen Publishing Group
Edgar Badger's Balloon Day	K	F	864	Kulling, Monica	Mondo
Edgar Badger's Butterfly Day	K	F	250+	Kulling, Monica	Mondo
Edgar Badger's Fishing Day	K	F	250+	Kulling, Monica	Mondo
Edgar Badger's Fix-it Day	K	F	250+	Kulling, Monica	Mondo
Edwin and Emily	K	RF	250+	Williams, Suzanne	Hyperion
Effie	K	F	250+	Allison, Beverly	Scholastic
Egg	K	F	250+	Logan, Dick	Cypress
Eggs, Larvae, and Flies	K	I	450	Sunshine	Wright Group/McGraw Hill
Elephants	K	I	250+	PM Animal Facts: Turquoise	Rigby
Elizabite: Adventures of a Carnivorous Plant	K	F	250+	Rey, H. A.	Houghton Mifflin
Elves and the Shoemaker, The: A Tale by the Brothers Grimm	K	TL	250+	Rigby Literacy	Rigby
*Elves and the Shoemaker,The	K	TL	622	New Way Orange	Steck-Vaughn
Emergency Vehicles	K	I	250+	PM Plus	Rigby
Endangered Animals	K	I	148	Early Connections	Benchmark Education
Even Steven and Odd Todd	K	F	250+	Cristaldi, Kathryn	Scholastic
Every Flower is Beautiful	K	TL	250+	Turner, Teresa	Steck-Vaughn
*Fables by Aesop	K	TL	250+	Reading Unlimited	Pearson Learning Group
Fabulous Animal Families	K	I	250+	Home Connection Collection	Rigby
Fabulous Fish	K	I	178	Rigby Focus	Rigby
Fabulous Freckles	K	RF	250+	Literacy 2000	Rigby
Fair Swap, A	K	TL	250+	PM Story Books-Silver	Rigby
Families Are Different	K	RF	250+	Pellegrini, Nina	Scholastic
Family Tree, The	K	RF	250+	PM Plus Story Books	Rigby
Fantastic Fungi	K	I	234	Rigby Focus	Rigby
Farm for Wild Animals, A	K	I	161	Vocabulary Readers	Houghton Mifflin
Farm Friends	K	I	197	Spyglass Books	Compass Point Books
Farmer in the Dell, The	K	TL	250+	Traditional Songs	Picture Window Books

* Collection of short stories

TITLE	LEVEL	GENRE	WORD COUNT	AUTHOR / SERIES	PUBLISHER / DISTRIBUTOR
Farmer in the Soup, The	K	TL	250+	Littledale, Freya	Scholastic
Father Who Walked on Hands	K	RF	344	Literacy 2000	Rigby
Feel the Power: Energy All Around	K	I	250+	Spyglass Books	Compass Point Books
Fergus and Bridey	K	F	250+	Little Celebrations	Pearson Learning Group
Figaro	K	F	250+	Voyages	SRA/McGraw Hill
Fight in the Schoolyard, The	K	RF	129	City Kids	Rigby
Fighter Planes	K	I	115	Mighty Machines	Capstone Press
Fire!	K	F	250+	Rigby Literacy	Rigby
First Fire, The	K	F	250+	Little Celebrations	Pearson Learning Group
First Fire: A Traditional Native American Tale	K	TL	250+	Rigby Literacy	Rigby
First Flight	K	B	250+	Shea, George	HarperTrophy
Fish for Sale	K	RF	250+	SupaDoopers	Sundance
Fishing Trip, The	K	RF	250+	PM Plus Story Books	Rigby
Five Days to Go!	K	RF	250+	Rigby Literacy	Rigby
*Five Funny Frights	K	RF	250+	Bauer, Judith	Scholastic
Five Senses, The	K	I	280	Story Box	Wright Group/McGraw Hill
Floating	K	RF	250+	Sunshine	Wright Group/McGraw Hill
Flood!	K	RF	250+	Rigby Literacy	Rigby
Florence Griffith-Joyner: Olympic Champion	K	B	184	Leveled Readers	Houghton Mifflin
Flour	K	I	174	Wonder World	Wright Group/McGraw Hill
Flows & Quakes and Spinning Winds	K	I	250+	Home Connection Collection	Rigby
Fluffy's Trip	K	F	250+	Sunshine	Wright Group/McGraw Hill
Flying Fingers	K	RF	250+	Literacy 2000	Rigby
Follow Me, Be a Bee	K	I	428	Independent Readers Science	Houghton Mifflin
Follow That Fish	K	F	250+	Bank Street	Bantam
Food Journey, The	K	I	116	Home Connection Collection	Rigby
Forty-Three Cats	K	RF	232	Sunshine	Wright Group/McGraw Hill
Fossils	K	I	238	Windows on Literacy	National Geographic
Fourth Little Pig, The	K	TL	250+	Ready Set Read	Steck-Vaughn
Fox and The Crow, The	K	TL	250+	Ready Readers	Pearson Learning Group
Franklin Goes To School	K	F	250+	Bourgeois, Paulette; Clark, Brenda	Scholastic
Franklin Plays the Game	K	F	250+	Bourgeois, Paulette; Clark, Brenda	Scholastic
Freddy's Train Ride	K	RF	573	Pair-It Books	Steck-Vaughn
Friends are Forever	K	F	585	Literacy 2000	Rigby
Friends Forever	K	RF	559	Leveled Readers	Houghton Mifflin
Friendship Garden, The	K	RF	250+	Little Celebrations	Pearson Learning Group
*Frog and Toad All Year	K	F	250+	Little Readers	Houghton Mifflin
*Frog and Toad Are Friends	K	F	250+	Lobel, Arnold	Harper & Row
Frog and Toad Together	K	F	250+	Little Readers	Houghton Mifflin
Frog and Toad Together	K	F	1927	Lobel, Arnold	HarperCollins
Frog Prince, The	K	TL	250+	Tarcov, Edith H.	Scholastic
Frog Princess, The	K	TL	206	Literacy 2000	Rigby
Frog Report, The	K	I	184	Rigby Focus	Rigby
Frogs	K	I	311	Wonder World	Wright Group/McGraw Hill
Frogs	K	I	170	Windows on Literacy	National Geographic
From a Tree	K	I	351	Rigby Focus	Rigby
From the Mountain to the Ocean	K	I	99	Independent Readers Social Studies	Houghton Mifflin
Frown, The	K	RF	228	Read Alongs	Rigby
Fun with Fingerprints	K	I	250+	How-To Series	Benchmark Education
Gargoyles On Guard	K	I	269	Books for Young Learners	Richard C. Owen
*Gaston the Giant	K	F	331	New Way Orange	Steck-Vaughn

* Collection of short stories

TITLE	LEVEL	GENRE	WORD COUNT	AUTHOR / SERIES	PUBLISHER / DISTRIBUTOR
George the Drummer Boy	K	HF	250+	Benchley, Nathaniel	HarperTrophy
Getting Cold! Getting Hot!	K	RF	753	Sunshine	Wright Group/McGraw Hill
Getting To Know Sharks	K	I	379	Little Books	Sadlier-Oxford
Ghost Tree, The	K	RF	250+	Voyages	SRA/McGraw Hill
Giant Games	K	F	250+	Phonics and Friends	Hampton-Brown
Giant Jam Sandwich, The	K	F	250+	Vernon Lord, John	Houghton Mifflin
Giant Seeds, The	K	RF	507	PM Plus Story Books	Rigby
Gibbon Island	K	RF	444	PM Plus Story Books	Rigby
Gift to Share, A	K	RF	544	Pair-It Books	Steck-Vaughn
Gifts to Make	K	I	509	Pair-It Books	Steck-Vaughn
Gigantic Bell, The	K	TL	250+	PM Plus Story Books	Rigby
Girl Named Helen Keller, A	K	B	250+	Lundell, Margo	Scholastic
Gluepots	K	RF	205	Book Bank	Wright Group/McGraw Hill
Gnu Named Blue, A	K	F	250+	Phonics and Friends	Hampton-Brown
Go and Hush the Baby	K	RF	250+	Byars, Betsy	Viking
Go Annie, Go!	K	RF	250+	Pacific Literacy	Pacific Learning
Go-cart Day	K	RF	165	City Kids	Rigby
Going Places	K	I	410	Early Connections	Benchmark Education
Going to America	K	HF	250+	Leveled Readers Language Support	Houghton Mifflin
Going Up the Mountain	K	I	251	Windows on Literacy	National Geographic
Goldilocks and the Three Bears	K	TL	250+	New Way Literature	Steck-Vaughn
Goldilocks and the Three Bears	K	TL	250+	Once Upon a Time	Wright Group/McGraw Hill
Golly Sisters Go West, The	K	RF	250+	Byars, Betsy	HarperTrophy
Golly Sisters Ride Again, The	K	RF	250+	Byars, Betsy	HarperTrophy
Good Morning Mrs. Martin	K	F	156	Book Bank	Wright Group/McGraw Hill
Good Vibrations: Experimenting with Sound	K	I	250+	Rigby Literacy	Rigby
Gorgo Meets Her Match	K	HF	453	PM Story Books	Rigby
Grandad's Dinosaur	K	F	250+	Girling, Brough	Wright Group/McGraw Hill
Grandad's Mask	K	RF	250+	PM Turquoise	Rigby
Grandfather Horned Toad	K	F	250+	Little Celebrations	Pearson Learning Group
Grandma Mixup, The	K	RF	250+	Little Readers	Houghton Mifflin
Grandma Mix-Up, The	K	RF	250+	McCully, Emily Arnold	HarperTrophy
Grandmas At Bat	K	RF	250+	McCully, Emily Arnold	HarperTrophy
Grandmas at the Lake	K	RF	250+	McCully, Emily Arnold	HarperTrophy
Grandma's Cookie Cutters	K	RF	577	Leveled Readers	Houghton Mifflin
Grandma's Garden	K	I	340	Rigby Focus	Rigby
Grandma's Heart	K	I	90	Wonder World	Wright Group/McGraw Hill
Grandma's Table	K	RF	287	Leveled Readers	Houghton Mifflin
Graph It	K	I	250+	Yellow Umbrella Books	Capstone Press
Grass Circles Mystery, The	K	F	250+	Talking Points	Pearson Learning Group
Grasshopper and the Ants	K	TL	452	Sunshine	Wright Group/McGraw Hill
Grasshopper on the Road	K	F	250+	Lobel, Arnold	HarperTrophy
Great Bean Race, The	K	RF	295	Pacific Literacy	Pacific Learning
Great Day for Snorkeling, A	K	RF	238	Leveled Readers	Houghton Mifflin
Great Green Place, The	K	I	242	Story Box	Wright Group/McGraw Hill
Great Grumbler and the Wonder Tree, The	K	F	250+	Mahy, Margaret	Pacific Learning
Great Ocean, The	K	I	250+	Spyglass Books	Compass Point Books
Green Grasshoppers	K	F	229	Sunshine	Wright Group/McGraw Hill
Greg's Microscope	K	I	250+	Selsam, Millicent E.	HarperTrophy
Guessing Jar, The	K	I	395	Early Connections	Benchmark Education
Guide Dog, The	K	I	338	Foundations	Wright Group/McGraw Hill
Gumshoe Goose Private Eye	K	F	250+	Kwitz, Mary DeBall	Puffin Books
Half for You, Half for Me	K	TL	399	Literacy 2000	Rigby

* Collection of short stories

TITLE	LEVEL	GENRE	WORD COUNT	AUTHOR / SERIES	PUBLISHER / DISTRIBUTOR
Hansel and Gretel	K	TL	250+	Enrichment	Wright Group/McGraw Hill
Happy Birthday, Dear Duck	K	F	250+	Bunting, Eve	Clarion
Happy Valentine's Day, Miss Hildy!	K	RF	250+	Grambling, Lois	Random House
Hare and the Tortoise, The	K	TL	250+	Literacy 2000	Rigby
Hare and the Tortoise, The	K	TL	250+	PM Tales and Plays-Purple	Rigby
Harold and the Purple Crayon	K	F	660	Johnson, Crockett	Harper & Row
Harriet Tubman: A Woman of Courage	K	B	170	Independent Readers Social Studies	Houghton Mifflin
Harry and Willy and Carrothead	K	RF	250+	Caseley, Judith	Scholastic
Harry Hates Shopping!	K	F	250+	Armitage, Ronda & David	Scholastic
Hat Came Back, The	K	RF	250+	Literacy 2000	Rigby
Have You Seen a Javelina?	K	F	250+	Literacy 2000	Rigby
Have You Seen Birds?	K	I	250+	Oppenheim, Joanne; Reid, Barbara	Scholastic
Hawkers' Amazing Machines, The: A Play	K	F	250+	Phonics and Friends	Hampton-Brown
He Who Listens	K	RF	250+	Literacy 2000	Rigby
Heather's Book	K	RF	250+	Ready Readers	Pearson Learning Group
Hello Creatures!	K	I	250+	Literacy 2000	Rigby
Henry and the Fox	K	RF	388	Leveled Readers	Houghton Mifflin
Here Comes the Strikeout	K	RF	250+	Kessler, Leonard	HarperTrophy
Hide and Seek	K	I	250+	World Quest Adventures	World Quest Learning
Highway Turtles, The	K	RF	250+	PM Plus Story Books	Rigby
Hippos	K	I	250+	PM Animal Facts: Turquoise	Rigby
Hit By a Blade	K	RF	250+	Foundations	Wright Group/McGraw Hill
Home for Diggory, A	K	RF	250+	Pacific Literacy	Pacific Learning
Home in the Sky	K	RF	250+	Baker, Jeannie	Scholastic
Hooray for the Golly Sisters!	K	RF	250+	Byars, Betsy	HarperTrophy
Horrie the Hoarder	K	RF	250+	Voyages	SRA/McGraw Hill
Hot and Cold Weather	K	I	922	Sunshine	Wright Group/McGraw Hill
House Spider's Life, A	K	I	230	Himmelman, John	Scholastic
Houses That Move	K	I	250+	Voyages	SRA/McGraw Hill
How Big Is a Foot?	K	F	250+	Myller, Rolf	Bantam
How Does It Breathe?	K	I	250+	Home Connection Collection	Rigby
How Fire Came to Earth	K	TL	250+	Literacy 2000	Rigby
How Goods Are Moved	K	I	250+	People, Spaces & Places	Rand McNally
How Much Does This Hold?	K	RF	179	Coulton, Mia	Kaeden Books
How Spider Tricked Snake	K	TL	250+	Real Reading	Steck-Vaughn
*How the Tortoise Got His Shell and Other Stories	K	TL	250+	New Way Literature	Steck-Vaughn
How to Be Healthy	K	I	250+	Rosen Real Readers	Rosen Publishing Group
How to Make Cheese Muffins	K	I	220	Voyages	SRA/McGraw Hill
How to Weigh an Elephant	K	F	390	Pacific Literacy	Pacific Learning
Hugo Hogget: Story Based on an Ecuadoran Legend	K	TL	528	Cumpiano, Ina	Hampton-Brown
Hummingbird Garden	K	RF	252	Story Box	Wright Group/McGraw Hill
Hungry Red Hawk, A	K	I	2312	Independent Readers Science	Houghton Mifflin
I Am a Gypsy Pot	K	F	220	Evangeline Nicholas Collection	Wright Group/McGraw Hill
I Am Not Afraid	K	RF	250+	Mann, Kenny	Bantam
I Can See the Leaves	K	RF	368	Pacific Literacy	Pacific Learning
I Dream	K	RF	583	Sunshine	Wright Group/McGraw Hill
I Get the Creeps	K	RF	250+	Reading Corners	Pearson Learning Group
I Know an Old Lady	K	TL	250+	Traditional Songs	Picture Window Books
I Went to the Dentist	K	RF	152	City Kids	Rigby
Ibis: A True Whale Story	K	I	250+	Himmelman, John	Scholastic

* Collection of short stories

TITLE	LEVEL	GENRE	WORD COUNT	AUTHOR / SERIES	PUBLISHER / DISTRIBUTOR
Ice on the Move	K	I	362	Rigby Focus	Rigby
If You Give A Moose A Muffin	K	F	250+	Numeroff, Laura Joffe	HarperCollins
If You Give A Mouse A Cookie	K	F	291	Numeroff, Laura Joffe	HarperCollins
In a Faraway Forest	K	F	347	Kratky, Lada Josefa	Hampton-Brown
In Grandma Rita's Garden	K	RF	191	Books for Young Learners	Richard C. Owen
In the Days of the Dinosaurs: Arky, the Dinosaur With Feathers	K	HF	250+	PM Plus Story Books	Rigby
Insects All Around	K	I	229	Early Connections	Benchmark Education
Inside an Ant Colony	K	I	250+	Rookie Read-About Science	Children's Press
Is it a Fish?	K	I	606	Sunshine	Wright Group/McGraw Hill
Island to Island	K	RF	250+	Ready to Read	Pacific Learning
It's About Time	K	I	250+	Yellow Umbrella Books	Capstone Press
It's Halloween!	K	RF	250+	Prelutsky, Jack	Scholastic
Jack and the Beanstalk	K	TL	901	Hunia, Fran	Ladybird Books
Jack and the Beanstalk	K	TL	250+	Weisner, David	Scholastic
Jack and the Magic Harp	K	TL	250+	PM Tales and Plays-Gold	Rigby
Jade Emperor and the Four Dragons, The	K	TL	250+	Lighthouse	Rigby
Jake the Snake	K	F	250+	Supersonics	Rigby
Jamaica and Brianna	K	RF	250+	Little Readers	Houghton Mifflin
Jamaica's Find	K	RF	250+	Havill, Juanita	Scholastic
Japanese Garden, The	K	RF	250+	PM Plus Story Books	Rigby
Jimmy the Gymnast	K	RF	250+	Foundations	Wright Group/McGraw Hill
Jim's Dog Muffins	K	RF	250+	Cohen, Miriam	Bantam
*JJ Rabbit and the Monster	K	F	250+	Moon, Nicola	Wright Group/McGraw Hill
Jo the Model Maker	K	I	250+	Lighthouse	Rigby
Joe and Betsy the Dinosaur	K	F	250+	Hoban, Lillian	HarperTrophy
John H. Johnson, Business Leader	K	B	130	Independent Readers Social Studies	Houghton Mifflin
Johnny Appleseed	K	TL	250+	Moore, Eva	Scholastic
Jordan and the Northside Reps	K	RF	250+	PM Story Books-Silver	Rigby
Jordan's Lucky Day	K	RF	466	PM Story Books-Turquoise	Rigby
Joy Crowley Writes	K	B	250+	Sunshine	Wright Group/McGraw Hill
Julie's Mornings	K	F	250+	Ready Readers	Pearson Learning Group
June Bacon-Bercey: A Meteorologist Talks About the Weather	K	I	192	Leveled Readers Science	Houghton Mifflin
Jungle Life	K	I	268	Spyglass Books	Compass Point Books
Junk into Art	K	RF	587	Leveled Readers	Houghton Mifflin
Jupiter Spiders and Other Scary Creatures	K	SF	250+	Popcorn	Sundance
Just the Bee's Knees	K	I	250+	Story Steps	Rigby
Kalulu's Pumpkins	K	F	250+	Rigby Literacy	Rigby
Kangaroos	K	I	250+	PM Animal Facts: Turquoise	Rigby
Keep the Lights Burning Abbie	K	HF	250+	Roop, Peter & Connie	Scholastic
Keeping Warm! Keeping Cool!	K	I	946	Sunshine	Wright Group/McGraw Hill
Kerry	K	RF	250+	PM Story Books-Silver	Rigby
Kerry's Double	K	RF	250+	PM Story Books-Silver	Rigby
Key to Maps, The	K	I	222	Windows on Literacy	National Geographic
Kindest Family, The	K	TL	536	PM Plus Story Books	Rigby
King Midas and the Golden Touch	K	TL	721	PM Gold	Rigby
King, the Mice, and the Cheese, The	K	F	250+	Gurney, Nancy	Random House
Knock! Knock!	K	RF	250+	Carter, Jackie	Scholastic
Know-Nothing Birthday, A	K	RF	250+	Spirn, Michele Sobel	HarperTrophy
Know-Nothings, The	K	RF	250+	Spirn, Michele Sobel	HarperTrophy
Kwanzaa	K	I	225	Visions	Wright Group/McGraw Hill

* Collection of short stories

TITLE	LEVEL	GENRE	WORD COUNT	AUTHOR / SERIES	PUBLISHER / DISTRIBUTOR
Land and Water	K	I	106	Independent Readers Social Studies	Houghton Mifflin
Last Puppy, The	K	F	244	Asch, Frank	Simon & Schuster
Laughing Place, The	K	F	250+	Story Steps	Rigby
Lavender the Library Cat	K	RF	418	Jellybeans	Rigby
Law and Order	K	I	250+	Spyglass Books	Compass Point Books
Leaves	K	I	236	Pebble Books	Capstone Press
Legend of the Hummingbird, The	K	TL	250+	Folk Tales	Mondo
Legend of the Red Bird, The	K	TL	389	Sunshine	Wright Group/McGraw Hill
Lend a Hand	K	F	250+	Kratky, Lada	Hampton-Brown
Lenny and Tweek	K	F	250+	Bookshop	Mondo
Let's Eat: Foods of Our World	K	I	250+	Spyglass Books	Compass Point Books
Let's Get Dressed: What People Wear	K	I	250+	Spyglass Books	Compass Point Books
Let's Talk: How We Communicate	K	I	250+	Spyglass Books	Compass Point Books
Letter to Amy, A	K	RF	250+	Keats, Ezra Jack	Harper & Row
Life In the Arctic	K	I	293	Leveled Readers Science	Houghton Mifflin
Life Long Ago	K	I	250+	Spyglass Books	Compass Point Books
Lion and the Mouse, The	K	TL	557	Pair-It Books	Steck-Vaughn
*Lionel and His Friends	K	RF	250+	Krensky, Stephen	Puffin Books
*Lionel and Louise	K	RF	250+	Krensky, Stephen	Puffin Books
*Lionel at Large	K	RF	250+	Krensky, Stephen	Puffin Books
*Lionel In The Fall	K	RF	250+	Krensky, Stephen	Puffin Books
*Lionel In The Spring	K	RF	250+	Krensky, Stephen	Puffin Books
*Lionel In The Summer	K	RF	250+	Krensky, Stephen	Puffin Books
*Lionel In The Winter	K	RF	250+	Krensky, Stephen	Puffin Books
Lions & Tigers	K	I	250+	PM Animals in the Wild-Yellow	Rigby
Lions and Tigers	K	I	250+	PM Animal Facts: Turquoise	Rigby
Little Blue Big Blue	K	RF	250+	Rigby Literacy	Rigby
Little Brown Jay, The: A Tale from India	K	TL	366	Claire, Elizabeth	Mondo
Little Chief	K	F	250+	Hoff, Syd	HarperCollins
*Little Dancer and Other Short Stories, The	K	F	250+	New Way Literature	Steck-Vaughn
Little Dinosaur	K	F	250+	Voyages	SRA/McGraw Hill
Little Half Chick	K	F	250+	Literacy Tree	Rigby
Little Knight, The	K	F	250+	Reading Unlimited	Pearson Learning Group
*Little Leaf's Journey and the Lost Tooth, The	K	F	564	New Way Orange	Steck-Vaughn
Little One Inch	K	TL	384	Gibson, Akimi	Scholastic
Little Polar Bear and the Brave Little Hare	K	F	250+	de Beer, Hans	North-South Books
Little Red Riding Hood	K	TL	250+	Story Steps	Rigby
Little Red Riding Hood	K	TL	250+	Enrichment	Wright Group/McGraw Hill
Little Runner of the Longhouse	K	HF	250+	Baker, Betty	HarperTrophy
Little Soup's Birthday	K	RF	250+	Peck, Robert Newton	Bantam
Little Spider, The	K	F	250+	Literacy 2000	Rigby
Little Walrus Rising	K	F	250+	Young, Carol	Scholastic
Little Witch Goes to School	K	F	250+	Hautzig, Deborah	Random House
Little Witch's Big Night	K	F	250+	Hautzig, Deborah	Random House
Living in the Sky	K	RF	328	Sunshine	Wright Group/McGraw Hill
Lonely Giant, The	K	F	449	Literacy 2000	Rigby
Look at Both Sides	K	I	236	Yellow Umbrella Books	Capstone Press
Looking at Maps and Globes	K	I	250+	Brederson, Carmen	Scholastic
Looking for Shapes	K	I	289	Early Connections	Benchmark Education
Looking Through a Telescope	K	I	250+	Rookie Read-About Science	Children's Press
Lost in the Forest	K	RF	250+	Robinson, Fay	Wright Group/McGraw Hill
Lulu Goes to Witch School	K	F	250+	O'Connor, Jane	HarperTrophy
Lunch at the Joy House Café	K	RF	250+	Blackaby, Susan	Hampton-Brown

* Collection of short stories

TITLE	LEVEL	GENRE	WORD COUNT	AUTHOR / SERIES	PUBLISHER / DISTRIBUTOR
M & M and The Bad News Babies	K	RF	250+	Ross, Pat	Penguin Group
M & M and the Big Bag	K	RF	250+	Ross, Pat	Penguin Group
M & M and the Halloween Monster	K	RF	250+	Ross, Pat	Penguin Group
M & M and the Haunted House Game	K	RF	250+	Ross, Pat	Penguin Group
M & M and the Mummy Mess	K	RF	250+	Ross, Pat	Penguin Group
M & M and the Santa Secrets	K	RF	250+	Ross, Pat	Penguin Group
M & M and the Super Child Afternoon	K	RF	250+	Ross, Pat	Penguin Group
Madeline	K	F	250+	Bemelmans, Ludwig	Scholastic
Madeline's Rescue	K	F	250+	Bemelmans, Ludwig	Scholastic
Magic Box, The	K	F	250+	Brenner, Barbara	Bantam
Make a Sundial	K	I	250+	How-To Series	Benchmark Education
Make It! Ship It!	K	I	250+	Spyglass Books	Compass Point Books
Make Prints and Patterns	K	I	454	Sunshine	Wright Group/McGraw Hill
Making a Bug Habitat	K	I	250+	How-To Series	Benchmark Education
Making a Marionette	K	I	349	How-To Series	Benchmark Education
Making Music	K	I	174	Windows on Literacy	National Geographic
Making Shapes	K	I	250+	Yellow Umbrella Books	Capstone Press
Mammoth Mistake, A	K	RF	250+	Rigby Literacy	Rigby
Man from Mars, The	K	SF	250+	Popcorn	Sundance
Manatee Winter	K	RF	250+	Zoehfeld, Kathleen Weidnetz	Scholastic
Manly Ferry Pigeon, The	K	RF	250+	Sunshine	Wright Group/McGraw Hill
Mantu the Elephant	K	F	250+	Rigby Literacy	Rigby
Mapping Our World	K	I	250+	Spyglass Books	Compass Point Books
Maps	K	I	150	Phonics Readers	Compass Point Books
Martin and the Teacher's Pets	K	RF	250+	Chardiet, Bernice; Maccarone, Grace	Scholastic
Martin and the Tooth Fairy	K	RF	250+	Chardiet, Bernice; Maccarone, Grace	Scholastic
Martin Luther King, Jr. Day	K	I	138	Pebble Books	Capstone Press
Marvin's Birthday	K	RF	250+	Pacific Literacy	Pacific Learning
Mask Makers, The	K	RF	242	Leveled Readers	Houghton Mifflin
Matchbox Collection, A	K	I	250+	Stepping Stones	Nelson/Michaels Assoc.
Max and Mintie	K	F	250+	Home Connection Collection	Rigby
Max Visits London	K	RF	250+	Leveled Readers Language Support	Houghton Mifflin
Mazes Are Amazing!	K	I	220	Vocabulary Readers	Houghton Mifflin
Me Too	K	RF	136	Mayer, Mercer	Donovan
Meanest Thing to Say, The	K	RF	250+	Cosby, Bill	Scholastic
Measure Up!	K	I	303	Early Connections	Benchmark Education
Meat Eaters, Plant Eaters	K	I	156	Planet Earth	Rigby
Medal for Nickie, A	K	RF	262	Sunshine	Wright Group/McGraw Hill
Meet M & M	K	RF	250+	Ross, Pat	Penguin Group
Meet the Octopus	K	I	250+	Bookshop	Mondo
Messy Bessey's Closet	K	RF	92	Rookie Readers	Children's Press
Mickey's Secret	K	RF	250+	Rigby Literacy	Rigby
Middle of Nowhere, The	K	RF	250+	Rigby Literacy	Rigby
Mile High, A	K	F	331	Book Bank	Wright Group/McGraw Hill
Military Helicopters	K	I	106	Mighty Machines	Capstone Press
Miller Who Tried to Please Everyone, The	K	TL	250+	Aesop's Fables	Pearson Learning Group
Misha Disappears	K	RF	250+	Literacy 2000	Rigby
Miss Mouse Gets Married	K	TL	250+	Folk Tales	Wright Group/McGraw Hill
Missing Pet, The	K	RF	618	Pair-It Books	Steck-Vaughn
*Mollie Whuppie	K	TL	250+	New Way Orange	Steck-Vaughn
Molly the Brave and Me	K	RF	250+	O'Connor, Jane	Random House

* Collection of short stories

TITLE	LEVEL	GENRE	WORD COUNT	AUTHOR / SERIES	PUBLISHER / DISTRIBUTOR
Mom's Getting Married	K	RF	376	Sunshine	Wright Group/McGraw Hill
Monday Came	K	RF	250+	Voyages	SRA/McGraw Hill
Money Riddles That Count	K	I	250+	Fetty, Margaret	Steck-Vaughn
Monkeys & Apes	K	I	250+	PM Animal Facts: Turquoise	Rigby
Monster from the Sea, The	K	TL	250+	Bank Street	Bantam
Monster is Coming, The	K	F	250+	Rigby Literacy	Rigby
Monster Movie	K	F	250+	Cole, Joanna	Scholastic
Monster of Mirror Mountain, The	K	F	250+	Literacy 2000	Rigby
Monster Under The Bed, The	K	F	250+	Ready Readers	Pearson Learning Group
Monster's New Friend, The	K	F	250+	Rigby Literacy	Rigby
Moon, The	K	I	250+	Pebble Books	Red Brick Learning
Moonbeam Cow	K	TL	228	Books for Young Learners	Richard C. Owen
Morning Dance, The	K	RF	268	Jellybeans	Rigby
Mother Sea Turtle	K	I	240	Foundations	Wright Group/McGraw Hill
Mother's Helpers	K	RF	250+	Ready Readers	Pearson Learning Group
Mr. and Mrs. Murphy and Bernard	K	F	250+	Little Celebrations	Pearson Learning Group
Mr. Mancini's Rats	K	F	250+	Popcorn	Sundance
Mr. Merton's Vacation	K	RF	250+	Sails	Rigby
Mr. Pepperpot's Pet	K	F	250+	Literacy 2000	Rigby
Mrs. Huggins and Her Hen Hannah	K	F	250+	Dabcovich, Lydia	Dutton
Mrs. Sheep's Garden	K	F	953	Kratky, Lada	Hampton-Brown
Muscular System, The	K	I	131	Human Body Systems	Red Brick Learning
My First Business: Lemonade Stand	K	RF	548	Leveled Readers Social Studies	Houghton Mifflin
My Green Thumb	K	F	351	Leveled Readers	Houghton Mifflin
My Home	K	F	250+	Rhyme and Analogy	Oxford University Press
My Life	K	RF	250+	Pistone, Paul	Scholastic
My Neighborhood	K	I	250+	Early Connections	Benchmark Education
My New Mom	K	RF	282	Sunshine	Wright Group/McGraw Hill
My Pen Pal	K	RF	250+	Twig	Wright Group/McGraw Hill
My Scrapbook	K	I	312	Storyteller Nonfiction	Wright Group/McGraw Hill
My Sister's Getting Married	K	RF	300	Foundations	Wright Group/McGraw Hill
My Two Families	K	RF	250+	PM Story Books-Silver	Rigby
Mystery Man, The	K	RF	250+	Rigby Literacy	Rigby
Nate the Great	K	RF	250+	Sharmat, Marjorie Weinman	Bantam
Nate the Great and Me	K	RF	250+	Sharmat, Marjorie Weinman	Random House
Nate the Great and the Boring Beach Bag	K	RF	250+	Sharmat, Marjorie Weinman	Bantam
Nate the Great and the Crunchy Christmas	K	RF	250+	Sharmat, Marjorie Weinman	Bantam
Nate the Great and the Fishy Prize	K	RF	250+	Sharmat, Marjorie Weinman	Bantam
Nate the Great and the Halloween Hunt	K	RF	250+	Sharmat, Marjorie Weinman	Bantam
Nate the Great and the Lost List	K	RF	250+	Sharmat, Marjorie Weinman	Bantam
Nate the Great and the Missing Key	K	RF	250+	Sharmat, Marjorie Weinman	Bantam
Nate the Great and the Mushy Valentine	K	RF	250+	Sharmat, Marjorie Weinman	Bantam
Nate the Great and the Musical Note	K	RF	250+	Sharmat, Marjorie Weinman	Bantam
Nate the Great and the Phony Clue	K	RF	250+	Sharmat, Marjorie Weinman	Bantam
Nate the Great and the Pillowcase	K	RF	250+	Sharmat, Marjorie Weinman	Bantam
Nate the Great and the Snowy Trail	K	RF	250+	Sharmat, Marjorie Weinman	Bantam
Nate the Great and the Sticky Case	K	RF	250+	Sharmat, Marjorie Weinman	Bantam
Nate the Great and the Stolen Base	K	RF	250+	Sharmat, Marjorie Weinman	Bantam
Nate the Great and the Tardy Tortoise	K	RF	250+	Sharmat, Marjorie Weinman	Bantam
Nate the Great Goes Down in the Dumps	K	RF	250+	Sharmat, Marjorie Weinman	Bantam
Nate the Great Goes Undercover	K	RF	250+	Sharmat, Marjorie Weinman	Bantam
Nate the Great Saves the King of Sweden	K	RF	250+	Sharmat, Marjorie Weinman	Bantam
Nate the Great Stalks Stupidweed	K	RF	250+	Sharmat, Marjorie Weinman	Bantam
Nathan and Nicholas Alexander	K	F	250+	Delacre, Lulu	Scholastic

* Collection of short stories

TITLE	LEVEL	GENRE	WORD COUNT	AUTHOR / SERIES	PUBLISHER / DISTRIBUTOR
Natural History Museum, The	K	I	250+	Stepping Stones	Nelson/Michaels Assoc.
Nelson Gets a Fright	K	RF	387	PM Story Books	Rigby
Nesting Place, The	K	HF	356	PM Turquoise	Rigby
Nestor	K	F	250+	Bookshop	Mondo
New Car, The	K	RF	250+	Sunshine	Wright Group/McGraw Hill
New Girl, The	K	RF	250+	Pacific Literacy	Pacific Learning
Next Time I Will	K	RF	250+	Bank Street	Bantam
Nice New Neighbors	K	RF	250+	Brandenberg, Franz	Scholastic
Nicketty-Nacketty Noo-Noo-Noo	K	F	250+	Cowley, Joy	Mondo
Night Light, The	K	RF	554	Leveled Readers	Houghton Mifflin
No Fighting, No Biting!	K	RF	250+	Minarik, Else Holmelund	HarperTrophy
No Tooth, No Quarter!	K	F	250+	Buller, Jon	Random House
Not Your Usual Goat	K	F	656	Leveled Readers	Houghton Mifflin
Nothing to Be Scared About	K	RF	343	Sunshine	Wright Group/McGraw Hill
Now Listen, Stanley	K	F	250+	Literacy 2000	Rigby
Oh, Columbus!	K	F	250+	Literacy 2000	Rigby
Old Woman and Her Pig, The: An Old English Tale	K	TL	250+	Litzinger, Rosanne	OSI
Old Woman's Nose, The	K	F	250+	Sunshine	Wright Group/McGraw Hill
On Friday the Giant	K	F	240	The Giant	Wright Group/McGraw Hill
On Monday the Giant	K	F	250+	The Giant	Wright Group/McGraw Hill
On Sunday the Giant	K	F	250+	The Giant	Wright Group/McGraw Hill
On Thursday the Giant	K	F	250+	The Giant	Wright Group/McGraw Hill
On Tuesday the Giant	K	F	250+	The Giant	Wright Group/McGraw Hill
On Wednesday the Giant	K	F	250+	The Giant	Wright Group/McGraw Hill
One Drop of Water and a Million More	K	I	156	Book Bank	Wright Group/McGraw Hill
One Hundred Hungry Ants	K	F	250+	Pinczes, Elinor	Houghton Mifflin
One Piece Missing	K	SF	250+	Rigby Literacy	Rigby
Oogly Gum Chasing Game, The	K	F	250+	Literacy 2000	Rigby
Oops! Why Did I Do That?	K	RF	416	Early Connections	Benchmark Education
Opposite of Pig, The	K	F	250+	Little Celebrations	Pearson Learning Group
Orange: Seeing Orange All Around Us	K	I	250+	Colors	Capstone Press
Orca Song	K	RF	250+	Armour	Scholastic
Orphan Train	K	RF	250+	The Wright Skills	Wright Group/McGraw Hill
Our Busy Bodies	K	I	144	Home Connection Collection	Rigby
Our New Principal	K	RF	149	City Kids	Rigby
Our Senses	K	I	179	Spyglass Books	Compass Point Books
Out in the Big Wild World	K	F	430	Jellybeans	Rigby
Outside Dog, The	K	RF	250+	Pomerantz, Charlotte	HarperTrophy
Ovals: Seeing Ovals All Around Us	K	I	214	Shapes	Capstone Press
Owl and the Pussy	K	TL	250+	PM Animal Facts: Gold	Rigby
Owlbert	K	RF	250+	Soar To Success	Houghton Mifflin
Ox-Cart Man	K	HF	250+	Hall, Donald	Scholastic
Painting Lesson, The	K	F	250+	Pacific Literacy	Pacific Learning
Pancake, The	K	TL	250+	Lobel, Anita	Bantam
Paper Birds, The	K	RF	363	Foundations	Wright Group/McGraw Hill
Paper Crunch	K	I	250+	Rigby Literacy	Rigby
Paper Route, The	K	RF	314	New Way Green	Steck-Vaughn
Parade in Valencia	K	RF	214	Leveled Readers Language Support	Houghton Mifflin
Parents' Night Fright	K	RF	250+	Levy, Elizabeth	Scholastic
Parrot Talk	K	RF	250+	Cambridge Reading	Pearson Learning Group
Parts of a Plant	K	I	164	Phonics Readers	Compass Point Books
Peanut Butter Gang, The	K	F	250+	Siracusa, Catherine	Hyperion

* Collection of short stories

TITLE	LEVEL	GENRE	WORD COUNT	AUTHOR / SERIES	PUBLISHER / DISTRIBUTOR
Peanuts	K	I	250+	Rigby Literacy	Rigby
Penguins Are Waterbirds	K	I	250+	Bookshop	Mondo
Penny Candy	K	I	250+	Early Connections	Benchmark Education
People Are Living Things	K	I	250+	Home Connection Collection	Rigby
People of the Ice Age	K	I	286	Rigby Focus	Rigby
Perfect Paper	K	I	250+	Rigby Literacy	Rigby
Perfect Paper Planes	K	RF	250+	PM Plus Story Books	Rigby
Pet Dreams	K	F	410	Leveled Readers	Houghton Mifflin
Pet for You, A	K	I	531	Pair-It Books	Steck-Vaughn
Piano Recital, The	K	RF	250+	Rigby Literacy	Rigby
Picking Up Papers	K	RF	161	City Kids	Rigby
Pied Piper of Hamelin, The	K	TL	250+	Hautzig, Deborah	Random House
Pierre	K	RF	490	Sendak, Maurice	Scholastic
Piggle	K	F	250+	Bonsall, Crosby	HarperCollins
Pile in Pete's Room, The	K	RF	745	Sunshine	Wright Group/McGraw Hill
Pirate Traps	K	F	370	Story Box	Wright Group/McGraw Hill
Pizza for Everyone	K	I	251	Pair-It Books	Steck-Vaughn
Planets, The	K	I	250+	Out In Space	Red Brick Learning
Playhouse, The	K	RF	197	Pacific Literacy	Pacific Learning
Pocket for Corduroy, A	K	F	250+	Freeman, Don	Scholastic
Polar Bears	K	I	276	Wonder World	Wright Group/McGraw Hill
Pookie and Joe	K	F	250+	Literacy 2000	Rigby
Popcorn Book, The	K	I	208	Reading Unlimited	Pearson Learning Group
Poppy, The	K	I	152	Pacific Literacy	Pacific Learning
Pop's Truck	K	RF	250+	Voyages	SRA/McGraw Hill
Power of Nature, The	K	I	274	Early Connections	Benchmark Education
Prickles the Porcupine	K	RF	430	PM Plus Story Books	Rigby
Prince Among Donkeys, A	K	RF	250+	Rigby Literacy	Rigby
Princess and the Peas, The	K	TL	250+	Enrichment	Wright Group/McGraw Hill
Princess and the Wise Woman, The	K	TL	250+	Ready Readers	Pearson Learning Group
Princess Rosa's Winter	K	F	250+	Hindley, Judy	Wright Group/McGraw Hill
Priscilla and the Dinosaurs	K	RF	340	Sunshine	Wright Group/McGraw Hill
Prize for Purry, A	K	RF	250+	Literacy 2000	Rigby
Pterodactyl at the Airport	K	F	185	Wesley & the Dinosaurs	Wright Group/McGraw Hill
Public Library, The	K	I	250+	Stepping Stones	Nelson/Michaels Assoc.
Pueblo	K	I	114	Leveled Readers Social Studies	Houghton Mifflin
Purple: Seeing Purple All Around Us	K	I	250+	Colors	Capstone Press
Puss-in-Boots	K	TL	250+	PM Tales and Plays-Purple	Rigby
Pyjama Party, The	K	RF	250+	Cambridge Reading	Pearson Learning Group
Quiet World, The	K	RF	250+	Voyages	SRA/McGraw Hill
Quilt for Kiri, A	K	RF	367	Pacific Literacy	Pacific Learning
Rabbit Makes Toast	K	F	250+	Popcorn	Sundance
Rabbit's Tail	K	TL	250+	Cambridge Reading	Pearson Learning Group
Railroad Toad	K	F	178	Schade, Susan	Random House
Rain	K	I	263	Pebble Books	Capstone Press
Rainy Day Solution, A	K	I	161	Vocabulary Readers	Houghton Mifflin
Rats, Bats, and Black Puddings	K	F	714	Pacific Literacy	Pacific Learning
Ready, Set, Go!	K	RF	250+	Pacific Literacy	Pacific Learning
Rectangles: Seeing Rectangles All Around Us	K	I	199	Shapes	Capstone Press
Reduce, Reuse, and Recycle	K	I	326	Early Connections	Benchmark Education
Riches from Nature	K	I	382	Early Connections	Benchmark Education
Rick's Dream Adventure	K	F	250+	World Quest Adventures	World Quest Learning
Riding High	K	RF	529	PM Story Books	Rigby
Riding the Skateboard Ramps	K	RF	250+	PM Plus Story Books	Rigby

* Collection of short stories

TITLE	LEVEL	GENRE	WORD COUNT	AUTHOR / SERIES	PUBLISHER / DISTRIBUTOR
Right at Home	K	I	250+	Spyglass Books	Compass Point Books
Right Place for Jupiter, The	K	RF	250+	PM Story Books-Silver	Rigby
Rise and Shine, Mariko-chan	K	RF	250+	Tomioka, Chiyoko	Scholastic
Rita Moreno	K	B	250+	Leveled Readers Language Support	Houghton Mifflin
Robert Goddard	K	B	250+	Schaefer, Lola M.	Red Brick Learning
Robocat	K	F	295	Leveled Readers	Houghton Mifflin
Robot-a-cise	K	F	250+	Sunshine	Wright Group/McGraw Hill
Roller Coaster Ride	K	RF	484	PM Plus Story Books	Rigby
Rollercoaster	K	RF	250+	Rigby Literacy	Rigby
Rollo and Tweedy and the Ghost at Dougal Castle	K	F	250+	Allen, Laura Jean	HarperTrophy
Romana Acosta Banuelos	K	B	218	Leveled Readers Social Studies	Houghton Mifflin
Rosa's Tonsils	K	RF	337	Foundations	Wright Group/McGraw Hill
Rose Rest Home, The	K	RF	304	Sunshine	Wright Group/McGraw Hill
Roses for Anna	K	RF	250+	Rigby Literacy	Rigby
Rosie's House	K	RF	250+	Literacy 2000	Rigby
Royal Zookeeper, The	K	F	431	Early Connections	Benchmark Education
Ruby the Copycat	K	RF	250+	Rathman, Peggy	Scholastic
Rumpelstiltskin	K	TL	250+	PM Tales and Plays-Gold	Rigby
Runaway Ball, The	K	RF	250+	Rigby Literacy	Rigby
Running Shoes, The	K	RF	519	PM Plus Story Books	Rigby
Safe Harbor, A	K	I	167	Windows on Literacy	National Geographic
Sailing to a New Land	K	HF	250+	PM Plus Story Books	Rigby
Sam Who Never Forgets	K	F	281	Rice, Eve	Morrow
Sam's Big Clean-up	K	RF	287	Windmill Books	Rigby
Sam's Solution	K	RF	250+	Literacy 2000	Rigby
Sandwich Hero, The	K	RF	250+	Literacy 2000	Rigby
Sandy's Suitcase	K	RF	250+	Edwards, Elsy	SRA/McGraw Hill
Saturday Club, The	K	RF	250+	Melton, Holly	Hampton-Brown
Scaredy Bears	K	F	250+	Sunshine	Wright Group/McGraw Hill
Scaredy Dog	K	RF	250+	Thomas, Jane Resh	Hyperion
Scare-Kid	K	F	250+	Literacy 2000	Rigby
School in Colonial America	K	I	250+	Welcome Books	Children's Press
Scruffy	K	RF	250+	Parish, Peggy	HarperTrophy
Sea Animals	K	I	250+	Little Red Readers	Sundance
Sea of Animals, A	K	I	213	Spyglass Books	Compass Point Books
Sea Turtles	K	I	296	Marine Life For Young Readers	Pearson Learning Group
Sea Wall, The	K	I	251	Foundations	Wright Group/McGraw Hill
Seat Belt Song, The	K	RF	505	PM Turquoise	Rigby
Secret Hideaway, The	K	RF	618	PM Gold	Rigby
Secret Lives of Mr. and Mrs. Smith, The	K	F	395	Sunshine	Wright Group/McGraw Hill
Secret of Silk, The	K	I	234	Rigby Focus	Rigby
Secret, The: A Traditional Tale From Wales	K	TL	250+	Rigby Literacy	Rigby
Seeds	K	I	250+	Sunshine	Wright Group/McGraw Hill
Seeing	K	I	149	Pebble Books	Capstone Press
Seeing the School Doctor	K	RF	167	City Kids	Rigby
Selu and Kana Ti	K	TL	250+	Folk Tales	Mondo
Seven Foolish Fishermen	K	TL	250+	PM Tales and Plays-Gold	Rigby
Shadow Puppets	K	I	236	Rigby Focus	Rigby
Shape of Things, The	K	I	124	Spyglass Books	Compass Point Books
Shapes in the City	K	I	191	Twig	Wright Group/McGraw Hill
Sheila Rae, the Brave	K	F	250+	Henkes, Kevin	Scholastic
Shingo's Grandfather	K	RF	370	Sunshine	Wright Group/McGraw Hill

* Collection of short stories

TITLE	LEVEL	GENRE	WORD COUNT	AUTHOR / SERIES	PUBLISHER / DISTRIBUTOR
Ships at Sea	K	I	250+	PM Plus	Rigby
Shipwreck Saturday	K	RF	250+	Cosby, Bill	Scholastic
Shoe	K	RF	250+	Rigby Literacy	Rigby
Shortest Kid in the World	K	RF	250+	Bliss, Corinne Demas	Random House
Show and Tell	K	RF	201	City Kids	Rigby
Sidetrack Sam	K	RF	250+	Literacy 2000	Rigby
Silly Tilly's Valentine	K	F	250+	Hoban, Lillian	HarperTrophy
*Sing to the Moon	K	F	2448	Story Box	Wright Group/McGraw Hill
Singing Princess, The	K	F	250+	Rigby Literacy	Rigby
Skeletal System, The	K	I	166	Human Body Systems	Red Brick Learning
SkyScraper, The	K	I	252	Little Red Readers	Sundance
Sleeping Beauty	K	TL	250+	Enrichment	Wright Group/McGraw Hill
Slip and Slide	K	I	215	Spyglass Books	Compass Point Books
Slither McCreep and His Brother, Joe	K	RF	250+	Johnston, Tony	OSI
Sly Fox and Little Red Hen	K	TL	250+	PM Tales and Plays-Purple	Rigby
Smallest Cow in the World, The	K	RF	250+	Paterson, Katherine	HarperTrophy
Smallest Tree, The	K	F	250+	Literacy 2000	Rigby
Smile, The	K	RF	253	Read Alongs	Rigby
Snakes	K	I	259	Foundations	Wright Group/McGraw Hill
Sneakers	K	I	388	Sunshine	Wright Group/McGraw Hill
Snow White and Rose Red	K	TL	250+	Hunia, Fran	Ladybird Books
Snow White and the Seven Dwarfs	K	TL	250+	PM Tales and Plays-Gold	Rigby
Snowball War, The	K	RF	250+	Chardiet, Bernice	Scholastic
Snowshoe Thompson	K	HF	250+	Levinson, N. Smiler	HarperTrophy
Soap Soup and Other Verses	K	TL	250+	Kuskin, Karla	HarperTrophy
Soccer Cousins	K	RF	250+	Marzollo, Jean	Scholastic
Soil	K	I	381	Windows on Literacy	National Geographic
Solve It!	K	RF	250+	Goldish, Meish	Scholastic
Sounds All Around Us	K	I	168	Phonics Readers	Compass Point Books
Souvenirs	K	RF	179	Literacy 2000	Rigby
Space Cat	K	F	250+	Sails	Rigby
Spaghetti Party, The	K	RF	250+	Bank Street	Bantam
Special Cake, The	K	RF	250+	Cambridge Reading	Pearson Learning Group
Special Ride, The	K	RF	647	PM Gold	Rigby
Spider in My Bedroom, A	K	RF	477	PM Plus Story Books	Rigby
Spider Night	K	F	250+	Kunari, Anna	Hampton-Brown
Spiders and the Web	K	I	187	Animal Homes	Capstone Press
Spring Has Sprung	K	I	250+	Spyglass Books	Compass Point Books
Squares: Seeing Squares All Around Us	K	I	183	Shapes	Capstone Press
Stan the Hot Dog Man	K	RF	250+	Kessler, Ethel & Leonard	HarperTrophy
Star and Patches	K	RF	440	PM Plus Story Books	Rigby
Star Pictures	K	I	96	Books for Young Learners	Richard C. Owen
Starfish & Urchins	K	I	322	Marine Life For Young Readers	Pearson Learning Group
Stars, The	K	I	102	Pebble Books	Red Brick Learning
Statues Across America	K	I	293	Vocabulary Readers	Houghton Mifflin
Stems	K	I	231	Pebble Books	Capstone Press
Stone Mouse, The	K	F	250+	Rigby Literacy	Rigby
Stone Works	K	I	124	Wonder World	Wright Group/McGraw Hill
Story Box, The	K	RF	592	Leveled Readers	Houghton Mifflin
Story of Hungbu and Nolbu, The	K	TL	250+	Bookshop	Mondo
Strawberry Pop And Soda Crackers	K	RF	396	Little Celebrations	Pearson Learning Group
String Food	K	I	250+	Home Connection Collection	Rigby
Stump Hill	K	RF	627	Early Connections	Benchmark Education
Subtraction Fun	K	I	250+	Yellow Umbrella Books	Capstone Press

* Collection of short stories

TITLE	LEVEL	GENRE	WORD COUNT	AUTHOR / SERIES	PUBLISHER / DISTRIBUTOR
Sugar Bush, The	K	I	250+	Greetings	Rigby
Suki and the Case of the Lost Bunnies	K	RF	250+	Ready Readers	Pearson Learning Group
Sun, The	K	I	42	Pebble Books	Red Brick Learning
Sunflower That Went Flop, The	K	F	637	Story Box	Wright Group/McGraw Hill
Supermarket Chase, The	K	RF	438	Sunshine	Wright Group/McGraw Hill
Supermarket, The	K	I	255	Pebble Books	Capstone Press
Surf Carnival, The	K	RF	434	PM Story Books	Rigby
Surprise Party	K	I	333	Hutchins, Pat	Macmillan
Surprise Snow, The	K	RF	545	Leveled Readers	Houghton Mifflin
Swamp Monsters	K	F	250+	Christian, Mary Blount	Puffin Books
Take a Guess: A Look At Estimation	K	I	164	Spyglass Books	Compass Point Books
Talent Contest, The	K	RF	250+	PM Story Books-Silver	Rigby
Tall Tony	K	RF	383	Leveled Readers	Houghton Mifflin
Tarantula	K	I	144	Alphakids	Sundance
Tarantulas	K	I	97	Pebble Books	Red Brick Learning
Tea	K	I	267	Wonder World	Wright Group/McGraw Hill
Teddy Bears Cure a Cold	K	F	240	Gretz, Susanna	Scholastic
Teeth	K	I	470	Sunshine	Wright Group/McGraw Hill
Tell It to a Friend	K	I	250+	Home Connection Collection	Rigby
Ten-Gallon Hat, The	K	F	250+	Voyages	SRA/McGraw Hill
Terrible Fright, A	K	TL	291	Story Box	Wright Group/McGraw Hill
Terrific Trees	K	I	250+	Rigby Literacy	Rigby
That Fat Hat	K	F	250+	Barkan, Joanne	Scholastic
That Looks Different!	K	I	227	Windows on Literacy	National Geographic
That Old House	K	F	250+	Rigby Literacy	Rigby
That's Really Weird!	K	F	129	Read Alongs	Rigby
Thomas Edison	K	I	145	Windows on Literacy	National Geographic
Three Bears, The	K	TL	873	Galdone, Paul	Clarion
Three Billy Goats Gruff, The	K	TL	250+	Asbjornsen, P. C.; Moe, J. E.	Harcourt School Publishers
Three Billy Goats Gruff, The	K	TL	478	Stevens, Janet	Harcourt School Publishers
Three Days on a River in a Red Canoe	K	I	250+	Williams, Vera B.	Scholastic
Three Ducks Went Wandering	K	F	250+	Roy, Ron	Clarion
Three Magicians, The	K	F	250+	Literacy 2000	Rigby
*Three Stories You Can Read to Your Cat	K	F	250+	Miller, Sara Swan	Houghton Mifflin
*Three Stories You Can Read to Your Dog	K	F	250+	Miller, Sara Swan	Houghton Mifflin
Three Wishes, The	K	TL	501	Sunshine	Wright Group/McGraw Hill
Threw and Through	K	F	255	Sunshine	Wright Group/McGraw Hill
Thumbelina	K	TL	807	Tales from Hans Andersen	Wright Group/McGraw Hill
Thunder and Lightning	K	I	250+	Pfeffer, Wendy	Scholastic
Tiger, the Man, and the Jackal, The	K	F	520	Leveled Readers	Houghton Mifflin
Time for a Family	K	I	108	Literacy Tree	Rigby
Tippu	K	F	250+	Soar To Success	Houghton Mifflin
Too Many Babas	K	TL	250+	Croll, Carolyn	HarperTrophy
Too Many Babas	K	TL	250+	Little Readers	Houghton Mifflin
Too Much Trouble for Grandpa	K	F	250+	Lewis, Rob	Mondo
Tools Scientists Use	K	I	184	Windows on Literacy	National Geographic
Top Cat	K	F	250+	Story Steps	Rigby
Town Mouse and Country Mouse	K	TL	250+	PM Tales and Plays-Purple	Rigby
Trains on the Rails	K	I	250+	PM Plus	Rigby
Treasure of the Lost Lagoon, The	K	F	250+	Hayes, Geoffrey	Random House
Treasure on Fraser Street, The	K	RF	250+	Home Connection Collection	Rigby
Trees	K	I	388	Early Connections	Benchmark Education
Tricky Insects and Other Fun Creatures	K	I	250+	Spyglass Books	Compass Point Books
Trilobites	K	I	141	Books for Young Learners	Richard C. Owen

* Collection of short stories

TITLE	LEVEL	GENRE	WORD COUNT	AUTHOR / SERIES	PUBLISHER / DISTRIBUTOR
Trip to the Fire Station	K	I	182	Rosen Real Readers	Rosen Publishing Group
Truck Parade, The	K	RF	483	PM Plus Story Books	Rigby
Trucks on the Road	K	I	250+	PM Plus	Rigby
Truman's Aunt Farm	K	F	250+	Soar To Success	Houghton Mifflin
Tubes in My Ears: My Trip to the Hospital	K	I	250+	Bookshop	Mondo
Turtle Flies South	K	F	250+	Literacy 2000	Rigby
Tuttle's Shell	K	F	250+	Bookshop	Mondo
Two Foolish Cats, The	K	F	250+	Literacy 2000	Rigby
Two Languages	K	I	202	Vocabulary Readers	Houghton Mifflin
Unbelievable!	K	SF	250+	Shulman, Lisa	Hampton-Brown
Under the City	K	I	206	Sunshine	Wright Group/McGraw Hill
Under the Ground	K	I	250+	Pluckrose, Henry	Franklin Watts
Upside-Down Elephant, The	K	RF	396	Leveled Readers	Houghton Mifflin
Using Nature's Gifts	K	I	250+	People, Spaces & Places	Rand McNally
Using Rocks	K	I	167	Windows on Literacy	National Geographic
Using Your Safety Senses	K	I	413	Leveled Readers Science	Houghton Mifflin
Vehicles for Fun and Sports	K	I	439	PM Plus	Rigby
Vehicles in the Air	K	I	436	PM Plus	Rigby
Veterans Day	K	I	250+	Cotton, Jaqueline S.	Scholastic
Vicky the High Jumper	K	I	250+	Literacy 2000	Rigby
Visit to a Pueblo, A	K	I	129	Vocabulary Readers	Houghton Mifflin
Wagon Wheels	K	HF	250+	Brenner, Barbara	HarperTrophy
Wake Up, Scooterville	K	RF	250+	Stamper, Judith Bauer	Scholastic
Walkathon, The	K	RF	250+	PM Story Books-Silver	Rigby
Walking by the Rio	K	RF	118	Books for Young Learners	Richard C. Owen
Washington, D.C.	K	I	187	Windows on Literacy	National Geographic
Waste Not: Time to Recycle	K	I	250+	Spyglass Books	Compass Point Books
Watch It Grow	K	I	243	Spyglass Books	Compass Point Books
Water at Work	K	I	159	Instant Readers	Harcourt School Publishers
Water Can Change	K	I	138	Windows on Literacy	National Geographic
Water Goes Up! Water Goes Down!	K	I	299	Early Connections	Benchmark Education
Waterhole	K	I	149	Planet Earth	Rigby
We Scream for Ice Cream	K	RF	250+	Chardiet, Bernice; Maccarone, Grace	Scholastic
Weather Watcher, The	K	I	245	Spyglass Books	Compass Point Books
Weaver's Gift, The	K	RF	269	Leveled Readers	Houghton Mifflin
*Well I Never	K	F	2517	Story Box	Wright Group/McGraw Hill
Wetlands	K	I	175	Rigby Focus	Rigby
What a Day!	K	RF	621	Miranda, Anne	Hampton-Brown
What a Funny Thing to Do	K	RF	236	Stepping Stones	Nelson/Michaels Assoc.
What Angela Needs	K	RF	250+	Voyages	SRA/McGraw Hill
What Are Caves?	K	I	108	Pebble Books	Red Brick Learning
What Are Deserts?	K	I	105	Pebble Books	Capstone Press
What Are Forests?	K	I	114	Pebble Books	Capstone Press
What Are Lakes?	K	I	92	Pebble Books	Red Brick Learning
What Are Mountains?	K	I	70	Pebble Books	Capstone Press
What Are Oceans?	K	I	97	Pebble Books	Capstone Press
What Are Rivers?	K	I	111	Pebble Books	Red Brick Learning
What Are Volcanoes?	K	I	108	Pebble Books	Red Brick Learning
What Changes Our Earth?	K	I	273	People, Places & Spaces	Rand McNally
What Happens at the Bank?	K	I	388	Leveled Readers Social Studies	Houghton Mifflin
What Happens When You Recycle?	K	I	215	Discovery World	Rigby
What Is an Amphibian?	K	I	85	Pebble Books	Red Brick Learning
What Magnets Can Do	K	I	250+	Fowler, Allan	Scholastic

* Collection of short stories

TITLE	LEVEL	GENRE	WORD COUNT	AUTHOR / SERIES	PUBLISHER / DISTRIBUTOR
What Plants and Animals Need	K	I	200	Phonics Readers	Compass Point Books
What's Best for Red?	K	RF	444	Eggers, Casey	Hampton-Brown
What's for Dinner, Dad?	K	RF	459	Sunshine	Wright Group/McGraw Hill
What's Inside?	K	I	238	Wonder World	Wright Group/McGraw Hill
What's Missing?	K	I	252	Book Bank	Wright Group/McGraw Hill
What's Underneath?	K	I	200	Discovery World	Rigby
When I First Came to This Land	K	TL	250+	Ziefert, Harriet	Scholastic
When I Get Bigger	K	RF	205	Mayer, Mercer	Donovan
When Sophie Gets Angry - Really, Really Angry . . .	K	RF	166	Bang, Molly	Scholastic
When the Cookernup Store Burned Down	K	F	250+	Sunshine	Wright Group/McGraw Hill
When Will We Be Sisters?	K	RF	250+	Kroll, Virginia	Scholastic
Where Are the Bears?	K	F	250+	Winters, Kay	Bantam
Where Dinosaurs Walked	K	I	189	Phonics Readers	Compass Point Books
Where Does All the Garbage Go?	K	I	250+	Twig	Wright Group/McGraw Hill
Where Does Garbage Go?	K	I	250+	Soar To Success	Houghton Mifflin
Where Does the Butterfly Go When It Rains?	K	RF	250+	Bookshop	Mondo
Where Is the Bear?	K	F	250+	Nims, Bonnie	Whitman
Where is White Rabbit?	K	RF	250+	Pacific Literacy	Pacific Learning
Where Jeans Come From	K	I	250+	Ready Readers	Pearson Learning Group
White Horse, The	K	F	250+	Literacy 2000	Rigby
Who Grows Up on the Farm?: A Book About Farm Animals and Their Offspring	K	I	250+	Who Grows Up Here?	Picture Window Books
Who Likes It Hot?	K	F	250+	Bookshop	Mondo
Who Needs Math?	K	RF	349	Story Box	Wright Group/McGraw Hill
Who Passed Through?	K	RF	380	Leveled Readers	Houghton Mifflin
Who Pushed Humpty?	K	TL	250+	Literacy 2000	Rigby
Who Sank the Boat?	K	F	219	Allen, Pamela	Coward
Who's Afraid of the Big, Bad Bully?	K	RF	250+	Slater, Teddy	Scholastic
Whose Shoes?	K	RF	250+	Sunshine	Wright Group/McGraw Hill
Whose Side Are You On?	K	TL	250+	Cisco, Cheyenne	Sadlier-Oxford
Why Coyote Howls at Night	K	TL	274	Little Books	Sadlier-Oxford
Why People Move	K	I	250+	People, Places & Spaces	Rand McNally
Why the Kangaroo Hops	K	I	391	Sunshine	Wright Group/McGraw Hill
Why the Rooster Crows at Sunrise	K	TL	250+	Sunshine	Wright Group/McGraw Hill
Why There Are Shooting Stars	K	TL	362	Pacific Literacy	Pacific Learning
Why We Measure	K	I	178	Spyglass Books	Compass Point Books
Wild Weather	K	I	187	Rigby Focus	Rigby
Wind and Storms	K	I	868	Sunshine	Wright Group/McGraw Hill
Wind and the Sun, The	K	TL	399	Leveled Readers	Houghton Mifflin
Wind Eagle, The	K	RF	370	Wonders	Hampton-Brown
Wind, The	K	I	179	Spyglass Books	Compass Point Books
Winter Woollies	K	I	289	Storyteller Nonfiction	Wright Group/McGraw Hill
Wise Old Turtle, The	K	TL	250+	World Quest Adventures	World Quest Learning
Wizard and the Rainbow, The	K	F	250+	Sunshine	Wright Group/McGraw Hill
Wizard Came to Visit, A	K	F	250+	Sunshine	Wright Group/McGraw Hill
Wool Keeps Me Warm	K	I	214	Windows on Literacy	National Geographic
Wordsong	K	RF	192	Bobber Books	Wright Group/McGraw Hill
Work We Do, The	K	I	250+	Spyglass Books	Compass Point Books
Worm's Home, A	K	I	281	Independent Readers Science	Houghton Mifflin
Wright Brothers at Kitty Hawk, The	K	B	250+	Schaefer, Lola M.	Red Brick Learning
Yard Sale, The	K	RF	250+	Windows on Literacy	National Geographic
Yellow: Seeing Yellow All Around Us	K	I	250+	Colors	Capstone Press
You Are Special	K	I	250+	Sunshine	Wright Group/McGraw Hill

* Collection of short stories

TITLE	LEVEL	GENRE	WORD COUNT	AUTHOR / SERIES	PUBLISHER / DISTRIBUTOR
You Can Always Tell Cathy from Caitlin	K	RF	583	Sunshine	Wright Group/McGraw Hill
You Can Recycle!	K	I	219	Rigby Focus	Rigby
Yuck!	K	F	250+	Leveled Readers Language Support	Houghton Mifflin
Zack's Alligator	K	F	250+	Mozelle, Shirley	HarperTrophy
Zack's Alligator	K	F	250+	Little Readers	Houghton Mifflin
Zack's Alligator Goes to School	K	F	250+	Mozelle, Shirley	HarperTrophy
Abracadabra	L	RF	372	Reading Unlimited	Pearson Learning Group
Abraham Lincoln	L	B	235	Famous Americans	Capstone Press
Acid Rain	L	I	368	Wonder World	Wright Group/McGraw Hill
Adventures of a Kite	L	F	33	Jellybeans	Rigby
Adventures of Granny Gatman, The	L	RF	250+	Meadows, Graham	Pearson Learning Group
Adventures of the Buried Treasure, The	L	F	250+	McArthur, Nancy	Scholastic
Alexander and the Wind-Up Mouse	L	F	250+	Lionni, Leo	Scholastic
Alfie's Gift	L	F	250+	Literacy 2000	Rigby
All About Bicycles	L	I	250+	Sunshine	Wright Group/McGraw Hill
All About Me	L	I	250+	iOpeners	Pearson Learning Group
All About Plants	L	I	250+	Home Connection Collection	Rigby
All About Stacy	L	RF	250+	Giff, Patricia Reilly	Bantam
All Fall Down	L	I	206	Spyglass Books	Compass Point Books
All Kinds of Eyes	L	I	250+	Discovery World	Rigby
All Kinds of Flowers	L	I	250+	Turner, Teresa	Steck-Vaughn
*Amanda Pig and Her Big Brother Oliver	L	F	250+	Van Leeuwen, Jean	Puffin Books
Amazing Mr. Mulch, The	L	F	250+	Cambridge Reading	Pearson Learning Group
Amazing Trains	L	I	482	Pair-It Books	Steck-Vaughn
Amelia Bedelia	L	F	250+	Parish, Peggy	HarperTrophy
Amelia Bedelia and the Baby	L	F	250+	Parish, Peggy	Harper & Row
Amelia Bedelia and the Surprise Shower	L	F	250+	Parish, Peggy	Harper & Row
Amelia Bedelia Goes Camping	L	F	250+	Parish, Peggy	Avon Camelot
Amelia Bedelia Helps Out	L	F	250+	Parish, Peggy	Avon Camelot
Amelia Bedelia's Family Album	L	F	250+	Parish, Peggy	Avon
Anak the Brave	L	F	250+	Sunshine	Wright Group/McGraw Hill
And Then There Were Birds	L	TL	156	Books for Young Learners	Richard C. Owen
Androcles and the Lion	L	TL	250+	PM Tales and Plays-Silver	Rigby
Animal Mysteries	L	I	250+	Rigby Literacy	Rigby
Animal Pets	L	I	250+	Sunshine	Wright Group/McGraw Hill
Animal Reports	L	I	277	Little Red Readers	Sundance
Animal Tails	L	I	250+	Lighthouse	Rigby
Animal Tracks	L	I	250+	Dorros, Arthur	Scholastic
Animals at Night	L	I	520	Leveled Readers	Houghton Mifflin
Animals Building Homes	L	I	250+	Animal Behavior	Capstone Press
Animals Finding Food	L	I	250+	Animal Behavor	Capstone Press
Animals in Winter	L	I	250+	Soar To Success	Houghton Mifflin
Animals Raising Offspring	L	I	250+	Animal Behavior	Capstone Press
Animals Sleeping	L	I	250+	Animal Behavior	Capstone Press
Animals Staying Safe	L	I	250+	First Facts	Capstone Press
Annabel the Actress Starring in Gorilla My Dreams	L	RF	250+	Conford, Ellen	Simon & Schuster
Annie Bananie Moves To Barry Avenue	L	RF	250+	Komaiko, Leah	Bantam
Another Day, Another Challenge	L	RF	250+	Literacy 2000	Rigby
Ant and the Grasshopper, The	L	TL	250+	Little Celebrations	Pearson Learning Group
Antarctica	L	I	250+	Read-About Geography	Children's Press
Antarctica	L	RF	250+	Soar To Success	Houghton Mifflin
Antarctica	L	I	250+	Fowler, Allan	Scholastic

* Collection of short stories

TITLE	LEVEL	GENRE	WORD COUNT	AUTHOR / SERIES	PUBLISHER / DISTRIBUTOR
Armadillo, The	L	I	250+	Sunshine	Wright Group/McGraw Hill
Arnold Lobel: Words and Pictures Together	L	B	375	Leveled Readers	Houghton Mifflin
Arturo's Baton	L	RF	250+	Soar To Success	Houghton Mifflin
Ashley's World Record	L	F	250+	Little Celebrations	Pearson Learning Group
At the Coal Mine	L	I	317	Rigby Focus	Rigby
At the End of the Day	L	RF	250+	Pacific Literacy	Pacific Learning
Aunt Wilhelmina's Will	L	RF	250+	Voyages	SRA/McGraw Hill
Avalanche!	L	I	250+	Rosen Real Readers	Rosen Publishing Group
Awumpalema	L	TL	250+	Literacy 2000	Rigby
Backyard Camp-Out	L	RF	628	Leveled Readers	Houghton Mifflin
Bad Day for Benjamin, A	L	RF	250+	Reading Unlimited	Pearson Learning Group
Badgers	L	I	250+	Bridgestone Books	Capstone Press
Bad-Luck Penny, The	L	F	250+	O'Connor, Jane	Grosset & Dunlap
Baking Bread	L	I	426	How-To Series	Benchmark Education
*Bank Robbery and Jack and the Beanstalk, The	L	TL	250+	New Way Literature	Steck-Vaughn
Basketball Game, The	L	RF	607	Leveled Readers Science	Houghton Mifflin
Bat's Night Out	L	RF	172	Books for Young Learners	Richard C. Owen
Be a Plant Scientist	L	I	250+	Paul, Michele	Wright Group/McGraw Hill
Beans on the Roof	L	RF	250+	Byars, Betsy	Bantam
Bear and the Trolls, The	L	TL	250+	PM Tales and Plays-Silver	Rigby
Bear's Diet	L	RF	652	PM Gold	Rigby
Ben's Amazing Birthday	L	RF	250+	Cambridge Reading	Pearson Learning Group
Best Clown in Town, The	L	RF	250+	Bradley, Tom	Pearson Learning Group
B-E-S-T Friends	L	RF	250+	Giff, Patricia Reilly	Bantam
Best Older Sister, The	L	RF	250+	Choi, Sook Nyul	Bantam
Best Worst Day, The	L	RF	250+	Graves, Bonnie	Hyperion
Best-Loved Doll, The	L	RF	250+	Caudill, Rebecca	Henry Holt & Co.
Betsy Ross	L	B	250+	Pebble Books	Red Brick Learning
Big Al	L	F	250+	Yoshi, Andrew C.	Scholastic
Big Balloon Festival, The	L	RF	625	PM Gold	Rigby
Big Beet, The	L	F	250+	Ready Readers	Pearson Learning Group
Big Orange Spot, The	L	F	250+	Pinkwater, Daniel Manus	Scholastic
Big Race, The	L	RF	250+	Pattrick, Steve	Rigby
Big Shrink, The	L	F	250+	Cambridge Reading	Pearson Learning Group
Bill Cosby's Little Bill: The Best Way to Play	L	F	250+	Cosby, Bill	Scholastic
Billy the Ghost and Me	L	F	250+	Greer, Gery; Ruddick, Bob	HarperTrophy
Birds at My Barn, The	L	RF	230	Books for Young Learners	Richard C. Owen
Birthday Wishes	L	RF	250+	Voyages	SRA/McGraw Hill
Black Bear Cub	L	F	250+	Lind, Alan	Scholastic
Black: Seeing Black All Around Us	L	I	250+	Colors	Capstone Press
Blackbirds	L	I	250+	Sunshine	Wright Group/McGraw Hill
Blue: Seeing Blue All Around Us	L	I	250+	Colors	Capstone Press
Bluebird Out My Window	L	RF	633	Leveled Readers Science	Houghton Mifflin
Bobo's Magic Wishes	L	F	250+	Little Readers	Houghton Mifflin
Boston Coffee Party, The	L	HF	250+	Rappaport, Doreen	HarperCollins
Boy Who Cried Wolf, The	L	TL	250+	Literacy Tree	Rigby
Boy Who Turned Into a T.V. Set, The	L	F	250+	Manes, Stephen	Avon Camelot
Boy Who Went to the North Wind, The	L	TL	250+	Literacy 2000	Rigby
Brachiosaurus in the River	L	F	200	Wesley & The Dinosaurs	Wright Group/McGraw Hill
Brand New Butterfly, A	L	I	186	Literacy 2000	Rigby
Bravest Dog Ever, The: The True Story of Balto	L	I	250+	Standiford, Natalie	Random House
Bravo Amelia Bedelia!	L	F	250+	Parish, Herman	Avon
Breathing	L	I	106	Bookshop	Mondo
Bright Lights and Shadowy Shapes	L	I	250+	Spyglass Books	Compass Point Books

* Collection of short stories

TITLE	LEVEL	GENRE	WORD COUNT	AUTHOR / SERIES	PUBLISHER / DISTRIBUTOR
Brigid Beware	L	RF	250+	Leverich, Kathleen	Random House
Brigid Bewitched	L	RF	250+	Leverich, Kathleen	Random House
Brigid the Bad	L	RF	250+	Leverich, Kathleen	Random House
Bringing the Sea Back Home	L	F	250+	Literacy 2000	Rigby
Brothers are Forever	L	RF	536	Leveled Readers	Houghton Mifflin
Brown: Seeing Brown All Around Us	L	I	250+	Colors	Capstone Press
Bug Off!	L	F	250+	Dussling, Jennifer	Grosset & Dunlap
Bugs!	L	I	250+	Phonics and Friends	Hampton-Brown
Building a Castle	L	I	250+	Early Connections	Benchmark Education
Bully, The	L	RF	250+	PM Story Books	Rigby
Bumps in the Night	L	F	250+	Allard, Harry	Bantam
Burger Time	L	I	250+	Voyages	SRA/McGraw Hill
Butterflies and Moths	L	I	250+	Early Connections	Benchmark Education
Butterflies of the Sea	L	I	250+	Swartz, Stanley L.	Pearson Learning Group
Cam Jansen and the Chocolate Fudge Mystery	L	RF	250+	Adler, David A.	Puffin Books
Cam Jansen and the Ghostly Mystery	L	RF	250+	Adler, David A.	Puffin Books
Cam Jansen and the Mystery at the Haunted House	L	RF	250+	Adler, David A.	Puffin Books
Cam Jansen and the Mystery at the Monkey House	L	RF	250+	Adler, David A.	Puffin Books
Cam Jansen and the Mystery of Flight 54	L	RF	250+	Adler, David A.	Puffin Books
Cam Jansen and the Mystery of the Babe Ruth Baseball	L	RF	250+	Adler, David A.	Puffin Books
Cam Jansen and the Mystery of the Carnival Prize	L	RF	250+	Adler, David A.	Puffin Books
Cam Jansen and the Mystery of the Circus Clown	L	RF	250+	Adler, David A.	Puffin Books
Cam Jansen and the Mystery of the Dinosaur Bones	L	RF	250+	Adler, David A.	Puffin Books
Cam Jansen and the Mystery of the Gold Coins	L	RF	250+	Adler, David A.	Puffin Books
Cam Jansen and the Mystery of the Monkey House	L	RF	250+	Adler, David A.	Puffin Books
Cam Jansen and the Mystery of the Monster Movie	L	RF	250+	Adler, David A.	Puffin Books
Cam Jansen and the Mystery of the Stolen Corn Popper	L	RF	250+	Adler, David A.	Puffin Books
Cam Jansen and the Mystery of the Stolen Diamonds	L	RF	250+	Adler, David A.	Puffin Books
Cam Jansen and the Mystery of the Television Dog	L	RF	250+	Adler, David A.	Puffin Books
Cam Jansen and the Mystery of the U.F.O.	L	RF	250+	Adler, David A.	Puffin Books
Cam Jansen and the Scary Snake Mystery	L	RF	250+	Adler, David A.	Puffin Books
Cam Jansen and the Triceratops Pops Mystery	L	RF	250+	Adler, David A.	Puffin Books
Camping with Our Dad	L	RF	250+	Sunshine	Wright Group/McGraw Hill
Can I Have a Dinosaur?	L	RF	250+	Literacy 2000	Rigby
Candy Corn Contest, The	L	RF	250+	Giff, Patricia Reilly	Bantam
Cannonball Chris	L	RF	250+	Marzollo, J.	Random House
Captain Felonius	L	F	250+	Literacy 2000	Rigby
Car Trouble	L	RF	724	PM Gold	Rigby
Caring	L	I	250+	Character Education	Red Brick Learning
Carlita Ropes the Twister	L	F	363	Pair-It Books	Steck-Vaughn
Carpenters	L	I	250+	Community Workers	Compass Point Books
Case of the Cool-Itch Kid, The	L	RF	250+	Giff, Patricia Reilly	Bantam
Cass Becomes a Star	L	B	250+	Literacy 2000	Rigby

* Collection of short stories

TITLE	LEVEL	GENRE	WORD COUNT	AUTHOR / SERIES	PUBLISHER / DISTRIBUTOR
Cassie's Castle	L	RF	250+	Rigby Literacy	Rigby
Cat Called Tim, A	L	RF	250+	New Way Literature	Steck-Vaughn
Cat for Keeps, A	L	RF	250+	Cambridge Reading	Pearson Learning Group
Cattle	L	I	250+	PM Animal Facts: Purple	Rigby
Celebrations	L	I	199	Yellow Umbrella Books	Capstone Press
Cesar Chavez	L	B	262	Pebble Books	Capstone Press
Chameleons	L	I	201	Twig	Wright Group/McGraw Hill
Chang's Paper Pony	L	RF	250+	Coerr, Eleanor	HarperTrophy
Charles M. Schulz	L	B	186	First Biographies	Red Brick Learning
Charlie	L	F	250+	Literacy 2000	Rigby
Chefs	L	I	250+	Community Workers	Compass Point Books
Chicken Little	L	TL	587	Traditional Tales & More	Rigby
Chickens	L	I	250+	PM Animal Facts: Purple	Rigby
Chocolate	L	I	191	Windows on Literacy	National Geographic
Chomp	L	I	250+	Berger, Melvin	Scholastic
Circles: Seeing Circles All Around Us	L	I	198	Shapes	Capstone Press
City Green	L	RF	250+	DiSalvo-Ryan, DyAnne	Scholastic
Clarence the Crocodile	L	F	250+	New Way Literature	Steck-Vaughn
Claudine's Concert	L	RF	250+	Literacy 2000	Rigby
Clay Dog, The	L	HF	250+	Lighthouse	Rigby
Clean Machine, The	L	RF	250+	Home Connection Collection	Rigby
Clementine	L	TL	101	Traditional Songs	Picture Window Books
Clothes	L	I	386	Wonder World	Wright Group/McGraw Hill
Clouds	L	I	40	iOpeners	Pearson Learning Group
Clouds of Terror	L	HF	250+	Soar To Success	Houghton Mifflin
Clouds of Terror	L	HF	250+	Welsh, Catherine A.	Carolrhoda Books
Clue at the Zoo, The	L	RF	250+	Giff, Patricia Reilly	Bantam
Code that No One Broke, The	L	I	90	Independent Readers Social Studies	Houghton Mifflin
Coin Magic	L	I	250+	How-To Series	Benchmark Education
Colonial Teachers	L	I	250+	Rosen Real Readers	Rosen Publishing Group
Come Back, Amelia Bedelia	L	F	250+	Parish, Peggy	Harper & Row
Coming to America	L	I	185	Vocabulary Readers	Houghton Mifflin
Computer Error	L	F	250+	Rigby Literacy	Rigby
Concrete Jungle	L	RF	250+	Pacific Literacy	Pacific Learning
Consideration	L	I	250+	Character Education	Red Brick Learning
Conversation Club, The	L	F	250+	Stanley, Diane	Aladdin
*Cooking Pot	L	TL	250+	The Story Box	Rigby
Cool	L	RF	137	Books for Young Learners	Richard C. Owen
Coolest Rock, The	L	I	250+	Chanek, Sherilin	Hampton-Brown
Cotton Plant to Cotton Shirt	L	I	250+	Schaefer, Lola M.	Benchmark Education
*Coyote in Trouble	L	TL	250+	Beveridge, Barbara	Pacific Learning
Coyotes	L	I	250+	Story Box	Wright Group/McGraw Hill
Crabs	L	I	501	Sunshine	Wright Group/McGraw Hill
Crabs, Shrimp & Lobsters	L	I	322	Marine Life For Young Readers	Pearson Learning Group
Crafty Jackal	L	TL	250+	Folk Tales	Wright Group/McGraw Hill
Creep Show	L	F	250+	Dussling, Jennifer	Grosset & Dunlap
*Cricket Boy and Other Stories, The	L	TL	250+	New Way Literature	Steck-Vaughn
Crocodile in the Garden, A	L	F	250+	Ready to Read	Pacific Learning
Crocodile in the Library, A	L	F	250+	Pacific Literacy	Pacific Learning
Crocodiles	L	I	250+	Sunshine	Wright Group/McGraw Hill
Crocodile's Christmas Jandals, The	L	F	250+	Pacific Literacy	Pacific Learning
Curse of the Cobweb Queen, The	L	F	250+	Hayes, Geoffrey	Random House
Dad's Pasta	L	RF	250+	Sails	Rigby

* Collection of short stories

TITLE	LEVEL	GENRE	WORD COUNT	AUTHOR / SERIES	PUBLISHER / DISTRIBUTOR
Dad's Promise	L	RF	250+	Cambridge Reading	Pearson Learning Group
Dance My Dance	L	TL	250+	Foundations	Wright Group/McGraw Hill
Dancing in Soot	L	RF	250+	Cambridge Reading	Pearson Learning Group
Dangerous Droughts	L	I	250+	Rosen Real Readers	Rosen Publishing Group
Danny's Big Jump	L	RF	250+	Reeder, Tracey	Wright Group/McGraw Hill
Day in Space, A	L	SF	250+	Lord, Suzanne; Epstein, Jolie	Scholastic
Day in the Life of a Librarian, A	L	I	250+	First Facts	Capstone Press
Day in the Life of a Zoo Keeper, A	L	I	250+	First Facts	Capstone Press
Day of the Rain, The	L	F	250+	Cowley, Joy	Pearson Learning Group
Day of the Snow, The	L	F	250+	Cowley, Joy	Pearson Learning Group
Day of the Wind, The	L	F	250+	Cowley, Joy	Pearson Learning Group
Dear Butterflies . . .	L	RF	414	Leveled Readers	Houghton Mifflin
December Secrets	L	RF	250+	Giff, Patricia Reilly	Bantam
Deputy Dan and the Bank Robbers	L	RF	250+	Rosenbloom, Joseph	Random House
Deputy Dan Gets His Man	L	RF	250+	Rosenbloom, Joseph	Random House
Desert Giant: The World of the Saguaro Cactus	L	I	250+	Bash, Barbara	Scholastic
Diary of a Honeybee	L	I	250+	Literacy 2000	Rigby
Diary of a Sunflower	L	I	250+	Story Steps	Rigby
Dick Whittington	L	TL	250+	PM Tales and Plays-Silver	Rigby
Did You Know?	L	I	250+	Sunshine	Wright Group/McGraw Hill
Diego Rivera: An Artist's Life	L	B	250+	Pair-It Books	Steck-Vaughn
Digestive System, The	L	I	173	Human Body Systems	Red Brick Learning
Dinosaur Babies	L	I	250+	Penner, Lucille Recht	Random House
Dinosaur Days	L	I	250+	Milton, Joyce	Random House
Dinosaur Hunters	L	I	250+	McMullan, Kate	Random House
Dinosaur Reports	L	I	324	Little Red Readers	Sundance
Doctors	L	I	250+	Community Workers	Compass Point Books
Doctor's Busy Day, A	L	I	250+	Rosen Real Readers	Rosen Publishing Group
Dog that Pitched a No-Hitter, The	L	F	250+	Christopher, Matt	Little, Brown & Co.
Dog that Stole Football Plays, The	L	F	250+	Christopher, Matt	Little, Brown & Co.
Dog that Stole Home, The	L	F	250+	Christopher, Matt	Little, Brown & Co.
Dog-Gone Hollywood	L	F	250+	Sharmat, Marjorie Weinman	Random House
Doing the Dishes	L	RF	136	City Kids	Rigby
Dolley Madison, First Lady	L	B	330	Leveled Readers Social Studies	Houghton Mifflin
Dolphin	L	I	250+	Morris, Robert A.	HarperTrophy
Dolphins!	L	I	250+	Bokoske, Sharon	Random House
Dolphins!	L	I	250+	Bokoske, Sharon; Davidson, M.	Random House
Dolphins, The	L	RF	721	PM Gold	Rigby
Dom's Handplant	L	RF	250+	Literacy 2000	Rigby
Donna O'Neeshuck Was Chased By Some Cows	L	RF	250+	Grossman, Bill	HarperTrophy
Don't Be Late!	L	RF	250+	Cambridge Reading	Pearson Learning Group
Don't Forget Fun	L	RF	250+	Little Celebrations	Pearson Learning Group
Double Trouble	L	RF	250+	Sunshine	Wright Group/McGraw Hill
Dr. Seuss	L	B	184	First Biographies	Red Brick Learning
Dragon Breath	L	F	250+	O'Connor, Jane	Grosset & Dunlap
Dragon of Krakow, The: A Polish Folktale	L	TL	366	Leveled Readers	Houghton Mifflin
Dragons of Blueland, The	L	F	250+	Gannett, Ruth	Random House
Eagle in the Sky	L	RF	250+	Little Celebrations	Pearson Learning Group
Earning Money	L	I	250+	First Facts	Capstone Press
Earth on Turtle's Back, The	L	TL	508	Early Connections	Benchmark Education
Earthworm's Life, An	L	I	250+	Himmelman, John	Scholastic
Earthworm's Life, An	L	I	250+	Nature Up Close	Children's Press
Eat and Run!	L	I	289	Vocabulary Readers	Houghton Mifflin
Ed and Me	L	RF	250+	McPhail, David	OSI

* Collection of short stories

TITLE	LEVEL	GENRE	WORD COUNT	AUTHOR / SERIES	PUBLISHER / DISTRIBUTOR
Eggs	L	I	250+	Rigby Literacy	Rigby
Ellen Ochoa	L	B	250+	Biography	Benchmark Education
Emily and Alice	L	RF	250+	Champion, Joyce	Harcourt Trade
Emily at School	L	RF	250+	Williams, Suzanne	Hyperion
Emma	L	RF	250+	Kesselman, Wendy	HarperTrophy
Emperor and the Nightingale, The	L	TL	250+	Literacy 2000	Rigby
Environmentally Friendly World	L	F	929	Early Connections	Benchmark Education
Erosion	L	I	300	Independent Readers Social Studies	Houghton Mifflin
Evening Song	L	RF	115	Books for Young Learners	Richard C. Owen
Everyone Knows About Cars	L	I	176	Bookshop	Mondo
Everything Changes	L	I	250+	Discovery World	Rigby
Everything Is Matter!	L	I	226	Yellow Umbrella Books	Capstone Press
Exotic Tropical Fish	L	I	250+	Swartz, Stanley L.	Pearson Learning Group
Exploring National Parks	L	I	250+	Rigby Literacy	Rigby
Exploring Saturn	L	I	250+	Rosen Real Readers	Rosen Publishing Group
Facts About Magnets	L	I	237	Leveled Readers Science	Houghton Mifflin
Facts About Tornadoes	L	I	250+	Rosen Real Readers	Rosen Publishing Group
Families of 1608 Ash Street, The	L	RF	571	Leveled Readers	Houghton Mifflin
Fancy Feet	L	RF	250+	Giff, Patricia Reilly	Bantam
Farm Life Long Ago	L	I	436	Pair-It Books	Steck-Vaughn
Festival in Valencia	L	RF	301	Leveled Readers	Houghton Mifflin
Fighting Fires Then and Now	L	I	381	Leveled Readers	Houghton Mifflin
Fire and Wind	L	TL	250+	PM Story Books-Silver	Rigby
Fire Fighters	L	I	250+	Community Workers	Compass Point Books
Firefighters	L	I	250+	Mitten, Christopher	Scholastic
Fireflies!	L	I	250+	Twig	Wright Group/McGraw Hill
Firefly Named Torchy, A	L	F	250+	Waber, Bernard	Houghton Mifflin
First, Take the Flour	L	I	186	Rigby Literacy	Rigby
Fish	L	I	250+	Rigby Literacy	Rigby
Fish	L	I	298	Marine Life For Young Readers	Pearson Learning Group
Fish that Hide	L	I	250+	Swartz, Stanley L.	Pearson Learning Group
Fishing Family	L	I	281	Independent Readers Science	Houghton Mifflin
Fishy Story, A	L	F	174	Books for Young Learners	Richard C. Owen
Flag Day	L	I	116	National Holidays	Red Brick Learning
Flea Story, A	L	F	250+	Lionni, Leo	Scholastic
Flight of the Union, The	L	B	250+	White, Tekla	Carolrhoda Books
Floating Markets of Bangkok, The	L	I	250+	Sunshine	Wright Group/McGraw Hill
Flower Girls # 1: Violet	L	RF	250+	Leverich, Kathleen	HarperTrophy
Flower Girls # 2: Daisy	L	RF	250+	Leverich, Kathleen	HarperTrophy
Flower Girls # 3: Heather	L	RF	250+	Leverich, Kathleen	HarperTrophy
Flower Girls # 4: Rose	L	RF	250+	Leverich, Kathleen	HarperTrophy
Flower of Sheba, The	L	TL	250+	Orgel, Doris; Schecter, Ellen	Bantam
Flowers	L	I	270	Pebble Books	Capstone Press
Fly Trap	L	F	250+	Anastasio, Dina	Grosset & Dunlap
Follow a River	L	I	198	iOpeners	Pearson Learning Group
Food Found All Around	L	I	220	Spyglass Books	Compass Point Books
Food Pyramid, The	L	I	155	Spyglass Books	Compass Point Books
Football Friends	L	RF	250+	Marzollo, Jean, Dan & Dave	Scholastic
Forest, The	L	I	250+	Cambridge Reading	Pearson Learning Group
Forget It!	L	RF	250+	Rigby Literacy	Rigby
Forgotten Princess, The	L	TL	250+	Literacy 2000	Rigby
Fossil Hunting	L	I	170	Rigby Focus	Rigby
Fossils	L	I	250+	Early Connections	Benchmark Education

* Collection of short stories

TITLE	LEVEL	GENRE	WORD COUNT	AUTHOR / SERIES	PUBLISHER / DISTRIBUTOR
Four Days in the Life of Zoe Coznaut	L	SF	250+	Foundations	Wright Group/McGraw Hill
*Four Friends and Other Stories, The	L	TL	250+	New Way Literature	Steck-Vaughn
Fox and the Little Red Hen, The	L	TL	250+	Traditional Tales & More	Rigby
Frances the Fairy Dressmaker	L	F	736	Early Connections	Benchmark Education
Freedom	L	RF	250+	Rigby Literacy	Rigby
Friendliness	L	I	250+	Character Education	Red Brick Learning
Frog Who Thought He Was A Horse, The	L	F	250+	Literacy 2000	Rigby
From Camel Cart to Canoe	L	I	250+	Sunshine	Wright Group/McGraw Hill
From Cotton Plant to Cotton Shirt	L	I	250+	Schaefer, Lola M.	Benchmark Education
Frozen Music	L	TL	432	Books for Young Learners	Richard C. Owen
Fun with Magnets	L	I	394	Rigby Focus	Rigby
Gail & Me	L	RF	250+	Literacy 2000	Rigby
Gannets	L	I	250+	Sunshine	Wright Group/McGraw Hill
Garden on Green Street, The	L	RF	250+	Meish Goldish	Scholastic
Gasp!	L	F	250+	Bookshop	Mondo
Gator Girls, The	L	F	250+	Calmenson, Stephanie & Cole	Beech Tree Books
Genghis Khan: A Dog Star is Born	L	RF	250+	Sharmat, Marjorie Weinman	Random House
George and Martha	L	F	250+	Marshall, James	Houghton Mifflin
George and Martha Back in Town	L	F	250+	Marshall, James	Houghton Mifflin
George and Martha Encore	L	F	250+	Marshall, James	Houghton Mifflin
George and Martha One Fine Day	L	F	250+	Marshall, James	Houghton Mifflin
George and Martha Rise and Shine	L	F	250+	Marshall, James	Houghton Mifflin
George and Martha Round and Round	L	F	250+	Marshall, James	Houghton Mifflin
George and the Whopper	L	F	250+	Rigby Literacy	Rigby
George Washington	L	B	270	Pebble Books	Capstone Press
Germs	L	I	250+	Twig	Wright Group/McGraw Hill
Germs! Germs! Germs!	L	F	250+	Katz, Bobbi	Scholastic
Ginger Brown: The Nobody Boy	L	RF	250+	Wyeth, Sharon Dennis	Random House
Ginger Brown: Too Many Houses	L	RF	250+	Wyeth, Sharon Dennis	Random House
Gingerbread Boy, The	L	TL	1097	Galdone, Paul	Clarion
Girl Who Climbed to the Moon, The	L	F	604	Sunshine	Wright Group/McGraw Hill
*Goat Monster and Other Stories, The	L	F	250+	New Way Literature	Steck-Vaughn
Goats	L	I	250+	PM Animal Facts: Purple	Rigby
Going to Be a Butterfly	L	I	250+	Sunshine	Wright Group/McGraw Hill
Golden Goose, The	L	TL	731	Sunshine	Wright Group/McGraw Hill
Golden Land, The	L	HF	505	Leveled Readers	Houghton Mifflin
Goldsworthy and Mort Blast Off	L	F	250+	Little Celebrations	Pearson Learning Group
Goliath and the Burglar	L	RF	250+	Dicks, Terrance	Barron's Educational
Goliath and the Buried Treasure	L	RF	250+	Dicks, Terrance	Barron's Educational
Goliath and the Cub Scouts	L	RF	250+	Dicks, Terrance	Barron's Educational
Goliath at the Dog Show	L	RF	250+	Dicks, Terrance	Barron's Educational
Goliath at the Seaside	L	RF	250+	Dicks, Terrance	Barron's Educational
Goliath Goes to Summer School	L	RF	250+	Dicks, Terrance	Barron's Educational
Goliath on Vacation	L	RF	250+	Dicks, Terrance	Barron's Educational
Goliath's Birthday	L	RF	250+	Dicks, Terrance	Barron's Educational
Goliath's Christmas	L	RF	250+	Dicks, Terrance	Barron's Educational
Goliath's Easter Parade	L	RF	250+	Dicks, Terrance	Barron's Educational
Good As New	L	RF	250+	Douglass, Barbara	Scholastic
Good Driving, Amelia Bedelia	L	F	250+	Parish, Peggy	Harper & Row
Good Work, Amelia Bedelia	L	F	250+	Parish, Peggy	Avon Camelot
Goodbye Goose	L	F	264	Books for Young Learners	Richard C. Owen
Gooey Chewy Contest, The	L	F	1512	Goldsmith, Howard	Mondo
Gorilla Families	L	I	250+	Rosen Real Readers	Rosen Publishing Group
Gorilla Guardian	L	RF	250+	World Quest Adventures	World Quest Learning

* Collection of short stories

TITLE	LEVEL	GENRE	WORD COUNT	AUTHOR / SERIES	PUBLISHER / DISTRIBUTOR
Gorillas: Gentle Giants on the Forest	L	I	250+	Milton, Joyce	Random House
Grabbing Bird, The	L	F	250+	Cambridge Reading	Pearson Learning Group
Grandad	L	RF	250+	Literacy 2000	Rigby
Great Dinosaur Race, The	L	F	250+	Popcorn	Sundance
Great Escape, The	L	RF	250+	Rigby Literacy	Rigby
Great Genghis Khan Look-Alike Contest, The	L	RF	250+	Sharmat, Marjorie Weinman	Random House
Great Ghosts	L	F	250+	Cohen, Daniel	Scholastic
Greatest of All, The: A Japanese Folktale	L	TL	250+	Kimmel, Eric A.	Holiday House
Greedy Goat, The	L	TL	250+	Bookshop	Mondo
Green: Seeing Green All Around Us	L	I	250+	Colors	Capstone Press
Gregory, the Terrible Eater	L	F	250+	Sharmat, Marjorie Weinman	Scholastic
Guard Dog Diggory	L	RF	250+	Pacific Literacy	Pacific Learning
Guess Who?	L	I	250+	Home Connection Collection	Rigby
Gurgles and Growls: Learning About Your Stomach	L	I	250+	Amazing Body	Picture Window Books
Hands Up, Wolf	L	F	250+	Pacific Literacy	Pacific Learning
Happy Birthday, Martin Luther King	L	B	250+	Marzollo, Jean	Scholastic
Happy Birthday, Moon	L	F	345	Asch, Frank	Simon & Schuster
Happy Birthday, Mrs. Boedecker	L	RF	250+	Little Celebrations	Pearson Learning Group
Haunted Bike, The	L	F	250+	Herman, Gail	Grosset & Dunlap
Hawaii	L	I	240	Windows on Literacy	National Geographic
Haystack, The	L	RF	250+	Cambridge Reading	Pearson Learning Group
Headfirst into the Oatmeal	L	F	250+	Rigby Literacy	Rigby
Headless Horseman, The	L	TL	250+	Standiford, Natalie	Random House
Hello, Peter-Bonjour, Remy	L	F	250+	Little Celebrations	Pearson Learning Group
Helpful Change, A	L	RF	250+	Behr, Alexandra	Hampton-Brown
*Helpful Harry and Other Stories	L	RF	250+	New Way Literature	Steck-Vaughn
Helping Out	L	RF	317	Independent Readers Social Studies	Houghton Mifflin
Here Come the Bison	L	I	212	Sunshine	Wright Group/McGraw Hill
Here's Bobby's World! How a TV Cartoon Is	L	I	250+	Little Celebrations	Pearson Learning Group
Here's to Hats	L	I	250+	Sunshine	Wright Group/McGraw Hill
Hide to Survive	L	I	250+	Home Connection Collection	Rigby
Hill of Fire	L	RF	1099	Lewis, Thomas P.	HarperCollins
Honesty	L	I	250+	Character Education	Red Brick Learning
Honey Tree, The	L	F	250+	Literacy 2000	Rigby
Hoop Dancers	L	I	250+	Phonics and Friends	Hampton-Brown
Horrible Harry and the Ant Invasion	L	RF	250+	Kline, Suzy	Scholastic
Horrible Harry and the Christmas Surprise	L	RF	250+	Kline, Suzy	Scholastic
Horrible Harry and the Drop of Doom	L	RF	250+	Kline, Suzy	Puffin Books
Horrible Harry and the Dungeon	L	RF	250+	Kline, Suzy	Penguin Group
Horrible Harry and the Green Slime	L	RF	250+	Kline, Suzy	Penguin Group
Horrible Harry and the Kickball Wedding	L	RF	250+	Kline, Suzy	Penguin Group
Horrible Harry and the Purple People	L	F	250+	Kline, Suzy	Puffin Books
Horrible Harry in Room 2B	L	RF	250+	Kline, Suzy	Penguin Group
Horrible Harry Moves Up to Third Grade	L	RF	250+	Kline, Suzy	Puffin Books
Horrible Harry's Secret	L	RF	250+	Kline, Suzy	Penguin Group
Horses	L	I	250+	PM Animal Facts: Purple	Rigby
Hospitals	L	I	177	Bookshop	Mondo
Hot Air Balloons	L	I	479	Pair-It Books	Steck-Vaughn
Hot Fudge Hero	L	RF	250+	Brisson, Pat	Henry Holt & Co.
How Animals Move	L	I	250+	First Facts	Capstone Press
How Animals Move	L	I	132	Discovery World	Rigby
How Animals Move Around	L	I	593	PM Plus Nonfiction	Rigby

* Collection of short stories

TITLE	LEVEL	GENRE	WORD COUNT	AUTHOR / SERIES	PUBLISHER / DISTRIBUTOR
How Chocolate Is Made	L	I	250+	Lighthouse	Rigby
How Do Plants Get Food?	L	I	250+	Goldish, Meish	Steck-Vaughn
How Do Plants Grow?	L	I	250+	Rosen Real Readers	Rosen Publishing Group
How Do Trees Grow?	L	I	250+	Rosen Real Readers	Rosen Publishing Group
How Do You Feel Today?	L	I	250+	Rosen Real Readers	Rosen Publishing Group
How Does It Grow?	L	I	250+	Home Connection Collection	Rigby
How Does This Sound?	L	I	260	Independent Readers Science	Houghton Mifflin
How Far Is It?	L	I	250+	Rosen Real Readers	Rosen Publishing Group
How Kittens Grow	L	I	250+	Selsam, Millicent E.	Scholastic
How Much Is That Guinea Pig in the Window?	L	RF	250+	Rocklin, Joanne	Scholastic
How People Move Around	L	I	541	PM Plus Nonfiction	Rigby
How Spiders Got Eight Legs	L	F	884	Pair-It Books	Steck-Vaughn
How the Animals Got Their Tails	L	TL	250+	Cambridge Reading	Pearson Learning Group
How the Donosaurs Disappeared	L	I	250+	Rosen Real Readers	Rosen Publishing Group
How the Rattlesnake Got Its Rattle	L	TL	1006	Pair-It Books	Steck-Vaughn
How the Water Got to the Plains	L	TL	250+	Home Connection Collection	Rigby
How To Choose a Pet	L	I	250+	Discovery World	Rigby
How We Vote	L	I	314	Independent Readers Social Studies	Houghton Mifflin
Huberta the Hiking Hippo	L	RF	250+	Literacy 2000	Rigby
Hungry, Hungry Sharks	L	I	250+	Cole, Joanna	Random House
Hush Up!	L	F	250+	Little Celebrations	Pearson Learning Group
I Can Read! I Can Read!	L	RF	250+	Little Celebrations	Pearson Learning Group
I Don't Believe It!	L	RF	250+	Home Connection Collection	Rigby
I Hate English	L	RF	250+	Levine, Ellen	Scholastic
I Hate My Best Friend	L	RF	250+	Rosner, Ruth	Hyperion
I Know a Lady	L	RF	221	Zolotow, Charlotte	Penguin Group
I Live in the Rockies	L	I	259	Windows on Literacy	National Geographic
Ice Man, The: A Traditional Native American Tale	L	TL	250+	Rigby Literacy	Rigby
Icebergs	L	I	250+	Sunshine	Wright Group/McGraw Hill
If Anything Ever Goes Wrong at the Zoo	L	F	250+	Hendrick, Mary Jean	Harcourt Trade
Imogene's Antlers	L	F	191	Small, David	Scholastic
In a New Land	L	HF	378	Sunshine	Wright Group/McGraw Hill
In City Gardens	L	I	250+	Little Celebrations	Pearson Learning Group
In Hiding, Animals Under Cover	L	I	250+	Burke, Melissa Blackwell	Steck-Vaughn
In Search of Treasure	L	TL	250+	PM Story Books	Rigby
In the Forest	L	I	581	Leveled Readers	Houghton Mifflin
Incredible, Edible Plants	L	I	250+	Early Connections	Benchmark Education
Independence Day	L	I	182	Pebble Books	Red Brick Learning
Into the Jungle: Searching for the Rare Mountain Gorilla	L	I	250+	World Quest Adventures	World Quest Learning
Inventing the Telephone	L	I	250+	iOpeners	Pearson Learning Group
Is Your Mama a Llama?	L	F	250+	Guarino, Deborah	Scholastic
It Smells Like Friday	L	F	250+	Popcorn	Sundance
It Takes A Village	L	RF	250+	Cowen-Fletcher, J.	Scholastic
It Wasn't My Fault	L	RF	250+	Lester, Helen	Houghton Mifflin
It's a Blizzard!	L	I	250+	Rosen Real Readers	Rosen Publishing Group
Jacques Cousteau	L	B	250+	Biography	Benchmark Education
Jane Goodall and the Chimps	L	B	250+	Twig	Wright Group/McGraw Hill
Jane Goodall and the Wild Chimpanzees	L	B	250+	Birnbaum, Bette	Steck-Vaughn
Jennifer, Too	L	RF	250+	Havill, Juanita	Hyperion
Jenny and the Cornstalk	L	TL	890	Pair-It Books	Steck-Vaughn
Joey's Head	L	F	250+	Cretan, G.	Simon & Schuster

* Collection of short stories

TITLE	LEVEL	GENRE	WORD COUNT	AUTHOR / SERIES	PUBLISHER / DISTRIBUTOR
John F. Kennedy	L	B	250+	Pebble Books	Red Brick Learning
Jonathan and His Mommy	L	RF	250+	Smalls, Irene	Scholastic
Josefina Story Quilt	L	F	250+	Coerr, Eleanor	HarperTrophy
Josephine's Imagination	L	RF	250+	Dobrin, Arnold	Scholastic
Joshua Poole and Sunrise	L	RF	250+	Rigby Literacy	Rigby
Judy Moody	L	RF	250+	McDonald, Megan	Candlewick Press
Judy Moody Saves the World	L	RF	250+	McDonald, Megan	Candlewick Press
Jumble Power	L	F	250+	Cambridge Reading	Pearson Learning Group
Jump the Broom	L	RF	119	Books For Young Learners	Richard C. Owen
Junkpile Robot, The	L	F	250+	Ready Readers	Pearson Learning Group
Katy and the Big Snow	L	F	250+	Burton, Virginia L.	Scholastic
Kelly's Trip	L	RF	250	Sunshine	Wright Group/McGraw Hill
Kerri Strug: Heart of Gold	L	B	250+	Strug, K.; Brown, G.	Scholastic
Kids in the Circus	L	I	250+	Robinson, Fay	Wright Group/McGraw Hill
Kilmer's Pet Monster	L	RF	250+	Dadey, Debbie; Jones, Marcia Thornton	Scholastic
*Kind Prince and Rupert, The	L	F	250+	New Way Literature	Steck-Vaughn
King Beast's Birthday	L	F	250+	Literacy 2000	Rigby
*King's Dream and Sammy's New Yellow Sweater, The	L	TL	250+	New Way Literature	Steck-Vaughn
*King's Race and Other Stories, The	L	F	250+	New Way Literature	Steck-Vaughn
Kit's Castle	L	RF	250+	Powling, Chris	Wright Group/McGraw Hill
Kyle's First Kwanzaa	L	RF	250+	Little Celebrations	Pearson Learning Group
Labor Day	L	I	125	National Holidays	Red Brick Learning
Lacey's Loud Voice	L	RF	589	Leveled Readers	Houghton Mifflin
Land of the Great Big "No!"	L	RF	250+	Trussell-Cullen, Alan	Pearson Learning Group
Langston Hughes	L	B	168	Vocabulary Readers	Houghton Mifflin
Laura Ingalls Wilder	L	B	250+	Biography	Benchmark Education
Leaping Lena	L	F	250+	Rigby Literacy	Rigby
Left Behind	L	RF	250+	Carrick, Carol	Clarion
Leo and Lester	L	F	250+	Bookshop	Mondo
Let's Look After Our World	L	I	250+	Sunshine	Wright Group/McGraw Hill
Let's Look at Venus	L	I	250+	Rosen Real Readers	Rosen Publishing Group
Letter Carriers	L	I	250+	Community Workers	Compass Point Books
Letter to a Friend	L	I	250+	Early Connections	Benchmark Education
Librarians	L	I	250+	Community Workers	Compass Point Books
Life at Plimouth	L	I	210	Leveled Readers Social Studies	Houghton Mifflin
Life in a Coral Reef	L	I	250+	Rosen Real Readers	Rosen Publishing Group
Life in Colonial America	L	I	405	Leveled Readers Social Studies	Houghton Mifflin
Life in the Desert	L	I	250+	Sails	Rigby
Life in the Rain Forest	L	I	250+	Rosen Real Readers	Rosen Publishing Group
Lightning	L	I	279	Pebble Books	Capstone Press
Lila the Fair	L	RF	250+	Social Studies Connects	The Kane Press
Lilacs, Lotuses, and Ladybugs	L	RF	402	Evangeline Nicholas Collection	Wright Group/McGraw Hill
Lionel and Amelia	L	F	250+	Bookshop	Mondo
Lions	L	I	644	Pair-It Books	Steck-Vaughn
Lisa's Diary	L	RF	250+	Home Connection Collection	Rigby
Little Bill	L	RF	250+	Cosby, Bill	Scholastic
Little Bit Hotter Can't Hurt, A	L	RF	466	Leveled Readers	Houghton Mifflin
Little Penguin's Tale	L	F	250+	Wood, Audrey	Scholastic
Little Princess, A	L	RF	250+	All Aboard Reading	Grosset & Dunlap
Little Vampire and the Midnight Bear	L	F	250+	Kwitz, Mary DeBall	Puffin Books
Lizards	L	I	356	Wonder World	Wright Group/McGraw Hill
Lizzie's Lizard	L	I	289	Storyteller Nonfiction	Wright Group/McGraw Hill

* Collection of short stories

TITLE	LEVEL	GENRE	WORD COUNT	AUTHOR / SERIES	PUBLISHER / DISTRIBUTOR
Long Way to a New Land, A	L	HF	250+	Sandin, Joan	HarperTrophy
Long Way Westward, The	L	HF	250+	Sandin, Joan	HarperTrophy
Look Who's Talking!	L	I	250+	Rigby Literacy	Rigby
Looking at Insects	L	I	250+	Discovery World	Rigby
Looking for Lions	L	I	250+	World Quest Adventures	World Quest Learning
Looking into Space	L	I	345	Early Connections	Benchmark Education
Loose Laces	L	RF	209	Reading Unlimited	Pearson Learning Group
Lost at the White House: A 1909 Easter Story	L	HF	250+	Griest, Lisa	Carolrhoda Books
Lost!	L	F	57	Home Connection Collection	Rigby
Louis Agassiz Fuertes, Painter of the Bird	L	B	250+	Independent Readers Science	Houghton Mifflin
Lucky Feather, The	L	F	250+	Literacy 2000	Rigby
Lucky Stars	L	RF	250+	Adler, David A.	Random House
Lucy Meets a Dragon	L	F	250+	Literacy 2000	Rigby
Luke's Go-cart	L	RF	656	PM Gold	Rigby
Luna	L	F	371	Leveled Readers	Houghton Mifflin
Lying as Still as I Can	L	RF	250+	Greetings	Rigby
Mack's Big Day	L	RF	464	PM Plus Story Books	Rigby
Made's Birthday	L	RF	250+	Little Celebrations	Pearson Learning Group
Magic All Around	L	F	250+	Literacy 2000	Rigby
Magic Fish, The	L	TL	870	Littledale, Freya	Scholastic
Magic Money	L	RF	250+	Adler, David A.	Random House
Magic Porridge Pot, The	L	TL	497	Sunshine	Wright Group/McGraw Hill
Magic Sword, The	L	F	250+	Cambridge Reading	Pearson Learning Group
Magpie's Tail, The	L	F	543	Pacific Literacy	Pacific Learning
Mailman Mario & His Boris-Busters	L	RF	250+	Parker, John	Pearson Learning Group
Maisie's Race	L	RF	250+	Mawter, Jeni	Wright Group/McGraw Hill
Make a Bottle Garden	L	I	250+	Lighthouse	Rigby
Make a Shake and a Bakeless Cake	L	I	250+	Cole, Sally	Wright Group/McGraw Hill
Make Way For Ducklings	L	RF	250+	McCloskey, Robert	Puffin Books
Making a Map	L	I	293	Rigby Focus	Rigby
Making a Terrarium	L	I	250+	How-To Series	Benchmark Education
Making Patterns	L	I	250+	Early Connections	Benchmark Education
Man Who Rode the Tiger, The	L	TL	250+	PM Story Books	Rigby
Manners at a Friend's Home	L	I	250+	First Facts	Capstone Press
Manners at a Restaurant	L	I	250+	First Facts	Capstone Press
Manners at the Library	L	I	250+	First Facts	Capstone Press
Manners in the Classroom	L	I	250+	First Facts	Capstone Press
Manners on the Playground	L	I	250+	First Facts	Capstone Press
Manners on the Telephone	L	I	250+	First Facts	Capstone Press
Maple Thanksgiving, The	L	F	250+	Little Celebrations	Pearson Learning Group
Marcella	L	RF	250+	Literacy 2000	Rigby
Mare for Young Wolf, A	L	HF	250+	Shefelman, Janice	Random House
Margaret Mahy	L	B	250+	Sunshine	Wright Group/McGraw Hill
Margarito's Carvings	L	I	250+	Little Celebrations	Pearson Learning Group
Marie-Maud Becomes a Citizen	L	RF	563	Leveled Readers Social Studies	Houghton Mifflin
Mars	L	I	220	Rigby Focus	Rigby
Mars: The Red Planet	L	I	250+	Rosen Real Readers	Rosen Publishing Group
Martin Luther King Day	L	I	250+	Lowery, Linda	Scholastic
Martin Luther King, Jr.	L	B	290	Pebble Books	Capstone Press
Mask Book, The	L	I	217	Twig	Wright Group/McGraw Hill
Materials	L	I	250+	Discovery World	Rigby
Math Counts	L	I	250+	Pluckrose, Henry	Scholastic
Matter of Balance, A	L	B	250+	Voyages	SRA/McGraw Hill
Matthew and Tilly	L	RF	250+	Jones, Rebecca C.	Penguin Group

* Collection of short stories

TITLE	LEVEL	GENRE	WORD COUNT	AUTHOR / SERIES	PUBLISHER / DISTRIBUTOR
Matthew Henson	L	B	250+	Biography	Benchmark Education
Maurice Sendak	L	B	201	First Biographies	Red Brick Learning
Max's Glasses	L	RF	250+	Navigators Fiction Series	Benchmark Education
Mayors	L	I	250+	Community Workers	Compass Point Books
McGinty's Friend	L	F	250+	Sails	Rigby
Measure	L	I	229	Spyglass Books	Compass Point Books
Meerkat Chat	L	I	250+	Story Steps	Rigby
Meet the Lincoln Lions Band	L	RF	250+	Giff, Patricia Reilly	Bantam
Meet the Meerkats	L	I	250+	World Quest Adventures	World Quest Learning
*Meet the Molesons	L	F	250+	Bos, Burny	North-South Books
Memorial Day	L	I	250+	Frost, Helen	Red Brick Learning
Mermaid Island	L	F	250+	Frith, Margaret	Grosset & Dunlap
Merry Christmas, Amelia Bedelia	L	F	250+	Parish, Peggy	William Morrow
Milkshake Man, The	L	F	250+	Cole, Sally	Wright Group/McGraw Hill
Minh's New Life	L	RF	250+	PM Plus Story Books	Rigby
Mirounga's Pup	L	RF	250+	Books for Young Learners	Richard C. Owen
Miss Nelson Has a Field Day	L	RF	250+	Allard, Harry	Scholastic
Miss Nelson is Missing	L	RF	598	Allard, Harry	Houghton Mifflin
Missing Fossil Mystery, The	L	RF	250+	Herman, Emily	Hyperion
Mog at the Zoo	L	F	250+	Nicoll, Helen	Penguin Group
Mog's Mumps	L	F	250+	Nicoll, Helen	Penguin Group
Mom Named Dad, A	L	RF	250+	Rigby Literacy	Rigby
Mondo and Gordo Weather the Storm	L	F	759	Early Connections	Benchmark Education
Monster from Mercury, The	L	F	250+	Popcorn	Sundance
Monsters Next Door, The	L	RF	250+	Dadey, Debbie; Jones, Marcia Thornton	Scholastic
Monsters of the Deep	L	I	250+	Swartz, Stanley L.	Pearson Learning Group
Moon Journal	L	RF	250+	Rigby Literacy	Rigby
Moon, The	L	I	139	Twig	Wright Group/McGraw Hill
More Places to Visit	L	I	238	Windows on Literacy	National Geographic
*More Tales of Amanda Pig	L	F	1939	Van Leeuwen, Jean	Penguin Group
*More Tales of Oliver Pig	L	F	250+	Van Leeuwen, Jean	Puffin Books
Mother Hippopotamus Goes Canoeing	L	F	250+	Foundations	Wright Group/McGraw Hill
Mountains	L	I	250+	Early Connections	Benchmark Education
Move It!	L	I	268	Spyglass Books	Compass Point Books
Mr. Bumbleticker Goes to the Zoo	L	RF	250+	Foundations	Wright Group/McGraw Hill
Mr. Gumpy's Motor Car	L	RF	250+	Burningham, John	HarperCollins
Mr. Gumpy's Outing	L	RF	283	Burningham, John	Henry Holt & Co.
Mr. Mulch's Magic Mixtures	L	F	250+	Cambridge Reading	Pearson Learning Group
Mr. Sun and Mr. Sea	L	F	506	Sunshine	Wright Group/McGraw Hill
Mrs. Jeepers' Batty Vacation	L	RF	250+	Dadey, Debbie; Jones, Marcia Thornton	Scholastic
Mud Pony, The	L	TL	764	Sunshine	Wright Group/McGraw Hill
Mummy's Gold, The	L	F	250+	McMullan, Kate	Grosset & Dunlap
My Grandma, the Rock Star	L	RF	250+	Rigby Literacy	Rigby
Mystery in the Attic, The	L	RF	250+	Leveled Readers Language Support	Houghton Mifflin
Mystery of the Blue Ring, The	L	RF	250+	Giff, Patricia Reilly	Bantam
Mystery of the Pirate Ghost, The	L	F	250+	Hayes, Geoffrey	Random House
Mystery of the Tooth Gremlin	L	RF	250+	Graves, Bonnie	Hyperion
Mystery Seeds	L	RF	250+	Reading Unlimited	Pearson Learning Group
Naming the Cat	L	RF	250+	Soar To Success	Houghton Mifflin
Native American Baskets	L	I	195	Phonics Readers	Compass Point Books
New Citizens	L	I	250+	Twig	Wright Group/McGraw Hill

* Collection of short stories

TITLE	LEVEL	GENRE	WORD COUNT	AUTHOR / SERIES	PUBLISHER / DISTRIBUTOR
New Light for the Lodge, A	L	F	250+	Smith, Ben	Wright Group/McGraw Hill
Niagra Falls	L	I	184	Rosen Real Readers	Rosen Publishing Group
Nicest Day, The	L	RF	400	Leveled Readers	Houghton Mifflin
Night Cat	L	I	250+	World Quest Adventures	World Quest Learning
Night Walk, The	L	RF	667	PM Story Books-Gold	Rigby
Nine Lives of Adventure Cat, The	L	F	250+	Clymer, Susan	Scholastic
No Copycats Allowed!	L	RF	250+	Graves, Bonnie	Hyperion
No Jumping On The Bed!	L	F	250+	Arnold, Tedd	Scholastic
No Money? No Problem!	L	RF	250+	Social Studies Connects	The Kane Press
No Rules For Rex!	L	RF	250+	Social Studies Connects	The Kane Press
*Not Too Young and Other Stories	L	RF	250+	New Way Literature	Steck-Vaughn
Noura Comes to Cleveland	L	RF	717	Leveled Readers Social Studies	Houghton Mifflin
Now and Long Ago	L	I	189	Phonics Readers	Compass Point Books
Number Cruncher, The	L	F	250+	Sunshine	Wright Group/McGraw Hill
Numbers: Counting It Up	L	I	250+	Exploring Math	Capstone Press
Obstacles in Our Way	L	RF	250+	Home Connection Collection	Rigby
Octopuses, Squid & Cuttlefish	L	I	231	Marine Life For Young Readers	Pearson Learning Group
Oh, What a Daughter!	L	F	250+	Literacy 2000	Rigby
Oil Spill!	L	I	250+	Soar To Success	Houghton Mifflin
Old Enough for Magic	L	F	250+	Pickett, A.	HarperTrophy
Old Recipe Book, The	L	F	250+	Smith, Ben	Wright Group/McGraw Hill
*Oliver and Amanda's Halloween	L	F	250+	Van Leeuwen, Jean	Puffin Books
*Oliver Pig at School	L	F	250+	Van Leeuwen, Jean	Puffin Books
*Oliver, Amanda, and Grandmother Pig	L	F	250+	Van Leeuwen, Jean	Puffin Books
On the Air	L	I	250+	Rigby Literacy	Rigby
On the Silk Road: Ancient Baghdad	L	I	250+	Leveled Readers Language Support	Houghton Mifflin
Once When I Was Shipwrecked	L	F	250+	Literacy 2000	Rigby
Onion Sundaes	L	RF	250+	Adler, David A.	Random House
Open Door Club, The	L	RF	570	Leveled Readers	Houghton Mifflin
Origami	L	I	250+	How-To Series	Benchmark Education
Other Side of the Lake, The	L	F	250+	Little Celebrations	Pearson Learning Group
Ouch!	L	RF	250+	Noonan, Diana	Pearson Learning Group
Our Adobe House	L	I	250+	Greetings	Rigby
Our Four Walls	L	RF	422	Leveled Readers	Houghton Mifflin
Out in Space	L	I	224	Spyglass Books	Compass Point Books
Outwitting the Tiger	L	TL	250+	Voyages	SRA/McGraw Hill
Owl and the Pussy Cat	L	TL	215	Lear, Edward	Scholastic
Owls in the Garden	L	RF	670	PM Gold	Rigby
Paloma's Party	L	I	250+	Little Celebrations	Pearson Learning Group
Panda, The	L	I	250+	Sunshine	Wright Group/McGraw Hill
Parrots	L	I	250+	Bridgestone Books	Capstone Press
Partners	L	I	159	Home Connection Collection	Rigby
Pat Mora, the Storyteller	L	B	278	Vocabulary Readers	Houghton Mifflin
Patrick and the Leprechaun	L	F	677	PM Gold	Rigby
Patterns: What Comes Next?	L	I	250+	Exploring Math	Capstone Press
Peace Ring, The	L	F	250+	Cambridge Reading	Pearson Learning Group
Peacefulness	L	I	250+	Character Education	Red Brick Learning
Pee Wee Scouts	L	RF	250+	Delton, Judy	Yearling
Pee Wee Scouts on First	L	RF	250+	Delton, Judy	Bantam
Pee Wee Scouts on Parade	L	RF	250+	Delton, Judy	Bantam
Pee Wee Scouts on Skis	L	RF	250+	Delton, Judy	Bantam
Pee Wee Scouts: A Big Box of Memories	L	RF	250+	Delton, Judy	Bantam
Pee Wee Scouts: A Pee Wee Christmas	L	RF	250+	Delton, Judy	Bantam

* Collection of short stories

TITLE	LEVEL	GENRE	WORD COUNT	AUTHOR / SERIES	PUBLISHER / DISTRIBUTOR
Pee Wee Scouts: Bad, Bad Bunnies	L	RF	250+	Delton, Judy	Bantam
Pee Wee Scouts: Blue Skies, French Fries	L	RF	250+	Delton, Judy	Bantam
Pee Wee Scouts: Bookworm Buddies	L	RF	250+	Delton, Judy	Bantam
Pee Wee Scouts: Camp Ghost Away	L	RF	250+	Delton, Judy	Bantam
Pee Wee Scouts: Computer Clues	L	RF	250+	Delton, Judy	Bantam
Pee Wee Scouts: Cookies and Crutches	L	RF	250+	Delton, Judy	Bantam
Pee Wee Scouts: Eggs with Legs	L	RF	250+	Delton, Judy	Bantam
Pee Wee Scouts: Fishy Wishes	L	RF	250+	Delton, Judy	Bantam
Pee Wee Scouts: Greedy Groundhogs	L	RF	250+	Delton, Judy	Bantam
Pee Wee Scouts: Grumpy Pumpkins	L	RF	250+	Delton, Judy	Bantam
Pee Wee Scouts: Halloween Helpers	L	RF	250+	Delton, Judy	Bantam
Pee Wee Scouts: Lights, Action, Land-Ho!	L	RF	250+	Delton, Judy	Bantam
Pee Wee Scouts: Lucky Dog Days	L	RF	250+	Delton, Judy	Bantam
Pee Wee Scouts: Moans and Groans and Dinosaur Bones	L	RF	250+	Delton, Judy	Bantam
Pee Wee Scouts: Molly for Mayor	L	RF	250+	Delton, Judy	Bantam
Pee Wee Scouts: Peanut-Butter Pilgrims	L	RF	250+	Delton, Judy	Bantam
Pee Wee Scouts: Pedal Power	L	RF	250+	Delton, Judy	Bantam
Pee Wee Scouts: Pee Wee Pool Party	L	RF	250+	Delton, Judy	Bantam
Pee Wee Scouts: Piles of Pets	L	RF	250+	Delton, Judy	Bantam
Pee Wee Scouts: Planet Pee Wee	L	RF	250+	Delton, Judy	Bantam
Pee Wee Scouts: Rosy Noses, Freezing Toes	L	RF	250+	Delton, Judy	Bantam
Pee Wee Scouts: Send in the Clowns	L	RF	250+	Delton, Judy	Bantam
Pee Wee Scouts: Sky Babies	L	RF	250+	Delton, Judy	Bantam
Pee Wee Scouts: Sonny's Secret	L	RF	250+	Delton, Judy	Bantam
Pee Wee Scouts: Spring Sprouts	L	RF	250+	Delton, Judy	Bantam
Pee Wee Scouts: Stage Frightened	L	RF	250+	Delton, Judy	Bantam
Pee Wee Scouts: Super Duper Pee Wee!	L	RF	250+	Delton, Judy	Bantam
Pee Wee Scouts: Teeny Weeny Zucchinis	L	RF	250+	Delton, Judy	Bantam
Pee Wee Scouts: That Mushy Stuff	L	RF	250+	Delton, Judy	Bantam
Pee Wee Scouts: The Pee Wee Jubilee	L	RF	250+	Delton, Judy	Bantam
Pee Wee Scouts: The Pooped Troop	L	RF	250+	Delton, Judy	Bantam
Pee Wee Scouts: Trash Bash	L	RF	250+	Delton, Judy	Bantam
Pee Wee Scouts: Tricks and Treats	L	RF	250+	Delton, Judy	Bantam
Pee Wee Scouts: Wild, Wild West	L	RF	250+	Delton, Judy	Bantam
Penguin Pete	L	F	250+	Pfister, Marcus	North-South Books
Penguin Rescue	L	RF	250+	PM Story Books	Rigby
Penguins	L	I	250+	Reed, Janet	Scholastic
Perfect Pretzels	L	I	232	Twig	Wright Group/McGraw Hill
Perfect the Pig	L	F	250+	Jeschke, Susan	Scholastic
Pet Sitters Plus Five	L	RF	250+	Springstubb, Tricia	Scholastic
Peter and the North Wind	L	TL	250+	Littledale, Freya	Scholastic
Pete's Story	L	F	250+	Literacy 2000	Rigby
Pets Lost-and-Found	L	I	250+	Rigby Literacy	Rigby
Pheasant and Kingfisher	L	TL	250+	Bookshop	Mondo
Picked for the Team	L	RF	709	PM Gold	Rigby
Picking Apples and Pumpkins	L	I	250+	Hutchings, Amy & Richard	Scholastic
Pickle Puss	L	RF	250+	Giff, Patricia Reilly	Bantam
Pied Piper	L	TL	250+	Hunia, Fran	Ladybird Books
Pignocchio	L	F	250+	Pair-It Books	Steck-Vaughn
Pigs	L	I	250+	PM Animal Facts: Purple	Rigby
Pigs at Odds	L	F	250+	Axelrod, Amy	Aladdin
Pink: Seeing Pink All around Us	L	I	250+	Colors	Capstone Press
Pinky and Rex	L	RF	250+	Howe, James	Simon & Schuster

TITLE	LEVEL	GENRE	WORD COUNT	AUTHOR / SERIES	PUBLISHER / DISTRIBUTOR
Pinky and Rex and the Bully	L	RF	250+	Howe, James	Simon & Schuster
Pinky and Rex and the Double-Dad Weekend	L	RF	250+	Howe, James	Simon & Schuster
Pinky and Rex and the Mean Old Witch	L	RF	250+	Howe, James	Simon & Schuster
Pinky and Rex and the New Baby	L	RF	250+	Howe, James	Simon & Schuster
Pinky and Rex and the New Neighbors	L	RF	250+	Howe, James	Simon & Schuster
Pinky and Rex and the Perfect Pumpkin	L	RF	250+	Howe, James	Simon & Schuster
Pinky and Rex and the School Play	L	RF	250+	Howe, James	Simon & Schuster
Pinky and Rex and the Spelling Bee	L	RF	250+	Howe, James	Simon & Schuster
Pinky and Rex Get Married	L	RF	250+	Howe, James	Simon & Schuster
Pinky and Rex Go to Camp	L	RF	250+	Howe, James	Aladdin
Pioneer Bear	L	F	250+	Sandin, Joan	Random House
Pioneer Families	L	I	250+	Rosen Real Readers	Rosen Publishing Group
Places to Visit	L	I	202	Windows on Literacy	National Geographic
Planet Earth	L	I	197	Rigby Focus	Rigby
Planet X	L	SF	250+	Popcorn	Sundance
Plants that Eat Animals	L	I	250+	Read-About Science	Children's Press
Play Ball, Amelia Bedelia	L	F	250+	Parish, Peggy	Harper & Row
Play, The	L	RF	588	Leveled Readers	Houghton Mifflin
Pocket Full of Acorns, A	L	RF	250+	Beames, Michael	Pearson Learning Group
Polar Bears: In Living Color	L	I	250+	Rigby Literacy	Rigby
Police Officers	L	I	250+	Community Workers	Compass Point Books
Pony Trouble	L	RF	250+	Gasque, Dale Blackwell	Hyperion
*Pot of Gold, A/Clever Farmer, The	L	TL	250+	Pacific Literacy	Pacific Learning
Pot of Stone Soup, A	L	TL	250+	Ready Readers	Pearson Learning Group
Potato: A Tale From the Great Depression	L	HF	250+	Soar To Success	Houghton Mifflin
Powder Puff Puzzle, The	L	RF	250+	Giff, Patricia Reilly	Bantam
Power of Water, The	L	I	250+	Home Connection Collection	Rigby
Prairie Dogs	L	I	212	Twig	Wright Group/McGraw Hill
Present for LaNita, A	L	RF	835	Leveled Readers Social Studies	Houghton Mifflin
Presidents' Day	L	I	250+	Frost, Helen	Red Brick Learning
Princess Josie's Pets	L	RF	250+	Macdonald, Maryann	Hyperion
Puppy Who Wanted a Boy, The	L	F	250+	Thayer, Jane	Scholastic
Push or Pull	L	I	316	Independent Readers Science	Houghton Mifflin
Putting on a Concert and The Television News	L	RF	250+	Voyages	SRA/McGraw Hill
Quiet TV Lunch, A	L	F	250+	Popcorn	Sundance
Quilt Story, The	L	HF	250+	Johnston, Tony; DePaola, Tomie	Scholastic
Quork Attack	L	F	250+	Rigby Literacy	Rigby
Rabbit Stew	L	F	250+	Literacy 2000	Rigby
Rabbit's Robber	L	F	250+	Popcorn	Sundance
Rain Forest Adventure	L	F	482	Pair-It Books	Steck-Vaughn
Rainbows	L	I	250+	Rigby Literacy	Rigby
Rainbows of the Sea	L	I	250+	Thomas, Meredith	Mondo
Rapunzel	L	TL	250+	Literacy 2000	Rigby
Raven's Gift	L	F	160	Books For Young Learners	Richard C. Owen
Red Nose Frost: A Traditional Tale From Russia	L	TL	250+	Rigby Literacy	Rigby
*Red Riding Hood and the Flower in the Woods	L	TL	250+	New Way Literature	Steck-Vaughn
Red Shoes, The	L	RF	250+	Sails	Rigby
Red: Seeing Red All Around Us	L	I	250+	Colors	Capstone Press
Red-Tailed Hawk, The	L	RF	197	Books For Young Learners	Richard C. Owen
Reptiles and Amphibians	L	I	250+	Rosen Real Readers	Rosen Publishing Group
Rescue, The	L	RF	176	Pacific Literacy	Pacific Learning
Respect	L	I	250+	Character Education	Red Brick Learning
Responsibility	L	I	250+	Character Education	Red Brick Learning
Rice	L	I	132	Literacy Tree	Rigby

TITLE	LEVEL	GENRE	WORD COUNT	AUTHOR / SERIES	PUBLISHER / DISTRIBUTOR
Riddle of The Red Purse, The	L	RF	250+	Giff, Patricia Reilly	Bantam
Riding the Steam Train	L	I	250+	Pacific Literacy	Pacific Learning
Rising Up, Falling Down	L	I	205	Spyglass Books	Compass Point Books
Robin Hood and the Silver Trophy	L	TL	250+	PM Tales and Plays-Silver	Rigby
Robin Hood Meets Little John	L	TL	250+	PM Story Books	Rigby
Rocket Surpise, A	L	RF	250+	Sunshine	Wright Group/McGraw Hill
Rockin' Reptiles	L	F	250+	Calmenson, Stephanie & Cole	Beech Tree Books
Rocks	L	I	157	Early Connections	Benchmark Education
Rosie's Story	L	RF	250+	Bookshop	Mondo
Royal Drum, The	L	TL	250+	Bookshop	Mondo
Runaround Rowdy	L	RF	250+	PM Story Books	Rigby
Sadie and the Snowman	L	RF	250+	Morgan, Allen	Scholastic
Sadie, Remember	L	HF	250+	Kline, Carol	Sundance
Sally Ride in Space	L	B	235	Vocabulary Readers	Houghton Mifflin
Salty Dog	L	RF	250+	Rand, Gloria	Henry Holt & Co.
Sam King and Little Bull	L	RF	250+	Wilson, Trevor	Pearson Learning Group
Save the Rain Forests	L	I	250+	Read-About Science	Children's Press
Save the Rain Forests	L	I	250+	Fowler, Allan	Scholastic
Say "Cheese"	L	RF	250+	Giff, Patricia Reilly	Bantam
Scarecrow, The	L	RF	250+	Pacific Literacy	Pacific Learning
School Mural, The	L	RF	250+	Pair-It Books	Steck-Vaughn
School Recyclers	L	RF	380	Leveled Readers Science	Houghton Mifflin
Schoolyard Mystery, The	L	RF	250+	Levy, Elizabeth	Scholastic
Science - Just Add Salt	L	I	250+	Markle, Sandra	Scholastic
Sculpture	L	I	250+	Little Celebrations	Pearson Learning Group
Sea Lights	L	I	128	Books for Young Learners	Richard C. Owen
Sea Otters	L	I	406	Storyteller Nonfiction	Wright Group/McGraw Hill
Sea Turtles	L	I	553	Leveled Readers	Houghton Mifflin
Seashells	L	I	186	Marine Life For Young Readers	Pearson Learning Group
Second Birthday, A	L	I	250+	Greetings	Rigby
Secondhand Star	L	RF	250+	Macdonald, Maryann	Hyperion
Secret of Foghorn Island, The	L	F	250+	Step into Reading	Random House
Selfish Giant, The	L	F	250+	Literacy 2000	Rigby
Sets: Sorting into Groups	L	I	250+	Exploring Math	Capstone Press
Seven Continents	L	I	202	Windows on Literacy	National Geographic
Shapes: Discovering Flats and Solids	L	I	250+	Exploring Math	Capstone Press
Shaping the Earth	L	I	233	Rigby Focus	Rigby
Shark!	L	I	479	Leveled Readers Science	Houghton Mifflin
Sharks	L	I	238	Wonder World	Wright Group/McGraw Hill
Sharks and Rays	L	I	250+	Marine Life For Young Readers	Pearson Learning Group
Sheeba	L	F	250+	Noonan, Diana	Pearson Learning Group
Sheep	L	I	250+	PM Animal Facts: Purple	Rigby
Ships	L	I	275	Wonder World	Wright Group/McGraw Hill
Shoot of Corn, A	L	RF	250+	Cambridge Reading	Pearson Learning Group
Shopping with a Crocodile	L	F	250+	Pacific Literacy	Pacific Learning
Show Me a Snake Hole	L	RF	250+	Frederick, Shirley	Hampton-Brown
Show Must Go On!, The	L	RF	586	Leveled Readers	Houghton Mifflin
Show of Hands, A	L	I	250+	Rigby Literacy	Rigby
Silent World, A	L	RF	250+	Literacy 2000	Rigby
Silver and Prince	L	RF	250+	PM Story Books-Silver	Rigby
Simple Machines	L	I	250+	Early Connections	Benchmark Education
Sing-Song Tree, The	L	I	250+	Sunshine	Wright Group/McGraw Hill
Six Foolish Fishermen	L	TL	715	Elkin, Benjamin	Children's Press
Six Things to Make	L	I	250+	Bookshop	Mondo

* Collection of short stories

TITLE	LEVEL	GENRE	WORD COUNT	AUTHOR / SERIES	PUBLISHER / DISTRIBUTOR
Size: Many Ways to Measure	L	I	250+	Exploring Math	Capstone Press
Sky High	L	F	619	Pair-It Books	Steck-Vaughn
Sleeping Beauty, The	L	TL	250+	PM Tales and Plays-Silver	Rigby
Slim Shorty and the Mules	L	RF	411	Reading Unlimited	Pearson Learning Group
Slippery Planet, The	L	F	250+	Cambridge Reading	Pearson Learning Group
Snakes	L	I	252	Wonder World	Wright Group/McGraw Hill
Snakes!	L	I	250+	Recht Penner, Lucille	Random House
Snow Daughter, The	L	TL	505	Sunshine	Wright Group/McGraw Hill
Snow Goes To Town	L	F	250+	Literacy 2000	Rigby
Snow in the Kitchen	L	RF	250+	Cambridge Reading	Pearson Learning Group
Snow Walker, The	L	HF	250+	Wetterer, Margaret K. & Charles M.	Carolrhoda Books
Sojourner Truth	L	B	250+	Pebble Books	Red Brick Learning
Solo Flyer	L	RF	605	PM Gold	Rigby
Something Else	L	F	250+	Cave, Kathryn	Mondo
Song Lee and the Hamster Hunt	L	RF	250+	Kline, Suzy	Penguin Group
Song Lee and the Leech Man	L	RF	250+	Kline, Suzy	Penguin Group
Song Lee In Room 2B	L	RF	250+	Kline, Suzy	Penguin Group
Sound, Heat & Light: Energy at Work	L	I	250+	Berger, Melvin	Scholastic
Space Dog and Roy	L	F	250+	Standiford, Natalie	Random House
Space Dog and the Pet Show	L	F	250+	Standiford, Natalie	Random House
Space Dog in Trouble	L	F	250+	Standiford, Natalie	Random House
Space Dog the Hero	L	F	250+	Standiford, Natalie	Random House
Space Rock	L	F	250+	Buller, Jon	Random House
Space Station Orion	L	F	250+	Rigby Literacy	Rigby
Spanish Omelette	L	RF	250+	PM Story Books-Silver	Rigby
Special Present, The	L	RF	250+	Cole, Sally	Wright Group/McGraw Hill
Spectacular Stone Soup	L	RF	250+	Giff, Patricia Reilly	Yearling
Spending Money	L	I	250+	First Facts	Capstone Press
Spider and the King, The	L	TL	250+	Literacy 2000	Rigby
Spider Bank, The	L	I	250+	Story Steps	Rigby
Spider's Web, A	L	I	323	Wonder World	Wright Group/McGraw Hill
Spike and the Concert	L	RF	250+	Cambridge Reading	Pearson Learning Group
Spoiled Rotten	L	RF	250+	DeClements, Barthe	Hyperion
Sports Matters: A Magazine for Kids	L	I	250+	Rigby Literacy	Rigby
Squanto and the First Thanksgiving	L	HF	250+	Celsi, Teresa	Steck-Vaughn
Stacy Says Good-Bye	L	RF	250+	Giff, Patricia Reilly	Bantam
Steam Power	L	I	308	Rigby Focus	Rigby
Stone in the Road, A	L	TL	250+	Bookshop	Mondo
*Stone Soup and Other Stories	L	TL	250+	New Way Literature	Steck-Vaughn
Storm Chasers	L	RF	250+	Navigators Fiction Series	Benchmark Education
Storms!	L	I	359	Pair-It Books	Steck-Vaughn
Story of a Book, The	L	I	250+	Reeder, Paul	Wright Group/McGraw Hill
Storytellers	L	I	506	Storyteller Nonfiction	Wright Group/McGraw Hill
Strange Day in Mayville, A	L	TL	250+	Leveled Readers Language Support	Houghton Mifflin
Strange Shoe, The	L	TL	250+	PM Tales and Plays-Silver	Rigby
Strange Things	L	RF	289	Books for Young Learners	Richard C. Owen
Stranger's Gift, The	L	TL	250+	Literacy 2000	Rigby
Strike Me Down with a Stringbean	L	F	404	Read Alongs	Rigby
Sun's Family of Planets, The	L	I	250+	Read-About Science	Children's Press
Sunshine	L	I	307	Pebble Books	Capstone Press
Surprise Dinner, The	L	RF	680	PM Gold	Rigby
Survivors in the Frozen North	L	RF	250+	PM Plus Story Books	Rigby

* Collection of short stories

TITLE	LEVEL	GENRE	WORD COUNT	AUTHOR / SERIES	PUBLISHER / DISTRIBUTOR
Table for Two	L	TL	250+	Little Celebrations	Pearson Learning Group
Tale of Peter Rabbit, The	L	TL	250+	Potter, Beatrix	Scholastic
Tale of the Golden Goose, The	L	TL	250+	Behr, Alexandra	Hampton-Brown
*Tales of Amanda Pig	L	F	250+	Van Leeuwen, Jean	Puffin Books
*Tales of Oliver Pig	L	F	250+	Van Leeuwen, Jean	Puffin Books
Tame and Wild	L	I	306	Spyglass Books	Compass Point Books
Teach Us, Amelia Bedelia	L	F	250+	Parish, Peggy	Scholastic
Teachers	L	I	250+	Community Workers	Compass Point Books
Teacher's Pet	L	F	250+	Dicks, Terrance	Scholastic
Tell Me a Story, Grandpa	L	RF	250+	Little Celebrations	Pearson Learning Group
Ten Easy Tips for Staying Safe	L	I	250+	Rosen Real Readers	Rosen Publishing Group
*Terrible Tiger and Sleeping Beauty	L	TL	250+	New Way Literature	Steck-Vaughn
Thank You, Amelia Bedelia	L	F	250+	Little Readers	Houghton Mifflin
Thanksgiving Day	L	I	132	National Holidays	Red Brick Learning
That's Determination!	L	RF	250+	Rigby Literacy	Rigby
That's HOT!	L	I	250+	Spyglass Books	Compass Point Books
Therapy Dogs to the Rescue	L	I	250+	Rigby Literacy	Rigby
There's a Dinosaur!	L	I	250+	Stone, Evelyn	Hampton-Brown
There's a Rainbow in the River	L	RF	250+	Home Connection Collection	Rigby
Things Don't Change Much	L	RF	250+	Home Connection Collection	Rigby
Things That Go: A Traveling Alphabet	L	I	250+	Reit, Seymour	Bantam
Thinking About Ants	L	I	250+	Bookshop	Mondo
This Is My House	L	I	250+	Dorros, Arthur	Scholastic
Three Blind Mice Mystery, The	L	F	250+	Krensky, Stephen	Bantam
Three Little Pigs	L	TL	250+	Once Upon a Time	Wright Group/McGraw Hill
Three Little Pigs	L	TL	919	Galdone, Paul	Houghton Mifflin
Three Little Pigs, The	L	TL	250+	Marshall, James	Scholastic
Three Sillies, The	L	F	250+	Literacy 2000	Rigby
Three Smart Pals	L	RF	250+	Rocklin, Joanne	Scholastic
Three Wishes	L	F	250+	Popcorn	Sundance
Three Wishes, The	L	TL	250+	Bookshop	Mondo
Thurgood Marshall	L	B	250+	Pebble Books	Red Brick Learning
Tiger & the Mad Millionaire, The	L	F	250+	Voyages	SRA/McGraw Hill
Time to Estimate	L	I	250+	Yellow Umbrella Books	Capstone Press
Time to Tell Time	L	I	116	Spyglass Books	Compass Point Books
Time's Up!	L	F	250+	Sunshine	Wright Group/McGraw Hill
Tiny Dinosaurs	L	RF	250+	PM Story Books	Rigby
To Tell the Truth, A Native American Cinderella Tale	L	TL	250+	Leveled Readers Language Support	Houghton Mifflin
Toes	L	I	250+	Sunshine	Wright Group/McGraw Hill
Tolerance	L	I	250+	Character Education	Red Brick Learning
Tomato Picking Day	L	I	250+	Pipher, Tom	Wright Group/McGraw Hill
Tomie dePaola	L	B	196	First Biographies	Red Brick Learning
Tongues Are for Tasting, Licking, Tricking	L	I	250+	Literacy 2000	Rigby
Tooter Pepperday	L	RF	250+	Spinelli, Jerry	Random House
Tornado, The	L	RF	250+	PM Story Books	Rigby
Totem Poles	L	I	246	Twig	Wright Group/McGraw Hill
Touch the Earth	L	RF	250+	Bookshop	Mondo
Toy Shop, The	L	RF	250+	Book Project	Sundance
Tracks	L	I	250+	Voyages	SRA/McGraw Hill
Tracks in the Sand	L	I	250+	Sunshine	Wright Group/McGraw Hill
Train Time	L	I	250+	Baehr, Lisa	Hampton-Brown
Training My Dog	L	I	917	Leveled Readers Science	Houghton Mifflin
Trapped!	L	RF	250+	New Way Literature	Steck-Vaughn

* Collection of short stories

TITLE	LEVEL	GENRE	WORD COUNT	AUTHOR / SERIES	PUBLISHER / DISTRIBUTOR
Treasure Cave, The	L	F	250+	Cambridge Reading	Pearson Learning Group
Treasures	L	RF	263	Books for Young Learners	Richard C. Owen
Trees	L	I	158	Bookshop	Mondo
Trees Belong To Everyone	L	I	250+	Literacy 2000	Rigby
Triceratops on the Farm	L	F	208	Wesley & the Dinosaurs	Wright Group/McGraw Hill
Trip on the Erie Canal, A	L	RF	260	Independent Readers Social Studies	Houghton Mifflin
Trip Through Our Solar System, A	L	I	250+	Rosen Real Readers	Rosen Publishing Group
Trip Through the Airport, A	L	I	250+	Rigby Literacy	Rigby
Triplet Trouble and the Bicycle Race	L	RF	250+	Dadey, Debbie; Jones, Marcia Thornton	Scholastic
Triplet Trouble and the Class Trip	L	RF	250+	Dadey, Debbie; Jones, Marcia Thornton	Scholastic
Triplet Trouble and the Cookie Contest	L	RF	250+	Dadey, Debbie; Jones, Marcia Thornton	Scholastic
Triplet Trouble and the Field Day Disaster	L	RF	250+	Dadey, Debbie; Jones, Marcia Thornton	Scholastic
Triplet Trouble and the Pizza Party	L	RF	250+	Dadey, Debbie; Jones, Marcia Thornton	Scholastic
Triplet Trouble and the Red Heart Race	L	RF	250+	Dadey, Debbie; Jones, Marcia Thornton	Scholastic
Triplet Trouble and the Runaway Reindeer	L	RF	250+	Dadey, Debbie; Jones, Marcia Thornton	Scholastic
Triplet Trouble and the Talent Show Mess	L	RF	250+	Dadey, Debbie; Jones, Marcia Thornton	Scholastic
Trixie	L	RF	250+	Voyages	SRA/McGraw Hill
Trouble with Herbert, The	L	F	1830	Eyles, Heather	Mondo
True Story of Balto, The	L	I	250+	Standiford, Natalie	Random House
T-Shirt Triplets, The	L	RF	344	Literacy 2000	Rigby
Tunnels	L	I	262	Windows on Literacy	National Geographic
Turn on a Faucet	L	I	238	Windows on Literacy	National Geographic
Turtles Take Their Time	L	I	250+	Read-About Science	Children's Press
Twiddle Twins' Haunted House, The	L	F	1141	Goldsmith, Howard	Mondo
Twiddle Twins' Music Box Mystery, The	L	F	250+	Goldsmith, Howard	Mondo
Twiddle Twins' Single Footprint Mystery, The	L	F	250+	Goldsmith, Howard	Mondo
Two Plus One Goes A.P.E.	L	RF	250+	Springstubb, Tricia	Scholastic
Two Red Tugs	L	F	547	PM Story Books	Rigby
*Two Tricky Tales	L	TL	250+	Pacific Literacy	Pacific Learning
Tyrannosaurus the Terrible	L	F	182	Wesley & the Dinosaurs	Wright Group/McGraw Hill
Ty's One-man Band	L	RF	250+	Walter, Mildred Pitts	Scholastic
Umbrellas	L	I	430	Sunshine	Wright Group/McGraw Hill
Underwater with Jacques Cousteau	L	B	633	Leveled Readers Science	Houghton Mifflin
Upside-Down Reader, The	L	F	250+	Gruber, Wolfram	North-South Books
Using the Library	L	I	291	Wonder World	Wright Group/McGraw Hill
Vampire Trouble	L	F	250+	Dadey, Debbie; Jones, Marcia Thornton	Scholastic
Very Strange Dollhouse, A	L	F	250+	Dussling, Jennifer	Grosset & Dunlap
Very Thin Cat of Alloway Road, The	L	RF	250+	Literacy 2000	Rigby
Veterans Day	L	I	96	National Holidays	Red Brick Learning
Veterinarians	L	I	250+	Ready, Dee	Red Brick Learning
Viva Mexico	L	I	432	Leveled Readers Social Studies	Houghton Mifflin
Volcanoes	L	I	250+	Sunshine	Wright Group/McGraw Hill
Wacky Jacks	L	RF	250+	Adler, David A.	Random House
Walk With Grandpa, A	L	RF	388	Read Alongs	Rigby

* Collection of short stories

TITLE	LEVEL	GENRE	WORD COUNT	AUTHOR / SERIES	PUBLISHER / DISTRIBUTOR
Walter and the Inventor's Garden	L	F	250+	Pacific Literacy	Pacific Learning
Walter Hottle Bottle	L	RF	250+	Voyages	SRA/McGraw Hill
Walter's Worries	L	F	250+	Pacific Literacy	Pacific Learning
Washington, D.C.	L	I	163	Rosen Real Readers	Rosen Publishing Group
Watch by the Sea, The	L	RF	250+	Cambridge Reading	Pearson Learning Group
Watch Out, Man-Eating Snake	L	RF	250+	Giff, Patricia Reilly	Bantam
Watching the Whales	L	RF	267	Foundations	Wright Group/McGraw Hill
Water as a Gas	L	I	127	Pebble Books	Capstone Press
Water Cycle, The	L	I	146	Pebble Books	Capstone Press
*Water Lilies and Other Stories	L	TL	250+	New Way Literature	Steck-Vaughn
Waterhole, The	L	F	250+	Sunshine	Wright Group/McGraw Hill
Wax Museum	L	I	250+	Cook, Donald	Grosset & Dunlap
Weather Watching	L	I	339	Rigby Focus	Rigby
Weather Wise	L	I	250+	Spyglass Books	Compass Point Books
Welcome Home	L	I	250+	Early Connections	Benchmark Education
Welsh Lamb, A	L	RF	250+	Cambridge Reading	Pearson Learning Group
We're Off to Thunder Mountain	L	RF	250+	Bookshop	Mondo
Whales - The Gentle Giants	L	I	250+	Milton, Joyce	Random House
What a Great Idea!	L	RF	250+	Home Connection Collection	Rigby
What a Load of Garbage	L	I	250+	Lighthouse	Rigby
What a Trip, Amber Brown	L	RF	250+	Danziger, Paula	Puffin Books
What Did You Eat Today?	L	F	250+	Literacy Tree	Rigby
What Does a Governor Do?	L	I	288	Independent Readers Social Studies	Houghton Mifflin
What Is Matter?	L	I	250+	Schaefer, Lola M.	Benchmark Education
What Joy Found	L	RF	250+	Ready Readers	Pearson Learning Group
What Keeps Them Warm?	L	I	156	Pacific Literacy	Pacific Learning
What Kind of Babysitter Is This?	L	RF	250+	Johnson, Dolores	Scholastic
What My Dog Knows	L	RF	866	Leveled Readers Science	Houghton Mifflin
What Next, Baby Bear?	L	F	313	Murphy, Jill	Dial Books
What's It Like to Be a Fish?	L	I	250+	Little Readers	Houghton Mifflin
What's the Address?	L	I	186	iOpeners	Pearson Learning Group
When I Broke the Office Window	L	RF	257	City Kids	Rigby
*When the Giants Came to Town	L	F	250+	Leonard, Marcia	Scholastic
When Tony Got Lost at the Zoo	L	RF	122	City Kids	Rigby
Where Do the Puddles Go?	L	I	170	Windows on Literacy	National Geographic
Where Do You Live?	L	I	250+	Twig	Wright Group/McGraw Hill
Where Does the Water Go?	L	I	189	Windows on Literacy	National Geographic
Where's the Bus?	L	F	250+	Sunshine	Wright Group/McGraw Hill
Whistle for Willie	L	RF	380	Keats, Ezra Jack	Penguin Group
White Elephants	L	RF	250+	Sunshine	Wright Group/McGraw Hill
White: Seeing White All Around Us	L	I	250+	Colors	Capstone Press
Whizz! Click!	L	RF	285	Pacific Literacy	Pacific Learning
Who Grows Up in the Desert?: A Book About Desert Animals and Their Offspring	L	I	250+	Who Grows Up Here?	Picture Window Books
Who Grows Up in the Forest?: A Book About Forest Animals and Their Offspring	L	I	250+	Who Grows Up Here?	Picture Window Books
Who Grows Up in the Ocean?: A Book About Ocean Animals and Their Offspring	L	I	250+	Who Grows Up Here?	Picture Window Books
Who Grows Up in the Rain Forest?: A Book About Rain Forest Animals and Their Offspring	L	I	250+	Who Grows Up Here?	Picture Window Books
Who Grows Up in the Snow?: A Book About Polar Animals and Their Offspring	L	I	250+	Who Grows Up Here?	Picture Window Books
Why Bear Sleeps All Winter	L	TL	647	Leveled Readers	Houghton Mifflin

* Collection of short stories

TITLE	LEVEL	GENRE	WORD COUNT	AUTHOR / SERIES	PUBLISHER / DISTRIBUTOR
Why Rabbits Have Long Ears	L	TL	250+	Literacy 2000	Rigby
Why the Leopard Has Spots	L	I	250+	Pair-It Books	Steck-Vaughn
Why The Sea Is Salty	L	TL	250+	Literacy 2000	Rigby
Wild Swans, The	L	TL	754	Tales from Hans Andersen	Wright Group/McGraw Hill
Wild Wicked Winifred and Horrible Hank	L	F	250+	Popcorn	Sundance
Wild Wicked Winifred and the Pirates	L	F	250+	Popcorn	Sundance
Wild Wicked Winifred and the Sea Serpent	L	F	250+	Popcorn	Sundance
Wild Wicked Winifred and the Treasure Map	L	F	250+	Popcorn	Sundance
Winter on the Ice	L	F	506	PM Plus Story Books	Rigby
Wizard of Oz, The	L	TL	903	Hunia, Fran	Ladybird Books
Wolf and the Seven Little Kids	L	TL	250+	Hunia, Fran	Ladybird Books
Working on Water	L	I	250+	Home Connection Collection	Rigby
Working with Metal	L	I	299	Rigby Focus	Rigby
World in Your Kitchen, The	L	I	347	Independent Readers Social Studies	Houghton Mifflin
Worms, Wonderful Worms	L	I	250+	Voyages	SRA/McGraw Hill
Yellow Overalls	L	F	250+	Literacy 2000	Rigby
You Don't Look Like Your Mother	L	F	250+	Bookshop	Mondo
Young Arthur Ashe: Brave Champion	L	B	250+	First-Start Biography	Troll Associates
Young Clara Barton: Battlefield Nurse	L	B	250+	First-Start Biography	Troll Associates
Young Davy Crockett: Frontier Fighter	L	B	250+	First-Start Biography	Troll Associates
Young Helen Keller: Woman of Courage	L	B	250+	First-Start Biography	Troll Associates
Young Jackie Robinson: Baseball Hero	L	B	250+	First-Start Biography	Troll Associates
Young Jim Thorpe: All-American Athlete	L	B	250+	First-Start Biography	Troll Associates
Young Orville and Wilbur Wright: First to Fly	L	B	250+	First-Start Biography	Troll Associates
Young Reggie Jackson: Hall of Fame Champion	L	B	250+	First-Start Biography	Troll Associates
Young Rosa Parks: Civil Rights Heroine	L	B	250+	First-Start Biography	Troll Associates
Young Squanto: The First Thanksgiving	L	B	250+	First-Start Biography	Troll Associates
Young Thurgood Marshall: Fighter for Equality	L	B	250+	First-Start Biography	Troll Associates
Young Tom Edison: Great Inventor	L	B	250+	First-Start Biography	Troll Associates
Your Heart	L	I	250+	Early Connections	Benchmark Education
Zemti	L	TL	250+	Books for Young Learners	Richard C. Owen
Zoo Overnight	L	RF	250+	Pacific Literacy	Pacific Learning
Abby	M	RF	250+	Hanel, Wolfram	North-South Books
Abe Lincoln's Hat	M	B	250+	Brenner, Martha	Random House
About How Many?	M	I	250+	Early Connections	Benchmark Education
Abraham Lincoln: Lawyer, President, Emancipator	M	B	250+	Biographies	Picture Window Books
Adventure Vacations	M	I	250+	Rigby Literacy	Rigby
Adventures of Ratman	M	F	250+	Weiss, Ellen; Freidman, Mel	Random House
African Giants	M	I	250+	World Quest Adventures	World Quest Learning
African Hunting Dog, The	M	I	250+	Sunshine	Wright Group/McGraw Hill
Afternoon on the Amazon	M	F	250+	Osborne, Mary Pope	Random House
Air: Outside, Inside, and All Around	M	I	250+	Amazing Science	Picture Window Books
Airplanes	M	I	250+	Transportation	Compass Point Books
Alexander and the Stallion	M	HF	434	Books for Young Learners	Richard C. Owen
Alexander Graham Bell	M	B	250+	Rosen Real Readers	Rosen Publishing Group
Aliens Don't Wear Braces	M	F	250+	Dadey, Debbie; Jones, Marcia Thornton	Scholastic
Aliens for Breakfast	M	F	250+	Etra, Jonathan; Spinner, Stephanie	Random House
Aliens for Dinner	M	F	250+	Spinner, Stephanie	Random House
Aliens for Lunch	M	F	250+	Spinner, Stephanie; Etra, Jonathan	Random House

* Collection of short stories

TITLE	LEVEL	GENRE	WORD COUNT	AUTHOR / SERIES	PUBLISHER / DISTRIBUTOR
All About Drums	M	I	250+	Rosen Real Readers	Rosen Publishing Group
All About Potbellied Pigs	M	I	250+	Rigby Literacy	Rigby
Alligator Alley	M	RF	250+	Schultz, Irene	Wright Group/McGraw Hill
Alligator, The	M	I	250+	Crewe, Sabrina	Steck-Vaughn
Allosaurus	M	I	250+	Discovering Dinosaurs	Capstone Press
All-Star Fever	M	RF	250+	Christopher, Matt	Little, Brown & Co.
Always Elephant: A Traditional Tale	M	TL	250+	Rigby Literacy	Rigby
Amazing Ant, The	M	I	250+	Story Box	Wright Group/McGraw Hill
Amazing Birds of the Rain Forest	M	I	250+	Daniel, Claire	Steck-Vaughn
Amazing Silkworm, The	M	I	250+	Windows on Literacy	National Geographic
American Heroes	M	I	189	Phonics Readers	Compass Point Books
Among the Flowers	M	I	250+	Look Once Look Again	Creative Teaching Press
Amphibians	M	I	250+	First Facts	Capstone Press
Andrew's Angry Words	M	F	250+	Lachner, Dorothea	North-South Books
Angels Don't Know Karate	M	F	250+	Dadey, Debbie; Jones, Marcia Thornton	Scholastic
Animal Adventures	M	RF	250+	Navigators Fiction Series	Benchmark Education
Animal Eyes	M	I	250+	Look Once Look Again	Creative Teaching Press
Animal Feathers and Fur	M	I	250+	Look Once Look Again	Creative Teaching Press
Animal Mouths	M	I	250+	Look Once Look Again	Creative Teaching Press
Animal Noses	M	I	250+	Look Once Look Again	Creative Teaching Press
Animal Senses	M	I	250+	Cambridge Reading	Pearson Learning Group
Animal Trackers, The	M	I	333	Independent Readers Science	Houghton Mifflin
Animals and Air	M	I	250+	Sunshine	Wright Group/McGraw Hill
Animals at Work	M	I	250+	Home Connection Collection	Rigby
Animals Communicating	M	I	250+	First Facts	Capstone Press
Animals in Danger	M	I	250+	Pair-It Books	Steck-Vaughn
Animals of the Savanna	M	I	250+	Rosen Real Readers	Rosen Publishing Group
Animals of the Tropical Forest	M	I	250+	Rosen Real Readers	Rosen Publishing Group
Animals of the Tropical Rain Forest	M	I	250+	Sunshine	Wright Group/McGraw Hill
Animals on the Loose	M	F	642	Leveled Readers	Houghton Mifflin
Animals Say	M	F	250+	Sails	Rigby
Animals With Backbones	M	I	177	Windows on Literacy	National Geographic
Ankylosaurus	M	I	250+	Discovering Dinosaurs	Capstone Press
Annie's Secret Diary	M	RF	250+	Little Celebrations	Pearson Learning Group
Antarctic Adventure, An	M	I	296	Vocabulary Readers	Houghton Mifflin
Antarctic Diary	M	I	250+	Voyages	SRA/McGraw Hill
April Fool's Day Mystery, The	M	RF	250+	Soar To Success	Houghton Mifflin
Arctic Life	M	I	250+	Robinson, F. R.	Steck-Vaughn
Arctic Tundra	M	I	250+	Forman, Michael H.	Children's Press
Armadillo	M	RF	134	Books for Young Learners	Richard C. Owen
Armies of Ants	M	I	250+	Retan, Walter	Scholastic
Art Around the World	M	I	250+	Discovery World	Rigby
Art Lesson, The	M	B	246	DePaola, Tomie	Putnam
Arthur Accused!	M	F	250+	Brown, Marc	Little, Brown & Co.
Arthur and the Big Blow-Up	M	F	250+	Brown, Marc	Little, Brown & Co.
Arthur and the Cootie-Catcher	M	F	250+	Brown, Marc	Little, Brown & Co.
Arthur and the Crunch Cereal Contest	M	F	250+	Brown, Marc	Little, Brown & Co.
Arthur and the Lost Diary	M	F	250+	Brown, Marc	Little, Brown & Co.
Arthur and the Poetry Contest	M	F	250+	Brown, Marc	Little, Brown & Co.
Arthur and the Popularity Test	M	F	250+	Brown, Marc	Little, Brown & Co.
Arthur and the Scare-Your-Pants-Off Club	M	F	250+	Brown, Marc	Little, Brown & Co.
Arthur and the TL Contest	M	F	250+	Brown, Marc	Little, Brown & Co.
Arthur Makes the Team	M	F	250+	Brown, Marc	Little, Brown & Co.

* Collection of short stories

TITLE	LEVEL	GENRE	WORD COUNT	AUTHOR / SERIES	PUBLISHER / DISTRIBUTOR
Arthur Rocks with BINKY	M	F	250+	Brown, Marc	Little, Brown & Co.
Arthur's Mystery Envelope	M	F	250+	Brown, Marc	Little, Brown & Co.
Assembly Line, The	M	I	501	Leveled Readers Social Studies	Houghton Mifflin
Asteroid, The	M	F	752	PM Gold	Rigby
Astronauts	M	I	250+	Deedrick, Tami	Red Brick Learning
At the Art Museum	M	I	250+	Rosen Real Readers	Rosen Publishing Group
At the Edge of the Sea	M	I	693	Sunshine	Wright Group/McGraw Hill
At the Farm	M	I	250+	Look Once Look Again	Creative Teaching Press
At the Pond	M	I	250+	Look Once Look Again	Creative Teaching Press
At the Zoo	M	I	250+	Look Once Look Again	Creative Teaching Press
Aunt Flossie's Hats (and Crab Cakes Later)	M	RF	250+	Howard, Elizabeth	Scholastic
Auto Mechanics	M	I	250+	Boraas, Tracey	Red Brick Learning
Autumn	M	I	225	Pebble Books	Red Brick Learning
Baboon Troops	M	I	250+	Sails	Rigby
Baby Whales Drink Milk	M	I	250+	Soar To Success	Houghton Mifflin
Back to the Dentist	M	RF	199	City Kids	Rigby
Bad Dad List, The	M	RF	250+	Kenna, Anna	Pacific Learning
Bakers	M	I	250+	Deedrick, Tami	Red Brick Learning
Balloons	M	I	57	iOpeners	Pearson Learning Group
Bank Tellers	M	I	250+	Community Workers	Compass Point Books
Baseball Flyhawk	M	RF	250+	Christopher, Matt	Little, Brown & Co.
Baseball Heroes, The	M	RF	250+	Schultz, Irene	Wright Group/McGraw Hill
Baseball Pals	M	RF	250+	Christopher, Matt	Little, Brown & Co.
Basket Counts, The	M	RF	250+	Christopher, Matt	Little, Brown & Co.
Bats	M	I	250+	PM Animal Facts: Gold	Rigby
Bear, The	M	I	250+	Life Cycles	Steck-Vaughn
Bear's Christmas	M	F	250+	Berenstain, Stan & Jan	Random House
Bears Have Cubs	M	I	250+	Animals and Their Young	Compass Point Books
Bears On Hemlock Mountain, The	M	RF	250+	Dalgliesh, Alice	Aladdin
Bears' Picnic	M	F	250+	Berenstain, Stan & Jan	Random House
Beast and the Halloween Horror	M	RF	250+	Giff, Patricia Reilly	Bantam
Beast in Ms. Rooney's Room, The	M	RF	250+	Giff, Patricia Reilly	Bantam
Beating the Drought	M	RF	250+	Noonan, Diana	Pacific Learning
Beauregard the Cat	M	RF	250+	Bookshop	Mondo
Beaver, The	M	I	250+	Crewe, Sabrina	Steck-Vaughn
Bee, The	M	I	250+	Crewe, Sabrina	Steck-Vaughn
Beekeeper, The	M	I	250+	Literacy 2000	Rigby
Bend and Stretch: Learning About Your Bones and Muscles	M	I	250+	Amazing Body	Picture Window Books
Benjamin Franklin: Writer, Inventor, Statesman	M	B	250+	Biographies	Picture Window Books
Berenstain Bear Scouts and the Coughing Catfish	M	F	250+	Berenstain, Stan & Jan	Scholastic
Berenstain Bear Scouts, The: Ghost Versus Ghost	M	F	250+	Berenstain, Stan & Jan	Scholastic
Berenstain Bears and the Ghost of the Auto Graveyard, The	M	F	250+	Berenstain, Stan & Jan	Random House
Berenstain Bears and the Missing Honey	M	F	531	Berenstain, Stan & Jan	Random House
Best Friends Don't Fight	M	RF	250+	Bookshop	Mondo
Best Wishes for Eddie	M	RF	250+	Nayer, Judy	Pearson Learning Group
Bicycle for Rosaura, A	M	F	250+	Soar To Success	Houghton Mifflin
Bicycles	M	I	250+	Windows on Literacy	National Geographic
Big Bulgy Fat Black Slugs	M	F	250+	Stepping Stones	Nelson/Michaels Assoc.
Big Chase, The	M	F	250+	SupaDoopers	Sundance
Big Dipper, The	M	I	585	Leveled Readers Science	Houghton Mifflin

* Collection of short stories

TITLE	LEVEL	GENRE	WORD COUNT	AUTHOR / SERIES	PUBLISHER / DISTRIBUTOR
Big Fish, The	M	RF	301	Yukish, Joe	Kaeden Books
Big Rigs	M	I	250+	Transportation	Compass Point Books
Bigfoot Doesn't Square Dance	M	F	250+	Dadey, Debbie; Jones, Marcia Thornton	Scholastic
Bird Behavior: Living Together	M	I	631	Sunshine	Wright Group/McGraw Hill
Bird Chain, The	M	F	250+	Voyages	SRA/McGraw Hill
Bird for You, A: Caring for Your Bird	M	I	250+	Pet Care	Picture Window Books
Bird in the Basket, The	M	RF	250+	Beveridge, Barbara	Pacific Learning
Birds	M	I	68	First Facts	Capstone Press
Birds of the City	M	I	840	Sunshine	Wright Group/McGraw Hill
Birdwoman Interview	M	RF	250+	Sails	Rigby
Birthdays Around the World	M	I	250+	Early Connections	Benchmark Education
Blast Off with Ellen Ochoa!	M	B	250+	Greetings	Rigby
Blizzards!	M	HF	250+	Hopping, Lorraine Jean	Scholastic
*Blue Hill Meadows, The	M	RF	250+	Rylant, Cynthia	Harcourt Trade
Blue Ribbon Blues	M	RF	250+	Spinelli, Jerry	Random House
Blueberries for Sal	M	RF	250+	McCloskey, Robert	Scholastic
BMX Freestyle	M	I	250+	Blazers	Capstone Press
Boats	M	I	250+	Transportation	Compass Point Books
Boats Afloat	M	I	752	Sunshine	Wright Group/McGraw Hill
Bogeymen Don't Play Football	M	F	250+	Dadey, Debbie; Jones, Marcia Thornton	Scholastic
Bone Museum, The	M	RF	250+	Sunshine	Wright Group/McGraw Hill
Book About Your Skeleton, A	M	I	250+	Gross, Ruth Belov	Scholastic
Booker T. Washington	M	B	250+	Schaefer, Lola M.	Steck-Vaughn
Boundless Grace	M	RF	250+	Hoffman, Mary	Scholastic
Boy Who Stretched to the Sky, The	M	F	463	Book Bank	Wright Group/McGraw Hill
Brachiosaurus	M	I	250+	Discovering Dinosaurs	Capstone Press
Brain-in-a-Box	M	F	250+	Matthews, Steve	Sundance
Brave Maddie Egg	M	RF	250+	Standiford, Natalie	Random House
*Breakfast Bird and Other Animal Stories	M	F	250+	Bookshop	Mondo
Breathe In, Breathe Out: Learning About Your Lungs	M	I	250+	Amazing Body	Picture Window Books
Bridge, The	M	I	250+	Cambridge Reading	Pearson Learning Group
Brith The Terrible	M	F	250+	Literacy 2000	Rigby
Bubbles	M	I	250+	Cambridge Reading	Pearson Learning Group
Buddy: The First Seeing Eye Dog	M	I	250+	Moore, Eva	Scholastic
Buds and Blossoms: A Book About Flowers	M	I	250+	Growing Things	Picture Window Books
Buffalo Before Breakfast	M	F	250+	Osborne, Mary Pope	Random House
Buffalo, The	M	I	250+	Crewe, Sabrina	Steck-Vaughn
Bug-head and Me	M	RF	250+	Rigby Literacy	Rigby
Bugs on the Menu	M	I	250+	Sails	Rigby
Build It Strong!	M	I	250+	First Science	Children's Press
Build, Build, Build	M	I	470	Sunshine	Wright Group/McGraw Hill
Building Strong Bridges	M	I	250+	Twig	Wright Group/McGraw Hill
Bull Harris and the Purple Ooze	M	RF	250+	SupaDoopers	Sundance
Buried Eye, The	M	F	250+	Schultz, Irene	Wright Group/McGraw Hill
Bush Tucker	M	I	250+	Sunshine	Wright Group/McGraw Hill
Buster	M	F	250+	Bookshop	Mondo
Buster Baxter, Cat Saver	M	F	250+	Brown, Marc	Little, Brown & Co.
Buster Makes the Grade	M	F	250+	Brown, Marc	Little, Brown & Co.
Buster's Dino Dilemma	M	F	250+	Brown, Marc	Little, Brown & Co.
Busy Bees	M	I	514	Leveled Readers	Houghton Mifflin
Butterfly Farm Burglar, The	M	RF	250+	Schultz, Irene	Wright Group/McGraw Hill

* Collection of short stories

TITLE	LEVEL	GENRE	WORD COUNT	AUTHOR / SERIES	PUBLISHER / DISTRIBUTOR
Butterfly, The	M	I	250+	Crewe, Sabrina	Steck-Vaughn
Buttons for General Washington	M	HF	250+	Roop, Peter & Connie	Carolrhoda Books
Cake Walk	M	RF	250+	Books for Young Learners	Richard C. Owen
Cake, The	M	RF	250+	Read Alongs	Rigby
Camouflage	M	I	250+	Cambridge Reading	Pearson Learning Group
Camp Sink or Swim	M	RF	250+	Davis, Gibbs	Random House
Can Do, Jenny Archer	M	RF	250+	Conford, Ellen	Random House
Can You Eat a Fraction?	M	I	250+	Yellow Umbrella Books	Capstone Press
Cape of Rushes, The	M	TL	250+	Cambridge Reading	Pearson Learning Group
Caribbean Cats	M	RF	250+	Books for Young Learners	Richard C. Owen
Carlos and his Friends	M	RF	250+	Sunflower	Intercultural Center for Research in Education
Carpenters	M	I	250+	Community Helpers	Red Brick Learning
Case for Jenny Archer, A	M	RF	250+	Conford, Ellen	Random House
Case of the Elevator Duck, The	M	RF	250+	Berends, Polly Berrien	Random House
Cat and Rat	M	TL	250+	Young, Ed	Henry Holt & Co.
Cat Burglar, The	M	RF	250+	Krailing, Tessa	Barron's Educational
Cat for You, A: Caring for Your Cat	M	I	250+	Pet Care	Picture Window Books
Catch Me If You Can!: The Roadrunner	M	I	250+	Chukran, Bobbi A.	Wright Group/McGraw Hill
Catch That Pass!	M	RF	250+	Christopher, Matt	Little, Brown & Co.
Catcher With a Glass Arm	M	RF	250+	Christopher, Matt	Little, Brown & Co.
Catcher's Mask, The	M	RF	250+	Christopher, Matt	Little, Brown & Co.
Catching Sunlight: A Book About Leaves	M	I	250+	Growing Things	Picture Window Books
*Catching the Sun	M	TL	250+	Paul, Michele	Wright Group/McGraw Hill
Caterpillars	M	I	114	Bookshop	Mondo
Cat's Diary	M	F	250+	Sails	Rigby
Cats Have Kittens	M	I	250+	Animals and Their Young	Compass Point Books
Caves	M	I	250+	Discovery World	Rigby
Celebrate Art	M	I	228	Twig	Wright Group/McGraw Hill
Center Court Sting	M	RF	250+	Christopher, Matt	Little, Brown & Co.
Centerfield Ballhawk	M	RF	250+	Christopher, Matt	Little, Brown & Co.
Cesar Chavez	M	B	295	Independent Readers Social Studies	Houghton Mifflin
Chair For My Mother, A	M	RF	250+	Williams, Vera B.	Scholastic
Challenge at Second Base	M	RF	250+	Christopher, Matt	Little, Brown & Co.
Changing Colors	M	I	247	Vocabulary Readers	Houghton Mifflin
Cherries and Cherry Pits	M	RF	250+	Williams, Vera B.	Houghton Mifflin
Cherry Blossoms Everywhere	M	I	370	Independent Readers Social Studies	Houghton Mifflin
Chester the Wizard	M	F	250+	Reading Unlimited	Pearson Learning Group
Chester's Good Idea	M	B	250+	Leveled Readers Language Support	Houghton Mifflin
Chicken	M	I	250+	Life Cycles	Creative Teaching Press
Chicken Soup with Rice	M	F	310	Sendak, Maurice	HarperCollins
Chickens Have Chicks	M	I	250+	Animals and Their Young	Compass Point Books
Children Around the World	M	I	250+	People, Spaces & Places	Rand McNally
Chimpanzees	M	I	250+	The Wild World of Animals	Capstone Press
China Teacup, The	M	F	250+	Voyages	SRA/McGraw Hill
Christa McAuliffe	M	B	250+	Explore Space!	Capstone Press
Christopher Columbus	M	B	250+	First Biographies	Red Brick Learning
Circulatory System, The	M	I	171	Human Body Systems	Red Brick Learning
Circus Mystery, The	M	RF	250+	Schultz, Irene	Wright Group/McGraw Hill
Cities Around the World	M	I	250+	Pair-It Books	Steck-Vaughn
Cities Then, Cities Now	M	I	406	Leveled Readers Social Studies	Houghton Mifflin

* Collection of short stories

TITLE	LEVEL	GENRE	WORD COUNT	AUTHOR / SERIES	PUBLISHER / DISTRIBUTOR
Civil War on Sunday	M	F	250+	Osborne, Mary Pope	Random House
Clara Barton	M	B	320	Independent Readers Social Studies	Houghton Mifflin
Clara Barton: Angel of the Battlefield	M	B	250+	Rosen Real Readers	Rosen Publishing Group
Clay	M	I	250+	First Facts	Capstone Press
Close Call, A	M	RF	250+	Kenna, Anna	Pacific Learning
Cloudy With a Chance of Meatballs	M	F	250+	Barrett, Judi	Atheneum
Clue Club, The	M	RF	660	Leveled Readers	Houghton Mifflin
Clue in the Castle, The	M	RF	250+	Schultz, Irene	Wright Group/McGraw Hill
Clues in the Woods	M	RF	250+	Parrish, Peggy	Bantam
Cobwebs, Elephants, and Stars	M	F	779	Sunshine	Wright Group/McGraw Hill
Color	M	I	250+	Early Connections	Benchmark Education
Color of Light, The	M	I	558	Leveled Readers Science	Houghton Mifflin
Colorful Animals	M	I	250+	Sunshine	Wright Group/McGraw Hill
Comeback Challenge, The	M	RF	250+	Christopher, Matt	Little, Brown & Co.
Commuter	M	I	343	Independent Readers Social Studies	Houghton Mifflin
Connie's Dance	M	RF	361	Windmill Books	Rigby
Construction Workers	M	I	250+	Deedrick, Tami	Red Brick Learning
Continents, The	M	I	250+	Spyglass Books	Compass Point Books
Cookie Count!	M	I	250+	Early Connections	Benchmark Education
Copper Lady, The	M	HF	250+	Ross, Alice & Kent	Carolrhoda Books
Cora at Camp	M	RF	250+	Leveled Readers Language Support	Houghton Mifflin
Corey's Christmas Wish	M	RF	250+	Pony Tails	Skylark
Corn: An American Indian Gift	M	I	690	Pair-It Books	Steck-Vaughn
Count Your Money with the Polk Street School	M	RF	250+	Giff, Patricia Reilly	Bantam
Counterfeit Tackle, The	M	RF	250+	Christopher, Matt	Little, Brown & Co.
Cows Have Calves	M	I	250+	Animals and Their Young	Compass Point Books
Coyote Girl	M	TL	250+	Cambridge Reading	Pearson Learning Group
Crabs	M	I	272	Wonder World	Wright Group/McGraw Hill
CrackerJack Halfback	M	RF	250+	Christopher, Matt	Little, Brown & Co.
Crane Wife, The	M	F	620	Pair-It Books	Steck-Vaughn
Creatures of the Night	M	I	250+	Rigby Focus	Rigby
Creatures of the Night	M	I	250+	Murdock & Ray	Mondo
*Crinkum Crankum	M	F	250+	Pacific Literacy	Pacific Learning
Cupids Don't Flip Hamburgers	M	F	250+	Dadey, Debbie; Jones, Marcia Thornton	Scholastic
Custodians	M	I	250+	Community Helpers	Red Brick Learning
Cyclops Doesn't Roller-Skate	M	F	250+	Dadey, Debbie; Jones, Marcia Thornton	Scholastic
Dad Still Smiles	M	RF	212	Books for Young Learners	Richard C. Owen
Daddy Saved the Day	M	RF	250+	Greetings	Rigby
Daily Meow, The	M	F	250+	Sails	Rigby
Daisy Divine, Dancing Dog	M	F	763	Leveled Readers	Houghton Mifflin
Dancing with the Indians	M	HF	250+	Medearis, Angela	Scholastic
Dark Side of the Creek, The	M	RF	250+	Harlow, Joan Hiatt	Wright Group/McGraw Hill
Day and Night	M	TL	250+	Orbit Chapter Books	Pacific Learning
Day at the Races, A	M	RF	250+	Michaels, Eric	Pearson Learning Group
Day for J. J. and Me, A	M	RF	371	Evangeline Nicholas Collection	Wright Group/McGraw Hill
Day Martin Luther King, Jr., Died, The	M	RF	250+	Story Vines	Wright Group/McGraw Hill
Day of Ahmed's Secret, A	M	RF	250+	Heide, Florence Perry; Gilliland, Judith Heide	Scholastic
Day of the Dragon King	M	F	250+	Osborne, Mary Pope	Random House

* Collection of short stories

TITLE	LEVEL	GENRE	WORD COUNT	AUTHOR / SERIES	PUBLISHER / DISTRIBUTOR
Day the Sky Turned Green, The	M	F	250+	Reeves, Barbara	Pearson Learning Group
Dayton and the Happy Tree	M	RF	1237	Sunshine	Wright Group/McGraw Hill
Dear Grandma	M	I	264	Storyteller Nonfiction	Wright Group/McGraw Hill
Deer Have Fawns	M	I	250+	Animals and Their Young	Compass Point Books
Dentists	M	I	250+	Ready, Dee	Red Brick Learning
Desert Treasure	M	RF	250+	Pair-It Books	Steck-Vaughn
Deserts	M	I	250+	PM Plus Nonfiction	Rigby
Diamond Champs, The	M	RF	250+	Christopher, Matt	Little, Brown & Co.
Diamond of Doom, The	M	RF	250+	Schultz, Irene	Wright Group/McGraw Hill
Dingoes at Dinnertime	M	F	250+	Osborne, Mary Pope	Random House
Dinosaur	M	I	250+	Cambridge Reading	Pearson Learning Group
Dinosaurs	M	I	250+	Gibbons, Gail	Holiday House
Dinosaurs Before Dark	M	F	250+	Osborne, Mary Pope	Random House
Dirt Bike Racer	M	RF	250+	Christopher, Matt	Little, Brown & Co.
Dirt Bike Runaway	M	RF	250+	Christopher, Matt	Little, Brown & Co.
Dirt Bikes	M	I	250+	Blazers	Capstone Press
Dirt: The Scoop on Soil	M	I	250+	Amazing Science	Picture Window Books
Discovering Dinosaurs	M	F	335	Little Books	Sadlier-Oxford
Diving at the Pool	M	RF	519	PM Plus Story Books	Rigby
Diving for Treasure	M	I	284	Books for Young Learners	Richard C. Owen
Do Bears Buzz?: A Book About Animal Sounds	M	I	250+	Animals All Around	Picture Window Books
Do Bees Make Butter?: A Book About Things Animals Make	M	I	250+	Animals All Around	Picture Window Books
Do Cows Eat Cake?: A Book About What Animals Eat	M	I	250+	Animals All Around	Picture Window Books
Do Dogs Make Dessert?: A Book About How Animals Help Humans	M	I	250+	Animals All Around	Picture Window Books
Do Ducks Live in the Desert?: A Book About Where Animals Live	M	I	250+	Animals All Around	Picture Window Books
Do Frogs Have Fur?: A Book About Animal Coats and Coverings	M	I	250+	Animals All Around	Picture Window Books
Do Goldfish Gallop?: A Book About Animal Movement	M	I	250+	Animals All Around	Picture Window Books
Do Parrots Have Pillows?: A Book About Where Animals Sleep	M	I	250+	Animals All Around	Picture Window Books
Do Penguins Have Puppies?: A Book About Animal Babies	M	I	250+	Animals All Around	Picture Window Books
Do Salamanders Spit?: A Book About How Animals Protect Themselves	M	I	250+	Animals All Around	Picture Window Books
Do Squirrels Swarm?: A Book About Animal Groups	M	I	250+	Animals All Around	Picture Window Books
Do Whales Have Wings?: A Book About Animal Bodies	M	I	250+	Animals All Around	Picture Window Books
Doctors	M	I	250+	Ready, Dee	Red Brick Learning
Dog for You, A: Caring for Your Dog	M	I	250+	Pet Care	Picture Window Books
Dog Who Wanted to Be a Tiger!, The	M	F	250+	Little Celebrations	Pearson Learning Group
Dog's Best Friend, A	M	RF	647	Pair-It Books	Steck-Vaughn
Dog's Diary	M	F	250+	Sails	Rigby
Dogs Have Puppies	M	I	250+	Animals and Their Young	Compass Point Books
Dolphins at Daybreak	M	F	250+	Osborne, Mary Pope	Random House
Donkey	M	F	250+	Literacy 2000	Rigby
Donkey Rescue	M	RF	250+	Krailing, Tessa	Barron's Educational
Donkeys	M	I	250+	Voyages	SRA/McGraw Hill
Don't Forget the Bacon	M	RF	174	Hutchins, Pat	Puffin Books

* Collection of short stories

TITLE	LEVEL	GENRE	WORD COUNT	AUTHOR / SERIES	PUBLISHER / DISTRIBUTOR
Double Play at Short	M	RF	250+	Christopher, Matt	Little, Brown & Co.
Double Switch	M	RF	250+	Noonan, Diana	Pacific Learning
Double Trouble	M	TL	250+	Literacy 2000	Rigby
Douglas Florian, Poet and Artist	M	B	484	Leveled Readers	Houghton Mifflin
Dracula Doesn't Drink Lemonade	M	F	250+	Dadey, Debbie; Jones, Marcia Thornton	Scholastic
Dragons Don't Cook Pizza	M	F	250+	Dadey, Debbie; Jones, Marcia Thornton	Scholastic
Dragons Don't Read Books	M	RF	250+	Bookshop	Mondo
Dragsters	M	I	250+	Blazers	Capstone Press
Dream Boat	M	RF	250+	Action Packs	Rigby
Dream Catcher	M	TL	159	Books for Young Learners	Richard C. Owen
Dream Catchers	M	RF	176	Storyteller-Night Crickets	Wright Group/McGraw Hill
Drinking Gourd, The	M	HF	250+	Monjo, F. N.	HarperTrophy
Drought Marker, The	M	F	250+	Literacy 2000	Rigby
Duck in the Gun, The	M	F	250+	Literacy 2000	Rigby
Ducks Crossing	M	RF	250+	Wilson, Trevor	Pacific Learning
Ducks Have Ducklings	M	I	250+	Animals and Their Young	Compass Point Books
Eagles: Birds of Prey	M	I	250+	The Wild World of Animals	Red Brick Learning
Early Inventions	M	I	250+	Rigby Focus	Rigby
Earth Is Mostly Ocean, The	M	I	250+	Rookie Read About Science	Children's Press
Earthquake	M	RF	415	Jellybeans	Rigby
Eat!	M	RF	250+	Kroll, Steven	Hyperion
Edward's Night Light	M	RF	622	Reading Corners	Pearson Learning Group
Eeny, Meeny, Miney Mole	M	F	250+	Yolen, Jane	OSI
Eggs and Baby Birds	M	I	539	Sunshine	Wright Group/McGraw Hill
Elaine and the Flying Frog	M	RF	250+	Chang, Heidi	Scholastic
Elbert's Bad Word	M	RF	250+	Wood, Audrey	Harcourt Trade
Elena's Two Homes	M	HF	250+	Leveled Readers Language Support	Houghton Mifflin
Eliza Pinckney	M	B	325	Independent Readers Social Studies	Houghton Mifflin
Eliza the Hypnotizer	M	RF	250+	Granger, Michele	Scholastic
Ellen Ochoa, Astronaut	M	B	726	Leveled Readers Science	Houghton Mifflin
Elmer and the Dragon	M	F	250+	Gannett, Ruth	Random House
Elves Don't Wear Hard Hats	M	F	250+	Dadey, Debbie; Jones, Marcia Thornton	Scholastic
Emily Arrow Promises to Do Better This Year	M	RF	250+	Giff, Patricia Reilly	Bantam
Emily Eyefinger	M	F	250+	Ball, Duncan	Aladdin
Emma, the Birthday Clown	M	RF	1887	Sunshine	Wright Group/McGraw Hill
Empty Lot, The	M	RF	606	Leveled Readers	Houghton Mifflin
Energy	M	I	250+	First Facts	Capstone Press
Energy: Heat, Light, and Fuel	M	I	250+	Amazing Science	Picture Window Books
Er-Lang and the Suns: A Tale from China	M	TL	250+	Folk Tales	Mondo
Erosion	M	I	250+	Schaefer, Lola	Benchmark Education
Escape from Death Valley	M	I	419	Books for Young Learners	Richard C. Owen
Everglades, The	M	I	250+	Early Connections	Benchmark Education
Everybody Cooks Rice	M	I	250+	Dooley, Norah	Scholastic
Everyday Forces	M	I	250+	Discovery World	Rigby
Explorers: Searching for Adventure	M	I	250+	Pair-It Books	Steck-Vaughn
Expressway Jewels	M	RF	368	Evangeline Nicholas Collection	Wright Group/McGraw Hill
Farmer Boy Days	M	HF	250+	Wilder, Laura Ingalls	HarperTrophy
Farmers	M	I	250+	Community Workers	Compass Point Books
Farmers	M	I	250+	Ready, Dee	Red Brick Learning

* Collection of short stories

TITLE	LEVEL	GENRE	WORD COUNT	AUTHOR / SERIES	PUBLISHER / DISTRIBUTOR
Farmer's Journey, The	M	RF	250+	Little Celebrations	Pearson Learning Group
Father Fights Back: Franklin Delano Roosevelt and Polio	M	B	250+	Twig	Wright Group/McGraw Hill
Festival Foods Around the World	M	I	250+	Stull, Becky	Steck-Vaughn
Fibers Made by People	M	I	442	Sunshine	Wright Group/McGraw Hill
*Fiddle and the Gun, The	M	F	250+	Literacy 2000	Rigby
Fiesta!	M	I	250+	Festivals and Holidays	Children's Press
Fighting Fire With Fire	M	I	250+	Rigby Literacy	Rigby
Fighting Tackle	M	RF	250+	Christopher, Matt	Little, Brown & Co.
Fiji Flood, The	M	F	250+	Schultz, Irene	Wright Group/McGraw Hill
*Finch Family Summer	M	F	250+	Sunshine	Wright Group/McGraw Hill
Fire Fighters	M	I	250+	Ready, Dee	Red Brick Learning
Fire Safety Day	M	RF	749	Leveled Readers	Houghton Mifflin
Fire Trucks	M	I	250+	Transportation	Compass Point Books
Fireflies in the Night	M	I	250+	Hawes, Judy	HarperTrophy
First Hot-Air Balloons, The	M	I	250+	Moore, Philip	Wright Group/McGraw Hill
Fish	M	I	250+	First Facts	Capstone Press
Fish Face	M	RF	250+	Giff, Patricia Reilly	Bantam
Fish for You: Caring for Your Fish	M	I	250+	Pet Care	Picture Window Books
Fishing Off the Wharf	M	RF	274	Pacific Literacy	Pacific Learning
Fishy, Flashy Fourth, The	M	RF	250+	Schultz, Irene	Wright Group/McGraw Hill
*Five True Dog Stories	M	I	250+	Davidson, Margaret	Scholastic
*Five True Horse Stories	M	I	250+	Davidson, Margaret	Scholastic
Flakes and Flurries: A Book About Snow	M	I	250+	Amazing Science	Picture Window Books
Flat Stanley	M	F	250+	Brown, Jeff	HarperTrophy
Flowers for Mrs. Falepau	M	RF	857	Book Bank	Wright Group/McGraw Hill
Fly-away Umbrella, The	M	F	250+	Voyages	SRA/McGraw Hill
Flying Trunk,The	M	TL	644	Tales from Hans Andersen	Wright Group/McGraw Hill
Food Service Workers	M	I	250+	Community Helpers	Red Brick Learning
Football Fugitive	M	RF	250+	Christopher, Matt	Little, Brown & Co.
For the Love of Turtles	M	RF	250+	Greetings	Rigby
Forests	M	I	250+	PM Plus Nonfiction	Rigby
Forests, Grasslands, Deserts	M	I	250+	People, Spaces & Places	Rand McNally
Forgiveness	M	I	250+	Character Education	Red Brick Learning
Forgotten Hiding Place, The	M	RF	250+	Schultz, Irene	Wright Group/McGraw Hill
Fossil Fuels	M	I	250+	Rigby Focus	Rigby
Four Faces in Rock	M	I	300	Early Connections	Benchmark Education
Fox and the Crow, The	M	TL	614	Leveled Readers	Houghton Mifflin
Fox Steals Home, The	M	RF	250+	Christopher, Matt	Little, Brown & Co.
Foxes	M	I	250+	PM Animal Facts: Gold	Rigby
Foxes: Clever Hunters	M	I	250+	The Wild World of Animals	Red Brick Learning
Fractions: Making Fair Shares	M	I	250+	Exploring Math	Capstone Press
Francis Scott Key and "The Star-Spangled Banner"	M	I	250+	Bookshop	Mondo
Frank and Sam's Summer at Aramoana	M	RF	250+	Voyages	SRA/McGraw Hill
Frankenstein Doesn't Plant Petunias	M	F	250+	Dadey, Debbie; Jones, Marcia Thornton	Scholastic
Frankenstein Doesn't Slam Hockey Pucks	M	F	250+	Dadey, Debbie; Jones, Marcia Thornton	Scholastic
Frankenstein Moved on to the 4th Floor	M	RF	250+	Levy, Elizabeth	Harper & Row
Franklin Chang-Diaz in Space	M	B	250	Vocabulary Readers	Houghton Mifflin
Freckle Juice	M	RF	250+	Blume, Judy	Bantam
Frederick Douglass	M	B	250+	First Biographies	Red Brick Learning

* Collection of short stories

TITLE	LEVEL	GENRE	WORD COUNT	AUTHOR / SERIES	PUBLISHER / DISTRIBUTOR
Frederick Douglass: Fights For Freedom	M	B	250+	Davidson, Margaret	Language for Learning Assoc.
Freedom Quilt	M	HF	300	Books for Young Learners	Richard C. Owen
Freeze, Goldilocks!	M	F	250+	Pacific Literacy	Pacific Learning
Freight Trains	M	I	250+	Transportation	Compass Point Books
Frida María: A Story of the Old Southwest	M	RF	250+	Lattimore, Deborah Nourse	Harcourt Trade
Frog, The	M	I	250+	Crewe, Sabrina	Steck-Vaughn
From Apples to Applesauce	M	I	250+	First Facts	Capstone Press
From Cow to Milk Carton	M	I	250+	Miles, Annie	Wright Group/McGraw Hill
From Here to There	M	I	250+	Sails	Rigby
From Maple Trees to Maple Syrup	M	I	250+	First Facts	Capstone Press
From Milk to Ice Cream	M	I	250+	First Facts	Capstone Press
From Oranges to Orange Juice	M	I	250+	First Facts	Capstone Press
From Peanuts to Peanut Butter	M	I	250+	First Facts	Capstone Press
From Seed to Plant	M	I	250+	Gibbons, Gail	Holiday House
From Wheat to Bread	M	I	250+	First Facts	Capstone Press
Fruit Group, The	M	I	96	Pebble Books	Red Brick Learning
Fun with Fingerprints	M	I	250+	Sokoloff, Myka-Lynne	Wright Group/McGraw Hill
Fun With Magnets	M	I	250+	Early Connections	Benchmark Education
Fun With Shadows	M	I	250+	iOpeners	Pearson Learning Group
Funny Old Man and the Funny Old Woman, The	M	F	250+	Bookshop	Mondo
Funny, Funny Clown Face, The	M	F	250+	Sunshine	Wright Group/McGraw Hill
Fuzz and the Glass Eye	M	RF	250+	Literacy Tree	Rigby
Gail Devers: A Runner's Dream	M	B	250+	Pair-It Books	Steck-Vaughn
Game for Jamie, A	M	RF	572	Sunshine	Wright Group/McGraw Hill
Garbage Collectors	M	I	250+	Deedrick, Tami	Red Brick Learning
Gargoyles Don't Drive School Buses	M	F	250+	Dadey, Debbie; Jones, Marcia Thornton	Scholastic
Genies Don't Ride Bicycles	M	F	250+	Dadey, Debbie; Jones, Marcia Thornton	Scholastic
George Washington Carver	M	B	521	Leveled Readers	Houghton Mifflin
George Washington Carver	M	B	250+	Biography	Benchmark Education
George Washington: Farmer, Soldier, President	M	B	250+	Biographies	Picture Window Books
George Washington: Our First President	M	B	200	Rosen Real Readers	Rosen Publishing Group
George Washington's Mother	M	B	250+	Fritz, Jean	Scholastic
Georgia O'Keeffe	M	B	250+	Lowery, Linda	Carolrhoda Books
Gerard Giraffe: Private Investigator	M	F	250+	Foundations	Wright Group/McGraw Hill
Ghost Dog	M	F	250+	Allen, Eleanor	Scholastic
Ghost in Tent 19, The	M	F	250+	O'Connor, Jim	Random House
Ghost School	M	F	250+	Clifford, Eth	Scholastic
Ghost Town at Sundown	M	F	250+	Osborne, Mary Pope	Random House
Ghost Town Treasure	M	RF	250+	Bulla, Clyde Robert	Penguin Group
Ghosts Don't Eat Potato Chips	M	F	250+	Dadey, Debbie; Jones, Marcia Thornton	Scholastic
Ghouls Don't Scoop Ice Cream	M	F	250+	Dadey, Debbie; Jones, Marcia Thornton	Scholastic
Giant Jack's Boots	M	F	420	Book Bank	Wright Group/McGraw Hill
Giant, The	M	F	250+	Voyages	SRA/McGraw Hill
Giant's Cake	M	F	250+	Learning Media	Mondo
Giants Don't Go Snowboarding	M	F	250+	Dadey, Debbie; Jones, Marcia Thornton	Scholastic
Girl Who Loved Meerkats, The	M	F	250+	World Quest Adventures	World Quest Learning
Gladys and Max Love Bob	M	RF	459	Book Bank	Wright Group/McGraw Hill
Glass	M	I	250+	First Facts	Capstone Press

* Collection of short stories

TITLE	LEVEL	GENRE	WORD COUNT	AUTHOR / SERIES	PUBLISHER / DISTRIBUTOR
Goblins Don't Play Video Games	M	RF	250+	Dadey, Debbie; Jones, Marcia Thornton	Scholastic
Going Outside	M	F	118	Voyages	SRA/McGraw Hill
Golden Goose, The	M	TL	250+	Literacy 2000	Rigby
Golden Locket, The	M	F	250+	Greene, Carol	OSI
Good Night	M	RF	753	Leveled Readers	Houghton Mifflin
Good-for-Nothing Dog, The	M	RF	250+	Schultz, Irene	Wright Group/McGraw Hill
Grandfather's Ghost	M	F	250+	Sunshine	Wright Group/McGraw Hill
Great Dinosaur Hunt, The	M	F	250+	Schultz, Irene	Wright Group/McGraw Hill
Great Houdini, The: World Famous Magician and Escape Artist	M	B	250+	Kulling, Monica	Random House
Great Ice Battle, The	M	F	250+	Abbott, Tony	Scholastic
Great Quarterback Switch, The	M	RF	250+	Christopher, Matt	Little, Brown & Co.
Great Riddle Mystery, The	M	RF	250+	MacClean, James R.	Pearson Learning Group
Greatest Binnie in the World, The	M	RF	709	Sunshine	Wright Group/McGraw Hill
Greedy Cat and the Birthday Cake	M	F	250+	Cowley, Joy	Pacific Learning
Greedy Crows, The	M	TL	250+	Story Vines	Wright Group/McGraw Hill
Greeks, The	M	I	250+	Footsteps in Time	Children's Press
Green and Growing: A Book About Plants	M	I	250+	Growing Things	Picture Window Books
Gremlins Don't Chew Bubble Gum	M	F	250+	Dadey, Debbie; Jones, Marcia Thornton	Scholastic
Growing Tomatoes	M	I	626	Leveled Readers Science	Houghton Mifflin
Guinea Pig for You, A: Caring for Your Guinea Pig	M	I	250+	Pet Care	Picture Window Books
Gusts and Gales: A Book About Wind	M	I	250+	Amazing Science	Picture Window Books
Hand Tools	M	I	367	Wonder World	Wright Group/McGraw Hill
Happy New Year!	M	I	114	Independent Readers Social Studies	Houghton Mifflin
Harbour, The	M	I	250+	Cambridge Reading	Pearson Learning Group
Hard Drive to Short	M	RF	250+	Christopher, Matt	Little, Brown & Co.
Harriet Tubman: A Lesson in Bravery	M	B	250+	Rosen Real Readers	Rosen Publishing Group
Haunted Halloween, The	M	F	250+	Schultz, Irene	Wright Group/McGraw Hill
Henry's Choice	M	RF	527	Reading Unlimited	Pearson Learning Group
Hercules Doesn't Pull Teeth	M	F	250+	Dadey, Debbie; Jones, Marcia Thornton	Scholastic
Hero in the Mirror, The	M	RF	250+	Rigby Literacy	Rigby
Hiawatha, American Leader	M	B	535	Leveled Readers Social Studies	Houghton Mifflin
Hidden Hand, The	M	RF	250+	Schultz, Irene	Wright Group/McGraw Hill
Hiders, The	M	I	250+	Sails	Rigby
Hilary and the Lions	M	F	250+	Desaix, Frank	Farrar, Straus and Giroux
Hippo from Another Planet	M	F	250+	Little Celebrations	Pearson Learning Group
History Walk	M	RF	250+	Pacific Literacy	Pacific Learning
Hit-Away Kid, The	M	RF	250+	Christopher, Matt	Little, Brown & Co.
Hocus Pocus	M	I	250+	Wildcats	Wright Group/McGraw Hill
Home	M	RF	250+	Voyages	SRA/McGraw Hill
Homes Are for Living	M	I	417	Cumpiano, Ina	Hampton-Brown
Honey Bees	M	I	250+	Kahkonen, Sharon	Steck-Vaughn
Hoopstars: Go to the Hoop!	M	RF	250+	Hughes, Dean	Random House
*Horrakapotchkin	M	F	250+	Pacific Literacy	Pacific Learning
Horse	M	I	250+	Life Cycles	Creative Teaching Press
Horse Called Sky, A	M	RF	250+	Leveled Readers Language Support	Houghton Mifflin
Horses Have Foals	M	I	250+	Animals and Their Young	Compass Point Books
Hour of the Olympics	M	F	250+	Osborne, Mary Pope	Random House

TITLE	LEVEL	GENRE	WORD COUNT	AUTHOR / SERIES	PUBLISHER / DISTRIBUTOR
House for Sergin, A	M	RF	250+	Greetings	Rigby
House of Mirrors, The	M	F	250+	Weaver, Betty-May	Wright Group/McGraw Hill
House of the Horrible Ghosts	M	F	250+	Hayes, Geoffrey	Random House
Houses	M	I	279	Wonder World	Wright Group/McGraw Hill
How a House is Built	M	I	250+	Gibbons, Gail	Scholastic
How a Volcano is Formed	M	I	135	Wonder World	Wright Group/McGraw Hill
How Bullfrog Found His Sound	M	F	250+	Michaels, Eric	Pearson Learning Group
How Did This City Grow?	M	I	250+	Schaefer, Lola M.	Benchmark Education
How Do You Measure a Dinosaur?	M	F	257	Pacific Literacy	Pacific Learning
How Flamingos Came to Have Red Legs: A South American Folk Tale	M	TL	250+	Jensen, Ned	Wright Group/McGraw Hill
How Flexible Are You?	M	I	250+	Marks, Ashley	Wright Group/McGraw Hill
How I Met Archie	M	RF	250+	Kenna, Anna	Pacific Learning
How Leaves Change Color	M	I	250+	Rosen Real Readers	Rosen Publishing Group
How Long Is a Foot?	M	I	250+	Twig	Wright Group/McGraw Hill
How News Travels	M	I	250+	PM Plus Nonfiction	Rigby
How the Giraffe Became a Giraffe	M	TL	648	Sunshine	Wright Group/McGraw Hill
How To Make a Kite	M	I	250+	Reeder, Paul	Wright Group/McGraw Hill
How to Stay Safe at Home and On-Line	M	I	250+	Rosen Real Readers	Rosen Publishing Group
How Wisdom Came to the World: An Ashanti Tale	M	TL	250+	Khan, Benjamin	Houghton Mifflin
Howie Merton and the Magic Dust	M	F	250+	Reeves, Faye Couch	Random House
Howling at the Hauntly's	M	RF	250+	Dadey, Debbie; Jones, Marcia Thornton	Scholastic
Hue Boy	M	RF	250+	Mitchell, Rita Phillips	Penguin Group
Humphrey	M	RF	250+	Literacy Tree	Rigby
Hunt for Pirate Gold, The	M	F	250+	Schultz, Irene	Wright Group/McGraw Hill
Hunting Sharks	M	I	250+	Pull Ahead Books	Lerner Publishing
Hurdles and Jumps	M	I	250+	Reeder, Tracey	Wright Group/McGraw Hill
Hurricanes and Storms	M	I	250+	Rosen Real Readers	Rosen Publishing Group
I Can't Said the Ant	M	F	250+	Cameron, Polly	Scholastic
I Hate Camping	M	RF	250+	Petersen, P. J.	Penguin Group
I Hate Company	M	RF	250+	Petersen, P. J.	Penguin Group
I Love the Beach	M	I	250+	Literacy 2000	Rigby
I Need Glasses: My Visit to the Optometrist	M	RF	250+	Bookshop	Mondo
I Said to Sam	M	F	250+	Molnar, Gwen	Scholastic
I See Animals Hiding	M	I	250+	Arnosky, Jim	Scholastic
I. M. Pei	M	B	250+	Biography	Benchmark Education
*Ice Dove and Other Stories, The	M	RF	250+	deAnda, Diane	Arte Publico
Ice Magic	M	RF	250+	Christopher, Matt	Little, Brown & Co.
Iguanodon	M	I	250+	Discovering Dinosaurs	Capstone Press
I'm a Chef	M	I	250+	Literacy 2000	Rigby
I'm No One Else But Me	M	RF	1010	Book Bank	Wright Group/McGraw Hill
I'm So Hungry and Other Plays	M	F	250+	Orbit Chapter Books	Pacific Learning
In a Pickle	M	RF	250+	SupaDoopers	Sundance
In a Tree	M	I	250+	Look Once Look Again	Creative Teaching Press
In Aunt Lucy's Kitchen	M	RF	250+	Rylant, Cynthia	Aladdin
In Danger	M	I	250+	Home Connection Collection	Rigby
In the Clouds	M	RF	250+	Literacy 2000	Rigby
In the Desert	M	I	250+	Look Once Look Again	Creative Teaching Press
In the Dinosaur's Paw	M	RF	250+	Giff, Patricia Reilly	Bantam
In the Garden	M	I	250+	Look Once Look Again	Creative Teaching Press
In the Meadow	M	I	250+	Look Once Look Again	Creative Teaching Press
In the Park	M	I	250+	Look Once Look Again	Creative Teaching Press

* Collection of short stories

TITLE	LEVEL	GENRE	WORD COUNT	AUTHOR / SERIES	PUBLISHER / DISTRIBUTOR
In the Treetops	M	I	250+	Woolley, M.; Pigdon, K.	Mondo
Incredible Insects	M	I	250+	Sunshine	Wright Group/McGraw Hill
Insects	M	I	250+	First Facts	Capstone Press
Inside a Rain Forest	M	I	353	Pair-It Books	Steck-Vaughn
Inventor's Diary, The	M	RF	271	Pacific Literacy	Pacific Learning
Inventors: Making Things Better	M	I	250+	Pair-It Books	Steck-Vaughn
Invisible Dog, The	M	F	250+	King-Smith, Dick	Alfred A. Knopf
Invisible in the Third Grade	M	RF	250+	Cuyler, Margery	Scholastic
Irniq and the Eagles	M	TL	250+	Orbit Chapter Books	Pacific Learning
Island Baby	M	RF	250+	Keller, Holly	Scholastic
Island of the Skog, The	M	F	250+	Kellogg, Steven	Dial Books
It's About Time	M	I	481	Storyteller Nonfiction	Wright Group/McGraw Hill
Jaime Escalante, A Great Teacher	M	B	273	Independent Readers Social Studies	Houghton Mifflin
Jake Was a Pirate	M	F	250+	Voyages	SRA/McGraw Hill
Jane Goodall: Living With Chimpanzees	M	I	250+	Rigby Literacy	Rigby
Japan	M	I	488	Pair-It Books	Steck-Vaughn
Jelly Beans	M	I	250+	Stadler, Charlotte	Benchmark Education
Jenny Archer to the Rescue	M	RF	250+	Conford, Ellen	Little, Brown & Co.
Jenny Archer, Author	M	RF	250+	Conford, Ellen	Little, Brown & Co.
Jigsaw Jones Mystery: The Case of the Christmas Snowman	M	RF	250+	Ruller, James	Scholastic
Jilly the Kid	M	RF	250+	Krailing, Tessa	Barron's Educational
Jo Jo's Flying Side Kick	M	RF	250+	Soar To Success	Houghton Mifflin
Job for Jenny Archer, A	M	RF	250+	Conford, Ellen	Random House
John Glenn	M	B	250+	Explore Space!	Capstone Press
John James Audubon	M	B	250+	Biography	Benchmark Education
John James Audubon, American Painter	M	B	538	Leveled Readers Social Studies	Houghton Mifflin
Johnny Appleseed	M	B	250+	First Biographies	Red Brick Learning
Johnny Long Legs	M	RF	250+	Christopher, Matt	Little, Brown & Co.
Journey to a New Land	M	HF	250+	Rigby Literacy	Rigby
Joy's Great Idea	M	RF	250+	Ellis, Veronica Freeman	Houghton Mifflin
Julie Rescues Big Mack	M	RF	250+	Voyages	SRA/McGraw Hill
Jump Ball!: You Can Play Basketball	M	I	250+	Game Day	Picture Window Books
Jumping Into Nothing	M	RF	250+	Willner-Pardo, Gina	Houghton Mifflin
Jungle Sun, The	M	F	250+	Sails	Rigby
Junie B. Jones and a Little Monkey Business	M	RF	250+	Park, Barbara	Random House
Junie B. Jones and Her Big Fat Mouth	M	RF	250+	Park, Barbara	Random House
Junie B. Jones and Some Sneaky Peeky Spying	M	RF	250+	Park, Barbara	Random House
Junie B. Jones and that Meanie Jim's Birthday	M	RF	250+	Park, Barbara	Random House
Junie B. Jones and the Mushy Gushy Valentine	M	RF	250+	Park, Barbara	Random House
Junie B. Jones and the Stupid Smelly Bus	M	RF	250+	Park, Barbara	Random House
Junie B. Jones and the Yucky Blucky Fruitcake	M	RF	250+	Park, Barbara	Random House
Junie B. Jones Has a Monster Under Her Bed	M	RF	250+	Park, Barbara	Random House
Junie B. Jones Has a Peep in Her Pocket	M	RF	250+	Park, Barbara	Random House
Junie B. Jones is (almost) a Flower Girl	M	RF	250+	Park, Barbara	Random House
Junie B. Jones Is a Beauty Shop Guy	M	RF	250+	Park, Barbara	Random House
Junie B. Jones Is a Party Animal	M	RF	250+	Park, Barbara	Random House
Junie B. Jones Is Not a Crook	M	RF	250+	Park, Barbara	Random House
Junie B. Jones Loves Handsome Warren	M	RF	250+	Park, Barbara	Random House
Junie B. Jones Smells Something Fishy	M	RF	250+	Park, Barbara	Random House
Junior Gymnasts: Katie's Big Move	M	RF	250+	Slater, Teddy	Scholastic
Kangaroo, The	M	I	250+	Crewe, Sabrina	Steck-Vaughn
Kangaroos Have Joeys	M	I	250+	Animals and Their Young	Compass Point Books

* Collection of short stories

TITLE	LEVEL	GENRE	WORD COUNT	AUTHOR / SERIES	PUBLISHER / DISTRIBUTOR
Kangaroos in the Land Down Under	M	I	250+	Rosen Real Readers	Rosen Publishing Group
Kantjil and Tiger	M	TL	250+	Story Vines	Wright Group/McGraw Hill
Kate Shelley and the Midnight Express	M	B	250+	Wetterer, Margaret	Carolrhoda Books
Katydid's Life, A	M	I	250+	Twig	Wright Group/McGraw Hill
Keep Ms. Sugarman in the Fourth Grade	M	RF	250+	Levy, Elizabeth	HarperTrophy
Kid Who Only Hit Homers, The	M	RF	250+	Christopher, Matt	Little, Brown & Co.
Kids Can Cook	M	I	250+	Literacy 2000	Rigby
Kids in Ms. Colman's Class: Author Day	M	RF	250+	Martin, Ann M.	Scholastic
King Arthur	M	F	250+	Brown, Marc	Little, Brown & Co.
King Who Had Dirty Feet, The: A Play	M	TL	250+	Rigby Literacy	Rigby
Kitchen Science	M	I	250+	Windows on Literacy	National Geographic
Knight at Dawn, The	M	F	250+	Osborne, Mary Pope	Random House
Knights Don't Teach Piano	M	F	250+	Dadey, Debbie; Jones, Marcia Thornton	Scholastic
Know Where to Go	M	I	250+	Pacific Literacy	Pacific Learning
Korky Paul: Biography of an Illustrator	M	B	250+	Discovery World	Rigby
Laura and Mr. Edwards	M	HF	250+	Wilder, Laura Ingalls	HarperTrophy
Laura and Nellie	M	HF	250+	Wilder, Laura Ingalls	HarperTrophy
Laura's Ma	M	HF	250+	Wilder, Laura Ingalls	HarperTrophy
Laura's Pa	M	HF	250+	Wilder, Laura Ingalls	HarperTrophy
Lazy Jackal, The	M	F	561	Sunshine	Wright Group/McGraw Hill
Lazy Lions, Lucky Lambs	M	RF	250+	Giff, Patricia Reilly	Bantam
Leaf Raker, The	M	RF	250+	Voyages	SRA/McGraw Hill
Leaping Lizards	M	I	250+	Stadler, Charlotte	Benchmark Education
Lemurs	M	I	250+	The Wild World of Animals	Capstone Press
Lentil	M	RF	250+	McCloskey, Robert	Scholastic
Leprechauns Don't Play Basketball	M	F	250+	Dadey, Debbie; Jones, Marcia Thornton	Scholastic
Let's Get Moving	M	I	250+	Literacy 2000	Rigby
Let's Go Fishing	M	RF	250+	Voyages	SRA/McGraw Hill
Let's Go, Philadelphia!	M	RF	250+	Giff, Patricia Reilly	Bantam
Let's Graph	M	I	239	Yellow Umbrella Books	Capstone Press
Letting Swift River Go	M	HF	250+	Yolen, Jane	Little, Brown & Co.
Librarians	M	I	250+	Ready, Dee	Red Brick Learning
Life in the Arctic	M	I	250+	Rosen Real Readers	Rosen Publishing Group
Life in the Desert	M	I	250+	Pair-It Books	Steck-Vaughn
Life in the Ocean	M	I	250+	Windows on Literacy	National Geographic
Life of Abraham Lincoln, The	M	B	250+	Rosen Real Readers	Rosen Publishing Group
Lifeguards	M	I	250+	Community Helpers	Red Brick Learning
Light: Shadows, Mirrors, and Rainbows	M	I	250+	Amazing Science	Picture Window Books
Lighthouse Mermaid, The	M	F	250+	Karr, Kathleen	Hyperion
Lions at Lunchtime	M	F	250+	Osborne, Mary Pope	Random House
Listening in Bed	M	RF	116	Book Bank	Wright Group/McGraw Hill
Little Firefighter, The	M	RF	867	Sunshine	Wright Group/McGraw Hill
Little Hawk's New Name	M	HF	250+	Bolognese, Don	Scholastic
Little House Farm Days	M	HF	250+	Wilder, Laura Ingalls	HarperTrophy
Little House Friends	M	HF	250+	Wilder, Laura Ingalls	HarperTrophy
Little Lefty	M	RF	250+	Christopher, Matt	Little, Brown & Co.
Little Old Lady Who Danced on the Moon, The	M	RF	711	Sunshine	Wright Group/McGraw Hill
Little Painter of Sabana Grande, The	M	RF	250+	Soar To Success	Houghton Mifflin
Little Shopping, A	M	RF	250+	Rylant, Cynthia	Aladdin
Little Swan	M	RF	250+	Geras, Adele	Random House
Little Tin Soldier, The	M	TL	766	Tales from Hans Andersen	Wright Group/McGraw Hill
Little Whale, The	M	F	1057	Sunshine	Wright Group/McGraw Hill

* Collection of short stories

TITLE	LEVEL	GENRE	WORD COUNT	AUTHOR / SERIES	PUBLISHER / DISTRIBUTOR
Little Women	M	HF	250+	Bullseye	Random House
Little, Little Man, The	M	F	741	Book Bank	Wright Group/McGraw Hill
Littles and the Great Halloween Scare, The	M	F	250+	Peterson, John	Scholastic
Littles and the Lost Children, The	M	F	250+	Peterson, John	Scholastic
Littles and the Terrible Tiny Kid, The	M	F	250+	Peterson, John	Scholastic
Littles and the Trash Tinies, The	M	F	250+	Peterson, John	Scholastic
Littles Give a Party, The	M	F	250+	Peterson, John	Scholastic
Littles Go Exploring, The	M	F	250+	Peterson, John	Scholastic
Littles Go to School, The	M	F	250+	Peterson, John	Scholastic
Littles Have a Wedding, The	M	F	250+	Peterson, John	Scholastic
Littles Take a Trip, The	M	F	250+	Peterson, John	Scholastic
Littles to the Rescue, The	M	F	250+	Peterson, John	Scholastic
Littles, The	M	F	250+	Peterson, John	Scholastic
Lizards and Salamanders	M	I	250+	Reading Unlimited	Pearson Learning Group
Lizard's Song	M	TL	250+	Voyages	SRA/McGraw Hill
Locked in the Library!	M	F	250+	Brown, Marc	Little, Brown & Co.
Log Garfish	M	TL	114	Books for Young Learners	Richard C. Owen
Long Grass of Tumbledown Road	M	F	283	Read Alongs	Rigby
Long Shot for Paul	M	RF	250+	Christopher, Matt	Little, Brown & Co.
Long, Long Ago	M	I	250+	Literacy 2000	Rigby
Long-Lost Friends, The	M	RF	250+	Schultz, Irene	Wright Group/McGraw Hill
Look at Australia, A	M	I	250+	Pebble Books	Red Brick Learning
Look at Canada, A	M	I	250+	Pebble Books	Red Brick Learning
Look at China, A	M	I	178	Pebble Books	Capstone Press
Look at Dogs, A	M	I	551	Pair-It Books	Steck-Vaughn
Look at France, A	M	I	250+	Pebble Books	Red Brick Learning
Look at Japan, A	M	I	250+	Pebble Books	Red Brick Learning
Look at Kenya, A	M	I	161	Pebble Books	Capstone Press
Look at Lady Liberty, A	M	B	250+	Rosen Real Readers	Rosen Publishing Group
Look at Mexico, A	M	I	159	Pebble Books	Capstone Press
Look at Russia, A	M	I	161	Pebble Books	Capstone Press
Look at Snakes, A	M	I	250+	Pair-It Books	Steck-Vaughn
Look at Spiders, A	M	I	785	Pair-It-Books	Steck-Vaughn
Look What I Made!	M	I	250+	Literacy 2000	Rigby
Look Who's Playing First Base	M	RF	250+	Christopher, Matt	Little, Brown & Co.
Look, Listen, Taste, Touch, and Smell: Learning About Your Five Senses	M	I	250+	Amazing Body	Picture Window Books
Looking at Low Tide	M	RF	642	Leveled Readers	Houghton Mifflin
Looking for Dad	M	RF	250+	SupaDoopers	Sundance
Lord Mount Dragon, The	M	TL	250+	Cambridge Reading	Pearson Learning Group
Lost and Found Game, The	M	RF	250+	Nayer, Judy	Pearson Learning Group
Lost Children, The	M	TL	250+	Goble, Paul	Aladdin
Lost in Space	M	SF	250+	Pacific Literacy	Pacific Learning
Lost Lake, The	M	RF	250+	Soar To Success	Houghton Mifflin
Lucky Baseball Bat, The	M	RF	250+	Christopher, Matt	Little, Brown & Co.
Lucky Last Luke	M	RF	250+	Clark, Margaret	Sundance
Lucy Takes A Holiday	M	F	250+	Bookshop	Mondo
Lumberjacks	M	I	255	Vocabulary Readers	Houghton Mifflin
Lunch Room, The	M	F	259	Leveled Readers	Houghton Mifflin
Mad Scientist, The	M	F	250+	Schultz, Irene	Wright Group/McGraw Hill
Mae Jemison	M	B	250+	Explore Space!	Capstone Press
Magic Ride, The	M	F	170	Book Bank	Wright Group/McGraw Hill
Magnets: Pulling Together, Pushing Apart	M	I	250+	Amazing Science	Picture Window Books
Mail Carriers	M	I	250+	Ready, Dee	Red Brick Learning

TITLE	LEVEL	GENRE	WORD COUNT	AUTHOR / SERIES	PUBLISHER / DISTRIBUTOR
Make a Cloud, Measure the Wind	M	I	250+	Reimer, Luther	Wright Group/McGraw Hill
Making a Weather Station	M	I	250+	How-To Series	Benchmark Education
Making Friends on Beacon Street	M	RF	250+	Literacy 2000	Rigby
Making Lily Laugh!	M	RF	250+	Dreyer, Ellen	Pearson Learning Group
Making Mount Rushmore	M	I	250+	Twig	Wright Group/McGraw Hill
Mall Mystery, The	M	F	250+	Schultz, Irene	Wright Group/McGraw Hill
Mammals	M	I	134	First Facts	Capstone Press
Man Out at First	M	RF	250+	Christopher, Matt	Little, Brown & Co.
Manatees and Dugongs	M	I	250+	Cole, Sally	Wright Group/McGraw Hill
Map Mysteries	M	I	250+	Home Connection Collection	Rigby
Mapping North America	M	I	148	Windows on Literacy	National Geographic
Marigolds for Dona Remedios	M	RF	250+	Story Vines	Wright Group/McGraw Hill
Mario Mixwell	M	B	250+	Reimer, Luther	Wright Group/McGraw Hill
Marion Anderson, American Hero	M	B	645	Leveled Readers Social Studies	Houghton Mifflin
Martians Don't Take Temperatures	M	F	250+	Dadey, Debbie; Jones, Marcia Thornton	Scholastic
Martin Luther King, Jr.: Preacher, Freedom Fighter, Peacemaker	M	B	250+	Biographies	Picture Window Books
Martin's Mighty Hit	M	RF	390	Windmill Books	Rigby
Marvelous Treasure, The	M	RF	481	Sunshine	Wright Group/McGraw Hill
Marvin and the Mean Words	M	RF	250+	Kline, Suzy	PaperStar
Marvin Redpost (Class President)	M	RF	250+	Sachar, Louis	Random House
Marvin Redpost, Super Fast, Out of Control!	M	RF	250+	Sachar, Louis	Random House
Marvin Redpost: A Flying Birthday Cake?	M	RF	250+	Sachar, Louis	Random House
Marvin Redpost: Alone in His Teacher's House	M	RF	250+	Sachar, Louis	Random House
Marvin Redpost: Is He a Girl?	M	RF	250+	Sachar, Louis	Random House
Marvin Redpost: Kidnapped at Birth?	M	RF	250+	Sachar, Louis	Random House
Marvin Redpost: Why Pick on Me?	M	RF	250+	Sachar, Louis	Random House
Mary Marony and the Chocolate Surprise	M	RF	250+	Kline, Suzy	Bantam
Mary Marony and the Snake	M	RF	250+	Kline, Suzy	Bantam
Mary Marony Hides Out	M	RF	250+	Kline, Suzy	Bantam
Mary Marony, Mummy Girl	M	RF	250+	Kline, Suzy	Bantam
Masks	M	I	250+	Literacy 2000	Rigby
Math Chat: A Glossary of Terms	M	I	250+	Twig	Wright Group/McGraw Hill
Maui and the Sun	M	TL	359	Pacific Literacy	Pacific Learning
Maybe Yes, Maybe No, Maybe Maybe	M	RF	250+	Patron, Susan	Bantam
Measuring Tools	M	I	250+	Daronco, Mickey; Presti, Lori	Benchmark Education
Meet the Villarreals	M	B	387	Kratky, Lada Josefa	Hampton-Brown
Mermaids Don't Run Track	M	F	250+	Dadey, Debbie; Jones, Marcia Thornton	Scholastic
Meteorologists	M	I	250+	Community Helpers	Red Brick Learning
Mexico City Is Muy Grande	M	I	250+	Twig	Wright Group/McGraw Hill
Michael Jordan	M	B	250+	Edwards, Nick	Scholastic
Mickey Maloney's Mail	M	RF	250+	Sails	Rigby
Midnight on the Moon	M	F	250+	Osborne, Mary Pope	Random House
Midnight Pig, The	M	F	250+	Action Packs	Rigby
Miles on the Mississippi	M	I	337	Independent Readers Social Studies	Houghton Mifflin
Milo's Great Invention	M	RF	250+	Pair-It Books	Steck-Vaughn
Minerva's Dream	M	F	250+	Pair-It Books	Steck-Vaughn
Miracle at the Plate	M	RF	250+	Christopher, Matt	Little, Brown & Co.
Mischief	M	RF	250+	Pacific Literacy	Pacific Learning
Miss Rumphius	M	RF	250+	Cooney, Barbara	Penguin Group
Missing Will, The	M	RF	250+	Schultz, Irene	Wright Group/McGraw Hill

* Collection of short stories

TITLE	LEVEL	GENRE	WORD COUNT	AUTHOR / SERIES	PUBLISHER / DISTRIBUTOR
Mitten, The	M	TL	250+	Brett, Jan	Scholastic
Molly's Pilgrim	M	RF	250+	Cohen, Barbara	Bantam
Momotaro	M	F	631	Sunshine	Wright Group/McGraw Hill
Money	M	I	250+	Early Connections	Benchmark Education
Money	M	I	250+	Spyglass Books	Compass Point Books
Monica and the Summer Party	M	RF	250+	Sunflower	Intercultural Center for Research in Education
Monica goes to the Zoo	M	RF	250+	Sunflower	Intercultural Center for Research in Education
Monster for Hire	M	F	250+	Wilson, Trevor	Mondo
Monster Rabbit Runs Amuck!	M	RF	250+	Giff, Patricia Reilly	Bantam
Monster Trucks	M	I	250+	Blazers	Capstone Press
Monsters Don't Scuba Dive	M	F	250+	Dadey, Debbie; Jones, Marcia Thornton	Scholastic
Moon and the Mirror, The	M	TL	250+	Literacy 2000	Rigby
Moonhorse	M	F	250+	Osborne, Mary Pope	Alfred A. Knopf
*More! More! More!	M	TL	250+	Story Box	Wright Group/McGraw Hill
Most Beautiful Child, The	M	TL	250+	Cambridge Reading	Pearson Learning Group
Most Terrible Creature in the World, The	M	F	340	Pacific Literacy	Pacific Learning
Mother Teresa	M	B	250+	First Biographies	Red Brick Learning
Motorcross Freestyle	M	I	250+	Blazers	Capstone Press
Mountains of Fire	M	I	153	Windows on Literacy	National Geographic
Mountains, Hills, and Cliffs	M	I	250+	PM Plus Nonfiction	Rigby
Mouse Manual	M	F	250+	Sails	Rigby
Mouse Party!	M	F	250+	Little Celebrations	Pearson Learning Group
Moving Things	M	I	250+	Sunshine	Wright Group/McGraw Hill
Mr. Beep	M	F	250+	Read Alongs	Rigby
Mr. McGillicuddy's Clocks	M	RF	250+	Voyages	SRA/McGraw Hill
Mrs. Always Goes Shopping	M	RF	423	Sunshine	Wright Group/McGraw Hill
Mrs. Bubble's Baby	M	F	250+	Pacific Literacy	Pacific Learning
Mrs. Jeepers in Outer Space	M	RF	250+	Dadey, Debbie; Jones, Marcia Thornton	Scholastic
Mud Pony, The	M	TL	250+	Reading Rainbow	Scholastic
Muddledy Fuddledy Mixed-Up Day, The	M	F	250+	Redhead, Janet Slater	Steck-Vaughn
Muffy's Secret Admirer	M	RF	250+	Brown, Marc	Little, Brown & Co.
Mummies	M	I	250+	All Aboard Reading	Grosset & Dunlap
Mummies Don't Coach Softball	M	F	250+	Dadey, Debbie; Jones, Marcia Thornton	Scholastic
Mummies in the Morning	M	F	250+	Osborne, Mary Pope	Random House
Mutt and the Lifeguards	M	RF	754	Sunshine	Wright Group/McGraw Hill
My Body	M	I	250+	Schaefer, Lola M.	Benchmark Education
My Brother, the Knight	M	RF	250+	Social Studies Connects	The Kane Press
My First Book About the Internet	M	I	250+	Cromwell, Sharon	Troll Associates
My Prairie Summer	M	RF	250+	Pair-It Books	Steck-Vaughn
My Town at Work	M	I	250+	Windows on Literacy	National Geographic
My Weird Mother	M	RF	250+	SupaDoopers	Sundance
My Wonderful Aunt, Story Five	M	F	493	Sunshine	Wright Group/McGraw Hill
My Wonderful Aunt, Story Four	M	F	436	Sunshine	Wright Group/McGraw Hill
My Wonderful Aunt, Story One	M	F	193	Sunshine	Wright Group/McGraw Hill
My Wonderful Aunt, Story Six	M	F	432	Sunshine	Wright Group/McGraw Hill
My Wonderful Aunt, Story Three	M	F	392	Sunshine	Wright Group/McGraw Hill
My Wonderful Aunt, Story Two	M	F	199	Sunshine	Wright Group/McGraw Hill
Mysterious I.O.U., The	M	RF	250+	Schultz, Irene	Wright Group/McGraw Hill
Mystery in the Night Woods	M	F	250+	Peterson, John	Scholastic

* Collection of short stories

TITLE	LEVEL	GENRE	WORD COUNT	AUTHOR / SERIES	PUBLISHER / DISTRIBUTOR
Mystery of Mrs. Kim, The	M	RF	250+	Rigby Literacy	Rigby
Mystery of the Dark Old House, The	M	F	250+	Schultz, Irene	Wright Group/McGraw Hill
Mystery of the Missing Dog, The	M	RF	250+	Schultz, Irene	Wright Group/McGraw Hill
Mystery of the Missing Malamute, The	M	RF	250+	Kleinhenz, Sydnie Meltzer	Wright Group/McGraw Hill
Mystery of the Stolen Bike, The	M	F	250+	Brown, Marc	Little, Brown & Co.
Mystery of the Talking Tail, The	M	F	250+	SupaDoopers	Sundance
Mystery of the Three Keys, The	M	RF	250+	Schultz, Irene	Wright Group/McGraw Hill
Nadia Comaneci	M	B	250+	Cole, Sally	Wright Group/McGraw Hill
Nana's in the Plum Tree	M	RF	250+	Pacific Literacy	Pacific Learning
Nana's Tomatoes	M	RF	587	Leveled Readers Science	Houghton Mifflin
Nannies for Hire	M	RF	250+	Hest, Amy	William Morrow
Nature's Celebration	M	I	250+	Literacy 2000	Rigby
Nature's Fireworks: A Book About Lightning	M	I	250+	Amazing Science	Picture Window Books
Neil Armstrong	M	B	250+	Explore Space!	Capstone Press
Nelson is Kidnapped	M	RF	250+	PM Story Books-Silver	Rigby
Nervous System, The	M	I	213	Human Body Systems	Red Brick Learning
Nests	M	I	222	Vocabulary Readers	Houghton Mifflin
New Land, The: A First Year on the Prairie	M	I	250+	Reynolds, Marilynn	Orca Book Publishers
Newspaper Carriers	M	I	250+	Community Helpers	Red Brick Learning
Nibble, Nibble, Jenny Archer	M	RF	250+	Conford, Ellen	Little, Brown & Co.
Nice Hit!: You Can Play Baseball	M	I	250+	Game Day	Picture Window Books
Night of the Ninjas	M	F	250+	Osborne, Mary Pope	Random House
Night Out, The	M	RF	250+	Sails	Rigby
Night Owls, The	M	I	368	Wonder World	Wright Group/McGraw Hill
Nightmare	M	RF	250+	Action Packs	Rigby
*Nine True Dolphin Stories	M	I	250+	Davidson, Margaret	Scholastic
Ninjas Don't Bake Pumpkin Pies	M	RF	250+	Dadey, Debbie; Jones, Marcia Thornton	Scholastic
No Arm in Left Field	M	RF	250+	Christopher, Matt	Little, Brown & Co.
No Trouble at All!	M	RF	250+	Literacy Tree	Rigby
Nobody Owns the Sky: The Story of "Brave Bessie" Coleman	M	B	250+	Lindbergh, Reeve	Candlewick Press
Now You See It, Now You Don't	M	I	204	Independent Readers Science	Houghton Mifflin
Nurses	M	I	250+	Community Workers	Compass Point Books
Nurses	M	I	250+	Ready, Dee	Red Brick Learning
Ocean Tides	M	I	250+	Rosen Real Readers	Rosen Publishing Group
Oceans, Seas, and Coasts	M	I	250+	PM Plus Nonfiction	Rigby
Old Bones	M	RF	848	Sunshine	Wright Group/McGraw Hill
Old Friends	M	RF	345	Literacy 2000	Rigby
Old Man and the Bear, The	M	RF	250+	Hanel, Wolfram	North-South Books
Old Red Rocking Chair, The	M	RF	250+	Root, Phyllis	Scholastic
Old Tom and the Rogue	M	HF	250+	Wilson, Trevor	Pearson Learning Group
Old Woman Who Lived in a Vinegar Bottle	M	TL	1161	Douglas, Ann	Mondo
On and Off the Road	M	I	250+	Wildcats	Wright Group/McGraw Hill
On With the Show!	M	I	250+	Pair-It Books	Steck-Vaughn
Once upon a Rhyme	M	F	250+	Pacific Literacy	Pacific Learning
Once Upon a Story	M	I	227	Vocabulary Readers	Houghton Mifflin
One Bad Thing About Father, The	M	RF	250+	Monjo, F. N.	HarperTrophy
One- Eyed Jake	M	F	547	Hutchins, Pat	Morrow
One in the Middle Is the Green Kangaroo, The	M	RF	250+	Blume, Judy	Bantam
Oni Wa Soto	M	TL	250+	Story Vines	Wright Group/McGraw Hill
Opening Night	M	RF	250+	Navigators Fiction Series	Benchmark Education
Osprey	M	I	250+	Cambridge Reading	Pearson Learning Group
Ostriches	M	I	250+	Sails	Rigby

* Collection of short stories

TITLE	LEVEL	GENRE	WORD COUNT	AUTHOR / SERIES	PUBLISHER / DISTRIBUTOR
Our Flag	M	HF	250+	Rothman, Cynthia	Scholastic
Our Government	M	I	250+	People, Spaces & Places	Rand McNally
Our Natural Resources	M	I	1234	Leveled Readers Social Studies	Houghton Mifflin
Our Town Mural	M	RF	660	Leveled Readers	Houghton Mifflin
Owls	M	I	250+	PM Animal Facts: Gold	Rigby
Paint Brush Kid, The	M	RF	250+	Bulla, Clyde Robert	Random House
Pajama Party	M	RF	250+	Hest, Amy	William Morrow
Pandas Have Cubs	M	I	250+	Animals and Their Young	Compass Point Books
Pandas in the Mountains	M	F	735	PM Gold	Rigby
Paper Crane, The	M	F	250+	Soar To Success	Houghton Mifflin
Park Rangers	M	I	250+	Community Helpers	Red Brick Learning
Parts of a Whole	M	I	250+	Yellow Umbrella Books	Capstone Press
Patches	M	RF	250+	Szymanski, Lois	Avon Camelot
Pet Peeves	M	RF	250+	Social Studies Connects	The Kane Press
Pete Discovers Gravity	M	RF	947	Early Connections	Benchmark Education
Pete for President	M	RF	250+	Social Studies Connects	The Kane Press
Peter the Pumpkin-Eater	M	RF	250+	Action Packs	Rigby
Pets Need People	M	I	250+	Literacy 2000	Rigby
Phantoms Don't Drive Sports Cars	M	F	250+	Dadey, Debbie; Jones, Marcia Thornton	Scholastic
Picture Book of Abraham Lincoln, A	M	B	250+	Adler, David A.	Holiday House
Picture Book of Amelia Earhart, A	M	B	250+	Adler, David A.	Holiday House
Picture Book of Anne Frank, A	M	B	250+	Adler, David A.	Holiday House
Picture Book of Benjamin Franklin, A	M	B	250+	Adler, David A.	Holiday House
Picture Book of Christopher Columbus, A	M	B	250+	Adler, David A.	Holiday House
Picture Book of Davy Crockett, A	M	B	250+	Adler, David A.	Holiday House
Picture Book of Eleanor Roosevelt, A	M	B	250+	Adler, David A.	Holiday House
Picture Book of Florence Nightingale, A	M	B	250+	Adler, David A.	Holiday House
Picture Book of Frederick Douglass, A	M	B	250+	Adler, David A.	Holiday House
Picture Book of George Washington Carver, A	M	B	250+	Adler, David A.	Holiday House
Picture Book of George Washington, A	M	B	250+	Adler, David A.	Holiday House
Picture Book of Harriet Tubman, A	M	B	250+	Adler, David A.	Holiday House
Picture Book of Helen Keller, A	M	B	250+	Adler, David A.	Holiday House
Picture Book of Jackie Robinson, A	M	B	250+	Adler, David A.	Holiday House
Picture Book of Louis Braille, A	M	B	250+	Adler, David A.	Holiday House
Picture Book of Martin Luther King, Jr., A	M	B	250+	Adler, David A.	Holiday House
Picture Book of Patrick Henry, A	M	B	250+	Adler, David A.	Holiday House
Picture Book of Paul Revere, A	M	B	250+	Adler, David A.	Holiday House
Picture Book of Rosa Parks, A	M	B	250+	Adler, David A.	Holiday House
Picture Book of Sacagawea, A	M	B	250+	Adler, David A.	Holiday House
Picture Book of Sitting Bull, A	M	B	250+	Adler, David A.	Holiday House
Picture Book of Sojourner Truth, A	M	B	250+	Adler, David A.	Holiday House
Picture Book of Thomas Alva Edison, A	M	B	250+	Adler, David A.	Holiday House
Picture Book of Thomas Jefferson, A	M	B	250+	Adler, David A.	Holiday House
Picture Book of Thurgood Marshall, A	M	B	250+	Adler, David A.	Holiday House
Pied Piper, The	M	TL	585	Sunshine	Wright Group/McGraw Hill
Pigeon Feathers	M	TL	250+	Books for Young Learners	Richard C. Owen
Pigs Have Piglets	M	I	250+	Animals and Their Young	Compass Point Books
Pilots	M	I	250+	Community Workers	Compass Point Books
Pirate Pie	M	F	250+	Vaughan, Marcia	Pacific Learning
Pirates Don't Wear Pink Sunglasses	M	F	250+	Dadey, Debbie; Jones, Marcia Thornton	Scholastic
Pirates Past Noon	M	F	250+	Osborne, Mary Pope	Scholastic
Planets of Our Solar System	M	I	250+	Rigby Focus	Rigby

* Collection of short stories

TITLE	LEVEL	GENRE	WORD COUNT	AUTHOR / SERIES	PUBLISHER / DISTRIBUTOR
Plant and Animal Partners	M	I	587	Early Connections	Benchmark Education
Plant Blossoms	M	I	250+	Look Once Look Again	Creative Teaching Press
Plant Fruits and Seeds	M	I	250+	Look Once Look Again	Creative Teaching Press
Plant Packages: A Book About Seeds	M	I	250+	Growing Things	Picture Window Books
Plant Plumbing: A Book About Roots and Stems	M	I	250+	Growing Things	Picture Window Books
Plants and Flowers	M	I	250+	It's Science!	Children's Press
Plumbers	M	I	250+	Boraas, Tracey	Red Brick Learning
Pocahontas	M	B	250+	First Biographies	Red Brick Learning
Pocahontas: Peacemaker and Friend to the Colonists	M	B	250+	Biographies	Picture Window Books
Pocahontas: The Life of an Indian Princess	M	B	250+	Rosen Real Readers	Rosen Publishing Group
Poem for Grandma, A	M	RF	250+	Leveled Readers Language Support	Houghton Mifflin
Polar Bears Past Bedtime	M	F	250+	Osborne, Mary Pope	Random House
Police Cars	M	I	250+	Transportation	Compass Point Books
Police Officers	M	I	250+	Ready, Dee	Red Brick Learning
Politeness	M	I	250+	Character Education	Red Brick Learning
Postcard Pest, The	M	RF	250+	Giff, Patricia Reilly	Bantam
Present From Aunt Skidoo, The	M	RF	250+	Literacy 2000	Rigby
Princess Who Loved to Cook, The	M	F	250+	Cartwright, Pauline	Pearson Learning Group
Princess Who Wanted the Moon, The	M	F	250+	Lane, Sheila; Kemp, Marion	Wood Lock Educational
Princesses Don't Wear Jeans	M	RF	250+	Bookshop	Mondo
Pumpkins	M	I	250+	Ray, Mary Lyn	Harcourt Trade
Purple Climbing Days	M	RF	250+	Giff, Patricia Reilly	Bantam
Qillak	M	RF	250+	Jensen, Ned	Wright Group/McGraw Hill
Quackers, the Troublesome Duck	M	F	250+	Ellen, Leslie	Pearson Learning Group
Rabbit Catches the Sun	M	F	621	Sunshine	Wright Group/McGraw Hill
Rabbit for You, A: Caring for your Rabbit	M	I	250+	Pet Care	Picture Window Books
Rabbits Have Bunnies	M	I	250+	Animals and Their Young	Compass Point Books
Raccoons	M	I	250+	PM Animal Facts: Gold	Rigby
Race Cars	M	I	250+	Transportation	Compass Point Books
Rain Forest Plants	M	I	580	Lundberg, Linda	Harcourt School Publishers
Rain, Rivers, and Rain Again	M	I	250+	Sunshine	Wright Group/McGraw Hill
Rainbow Wings	M	F	250+	Nevinski, Margaret	Wright Group/McGraw Hill
Rainbows All Around	M	RF	250+	Hardin, Suzanne	Pacific Learning
Rashee and the Seven Elephants	M	RF	250+	Little Celebrations	Pearson Learning Group
Reading a Map	M	I	250+	Rosen Real Readers	Rosen Publishing Group
Ready, Set, Jump!	M	I	250+	Rigby Literacy	Rigby
Recycling a Can	M	I	250+	Rosen Real Readers	Rosen Publishing Group
Red and Blue Mittens	M	RF	250+	Reading Unlimited	Pearson Learning Group
Red Egg and Ginger	M	RF	250+	Greetings	Rigby
Red Ribbon Rosie	M	RF	250+	Marzollo, Jean	Random House
Reptiles	M	I	250+	First Facts	Capstone Press
Respect the Winds	M	TL	250+	Reeder, Paul	Wright Group/McGraw Hill
Respiratory System, The	M	I	212	Human Body Systems	Red Brick Learning
Return of Rinaldo, the Sly Fox	M	TL	250+	Scheffler, Ursel	North-South Books
Return of the Third-Grade Ghosthunters, The	M	RF	250+	Maccarone, Grace	Scholastic
Revolutionary War on Wednesday	M	F	250+	Osborne, Mary Pope	Random House
Rinaldo the Sly Fox	M	TL	250+	Scheffler, Ursel	North-South Books
*Rip-Roaring Russell	M	RF	250+	Hurwitz, Johanna	Penguin Group
Rita Moreno: Shining Star	M	B	593	Leveled Readers	Houghton Mifflin
River Runners	M	RF	250+	Literacy Tree	Rigby
Rivers, Streams, and Lakes	M	I	250+	PM Plus Nonfiction	Rigby
Robber Pig and the Ginger Bear	M	F	403	Read Alongs	Rigby

* Collection of short stories

TITLE	LEVEL	GENRE	WORD COUNT	AUTHOR / SERIES	PUBLISHER / DISTRIBUTOR
Robber Pig and the Green Eggs	M	F	250+	Read Alongs	Rigby
Robber, The	M	RF	1255	Sunshine	Wright Group/McGraw Hill
Rock	M	I	250+	First Facts	Capstone Press
Rocks and Fossils	M	I	250+	Rosen Real Readers	Rosen Publishing Group
Rocks From Space	M	I	250+	Rigby Focus	Rigby
Rooster's Gift, The	M	F	250+	Conrad, Pam	HarperCollins
Rosa and Fredo	M	F	250+	SupaDoopers	Sundance
Rosa Parks	M	B	250+	First Biographies	Red Brick Learning
Rubber	M	I	250+	First Facts	Capstone Press
Rumpelstiltskin	M	TL	250+	Once Upon a Time	Wright Group/McGraw Hill
*Russell and Elisa	M	RF	250+	Hurwitz, Johanna	Penguin Group
*Russell Rides Again	M	RF	250+	Hurwitz, Johanna	Penguin Group
*Russell Sprouts	M	RF	250+	Hurwitz, Johanna	Penguin Group
Sacagawea's Journey	M	B	250+	Leveled Readers Language Support	Houghton Mifflin
Salamanders and Alligators	M	I	710	Leveled Readers Science	Houghton Mifflin
Sally Ride: Astronaut, Scientist, Teacher	M	B	250+	Biographies	Picture Window Books
Sam's Glasses	M	RF	250+	Literacy 2000	Rigby
Sand	M	I	250+	Windows on Literacy	National Geographic
Santa Claus Doesn't Mop Floors	M	F	250+	Dadey, Debbie; Jones, Marcia Thornton	Scholastic
Save the River!	M	SF	250+	Pair-It Books	Steck-Vaughn
Save the Sea Turtles!	M	I	250+	Leonhardt, Alice	Steck-Vaughn
Saving Money	M	I	250+	First Facts	Capstone Press
School Bus Drivers	M	I	250+	Ready, Dee	Red Brick Learning
School Principals	M	I	250+	Boraas, Tracey	Red Brick Learning
School Secretaries	M	I	250+	Community Helpers	Red Brick Learning
Score!: You Can Play Soccer	M	I	250+	Game Day	Picture Window Books
Scots Pine, The	M	I	250+	Cambridge Reading	Pearson Learning Group
Scruncher Goes Wandering	M	RF	250+	Krailing, Tessa	Barron's Educational
Sea Monsters Don't Ride Motorcycles	M	RF	250+	Dadey, Debbie; Jones, Marcia Thornton	Scholastic
Seahorses	M	I	250+	Bookshop	Mondo
Seal	M	I	250+	Cambridge Reading	Pearson Learning Group
Search for the Lost Cave, The	M	F	250+	Schultz, Irene	Wright Group/McGraw Hill
Seasons and Weather	M	I	250+	PM Plus Nonfiction	Rigby
Second Grade - Friends Again!	M	RF	250+	Cohen, Miriam	Scholastic
Second-Grade Friends	M	RF	250+	Cohen, Miriam	Scholastic
Secret at the Polk Street School, The	M	RF	250+	Giff, Patricia Reilly	Bantam
Secret of the Monster Book, The	M	F	250+	Schultz, Irene	Wright Group/McGraw Hill
Secret of the Old Oak Trunk, The	M	F	250+	Schultz, Irene	Wright Group/McGraw Hill
Secret of the Song, The	M	F	250+	Schultz, Irene	Wright Group/McGraw Hill
Security Guards	M	I	250+	Community Helpers	Red Brick Learning
Self-Respect	M	I	250+	Character Education	Red Brick Learning
Seven Treasure Hunts, The	M	RF	250+	Byars, Betsy	HarperTrophy
Shadow Over Second	M	RF	250+	Christopher, Matt	Little, Brown & Co.
Shapes in the Sky: A Book About Clouds	M	I	250+	Amazing Science	Picture Window Books
Sharks	M	I	250+	Gibbons, Gail	Holiday House
Sheep Have Lambs	M	I	250+	Animals and Their Young	Compass Point Books
Shooting Star, The	M	RF	661	PM Gold	Rigby
Shortstop from Tokyo	M	RF	250+	Christopher, Matt	Little, Brown & Co.
Shorty	M	RF	250+	Literacy 2000	Rigby
Show Time at the Polk Street School	M	RF	250+	Giff, Patricia Reilly	Bantam
Shy People's Picnic, The	M	F	250+	Little Celebrations	Pearson Learning Group

* Collection of short stories

TITLE	LEVEL	GENRE	WORD COUNT	AUTHOR / SERIES	PUBLISHER / DISTRIBUTOR
Si Won's Victory	M	RF	250+	Little Celebrations	Pearson Learning Group
Silly Willy	M	RF	250+	Bookshop	Mondo
Simple Machines	M	I	250+	Rosen Real Readers	Rosen Publishing Group
Skateboard Tough	M	RF	250+	Christopher, Matt	Little, Brown & Co.
Skateboarding	M	I	250+	Blazers	Capstone Press
Skeletons Don't Play Tubas	M	F	250+	Dadey, Debbie; Jones, Marcia Thornton	Scholastic
Skunks	M	I	250+	PM Animal Facts: Gold	Rigby
Sky Changes	M	I	250+	PM Plus Nonfiction	Rigby
Slam Dunk Saturday	M	RF	250+	Marzollo, Jean	Random House
Smokey the Dragon	M	F	250+	Bennett, Jean	Pearson Learning Group
Smudge-Face: A Native American Cinderella Tale	M	TL	580	Leveled Readers	Houghton Mifflin
Snaggle Doodles	M	RF	250+	Giff, Patricia Reilly	Bantam
Snake Alarm	M	RF	250+	Krailing, Tessa	Barron's Educational
Snake!	M	RF	641	Sunshine	Wright Group/McGraw Hill
Snakes: Cold-Blooded Crawlers	M	I	250+	The Wild World of Animals	Red Brick Learning
Snow Bright and the Seven Sumos	M	F	250+	SupaDoopers	Sundance
Snow Bright and the Tooth Magician	M	F	250+	SupaDoopers	Sundance
So Long Stinky Queen	M	RF	250+	First Flight	Fitzhenry & Whiteside
So You Want to Move a Building?	M	I	380	Pacific Literacy	Pacific Learning
Soccer	M	I	250+	Little Celebrations	Pearson Learning Group
Soccer Mania!	M	RF	250+	Tamar, Erika	Random House
Soccer Sam	M	RF	250+	Marzollo, Jean	Random House
*Sock Gobbler and Other Stories, The	M	F	250+	Learning Media	Pacific Learning
Soddies	M	I	250+	Twig	Wright Group/McGraw Hill
Solo Girl	M	RF	250+	Pinkey, Andrea Davis	Hyperion
Something Soft for Danny Bear	M	F	493	Literacy 2000	Rigby
Sometimes I Feel Like a Storm Cloud	M	RF	250+	Bookshop	Mondo
Sophie Hits Six	M	F	250+	King-Smith, Dick	Candlewick Press
Sophie in the Saddle	M	F	250+	King-Smith, Dick	Candlewick Press
Sophie Is Seven	M	F	250+	King-Smith, Dick	Candlewick Press
Sophie's Lucky	M	F	250+	King-Smith, Dick	Candlewick Press
Sophie's Snail	M	F	250+	King-Smith, Dick	Candlewick Press
Sophie's Tom	M	F	250+	King-Smith, Dick	Candlewick Press
Sound: Loud, Soft, High, and Low	M	I	250+	Amazing Science	Picture Window Books
Space Rocks: A Look at Asteroids and Comets	M	I	250+	Rosen Real Readers	Rosen Publishing Group
Space Walks	M	I	250+	Explore Space	Red Brick Learning
Special Gifts	M	RF	250+	Rylant, Cynthia	Aladdin
Spencer School Sleepover, The	M	RF	250+	Floyd, Lucy	Wright Group/McGraw Hill
Spider Man	M	I	250+	Literacy 2000	Rigby
Spiders	M	I	250+	Bookshop	Mondo
Splish! Splash!: A Book About Rain	M	I	250+	Amazing Science	Picture Window Books
Spooky Tail of Prewitt Peacock, The	M	F	250+	Peet, Bill	Houghton Mifflin
Sports Cars	M	I	250+	Blazers	Capstone Press
Sportsmanship	M	I	250+	Character Education	Red Brick Learning
Spring in the City	M	F	46	Leveled Readers	Houghton Mifflin
Springs	M	I	245	Books for Young Learners	Richard C. Owen
Spy Down the Street, The	M	F	250+	Schultz, Irene	Wright Group/McGraw Hill
Spy in the Attic, The	M	RF	250+	Scheffler, Ursel	North-South Books
Spy Manual	M	I	250+	Sails	Rigby
Spy on Third Base, The	M	RF	250+	Christopher, Matt	Little, Brown & Co.
Squirrels: Furry Scurriers	M	I	250+	The Wild World of Animals	Red Brick Learning
Star	M	RF	250+	Simon, Jo Ann	Random House

* Collection of short stories

TITLE	LEVEL	GENRE	WORD COUNT	AUTHOR / SERIES	PUBLISHER / DISTRIBUTOR
Starfishers to the Rescue	M	SF	250+	Dreyer, Ellen	Pearson Learning Group
Stick to It!: The Story of Wilma Rudolph	M	B	250+	Spyglass Books	Compass Point Books
Stop, Stop	M	F	250+	Hurd, Edith Thacher	HarperCollins
Stories in Stone	M	I	250+	Pacific Literacy	Pacific Learning
Storm at Coldwater Creek	M	HF	250+	Blackaby, Susan	Wright Group/McGraw Hill
Story of Big Bess Call, The	M	TL	250+	Bovetz, Marcie	Wright Group/McGraw Hill
Story of Jeans, The	M	I	250+	Discovery World	Rigby
Story of the Mexican Jumping Bean, The	M	TL	250+	Story Vines	Wright Group/McGraw Hill
Story of William Tell, The	M	TL	250+	PM Story Books-Silver	Rigby
Story of You, The	M	I	482	Sunshine	Wright Group/McGraw Hill
Story, a Story, A: An African Tale	M	TL	250+	Haley, Gail E.	Aladdin
Strike Out!	M	RF	250+	Howard, Tristan	Scholastic
Stuck in the Ice	M	I	250+	Leveled Readers Language Support	Houghton Mifflin
Studying a Glacier	M	I	501	Leveled Readers Science	Houghton Mifflin
Sugar Cakes Cyril	M	RF	4022	Gershator, Phillis	Mondo
Summer Sands	M	RF	839	Evangeline Nicholas Collection	Wright Group/McGraw Hill
Sunny-Side Up	M	RF	250+	Giff, Patricia Reilly	Bantam
Sunset of the Sabertooth	M	F	250+	Osborne, Mary Pope	Random House
Sunshine: A Book About Sunlight	M	I	250+	Amazing Science	Picture Window Books
Super Space Stations	M	I	250+	Rosen Real Readers	Rosen Publishing Group
Supercharged Infield	M	RF	250+	Christopher, Matt	Little, Brown & Co.
Supermarket Managers	M	I	250+	Community Helpers	Red Brick Learning
Survival of Fish, The	M	I	946	Science	Wright Group/McGraw Hill
Swamp of the Hideous Zombies	M	F	250+	Hayes, Geoffrey	Random House
Take Care of Our Earth	M	I	250+	Pair-It Books	Steck-Vaughn
Taken by the Wind	M	RF	250+	Wahman, Joe	Wright Group/McGraw Hill
Taking Photographs	M	I	788	Early Connections	Benchmark Education
Tale of Veruschka Babuschka, The	M	TL	250+	Literacy 2000	Rigby
Tasmanian Devils	M	I	250+	PM Animal Facts: Gold	Rigby
Tattercoat and the Magical Flute, A Cinderella Tale from England	M	TL	692	Leveled Readers Language Support	Houghton Mifflin
Teachers	M	I	250+	Deedrick, Tami	Red Brick Learning
Temperature	M	I	250+	First Facts	Capstone Press
Temperature: Heating Up and Cooling Down	M	I	250+	Amazing Science	Picture Window Books
Thao Kham, the Pebble Shooter	M	TL	250+	Story Vines	Wright Group/McGraw Hill
*That's a Laugh: Four Funny Fables	M	TL	250+	Literacy 2000	Rigby
These Old Rags	M	RF	352	Evangeline Nicholas Collection	Wright Group/McGraw Hill
Things Change	M	I	569	Bourne, Phyllis Montenegro	Hampton-Brown
Think, Think, Think: Learning About Your Brain	M	I	250+	Amazing Body	Picture Window Books
Those Tricky Animals	M	I	250+	Literacy Tree	Rigby
Three Little Pigs Wise Up and The Princess, the Prince, and the Vegetables, The	M	F	250+	Navigators Fiction Series	Benchmark Education
Through the Garden Door	M	F	250+	Reeves, Barbara	Pearson Learning Group
Thump-Thump: Learning About Your Heart	M	I	250+	Amazing Body	Picture Window Books
Tigers at Twilight	M	F	250+	Osborne, Mary Pope	Random House
Tigers: Striped Stalkers	M	I	250+	The Wild World of Animals	Red Brick Learning
Tight End	M	RF	250+	Christopher, Matt	Little, Brown & Co.
Timber Box, The	M	TL	250+	Enrichment	Wright Group/McGraw Hill
Time Capsule, The	M	SF	257	Book Bank	Wright Group/McGraw Hill
Time to Celebrate!	M	I	250+	iOpeners	Pearson Learning Group
Timothy's Five-City Tour	M	F	250+	Pair-It Books	Steck-Vaughn
Tin Lizzy	M	RF	425	Windmill Books	Rigby
Tom, the Dragon	M	F	522	New Way Orange	Steck-Vaughn

* Collection of short stories

TITLE	LEVEL	GENRE	WORD COUNT	AUTHOR / SERIES	PUBLISHER / DISTRIBUTOR
Tomatoes	M	I	250+	Cole, Sally	Wright Group/McGraw Hill
Tom's Friend	M	RF	250+	Voyages	SRA/McGraw Hill
Tonight on the Titanic	M	F	250+	Osborne, Mary Pope	Random House
Too Hot to Handle	M	RF	250+	Christopher, Matt	Little, Brown & Co.
Too Many Tamales	M	RF	250+	Soto, Gary	Putnam & Grosset
Totara Tree, The	M	RF	391	Book Bank	Wright Group/McGraw Hill
*Touch of Gold and Other Stories, The	M	TL	250+	Lane, Sheila; Kemp, Marion	Wood Lock Educational
Touch of Sepia, A	M	RF	250+	Voyages	SRA/McGraw Hill
Touchdown for Tommy	M	RF	250+	Christopher, Matt	Little, Brown & Co.
Touchdown!: You Can Play Football	M	I	250+	Game Day	Picture Window Books
Towers	M	I	250+	Rigby Literacy	Rigby
Tracey and the Sun	M	F	250+	Sails	Rigby
Tractors	M	I	250+	Transportation	Compass Point Books
Transportation Yesterday and Today	M	I	659	Relf, Coco	Harcourt School Publishers
Treasure Hunting	M	RF	250+	Literacy 2000	Rigby
Tree Falls Down, A	M	F	250+	Orbit Double Takes	Pacific Learning
Tricksters	M	RF	250+	SupaDoopers	Sundance
Trip Around the Gulf of Mexico, A	M	I	250+	People, Spaces & Places	Rand McNally
Trip to Freedom	M	B	250+	Greetings	Rigby
Trip to Japan, A	M	I	250+	Rosen Real Readers	Rosen Publishing Group
Trixie and the Cyber Pet	M	F	250+	Krailing, Tessa	Barron's Educational
Trolls Don't Ride Roller Coasters	M	F	250+	Dadey, Debbie; Jones, Marcia Thornton	Scholastic
Troublemaker	M	RF	250+	SupaDoopers	Sundance
Truth About the Moon, The	M	TL	250+	Bess, Clayton	Houghton Mifflin
Turkey Trouble	M	RF	250+	Giff, Patricia Reilly	Bantam
TV Reporters	M	I	250+	Boraas, Tracey	Red Brick Learning
TV Time-Out	M	RF	250+	Blackaby, Susan	Wright Group/McGraw Hill
Twelve Dancing Princesses	M	I	250+	Enrichment	Wright Group/McGraw Hill
Twisters	M	I	250+	Early Connections	Benchmark Education
Two Hungry Hippos	M	I	250+	Adams, Alison	Benchmark Education
Two Runaways, The	M	RF	250+	Schultz, Irene	Wright Group/McGraw Hill
Tyler Toad and Thunder	M	F	250+	Crowe, Robert	Dutton
Tyrannosaurus Rex	M	I	250+	Prehistoric Creatures Then and Now	Steck-Vaughn
Tyrannosaurus Rex	M	I	250+	Discovering Dinosaurs	Capstone Press
Unicorns Don't Give Sleigh Rides	M	F	250+	Dadey, Debbie; Jones, Marcia Thornton	Scholastic
Up, Up, and Away	M	I	250+	Twig	Wright Group/McGraw Hill
Using a Beak	M	I	250+	Sails	Rigby
Using a Tail	M	I	250+	Sails	Rigby
Using the River	M	I	250+	Rigby Literacy	Rigby
Vacation Journal, A	M	B	250+	Discovery World	Rigby
Vacation Under the Volcano	M	F	250+	Osborne, Mary Pope	Random House
Valentine Star, The	M	RF	250+	Giff, Patricia Reilly	Bantam
Vampires Don't Wear Polka Dots	M	F	250+	Dadey, Debbie; Jones, Marcia Thornton	Scholastic
Very Happy Birthday, A	M	RF	1017	Jellybeans	Rigby
Veterinarians	M	I	250+	Community Workers	Compass Point Books
View from Above, A	M	I	250+	Rigby Literacy	Rigby
Viking Ships at Sunrise	M	F	250+	Osborne, Mary Pope	Random House
Visiting the Eagle Hotel	M	I	250+	Rigby Literacy	Rigby
Volcano Woman	M	TL	250+	Cambridge Reading	Pearson Learning Group
Voyage, The	M	F	250+	Pair-It Books	Steck-Vaughn

* Collection of short stories

TITLE	LEVEL	GENRE	WORD COUNT	AUTHOR / SERIES	PUBLISHER / DISTRIBUTOR
Wake Up, Emily, It's Mother's Day	M	RF	250+	Giff, Patricia Reilly	Yearling
Walking	M	I	250+	Literacy 2000	Rigby
Walter the Warlock	M	F	250+	Hautzig, Deborah	Random House
War Shirt, The	M	RF	250+	Greetings	Rigby
Waste of Space, A	M	RF	250+	SupaDoopers	Sundance
Watching Every Drop	M	I	250+	Home Connection Collection	Rigby
Water for the World	M	I	250+	Home Connection Collection	Rigby
Water: Liquid, Solid, Gas	M	I	240	Twig	Wright Group/McGraw Hill
Water: Up, Down, and All Around	M	I	250+	Amazing Science	Picture Window Books
Waterfalls, Glaciers, and Avalanches	M	I	250+	PM Plus Nonfiction	Rigby
We Are All Alike	M	I	250+	Schaefer, Lola M.	Benchmark Education
Weather Drum, The	M	TL	250+	Cambridge Reading	Pearson Learning Group
Wedding Day Disaster	M	RF	250+	SupaDoopers	Sundance
Welcome to Brazil	M	I	250+	Spyglass Books	Compass Point Books
Welcome to Canada	M	I	250+	Spyglass Books	Compass Point Books
Welcome to Japan	M	I	250+	Spyglass Books	Compass Point Books
Welcome to Kenya	M	I	250+	Spyglass Books	Compass Point Books
Welcome to Mexico	M	I	250+	Spyglass Books	Compass Point Books
Welcome to Russia	M	I	250+	Spyglass Books	Compass Point Books
Werewolves Don't Go To Summer Camp	M	F	250+	Dadey, Debbie; Jones, Marcia Thornton	Scholastic
Whales	M	I	333	Wonder World	Wright Group/McGraw Hill
Whales: Giants of the Deep	M	I	250+	The Wild World of Animals	Red Brick Learning
What a Job!	M	I	250+	Rigby Literacy	Rigby
What are Inclined Planes?	M	I	70	Pebble Books	Red Brick Learning
What are Levers?	M	I	66	Pebble Books	Red Brick Learning
What are Pulleys?	M	I	88	Pebble Books	Red Brick Learning
What are Screws?	M	I	65	Pebble Books	Red Brick Learning
What are Wedges?	M	I	60	Pebble Books	Red Brick Learning
What are Wheels and Axles?	M	I	70	Pebble Books	Red Brick Learning
What Dinah Saw	M	F	250+	Lighthouse	Rigby
What Is a Fly?	M	I	561	Sunshine	Wright Group/McGraw Hill
What is a Reptile?	M	I	183	Now I Know	Troll Associates
What Is Money?	M	I	250+	First Facts	Capstone Press
What Made Teddalik Laugh	M	TL	250+	Folk Tales	Wright Group/McGraw Hill
What Shall I Do?	M	RF	584	Sunshine	Wright Group/McGraw Hill
What Would You Do?	M	I	392	Vocabulary Readers	Houghton Mifflin
Whatcha Got?	M	RF	250+	Social Studies Connects	The Kane Press
Whatever Am I Going to Do Now?	M	RF	250+	Little Celebrations	Pearson Learning Group
What's Cooking, Jenny Archer?	M	RF	250+	Conford, Ellen	Little, Brown & Co.
When I Go to Grandma's House	M	RF	199	Cleary, Brian	Kaeden Books
When My Dad Came to School	M	RF	230	City Kids	Rigby
When The Truck Got Stuck!	M	RF	250+	Cowley, Joy	Pacific Learning
Where Does the Garbage Go?	M	I	250+	Soar To Success	Houghton Mifflin
Where Does the Wind Go?	M	I	95	Bookshop	Mondo
Where There Was Smoke	M	I	250+	Martinucci, Suzanne	Scholastic
Which Way, Wendy	M	RF	250+	Social Studies Connects	The Kane Press
Who Looks After Me?	M	I	250+	Literacy 2000	Rigby
Who Makes the Rules?	M	I	250+	Schafer, Lola M.	Benchmark Education
Who Was Betsy Ross?	M	B	250+	Rosen Real Readers	Rosen Publishing Group
Who Was Paul Revere?	M	B	250+	Rosen Real Readers	Rosen Publishing Group
Who's in Love with Arthur?	M	F	250+	Brown, Marc	Little, Brown & Co.
Whose Ears Are These?: A Look at Aminal Ears - Short, Flat, and Floppy	M	I	250+	Whose Is It? Science	Picture Window Books

* Collection of short stories

TITLE	LEVEL	GENRE	WORD COUNT	AUTHOR / SERIES	PUBLISHER / DISTRIBUTOR
Whose Eyes Are These?: A Look at Animal Eyes - Big, Round, and Narrow	M	I	250+	Whose Is It? Science	Picture Window Books
Whose Feet Are These? A Look at Hooves, Paws, and Claws	M	I	250+	Whose Is It? Science	Picture Window Books
Whose Legs Are These?: A Look at Animal Legs - Kicking, Running, and Hopping	M	I	250+	Whose Is It? Science	Picture Window Books
Whose Mouth Is This?: A Look at Bills, Suckers, and Tubes	M	I	250+	Whose Is It? Science	Picture Window Books
Whose Nose Is This?: A Look at Beaks, Snouts, and Trunks	M	I	250+	Whose Is It? Science	Picture Window Books
Whose Skin Is This?: A Look at Animal Skin - Scaly, Furry, and Prickly	M	I	250+	Whose Is It? Science	Picture Window Books
Whose Tail Is This?: A Look at Tails - Swishing, Wiggling, and Rattling	M	I	250+	Whose Is It? Science	Picture Window Books
Whose Way Today?	M	RF	683	Leveled Readers	Houghton Mifflin
Wilamina and the Weather Conditions	M	F	250+	Reimer, Luther	Wright Group/McGraw Hill
Wild Cat Guide, The	M	I	250+	Lighthouse	Rigby
Wild Weather, Tall Tales	M	F	321	Vocabulary Readers	Houghton Mifflin
Wild, Wild Wolves	M	I	250+	Milton, Joyce	Random House
Wilde Street Club and Molly, The	M	RF	965	Sunshine	Wright Group/McGraw Hill
Wilde Street Club and the Duck Man, The	M	RF	1057	Sunshine	Wright Group/McGraw Hill
Wind That Would Not Blow, The	M	TL	250+	Kunari, Anna	Hampton-Brown
Wingman on Ice	M	RF	250+	Christopher, Matt	Little, Brown & Co.
Winklepoo the Wicked	M	F	1614	Sunshine	Wright Group/McGraw Hill
Wishes Don't Come True	M	RF	250+	Bookshop	Mondo
Witches Don't Do Backflips	M	F	250+	Dadey, Debbie; Jones, Marcia Thornton	Scholastic
Wizards Don't Need Computers	M	F	250+	Dadey, Debbie; Jones, Marcia Thornton	Scholastic
Wolf Who Cried Boy, The	M	F	250+	Hartman, Bob	Scholastic
Wolfmen Don't Hula Dance	M	RF	250+	Dadey, Debbie; Jones, Marcia Thornton	Scholastic
Wolf's First Deer	M	RF	434	Book Bank	Wright Group/McGraw Hill
Wolves Have Pups	M	I	250+	Animals and Their Young	Compass Point Books
Wonder Kid Meets the Evil Lunch Snatcher	M	RF	250+	Duncan, Lois	Little, Brown & Co.
Wonder of Bald Eagles, The	M	I	250+	Soar To Success	Houghton Mifflin
Wonder of Wolves, The	M	I	250+	Soar To Success	Houghton Mifflin
Wonderful Eyes	M	I	1070	Science	Wright Group/McGraw Hill
Woodcutter and the Bear, The: A Play	M	TL	250+	Rigby Literacy	Rigby
Woodlanders Begin, The	M	F	250+	Schultz, Irene	Wright Group/McGraw Hill
Words	M	I	578	Pacific Literacy	Pacific Learning
World of Kites, A	M	I	272	Vocabulary Readers	Houghton Mifflin
World of Snow, A	M	RF	250+	Livorse, Kay	Houghton Mifflin
World's Greatest Toe Show, The	M	RF	250+	Lamb, Nancy; Singer, Muff	Troll Associates
World's Largest Plants, The: A Book About Trees	M	I	250+	Growing Things	Picture Window Books
Worrisome Wombat, The	M	F	250+	Voyages	SRA/McGraw Hill
Wright Brothers, The	M	B	250+	Biography	Benchmark Education
Write Up a Storm with the Polk Street School	M	RF	250+	Giff, Patricia Reilly	Bantam
Year Mom Won the Pennant, The	M	RF	250+	Christopher, Matt	Little, Brown & Co.
Yonder	M	RF	250+	Johnston, Tony	Penguin Group
You Can Cook	M	I	250+	Woo, Lornette	Steck-Vaughn
Young Wolf's First Hunt	M	RF	250+	Shefelman, Janice	Random House
Your Heart and Blood	M	I	250+	Rigby Focus	Rigby
Your Nervous System	M	I	366	Early Connections	Benchmark Education

* Collection of short stories

TITLE	LEVEL	GENRE	WORD COUNT	AUTHOR / SERIES	PUBLISHER / DISTRIBUTOR
You're My Nikki	M	RF	250+	Eisenberg, Phyllis Rose	Penguin Group
You've Got Cheetah-Mail	M	I	250+	World Quest Adventures	World Quest Learning
Zero's Slider	M	RF	250+	Christopher, Matt	Little, Brown & Co.
Zombies Don't Play Soccer	M	F	250+	Dadey, Debbie; Jones, Marcia Thornton	Scholastic
Zomo the Rabbit: A Trickster Tale from West Africa	M	TL	250+	McDermott, Gerald	Harcourt Trade
Zoo Keepers	M	I	250+	Deedrick, Tami	Red Brick Learning
1 Potato 2 Potato	N	I	250+	Literacy 2000	Rigby
26 Fairmount Avenue	N	B	250+	DePaola, Tomie	Putnam
Abraham Lincoln	N	B	235	First Biographies	Capstone Press
Absent Author, The	N	RF	250+	Roy, Ron	Random House
Adam Joshua Capers: Halloween Monster	N	RF	250+	Smith, Janice Lee	HarperTrophy
*Adam Joshua Capers: Kid Next Door, The	N	RF	250+	Smith, Janice Lee	HarperTrophy
*Adam Joshua Capers: Monster in the Third	N	RF	250+	Smith, Janice Lee	HarperTrophy
Adam Joshua Capers: Nelson in Love	N	RF	250+	Smith, Janice Lee	HarperTrophy
Adam Joshua Capers: Show-and-Tell War, The	N	RF	250+	Smith, Janice Lee	HarperTrophy
Adam Joshua Capers: Superkid!	N	RF	250+	Smith, Janice Lee	HarperTrophy
Adam Joshua Capers: Turkey Trouble	N	RF	250+	Smith, Janice Lee	HarperTrophy
Adios, Anna	N	RF	250+	Giff, Patricia Reilly	Bantam
Adventures of George Washington, The	N	B	250+	Davidson, Margaret	Scholastic
Adventures of Max and Ned, The	N	F	250+	Little Celebrations	Pearson Learning Group
Africa	N	I	250+	Continents	Capstone Press
Alexander Graham Bell	N	B	250+	First Biographies	Red Brick Learning
Alien in the Classroom	N	F	250+	Keene, Carolyn	Pocket Books
All About Bears	N	I	250+	Voyages	SRA/McGraw Hill
All About Cats and Kittens	N	I	250+	Neye, Emily	Grosset & Dunlap
All From a Bottle	N	F	250+	Phonics and Friends	Hampton-Brown
All Kinds of Maps	N	I	163	Windows on Literacy	National Geographic
All Kinds of Museums	N	I	250+	Ramsey, Joe	Wright Group/McGraw Hill
All Pigs Are Beautiful	N	I	250+	King-Smith, Dick	Candlewick Press
Alligator in the Bathtub	N	F	628	Leveled Readers	Houghton Mifflin
Alvin Ailey, an American Dancer	N	B	326	Vocabulary Readers	Houghton Mifflin
Always My Dad	N	RF	250+	Wyeth, Sharon Dennis	Alfred A. Knopf
Amazon, The	N	I	250+	Early Connections	Benchmark Education
Amber Brown Goes Fourth	N	RF	250+	Danziger, Paula	Scholastic
Amber Brown is Feeling Blue	N	RF	250+	Danziger, Paula	Scholastic
Amber Brown is Green with Envy	N	RF	250+	Danziger, Paula	Scholastic
Amber Brown is Not a Crayon	N	RF	250+	Danziger, Paula	Scholastic
Amber Brown Sees Red	N	RF	250+	Danziger, Paula	Scholastic
Amber Brown Wants Extra Credit	N	RF	250+	Danziger, Paula	Scholastic
American Flag, The	N	I	250+	American Symbols	Capstone Press
American Flag, The	N	I	250+	A True Book	Children's Press
And Then It Was Sugar	N	RF	250+	Story Vines	Wright Group/McGraw Hill
Andy and Tamika	N	RF	250+	Adler, David A.	Harcourt Trade
Animal Adventures	N	HF	250+	Little House	HarperTrophy
Animal Advertisements	N	F	250+	Sails	Rigby
Animal Communication	N	I	250+	Cambridge Reading	Pearson Learning Group
Animal Ears	N	I	250+	Look Once Look Again	Creative Teaching Press
Animal Farmers	N	I	250+	Literacy Tree	Rigby
Animal Fathers	N	I	250+	Literacy 2000 Satellites	Rigby
Animal Friends	N	I	250+	Literacy 2000	Rigby
Animal Shelters	N	I	250+	Bookshop	Mondo
Animal Skin and Scales	N	I	250+	Look Once Look Again	Creative Teaching Press

* Collection of short stories

TITLE	LEVEL	GENRE	WORD COUNT	AUTHOR / SERIES	PUBLISHER / DISTRIBUTOR
Animal Tails	N	I	250+	Look Once Look Again	Creative Teaching Press
Animals and Their Young	N	I	484	Kratky, Lada Josefa	Hampton-Brown
Animals from the Past	N	I	304	Independent Readers Science	Houghton Mifflin
Animals of Long Ago	N	I	250+	Ring, Susan	Scholastic
Animals of the Tundra	N	I	250+	Little Celebrations	Pearson Learning Group
Animals Talk, Too	N	I	250+	Literacy 2000	Rigby
Anna, Grandpa, and the Big Storm	N	RF	250+	Stevens, Carla	Penguin Group
Antarctic Penguins	N	I	250+	PM Animal Facts: Silver	Rigby
Antarctic Seals	N	I	250+	PM Animal Facts: Silver	Rigby
Antarctica	N	I	250+	Continents	Capstone Press
Antarctica: Ice-Covered Continent	N	I	250+	Phonics and Friends	Hampton-Brown
Ants	N	I	250+	Nature's Friends	Compass Point Books
Ants	N	I	250+	Daronco, Mickey; Presti, Lori	Benchmark Education
Asia	N	I	250+	Continents	Capstone Press
Ask Einstein!	N	RF	250+	Trussell-Cullen, Alan	Pacific Learning
Astronauts at Work	N	I	250+	Explore Space	Red Brick Learning
At Home on the Prairie	N	I	436	Vocabulary Readers	Houghton Mifflin
At the Seashore	N	I	250+	Look Once Look Again	Creative Teaching Press
Attack of the Giant Squirrel!	N	F	653	Leveled Readers	Houghton Mifflin
Australia	N	I	250+	Continents	Capstone Press
Australia	N	I	250+	A True Book	Children's Press
Baba Yaga: A Russian Folktale	N	TL	250+	Phinney, Margaret Y.	Mondo
Bad Day for Ballet	N	RF	250+	Keene, Carolyn	Pocket Books
Bald Bandit, The	N	RF	250+	Roy, Ron	Random House
Bald Eagle, The	N	I	250+	American Symbols	Capstone Press
Bald Eagle, The	N	I	250+	A True Book	Children's Press
Bart's Amazing Charts	N	RF	250+	Ochiltree, Dianne	Scholastic
Baseball Math	N	I	250+	Early Connections	Benchmark Education
Bats and Burglars	N	RF	250+	First Flight	Fitzhenry & Whiteside
Be A Perfect Person In Just Three Days!	N	RF	250+	Manes, Stephen	Dell
Bean	N	I	250+	Life Cycles	Creative Teaching Press
Bear Collection, The	N	I	250+	PM Ruby	Rigby
Beatles, The	N	B	250+	Venezia, Mike	Children's Press
Beaver Engineers	N	I	250+	Reeder, Tracey	Wright Group/McGraw Hill
Beavers	N	I	250+	Bookshop	Mondo
Because of Walter	N	RF	250+	Action Packs	Rigby
Beeman Interview	N	F	250+	Sails	Rigby
Bees	N	I	250+	Nature's Friends	Compass Point Books
Bees	N	I	250+	A True Book	Children's Press
Beetles	N	I	250+	Minibeasts	Franklin Watts
Behind the Couch	N	F	250+	Gerstein, Mordicai	Hyperion
Behind the Scenes with Sammy	N	I	250+	Little Celebrations	Pearson Learning Group
Below the Green Pond	N	I	250+	Read All About It	Steck-Vaughn
Benjamin Franklin	N	B	250+	Pebble Books	Capstone Press
Benjamin Franklin	N	B	250+	Biography	Benchmark Education
Benjamin Franklin: American Inventor	N	B	250+	Rosen Real Readers	Rosen Publishing Group
Ben's Tune	N	RF	250+	PM Ruby	Rigby
Berlioz The Bear	N	F	250+	Brett, Jan	Scholastic
Berta: A Remarkable Dog	N	RF	250+	Lottridge, Celia Barker	Groundwood Books
Best Detective, The	N	RF	250+	Keene, Carolyn	Pocket Books
Beware!	N	RF	250+	Cartwright, Pauline	Pacific Learning
Big Cat Trouble	N	RF	250+	World Quest Adventures	World Quest Learning
Big Fish, The	N	RF	250+	Sunshine	Wright Group/McGraw Hill
Big Gold Mountain	N	RF	250+	Bookweb	Rigby

* Collection of short stories

TITLE	LEVEL	GENRE	WORD COUNT	AUTHOR / SERIES	PUBLISHER / DISTRIBUTOR
Big Gust, The	N	F	650	Leveled Readers	Houghton Mifflin
Big Race, The	N	F	250+	Pye, Trevor	Pacific Learning
Big Toe Robbery, The	N	F	250+	PM Ruby	Rigby
Bill of Rights, The	N	I	250+	A True Book	Children's Press
Billie the Hippo	N	I	250+	Pacific Literacy	Pacific Learning
Billy's Truck Diary	N	I	250+	Sunshine	Wright Group/McGraw Hill
Birds	N	I	250+	Nature's Friends	Compass Point Books
Birds and How They Grow	N	I	250+	National Geographic Society	National Geographic
Birds of a Feather	N	RF	250+	Literacy 2000	Rigby
Birthday	N	RF	250+	Steptoe, John	Henry Holt & Co.
Birthday Party for Cornelius, A	N	RF	250+	Leveled Readers Language Support	Houghton Mifflin
Black Elk: A Man with a Vision	N	B	250+	Rookie Biographies	Children's Press
Black Holes	N	I	250+	A True Book	Children's Press
Black Velvet Mystery, The	N	RF	250+	Keene, Carolyn	Pocket Books
Blackberries in the Dark	N	RF	250+	Jukes, Mavis	Alfred A. Knopf
Blast Off!	N	I	250+	Home Connection Collection	Rigby
Blast to the Past	N	SF	250+	Orbit Chapter Books	Pacific Literacy
Blimps	N	I	250+	A True Book	Children's Press
Blue Layer, The	N	I	250+	Voyages	SRA/McGraw Hill
Bone Tree, The	N	F	250+	Voyages	SRA/McGraw Hill
Boom!	N	I	250+	Gutner, Howard	Scholastic
Boonsville Bombers, The	N	RF	250+	Herzig, Alison	Puffin Books
Boy in the Doghouse, A	N	RF	250+	Duffey, Betsy	Simon & Schuster
Boy of the Three-Year Nap, The	N	TL	250+	Soar To Success	Houghton Mifflin
Boy Who Ate Dog Biscuits, The	N	RF	250+	Sachs, Betsy	Random House
Boy Who Cried Bigfoot, The	N	F	250+	The Zack Files	Grosset & Dunlap
Bozo the Clone	N	SF	250+	The Zack Files	Grosset & Dunlap
Brachiosaurus	N	I	250+	Discovering Dinosaurs	Red Brick Learning
Brad and Butter Play Ball!	N	RF	250+	Hughes, Dean	William Morrow
Brazil	N	I	250+	A True Book	Children's Press
Bridges	N	I	250+	Wildcats	Wright Group/McGraw Hill
Brilliant Bugologist, The	N	RF	250+	Orbit Chapter Books	Pacific Literacy
Bringing Up Baby Chimp	N	I	495	Independent Readers Science	Houghton Mifflin
Brookfield Days	N	HF	250+	Little House	HarperTrophy
Bryce Canyon National Park	N	I	250+	A True Book	Children's Press
Buffalo Woman	N	TL	250+	Goble, Paul	Aladdin
Building a Case	N	I	379	Vocabulary Readers	Houghton Mifflin
Burrows, Tunnels, and Chambers	N	I	250+	Sails	Rigby
*Busybody Nora	N	RF	250+	Hurwitz, Johanna	Penguin Group
Butterflies and Moths	N	I	250+	Kalman, Bobbie	Crabtree
Butterfly Pyramid, The	N	TL	250+	Story Vines	Wright Group/McGraw Hill
By Lakes and Rivers	N	I	250+	Animal Trackers	Crabtree
By the Seashore	N	I	250+	Animal Trackers	Crabtree
California or Bust!	N	HF	250+	Stamper, Judith	Scholastic
Canary Caper, The	N	RF	250+	Roy, Ron	Random House
Candy Creations from the "Candy Queen"	N	I	250+	Bookshop	Mondo
Caribou (Reindeer)	N	I	250+	PM Animal Facts: Silver	Rigby
Case of Hermie the Missing Hamster, The	N	RF	250+	Preller, James	Scholastic
Case of the Christmas Snowman, The	N	RF	250+	Preller, James	Scholastic
Case of the Disappearing Bones	N	RF	250+	SupaDoopers	Sundance
Case of the Nervous Newsboy, The	N	RF	250+	Hildick, E. W.	Sundance
Case of the Secret Valentine, The	N	RF	250+	Preller, James	Scholastic
Case of the Spooky Sleepover, The	N	RF	250+	Preller, James	Scholastic

* Collection of short stories

TITLE	LEVEL	GENRE	WORD COUNT	AUTHOR / SERIES	PUBLISHER / DISTRIBUTOR
Case of the Stolen Baseball Cards, The	N	RF	250+	Preller, James	Scholastic
Cat Burglar of Pethaven Drive, The	N	F	250+	Literacy 2000	Rigby
Cat Talk	N	I	250+	Long, Don	Pacific Learning
Cat Who Wore a Pot on Her Head, The	N	F	250+	Slepian, Jan; Seidler, Ann	Scholastic
Catching the Wind	N	I	250+	iOpeners	Pearson Learning Group
Caterpillars	N	I	250+	Minibeasts	Franklin Watts
Catwings	N	F	250+	Le Guin, Ursula K.	Scholastic
Catwings Return	N	F	250+	Le Guin, Ursula K.	Scholastic
Caught by the Sea	N	RF	250+	Keating, Rosemary	Pacific Learning
Cesar Chavez	N	B	262	Biography	Benchmark Education
Chalk Box Kid, The	N	RF	250+	Bulla, Clyde Robert	Random House
Cheyenne, The	N	I	250+	A New True Book	Children's Press
Chicken Sunday	N	RF	250+	Polacco, Patricia	Scholastic
Chief Great Raven	N	TL	250+	Orbit Double Takes	Pacific Learning
China	N	I	250+	A True Book	Children's Press
Chocolate	N	I	250+	What's For Lunch?	Children's Press
Chocolate Touch, The	N	F	250+	Catling, Patrick Skene	Bantam
Chocolate Trail, The	N	I	250+	Rigby Focus	Rigby
Circulatory System, The	N	I	250+	A True Book	Children's Press
City by the Lake	N	I	250+	Early Connections	Benchmark Education
City Lights	N	RF	250+	Orbit Double Takes	Pacific Learning
Cloud Book, The	N	I	250+	DePaola, Tomie	Scholastic
Clouds	N	I	250+	Literacy 2000	Rigby
Clue in the Glue, The	N	RF	250+	Keene, Carolyn	Pocket Books
Clyde Tombaugh and the Search for Planet X	N	B	250+	Wetterer, Margaret K.	Carolrhoda Books
Coast to Coast	N	I	250+	People, Spaces & Places	Rand McNally
Coconut Seed or Fruit?	N	I	250+	iOpeners	Pearson Learning Group
Codes and Signals	N	I	250+	Cambridge Reading	Pearson Learning Group
Colorful Facts	N	I	561	Leveled Readers Science	Houghton Mifflin
Comets and Meteor Showers	N	I	250+	A True Book	Children's Press
Communication	N	I	250+	Literacy 2000	Rigby
Congress	N	I	250+	A True Book	Children's Press
Constellations	N	I	250+	A True Book	Children's Press
Constitution, The	N	I	250+	A True Book	Children's Press
Cool Treasure, The	N	RF	250+	Orbit Chapter Books	Pacific Literacy
Cora at Camp Blue Waters	N	RF	772	Leveled Readers	Houghton Mifflin
Coral Reef Hunters	N	I	250+	Soar To Success	Houghton Mifflin
Cottle Street	N	RF	250+	Action Packs	Rigby
Courage of Helen Keller, The	N	B	250+	Rosen Real Readers	Rosen Publishing Group
*Coyote Not-So-Clever	N	TL	250+	Beveridge, Barbara	Pacific Learning
Cranes	N	I	250+	Cole, Sally	Wright Group/McGraw Hill
Creature of Cassidy's Creek, The	N	RF	250+	PM Emerald	Rigby
Creatures of the Dark	N	I	250+	Literacy 2000	Rigby
Crossing the Atlantic: One Family's Story	N	I	250+	iOpeners	Pearson Learning Group
Crystal Unicorn, The	N	RF	250+	PM Emerald	Rigby
Curse of the Squirrel, The	N	F	250+	Yep, Laurence	Random House
Dance Wth Rosie	N	RF	250+	Giff, Patricia Reilly	Penguin Group
Dancing with Manatees	N	I	250+	McNulty, Faith	Scholastic
Danger Guys	N	RF	250+	Abbott, Tony	HarperTrophy
Danger Guys Blast Off	N	RF	250+	Abbott, Tony	HarperTrophy
Danger Guys on Ice	N	RF	250+	Abbott, Tony	HarperTrophy
Dark and Full of Secrets	N	RF	250+	Carrick, Carol	Houghton Mifflin
Day Miss Francie Got Skunked, The	N	RF	250+	DeFord, Diane	Pearson Learning Group
Day with the Mayor, A	N	RF	704	Leveled Readers Social Studies	Houghton Mifflin

* Collection of short stories

TITLE	LEVEL	GENRE	WORD COUNT	AUTHOR / SERIES	PUBLISHER / DISTRIBUTOR
Day with Wilbur Robinson, A	N	RF	250+	Joyce, William	HarperTrophy
Deadbolts and Dinkles	N	RF	250+	Tapp, Kathy Kennedy	Mondo
Deadly Dungeon, The	N	RF	250+	Roy, Ron	Random House
Dear Diary	N	RF	250+	Literacy 2000 Satellites	Rigby
Declaration of Independence, The	N	I	250+	A True Book	Children's Press
Desert Birds	N	I	250+	A New True Book	Children's Press
Desert Life	N	I	250+	Mann, Rachel	Scholastic
Deserts	N	I	250+	Habitats of the World	Pearson Learning Group
Deserts	N	I	250+	A True Book	Children's Press
Did You Carry The Flag Today, Charley?	N	RF	250+	Caudill, Rebecca	Bantam
Did You Hear Wind Sing Your Name?	N	TL	182	Bookshop	Mondo
Digestive System, The	N	I	250+	A True Book	Children's Press
Dinosaur Girl	N	RF	250+	Literacy Tree	Rigby
Dinosaur Hunting	N	I	579	Leveled Readers Science	Houghton Mifflin
Diplodocus	N	I	250+	Discovering Dinosaurs	Red Brick Learning
Dog I Share, The	N	RF	250+	Marriott, Janice	Pacific Learning
Dolphins	N	I	250+	Kalman, Bobbie	Crabtree
Dolphin's First Day: The Story of a Bottlenose Dolphin	N	I	250+	Zoehfeld, Kathleen Weidnetz	Scholastic
Donavan's Word Jar	N	RF	250	DeGross, Monalisa	HarperCollins
Don't Call Me Beanhead!	N	RF	250+	Wojciechowski, Susan	Candlewick Press
Dr. Jekyll, Orthodontist	N	RF	250+	The Zack Files	Grosset & Dunlap
Dr. MacTavish's Creature	N	RF	250+	PM Emerald	Rigby
Dr. Seuss and His Stories	N	B	250+	Colgon, Kari	Wright Group/McGraw Hill
Dragon Trouble	N	F	250+	SupaDoopers	Sundance
Dragons Galore	N	F	250+	Wildcats	Wright Group/McGraw Hill
Dream Eater, The	N	F	250+	Garrison, Christian	Aladdin
Duck Magic	N	I	250+	Literacy 2000 Satellites	Rigby
*E is for Elisa	N	RF	250+	Hurwitz, Johanna	Puffin Books
Eagle Feathers	N	TL	250+	Story Vines	Wright Group/McGraw Hill
Eagle Watchers	N	RF	765	Leveled Readers	Houghton Mifflin
Earth	N	I	250+	A True Book	Children's Press
Earthquake in the Third Grade	N	RF	250+	Myers, Laurie	Clarion
Earthquake!	N	RF	250+	Bookweb	Rigby
Earthquakes	N	I	250+	A True Book	Children's Press
Egg Saga, The	N	RF	250+	Sails	Rigby
Einstein: Champion of the World	N	RF	250+	Trussell-Cullen, Alan	Pacific Learning
Eleanor Roosevelt	N	B	250+	Pebble Books	Capstone Press
Electricity Makes Things Work	N	I	250+	PM Plus Nonfiction	Rigby
Electricity: Bulbs, Batteries, and Sparks	N	I	250+	Amazing Science	Picture Window Books
Elephants	N	I	250+	Meadows, Graham; Vial, Claire	Pearson Learning Group
*Elisa in the Middle	N	RF	250+	Hurwitz, Johanna	Penguin Group
Ellen Ochoa	N	B	703	Leveled Readers Science	Houghton Mifflin
Ellis Island	N	I	250+	Early Connections	Benchmark Education
Ellis Island	N	I	250+	A True Book	Children's Press
Ellis Island	N	I	263	Independent Readers Social Studies	Houghton Mifflin
Elvis the Turnip and Me	N	F	250+	The Zack Files	Gosset & Dunlap
Emma's Emu	N	F	250+	First Flight	Fitzhenry & Whiteside
Empty Envelope, The	N	RF	250+	Roy, Ron	Random House
Endangered Animals	N	I	250+	A New True Book	Children's Press
Enormous Crocodile, The	N	F	250+	Dahl, Roald	Penguin Group
Escape!	N	SF	250+	Cartwright, Pauline	Pacific Learning
Europe	N	I	250+	Continents	Capstone Press

* Collection of short stories

TITLE	LEVEL	GENRE	WORD COUNT	AUTHOR / SERIES	PUBLISHER / DISTRIBUTOR
Evil Queen Tut and the Great Ant Pyramids	N	F	250+	The Zack Files	Grosset & Dunlap
Extreme Lives	N	I	250+	Wildcats	Wright Group/McGraw Hill
*Fables	N	TL	250+	Lobel, Arnold	HarperCollins
Falcon, The	N	RF	250+	PM Emerald	Rigby
Falcon's Feathers, The	N	RF	250+	Roy, Ron	Random House
Fangs and Me	N	RF	250+	Gilmore, Rachna	Fitzhenry & Whiteside
Farms	N	I	606	Wonders	Hampton-Brown
Festival Fun	N	I	250+	Wildcats	Wright Group/McGraw Hill
Finding Gold	N	I	848	Leveled Readers Science	Houghton Mifflin
First Apple	N	RF	250+	Russell, Ching Yueng	Penguin Group
First Morning, The	N	TL	250+	Literacy 2000	Rigby
First Things	N	RF	250+	Stepping Stones	Nelson/Michaels Assoc.
Fishy Mystery, The	N	RF	250+	Orbit Chapter Books	Pacific Literacy
Flag For Our Country, A	N	I	250+	Spencer, Eve	Steck-Vaughn
Flamingos	N	I	250+	Cole, Sally	Wright Group/McGraw Hill
Flies	N	I	250+	A True Book	Children's Press
Floating and Paddling	N	I	250+	Strebor, Leon	Wright Group/McGraw Hill
Floods	N	I	250+	A True Book	Children's Press
Florence Nightingale	N	B	228	Pebble Books	Capstone Press
Fly Homer Fly	N	F	250+	Peet, Bill	Houghton Mifflin
Folktales from China	N	TL	250+	Lawson, Barbara	Scholastic
For the Love of Pooch	N	RF	250+	Literacy 2000	Rigby
For the Love of Turtles	N	RF	250+	Greetings	Rigby
Forests	N	I	250+	Habitats of the World	Pearson Learning Group
Forever Amber Brown	N	RF	250+	Danziger, Paula	Scholastic
*Four-Legged Friends	N	TL	250+	Literacy 2000	Rigby
Franklin D. Roosevelt	N	B	223	Pebble Books	Capstone Press
Freshwater Habitats	N	I	250+	Habitats of the World	Pearson Learning Group
Frog Who Would Be King, The	N	TL	250+	Walker, Kate	Mondo
Frogs	N	I	250+	Nature's Friends	Compass Point Books
Frogs	N	I	250+	Bookshop	Mondo
Frogs of Betts, The	N	RF	250+	SupaDoopers	Sundance
Fun Zone	N	F	250+	Sails	Rigby
Funny Bananas: The Mystery in the Museum	N	RF	250+	McHargue, Georgess	Dell
Gadget War, The	N	RF	250+	Duffey, Betsy	Penguin Group
Galaxies	N	I	250+	A True Book	Children's Press
George Washington Carver	N	B	224	Pebble Books	Capstone Press
George Washington: First President of the U.S.	N	B	250+	Rookie Biographies	Children's Press
Ghost Named Wanda, A	N	F	250+	The Zack Files	Grosset & Dunlap
Ghost of Popcorn Hill, The	N	F	250+	Wright, Betty Ren	Scholastic
Gift for Mama, A	N	RF	250+	Hautzig, Esther	Penguin Group
Gift, The	N	TL	250+	Story Vines	Wright Group/McGraw Hill
Ginger's War	N	HF	250+	Daniel, Lea	Wright Group/McGraw Hill
Giraffes	N	I	250+	Meadows, Graham; Vial, Claire	Pearson Learning Group
Glass Slipper for Rosie, A	N	RF	250+	Giff, Patricia Reilly	Penguin Group
Going to America	N	RF	250+	Orbit Chapter Books	Pacific Literacy
Going West	N	I	428	Vocabulary Readers	Houghton Mifflin
Gold Dust Kids, The	N	HF	250+	Dionetti, Michelle	Wright Group/McGraw Hill
Gold Fever!	N	HF	250+	Step into Reading	Random House
Good Dog, Bonita	N	RF	250+	Giff, Patricia Reilly	Bantam
Good Place for a City, A	N	I	194	Windows on Literacy	National Geographic
Goose's Gold, The	N	RF	250+	Roy, Ron	Random House
Grandma Moses	N	B	250+	Biography	Benchmark Education
Grasshoppers	N	I	250+	Nature's Friends	Compass Point Books

* Collection of short stories

TITLE	LEVEL	GENRE	WORD COUNT	AUTHOR / SERIES	PUBLISHER / DISTRIBUTOR
Grasslands	N	I	250+	A True Book	Children's Press
Great Wall of China, The	N	I	141	Vocabulary Readers	Houghton Mifflin
Great-Grandpa's In The Litter Box	N	F	250+	The Zack Files	Grosset & Dunlap
Green Snake	N	I	250+	Life Cycles	Creative Teaching Press
Green Thumbs, Everyone	N	RF	250+	Giff, Patricia Reilly	Bantam
Green with Red Spots Horrible	N	RF	250+	SupaDoopers	Sundance
Gribblegrot from Outer Space, The	N	F	250+	Literacy 2000 Satellites	Rigby
Grizzly Bears	N	I	250+	Woolley, M.; Pigdon, K.	Mondo
Guess How Many	N	I	250+	Rosen Real Readers	Rosen Publishing Group
Gung Hay Fat Choy	N	I	250+	Behrens, June	Children's Press
Hang a Left at Venus	N	F	250+	The Zack Files	Grosset & Dunlap
Hang in there, Oscar Martin!	N	RF	250+	Noonan, Diana	Pacific Learning
Hannah	N	RF	250+	Whelan, Gloria	Random House
Hans Christian Andersen: Prince of Storytellers	N	B	250+	Rookie Biographies	Children's Press
Hanukkah	N	I	250+	Festivals and Holidays	Children's Press
Happy Birthday, Anna, Sorpresa!	N	RF	250+	Giff, Patricia Reilly	Bantam
Harriet Tubman	N	B	239	Pebble Books	Capstone Press
Harry Houdini: Wonderdog!	N	RF	250+	Taylor, William	Pacific Learning
Helen Keller	N	B	250+	Davidson, Margaret	Scholastic
Helen Keller: Courage in the Dark	N	B	250+	Hurwitz, Johanna	Random House
Helen Keller's Teacher	N	B	250+	Davidson, Margaret	Scholastic
Helicopters	N	I	250+	A True Book	Children's Press
Henry Gonzales, U.S. Representative	N	B	491	Leveled Readers Social Studies	Houghton Mifflin
Herbie Jones	N	RF	250+	Kline, Suzy	Penguin Group
Herbie Jones and Hamburger Head	N	RF	250+	Kline, Suzy	Penguin Group
Herbie Jones and the Birthday Showdown	N	RF	250+	Kline, Suzy	Penguin Group
Herbie Jones and the Class Gift	N	RF	250+	Kline, Suzy	Penguin Group
Herbie Jones and the Dark Attic	N	RF	250+	Kline, Suzy	Puffin Books
Herbie Jones and the Monster Ball	N	RF	250+	Kline, Suzy	Penguin Group
Here We All Are	N	B	250+	DePaola, Tomie	Penguin Group
Heroes	N	I	250+	Wildcats	Wright Group/McGraw Hill
Hey, Al	N	F	250+	Yorinks, Arthur	Farrar, Straus and Giroux
Hey, New Kid!	N	RF	250+	Duffey, Betsy	Penguin Group
High Wire	N	RF	250+	Orbit Double Takes	Pacific Learning
High-Flying Contest, The: An African American	N	F	639	Leveled Readers	Houghton Mifflin
History Behind the Holidays	N	I	250+	Early Connections	Benchmark Education
Ho, Ho, Benjamin, Feliz Navidad	N	RF	250+	Giff, Patricia Reilly	Bantam
Hole in the Hill, The	N	RF	250+	Action Packs	Rigby
Holly & Mac	N	RF	250+	SupaDoopers	Sundance
Home Sweet Home	N	I	250+	Literacy 2000	Rigby
Horses	N	I	250+	A New True Book	Children's Press
Horses of the Air	N	I	250+	Little Celebrations	Pearson Learning Group
House on Walenska Street, The	N	RF	250+	Herman, Charlotte	Penguin Group
How a Book is Made	N	I	250+	Aliki	Harper & Row
How I Fixed the Year 1000 Problem	N	F	250+	The Zack Files	Grosset & Dunlap
How I Went from Bad to Verse	N	F	250+	The Zack Files	Grosset & Dunlap
How People Got Wisdom: An Ashanti Tale	N	TL	891	Leveled Readers	Houghton Mifflin
How To Be Cool in the Third Grade	N	RF	250+	Duffey, Betsy	Penguin Group
How To Speak Dolphin in Three Easy Lessons	N	F	250+	The Zack Files	Grosset & Dunlap
How's the Weather?	N	I	250+	Berger, Melvin & Gilda	Ideals Children's Books
Hubble Space Telescope, The	N	I	250+	A True Book	Children's Press
Hummingbird	N	I	250+	Life Cycles	Creative Teaching Press
Hurricanes!	N	I	250+	Hopping, Jean	Scholastic
I Was a Third Grade Science Project	N	RF	250+	Auch, Mary Jane	Yearling

TITLE	LEVEL	GENRE	WORD COUNT	AUTHOR / SERIES	PUBLISHER / DISTRIBUTOR
I, Amber Brown	N	RF	250+	Danziger, Paula	Scholastic
Iceberg Rescue	N	I	464	Leveled Readers	Houghton Mifflin
Ichthyosaurus	N	I	250+	Discovering Dinosaurs	Red Brick Learning
I'm an Artist	N	I	250+	Literacy 2000	Rigby
I'm an Entrepreneur	N	B	501	Independent Readers Social Studies	Houghton Mifflin
I'm Out of My Body . . . Please Leave a Message	N	F	250+	The Zack Files	Grosset & Dunlap
Impossible Bridge, The	N	I	250+	Pacific Literacy	Pacific Learning
In the Forest	N	I	250+	Look Once Look Again	Creative Teaching Press
*Incredible Animal Adventures	N	I	250+	George, Jean Craighead	HarperCollins
Insects	N	I	250+	A New True Book	Children's Press
Inspector Grub and the Fizzer-X Spy	N	RF	250+	Bookweb	Rigby
Irritating Irma	N	F	250+	Literacy 2000	Rigby
Island of Wingo, The	N	F	250+	Sails	Rigby
It Takes All Kinds	N	I	250+	Voyages	SRA/McGraw Hill
It's a Fiesta, Benjamin	N	RF	250+	Giff, Patricia Reilly	Bantam
Jackie Robinson	N	B	250+	Soar To Success	Houghton Mifflin
Jackie Robinson and the Story of All-Black Baseball	N	I	250+	O'Connor, Jim	Random House
Jane Goodall	N	B	250+	Biography	Benchmark Education
Jane Goodall	N	B	250+	Pebble Books	Capstone Press
Jane's Mansion	N	I	250+	Literacy 2000	Rigby
Japan	N	I	250+	A True Book	Children's Press
Jenius: The Amazing Guinea Pig	N	F	250+	King-Smith, Dick	Hyperion
Joe Cocker Spaniel	N	RF	250+	SupaDoopers	Sundance
John Chapman: The Man Who Was Johnny	N	B	250+	Rookie Biographies	Children's Press
John F. Kennedy	N	B	250+	Pebble Books	Capstone Press
John Henry	N	TL	250+	Tall Tales	Compass Point Books
John Muir: Man of the Wild Places	N	B	250+	Rookie Biographies	Children's Press
John Philip Sousa: The March King	N	B	250+	Rookie Biographies	Children's Press
Johnny Appleseed	N	TL	250+	Tall Tales	Compass Point Books
Journey West, The	N	I	250+	Rigby Literacy	Rigby
Joy of Making Music, The	N	I	280	Vocabulary Readers	Houghton Mifflin
Judge Rabbit Helps the Fish	N	TL	250+	Story Vines	Wright Group/McGraw Hill
Julian, Dream Doctor	N	RF	250+	Cameron, Ann	Random House
Julian, Secret Agent	N	RF	250+	Cameron, Ann	Random House
Julian's Glorious Summer	N	RF	250+	Cameron, Ann	Random House
Junkyard Dog, The	N	RF	250+	PM Emerald	Rigby
Jupiter	N	I	250+	A True Book	Children's Press
Just a Few Words, Mr. Lincoln	N	I	250+	Fritz, Jean	Putnam
Kangaroos	N	I	250+	A New True Book	Children's Press
Katherine Dunham, Black Dancer	N	B	250+	Rookie Biographies	Children's Press
Keelboat Annie	N	TL	250+	Johnson, Janet P.	Troll Associates
Keeping Tadpoles	N	I	250+	Discovery World	Rigby
Key to the Treasure	N	RF	250+	Parish, Peggy	Bantam
Kid Next Door, The	N	RF	250+	Smith, Janice Lee	HarperTrophy
Kids Say	N	F	250+	Sails	Rigby
Kites	N	I	250+	Literacy 2000	Rigby
Knife, The	N	RF	250+	Cartwright, Pauline	Pacific Learning
Koalas	N	I	250+	A New True Book	Children's Press
Ladybug	N	I	250+	Life Cycles	Creative Teaching Press
Ladybugs	N	I	250+	Minibeasts	Franklin Watts
Ladybugs	N	I	250+	Nature's Friends	Compass Point Books
Laura Ingalls Wilder: An Author's Story	N	B	250+	Glasscock, Sarah	Steck-Vaughn

* Collection of short stories

TITLE	LEVEL	GENRE	WORD COUNT	AUTHOR / SERIES	PUBLISHER / DISTRIBUTOR
Leftovers, The: Catch Flies!	N	RF	250+	Howard, Tristan	Scholastic
Leftovers, The: Fast Break	N	RF	250+	Howard, Tristan	Scholastic
Leftovers, The: Get Jammed	N	RF	250+	Howard, Tristan	Scholastic
Leftovers, The: Reach Their Goal	N	RF	250+	Howard, Tristan	Scholastic
Leftovers, The: Strike Out!	N	RF	250+	Howard, Tristan	Scholastic
Leftovers, The: Use Their Heads!	N	RF	250+	Howard, Tristan	Scholastic
Legendary Places	N	I	250+	Wildcats	Wright Group/McGraw Hill
Leontyne Price: Opera Superstar	N	B	250+	Williams, Sylvia B.	Children's Press
Let's Go Rock Collecting	N	I	250+	Soar To Success	Houghton Mifflin
Let's Go to the Theater!	N	I	320	Vocabulary Readers	Houghton Mifflin
Letter from Fish Bay, A	N	B	250+	Cowley, Joy	Pacific Learning
Liberty Bell, The	N	I	250+	American Symbols	Capstone Press
Life of a Dollar Bill, The	N	I	301	Leveled Readers Social Studies	Houghton Mifflin
Light at Tern Rock, The	N	RF	250+	Sauer, Julia L.	Scholastic
Lili the Brave	N	RF	250+	Armstrong, Jennifer	Random House
Lily and Miss Liberty	N	HF	250+	Stephens, Carla	Scholastic
Limestone Caves	N	I	250+	A First Book	Franklin Watts
Limestone Caves	N	I	250+	Davis, Gary	Children's Press
Lion Dancer: Ernie Wan's Chinese New Year	N	B	250+	Waters, Kate; Slovenz-Low, Madeline	Scholastic
Lions	N	I	250+	Meadows, Graham; Vial, Claire	Pearson Learning Group
Little Caribou	N	I	250+	Fox-Davies, Sarah	Candlewick Press
Little Sea Pony, The	N	F	250+	Cresswell, Helen	HarperTrophy
Llama Pajamas	N	RF	250+	Clymer, Susan	Scholastic
Look at the Moon	N	I	250+	Bookshop	Mondo
Looking at Animals in Hot Places	N	I	250+	Butterfield, Moira	Steck-Vaughn
Looking for Buddy	N	RF	250+	Leveled Readers Language Support	Houghton Mifflin
Lost Sandals, The	N	RF	250+	Bennett, Jean	Pacific Learning
Louis Braille: Boy Who Invented Books for the Blind	N	B	250+	Davidson, Margaret	Scholastic
Louis Pasteur	N	B	250+	Biography	Benchmark Education
Lucky Candlesticks, The	N	RF	764	Leveled Readers	Houghton Mifflin
Ludwig van Beethoven: Musical Pioneer	N	B	250+	Rookie Biographies	Children's Press
Luke's Bully	N	RF	250+	Winthrop, Elizabeth	Puffin Books
Lunchbox Mystery, The	N	RF	250+	Lohans, Alison	Scholastic
MacGregors and the MacDougalls, The	N	RF	250+	Bookweb	Rigby
Machines in the Home	N	I	250+	Home Connection Collection	Rigby
Mae Jemison: Making Dreams Come True	N	B	540	Leveled Readers	Houghton Mifflin
Magic Finger, The	N	F	250+	Dahl, Roald	Penguin Group
Magic Noodle Show, The	N	RF	250+	Orbit Chapter Books	Pacific Literacy
Magic Passport, The	N	F	250+	Navigators Fiction Series	Benchmark Education
Make It Move!	N	I	215	Yellow Umbrella Books	Capstone Press
*Make Room For Elisa	N	RF	250+	Hurwitz, Johanna	Penguin Group
Making Pop-ups	N	I	250+	Bookshop	Mondo
Mammals	N	I	250+	Simply Science	Compass Point Books
Man in the Moon and Other Moon Tales, The	N	RF	322	Independent Readers Science	Houghton Mifflin
Man Who Tricked a Ghost, The	N	TL	250+	Yep, Laurence	Troll Associates
Marie Curie	N	B	182	Pebble Books	Capstone Press
Marina Silva: Conserving the Rain Forest	N	B	812	Leveled Readers Science	Houghton Mifflin
Marjorie Stoneman Douglas	N	B	294	Independent Readers Social Studies	Houghton Mifflin
Martians Are People, Too	N	F	250+	Navigators Fiction Series	Benchmark Education
Marvelous Menus	N	F	250+	Sails	Rigby

* Collection of short stories

TITLE	LEVEL	GENRE	WORD COUNT	AUTHOR / SERIES	PUBLISHER / DISTRIBUTOR
Math Wiz, The	N	RF	250+	Duffey, Betsy	Penguin Group
Matter	N	I	250+	Our Physical World	Capstone Press
Matter: See It, Touch It, Taste It, Smell It	N	I	250+	Amazing Science	Picture Window Books
Max Malone and the Great Cereal Rip-off	N	RF	250+	Herman, Charlotte	Henry Holt & Co.
Max Malone Makes a Million	N	RF	250+	Herman, Charlotte	Henry Holt & Co.
Max Malone the Magnificent	N	RF	250+	Herman, Charlotte	Scholastic
Max Malone, Superstar	N	RF	250+	Herman, Charlotte	Scholastic
Maya, The	N	I	250+	A New True Book	Children's Press
Medal for Molly, A	N	RF	250+	PM Emerald	Rigby
Meeting Sqauwky	N	I	250+	Books for Young Learners	Richard C. Owen
Mercury	N	I	250+	A True Book	Children's Press
Metropolitan Cow	N	F	250+	Egan, Tim	Houghton Mifflin
Michelle Kwan	N	B	250+	Biography	Benchmark Education
Midnight Rescue	N	RF	250+	Literacy Tree	Rigby
Min-Yo and the Moon Dragon	N	TL	250+	Hillman, Elizabeth	OSI
Miriam Dives Into a Good Book	N	F	653	Leveled Readers	Houghton Mifflin
Misfortune Cookie, The	N	F	250+	The Zack Files	Grosset & Dunlap
Mishmash	N	RF	250+	Cone, Molly	Pocket Books
Mission Control	N	I	250+	Explore Space	Red Brick Learning
Monarch Butterfly	N	I	250+	Life Cycles	Creative Teaching Press
Money Boot, The	N	RF	250+	Russell, Ginny	Fitzhenry & Whiteside
Moon, The	N	I	250+	Literacy 2000	Rigby
More Monsters in School	N	RF	250+	Godfrey, M.	Fitzhenry & Whiteside
*More Stories Huey Tells	N	RF	250+	Cameron, Ann	Alfred A. Knopf
*More Stories Julian Tells	N	RF	250+	Cameron, Ann	Random House
Morse and the Telegraph	N	B	524	Leveled Readers Science	Houghton Mifflin
Motion	N	I	250+	Our Physical World	Capstone Press
Motion: Push and Pull, Fast and Slow	N	I	250+	Amazing Science	Picture Window Books
Mountain Gorillas in Danger	N	I	250+	Soar To Success	Houghton Mifflin
Mountains of Quilt, The	N	F	250+	Willard, Nancy	OSI
Mr. Potter's Pet	N	F	250+	King-Smith, Dick	Hyperion
Mufaro's Beautiful Daughters: An African Tale	N	TL	250+	Steptoe, John	Scholastic
Murals for Joy	N	RF	745	Leveled Readers	Houghton Mifflin
My Brother, the Spy	N	RF	250+	SupaDoopers	Sundance
My Family & the Wasps	N	F	250+	Parker, John	Pearson Learning Group
My Farm	N	RF	250+	Lester, Alison	Houghton Mifflin
My Father's Dragon	N	F	250+	Gannett, Ruth Stiles	Random House
My Friend the Monster	N	F	250+	Bulla, Clyde Robert	Harper & Row
My Great-Aunt Arizona	N	RF	250+	Houston, Gloria	HarperCollins
My Name is Maria Isabel	N	RF	250+	Ada, Alma Flor	Aladdin
My Name is Yun Jim	N	RF	250+	Murphy, Catherine	Wright Group/McGraw Hill
My Son, the Time Traveler	N	F	250+	The Zack Files	Grosset & Dunlap
Mystery of Pony Hollow, The	N	F	250+	Hall, Lynn	Random House
Mystery of the Blue Box, The	N	I	841	Independent Readers Science	Houghton Mifflin
Mystery of the Noises in the Attic, The	N	F	606	Leveled Readers	Houghton Mifflin
Mystery of the Phantom Pony, The	N	RF	250+	Stepping Stone	Random House
Natalia and her Grandma	N	RF	250+	Sunflower	Intercultural Center for Research in Education
National Anthem, The	N	I	250+	A True Book	Children's Press
Neighbor From Outer Space, The	N	F	250+	George, Maureen	Scholastic
Neptune	N	I	250+	A True Book	Children's Press
Nervous System, The	N	I	250+	A True Book	Children's Press
Never Hitch a Ride With a Martian!	N	SF	250+	Clark, Tony	Pacific Learning
Never Trust a Cat Who Wears Earrings	N	F	250+	The Zack Files	Grosset & Dunlap

* Collection of short stories

TITLE	LEVEL	GENRE	WORD COUNT	AUTHOR / SERIES	PUBLISHER / DISTRIBUTOR
New Friends in a New Land: A Thanksgiving Story	N	I	250+	Stamper, Judith Bauer	Steck-Vaughn
New Kid in Town	N	RF	250+	Kroll, Stephen	Avon Camelot
Newf	N	TL	250+	Killilea, Marie	Putnam & Grosset
Next Spring an Oriole	N	HF	250+	Whelan, Gloria	Random House
No Room For a Dog	N	RF	250+	Nichols, Joan Kane	Hearst
No Way, Winky Blue!	N	F	4053	Jane, Pamela	Mondo
North America	N	I	250+	Continents	Capstone Press
Not-So-Perfect Rosie	N	RF	250+	Giff, Patricia Reilly	Penguin Group
Now You See Me . . . Now You Don't	N	F	250+	The Zack Files	Grosset & Dunlap
Oak Tree Controversy	N	RF	250+	Bookweb	Rigby
Obadiah the Bold	N	RF	250+	Turkle, Brinton	Penguin Group
Ocean by the Lake, The	N	I	250+	Little Celebrations	Pearson Learning Group
Off To Squintum's/The Four Musicians	N	TL	1268	Collins, Gillian	Mondo
Ogs Discover Fire and Other Stuff, The	N	F	250+	Navigators Drama Series	Benchmark Education
Olympics and the Mini Olympics, The	N	I	250+	Mack, Rachel	Wright Group/McGraw Hill
On My Way	N	B	250+	DePaola, Tomie	Penguin Group
On Safari	N	I	250+	Windows on Literacy	National Geographic
On the Beams	N	I	328	Independent Readers Social Studies	Houghton Mifflin
On the Farm	N	I	250+	iOpeners	Pearson Learning Group
On the List	N	F	250+	Sails	Rigby
On the Menu	N	F	250+	Sails	Rigby
On the Right Track	N	I	250+	Home Connection Collection	Rigby
One Day in May	N	F	710	Leveled Readers	Houghton Mifflin
One Day, Two Stars	N	RF	250+	Leveled Readers Language Support	Houghton Mifflin
Oscar & Tatiana	N	RF	250+	Literacy 2000	Rigby
Our Book of Maps	N	I	250+	Discovery World	Rigby
Our Star, the Sun	N	I	599	Leveled Readers Science	Houghton Mifflin
Papagayo the Mischief Maker	N	TL	250+	McDermott, Gerald	Harcourt Trade
Paper Shapes	N	I	250+	Voyages	SRA/McGraw Hill
Pasta	N	I	250+	Little Celebrations	Pearson Learning Group
Paul Bunyan	N	TL	250+	Tall Tales	Compass Point Books
Pecos Bill	N	TL	250+	Tall Tales	Compass Point Books
People Who Traveled with Lewis and Clark, The	N	B	555	Leveled Readers Social Studies	Houghton Mifflin
Pet for Sol, A	N	F	619	Leveled Readers	Houghton Mifflin
Pet Vet	N	I	250+	Pacific Literacy	Pacific Learning
Phan's Diary	N	RF	250+	PM Ruby	Rigby
Photos, Photos	N	I	250+	Wildcats	Wright Group/McGraw Hill
Phyllis Wheatley: First African-American Poet	N	B	250+	Rookie Biographies	Children's Press
Picture Book of Jesse Owens, A	N	B	250+	Adler, David A.	Holiday House
Picture Book of John F. Kennedy, A	N	B	250+	Adler, David A.	Holiday House
Picture Book of Robert E. Lee, A	N	B	250+	Adler, David A.	Holiday House
Pie Magic	N	F	250+	Cornell, Laura	Beech Tree Books
Pioneer Cat	N	HF	250+	Hooks, William H.	Random House
Pirate's Promise	N	RF	250+	Bulla, Clyde Robert	HarperTrophy
Pitching Trouble	N	RF	250+	Kroll, Stephen	Avon Camelot
Planning a Birthday Party	N	I	250+	Bookshop	Mondo
Plant Leaves	N	I	250+	Look Once Look Again	Creative Teaching Press
Plant Stems and Roots	N	I	250+	Look Once Look Again	Creative Teaching Press
Playing Favorites	N	RF	250+	Kroll, Steven	Avon Camelot
Pledge of Allegiance, The	N	I	250+	American Symbols	Capstone Press
Pluto	N	I	250+	A True Book	Children's Press

* Collection of short stories

TITLE	LEVEL	GENRE	WORD COUNT	AUTHOR / SERIES	PUBLISHER / DISTRIBUTOR
Pluto	N	I	250+	A First Book	Franklin Watts
Pocahontas: Daughter of a Chief	N	B	250+	Rookie Biographies	Children's Press
Poet from the Plains, A	N	B	353	Vocabulary Readers	Houghton Mifflin
Polar Bears	N	I	250+	PM Animal Facts: Silver	Rigby
Polar Regions	N	I	250+	Habitats of the World	Pearson Learning Group
Police Files	N	RF	250+	Sails	Rigby
Pompeii . . . Buried Alive!	N	I	250+	Kunhardt, Edith	Random House
Popcorn Book, The	N	I	250+	DePaola, Tomie	Holiday House
Portia and the Math Problems	N	B	250+	Leveled Readers Language Support	Houghton Mifflin
Possum's Bare Tail	N	TL	770	Leveled Readers	Houghton Mifflin
Postcards From France	N	I	250+	Arnold, Helen	Steck-Vaughn
Postcards From Kenya	N	I	250+	Arnold, Helen	Steck-Vaughn
Postcards From South Africa	N	I	250+	Dawson, Zoe	Steck-Vaughn
Postcards From Vietnam	N	I	250+	Allard, Denise	Steck-Vaughn
Potato	N	RF	250+	Peirce, Robin	Wright Group/McGraw Hill
Potter in Fiji, A	N	I	453	Wonder World	Wright Group/McGraw Hill
Pourquoi Tales	N	TL	523	Vocabulary Readers	Houghton Mifflin
Power Machines	N	I	250+	Robbins, Ken	Henry Holt & Co.
Prehistoric Record Breakers	N	I	250+	Discovery World	Rigby
Presidency, The	N	I	250+	A True Book	Children's Press
Pride of the Rockets	N	RF	250+	Kroll, Stephen	Avon Camelot
Princess Euphorbia	N	RF	250+	SupaDoopers	Sundance
Problems with My Pudding	N	I	950	Leveled Readers Science	Houghton Mifflin
Project Apollo	N	I	250+	A True Book	Children's Press
Project Gemini	N	I	250+	A True Book	Children's Press
Project Mercury	N	I	250+	A True Book	Children's Press
Prudence	N	I	250+	Raatma, Lucia	Red Brick Learning
Pudding Problems	N	RF	921	Leveled Readers Science	Houghton Mifflin
Puppy Love	N	RF	250+	Duffey, Betsy	Puffin Books
Queen of the Bean	N	RF	250+	Action Packs	Rigby
Queen of the Pool	N	RF	250+	PM Emerald	Rigby
Quilt with a Difference, A	N	I	250+	Pacific Literacy	Pacific Learning
Rabbits	N	I	250+	Literacy 2000	Rigby
Rachel Carson, Scientist and Writer	N	B	370	Independent Readers Social Studies	Houghton Mifflin
Rachel Carson: Friend of Nature	N	B	250+	Rookie Biographies	Children's Press
Rain Forest, The	N	I	191	Windows on Literacy	National Geographic
Rainbow Solution, The	N	RF	250+	Literacy 2000	Rigby
Return of the Home Run Kid	N	RF	250+	Christopher, Matt	Scholastic
Rhythm and Shoes	N	I	250+	Pacific Literacy	Pacific Learning
River Life	N	I	250+	Windows on Literacy	National Geographic
River Race	N	HF	250+	Leveled Readers Language Support	Houghton Mifflin
River's Journey, The	N	I	221	Windows on Literacy	National Geographic
Roberto Clemente: Baseball Superstar	N	B	250+	Rookie Biographies	Children's Press
Rocks	N	I	250+	Simply Science	Compass Point Books
Rocks: Hard, Soft, Smooth, and Rough	N	I	250+	Amazing Science	Picture Window Books
Rodeo!	N	I	1186	Leveled Readers Social Studies	Houghton Mifflin
Rodney, the Surfing Duck	N	F	250+	SupaDoopers	Sundance
Rollerama	N	RF	250+	SupaDoopers	Sundance
Rollercoaster Science	N	I	250+	Rigby Literacy	Rigby
Rosie: A Visiting Dog's Story	N	I	250+	Soar To Success	Houghton Mifflin
Rosie's Big City Ballet	N	RF	250+	Giff, Patricia Reilly	Penguin Group

* Collection of short stories

TITLE	LEVEL	GENRE	WORD COUNT	AUTHOR / SERIES	PUBLISHER / DISTRIBUTOR
Rosie's Nutcracker Dreams	N	RF	250+	Giff, Patricia Reilly	Penguin Group
Round and Round: The Story of Wheels	N	I	250+	Home Connection Collection	Rigby
Rumpelstiltskin	N	TL	250+	Zelinsky, Paul O.	Scholastic
Ruthie's Perfect Poem	N	RF	744	Leveled Readers	Houghton Mifflin
Sacagawea	N	I	242	Leveled Readers	Houghton Mifflin
Sacajawea	N	B	250+	Biography	Benchmark Education
Salmon	N	I	250+	Bookshop	Mondo
Sam and the Lucky Money	N	RF	250+	Soar To Success	Houghton Mifflin
Sam Houston	N	B	248	Pebble Books	Capstone Press
Saturn	N	I	250+	A First Book	Franklin Watts
Saturn	N	I	250+	A True Book	Children's Press
Save the Manatee	N	I	250+	Friesinger, Alison	Random House
Saving the Park	N	RF	250+	Wilson, Sarah	Pacific Learning
Say Hola, Sarah	N	RF	250+	Giff, Patricia Reilly	Bantam
Scare in the City, A	N	RF	250+	Chanek, Sherilin	Hampton-Brown
Scary Day, The	N	RF	250+	Bennett, Jean	Pacific Learning
School's Out	N	RF	250+	Hurwitz, Johanna	Scholastic
Seals and Sea Lions	N	I	250+	Cole, Sally	Wright Group/McGraw Hill
Seasons	N	I	250+	Simply Science	Compass Point Books
Seasons	N	I	250+	A True Book	Children's Press
Second Chance	N	RF	250+	Kroll, Stephen	Avon Camelot
Second Story Sally	N	RF	250+	SupaDoopers	Sundance
Second-Grade Star	N	RF	250+	Alberts, Nancy	Scholastic
Secret Land of the Past	N	F	250+	Schlein, Miriam	Scholastic
Secret, The	N	RF	250+	PM Emerald	Rigby
Self-Discipline	N	I	250+	Raatma, Lucia	Red Brick Learning
Shadow of the Wolf	N	I	250+	Whelan, Gloria	Random House
Shapes of Water, The: Stories About Patterns and Shapes	N	I	250+	Shannan, Gillian	Pacific Learning
Shark in School	N	RF	250+	Giff, Patricia Reilly	Bantam
Sharks	N	I	250+	Bookshop	Mondo
Shoeshine Girl	N	RF	250+	Bulla, Clyde Robert	HarperTrophy
Should We Have Pets?: A Persuasive Text	N	I	250+	Bookshop	Mondo
Show-and-Tell War, The	N	RF	250+	Smith, Janice Lee	HarperTrophy
Sidewalk Story	N	RF	250+	Mathis, Sharon Bell	Penguin Group
Silkworms	N	I	250+	Blackburn, Rachel	Wright Group/McGraw Hill
Silver	N	RF	250+	Whelan, Gloria	Random House
Simon and the Aliens	N	SF	250+	SupaDoopers	Sundance
Sitting Bull	N	B	217	Pebble Books	Capstone Press
Skirt, The	N	RF	250+	Soto, Gary	Bantam
Sky	N	RF	506	Leveled Readers	Houghton Mifflin
Slugs and Snails	N	I	250+	Bookshop	Mondo
Slump, The	N	RF	250+	Kroll, Stephen	Avon Camelot
Smartest Bear and His Brother Oliver, The	N	F	250+	Bach, Alice	Bantam
Soccer Fun!	N	RF	661	Leveled Readers	Houghton Mifflin
Sod Houses on the Great Plains	N	I	250+	Rounds, Glen	Holiday House
Soil	N	I	250+	Simply Science	Compass Point Books
Solar System, The	N	I	250+	Simply Science	Compass Point Books
Solar System, The	N	I	250+	A True Book	Children's Press
Solids, Liquids, Gases	N	I	250+	Simply Science	Compass Point Books
Someday Cyril	N	RF	250+	Gershator, Phillis	Mondo
Someone is Following Pip Ramsey	N	RF	250+	Roy, Ron	Random House
Something Queer at the Ball Park	N	RF	250+	Levy, Elizabeth	Bantam
Something Queer at the Haunted School	N	RF	250+	Levy, Elizabeth	Bantam

* Collection of short stories

TITLE	LEVEL	GENRE	WORD COUNT	AUTHOR / SERIES	PUBLISHER / DISTRIBUTOR
Something Queer at the Lemonade Stand	N	RF	250+	Levy, Elizabeth	Bantam
Something Queer at the Library	N	RF	250+	Levy, Elizabeth	Bantam
Something Queer at the Scary Movie	N	RF	250+	Levy, Elizabeth	Hyperion
Something Queer in Outer Space	N	RF	250+	Levy, Elizabeth	Hyperion
Something Queer in the Cafeteria	N	RF	250+	Levy, Elizabeth	Hyperion
Something Queer in the Wild West	N	RF	250+	Levy, Elizabeth	Hyperion
Something Queer Is Going On	N	RF	250+	Levy, Elizabeth	Bantam
Something Queer on Vacation	N	RF	250+	Levy, Elizabeth	Bantam
Sound	N	I	250+	Windows on Literacy	National Geographic
Sounds	N	I	250+	Lighthouse	Rigby
South America	N	I	250+	Continents	Capstone Press
Space Missions	N	I	250+	Explore Space!	Red Brick Learning
Space Stations	N	I	250+	A True Book	Children's Press
Space Suits	N	I	250+	Explore Space	Red Brick Learning
Spiders	N	I	250+	Minibeasts	Franklin Watts
Spider's Web	N	I	250+	Back, Christine	Silver Burdett Press
Spirit of Hope	N	F	250+	Bookshop	Mondo
Splatter	N	RF	250+	Marriott, Janice	Pacific Learning
Spy Maps	N	F	250+	Sails	Rigby
Squirrels	N	I	460	Storyteller Nonfiction	Wright Group/McGraw Hill
Stage Fright	N	RF	250+	Martin, Ann M.	Scholastic
Starring Rosie	N	RF	250+	Giff, Patricia Reilly	Penguin Group
Stars	N	I	250+	A True Book	Children's Press
Statue of Liberty, The	N	I	250+	American Symbols	Capstone Press
Statue of Liberty, The	N	I	250+	A True Book	Children's Press
Stepping Through Time	N	I	250+	Rigby Literacy	Rigby
Stomachs	N	I	250+	Sails	Rigby
*Stories Huey Tells, The	N	RF	250+	Cameron, Ann	Alfred A. Knopf
*Stories Julian Tells, The	N	RF	250+	Cameron, Ann	Alfred A. Knopf
Storm in the Night	N	RF	250+	Stolz, Mary	HarperCollins
Storms	N	I	250+	Windows on Literacy	National Geographic
Storms	N	I	250+	PM Plus Story Books	Rigby
Strange Creatures	N	SF	250+	Cartwright, Pauline	Pacific Learning
Streak, The	N	RF	250+	Kroll, Stephen	Avon Camelot
Striped Ice Cream	N	RF	250+	Lexau, Joan M.	Scholastic
Sun, The	N	I	250+	Windows on Literacy	National Geographic
Sun, The	N	I	573	Leveled Readers Science	Houghton Mifflin
Sun, The	N	I	250+	Literacy 2000	Rigby
Sunday Horse	N	RF	250+	Literacy Tree	Rigby
Sunflower	N	I	250+	Life Cycles	Creative Teaching Press
Supernova	N	RF	250+	PM Ruby	Rigby
Super-tuned!	N	RF	250+	PM Emerald	Rigby
Supreme Court, The	N	I	250+	A True Book	Children's Press
Susan B. Anthony	N	B	237	Pebble Books	Capstone Press
Susan B. Anthony, Fighter for Women's Rights	N	I	381	Independent Readers Social Studies	Houghton Mifflin
Take A Look	N	I	250+	Wildcats	Wright Group/McGraw Hill
Talk! Talk! Talk!	N	I	50	Little Celebrations	Pearson Learning Group
Tall Tale of John Henry, The	N	TL	250+	Neufeld, David	Scholastic
Tattercoat, A Cinderella Tale from England	N	TL	250+	Leveled Readers	Houghton Mifflin
Tchin the Storyteller	N	B	269	Vocabulary Readers	Houghton Mifflin
Teeth	N	I	250+	Rigby Literacy	Rigby
Telling Stories Through Art	N	I	250+	Reimer, Luther	Wright Group/McGraw Hill
Ten O'Clock Club, The	N	F	250+	York, Carol Beach	Scholastic

* Collection of short stories

TITLE	LEVEL	GENRE	WORD COUNT	AUTHOR / SERIES	PUBLISHER / DISTRIBUTOR
Thank You, Sandra Cisneros	N	RF	250+	Leveled Readers	Houghton Mifflin
Theodore Roosevelt	N	B	208	Pebble Books	Capstone Press
Third Grade Bullies	N	RF	250+	Levy, Elizabeth	Hyperion
Thomas Jefferson	N	I	157	Independent Readers Social Studies	Houghton Mifflin
Thomas Jefferson: Author, Inventor, President	N	B	250+	Rookie Biographies	Children's Press
Three Ships for Columbus	N	I	250+	Stories of America	Steck-Vaughn
Through the Medicine Cabinet	N	F	250+	The Zack Files	Grosset & Dunlap
Throw-Away Pets	N	RF	250+	Duffey, Betsy	Puffin Books
Thunderstorms	N	I	250+	A True Book	Children's Press
Thurgood Marshall: First Black Supreme Court Justice	N	B	250+	Rookie Biographies	Children's Press
Tiger Woods	N	B	250+	Biography	Benchmark Education
Tikki Tikki Tembo	N	TL	250+	Mosel, Arlene	Scholastic
Timedetectors	N	SF	250+	SupaDoopers	Sundance
Titanic, The: Lost . . . and Found	N	I	250+	Donnelly, Judy	Random House
To the Top!: Climbing the World's Highest Mountain	N	B	250+	Kramer, Sydelle	Random House
Tom Edison's Bright Idea	N	B	250+	Keller, Jack	Steck-Vaughn
Toothwalkers	N	I	250+	Sails	Rigby
Tornadoes!	N	I	250+	Hopping, Lorraine Jean	Scholastic
*Tortoise Shell and Other African Stories, The	N	TL	250+	Smith, Geof	Scholastic
Tractor Trailers	N	I	250+	Schaefer, Lola M.	Red Brick Learning
Treehouse Club, The	N	RF	250+	Navigators Fiction Series	Benchmark Education
Trojan Horse, The	N	I	250+	Literacy 2000	Rigby
Trojan Horse, The: How the Greeks Won the War	N	HF	250+	Little, Emily	Random House
Tropical Rainforests	N	I	250+	Habitats of the World	Pearson Learning Group
Trouble with Buster, The	N	RF	250+	Lorimer, Janet	Scholastic
Trouble with Parents, The	N	RF	250+	SupaDoopers	Sundance
*True-Life Treasure Hunts	N	I	250+	Donnelly, Judy	Random House
Turkeys' Side of It, The	N	RF	250+	Smith, Janice Lee	HarperTrophy
U.S. Airforce, The	N	I	250+	The U.S. Armed Forces	Capstone Press
U.S. Army, The	N	I	250+	The U.S. Armed Forces	Capstone Press
U.S. Marine Corps, The	N	I	250+	The U.S. Armed Forces	Capstone Press
U.S. Navy, The	N	I	250+	The U.S. Armed Forces	Capstone Press
Unbelievable Johnny Appleseed, The	N	B	250+	Leveled Readers Language Support	Houghton Mifflin
Uncle Tease	N	RF	250+	Literacy Tree	Rigby
Underfoot	N	I	250+	Look Once Look Again	Creative Teaching Press
Underground Railroad, The	N	I	250+	Twig	Wright Group/McGraw Hill
Unusual Spiders	N	I	250+	Jensen, Ned	Wright Group/McGraw Hill
Up and Away!: Taking a Flight	N	RF	250+	Bookshop	Mondo
Up High in the Mountains	N	RF	250+	Wildcats	Wright Group/McGraw Hill
Uranus	N	I	250+	A True Book	Children's Press
Venus	N	I	250+	A True Book	Children's Press
Very Best Fish, The	N	RF	250+	Leveled Readers Language Support	Houghton Mifflin
Veterans Day	N	I	250+	Leveled Readers Social Studies	Houghton Mifflin
Veterans' Day	N	I	555	Leveled Readers Social Studies	Houghton Mifflin
Victor Takes a Sewing Class	N	RF	250+	Leveled Readers Language Support	Houghton Mifflin
Visit to a Museum	N	I	306	Leveled Readers Social Studies	Houghton Mifflin
Volcano Goddess Will See You Now, The	N	F	250+	The Zack Files	Grosset & Dunlap

TITLE	LEVEL	GENRE	WORD COUNT	AUTHOR / SERIES	PUBLISHER / DISTRIBUTOR
Volcanoes	N	I	250+	Early Connections	Benchmark Education
Volcanoes	N	I	250+	A True Book	Children's Press
Wacky Wheels	N	I	250+	Pacific Literacy	Pacific Learning
Walking on the Moon	N	I	250+	Explore Space	Red Brick Learning
Water	N	I	250+	Simply Science	Compass Point Books
Water and Wind	N	I	250+	PM Plus Story Books	Rigby
Water Wise	N	I	250+	iOpeners	Pearson Learning Group
We Need Insects	N	I	250+	iOpeners	Pearson Learning Group
Weather	N	I	250+	Literacy 2000	Rigby
Weather	N	I	250+	Simply Science	Compass Point Books
Weather Alert!	N	I	314	Independent Readers Social Studies	Houghton Mifflin
Weather Watch	N	I	624	Wonders!	Hampton-Brown
Whale Music	N	RF	771	Leveled Readers	Houghton Mifflin
Whale Tales	N	I	250+	Westerskov, Kim	Pacific Learning
Whales	N	I	250+	PM Animal Facts: Silver	Rigby
Whales on the Move	N	I	250+	Little Celebrations	Pearson Learning Group
Whales' Song, The	N	I	250+	Sheldon, Dyan	Penguin Group
What a Year	N	RF	250+	DePaola, Tomie	Penguin Group
What Am I Made Of?	N	I	250+	Bennett, David	Scholastic
What Can It Be?	N	I	250+	Schaefer, Lola M.	Benchmark Education
What Causes Forest Fires?	N	I	868	Leveled Readers Science	Houghton Mifflin
What Lives on a Prairie?	N	I	250+	Rosen Real Readers	Rosen Publishing Group
What's the Matter with Herbie Jones?	N	RF	250+	Kline, Suzy	Penguin Group
What's the Matter, Kelly Beans?	N	RF	250+	Enderle, Judith R.; Tessler, S. G.	Candlewick Press
What's This?	N	I	250+	Literacy 2000	Rigby
When Children Worked	N	I	292	Independent Readers Social Studies	Houghton Mifflin
When I Forgot	N	RF	250+	Marriott, Janice	Pacific Learning
Where Do You Live?	N	I	250+	People, Places & Spaces	Rand McNally
Where Does Rain Come From?	N	I	250+	Rosen Real Readers	Rosen Publishing Group
White Bird	N	RF	250+	Bulla, Clyde Robert	Random House
White House, The	N	I	250+	American Symbols	Capstone Press
Whiteout	N	RF	1029	Leveled Readers	Houghton Mifflin
Who Eats What?	N	I	697	Leveled Readers Science	Houghton Mifflin
Why Did They Come?	N	I	157	Windows on Literacy	National Geographic
Why Mosquitoes Buzz in People's Ears	N	TL	250+	Aardema, Verna	Scholastic
Wild Baby Animals	N	I	250+	Little Celebrations	Pearson Learning Group
Wild Willie and King Kyle Detectives	N	F	250+	Joosse, Barbara M.	Bantam
Wildfires	N	I	250+	A True Book	Children's Press
William's Journal	N	HF	250+	Early Connections	Benchmark Education
Winslow Homer, American Painter	N	I	348	Independent Readers Social Studies	Houghton Mifflin
Wolfgang Amadeus Mozart: Musical Genius	N	B	250+	Rookie Biographies	Children's Press
Wolves	N	I	250+	PM Animal Facts: Silver	Rigby
Wonderful Alexander and the Catwings	N	F	250+	LeGuin, Ursula	Scholastic
Wonders of the World	N	I	250+	Sunshine	Wright Group/McGraw Hill
Wood Stork Swamp	N	RF	250+	Orbit Double Takes	Pacific Learning
Working Cotton	N	RF	250+	Williams, Sherley Anne	Harcourt Trade
Writer's Work, A	N	I	481	Wonder World	Wright Group/McGraw Hill
Wrong Way Around Magic	N	F	250+	Chew, Ruth	Scholastic
X Marks the Spot	N	I	250+	Home Connection Collection	Rigby
Yabby Tale, A	N	RF	250+	Sunshine	Wright Group/McGraw Hill
Year of the Panda, The	N	RF	250+	Soar To Success	Houghton Mifflin

* Collection of short stories

TITLE	LEVEL	GENRE	WORD COUNT	AUTHOR / SERIES	PUBLISHER / DISTRIBUTOR
Yellowstone: Our First National Park	N	I	250+	Rosen Real Readers	Rosen Publishing Group
Yikes! Grandma's a Teenager	N	F	250+	The Zack Files	Grosset & Dunlap
You Can't Eat Your Chicken Pox, Amber Brown	N	RF	250+	Danziger, Paula	Scholastic
Young Martin's Promise	N	B	250+	Stories of America	Steck-Vaughn
You're Out	N	RF	250+	Kroll, Stephen	Avon Camelot
Zap! I'm a Mind Reader	N	SF	250+	The Zack Files	Grosset & Dunlap
Zebras	N	I	250+	Meadows, Graham; Vial, Claire	Pearson Learning Group
Zipping, Zapping, Zooming Bats	N	I	250+	Soar To Success	Houghton Mifflin
89th Kitten, The	O	RF	250+	Nilsson, Eleanor	Scholastic
Abraham Lincoln	O	B	250+	Early Biographies	Compass Point Books
Abraham Lincoln: President of a Divided Country	O	B	250+	Greene, Carol	Children's Press
Adventure In Alaska	O	I	250+	Kramer, S. A.	Random House
*Adventures of Ali Baba Bernstein, The	O	RF	250+	Hurwitz, Johanna	Scholastic
*Aesop & Company: With Scenes from His Legendary Life	O	TL	250+	Bader, Barbara	Houghton Mifflin
*African-American Scientists	O	B	250+	St. John, Jetty	Red Brick Learning
Aldo Ice Cream	O	RF	250+	Hurwitz, Johanna	Penguin Group
Aldo Peanut Butter	O	RF	250+	Hurwitz, Johanna	Penguin Group
Alfred the Curious	O	RF	250+	PM Emerald	Rigby
*Ali Baba Bernstein, Lost and Found	O	RF	250+	Hurwitz, Johanna	Avon
All About Bikes	O	I	250+	iOpeners	Pearson Learning Group
All About Money	O	I	250+	Let's See	Compass Point Books
All Kinds of Animals	O	I	250+	It's Science	Children's Press
All the World's a Stage	O	I	250+	Literacy Tree	Rigby
Allen Jay and the Underground Railroad	O	HF	250+	Brill, Marlene Targ	Carolrhoda Books
Almost Starring Skinnybones	O	RF	250+	Park, Barbara	Random House
Alroy's Very Nearly Clean Bedroom	O	RF	250+	SupaDoopers	Sundance
Amazing Adaptations	O	I	453	Independent Readers Science	Houghton Mifflin
Amelia's Road	O	RF	250+	Soar To Success	Houghton Mifflin
Amigo	O	F	250+	Baylor, Byrd	Aladdin
Anansi Does the Impossible	O	TL	250+	Aardema, Verna	Simon & Schuster
Angel Park Hoopstars: Nothing But Net	O	RF	250+	Hughes, Dean	Alfred A. Knopf
Angel Park Hoopstars: Point Guard	O	RF	250+	Hughes, Dean	Alfred A. Knopf
Angel Park Soccer Stars: Backup Goalie	O	RF	250+	Hughes, Dean	Random House
Angel Park Soccer Stars: Defense!	O	RF	250+	Hughes, Dean	Alfred A. Knopf
Angel Park Soccer Stars: Psyched!	O	RF	250+	Hughes, Dean	Random House
Angel Park Soccer Stars: Total Soccer	O	RF	250+	Hughes, Dean	Alfred A. Knopf
Angel Park Soccer Stars: Victory Goal	O	RF	250+	Hughes, Dean	Alfred A. Knopf
Angel's Mother's Boyfriend	O	RF	250+	Delton, Judy	Houghton Mifflin
*Angry Bull and Other Cases, The	O	RF	250+	Simon, Seymour	Avon
Animal Champions	O	I	250+	Jones, Teri Crawford	Pearson Learning Group
Animal Hiding Places	O	I	250+	Windows on Literacy	National Geographic
Animal Look-Alikes	O	I	250+	iOpeners	Pearson Learning Group
Animals Nearby	O	I	943	Leveled Readers Science	Houghton Mifflin
Animals of the Ice and Snow	O	I	250+	Literacy 2000	Rigby
Ant	O	I	250+	Chinery, Michael	Troll Associates
Ant Cities	O	I	250+	Dorros, Arthur	HarperCollins
Antarctica: The Last Great Wilderness	O	I	250+	Rigby Literacy	Rigby
Apache Indian Community, An	O	I	250+	Rosen Real Readers	Rosen Publishing Group
Ark, The	O	HF	250+	Geisert, Arthur	Houghton Mifflin
At 1600 Pennsylvania Avenue	O	I	250+	Wirth, Crystal	Scholastic
Australia	O	I	250+	Countries of the World	Red Brick Learning
Baby Animal Zoo	O	I	250+	Martin, Ann M.	Scholastic

* Collection of short stories

TITLE	LEVEL	GENRE	WORD COUNT	AUTHOR / SERIES	PUBLISHER / DISTRIBUTOR
Baby-Sitters Club Mystery: Beware, Dawn!	O	RF	250+	Martin, Ann M.	Scholastic
Baby-Sitters Club Mystery: Claudia, Clue in the Photograph	O	RF	250+	Martin, Ann M.	Scholastic
Baby-Sitters Club Mystery: Claudia, Mystery at the Museum	O	RF	250+	Martin, Ann M.	Scholastic
Baby-Sitters Club Mystery: Claudia, Recipe for Danger	O	RF	250+	Martin, Ann M.	Scholastic
Baby-Sitters Club Mystery: Dawn, Disappearing Dogs	O	RF	250+	Martin, Ann M.	Scholastic
Baby-Sitters Club Mystery: Dawn, Halloween Mystery	O	RF	250+	Martin, Ann M.	Scholastic
Baby-Sitters Club Mystery: Dawn, Surfer Ghost	O	RF	250+	Martin, Ann M.	Scholastic
Baby-Sitters Club Mystery: Jessi, Jewel Thieves	O	RF	250+	Martin, Ann M.	Scholastic
Baby-Sitters Club Mystery: Kristy, Haunted Mansion	O	RF	250+	Martin, Ann M.	Scholastic
Baby-Sitters Club Mystery: Kristy, Missing Child	O	RF	250+	Martin, Ann M.	Scholastic
Baby-Sitters Club Mystery: Kristy, Missing Fortune	O	RF	250+	Martin, Ann M.	Scholastic
Baby-Sitters Club Mystery: Kristy, Vampires	O	RF	250+	Martin, Ann M.	Scholastic
Baby-Sitters Club Mystery: Mallory, Ghost Cat	O	RF	250+	Martin, Ann M.	Scholastic
Baby-Sitters Club Mystery: Mary Anne, Library Mystery	O	RF	250+	Martin, Ann M.	Scholastic
Baby-Sitters Club Mystery: Mary Anne, Secret in the Attic	O	RF	250+	Martin, Ann M.	Scholastic
Baby-Sitters Club Mystery: Mary Anne, Zoo Mystery	O	RF	250+	Martin, Ann M.	Scholastic
Baby-Sitters Club Mystery: Mystery at Claudia's House	O	RF	250+	Martin, Ann M.	Scholastic
Baby-Sitters Club Mystery: Stacey and the Mystery Money	O	RF	250+	Martin, Ann M.	Scholastic
Baby-Sitters Club Mystery: Stacey, Haunted Masquerade	O	RF	250+	Martin, Ann M.	Scholastic
Baby-Sitters Club Mystery: Stacey, Missing Ring	O	RF	250+	Martin, Ann M.	Scholastic
Baby-Sitters Club Mystery: Stacey, Mystery at the Empty House	O	RF	250+	Martin, Ann M.	Scholastic
Baby-Sitters Club Mystery: Stacey, Mystery at the Mall	O	RF	250+	Martin, Ann M.	Scholastic
Baby-Sitters Club Special Edition, The: Readers' Request	O	RF	250+	Martin, Ann M.	Scholastic
Baby-Sitters Club: Abby and the Best Kid Ever	O	RF	250+	Martin, Ann M.	Scholastic
Baby-Sitters Club: Abby, the Bad Sport	O	RF	250+	Martin, Ann M.	Scholastic
Baby-Sitters Club: Claudia and the Bad Joke	O	RF	250+	Martin, Ann M.	Scholastic
Baby-Sitters Club: Claudia and the Little Liar	O	RF	250+	Martin, Ann M.	Scholastic
Baby-Sitters Club: Claudia and the New Girl	O	RF	250+	Martin, Ann M.	Scholastic
Baby-Sitters Club: Claudia and the Phantom Phone Calls	O	RF	250+	Martin, Ann M.	Scholastic
Baby-Sitters Club: Dawn and Too Many Sitters	O	RF	250+	Martin, Ann M.	Scholastic
Baby-Sitters Club: Dawn's Big Move	O	RF	250+	Martin, Ann M.	Scholastic
Baby-Sitters Club: Dawn's Wicked Stepsister	O	RF	250+	Martin, Ann M.	Scholastic
Baby-Sitters Club: Get Well Soon, Mallory	O	RF	250+	Martin, Ann M.	Scholastic
Baby-Sitters Club: Ghost at Dawn's House, The	O	RF	250+	Martin, Ann M.	Scholastic
Baby-Sitters Club: Good-bye Stacey, Good-bye	O	RF	250+	Martin, Ann M.	Scholastic
Baby-Sitters Club: Hello, Mallory	O	RF	250+	Martin, Ann M.	Scholastic
Baby-Sitters Club: Jessi and the Bad Baby-Sitter	O	RF	250+	Martin, Ann M.	Scholastic

* Collection of short stories

TITLE	LEVEL	GENRE	WORD COUNT	AUTHOR / SERIES	PUBLISHER / DISTRIBUTOR
Baby-Sitters Club: Jessi and the Superbrat	O	RF	250+	Martin, Ann M.	Scholastic
Baby-Sitters Club: Jessi Ramsey, Pet-sitter	O	RF	250+	Martin, Ann M.	Scholastic
Baby-Sitters Club: Kristy and the Snobs	O	RF	250+	Martin, Ann M.	Scholastic
Baby-Sitters Club: Kristy's Big Day	O	RF	250+	Martin, Ann M.	Scholastic
Baby-Sitters Club: Kristy's Great Idea	O	RF	250+	Martin, Ann M.	Scholastic
Baby-Sitters Club: Mary Anne and Camp BSC	O	RF	250+	Martin, Ann M.	Scholastic
Baby-Sitters Club: Mary Anne Saves the Day	O	RF	250+	Martin, Ann M.	Scholastic
Baby-Sitters Club: Welcome to the BSC, Abby	O	RF	250+	Martin, Ann M.	Scholastic
Baby-Sitter's Little Sister	O	RF	250+	Martin, Ann M.	Scholastic
Baby-Sitter's Little Sister : Karen's Accident	O	RF	250+	Martin, Ann M.	Scholastic
Baby-Sitter's Little Sister : Karen's Big Fight	O	RF	250+	Martin, Ann M.	Scholastic
Baby-Sitter's Little Sister : Karen's Big Sister	O	RF	250+	Martin, Ann M.	Scholastic
Baby-Sitter's Little Sister : Karen's Copycat	O	RF	250+	Martin, Ann M.	Scholastic
Baby-Sitter's Little Sister : Karen's Dinosaur	O	RF	250+	Martin, Ann M.	Scholastic
Baby-Sitter's Little Sister : Karen's Monsters	O	RF	250+	Martin, Ann M.	Scholastic
Baby-Sitter's Little Sister: Karen's Campout	O	RF	250+	Martin, Ann M.	Scholastic
Baby-Sitter's Little Sister: Karen's Mystery, Super Special	O	RF	250+	Martin, Ann M.	Scholastic
Baby-Sitter's Little Sister: Karen's Nanny	O	RF	250+	Martin, Ann M.	Scholastic
Baby-Sitter's Little Sister: Karen's Stepmother	O	RF	250+	Martin, Ann M.	Scholastic
Baby-Sitter's Little Sister: Karen's Two Families	O	RF	250+	Martin, Ann M.	Scholastic
Back Home	O	RF	250+	Pinkney, Gloria Jean	Penguin Group
Backyard Angel	O	RF	250+	Delton, Judy	Houghton Mifflin
Bad Luck of King Fred, The	O	F	250+	Literacy Tree	Rigby
Bagels for Kids	O	I	250+	Pacific Literacy	Pacific Learning
Baseball Fever	O	RF	250+	Hurwitz, Johanna	William Morrow
Baseball Megastars	O	I	250+	Weber, Bruce	Scholastic
*Baseball Pitching Challenge and Other Cases, The	O	RF	250+	Simon, Seymour	Avon
Baseball Saved Us	O	HF	250+	Mochizuki, Ken	Scholastic
*Baseball's Best: Five True Stories	O	B	250+	Step into Reading	Random House
Bats	O	I	250+	Gibbons, Gail	Holiday House
Bats	O	I	250+	Holmes, Kevin J.	Red Brick Learning
Bats Out the Window	O	RF	250+	First Flight	Fitzhenry & Whiteside
Battle of Words, A	O	RF	250+	Literacy 2000	Rigby
Beacons of Light: Lighthouses	O	I	250+	Gibbons, Gail	Scholastic
Bears	O	I	59	Holmes, Kevin J.	Red Brick Learning
Beatrix Potter	O	B	250+	Wallner, Alexandra	Holiday House
Bees	O	I	250+	Holmes, Kevin J.	Red Brick Learning
Beezus & Ramona	O	RF	250+	Cleary, Beverly	Avon
Beneath Earth's Surface	O	I	250+	Rosen Real Readers	Rosen Publishing Group
Benjamin Franklin: A Man with Many Jobs	O	B	250+	Greene, Carol	Children's Press
Bessie Coleman	O	B	250+	Brager, Bruce	Scholastic
Best Fish Ever, The	O	RF	884	Leveled Readers	Houghton Mifflin
Best Wishes	O	B	250+	Rylant, Cynthia	Richard C. Owen
Bicycle Book, The	O	I	250+	PM Nonfiction-Emerald	Rigby
Bicycle Rider	O	B	250+	Scioscia, Mary	HarperTrophy
Big Boy	O	TL	250+	Mollel, Tololwa M.	Houghton Mifflin
Bill Clinton: Forty-Second President of the U.S.	O	B	250+	Greene, Carol	Children's Press
Birds of Prey	O	I	250+	Woolley, M.; Pigdon, K.	Mondo
Birthday Party, The	O	F	797	Leveled Readers	Houghton Mifflin
Book of Hours, A	O	I	250+	Cambridge Reading	Pearson Learning Group
Bookworm Who Hatched, A	O	B	250+	Aardema, Verna	Richard C. Owen
Boot Balancers Wanted	O	F	250+	Sails	Rigby

* Collection of short stories

TITLE	LEVEL	GENRE	WORD COUNT	AUTHOR / SERIES	PUBLISHER / DISTRIBUTOR
Borreguita and the Coyote	O	TL	250+	Aardema, Verna	Scholastic
Boxcar Children Return, The	O	RF	250+	Warner, Gertrude Chandler	Albert Whitman & Co.
Boxcar Children Special: The Mystery at Snowflake Inn	O	RF	250+	Warner, Gertrude Chandler	Albert Whitman & Co.
Boxcar Children Special: The Mystery at the Ballpark	O	RF	250+	Warner, Gertrude Chandler	Albert Whitman & Co.
Boxcar Children Special: The Mystery at the Fair	O	RF	250+	Warner, Gertrude Chandler	Albert Whitman & Co.
Boxcar Children Special: The Pilgrim Village Mystery	O	RF	250+	Warner, Gertrude Chandler	Albert Whitman & Co.
Boxcar Children: Amusement Park Mystery, The	O	RF	250+	Warner, Gertrude Chandler	Albert Whitman & Co.
Boxcar Children: Animal Shelter Mystery, The	O	RF	250+	Warner, Gertrude Chandler	Albert Whitman & Co.
Boxcar Children: Basketball Mystery, The	O	RF	250+	Warner, Gertrude Chandler	Albert Whitman & Co.
Boxcar Children: Benny Uncovers a Mystery	O	RF	250+	Warner, Gertrude Chandler	Albert Whitman & Co.
Boxcar Children: Bicycle Mystery	O	RF	250+	Warner, Gertrude Chandler	Albert Whitman & Co.
Boxcar Children: Black Pearl Mystery, The	O	RF	250+	Warner, Gertrude Chandler	Albert Whitman & Co.
Boxcar Children: Blue Bay Mystery	O	RF	250+	Warner, Gertrude Chandler	Albert Whitman & Co.
Boxcar Children: Boxcar Children, The	O	RF	250+	Warner, Gertrude Chandler	Albert Whitman & Co.
Boxcar Children: Bus Station Mystery	O	RF	250+	Warner, Gertrude Chandler	Albert Whitman & Co.
Boxcar Children: Caboose Mystery	O	RF	250+	Warner, Gertrude Chandler	Albert Whitman & Co.
Boxcar Children: Camp-Out Mystery, The	O	RF	250+	Warner, Gertrude Chandler	Albert Whitman & Co.
Boxcar Children: Canoe Trip Mystery, The	O	RF	250+	Warner, Gertrude Chandler	Albert Whitman & Co.
Boxcar Children: Castle Mystery, The	O	TL	250+	Warner, Gertrude Chandler	Albert Whitman & Co.
Boxcar Children: Cereal Box Mystery, The	O	RF	250+	Warner, Gertrude Chandler	Albert Whitman & Co.
Boxcar Children: Chocolate Sundae Mystery, The	O	RF	250+	Warner, Gertrude Chandler	Albert Whitman & Co.
Boxcar Children: Deserted Library Mystery, The	O	RF	250+	Warner, Gertrude Chandler	Albert Whitman & Co.
Boxcar Children: Dinosaur Mystery, The	O	RF	250+	Warner, Gertrude Chandler	Albert Whitman & Co.
Boxcar Children: Disappearing Friend Mystery, The	O	RF	250+	Warner, Gertrude Chandler	Albert Whitman & Co.
Boxcar Children: Firehouse Mystery, The	O	RF	250+	Warner, Gertrude Chandler	Albert Whitman & Co.
Boxcar Children: Ghost Ship Mystery, The	O	RF	250+	Warner, Gertrude Chandler	Albert Whitman & Co.
Boxcar Children: Growling Bear Mystery, The	O	RF	250+	Warner, Gertrude Chandler	Albert Whitman & Co.
Boxcar Children: Haunted Cabin Mystery, The	O	RF	250+	Warner, Gertrude Chandler	Albert Whitman & Co.
Boxcar Children: Lighthouse Mystery, The	O	RF	250+	Warner, Gertrude Chandler	Albert Whitman & Co.
Boxcar Children: Mike's Mystery	O	TL	250+	Aardema, Gertrude Chandler	Scholastic
Boxcar Children: Mountain Top Mystery	O	RF	250+	Warner, Gertrude Chandler	Albert Whitman & Co.
Boxcar Children: Mystery at Snowflake Inn, The	O	RF	250+	Warner, Gertrude Chandler	Albert Whitman & Co.
Boxcar Children: Mystery at the Alamo, The	O	RF	250+	Warner, Gertrude Chandler	Albert Whitman & Co.
Boxcar Children: Mystery at the Ballpark, The	O	RF	250+	Warner, Gertrude Chandler	Albert Whitman & Co.
Boxcar Children: Mystery at the Dog Show, The	O	RF	250+	Warner, Gertrude Chandler	Albert Whitman & Co.
Boxcar Children: Mystery at the Fair	O	RF	250+	Warner, Gertrude Chandler	Albert Whitman & Co.
Boxcar Children: Mystery Behind the Wall	O	RF	250+	Warner, Gertrude Chandler	Albert Whitman & Co.
Boxcar Children: Mystery Bookstore, The	O	RF	250+	Warner, Gertrude Chandler	Albert Whitman & Co.
Boxcar Children: Mystery Cruise, The	O	RF	250+	Warner, Gertrude Chandler	Albert Whitman & Co.
Boxcar Children: Mystery Girl, The	O	RF	250+	Warner, Gertrude Chandler	Albert Whitman & Co.
Boxcar Children: Mystery Horse, The	O	RF	250+	Warner, Gertrude Chandler	Albert Whitman & Co.
Boxcar Children: Mystery in San Francisco, The	O	RF	250+	Warner, Gertrude Chandler	Albert Whitman & Co.
Boxcar Children: Mystery in the Cave, The	O	RF	250+	Warner, Gertrude Chandler	Albert Whitman & Co.
Boxcar Children: Mystery in the Old Attic, The	O	RF	250+	Warner, Gertrude Chandler	Albert Whitman & Co.
Boxcar Children: Mystery in the Sand	O	RF	250+	Warner, Gertrude Chandler	Albert Whitman & Co.
Boxcar Children: Mystery in Washington, DC, The	O	RF	250+	Warner, Gertrude Chandler	Albert Whitman & Co.
Boxcar Children: Mystery of the Hidden Beach	O	RF	250+	Warner, Gertrude Chandler	Albert Whitman & Co.
Boxcar Children: Mystery of the Lost Mine, The	O	RF	250+	Warner, Gertrude Chandler	Albert Whitman & Co.

* Collection of short stories

TITLE	LEVEL	GENRE	WORD COUNT	AUTHOR / SERIES	PUBLISHER / DISTRIBUTOR
Boxcar Children: Mystery of the Lost Village, The	O	RF	250+	Warner, Gertrude Chandler	Albert Whitman & Co.
Boxcar Children: Mystery of the Missing Cat, The	O	RF	250+	Warner, Gertrude Chandler	Albert Whitman & Co.
Boxcar Children: Mystery of the Mixed-Up Zoo, The	O	RF	250+	Warner, Gertrude Chandler	Albert Whitman & Co.
Boxcar Children: Mystery of the Stolen Boxcar, The	O	RF	250+	Warner, Gertrude Chandler	Albert Whitman & Co.
Boxcar Children: Mystery of the Stolen Music, The	O	RF	250+	Warner, Gertrude Chandler	Albert Whitman & Co.
Boxcar Children: Mystery on Stage, The	O	RF	250+	Warner, Gertrude Chandler	Albert Whitman & Co.
Boxcar Children: Mystery on the Train, The	O	RF	250+	Warner, Gertrude Chandler	Albert Whitman & Co.
Boxcar Children: Mystery Ranch	O	RF	250+	Warner, Gertrude Chandler	Albert Whitman & Co.
Boxcar Children: Outer Space Mystery, The	O	RF	250+	Warner, Gertrude Chandler	Albert Whitman & Co.
Boxcar Children: Pizza Mystery, The	O	RF	250+	Warner, Gertrude Chandler	Albert Whitman & Co.
Boxcar Children: Schoolhouse Mystery	O	RF	250+	Warner, Gertrude Chandler	Albert Whitman & Co.
Boxcar Children: Snowbound Mystery	O	RF	250+	Warner, Gertrude Chandler	Albert Whitman & Co.
Boxcar Children: Soccer Mystery, The	O	RF	250+	Warner, Gertrude Chandler	Albert Whitman & Co.
Boxcar Children: Surprise Island	O	RF	250+	Warner, Gertrude Chandler	Albert Whitman & Co.
Boxcar Children: Woodshed Mystery, The	O	RF	250+	Warner, Gertrude Chandler	Albert Whitman & Co.
Boxcar Children: Yellow House Mystery, The	O	RF	250+	Warner, Gertrude Chandler	Albert Whitman & Co.
Brave Little Tailor, The: A German Folktale	O	TL	660	Leveled Readers	Houghton Mifflin
Brazil	O	I	250+	Dahl, Michael	Red Brick Learning
*Broken Window and Other Cases, The	O	RF	250+	Simon, Seymour	Avon
Brown Sunshine of Sawdust Valley	O	RF	250+	Henry, Marguerite	Aladdin
Bugs	O	I	250+	Parker, Nancy Winslow; Wright, Joan Richards	Mulberry Books
Bugs and Other Insects	O	I	250+	Kalman, Bobbie	Crabtree
Building Homes, Building Hope	O	I	250+	Bovez, Marcie	Wright Group/McGraw Hill
Bungy 70528	O	RF	250+	Belcher, Angie	Pacific Learning
Butterflies	O	I	250+	Holmes, Kevin J.	Red Brick Learning
Butterflies	O	I	250+	Nature's Friends	Compass Point Books
Butterflies!	O	I	725	Leveled Readers	Houghton Mifflin
Can You Imagine?	O	B	250+	McKissack, Patricia	Richard C. Owen
Canada	O	I	250+	Dahl, Michael	Red Brick Learning
Candlelight Service	O	RF	250+	Literacy 2000	Rigby
Canoe Diary	O	I	250+	Bishop, Nic	Pacific Learning
Case of the Dirty Bird, The	O	RF	250+	Paulsen, Gary	Bantam
Cat Crazy	O	RF	250+	Baglio, Ben M.	Scholastic
Cat's Meow, The	O	F	250+	Soto, Gary	Scholastic
Caves and Caverns	O	I	250+	Gibbons, Gail	Harcourt Trade
Changing Shores	O	I	250+	iOpeners	Pearson Learning Group
Charles Lindbergh	O	B	250+	Early Biographies	Compass Point Books
Chick Challenge	O	RF	250+	Baglio, Ben M.	Scholastic
China	O	I	250+	Many Cultures, One World	Capstone Press
China	O	I	250+	Dahl, Michael	Red Brick Learning
China's Bravest Girl: The Legend of Hua Mu Lan	O	TL	250+	Chin, Charlie	Children's Press
Chinese New Year	O	I	250+	Holidays and Festivals	Compass Point Books
Chocolate Fever	O	F	250+	Smith, Robert	Bantam
Christmas	O	I	250+	Holidays and Festivals	Compass Point Books
Christopher Columbus: A Great Explorer	O	B	250+	Greene, Carol	Children's Press
Cinco de Mayo	O	I	250+	Holidays and Festivals	Compass Point Books
Cities: Then and Now	O	I	250+	People, Spaces & Places	Rand McNally
Class Clown	O	RF	250+	Hurwitz, Johanna	Scholastic

* Collection of short stories

TITLE	LEVEL	GENRE	WORD COUNT	AUTHOR / SERIES	PUBLISHER / DISTRIBUTOR
Class President	O	RF	250+	Hurwitz, Johanna	Scholastic
Cloak of the Wind	O	HF	250+	Voyages in Time	Wright Group/McGraw Hill
Clue, Jr.: The Case of the Chocolate Fingerprints	O	RF	250+	Hinter, Parker C.	Scholastic
Comeback Dog, The	O	RF	250+	Thomas, Jane Resh	Bantam
Connecting to the Internet	O	I	250+	Rigby Literacy	Rigby
Cool Cat, A	O	RF	250+	Leveled Readers	Houghton Mifflin
Cool School	O	F	250+	Sails	Rigby
Corn Is Maize: The Gift of the Indians	O	I	250+	Aliki	Steck-Vaughn
Could We Live on the Moon?	O	I	250+	iOpeners	Pearson Learning Group
Courage of Sarah Noble, The	O	HF	250+	Dalgliesh, Alice	Aladdin
Cow	O	I	250+	Older, Jules	Charlesbridge
Cowpokes and Desperadoes	O	RF	250+	Paulsen, Gary	Bantam
*Creature from Beneath the Ice and Other Cases, The	O	RF	250+	Simon, Seymour	Avon
Crocodilians	O	I	250+	Literacy 2000	Rigby
*Crowded Dock and Other Cases, The	O	RF	250+	Simon, Seymour	Avon
*Crying Rocks and Other Cases, The	O	RF	250+	Simon, Seymour	Avon
Cuba	O	I	250+	Mara, William P.	Red Brick Learning
Culpepper's Canyon	O	RF	250+	Paulsen, Gary	Bantam
Danger on Midnight River	O	RF	250+	Paulsen, Gary	Bantam
*Dangerous Comet and Other Cases, The	O	RF	250+	Simon, Seymour	Avon
Daniel Boone: Man of the Forests	O	B	250+	Greene, Carol	Children's Press
Dear Prime Minister	O	I	250+	Roberts, Chris	Fitzhenry & Whiteside
DeDe Takes Charge!	O	RF	250+	Hurwitz, Johanna	Morrow
Deserts	O	I	250+	Gibbons, Gail	Holiday House
Diego Rivera	O	B	250+	First Biographies	Steck-Vaughn
Different Dragons	O	RF	250+	Little, Jean	Penguin Group
Dinosaur Connection, The	O	I	250+	Literacy Tree	Rigby
Dinosaur Detective	O	I	250+	Wildcats	Wright Group/McGraw Hill
Dirty Beasts	O	F	250+	Dahl, Roald	Penguin Group
*Disappearing Cookies and Other Cases, The	O	RF	250+	Simon, Seymour	Avon
*Disappearing Ice Cream and Other Cases, The	O	RF	250+	Simon, Seymour	Avon
*Disappearing Snowball and Other Cases, The	O	RF	250+	Simon, Seymour	Avon
Discovering the Titanic	O	I	250+	Trumbore, Cindy	Pearson Learning Group
*Distant Stars and Other Cases, The	O	RF	250+	Simon, Seymour	Avon
Does Third Grade Last Forever?	O	RF	250+	Schanback, Mindy	Troll Associates
Doggy Dare	O	RF	250+	Baglio, Ben M.	Scholastic
Dogs Don't Tell Jokes	O	RF	250+	Sachar, Louis	Alfred A. Knopf
Dolphins	O	I	250+	Holmes, Kevin J.	Red Brick Learning
Douglas Fir	O	I	250+	Davis, Wendy	Children's Press
Dragon Bones	O	F	250+	Hindman, Paul	Random House
Dragon Parade: A Chinese New Year Story	O	I	250+	Chin, Steven A.	Steck-Vaughn
Dream Come True, A	O	B	250+	Hurwitz, Johanna	Richard C. Owen
Dream of Flight, The	O	I	250+	Rigby Focus	Rigby
Drum Beats On, The	O	I	250+	Cherrington, Janelle	Scholastic
Duckling Diary	O	RF	250+	Baglio, Ben M.	Scholastic
Dunkin' Dazza's Daring Dribble	O	RF	250+	SupaDoopers	Sundance
Dunkin' Dazza's Soaring Slammer	O	RF	250+	SupaDoopers	Sundance
Eagle Has Landed, The	O	I	250+	Merchant, Peter	Scholastic
Earning Money	O	I	250+	Let's See	Compass Point Books
Earthquakes	O	I	250+	Branley, Franklyn M.	HarperCollins
Earthquakes and Tsunamis	O	I	250+	PM Plus Story Books	Rigby
Earthworms	O	I	250+	Holmes, Kevin J.	Red Brick Learning

* Collection of short stories

TITLE	LEVEL	GENRE	WORD COUNT	AUTHOR / SERIES	PUBLISHER / DISTRIBUTOR
Eleanor Everywhere: The Life of Eleanor Roosevelt	O	B	250+	Step into Reading	Random House
Eleanor Roosevelt: Fighter for Social Justice	O	B	250+	Childhood of Famous Americans	Aladdin
*Electric Spark and Other Cases, The	O	RF	250+	Simon, Seymour	Avon
Electricity	O	I	250+	Winkelman, Barbara Gaines	Wright Group/McGraw Hill
*Electrifying Cows and Other Cases, The	O	RF	250+	Simon, Seymour	Avon
Elena in America	O	HF	575	Leveled Readers	Houghton Mifflin
Eleven Kids, One Summer	O	RF	250+	Martin, Ann M.	Scholastic
Elizabeth Blackwell: First Woman Doctor	O	B	250+	Greene, Carol	Children's Press
Elizabeth Blackwell: Girl Doctor	O	B	250+	Henry, Joanne Landers	Simon & Schuster
Elizabeth the First: Queen of England	O	B	250+	Greene, Carol	Children's Press
Eloise Greenfield: The Music of Poetry	O	B	250+	Leveled Readers Language Support	Houghton Mifflin
Emily Dickinson: American Poet	O	B	250+	Greene, Carol	Children's Press
Encyclopedia of a Rain Forest	O	I	250+	Rigby Literacy	Rigby
England	O	I	250+	Many Cultures, One World	Capstone Press
Exercise Time	O	F	250+	Sails	Rigby
Exploring with Lewis and Clark	O	I	250+	People, Spaces & Places	Rand McNally
Face-Off	O	RF	250+	Christopher, Matt	Little, Brown & Co.
Facts About Earthquakes	O	I	250+	Rosen Real Readers	Rosen Publishing Group
*Famous Children	O	I	250+	Literacy 2000	Rigby
Fanfare for Food	O	I	497	Vocabulary Readers	Houghton Mifflin
*Fantastic Water Pot and Other Cases, The	O	RF	250+	Simon, Seymour	Avon
*Far-Out Frisbee and Other Cases, The	O	RF	250+	Simon, Seymour	Avon
Fascinating Families	O	I	717	Leveled Readers	Houghton Mifflin
*Fastest Ketchup in the Cafeteria and Other Cases, The	O	RF	250+	Simon, Seymour	Avon
*Fearless Explorer and Other Cases, The	O	RF	250+	Simon, Seymour	Avon
Ferret Fun	O	RF	250+	Baglio, Ben M.	Scholastic
Fighting Fish	O	I	250+	Life Cycles	Creative Teaching Press
Finches' Fabulous Furnace, The	O	F	250+	Drury, Roger	Scholastic
Fine Lines	O	B	250+	Heller, Ruth	Richard C. Owen
Fire! Fire!	O	I	250+	Wildcats	Wright Group/McGraw Hill
Fire! in Yellowstone: A True Adventure	O	I	250+	Soar To Success	Houghton Mifflin
Firelight Secrets	O	RF	250+	PM Ruby	Rigby
Firetalking	O	B	250+	Polacco, Patricia	Richard C. Owen
First Americans, The	O	I	250+	People, Spaces & Places	Rand McNally
Fish	O	I	250+	Nature's Friends	Compass Point Books
Flash Flood!	O	I	1784	Independent Readers Science	Houghton Mifflin
Flicking the Switch	O	I	250+	Pacific Literacy	Pacific Learning
Flossie and the Fox	O	F	250+	McKissack, Patricia	Scholastic
Fly-Fishing with Grandpa	O	RF	1029	Leveled Readers	Houghton Mifflin
*Flying-Saucer People and Other Cases, The	O	RF	250+	Simon, Seymour	Avon
*Folktales from Asia	O	TL	250+	Bookshop	Mondo
Food and Festivals: Israel	O	I	250+	Randall, Ronne	Steck-Vaughn
Food and Festivals: Italy	O	I	250+	Pirotta, Saviour	Steck-Vaughn
Food Chains	O	I	677	Leveled Readers Science	Houghton Mifflin
Foolish Gretel	O	TL	250+	Armstrong, Jennifer	Random House
Forced Out	O	I	889	Independent Readers Science	Houghton Mifflin
Forest Fire!	O	I	769	Leveled Readers Science	Houghton Mifflin
Fortune-Tellers, The	O	TL	250+	Alexander, Lloyd	Puffin Books
Fossils Tell of Long Ago	O	I	250+	Soar To Success	Houghton Mifflin
France	O	I	250+	Dahl, Michael	Red Brick Learning

* Collection of short stories

TITLE	LEVEL	GENRE	WORD COUNT	AUTHOR / SERIES	PUBLISHER / DISTRIBUTOR
Frank Lloyd Wright	O	B	346	Independent Readers Social Studies	Houghton Mifflin
Fresh Air	O	RF	250+	Leveled Readers Language Support	Houghton Mifflin
Friendship in Action	O	I	250+	Literacy Tree	Rigby
Frogs	O	I	250+	Holmes, Kevin J.	Red Brick Learning
From Paper Airplanes to Outer Space	O	B	250+	Simon, Seymour	Richard C. Owen
Fudge	O	RF	250+	Graeber, Charlotte Towner	Simon & Schuster
Garden in Your Bedroom, A	O	I	250+	Sunshine	Wright Group/McGraw Hill
General Butterfingers	O	RF	250+	Gardiner, John Reynolds	Puffin Books
George Washington	O	B	250+	Early Biographies	Compass Point Books
George Washington Carver: Scientist and Teacher	O	B	250+	Greene, Carol	Children's Press
George Washington: Young Leader	O	B	250+	Childhood of Famous Americans	Aladdin
Gerbil Genius	O	RF	250+	Baglio, Ben M.	Scholastic
Germany	O	I	250+	Dahl, Michael	Red Brick Learning
Gertie's Green Thumb	O	F	250+	Dexter, Catherine	Dell
Ghana	O	I	250+	Davis, Lucile	Red Brick Learning
Giants, Monsters & Mythical Beasts	O	I	250+	Literacy 2000	Rigby
*Gigantic Ants and Other Cases, The	O	RF	250+	Simon, Seymour	Avon
Giraffes	O	I	250+	Reeder, Tracey	Wright Group/McGraw Hill
Glorious Flight, The: Across the Channel with Louis Blériot	O	B	250+	Provensen, Alice & Martin	Puffin Books
Go-cart Team, The	O	I	250+	PM Nonfiction-Emerald	Rigby
Godzilla Ate My Homework	O	F	250+	Jones, Marcia	Scholastic
Going Lobstering	O	I	250+	Pallotta, Jerry; Bolster, Rob	Charlesbridge
Going to School	O	I	21	iOpeners	Pearson Learning Group
Going West	O	HF	250+	Van Leeuwen, Jean	Penguin Group
Good Grief . . . Third Grade	O	RF	250+	McKenna, Colleen	Scholastic
Gorganzola Zombies in the Park	O	F	250+	Levy, Elizabeth	HarperTrophy
Grace the Pirate	O	F	250+	Lasky, Kathryn	Hyperion
Gravity	O	I	250+	Early Connections	Benchmark Education
Gravity and the Solar System	O	I	250+	PM Plus Story Books	Rigby
Great Dog Wash, The	O	RF	250+	Rigby Focus	Rigby
*Grizzly Mistake and Other Cases, The	O	RF	250+	Simon, Seymour	Avon
Growing a Kitchen Garden	O	I	250+	Navigators Fiction Series	Benchmark Education
Growing Ideas	O	B	250+	Van Leeuwen, Jean	Richard C. Owen
Guatemala	O	I	250+	Dahl, Michael	Red Brick Learning
Guinea Pig Gang	O	RF	250+	Baglio, Ben M.	Scholastic
Habitat Rescue	O	I	250+	Navigators Fiction Series	Benchmark Education
Hairy Little Critters	O	I	250+	Literacy Tree	Rigby
Halloween	O	I	250+	Holidays and Festivals	Compass Point Books
*Halloween Horror and Other Cases, The	O	RF	250+	Simon, Seymour	Avon
Hamster Hotel	O	RF	250+	Baglio, Ben M.	Scholastic
Happily Ever After	O	F	250+	Quindlen, Anna	Penguin Group
Harriet Tubman	O	B	250+	Early Biographies	Compass Point Books
Harriet's Hare	O	F	250+	King-Smith, Dick	Alfred A. Knopf
Harry Houdini: Young Magician	O	B	250+	Childhood of Famous Americans	Aladdin
Harvest Festivals	O	I	250+	Windows on Literacy	National Geographic
Hau Kola Hello Friend	O	B	250+	Goble, Paul	Richard C. Owen
Haunting of Grade Three, The	O	RF	250+	Maccarone, Grace	Scholastic
Head For the Hills!	O	I	250+	Walker, Paul Robert	Random House
*Heavy Weight and Other Cases, The	O	RF	250+	Simon, Seymour	Avon
Heavyweights	O	I	250+	Paul, Michele	Wright Group/McGraw Hill

* Collection of short stories

TITLE	LEVEL	GENRE	WORD COUNT	AUTHOR / SERIES	PUBLISHER / DISTRIBUTOR
Helen Keller: From Tragedy to Triumph	O	B	250+	Childhood of Famous Americans	Aladdin
*Hello, Mrs. Piggle-Wiggle	O	F	250+	MacDonald, Betty	HarperTrophy
Helpful or Harmful?	O	I	250+	Orbit Double Takes	Pacific Learning
Henry and Beezus	O	RF	250+	Cleary, Beverly	Avon
Henry and Ribsy	O	RF	250+	Cleary, Beverly	Hearst
Henry and the Clubhouse	O	RF	250+	Cleary, Beverly	Avon
Henry and the Paper Route	O	RF	250+	Cleary, Beverly	Hearst
Henry Ford: Young Man with Ideas	O	B	250+	Childhood of Famous Americans	Aladdin
Henry Huggins	O	RF	250+	Cleary, Beverly	Avon
Her Seven Brothers	O	TL	250+	Goble, Paul	Aladdin
*Here Comes McBroom	O	F	250+	Fleischman, Sid	Beech Tree Books
History Nook, The	O	SF	250+	Phonics and Friends	Hampton-Brown
History of Machines, The	O	I	250+	Home Connection Collection	Rigby
Hop to it, Minty!	O	RF	250+	PM Ruby	Rigby
Horse Power	O	I	250+	Pacific Literacy	Pacific Learning
Hot and Cold Summer	O	RF	250+	Hurwitz, Johanna	Scholastic
Houdini's Last Trick	O	B	250+	Hass, Elizabeth	Random House
How a Plant Grows	O	I	250+	Kalman, Bobbie	Crabtree
How My Family Lives in America	O	I	250+	Kuklin, Susan	Aladdin
*Howling Dog and Other Cases, The	O	RF	250+	Simon, Seymour	Avon
Hundred Dresses, The	O	RF	250+	Estes, Eleanor	Scholastic
Hunted, The	O	I	250+	Rigby Focus	Rigby
*Hurray For Ali Baba Bernstein	O	RF	250+	Hurwitz, Johanna	Scholastic
*Hurricane Machine and Other Cases, The	O	RF	250+	Simon, Seymour	Avon
Hyenas	O	I	250+	Holmes, Kevin J.	Red Brick Learning
*Hypnotized Frog and Other Cases, The	O	RF	250+	Simon, Seymour	Avon
I Am Rosa Parks	O	B	250+	Parks, Rosa	Dial Books
I Love Guinea Pigs	O	I	250+	King-Smith, Dick	Candlewick Press
I Wonder Why Snakes Shed Their Skins and Other Questions About Reptiles	O	I	250+	O'Neill, Amanda	Scholastic
I Wonder Why the Sky is Blue	O	I	250+	Rosen Real Readers	Rosen Publishing Group
*Icy Question and Other Cases, The	O	RF	250+	Simon, Seymour	Avon
*Impossible Bend and Other Cases, The	O	RF	250+	Simon, Seymour	Avon
*Incredible Shrinking Machine and Other Cases, The	O	RF	250+	Simon, Seymour	Avon
India	O	I	250+	Dahl, Michael	Red Brick Learning
*Indian-Head Pennies and Other Cases, The	O	RF	250+	Simon, Seymour	Avon
Indonesia	O	I	250+	Countries of the World	Red Brick Learning
Inside the Sun	O	I	250+	Rosen Real Readers	Rosen Publishing Group
Invisible Stanley	O	F	250+	Brown, Jeff	HarperTrophy
Iron Giant, The	O	SF	250+	Hughes, Ted	Alfred A. Knopf
Is There Life in Outer Space	O	I	250+	Branley, Franklyn M.	HarperCollins
Israel	O	I	250+	Thoennes, Kristin	Red Brick Learning
It Came Through the Wall	O	F	1182	Healey, Tim	Mondo
Italy	O	I	250+	Thoennes, Kristin	Red Brick Learning
It's Easy!	O	RF	250+	Leveled Readers Language Support	Houghton Mifflin
It's Just a Trick	O	RF	250+	Literacy 2000	Rigby
Jackie Robinson	O	B	250+	Early Biographies	Compass Point Books
Jackie Robinson: Baseball's First Black Major Leaguer	O	B	250+	Greene, Carol	Children's Press
Jaguars	O	I	250+	First Reports	Compass Point Books
Jane Addams	O	B	586	Leveled Readers Social Studies	Houghton Mifflin
Japan	O	I	250+	Countries of the World	Red Brick Learning

TITLE	LEVEL	GENRE	WORD COUNT	AUTHOR / SERIES	PUBLISHER / DISTRIBUTOR
Japan	O	I	250+	Many Cultures, One World	Capstone Press
Jason and the Aliens Down the Street	O	F	250+	Greer, Greg; Ruddick, Bob	HarperTrophy
Jo Jo Winnie Again	O	RF	250+	Sachs, Marilyn	Dutton
Johann Sebastian Bach: Great Man of Music	O	B	250+	Greene, Carol	Children's Press
John F. Kennedy: America's Youngest President	O	B	250+	Childhood of Famous Americans	Aladdin
Johnny Appleseed	O	B	622	Leveled Readers	Houghton Mifflin
Jokes and Riddles	O	I	250+	Literacy 2000	Rigby
Jumping Spider	O	I	250+	Life Cycles	Creative Teaching Press
Just Like Mom and Dad	O	I	1099	Leveled Readers Science	Houghton Mifflin
Just Plain Cat	O	RF	250+	Robinson, Nancy K.	Scholastic
Just Tell Me When We're Dead!	O	RF	250+	Clifford, Eth	Scholastic
Kenya	O	I	250+	Dahl, Michael	Red Brick Learning
Key to the Playhouse, The	O	RF	250+	York, Carol	Scholastic
Kid in the Red Jacket, The	O	RF	250+	Park, Barbara	Random House
Kids' Guide to Family Reunions, A	O	I	351	Vocabulary Readers	Houghton Mifflin
Kids Rule!	O	I	250+	Bookshop	Mondo
King's Equal, The	O	TL	250+	Paterson, Katherine	HarperTrophy
Kites	O	I	250+	PM Nonfiction-Emerald	Rigby
Kitesurfing	O	I	250+	Sails	Rigby
Kitten Crowd	O	RF	250+	Baglio, Ben M.	Scholastic
Knights in Shining Armor	O	I	250+	Gibbons, Gail	Little, Brown & Co.
Kristy and the Walking Disaster	O	RF	250+	Martin, Ann M.	Scholastic
Kwanzaa	O	I	250+	Chocolate, Deborah M. Newton	Children's Press
Ladybug and the Legislature, The	O	I	484	Independent Readers Social Studies	Houghton Mifflin
Ladybug, The	O	I	250+	Crewe, Sabrina	Steck-Vaughn
Ladybug, The	O	I	250+	Exploring History & Geography	Rigby
Lake Critter Journal	O	RF	250+	Little Celebrations	Pearson Learning Group
Lamb Lessons	O	RF	250+	Baglio, Ben M.	Scholastic
Langston Hughes: Young Black Poet	O	B	250+	Childhood of Famous Americans	Aladdin
Laura Ingalls Wilder	O	B	250+	Allen, Thomas B.	Putnam
Laura Ingalls Wilder: Author of the Little House Books	O	B	250+	Greene, Carol	Children's Press
Lavender	O	RF	250+	Hesse, Karen	Henry Holt & Co.
Legend of the Bluebonnet, The	O	TL	250+	DePaola, Tomie	Scholastic
Legend of the Indian Paintbrush, The	O	TL	250+	DePaola, Tomie	Scholastic
Let's Build a Playground	O	I	250+	Myers, Edward	Pearson Learning Group
Let's Find Out about Money	O	I	250+	Barabas, Kathy	Scholastic
Let's Play Games Around the World	O	I	250+	iOpeners	Pearson Learning Group
Letter From Phoenix Farm, A	O	B	250+	Yolen, Jane	Richard C. Owen
Liar, Liar, Pants on Fire	O	RF	250+	Korman, Gordon	Scholastic
*Lightweight Rocket and Other Cases, The	O	RF	250+	Simon, Seymour	Avon
Like Jake and Me	O	RF	250+	Jukes, Mavis	Alfred A. Knopf
Lions	O	I	250+	Holmes, Kevin J.	Red Brick Learning
Little Icicle	O	RF	250+	Szymanski, Lois	Avon Camelot
Little Miss Stoneybrook and Dawn	O	RF	250+	Martin, Ann M.	Scholastic
*Little Pear	O	HF	250+	Lattimore, Eleanor F.	Harcourt Trade
*Little Pear and His Friends	O	HF	250+	Lattimore, Eleanor F.	Harcourt Trade
Little Sparrow, The: A Cinderella Story From Italy	O	TL	795	Leveled Readers	Houghton Mifflin
Living in Space	O	I	250+	Nayer, Judy	Pearson Learning Group
Lizards and Snakes	O	I	250+	Rigby Literacy	Rigby
Llama in the Family, A	O	RF	250+	Hurwitz, Johanna	Scholastic
Look Out, Washington D.C.!	O	RF	250+	Giff, Patricia Reilly	Bantam

* Collection of short stories

TITLE	LEVEL	GENRE	WORD COUNT	AUTHOR / SERIES	PUBLISHER / DISTRIBUTOR
Look What Came from China	O	I	250+	Harvey, Miles	Franklin Watts
Look What Came from Egypt	O	I	250+	Harvey, Miles	Franklin Watts
Look What Came from France	O	I	250+	Harvey, Miles	Franklin Watts
Look What Came from Italy	O	I	250+	Harvey, Miles	Franklin Watts
Look What Came from Mexico	O	I	250+	Harvey, Miles	Franklin Watts
Look What Came from Russia	O	I	250+	Harvey, Miles	Franklin Watts
Look What Came from the United States	O	I	250+	Davis, Kevin	Franklin Watts
Looking at Animals in Cold Places	O	I	250+	Butterfield, Moira	Steck-Vaughn
Looking at Animals in the Ocean	O	I	250+	Butterfield, Moira	Steck-Vaughn
Looking for the Queen	O	I	250+	Frederick, Shirley	Hampton-Brown
Loose Bolts	O	SF	250+	Neufeld, David	Wright Group/McGraw Hill
*Lost Continent and Other Cases, The	O	RF	250+	Simon, Seymour	Avon
*Lost Hikers and Other Cases, The	O	RF	250+	Simon, Seymour	Avon
Lou Gehrig: One of Baseball's Greatest	O	B	250+	Childhood of Famous Americans	Aladdin
Louisa May Alcott: Young Novelist	O	B	250+	Childhood of Famous Americans	Aladdin
Luther Burbank	O	B	250+	Faber, Doris	Garrard Publishing Co.
Ma and Pa Dracula	O	F	250+	Martin, Ann M.	Scholastic
Make A Wish, Molly	O	RF	250+	Cohen, Barbara	Bantam
Make Things That Move	O	I	250+	Sunshine	Wright Group/McGraw Hill
Making a Magazine	O	I	496	Vocabulary Readers	Houghton Mifflin
Making Clay	O	I	792	Leveled Readers Science	Houghton Mifflin
Making Crafts From Around the World	O	I	250+	Navigators Fiction Series	Benchmark Education
Making Pop-ups	O	I	250+	Brian, Janeen	Mondo
Man Who Paints Nature, The	O	B	250+	Locker, Thomas	Richard C. Owen
Manual of House Monsters, A	O	F	250+	Marijanovic, Stanislav	Mondo
Maple Tree	O	I	250+	Life Cycles	Creative Teaching Press
Margaret Bourke-White	O	B	250+	Welch, Catherine	Carolrhoda Books
Margaret Wise Brown	O	B	250+	Greene, Carol	Children's Press
Maria Mitchell	O	B	291	Independent Readers Science	Houghton Mifflin
Marie Curie	O	B	250+	Early Biographies	Compass Point Books
Marie Mitchell	O	B	250+	Independent Readers Science	Houghton Mifflin
Marjorie Harris Carr	O	B	546	Leveled Readers Science	Houghton Mifflin
Mark Twain: Young Writer	O	B	250+	Childhood of Famous Americans	Aladdin
Martha Washington: America's First First Lady	O	B	250+	Childhood of Famous Americans	Aladdin
Martin Luther King, Jr.	O	B	250+	Rookie Biographies	Children's Press
Martin Luther King, Jr., A Man Who Changed Things	O	B	250+	Greene, Carol	Children's Press
Martin Luther King, Jr.: Young Man with a Dream	O	B	250+	Childhood of Famous Americans	Aladdin
Mary McLeod Bethune	O	B	250+	Greenfield, Eloise	HarperTrophy
Mary Todd Lincoln: Girl of the Bluegrass	O	B	250+	Childhood of Famous Americans	Aladdin
Math on the Moon	O	I	250+	Navigators Fiction Series	Benchmark Education
Matilda's Plans	O	F	250+	Sails	Rigby
Matthew Henson: Arctic Explorer	O	B	250+	Podojil, Catherine	Wright Group/McGraw Hill
Maxie, Rosie, and Earl - Partners in Grime	O	RF	250+	Park, Barbara	Random House
*McBroom's Wonderful One-Acre Farm	O	RF	250+	Fleischman, Sid	Beech Tree Books
Meerkats	O	I	250+	Weaver, Robyn	Red Brick Learning
Meet Abraham Lincoln	O	B	250+	Cary, Barbara	Step-Up Books
Meet Benjamin Franklin	O	B	250+	Scarf, Maggi	Step-Up Books
Meet George Washington	O	B	250+	Heilbroner, Joan	Random House
Meet Thomas Jefferson	O	B	250+	Barrett, Marvin	Step-Up Books
Meg Mackintosh and The Case of the Curious Whale Watch	O	RF	250+	Landon, Lucinda	Secret Passage Press

* Collection of short stories

TITLE	LEVEL	GENRE	WORD COUNT	AUTHOR / SERIES	PUBLISHER / DISTRIBUTOR
Meg Mackintosh and The Case of the Missing Babe Ruth Baseball	O	RF	250+	Landon, Lucinda	Secret Passage Press
Meg Mackintosh and The Mystery at Camp Creepy	O	RF	250+	Landon, Lucinda	Secret Passage Press
Meg Mackintosh and The Mystery at the Medieval Castle	O	RF	250+	Landon, Lucinda	Secret Passage Press
Meg Mackintosh and The Mystery at the Soccer Match	O	RF	250+	Landon, Lucinda	Secret Passage Press
Meg Mackintosh and The Mystery in the Locked Library	O	RF	250+	Landon, Lucinda	Secret Passage Press
*Melting Snow Sculptures and Other Cases, The	O	RF	250+	Simon, Seymour	Avon
Mexico	O	I	250+	Many Cultures, One World	Capstone Press
Mexico	O	I	250+	Dahl, Michael	Red Brick Learning
Mice	O	I	250+	Holmes, Kevin J.	Red Brick Learning
Mieko and the Fifth Treasure	O	HF	250+	Coerr, Eleanor	Bantam
Mitch and Amy	O	RF	250+	Cleary, Beverly	HarperCollins
Molly Pitcher: Young Patriot	O	B	250+	Childhood of Famous Americans	Aladdin
Mom, You're Fired!	O	RF	250+	Robinson, Nancy K.	Scholastic
Money, Money, Money!	O	I	250+	Bookweb	Rigby
Moonwalk: The First Trip to the Moon	O	I	250+	Donnelly, Judy	Random House
*More Stories from Grandma's Attic	O	RF	250+	Richardson, Arleta	Chariot Victor Publishing
Most Beautiful Place in the World, The	O	RF	250+	Cameron, Ann	Alfred A. Knopf
Most Wonderful Doll in the World, The	O	RF	250+	McGinley, Phyllis	Scholastic
Mount St. Helens	O	I	250+	Early Connections	Benchmark Education
Mountain Bike Mania	O	RF	250+	Action Packs	Rigby
Mountain Gorillas	O	I	250+	Wonder World	Wright Group/McGraw Hill
Mountain Lion, The	O	I	250+	Crewe, Sabrina	Steck-Vaughn
Mouse and the Motorcycle, The	O	F	250+	Cleary, Beverly	Avon Camelot
Mouse Called Wolf, A	O	F	250+	King-Smith, Dick	Alfred A. Knopf
Mouse Magic	O	RF	250+	Baglio, Ben M.	Scholastic
Mr. Ape	O	F	250+	King-Smith, Dick	Alfred A. Knopf
*Mrs. Piggle-Wiggle	O	F	250+	MacDonald, Betty	Scholastic
*Mrs. Piggle-Wiggle's Farm	O	F	250+	MacDonald, Betty	Scholastic
*Mrs. Piggle-Wiggle's Magic	O	F	250+	MacDonald, Betty	Scholastic
Much Ado About Aldo	O	RF	250+	Hurwitz, Johanna	Penguin Group
Muggie Maggie	O	RF	250+	Cleary, Beverly	Avon Camelot
Mummy's Curse, The	O	F	250+	SupaDoopers	Sundance
Mural, The	O	RF	801	Leveled Readers	Houghton Mifflin
My Mysterious World	O	B	250+	Mahy, Margaret	Richard C. Owen
My Teacher Turns into a Tyrannosaurus	O	F	250+	SupaDoopers	Sundance
My Writing Day	O	B	250+	Adler, David A.	Richard C. Owen
*Mysterious Green Swimmer and Other Cases, The	O	RF	250+	Simon, Seymour	Avon
*Mysterious Tracks and Other Cases, The	O	RF	250+	Simon, Seymour	Avon
Mystery on October Road	O	RF	250+	Herzig, A. C.; Mali, Jane	Scholastic
Native American Art	O	I	250+	Motil, Rebecca	Scholastic
Native American Foods and Recipes	O	I	250+	Rosen Real Readers	Rosen Publishing Group
Native Americans	O	I	250+	Navigators Fiction Series	Benchmark Education
Nature Club, The	O	RF	755	Leveled Readers	Houghton Mifflin
Nature! Wild and Wonderful	O	B	250+	Pringle, Laurence	Richard C. Owen
Neil Armstrong: Young Flyer	O	B	250+	Childhood of Famous Americans	Aladdin
Nemo and the Ship of Gold	O	I	250+	Leveled Readers Language Support	Houghton Mifflin
Netherlands, The	O	I	250+	Dahl, Michael	Red Brick Learning

* Collection of short stories

TITLE	LEVEL	GENRE	WORD COUNT	AUTHOR / SERIES	PUBLISHER / DISTRIBUTOR
Never Bored on Boards	O	I	250+	Literacy 2000	Rigby
Never Hit a Ghost with a Baseball Bat	O	RF	250+	Clifford, Eth	Scholastic
New Year's Around the World	O	I	250+	Trumbore, Cindy	Pearson Learning Group
Next Stop, New York City!	O	RF	250+	Giff, Patricia Reilly	Bantam
Nicaragua	O	I	250+	Countries of the World	Red Brick Learning
Nigeria	O	I	250+	Thoennes, Kristin	Red Brick Learning
Night Crossing, The	O	HF	250+	Ackerman, Karen	Alfred A. Knopf
Nikki Giovanni: A Special Poet	O	B	605	Leveled Readers	Houghton Mifflin
*No Dogs Allowed	O	RF	73	Cutler, Jane	Farrar, Straus and Giroux
No One is Going to Nashville	O	RF	250+	Jukes, Mavis	Alfred A. Knopf
*Not-So-Dead Fish and Other Cases, The	O	RF	250+	Simon, Seymour	Avon
Oceans of Grass: The Prairie	O	I	707	Leveled Readers Social Studies	Houghton Mifflin
Octopuses and Squids	O	I	328	Wonder World	Wright Group/McGraw Hill
Oh Boy, Boston!	O	RF	250+	Giff, Patricia Reilly	Bantam
Olympic Dreams	O	RF	250+	Navigators Fiction Series	Benchmark Education
Olympics, The	O	I	250+	Windows on Literacy	National Geographic
On the Way to the Moon	O	F	250+	Gold, Becky	Pearson Learning Group
Once Upon a Time	O	B	250+	Bunting, Eve	Richard C. Owen
One Lucky Summer	O	RF	250+	Kvasnosky, Laura McGee	Penguin Group
One Man Show	O	B	250+	Asch, Frank	Richard C. Owen
*On-Line Spaceman and Other Cases, The	O	RF	250+	Simon, Seymour	Avon
Otis Spofford	O	RF	250+	Cleary, Beverly	Avon
Our American Flag	O	I	250+	McCloskey, Susan	Wright Group/McGraw Hill
Our National Treasures	O	I	250+	Bookshop	Mondo
Owl Moon	O	B	250+	Yolen, Jane	Scholastic
Owls	O	I	250+	Holmes, Kevin J.	Red Brick Learning
Panning for Gold	O	RF	825	Leveled Readers Science	Houghton Mifflin
Passover	O	I	250+	Holidays and Festivals	Compass Point Books
Patrick Doyle is Full of Blarney	O	HF	250+	Armstrong, Jennifer	Random House
Penguin, The	O	I	250+	Crewe, Sabrina	Steck-Vaughn
Penguins	O	I	250+	First Reports	Compass Point Books
Penguins	O	I	250+	Holmes, Kevin J.	Red Brick Learning
Penguins	O	I	250+	Woolley, M.; Pigdon, K.	Mondo
Penguins on Parade	O	F	250+	Little Celebrations	Pearson Learning Group
People in the Rain Forest	O	I	250+	Pirotta, Saviour	Steck-Vaughn
Perfect Instrument, The	O	RF	786	Leveled Readers	Houghton Mifflin
Perfect Pony, A	O	RF	250+	Szymanski, Lois	Avon Camelot
Peru	O	I	250+	Thoennes, Kristin	Red Brick Learning
Pet Parade	O	RF	250+	Giff, Patricia Reilly	Bantam
Philippines, The	O	I	250+	Davis, Lucile	Red Brick Learning
Photo Contest, The	O	RF	250+	Leveled Readers Language Support	Houghton Mifflin
Photographic Memory	O	RF	250+	PM Ruby	Rigby
Pippi Goes on Board	O	F	250+	Lindgren, Astrid	Puffin Books
Pippi in the South Seas	O	F	250+	Lindgren, Astrid	Puffin Books
Pippi Longstocking	O	F	250+	Lindgren, Astrid	Penguin Group
Pizza Parts	O	I	250+	Early Connections	Benchmark Education
Plants	O	I	250+	Rigby Focus	Rigby
Playing with Words	O	B	250+	Howe, James	Richard C. Owen
Pony Pals: A Pony for Keeps	O	RF	250+	Betancourt, Jeanne	Scholastic
Pony Pals: A Pony in Trouble	O	RF	250+	Betancourt, Jeanne	Scholastic
Pony Pals: Detective Pony	O	RF	250+	Betancourt, Jeanne	Scholastic
Pony Pals: Don't Hurt My Pony	O	RF	250+	Betancourt, Jeanne	Scholastic
Pony Pals: Give Me Back My Pony	O	RF	250+	Betancourt, Jeanne	Scholastic

* Collection of short stories

TITLE	LEVEL	GENRE	WORD COUNT	AUTHOR / SERIES	PUBLISHER / DISTRIBUTOR
Pony Pals: Good-bye Pony	O	RF	250+	Betancourt, Jeanne	Scholastic
Pony Pals: I Want a Pony	O	RF	250+	Betancourt, Jeanne	Scholastic
Pony Pals: Keep Out, Pony!	O	RF	250+	Betancourt, Jeanne	Scholastic
Pony Pals: Pony to the Rescue	O	RF	250+	Betancourt, Jeanne	Scholastic
Pony Pals: Pony-Sitters	O	RF	250+	Betancourt, Jeanne	Scholastic
Pony Pals: Runaway Pony	O	RF	250+	Betancourt, Jeanne	Scholastic
Pony Pals: The Blind Pony	O	RF	250+	Betancourt, Jeanne	Scholastic
Pony Pals: The Ghost Pony	O	RF	250+	Betancourt, Jeanne	Scholastic
Pony Pals: The Girl Who Hated Ponies	O	RF	250+	Betancourt, Jeanne	Scholastic
Pony Pals: The Lonely Pony	O	RF	250+	Betancourt, Jeanne	Scholastic
Pony Pals: The Wild Pony	O	RF	250+	Betancourt, Jeanne	Scholastic
Pony Pals: Too Many Ponies	O	RF	250+	Betancourt, Jeanne	Scholastic
Pony Parade	O	RF	250+	Baglio, Ben M.	Scholastic
Predators in the Rain Forest	O	I	250+	Pirotta, Saviour	Steck-Vaughn
PS, I Love You Gramps	O	RF	250+	Literacy Tree	Rigby
Puppy Puzzle	O	RF	250+	Baglio, Ben M.	Scholastic
Purple Walrus and Other Perfect Pets	O	RF	250+	Wildcats	Wright Group/McGraw Hill
Rabbit Race	O	RF	250+	Baglio, Ben M.	Scholastic
Rachel to the Rescue	O	RF	250+	SupaDoopers	Sundance
Radio	O	I	250+	Let's See	Compass Point Books
Ralph S. Mouse	O	F	250+	Cleary, Beverly	HarperTrophy
Ramona and Her Father	O	RF	250+	Cleary, Beverly	Avon
Ramona and Her Mother	O	RF	250+	Cleary, Beverly	Avon
Ramona Forever	O	RF	250+	Cleary, Beverly	Hearst
Ramona Quimby, Age 8	O	RF	250+	Cleary, Beverly	Hearst
Ramona the Brave	O	RF	250+	Cleary, Beverly	Hearst
Ramona the Pest	O	RF	250+	Cleary, Beverly	Avon
*Rats on the Range and Other Stories	O	F	250+	Marshall, James	Penguin Group
*Rats on the Roof and Other Stories	O	F	250+	Marshall, James	Penguin Group
*Rats!	O	RF	250+	Cutler, Jane	Farrar, Straus and Giroux
Red Sox and the World Series, The	O	I	460	Vocabulary Readers	Houghton Mifflin
Rent a Third Grader	O	RF	250+	Hiller, B. B.	Scholastic
Rescue!	O	RF	250+	Wildcats	Wright Group/McGraw Hill
Rhinos	O	I	250+	Holmes, Kevin J.	Red Brick Learning
Ribsy	O	RF	250+	Cleary, Beverly	Hearst
Rice	O	I	250+	Windows on Literacy	National Geographic
Right or Wrong?	O	RF	250+	Wildcats	Wright Group/McGraw Hill
Riptide	O	RF	250+	Weller, Frances Ward	Putnam & Grosset
River Rats	O	RF	250+	Belcher, Angie	Pacific Learning
Rivers in the Rain Forest	O	I	250+	Pirotta, Saviour	Steck-Vaughn
Roaring Down the Rapids	O	RF	634	Leveled Readers	Houghton Mifflin
Rock Climbing	O	I	250+	Sunshine	Wright Group/McGraw Hill
*Rotating Rollerblades and Other Cases, The	O	RF	250+	Simon, Seymour	Avon
Rubbery Arms and Baggy Bodies	O	I	250+	Sails	Rigby
Runaway Ralph	O	F	250+	Cleary, Beverly	Hearst
Russia	O	I	250+	Thoennes, Kristin	Red Brick Learning
Sable	O	RF	250+	Hesse, Karen	Henry Holt & Co.
Sam and Kim	O	I	250+	Pacific Literacy	Pacific Learning
San Francisco Exploratorium, The	O	I	250+	Little Celebrations	Pearson Learning Group
Sandra Day O'Connor	O	I	318	Independent Readers Social Studies	Houghton Mifflin
Sara Crewe	O	HF	250+	Burnett, Frances Hodgson	Scholastic
Satellites	O	I	250+	Let's See	Compass Point Books
Saving Money	O	I	250+	Let's See	Compass Point Books

* Collection of short stories

TITLE	LEVEL	GENRE	WORD COUNT	AUTHOR / SERIES	PUBLISHER / DISTRIBUTOR
Scary Sharks	O	I	250+	Fearsome, Scary, and Creepy Animals	Enslow Publishers, Inc.
School Newspaper, The	O	I	250+	Sunshine	Wright Group/McGraw Hill
Sea Otter Inlet	O	I	250+	Godkin, Celia	Fitzhenry & Whiteside
Search and Discover	O	I	250+	Discovery Links	Newbridge
Seawall	O	RF	250+	PM Ruby	Rigby
Secret Soldier, The: The Story of Deborah Sampson	O	B	250+	McGovern, Ann	Scholastic
Secret Valley, The	O	HF	250+	Bulla, Clyde Robert	Scholastic
Secrets of the Fun Park	O	I	250+	Home Connection Collection	Rigby
Secrets of the Rain Forest	O	I	250+	Myers, Edward	Pearson Learning Group
Seed is a Promise, A	O	I	250+	Merrill, Claire	Scholastic
Seeing the Circle	O	B	250+	Bruchac, Joseph	Richard C. Owen
Sequoyah	O	B	865	Leveled Readers Social Studies	Houghton Mifflin
Seven Kisses in a Row	O	RF	250+	MacLachlan, Patricia	HarperCollins
Seven Stones of Sligo	O	TL	250+	PM Ruby	Rigby
Shark Lady: The Adventures of Eugenie Clark	O	B	250+	McGovern, Ann	Scholastic
Sharks	O	I	250+	First Reports	Compass Point Books
Sharks	O	I	250+	Holmes, Kevin J.	Red Brick Learning
*Shining Blue Planet and Other Cases, The	O	RF	250+	Simon, Seymour	Avon
Silent Hero, The	O	I	250+	Shea, George	Random House
Simple Machines	O	I	250+	Windows on Literacy	National Geographic
Skateboarding	O	I	250+	PM Nonfiction-Emerald	Rigby
Sky Rider	O	RF	250+	Belcher, Angie	Pacific Learning
Smasher	O	RF	250+	King-Smith, Dick	Random House
Snails	O	I	67	Holmes, Kevin J.	Red Brick Learning
Snake, The	O	I	250+	Crewe, Sabrina	Steck-Vaughn
Snakes	O	I	250+	First Reports	Compass Point Books
Snowboarding Diary	O	I	250+	PM Nonfiction-Emerald	Rigby
Socks	O	RF	250+	Cleary, Beverly	Avon
Sojourner Truth, Speaker for Equal Rights	O	B	374	Independent Readers Social Studies	Houghton Mifflin
Somalia	O	I	250+	Countries of the World	Red Brick Learning
Some Dog!	O	RF	250+	PM Ruby	Rigby
Song of the Giraffe	O	RF	250+	Jacobs, Shannon K.	Little, Brown & Co.
Sor Juana Inez de la Cruz	O	B	693	Leveled Readers Social Studies	Houghton Mifflin
South Africa	O	I	250+	Countries of the World	Red Brick Learning
South Korea	O	I	250+	Davis, Lucile	Red Brick Learning
South Pole Bound	O	RF	788	Leveled Readers	Houghton Mifflin
Space Junk	O	RF	250+	Wildcats	Wright Group/McGraw Hill
Space Quest	O	I	250+	Discovery World	Rigby
*Space Station Plot and Other Cases, The	O	RF	250+	Simon, Seymour	Avon
Space Stations	O	I	250+	Ryan, Cheryl	Wright Group/McGraw Hill
Special Trip, A	O	RF	910	Leveled Readers Science	Houghton Mifflin
*Speeding Sleigh and Other Cases, The	O	RF	250+	Simon, Seymour	Avon
*Speedy Pasta and Other Cases, The	O	RF	250+	Simon, Seymour	Avon
*Speedy Snake and Other Cases, The	O	RF	250+	Simon, Seymour	Avon
*Speedy Soapbox Car and Other Cases, The	O	RF	250+	Simon, Seymour	Avon
Spending Money	O	I	250+	Let's See	Compass Point Books
Spider Kane and the Mystery at Jumbo Nightcrawler's	O	F	250+	Osborne, Mary Pope	Random House
Spider Kane and the Mystery Under the May-Apple	O	F	250+	Osborne, Mary Pope	Random House
Spider, The	O	I	250+	Crewe, Sabrina	Steck-Vaughn

TITLE	LEVEL	GENRE	WORD COUNT	AUTHOR / SERIES	PUBLISHER / DISTRIBUTOR
Spiders	O	I	250+	Holmes, Kevin J.	Red Brick Learning
*Sports Hall of Fame	O	B	250+	Bookshop	Mondo
Sports Legends	O	B	250+	Navigators Fiction Series	Benchmark Education
Spray-Paint Mystery, The	O	RF	250+	Medearis, Angela Shelf	Scholastic
Squanto: Friend of the Pilgrims	O	B	250+	Bulla, Clyde Robert	Scholastic
St. Lawrence Seaway, The	O	I	371	Independent Readers Social Studies	Houghton Mifflin
Stacey and the Haunted Masquerade	O	RF	250+	Martin, Ann M.	Scholastic
Stacey and the Missing Ring	O	RF	250+	Martin, Ann M.	Scholastic
Stacey and the Mystery at the Mall	O	RF	250+	Martin, Ann M.	Scholastic
Stacey and the Mystery Money	O	RF	250+	Martin, Ann M.	Scholastic
Stage Fright	O	RF	250+	Orbit Double Takes	Pacific Learning
Stay Away from Simon!	O	RF	250+	Carrick, Carol	Clarion
Staying Healthy: Eating Right	O	I	250+	McGinty, Alice B.	Franklin Watts
Staying Nine	O	RF	250+	Conrad, Pam	HarperTrophy
Still Standing	O	I	388	Independent Readers Science	Houghton Mifflin
Stormy Weather	O	I	250+	Navigators Fiction Series	Benchmark Education
Story of Alexander Graham Bell, Inventor of the Telephone	O	B	250+	Davidson, Margaret	Scholastic
Story of Benjamin Franklin, Amazing American	O	B	250+	Davidson, Margaret	Scholastic
Story of Books, The	O	I	250+	Sunshine	Wright Group/McGraw Hill
Story of Jackie Robinson, The: Bravest Man in Baseball	O	B	250+	Davidson, Margaret	Scholastic
Story of Ruby Bridges, The	O	B	250+	Coles, Robert	Scholastic
Story of Sacagawea, The	O	B	250+	Rosen Real Readers	Rosen Publishing Group
Story of Walt Disney, Maker of Magical Worlds, The	O	B	250+	Selden, Bernice	Bantam
Story Teller's Story, A	O	B	250+	Martin, Rafe	Richard C. Owen
*Strange Clues and Other Cases, The	O	RF	250+	Simon, Seymour	Avon
*Strange Museum and Other Cases, The	O	RF	250+	Simon, Seymour	Avon
Strange Plants	O	I	250+	Windows on Literacy	National Geographic
Street Action	O	I	250+	Wildcats	Wright Group/McGraw Hill
Strike	O	I	250+	Pacific Literacy	Pacific Learning
Summer Wheels	O	B	250+	Bunting, Eve	Harcourt Trade
Sun	O	I	250+	Vogt, Gregory L.	Red Brick Learning
Surprise Feast, The	O	I	250+	Rigby Focus	Rigby
Surprising Myself	O	B	250+	Fritz, Jean	Richard C. Owen
Switzerland	O	I	250+	Countries of the World	Red Brick Learning
Symmetry in Our World	O	I	250+	Early Connections	Benchmark Education
Tadpole Diary	O	I	250+	Literacy Tree	Rigby
Talented Alex	O	RF	772	Leveled Readers	Houghton Mifflin
Talk About a Family	O	RF	250+	Greenfield, Eloise	HarperTrophy
*Tall Tale and Other Cases, The	O	RF	250+	Simon, Seymour	Avon
Tall Tale to Tell, A	O	I	860	Independent Readers Social Studies	Houghton Mifflin
Tall Tales	O	TL	615	Vocabulary Readers	Houghton Mifflin
Tall Tales	O	RF	250+	PM Emerald	Rigby
Tamika and the Wisdom Rings	O	RF	250+	Yarbrough, Camille	Random House
Teacher's Pet	O	RF	250+	Hurwitz, Johanna	Scholastic
Telephones	O	I	250+	Let's See	Compass Point Books
Television	O	I	250+	Let's See	Compass Point Books
Tell Me a Story	O	B	250+	London, Jonathan	Richard C. Owen
Tell Me Why Planes Have Wings	O	I	250+	Whiz Kids	Franklin Watts
*Ten True Animal Rescues	O	I	250+	Betancourt, Jeanne	Scholastic

* Collection of short stories

TITLE	LEVEL	GENRE	WORD COUNT	AUTHOR / SERIES	PUBLISHER / DISTRIBUTOR
*Terrible Test Mark and Other Cases, The	O	RF	250+	Simon, Seymour	Avon
Terror In the Towers	O	B	250+	Kerson, Adrian	Random House
Thailand	O	I	250+	Thoennes, Kristin	Red Brick Learning
Thanks to Sandra Cisneros	O	RF	940	Leveled Readers Language Support	Houghton Mifflin
Thanksgiving	O	I	250+	Holidays and Festivals	Compass Point Books
There's a Ship Outside My Window	O	RF	250+	PM Ruby	Rigby
*They Led The Way: 14 American Women	O	B	250+	Johnston, Johanna	Scholastic
They Survived Mount St. Helens!	O	I	250+	Stine, Megan	Random House
They Worked Together	O	I	250+	iOpeners	Pearson Learning Group
Those Amazingly Useful Ears	O	I	250+	Frederick, Shirley	Hampton-Brown
Thoughts, Pictures, and Words	O	B	250+	Kuskin, Karla	Richard C. Owen
*Three Wishes, The	O	TL	250+	Literacy 2000	Rigby
Tiger Tales	O	F	250+	Little Celebrations	Pearson Learning Group
*Time Machine and Other Cases, The	O	RF	250+	Simon, Seymour	Avon
Toad for Tuesday, A	O	F	250+	Erickson, Russell E.	Beech Tree Books
Today's Weather Is . . . A Book of Experiments	O	I	250+	Bookshop	Mondo
Top Cat	O	I	250+	Byars, Betsy	Penguin Group
Tornado	O	I	250+	Byars, Betsy	HarperTrophy
Trailblazers!	O	RF	250+	Action Packs	Rigby
Train to the West?	O	I	279	Vocabulary Readers	Houghton Mifflin
Trapped!	O	RF	250+	SupaDoopers	Sundance
Traveling Across Australia	O	I	250+	Windows on Literacy	National Geographic
Traveling by Train	O	I	485	Leveled Readers Social Studies	Houghton Mifflin
Traveling Guitar, The	O	RF	674	Leveled Readers	Houghton Mifflin
Treasure Hunt	O	I	250+	Early Connections	Benchmark Education
Trees and Plants in the Rain Forest	O	I	250+	Pirotta, Saviour	Steck-Vaughn
Trevor's New Home	O	RF	250+	Leveled Readers Language Support	Houghton Mifflin
Trickster Ghost, The	O	F	250+	Showell, E.	Scholastic
Trouble with Oatmeal, The	O	RF	250+	PM Emerald	Rigby
Trouble with Patrick, The	O	RF	250+	Action Packs	Rigby
True Stories about Abraham Lincoln	O	B	250+	Gross, Ruth Belov	Scholastic
Tugboats	O	I	250+	Schaefer, Lola M.	Red Brick Learning
Two Cold Ears	O	B	560	Leveled Readers	Houghton Mifflin
Two-Star Day	O	RF	446	Leveled Readers	Houghton Mifflin
Tyrannosaurus Rex	O	I	250+	True Books	Children's Press
Under My Nose	O	B	250+	Ehlert, Lois	Richard C. Owen
Undercover Tailback	O	RF	250+	Christopher, Matt	Scholastic
*Universal Solvent and Other Cases, The	O	RF	250+	Simon, Seymour	Avon
Unusual Coin, The	O	F	951	Leveled Readers	Houghton Mifflin
Uranus	O	I	250+	Vogt, Gregory L.	Red Brick Learning
Valentine's Day	O	I	250+	Holidays and Festivals	Compass Point Books
Very Special Kwanzaa, A	O	I	250+	Chocolate, Deborah M. Newton	Scholastic
Vicar of Nibbleswick, The	O	RF	250+	Dahl, Roald	Puffin Books
Vietnam	O	I	250+	Dahl, Michael	Red Brick Learning
Virtual Fred	O	SF	250+	Courtney, Vincent	Random House
Visit to Vancouver Island, A	O	RF	1261	Leveled Readers Social Studies	Houghton Mifflin
Volcanoes and Geysers	O	I	250+	PM Plus Story Books	Rigby
Volcanoes Around the World	O	I	380	Vocabulary Readers	Houghton Mifflin
Wacky Plant Cycles	O	I	250+	Bookshop	Mondo
Warning: Volcano!: The Story of Mount St. Helens	O	I	250+	Rosen Real Readers	Rosen Publishing Group
Warthogs	O	I	250+	Holmes, Kevin J.	Red Brick Learning

* Collection of short stories

TITLE	LEVEL	GENRE	WORD COUNT	AUTHOR / SERIES	PUBLISHER / DISTRIBUTOR
Warton and the King of the Skies	O	F	250+	Erickson, Russell E.	Houghton Mifflin
Weather	O	I	250+	Fleisher, Julian	Scholastic
*Weaving Contest, The	O	TL	250+	Literacy 2000	Rigby
Welcome, Wilma	O	F	667	Leveled Readers	Houghton Mifflin
West Virginia: Facts and Symbols	O	I	250+	Feeney, Kathy	Red Brick Learning
Whale, The	O	I	250+	Crewe, Sabrina	Steck-Vaughn
Whales	O	I	250+	Holmes, Kevin J.	Red Brick Learning
Whales	O	I	250+	Soar To Success	Houghton Mifflin
Whales	O	I	250+	Bookshop	Mondo
Whales	O	I	250+	Simon, Seymour	Houghton Mifflin
What a Wonderful Idea	O	RF	1059	Leveled Readers	Houghton Mifflin
What Do You Think?	O	I	250+	Wildcats	Wright Group/McGraw Hill
What Makes a Bird a Bird?	O	I	250+	Garelick, May	Mondo
What's the Big Idea, Ben Franklin?	O	B	250+	Fritz, Jean	Scholastic
Where is Blackbeard's Ship?	O	I	286	Vocabulary Readers	Houghton Mifflin
Where to Look for a Dinosaur	O	F	250+	Most, Bernard	OSI
Which Way, Jack?	O	F	250+	Action Packs	Rigby
White Elephants and Yellow Jackets	O	I	250+	Action Packs	Rigby
Who Was Marjorie Harris Carr?	O	B	597	Leveled Readers Science	Houghton Mifflin
Whoops! It Works!	O	I	250+	Lopez, Orlando	Pearson Learning Group
Why Polar Bears Like Snow . . . and Flamingos Don't	O	I	250+	Navigators Fiction Series	Benchmark Education
Wild Babies	O	I	250+	Simon, Seymour	HarperCollins
*Wild Bird and Other Stories of Adventure	O	RF	250+	Belcher, Angie	Pacific Learning
Wild Culpepper Cruise, The	O	RF	250+	Paulsen, Gary	Bantam
Will Rogers	O	B	250+	Schott, Jane A.	Carolrhoda Books
Wingman	O	F	250+	Pinkwater, Daniel	Bantam
Winter in Alaska	O	I	347	Vocabulary Readers	Houghton Mifflin
Winter Survival	O	I	250+	Literacy Tree	Rigby
Wolfman Sam	O	RF	250+	Levy, Elizabeth	HarperTrophy
Woman Who Flummoxed the Fairies, The	O	TL	250+	Forest, Heather	Harcourt Trade
*Women Inventors	O	B	250+	Blashfield, Jean	Red Brick Learning
Wood Frog	O	I	250+	Life Cycles	Creative Teaching Press
Wordful Child, A	O	B	250+	Lyon, George Ella	Richard C. Owen
Writing Bug, The	O	B	250+	Hopkins, Lee Bennett	Richard C. Owen
Wyoming: Facts and Symbols	O	I	250+	Dubois, Muriel L.	Red Brick Learning
X-Rays	O	I	250+	Voyages	SRA/McGraw Hill
You Can Canoe!: A Book of Sporting Activities	O	I	250+	Literacy Tree	Rigby
Young Geographers	O	I	250+	People, Spaces & Places	Rand McNally
Young Mozart	O	B	250+	Isadora, Rachel	Penguin Group
Yo-Yo's	O	I	250+	PM Nonfiction-Emerald	Rigby
Zacharys' Plans, The	O	F	250+	Sails	Rigby
Zebras	O	I	250+	Holmes, Kevin J.	Red Brick Learning
15 Facts about the Solar System	P	I	474	Independent Readers Science	Houghton Mifflin
Accident Prone	P	RF	250+	Bookweb	Rigby
Accidental Angel (Secret Sisters)	P	RF	250+	Byrd, Sandra	WaterBrook Press
Ad Break	P	RF	250+	Bookweb	Rigby
Afghanistan	P	I	250+	Fact Finders	Capstone Press
Against the Odds	P	I	250+	Layden, Joe	Scholastic
Albert Einstein	P	B	250+	Early Biographies	Compass Point Books
Alexander Graham Bell	P	B	250+	Bridgestone Books	Red Brick Learning
Alexander Graham Bell and the Telephone	P	B	250+	Windows on Literacy	National Geographic
All About Eggs	P	I	250+	Sunshine	Wright Group/McGraw Hill
All-Pro Biographies: Dan Marino	P	B	250+	Stewart, Mark	Children's Press

* Collection of short stories

TITLE	LEVEL	GENRE	WORD COUNT	AUTHOR / SERIES	PUBLISHER / DISTRIBUTOR
All-Pro Biographies: Gwen Torrence	P	B	250+	Stewart, Mark	Children's Press
Alvin Ailey	P	B	250+	Pinkney, Andrea Davis	Hyperion
Amazing Journeys	P	I	250+	Literacy 2000	Rigby
Amber Cat, The	P	RF	250+	McKay, Hilary	Simon & Schuster
Amelia Earhart	P	B	250+	Parlin, John	Bantam
Amelia Earhart	P	B	250+	Rosenthal, Marilyn; Freeman, Daniel	Red Brick Learning
American Beginnings: You're Right There!	P	HF	250+	Navigators Drama Series	Benchmark Education
Americans of the Midwest: The Potawatomi	P	I	701	Leveled Readers Social Studies	Houghton Mifflin
Andrew Carnegie	P	B	530	Leveled Readers Social Studies	Houghton Mifflin
Andrew Carnegie: Builder of Libraries	P	B	250+	Community Builders	Children's Press
Animal Behaviorists	P	B	250+	Navigators Biography Series	Benchmark Education
Anna Allen Faces the White Dragon	P	I	250+	Leveled Readers Language Support	Houghton Mifflin
Another Point of View	P	RF	250+	Wildcats	Wright Group/McGraw Hill
Apache Indians, The	P	I	250+	Lund, Bill	Red Brick Learning
Apple Man, The	P	F	1094	Leveled Readers	Houghton Mifflin
Apples for America	P	B	824	Leveled Readers	Houghton Mifflin
Appointment with Action	P	RF	250+	Wildcats	Wright Group/McGraw Hill
Apsaalooke (Crow) Nation, The	P	I	250+	Native Peoples	Red Brick Learning
Archaeologists Dig for Clues	P	I	250+	Duke, Kate	HarperCollins
Arctic Babies	P	I	250+	Darling, Kathy	Scholastic
Arctic Food Web, The	P	I	250+	Rigby Literacy	Rigby
Artful Stories	P	I	250+	Rigby Literacy	Rigby
Asteroids	P	I	250+	The Galaxy	Red Brick Learning
Attaboy, Sam	P	RF	250+	Lowry, Lois	Bantam
Aunt Clara Brown: Official Pioneer	P	B	250+	Lowery, Linda	Lerner Publishing
Baba Nangko	P	F	250+	Voyages	SRA/McGraw Hill
Baby Grand, the Moon in July, and Me, The	P	RF	250+	Barnes, Joyce Annette	Penguin Group
Baby Island	P	RF	250+	Brink, Carol Ryrie	Simon & Schuster
Baby Whale Rescue: The True Story of J.J.	P	I	250+	Arnold, Caroline; Hewett, Richard	Troll Associates
Backyard Hunter: The Praying Mantis	P	I	250+	Lavies, Bianca	Penguin Group
Bad Spell for the Worst Witch, A	P	F	250+	Murphy, Jill	Puffin Books
Bald Eagle Free Again!, The	P	I	250+	Young Readers' Series	Barron's Educational
Ballad of Robin Hood, The	P	HF	250+	Literacy 2000	Rigby
Balto and the Great Race	P	RF	250+	Kimmel, Elizabeth Cody	Random House
Bargains for Everyone	P	RF	1025	Leveled Readers	Houghton Mifflin
Barney	P	RF	250+	Literacy 2000	Rigby
Baseball in the Barrios	P	I	250+	Horenstein, Henry	Harcourt Trade
*Baseball's Greatest Pitchers	P	B	250+	Kramer, S. A.	Random House
Bats	P	I	250+	Literacy 2000	Rigby
Battle for Survival, The	P	I	250+	Sunshine	Wright Group/McGraw Hill
Battle for the Castle, The	P	F	250+	Winthrop, Elizabeth	Yearling
Bear That Heard Crying, The	P	HF	250+	Kinsey-Warnock, Natalie; Kinsey, Helen	Penguin Group
Bears	P	I	3286	Leveled Readers Science	Houghton Mifflin
Becoming a Citizen	P	I	209	Vocabulary Readers	Houghton Mifflin
Ben Franklin Remembers	P	B	493	Vocabulary Readers	Houghton Mifflin
Bess's Log Cabin Quilt	P	HF	250+	Love, D. Anne	Bantam
Best Enemies	P	RF	250+	Leverich, Kathleen	Beech Tree Books
Best Enemies Again	P	RF	250+	Leverich, Kathleen	Alfred A. Knopf
Best Enemies Forever	P	RF	250+	Leverich, Kathleen	William Morrow
Best School Year Ever, The	P	RF	250+	Robinson, Barbara	HarperTrophy
Betsy and the Boys	P	RF	250+	Haywood, Carolyn	Harcourt Trade

TITLE	LEVEL	GENRE	WORD COUNT	AUTHOR / SERIES	PUBLISHER / DISTRIBUTOR
Bicycle Man, The	P	RF	250+	Say, Allen	Houghton Mifflin
Bill Gates: Helping People Use Computers	P	B	250+	Community Builders	Children's Press
Bison Are Back!, The	P	RF	743	Leveled Readers	Houghton Mifflin
Blackout!	P	RF	250+	Bookweb	Rigby
Blind Outlaw, The	P	RF	250+	Rounds, Glen	Scholastic
Body Battles	P	I	250+	Gelman, Rita G.	Scholastic
*Book of Black Heroes from A to Z	P	B	250+	Hudson, Wade; Wesley, Valerie Wilson	Scholastic
Book of Monsters, The	P	I	250+	Sunshine	Wright Group/McGraw Hill
*Brainstorm!: The Stories of Twenty American Kid Inventors	P	B	250+	Tucker, Tom	Farrar, Straus and Giroux
Brave As	P	RF	250+	Marriott, Janice	Pacific Learning
Brazil	P	I	250+	Fact Finders	Capstone Press
Breath of Fresh Air, A	P	RF	961	Leveled Readers	Houghton Mifflin
Breath of the Dragon	P	RF	250+	Giles, Gail	Bantam
Brian's Brilliant Career	P	RF	250+	Literacy 2000	Rigby
Bright Paddles	P	HF	250+	Downi, Mary Alice	Fitzhenry & Whiteside
Canada	P	I	250+	Fact Finders	Capstone Press
Canada Geese Quilt, The	P	RF	250+	Kinsey-Warnock, Natalie	Bantam
Capsize!	P	RF	250+	Bookweb	Rigby
Carnival	P	I	250+	Holidays and Festivals	Compass Point Books
Case of the Measled Cowboy, The	P	F	250+	Erickson, John R.	Puffin Books
Case of the Midnight Rustler, The	P	F	250+	Erickson, John R.	Puffin Books
Case of the Missing Cat, The	P	F	250+	Erickson, John R.	Puffin Books
Case of the Missing Key, The	P	F	1198	Leveled Readers	Houghton Mifflin
Caterpillars	P	I	250+	Mini Pets	Steck-Vaughn
Caught in a Flash	P	I	250+	Bishop, Nic	Pacific Learning
Cesar Chavez	P	B	262	Davis, Lucile	Red Brick Learning
Champion Billy Mills	P	B	725	Leveled Readers	Houghton Mifflin
Changing Earth, The	P	I	250+	iOpeners	Pearson Learning Group
Charlie Is a Chicken	P	RF	250+	Smith, Jane Denitz	HarperTrophy
Charlotte's Web Page	P	RF	250+	Action Packs	Rigby
Chasing the Train	P	HF	768	Leveled Readers	Houghton Mifflin
Chasing Tornadoes	P	I	250+	Gold, Becky	Pearson Learning Group
Chasing Tornadoes!	P	I	250+	Rigby Literacy	Rigby
Cherokee Indians, The	P	I	250+	Lund, Bill	Red Brick Learning
Chicago Fire, The	P	I	250+	Gutner, Howard	Scholastic
Chief Joseph of the Nez Percé	P	B	250+	McAuliffe, Bill	Red Brick Learning
Children Around the World	P	I	250+	Rigby Focus	Rigby
Children of Ancient Greece	P	I	250+	Rosen Real Readers	Rosen Publishing Group
*Children of the Earth and Sky	P	I	250+	Krensky, Stephen	Scholastic
Children of the Fire	P	HF	250+	Robinet, Harriette	Aladdin
China	P	I	250+	Fact Finders	Capstone Press
Chinese Foods and Recipes	P	I	250+	Rosen Real Readers	Rosen Publishing Group
Chocolate!	P	I	250+	Action Packs	Rigby
Christmas	P	I	250+	Let's See	Compass Point Books
Christmas: Why We Celebrate It the Way We Do	P	I	250+	Hintz, Martin & Kate	Red Brick Learning
*Cinderella's Big Night and Other Fractured Fairy Tales	P	TL	250+	Action Packs	Rigby
Clara Barton	P	B	250+	Photo-Illustrated Biographies	Red Brick Learning
Clean Air	P	I	250+	Independent Readers Social Studies	Houghton Mifflin
Clean and Clear	P	I	806	Independent Readers Social Studies	Houghton Mifflin

* Collection of short stories

TITLE	LEVEL	GENRE	WORD COUNT	AUTHOR / SERIES	PUBLISHER / DISTRIBUTOR
Cloud Catcher	P	F	250+	Action Packs	Rigby
Colors of Australia	P	I	250+	Colors of the World	Carolrhoda Books
Colors of Germany	P	I	250+	Colors of the World	Carolrhoda Books
Colors of Ghana	P	I	250+	Colors of the World	Carolrhoda Books
Colors of India	P	I	250+	Colors of the World	Carolrhoda Books
Colors of Kenya	P	I	250+	Colors of the World	Carolrhoda Books
Colors of Mexico	P	I	250+	Colors of the World	Carolrhoda Books
Comanche Indians, The	P	I	250+	Lund, Bill	Red Brick Learning
Comets	P	I	250+	The Galaxy	Red Brick Learning
Constellations	P	I	250+	Bridgestone Books	Capstone Press
Coral Reef	P	I	250+	Habitats	Children's Press
Coral Reef: Inside Australia's Great Barrier Reef	P	I	250+	Cambridge Reading	Pearson Learning Group
Creepy Crawlies	P	I	250+	Literacy 2000	Rigby
Curious Kat	P	RF	250+	Leveled Readers	Houghton Mifflin
Curse of Being Pharaoh, The	P	RF	250+	Marriott, Janice	Pacific Learning
Dancing with Jacques	P	HF	250+	Voyages in Time	Wright Group/McGraw Hill
Daniel Inouye: Senator from Hawaii	P	B	799	Leveled Readers Social Studies	Houghton Mifflin
Daring Rescue of Marlon the Swimming Pig, The	P	F	250+	Saunders, S.	Random House
Davy Crockett	P	B	250+	Photo-Illustrated Biographies	Red Brick Learning
Day of the Tornadoes	P	I	552	Vocabulary Readers	Houghton Mifflin
Deborah Sampson, Soldier of the American Revolution	P	B	250+	Leveled Readers Language Support	Houghton Mifflin
Delaware People, The	P	I	250+	Native Peoples	Red Brick Learning
Desert Run, The	P	I	250+	Bonallack, John	Pacific Learning
Desert: Inside Australia's Simpson Desert	P	I	250+	Cambridge Reading	Pearson Learning Group
Destination Disaster	P	RF	250+	Action Packs	Rigby
DeWitt and Lila Wallace: Charity for All	P	B	250+	Community Builders	Children's Press
Digging Dinosaurs	P	I	250+	Nayer, Judy	Pearson Learning Group
Digging Up Tyrannosaurus Rex	P	I	250+	Horner, John; Lessem, Don	Crown
Dinosaur Named Sue, A	P	F	250+	Robinson, Fay	Scholastic
Divers' Dream	P	I	250+	Pacific Literacy	Pacific Learning
Dolphin Adventure	P	RF	250+	Grover, Wayne	Beech Tree Books
Dolphin Treasure	P	RF	250+	Grover, Wayne	Beech Tree Books
Dolphin, The	P	I	250+	Animal Close-Ups	Charlesbridge
Dominoes	P	I	250+	Games Around the World	Compass Point Books
Double Danger	P	F	250+	Hager, Mandy	Pacific Learning
Down on the Ice	P	I	250+	Alchin, Rupert	Pacific Learning
Dragon Fire	P	F	250+	Cowley, Joy	Pacific Learning
Dragon Prince, The: A Chinese Beauty and the Beast Tale	P	TL	250+	Yep, Laurence	HarperCollins
Dragon Slayer	P	F	250+	Cowley, Joy	Pacific Learning
Draw Me a Story	P	B	250+	Winter, Max	Scholastic
Duke Ellington: Man of Music	P	B	250+	Leveled Readers Language Support	Houghton Mifflin
Dust Bowl, The	P	I	1204	Leveled Readers Social Studies	Houghton Mifflin
Dynamic Duos	P	F	250+	Moore, David	Scholastic
*Eagle's Reflection and Other Northwest Coast Stories	P	TL	250+	Challenger, James Robert	Heritage House
East of the Sun & West of the Moon	P	TL	250+	Mayer, Mercer	Aladdin
Eddie and the Fire Engine	P	RF	250+	Haywood, Carolyn	Beech Tree Books
Egypt	P	I	250+	Fact Finders	Capstone Press
El Chino	P	B	250+	Say, Allen	Houghton Mifflin
Eleanor Roosevelt	P	B	250+	Early Biographies	Compass Point Books

TITLE	LEVEL	GENRE	WORD COUNT	AUTHOR / SERIES	PUBLISHER / DISTRIBUTOR
Eleanor Roosevelt	P	B	250+	Davis, Lucile	Red Brick Learning
Elizabeth Cady Stanton	P	B	250+	Davis, Lucile	Red Brick Learning
Ellen Tebbits	P	RF	250+	Cleary, Beverly	Dell
Ellis Island: Welcome to America	P	I	250+	Rosen Real Readers	Rosen Publishing Group
Eloise Greenfield: Poetry to Grow On	P	B	886	Leveled Readers	Houghton Mifflin
Emily's Runaway Imagination	P	F	250+	Cleary, Beverly	Avon Camelot
*Encyclopedia Brown Boy Detective	P	RF	250+	Sobol, Donald J.	Bantam
*Encyclopedia Brown Carries On	P	RF	250+	Sobol, Donald J.	Bantam
*Encyclopedia Brown Finds the Clues	P	RF	250+	Sobol, Donald J.	Bantam
*Encyclopedia Brown Gets His Man	P	RF	250+	Sobol, Donald J.	Bantam
*Encyclopedia Brown Keeps the Peace	P	RF	250+	Sobol, Donald J.	Bantam
*Encyclopedia Brown Lends a Hand	P	RF	250+	Sobol, Donald J.	Bantam
*Encyclopedia Brown Saves the Day	P	RF	250+	Sobol, Donald J.	Bantam
*Encyclopedia Brown Sets the Pace	P	RF	250+	Sobol, Donald J.	Bantam
*Encyclopedia Brown Shows the Way	P	RF	250+	Sobol, Donald J.	Bantam
*Encyclopedia Brown Solves Them All	P	RF	250+	Sobol, Donald J.	Bantam
Encyclopedia Brown Takes the Cake	P	RF	250+	Sobol, Donald J.	Bantam
*Encyclopedia Brown Takes the Case	P	RF	250+	Sobol, Donald J.	Bantam
*Encyclopedia Brown Tracks Them Down	P	RF	250+	Sobol, Donald J.	Bantam
*Encyclopedia Brown: Case of Pablo's Nose	P	RF	250+	Sobol, Donald J.	Scholastic
*Encyclopedia Brown: Case of the Dead Eagles	P	RF	250+	Sobol, Donald J.	Bantam
*Encyclopedia Brown: Case of the Disgusting Sneakers	P	RF	250+	Sobol, Donald J.	Bantam
*Encyclopedia Brown: Case of the Midnight Visitor	P	RF	250+	Sobol, Donald J.	Bantam
*Encyclopedia Brown: Case of the Mysterious Handprints	P	RF	250+	Sobol, Donald J.	Bantam
*Encyclopedia Brown: Case of the Secret Pitch	P	RF	250+	Sobol, Donald J.	Bantam
*Encyclopedia Brown: Case of the Sleeping Dog	P	RF	250+	Sobol, Donald J.	Scholastic
*Encyclopedia Brown: Case of the Slippery Salamander	P	RF	250+	Sobol, Donald J.	Scholastic
*Encyclopedia Brown: Case of the Treasure Hunt	P	RF	250+	Sobol, Donald J.	Bantam
*Encyclopedia Brown: Case of the Two Spies	P	RF	250+	Sobol, Donald J.	Bantam
Encyclopedia Brown's Book of Strange But True Crimes	P	RF	250+	Sobol, Donald J.; Sobol, Rose	Scholastic
England	P	I	250+	Fact Finders	Capstone Press
Escape to Canada	P	I	513	Vocabulary Readers	Houghton Mifflin
Eureka! Stories of Everyday Inventions	P	I	250+	Literacy 2000	Rigby
Exploring Freshwater Habitats	P	I	250+	Snowball, Diane	Mondo
Exploring Land Habitats	P	I	250+	Phinney, Margaret Yatsevitch	Mondo
Exploring Saltwater Habitats	P	I	250+	Smith, Sue	Mondo
Exploring Tree Habitats	P	I	250+	Seifert, Patti	Mondo
Extreme Sports	P	I	250+	Wildcats	Wright Group/McGraw Hill
Eye in the Sky	P	F	250+	Marriott, Janice	Pacific Learning
Eye Spy	P	I	250+	Wildcats	Wright Group/McGraw Hill
Face to Face	P	RF	250+	Bookweb	Rigby
Falcons Nest on Skyscrapers	P	I	250+	Soar To Success	Houghton Mifflin
Families of the Deep Blue Sea	P	I	250+	Mallory, Kenneth	Charlesbridge
Fantastic Mr. Fox	P	F	250+	Dahl, Roald	Penguin Group
*Feathery Fables	P	TL	250+	Action Packs	Rigby
Feelings	P	I	250+	Sunshine	Wright Group/McGraw Hill
Felicia the Critic	P	RF	250+	Conford, Ellen	Little, Brown & Co.
Felita	P	RF	250+	Mohr, Nicholas	Dell

* Collection of short stories

TITLE	LEVEL	GENRE	WORD COUNT	AUTHOR / SERIES	PUBLISHER / DISTRIBUTOR
Finding Providence: The Story of Roger Williams	P	B	250+	Avi	HarperTrophy
Fire at the Triangle Factory	P	HF	250+	Littlefield, Holly	Carolrhoda Books
Fireworks!	P	I	889	Leveled Readers Science	Houghton Mifflin
First Day For Carlos	P	RF	764	Leveled Readers	Houghton Mifflin
First Family on Mars, The	P	SF	250+	Orbit Double Takes	Pacific Learning
Five-Dog Night, The	P	RF	250+	Christelow, Eileen	Clarion
Florence Kelley	P	B	250+	Saller, Carol	Carolrhoda Books
Florence Nightingale	P	B	250+	Davis, Lucile	Red Brick Learning
Follow That Spy!	P	RF	250+	Action Packs	Rigby
Fossils	P	I	250+	Simply Science	Compass Point Books
Fourth Grade Is a Jinx	P	RF	250+	McKenna, Colleen	Scholastic
Fourth-Graders Don't Believe In Witches	P	F	250+	Fields, Terri	Scholastic
France	P	I	250+	Fact Finders	Capstone Press
Frederick Douglass	P	B	250+	Early Biographies	Compass Point Books
Frederick Douglass	P	B	250+	McLoone, Margo	Red Brick Learning
Frogs and Toads	P	I	250+	Crabapples	Crabtree
From Here to There: Transportation Timelines	P	I	250+	Discovery World	Rigby
Fun with Fractions	P	I	250+	Rosen Real Readers	Rosen Publishing Group
Galapagos Giants	P	I	250+	Orbit Double Takes	Pacific Learning
Gampy's Lamps	P	RF	1296	Leveled Readers	Houghton Mifflin
George Armstrong Custer	P	B	250+	Early Biographies	Compass Point Books
George Washington Carver	P	B	250+	McLoone, Margo	Red Brick Learning
George Washington's Breakfast	P	B	250+	Fritz, Jean	Putnam & Grosset
George's Marvelous Medicine	P	F	250+	Dahl, Roald	Penguin Group
Gerbilitis	P	RF	250+	Soar To Success	Houghton Mifflin
Gerbilitis	P	RF	250+	Spinner, Stephanie; Weiss, Ellen	HarperTrophy
Germany	P	I	250+	Fact Finders	Capstone Press
Get A Grip, Pip!	P	RF	250+	Literacy 2000	Rigby
Ghost Fox, The	P	F	250+	Yep, Laurence	Scholastic
Ghost Twins: Mystery at Kickingbird Lake	P	F	250+	Regan, Diane Curtis	Scholastic
Giraffe and the Pelly and Me, The	P	F	250+	Dahl, Roald	Penguin Group
Giraffe, The	P	I	250+	Animal Close-Ups	Charlesbridge
Giraffes	P	I	250+	Crabapples	Crabtree
Girl Called Al, A	P	RF	250+	Greene, Constance C.	Puffin Books
Glenda	P	F	250+	Udry, Janice May	HarperTrophy
Glenda Glinka: Witch-At-Large	P	F	250+	Udry, Janice May	HarperTrophy
Going Back to Harlem	P	I	522	Vocabulary Readers	Houghton Mifflin
Going for Gold!	P	B	250+	Eyewitness Readers	DK Publishing
Good Night's Sleep, A	P	RF	1091	Leveled Readers	Houghton Mifflin
Gooseberry Park	P	F	250+	Rylant, Cynthia	Scholastic
Grace's Letter to Lincoln	P	HF	250+	Roop, Peter & Connie	Hyperion
Grain of Rice, A	P	TL	250+	Pittman, Helena Clare	Bantam
Grandpa's Baseball Card	P	RF	1022	Leveled Readers	Houghton Mifflin
Great Inventions and Where They Came From	P	I	250+	Navigators Social Studies Series	Benchmark Education
Growing Up	P	I	250+	It's Science	Children's Press
Gwen Torrence	P	B	250+	Stewart, Mark	Children's Press
Halloween	P	I	250+	Let's See	Compass Point Books
Halloween: Why We Celebrate It the Way We Do	P	I	250+	Hintz, Martin & Kate	Red Brick Learning
Hanukkah	P	I	250+	Let's See	Compass Point Books
Happy Birthday Book, The	P	I	250+	Sunshine	Wright Group/McGraw Hill
Harriet Tubman	P	B	250+	McLoone, Margo	Red Brick Learning
Harry's Mad	P	F	250+	King-Smith, Dick	Alfred A. Knopf
Helen Keller	P	B	250+	Photo-Illustrated Biographies	Red Brick Learning

TITLE	LEVEL	GENRE	WORD COUNT	AUTHOR / SERIES	PUBLISHER / DISTRIBUTOR
Helen Keller: Crusader for the Blind and Deaf	P	B	250+	Graff, Stewart & Polly Anne	Bantam
Hindu Holiday	P	I	494	Independent Readers Social Studies	Houghton Mifflin
Hometown Turtles	P	RF	1175	Leveled Readers	Houghton Mifflin
Hopi, The	P	I	250+	Native Peoples	Red Brick Learning
Hopscotch	P	I	250+	Games Around the World	Compass Point Books
Horses	P	I	250+	Crabapples	Crabtree
Horses of the Sea	P	I	250+	Rigby Literacy	Rigby
House Gobbaleen, The	P	F	250+	Alexander, Lloyd	Penguin Group
How Is a Crayon Made?	P	I	250+	Oz, Charles	Scholastic
How To Grow Crystals	P	I	250+	Bookshop	Mondo
Howliday Inn	P	F	250+	Howe, James	Atheneum
Hundred Penny Box, The	P	RF	250+	Mathis, Sharon Bell	Puffin Books
Ice Age Safari	P	I	250+	Rigby Focus	Rigby
Ice Mummy: The Discovery of a 5,000-Year-Old Man	P	I	250+	Dubowski, Mark & Cathy East	Random House
Imagine This, James Robert	P	F	250+	Action Packs	Rigby
In-Between Days, The	P	RF	250+	Bunting, Eve	HarperTrophy
Incredible Creatures	P	I	250+	Explorers	Wright Group/McGraw Hill
Incredible Places	P	I	250+	Wildcats	Wright Group/McGraw Hill
Incredible Shrinking Kid, The	P	F	250+	Abbott, Tony	Scholastic
Indian School, The	P	RF	250+	Whelan, Gloria	HarperTrophy
Interrupting The Big Sleep	P	RF	250+	Marriott, Janice	Pacific Learning
Iraq	P	I	250+	Fact Finders	Capstone Press
Iroquois Indians, The	P	I	250+	Lund, Bill	Red Brick Learning
Ishi's Tale of Lizard	P	TL	250+	Hinton, Leanne; Roth, Susan L.	Farrar, Straus and Giroux
It's All in Your Mind, James Robert	P	F	250+	Literacy 2000	Rigby
It's Mine!	P	F	250+	Lionni, Leo	Scholastic
Jacks	P	I	250+	Games Around the World	Compass Point Books
Jacob Two-Two and the Dinosaur	P	F	250+	Richler, Mordecai	Tundra Books
Jacob Two-Two Meets the Hooded Fang	P	F	250+	Richler, Mordecai	Seal Books
Jaguar Attack!	P	RF	250+	Bookweb	Rigby
Jane Addams	P	B	250+	Community Builders	Children's Press
Japan	P	I	250+	Fact Finders	Capstone Press
Jason Kidd Story, The	P	RF	250+	Moore, David	Scholastic
Jazz, Pizzazz, and the Silver Threads	P	RF	250+	Quattlebaum, Mary	Bantam
Jesse Jackson	P	B	250+	Simon, Charnan	Children's Press
Jesse Owens: Olympic Hero	P	B	250+	Sabin, Francene	Troll Associates
Journey of a Butterfly, The	P	I	250+	Scrace, Carolyn	Scholastic
Juggling	P	I	250+	Games Around the World	Compass Point Books
Jumping into the Flames	P	I	675	Vocabulary Readers	Houghton Mifflin
Jupiter	P	I	250+	Bridgestone Books	Capstone Press
Justin and the Best Biscuits in the World	P	RF	250+	Pitts, Walter & Mildred	Alfred A. Knopf
Keep Out: Our Dog Buries What It Can't Eat	P	RF	250+	Beale, Fleur	Pacific Learning
Keeping Warm in Winter	P	I	516	Vocabulary Readers	Houghton Mifflin
Ketchup Deal, The	P	F	250+	Marriott, Janice	Pacific Learning
Kid Power	P	RF	250+	Pfeffer, Susan Beth	Scholastic
Kids from Quiller's Bend	P	RF	250+	Action Packs	Rigby
Kitchen Science	P	I	958	Independent Readers Science	Houghton Mifflin
Knightly News	P	RF	250+	Kenna, Anna	Pacific Learning
Knots on a Counting Rope	P	RF	250+	Martin, Jr., B.; Archambault, J.	Henry Holt & Co.
Koala Is Not a Bear, A	P	I	250+	Crabapples	Crabtree
Koi's Python	P	RF	250+	Moore, Miriam	Hyperion
Koya DeLaney and the Good Girl Blues	P	RF	250+	Greenfield, Eloise	Scholastic

* Collection of short stories

TITLE	LEVEL	GENRE	WORD COUNT	AUTHOR / SERIES	PUBLISHER / DISTRIBUTOR
Land I Lost, The	P	I	250+	Nhuong, Huynh Quang	HarperTrophy
Land of the Dragons	P	I	250+	Morris, Rod	Pacific Learning
Last Chance for Magic	P	F	250+	Chew, Ruth	Scholastic
Last Look	P	RF	250+	Bulla, Clyde Robert	Puffin Books
Laughter Is the Best Medicine	P	I	250+	Literacy Tree	Rigby
Laura Ingalls Wilder	P	B	250+	Blair, Gwenda; Allen, Thomas	Lerner Publishing
Laura Ingalls Wilder: Growing Up in the Little House	P	B	250+	Giff, Patricia Reilly	Puffin Books
Lazy Bones Jones	P	F	250+	Welch, Sheila Kelly	Pacific Learning
Lion to Guard Us, A	P	HF	250+	Bulla, Clyde Robert	HarperTrophy
Little Cats	P	I	250+	Crabapples	Crabtree
Living with Salties	P	I	250+	Orbit Double Takes	Pacific Learning
Long Walk Home, The	P	RF	250+	Action Packs	Rigby
Lotus Seed, The	P	HF	250+	Garland, Sherry	Harcourt Trade
Lucky Stone, The	P	RF	250+	Clifton, Lucille	Bantam
Mad Scientist's Secret, The	P	SF	250+	Miller, Marvin	Scholastic
Magic Moscow, The	P	RF	250+	Pinkwater, Daniel	Aladdin
Magic School Bus	P	F	250+	Cole, Joanna; Degen, Bruce	Scholastic
Magic School Bus and the Electric Field Trip, The	P	F	250+	Cole, Joanna; Degen, Bruce	Scholastic
Magic School Bus Answers Questions, The	P	F	250+	Cole, Joanna; Degen, Bruce	Scholastic
Magic School Bus At the Waterworks, The	P	F	250+	Cole, Joanna; Degen, Bruce	Scholastic
Magic School Bus Blows Its Top, The	P	F	250+	Cole, Joanna; Degen, Bruce	Scholastic
Magic School Bus Briefcase, The	P	F	250+	Cole, Joanna; Degen, Bruce	Scholastic
Magic School Bus Butterfly and the Bog Beast, The	P	F	250+	Cole, Joanna; Degen, Bruce	Scholastic
Magic School Bus Explores the Senses, The	P	F	250+	Cole, Joanna; Degen, Bruce	Scholastic
Magic School Bus Explores the World of Animals, The	P	F	250+	Cole, Joanna; Degen, Bruce	Scholastic
Magic School Bus Gets a Bright Idea, The	P	F	250+	Cole, Joanna; Degen, Bruce	Scholastic
Magic School Bus Gets All Dried Up, The	P	F	250+	Cole, Joanna; Degen, Bruce	Scholastic
Magic School Bus Gets Ants in Its Pants, The	P	F	250+	Cole, Joanna; Degen, Bruce	Scholastic
Magic School Bus Gets Baked in a Cake, The	P	F	250+	Cole, Joanna; Degen, Bruce	Scholastic
Magic School Bus Gets Cold Feet, The	P	F	250+	Cole, Joanna; Degen, Bruce	Scholastic
Magic School Bus Gets Eaten, The	P	F	250+	Cole, Joanna; Degen, Bruce	Scholastic
Magic School Bus Gets Programmed, The	P	F	250+	Cole, Joanna; Degen, Bruce	Scholastic
Magic School Bus Goes Upstream, The	P	F	250+	Cole, Joanna; Degen, Bruce	Scholastic
Magic School Bus Going Batty, The	P	F	250+	Cole, Joanna; Degen, Bruce	Scholastic
Magic School Bus Hops Home, The	P	F	250+	Cole, Joanna; Degen, Bruce	Scholastic
Magic School Bus in a Pickle, The	P	F	250+	Cole, Joanna; Degen, Bruce	Scholastic
Magic School Bus in the Arctic, The	P	F	250+	Cole, Joanna; Degen, Bruce	Scholastic
Magic School Bus in the Haunted Museum, The	P	F	250+	Cole, Joanna; Degen, Bruce	Scholastic
Magic School Bus in the Rain Forest, The	P	F	250+	Cole, Joanna; Degen, Bruce	Scholastic
Magic School Bus in the Time of the Dinosaurs, The	P	F	250+	Cole, Joanna; Degen, Bruce	Scholastic
Magic School Bus Inside a Beehive, The	P	F	250+	Cole, Joanna; Degen, Bruce	Scholastic
Magic School Bus Inside a Hurricane, The	P	F	250+	Cole, Joanna; Degen, Bruce	Scholastic
Magic School Bus Inside Ralphie, The	P	HF	250+	Cole, Joanna; Degen, Bruce	Scholastic
Magic School Bus Inside the Earth, The	P	F	250+	Cole, Joanna; Degen, Bruce	Scholastic
Magic School Bus Inside the Human Body, The	P	SF	250+	Cole, Joanna; Degen, Bruce	Scholastic
Magic School Bus Kicks Up a Storm, The	P	F	250+	Cole, Joanna; Degen, Bruce	Scholastic
Magic School Bus Liz Sorts It Out, The	P	F	250+	Cole, Joanna; Degen, Bruce	Scholastic
Magic School Bus Lost in the Solar System, The	P	F	250+	Cole, Joanna; Degen, Bruce	Scholastic
Magic School Bus Makes a Rainbow, The	P	F	250+	Cole, Joanna; Degen, Bruce	Scholastic

TITLE	LEVEL	GENRE	WORD COUNT	AUTHOR / SERIES	PUBLISHER / DISTRIBUTOR
Magic School Bus Meets the Rot Squad, The	P	F	250+	Cole, Joanna; Degen, Bruce	Scholastic
Magic School Bus on the Ocean Floor, The	P	F	250+	Cole, Joanna; Degen, Bruce	Scholastic
Magic School Bus Out of This World, The	P	F	250+	Cole, Joanna; Degen, Bruce	Scholastic
Magic School Bus Plants Seeds, The	P	F	250+	Cole, Joanna; Degen, Bruce	Scholastic
Magic School Bus Plays Ball, The	P	F	250+	Cole, Joanna; Degen, Bruce	Scholastic
Magic School Bus Science Explorations, The	P	F	250+	Cole, Joanna; Degen, Bruce	Scholastic
Magic School Bus Search for the Missing Bones, The	P	F	250+	Cole, Joanna; Degen, Bruce	Scholastic
Magic School Bus Sees Stars, The	P	F	250+	Cole, Joanna; Degen, Bruce	Scholastic
Magic School Bus Shows and Tells, The	P	F	250+	Cole, Joanna; Degen, Bruce	Scholastic
Magic School Bus Space Explorers, The	P	F	250+	Cole, Joanna; Degen, Bruce	Scholastic
Magic School Bus Spins a Web, The	P	F	250+	Cole, Joanna; Degen, Bruce	Scholastic
Magic School Bus Takes a Dive, The	P	F	250+	Cole, Joanna; Degen, Bruce	Scholastic
Magic School Bus Taking Flight, The	P	F	250+	Cole, Joanna; Degen, Bruce	Scholastic
Magic School Bus The Truth About Bats, The	P	F	250+	Cole, Joanna; Degen, Bruce	Scholastic
Magic School Bus The Wild Whale Watch, The	P	F	250+	Cole, Joanna; Degen, Bruce	Scholastic
Magic School Bus Twister Trouble, The	P	F	250+	Cole, Joanna; Degen, Bruce	Scholastic
Magic School Bus Ups and Downs, The	P	F	250+	Cole, Joanna; Degen, Bruce	Scholastic
Magic School Bus Visits the Planets, The	P	F	250+	Cole, Joanna; Degen, Bruce	Scholastic
Magic School Bus Wet All Over, The	P	F	250+	Cole, Joanna; Degen, Bruce	Scholastic
Magic Squad and the Dog of Great Potential, The	P	RF	250+	Quattlebaum, Mary	Bantam
Magic Tricks	P	I	250+	Games Around the World	Compass Point Books
Magic Wheel, The	P	I	250+	Voyages	SRA/McGraw Hill
Make It, Wear It	P	I	250+	iOpeners	Pearson Learning Group
Make Your Own Terrarium	P	I	1380	Leveled Readers Science	Houghton Mifflin
Making Sense of Your Senses	P	I	250+	Navigators Science Series	Benchmark Education
Maps and Codes	P	I	250+	Wildcats	Wright Group/McGraw Hill
Marbles	P	I	250+	Games Around the World	Compass Point Books
March on Washington, The	P	I	304	Vocabulary Readers	Houghton Mifflin
Marching to Freedom: The Story of Martin Luther King, Jr.	P	B	250+	Milton, Joyce	Bantam
Margaret Bourke-White: A Photographer's Life	P	B	250+	Keller, Emily	Lerner Publishing
Mario's Mayan Journey	P	F	250+	Bookshop	Mondo
Mark McGuire, Home Run King	P	B	250+	Leveled Readers Language Support	Houghton Mifflin
Martha Graham, Modern Dancer	P	B	982	Leveled Readers	Houghton Mifflin
Martin Luther King, Jr.	P	B	250+	Photo-Illustrated Biographies	Red Brick Learning
Martin's Mice	P	F	250+	King-Smith, Dick	Alfred A. Knopf
Matchlock Gun, The	P	HF	250+	Edmonds, Walter D.	Putnam & Grosset
Math Bee, The	P	B	795	Leveled Readers	Houghton Mifflin
Medical Pioneers	P	B	250+	Navigators Biography Series	Benchmark Education
Meet Erdene	P	I	250+	iOpeners	Pearson Learning Group
Meet Samuel Adams	P	B	447	Vocabulary Readers	Houghton Mifflin
Mei Fuh: Memories From China	P	B	250+	Schaeffer, Edith	Houghton Mifflin
Memories for Mom	P	RF	1517	Leveled Readers	Houghton Mifflin
Meteors and Meteorites	P	I	250+	The Galaxy	Red Brick Learning
Mexican Feast, A: The Foods and Recipes of Mexico	P	I	250+	Rosen Real Readers	Rosen Publishing Group
Mexico	P	I	250+	Fact Finders	Capstone Press
Milton Hershey: Chocolate King Town Builder	P	B	250+	Simon, Charnan	Children's Press
Minpins, The	P	F	250+	Dahl, Roald	Penguin Group
Miss Geneva's Lantern	P	RF	250+	Bookshop	Mondo

* Collection of short stories

TITLE	LEVEL	GENRE	WORD COUNT	AUTHOR / SERIES	PUBLISHER / DISTRIBUTOR
Mound Builders, The	P	I	426	Independent Readers Social Studies	Houghton Mifflin
Mushrooms and Other Fungi	P	I	250+	Sunshine	Wright Group/McGraw Hill
Music Counts	P	I	250+	Navigators Math Series	Benchmark Education
My Father The Mad Professor	P	F	250+	Action Packs	Rigby
*My First Book of Biographies: Great Men and Women Every Child Should Know	P	B	250+	Marzollo, Jean	Scholastic
My Mother Got Married (And Other Disasters)	P	RF	250+	Park, Barbara	Random House
Mystery Bay	P	RF	250+	Krueger, Carol	Rigby
Mystery of Lighthouse Cave, The	P	RF	250+	Leveled Readers Language Support	Houghton Mifflin
Mystery of Magnets, The	P	I	250+	iOpeners	Pearson Learning Group
Mystery Valley	P	SF	250+	Bookweb	Rigby
Native American Art from the Pueblos	P	I	250+	Rosen Real Readers	Rosen Publishing Group
Native Americans	P	I	250+	Explorers	Wright Group/McGraw Hill
Neighborhood Party, The	P	RF	250+	Leveled Readers Language Support	Houghton Mifflin
New Kind of Magic, The	P	F	250+	Szymanski, Lois	Avon Camelot
Nez Perce Tribe, The	P	I	250+	Lassieur, Allison	Red Brick Learning
Night Crossing, The	P	SF	250+	Bookweb	Rigby
Night Music	P	HF	250+	Voyages in Time	Wright Group/McGraw Hill
No Flying in the House	P	F	250+	Brock, Betty	HarperCollins
No Safe Place	P	SF	250+	Orbit Double Takes	Pacific Learning
Nose for Trouble, A	P	RF	250+	Wilson, Nancy Hope	Avon
Not What It Seems	P	RF	250+	Wildcats	Wright Group/McGraw Hill
Not-Just-Anybody Family, The	P	RF	250+	Byars, Betsy	Dell
Ocean Tide Pool	P	I	250+	L'Hommedieu, Arthur John	Grolier Press
Odds on Oliver	P	RF	250+	Greene, Carol	Puffin Books
Oh, Brother	P	RF	250+	Wilson, Johnniece M.	Scholastic
Oil on Water	P	I	250+	Sails	Rigby
Oil Spills	P	I	250+	Rigby Focus	Rigby
Oil!	P	I	450	Independent Readers Social Studies	Houghton Mifflin
Ojibwa Indians, The	P	I	250+	Lund, Bill	Red Brick Learning
One Day in the Alpine Tundra	P	I	250+	George, Jean Craighead	HarperCollins
One Day in the Desert	P	I	250+	George, Jean Craighead	HarperCollins
One Day in the Woods	P	I	250+	George, Jean Craighead	HarperTrophy
*Orca's Family and More Northwest Coast Stories	P	TL	250+	Challenger, James Robert	Heritage House
Our Magazine Article	P	I	250+	Rigby Focus	Rigby
Owls in the Family	P	F	250+	Mowat, Farley	Bantam
Pablo Picasso	P	B	250+	Lowery, Linda	Lerner Publishing
Pagemaster, The	P	F	250+	Horowitz, Jordan	Scholastic
Pan Woman	P	RF	1145	Leveled Readers	Houghton Mifflin
Pat Mora: Two Languages, One Poet	P	B	769	Leveled Readers	Houghton Mifflin
Pathfinder: Mission to Mars	P	I	250+	Rigby Literacy	Rigby
Paul the Artist	P	RF	1356	Leveled Readers	Houghton Mifflin
Pawnee Nation, The	P	I	250+	Walters, Anna Lee	Red Brick Learning
Penguins of the Galápagos	P	I	250+	Young Readers' Series	Barron's Educational
Piglet in a Playpen	P	RF	250+	Daniels, Lucy	Barron's Educational
Planet Boring	P	F	250+	Cook, Nathan	Pacific Learning
Plants	P	I	250+	Simply Science	Compass Point Books
Platypus	P	I	1098	Short, Joan.; Green, J.; Bird, Bettina	Mondo

TITLE	LEVEL	GENRE	WORD COUNT	AUTHOR / SERIES	PUBLISHER / DISTRIBUTOR
Poetry of Basketball, The	P	RF	250+	Leveled Readers Language Support	Houghton Mifflin
Pony Named Shawney, A	P	RF	3075	Small, Mary	Mondo
Pony Tails: Jasmine and the Jumping Pony	P	RF	250+	Bryant, Bonnie	Bantam
Pony Tails: Jasmine's Christmas Ride	P	RF	250+	Bryant, Bonnie	Bantam
Pony Tails: May Takes the Lead	P	RF	250+	Bryant, Bonnie	Bantam
Poopsie Pomerantz Pick Up Your Feet	P	RF	250+	Giff, Patricia Reilly	Dell
Poor Little Kittens	P	RF	1173	Leveled Readers	Houghton Mifflin
Potato Pride	P	RF	1000	Leveled Readers	Houghton Mifflin
Private Notebook of Katie Roberts, Age 11, The	P	RF	250+	Hest, Amy	Candlewick Press
Probability	P	I	250+	Early Connections	Benchmark Education
Pueblo Indians, The	P	I	250+	Ross, Pamela	Red Brick Learning
Puppets	P	I	250	Literacy Tree	Rigby
Quarters Toss, The	P	RF	250+	Leveled Readers Language Support	Houghton Mifflin
Questions and Answers About Forest Animals	P	I	250+	Chinery, Michael	Kingfisher
Questions and Answers About Freshwater Animals	P	I	250+	Chinery, Michael	Kingfisher
Race of the River Runner	P	HF	540	Leveled Readers	Houghton Mifflin
*Raven's Call and More Northwest Coast Stories	P	TL	250+	Challenger, James Robert	Heritage House
Refugees, The	P	RF	250+	Marriott, Janice	Pacific Learning
Regina's Ride	P	RF	1017	Leveled Readers	Houghton Mifflin
Return to Howliday Inn	P	F	250+	Howe, James	Avon Camelot
Revenge of the Mummy	P	RF	250+	Parker, A. E.	Scholastic
Riding Freedom	P	HF	250+	Ryan, Pam Munoz	Scholastic
Rising Stars of the NBA	P	B	250+	Layden, Joe	Scholastic
Robinson Crusoe	P	TL	250+	Dolch, E. W.; Marguerite, P.	Scholastic
Rogue Robot	P	F	250+	Bookweb	Rigby
Rosa Parks	P	B	250+	Greenfield, Eloise	HarperTrophy
Rules of the Ride	P	RF	1023	Leveled Readers	Houghton Mifflin
Russia	P	I	250+	Fact Finders	Capstone Press
Ryan's Dog Ringo	P	RF	250+	Literacy 2000	Rigby
Sacagawea	P	B	250+	Photo-Illustrated Biographies	Red Brick Learning
*Salmon's Journey and More Northwest Coast Stories	P	TL	250+	Challenger, James Robert	Heritage House
San Francisco: Then and Now	P	I	476	Independent Readers Social Studies	Houghton Mifflin
Saving The Yellow Eye	P	I	250+	Darby, John	Pacific Learning
School Mouse, The	P	F	250+	King-Smith, Dick	Hyperion
Scoring Points	P	RF	250+	Leveled Readers Language Support	Houghton Mifflin
Searching for Sea Lions	P	I	250+	Westerskov, Kim	Pacific Learning
Secret of the Seal, The	P	RF	250+	Davis, Deborah	Alfred A. Knopf
Secret Secret Passage, The	P	RF	250+	Parker, A. E.	Scholastic
Seminole Indians, The	P	I	250+	Lund, Bill	Red Brick Learning
Shoebag	P	F	250+	James, Mary	Scholastic
*Sideways Stories from Wayside School	P	F	250+	Sachar, Louis	Hearst
Sioux Indians, The	P	I	250+	Lund, Bill	Red Brick Learning
Sir Arthur	P	B	250+	Apte, Sunita	Scholastic
Skate Jam, The	P	RF	250+	Orbit Double Takes	Pacific Learning
Skates of Uncle Richard, The	P	RF	250+	Fenner, Carol	Random House
Skinny-Bones	P	RF	250+	Park, Barbara	Random House
Sky's the Limit, The	P	I	250+	Christiansen, Tony	Pacific Learning
Slugs and Snails	P	I	250+	Mini Pets	Steck-Vaughn

* Collection of short stories

TITLE	LEVEL	GENRE	WORD COUNT	AUTHOR / SERIES	PUBLISHER / DISTRIBUTOR
Slumber Party Organizer, The	P	I	250+	Sunshine	Wright Group/McGraw Hill
Snot Stew	P	F	250+	Wallace, Bill	Pocket Books
Sojourner Truth	P	B	250+	McLoone, Margo	Red Brick Learning
Solar System, The	P	I	250+	Bridgestone Books	Capstone Press
Someday a Tree	P	RF	250+	Bunting, Eve	Clarion
Space Animals	P	I	474	Independent Readers Science	Houghton Mifflin
Special Effects	P	I	250+	Wildcats	Wright Group/McGraw Hill
Speech, The	P	RF	250+	Leveled Readers Language Support	Houghton Mifflin
Spiders	P	I	250+	Mini Pets	Steck-Vaughn
Sports Bloopers	P	I	250+	Hollander, Phyllis & Zander	Scholastic
Sports Mysteries: Case of the Basketball Video	P	RF	250+	Edwards, T. J.	Scholastic
Sports Mysteries: Case Of The Missing Pitcher	P	RF	250+	Edwards, T. J.	Scholastic
St. Patrick's Day	P	I	250+	Let's See	Compass Point Books
Stanley and the Magic Lamp	P	F	250+	Brown, Jeff	HarperTrophy
Star Thief	P	RF	250+	Bilbrough, Norman	Pacific Learning
Stars	P	I	250+	The Galaxy	Red Brick Learning
Sticks and Stones, Bobbie Bones	P	RF	250+	Roberts, Brenda C.	Scholastic
Stone Fox	P	RF	250+	Gardiner, John Reynolds	HarperTrophy
Storm Book, The	P	I	250+	Zolotow, Charlotte	HarperCollins
Story of Doña Chila, The	P	B	250+	Moore, Eva	Scholastic
Story of My Life, The	P	B	250+	Leveled Readers Language Support	Houghton Mifflin
Story of Small Fry, The	P	I	250+	Action Packs	Rigby
Story of the Pony Express, The	P	I	250+	Windows on Literacy	National Geographic
Storytelling Around the World	P	I	573	Vocabulary Readers	Houghton Mifflin
Straight From the Horses Mouth	P	I	250+	Sunshine	Wright Group/McGraw Hill
Strange Bird, A	P	F	1024	Leveled Readers	Houghton Mifflin
Stumpy's Secret	P	RF	250+	Hager, Mandy	Pacific Learning
Sub, The	P	RF	250+	Peterson, P. J.	Puffin Books
Sun Power	P	I	250+	Rigby Focus	Rigby
Sunken Treasure	P	I	250+	Gibbons, Gail	Houghton Mifflin
Surf's Up	P	RF	250+	Wildcats	Wright Group/McGraw Hill
Surrender at Yorktown	P	I	250+	Leveled Readers	Houghton Mifflin
Susan B. Anthony	P	B	250+	Davis, Lucile	Red Brick Learning
Tales of Olga da Polga, The	P	F	250+	Bond, Michael	Houghton Mifflin
Tar Beach	P	HF	250+	Ringgold, Faith	Crown
Team of Two, A	P	I	566	Vocabulary Readers	Houghton Mifflin
Thank You, Jackie Robinson	P	B	250+	Cohen, Barbara	Scholastic
Thanksgiving	P	I	250+	Let's See	Compass Point Books
Thanksgiving: Why We Celebrate It the Way We Do	P	I	250+	Hintz, Martin & Kate	Red Brick Learning
Theodore Roosevelt: Friend of Nature	P	B	756	Leveled Readers	Houghton Mifflin
Third Grade Stars	P	RF	250+	Ransom, Candice	Troll Associates
Thomas Edison	P	B	250+	Linder, Greg	Red Brick Learning
Through Grandpa's Eyes	P	RF	250+	MacLachlan, Patricia	HarperTrophy
Thurgood Marshall	P	B	250+	Photo-Illustrated Biographies	Red Brick Learning
Time Warp Kids: Summer Reading is Killing Me!	P	F	250+	Scieszka, Jon	Puffin Books
Time Warp Trio: 2095	P	SF	250+	Scieszka, Jon	Penguin Group
Time Warp Trio: Good, the Bad, and the Goofy, The	P	SF	250+	Scieszka, Jon	Penguin Group
Time Warp Trio: Knights of the Kitchen Table, The	P	F	250+	Scieszka, Jon	Penguin Group

* Collection of short stories

TITLE	LEVEL	GENRE	WORD COUNT	AUTHOR / SERIES	PUBLISHER / DISTRIBUTOR
Time Warp Trio: Not-So-Jolly Roger, The	P	F	250+	Scieszka, Jon	Penguin Group
Time Warp Trio: Tut Tut	P	F	250+	Scieszka, Jon	Penguin Group
Time Warp Trio: Your Mother Was a Neanderthal	P	F	250+	Scieszka, Jon	Penguin Group
To JJ From CC	P	RF	250+	Literacy 2000	Rigby
Tommy Thompson's Ship of Gold	P	I	685	Leveled Readers	Houghton Mifflin
Tower, The	P	SF	250+	Orbit Double Takes	Pacific Learning
Town in Trouble, A	P	F	1019	Leveled Readers	Houghton Mifflin
Tracing the Anasazi	P	I	830	Independent Readers Social Studies	Houghton Mifflin
Tradition of the Harvest, The	P	RF	250+	Leveled Readers Language Support	Houghton Mifflin
Transportation Time Line, A	P	I	250+	Discovery World	Rigby
Travel Smart	P	I	250+	iOpeners	Pearson Learning Group
Trouble Dolls	P	F	250+	Buffett, Jimmy; Savannah, Jane	Harcourt School Publishers
Trucker	P	RF	250+	Beale, Fleur	Pacific Learning
True Cortez, A	P	RF	685	Leveled Readers	Houghton Mifflin
Tut's Mummy: Lost and Found	P	I	250+	Donnelly, Judy	Random House
Twisters and Other Wind Storms	P	I	250+	Wildcats	Wright Group/McGraw Hill
Two Traditions of Dance	P	I	382	Vocabulary Readers	Houghton Mifflin
Ugly Mug	P	RF	250+	Joseph, Vivienne	Pacific Learning
Under the Ground	P	I	250+	Literacy 2000	Rigby
Understudies	P	RF	250+	Bookweb	Rigby
Up in the Air	P	I	250+	Wildcats	Wright Group/McGraw Hill
Utes, The	P	I	250+	Native Peoples	Red Brick Learning
Valentine's Day	P	I	250+	Let's See	Compass Point Books
Vanished!: The Mysterious Disappearance of Amelia Earhart	P	B	250+	Kulling, Monica	Random House
Victor Sews	P	RF	1323	Leveled Readers	Houghton Mifflin
Wall of Names, A: The Story of the Vietnam Veterans Memorial	P	I	250+	Donnelly, Judy	Random House
Wall, The	P	HF	250+	Bunting, Eve	Clarion
Wanted . . . Mud Blossom	P	RF	250+	Byars, Betsy	Dell
Wanted Dead or Alive: The True Story of Harriet Tubman	P	B	250+	McGovern, Ann	Scholastic
Water Buffalo Days	P	B	250+	Huynh, Quong Nhuong	HarperTrophy
Water: A Natural Resource	P	I	250+	Rigby Focus	Rigby
*Wayside School Gets a Little Stranger	P	F	250+	Sachar, Louis	Avon Camelot
*Wayside School is Falling Down	P	F	250+	Sachar, Louis	Avon
Whale Is Not A Fish, A: And Other Animal Mix-ups	P	I	250+	Berger, Melvin	Scholastic
What Are You Figuring Now?	P	B	250+	Ferris, Jeri	Scholastic
What Grows There	P	I	448	Independent Readers Social Studies	Houghton Mifflin
What is Congress?	P	I	628	Leveled Readers Social Studies	Houghton Mifflin
*When I Was Young and Wild Bill's Secret Wish	P	RF	250+	Miggs, W. B.	Pacific Learning
When the Earth Was Bare	P	TL	250+	Voyages	SRA/McGraw Hill
Where Did the Maya Go?	P	F	250+	Action Packs	Rigby
Where in the World is the Perfect Family?	P	RF	250+	Hest, Amy	Penguin Group
Who Killed Mr. Boddy?	P	RF	250+	Parker, A. E.	Scholastic
Who Shot the President?: The Death of John F. Kennedy	P	I	250+	Donnelly, Judy	Random House
Who Stole the Wizard of Oz?	P	RF	250+	Avi	Alfred A. Knopf
Wild Adaptations	P	I	924	Independent Readers Science	Houghton Mifflin

* Collection of short stories

TITLE	LEVEL	GENRE	WORD COUNT	AUTHOR / SERIES	PUBLISHER / DISTRIBUTOR
Wild and Wooly Mammoths	P	I	250+	Aliki	HarperCollins
Willow Pattern, The	P	TL	250+	Action Packs	Rigby
Wilma Mankiller	P	B	250+	Lowery, Linda	Carolrhoda Books
*Wish Fish, The	P	TL	250+	Action Packs	Rigby
Witch's Cat	P	F	250+	Chew, Ruth	Scholastic
With a Dance and a Roar	P	I	663	Leveled Readers	Houghton Mifflin
Women Inventors	P	I	996	Leveled Readers Science	Houghton Mifflin
World of Games, A	P	RF	676	Leveled Readers	Houghton Mifflin
Worm Work	P	I	250+	Sails	Rigby
Worms	P	I	250+	Mini Pets	Steck-Vaughn
Worst Witch at Sea, The	P	F	250+	Murphy, Jill	Candlewick Press
Worst Witch Strikes Again, The	P	F	250+	Murphy, Jill	Candlewick Press
Worst Witch, The	P	F	250+	Murphy, Jill	Puffin Books
Yang the Eldest and His Odd Jobs	P	RF	250+	Namioka, Lensey	Bantam
Yang the Second and Her Secret Admirer	P	RF	250+	Namioka, Lensey	Bantam
Yang the Third and Her Impossible Family	P	RF	250+	Namioka, Lensey	Bantam
Yang the Youngest and His Terrible Ear	P	RF	250+	Namioka, Lensey	Bantam
Your Bones	P	I	250+	Your Body	Red Brick Learning
Your Brain	P	I	250+	Your Body	Red Brick Learning
Your Heart	P	I	250+	Your Body	Red Brick Learning
Your Lungs	P	I	250+	Your Body	Red Brick Learning
Your Muscles	P	I	250+	Your Body	Red Brick Learning
Your Stomach	P	I	250+	Your Body	Red Brick Learning
Yo-Yo Tricks	P	I	250+	Games Around the World	Compass Point Books
Zachary and the Pony Express	P	HF	250+	Leveled Readers Language Support	Houghton Mifflin
Zooman Sam	P	RF	250+	Lowry, Lois	Houghton Mifflin
Abraham Lincoln	Q	B	250+	Gross, Ruth Belov	Scholastic
Addy Learns a Lesson: A School Story	Q	HF	250+	The American Girls Collection	Pleasant Company
Addy Saves the Day: A Summer Story	Q	HF	250+	The American Girls Collection	Pleasant Company
Addy's Surprise: A Christmas Story	Q	HF	250+	The American Girls Collection	Pleasant Company
Adventures of the Shark Lady	Q	I	250+	McGovern, Ann	Scholastic
Aliens Ate My Homework	Q	F	250+	Coville, Bruce	Pocket Books
All About Codes	Q	I	250+	Riley, Gail Blasser	Steck-Vaughn
All About Deer	Q	I	250+	Arnosky, Jim	Scholastic
All About Frogs	Q	TL	250+	Arnosky, Jim	Scholastic
All About Owls	Q	I	250+	Arnosky, Jim	Scholastic
All About Rattlesnakes	Q	I	250+	Aronsky, Jim	Scholastic
All About Sam	Q	RF	250+	Lowry, Lois	Bantam
All About Seeds	Q	I	250+	Berger, Melvin	Scholastic
All-of-a-Kind Family	Q	RF	250+	Taylor, Sydney	Bantam
Amazing Animal Rescue Team, The	Q	I	250+	Blankenhorn, Rebecca	Steck-Vaughn
*Amazing But True Sports Stories	Q	I	250+	Hollander, Phyllis & Zander	Scholastic
Amazing Spiders	Q	I	250+	Eyewitness Juniors	Alfred A. Knopf
Amelia Earhart	Q	B	250+	Literacy Tree	Rigby
American Dream, An	Q	HF	250+	Leveled Readers Language Support	Houghton Mifflin
American Flag, The	Q	I	250+	Let's See	Compass Point Books
Amy's True Prize	Q	HF	250+	The Little Women Journals	Avon
Anastasia Again!	Q	RF	250+	Lowry, Lois	Bantam
Anastasia At This Address	Q	RF	250+	Lowry, Lois	Bantam
Anastasia At Your Service	Q	RF	250+	Lowry, Lois	Bantam
Anastasia Has the Answers	Q	RF	250+	Lowry, Lois	Bantam
Anastasia Krupnik	Q	RF	250+	Lowry, Lois	Bantam

TITLE	LEVEL	GENRE	WORD COUNT	AUTHOR / SERIES	PUBLISHER / DISTRIBUTOR
Anastasia On Her Own	Q	RF	250+	Lowry, Lois	Bantam
Anastasia, Absolutely	Q	RF	250+	Lowry, Lois	Bantam
Anastasia, Ask Your Analyst	Q	RF	250+	Lowry, Lois	Bantam
Anastasia's Chosen Career	Q	RF	250+	Lowry, Lois	Bantam
Ancient Greeks	Q	I	250+	Worldwise	Grolier Press
Ancient Romans	Q	I	250+	Worldwise	Grolier Press
And Still the Turtle Watched	Q	RF	250+	MacGill-Callahan, Sheila	Penguin Group
Animal Neighbors	Q	I	250+	Orbit Double Takes	Pacific Learning
*Animal Stories	Q	F	250+	King-Smith, Dick	Penguin Group
Art Riddle Contest, The	Q	RF	250+	Medearis, Angela Shelf	Steck-Vaughn
*Artists and Their Art	Q	I	250+	Medearis, Michael	Steck-Vaughn
Astronauts Take Flight	Q	I	250+	iOpeners	Pearson Learning Group
At the Root of It	Q	I	250+	iOpeners	Pearson Learning Group
Attack and Defense	Q	I	250+	Explorers	Wright Group/McGraw Hill
Australia	Q	I	250+	First Reports	Compass Point Books
Awfully Short for the Fourth Grade	Q	RF	250+	Woodruff, Elvira	Bantam
Badger in the Basement	Q	RF	250+	Daniels, Lucy	Barron's Educational
Bald Eagles	Q	I	250+	Action Packs	Rigby
Beetles, Lightly Toasted	Q	RF	250+	Naylor, Phyllis Reynolds	Bantam
Bermuda Triangle, The	Q	I	250+	The Unexplained	Capstone Press
Beth's Snow Dancer	Q	HF	250+	The Little Women Journals	Avon
Betsy and Tacy Go Downtown	Q	HF	250+	Lovelace, Maud Hart	HarperTrophy
Betsy and Tacy Go Over the Big Hill	Q	HF	250+	Lovelace, Maud Hart	HarperTrophy
Betsy and Tacy: 60th Anniversary Edition	Q	HF	250+	Lovelace, Maud Hart	HarperTrophy
Beyond the Beyond	Q	I	250+	Wildcats	Wright Group/McGraw Hill
Beyond the Black Hole	Q	SF	250+	Bookweb	Rigby
Bicycle, The	Q	I	250+	Great Inventions	Capstone Press
Big Dipper and You, The	Q	I	250+	Krupp, E. C.	Mulberry Books
Big Storm, The	Q	I	250+	Hiscock, Bruce	Aladdin
Big Wave, The	Q	RF	250+	Buck, Pearl S.	Scholastic
Birthday Disaster	Q	RF	250+	Literacy 2000	Rigby
Black Diamond: Story of the Negro Baseball Leagues	Q	I	250+	McKissack, Patricia & Fred	Scholastic
Black-Eyed Susan	Q	HF	250+	Armstrong, Jennifer	Alfred A. Knopf
Boodil My Dog	Q	RF	250+	Lindenbaum, Pija	Henry Holt & Co.
Brazil	Q	I	250+	First Reports	Compass Point Books
Bridging the Gap	Q	I	250+	Miller, Steve	Pacific Learning
Bright Ideas	Q	I	250+	Explorers	Wright Group/McGraw Hill
Buck Leonard, Baseball Hero	Q	B	250+	Leveled Readers Language Support	Houghton Mifflin
Buddy	Q	RF	1522	Leveled Readers	Houghton Mifflin
Bunnicula	Q	F	250+	Howe, James	Avon
Bunnicula Strikes Again!	Q	F	250+	Howe, James	Simon & Schuster
Bunnies in the Bathroom	Q	RF	250+	Baglio, Ben M.	Scholastic
By E-mail with Love	Q	RF	250+	Leveled Readers	Houghton Mifflin
By the Shores of Silver Lake	Q	HF	250+	Wilder, Laura Ingalls	HarperTrophy
Calamity Kate	Q	RF	250+	Deary, Terry	HarperTrophy
California	Q	I	250+	One Nation	Capstone Press
Call of the Selkie	Q	RF	250+	Action Packs	Rigby
Camera, The	Q	I	250+	Great Inventions	Capstone Press
Canada	Q	I	250+	First Reports	Compass Point Books
Caribou Journey, A	Q	I	250+	Miller, Debbie S.	Little, Brown & Co.
Cars	Q	I	250+	Early Connections	Benchmark Education
Case of the Invisible Cat, The	Q	RF	250+	Parker, A. E.	Scholastic

* Collection of short stories

TITLE	LEVEL	GENRE	WORD COUNT	AUTHOR / SERIES	PUBLISHER / DISTRIBUTOR
Casey's Case	Q	RF	250+	Literacy 2000	Rigby
Casey's Code	Q	RF	250+	Riley, Gail Blasser	Steck-Vaughn
Cats, Cats, Cats	Q	I	250+	Literacy 2000	Rigby
Cave Creatures	Q	I	872	Independent Readers Science	Houghton Mifflin
*Centerburg Tales: More Adventures of Homer Price	Q	RF	250+	McCloskey, Robert	Puffin Books
Changes for Addy	Q	HF	250+	The American Girls Collection	Pleasant Company
Changes For Addy: A Winter Story	Q	HF	250+	The American Girls Collection	Pleasant Company
Changes For Felicity: A Winter Story	Q	HF	250+	The American Girls Collection	Pleasant Company
Changes For Josefina: A Winter Story	Q	HF	250+	The American Girls Collection	Pleasant Company
Changes For Kirsten: A Winter Story	Q	HF	250+	The American Girls Collection	Pleasant Company
Changes For Molly: A Winter Story	Q	HF	250+	The American Girls Collection	Pleasant Company
Changes For Samantha: A Winter Story	Q	HF	250+	The American Girls Collection	Pleasant Company
Changing Times	Q	RF	250+	Treasured Horses Collection	Scholastic
Child's Portrait of Shakespeare, A	Q	B	250+	Burdett, Lois	Firefly Books
Chile	Q	I	250+	First Reports	Compass Point Books
China	Q	I	250+	First Reports	Compass Point Books
Cities: The Building of America	Q	I	250+	Thompson, Gare	Children's Press
Class Trip to the Cave of Doom	Q	F	250+	McMullan, Kate	Grosset & Dunlap
Computer Evidence	Q	I	250+	Forensic Crime Solvers	Capstone Press
Coral Reefs	Q	I	250+	First Reports	Compass Point Books
Countess Veronica	Q	RF	250+	Robinson, Nancy K.	Scholastic
Creepy Creatures	Q	I	250+	Explorers	Wright Group/McGraw Hill
Cub in the Cupboard	Q	RF	250+	Baglio, Ben M.	Scholastic
Cuckoo Child, The	Q	F	250+	King-Smith, Dick	Hyperion
Danger, Landslides!	Q	I	250+	Leveled Readers Language Support	Houghton Mifflin
Dangerous Waters	Q	I	250+	Leveled Readers	Houghton Mifflin
David McCord: Poet	Q	B	407	Vocabulary Readers	Houghton Mifflin
Day in the Life of the Great Plains, A	Q	I	1287	Leveled Readers Social Studies	Houghton Mifflin
Day of the Blizzard	Q	I	250+	Moskin, Marietta	Scholastic
Day the Fifth Grade Disappeared, The	Q	F	250+	Fields, Terri	Scholastic
Dear Future	Q	RF	250+	Literacy 2000	Rigby
Dear Mr. Henshaw	Q	RF	250+	Cleary, Beverly	HarperCollins
Dennis Tito: First Space Tourist	Q	I	250+	Rosen Real Readers	Rosen Publishing Group
Deserts	Q	I	250+	First Reports	Compass Point Books
Deserts of the World	Q	I	1288	Leveled Readers Science	Houghton Mifflin
Diary of a Pioneer Boy	Q	HF	250+	Massie, Elizabeth	Steck-Vaughn
Disappearing Bike Shop, The	Q	SF	250+	Woodruff, Elvira	Bantam
Do You Know Me?	Q	RF	250+	Farmer, Nancy	Penguin Group
Donner Party, The	Q	HF	250+	Werther, Scott P.	Scholastic
Double Trouble	Q	RF	250+	Leveled Readers Language Support	Houghton Mifflin
Dragon for Sale	Q	F	250+	MacDonald, Marianne	Troll Associates
Dragon in the Family, A	Q	F	250+	Koller, Jackie French	Pocket Books
Dragon Quest	Q	F	250+	Koller, Jackie French	Pocket Books
Dragon Trouble	Q	F	250+	Koller, Jackie French	Pocket Books
Dragonling, The	Q	F	250+	Koller, Jackie French	Pocket Books
Dragons and Kings	Q	F	250+	Koller, Jackie French	Pocket Books
Dragons of Krad	Q	F	250+	Koller, Jackie French	Pocket Books
Driscoll and the Singing Fish	Q	F	1005	Leveled Readers	Houghton Mifflin
Droughts	Q	I	250+	Natural Disasters	Red Brick Learning
Drum Dancers: An Inuit Story	Q	RF	873	Leveled Readers	Houghton Mifflin
Duke Ellington: A Life in Music	Q	B	905	Leveled Readers	Houghton Mifflin

TITLE	LEVEL	GENRE	WORD COUNT	AUTHOR / SERIES	PUBLISHER / DISTRIBUTOR
Easter Bunny that Ate My Sister, The	Q	F	250+	Marney, Dean	Scholastic
Egypt	Q	I	250+	First Reports	Compass Point Books
England	Q	I	250+	First Reports	Compass Point Books
Errol the Peril	Q	F	250+	Literacy 2000	Rigby
Escape From Slavery: Five Journeys to Freedom	Q	B	250+	Rappaport, Doreen	HarperTrophy
Escape from the Comics	Q	RF	250+	Bookweb	Rigby
Everest Challenge	Q	I	489	Vocabulary Readers	Houghton Mifflin
Expect the Unexpected	Q	I	250+	Orbit Double Takes	Pacific Learning
Experiment with Movement	Q	I	250+	Murphy, Bryan	Scholastic
Experiment with Water	Q	I	250+	Murphy, Bryan	Scholastic
Exploring the Grand Canyon	Q	I	250+	Rosen Real Readers	Rosen Publishing Group
Exploring the Titanic	Q	I	250+	Ballard, Robert D.	Scholastic
Facing the Flood	Q	RF	250+	Kleinhenz, Sydnie Meltzer	Steck-Vaughn
Falling Off a Log	Q	RF	1290	Leveled Readers	Houghton Mifflin
Family Dinner	Q	RF	250+	Cutler, Jane	Farrar, Straus and Giroux
*Famous Animals	Q	I	250+	Literacy Tree	Rigby
Famous Rocks	Q	I	578	Independent Readers Science	Houghton Mifflin
Fantastic Animal Features	Q	I	250+	Parker, Heather	Steck-Vaughn
Farmer Boy	Q	HF	250+	Wilder, Laura Ingalls	HarperTrophy
Favorite Games Around the World	Q	I	250+	Sunshine	Wright Group/McGraw Hill
Feathers and Flight	Q	I	250+	Explorers	Wright Group/McGraw Hill
Felicity Learns a Lesson	Q	HF	250+	The American Girls Collection	Pleasant Company
Felicity Saves the Day	Q	HF	250+	The American Girls Collection	Pleasant Company
Felicity's Surprise	Q	HF	250+	The American Girls Collection	Pleasant Company
Finding the Titanic	Q	I	250+	Ballard, Robert D.	Scholastic
First Book About Africa: An Introduction for Young Readers	Q	I	250+	Ellis, Veronica Freeman	Just Us Books
*Five Brave Explorers	Q	B	250+	Hudson, Wade	Scholastic
*Five Brilliant Scientists	Q	B	250+	Steward, Susan McKinney	Scholastic
*Five Notable Inventors	Q	B	250+	Hudson, Wade	Scholastic
Floating on Air	Q	F	1332	Leveled Readers	Houghton Mifflin
Florida	Q	I	250+	One Nation	Capstone Press
Flunking of Joshua T. Bates, The	Q	RF	250+	Shreve, Susan	Alfred A. Knopf
Flying Ace: The Story of Amelia Earhart	Q	B	250+	Eyewitness Readers	DK Publishing
Forest Community, A	Q	I	250+	Massie, Elizabeth	Steck-Vaughn
Fort Sumter: Where the Civil War Began	Q	I	250+	Rosen Real Readers	Rosen Publishing Group
*Fortune's Friend: Tales of Rivalry and Riches	Q	TL	250+	Literacy 2000	Rigby
Fossils Alive!	Q	I	250+	Daniel, Claire	Steck-Vaughn
Fossils: Pictures from the Past	Q	I	250+	Daniel, Claire	Steck-Vaughn
Four A's, The	Q	RF	250+	Wildcats	Wright Group/McGraw Hill
Fourth Grade Celebrity	Q	RF	250+	Giff, Patricia Reilly	Bantam
Fourth Grade Wizards, The	Q	RF	250+	DeClements, Barthe	Penguin Group
Fox in the Frost	Q	RF	250+	Baglio, Ben M.	Scholastic
Free Fall	Q	I	250+	Basalaj, Kathy	Pacific Learning
Friendship Pact, The	Q	RF	250+	Pfeffer, Susan Beth	Scholastic
From Axes to Zippers: Simple Machines	Q	I	250+	Navigators Social Studies Series	Benchmark Education
Fudge-a-Mania	Q	RF	250+	Blume, Judy	Bantam
Full House: Club Stephanie	Q	RF	250+	Herman, Gail	Pocket Books
Full House; Stephanie	Q	RF	250+	Herman, Gail	Pocket Books
Galileo Galilee, Astronomer	Q	B	455	Independent Readers Science	Houghton Mifflin
Garfield and the Beast in the Basement	Q	F	250+	Davis, Jim	Troll Associates
Garfield and the Mysterious Mummy	Q	F	250+	Davis, Jim	Troll Associates
Gathering: A Northwoods Counting Book	Q	I	250+	Bowen, Betsy	Houghton Mifflin
Georgia	Q	I	250+	One Nation	Capstone Press

TITLE	LEVEL	GENRE	WORD COUNT	AUTHOR / SERIES	PUBLISHER / DISTRIBUTOR
Germany	Q	I	250+	First Reports	Compass Point Books
Getting Rid of Katherine	Q	RF	250+	Wright, Betty Ren	Troll Associates
Ghost Comes Calling, The	Q	F	250+	Wright, Betty	Scholastic
Ghost On Saturday Night, The	Q	F	250+	Fleischman, Sid	Beech Tree Books
Giant Rock of Yosemite, The: A Sierra Miwok Tale	Q	F	1028	Leveled Readers	Houghton Mifflin
Gifts of the Dineh	Q	RF	1301	Leveled Readers	Houghton Mifflin
Girl in the Golden Bower, The	Q	TL	250+	Yolen, Jane	Little, Brown & Co.
Girl Who Knew it All, The	Q	RF	250+	Giff, Patricia Reilly	Bantam
Girl Who Loved the Wind, The	Q	TL	250+	Yolen, Jane	HarperTrophy
*Girls to the Rescue, Book #3	Q	RF	250+	Lansky, Bruce	Meadowbrook Press
*Girls to the Rescue, Book #4	Q	RF	250+	Lansky, Bruce	Meadowbrook Press
*Girls to the Rescue, Book #6	Q	RF	250+	Lansky, Bruce	Meadowbrook Press
Global Alert	Q	I	250+	Navigators Social Studies Series	Benchmark Education
Glumly	Q	F	250+	Literacy 2000	Rigby
Goat in the Garden	Q	RF	250+	Baglio, Ben M.	Scholastic
Golden Games	Q	I	250+	Zemanski, Stella	Scholastic
Golden Sword of Dragonwalk	Q	F	250+	Stine, R. L.	Scholastic
Good-Bye, Chicken Little	Q	RF	250+	Byars, Betsy	HarperTrophy
Goose on the Loose	Q	RF	250+	Baglio, Ben M.	Scholastic
Grand Coulee Dam, The	Q	I	793	Leveled Readers Social Studies	Houghton Mifflin
Grandpa's Face	Q	RF	250+	Greenfield, Eloise	Putnam & Grosset
Grasslands	Q	I	250+	First Reports	Compass Point Books
Great Wall of China, The	Q	I	250+	Rosen Real Readers	Rosen Publishing Group
Great Wall of China, The	Q	I	250+	Fisher, Leonard Everett	Aladdin
Green Thumbs	Q	I	250+	Literacy 2000	Rigby
Gulliver's Stories	Q	F	250+	Dolch, E. W.; Marguerite, P.	Scholastic
Hamster in a Handbasket	Q	RF	250+	Baglio, Ben M.	Scholastic
Hannah and the Angels	Q	F	250+	Lowery, Linda	Random House
Hannah of Fairfield	Q	HF	250+	Pioneer Daughters	Puffin Books
Hannah's Helping Hands	Q	HF	250+	Van Leeuwen, Jean	Puffin Books
Hannah's Winter of Hope	Q	HF	250+	Van Leeuwen, Jean	Puffin Books
Happy Accidents!	Q	I	250+	Action Packs	Rigby
Happy Birthday, Addy!	Q	HF	250+	The American Girls Collection	Pleasant Company
Happy Birthday, Felicity!	Q	HF	250+	The American Girls Collection	Pleasant Company
Happy Birthday, Josefina!	Q	HF	250+	The American Girls Collection	Pleasant Company
Happy Birthday, Kirsten!	Q	HF	250+	The American Girls Collection	Pleasant Company
Happy Birthday, Molly!	Q	HF	250+	The American Girls Collection	Pleasant Company
Happy Birthday, Samantha!	Q	HF	250+	The American Girls Collection	Pleasant Company
Haunted	Q	F	250+	Ragged Island Mysteries	Wright Group/McGraw Hill
Hawaii: The Aloha State	Q	I	250+	Rosen Real Readers	Rosen Publishing Group
Headlines from Space	Q	I	250+	Rigby Focus	Rigby
Heather and the Pink Poodles	Q	RF	250+	Engle, Marion	Magic Attic
Heather at the Barre	Q	RF	250+	Sinykin, Sheri Cooper	Magic Attic
Heather Goes to Hollywood	Q	RF	250+	Sinykin, Sheri Cooper	Magic Attic
Heather Takes the Reins	Q	RF	250+	Sinykin, Sheri Cooper	Magic Attic
Heather, Belle of the Ball	Q	RF	250+	Sinykin, Sheri Cooper	Magic Attic
Hedgehog in the Hall	Q	RF	250+	Daniels, Lucy	Barron's Educational
Help Is on the Way	Q	I	372	Vocabulary Readers	Houghton Mifflin
Help! I'm a Prisoner in the Library	Q	RF	250+	Clifford, Eth	Scholastic
Help! I'm Trapped in an Alien's Body	Q	F	250+	Strasser, Todd	Scholastic
Help! I'm Trapped in My Lunch Lady's Body	Q	F	250+	Strasser, Todd	Scholastic
Help! I'm Trapped in My Teacher's Body	Q	F	250+	Strasser, Todd	Scholastic
Help! I'm Trapped in Obedience School	Q	F	250+	Strasser, Todd	Scholastic

* Collection of short stories

TITLE	LEVEL	GENRE	WORD COUNT	AUTHOR / SERIES	PUBLISHER / DISTRIBUTOR
Help! I'm Trapped in Obedience School Again	Q	F	250+	Strasser, Todd	Scholastic
Help! I'm Trapped in Santa's Body	Q	F	250+	Strasser, Todd	Scholastic
Help! I'm Trapped in the First Day of School	Q	F	250+	Strasser, Todd	Scholastic
Help! I'm Trapped in the First Day of Summer Camp	Q	F	250+	Strasser, Todd	Scholastic
Help! I'm Trapped in the President's Body	Q	F	250+	Strasser, Todd	Scholastic
*Homer Price	Q	RF	250+	McCloskey, Robert	Puffin Books
Horrors of the Haunted Museum	Q	RF	250+	Stine, R. L.	Scholastic
Horse, of Course, The	Q	I	250+	Action Packs	Rigby
How Do Airplanes Fly?	Q	I	250+	Rosen Real Readers	Rosen Publishing Group
Human Body, The	Q	I	250+	Explorers	Wright Group/McGraw Hill
Hushtown: A Peaceful Community	Q	RF	250+	Massie, Elizabeth	Steck-Vaughn
I Have a Dream	Q	B	250+	Davidson, Margaret	Scholastic
Ice Storms	Q	I	250+	Natural Disasters	Red Brick Learning
Iditarod: Dogsled Race Across Alaska	Q	I	250+	Fuerst, Jeffery B.	Wright Group/McGraw Hill
If You Grew Up with Abraham Lincoln	Q	I	250+	McGovern, Ann	Scholastic
If You Grew Up with George Washington	Q	I	250+	Gross, Ruth Belov	Scholastic
If You Lived 100 Years Ago	Q	I	250+	McGovern, Ann	Scholastic
If You Lived at the Time of Martin Luther King	Q	I	250+	Levine, Ellen	Scholastic
If You Lived at the Time of the American Revolution	Q	I	250+	Moore, Kay	Scholastic
If You Lived at the Time of the Civil War	Q	I	250+	Moore, Kay	Scholastic
If You Lived at the Time of the Great San Francisco Earthquake	Q	I	250+	Levine, Ellen	Scholastic
If You Lived in Colonial Times	Q	I	250+	McGovern, Ann	Scholastic
If you Lived in the Alaska Territory	Q	I	250+	Levinson, Nancy Smiler	Scholastic
If You Lived with the Cherokee	Q	I	250+	Roop, Peter & Connie	Scholastic
If You Lived with the Hopi	Q	I	250+	Kamma, Anne	Scholastic
If You Lived with the Iroquois	Q	I	250+	Levine, Ellen	Scholastic
If You Lived with the Sioux Indians	Q	I	250+	McGovern, Ann	Scholastic
If You Sailed on the Mayflower in 1620	Q	I	250+	McGovern, Ann	Scholastic
If You Traveled on the Underground Railroad	Q	I	250+	Levine, Ellen	Scholastic
If You Traveled West in a Covered Wagon	Q	I	250+	Levine, Ellen	Scholastic
If You Were There When They Signed the Constitution	Q	I	250+	Levy, Elizabeth	Scholastic
If Your Name was Changed at Ellis Island	Q	I	250+	Levine, Ellen	Scholastic
Illinois	Q	I	250+	One Nation	Capstone Press
In the News	Q	I	250+	Wildcats	Wright Group/McGraw Hill
In the Rain Forest	Q	I	250+	Wildcats	Wright Group/McGraw Hill
India	Q	I	250+	First Reports	Compass Point Books
Inspector Grub and the Gourmet Mystery	Q	F	250+	Bookweb	Rigby
Iroquois League, The	Q	I	250+	Rosen Real Readers	Rosen Publishing Group
Isabella: A Wish for Miguel	Q	HF	250+	Childhood Journeys	Aladdin
Italy	Q	I	250+	First Reports	Compass Point Books
It'll Be All Right on the Night!	Q	I	250+	Quinn, Pat	Pacific Learning
It's a Frog's Life	Q	I	250+	Literacy 2000 Satellites	Rigby
It's a Mammal!	Q	I	250+	iOpeners	Pearson Learning Group
It's All in the Soil	Q	I	250+	iOpeners	Pearson Learning Group
It's New, It's Improved, It's Terrible!	Q	RF	250+	Manes, Stephen	Bantam
J. T.	Q	RF	250+	Wagner, Jane	Bantam
James and the Giant Peach	Q	F	250+	Dahl, Roald	Penguin Group
James Madison: Founding Father	Q	B	250+	Rosen Real Readers	Rosen Publishing Group
Jane and the Beanstalk	Q	TL	1534	Leveled Readers	Houghton Mifflin
Japan	Q	I	250+	First Reports	Compass Point Books

* Collection of short stories

TITLE	LEVEL	GENRE	WORD COUNT	AUTHOR / SERIES	PUBLISHER / DISTRIBUTOR
Jim Ugly	Q	RF	250+	Fleischman, Sid	Bantam
John Henry and the Steam Drill	Q	F	1203	Leveled Readers	Houghton Mifflin
Jon Scieszka Gets Kids Reading	Q	B	1155	Leveled Readers	Houghton Mifflin
Jo's Troubled Heart	Q	HF	250+	The Little Women Journals	Avon
Josefina Learns a Lesson	Q	HF	250+	The American Girls Collection	Pleasant Company
Josefina Saves the Day	Q	HF	250+	The American Girls Collection	Pleasant Company
Josefina's Surprise	Q	HF	250+	The American Girls Collection	Pleasant Company
Joshua T. Bates	Q	RF	250+	Shreve, Susan	Alfred A. Knopf
Joshua T. Bates in Trouble Again	Q	RF	250+	Shreve, Susan	Alfred A. Knopf
Joshua T. Bates Takes Charge	Q	RF	250+	Shreve, Susan	Alfred A. Knopf
Journal, The: Dear Future II	Q	SF	250+	Literacy 2000	Rigby
Journey to the Undersea Gardens	Q	I	250+	iOpeners	Pearson Learning Group
Juan Ponce De Leon	Q	B	250+	Biographies-Great Explorers	Capstone Press
Julia Alvarez: One Author, Two Cultures	Q	B	1029	Leveled Readers	Houghton Mifflin
Junebug	Q	RF	250+	Mead, Alice	Bantam
Juneteenth: Celebrating the End of Slavery	Q	I	250+	Rosen Real Readers	Rosen Publishing Group
Just Juice	Q	RF	250+	Hesse, Karen	Scholastic
Kayaking	Q	I	250+	Lund, Bill	Red Brick Learning
Keep Calm!	Q	RF	250+	Bookweb	Rigby
Keisha Discovers Harlem	Q	RF	250+	Lewis, Zoe	Magic Attic
Keisha Leads the Way: Magic Attic Club	Q	RF	250+	Reed, Teresa	Magic Attic
Keisha the Fairy Snow Queen: Magic Attic Club	Q	RF	250+	Reed, Teresa	Magic Attic
Keisha to the Rescue: Magic Attic Club	Q	RF	250+	Reed, Teresa	Magic Attic
Keisha's Maze Mystery: Magic Attic Club	Q	RF	250+	Benson, Lauren	Magic Attic
Kenya	Q	I	250+	First Reports	Compass Point Books
Kid Heroes of the Environment	Q	I	250+	Dee, Catherine	Scholastic
Kids in Pioneer Times	Q	I	250+	Kids Throughout History	Rosen Publishing Group
King Max	Q	F	250+	King-Smith, Dick	Troll Associates
Kirsten Learns a Lesson	Q	HF	250+	The American Girls Collection	Pleasant Company
Kirsten Saves the Day	Q	HF	250+	The American Girls Collection	Pleasant Company
Kirsten's Surprise	Q	HF	250+	The American Girls Collection	Pleasant Company
Kitten in the Cold	Q	RF	250+	Baglio, Ben M.	Scholastic
Kitten That Won First Prize, The	Q	RF	250+	Baglio, Ben M.	Scholastic
Kittens in the Kitchen	Q	RF	250+	Daniels, Lucy	Barron's Educational
Knights & Armor	Q	I	250+	Worldwise	Grolier Press
Knitwits	Q	RF	250+	Taylor, William	Scholastic
Lady Bird Johnson	Q	B	250+	Simon, Charnan	Children's Press
Lamb in the Laundry	Q	RF	250+	Baglio, Ben M.	Scholastic
Landslides	Q	I	250+	Natural Disasters	Red Brick Learning
Last Summer with Maizon	Q	RF	250+	Woodson, Jacqueline	G.P. Putnam's Sons
Learning from Fossils	Q	I	3234	Leveled Readers Science	Houghton Mifflin
Leif Eriksson	Q	B	250+	Biographies-Great Explorers	Capstone Press
Lemonade Trick, The	Q	RF	250+	Corbett, Scott	Scholastic
Lewis and Clark	Q	B	250+	Biographies-Great Explorers	Capstone Press
Life on a Wagon Train	Q	I	250+	Rosen Real Readers	Rosen Publishing Group
Lincoln Memorial, The	Q	I	250+	National Landmarks	Red Brick Learning
Little Clearing in the Woods	Q	HF	250+	Wilkes, Maria D.	HarperTrophy
Little House by Boston Bay	Q	HF	250+	Wiley, Melissa	HarperTrophy
Little House in Brookfield	Q	HF	250+	Wilkes, Maria D.	HarperTrophy
Little House in the Big Woods	Q	HF	250+	Wilder, Laura Ingalls	HarperTrophy
Little House in the Highlands	Q	HF	250+	Wiley, Melissa	HarperTrophy
Little House on the Prairie	Q	HF	250+	Wilder, Laura Ingalls	HarperTrophy
Little Town at the Crossroads	Q	HF	250+	Wilkes, Maria D.	HarperTrophy
Little Town on the Prairie	Q	HF	250+	Wilder, Laura Ingalls	HarperTrophy

* Collection of short stories

TITLE	LEVEL	GENRE	WORD COUNT	AUTHOR / SERIES	PUBLISHER / DISTRIBUTOR
Loch Ness Monster, The	Q	I	250+	The Unexplained	Capstone Press
Long Arrow and the Elk Dogs	Q	TL	250+	Leveled Readers Language Support	Houghton Mifflin
Long Winter, The	Q	HF	250+	Wilder, Laura Ingalls	HarperTrophy
Lost Flower Children, The	Q	RF	250+	Lisle, Janet Taylor	Philomel Books
Lost in the Dark	Q	I	250+	Orbit Double Takes	Pacific Learning
Lost in the Wilderness!	Q	I	660	Vocabulary Readers	Houghton Mifflin
Love, from the Fifth-Grade Celebrity	Q	RF	250+	Giff, Patricia Reilly	Bantam
Madame C. J. Walker	Q	B	494	Independent Readers Social Studies	Houghton Mifflin
Mammals of the Sea	Q	I	250+	Explorers	Wright Group/McGraw Hill
Maps	Q	I	250+	Rigby Focus	Rigby
Maps and Our World	Q	I	250+	Explorers	Wright Group/McGraw Hill
Marcie's Birthday Dig	Q	RF	250+	Leveled Readers Language Support	Houghton Mifflin
Marie: Summer in the Country	Q	HF	250+	Girlhood Journeys	Aladdin
Mark McGwire: Home Run Hero	Q	B	960	Leveled Readers	Houghton Mifflin
Mary by Myself	Q	F	250+	Smith, Jane Denitz	HarperTrophy
*Mary on Horseback	Q	RF	250+	Wells, Rosemary	Puffin Books
Max the Man Mountain	Q	RF	250+	McFarlane, Peter	HarperCollins
Medieval Feast, A	Q	I	250+	Aliki	HarperCollins
Medieval Town	Q	I	250+	Worldwise	Grolier Press
Meet Addy	Q	HF	250+	The American Girls Collection	Pleasant Company
Meet Felicity	Q	HF	250+	The American Girls Collection	Pleasant Company
Meet Hillary Rodham Clinton	Q	B	250+	Spain, Valerie	Random House
Meet John F. Kennedy	Q	B	250+	White, Nancy Bean	Random House
Meet Josefina	Q	HF	250+	The American Girls Collection	Pleasant Company
Meet Kirsten	Q	HF	250+	The American Girls Collection	Pleasant Company
Meet Molly	Q	HF	250+	The American Girls Collection	Pleasant Company
Meet Samantha	Q	HF	250+	The American Girls Collection	Pleasant Company
Megan in Ancient Greece	Q	HF	250+	Korman, Susan	Magic Attic
Megan's Balancing Act	Q	RF	250+	Korman, Susan	Magic Attic
Meg's Dearest Wish	Q	HF	250+	The Little Women Journals	Avon
Messages Without Words	Q	I	250+	Sunshine	Wright Group/McGraw Hill
Mexico	Q	I	250+	First Reports	Compass Point Books
Mia Hamm: Soccer Star	Q	B	250+	Leveled Readers Language Support	Houghton Mifflin
Michael Jordan	Q	B	250+	Lovitt, Chip	Scholastic
Michigan	Q	I	250+	One Nation	Capstone Press
Mighty Mammals	Q	I	250+	Explorers	Wright Group/McGraw Hill
Miguel Hidalgo, Father of Mexican Independence	Q	B	1145	Leveled Readers Social Studies	Houghton Mifflin
Minibeasts	Q	I	250+	The News	Richard C. Owen
Missing Osprey Nest, The	Q	RF	250+	Ragged Island Mysteries	Wright Group/McGraw Hill
Mixed-up Max	Q	F	250+	King-Smith, Dick	Troll Associates
Miyu and the Cranes for Peace	Q	RF	949	Leveled Readers	Houghton Mifflin
Moki	Q	HF	250+	Penny, Grace Jackson	Penguin Group
Molly Learns a Lesson	Q	HF	250+	The American Girls Collection	Pleasant Company
Molly Saves the Day	Q	HF	250+	The American Girls Collection	Pleasant Company
Molly's Surprise	Q	HF	250+	The American Girls Collection	Pleasant Company
Moon, The	Q	I	250+	Eye on the Universe	Crabtree
Morgan's Zoo	Q	F	250+	Howe, James	Aladdin
Mostly Michael	Q	RF	250+	Smith, Robert Kimmel	Bantam
Motion	Q	I	250+	Simply Science	Compass Point Books

* Collection of short stories

TITLE	LEVEL	GENRE	WORD COUNT	AUTHOR / SERIES	PUBLISHER / DISTRIBUTOR
Mount Rushmore	Q	I	250+	Let's See	Compass Point Books
Mountain Bike Challenge, The	Q	I	250+	Morgan, Patrick	Pacific Learning
Mountain Man and the President, The	Q	B	250+	First Reports	Compass Point Books
Mountains	Q	I	250+	First Reports	Compass Point Books
Mouse of Amherst, The	Q	F	250+	Spires, Elizabeth	Farrar, Straus and Giroux
Mr. Popper's Penguins	Q	F	250+	Atwater, Richard & Florence	Dell
Mystery of Moody Manor, The	Q	F	250+	Ragged Island Mysteries	Wright Group/McGraw Hill
Mystery of the Fire in the Sky	Q	RF	250+	Mystery Solvers	Troll Associates
Mystery of the Missing Leopard, The	Q	F	250+	Leonhardt, Alice	Steck-Vaughn
Myth or Mystery?	Q	F	250+	Literacy Tree	Rigby
*Native American Stories	Q	TL	250+	Bruchac, Joseph	Fulcrum Publishing
Nature's Power	Q	I	250+	Hummer, Patricia K.	Steck-Vaughn
Nelson Mandela	Q	B	250+	First Biographies	Steck-Vaughn
Nero Hawley's Fight for Freedom	Q	B	545	Vocabulary Readers	Houghton Mifflin
Netherlands	Q	I	250+	First Reports	Compass Point Books
New England's Whales	Q	I	856	Independent Readers Social Studies	Houghton Mifflin
New Jersey	Q	I	250+	Kummer, Patricia K.	Red Brick Learning
New Language, New Friends	Q	I	250+	iOpeners	Pearson Learning Group
New York	Q	I	250+	One Nation	Capstone Press
Newspaper Kids, The	Q	RF	250+	Phillips, Juanita	HarperCollins
Night Quee's Blue Velvet Dress, The	Q	F	250+	Pair-It Books	Steck-Vaughn
No Laughing Matter	Q	RF	250+	Ragged Island Mysteries	Wright Group/McGraw Hill
Norman Newman and the Werewolf of Walnut Street	Q	F	250+	Conford, Ellen	Troll Associates
North America	Q	I	250+	Petersen, David	Grolier Publishing
Nothing But Trouble, Trouble, Trouble	Q	RF	250+	Hermes, Patricia	Scholastic
Ocean Life	Q	I	250+	Explorers	Wright Group/McGraw Hill
Ocean Life: Tide Pool Creatures	Q	I	250+	Leonhardt, Alice	Steck-Vaughn
Oceanography	Q	I	2127	Independent Readers Social Studies	Houghton Mifflin
Oceans	Q	I	250+	First Reports	Compass Point Books
Oceans	Q	I	250+	The Wonders of our World	Crabtree
Officially Interesting	Q	RF	1460	Leveled Readers	Houghton Mifflin
Ohio	Q	I	250+	One Nation	Capstone Press
On the Banks of Plum Creek	Q	HF	250+	Wilder, Laura Ingalls	HarperCollins
On the Banks of the Bayou	Q	HF	250+	MacBride, Roger Lea	HarperCollins
On Top of Concord Hill	Q	HF	250+	Wilkes, Maria D.	HarperCollins
On Top of the World	Q	I	588	Vocabulary Readers	Houghton Mifflin
Once I Was a Plum Tree	Q	RF	250+	Hurwitz, Johanna	Beech Tree Books
Onion Tears	Q	RF	250+	Kidd, Diana	William Morrow
Original Adventures of Hank the Cowdog, The	Q	F	250+	Erickson, John R.	Gulf
Orphan Train Children: Aggie's Home	Q	HF	250+	Nixon, Joan Lowery	Yearling
Our National Holidays	Q	I	250+	Let's See	Compass Point Books
Our National Parks	Q	I	250+	Let's See	Compass Point Books
Our World of Wonders	Q	I	250+	Canetti, Yanitzia	Steck-Vaughn
Out and About	Q	I	250+	Explorers	Wright Group/McGraw Hill
Outside and Inside Bats	Q	I	250+	Markle, Sandra	Simon & Schuster
Outside and Inside Kangaroos	Q	I	250+	Markle, Sandra	Atheneum
Outside and Inside Sharks	Q	I	250+	Markle, Sandra	Simon & Schuster
Outside and Inside Snakes	Q	I	250+	Markle, Sandra	Simon & Schuster
Outside and Inside Spiders	Q	I	250+	Markle, Sandra	Simon & Schuster
Overcoming Challenges: The Life of Charles F. Bolden, Jr.	Q	B	250+	Walton, Darwin McBeth	Steck-Vaughn

TITLE	LEVEL	GENRE	WORD COUNT	AUTHOR / SERIES	PUBLISHER / DISTRIBUTOR
Owl in the Office	Q	RF	250+	Baglio, Ben M.	Scholastic
P. W. Cracker Sees the World	Q	F	250+	Yoshizawa, Linda	Steck-Vaughn
Paintball	Q	I	250+	X-Sports	Capstone Press
Pandora's Box	Q	RF	250+	Literacy 2000	Rigby
Peanut	Q	I	250+	Selsam, Millicent	William Morrow
Pedro's Journal	Q	HF	250+	Conrad, Pam	Scholastic
Pennsylvania	Q	I	250+	One Nation	Capstone Press
People on the Move	Q	I	250+	iOpeners	Pearson Learning Group
Perfect Person, The	Q	SF	250+	Bookweb	Rigby
Peter Tchaikovsky	Q	B	250+	Venezia, Mike	Children's Press
Peter's Harvest	Q	RF	1085	Leveled Readers	Houghton Mifflin
Picture Book of Simon Bolivar, A	Q	B	250+	Adler, David A.	Bantam
Piglet in a Playpen	Q	RF	250+	Baglio, Ben M.	Scholastic
Pioneer Way, The	Q	I	250+	Kummer, Patricia K.	Steck-Vaughn
Plain Girl	Q	RF	250+	Sorensen, Virginia	Harcourt Trade
Planets, The	Q	I	101	Explorers	Wright Group/McGraw Hill
Plant Kingdom, The	Q	I	250+	Explorers	Wright Group/McGraw Hill
Pocahantas	Q	B	838	Independent Readers Social Studies	Houghton Mifflin
Pocketful of Goobers, A: Story of George Washington Carver	Q	B	250+	Mitchell, Barbara	Carolrhoda Books
Ponies at the Point	Q	RF	250+	Baglio, Ben M.	Scholastic
Pony on the Porch	Q	RF	250+	Baglio, Ben M.	Scholastic
Prairie School	Q	I	505	Vocabulary Readers	Houghton Mifflin
Prairie Songs	Q	HF	250+	Conrad, Pam	HarperTrophy
Preparing for Lift-Off	Q	I	453	Vocabulary Readers	Houghton Mifflin
Presidency, The	Q	I	250+	Let's See	Compass Point Books
Pretty Cool, For a Cat	Q	RF	1707	Leveled Readers	Houghton Mifflin
Prince William	Q	B	250+	Rand, Gloria	Henry Holt & Co.
Proof of Magic	Q	F	250+	Ragged Island Mysteries	Wright Group/McGraw Hill
Pueblo Ruins	Q	I	250+	Rigby Literacy	Rigby
Puppies in the Pantry	Q	RF	250+	Baglio, Ben M.	Scholastic
Putting on a Play	Q	I	424	Vocabulary Readers	Houghton Mifflin
Rabbit and the Coyote, The	Q	F	979	Leveled Readers	Houghton Mifflin
Racing Danger	Q	I	737	Leveled Readers	Houghton Mifflin
Racing with the Sun	Q	I	250+	Orbit Double Takes	Pacific Learning
Rain Forest Tree, A	Q	I	250+	Kite, Lorien	Crabtree
Rain Forest, The	Q	I	191	Action Packs	Rigby
Rain Forests	Q	I	250+	First Reports	Compass Point Books
Rain or Shine	Q	I	250+	Explorers	Wright Group/McGraw Hill
Reason to Run, A	Q	RF	250+	Leveled Readers Language Support	Houghton Mifflin
Revolutionary Poet: A Story About Phillis Wheatley	Q	B	250+	Weidt, Maryann N.	Carolrhoda Books
Rock Climbing	Q	I	250+	Lund, Bill	Red Brick Learning
Rosa Parks	Q	B	250+	Photo-Illustrated Biographies	Red Brick Learning
Rupert and the Griffin	Q	F	250+	Literacy 2000	Rigby
Russia	Q	I	250+	First Reports	Compass Point Books
Safe Return	Q	RF	250+	Dexter, Catherine	Candlewick Press
Samantha Saves the Day	Q	RF	250+	The American Girls Collection	Pleasant Company
Samantha's Surprise	Q	RF	250+	The American Girls Collection	Pleasant Company
Same, But Different, The	Q	RF	1205	Leveled Readers	Houghton Mifflin
Samuel Eaton's Day: A Day in the Life of a Pilgrim Boy	Q	I	250+	Waters, Kate	Scholastic

* Collection of short stories

TITLE	LEVEL	GENRE	WORD COUNT	AUTHOR / SERIES	PUBLISHER / DISTRIBUTOR
Samurai's Daughter, The	Q	TL	250+	San Souci, Robert D.	Penguin Group
San Francisco Earthquake, The	Q	I	618	Vocabulary Readers	Houghton Mifflin
Sarah Morton's Day: Day in the Life of a Pilgrim Girl, A	Q	B	250+	Waters, Kate	Scholastic
Saving America's Wild Horses	Q	I	494	Vocabulary Readers	Houghton Mifflin
Scaly Things	Q	I	250+	Explorers	Wright Group/McGraw Hill
School Days in 1700	Q	I	975	Independent Readers Social Studies	Houghton Mifflin
Science Fair Surprise, The	Q	RF	250+	Burke, Melissa Blackwell	Steck-Vaughn
Scrappers No Easy Out	Q	RF	250+	Hughes, Dean	Aladdin
Scrappers No Fear	Q	RF	250+	Hughes, Dean	Aladdin
Secret of Bunratty Castle, The	Q	F	250+	Action Packs	Rigby
Secret of the Silver Shoes, The	Q	F	250+	Massie, Elizabeth	Steck-Vaughn
Secret Silver Lining, A	Q	RF	250+	Ragged Island Mysteries	Wright Group/McGraw Hill
Secrets of the Desert	Q	I	250+	Literacy 2000	Rigby
Seven Natural Wonders, The	Q	I	250+	Navigators Social Studies Series	Benchmark Education
Sewing Machine, The	Q	I	250+	Great Inventions	Capstone Press
*Shady Deal, The: Tales of Cleverness and Cunning	Q	TL	250+	Literacy 2000	Rigby
Sharks and Rays	Q	I	250+	Explorers	Wright Group/McGraw Hill
Sheepdog in the Snow	Q	RF	250+	Baglio, Ben M.	Scholastic
Ship in a Bottle, The	Q	RF	250+	Ragged Island Mysteries	Wright Group/McGraw Hill
Shipwrecked!	Q	F	250+	Bookweb	Rigby
Shoes Through the Ages	Q	I	250+	Brill, Marlene Targ	Steck-Vaughn
Sierra	Q	I	250+	Siebert, Diane	HarperCollins
Sieur de La Salle	Q	B	250+	Biographies-Great Explorers	Capstone Press
Simon's Big Challenge	Q	RF	250+	Day, Mark	Steck-Vaughn
Skateboarding	Q	I	250+	X-Sports	Capstone Press
Skating to Fame	Q	I	524	Vocabulary Readers	Houghton Mifflin
Sky Watch	Q	I	250+	Explorers	Wright Group/McGraw Hill
Sky's the Limit, The	Q	RF	250+	Wildcats	Wright Group/McGraw Hill
Snakes	Q	I	250+	Explorers	Wright Group/McGraw Hill
Snowboarding	Q	I	250+	X-Sports	Capstone Press
Snowboarding	Q	I	250+	To the Extreme	Capstone Press
Soup	Q	RF	250+	Peck, Robert Newton	Bantam
South Africa	Q	I	250+	First Reports	Compass Point Books
Space Station	Q	I	250+	Orbit Double Takes	Pacific Learning
Spider Relatives	Q	I	250+	Literacy 2000	Rigby
Sports for All	Q	I	250+	Explorers	Wright Group/McGraw Hill
Spreading the Word	Q	I	250+	Wildcats	Wright Group/McGraw Hill
Squirrels in the School	Q	RF	250+	Baglio, Ben M.	Scholastic
Statue of Liberty, The	Q	I	250+	Let's See	Compass Point Books
Statue of Liberty, The	Q	I	250+	National Landmarks	Red Brick Learning
Story of George Washington Carver, The	Q	B	250+	Moore, Eva	Bantam
Story of Laura Ingalls Wilder, Pioneer Girl, The	Q	B	250+	Stine, Megan	Bantam
Strange Jobs	Q	I	250+	Sunshine	Wright Group/McGraw Hill
Strange Meetings	Q	F	250+	Literacy 2000	Rigby
Street Skating: Grinds and Grabs	Q	I	250+	Skateboarding	Capstone Press
Summer I Shrank My Grandmother, The	Q	F	250+	Woodruff, Elvira	Bantam
Summer in the South, A	Q	F	250+	Marshall, James	Houghton Mifflin
Superfudge	Q	RF	250+	Blume, Judy	Bantam
Survive!	Q	RF	250+	Wildcats	Wright Group/McGraw Hill
Sweet Memories Still	Q	RF	250+	Kinsey-Warnock, Natalie	Bantam
Taking to the Air	Q	I	250+	Literacy Tree	Rigby

* Collection of short stories

TITLE	LEVEL	GENRE	WORD COUNT	AUTHOR / SERIES	PUBLISHER / DISTRIBUTOR
Tales of a Fourth Grade Nothing	Q	RF	250+	Blume, Judy	Bantam
Team Players	Q	I	555	Vocabulary Readers	Houghton Mifflin
Television Drama	Q	RF	250+	Literacy 2000	Rigby
Television, The	Q	I	250+	Great Inventions	Capstone Press
Tell Me No Lies	Q	RF	250+	Ragged Island Mysteries	Wright Group/McGraw Hill
Telling Time Through the Ages	Q	I	250+	Navigators Social Studies Series	Benchmark Education
Texas	Q	I	250+	One Nation	Capstone Press
There's A Boy In The Girls' Bathroom	Q	RF	250+	Sachar, Louis	Alfred A. Knopf
There's an Owl in the Shower	Q	RF	250+	George, Jean Craighead	HarperCollins
Think Like a Scientist	Q	I	250+	Burke, Melissa Blackwell	Steck-Vaughn
Thomas Alva Edison: Great Inventor	Q	B	250+	Levinson, Nancy Smiler	Scholastic
Thomas Edison and the Light Bulb	Q	I	619	Independent Readers Science	Houghton Mifflin
Three Kinds of Bears	Q	I	3256	Leveled Readers Science	Houghton Mifflin
Time for Sale	Q	F	250+	Literacy 2000	Rigby
Toilet Paper Tigers, The	Q	RF	250+	Korman, Gordon	Bantam
Tony Hawk: Skateboarding Legend	Q	I	250+	Skateboarding	Capstone Press
Trains	Q	I	250+	Literacy 2000	Rigby
Transportation Through Time	Q	I	250+	Rigby Focus	Rigby
Trapped By a Teacher	Q	RF	250+	Action Packs	Rigby
Travelers and Traders	Q	I	250+	Explorers	Wright Group/McGraw Hill
Tree, the Trunk, and the Tuba, The	Q	RF	250+	Literacy 2000	Rigby
Trevor from Trinidad	Q	RF	1685	Leveled Readers	Houghton Mifflin
Triathlon	Q	I	250+	Lund, Bill	Red Brick Learning
True Story of the Three Little Pigs, The	Q	TL	250+	Scieszka, Jon	Scholastic
Tsunami!	Q	I	784	Independent Readers Science	Houghton Mifflin
Tundra	Q	I	250+	First Reports	Compass Point Books
Turkey That Ate My Father, The	Q	F	250+	Marney, Dean	Scholastic
U.S. Congress, The	Q	I	250+	Let's See	Compass Point Books
U.S. Supreme Court, The	Q	I	250+	Let's See	Compass Point Books
Under the Ground	Q	I	250+	Wildcats	Wright Group/McGraw Hill
Underwater Animals	Q	I	250+	Explorers	Wright Group/McGraw Hill
Unexpected Treasure	Q	RF	250+	Ragged Island Mysteries	Wright Group/McGraw Hill
Universe, The	Q	I	250+	Pair-It-Books	Steck-Vaughn
Up and Away	Q	I	250+	Explorers	Wright Group/McGraw Hill
Up the Amazon	Q	I	250+	Windows on Literacy	National Geographic
Vampire Who Came For Christmas, The	Q	F	250+	Regan, Diane Curtis	Bantam
Velveteen Rabbit, The	Q	F	250+	Williams, Margery	Hearst
Venus	Q	I	250+	Vogt, Gregory L.	The Millbrook Press
Vert Skating: Mastering the Ramp	Q	I	250+	Skateboarding	Capstone Press
Vietnam	Q	I	250+	First Reports	Compass Point Books
Vietnam Veterans Memorial, The	Q	I	250+	National Landmarks	Red Brick Learning
Viva México!: A Story of Benito Juárez and Cinco de Mayo	Q	B	250+	Stories of America	Steck-Vaughn
Volcanoes	Q	I	250+	Windows on Literacy	National Geographic
Volcanoes	Q	I	250+	Explorers	Wright Group/McGraw Hill
Volcanoes	Q	I	250+	Worldwise	Grolier Press
Voting and Elections	Q	I	250+	Let's See	Compass Point Books
Voyager: An Adventure Through Space	Q	I	250+	Gustafson, John	Scholastic
Walk Through History on the Freedom Trail	Q	I	828	Leveled Readers Social Studies	Houghton Mifflin
Walking the Road to Freedom: A Story About Sojourner Truth	Q	B	250+	Ferris, Jeri	Dell
Washington Monument, The	Q	I	250+	National Landmarks	Red Brick Learning
Watching Josh	Q	RF	250+	Ragged Island Mysteries	Wright Group/McGraw Hill
Weather Watching	Q	I	250+	Explorers	Wright Group/McGraw Hill

* Collection of short stories

TITLE	LEVEL	GENRE	WORD COUNT	AUTHOR / SERIES	PUBLISHER / DISTRIBUTOR
Weight Lifting	Q	I	250+	Lund, Bill	Red Brick Learning
We'll Never Forget You, Roberto Clemente	Q	B	250+	Engel, Trudie	Scholastic
Wetland Home, A	Q	I	250+	Sunshine	Wright Group/McGraw Hill
Wetlands	Q	I	250+	First Reports	Compass Point Books
What Happened at the Boston Tea Party?	Q	I	250+	Rosen Real Readers	Rosen Publishing Group
What's Cooking?	Q	I	250+	Cartwright, Pauline	Pacific Learning
What's for Dinner	Q	I	250+	Sunshine	Wright Group/McGraw Hill
What's Happening?: A Book of Explanations	Q	I	250+	Bookshop	Mondo
What's Living at Your Place?	Q	I	250+	Chapman, Bruce	Pacific Learning
White House, The	Q	I	250+	Let's See	Compass Point Books
Who Stole the Tiger's Eye?	Q	F	250+	Sunshine	Wright Group/McGraw Hill
Whose Side Are You On?	Q	RF	250+	Moore, Emily	Bantam
Why Bears Have Short Tails, A Norwegian Tale	Q	F	1093	Leveled Readers	Houghton Mifflin
Why Coyote Howls at Night	Q	TL	250+	Moore, Emily	Farrar, Straus and Giroux
Why the Ocean Is Salty	Q	I	250+	Leonhardt, Alice	Steck-Vaughn
Wild Cats	Q	I	250+	Leonhardt, Alice	Steck-Vaughn
Wing High, Goofah	Q	RF	250+	Literacy 2000	Rigby
Wings	Q	F	250+	Brittain, Bill	HarperTrophy
Winter Solstice, The	Q	I	250+	Jackson, Ellen	Millbrook Press
Witch Hunt: It Happened in Salem Village	Q	I	250+	Krensky, Stephen	Random House
Wolves	Q	I	250+	Literacy 2000	Rigby
World of Dogs, The	Q	I	250+	Pair-It Books	Steck-Vaughn
World's Best Dog-Walker, The	Q	RF	250+	Zollman, Pam	Steck-Vaughn
Writer of the Plains: A Story about Willa Cather	Q	B	250+	Streissguth, Tom	Carolrhoda Books
X-Games, The: Skateboarding's Greatest Event	Q	I	250+	Skateboarding	Capstone Press
Yao's Wild Ride	Q	HF	250+	Leveled Readers Language Support	Houghton Mifflin
*You Be The Detective	Q	RF	250+	Miller, Marvin	Scholastic
*You Be The Detective II	Q	RF	250+	Miller, Marvin	Scholastic
*You Be The Jury	Q	I	250+	Miller, Marvin	Scholastic
*You Be The Jury: Courtroom V	Q	I	250+	Miller, Marvin	Bantam
Yo-Yo Ma: Musical Superstar	Q	B	250+	Leveled Readers Language Support	Houghton Mifflin
18th Emergency, The	R	RF	250+	Byars, Betsy	Bantam
1980s, The	R	I	1144	Leveled Readers Social Studies	Houghton Mifflin
Abigail Adams: Girl of Colonial Days	R	B	250+	Wagoner, Jean Brown	Aladdin
Abraham Lincoln: The Great Emancipator	R	B	250+	Stevenson, Augusta	Aladdin
Absolutely True Story, The: How I Visited Yellowstone Park With the Terrible Rupes	R	RF	250+	Roberts, Willo Davis	Aladdin
Ace: The Very Important Pig	R	F	250+	King-Smith, Dick	Alfred A. Knopf
Adventures of Spider, The	R	TL	250+	Arkhurst, Joyce C.	Scholastic
After the Goat Man	R	RF	250+	Byars, Betsy	Puffin Books
Against the Odds	R	I	250+	Wildcats	Wright Group/McGraw Hill
Against the Rules	R	RF	250+	Costello, Emily	Dell
Aggressive In-Line Skating	R	I	250+	X-Sports	Capstone Press
Agnes the Sheep	R	F	250+	Taylor, William	Bantam
Alabama	R	I	250+	This Land Is Your Land	Compass Point Books
Alaska	R	I	250+	This Land Is Your Land	Compass Point Books
All for the Better: A Story of El Barrio	R	RF	250+	Mohr, Nicholasa	Steck-Vaughn
All Is Well	R	HF	250+	Litchman, Kristin Embry	Bantam
Alone in the Storm	R	RF	250+	Leveled Readers Language Support	Houghton Mifflin
Alphabet, The	R	I	250+	Literacy 2000	Rigby
Amanda Joins the Circus	R	F	250+	Avi	Bantam

TITLE	LEVEL	GENRE	WORD COUNT	AUTHOR / SERIES	PUBLISHER / DISTRIBUTOR
Amelia Earhart: Young Aviator	R	B	250+	Gormley, Beatrice	Aladdin
*America Street: A Multicultural Anthology of Stories	R	RF	250+	Mazer, Anne	Persea Books
America: A Dream	R	HF	1620	Leveled Readers	Houghton Mifflin
American Alligator, The	R	I	250+	Potts, Steve	Red Brick Learning
American Bison, The	R	I	250+	Potts, Steve	Red Brick Learning
America's Most Wanted Fifth-Graders	R	RF	250+	Lawrence, Jan; Raskin, Linda	Scholastic
Amos and the Alien	R	F	250+	Paulsen, Gary	Bantam
Amos Binder, Secret Agent	R	F	250+	Paulsen, Gary	Bantam
Amos Gets Famous	R	F	250+	Paulsen, Gary	Bantam
Amos Gets Married	R	F	250+	Paulsen, Gary	Bantam
Amos Goes Bananas	R	F	250+	Paulsen, Gary	Bantam
Amos's Killer Concert Caper	R	F	250+	Paulsen, Gary	Bantam
An Wang: A Mind for Computers	R	B	3495	Leveled Readers Science	Houghton Mifflin
And Then What Happened, Paul Revere?	R	B	250+	Fritz, Jean	Bantam
Animal Babies	R	I	250+	Kalman, Bobbie	Crabtree
*Animal Stories by Young Writers	R	F	250+	Rubel, William; Mandel, Gerry	Tricycle Press
Animal, the Vegetable, and John D. Jones, The	R	RF	250+	Byars, Betsy	Bantam
Animals of the Amazon	R	I	683	Vocabulary Readers	Houghton Mifflin
Anne Bradstreet	R	B	548	Independent Readers Science	Houghton Mifflin
Annie Oakley	R	B	250+	Wilson, Ellen	Aladdin
Ansel Adams, Photographer	R	B	1763	Leveled Readers Social Studies	Houghton Mifflin
Apache, The	R	I	250+	First Reports	Compass Point Books
Arctic	R	I	250+	The Heinle Reading Library	Thomson Learning
Arkansas	R	I	250+	This Land Is Your Land	Compass Point Books
Armadillo, The	R	I	250+	Potts, Steve	Red Brick Learning
Arthur, For the Very First Time	R	RF	250+	MacLachlan, Patricia	Bantam
A-Z Fascinating Facts About Animals	R	I	250+	Literacy 2000	Rigby
Babe Didrikson: Athlete of the Century	R	B	250+	Knudson, R. Rozanne	Bantam
Babe Ruth: One of Baseball's Greatest	R	B	250+	Van Riper, Guernsey	Aladdin
Babe the Gallant Pig	R	F	250+	King-Smith, Dick	Random House
Backward Bird Dog, The	R	F	250+	Wallace, Bill	Bantam
Bald Eagle, The	R	I	250+	Potts, Steve	Red Brick Learning
Barbara Esbensen: Words into Pictures	R	B	1043	Leveled Readers	Houghton Mifflin
Barrel in the Basement, The	R	F	250+	Wallace, Barbara Brooks	Aladdin
Because of Winn-Dixie	R	RF	250+	DiCamillo, Kate	Candlewick Press
Beginnings of Sports	R	I	250+	PM Nonfiction-Ruby	Rigby
Behind the Scenes	R	I	250+	Literacy 2000	Rigby
Benjamin Franklin: Young Printer	R	B	250+	Stevenson, Augusta	Aladdin
Betsy Ross: Designer of Our Flag	R	B	250+	Weil, Ann	Aladdin
Big Picture, The	R	I	250+	Bennett, Mary	Pacific Learning
Bighorn Sheep, The	R	I	250+	Mattern, Joanne	Red Brick Learning
Birds At My Feeder	R	I	250+	Kalman, Bobbie	Crabtree
Birthday Dig, The	R	F	1216	Leveled Readers	Houghton Mifflin
*Birthday Surprises: Ten Great Stories to Unwrap	R	RF	250+	Hurwitz, Johanna	William Morrow
Black Gold	R	RF	250+	Henry, Marguerite	Aladdin
Blackfeet, The	R	I	250+	First Reports	Compass Point Books
Blossom Promise, A	R	RF	250+	Byars, Betsy	Bantam
Blossoms and the Green Phantom, The	R	RF	250+	Byars, Betsy	Dell
Blossoms Meet the Vulture Lady, The	R	RF	250+	Byars, Betsy	Bantam
Book About Planets and Stars, A	R	I	250+	Reigot, Betty Polisar	Scholastic
Born To Trot	R	RF	250+	Henry, Marguerite	Aladdin
Botticelli	R	B	250+	Venezia, Mike	Children's Press

* Collection of short stories

TITLE	LEVEL	GENRE	WORD COUNT	AUTHOR / SERIES	PUBLISHER / DISTRIBUTOR
Bow Down, Shadrach	R	RF	250+	Cowley, Joy	Wright Group/McGraw Hill
Boy Who Lost His Face, The	R	RF	250+	Sachar, Louis	Alfred A. Knopf
Bracelet, The	R	HF	250+	Uchida, Yoshiko	Philomel Books
Bread and Roses: How an Orphan Girl Helped American Women Win the Vote	R	I	250+	Navigators Fiction Series	Benchmark Education
Brendan the Navigator: A History Mystery about the Discovery of America	R	I	250+	Fritz, Jean	Penguin Group
Brian's Winter	R	RF	250+	Paulsen, Gary	Bantam
Brighty of the Grand Canyon	R	RF	250+	Henry, Marguerite	Aladdin
Buck Leonard, Baseball's Greatest Gentleman	R	B	1419	Leveled Readers	Houghton Mifflin
Building a Dream: Mary Bethune's School	R	B	250+	Kelso, Richard	Steck-Vaughn
Bully of Barkham Street	R	RF	250+	Stolz, Mary	HarperTrophy
Cabin Faced West, The	R	HF	250+	Fritz, Jean	Bantam
Caddie Woodlawn	R	HF	250+	Brink, Carol Ryrie	Bantam
California	R	I	250+	This Land Is Your Land	Compass Point Books
Call Me Ruth	R	RF	250+	Sachs, Marilyn	Beech Tree Books
Can It Rain Cats and Dogs?	R	I	250+	Berger, Melvin & Gilda	Scholastic
Can't You Make Them Behave, King George?	R	I	250+	Fritz, Jean	Putnam & Grosset
Carole: The Inside Story	R	RF	250+	Bryant, Bonnie	Skylark
Case of the Sabotaged School Play, The	R	RF	250+	Singer, Marilyn	Bantam
Castle in the Attic, The	R	F	250+	Winthrop, Elizabeth	Bantam
Cat Walk	R	F	250+	Stolz, Mary	Bantam
Caves	R	I	250+	The Wonders of our World	Crabtree
Caves	R	I	250+	Wood, Jenny	Scholastic
Celery Stalks at Midnight, The	R	F	250+	Howe, James	Atheneum
Cells	R	I	1649	Leveled Readers Science	Houghton Mifflin
Chancy and the Grand Rascal	R	F	250+	Fleischman, Sid	Beech Tree Books
Charlie and the Chocolate Factory	R	F	250+	Dahl, Roald	Bantam
Charlie and the Great Glass Elevator	R	F	250+	Dahl, Roald	Bantam
Charlie Malarkey and the Singing Moose	R	F	250+	Kennedy, William & Brendan	Puffin Books
Charlotte's Web	R	F	250+	White, E. B.	HarperTrophy
Cherokee, The	R	I	250+	First Reports	Compass Point Books
Cherokee, The: Native Basket Weavers	R	I	250+	America's First Peoples	Capstone Press
Chesapeake Bay	R	I	1192	Leveled Readers Social Studies	Houghton Mifflin
Cheyenne, The	R	I	250+	First Reports	Compass Point Books
*Children of Christmas: Stories for the Season	R	RF	250+	Rylant, Cynthia	Orchard Books
Chocolate by Hershey: A Story about Milton S. Hershey	R	B	250+	Burford, Betty	Carolrhoda Books
Chocolate Flier, The	R	I	250+	Action Packs	Rigby
Christina's Ghost	R	F	250+	Wright, Betty Ren	Bantam
Christmas Spurs, The	R	RF	250+	Wallace, Bill	Bantam
Christopher Reeve: Still a Hero	R	B	250+	Leveled Readers Language Support	Houghton Mifflin
Circle of Gold	R	RF	250+	Boyd, Candy Dawson	Bantam
Cities of Splendor: The Facts and the Fables	R	TL	250+	Landscapes of Legend	Children's Press
City on a Lake, The	R	I	642	Vocabulary Readers	Houghton Mifflin
Clara Barton: Founder of the American Red Cross	R	B	250+	Stevenson, Augusta	Aladdin
Close to Home: A Story of the Polio Epidemic	R	I	250+	Weaver, Lydia	Bantam
Coach Amos	R	RF	250+	Paulsen, Gary	Bantam
Colorado	R	I	250+	This Land Is Your Land	Compass Point Books
Combat Rescue Helicopters: The MH-53 Pave Lows	R	I	250+	War Planes	Red Brick Learning
Computer Nut, The	R	SF	250+	Byars, Betsy	Bantam

* Collection of short stories

TITLE	LEVEL	GENRE	WORD COUNT	AUTHOR / SERIES	PUBLISHER / DISTRIBUTOR
Connecticut	R	I	250+	This Land Is Your Land	Compass Point Books
Contemporary Age, The	R	I	250+	Journey Through History	Barron's Educational
Coronado's Golden Quest	R	F	250+	Weisberg, Barbara	Steck-Vaughn
Cougars	R	I	250+	Predators in the Wild	Capstone Press
Coyote, The	R	I	250+	Mattern, Joanne	Red Brick Learning
Crispus Attucks: Black Leader of Colonial Patriots	R	B	250+	Millender, Dharathula H.	Aladdin
Da Vinci	R	B	250+	Venezia, Mike	Children's Press
Dame Shirley and the Gold Rush	R	B	250+	Rawls, Jim	Steck-Vaughn
Danger on Panther Peak	R	RF	250+	Wallace, Bill	Pocket Books
Dangerous Animals	R	I	250+	Explorers	Wright Group/McGraw Hill
*Dark-Thirty: Southern Tales of the Supernatural	R	F	250+	McKissack, Patricia C.	Alfred A. Knopf
Davin	R	F	250+	Gordon, Dan; Gordon, Zaki	Bantam
Days of Courage: The Little Rock Story	R	I	250+	Kelso, Richard	Steck-Vaughn
Days to Remember	R	I	250+	iOpeners	Pearson Learning Group
Declaration of Independence and Benjamin Franklin of Pennsylvania, The	R	B	250+	Framers of the Declaration of Independence	Rosen Publishing Group
Declaration of Independence and John Adams of Massachusetts, The	R	B	250+	Framers of the Declaration of Independence	Rosen Publishing Group
Declaration of Independence and Richard Henry Lee of Virginia, The	R	B	250+	Framers of the Declaration of Independence	Rosen Publishing Group
Declaration of Independence and Robert Livingston of New York, The	R	B	250+	Framers of the Declaration of Independence	Rosen Publishing Group
Declaration of Independence and Roger Sherman of Connecticut, The	R	B	250+	Framers of the Declaration of Independence	Rosen Publishing Group
Declaration of Independence and Thomas Jefferson of Virginia, The	R	B	250+	Framers of the Declaration of Independence	Rosen Publishing Group
Delaware	R	I	250+	This Land Is Your Land	Compass Point Books
Deserts	R	I	250+	The Wonders of our World	Crabtree
Devil's Bridge	R	RF	250+	DeFelice, Cynthia	Avon
Diego Rivera	R	B	250+	Venezia, Mike	Children's Press
Dirty Socks Don't Win Games	R	RF	250+	Marney, Dean	Scholastic
Disaster, The	R	RF	1309	Leveled Readers	Houghton Mifflin
Do Stars Have Points?	R	I	250+	Berger, Melvin & Gilda	Scholastic
Dog Called Kitty, A	R	RF	250+	Wallace, Bill	Pocket Books
Dog on Barkham Street, A	R	RF	250+	Stolz, Mary	HarperTrophy
Dog Years	R	RF	250+	Warner, Sally	Alfred A. Knopf
Dogs Dogs Dogs	R	I	250+	Literacy 2000	Rigby
Doll's House, The	R	RF	250+	Godden, Rumer	Penguin Group
Dominic	R	F	250+	Steig, William	Farrar, Straus and Giroux
Dunc and Amos and the Red Tattoos	R	RF	250+	Paulsen, Gary	Bantam
Dunc and Amos Go to the Dogs	R	RF	250+	Paulsen, Gary	Bantam
Dunc and Amos Hit the Big Top	R	RF	250+	Paulsen, Gary	Bantam
Dunc and Amos Meet the Slasher	R	RF	250+	Paulsen, Gary	Bantam
Dunc and the Flaming Ghost	R	F	250+	Paulsen, Gary	Bantam
Dunc and the Greased Sticks of Doom	R	RF	250+	Paulsen, Gary	Bantam
Dunc and the Haunted Castle	R	RF	250+	Paulsen, Gary	Bantam
Dunc and the Scam Artists	R	RF	250+	Paulsen, Gary	Bantam
Dunc Breaks the Record	R	RF	250+	Paulsen, Gary	Bantam
Dunc Gets Tweaked	R	RF	250+	Paulsen, Gary	Bantam
Dunc's Doll	R	RF	250+	Paulsen, Gary	Bantam
Dunc's Dump	R	RF	250+	Paulsen, Gary	Bantam
Dunc's Halloween	R	RF	250+	Paulsen, Gary	Bantam

* Collection of short stories

TITLE	LEVEL	GENRE	WORD COUNT	AUTHOR / SERIES	PUBLISHER / DISTRIBUTOR
Dunc's Undercover Christmas	R	RF	250+	Paulsen, Gary	Bantam
Earthquake!: San Francisco, 1906	R	I	250+	Wilson, Kate	Steck-Vaughn
Earthquakes	R	I	250+	The Wonders of our World	Crabtree
Earthquakes	R	I	250+	Explorers	Wright Group/McGraw Hill
East of the Sun and West of the Moon	R	TL	250+	Hague, Kathleen & Michael	Harcourt Trade
El Greco	R	B	250+	Venezia, Mike	Children's Press
Eleanor Roosevelt: First Lady of the World	R	B	250+	Faber, Doris	Penguin Group
Ellie Brader Hates Mr. G.	R	RF	250+	Johnston, Janet	Pocket Books
Enchanted Horse, The	R	F	250+	Nabb, Magdalen	Hyperion
Endangered Desert Animals	R	I	250+	Taylor, Dave	Crabtree
Endangered Forest Animals	R	I	250+	Taylor, Dave	Crabtree
Endangered Grassland Animals	R	I	250+	Taylor, Dave	Crabtree
Endangered Island Animals	R	I	250+	Taylor, Dave	Crabtree
Endangered Mountain Animals	R	I	250+	Taylor, Dave	Crabtree
Endangered Ocean Animals	R	I	250+	Taylor, Dave	Crabtree
Endangered Savannah Animals	R	I	250+	Taylor, Dave	Crabtree
Endangered Wetland Animals	R	I	250+	Taylor, Dave	Crabtree
Enormous Egg, The	R	F	250+	Butterworth, Oliver	Little, Brown & Co.
Eruption	R	I	250+	Wildcats	Wright Group/McGraw Hill
ESP TV	R	SF	250+	Rodgers, Mary	HarperTrophy
Every Body Tells a Story	R	I	250+	Explorers	Wright Group/McGraw Hill
*Every Living Thing	R	RF	250+	Rylant, Cynthia	Aladdin
Everything Cat: What Kids Really Want to Know About Cats	R	I	250+	Crisp, Marty	NorthWord Press
Everywhere	R	RF	250+	Brooks, Bruce	Scholastic
Exploring Space	R	I	250+	Explorers	Wright Group/McGraw Hill
Extreme Sports	R	I	250+	PM Nonfiction-Ruby	Rigby
Eyes in the Sky	R	I	250+	Literacy 2000	Rigby
Family Picture, A	R	RF	1570	Leveled Readers	Houghton Mifflin
Family Under the Bridge, The	R	RF	250+	Savage Carlson, Natalie	Scholastic
Fernitickles	R	HF	250+	Literacy 2000	Rigby
Fig Pudding	R	RF	250+	Fletcher, Ralph	Clarion
Finding Your Way	R	I	250+	Bonallack, John	Pacific Learning
Fire in the Sky	R	HF	250+	Ransom, Candice F.	Carolrhoda Books
Fire! The Beginnings of the Labor Movement	R	HF	250+	Goldin, Barbara Diamond	Puffin Books
First Four Years, The	R	HF	250+	Wilder, Laura Ingalls	HarperTrophy
First Thanksgiving, The	R	I	250+	The Library of the Pilgrims	Rosen Publishing Group
Flags	R	I	250+	Action Packs	Rigby
Flight: The Journey of Charles Lindbergh	R	I	250+	Burleigh, Robert	Putnam & Grosset
Floods	R	I	1142	Leveled Readers	Houghton Mifflin
Florida	R	I	250+	This Land Is Your Land	Compass Point Books
Flying High	R	RF	250+	Orbit Double Takes	Pacific Learning
Food and Recipes of the Pilgrims	R	I	250+	Cooking Throughout American History	Rosen Publishing Group
Food and Recipes of the Thirteen Colonies	R	I	250+	Cooking Throughout American History	Rosen Publishing Group
Food and Recipes of the Westward Expansion	R	I	250+	Cooking Throughout American History	Rosen Publishing Group
Forest Mammals	R	I	250+	Kalman, Bobbie	Crabtree
Forests	R	I	250+	The Wonders of Our World	Crabtree
Fortune Branches Out, A	R	RF	250+	Mahy, Margaret	Bantam
Fossils	R	I	1272	Leveled Readers Science	Houghton Mifflin
Foul Play on the Sidelines	R	RF	250+	Costello, Emily	Dell
Francisco Goya	R	B	250+	Venezia, Mike	Children's Press

* Collection of short stories

TITLE	LEVEL	GENRE	WORD COUNT	AUTHOR / SERIES	PUBLISHER / DISTRIBUTOR
Freaky Friday	R	F	250+	Rodgers, Mary	HarperTrophy
Frederick Douglass: The Last Days of Slavery	R	B	250+	Miller, William	Lee & Low Books Inc.
Freedom Crossing	R	HF	250+	Clark, Margaret Goff	Scholastic
Frida Kahlo	R	B	250+	Venezia, Mike	Children's Press
Friends or Enemies?	R	I	250+	Leveled Readers Language Support	Houghton Mifflin
Frindle	R	RF	250+	Clements, Andrew	Aladdin
Galapagos Islands, The	R	I	250+	Rosen Real Readers	Rosen Publishing Group
Galileo: Man of Science	R	B	250+	Rosen Real Readers	Rosen Publishing Group
Gentle Annie: The True Story of a Civil War Nurse	R	I	250+	Shura, Mary Frances	Scholastic
George Handel	R	B	250+	Venezia, Mike	Children's Press
George Washington: A Picture Book Biography	R	B	250+	Giblin, James Cross	Scholastic
George Washington: Young Leader	R	B	250+	Santrey, Laurence	Troll Associates
Georgia	R	I	250+	This Land Is Your Land	Compass Point Books
Georgia O'Keeffe	R	B	250+	Venezia, Mike	Children's Press
Ghosts Beneath Our Feet	R	F	250+	Wright, Betty Ren	Scholastic
Girl-Son, The	R	HF	250+	Neuberger, Anne E.	Carolrhoda Books
Gladly, Here I Come	R	RF	250+	Cowley, Joy	Wright Group/McGraw Hill
Glorious Days, Dreadful Days: The Battle of Bunker Hill	R	I	250+	Kirby, Philippa	Steck-Vaughn
Go Free or Die: A Story About Harriet Tubman	R	B	250+	Ferris, Jeri	Carolrhoda Books
Goldfish Charlie and the Case of the Missing Planet	R	SF	250+	Mazer, Anne	Troll Associates
Good, the Bad, and Everything Else, The	R	RF	250+	Action Packs	Rigby
Goodbye to Angel Island	R	HF	1055	Leveled Readers	Houghton Mifflin
Grant Wood	R	B	250+	Venezia, Mike	Children's Press
Great Kapok Tree, The	R	I	250+	Cherry, Lynne	Scholastic
Great Migration, The	R	I	250+	Lawrence, Jacob	HarperCollins
Great Sporting Events	R	I	250+	PM Nonfiction-Ruby	Rigby
Greatest, The	R	I	250+	Literacy 2000	Rigby
Greek and Roman Eras, The	R	I	250+	Journey Through History	Barron's Educational
Grizzly Bear, The	R	I	250+	Potts, Steve	Red Brick Learning
Grizzly Bears	R	I	250+	Predators in the Wild	Red Brick Learning
Growin'	R	RF	250+	Grimes, Nikki	Puffin Books
Gwendolyn Brooks: A Life of Poetry	R	B	811	Leveled Readers	Houghton Mifflin
Hannah's Fancy Notions: A Story of Industrial New England	R	HF	250+	Ross, Pat	Penguin Group
Harry Cat's Pet Puppy	R	F	250+	Selden, George	Bantam
Harry Houdini: Master of Magic	R	B	250+	Kraske, Robert	Scholastic
Hatchet	R	RF	250+	Paulsen, Gary	Aladdin
Have You Seen Hyacinth Macaw?	R	RF	250+	Giff, Patricia Reilly	Dell
Hawaii	R	I	250+	This Land Is Your Land	Compass Point Books
Hawaiian Magic	R	I	250+	Morris, Rod	Pacific Learning
Hawks	R	I	250+	Predators in the Wild	Red Brick Learning
Heather's Story	R	I	250+	Orbit Double Takes	Pacific Learning
Helen Keller: A Light For The Blind	R	B	250+	Kudlinski, Kathleen V.	Penguin Group
Hello, My Name Is Scrambled Eggs	R	RF	250+	Gilson, Jamie	Pocket Books
Helping Wild Animals	R	I	582	Vocabulary Readers	Houghton Mifflin
Henri de Toulouse-Lautrec	R	B	250+	Venezia, Mike	Children's Press
Henri Matisse	R	B	250+	Venezia, Mike	Children's Press
Her Piano Sang: A Story About Clara Schumann	R	B	250+	Allman, Barbara	Carolrhoda Books
Hidden World	R	I	250+	Explorers	Wright Group/McGraw Hill
High Flying	R	I	250+	Explorers	Wright Group/McGraw Hill

* Collection of short stories

TITLE	LEVEL	GENRE	WORD COUNT	AUTHOR / SERIES	PUBLISHER / DISTRIBUTOR
Home Sweet Home, Goodbye	R	RF	250+	Stowe, Cynthia	Scholastic
Home: A Journey Through America	R	I	250+	Locker, Thomas	Voyager Books
House of Wings, The	R	RF	250+	Byars, Betsy	Penguin Group
How Did the Lights Go Out? The Story of the New York City Blackout	R	I	1175	Independent Readers Science	Houghton Mifflin
How Do Flies Walk Upside Down?	R	I	250+	Berger, Melvin & Gilda	Scholastic
How Do Frogs Swallow with Their Eyes?	R	I	250+	Berger, Melvin	Scholastic
How Things Work	R	I	250+	Explorers	Wright Group/McGraw Hill
How To Eat Fried Worms	R	RF	250+	Rockwell, Thomas	Bantam
Hunting the Horned Lizard	R	I	250+	Bishop, Nic	Pacific Learning
Hurricanes & Tornadoes	R	I	250+	The Wonders of our World	Crabtree
Hyrax, The: An Interesting Puzzle	R	I	250+	Leveled Readers Language Support	Houghton Mifflin
I Can Measure an Elephant	R	I	521	Independent Readers Science	Houghton Mifflin
Idaho	R	I	250+	This Land Is Your Land	Compass Point Books
Iggie's House	R	RF	250+	Blume, Judy	Bantam
Immigrants: Coming to America	R	I	250+	Thompson, Gare	Children's Press
In the Fast Lane	R	I	250+	Literacy 2000	Rigby
Indian in the Cupboard, The	R	F	250+	Banks, Lynne Reid	Avon
Indiana	R	I	250+	This Land Is Your Land	Compass Point Books
Insects & Spiders	R	I	250+	Worldwise	Franklin Watts
Iowa	R	I	250+	This Land Is Your Land	Compass Point Books
Iroquois, The	R	I	250+	First Reports	Compass Point Books
Island Life	R	I	250+	iOpeners	Pearson Learning Group
Island, The	R	RF	250+	Paulsen, Gary	Bantam
Isn't It Cool?	R	I	250+	Action Packs	Rigby
It Came From Ohio!: My Life as a Writer	R	B	250+	Stine, R. L.	Scholastic
Ivy's Journal: A Trip to the Yucatán	R	RF	250+	Bookshop	Mondo
Jar of Dreams, A	R	RF	250+	Uchida, Yoshiko	Aladdin
Jennifer, Hecate, Macbeth, William McKinley, and Me, Elizabeth	R	RF	250+	Konigsburg, E. L.	Yearling
Jeremy Thatcher, Dragon Hatcher	R	F	250+	Coville, Bruce	Aladdin
Jerry on the Line	R	RF	250+	Seabrooke, Brenda	Puffin Books
Journey to a New Land: An Oral History	R	B	250+	Bookshop	Mondo
Journey to Kansas	R	HF	250+	Leveled Readers Language Support	Houghton Mifflin
Journeys of Sojourner Truth, The	R	B	1217	Leveled Readers Social Studies	Houghton Mifflin
Jump Jets: The AV-88 Harriers	R	I	250+	War Planes	Red Brick Learning
Just Call Me Stupid	R	RF	250+	Birdseye, Tom	Puffin Books
Justin Morgan Had a Horse	R	HF	250+	Henry, Marguerite	Scholastic
Kansas	R	I	250+	This Land Is Your Land	Compass Point Books
Kat the Curious	R	RF	1723	Leveled Readers	Houghton Mifflin
Keep Your Eye On Amanda!	R	F	250+	Avi	Avon
Kentucky	R	I	250+	This Land Is Your Land	Compass Point Books
Killer Whales	R	I	250+	Predators in the Wild	Red Brick Learning
King Emmett the Second	R	RF	250+	Stolz, Mary	Bantam
King of the Wind	R	HF	250+	Henry, Marguerite	Aladdin
Komodo Dragons	R	I	250+	Predators in the Wild	Red Brick Learning
Landry News, The	R	RF	250+	Clements, Andrew	Simon & Schuster
Landslides	R	I	1127	Leveled Readers	Houghton Mifflin
Later, Gator	R	RF	250+	Yep, Laurence	Hyperion
Laura Ingalls Wilder, Pioneer Girl	R	B	250+	Stine, Megan	Bantam
Laura Ingalls Wilder: A Biography	R	B	250+	Anderson, William	HarperTrophy
Leaders: People Who Make a Difference	R	B	250+	You Are There	Children's Press

* Collection of short stories

TITLE	LEVEL	GENRE	WORD COUNT	AUTHOR / SERIES	PUBLISHER / DISTRIBUTOR
Leonard Bernstein	R	B	250+	Venezia, Mike	Children's Press
Letter to Mrs. Roosevelt, A	R	HF	250+	DeYoung, C. Coco	Delacorte
Library Card, The	R	RF	250+	Spinelli, Jerry	Scholastic
Listening to Crickets: A Story about Rachel Carson	R	HF	250+	Ransom, Candice F.	Carolrhoda Books
Little Farm in the Ozarks	R	HF	250+	MacBride, Roger Lea	HarperTrophy
Little House on Rocky Ridge	R	HF	250+	MacBride, Roger Lea	HarperTrophy
Little Town in the Ozarks	R	HF	250+	MacBride, Roger Lea	HarperTrophy
Log Cabin in the Woods	R	HF	250+	Henry, Joanne Landers	Scholastic
Long Way to Go, A	R	I	250+	O'Neal, Zibby	Penguin Group
Look Up	R	I	250+	iOpeners	Pearson Learning Group
Lost on a Mountain in Maine	R	RF	250+	Fendler, Donn	Peter Smith Publications
Louisiana	R	I	250+	This Land Is Your Land	Compass Point Books
Love You, Soldier	R	HF	250+	Hest, Amy	Puffin Books
Luis W. Alvarez	R	B	250+	Hispanic Stories	Steck-Vaughn
Mae Jemison	R	B	250+	Bookshop	Mondo
Maine	R	I	250+	This Land Is Your Land	Compass Point Books
Many Happy Returns: A Review of Recycling	R	I	250+	Literacy 2000	Rigby
Maria Tallchief	R	B	250+	Native American Stories	Steck-Vaughn
Maria: A Christmas Story	R	RF	250+	Taylor, Theodore	Avon Camelot
Marion Jones: Quest for Gold	R	B	1337	Leveled Readers	Houghton Mifflin
Martial Arts	R	I	250+	Malane, Donna	Pacific Learning
Martin Luther King, Jr. and the March Toward Freedom	R	B	250+	Hakim, Rita	The Millbrook Press
Mary Anning, Fossil Hunter	R	B	1307	Independent Readers Science	Houghton Mifflin
Maryland	R	I	250+	This Land Is Your Land	Compass Point Books
Massachusetts	R	I	250+	This Land Is Your Land	Compass Point Books
Math in the Garden	R	I	250+	Navigators Math Series	Benchmark Education
Maya, The	R	I	250+	First Reports	Compass Point Books
Mayflower, The	R	I	250+	The Library of the Pilgrims	Rosen Publishing Group
Measuring the Weather	R	I	250+	Gaynor, Bill	Pacific Learning
Meet Calliope Day	R	F	250+	Haddad, Charles	Random House
Meet Martin Luther King, Jr.	R	B	250+	DeKay, James T.	Random House
Meet Yo-Yo Ma	R	B	1406	Leveled Readers	Houghton Mifflin
Megan's Island	R	RF	250+	Roberts, Willo Davis	Aladdin
Message, The	R	F	250+	Applegate, K. A.	Scholastic
Michelangelo: His Life and Art	R	B	250+	Rosen Real Readers	Rosen Publishing Group
Michigan	R	I	250+	This Land Is Your Land	Compass Point Books
Middle Ages, The	R	I	250+	Journey Through History	Barron's Educational
Midnight Fox, The	R	RF	250+	Byars, Betsy	Scholastic
Mini Mammals	R	I	250+	Explorers	Wright Group/McGraw Hill
Minnesota	R	I	250+	This Land Is Your Land	Compass Point Books
Miracles on Maple Hill	R	RF	250+	Sorensen, Virginia	Scholastic
Mirandy and Brother Wind	R	F	250+	McKissack, Patricia	Alfred A. Knopf
Mississippi	R	I	250+	This Land Is Your Land	Compass Point Books
Missouri	R	I	250+	This Land Is Your Land	Compass Point Books
Misty of Chincoteague	R	RF	250+	Henry, Marguerite	Aladdin
Misty's Twilight	R	RF	250+	Henry, Marguerite	Aladdin
Modern Times	R	I	250+	Journey Through History	Barron's Educational
Monet	R	B	250+	Venezia, Mike	Children's Press
Monster's Ring, The	R	F	250+	Coville, Bruce	Pocket Books
Montana	R	I	250+	This Land Is Your Land	Compass Point Books
Moonlight on the River	R	RF	250+	Kovacs, Deborah	Penguin Group
Moose, The	R	I	250+	Hemstock, Annie	Red Brick Learning

* Collection of short stories

TITLE	LEVEL	GENRE	WORD COUNT	AUTHOR / SERIES	PUBLISHER / DISTRIBUTOR
More Perfect than the Moon	R	HF	250+	MacLachlan, Patricia	HarperCollins
Mr. Mysterious & Company	R	F	250+	Fleischman, Sid	Beech Tree Books
Mummies Made in Egypt	R	I	250+	Aliki	HarperCollins
My Dream of Martin Luther King	R	I	250+	Ringgold, Faith	Crown
My Sister the Witch	R	RF	250+	Conford, Ellen	Troll Associates
Mysteries of the Deep	R	I	531	Vocabulary Readers	Houghton Mifflin
Mystery of the Cupboard	R	F	250+	Banks, Lynne Reid	Avon Camelot
*Mystery Stories	R	RF	250+	Higgins, James	Houghton Mifflin
Nasty, Stinky Sneakers	R	RF	250+	Bunting, Eve	HarperTrophy
Nebraska	R	I	250+	This Land Is Your Land	Compass Point Books
Nevada	R	I	250+	This Land Is Your Land	Compass Point Books
New Hampshire	R	I	250+	This Land Is Your Land	Compass Point Books
New Jersey	R	I	250+	This Land Is Your Land	Compass Point Books
New Mexico	R	I	250+	This Land Is Your Land	Compass Point Books
New York	R	I	250+	This Land Is Your Land	Compass Point Books
News Flash!	R	I	250+	Hill, Sharon	Pacific Learning
Nez Perce, The	R	I	250+	First Reports	Compass Point Books
Night Lights, A Cruise Around the Solar System	R	I	250+	Hill, David	Pacific Learning
Nighty-Nightmare	R	F	250+	Howe, James	Avon Camelot
No More Magic	R	SF	250+	Avi	Alfred A. Knopf
Noonday Friends, The	R	RF	250+	Stolz, Mary	Scholastic
North Carolina	R	I	250+	This Land Is Your Land	Compass Point Books
North Dakota	R	I	250+	This Land Is Your Land	Compass Point Books
North Pole Walk	R	I	250+	Orbit Double Takes	Pacific Learning
Nothing's Fair in Fifth Grade	R	RF	250+	DeClements, Barthe	Scholastic
Ohio	R	I	250+	This Land Is Your Land	Compass Point Books
Ojibwa, The: Wild Rice Gatherers	R	I	250+	America's First Peoples	Capstone Press
Oklahoma	R	I	250+	This Land Is Your Land	Compass Point Books
Ola's Wake	R	RF	250+	Stone, B. J.	Henry Holt & Co.
Olympic Softball Stars	R	I	577	Vocabulary Readers	Houghton Mifflin
On Guard	R	RF	250+	Napoli, Donna Jo	Puffin Books
One Hundredth Thing about Caroline, The	R	RF	250+	Lowry, Lois	Bantam
One Thing I'm Good At	R	RF	250+	Williams, Karen Lynn	William Morrow
Oregon	R	I	250+	This Land Is Your Land	Compass Point Books
Otherwise Known As Sheila the Great	R	RF	250+	Blume, Judy	Bantam
Our Changing Earth	R	I	250+	Belcher, Angie	Pacific Learning
Our Only May Amelia	R	HF	250+	Holm, Jennifer	HarperCollins
Our Planet	R	I	250+	Worldwise	Grolier Press
Owls	R	I	250+	Kalman, Bobbie	Crabtree
Passing Poetry	R	RF	785	Leveled Readers	Houghton Mifflin
Paul Cezanne	R	B	250+	Venezia, Mike	Children's Press
Paul Gauguin	R	B	250+	Venezia, Mike	Children's Press
Paul Klee	R	B	250+	Venezia, Mike	Children's Press
Pennsylvania	R	I	250+	This Land Is Your Land	Compass Point Books
People and Places	R	I	250+	Rigby Focus	Rigby
People from the Past	R	I	250+	Explorers	Wright Group/McGraw Hill
Phoebe The Spy	R	HF	250+	Griffin, Judith Berry	Scholastic
Picasso	R	B	250+	Venezia, Mike	Children's Press
Pierre August Renoir	R	B	250+	Venezia, Mike	Children's Press
Pigs Might Fly	R	F	250+	King-Smith, Dick	Scholastic
Pike River Phantom, The	R	F	250+	Wright, Betty	Scholastic
Pilgrims, The	R	I	250+	The Heinle Reading Library	Thomson Learning
Pioneer Girl, The Story of Laura Ingalls Wilder	R	B	250+	Anderson, William	HarperCollins
Play Ball!	R	I	250+	Explorers	Wright Group/McGraw Hill

* Collection of short stories

TITLE	LEVEL	GENRE	WORD COUNT	AUTHOR / SERIES	PUBLISHER / DISTRIBUTOR
Playground Science	R	I	250+	iOpeners	Pearson Learning Group
Please Don't Be Mine, Julie Valentine!	R	RF	250+	Strasser, Todd	Scholastic
Plymouth Partnership, A: Pilgrims and Native Americans	R	I	250+	The Library of the Pilgrims	Rosen Publishing Group
Plymouth: Surviving the First Winter	R	I	250+	The Library of the Pilgrims	Rosen Publishing Group
Pony For Jeremiah, A	R	HF	250+	Miller, Robert H.	Silver Burdett Press
Prehistory to Egypt	R	I	250+	Journey Through History	Barron's Educational
Prince Amos	R	RF	250+	Paulsen, Gary	Bantam
Protecting Sea Turtles	R	I	250+	Leveled Readers Language Support	Houghton Mifflin
Pueblo, The	R	I	250+	First Reports	Compass Point Books
Pueblo, The: Southwestern Potters	R	I	250+	America's First Peoples	Capstone Press
Puerto Rico	R	I	250+	This Land Is Your Land	Compass Point Books
Race to the Pole	R	I	250+	Windows on Literacy	National Geographic
Radar Jammers: The EA-6B Prowlers	R	I	250+	War Planes	Red Brick Learning
Railroad Revolution	R	I	618	Vocabulary Readers	Houghton Mifflin
Rain Forest	R	I	250+	Worldwise	Grolier Press
Raptors: Hunters in the Sky	R	I	250+	Rauzon, Mark J.	Wright Group/McGraw Hill
Real Team Soccer	R	RF	1207	Leveled Readers	Houghton Mifflin
Relationships of Living Things	R	I	250+	Atwater, Mary et al.	Macmillan/McGraw Hill
Rella's Wish	R	TL	1207	Leveled Readers	Houghton Mifflin
Remembering the Big Quake	R	I	250+	Trussell-Cullen, Alan	Pacific Learning
Reptiles and Amphibians	R	I	250+	Explorers	Wright Group/McGraw Hill
Rhode Island	R	I	250+	This Land Is Your Land	Compass Point Books
River, The	R	RF	250+	Paulsen, Gary	Dell
Road to Seneca Falls, The	R	B	250+	Swain, Gwenyth	Carolrhoda Books
Roald Dahl's Revolting Rhymes	R	F	250+	Dahl, Roald	Puffin Books
Robert Frost: New England Poet	R	B	250+	Leveled Readers Language Support	Houghton Mifflin
Rocks & Minerals	R	I	250+	The Wonders of our World	Crabtree
Roll On, Columbia	R	I	826	Independent Readers Social Studies	Houghton Mifflin
Rube Goldberg's Silly Machines	R	B	438	Independent Readers Science	Houghton Mifflin
Sadako and the Thousand Paper Cranes	R	HF	250+	Coerr, Eleanor	Bantam
San Domingo	R	I	250+	Henry, Marguerite	Scholastic
Sarah, Plain and Tall	R	HF	250+	MacLachlan, Patricia	HarperTrophy
Save the Everglades	R	I	250+	Stamper, Judith Bauer	Steck-Vaughn
Sea Star	R	RF	250+	Henry, Marguerite	Aladdin
Seeing with Heat	R	I	436	Independent Readers Science	Houghton Mifflin
Seminole, The	R	I	250+	First Reports	Compass Point Books
Seminole, The: Patchworkers of the Everglades	R	I	250+	America's First Peoples	Capstone Press
Shawnee, The	R	I	250+	First Reports	Compass Point Books
Shell-Flower and the Strangers	R	I	250+	Leveled Readers	Houghton Mifflin
Shiloh	R	RF	250+	Naylor, Phyllis Reynolds	Bantam
Shoes for Everyone: A Story About Jan Matzeliger	R	B	250+	Mitchell, Barbara	Carolrhoda Books
Shooting Stars	R	RF	250+	Costello, Emily	Dell
Sioux, The	R	I	250+	First Reports	Compass Point Books
Sioux, The: Nomadic Buffalo Hunters	R	I	250+	America's First Peoples	Capstone Press
Six Voyages of Pleasant Fieldmouse, The	R	F	250+	Wahl, Jan	Tom Doherty
Sixth-Grade Sleepover	R	RF	250+	Bunting, Eve	Scholastic
Skateboarding Greats: Champs of the Ramps	R	I	250+	Skateboarding	Red Brick Learning
Skateboarding History: From the Backyard to the Big Time	R	I	250+	Skateboarding	Red Brick Learning

* Collection of short stories

TITLE	LEVEL	GENRE	WORD COUNT	AUTHOR / SERIES	PUBLISHER / DISTRIBUTOR
Skateboards: Designs and Equipment	R	I	250+	Skateboarding	Red Brick Learning
Skateparks: Grab Your Skateboard	R	I	250+	Skateboarding	Red Brick Learning
Skylark	R	HF	250+	MacLachlan, Patricia	HarperTrophy
Snow Treasure	R	HF	250+	McSwigan, Marie	Scholastic
Soccer Stars, Best Friend Face-off	R	RF	250+	Costello, Emily	Dell
Solar Storms	R	I	250+	Rosen Real Readers	Rosen Publishing Group
Solid, Liquid, Gas: What Is Matter?	R	I	250+	Rosen Real Readers	Rosen Publishing Group
Some Friend	R	RF	250+	Warner, Sally	Alfred A. Knopf
Something for Everyone	R	RF	1371	Leveled Readers	Houghton Mifflin
Something Very Sorry	R	RF	250+	Bohlmeijer, Arno	Putnam & Grosset
Song of the Trees	R	HF	250+	Taylor, Mildred	Bantam
South Carolina	R	I	250+	This Land Is Your Land	Compass Point Books
South Dakota	R	I	250+	This Land Is Your Land	Compass Point Books
Space	R	I	250+	Worldwise	Grolier Press
Space Math	R	I	250+	Rosen Real Readers	Rosen Publishing Group
Spell Casters, Phoebe's Fortune	R	F	250+	Warriner, Holly	Aladdin
Spider Boy	R	RF	250+	Fletcher, Ralph	Bantam
Sports Heroes	R	I	250+	PM Nonfiction-Ruby	Rigby
Sports on Wheels	R	I	250+	PM Nonfiction-Ruby	Rigby
Sports Technology	R	I	250+	PM Nonfiction-Ruby	Rigby
Storm at Sea, A	R	HF	1145	Leveled Readers	Houghton Mifflin
Stormy, Misty's Foal	R	RF	250+	Henry, Marguerite	Aladdin
Story of Amy Johnson, The: Pioneering Woman Navigator	R	B	250+	Literacy 2000	Rigby
Story of Bunker's Cove	R	I	250+	Leveled Readers Language Support	Houghton Mifflin
Story of Thomas Alva Edison, Inventor, The	R	B	250+	Davidson, Margaret	Scholastic
Stray, The	R	RF	250+	King-Smith, Dick	Alfred A. Knopf
Strider	R	RF	250+	Cleary, Beverly	HarperCollins
Strike Fighters: The F/A-18E/F Super Hornets	R	I	250+	War Planes	Red Brick Learning
Stuart Little	R	F	250+	White, E. B.	HarperTrophy
Summer Switch	R	F	250+	Rodgers, Mary	HarperTrophy
Sun & Spoon	R	RF	250+	Henkes, Kevin	Penguin Group
Super Amos	R	RF	250+	Paulsen, Gary	Bantam
Surprising Swimmers: Nature's Most Amazing Animals	R	I	250+	Fredericks, Anthony D.	NorthWord Press
Survival!: Fire	R	HF	250+	Duey, Kathleen; Bale, Karen A.	Aladdin
Susan B. Anthony: Champion of Women's Rights	R	B	250+	Monsell, Helen Albee	Simon & Schuster
Switcharound	R	RF	250+	Lowry, Lois	Random House
Sydney - Where Biscuits Go Surfing	R	RF	250+	Coy, Michael	Scholastic
Taking Care of Yoki	R	RF	250+	Campbell, Barbara	HarperTrophy
Tasmanian Devils	R	I	250+	Morris, Rod	Pacific Learning
Tennessee	R	I	250+	This Land Is Your Land	Compass Point Books
Tennessee Summer	R	RF	2198	Leveled Readers	Houghton Mifflin
Texas	R	I	250+	This Land Is Your Land	Compass Point Books
There's a Frog in My Sleeping Bag	R	RF	250+	Clymer, Susan	Scholastic
There's a Hamster in My Lunchbox	R	RF	250+	Clymer, Susan	Scholastic
There's a Tarantula in My Homework	R	RF	250+	Clymer, Susan	Scholastic
There's No Place Like Home	R	I	250+	Hill, David	Pacific Learning
They Came From Center Field	R	RF	250+	Gutman, Dan	Scholastic
They Changed the World	R	I	250+	iOpeners	Pearson Learning Group
Thirteen	R	RF	250+	Ransom, Candice	Scholastic
This Place is Dry	R	I	250+	Cobb, Vicki	Walker & Company

* Collection of short stories

TITLE	LEVEL	GENRE	WORD COUNT	AUTHOR / SERIES	PUBLISHER / DISTRIBUTOR
This Place is Wet	R	I	250+	Cobb, Vicki	Walker & Company
Tiger Woods: An American Master	R	B	250+	Edwards, Nicholas	Scholastic
Till's Christmas	R	RF	250+	Thacker, Nola	Scholastic
Time Flies	R	I	250+	Literacy 2000	Rigby
Time Line of the American Revolution, A	R	I	250+	Rosen Real Readers	Rosen Publishing Group
Titanic Crossing	R	HF	250+	Williams, Barbara	Scholastic
Tomorrow's Wizard	R	F	250+	MacLachlan, Patricia	Scholastic
Too Much Magic	R	F	250+	Sterman, Betsy & Samuel	HarperTrophy
Tornado!	R	RF	1470	Leveled Readers Social Studies	Houghton Mifflin
Tournament Trouble	R	RF	250+	Costello, Emily	Dell
Triffic the Extraordinary Pig	R	F	250+	King-Smith, Dick	Bantam
Troquois, The: Longhouse Builders	R	I	250+	America's First Peoples	Capstone Press
Trouble with Tuck, The	R	RF	250+	Taylor, Theodore	Avon
Trumpet of the Swan, The	R	F	250+	White, E. B.	Scholastic
Turn Up the Radio	R	I	795	Independent Readers Social Studies	Houghton Mifflin
Tutankhamen's Gift	R	I	250+	Sabuda, Robert	Simon & Schuster
TV Kid, The	R	RF	250+	Byars, Betsy	Puffin Books
Twisters and Other Terrible Storms	R	I	250+	Osborne, Will; Osborne, Mary Pope	Random House
Twisting Up a Storm	R	I	250+	Duksta, Cheryl	Pacific Learning
Under the Bright Lights	R	I	466	Vocabulary Readers	Houghton Mifflin
United Nations, The	R	I	250+	Rigby Focus	Rigby
Upstate Autumn	R	RF	1676	Leveled Readers	Houghton Mifflin
Urban Wildlife	R	I	1212	Leveled Readers	Houghton Mifflin
Utah	R	I	250+	This Land Is Your Land	Compass Point Books
Vermont	R	I	250+	This Land Is Your Land	Compass Point Books
Virginia	R	I	250+	This Land Is Your Land	Compass Point Books
Voice of the Pioneer: Carrie Chapman Catt	R	B	1916	Leveled Readers Social Studies	Houghton Mifflin
Voyage of the Fram, The	R	I	611	Vocabulary Readers	Houghton Mifflin
W.E.B. DuBois and the Fight for a Just Society	R	B	904	Leveled Readers Social Studies	Houghton Mifflin
Wake Up, Young Soldier	R	I	864	Independent Readers Social Studies	Houghton Mifflin
Walking For Freedom: The Montgomery Bus Boycott	R	I	250+	Kelso, Richard	Steck-Vaughn
Washington	R	I	250+	This Land Is Your Land	Compass Point Books
Washington, D.C.	R	I	250+	This Land Is Your Land	Compass Point Books
Way West, The: Journal of a Pioneer Woman	R	B	250+	Knight, Amelia Stewart	Simon & Schuster
We Want Jobs!: A Story of the Great Depression	R	I	250+	Norrell, Robert J.	Steck-Vaughn
Weather Words and What They Mean	R	I	250+	Gibbons, Gail	Scholastic
Week of the Jellyhoppers, The	R	F	250+	Literacy 2000	Rigby
Weird Walkers	R	I	250+	Fredericks, Anthony D.	NorthWord Press
West Side Kids: Don't Call Me Slob-o	R	RF	250+	Orgel, Doris	Hyperion
West Side Kids: The Big Idea	R	RF	250+	Schecter, Ellen	Hyperion
West Side Kids: The Pet Sitters	R	RF	250+	Schecter, Ellen	Hyperion
West Virginia	R	I	250+	This Land Is Your Land	Compass Point Books
What Can You Do with an Elephant House?	R	I	250+	Gaynor, Miriam; Goodwin, A.	Pacific Learning
What Is the U.S. Constitution?	R	I	250+	Rosen Real Readers	Rosen Publishing Group
What Were Castles For?	R	I	250+	Usborne Starting Point History	EDC Publishing
When the Circus Came to Town	R	RF	250+	Horvath, Polly	Sunburst
When the Water Closes Over My Head	R	RF	250+	Napoli, Donna	Puffin Books
Where Are the Wolves?	R	I	250+	Motil, Rebecca	Scholastic
Where Was Patrick Henry on the 29th of May?	R	B	250+	Fritz, Jean	Scholastic
Whipping Boy, The	R	F	250+	Fleischman, Sid	Troll Associates

* Collection of short stories

TITLE	LEVEL	GENRE	WORD COUNT	AUTHOR / SERIES	PUBLISHER / DISTRIBUTOR
White Dragon: Anna Allen in the Face of Danger	R	I	1253	Leveled Readers	Houghton Mifflin
White-Tailed Deer, The	R	I	250+	Zwaschka, Michael	Red Brick Learning
Who Were the First People?	R	I	250+	Usborne Starting Point History	EDC Publishing
Who Were the Romans?	R	I	250+	Usborne Starting Point History	EDC Publishing
Who Were the Vikings?	R	I	250+	Usborne Starting Point History	EDC Publishing
Who's That Stepping on Plymouth Rock?	R	I	250+	Fritz, Jean	Putnam & Grosset
Why Don't You Get a Horse, Sam Adams?	R	B	250+	Fritz, Jean	G.P. Putnam's Sons
Wild Horses	R	I	250+	Action Packs	Rigby
William Bradford and Plymouth: A Colony Grows	R	I	250+	The Library of the Pilgrims	Rosen Publishing Group
Wind, Water and Ice	R	I	1829	Independent Readers Science	Houghton Mifflin
Wisconsin	R	I	250+	This Land Is Your Land	Compass Point Books
Witches, The	R	F	250+	Dahl, Roald	Penguin Group
Women Pioneers of Medicine	R	B	2018	Leveled Readers Science	Houghton Mifflin
Woods, Irons, and Greens	R	I	250+	Wildcats	Wright Group/McGraw Hill
World of Imagination, A	R	I	250+	Literacy 2000	Rigby
Wyoming	R	I	250+	This Land Is Your Land	Compass Point Books
Year in Antartica, A	R	I	250+	iOpeners	Pearson Learning Group
Yellowstone, Our First National Park	R	I	1288	Leveled Readers Social Studies	Houghton Mifflin
Your Move, J. P.!	R	RF	250+	Lowry, Lois	Random House
Zachary's Ride	R	HF	1780	Leveled Readers	Houghton Mifflin
Zeely	R	RF	250+	Hamilton, Virginia	Macmillan
Zuni, The	R	I	250+	First Reports	Compass Point Books
15 Facts about Atoms	S	I	654	Independent Readers Science	Houghton Mifflin
Abraham Lincoln	S	B	250+	Parin d'Aulaire, Ingri & Edgar	Bantam
Afternoon of the Elves	S	F	250+	Lisle, Janet Taylor	Scholastic
Ahyoka and the Talking Leaves	S	HF	250+	Roop, Peter & Connie	Beech Tree Books
Ajeemah and his Son	S	HF	250+	Berry, James	HarperTrophy
Alabama	S	I	250+	Land of Liberty	Red Brick Learning
Alaska	S	I	250+	Land of Liberty	Red Brick Learning
Alice's Diary, Living With Diabetes	S	I	250+	Gibson, Marie	Pacific Learning
All Alone in the Universe	S	RF	250+	Perkins, Lynne Rae	Greenwillow
*Altogether, One at a Time	S	RF	250+	Konigsburg, E. L.	Simon & Schuster
Amazing Impossible Erie Canal, The	S	I	250+	Harness, Cheryl	Simon & Schuster
Amazing Skyscrapers	S	I	2047	Independent Readers Social Studies	Houghton Mifflin
Amelia Earhart: Challenging the Skies	S	B	250+	Sloate, Susan	Fawcett Columbine
Amelia Earhart: Courage in the Sky	S	B	250+	Kerby, Mona	Puffin Books
Amelia Earhart: Flying for Adventure	S	B	250+	Wade, Mary Dodson	The Millbrook Press
America's First Traitor: Benedict Arnold Betrays the Colonies	S	I	250+	Headlines from History	Rosen Publishing Group
Ancient Greece	S	I	250+	Journey Into Civilization	Chelsea House
Animals of Alaska	S	I	517	Vocabulary Readers	Houghton Mifflin
Animated Illusions	S	I	250+	Sunshine	Wright Group/McGraw Hill
Anne Frank	S	B	250+	Epstein, Rachel	Franklin Watts
Ants Aren't Antisocial	S	I	250+	Action Packs	Rigby
Apache, The: Nomadic Hunters of the Southwest	S	I	250+	American Indian Nations	Capstone Press
Arapaho, The: Hunters of the Great Plains	S	I	250+	American Indian Nations	Capstone Press
Arizona	S	I	250+	Land of Liberty	Red Brick Learning
Arkansas	S	I	250+	Land of Liberty	Red Brick Learning
Asli's Story	S	I	250+	Jansen, Adrienne	Pacific Learning
Awake and Dreaming	S	F	250+	Person, Kit	Puffin Books
Baby-Sitter Burglaries, The	S	RF	250+	Keene, Carolyn	Pocket Books

TITLE	LEVEL	GENRE	WORD COUNT	AUTHOR / SERIES	PUBLISHER / DISTRIBUTOR
Back To The Day Lincoln Was Shot!	S	I	250+	Gormley, Beatrice	Scholastic
Back To The Titanic!	S	F	250+	Gormley, Beatrice	Scholastic
Barefoot: Escape on the Underground Railroad	S	HF	250+	Edwards, Pamela Duncan	HarperTrophy
Baseball for Fun	S	I	250+	Sports for Fun	Compass Point Books
Basket of Beethoven	S	RF	250+	Currie, Susan	Fitzhenry & Whiteside
Basketball for Fun	S	I	250+	Sports for Fun	Compass Point Books
Bat-Poet, The	S	F	250+	Jarrell, Randall	HarperCollins
Bats: The Amazing Upside-Downers	S	I	250+	A First Book	Franklin Watts
Beating Diabetes	S	I	250+	Orbit Double Takes	Pacific Learning
Beautiful Land: A Story of the Oklahoma Land Rush	S	I	250+	Antle, Nancy	Penguin Group
Beethoven Lives Upstairs	S	I	250+	Nichol, Barbara	Orchard Books
Bell, the Book, and the Spellbinder, The	S	F	250+	Strickland, Brad	Puffin Books
Ben and Me	S	HF	250+	Lawson, Robert	Little, Brown & Co.
Bicycle Patrol Officers	S	I	250+	Law Enforcement	Capstone Press
Birds of Prey	S	I	250+	Peterson Field Guides	Houghton Mifflin
Bird-Watching	S	I	250+	iOpeners	Pearson Learning Group
Bite of the Gold Bug, The: A Story of the Alaskan Gold Rush	S	I	250+	DeClements, Barthe	Penguin Group
Blackfeet, The: People of the Dark Moccasins	S	I	250+	American Indian Nations	Capstone Press
Blister	S	RF	250+	Shreve, Susan	Scholastic
Blizzard	S	HF	250+	Duey, Kathleen	Simon & Schuster
BMX Racing	S	I	250+	X-Sports	Capstone Press
Bomb Detection Squads	S	I	250+	Law Enforcement	Capstone Press
Boomtowns of the West	S	I	250+	Kalman, Bobbie	Crabtree
Borrowers, The	S	F	250+	Norton, Mary	Harcourt Trade
Boston Massacre, The: Five Colonists Killed by British Soldiers	S	I	250+	Headlines from History	Rosen Publishing Group
Boston Tea Party, The: Angry Colonists Dump British Tea	S	I	250+	Headlines from History	Rosen Publishing Group
Boy Called Slow, A	S	B	250+	Bruchac, Joseph	Putnam & Grosset
Boys Against Girls	S	RF	250+	Naylor, Phyllis Reynolds	Bantam
Boys Start the War and the Girls Get Even, The	S	RF	250+	Naylor, Phyllis Reynolds	Bantam
Boy's Will, A	S	HF	250+	Haugaard, Erik Christian	Houghton Mifflin
Brave Irene	S	F	250+	Steig, William	Farrar, Straus and Giroux
Breakfast Around the World	S	I	1894	Leveled Readers Social Studies	Houghton Mifflin
Broccoli Tapes, The	S	RF	250+	Slepian, Jan	Scholastic
Building Bridges	S	I	250+	Navigators Science Series	Benchmark Education
Bunker's Cove	S	I	1125	Leveled Readers	Houghton Mifflin
Cajun Country	S	I	2013	Leveled Readers Social Studies	Houghton Mifflin
Caleb's Choice	S	HF	250+	Wisler, Clifton G.	Penguin Group
Calico Captive	S	HF	250+	Speare, Elizabeth George	Yearling
California	S	I	250+	Land of Liberty	Red Brick Learning
Canoeing	S	I	250+	The Great Outdoors	Red Brick Learning
Cartoonist, The	S	RF	250+	Byars, Betsy	Puffin Books
Case of Capital Intrigue, The	S	RF	250+	Keene, Carolyn	Pocket Books
Case of the Captured Queen	S	RF	250+	Keene, Carolyn	Pocket Books
Case of the Dangerous Solution, The	S	RF	250+	Keene, Carolyn	Pocket Books
Case of the Floating Crime, The	S	RF	250+	Keene, Carolyn	Pocket Books
Case of the Missing Cutthroats, The	S	RF	250+	George, Jean Craighead	HarperTrophy
Case of the Twin Teddy Bears, The	S	RF	250+	Keene, Carolyn	Pocket Books
Cassidy's Magic	S	F	250+	Literacy 2000	Rigby
Cat Who Went To Heaven, The	S	F	250+	Coatsworth, Elizabeth	Aladdin
Cat!	S	I	250+	Kroll, Virginia L.	Dawn

* Collection of short stories

TITLE	LEVEL	GENRE	WORD COUNT	AUTHOR / SERIES	PUBLISHER / DISTRIBUTOR
Change The Locks	S	RF	250+	French, Simon	Scholastic
Changing Seasons	S	I	1936	Leveled Readers Science	Houghton Mifflin
Changing the Rules	S	RF	1908	Leveled Readers	Houghton Mifflin
Cheerleading for Fun!	S	I	250+	Activities for Fun	Compass Point Books
Chester Cricket's New Home	S	F	250+	Selden, George	Bantam
Chester Cricket's Pigeon Ride	S	F	250+	Selden, George	Bantam
Children of Clay: A Family of Pueblo Potters	S	I	250+	Swentzell, Rina	Lerner Publishing
Children of the Longhouse	S	HF	250+	Bruchac, Joseph	Penguin Group
Children's Clothing of the 1800's	S	I	250+	Historic Communities	Crabtree
Chimpanzees	S	I	1605	Leveled Readers Science	Houghton Mifflin
China's Huang River	S	I	2036	Independent Readers Social Studies	Houghton Mifflin
Chocolate-Covered Contest, The	S	RF	250+	Keene, Carolyn	Pocket Books
Clue of the Gold Doubloons, The	S	RF	250+	Keene, Carolyn	Pocket Books
Colin Powell: Straight to the Top	S	B	250+	Blue, Rose; Naden, Corinne J.	The Millbrook Press
Colorado	S	I	250+	Land of Liberty	Red Brick Learning
Comets, Asteroids, and Meteoroids	S	I	250+	Our Solar System	Compass Point Books
Connecticut	S	I	250+	Land of Liberty	Red Brick Learning
Cookcamp, The	S	RF	250+	Paulsen, Gary	Bantam
Cowboy Trade, The	S	I	250+	Rounds, Glen	Holiday House
Crazy Horse	S	I	515	Vocabulary Readers	Houghton Mifflin
Creatures of the Reef	S	I	250+	Belcher, Angie	Pacific Learning
Creek, The: Farmers of the Southeast	S	I	250+	American Indian Nations	Capstone Press
Cricket in Times Square, The	S	F	250+	Selden, George	Bantam
Crime At the Chat Café	S	RF	250+	Keene, Carolyn	Pocket Books
Crime for Christmas, A	S	RF	250+	Keene, Carolyn	Pocket Books
Crime in the Queen's Court	S	RF	250+	Keene, Carolyn	Pocket Books
Crocodilians: Reminders of the Age of Dinosaurs	S	I	250+	A First Book	Franklin Watts
Cry of the Crow, The	S	RF	250+	George, Jean Craighead	HarperTrophy
Cuauhtemoc, the Last Aztec Ruler	S	B	1598	Leveled Readers Social Studies	Houghton Mifflin
Cumberland Gap, The	S	I	1262	Leveled Readers Social Studies	Houghton Mifflin
Customs Service	S	I	250+	Law Enforcement	Capstone Press
Cyberspace	S	SF	250+	Wildcats	Wright Group/McGraw Hill
Cybil War, The	S	RF	250+	Byars, Betsy	Scholastic
Dance for Fun!	S	I	250+	Activities for Fun	Compass Point Books
Daughters of Liberty	S	B	1620	Independent Readers Social Studies	Houghton Mifflin
Day in the Life of a Colonial Cabinetmaker, A	S	I	250+	The Library of Living and Working in Colonial Times	Rosen Publishing Group
Day in the Life of a Colonial Dressmaker, A	S	I	250+	The Library of Living and Working in Colonial Times	Rosen Publishing Group
Day in the Life of a Colonial Glassblower, A	S	I	250+	The Library of Living and Working in Colonial Times	Rosen Publishing Group
Day in the Life of a Colonial Sea Captain, A	S	I	250+	The Library of Living and Working in Colonial Times	Rosen Publishing Group
Day in the Life of a Colonial Soldier, A	S	I	250+	The Library of Living and Working in Colonial Times	Rosen Publishing Group
Day in the Life of a Colonial Surveyor, A	S	I	250+	The Library of Living and Working in Colonial Times	Rosen Publishing Group
Day It Rained Forever, The: A Story of the Johnstown Flood	S	I	250+	Gross, Virginia T.	Penguin Group
Dead Letter	S	RF	250+	Byars, Betsy	Puffin Books
Death Valley	S	HF	250+	Duey, Kathleen; Bale, Karen A.	Simon & Schuster
Deborah Sampson: Soldier of the Revolution	S	B	1207	Leveled Readers	Houghton Mifflin

TITLE	LEVEL	GENRE	WORD COUNT	AUTHOR / SERIES	PUBLISHER / DISTRIBUTOR
Delaware	S	I	250+	Land of Liberty	Red Brick Learning
Diary of a Hurricane	S	RF	3402	Leveled Readers Science	Houghton Mifflin
Disappearing Acts	S	RF	250+	Byars, Betsy	Puffin Books
Discovering the Past	S	I	250+	Literacy 2000	Rigby
Discovery of the Americas, The	S	I	250+	Maestro, Betsy & Giulio	William Morrow
Divers of the Deep Sea	S	I	250+	Windows on Literacy	National Geographic
Do Tornadoes Really Twist?	S	I	250+	Berger, Melvin	Scholastic
Dollhouse Murders, The	S	RF	250+	Wright, Betty Ren	Scholastic
*Don't Split the Pole: Tales of Down-Home Folk Wisdom	S	RF	250+	Tate, Eleanora E.	Bantam
Dr. Charles Drew and the Blood Banks	S	B	1515	Independent Readers Science	Houghton Mifflin
Drummer Boy, The	S	I	1164	Leveled Readers	Houghton Mifflin
Eagle Song	S	RF	250+	Bruchac, Joseph	Puffin Books
Earth	S	I	250+	Our Solar System	Compass Point Books
Earthquake	S	HF	250+	Duey, Kathleen; Bale, Karen A.	Simon & Schuster
Earthquake!	S	HF	2376	Leveled Readers	Houghton Mifflin
Earthquake!	S	I	2075	Leveled Readers Science	Houghton Mifflin
Earthquake!: A Story of Old San Francisco	S	I	250+	Kudlinski, Kathleen V.	Penguin Group
Eenie, Meanie, Murphy, NO!	S	RF	250+	McKenna, Colleen O'Shaughnessy	Scholastic
Eleanor	S	B	250+	Cooney, Barbara	Puffin Books
Endurance: Shackleton's Antarctic Expedition	S	I	250+	Marriott, Janice	Pacific Learning
Extinct	S	I	2101	Leveled Readers Science	Houghton Mifflin
Facing West: A Story of the Oregon Trail	S	I	250+	Kudlinski, Kathleen V.	Penguin Group
Facts and Fun About the Presidents	S	I	250+	Sullivan, George	Scholastic
Faith's Journey	S	HF	1263	Leveled Readers	Houghton Mifflin
Family Tree	S	RF	250+	Ayres, Katherine	Bantam
Favorite Medieval Tales	S	TL	250+	Pope, Mary Osborne	Scholastic
Fear of White Water	S	RF	250+	Leveled Readers Language Support	Houghton Mifflin
Fifth Grade: Here Comes Trouble	S	RF	250+	McKenna, Colleen O'Shaughnessy	Scholastic
Figure in the Shadows, The	S	F	250+	Bellairs, John	Penguin Group
Finding Buck McHenry	S	RF	250+	Slote, Alfred	Scholastic
Fire	S	HF	250+	Duey, Kathleen; Bale, Karen A.	Simon & Schuster
Fire Bug Connection, The	S	RF	250+	George, Jean Craighead	HarperTrophy
First-Aid Handbook	S	I	250+	iOpeners	Pearson Learning Group
Flood	S	HF	250+	Duey, Kathleen; Bale, Karen A.	Simon & Schuster
Florida	S	I	250+	Land of Liberty	Red Brick Learning
Fly Away, Children	S	I	548	Vocabulary Readers	Houghton Mifflin
Flying Flea, Callie, and Me, The	S	F	250+	Wallace, Carol & Bill	Pocket Books
Flying Solo	S	RF	250+	Fletcher, Ralph	Bantam
Football for Fun	S	I	250+	Sports for Fun	Compass Point Books
Fountains of Life: The Story of Deep-Sea Vents	S	I	250+	A First Book	Franklin Watts
Four Seasons, The	S	I	1820	Leveled Readers Science	Houghton Mifflin
Freshwater Giants: Hippopatamus, River Dolphins, and Manatees	S	I	250+	Perry, Phyllis J.	Franklin Watts
Freshwater Seas: The Great Lakes	S	I	1905	Independent Readers Social Studies	Houghton Mifflin
Friendship and the Gold Cadillac, The	S	HF	250+	Taylor, Mildred	Bantam
Friendship, The	S	HF	250+	Taylor, Mildred	Puffin Books
From Barbadoes to Brooklyn: The Story of Shirley Chisholm	S	B	2374	Leveled Readers Social Studies	Houghton Mifflin
From Idea to Law: The Legislative Process	S	I	1625	Leveled Readers Social Studies	Houghton Mifflin
From the Mixed-up Files of Mrs. Basil E. Frankweiler	S	RF	250+	Konigsburg, E. L.	Bantam

* Collection of short stories

TITLE	LEVEL	GENRE	WORD COUNT	AUTHOR / SERIES	PUBLISHER / DISTRIBUTOR
Fun Facts About Fossils	S	I	1129	Leveled Readers Science	Houghton Mifflin
*Future-Telling Lady and Other Stories, The	S	RF	250+	Berry, James	HarperTrophy
George Washington Elected: How America's First President Was Chosen	S	I	250+	Headlines from History	Rosen Publishing Group
Georgia	S	I	250+	Land of Liberty	Red Brick Learning
Ghostmobile, The	S	F	250+	Tapp, Kathy Kennedy	Scholastic
Gift of the Pirate Queen, The	S	RF	250+	Giff, Patricia Reilly	Yearling
Gift-Giver, The	S	RF	250+	Hansen, Joyce	Houghton Mifflin
Glory Girl, The	S	RF	250+	Byars, Betsy	Penguin Group
Glow from Lighthouse Cove, The	S	RF	2501	Leveled Readers	Houghton Mifflin
Going West: Trials and Tradeoffs	S	I	2572	Independent Readers Social Studies	Houghton Mifflin
Gold Cadillac, The	S	HF	250+	Taylor, Mildred D.	Puffin Books
Gold Dust Letters, The	S	RF	250+	Lisle, Janet Taylor	Avon Camelot
Golf for Fun!	S	I	250+	Sports for Fun	Compass Point Books
Good Dog, The	S	F	250+	Avi	Simon & Schuster
Good Master, The	S	RF	250+	Seredy, Kate	Scholastic
Good-Bye My Wishing Star	S	RF	250+	Grove, Vicki	Scholastic
Grand Escape, The	S	F	250+	Naylor, Phyllis Reynolds	Bantam
Great Apes, The	S	I	250+	A First Book	Franklin Watts
Great Dimpole Oak, The	S	RF	250+	Lisle, Janet Taylor	Puffin Books
Great Expectations	S	HF	250+	Bullseye Step Into Classics	Random House
Great Gilly Hopkins, The	S	RF	250+	Paterson, Katherine	Hearst
Great Pyramid, The	S	I	250+	Windows on Literacy	National Geographic
Guinea Pigs	S	I	250+	Hansen, Elvig	Carolrhoda Books
Harry and Chicken	S	F	250+	Sheldon, Dyan	Candlewick Press
Harry On Vacation	S	SF	250+	Sheldon, Dyan	Candlewick Press
Harry the Explorer	S	F	250+	Sheldon, Dyan	Candlewick Press
Hawaii	S	I	250+	Land of Liberty	Red Brick Learning
Head Full of Notions, A: A Story about Robert Fulton	S	B	250+	Russell Bowen, Andy	Carolrhoda Books
Helping the Hoiho	S	I	250+	Literacy 2000	Rigby
Heros and Heroines	S	I	250+	Literacy 2000	Rigby
*Hey World, Here I Am!	S	RF	250+	Little, Jean	HarperTrophy
Hillary Rodham Clinton: A New Kind of First Lady	S	B	250+	Guernsey, JoAnn Bren	Lerner Publishing
Hiram Fong, Hawaii's First Senator	S	B	1726	Leveled Readers Social Studies	Houghton Mifflin
Hiroshima	S	HF	250+	Yep, Laurence	Scholastic
History of Electricity, A	S	I	794	Leveled Readers Science	Houghton Mifflin
History of the Blues, The	S	I	250+	Rosen Real Readers	Rosen Publishing Group
Hockey for Fun!	S	I	250+	Sports for Fun	Compass Point Books
Home for the Howl-idays	S	F	250+	Regan, Diane Curtis	Scholastic
Homegirl on the Range (Sister Sister)	S	RF	250+	Quin-Harkin, Janet	Pocket Books
Horseback Riding for Fun!	S	I	250+	Activities for Fun	Compass Point Books
House in the Snow, The	S	RF	250+	Engh, M. J.	Scholastic
House with a Clock in its Walls, The	S	F	250+	Bellairs, John	Penguin Group
How I Met Einstein: A Character Comes to Life	S	I	250+	Trussell-Cullen, Alan	Pacific Learning
How Many Days to America?: A Thanksgiving Story	S	I	250+	Bunting, Eve	Houghton Mifflin
Humpback Whale, The	S	I	250+	Frahm, Randy	Red Brick Learning
Hunting with My Camera	S	I	250+	Literacy 2000	Rigby
Hurricane	S	HF	250+	Duey, Kathleen; Bale, Karen A.	Simon & Schuster
Hyrax of Top-Knot Island, The	S	I	1762	Leveled Readers	Houghton Mifflin
I Am the Ice Worm	S	F	250+	Easley, Mary Ann	Yearling

* Collection of short stories

TITLE	LEVEL	GENRE	WORD COUNT	AUTHOR / SERIES	PUBLISHER / DISTRIBUTOR
I Care: American Reformers	S	I	914	Independent Readers Social Studies	Houghton Mifflin
I Double Dare You	S	RF	1910	Leveled Readers	Houghton Mifflin
I Was a Sixth Grade Alien	S	F	250+	Coville, Bruce	Pocket Books
Ice Fishing	S	I	250+	The Great Outdoors	Red Brick Learning
Ida Lewis and the Lighthouse	S	I	973	Leveled Readers	Houghton Mifflin
Idaho	S	I	250+	Land of Liberty	Red Brick Learning
Illinois	S	I	250+	Land of Liberty	Red Brick Learning
In Search of the Great Bears	S	I	250+	Literacy 2000	Rigby
In the Shade of the Nispero Tree	S	HF	250+	Bernier-Grand, Carmen T.	Orchard Books
In the Year of the Boar and Jackie Robinson	S	HF	250+	Lord, Bette Bao	HarperTrophy
Indiana	S	I	250+	Land of Liberty	Red Brick Learning
Inside a Cell	S	I	1651	Leveled Readers Science	Houghton Mifflin
Iowa	S	I	250+	Land of Liberty	Red Brick Learning
It's Not Easy Being George	S	RF	250+	Smith, Janice Lee	HarperTrophy
It's the Fashion	S	I	250+	Literacy 2000	Rigby
Jackie Robinson and the Breaking of the Color Barrier	S	B	250+	Shorto, Russell	Millbrook Press
Jean Craighead George	S	B	250+	Cary, Alice	Learning Works, The
John Adams	S	B	250+	Photo-Illustrated Biographies	Red Brick Learning
Journey	S	RF	250+	MacLachlan, Patricia	Yearling
Journey Home, The	S	RF	250+	Holland, Isabelle	Scholastic
Journey to a Free Town	S	HF	1747	Leveled Readers	Houghton Mifflin
Journey to Jo'burg	S	HF	250+	Naidoo, Beverly	HarperTrophy
Journey to the New World	S	HF	250+	Action Packs	Rigby
Jupiter	S	I	250+	Our Solar System	Compass Point Books
Kansas	S	I	250+	Land of Liberty	Red Brick Learning
Katherine Paterson	S	B	250+	Cary, Alice	Learning Works, The
Kentucky	S	I	250+	Land of Liberty	Red Brick Learning
Kickboxing	S	I	250+	X-Sports	Capstone Press
Killer Bees	S	I	250+	Blau, Melinda	Steck-Vaughn
Klondike Gold Rush, The	S	I	250+	A First Book	Franklin Watts
Knee Knock Rise	S	F	250+	Babbitt, Natalie	Farrar, Straus and Giroux
Lamp from the Warlock's Tomb, The	S	F	250+	Bellairs, John	Puffin Books
*Legends	S	TL	250+	Goodman, R.; Pierce, R.; Wagner, Betty Jane	Houghton Mifflin
Leonardo da Vinci	S	B	250+	Masterpieces: Artists and Their Works	Capstone Press
Let's Graph It!	S	I	250+	Rosen Real Readers	Rosen Publishing Group
Letter, the Witch, and the Ring, The	S	F	250+	Bellairs, John	Penguin Group
Letters from Rifka	S	HF	250+	Hesse, Karen	Puffin Books
Letters from the Sea	S	I	250+	Voyages in Time	Wright Group/McGraw Hill
Lewis & Clark: Explorers of the American West	S	I	250+	Kroll, Steven	Holiday House
Lewis and Clark's Voyage of Discovery	S	I	250+	The Library of the Westward Expansion	Rosen Publishing Group
Lightning	S	I	1110	Leveled Readers	Houghton Mifflin
Lights On!	S	I	1450	Independent Readers Science	Houghton Mifflin
Lily's Crossing	S	HF	250+	Giff, Patricia Reilly	Delacorte
*Little Boy with Three Names and Other Short Stories	S	TL	250+	Clark, Ann Nolan	Kiva Publishing
Living in Hard Times	S	I	594	Vocabulary Readers	Houghton Mifflin
Living Rain Forest, The	S	I	250+	Bishop, Nic	Pacific Learning
Loch Ness Monster Mystery, The	S	I	250+	Literacy 2000	Rigby

* Collection of short stories

TITLE	LEVEL	GENRE	WORD COUNT	AUTHOR / SERIES	PUBLISHER / DISTRIBUTOR
Lon Po Po: A Red-Riding Hood Story from China	S	TL	250+	Young, Ed	Scholastic
Look at Minerals, A: From Galena to Gold	S	I	250+	A First Book	Franklin Watts
Look at Rocks, A: From Coal to Kimerlite	S	I	250+	A First Book	Franklin Watts
Louisiana	S	I	250+	Land of Liberty	Red Brick Learning
Love Me, Love My Broccoli	S	RF	250+	Peters, Julie Anne	Avon Camelot
Luis Alvarez	S	B	871	Leveled Readers Science	Houghton Mifflin
Luis Rodriguez	S	B	250+	Schwartz, Michael	Steck-Vaughn
Maine	S	I	250+	Land of Liberty	Red Brick Learning
Making Flavors and Fragrances	S	I	2032	Leveled Readers Science	Houghton Mifflin
Man From The Sky	S	RF	250+	Avi	Beech Tree Books
Man Who Kept His Heart in a Bucket, The	S	TL	250+	Levitin, Sonia	Penguin Group
Mansion in the Mist, The	S	F	250+	Bellairs, John	Puffin Books
Marian Wright Edelman: For Every Child	S	B	2406	Leveled Readers	Houghton Mifflin
Marie Curie	S	B	1924	Independent Readers Science	Houghton Mifflin
Mars	S	I	250+	Our Solar System	Compass Point Books
Mars, Our Closest Neighbor	S	I	1366	Leveled Readers Science	Houghton Mifflin
Martial Arts for Fun!	S	I	250+	Activities for Fun	Compass Point Books
Mary Cassatt	S	B	250+	Masterpieces: Artists and Their Works	Capstone Press
Mary McLeod Bethune - Voice of Black Hope	S	B	250+	Meltzer, Milton	Puffin Books
Maryland	S	I	250+	Land of Liberty	Red Brick Learning
Massachusetts	S	I	250+	Land of Liberty	Red Brick Learning
Matchbox, The	S	HF	250+	Literacy 2000	Rigby
Matilda	S	F	250+	Dahl, Roald	Penguin Group
Matisse	S	B	250+	Masterpieces: Artists and Their Works	Capstone Press
Maya, The	S	I	250+	Journey Into Civilization	Chelsea House
Me, Mop, and the Moondance Kid	S	RF	250+	Myers, Walter Dean	Bantam
Mercury	S	I	250+	Our Solar System	Compass Point Books
Message to the World, A	S	I	813	Vocabulary Readers	Houghton Mifflin
Mia Hamm, Journey of a Soccer Champion	S	B	1730	Leveled Readers	Houghton Mifflin
Michelangelo	S	B	250+	Masterpieces: Artists and Their Works	Red Brick Learning
Michigan	S	I	250+	Land of Liberty	Red Brick Learning
Mina's Spring of Colors	S	RF	250+	Gilmore, Rachna	Fitzhenry & Whiteside
Missing 'Gator of Gumbo Limbo, The	S	RF	250+	George, Jean Craighead	HarperTrophy
Mississippi Bridge	S	HF	250+	Taylor, Mildred	Bantam
Monet	S	B	250+	Masterpieces: Artists and Their Works	Red Brick Learning
Mongols, The	S	I	250+	Journey Into Civilization	Chelsea House
Monster of the Year	S	F	250+	Coville, Bruce	Pocket Books
Moon	S	I	250+	Our Solar System	Compass Point Books
More Perfect Union: The Story of Our Constitution	S	I	250+	Maestro, Betsy & Giulio	William Morrow
Morning Girl	S	HF	250+	Dorris, Michael	Hyperion
Motorcycle Police	S	I	250+	Law Enforcement	Capstone Press
Mountain Men of the West	S	I	250+	The Library of the Westward Expansion	Rosen Publishing Group
Mountains	S	I	250+	Weitzman, David	Steck-Vaughn
Mounted Police	S	I	250+	Law Enforcement	Capstone Press
*Mr. President: A Book of U.S. Presidents	S	B	250+	Sullivan, George	Scholastic
Mt. St. Helens	S	I	1492	Independent Readers Science	Houghton Mifflin
My Brother is a Superhero	S	RF	250+	Sheldon, Dyan	Candlewick Press

* Collection of short stories

TITLE	LEVEL	GENRE	WORD COUNT	AUTHOR / SERIES	PUBLISHER / DISTRIBUTOR
My Brother is a Visitor From Another Planet	S	RF	250+	Sheldon, Dyan	Candlewick Press
My Life in Dog Years	S	B	250+	Paulsen, Gary	Bantam
My Sister Annie	S	RF	250+	Dodds, Bill	Boyds Mills Press
My Teacher Flunked the Planet	S	F	250+	Coville, Bruce	Pocket Books
My Teacher Fried My Brains	S	F	250+	Coville, Bruce	Pocket Books
My Teacher Glows in the Dark	S	F	250+	Coville, Bruce	Pocket Books
My Teacher Is an Alien	S	F	250+	Coville, Bruce	Pocket Books
*Myths	S	TL	250+	Goodman, Ronald; Pierce, Robert; Wagner, Betty Jane	Houghton Mifflin
Nation of Nations, A	S	HF	1931	Leveled Readers Social Studies	Houghton Mifflin
National Parks	S	I	250+	iOpeners	Pearson Learning Group
Navajo Longwalk	S	HF	250+	Armstrong, Nancy M.	Scholastic
Necklace of Raindrops and Other Stories, A	S	TL	250+	Aiken, Joan	Random House
Neptune	S	I	250+	Our Solar System	Compass Point Books
Never Turn Back: Father Serra's Mission	S	B	250+	Rawls, Jim	Steck-Vaughn
New Mexico	S	I	250+	Thompson, Kathleen	Steck-Vaughn
New York	S	I	250+	Land of Liberty	Red Brick Learning
New York	S	I	250+	Thompson, Kathleen	Steck-Vaughn
Night Swimmers, The	S	RF	250+	Byars, Betsy	Dell
Night Without Stars, A	S	RF	250+	Howe, James	Aladdin
North Carolina	S	I	250+	Portrait of America	Steck-Vaughn
Off and Running	S	RF	250+	Soto, Gary	Dell
Ohio	S	I	250+	Land of Liberty	Red Brick Learning
Ohio	S	I	250+	Thompson, Kathleen	Steck-Vaughn
Old Meadow, The	S	F	250+	Selden, George	Farrar, Straus and Giroux
Olympic Champions	S	I	250+	iOpeners	Pearson Learning Group
On My Honor	S	RF	250+	Bauer, Marion Dane	Bantam
On Site	S	I	250+	Pollock, John	Mondo
On the Air	S	I	250+	Wonder World	Wright Group/McGraw Hill
On the Edge	S	I	250+	Action Packs	Rigby
On the Move	S	I	250+	Sunshine	Wright Group/McGraw Hill
On the Way Home	S	HF	250+	Wilder, Laura Ingalls	HarperCollins
Once on this Island	S	HF	250+	Whelan, Gloria	HarperTrophy
One Day in the Tropical Rain Forest	S	I	250+	George, Jean Craighead	HarperTrophy
One Giant Leap	S	I	250+	Fraser, Mary Ann	Henry Holt & Co.
One-Eyed Cat	S	RF	250+	Fox, Paula	Bantam
Oregon Trail, The	S	I	250+	The Library of the Westward Expansion	Rosen Publishing Group
Orphan of Ellis Island, The	S	HF	250+	Woodruff, Elvira	Scholastic
Orphan Train Journey	S	HF	1247	Leveled Readers	Houghton Mifflin
Out of Darkness: The Story of Louis Braille	S	B	250+	Freedman, Russell	Houghton Mifflin
Paul Laurence Dunbar, Poet	S	B	542	Vocabulary Readers	Houghton Mifflin
Paul Revere's Ride	S	HF	250+	Literacy 2000	Rigby
Pheasant Hunting	S	I	250+	The Great Outdoors	Red Brick Learning
Picasso	S	B	250+	Masterpieces: Artists and Their Works	Red Brick Learning
Pinballs, The	S	RF	250+	Byars, Betsy	HarperTrophy
Plant That Ate Dirty Socks Goes Up in Space	S	F	250+	McArthur, Nancy	Avon Camelot
Playing with Words	S	I	250+	Action Packs	Rigby
Pluto	S	I	250+	Our Solar System	Compass Point Books
Polar Bear, The	S	I	250+	Hemstock, Annie	Red Brick Learning
Poppy	S	F	250+	Avi	Avon
Poppy and Rye	S	F	250+	Avi	Avon

* Collection of short stories

TITLE	LEVEL	GENRE	WORD COUNT	AUTHOR / SERIES	PUBLISHER / DISTRIBUTOR
Powhatan, The: A Confederacy of Native American Tribes	S	I	250+	American Indian Nations	Capstone Press
Powwow Summer: A Family Celebrates the Circle of Life	S	I	250+	Rendon, Marcie R.	Carolrhoda Books
Puppies, Dogs, and Blue Northers	S	I	250+	Paulsen, Gary	Delacorte
Pyramids of Egypt, The	S	I	250+	Rosen Real Readers	Rosen Publishing Group
Quarters for Everyone	S	RF	1798	Leveled Readers	Houghton Mifflin
Quest for California's Gold, The	S	I	250+	The Library of the Westward Expansion	Rosen Publishing Group
Rain Forests	S	I	250+	The Heinle Reading Library	Thomson Learning
Rairarubia	S	F	250+	Adams, W. Royce	Lost Coast Press
Red Means Good Fortune: A Story of San Francisco's Chinatown	S	I	250+	Goldin, Barbara Diamond	Penguin Group
Red Planet, The	S	I	250+	Orbit Double Takes	Pacific Learning
Rembrandt	S	B	250+	Masterpieces: Artists and Their Works	Capstone Press
Rescuers, The	S	F	250+	Sharp, Margery	Dell
Riddles of the Universe	S	I	250+	Bonallack, John	Pacific Learning
Riding Out the Storm	S	RF	1426	Leveled Readers	Houghton Mifflin
Robbie Hood, Hurricane Hunter	S	B	1150	Independent Readers Science	Houghton Mifflin
Robots	S	I	250+	iOpeners	Pearson Learning Group
Rocky Mountain Fur Trade, The	S	I	250+	The Library of the Westward Expansion	Rosen Publishing Group
Rough-Face Girl, The	S	TL	250+	Martin, Rafe; Shannon, David	Scholastic
Rubber Inventor: The Story of Charles Goodyear	S	B	912	Independent Readers Science	Houghton Mifflin
Sahara Special	S	RF	250+	Codell, Esme Raji	Hyperion
Samuel's Choice	S	HF	250+	Berleth, Richard	Scholastic
Saturn	S	I	250+	Our Solar System	Compass Point Books
Save Our Earth	S	I	250+	iOpeners	Pearson Learning Group
Saving Sea Turtles	S	I	1483	Leveled Readers	Houghton Mifflin
Seabirds	S	I	250+	A First Book	Franklin Watts
Secret of Kiribu Tapu Lagoon, The	S	I	250+	Literacy 2000	Rigby
Seventh Grade Weirdo	S	RF	250+	Wardlaw, Lee	Scholastic
Shell-Flower	S	I	1761	Leveled Readers	Houghton Mifflin
Sheriffs and Deputy Sheriffs	S	I	250+	Law Enforcement	Capstone Press
Should There Be Zoos?: A Persuasive Text	S	I	250+	Bookshop	Mondo
*Sideways Arithmetic from Wayside School	S	I	250+	Sachar, Louis	Scholastic
Sixth Grade Can Really Kill You	S	RF	250+	DeClements, Barthe	Scholastic
Sixth Grade Secrets	S	RF	250+	Sachar, Louis	Scholastic
Skeletons Inside and Out	S	I	250+	iOpeners	Pearson Learning Group
Smartest Man in Ireland, The	S	F	250+	Hunter, Mollie	OSI
Smoky the Cow Horse	S	RF	250+	James, Will	Scholastic
Snakes!: Deadly Predators or Harmless Pets?	S	I	250+	High Five Reading	Red Brick Learning
Snowboarding for Fun!	S	I	250+	Sports for Fun	Compass Point Books
Snowmobiling	S	I	250+	The Great Outdoors	Red Brick Learning
Soccer for Fun	S	I	250+	Sports for Fun	Compass Point Books
Song of the Mantis, The	S	I	250+	Literacy 2000	Rigby
Southern Sounds	S	I	2194	Independent Readers Social Studies	Houghton Mifflin
Space Exploration	S	I	250+	Our Solar System	Compass Point Books
Spirit Quest	S	RF	250+	Sharpe, Susan	Scholastic
Sports Skills	S	I	250+	Sunshine	Wright Group/McGraw Hill
Star Fisher, The	S	RF	250+	Yep, Lawrence	Scholastic

TITLE	LEVEL	GENRE	WORD COUNT	AUTHOR / SERIES	PUBLISHER / DISTRIBUTOR
Start of the American Revolutionary War, The: Paul Revere Rides at Midnight	S	I	250+	Headlines from History	Rosen Publishing Group
Starting a Business	S	I	596	Vocabulary Readers	Houghton Mifflin
Story of Harriet Tubman, The: Conductor of the Underground Railroad	S	B	250+	McMullan, Kate	Scholastic
Story of Muhammad Ali: Heavyweight Champion of the World, The	S	B	250+	Denenberg, Barry	Dell
Story of Pluto, The	S	I	2306	Leveled Readers Science	Houghton Mifflin
Story of the White House, The	S	I	250+	Waters, Kate	Scholastic
Sugaring Season (Making Maple Syrup)	S	I	250+	Burns, Diane	Carolrhoda Books
Sugaring Time	S	I	250+	Lasky, Kathryn	Macmillan
Sun	S	I	250+	Our Solar System	Compass Point Books
Surrender at Yorktown	S	I	600	Leveled Readers Social Studies	Houghton Mifflin
Survival!: Cave In	S	HF	250+	Duey, Kathleen; Bale, Karen A.	Simon & Schuster
SWAT Teams	S	I	250+	Law Enforcement	Capstone Press
Sweet Clara and the Freedom Quilt	S	HF	250+	Hopkinson, Deborah	Scholastic
Swimming for Fun	S	I	250+	Sports for Fun	Compass Point Books
*Sword of the Samurai: Adventure Stories From Japan	S	HF	250+	Kimmel, Eric A.	HarperCollins
Taking Care of Terrific	S	RF	250+	Lowry, Lois	Dell
Taking Sides	S	RF	250+	Soto, Gary	Harcourt Trade
*Tales from the Homeplace: Adventures of a Texas Farm Girl	S	RF	250+	Burandt, Harriet; Dale, Shelley	Bantam
*Tales from the Underground Railroad	S	HF	250+	Connell, Kate	Steck-Vaughn
Talking to Faith Ringgold	S	B	250+	Ringgold, Faith; Freeman, Linda; Roucher, Nancy	Crown
Taste of Blackberries, A	S	RF	250+	Smith, Doris Buchanan	Scholastic
Team Player, The	S	RF	1115	Leveled Readers	Houghton Mifflin
Texas	S	I	250+	Land of Liberty	Red Brick Learning
This Can't Be Happening at Macdonald Hall	S	RF	250+	Korman, Gordon	Scholastic
Thunder At Gettysburg	S	I	250+	Gauch, Patricia Lee	Bantam
Time for Andrew	S	F	250+	Hahn, Mary	Avon Camelot
Timeline of Electricity	S	I	948	Leveled Readers Science	Houghton Mifflin
Timothy Whuffenpuffen-Whippersnapper	S	F	250+	Literacy 2000	Rigby
Titanic	S	HF	250+	Duey, Kathleen; Bale, Karen A.	Simon & Schuster
To Fly with the Swallows: A Story of Old California	S	I	250+	deRuiz, Dana Catharine	Steck-Vaughn
To the Moon and Beyond	S	I	250+	Lott, Linda	Wright Group/McGraw Hill
Tomb of Nebamun, The	S	I	250+	Cambridge Reading	Pearson Learning Group
Too Soon to Say Goodbye	S	RF	250+	Kent, Deborah	Scholastic
Trail Home, The	S	RF	2004	Leveled Readers	Houghton Mifflin
Train Wreck	S	HF	250+	Duey, Kathleen; Bale, Karen A.	Simon & Schuster
Transcontinental Railroad, The	S	I	250+	The Library of the Westward Expansion	Rosen Publishing Group
Transforming Trash	S	I	250+	Quinn, Pat	Pacific Learning
Travels with Rainie Marie	S	B	250+	Martin, Patricia	Hyperion
Treasure of Alpheus Winterborn, The	S	F	250+	Bellairs, John	Penguin Group
*Treasury of Pirate Stories, A	S	F	250+	Bradman, Tony	Kingfisher
Trees and Leaves	S	I	250+	Nature Club	Troll Associates
Trouble River	S	HF	250+	Byars, Betsy	Scholastic
True Confessions	S	RF	250+	Tashjian, Janet	Scholastic
Turtles	S	I	250+	A First Book	Franklin Watts
Twinkie Squad, The	S	RF	250+	Korman, Gordon	Scholastic
Twits, The	S	F	250+	Dahl, Roald	Penguin Group

* Collection of short stories

TITLE	LEVEL	GENRE	WORD COUNT	AUTHOR / SERIES	PUBLISHER / DISTRIBUTOR
Two Tickets to Freedom: The True Story of Ellen and William Craft	S	HF	250+	Freedman, Florence	Scholastic
Ultimate Field Trip 1: Adventures in the Amazon Rain Forest	S	I	250+	Goodman, Susan E.	Simon & Schuster
United States Marshals Service	S	I	250+	Law Enforcement	Capstone Press
Uranus	S	I	250+	Our Solar System	Compass Point Books
Us and Uncle Fraud	S	RF	250+	Lowry, Lois	Houghton Mifflin
Van Gogh	S	B	250+	Masterpieces: Artists and Their Works	Red Brick Learning
Van Gogh Cafe, The	S	RF	250+	Rylant, Cynthia	Harcourt School Publishers
Venus	S	I	250+	Our Solar System	Compass Point Books
Vikings, The	S	I	250+	Journey Into Civilization	Chelsea House
Volcanoes National Park	S	I	1396	Leveled Readers Science	Houghton Mifflin
Voyage Across the Pacific	S	I	1250	Leveled Readers	Houghton Mifflin
Voyage of the Frog, The	S	RF	250+	Paulsen, Gary	Bantam
Wampanoag, The: The People of the First Light	S	I	250+	American Indian Nations	Capstone Press
*War Dog Heroes: True Stories of Dog Courage in Wartime	S	I	250+	Sanderson, Jeannette	Scholastic
War of 1812, The	S	I	250+	A First Book	Franklin Watts
War With Grandpa, The	S	RF	250+	Smith, Robert Kimmel	Bantam
Whale! Nantucket Whaling Days	S	I	2363	Independent Readers Social Studies	Houghton Mifflin
What a Pant!	S	I	250+	Sunshine	Wright Group/McGraw Hill
What Hearts	S	RF	250+	Brooks, Bruce	Language for Learning Assoc.
What in the World is the World Wide Web?	S	I	250+	Quinn, Pat	Pacific Learning
Where Do You Think You're Going, Christopher Columbus?	S	B	250+	Fritz, Jean	Putnam & Grosset
Which Witch?	S	F	250+	Ibbotson, Eva	Puffin Books
Who Will Look Out for Danny?	S	RF	250+	Action Packs	Rigby
William Problem, The	S	RF	250+	Baker, Barbara	Puffin Books
Windmills	S	I	783	Independent Readers Science	Houghton Mifflin
*Witch of Fourth Street, The	S	HF	250+	Levoy, Myron	Language for Learning Assoc.
Wolf, The	S	I	250+	Dahl, Michael	Red Brick Learning
Wonderful Sky Boat, The: And Other Native American Tales of the Southeast	S	TL	250+	Curry, Jane Louise	Simon & Schuster
Wreck Trek	S	I	250+	Belcher, Angie	Pacific Learning
Zeros and Ones	S	I	250+	Wildcats	Wright Group/McGraw Hill
52 Days by Camel: My Sahara Adventure	T	I	250+	Raskin, Lawrie	Annick Press
Abel's Island	T	F	250+	Steig, William	Farrar, Straus and Giroux
About The B'nai Bagels	T	RF	250+	Konigsburg, E. L.	Dell
Abraham's Battle: A Novel of Gettysburg	T	HF	250+	Banks, Sara Harrell	Atheneum
Addie's Dakota Winter	T	RF	250+	Lawlor, Laurie	Pocket Books
Admiral Perry	T	B	2451	Independent Readers Social Studies	Houghton Mifflin
Aircraft Carriers	T	I	250+	Land and Sea	Capstone Press
Alas My Albatross is Molting	T	I	250+	Literacy 2000	Rigby
Alex Rodriguez	T	B	250+	Sports Heroes	Red Brick Learning
Almost Home	T	RF	250+	Baskin, Nora Raleigh	Little, Brown & Co.
Amaze Us!	T	I	250+	Wildcats	Wright Group/McGraw Hill
Amazing Rocks	T	I	1894	Leveled Readers Science	Houghton Mifflin
American Revolution, The	T	I	250+	Bliven, Bruce, Jr.	Random House
Amphibious Ships	T	I	250+	Land and Sea	Capstone Press

* Collection of short stories

TITLE	LEVEL	GENRE	WORD COUNT	AUTHOR / SERIES	PUBLISHER / DISTRIBUTOR
Angel for Solomon Singer, An	T	RF	250+	Rylant, Cynthia	Orchard Books
*Angels and Other Strangers	T	RF	250+	Paterson, Katherine	HarperTrophy
Animal Dazzlers: The Role of Brilliant Colors in Nature	T	I	250+	Collard, Sneed B.	Franklin Watts
Antarctica	T	I	250+	Literacy 2000	Rigby
Arctic Investigations: Exploring the Frozen Ocean	T	I	250+	Young, Karen Romano	Steck-Vaughn
Are You There, God? It's Me, Margaret.	T	RF	250+	Blume, Judy	Bantam
Avi	T	B	250+	Markham, Lois	Learning Works, The
Baby	T	RF	250+	MacLachlan, Patricia	Language for Learning Assoc.
Ballad of the Civil War, A	T	HF	250+	Stolz, Mary	HarperTrophy
Bambi: A Life in the Woods	T	F	250+	Salten, Felix	Aladdin
Barn, The	T	RF	250+	Avi	Avon
Battles of Lexington & Concord, The	T	I	250+	We The People	Compass Point Books
Battleships	T	I	250+	Land and Sea	Capstone Press
Bear Called Paddington, A	T	F	250+	Bond, Michael	Bantam
Bears' House, The	T	RF	250+	Sachs, Marilyn	Puffin Books
Becoming A Real Hero	T	B	1650	Leveled Readers	Houghton Mifflin
Becoming Joe DiMaggio	T	HF	250+	Testa, Maria	Candlewick Press
Behind Rebel Lines	T	HF	250+	Reit, Seymour	Harcourt Trade
Best Bad Thing, The	T	RF	250+	Uchida, Yoshiko	Aladdin
Better Brown Stories, The	T	F	250+	Ahlberg, Allan	Penguin Group
Better Life, A	T	RF	1066	Independent Readers Social Studies	Houghton Mifflin
Bicentennial Gift, The	T	RF	1906	Leveled Readers	Houghton Mifflin
Big Lie, The: A True Story	T	B	250+	Leitner, Isabella	Scholastic
Birchbark House, The	T	HF	250+	Erdrich, Louise	Hyperion
Black Stallion, The	T	RF	250+	Farley, Walter	Language for Learning Assoc.
Blackwater Swamp	T	RF	250+	Wallace, Bill	Language for Learning Assoc.
Blowing in the Wind	T	I	250+	Literacy 2000	Rigby
Blubber	T	RF	250+	Blume, Judy	Bantam
Bonanza Girl	T	RF	250+	Beatty, Patricia	Scholastic
*Book of Monsters: Tales to Give You the Creeps	T	F	250+	Coville, Bruce	Scholastic
*Book of Spine Tinglers: Tales To Make You Shiver	T	F	250+	Coville, Bruce	Scholastic
Boston Tea Party, The	T	I	250+	We The People	Compass Point Books
Boston Tea Party: Rebellion in the Colonies	T	I	250+	Adventures in Colonial America	Troll Associates
Boy	T	B	250+	Dahl, Roald	Puffin Books
Boy and the Elk Dogs, The	T	TL	1688	Leveled Readers	Houghton Mifflin
Breath of Air, A	T	I	1356	Leveled Readers Science	Houghton Mifflin
Bridge to Terabithia	T	RF	250+	Paterson, Katherine	HarperTrophy
Bright Shadow	T	F	250+	Avi	Aladdin
Brinker's Isle	T	RF	2475	Leveled Readers	Houghton Mifflin
Broken Blade, The	T	HF	250+	Durbin, William	Yearling
Buck Stops Here, The	T	I	250+	Provensen, Alice	OSI
Bud, Not Buddy	T	RF	250+	Curtis, Christopher Paul	Random House
Built for Speed Aircraft	T	I	250+	Graham, Ian	Steck-Vaughn
California	T	I	250+	Sea To Shining Sea	Children's Press
California Gold Rush, The	T	I	250+	McNeer, May	Random House
California Gold Rush, The	T	I	250+	We The People	Compass Point Books
Camels: Ships of the Desert	T	I	667	Vocabulary Readers	Houghton Mifflin

* Collection of short stories

TITLE	LEVEL	GENRE	WORD COUNT	AUTHOR / SERIES	PUBLISHER / DISTRIBUTOR
Canada Celebrates Multiculturalism	T	I	250+	Kalman, Bobbie	Crabtree
Canada: The Culture	T	I	250+	Kalman, Bobbie	Crabtree
Canada: The Land	T	I	250+	Kalman, Bobbie	Crabtree
Canada: The People	T	I	250+	Kalman, Bobbie	Crabtree
Carolina Crow Girl	T	F	250+	Hobbs, Valerie	Puffin Books
Cassie Binegar	T	RF	250+	MacLachlan, Patricia	HarperTrophy
Catching Some Respect	T	RF	3009	Leveled Readers	Houghton Mifflin
Charting Your Course	T	I	250+	iOpeners	Pearson Learning Group
Children of Green Knowe, The	T	F	250+	Boston, L. M.	Harcourt Trade
Child's Day, A	T	I	250+	Historic Communities	Crabtree
China: The Culture	T	I	250+	Kalman, Bobbie	Crabtree
China: The Land	T	I	250+	Kalman, Bobbie	Crabtree
China: The People	T	I	250+	Kalman, Bobbie	Crabtree
China's Amazing Buildings	T	I	498	Vocabulary Readers	Houghton Mifflin
Citizens of the World	T	I	2642	Independent Readers Social Studies	Houghton Mifflin
Cleopatra	T	B	250+	Stanley, Diane; Vennema, Peter	Mulberry Books
Clothes & Crafts in Ancient Egypt	T	I	250+	Balkwill, Richard	Dillon Press
Clothes & Crafts in Ancient Greece	T	I	250+	Steele, Philip	Dillon Press
Clothes & Crafts in Aztec Times	T	I	250+	Dawson, Imogen	Dillon Press
Clothes & Crafts in Roman Times	T	I	250+	Steele, Philip	Dillon Press
Clothes & Crafts in the Middle Ages	T	I	250+	Dawson, Imogen	Dillon Press
Clothes & Crafts in Victorian Times	T	I	250+	Steele, Philip	Dillon Press
Cold As Ice	T	RF	250+	Keene, Carolyn	Pocket Books
Colonial Crafts	T	I	250+	Historic Communities	Crabtree
Colonial Life	T	I	250+	Historic Communities	Crabtree
Colonial Times from A to Z	T	I	250+	Kalman, Bobbie	Crabtree
Colonial Town, A: Williamsburg	T	I	250+	Historic Communities	Crabtree
Colony of Massachusetts, The	T	I	250+	The Library of the Thirteen Colonies and The Lost Colony	Rosen Publishing Group
Colony of New York, The	T	I	250+	The Library of the Thirteen Colonies and The Lost Colony	Rosen Publishing Group
Colony of Pennsylvania, The	T	I	250+	The Library of the Thirteen Colonies and The Lost Colony	Rosen Publishing Group
Colony of Virginia, The	T	I	250+	The Library of the Thirteen Colonies and The Lost Colony	Rosen Publishing Group
Colorado	T	I	250+	Sea To Shining Sea	Children's Press
Connecticut	T	I	250+	Sea To Shining Sea	Children's Press
Constitutional Convention, The	T	I	1267	Leveled Readers Social Studies	Houghton Mifflin
Corvettes	T	I	250+	Gronvall, Kal	Red Brick Learning
Cousins	T	RF	250+	Hamilton, Virginia	Language for Learning Assoc.
Cowboys	T	I	250+	Sandler, Martin W.	HarperTrophy
Cracker Jackson	T	RF	250+	Byars, Betsy	Puffin Books
Cranberries: Fruit of the Bogs	T	I	250+	Burns, Diane L.	Carolrhoda Books
Crazy Fish	T	RF	250+	Mazer, Norma Fox	Avon
Crossing Borders Stories of Immigrants	T	I	250+	iOpeners	Pearson Learning Group
Cruisers	T	I	250+	Land and Sea	Capstone Press
Cuckoo's Sacrifice, The: A Tale From the Yucatán	T	F	1900	Leveled Readers	Houghton Mifflin
Current in Your Home, The	T	I	554	Leveled Readers Science	Houghton Mifflin
*Cut From the Same Cloth: American Women of Myth, Legend, and Tall Tale	T	TL	250+	San Souci, Robert D.	Puffin Books
Dancing Around the World	T	I	250+	iOpeners	Pearson Learning Group

TITLE	LEVEL	GENRE	WORD COUNT	AUTHOR / SERIES	PUBLISHER / DISTRIBUTOR
Dancing in the Cadillac Light	T	HF	250+	Holt, Kimberly Willis	G.P. Putnam's Sons
Danger on Parade	T	RF	250+	Keene, Carolyn	Pocket Books
Danny, Champion of the World	T	RF	250+	Dahl, Roald	Language for Learning Assoc.
Darby	T	HF	250+	Fuqua, Jonathon Scott	Candlewick Press
Day the Earth Shook, The	T	I	1889	Leveled Readers Science	Houghton Mifflin
Dear Levi: Letters from the Overland Trail	T	HF	250+	Woodruff, Elvira	Alfred A. Knopf
Declaration of Independence, The	T	I	250+	We The People	Compass Point Books
Defenders, The	T	B	250+	McGovern, Ann	Language for Learning Assoc.
Delaware	T	I	250+	Hello U.S.A.	Lerner Publishing
Delaware	T	I	250+	Sea to Shining Sea	Children's Press
Destroyers	T	I	250+	Land and Sea	Capstone Press
Devil's Highway, The	T	HF	250+	Applegate, Stan	Peachtree
Discovering Jupiter: The Amazing Collision in Space	T	I	250+	Berger, Melvin	Scholastic
Dolley Madison: First Lady	T	B	250+	Let Freedom Ring	Capstone Press
Don't Bug Me!	T	RF	2224	Leveled Readers	Houghton Mifflin
Doodler, The	T	RF	2012	Leveled Readers	Houghton Mifflin
Dorothea Dix: Social Reformer	T	B	250+	Let Freedom Ring	Capstone Press
Dove Isabeau	T	F	250+	Yolen, Jane	OSI
Dr. Quinn, Medicine Woman	T	B	250+	McKenna, Colleen O'Shaughnessy	Language for Learning Assoc.
Dragon in the Ghetto Caper, The	T	RF	250+	Konigsburg, E. L.	Aladdin
*Dragon King's Palace, The	T	TL	250+	Literacy 2000	Rigby
Dragsters	T	I	250+	The World's Fastest	Red Brick Learning
Driving on Mars	T	I	936	Leveled Readers	Houghton Mifflin
DuSable - Chicago's First Citizen	T	B	1522	Leveled Readers Social Studies	Houghton Mifflin
Early Winter, An	T	RF	250+	Bauer, Marion Dane	Houghton Mifflin
Earthquakes	T	I	250+	Simon, Seymour	Mulberry Books
Eclipses: Nature's Blackouts	T	I	250+	Aronson, Billy	Franklin Watts
Election Connection	T	I	250+	Ring, Susan	Chronicle Books
Eli Whitney: American Inventor	T	B	250+	Let Freedom Ring	Capstone Press
Emma Rides on the Erie Canal	T	HF	1904	Leveled Readers	Houghton Mifflin
Empire Builders	T	I	250+	Rigby Focus	Rigby
Endurance: Shipwreck and Survival on a Sea of Ice	T	I	250+	High Five Reading	Red Brick Learning
Eureka! It's an Airplane	T	I	250+	Bendick, Jeanne	Scholastic
Eureka! It's Television!	T	I	250+	Bendick, Jeanne & Robert	Scholastic
Everglades	T	I	250+	George, Jean Craighead	HarperTrophy
Everybody Dances	T	I	250+	Literacy 2000	Rigby
Exploration and Conquest: The Americas After Columbus, 1500-1620	T	I	250+	Maestro, Betsy & Giulio	William Morrow
*Explorers: Women in Profile	T	B	250+	Hacker, Carolotta	Crabtree
*Fabulous Spotted Egg, The	T	TL	250+	Literacy 2000	Rigby
Ferret In The Bedroom, Lizards In The Fridge	T	RF	250+	Wallace, Bill	Language for learning Assoc.
Find Out About It!	T	I	250+	iOpeners	Pearson Learning Group
First Woman Doctor, The	T	B	250+	Rachel Baker	Scholastic
Flaming Arrows	T	HF	250+	Steele, William O.	Harcourt Trade
Flavors and Fragrances	T	I	1987	Leveled Readers Science	Houghton Mifflin
*Flying Free: America's First Black Aviators	T	B	250+	Hart, Philip S.	Lerner Publishing
Follow That Fin!: Studying Dolphin Behavior	T	I	250+	Samuels, Amy	Steck-Vaughn
Food & Feasts Between the Two World Wars	T	I	250+	Steele, Philip	Dillon Press
Food & Feasts In Ancient Egypt	T	I	250+	Balkwill, Richard	Dillon Press

* Collection of short stories

TITLE	LEVEL	GENRE	WORD COUNT	AUTHOR / SERIES	PUBLISHER / DISTRIBUTOR
Food & Feasts In Ancient Greece	T	I	250+	Steele, Philip	Dillon Press
Food & Feasts In Ancient Rome	T	I	250+	Steele, Philip	Dillon Press
Food & Feasts In the Middle Ages	T	I	250+	Dawson, Imogen	Dillon Press
Food & Feasts In Tudor Times	T	I	250+	Balkwill, Richard	Dillon Press
Food & Feasts With the Aztecs	T	I	250+	Dawson, Imogen	Dillon Press
Food & Feasts With the Vikings	T	I	250+	Martell, Hazel	Dillon Press
Forest Fires: Run for Your Life!	T	I	250+	Bookshop	Mondo
Forest's Life, A: From Meadow to Mature Woodland	T	I	250+	A First Book	Franklin Watts
Forgotten Door, The	T	SF	250+	Key, Alexander	Language for Learning Assoc.
Fort Life	T	I	250+	Historic Communities	Crabtree
Francis Scott Key: Patriotic Poet	T	B	250+	Let Freedom Ring	Capstone Press
Freedom Songs	T	HF	250+	Moore, Yvette	Language for Learning Assoc.
Freedom Train	T	B	250+	Sterling, Dorothy	Scholastic
Freshwater Pond, A	T	I	250+	Small Worlds	Crabtree
Friends, The	T	RF	250+	Yumoto, Kazumi	Yearling
Frozen Man	T	I	250+	Getz, David	Henry Holt & Co.
Fur, Feathers, and Flippers: How Animals Live Where They Do	T	I	250+	Lauber, Patricia	Scholastic
Galaxies	T	I	250+	Simon, Seymour	Mulberry Books
Games from Long Ago	T	I	250+	Historic Communities	Crabtree
Gentleman Outlaw and Me - Eli, The: A Story of the Old West	T	HF	250+	Hahn, Mary Downing	Avon Camelot
Geographic Information Systems: Locating Ourselves	T	I	1493	Leveled Readers Social Studies	Houghton Mifflin
George Washington's Socks	T	B	250+	Woodruff, Elvira	Language for Learning Assoc.
Georgia	T	I	250+	Sea to Shining Sea	Children's Press
Georgia	T	I	250+	LaDoux, Rita C.	Lerner Publishing
Gettysburg Address, The	T	I	250+	Lincoln, Abraham	Houghton Mifflin
Ghost Cadet	T	SF	250+	Alphin, Elaine Marie	Language for Learning Assoc.
Girl Who Chased Away Sorrow, The: The Diary of Sarah Nita, a Navajo Girl	T	HF	250+	Turner, Ann	Scholastic
Glaciers	T	I	250+	Gallant, Roy A.	Franklin Watts
Go Away, Tooth Decay	T	I	250+	Leveled Readers Language Support	Houghton Mifflin
Going Home	T	RF	250+	Mohr, Nicholas	Penguin Group
Going Solo	T	B	250+	Dahl, Roald	Puffin Books
Going Solo	T	I	250+	iOpeners	Pearson Learning Group
Going the Distance	T	RF	1626	Leveled Readers	Houghton Mifflin
Good-Bye Marianne	T	B	250+	Watts, Irene N.	Tundra Books
Goosebumps: It Came From Beneath the Sink	T	F	250+	Stine, R. L.	Language for Learning Assoc.
Gorillas	T	I	250+	Burgel, Paul H.; Hartwig, M.	Carolrhoda Books
Grand Trees of America: Our State and Champion Trees	T	I	250+	Jorgenson, Lisa	Roberts Rinehart
Grandma Moses: Painter of Rural America	T	B	250+	O'Neal, Zibby	Penguin Group
Grandpa's Mountain	T	RF	250+	Reeder, Carolyn	Avon Camelot
Grandpa's Rail Tales	T	F	1730	Leveled Readers	Houghton Mifflin
Gratefully Yours	T	HF	250+	Buchanan, Jane	Puffin Books

* Collection of short stories

TITLE	LEVEL	GENRE	WORD COUNT	AUTHOR / SERIES	PUBLISHER / DISTRIBUTOR
Gravity: Simple Experiments for Young Scientists	T	I	250+	White, Larry	Millbrook Press
*Great African Americans in Business	T	B	250+	Rediger, Pat	Crabtree
*Great African Americans in Civil Rights	T	B	250+	Rediger, Pat	Crabtree
*Great African Americans in Entertainment	T	B	250+	Rediger, Pat	Crabtree
*Great African Americans in Film	T	B	250+	Parker, Janice	Crabtree
*Great African Americans in Government	T	B	250+	Dudley, Karen	Crabtree
*Great African Americans in History	T	B	250+	Hacker, Carlotta	Crabtree
*Great African Americans in Jazz	T	B	250+	Hacker, Carlotta	Crabtree
*Great African Americans in Literature	T	B	250+	Rediger, Pat	Crabtree
*Great African Americans in Music	T	B	250+	Rediger, Pat	Crabtree
*Great African Americans in Sports	T	B	250+	Rediger, Pat	Crabtree
*Great African Americans in the Arts	T	B	250+	Hacker, Carlotta	Crabtree
*Great African Americans in the Olympics	T	B	250+	Hunter, Shaun	Crabtree
Great Brain at the Academy, The	T	RF	250+	Fitzgerald, John D.	Yearling
Great Brain Does It Again, The	T	RF	250+	Fitzgerald, John D.	Yearling
Great Brain Reforms, The	T	RF	250+	Fitzgerald, John D.	Yearling
Great Brain, The	T	RF	250+	Fitzgerald, John D.	Language for Learning Assoc.
Great Explorations	T	HF	250+	Neufeld, David	Scholastic
Gristmill, The	T	I	250+	Historic Communities	Crabtree
*Growing Up Stories	T	RF	250+	Byars, Betsy	Kingfisher
Guests	T	HF	250+	Dorris, Michael	Hyperion
Hamster of the Baskervilles, The: A Chet Gecko Mystery	T	F	250+	Hale, Bruce	Harcourt Trade
Hannibal	T	B	250+	Green, Robert	Franklin Watts
Harlem Globetrotters, The: Clown Princes of Basketball	T	I	250+	High Five Reading	Red Brick Learning
Harriet the Spy	T	RF	250+	Fitzhugh, Louise	HarperCollins
Hawaii	T	I	250+	Sea to Shining Sea	Children's Press
Haymeadow, The	T	RF	250+	Paulsen, Gary	Dell
Helicopters	T	I	250+	The World's Fastest	Red Brick Learning
Help with the Herd	T	RF	1830	Leveled Readers	Houghton Mifflin
Henri Rousseau	T	B	250+	Rabott, Ernest	HarperTrophy
Henry	T	RF	250+	Bawden, Nina	Bantam
Hercules and Other Greek Legends	T	TL	250+	Wildcats	Wright Group/McGraw Hill
Here's to You, Rachel Robinson	T	RF	250+	Blume, Judy	Bantam
High-Water Heroes	T	RF	2242	Leveled Readers	Houghton Mifflin
Hispaniola: Island of Two Nations	T	I	1871	Independent Readers Social Studies	Houghton Mifflin
Hoang Anh: A Vietnamese-American Boy	T	B	250+	Hoyt-Goldsmith, Diane	Scholastic
Home Crafts	T	I	250+	Historic Communities	Crabtree
Horse and His Boy, The	T	F	250+	Lewis, C. S.	Collier Books
Human Body Math	T	I	250+	Navigators Math Series	Benchmark Education
Hurricane Diary	T	RF	3392	Leveled Readers Science	Houghton Mifflin
Hurricanes	T	I	250+	iOpeners	Pearson Learning Group
Immigrants	T	I	250+	Sandler, Martin W.	HarperTrophy
Indy Cars	T	I	250+	The World's Fastest	Red Brick Learning
Into the Eye of a Hurricane	T	I	2712	Leveled Readers Science	Houghton Mifflin
Inventors	T	I	250+	Sandler, Martin W.	HarperTrophy
Iowa	T	I	250+	Sea to Shining Sea	Children's Press
Island Keeper	T	RF	250+	Mazer, Harry	Language for Learning Assoc.
Islander, The	T	F	250+	Rylant, Cynthia	Random House

* Collection of short stories

TITLE	LEVEL	GENRE	WORD COUNT	AUTHOR / SERIES	PUBLISHER / DISTRIBUTOR
It's Electric!	T	I	250+	Rosen Real Readers	Rosen Publishing Group
It's Not the End of the World	T	RF	250+	Blume, Judy	Dell
Jamestown Colony, The	T	I	250+	We The People	Compass Point Books
Jamestown: New World Adventure	T	I	250+	Adventures in Colonial America	Troll Associates
Jan Matzeliger, Inventor	T	B	1916	Leveled Readers Science	Houghton Mifflin
Jason's Gold	T	HF	250+	Hobbs, Will	William Morrow
Jazz Man, The	T	RF	250+	Weik, Mary Hays	Simon & Schuster
Jericho	T	RF	250+	Hickman, Janet	Hearst
Joey Pigza Loses Control	T	RF	250+	Gantos, Jack	Farrar, Straus and Giroux
Joey Pigza Swallowed the Key	T	RF	250+	Gantos, Jack	HarperTrophy
Journey to Ellis Island: How My Father Came to America	T	B	250+	Bierman, Carol	Scholastic
Journey to Mars	T	I	644	Vocabulary Readers	Houghton Mifflin
Journey to Nowhere	T	HF	250+	Auch, Mary Jane	Bantam
*Jump!: The Adventures of Brer Rabbit	T	TL	250+	Harris, Joel Chandler	OSI
Just As Long As We're Together	T	RF	250+	Blume, Judy	Bantam
Kalpana Chawla, Astronaut	T	B	250+	Independent Readers Science	Houghton Mifflin
Ken Griffey, Jr. & Ken Griffey, Sr.	T	B	250+	Star Families	Crestwood House
Kid Who Ran For President, The	T	RF	250+	Gutman, Dan	Language for Learning Assoc.
Kids at Work: Lewis Hine and the Crusade Against Child Labor	T	B	250+	Freedman, Russell	Clarion
Kitchen, The	T	I	250+	Historic Communities	Crabtree
Kobe Bryant	T	B	250+	Sports Heroes	Red Brick Learning
Lands of the Rainforest	T	I	1698	Leveled Readers Social Studies	Houghton Mifflin
Leonardo da Vinci	T	B	1776	Leveled Readers Science	Houghton Mifflin
Leon's Story	T	B	250+	Tillage, Leon Walter	Farrar, Straus and Giroux
Letters From a Mill Town	T	HF	1662	Leveled Readers Social Studies	Houghton Mifflin
Lewis and Clark	T	HF	250+	Sullivan, George	Scholastic
Lewis and Clark Expedition, The	T	I	250+	We The People	Compass Point Books
Life in the Ocean Depths	T	I	2165	Leveled Readers Science	Houghton Mifflin
Life in the Oceans: Animals, People, Plants	T	I	250+	Baker, Lucy	Scholastic
Life in the Rain Forests: Animals, People, Plants	T	I	250+	Baker, Lucy	Scholastic
Life of a Miner	T	I	250+	Life in the Old West	Crabtree
Life on a Plantation	T	I	250+	Historic Communities	Crabtree
Light in the Storm, A	T	HF	250+	Hesse, Karen	Scholastic
Lightning	T	I	250+	Kramer, Stephen	Carolrhoda Books
Lion, the Witch, and the Wardrobe, The	T	F	250+	Lewis, C. S.	HarperTrophy
Lizard Music	T	F	250+	Pinkwater, D. Manus	Bantam
Lois Lowry	T	B	250+	Markham, Lois	Learning Works, The
Long Ago and Far Away	T	I	250+	Wildcats	Wright Group/McGraw Hill
Lost Colony of Roanoke, The	T	I	1081	Leveled Readers Social Studies	Houghton Mifflin
Lost Star: The Story of Amelia Earhart	T	B	250+	Lauber, Patricia	Language for Learning Assoc.
Love That Dog	T	RF	250+	Creech, Sharon	HarperCollins
Magician's Nephew, The	T	F	250+	Lewis, C. S.	HarperTrophy
Magnet Book, The	T	I	250+	Levine, Shar; Johnstone, Leslie	Sterling
Man Who Was Poe, The	T	B	250+	Avi	Avon
Marrying Malcolm Murgatroyd	T	RF	250+	Farrell, Mame	Sunburst
Martin Luther King	T	B	250+	Bray, Rosemary L.	William Morrow
Math to Munch On	T	I	250+	Navigators Math Series	Benchmark Education
Mathew Brady: Civil War Photographer	T	B	250+	A First Book	Franklin Watts
Max and Me and the Time Machine	T	SF	250+	Greer, Gery; Ruddick, Bob	HarperTrophy
Me and My Little Brain	T	RF	250+	Fitzgerald, John D.	Dell

* Collection of short stories

TITLE	LEVEL	GENRE	WORD COUNT	AUTHOR / SERIES	PUBLISHER / DISTRIBUTOR
Meteors: The Truth Behind Shooting Stars	T	I	250+	Aronson, Billy	Franklin Watts
Metric Math	T	I	250+	Navigators Math Series	Benchmark Education
Michael Jordan: The Best Ever	T	B	250+	High Five Reading	Red Brick Learning
Middle Moffat, The	T	RF	250+	Estes, Eleanor	Language for Learning Assoc.
Mixed-Up Mystery, A	T	I	1541	Independent Readers Science	Houghton Mifflin
Monsters of the Myth	T	I	522	Vocabulary Readers	Houghton Mifflin
Monticello	T	I	250+	We The People	Compass Point Books
More Adventures of the Great Brain	T	RF	250+	Fitzgerald, John D.	Yearling
Movie Magic	T	I	250+	Sunshine	Wright Group/McGraw Hill
Mr. Fahrenheit and Mr. Celsius	T	I	1330	Leveled Readers Science	Houghton Mifflin
Muscles: Our Muscular System	T	I	250+	Simon, Seymour	HarperTrophy
*My Brother Louis Measures Worms and Other Louis Stories	T	RF	250+	Robinson, Barbara	HarperTrophy
My Daniel	T	HF	250+	Conrad, Pam	HarperTrophy
My Hiroshima	T	HF	250+	Morimoto, Junko	Penguin Group
My Life as a Fifth-Grade Comedian	T	RF	250+	Levy, Elizabeth	HarperTrophy
My Louisiana Sky	T	RF	250+	Holt, Kimberly Willis	Random House
Mysterious Ocean Highway: Benjamin Franklin and the Gulf Stream	T	B	250+	Heiligman, Deborah	Steck-Vaughn
Mystery at the Zoo	T	F	1733	Leveled Readers	Houghton Mifflin
Mythical Beasts	T	F	250+	Wildcats	Wright Group/McGraw Hill
Mythical Horse, The	T	I	250+	Sunshine	Wright Group/McGraw Hill
Mythmakers	T	I	250+	Wildcats	Wright Group/McGraw Hill
Nat Turner: Rebellious Slave	T	B	250+	Let Freedom Ring	Capstone Press
Natchez Under the Hill	T	HF	250+	Applegate, Stan	Peachtree
Nelson Mandela: Freedom for South Africa	T	B	250+	Dell, Pamela	Children's Press
Never Say Quit	T	RF	250+	Wallace, Bill	Pocket Books
New Kind of Art, A	T	I	527	Vocabulary Readers	Houghton Mifflin
New York	T	I	250+	Hello U.S.A.	Lerner Publishing
New York City	T	I	250+	Kent, Deborah	Children's Press
Niagra Falls, The Power of Water	T	I	1840	Independent Readers Science	Houghton Mifflin
Night Journey, The	T	HF	250+	Lasky, Kathryn	Puffin Books
Nikki Giovanni	T	B	1729	Leveled Readers	Houghton Mifflin
No Way, Tooth Decay!	T	F	1186	Leveled Readers	Houghton Mifflin
Noah's Ark	T	I	250+	Cambridge Reading	Pearson Learning Group
*Nobel Prize Winners	T	B	250+	Hacker, Carlotta	Crabtree
Norman Rockwell	T	B	250+	Cohen, Joel H.	Grolier Publishing
North Carolina	T	I	250+	Fradin, Dennis Brindell	Children's Press
North Carolina	T	I	250+	Hello U.S.A.	Lerner Publishing
Nory Ryan's Song	T	HF	250+	Giff, Patricia Reilly	Delacorte
Obee & Mungedeech	T	RF	250+	Martin, Trude	Aladdin
Off To Sea: An Inside Look at a Research Cruise	T	I	250+	Kovacs, Deborah	Steck-Vaughn
Ola Shakes It Up	T	RF	250+	Hyppolite, Joanne	Random House
*Old Key, The	T	TL	250+	Literacy 2000	Rigby
On Board the Santa Maria	T	I	2391	Independent Readers Social Studies	Houghton Mifflin
On Board The Titanic	T	I	250+	Tanaka, Shelley	Hyperion/Madison Press
Once Upon a Time	T	I	250+	Literacy 2000	Rigby
*One Potato, Tu	T	RF	250+	Pearson, Gayle	Scholastic
Ontario	T	I	250+	Hello Canada	Fitzhenry & Whiteside
Oregon Trail, The	T	I	250+	The Heinle Reading Library	Thomson Learning
Oregon Trail, The	T	I	250+	We The People	Compass Point Books
Osceola: Patriot and Warrior	T	B	250+	Jumper, Moses; Sonder, Ben	Steck-Vaughn

* Collection of short stories

TITLE	LEVEL	GENRE	WORD COUNT	AUTHOR / SERIES	PUBLISHER / DISTRIBUTOR
Our "Current" World	T	I	250+	Navigators Social Studies Series	Benchmark Education
Paul Revere's Ride	T	I	250+	We The People	Compass Point Books
Peter Salem: Hero of the Revolution	T	B	1096	Independent Readers Social Studies	Houghton Mifflin
Picture of Freedom, A	T	HF	250+	McKissack, Patricia C.	Scholastic
Pilar Speaks Up	T	RF	1354	Leveled Readers	Houghton Mifflin
Pilgrim Voices: Our First Year in the New World	T	HF	250+	Roop, Connie & Peter	Walker & Company
Pilgrims of Plimoth, The	T	I	250+	Sewall, Marcia	Simon & Schuster
Pioneers	T	I	250+	Sandler, Martin W.	HarperTrophy
Plymouth Colony, The	T	I	250+	We The People	Compass Point Books
Poor Girl, Rich Girl	T	RF	250+	Wilson, Johnniece Marshall	Language for Learning Assoc.
Power of Wind, The	T	I	1983	Leveled Readers Science	Houghton Mifflin
Prairie Danger	T	HF	1722	Leveled Readers	Houghton Mifflin
Preacher's Boy	T	RF	250+	Paterson, Katherine	Houghton Mifflin
Precious Stones	T	I	1331	Leveled Readers Science	Houghton Mifflin
Pro Stock Trucks	T	I	250+	The World's Fastest	Red Brick Learning
PT Boats	T	I	250+	Land and Sea	Capstone Press
Pyramids in the Bush: A Book about Mallee Fowl	T	I	250+	Sunshine	Wright Group/McGraw Hill
Quake!	T	RF	250+	Cottonwood, Joe	Language for Learning Assoc.
Rabble Starkey	T	RF	250+	Lowry, Lois	Bantam
Radio Scare	T	I	250+	Leveled Readers Language Support	Houghton Mifflin
Rat's Tale, A	T	F	250+	Seidler, Tor	HarperTrophy
Reefs	T	I	250+	iOpeners	Pearson Learning Group
Return of the Great Brain, The	T	RF	250+	Fitzgerald, John D.	Dell
Riding with the Vaqueros	T	HF	1790	Leveled Readers	Houghton Mifflin
Rifle, The	T	HF	250+	Paulsen, Gary	Dell
River of No Return	T	RF	1845	Leveled Readers	Houghton Mifflin
River Patrol Boats	T	I	250+	Land and Sea	Capstone Press
Roanoke: The Lost Colony	T	I	250+	The Library of the Thirteen Colonies and The Lost Colony	Rosen Publishing Group
Robert E. Lee	T	B	1940	Leveled Readers Social Studies	Houghton Mifflin
Robinson Crusoe	T	HF	250+	High-Fliers	Pacific Learning
Runaway to Freedom: A Story of the Underground Railway	T	I	250+	Smucker, Barbara	HarperTrophy
Salem Days: Life in a Colonial Seaport	T	I	250+	Adventures in Colonial America	Troll Associates
Sammy Keyes and the Art of Deception	T	RF	250+	Van Draanen, Wendelin	Random House
Sammy Keyes and the Curse of Moustache Mary	T	RF	250+	Van Draanen, Wendelin	Random House
Sammy Keyes and the Hotel Thief	T	RF	250+	Van Draanen, Wendelin	Random House
Sammy Keyes and the Runaway Elf	T	RF	250+	Van Draanen, Wendelin	Random House
Sammy Keyes and the Sisters of Mercy	T	RF	250+	Van Draanen, Wendelin	Random House
Sammy Keyes and the Skeleton Man	T	RF	250+	Van Draanen, Wendelin	Random House
Sandman to the Rescue	T	RF	1758	Leveled Readers	Houghton Mifflin
Santa Fe Trail, The	T	I	250+	We The People	Compass Point Books
Schernoff Discoveries, The	T	RF	250+	Paulsen, Gary	Dell
Second Mrs. Giaconda, The	T	HF	250+	Konigsburg, E. L.	Language for Learning Assoc.
Sees Behind Trees	T	HF	250+	Dorris, Michael	Language for Learning Assoc.
Serena and Venus Williams	T	B	250+	Sports Heroes	Red Brick Learning

* Collection of short stories

TITLE	LEVEL	GENRE	WORD COUNT	AUTHOR / SERIES	PUBLISHER / DISTRIBUTOR
Shaji in New York	T	RF	1906	Leveled Readers	Houghton Mifflin
Sharks	T	I	250+	Simon, Seymour	HarperTrophy
Shh! We're Writing the Constitution	T	I	250+	Fritz, Jean	G.P. Putnam's Sons
Sign of the Beaver	T	HF	250+	Speare, Elizabeth George	Bantam
Sing Down the Moon	T	HF	250+	O'Dell, Scott	Language for Learning Assoc.
*Singing Drum, The	T	TL	250+	Literacy 2000	Rigby
Sleepers, Wake	T	SF	250+	Jacobs, Paul Samuel	Language for Learning Assoc.
Sluefoot Sue's Wild Ride	T	F	1831	Leveled Readers	Houghton Mifflin
Soldier Boy	T	HF	250+	Burks, Brian	Harcourt Trade
Someone to Count On	T	RF	250+	Hermes, Patricia	Language for Learning Assoc.
Something Upstairs	T	RF	250+	Avi	Language for Learning Assoc.
Song of the Stranger	T	RF	250+	Tung, Angela	Lowell House
Sounder	T	RF	250+	Armstrong, William	Scholastic
Sports of the First Americans	T	I	1590	Leveled Readers Social Studies	Houghton Mifflin
Spring Fever!	T	F	250+	Lerangis, Peter	Language for Learning Assoc.
Standing in the Light	T	RF	250+	Osborne, Mary Pope	Scholastic
Starting a Rock Collection	T	I	250+	Independent Readers Science	Houghton Mifflin
Steps, The	T	RF	250+	Cohn, Rachel	Simon & Schuster
Stock Cars	T	I	250+	The World's Fastest	Red Brick Learning
Stonehenge: Still a Mystery	T	I	250+	Leveled Readers Language Support	Houghton Mifflin
Story of Geronimo, The	T	B	250+	Cornerstones of Freedom	Children's Press
Story of Harriet Tubman, The: Freedom Train	T	B	250+	Sterling, Dorothy	Bantam
Story of the Mayflower Compact, The	T	I	250+	Cornerstones of Freedom	Children's Press
Studying the Past	T	I	512	Vocabulary Readers	Houghton Mifflin
Submarines	T	I	250+	Land and Sea	Capstone Press
Summer to Die, A	T	RF	250+	Lowry, Lois	Dell
Superbikes	T	I	250+	The World's Fastest	Red Brick Learning
Susanna of the Alamo	T	B	250+	Jakes, John	Language for Learning Assoc.
Taste of America	T	I	250+	iOpeners	Pearson Learning Group
Tecumseh: Shawnee Leader	T	B	250+	Let Freedom Ring	Capstone Press
Tenement Writer, The: An Immigrant's Story	T	I	250+	Sonder, Ben	Steck-Vaughn
Tennessee Tornado, The: Wilma Rudolph	T	B	2097	Leveled Readers	Houghton Mifflin
Then Again, Maybe I Won't	T	RF	250+	Blume, Judy	Language for Learning Assoc.
These Lands Are Ours: Tecumseh's Fight For the Old Northwest	T	B	250+	Connell, Kate	Steck-Vaughn
They Shall Be Heard: Susan B. Anthony & Elizabeth Cady Stanton	T	B	250+	Connell, Kate	Steck-Vaughn
Three Lives to Live	T	F	250+	Lindbergh, Anne	Little, Brown & Co.
*Throwing Shadows	T	RF	250+	Konigsburg, E. L.	Language for Learning Assoc.
Thunder Valley	T	RF	250+	Paulsen, Gary	Bantam
Tiger Rising, The	T	RF	250+	DiCamillo, Kate	Candlewick Press
Time Apart, A	T	RF	250+	Stanley, Diane	William Morrow
Time Benders	T	SF	250+	Paulsen, Gary	Bantam
Titanic Sinks!, The	T	I	250+	Conklin, Thomas	Random House
To the Top of Mount Everest	T	I	2432	Leveled Readers Science	Houghton Mifflin

* Collection of short stories

TITLE	LEVEL	GENRE	WORD COUNT	AUTHOR / SERIES	PUBLISHER / DISTRIBUTOR
Toliver's Secret	T	HF	250+	Brady, Esther Wood	Alfred A. Knopf
*Tom, Babette & Simon	T	F	250+	Avi	Avon
Tools and Gadgets	T	I	250+	Historic Communities	Crabtree
Toothpaste Millionaire, The	T	RF	250+	Merrill, Jean	Houghton Mifflin
Tornado Chasers	T	RF	1520	Independent Readers Science	Houghton Mifflin
Tracker	T	RF	250+	Paulsen, Gary	Scholastic
Training for Space	T	I	508	Vocabulary Readers	Houghton Mifflin
Training for the Olympics	T	I	1381	Independent Readers Science	Houghton Mifflin
Trains	T	I	250+	The World's Fastest	Red Brick Learning
Travels of Marco Polo, The	T	I	250+	Explorers & Exploration	Steck-Vaughn
Treasure of El Patrón, The	T	RF	250+	Paulsen, Gary	Bantam
Trout Summer	T	RF	250+	Conly, Jane Leslie	Scholastic
Trucks	T	I	250+	The World's Fastest	Red Brick Learning
Try It!	T	I	250+	iOpeners	Pearson Learning Group
Turn Homeward, Hannalee	T	HF	250+	Beatty, Patricia	William Morrow
U.S. Constitution, The	T	I	250+	We The People	Compass Point Books
Under the Ocean	T	I	614	Vocabulary Readers	Houghton Mifflin
Ups and Downs of Carl Davis III, The	T	RF	250+	Guy, Rosa	Language for Learning Assoc.
Visiting a Village	T	I	250+	Kalman, Bobbie	Scholastic
Volcanoes and Earthquakes	T	I	250+	Lauber, Patricia	Language for Learning Assoc.
Voyage to Antartica	T	I	2505	Leveled Readers Science	Houghton Mifflin
Vulpes The Red Fox	T	F	250+	George, Jean Craighead	Puffin Books
Wainscott Weasel, The	T	F	250+	Seidler, Tor	HarperCollins
Week in the Woods, A	T	RF	250+	Clements, Andrew	Simon & Schuster
Well, The	T	HF	250+	Taylor, Mildred D.	Puffin Books
Werewolf Chronicles, The	T	F	250+	Philbrick, Rodman; Harnett, Lynn	Scholastic
What Does an Electrician Do?	T	I	1322	Independent Readers Science	Houghton Mifflin
What Is the Media?	T	I	2493	Independent Readers Social Studies	Houghton Mifflin
What Jamie Saw	T	RF	250+	Coman, Carolyn	Penguin Group
What People Wore During the American Revolution	T	I	250+	Clothing, Costumes and Uniforms Throughout American History	Rosen Publishing Group
What People Wore During the Westward Expansion	T	I	250+	Clothing, Costumes and Uniforms Throughout American History	Rosen Publishing Group
What People Wore in Colonial America	T	I	250+	Clothing, Costumes and Uniforms Throughout American History	Rosen Publishing Group
What People Wore in Early America	T	I	250+	Clothing, Costumes and Uniforms Throughout American History	Rosen Publishing Group
What Would Joey Do?	T	RF	250+	Gantos, Jack	Farrar, Straus and Giroux
Whistler's Hollow	T	HF	250+	Dadey, Debbie	Bloomsbury Children's Books
Wildlife Photographer Frank Greenway	T	I	250+	iOpeners	Pearson Learning Group
Wings for a Day	T	F	1842	Leveled Readers	Houghton Mifflin
Wish Giver, The	T	F	250+	Brittain, Bill	HarperTrophy
Wish on a Unicorn	T	RF	250+	Hesse, Karen	Penguin Group
Women Pioneers in Medicine	T	I	2664	Independent Readers Science	Houghton Mifflin
Women Writers: Voices from the 1800s	T	I	2535	Independent Readers Social Studies	Houghton Mifflin
Woodsong	T	B	250+	Paulsen, Gary	Dell
Work of Leonardo Da Vinci, The	T	I	1810	Leveled Readers Science	Houghton Mifflin
You Shouldn't Have to Say Good-bye	T	RF	250+	Hermes, Patricia	Scholastic
13th Floor, The: A Ghost Story	U	F	250+	Fleischman, Sid	Bantam

* Collection of short stories

TITLE	LEVEL	GENRE	WORD COUNT	AUTHOR / SERIES	PUBLISHER / DISTRIBUTOR
Abigail Adams, Patriot	U	B	2288	Leveled Readers Social Studies	Houghton Mifflin
Abraham Lincoln	U	B	250+	Let Freedom Ring	Red Brick Learning
Abraham Lincoln	U	B	250+	Profiles of the Presidents	Compass Point Books
Adam Canfield of the Slash	U	RF	250+	Winerip, Michael	Candlewick Press
African-Americans in the Colonies	U	I	250+	We The People	Compass Point Books
Agnes Macphail: Canada's Champion of the Poor	U	B	2412	Independent Readers Social Studies	Houghton Mifflin
Alexander Graham Bell: An Inventive Life	U	B	250+	MacLeod, Elizabeth	Kids Can Press Ltd.
Alice in Rapture: Sort of	U	RF	250+	Naylor, Phyllis Reynolds	Aladdin
Alice the Brave	U	RF	250+	Naylor, Phyllis Reynolds	Aladdin
Alice: Alice Alone	U	RF	250+	Naylor, Phyllis Reynolds	Simon & Schuster
All But Alice	U	RF	250+	Naylor, Phyllis Reynolds	Dell
Alligators & Crocodiles	U	I	250+	The Untamed World	Steck-Vaughn
Ancient Egypt	U	I	250+	Make It Work!	World Book
Andrew Jackson	U	B	250+	Profiles of the Presidents	Compass Point Books
Andrew Johnson	U	B	250+	Profiles of the Presidents	Compass Point Books
Animorphs	U	F	250+	Applegate, K. A.	Scholastic
Apprenticeship of Lucas Whitaker, The	U	HF	250+	DeFelice, Cynthia	Avon
Ariel of the Sea	U	F	250+	Calhoun, Dia	Winslow Press
Australia	U	I	250+	Countries and Cultures	Red Brick Learning
Bad Girls	U	RF	250+	Voigt, Cynthia	Scholastic
Bad, Badder, Baddest	U	RF	250+	Voigt, Cynthia	Scholastic
*Baseball in April and Other Stories	U	RF	250+	Soto, Gary	Harcourt Trade
Battle of Leyte, The	U	I	974	Leveled Readers Social Studies	Houghton Mifflin
Being Danny's Dog	U	RF	250+	Naylor, Phyllis Reynolds	Aladdin
Ben Franklin of Old Philadelphia	U	B	250+	Cousins, Margaret	Random House
Benjamin Franklin	U	B	250+	Kent, Deborah	Scholastic
Benjamin Harrison	U	B	250+	Profiles of the Presidents	Compass Point Books
*Beowulf	U	TL	250+	Literacy 2000	Rigby
Beyond the Burning Lands	U	F	250+	Christopher, John	Aladdin
BFG, The	U	F	250+	Dahl, Roald	Penguin Group
Birds of Prey: A Look at Daytime Raptors	U	I	250+	Collard III, Sneed B.	Franklin Watts
Blue Ice	U	RF	250+	Salata, Estelle	Fitzhenry & Whiteside
Blue Whales	U	I	250+	The Untamed World	Steck-Vaughn
Boggart and the Monster, The	U	F	250+	Cooper, Susan	Aladdin
Boggart, The	U	F	250+	Cooper, Susan	Simon & Schuster
Book of Three, The	U	F	250+	Alexander, Lloyd	Bantam
Boy Who Owned the School, The	U	RF	250+	Paulsen, Gary	Bantam
Boy Who Saved Baseball, The	U	RF	250+	Ritter, John H.	Penguin Group
*Boys Who Rocked the World: From King Tut to Tiger Woods	U	B	250+	Carlsmith, L.; Mann, B.; McCann, M. R.; & Strelow, E.	Beyond Words
Brave Pilot, A	U	B	660	Vocabulary Readers	Houghton Mifflin
Bronco Charlie and the Pony Express	U	B	1824	Leveled Readers	Houghton Mifflin
Bronze Bow, The	U	HF	250+	Speare, Elizabeth George	Houghton Mifflin
Buffalo Gal	U	RF	250+	Wallace, Bill	Simon & Schuster
Building an Ice Hotel	U	I	250+	iOpeners	Pearson Learning Group
Bye, Bye, Bali Kai	U	RF	250+	Luger, Harriett	OSI
Cabot: John Cabot and the Journey to North America	U	B	250+	Exploring the World	Compass Point Books
Calvin Coolidge	U	B	250+	Profiles of the Presidents	Compass Point Books
Captain Grey	U	HF	250+	Avi	HarperTrophy
Cartier: Jacques Cartier in Search of the Northwest Passage	U	B	250+	Exploring the World	Compass Point Books
Case of the Lion Dance	U	RF	250+	Yep, Laurence	HarperTrophy

* Collection of short stories

TITLE	LEVEL	GENRE	WORD COUNT	AUTHOR / SERIES	PUBLISHER / DISTRIBUTOR
Cat Ate My Gymsuit, The	U	RF	250+	Danziger, Paula	Putnam & Grosset
Cat Running	U	RF	250+	Snyder, Zilpha Keatley	Bantam
Ceiling of Stars, A	U	RF	250+	Creel, Ann Howard	Pleasant Company
Charley Skedaddle	U	HF	250+	Beatty, Patricia	Troll Associates
Chester A. Arthur	U	B	250+	Profiles of the Presidents	Compass Point Books
Child of the Wolves	U	RF	250+	Hall, Elizabeth	Bantam
Children of the Sierra Madre, The	U	I	250+	Staub, Frank	Carolrhoda Books
Chimp Communities	U	I	1618	Leveled Readers Science	Houghton Mifflin
Christmas Carol, A	U	F	250+	Dickens, Charles	Scholastic
City Through the Ages	U	I	250+	Steele, Philip	Troll Associates
Coal Miner's Son, A	U	RF	2652	Leveled Readers Science	Houghton Mifflin
Columbia	U	I	250+	Countries and Cultures	Red Brick Learning
Comets	U	I	250+	A First Book	Franklin Watts
Coming Home	U	HF	1920	Leveled Readers	Houghton Mifflin
Comstock Lode, The	U	I	2086	Leveled Readers Social Studies	Houghton Mifflin
Cook: Captain James Cook Charts the Pacific Ocean	U	B	250+	Exploring the World	Compass Point Books
Coronado: Francisco Vasquez de Coronado Explores the Southwest	U	B	250+	Exploring the World	Compass Point Books
Cousins in the Castle	U	F	250+	Wallace, Barbara Brooks	Aladdin
*Cow of No Color, The: Riddle Stories and Justice Tales From Around the World	U	TL	250+	Jaffe, Nina; Zeitlin, Steve	Henry Holt & Co.
Crafts and Games Around the World	U	I	250+	iOpeners	Pearson Learning Group
Crazy Lady!	U	RF	250+	Conly, Jane Leslie	HarperCollins
Crocodilians	U	I	250+	Short, Joan; Bird, Bettina	Mondo
Da Gama: Vasco da Gama Sails Around the Cape of Good Hope	U	B	250+	Exploring the World	Compass Point Books
Daily Life in a Plains Indian Village: 1868	U	I	250+	Terry, Michael Bad Hand	Clarion
Dancing Carl	U	RF	250+	Paulsen, Gary	Aladdin
Dangerous Wishes	U	F	250+	Sleator, William	Penguin Group
De Soto: Hernando de Soto Explores the Southeast	U	B	250+	Exploring the World	Compass Point Books
Different Beat, A	U	RF	250+	Boyd, Candy Dawson	Penguin Group
Do The Funky Pickle	U	RF	250+	Spinelli, Jerry	Scholastic
Dolores Huerta, Civil Rights Leader	U	B	1655	Leveled Readers Social Studies	Houghton Mifflin
Dolphins	U	I	250+	The Heinle Reading Library	Thomson Learning
Door in the Wall, The	U	HF	250+	De Angeli, Marguerite	Bantam
Double Life of Pocahontas, The	U	B	250+	Fritz, Jean	Language for Learning Assoc.
Dreadful Future of Blossom Culp, The	U	SF	250+	Peck, Richard	Bantam
Drew and the Homeboy Question	U	RF	250+	Armstrong, Robb	HarperTrophy
Dwight D. Eisenhower	U	B	250+	Profiles of the Presidents	Compass Point Books
Earth to Matthew	U	RF	250+	Danziger, Paula	PaperStar
Earthlings in Space	U	SF	250+	Sunshine	Wright Group/McGraw Hill
Earthquake Alaska	U	HF	2192	Leveled Readers	Houghton Mifflin
Egypt: The Culture	U	I	250+	Kalman, Bobbie	Crabtree
Egypt: The Land	U	I	250+	Kalman, Bobbie	Crabtree
Egypt: The People	U	I	250+	Kalman, Bobbie	Crabtree
Egyptian Town	U	I	250+	Steedman, Scott	Franklin Watts
Eleanor Roosevelt	U	B	250+	Blevins, Wiley	Scholastic
Elephants	U	I	250+	The Untamed World	Steck-Vaughn
Elijah McCoy	U	B	250+	Independent Readers Science	Houghton Mifflin
Elisha Otis's Ups and Downs	U	I	1759	Leveled Readers	Houghton Mifflin
Ella Enchanted	U	F	250+	Carson Levine, Gail	HarperTrophy

TITLE	LEVEL	GENRE	WORD COUNT	AUTHOR / SERIES	PUBLISHER / DISTRIBUTOR
Ellis Island	U	I	250+	We The People	Compass Point Books
End of the Ice Age, The	U	I	2221	Independent Readers Science	Houghton Mifflin
Everyone Else's Parents Said Yes	U	RF	250+	Danziger, Paula	PaperStar
Fab Four from Liverpool, The	U	B	1862	Leveled Readers	Houghton Mifflin
Factory Through the Ages	U	I	250+	Steele, Philip	Troll Associates
Facts and Fictions of Minna Pratt, The	U	RF	250+	MacLachlan, Patricia	HarperTrophy
Farm Through the Ages	U	I	250+	Steele, Philip	Troll Associates
Fire in the Wind	U	RF	250+	Levin, Betty	Beech Tree Books
*Fire-Bird, The	U	TL	250+	Literacy 2000	Rigby
First Family: The Roosevelts	U	B	2374	Independent Readers Social Studies	Houghton Mifflin
First Humans, The	U	I	1814	Leveled Readers Social Studies	Houghton Mifflin
First Ladies	U	B	250+	Cornerstones of Freedom	Children's Press
*First Ladies of the White House	U	B	250+	Skarmeas, Nancy	Ideals Publications Inc.
*First Ladies: Women Who Called the White House Home	U	B	250+	Gormley, Beatrice	Scholastic
Flags	U	I	250+	iOpeners	Pearson Learning Group
Flatboat Mondays	U	I	2452	Independent Readers Social Studies	Houghton Mifflin
Fledgling, The	U	F	250+	Langton, Jane	Scholastic
Flipped	U	RF	250+	Van Draanen, Wendelin	Random House
*Flying With the Eagle, Racing the Great Bear: Stories from Native North America	U	TL	250+	Bruchac, Joseph	Troll Associates
Fossil Seekers	U	I	250+	iOpeners	Pearson Learning Group
France	U	I	250+	Countries and Cultures	Red Brick Learning
Frances Hodgson Burnett: Beyond the Secret Garden	U	B	250+	Carpenter, Angelica Shirley; Shirley, Jean	Lerner Publishing
Franklin D. Roosevelt	U	B	250+	Profiles of the Presidents	Compass Point Books
Franklin Pierce	U	B	250+	Profiles of the Presidents	Compass Point Books
Frederick Douglass: His Story Made History	U	B	2008	Leveled Readers	Houghton Mifflin
Frightful's Mountain	U	RF	250+	George, Jean Craighead	Puffin Books
Gathering of Days, A: A New England Girl's Journal, 1830-32	U	HF	250+	Blos, Joan	Aladdin
George H. W. Bush	U	B	250+	Profiles of the Presidents	Compass Point Books
George W. Bush	U	B	250+	Profiles of the Presidents	Compass Point Books
George Washington	U	B	250+	Profiles of the Presidents	Compass Point Books
George Washington: The Man Who Would Not Be King	U	B	250+	Krensky, Stephen	Scholastic
Gerald R. Ford	U	B	250+	Profiles of the Presidents	Compass Point Books
Geronimo	U	B	1903	Leveled Readers Social Studies	Houghton Mifflin
Geysers: When Earth Roars	U	I	250+	A First Book	Franklin Watts
Ghost in the Tokaido Inn, The	U	F	250+	Hoobler, Dorothy & Thomas	Penguin Group
Giant Pandas	U	I	250+	The Untamed World	Steck-Vaughn
Gift of the Girl Who Couldn't Hear, The	U	RF	250+	Shreve, Susan	Beech Tree Books
Ginger Pye	U	RF	250+	Estes, Eleanor	Scholastic
Girl Called Boy, A	U	F	250+	Hurmence, Belinda	Clarion
Girl In the Window, The	U	RF	250+	Yeo, Wilma	Scholastic
*Girl Who Married the Moon, The: Tales from Native North America	U	TL	250+	Bruchac, Joseph; Ross, Gayle	Troll Associates
Girl With the Silver Eyes, The	U	F	250+	Roberts, Willo Davis	Scholastic
Gorillas	U	I	250+	The Untamed World	Steck-Vaughn
Grace	U	HF	250+	Walsh, Jill Paton	Farrar, Straus and Giroux
Graham Hawkes: Underwater Pilot	U	B	1492	Leveled Readers	Houghton Mifflin
Grams, Her Boyfriend, My Family, and Me	U	RF	250+	Derby, Pat	Sunburst

* Collection of short stories

TITLE	LEVEL	GENRE	WORD COUNT	AUTHOR / SERIES	PUBLISHER / DISTRIBUTOR
*Graven Images: Three Stories by Paul Fleischman	U	F	250+	Fleischman, Paul	HarperTrophy
Great Wheel, The	U	RF	250+	Lawson, Robert	Scholastic
Great White Sharks	U	I	250+	The Untamed World	Steck-Vaughn
Greece: The Culture	U	I	250+	Kalman, Bobbie	Crabtree
Greece: The Land	U	I	250+	Kalman, Bobbie	Crabtree
Greece: The People	U	I	250+	Kalman, Bobbie	Crabtree
Grover Cleveland	U	B	250+	Profiles of the Presidents	Compass Point Books
Gypsy Game, The	U	RF	250+	Snyder, Zilpha Keatly	Yearling
Haiti	U	I	250+	Countries and Cultures	Red Brick Learning
Handful of Time, A	U	F	250+	Pearson, Kit	Puffin Books
Harriet Tubman	U	B	250+	Let Freedom Ring	Red Brick Learning
Harry S. Truman	U	B	250+	Profiles of the Presidents	Compass Point Books
Heat Is On, The	U	I	250+	Tanaka, Shelley	Firefly Books
Herbert Hoover	U	B	250+	Profiles of the Presidents	Compass Point Books
Heroes & Idealists	U	B	250+	Real Lives	Troll Associates
Hitty: Her First Hundred Years	U	F	250+	Field, Rachel	Aladdin
House Through the Ages	U	I	250+	Steele, Philip	Troll Associates
*How Angel Peterson Got His Name: And Other Outrageous Tales About Extreme Sports	U	RF	250+	Paulsen, Gary	Random House
Hudson: Henry Hudson Searches for a Passage to Asia	U	B	250+	Exploring the World	Compass Point Books
Hurricane Opal: Into the Storm	U	RF	1931	Leveled Readers	Houghton Mifflin
I Am Regina	U	HF	250+	Keehn, Sally	Bantam
I Know, I Know!	U	RF	1820	Leveled Readers	Houghton Mifflin
If You Were There in 1492: Everyday Life in the Time of Columbus	U	I	250+	Brenner, Barbara	Aladdin
In the Line of Fire: Eight Women War Spies	U	B	250+	Sullivan, George	Scholastic
In the Mountains	U	I	250+	iOpeners	Pearson Learning Group
Indian Winter, An	U	I	250+	Freedman, Russell	Scholastic
Insects	U	I	250+	Bird, Bettina; Short, Joan	Mondo
Insects & Spiders	U	I	250+	World Book Looks at Science	World Book
Jaguars	U	I	250+	Green, Michael	Red Brick Learning
James A. Garfield	U	B	250+	Profiles of the Presidents	Compass Point Books
James Buchanan	U	B	250+	Profiles of the Presidents	Compass Point Books
James Earl Carter, Jr.	U	B	250+	Profiles of the Presidents	Compass Point Books
James K. Polk	U	B	250+	Profiles of the Presidents	Compass Point Books
James Madison	U	B	250+	Profiles of the Presidents	Compass Point Books
James Monroe	U	B	250+	Profiles of the Presidents	Compass Point Books
Jazz Great	U	RF	3296	Leveled Readers	Houghton Mifflin
Jefferson Davis	U	B	250+	Let Freedom Ring	Red Brick Learning
Jericho's Journey	U	RF	250+	Wisler, G. Clifton	Penguin Group
John Adams	U	B	250+	Profiles of the Presidents	Compass Point Books
John F. Kennedy	U	B	250+	Profiles of the Presidents	Compass Point Books
John Quincy Adams	U	B	250+	Profiles of the Presidents	Compass Point Books
John Tyler	U	B	250+	Profiles of the Presidents	Compass Point Books
Journal of Douglas Allen Deeds, The: The Donner Party Expedition, 1846	U	HF	250+	My Name is America	Scholastic
Journey Into Terror	U	RF	250+	Wallace, Bill	Simon & Schuster
Journey to America	U	HF	250+	Levitin, Sonia	Simon & Schuster
Journey to Topaz	U	HF	250+	Uchida, Yoshiko	Creative Arts Book Co.
Julie	U	RF	250+	George, Jean Craighead	HarperTrophy
Julie of the Wolves	U	RF	250+	George, Jean Craighead	HarperCollins
Julie's Wolf Pack	U	RF	250+	George, Jean Craighead	HarperTrophy

* Collection of short stories

TITLE	LEVEL	GENRE	WORD COUNT	AUTHOR / SERIES	PUBLISHER / DISTRIBUTOR
Jump Ship to Freedom	U	HF	250+	Collier, James & Christopher	Bantam
Jungle Book, The	U	F	250+	Kipling, Rudyard	Scholastic
K. C. at the Bat	U	F	1939	Leveled Readers	Houghton Mifflin
Kind of Thief, A	U	RF	250+	Alcock, Vivien	Bantam
Knots in My Yo-yo String: The Autobiography of a Kid	U	B	250+	Spinelli, Jerry	Alfred A. Knopf
La Causa: The Migrant Farmworkers' Story	U	I	250+	deRuiz, Dana Catharine	Steck-Vaughn
La Salle: La Salle and the Mississippi River	U	B	250+	Exploring the World	Compass Point Books
Lamborghinis	U	I	250+	Green, Michael	Red Brick Learning
Lampfish of Twill, The	U	F	250+	Lisle, Janet Taylor	Scholastic
Landslides, Slumps & Creep	U	I	250+	A First Book	Franklin Watts
Leaders of the People	U	B	250+	Real Lives	Troll Associates
Life at the Bottom of the Sea	U	I	250+	Leveled Readers Language Support	Houghton Mifflin
Life in the Sahara	U	I	1804	Leveled Readers Social Studies	Houghton Mifflin
Life in the Sahara	U	I	250+	Leveled Readers Social Studies	Houghton Mifflin
*Listen Children: An Anthology of Black Literature	U	RF	250+	Strickland, Dorothy S.	Bantam
Living in Space	U	I	250+	Leveled Readers Language Support	Houghton Mifflin
Loser	U	RF	250+	Spinelli, Jerry	HarperCollins
Lyndon Baines Johnson	U	B	250+	Profiles of the Presidents	Compass Point Books
Magellan: Ferdinand Magellan and the First Trip Around the World	U	B	250+	Exploring the World	Compass Point Books
Make Like a Tree and Leave	U	RF	250+	Danziger, Paula	PaperStar
Marco Polo: Marco Polo and the Silk Road to China	U	B	250+	Exploring the World	Compass Point Books
Martin Van Buren	U	B	250+	Profiles of the Presidents	Compass Point Books
Marvelous Metals	U	I	1616	Independent Readers Science	Houghton Mifflin
Mary McLeod Bethune	U	B	250+	Cornerstones of Freedom	Children's Press
Matter of Conscience, A: The Trial of Anne Hutchinson	U	I	250+	Nichols, Joan Kane	Steck-Vaughn
May Chinn: The Best Medicine	U	B	250+	Butts, Ellen; Schwartz, Joyce	W. H. Freeman & Co.
Merlin and the Dragons	U	F	250+	Yolen, Jane	Penguin Group
Midnight Magic	U	F	250+	Avi	Scholastic
Mighty Ironclads and Other Amazements	U	I	2454	Independent Readers Social Studies	Houghton Mifflin
Mighty Maya, The	U	I	250+	Leveled Readers Language Support	Houghton Mifflin
Millard Fillmore	U	B	250+	Profiles of the Presidents	Compass Point Books
Miranda and the Movies	U	HF	250+	Kendall, Jane	OSI
Moon, The	U	I	250+	A First Book	Franklin Watts
Mr. Revere and I	U	F	250+	Lawson, Robert	Little, Brown & Co.
Mr. Tucket	U	HF	250+	Paulsen, Gary	Bantam
Mustangs	U	I	250+	Gillespie, Lorraine	Red Brick Learning
My Side of the Mountain	U	RF	250+	George, Jean Craighead	Penguin Group
Navajo Code Talkers, The	U	I	2549	Independent Readers Social Studies	Houghton Mifflin
Navajo, The	U	I	250+	The Heinle Reading Library	Thomson Learning
Night Journeys	U	HF	250+	Avi	Avon
Night of the Twisters	U	RF	250+	Ruckman, Ivy	HarperTrophy
Nobody's Family Is Going to Change	U	RF	250+	Fitzhugh, Louise	Farrar, Straus and Giroux
North Star To Freedom	U	I	250+	Gorrell, Gena K.	Random House
Nothing But The Truth	U	RF	250+	Avi	Hearst

* Collection of short stories

TITLE	LEVEL	GENRE	WORD COUNT	AUTHOR / SERIES	PUBLISHER / DISTRIBUTOR
Number the Stars	U	HF	250+	Lowry, Lois	Bantam
Observations of Emma Boyle, The	U	RF	2623	Leveled Readers	Houghton Mifflin
Ocean of Story, The: Fairy Tales From India	U	TL	250+	Ness, Caroline	Lothrop, Lee & Shepard
Of Nightingales That Weep	U	HF	250+	Paterson, Katherine	HarperCollins
Off the Map: The Journals of Lewis and Clark	U	I	250+	Roop, Peter & Connie	Walker & Company
Ogden Nash: Playing with Words	U	B	1770	Leveled Readers	Houghton Mifflin
Once Upon a Time in Junior High	U	RF	250+	Norment, Lisa	Scholastic
Onion John	U	HF	250+	Krumgold, Joseph	Harper & Row
Oprah Winfrey, A Voice for the People	U	B	250+	Brooks, Philip	Grolier Publishing
Ordinary Genius, The Story of Albert Einstein	U	B	250+	McPherson, Stephanie S.	The Lerner Group
Outrageously Alice	U	RF	250+	Naylor, Phyllis Reynolds	Aladdin
P.S. Longer Letter Later	U	RF	250+	Danziger, Paula; Martin, Ann M.	Scholastic
Park's Quest	U	RF	250+	Paterson, Katherine	Puffin Books
Peril in the Bessledorf Parachute Factory	U	RF	250+	Naylor, Phyllis Reynolds	Atheneum
Perilous Road, The	U	HF	250+	Steele, William	Scholastic
Place Called Heartbreak, A: A Story of Vietnam	U	I	250+	Myers, Walter Dean	Steck-Vaughn
Place in the Sun, A	U	HF	250+	Rubalcaba, Jill	Puffin Books
Ponce de Leon: Juan Ponce de Leon Searches for the Fountain of Youth	U	B	250+	Exploring the World	Compass Point Books
Pony Express, The	U	I	250+	We The People	Compass Point Books
Popcorn Days & Buttermilk Nights	U	RF	250+	Paulsen, Gary	Penguin Group
Poppy's Timeline	U	RF	1759	Leveled Readers	Houghton Mifflin
Ragweed	U	F	250+	Avi	Avon
Reaction We Need, The	U	I	2708	Leveled Readers Science	Houghton Mifflin
Real Thief, The	U	F	250+	Steig, William	Farrar, Straus and Giroux
Red Dog	U	RF	250+	Wallace, Bill	Simon & Schuster
Regarding the Fountain: A Tale, in Letter, of Liars and Leaks	U	F	250+	Klise, Kate	Avon
REM World	U	F	250+	Philbrick, Rodman	Scholastic
Remember the Ladies: The First Women's Rights Convention	U	I	250+	Johnston, Norma	Scholastic
Report To the Principal's Office	U	RF	250+	Spinelli, Jerry	Scholastic
Richard M. Nixon	U	B	250+	Profiles of the Presidents	Compass Point Books
Right Fly, The	U	RF	1878	Leveled Readers	Houghton Mifflin
Righteous Revenge of Artemis Bonner, The	U	RF	250+	Myers, Walter Dean	HarperTrophy
River Through the Ages	U	I	250+	Steele, Philip	Troll Associates
Road Through the Ages	U	I	250+	Steele, Philip	Troll Associates
Robert E. Lee	U	B	250+	Let Freedom Ring	Red Brick Learning
Robert Frost: The Journey of a Poet	U	B	963	Leveled Readers	Houghton Mifflin
Ronald W. Reagan	U	B	250+	Profiles of the Presidents	Compass Point Books
Rosa Parks: My Story	U	B	250+	Parks, Rosa	Scholastic
Rutherford B. Hayes	U	B	250+	Profiles of the Presidents	Compass Point Books
Salem Witch Trials, The	U	I	1093	Leveled Readers Social Studies	Houghton Mifflin
Samuel de Champlain: Commander of New France	U	B	1694	Leveled Readers Social Studies	Houghton Mifflin
San Francisco Shakes	U	I	2116	Independent Readers Science	Houghton Mifflin
Sand On The Move: The Story of Dunes	U	I	250+	A First Book	Franklin Watts
School Days	U	I	250+	Literacy 2000	Rigby
Scientists in Space	U	I	3502	Leveled Readers Science	Houghton Mifflin
Search for Delicious, The	U	F	250+	Babbitt, Natalie	Farrar, Straus and Giroux
Secret Garden, The	U	RF	250+	Burnett, Frances H.	Scholastic
Seeing is Not Believing	U	I	250+	iOpeners	Pearson Learning Group
Seekers of Truth	U	B	250+	Real Lives	Troll Associates
Shadow of a Bull	U	RF	250+	Wojciechowska, Maia	Simon & Schuster

* Collection of short stories

TITLE	LEVEL	GENRE	WORD COUNT	AUTHOR / SERIES	PUBLISHER / DISTRIBUTOR
Sign of the Chrysanthemum, The	U	RF	250+	Paterson, Katherine	HarperTrophy
Silk Route, The	U	HF	250+	Major, John S.	HarperCollins
Silverwing: How One Small Bat Became a Noble Hero	U	F	250+	Oppel, Kenneth	Simon & Schuster
Single Shard, A	U	HF	250+	Park, Linda Sue	Clarion
Sky Dogs	U	RF	250+	Yolen, Jane	OSI
Smith: John Smith and the Settlement of Jamestown	U	B	250+	Exploring the World	Compass Point Books
Sojourner Truth	U	B	250+	Let Freedom Ring	Red Brick Learning
Solar System, The	U	I	250+	The Heinle Reading Library	Thomson Learning
*Some of the Kinder Planets	U	SF	250+	Wynne-Jones, Tim	Penguin Group
Space Commander: Eileen Collins	U	B	250+	Leveled Readers Language Support	Houghton Mifflin
Space Travel	U	I	250+	The Heinle Reading Library	Thomson Learning
*Spotted Pony, The: A Collection of Hanukkah Stories	U	TL	250+	Kimmel, Eric A.	Holiday House
Stand Tall	U	RF	250+	Bauer, Joan	Penguin Group
Stay! Keeper's Story	U	F	250+	Lowry, Lois	Random House
Stealing Freedom	U	HF	250+	Carbone, Lisa	Random House
Stonehenge: Mystery Unsolved?	U	I	1754	Leveled Readers	Houghton Mifflin
*Stories From the Days of Christopher Columbus	U	HF	250+	Young, Richard; Young, Judy Dockery	August House
Stories in Stone: The World of Animal Fossils	U	I	250+	A First Book	Franklin Watts
Strange Rocks	U	I	2135	Leveled Readers Science	Houghton Mifflin
Stranger at the Window	U	RF	250+	Alcock, Vivien	Houghton Mifflin
Stranger Came Ashore, A	U	F	250+	Hunter, Mollie	HarperTrophy
Streets of Gold	U	HF	1933	Leveled Readers	Houghton Mifflin
Summer of the Swans, The	U	RF	250+	Byars, Betsy	Penguin Group
Surrender at Appomattox, The	U	I	1530	Leveled Readers Social Studies	Houghton Mifflin
Tale of Despereaux, The	U	F	250+	DiCamillo, Kate	Candlewick Press
Talking Earth, The	U	RF	250+	George, Jean Craighead	HarperTrophy
Tangerine	U	RF	250+	Bloor, Edward	Scholastic
Tanya On Track	U	RF	1978	Leveled Readers	Houghton Mifflin
Tarantula in My Purse, The	U	B	250+	George, Jean Craighead	HarperCollins
That Wild Berries Should Grow	U	HF	250+	Whelan, Gloria	Books for Young Readers
Theodore Roosevelt	U	B	250+	Profiles of the Presidents	Compass Point Books
Thomas Jefferson	U	B	250+	Profiles of the Presidents	Compass Point Books
Thomas Jefferson: Man with a Vision	U	B	250+	Crisman, Ruth	Scholastic
Thunder Rolling in the Mountains	U	HF	250+	O'Dell, Scott; Hall, Elizabeth	Bantam
Ticket to Canada	U	RF	1904	Leveled Readers	Houghton Mifflin
Tiltawhirl John	U	RF	250+	Paulsen, Gary	Penguin Group
Treasures in the Dust	U	HF	250+	Porter, Tracey	HarperTrophy
Tucket's Gold	U	HF	250+	Paulsen, Gary	Bantam
Tucket's Ride	U	HF	250+	Paulsen, Gary	Bantam
Turn It Down!	U	I	250+	iOpeners	Pearson Learning Group
Ulysses S. Grant	U	B	250+	Let Freedom Ring	Red Brick Learning
Ulysses S. Grant	U	B	250+	Profiles of the Presidents	Compass Point Books
Under Wraps	U	I	250+	Goldish, Meish	Scholastic
Undying Glory: The Story of the Massachusetts 54th Regiment	U	HF	250+	Cox, Clinton	Scholastic
View from Saturday, The	U	F	250+	Konigsburg, E. L.	Atheneum
Village by the Sea, The	U	RF	250+	Fox, Paula	Bantam
Volcano	U	I	250+	Lauber, Patricia	Scholastic
Voyage of Patience Goodspeed, The	U	HF	250+	Frederick, Heather Vogel	Simon & Schuster

* Collection of short stories

TITLE	LEVEL	GENRE	WORD COUNT	AUTHOR / SERIES	PUBLISHER / DISTRIBUTOR
Wait Till Helen Comes	U	F	250+	Hahn, Mary Downing	Houghton Mifflin
Walk with John Muir, A	U	B	2237	Independent Readers Social Studies	Houghton Mifflin
War Comes to Willy Freeman	U	HF	250+	Collier, James & Christopher	Dell
Warren G. Harding	U	B	250+	Profiles of the Presidents	Compass Point Books
Watsons Go to Birmingham - 1963, The	U	HF	250+	Curtis, Christopher Paul	Bantam
What Ancient Astronomers Knew	U	I	2852	Leveled Readers Science	Houghton Mifflin
When Justice Failed: The Fred Korematsu Story	U	B	250+	Chin, Steven A.	Steck-Vaughn
When the Beginning Began: Stories About God, the Creatures, and Us	U	TL	250+	Lester, Julius	OSI
*Where the Flame Trees Bloom	U	B	250+	Ada, Alma Flor	Simon & Schuster
Who Really Killed Cock Robin?	U	RF	250+	George, Jean Craighead	HarperTrophy
William Henry Harrison	U	B	250+	Profiles of the Presidents	Compass Point Books
William Howard Taft	U	B	250+	Profiles of the Presidents	Compass Point Books
William Jefferson Clinton	U	B	250+	Profiles of the Presidents	Compass Point Books
William McKinley	U	B	250+	Profiles of the Presidents	Compass Point Books
Williamsburg	U	I	250+	We The People	Compass Point Books
Wind And Water: Two Great Powers	U	I	2567	Independent Readers Social Studies	Houghton Mifflin
Winged Cat, The: A Tale of Ancient Egypt	U	TL	250+	Lattimore, Deborah Nourse	HarperCollins
Winging It	U	I	250+	iOpeners	Pearson Learning Group
Winter Room, The	U	RF	250+	Paulsen, Gary	Bantam
Wired World: A Short History of the Internet	U	I	1527	Leveled Readers Social Studies	Houghton Mifflin
Witchcraft of Salem Village, The	U	I	250+	Jackson, Shirley	Random House
Wizard of Oz, The	U	F	250+	Baum, L. Frank	Scholastic
Wolves	U	I	250+	The Untamed World	Steck-Vaughn
Women in the Vietnam War	U	I	848	Independent Readers Social Studies	Houghton Mifflin
Women of Valor	U	B	250+	Real Lives	Troll Associates
*Wonderful Story of Henry Sugar, The: And Six More	U	F	250+	Dahl, Roald	Penguin Group
Woodrow Wilson	U	B	250+	Profiles of the Presidents	Compass Point Books
Words	U	RF	250+	Paulsen, Gary	Penguin Group
Words By Heart	U	HF	250+	Sebestyen, Ouida	Bantam Doubleday Dell
Wright Brothers, The	U	B	250+	Sobol, Donald J.	Scholastic
Wringer	U	RF	250+	Spinelli, Jerry	HarperTrophy
Write It Down!	U	I	250+	iOpeners	Pearson Learning Group
Zachary Taylor	U	B	250+	Profiles of the Presidents	Compass Point Books
12 Again	V	F	250+	Corbett, Sue	Penguin Group
5 Novels	V	F	250+	Pinkwater, Daniel	Farrar, Straus and Giroux
Absolutely Normal Chaos	V	RF	250+	Creech, Sharon	HarperTrophy
African-Americans in the Old West	V	I	250+	Cornerstones of Freedom	Children's Press
African-Americans in the Thirteen Colonies	V	I	250+	Cornerstones of Freedom	Children's Press
Alcatraz	V	I	250+	Cornerstones of Freedom	Bantam
Algonquin, The	V	I	3436	Leveled Readers Social Studies	Houghton Mifflin
Alice in Wonderland	V	F	250+	Carroll, Lewis	Scholastic
Alien Plant and Animal Invaders	V	I	3318	Leveled Readers Science	Houghton Mifflin
American Revolution, The	V	I	250+	Carter, Alden R.	Franklin Watts
Amos Fortune: Free Man	V	HF	250+	Yates, Elizabeth	Puffin Books
And One For All	V	RF	250+	Nelson, Theresa	Dell
Angel Island and the Land of Promise	V	I	2595	Independent Readers Social Studies	Houghton Mifflin
Anna and the King	V	HF	250+	Landon, Margaret	HarperTrophy
Anna Is Still Here	V	HF	250+	Vos, Ida	Puffin Books

* Collection of short stories

TITLE	LEVEL	GENRE	WORD COUNT	AUTHOR / SERIES	PUBLISHER / DISTRIBUTOR
Anne of Green Gables	V	RF	250+	Montgomery, L. M.	Scholastic
Are All The Giants Dead?	V	F	250+	Norton, Mary	Harcourt Trade
Arlington National Cemetery	V	I	250+	Cornerstones of Freedom	Bantam
Assassination of Abraham Lincoln, The	V	B	250+	Cornerstones of Freedom	Children's Press
Assassination of John F. Kennedy, The	V	B	250+	Cornerstones of Freedom	Children's Press
Assassination of Martin Luther King, Jr., The	V	B	250+	Cornerstones of Freedom	Children's Press
At Home in Space	V	I	2547	Leveled Readers	Houghton Mifflin
Atoms	V	I	250+	Simply Science	Compass Point Books
Aung San Suu Kyi	V	B	1980	Leveled Readers Social Studies	Houghton Mifflin
Austere Academy, The	V	F	250+	Snicket, Lemony	Scholastic
Autumn Street	V	HF	250+	Lowry, Lois	Bantam
Bad Beginning, The	V	F	250+	Snicket, Lemony	HarperTrophy
Bandit Moon	V	HF	250+	Fleischman, Sid	Dell Yearling
Barbara McClintock	V	B	1926	Independent Readers Science	Houghton Mifflin
Battle of Chancellorsville, The	V	I	250+	Cornerstones of Freedom	Children's Press
Battle of the Alamo, The	V	I	250+	Cornerstones of Freedom	Children's Press
Battle of the Little Bighorn, The	V	I	250+	Cornerstones of Freedom	Children's Press
Battle of Yorktown, The	V	I	250+	Let Freedom Ring	Red Brick Learning
Battles of Lexington and Concord, The	V	I	250+	Let Freedom Ring	Red Brick Learning
Bearstone	V	RF	250+	Hobbs, Will	Hearst
Beauty	V	RF	250+	Wallace, Bill	Holiday House
Behind The Bedroom Wall	V	HF	250+	Williams, Laura E.	Milkweed Editions
Belle Prater's Boy	V	RF	250+	White, Ruth	Bantam
Berlin Wall, The	V	I	2050	Independent Readers Social Studies	Houghton Mifflin
Beyond the Mango Tree	V	RF	250+	Zemser, Amy Bronwen	HarperTrophy
Beyond the Western Sea, Book II: Lord Kirkle's Money	V	HF	250+	Avi	Avon Camelot
Biggest Klutz in Fifth Grade, The	V	RF	250+	Wallace, Bill	Simon & Schuster
Bill of Rights, The	V	I	250+	Cornerstones of Freedom	Bantam
Bill Pickett, Rodeo King	V	B	3134	Leveled Readers	Houghton Mifflin
Biomes	V	I	1420	Independent Readers Science	Houghton Mifflin
Birthday Room, The	V	RF	250+	Henkes, Kevin	William Morrow
Black Hearts in Battersea	V	HF	250+	Aiken, Joan	Houghton Mifflin
Black Star, Bright Dawn	V	RF	250+	O'Dell, Scott	Ballantine Books
Bloomability	V	RF	250+	Creech, Sharon	HarperCollins
Blue Willow	V	RF	250+	Gates, Doris	Puffin Books
Boston Massacre, The	V	I	250+	Let Freedom Ring	Red Brick Learning
Boston Tea Party, The	V	I	250+	Let Freedom Ring	Red Brick Learning
Boston Tea Party, The	V	I	250+	Cornerstones of Freedom	Children's Press
Brady	V	HF	250+	Fritz, Jean	Puffin Books
Brain	V	I	250+	You And Your Body	Troll Associates
Brave Past, A	V	I	1931	Leveled Readers	Houghton Mifflin
Buffalo Bill's Wild West Show	V	B	1750	Leveled Readers	Houghton Mifflin
Building Bridges	V	I	250+	iOpeners	Pearson Learning Group
Building the Capital City	V	I	250+	Cornerstones of Freedom	Bantam
But I'll Be Back Again	V	B	250+	Rylant, Cynthia	Beech Tree Books
By the Great Horn Spoon!	V	HF	250+	Fleischman, Sid	Little, Brown & Co.
California Gold Rush, The	V	I	250+	Cornerstones of Freedom	Children's Press
California Gold Rush, The	V	I	250+	Let Freedom Ring	Red Brick Learning
Call Me Francis Tucket	V	HF	250+	Paulsen, Gary	Yearling
Canyons	V	F	250+	Paulsen, Gary	Laurel-Leaf Books
Capitol, The	V	I	250+	Cornerstones of Freedom	Bantam
Carnivorous Carnival, The	V	F	250+	Snicket, Lemony	Scholastic

* Collection of short stories

TITLE	LEVEL	GENRE	WORD COUNT	AUTHOR / SERIES	PUBLISHER / DISTRIBUTOR
Cay, The	V	HF	250+	Taylor, Theodore	Avon
CD and the Giant Cat	V	SF	250+	Action Packs	Rigby
Chasing Redbird	V	RF	250+	Creech, Sharon	HarperCollins
Chisholm Trail, The	V	I	250+	Cornerstones of Freedom	Bantam
Choosing Up Sides	V	RF	250+	Ritter, John H.	Puffin Books
Circle Unbroken, A	V	HF	250+	Leveled Readers Language Support	Houghton Mifflin
City of Gold & Lead, The	V	F	250+	Christopher, John	Aladdin
Civil Rights Marches	V	I	250+	Cornerstones of Freedom	Children's Press
Clay Marble, The	V	RF	250+	Ho, Minfong	Farrar, Straus and Giroux
Clearing the Dust	V	HF	2327	Leveled Readers	Houghton Mifflin
Cold Shoulder Road	V	RF	250+	Aiken, Joan	Bantam
Come Morning	V	HF	250+	Guccione, Leslie Davis	Lerner Publishing
Come Sing, Jimmy Jo	V	RF	250+	Paterson, Katherine	Penguin Group
Constitution, The	V	I	250+	Cornerstones of Freedom	Children's Press
Corrie's Important Decision	V	I	250+	Leveled Readers Language Support	Houghton Mifflin
Crash	V	RF	250+	Spinelli, Jerry	Alfred A. Knopf
Dark Stairs	V	RF	250+	Byars, Betsy	Puffin Books
Daughter of the Mountains	V	HF	250+	Rankin, Louise	Penguin Group
Davy Crockett: Frontier Hero	V	B	2127	Leveled Readers	Houghton Mifflin
Death's Door	V	RF	250+	Byars, Betsy	Puffin Books
Declaration of Independence, The	V	I	250+	Let Freedom Ring	Red Brick Learning
Declaration of Independence, The	V	I	250+	Cornerstones of Freedom	Children's Press
Deep Blue Lake, A	V	I	2270	Leveled Readers	Houghton Mifflin
Demolition	V	I	250+	iOpeners	Pearson Learning Group
Dive!: My Adventures in the Deep Frontier	V	B	250+	Earle, Sylvia A.	Scholastic
Dogsong	V	RF	250+	Paulsen, Gary	Simon & Schuster
Dragon Chronicles, The: Dragon's Milk	V	F	250+	Fletcher, Susan	Aladdin
Dragonsong	V	F	250+	McCaffrey, Anne	Bantam
Drylongso	V	RF	250+	Hamilton, Virginia	Harcourt Trade
Dustland	V	F	250+	Hamilton, Virginia	Scholastic
Early American Industrial Revolution, 1793-1850, The	V	I	250+	Let Freedom Ring	Capstone Press
Earth at Risk	V	I	250+	Sunshine	Wright Group/McGraw Hill
Eileen Collins: First Woman in Space	V	B	2488	Leveled Readers	Houghton Mifflin
El Sid and the Flea	V	RF	2632	Leveled Readers	Houghton Mifflin
Elements in Nature	V	I	1001	Leveled Readers Science	Houghton Mifflin
Elements, The	V	I	841	Leveled Readers Science	Houghton Mifflin
Ellis Island	V	I	250+	Cornerstones of Freedom	Children's Press
Emancipation Proclamation, The	V	I	250+	Cornerstones of Freedom	Children's Press
Emerald Cathedral, The	V	I	1983	Leveled Readers	Houghton Mifflin
Ersatz Elevator, The	V	F	250+	Snicket, Lemony	Scholastic
Escape to Freedom	V	HF	250+	Davis, Ossie	Puffin Books
Esperanza Rising	V	HF	250+	Ryan, Pam Munoz	Scholastic
Everything on a Waffle	V	RF	250+	Horvath, Polly	Farrar, Straus and Giroux
Explore Your World	V	I	250+	iOpeners	Pearson Learning Group
Extraordinary Life, An: The Story of a Monarch Butterfly	V	I	250+	Pringle, Laurence	Orchard Books
Eyes of the Amaryllis, The	V	RF	250+	Babbitt, Natalie	Farrar, Straus and Giroux
*Father Water, Mother Woods	V	RF	250+	Paulsen, Gary	Bantam
Father's Arcane Daughter	V	RF	250+	Konigsburg, E. L.	Aladdin
Fighting Ground, The	V	HF	250+	Avi	HarperTrophy
Final Freedom, The	V	RF	250+	Wallace, Bill	Pocket Books

* Collection of short stories

TITLE	LEVEL	GENRE	WORD COUNT	AUTHOR / SERIES	PUBLISHER / DISTRIBUTOR
Fort Sumter	V	I	250+	Cornerstones of Freedom	Children's Press
Foster's War	V	HF	250+	Reeder, Carolyn	Scholastic
Freedom Fighters: The Massachusetts 54th Regiment	V	I	2052	Leveled Readers Social Studies	Houghton Mifflin
From Caves to Canvas	V	I	250+	Navigators Social Studies Series	Benchmark Education
Gathering, The	V	F	250+	Hamilton, Virginia	OSI
George Rogers Clark and the American Revolution in the Midwest	V	B	2534	Leveled Readers Social Studies	Houghton Mifflin
Get on Board: The Story of the Underground Railroad	V	I	250+	Haskins, Jim	Scholastic
Getting Lincoln's Goat	V	RF	250+	Goldman, E. M.	Bantam
Getting Near to Baby	V	RF	250+	Couloumbis, Audrey	Penguin Group
Gettysburg Address, The	V	I	250+	Cornerstones of Freedom	Children's Press
Ghost Belonged to Me, The	V	F	250+	Peck, Richard	Penguin Group
Gib Rides Home	V	RF	250+	Snyder, Zilpha Keatley	Bantam
Glaciers	V	I	2117	Leveled Readers Social Studies	Houghton Mifflin
Golden Goblet, The	V	RF	250+	McGraw, Eloise Jarvis	Scholastic
Gone-Away Lake	V	RF	250+	Enright, Elizabeth	Harcourt Trade
Good-Bye, Billy Radish	V	HF	250+	Skurzynski, Gloria	Aladdin
Good-Bye, Vietnam	V	RF	250+	Whelan, Gloria	Alfred A. Knopf
Goody Hall	V	RF	250+	Babbitt, Natalie	Farrar, Straus and Giroux
Grab Hands and Run	V	RF	250+	Temple, Frances	HarperTrophy
Gray Blanket, The: Rabbits in Australia	V	I	1878	Leveled Readers Social Studies	Houghton Mifflin
Green Book, The	V	F	250+	Walsh, Jill Paton	Farrar, Straus and Giroux
Grim Grotto, The	V	F	250+	Snicket, Lemony	HarperCollins
Guardians of Ga'Hoole: The Journey	V	F	250+	Lasky, Kathryn	Scholastic
Habibi	V	B	250+	Nye, Naomi Shihab	Simon & Schuster
Hannah Brown, Union Army Spy	V	HF	2231	Leveled Readers	Houghton Mifflin
Harris and Me	V	RF	250+	Paulsen, Gary	Bantam
Harry Potter and the Chamber of Secrets	V	F	250+	Rowling, J. K.	Scholastic
Harry Potter and the Prisoner of Azkaban	V	F	250+	Rowling, J. K.	Scholastic
Harry Potter and the Sorcerer's Stone	V	F	250+	Rowling, J. K.	Scholastic
Hobby: The Young Merlin Trilogy	V	F	250+	Yolen, Jane	Scholastic
Holes	V	RF	250+	Sachar, Louis	Random House
Hostile Hospital, The	V	F	250+	Snicket, Lemony	Scholastic
House of Dies Drear	V	HF	250+	Hamilton, Virginia	Aladdin
I Rode a Horse of Milk White Jade	V	HF	250+	Wilson, Diane Lee	HarperTrophy
If I Forget, You Remember	V	RF	250+	Williams, Carol Lynch	Bantam
In the Days of the Dinosaur	V	I	3182	Leveled Readers Science	Houghton Mifflin
In the Path of Lewis & Clark: Traveling the Missouri	V	I	250+	Lourie, Peter	Silver Burdett Press
Incident at Hawk's Hill	V	F	250+	Eckert, Allen W.	Little, Brown & Co.
Incredible Journey, The	V	F	250+	Burnford, Sheila	Bantam
Island of the Blue Dolphins	V	HF	250+	O'Dell, Scott	Bantam
Jackie Robinson Breaks the Color Line	V	B	250+	Cornerstones of Freedom	Children's Press
Jamestown Colony, The	V	I	250+	Cornerstones of Freedom	Children's Press
Jericho Walls	V	HF	250+	Collier, Kristi	Henry Holt & Co.
Jewel of the Desert	V	HF	2994	Leveled Readers	Houghton Mifflin
Jingo Django	V	RF	250+	Fleischman, Sid	Bantam
Jip: His Story	V	HF	250+	Paterson, Katherine	Penguin Group
John Charles and Jessie Fremont: Pathfinders of the West	V	B	2453	Leveled Readers Social Studies	Houghton Mifflin
John F. Kennedy	V	B	250+	World Leaders: Past and Present	Chelsea House
John James Audubon: Wildlife Artist	V	B	250+	A First Book	Franklin Watts

* Collection of short stories

TITLE	LEVEL	GENRE	WORD COUNT	AUTHOR / SERIES	PUBLISHER / DISTRIBUTOR
John Peter Zenger and Freedom of the Press	V	B	2213	Leveled Readers Social Studies	Houghton Mifflin
Joseph: 1861 - A Rumble of War	V	HF	250+	Pryor, Bonnie	Avon
Journey Home	V	RF	250+	Uchida, Yoshika	Aladdin
Journey Outside	V	F	250+	Steele, Mary Q.	Penguin Group
Journey to an 800 Number	V	RF	250+	Konigsburg, E. L.	Aladdin
Juan's Three Wishes	V	F	1842	Leveled Readers	Houghton Mifflin
Keep Smiling Through	V	RF	250+	Rinaldi, Ann	Harcourt Trade
Keeping Room, The	V	HF	250+	Myers, Anna	Puffin Books
Kensuke's Kingdom	V	RF	250+	Morpurgo, Michael	Scholastic
Lake of Secrets	V	RF	250+	Little, Lael	Henry Holt & Co.
Lasers	V	I	250+	Sunshine	Wright Group/McGraw Hill
Letters From Camp: A Mystery	V	RF	250+	Klise, Kate	HarperTrophy
Lewis and Clark	V	B	250+	Cornerstones of Freedom	Children's Press
Lewis and Clark Expedition, The	V	I	250+	Let Freedom Ring	Red Brick Learning
Lexington and Concord	V	I	250+	Cornerstones of Freedom	Children's Press
Liberty Bell, The	V	I	250+	Cornerstones of Freedom	Children's Press
Library of Congress, The	V	I	250+	Cornerstones of Freedom	Children's Press
Life on the Serengeti	V	I	1811	Independent Readers Science	Houghton Mifflin
Lincoln Memorial, The	V	I	250+	Cornerstones of Freedom	Children's Press
Lincoln: A Photobiography	V	B	250+	Freedman, Russell	Clarion
Living History	V	I	250+	iOpeners	Pearson Learning Group
Locomotion	V	RF	250+	Woodson, Jacqueline	Penguin Group
Long Way from Chicago, A	V	HF	250+	Peck, Richard	Puffin Books
Lost World of the Olmec	V	I	2149	Independent Readers Social Studies	Houghton Mifflin
Louisiana Purchase, The	V	I	250+	Cornerstones of Freedom	Children's Press
Louisiana Purchase, The	V	I	250+	Let Freedom Ring	Red Brick Learning
Lyddie	V	HF	250+	Paterson, Katherine	Penguin Group
Manatee, The	V	I	250+	Silverstein, A.; Nunn, L.	The Millbrook Press
Many Waters	V	F	250+	L'Engle, Madeleine	Bantam
Marian Anderson: Singer	V	B	250+	American Women of Achievement	Chelsea House
Matthew's Meadow	V	RF	250+	Bliss, Corinne Demas	OSI
Maze, The	V	RF	250+	Hobbs, Will	Morrow Junior Books
Merlin: The Young Merlin Trilogy	V	TL	250+	Yolen, Jane	Scholastic
Mexican War, 1846-1848, The	V	I	250+	Let Freedom Ring	Capstone Press
Midnight Horse, The	V	F	250+	Fleischman, Sid	Bantam
Mighty, The	V	RF	250+	Philbrick, Rodman	Scholastic
Miserable Mill, The	V	F	250+	Snicket, Lemony	Scholastic
Monkey Island	V	RF	250+	Fox, Paula	Orchard Books
Monsoon Civilizations	V	I	2591	Independent Readers Social Studies	Houghton Mifflin
Monticello	V	I	250+	Cornerstones of Freedom	Children's Press
Mount Vernon	V	I	250+	Cornerstones of Freedom	Children's Press
Mrs. Frisby and the Rats of NIMH	V	F	250+	O'Brien, Robert C.	Aladdin
Multi-Tasker, The	V	RF	3226	Leveled Readers	Houghton Mifflin
Music of Dolphins, The	V	RF	250+	Hesse, Karen	Scholastic
My Brother, My Sister, and I	V	HF	250+	Watkins, Yoko Kawashima	Aladdin
My Name is Not Angelica	V	HF	250+	O'Dell, Scott	Bantam
My Wartime Summers	V	HF	250+	Cutler, Jane	HarperCollins
Negro Leagues of Baseball, The	V	I	3319	Leveled Readers Social Studies	Houghton Mifflin
Night Birds on Nantucket	V	HF	250+	Aiken, Joan	Houghton Mifflin
Ninjas, Piranhas, and Galileo	V	RF	250+	Smith, Greg Leitich	Little, Brown & Co.
Not That I Care	V	RF	250+	Vail, Rachel	Scholastic
Old Yeller	V	RF	250+	Gipson, Fred	Scholastic

TITLE	LEVEL	GENRE	WORD COUNT	AUTHOR / SERIES	PUBLISHER / DISTRIBUTOR
Olive's Ocean	V	RF	250+	Henkes, Kevin	HarperCollins
On The Far Side Of The Mountain	V	RF	250+	George, Jean Craighead	Puffin Books
One More River	V	HF	250+	Banks, Lynne Reid	Avon Camelot
Oregon Trail, The	V	I	250+	Let Freedom Ring	Red Brick Learning
Oregon Trail, The	V	I	250+	Cornerstones of Freedom	Children's Press
Orson Welles and The War of the Worlds	V	I	1917	Leveled Readers	Houghton Mifflin
Passager: The Young Merlin Trilogy	V	F	250+	Yolen, Jane	Scholastic
Paul Revere	V	B	250+	Cornerstones of Freedom	Children's Press
Perseus and Medusa	V	TL	250+	Leveled Readers Language Support	Houghton Mifflin
Pictures of Hollis Woods	V	RF	250+	Giff, Patricia Reilly	Scholastic
Pictures to Words: The Origins of Writing	V	I	2032	Independent Readers Social Studies	Houghton Mifflin
Pilgrims, The	V	I	250+	Cornerstones of Freedom	Children's Press
Pleasing the Ghost	V	F	250+	Creech, Sharon	HarperCollins
Pocket Full of Seeds, A	V	HF	250+	Sachs, Marilyn	Scholastic
Pony Express, The	V	I	250+	Cornerstones of Freedom	Children's Press
Pool of Fire, The	V	F	250+	Christopher, John	Aladdin
*Power of Light, The	V	TL	250+	Singer, Isaac Bashevis	Farrar, Straus and Giroux
Presidency of the United States, The	V	I	250+	American Civics	Red Brick Learning
Promise Me the Moon	V	RF	250+	Barnes, Joyce Annette	Penguin Group
Pullman Strike, The	V	I	1541	Leveled Readers Social Studies	Houghton Mifflin
Pyramids of Ancient Egypt, The	V	I	250+	Leveled Readers Language Support	Houghton Mifflin
*Rainbow People, The	V	F	250+	Yep, Lawrence	HarperTrophy
Rascal	V	HF	250+	North, Sterling	Scholastic
Remarkable Journey of Prince Jen, The	V	F	250+	Alexander, Lloyd	Bantam
Remember Not To Forget: A Memory of the Holocaust	V	I	250+	Finkelstein, Norman H.	William Morrow
Revolution!	V	HF	3239	Leveled Readers	Houghton Mifflin
Riddle of the Rosetta Stone, The	V	I	250+	Giblin, James Cross	HarperTrophy
Ring of Fire, The	V	I	2580	Leveled Readers Social Studies	Houghton Mifflin
Roberto Clemente, Baseball Superstar	V	B	1776	Leveled Readers	Houghton Mifflin
Root Cellar, The	V	HF	250+	Lunn, Janet	Penguin Group
Ruby Holler	V	RF	250+	Creech, Sharon	HarperCollins
Same Stuff as Stars, The	V	RF	250+	Paterson, Katherine	Clarion
Samuel de Champlain in Canada	V	B	3002	Leveled Readers	Houghton Mifflin
Santa Fe Trail, The	V	I	250+	Cornerstones of Freedom	Children's Press
Save Queen of Sheba	V	HF	250+	Moeri, Louise	Puffin Books
Saving Wild One	V	RF	2109	Leveled Readers	Houghton Mifflin
Scared Stiff	V	F	250+	Malcolm, Jahnna N.	Scholastic
Search for Oil	V	I	3343	Leveled Readers Science	Houghton Mifflin
Secret of NIMH, The	V	F	250+	O'Brien, Robert C.	Scholastic
*Shadows & Moonshine	V	TL	250+	Aiken, Joan	David R. Godine
Shane	V	HF	250+	Schaefer, Jack	Random House
Silent to the Bone	V	RF	250+	Konigsburg, E. L.	Atheneum
Simply Alice	V	RF	250+	Naylor, Phyllis Reynolds	Simon & Schuster
Skateway to Freedom	V	HF	250+	Alma, Ann	Orca Book Publishers
Slippery Slope, The	V	F	250+	Snicket, Lemony	Scholastic
So Far From the Bamboo Grove	V	HF	250+	Watkins, Yoko Kawashima	William Morrow
Sojourner Truth: Ain't I a Woman?	V	B	250+	McKissack, Fredrick & Patricia	Scholastic
Solar Energy	V	I	2068	Leveled Readers Science	Houghton Mifflin
Soldier's Heart	V	HF	250+	Paulsen, Gary	Random House
SOS Titanic	V	HF	250+	Bunting, Eve	Harcourt Trade

* Collection of short stories

TITLE	LEVEL	GENRE	WORD COUNT	AUTHOR / SERIES	PUBLISHER / DISTRIBUTOR
Spirit of St. Louis, The	V	I	250+	Cornerstones of Freedom	Children's Press
Stargirl	V	RF	250+	Spinelli, Jerry	Alfred A. Knopf
Statue of Liberty, The	V	I	250+	The Heinle Reading Library	Thomson Learning
Stealing Home: The Story of Jackie Robinson	V	B	250+	Denenberg, Barry	Scholastic
Stephen Hawking	V	B	2515	Leveled Readers Science	Houghton Mifflin
*Stories for Children	V	TL	250+	Singer, Isaac Bashevis	Farrar, Straus and Giroux
Story of The Surrender at Yorktown, The	V	I	250+	Cornerstones of Freedom	Children's Press
Story of The Women's Movement, The	V	I	250+	Cornerstones of Freedom	Children's Press
Story of Waltzing Matilda, The	V	I	2872	Independent Readers Social Studies	Houghton Mifflin
Summer Rays	V	RF	3077	Leveled Readers	Houghton Mifflin
Survival Animal Adaptations	V	I	250+	iOpeners	Pearson Learning Group
Swiftly Tilting Planet, A	V	F	250+	L'Engle, Madeleine	Bantam
Tea Overboard! The Boston Tea Party	V	I	1753	Leveled Readers	Houghton Mifflin
Tecumseh	V	B	250+	Cornerstones of Freedom	Children's Press
Tent, The	V	RF	250+	Paulsen, Gary	Bantam
Theft in Time, A: Timedetectors II	V	HF	250+	Action Packs	Rigby
*Thief in the Village, A	V	RF	250+	Berry, James	Puffin Books
Thief Lord, The	V	F	250+	Funke, Cornelia	Scholastic
Thief of Hearts	V	RF	250+	Yep, Laurence	HarperCollins
Things Not Seen	V	F	250+	Clements, Andrew	Scholastic
Through the Eyes of Your Ancestors: A Step-by-Step Guide to Uncovering Your Family's History	V	I	250+	Taylor, Maureen	Houghton Mifflin
Thurgood Marshall and Civil Rights	V	I	2540	Independent Readers Social Studies	Houghton Mifflin
Timedetectors	V	SF	250+	Literacy 2000	Rigby
Titanic, The	V	I	250+	Cornerstones of Freedom	Children's Press
Tom's Midnight Garden	V	F	250+	Pearce, Philippa	HarperTrophy
Trail of Tears, 1838, The	V	I	250+	Let Freedom Ring	Capstone Press
Transcontinental Railroad, The	V	I	250+	Cornerstones of Freedom	Children's Press
Tree by Leaf	V	F	250+	Voigt, Cynthia	Simon & Schuster
Troubling a Star	V	F	250+	L'Engle, Madeleine	Dell
True Confessions of Charlotte Doyle, The	V	HF	250+	Avi	Avon
Tuck Everlasting	V	F	250+	Babbitt, Natalie	Farrar, Straus and Giroux
Twenty-One Balloons, The	V	SF	250+	DuBois, William	Scholastic
Under the Royal Palms	V	B	250+	Ada, Alma Flor	Scholastic
Underground Railroad, The	V	I	250+	Cornerstones of Freedom	Children's Press
Underground Railroad, The	V	I	250+	Bial, Raymond	Houghton Mifflin
United States Constitution, The	V	I	250+	Let Freedom Ring	Red Brick Learning
Vile Village, The	V	F	250+	Snicket, Lemony	Scholastic
Voice of the People, The: American Democracy in Action	V	I	250+	Maestro, Betsy & Giulio	William Morrow
Volcanoes	V	I	250+	iOpeners	Pearson Learning Group
Wait Until Next Year	V	RF	2226	Leveled Readers	Houghton Mifflin
Walk Through a Rainforest, A: Life in the Ituri Forest of Zaire	V	RF	250+	Creech, Sharon	HarperCollins
Wanderer, The	V	RF	250+	Creech, Sharon	HarperCollins
War of 1812, The	V	I	250+	Let Freedom Ring	Capstone Press
Watchers: I.D.	V	SF	250+	Lerangis, Peter	Scholastic
Watchers: Island	V	SF	250+	Lerangis, Peter	Scholastic
Watchers: Lab 6	V	SF	250+	Lerangis, Peter	Scholastic
Watchers: Last Stop	V	SF	250+	Lerangis, Peter	Scholastic
Watchers: Rewind	V	SF	250+	Lerangis, Peter	Scholastic
Watchers: War	V	SF	250+	Lerangis, Peter	Scholastic

* Collection of short stories

TITLE	LEVEL	GENRE	WORD COUNT	AUTHOR / SERIES	PUBLISHER / DISTRIBUTOR
Westing Game, The	V	RF	250+	Raskin, Ellen	Penguin Group
What Every Girl (except me) Knows	V	RF	250+	Baskin, Nora Raleigh	Little, Brown & Co.
When the Tripods Came	V	F	250+	Christopher, John	Aladdin
White House, The	V	I	250+	Cornerstones of Freedom	Children's Press
White Mountain, The	V	F	250+	Christopher, John	Aladdin
Who Put That Hair in My Toothbrush?	V	RF	250+	Spinelli, Jerry	Little, Brown & Co.
Who Was Poor Richard? Colonials to Remember	V	I	2615	Independent Readers Social Studies	Houghton Mifflin
Wide Window, The	V	F	250+	Snicket, Lemony	Scholastic
Wild Weather	V	I	2411	Leveled Readers Science	Houghton Mifflin
Wilderness Road, 1775, The	V	I	250+	Let Freedom Ring	Capstone Press
William Penn	V	I	2200	Independent Readers Social Studies	Houghton Mifflin
Williamsburg	V	I	250+	Cornerstones of Freedom	Children's Press
Williwaw!	V	RF	250+	Bodett, Tom	Alfred A. Knopf
Wind in the Door, A	V	F	250+	L'Engle, Madeleine	Bantam
Window, The	V	RF	250+	Ingold, Jeanette	Harcourt Trade
Witches of Worm, The	V	F	250+	Snyder, Zilpha K.	Random House
Wolves of Willoughby Chase, The	V	HF	250+	Aiken, Joan	Bantam
Women Suffrage Movement, 1848-1920, The	V	I	250+	Let Freedom Ring	Capstone Press
Women Who Shaped the West	V	B	250+	Cornerstones of Freedom	Children's Press
Women's Voting Rights	V	I	250+	Cornerstones of Freedom	Children's Press
Words of Stone	V	RF	250+	Henkes, Kevin	Penguin Group
World in Grandfather's Hands, The	V	RF	250+	Strete, Craig Kee	Clarion
World Worth Keeping, A	V	I	250+	Sunshine	Wright Group/McGraw Hill
Wright Brothers, First Flyers, The	V	I	2700	Independent Readers Science	Houghton Mifflin
Year Down Yonder, A	V	RF	250+	Peck, Richard	Penguin Group
Yolonda's Genius	V	RF	250+	Fenner, Carol	Aladdin
Zulu Dog	V	RF	250+	Ferreira, Anton	Farrar, Straus and Giroux
15 Facts about Stars	W	I	1652	Independent Readers Science	Houghton Mifflin
Achilles	W	I	250+	World Mythology	Capstone Press
Across the Lines	W	HF	250+	Reeder, Carolyn	Avon Camelot
Adam of the Road	W	HF	250+	Gray, Elizabeth Janet	Scholastic
After the Dancing Days	W	HF	250+	Rostkowski, Margaret I.	HarperTrophy
After the War	W	HF	250+	Matas, Carol	Aladdin
Ancient Baghdad: City at the Crossroads of Trade	W	I	1989	Leveled Readers	Houghton Mifflin
Ancient Egypt	W	I	250+	Let's See	Compass Point Books
Ancient Greece	W	I	250+	Let's See	Compass Point Books
Ancient Indochina	W	I	2456	Independent Readers Social Studies	Houghton Mifflin
Ancient Mesopotamia	W	I	250+	Let's See	Compass Point Books
Ancient Rome	W	I	250+	Let's See	Compass Point Books
Animal Mummies of Ancient Egpyt	W	I	2896	Independent Readers Social Studies	Houghton Mifflin
Anne Frank: Life in Hiding	W	B	250+	Hurwitz, Johanna	Avon
Arkadians, The	W	F	250+	Alexander, Lloyd	Puffin Books
Around the World in a Hundred Years: From Henry the Navigator to Magellan	W	I	250+	Fritz, Jean	Putnam & Grosset
Art in Sub-Saharan Africa	W	I	2877	Independent Readers Social Studies	Houghton Mifflin
Athena	W	I	250+	World Mythology	Capstone Press
Bald Eagle Is Back, The	W	I	2691	Leveled Readers	Houghton Mifflin
Banished, The	W	F	250+	Levin, Betty	William Morrow

* Collection of short stories

TITLE	LEVEL	GENRE	WORD COUNT	AUTHOR / SERIES	PUBLISHER / DISTRIBUTOR
Battle for Iwo Jima, The	W	I	250+	Cornerstones of Freedom	Children's Press
Beating the Heat, Desert Style	W	I	1874	Leveled Readers	Houghton Mifflin
Bernardo de Gálvez	W	B	1818	Leveled Readers	Houghton Mifflin
Between the Dragon and the Eagle	W	HF	250+	Schneider, Mical	Carolrhoda Books
Blue Heron	W	RF	250+	Avi	Avon
Blue-Eyed Daisy, A	W	RF	250+	Rylant, Cynthia	Simon & Schuster
Building the Hoover Dam	W	I	1878	Leveled Readers Science	Houghton Mifflin
Calico Bush	W	HF	250+	Field, Rachel	Simon & Schuster
Cameras on the Battlefield: Photos of War	W	I	250+	High Five Reading	Red Brick Learning
Carved in Stone: Borglum and Mount Rushmore	W	I	2997	Leveled Readers	Houghton Mifflin
Castle of Llyr, The	W	F	250+	Alexander, Lloyd	Dell
Charlie Takes a Shot	W	RF	2507	Leveled Readers	Houghton Mifflin
Child of the Owl	W	RF	250+	Yep, Laurence	HarperTrophy
Christa McAuliffe: Teacher in Space	W	B	250+	Naden, Corinne J.; Blue, Rose	Millbrook Press
City of Ember, The	W	F	250+	DuPrau, Jeanne	Random House
Cleopatra	W	B	2055	Independent Readers Social Studies	Houghton Mifflin
Climbing Everest	W	I	250+	iOpeners	Pearson Learning Group
Climbing the Continents: Everest, McKinley, Kilimanjaro	W	I	3847	Leveled Readers Social Studies	Houghton Mifflin
Colibri	W	RF	250+	Cameron, Ann	Farrar, Straus and Giroux
Congress and Parliament	W	I	1803	Leveled Readers Social Studies	Houghton Mifflin
Congress of the United States, The	W	I	250+	American Civics	Red Brick Learning
Coraline	W	F	250+	Gaiman, Neil	HarperCollins
Corrie's Secret	W	I	1726	Leveled Readers	Houghton Mifflin
Crispin: The Cross of Lead	W	HF	250+	Avi	Hyperion
Cuba 15	W	RF	250+	Osa, Nancy	Delacorte
Danger In Quicksand Swamp	W	RF	250+	Wallace, Bill	Simon & Schuster
Daniel Inouye: Hero from Hawaii	W	B	3114	Leveled Readers	Houghton Mifflin
Day of Pleasure, A: Stories of a Boy Growing Up in Warsaw	W	B	250+	Singer, Isaac Bashevis	Farrar, Straus and Giroux
Dead Girls Don't Write Letters	W	RF	250+	Giles, Gail	Millbrook Press
Diana	W	I	250+	World Mythology	Capstone Press
Disability Rights Movement, The	W	I	250+	Cornerstones of Freedom	Children's Press
Dive to the Deep Ocean: Voyages of Exploration and Discovery	W	I	250+	Kovacs, Deborah	Steck-Vaughn
Dog in The Freezer, The	W	F	250+	Mazer, Harry	Simon & Schuster
Down to a Sunless Sea: The Strange World of Hydrothermal Vents	W	I	250+	Madin, Kate	Steck-Vaughn
Dragon Cauldron	W	F	250+	Yep, Laurence	HarperCollins
Dragon of the Lost Sea	W	F	250+	Yep, Laurence	HarperCollins
Dragon Steel	W	F	250+	Yep, Laurence	HarperCollins
Dragon War	W	F	250+	Yep, Laurence	HarperCollins
Dragon's Gate	W	HF	250+	Yep, Laurence	HarperCollins
Dragonwings	W	HF	250+	Yep, Lawrence	HarperTrophy
Dream Weaver	W	HF	3045	Leveled Readers	Houghton Mifflin
Drive-By	W	RF	250+	Ewing, Lynne	HarperCollins
Easter Island: Giant Stone Statues Tell of a Rich and Tragic Past	W	I	250+	Arnold, Caroline	Houghton Mifflin
Eleanor Roosevelt: A Life of Discovery	W	B	250+	Freedman, Russell	Clarion
Elections in the United States	W	I	250+	American Civics	Red Brick Learning
Exploring an Ocean Tide Pool	W	I	250+	Bendick, Jeanne	Henry Holt & Co.
*Extraordinary American Indians	W	B	250+	Avery, Susan; Skinner, Linda	Children's Press

* Collection of short stories

TITLE	LEVEL	GENRE	WORD COUNT	AUTHOR / SERIES	PUBLISHER / DISTRIBUTOR
*Extraordinary Black Americans: From Colonial to Contemporary Times	W	B	250+	Altman, Susan	Children's Press
*Extraordinary Jewish Americans	W	B	250+	Brooks, Philip	Children's Press
*Extraordinary People with Disabilities	W	B	250+	Kent, Deborah; Quinlan, Kathryn A.	Children's Press
*Extraordinary Women in Politics	W	B	250+	Gulatta, Charles	Children's Press
*Extraordinary Women Journalists	W	B	250+	Price-Groff, Claire	Children's Press
*Extraordinary Women of Medicine	W	B	250+	Stille, Darlene R.	Children's Press
*Extraordinary Women of the American West	W	B	250+	Alter, Judy	Children's Press
*Extraordinary Women Scientists	W	B	250+	Stille, Darlene R.	Children's Press
*Extraordinary Young People	W	B	250+	Brill, Marlene Targ	Children's Press
F is for Fabuloso	W	RF	250+	Lee, Marie G.	Avon
Face to Face	W	RF	250+	Bauer, Marion Dane	Bantam
Father Eusebio Francisco Kino: Changing the Colonial Southwest	W	I	2436	Independent Readers Science	Houghton Mifflin
Finding a Way: Six Historic U.S. Routes	W	I	250+	iOpeners	Pearson Learning Group
Flying Lessons	W	HF	250+	Matthews, Kezi	Cricket Books
Four Great Cities	W	I	250+	iOpeners	Pearson Learning Group
Four Great Inventions of Ancient China	W	I	2534	Independent Readers Social Studies	Houghton Mifflin
Francie	W	RF	250+	English, Karen	Farrar, Straus and Giroux
Franklin Delano Roosevelt	W	B	250+	Freedman, Russell	Clarion
Freak the Mighty	W	RF	250+	Philbrick, Rodman	Scholastic
Free Black Communities in the Time of Slavery	W	I	3120	Leveled Readers Social Studies	Houghton Mifflin
Garden of Eden Motel, The	W	RF	250+	Hamilton, Morse	William Morrow
Girl From Yamhill, A	W	B	250+	Cleary, Beverly	Bantam
Girls of Many Lands	W	HF	250+	Croutier, Alev Lytle	Pleasant Company
*Gone from Home	W	RF	250+	Johnson, Angela	Alfred A. Knopf
Grand Canyon Journey, A: Tracing Time in Stone	W	I	250+	A First Book	Franklin Watts
Great Whales: The Gentle Giants	W	I	250+	Lauber, Patricia	Henry Holt & Co.
Greatest Electrician in the World, The	W	B	1926	Leveled Readers	Houghton Mifflin
Greece	W	I	250+	Countries and Cultures	Capstone Press
Guardian of the Dark	W	F	250+	Spencer, Bev	Scholastic
Gunpowder and Tea	W	HF	3290	Leveled Readers	Houghton Mifflin
Hades	W	I	250+	World Mythology	Capstone Press
Harry Potter and the Goblet of Fire	W	F	250+	Rowling, J. K.	Scholastic
Harry Potter and the Half-Blood Prince	W	F	250+	Rowling, J. K.	Scholastic
Harry Potter and the Order of the Phoenix	W	F	250+	Rowling, J. K.	Scholastic
Heartbeat	W	RF	250+	Creech, Sharon	HarperCollins
Hercules	W	I	250+	World Mythology	Capstone Press
Honorable Prison, The	W	HF	250+	Becerra de Jenkins, Lyll	Penguin Group
Hoot	W	RF	250+	Hiaasen, Carl	Alfred A. Knopf
Hope Was Here	W	RF	250+	Bauer, Joan	G.P. Putnam's Sons
House on Mango Street, The	W	RF	250+	Cisneros, Sandra	Alfred A. Knopf
How I Came to Be a Writer	W	B	250+	Naylor, Phyllis Reynolds	Scholastic
Howard Carter: Searching for King Tut	W	B	250+	Ford, Barbara	W. H. Freeman & Co.
I Am A Star: Child of the Holocaust	W	I	250+	Auerbacher, Inge	Penguin Group
In Search of the Grand Canyon	W	I	250+	Fraser, Mary Ann	Henry Holt & Co.
India	W	I	250+	Countries and Cultures	Capstone Press
Introducing the Euro	W	I	1930	Leveled Readers Social Studies	Houghton Mifflin
Ireland	W	I	250+	Countries and Cultures	Capstone Press
Iron Ring, The	W	F	250+	Alexander, Lloyd	Puffin Books
Island Far From Home, An	W	HF	250+	Donahue, John	Carolrhoda Books

* Collection of short stories

TITLE	LEVEL	GENRE	WORD COUNT	AUTHOR / SERIES	PUBLISHER / DISTRIBUTOR
*Jack's New Power: Stories From a Caribbean Year	W	RF	250+	Gantos, Jack	Sunburst
John & Abigail Adams: An American Love Story	W	B	250+	St. George, Judith	Scholastic
John Paul Jones and the Battle at Sea	W	B	2095	Independent Readers Social Studies	Houghton Mifflin
Khyber Pass, The	W	I	1993	Leveled Readers Social Studies	Houghton Mifflin
Kingfisher's Gift, The	W	F	250+	Beckhorn, Susan Williams	Penguin Group
Kiss the Dust	W	RF	250+	Laird, Elizabeth	Penguin Group
Last Book in the Universe, The	W	SF	250+	Philbrick, Rodman	Scholastic
Letters to Julia	W	RF	250+	Holmes, Barbara Ware	HarperTrophy
Life and Words of Martin Luther King, Jr., The	W	B	250+	Peck, Ira	Scholastic
Lincoln-Douglas Debates, The	W	I	250+	Cornerstones of Freedom	Children's Press
Living Through a Natural Disaster	W	I	250+	iOpeners	Pearson Learning Group
Lobster's Tale, A	W	I	2114	Leveled Readers	Houghton Mifflin
*Local News	W	RF	250+	Soto, Gary	Scholastic
Lost Garden, The	W	B	250+	Yep, Laurence	Beech Tree Books
Magical Adventures of Pretty Pearl, The	W	F	250+	Hamilton, Virginia	HarperTrophy
Mama, Let's Dance	W	RF	250+	Hermes, Patricia	Scholastic
Maniac Magee	W	RF	250+	Spinelli, Jerry	Scholastic
Mark Twain	W	B	250+	Cox, Clinton	Scholastic
Mars	W	I	250+	World Mythology	Capstone Press
Mary Leakey	W	B	2174	Leveled Readers Social Studies	Houghton Mifflin
Max the Mighty	W	RF	250+	Philbrick, Rodman	Scholastic
Maya Angelou: Greeting the Morning	W	B	250+	King, Sarah E.	The Millbrook Press
Maya Angelou: Journey of the Heart	W	B	250+	Pettit, Jayne	Puffin Books
Medusa	W	I	250+	World Mythology	Capstone Press
Meet the Austins	W	RF	250+	L'Engle, Madeleine	Laurel-Leaf Books
Meteorite!: The Last Days of the Dinosaurs	W	I	250+	Norris, Richard	Steck-Vaughn
Mexico's Smoking Mountains	W	I	1955	Leveled Readers	Houghton Mifflin
Missing May	W	RF	250+	Rylant, Cynthia	Bantam
Moccasin Trail	W	RF	250+	McGraw, Eloise	Scholastic
Moon Bridge, The	W	HF	250+	Savin, Marcia	Scholastic
Moon Over Tennessee: A Boy's Civil War Journal	W	B	250+	Crist-Evans, Craig	Houghton Mifflin
Mouse Rap, The	W	RF	250+	Myers, Walter Dean	HarperTrophy
Mr. Lincoln's Drummer	W	HF	250+	Wisler, G. Clifton	Penguin Group
My Own Two Feet	W	B	250+	Cleary, Beverly	Avon
*Newbery Christmas, A: Fourteen Stories of Christmas by Newbery Award-Winning Authors	W	RF	250+	Greenberg, Martin H.; Waugh, Charles G.	Delacorte
*Newbery Halloween, A: A Dozen Scary Stories by Newbery Award-Winning Authors	W	F	250+	Greenberg, Martin H.; Waugh, Charles G.	Delacorte
Night Flyers, The	W	RF	250+	Jones, Elizabeth McDavid	Pleasant Company
Nightjohn	W	HF	250+	Paulsen, Gary	Bantam
*Nightmare Hour: Time for Terror	W	F	250+	Stine, R. L.	HarperCollins
Ocean Detectives: Solving Mysteries of the Sea	W	I	250+	Cerullo, Mary	Steck-Vaughn
Once Upon a Marigold	W	F	250+	Ferris, Jean	Harcourt Trade
Orphan Train Adventures: Caught in the Act	W	HF	250+	Nixon, Joan Lowery	Bantam
Orphan Train Adventures: Circle of Love	W	HF	250+	Nixon, Joan Lowery	Bantam
Orphan Train Adventures: Dangerous Promise, A	W	HF	250+	Nixon, Joan Lowery	Dell
Orphan Train Adventures: Family Apart, A	W	HF	250+	Nixon, Joan Lowery	Dell
Orphan Train Adventures: In the Face of Danger	W	HF	250+	Nixon, Joan Lowery	Dell
Orphan Train Adventures: Keeping Secrets	W	HF	250+	Nixon, Joan Lowery	Dell
Orphan Train Adventures: Place to Belong, A	W	HF	250+	Nixon, Joan Lowery	Dell
Our Endangered Planet (Oceans)	W	I	250+	Hoff, Mary; Rodgers, Mary	Lerner Publishing
Outdoor Adventures	W	I	250+	iOpeners	Pearson Learning Group

* Collection of short stories

TITLE	LEVEL	GENRE	WORD COUNT	AUTHOR / SERIES	PUBLISHER / DISTRIBUTOR
Pakistan	W	I	250+	Countries and Cultures	Capstone Press
Panama Canal, The	W	I	250+	Cornerstones of Freedom	Children's Press
Parvana's Journey	W	RF	250+	Ellis, Deborah	Douglas & McIntyre
Peter Stuyvesant: New Amsterdam and the Origins of New York	W	B	250+	The Library of American Lives and Times	Rosen Publishing Group
Pets in a Jar: Collecting and Caring for Small Wild Animals	W	I	250+	Simon, Seymour	Penguin Group
Phantom Tollbooth, The	W	F	250+	Juster, Norton	Bantam
Phoenix Rising	W	RF	250+	Hesse, Karen	Penguin Group
Pine Hollow: Changing Leads	W	RF	250+	Bryant, Bonnie	Bantam
Pine Hollow: Conformation Faults	W	RF	250+	Bryant, Bonnie	Bantam
Pine Hollow: Reining In	W	RF	250+	Bryant, Bonnie	Bantam
Pine Hollow: The Long Ride	W	RF	250+	Bryant, Bonnie	Bantam
Pine Hollow: The Trail Home	W	RF	250+	Bryant, Bonnie	Bantam
Plants of the Coral Reef	W	I	1832	Leveled Readers Science	Houghton Mifflin
Powers of Congress, The	W	I	250+	Cornerstones of Freedom	Children's Press
Presidential Elections	W	I	250+	Cornerstones of Freedom	Children's Press
Pride of Puerto Rico: The Life of Roberto Clemente	W	B	250+	Walker, Paul Robert	Harcourt Trade
Private Captain: A Story of Gettysburg	W	HF	250+	Crisp, Marty	Philomel Books
Proud Taste For Scarlet And Miniver	W	F	250+	Konigsburg, E. L.	Dell
Pure Dead Wicked	W	F	250+	Gliori, Debi	Random House
Pyramids of Giza, The	W	I	1718	Leveled Readers	Houghton Mifflin
Quest For Medusa's Head, The	W	TL	1385	Leveled Readers	Houghton Mifflin
Red and the Big Bad Wolf	W	F	1357	Leveled Readers	Houghton Mifflin
Red Cap	W	HF	250+	Wisler, G. Clifton	Penguin Group
Remnants	W	SF	250+	Applegate, K. A.	Scholastic
Ring of Endless Light, A	W	F	250+	L'Engle, Madeleine	Dell
Roll of Thunder, Hear My Cry	W	HF	250+	Taylor, Mildred D.	Penguin Group
Rosalyn Yalow	W	B	2138	Leveled Readers Science	Houghton Mifflin
Rough Riders, The	W	B	250+	Cornerstones of Freedom	Children's Press
Running Out of Time	W	SF	250+	Haddix, Margaret Peterson	Simon & Schuster
Sarny: A Life Remembered	W	HF	250+	Paulsen, Gary	Delacorte
Saturnalia	W	RF	250+	Fleischman, Paul	HarperCollins
Say Yes	W	RF	250+	Couloumbis, Audrey	Putnam
Scribe of Ancient China, A	W	HF	2134	Leveled Readers	Houghton Mifflin
Sea Otter Rescue: The Aftermath of an Oil Spill	W	I	250+	Smith, Roland	Scholastic
*Seedfolks	W	RF	250+	Fleishman, Paul	HarperTrophy
Selchie's Seed, The	W	F	250+	Oppenheim, Shulamith Levey	OSI
Serpent's Children, The	W	HF	250+	Yep, Laurence	HarperTrophy
Seventh Tower, The: The Fall	W	F	250+	Nix, Garth	Scholastic
Shades of Gray	W	HF	250+	Reeder, Carolyn	Avon Camelot
Simon Bolivar	W	B	1858	Leveled Readers Social Studies	Houghton Mifflin
Sing for Your Father, Su Phan	W	HF	250+	Pevsner, Stella; Tang, Fay	Bantam
Sister	W	RF	250+	Greenfield, Eloise	HarperCollins
Skin I'm In, The	W	RF	250+	Flake, Sharon G.	Hyperion
Slam!	W	RF	250+	Myers, Walter Dean	Scholastic
Solitary Blue, A	W	RF	250+	Voigt, Cynthia	Scholastic
Sonic Quest	W	F	250+	Roberts, Katherine	Scholastic
Space Wardrobe	W	I	1501	Independent Readers Science	Houghton Mifflin
Spanish-American War, The	W	I	250+	Cornerstones of Freedom	Children's Press
Spies on the Devil's Belt	W	HF	250+	Haynes, Betsy	Scholastic
Staying Healthy	W	I	250+	iOpeners	Pearson Learning Group
Stepping Back in Time	W	RF	2045	Leveled Readers	Houghton Mifflin

* Collection of short stories

TITLE	LEVEL	GENRE	WORD COUNT	AUTHOR / SERIES	PUBLISHER / DISTRIBUTOR
Stone in My Hand, A	W	RF	250+	Clinton, Cathryn	Candlewick Press
Story of The Persian Gulf War, The	W	I	250+	Cornerstones of Freedom	Children's Press
Story of The Sinking of the Battleship Maine, The	W	I	250+	Cornerstones of Freedom	Children's Press
Stowaway	W	HF	250+	Hesse, Karen	Simon & Schuster
Strange Life of Undersea Vents, The	W	I	2522	Leveled Readers	Houghton Mifflin
Stuck in the Tar Pits	W	I	250+	Independent Readers Science	Houghton Mifflin
Stuyvesant, Peter: New Amsterdam and the Origins of New York	W	B	250+	Power Plus	Rosen Publishing Group
Summer Mail	W	RF	3361	Leveled Readers	Houghton Mifflin
Sun's Strength, The: An Ancient Chinese Myth	W	TL	1972	Leveled Readers	Houghton Mifflin
Supreme Court of the United States, The	W	I	250+	American Civics	Red Brick Learning
Swimming Lessons	W	RF	2005	Leveled Readers	Houghton Mifflin
Tales Mummies Tell	W	I	250+	Lauber, Patricia	Scholastic
Taste of Salt: The Story of Modern Haiti	W	I	250+	Temple, Frances	HarperTrophy
Theseus and the Minotaur	W	I	250+	World Mythology	Capstone Press
Tiger Eyes	W	RF	250+	Blume, Judy	Bantam
Time of Angels, A	W	F	250+	Hesse, Karen	Hyperion
Torn Thread	W	HF	250+	Isaacs, Anne	Scholastic
Total Eclipse of the Sun	W	I	250+	Independent Readers Science	Houghton Mifflin
Twilight In Grace Falls	W	RF	250+	Honeycutt, Natalie	Avon
Under the Blood-Red Sun	W	HF	250+	Salisbury, Graham	Bantam
Underground Rescue	W	RF	2180	Leveled Readers	Houghton Mifflin
Unexpected Hero, An	W	RF	2407	Leveled Readers	Houghton Mifflin
United States Holocaust Memorial Museum, The	W	I	250+	Cornerstones of Freedom	Children's Press
Usborne Book of Inventors, The	W	B	250+	Reid, Struan; Fara, Patricia	Scholastic
Venus	W	I	250+	World Mythology	Capstone Press
Vietnam Women's Memorial, The	W	I	250+	Cornerstones of Freedom	Children's Press
Walk Two Moons	W	RF	250+	Creech, Sharon	HarperCollins
Weathering the Storm	W	RF	2125	Leveled Readers	Houghton Mifflin
*What Do Fish Have To Do With Anything?	W	RF	250+	Avi	Candlewick Press
What Is a Government?	W	I	250+	iOpeners	Pearson Learning Group
"What Shall Workers Do?"	W	I	2287	Independent Readers Social Studies	Houghton Mifflin
What Time Is It?	W	I	35	iOpeners	Pearson Learning Group
*When I Was Your Age: Original Stories About Growing Up (Vol. 1)	W	B	250+	Ehrlich, Amy (Ed.)	Candlewick Press
Where the River Runs: A Portrait of a Refugee Family	W	B	250+	Graff, Nancy Price	Scholastic
Who Is Carrie?	W	HF	250+	Collier, James & Christopher	Bantam
Wings	W	TL	250+	Yolen, Jane; Nolan, Dennis	OSI
Winterdance: The Fine Madness of Running the Iditarod	W	B	250+	Paulsen, Gary	Harcourt Trade
Witch of Blackbird Pond, The	W	HF	250+	Speare, Elizabeth George	Bantam
Wrinkle in Time, A	W	F	250+	L'Engle, Madeleine	Bantam Doubleday Dell
Xuanzang, Chinese Hero	W	B	3100	Leveled Readers Social Studies	Houghton Mifflin
Year of Impossible Goodbyes	W	HF	250+	Choi, Sook Nyui	Yearling
Yellowstone 1988: Summer of Fire	W	I	250+	Lauber, Patricia	Scholastic
You Want Women to Vote, Lizzie Stanton?	W	B	250+	Fritz, Jean	Penguin Group
Zeus	W	I	250+	World Mythology	Capstone Press
Zoos Back to Nature?	W	I	250+	iOpeners	Pearson Learning Group
1000 Facts about Space	X	I	250+	Beasant, Pam	Scholastic
13 Ghosts: Strange But True Stories	X	F	250+	Osborne, Will	Scholastic
Abracadabra Kid, The	X	B	250+	Fleischman, Sid	Beech Tree Books

TITLE	LEVEL	GENRE	WORD COUNT	AUTHOR / SERIES	PUBLISHER / DISTRIBUTOR
Acceptable Time, An	X	F	250+	L'Engle, Madeleine	Laurel-Leaf Books
Airborne	X	I	250+	iOpeners	Pearson Learning Group
Aksum: Heart of Ancient Ethiopia	X	I	2568	Independent Readers Social Studies	Houghton Mifflin
Alexander Graham Bell	X	B	250+	The Canadians	Fitzhenry & Whiteside
Amazing Amoeba, The	X	I	1290	Independent Readers Science	Houghton Mifflin
America's First City: Caral	X	I	2654	Independent Readers Social Studies	Houghton Mifflin
Angel Factory, The	X	SF	250+	Blacker, Terence	Simon & Schuster
Anne Frank: Beyond the Diary	X	I	250+	Van der Rol, Ruud; Verhoeven, Rian	Puffin Books
April Morning	X	HF	250+	Fast, Howard	Bantam
At Her Majesty's Request: An African Princess in Victorian England	X	HF	250+	Myers, Walter Dean	Scholastic
Band of Brave Men, A	X	I	250+	iOpeners	Pearson Learning Group
Beast	X	F	250+	Napoli, Donna Jo	Atheneum
Benjamin Franklin: A Scientist by Nature	X	B	2095	Leveled Readers	Houghton Mifflin
Beyond Providence	X	RF	250+	Schnur, Steven	OSI
Big Foot	X	I	250+	The Unexplained	Capstone Press
Bill Cosby: The Changing Black Image	X	B	250+	Rosenberg, Robert	Millbrook Press
Black Eagles: African Americans in Aviation	X	B	250+	Haskins, Jim	Scholastic
*Black Heroes of the American Revolution	X	B	250+	Davis, Burke	Harcourt Trade
Black Pearl, The	X	RF	250+	O'Dell, Scott	Bantam
Blue Door, The	X	HF	250+	Rinaldi, Ann	Scholastic
Bone Dance	X	RF	250+	Brooks, Martha	Random House
*Boys Will Be	X	I	250+	Brooks, Bruce	Hyperion
Break with Charity, A: A Story About the Salem Witch Trials	X	HF	250+	Rinaldi, Ann	Harcourt Trade
Bridging Beyond	X	F	250+	Duble, Kathleen Benner	Penguin Group
Bright Idea, A	X	I	250+	iOpeners	Pearson Learning Group
Buddha Boy	X	RF	250+	Koja, Kathe	Puffin Books
Build Your Own Web Site	X	I	250+	iOpeners	Pearson Learning Group
Bully for You, Teddy Roosevelt!	X	B	250+	Fritz, Jean	Penguin Group
C. W. Post: A Pioneer in His Time	X	B	2121	Leveled Readers	Houghton Mifflin
Call It Courage	X	RF	250+	Sperry, Armstrong	Aladdin
Caravan Boy	X	HF	3258	Leveled Readers	Houghton Mifflin
Castle	X	I	250+	Macaulay, David	Scholastic
Catherine, Called Birdy	X	HF	250+	Cushman, Karen	Clarion
Child in Prison Camp, A	X	HF	250+	Takashima, Shizuye	Tundra Books
Children of the River	X	RF	250+	Crew, Linda	Bantam
Children of the Wild West	X	I	250+	Freedman, Russell	Clarion
Childtimes: A Three-Generation Memoir	X	B	250+	Greenfield, Eloise; Little, Lessie Jones	HarperTrophy
Cleopatra	X	B	250+	Green, Robert	Franklin Watts
Conceived in Liberty: The Gettysburg Address	X	I	2069	Leveled Readers	Houghton Mifflin
Cowboys of the Wild West	X	I	250+	Freedman, Russell	Clarion
Crime Scene Clues	X	I	250+	Independent Readers Science	Houghton Mifflin
Crossing Jordan	X	RF	250+	Fogelin, Adrian	Peachtree
Crowfoot	X	B	250+	The Canadians	Fitzhenry & Whiteside
Danny's Desert Rats	X	RF	250+	Naylor, Phyllis Reynolds	Aladdin
Dark Is Rising, The	X	F	250+	Cooper, Susan	Macmillan
Daughter of Venice	X	HF	250+	Napoli, Donna Jo	Random House
Dawn of Fear	X	HF	250+	Cooper, Susan	Simon & Schuster
Definitely Cool	X	RF	250+	Wilkinson, Brenda	Scholastic

* Collection of short stories

TITLE	LEVEL	GENRE	WORD COUNT	AUTHOR / SERIES	PUBLISHER / DISTRIBUTOR
Dicey's Song	X	RF	250+	Voigt, Cynthia	Ballantine Books
Dragon's Blood	X	F	250+	Yolen, Jane	Harcourt Trade
Dred Scott Decision, The	X	I	250+	Cornerstones of Freedom	Children's Press
Dust from Old Bones	X	HF	250+	Forrester, Sandra	William Morrow
Earthquake Terror	X	RF	250+	Kehret, Peg	Puffin Books
Echohawk	X	HF	250+	Durrant, Lynda	Bantam
Egypt Game, The	X	RF	250+	Snyder, Zilpha Keatley	Bantam
Emily Carr	X	B	250+	The Canadians	Fitzhenry & Whiteside
Emily Murphy	X	B	250+	The Canadians	Fitzhenry & Whiteside
Europe: Geography of Conquest	X	I	1830	Leveled Readers Social Studies	Houghton Mifflin
Evvy's Civil War	X	HF	250+	Brenaman, Miriam	Putnam
Fall of Tenochtitlan	X	I	3489	Leveled Readers Social Studies	Houghton Mifflin
Find A Stranger, Say Goodbye	X	RF	250+	Lowry, Lois	Dell
First Journeys	X	I	250+	iOpeners	Pearson Learning Group
Forever Friends	X	RF	250+	Boyd, Candy Dawson	Puffin Books
Forgotten Heroes, The: The Story of the Buffalo Soldiers	X	I	250+	Cox, Clinton	Scholastic
Friends and Competitors	X	B	2333	Leveled Readers	Houghton Mifflin
Frost in the Night, A: A Girlhood on the Eve of the Third Reich	X	B	250+	Baer, Edith	Sunburst
Fur Traders of New France	X	I	2576	Independent Readers Social Studies	Houghton Mifflin
Gathering Blue	X	F	250+	Lowry, Lois	Houghton Mifflin
Geography of an Empire: Ancient Rome	X	I	2392	Independent Readers Social Studies	Houghton Mifflin
Ghost Canoe	X	HF	250+	Hobbs, Will	Avon Books
Ghosts	X	I	250+	The Unexplained	Capstone Press
*Gift From Zeus, A: Sixteen Favorite Myths	X	TL	250+	Steig, Jeanne	HarperCollins
Girl Named Disaster, A	X	RF	250+	Farmer, Nancy	Penguin Group
Girl Who Owned a City, The	X	F	250+	Nelson, O. T.	Laurel-Leaf Books
Glory Field, The	X	HF	250+	Myers, Walter Dean	Scholastic
Great Depression, The	X	I	250+	Cornerstones of Freedom	Children's Press
Great Little Madison, The	X	B	250+	Fritz, Jean	G.P. Putnam's Sons
Greenwitch	X	F	250+	Cooper, Susan	Scholastic
Grey King, The	X	F	250+	Cooper, Susan	Simon & Schuster
Growing Up in Coal Country	X	I	250+	Bartoletti, Susan Campbell	Houghton Mifflin
Gulf	X	F	250+	Westfall, Robert	Scholastic
Harriet Beecher Stowe and the Beecher Preachers	X	B	250+	Fritz, Jean	Penguin Group
Harriet Tubman and the Underground Railroad	X	B	2159	Leveled Readers	Houghton Mifflin
Hatshepsut and Nerfertiti: Egyptian Queens	X	B	2135	Leveled Readers Social Studies	Houghton Mifflin
Heart's Blood	X	F	250+	Yolen, Jane	Harcourt Trade
Henry Reed, Inc.	X	F	250+	Robertson, Keith	Puffin Books
High Tide	X	I	2084	Independent Readers Science	Houghton Mifflin
*Ho Yi the Archer and Other Classic Chinese Tales	X	TL	250+	Fu, Shelley	Linnet Books
Homecoming	X	RF	250+	Voigt, Cynthia	Ballantine Books
Homeless Bird	X	RF	250+	Whelan, Gloria	HarperCollins
Homesick, My Own Story	X	B	250+	Fritz, Jean	Penguin Group
Hoops	X	RF	250+	Myers, Walter Dean	Bantam
Iceberg Hermit, The	X	RF	250+	Roth, Arthur	Scholastic
Inventive Mind of Jules Verne, The	X	B	1828	Leveled Readers	Houghton Mifflin
Iqbal	X	RF	250+	D'Adamo, Francesco	Atheneum
Island on Bird Street, The	X	HF	250+	Orlev, Uri	Houghton Mifflin

TITLE	LEVEL	GENRE	WORD COUNT	AUTHOR / SERIES	PUBLISHER / DISTRIBUTOR
Izzy, Willy-Nilly	X	RF	250+	Voigt, Cynthia	Aladdin
Jacob Have I Loved	X	RF	250+	Paterson, Katherine	HarperTrophy
Jean Fritz Comes Home	X	B	2268	Leveled Readers	Houghton Mifflin
Jim Abbott: Making the Most of It	X	B	2451	Leveled Readers	Houghton Mifflin
John A. Macdonald	X	B	250+	The Canadians	Fitzhenry & Whiteside
Johnny Kelley's Tale	X	HF	2162	Leveled Readers	Houghton Mifflin
Journey to the Center of the Earth, A	X	SF	250+	Verne, Jules	HarperCollins
Kandake, The: Queens of Kush	X	I	2040	Independent Readers Social Studies	Houghton Mifflin
Katarina	X	HF	250+	Winter, Kathryn	Scholastic
*Knot in the Grain (and Other Stories)	X	F	250+	McKinley, Robin	HarperTrophy
Langston Hughes: An Illustrated Edition	X	B	250+	Meltzer, Milton	Millbrook Press
Let the Circle Be Unbroken	X	HF	250+	Taylor, Mildred D.	Penguin Group
Letters From a Slave Girl: The Story of Harriet Jacobs	X	HF	250+	Lyons, Mary E.	Simon & Schuster
Light and Shade	X	I	250+	iOpeners	Pearson Learning Group
Little Prince, The	X	F	250+	De Saint-Exupery, Antoine	Harcourt Trade
Living in Harsh Lands	X	I	250+	iOpeners	Pearson Learning Group
Looking Back: A Book of Memories	X	B	250+	Lowry, Lois	Delacorte
Looking the Part	X	I	2322	Leveled Readers	Houghton Mifflin
Louis Riel	X	B	250+	The Canadians	Fitzhenry & Whiteside
M. C. Higgins the Great	X	RF	250+	Hamilton, Virginia	Macmillan
Make Way for Sam Houston	X	B	250+	Fritz, Jean	Putnam & Grosset
Many Thousand Gone: African Americans From Slavery to Freedom	X	TL	250+	Hamilton, Virginia	Alfred A. Knopf
Margaret Bourke-White: Life Through the Lens	X	B	3041	Leveled Readers	Houghton Mifflin
Mario Molina: Above the Clouds	X	B	2464	Leveled Readers Science	Houghton Mifflin
Mars: Mysteries of the Red Planet	X	I	3297	Leveled Readers	Houghton Mifflin
Master Puppeteer, The	X	HF	250+	Paterson, Katherine	HarperCollins
Matilda Bone	X	HF	250+	Cushman, Karen	Clarion
Maura's Angel	X	F	250+	Banks, Lynne Reid	Avon
Memories of Anne Frank	X	B	250+	Gold, Alison Leslie	Scholastic
Mercy Otis Warren: A Woman of the Revolution	X	B	2210	Leveled Readers	Houghton Mifflin
Midwife's Apprentice, The	X	HF	250+	Cushman, Karen	HarperTrophy
Mound of the Dead: The City of Mohenjo-Daro	X	I	2018	Independent Readers Social Studies	Houghton Mifflin
Moving Mama to Town	X	RF	250+	Young, Ronder Thomas	Bantam
Mummies and Their Mysteries	X	I	250+	Wilcox, Charlotte	Carolrhoda Books
National Velvet	X	RF	250+	Bagnold, Enid	Avon Books
Near Death Experiences	X	I	250+	The Unexplained	Capstone Press
Nellie McClung	X	B	250+	The Canadians	Fitzhenry & Whiteside
Nelson Mandela: "No Easy Walk to Freedom"	X	B	250+	Denenberg, Barry	Scholastic
Nelson Mandela: South Africa's Silent Voice of Protest	X	B	250+	Hargrove, Jim	Children's Press
Nightmare Mountain	X	RF	250+	Kehret, Peg	Puffin Books
*Not Guilty	X	B	250+	Sullivan, George	Scholastic
Novio Boy	X	TL	250+	Soto, Gary	Harcourt Trade
*Oddballs	X	B	250+	Sleator, William	Puffin Books
*One More River to Cross	X	B	250+	Haskins, Jim	Scholastic
One Who Came Back, The	X	RF	250+	Mazzio, Joann	Houghton Mifflin
Opening Night	X	I	2265	Leveled Readers	Houghton Mifflin
*Our World of Mysteries: Fascinating Facts About the Planet Earth	X	I	250+	Lord, Suzanne	Scholastic
Out of the Dust	X	HF	250+	Hesse, Karen	Scholastic

* Collection of short stories

TITLE	LEVEL	GENRE	WORD COUNT	AUTHOR / SERIES	PUBLISHER / DISTRIBUTOR
Over Sea, Under Stone	X	F	250+	Cooper, Susan	Simon & Schuster
Pangaea	X	I	3186	Leveled Readers Science	Houghton Mifflin
*People Could Fly, American Black Folktales	X	TL	250+	Hamilton, Virginia	Alfred A. Knopf
Peter Pan	X	F	250+	Barrie, J. M.	Aladdin
Prohibition	X	I	2560	Independent Readers Social Studies	Houghton Mifflin
Pyramid	X	I	250+	Macaulay, David	Scholastic
Queen Eleanor: Independent Spirit in the Medieval World	X	B	250+	Brooks, Polly Schoyer	Houghton Mifflin
Rain Ghost, The	X	F	250+	Kilworth, Garry	Scholastic
Return of Wild Whoopers, The	X	I	3122	Leveled Readers	Houghton Mifflin
River Apart, A	X	HF	250+	Sutherland, Robert	Fitzhenry & Whiteside
Road to Memphis, The	X	HF	250+	Taylor, Mildred D.	Penguin Group
Sarah Bishop	X	HF	250+	O'Dell, Scott	Scholastic
Seaward	X	F	250+	Cooper, Susan	Simon & Schuster
*Standing Tall: The Stories of Ten Hispanic Americans	X	B	250+	Palacios, Argentina	Scholastic
Stones in Water	X	RF	250+	Napoli, Donna Jo	Puffin Books
Story of My Life, The	X	B	250+	Keller, Helen	Bantam
Story of Sue, The: T Rex	X	I	2391	Independent Readers Science	Houghton Mifflin
Survival in the Storm	X	HF	250+	Janke, Katelan	Scholastic
Take a Chance	X	RF	2464	Leveled Readers	Houghton Mifflin
Taking Liberty	X	HF	250+	Rinaldi, Ann	Simon & Schuster
Tales of Real Escape	X	B	250+	Dowswell, Paul	Scholastic
Ties That Bind, Ties That Break	X	HF	250+	Namioka, Lensey	Delacorte
Tiger Woods: Unbeatable!	X	B	2056	Leveled Readers	Houghton Mifflin
Traitor: The Case of Benedict Arnold	X	B	250+	Fritz, Jean	Putnam & Grosset
Travels of Alvar Nunez Cebeza de Vaca, The	X	B	3751	Leveled Readers Social Studies	Houghton Mifflin
UFOs	X	I	250+	The Unexplained	Capstone Press
Unclaimed Treasures	X	RF	250+	MacLachlan, Patricia	HarperTrophy
Usborne Book of Inventors, The: From Davinci to Biro	X	B	250+	Reid, Struan; Fara, Patricia	Scholastic
Walker's Crossing	X	RF	250+	Naylor, Phyllis Reynolds	Aladdin
Walls of the World	X	I	250+	iOpeners	Pearson Learning Group
Waterstone, The	X	F	250+	Rupp, Rebecca	Candlewick Press
Where the Red Fern Grows	X	RF	250+	Rawls, Wilson	Bantam
Who the Man	X	RF	250+	Lynch, Chris	HarperCollins
Wilfrid Laurier	X	B	250+	The Canadians	Fitzhenry & Whiteside
Wole Soyinka	X	B	1951	Leveled Readers Social Studies	Houghton Mifflin
X-rays	X	I	3158	Leveled Readers Science	Houghton Mifflin
Yearling, The	X	RF	250+	Rawlings, Marjorie Kinnan	Simon & Schuster
Young Joan	X	HF	250+	Dana, Barbara	HarperTrophy
Young Land Lords, The	X	RF	250+	Myers, Walter Dean	Penguin Group
Zlata's Diary	X	B	250+	Filipovic, Zlata	Puffin Books
Acid Rain	Y	I	1702	Independent Readers Science	Houghton Mifflin
Alida's Song	Y	RF	250+	Paulsen, Gary	Random House
All American Girl	Y	RF	250+	Cabot, Meg	HarperCollins
Amanda Miranda	Y	HF	250+	Peck, Richard	Penguin Group
Among the Volcanoes	Y	RF	250+	Castaneda, Omar S.	Bantam
Anne Frank Remembered: The Story of the Woman Who Helped Hide the Frank Family	Y	B	250+	Gies, Miep	Simon & Schuster
Anne Frank: The Diary of a Young Girl	Y	B	250+	Frank, Anne	Bantam
Anthony Burns: Defeat and Triumph of a Fugitive Slave	Y	B	250+	Hamilton, Virginia	Alfred A. Knopf

* Collection of short stories

TITLE	LEVEL	GENRE	WORD COUNT	AUTHOR / SERIES	PUBLISHER / DISTRIBUTOR
Artemis Fowl	Y	F	250+	Colfer, Eoin	Hyperion
Artemis Fowl: The Arctic Incident	Y	F	250+	Colfer, Eoin	Hyperion
Ashes of Roses	Y	HF	250+	Auch, Mary Jane	Random House
Avion My Uncle Flew, The	Y	RF	250+	Fisher, Cyrus	Penguin Group
Benedict Arnold at Saratoga	Y	HF	2151	Leveled Readers	Houghton Mifflin
Beware, Princess Elizabeth	Y	HF	250+	Meyer, Carolyn	Harcourt Trade
Biodiversity Hotspots	Y	I	250+	Independent Readers Science	Houghton Mifflin
*Black Pioneers of Science and Invention	Y	B	250+	Haber, Louis	Harcourt Trade
Blue Sword, The	Y	F	250+	McKinley, Robin	Puffin Books
Borning Room, The	Y	HF	250+	Fleischman, Paul	HarperCollins
Boy Who Reversed Himself, The	Y	SF	250+	Sleator, William	Puffin Books
Breathing Underwater: Adventures in Chemistry	Y	RF	1752	Leveled Readers Science	Houghton Mifflin
Bull Run	Y	HF	250+	Fleischman, Paul	HarperCollins
Call of the Wild	Y	RF	250+	London, Jack	Signet Classics
Carry on, Mr. Bowditch	Y	B	250+	Latham, Jean Lee	Houghton Mifflin
Cesar Chavez	Y	B	2023	Leveled Readers	Houghton Mifflin
Cesar Chavez	Y	B	250+	Rodriguez, Consuelo	Chelsea House
Charlemagne and the Holy Roman Empire	Y	B	3083	Leveled Readers Social Studies	Houghton Mifflin
Charters of Freedom	Y	I	2738	Independent Readers Social Studies	Houghton Mifflin
Chief Joseph	Y	B	2199	Leveled Readers	Houghton Mifflin
Children of the Dust Bowl	Y	I	250+	Stanley, Jerry	Crown
Circle of Time, A	Y	RF	250+	Montes, Marisa	Harcourt Trade
Confucius: The Golden Rule	Y	HF	250+	Russell Freedman	Scholastic
Corner of the Universe, A	Y	RF	250+	Martin, Ann M.	Scholastic
Coronado and the Cities of Gold	Y	B	2051	Leveled Readers	Houghton Mifflin
Count Karlstein	Y	F	250+	Pullman, Philip	Alfred A. Knopf
Day Martin Luther King, Jr., Was Shot, The	Y	B	250+	Haskins, Jim	Scholastic
Day the Women Got the Vote, The: A Photo History of the Women's Rights Movement	Y	B	250+	Sullivan, George	Scholastic
Devil's Arithmetic, The	Y	F	250+	Yolen, Jane	Puffin Books
Diary of Anne Frank, The	Y	B	250+	Frank, Anne	Pocket Books
Ear, the Eye, and the Arm, The	Y	SF	250+	Farmer, Nancy	Puffin Books
Endless Steppe, The	Y	B	250+	Hautzig, Esther	HarperTrophy
Face on the Milk Carton, The	Y	RF	250+	Cooney, Caroline B.	Bantam Doubleday Dell
Fast Sam, Cool Clyde, and Stuff	Y	RF	250+	Myers, Walter Dean	Puffin Books
*Favorite Greek Myths	Y	TL	250+	Pope, Mary Osborne	Scholastic
Fire in the Hills	Y	RF	250+	Myers, Anna	Puffin Books
First On The Moon	Y	I	250+	Hehner, Barbara	Hyperion/Madison Press
For The Life of Laetitia	Y	RF	250+	Hodge, Merle	Farrar, Straus and Giroux
Gary Soto	Y	B	2464	Leveled Readers	Houghton Mifflin
Geography of War, The: The Battle of Salamis	Y	I	2877	Independent Readers Social Studies	Houghton Mifflin
George Catlin, Frontier Painter	Y	B	3371	Leveled Readers	Houghton Mifflin
Get On Out of Here, Philip Hall	Y	RF	250+	Greene, Bette	Puffin Books
Ghana: Ancient Empire	Y	I	2070	Leveled Readers Social Studies	Houghton Mifflin
Gift of Light, The: A Japanese Myth	Y	TL	2018	Leveled Readers	Houghton Mifflin
Giver, The	Y	F	250+	Lowry, Lois	Bantam
Global Energy	Y	I	2359	Independent Readers Science	Houghton Mifflin
*Grand Mothers: Poems, Reminiscences, and Short Stories About Keepers of Our Traditions	Y	B	250+	Giovanni, Nikki	Henry Holt & Co.
Great Interactive Dream Machine, The	Y	SF	250+	Peck, Richard	Puffin Books
Hammurabi and the Glory of Mesopotamia	Y	B	2564	Independent Readers Social Studies	Houghton Mifflin

* Collection of short stories

TITLE	LEVEL	GENRE	WORD COUNT	AUTHOR / SERIES	PUBLISHER / DISTRIBUTOR
Hana's Suitcase	Y	I	250+	Levine, Karen	Albert Whitman & Co.
Hatshepsut Egypt's Woman King	Y	I	250+	iOpeners	Pearson Learning Group
Hear Our Stories	Y	I	250+	iOpeners	Pearson Learning Group
*Here There Be Dragons	Y	F	250+	Yolen, Jane	Harcourt Trade
*Here There Be Witches	Y	F	250+	Yolen, Jane	Harcourt Trade
Hurricane Music	Y	RF	2564	Leveled Readers	Houghton Mifflin
I Have Lived a Thousand Years	Y	B	250+	Bitton-Jackson, Livia	Simon & Schuster
Images of Nikki Grimes, The	Y	B	1974	Leveled Readers	Houghton Mifflin
*Instead of Three Wishes: Magical Short Stories	Y	F	250+	Turner, Megan Whalen	Penguin Group
Invaders!	Y	I	3289	Leveled Readers	Houghton Mifflin
It's Not All Ancient History	Y	I	250+	iOpeners	Pearson Learning Group
Jackaroo	Y	RF	250+	Voigt, Cynthia	Scholastic
Jacob's Rescue: A Holocaust Story	Y	HF	250+	Drucker, M.; Halperin, M.	Bantam
Jazz Kid, The	Y	RF	250+	Lincoln Collier, James	Penguin Group
Jesse	Y	RF	250+	Soto, Gary	Scholastic
John Adams and the Boston Massacre	Y	I	2307	Leveled Readers	Houghton Mifflin
Joseph Brant: Iroquois Leader in the Revolution	Y	B	1743	Leveled Readers	Houghton Mifflin
Julie Krone	Y	B	250+	The Achievers	Lerner Publishing
Just Ella	Y	F	250+	Haddix, Margaret Peterson	Simon & Schuster
Kindling, The (Fire-Us Trilogy: Book 1)	Y	SF	250+	Armstrong, Jennifer; Butcher, Nancy	HarperCollins
Kit's Wilderness	Y	RF	250+	Almond, David	Random House
Lan Xang, Kingdom of the Million Elephants	Y	I	2056	Leveled Readers Social Studies	Houghton Mifflin
Life and Death of Martin Luther King, Jr.,The	Y	B	250+	Haskins, James	Beech Tree Books
Light in the Forest, The	Y	HF	250+	Richter, Conrad	Random House
Lise Meitner	Y	B	3362	Leveled Readers Science	Houghton Mifflin
*Living Up The Street	Y	RF	250+	Soto, Gary	Bantam
Lone Wolf	Y	RF	2697	Leveled Readers	Houghton Mifflin
Losing Joe's Place	Y	RF	250+	Korman, Gordon	Scholastic
Lost in Cyberspace	Y	SF	250+	Peck, Richard	Puffin Books
Love from Your Friend, Hannah	Y	HF	250+	Skolsky, Mindy Warshaw	HarperTrophy
Magnets in Medicine	Y	I	2083	Leveled Readers Science	Houghton Mifflin
Manhattan Project, The: the Race to the Atomic Bomb	Y	I	2925	Leveled Readers Science	Houghton Mifflin
Messenger	Y	F	250+	Lowry, Lois	Houghton Mifflin
Milkweed	Y	HF	250+	Spinelli, Jerry	Random House
My Brother Sam is Dead	Y	HF	250+	Collier, James & Christopher	Scholastic
*New Kids In Town	Y	B	250+	Bode, Janet	Scholastic
Night of the Chupacabras	Y	RF	250+	Lee, Marie G.	Avon Camelot
Night the Heads Came, The	Y	SF	250+	Sleator, William	Puffin Books
Nissa's Place	Y	RF	250+	LaFaye, A.	Simon & Schuster
Now Is Your Time! The African-American Struggle	Y	I	250+	Myers, Walter Dean	HarperCollins
Numbering All the Bones	Y	HF	250+	Rinaldi, Ann	Hyperion
On Wings of a Dragon	Y	F	250+	Taylor, Cora	Fitzhenry & Whiteside
One Bird	Y	RF	250+	Mori, Kyoko	Ballantine Books
One Fat Summer	Y	RF	250+	Lipsyte, Robert	HarperCollins
Only Earth and Sky Last Forever	Y	HF	250+	Benchley, Nathaniel	HarperCollins
Ordinary Miracles	Y	RF	250+	Tolan, Stephanie S.	Morrow
Our Mysterious Universe	Y	I	250+	iOpeners	Pearson Learning Group
Pagan's Crusade	Y	HF	250+	Jinks, Catherine	Candlewick Press
Philip Hall Likes Me. I Reckon Maybe.	Y	RF	250+	Greene, Bette	Puffin Books
Place to Call Home, A	Y	RF	250+	Koller, Jackie French	Aladdin
Place To Hide, A	Y	B	250+	Petit, Jayne	Scholastic

* Collection of short stories

TITLE	LEVEL	GENRE	WORD COUNT	AUTHOR / SERIES	PUBLISHER / DISTRIBUTOR
Pool Boy	Y	RF	250+	Simmons, Michael	Roaring Book Press
Protectors, The	Y	RF	3223	Leveled Readers	Houghton Mifflin
Pushcart War, The	Y	F	250+	Merrill, Jean	Bantam
Randy Moss	Y	B	250+	Sports Heroes	Red Brick Learning
Red Midnight	Y	HF	250+	Mikaelsen, Ben	HarperTrophy
Rock Records	Y	I	250+	iOpeners	Pearson Learning Group
Rodzina	Y	HF	250+	Cushman, Karen	Clarion
Ruby and the Smoke, The	Y	F	250+	Pullman, Phillip	Laurel-Leaf Books
Sacajawea	Y	B	250+	Bruchac, Joseph	Harcourt Trade
Seeing Earth from Space	Y	I	250+	Lauber, Patricia	Scholastic
*Seven Strange and Ghostly Tales	Y	F	250+	Jacques, Brian	Penguin Group
Shelf Life	Y	RF	250+	Paulsen, Gary	Simon & Schuster
Shonto Begay: His Life and Work	Y	B	2196	Leveled Readers	Houghton Mifflin
Silent Boy, The	Y	RF	250+	Lowry, Lois	Houghton Mifflin
Slake's Limbo	Y	RF	250+	Holman, Felice	Aladdin
Slave Dancer, The	Y	HF	250+	Fox, Paula	Random House
Sons of Liberty	Y	RF	250+	Griffin, Adele	Hyperion
Starting Points	Y	I	250+	iOpeners	Pearson Learning Group
*Stories of the North	Y	RF	250+	London, Jack	Scholastic
Storyteller's Beads, The	Y	RF	250+	Kurtz, Jane	Harcourt Trade
Strawberry Hill	Y	RF	250+	LaFaye, A.	Simon & Schuster
Tell Them We Remember	Y	I	250+	Bachrach, Susan D.	Little, Brown & Co.
Three Investigators, The Mystery of the Fiery Eye	Y	RF	250+	Arthur, Robert	Random House
Three Twentieth-Century Dictators	Y	I	250+	Navigators Biography Series	Benchmark Education
Toning The Sweep	Y	RF	250+	Johnson, Angela	Scholastic
Touching Spirit Bear	Y	F	250+	Mikaelsen, Ben	HarperCollins
Turkey: Between Europe and Asia	Y	I	3597	Leveled Readers Social Studies	Houghton Mifflin
Understanding Newton's Laws	Y	I	2888	Leveled Readers Science	Houghton Mifflin
Unsinkable Madame C. J. Walker, The	Y	B	3573	Leveled Readers	Houghton Mifflin
*Walk in My World, A	Y	RF	250+	Mazer, Anne	Persea Books
Walking the Choctaw Road	Y	TL	250+	Tingle, Tim	Cinco Puntos Press
Watership Down	Y	F	250+	Adams, Richard	Avon
Waves and Rays	Y	I	2452	Independent Readers Science	Houghton Mifflin
We Remember the Holocaust	Y	I	250+	Adler, David A.	Henry Holt & Co.
We Were There, Too!: Young People in U.S. History	Y	B	250+	Hoose, Phillip	Farrar, Straus and Giroux
When Johnny Went Marching: Young Americans Fight the Civil War	Y	I	250+	Wisler, B. Clifton	HarperCollins
When Zachary Beaver Came to Town	Y	RF	250+	Holt, Kimberly Willis	Dell Yearling
Where the Ground Meets the Sky	Y	HF	250+	Davies, Jacqueline	Marshall Cavendish
Where the Lilies Bloom	Y	RF	250+	Cleavers, Vera & Bill	HarperTrophy
White Fang	Y	RF	250+	London, Jack	Scholastic
Why Does It Work?	Y	I	2160	Independent Readers Science	Houghton Mifflin
Wright Brothers, The	Y	B	250+	Freedman, Russell	Holiday House
Year of the Sawdust Man, The	Y	RF	250+	LaFaye, A.	Simon & Schuster
40 Nights to Knowing the Sky	Z	I	250+	Schaaf, Fred	Henry Holt & Co.
Abarat	Z	F	250+	Barker, Clive	HarperCollins
Abe Lincoln: Log Cabin To White House	Z	B	250+	North, Sterling	Random House
Across Five Aprils	Z	HF	250+	Hunt, Irene	Follett
Adventures of Huckleberry Finn, The	Z	HF	250+	Twain, Mark	Scholastic
Adventures of Tom Sawyer, The	Z	HF	250+	Twain, Mark	Scholastic
After the Rain	Z	RF	250+	Mazer, Norma Fox	Avon
Alien Visitors and Abductions	Z	I	250+	Innes, Brian	Steck-Vaughn

* Collection of short stories

TITLE	LEVEL	GENRE	WORD COUNT	AUTHOR / SERIES	PUBLISHER / DISTRIBUTOR
Amber Spyglass, The	Z	F	250+	Pullman, Phillip	Alfred A. Knopf
*American Dragons: Twenty-Five Asian American Voices	Z	RF	250+	Yep, Laurence	HarperTrophy
*American Eyes: New Asian-American Short Stories for Young Adults	Z	RF	250+	Carlson, Lori M.	Ballantine Books
American Plague, An	Z	I	250+	Murphy, Jim	Clarion
Among the Betrayed	Z	SF	250+	Haddix, Margaret Peterson	Simon & Schuster
Among the Hidden	Z	SF	250+	Haddix, Margaret Peterson	Aladdin
Ancient Heritage: The Arab-American Minority, An	Z	I	250+	Ashabranner, Brent	HarperCollins
. . . and Now Miguel	Z	RF	250+	Krumgold, Joseph	Scholastic
Angels on the Roof	Z	RF	250+	Moore, Martha	Bantam Doubleday Dell
Angus, Thongs and Full-Frontal Snogging: Confessions of Georgia Nicolson	Z	RF	250+	Rennison, Louise	HarperCollins
Animal Farm	Z	F	250+	Orwell, George	Harcourt Trade
Annie John	Z	RF	250+	Kincaid, Jamaica	Farrar, Straus and Giroux
Aphrodite's Blessings	Z	TL	250+	McLaren, Clemence	Atheneum
Baby-Snatcher	Z	RF	250+	Terris, Susan	Scholastic
Bat 6	Z	HF	250+	Wolff, Virginia Euwer	Scholastic
Bermuda Triangle, The	Z	I	250+	Innes, Brian	Steck-Vaughn
*Between Earth and Sky: Legends of Native American Sacred Places	Z	TL	250+	Bruchac, Joseph	Voyager Books
Beyond Belief	Z	I	250+	Steiger, Brad	Scholastic
Beyond the Myth: The Story of Joan of Arc	Z	B	250+	Brooks, Polly Schoyer	Houghton Mifflin
Black Boy	Z	RF	250+	Wright, Richard	HarperPerennial
Bless Me, Ultima	Z	RF	250+	Anaya, Rudolfo	Warner Books
Bomb, The	Z	HF	250+	Taylor, Theodore	Avon
*Bound for the North Star: True Stories of Fugitive Slaves	Z	B	250+	Fradin, Dennis Brindell	Houghton Mifflin
Bowman's Store: A Journey to Myself	Z	B	250+	Bruchac, Joseph	Lee & Low Books Inc.
Brian's Song	Z	I	250+	Blinn, William	Bantam
Broken Bridge, The	Z	RF	250+	Pullman, Philip	Alfred A. Knopf
Brooklyn Bridge: Eighth Wonder of the World, The	Z	I	3473	Leveled Readers	Houghton Mifflin
Brother To Shadows	Z	SF	250+	Norton, Andre	Avon
Bruises	Z	RF	250+	De Vries, Anke	Bantam
Cage, The	Z	B	250+	Sender, Ruth Minsky	Simon & Schuster
Catalyst	Z	RF	250+	Anderson, Laurie Halse	Penguin Group
Chill Wind	Z	RF	250+	McDonald, Janet	Farrar, Straus and Giroux
Circle of Quiet, A	Z	B	250+	L'Engle, Madeleine	HarperCollins
Circuit, The	Z	HF	250+	Francisco, Jimenez	University of New Mexico
Clockwork	Z	F	250+	Pullman, Philip	Scholastic
Constantinople in the Center of the World	Z	I	2840	Independent Readers Social Studies	Houghton Mifflin
Contender, The	Z	RF	250+	Lipsythe, Robert	HarperTrophy
Copán: City of the Maya	Z	I	3688	Leveled Readers	Houghton Mifflin
Cosmic Joker, The	Z	I	250+	Innes, Brian	Steck-Vaughn
Cracking the Code	Z	I	3314	Leveled Readers Science	Houghton Mifflin
Dancing on the Edge	Z	RF	250+	Nolan, Han	Harcourt School Publishers
Day No Pigs Would Die, A	Z	HF	250+	Peck, Robert Newton	Random House
*Detective Stories	Z	RF	250+	Pullman, Philip	Kingfisher
Disaster of the Hindenburg, The: The Last Flight of the Greatest Airship Ever Built	Z	I	250+	Tanaka, Shelley	Scholastic
Doomed Queen Anne	Z	HF	250+	Meyer, Carolyn	Harcourt Trade

* Collection of short stories

TITLE	LEVEL	GENRE	WORD COUNT	AUTHOR / SERIES	PUBLISHER / DISTRIBUTOR
Dreaming in Black and White	Z	HF	250+	Jung, Reinhardt	Penguin Group
Earthborn	Z	F	250+	Card, Orson Scott	Tor
Earthfall	Z	F	250+	Card, Orson Scott	Tor
Einstein, Father of Physics	Z	B	250+	Independent Readers Science	Houghton Mifflin
*EL Bronx Remembered	Z	RF	250+	Mohr, Nicholas	HarperTrophy
Ella Minnow Pea	Z	F	250+	Dunn, Mark	MacAdam/Cage Publishing
Ellie	Z	RF	250+	Borntrager, Mary Christner	Herald Press
Eva	Z	F	250+	Dickenson, Eva	Laurel-Leaf Books
Famous Friendships	Z	I	2538	Independent Readers Social Studies	Houghton Mifflin
Farewell to Manzanar	Z	B	250+	Houston, Jeanne; Houston, James D.	Houghton Mifflin
Farthest Shore, The	Z	F	250+	Le Guin, Ursula	Bantam
Fever 1793	Z	HF	250+	Anderson, Laurie Halse	Simon & Schuster
Flight #116 Is Down!	Z	RF	250+	Cooney, Caroline B.	Scholastic
Flowers For Algernon	Z	RF	250+	Keyes, Daniel	Harcourt Trade
Forged By Fire	Z	RF	250+	Draper, Sharon M.	Aladdin
Friedrich	Z	HF	250+	Richter, Hans Peter	Puffin Books
Friends, The	Z	RF	250+	Guy, Rosa	Bantam
From the Notebooks of Melanin Sun	Z	RF	250+	Woodson, Jacqueline	Scholastic
Galileo, Messenger of Modern Science	Z	B	3428	Leveled Readers	Houghton Mifflin
*Gathering of Flowers, A	Z	RF	250+	Thomas, Joyce Carol	HarperTrophy
Gentlehands	Z	RF	250+	Kerr, M. E.	HarperTrophy
Ghosts of Flight 401	Z	I	250+	Innes, Brian	Steck-Vaughn
Giant Humanlike Beasts	Z	I	250+	Innes, Brian	Steck-Vaughn
Glass Café, The	Z	RF	250+	Paulsen, Gary	Random House
Golden Compass, The	Z	F	250+	Pullman, Philip	Ballantine Books
Good Night, Mr. Tom	Z	HF	250+	Magorian, Michelle	HarperTrophy
*Gray Heroes Elder Tales from Around the World	Z	TL	250+	Yolen, Jane	Penguin Group
Great Chicago Fire, 1871, The	Z	HF	250+	Massie, Elizabeth	Pocket Books
*Great Escapes of World War II	Z	I	250+	Sullivan, George	Scholastic
Hanged Man, The	Z	RF	250+	Block, Francesca Lia	HarperCollins
Hero and the Crown, The	Z	F	250+	McKinley, Robin	Puffin Books
Hobbit, The	Z	F	250+	Tolkien, J.R.R.	Ballantine Books
House of Stairs	Z	F	250+	Sleator, William	Puffin Books
I Am an American: A True Story of Japanese Internment	Z	HF	250+	Stanley, Jerry	Scholastic
I Am the Cheese	Z	RF	250+	Cormier, Robert	Laurel-Leaf Books
I Hadn't Meant to Tell You This	Z	RF	250+	Woodson, Jacqueline	Bantam
I Heard the Owl Call My Name	Z	RF	250+	Craven, Margaret	Random House
I Will Plant You a Lilac Tree: A Memoir of a Schindler's List Survivor	Z	B	250+	Hillman, Laura	Atheneum
Iceman	Z	RF	250+	Lynch, Chris	HarperCollins
*In Short: A Collection of Brief Creative Nonfiction	Z	I	250+	Kitchen, J.; Jones, M. P.	W. W. Norton
Inn Keeper's Apprentice	Z	B	250+	Say, Allen	Penguin Group
Invincible Louisa	Z	B	250+	Meigs, Cornelia	Scholastic
Ironman	Z	RF	250+	Crutcher, Chris	Laurel-Leaf Books
Irrational Season, The	Z	B	250+	L'Engle, Madeleine	HarperCollins
*Island Like You, An: Stories of the Barrio	Z	RF	250+	Cofer, Judith Ortiz	Penguin Group
*It Was On Fire When I Lay Down On It	Z	I	250+	Fulghum, Robert	Ballantine Books
It's in the Air	Z	I	2025	Independent Readers Science	Houghton Mifflin
Jade Green	Z	F	250+	Naylor, Phyllis Reynolds	Simon & Schuster

* Collection of short stories

TITLE	LEVEL	GENRE	WORD COUNT	AUTHOR / SERIES	PUBLISHER / DISTRIBUTOR
Jazmin's Notebook	Z	RF	250+	Grimes, Nikki	Penguin Group
Jim Morrison	Z	B	250+	Rock Music Library	Capstone Press
Jinx	Z	RF	250+	Wild, Margaret	Walker & Company
John Lennon	Z	B	250+	Rock Music Library	Capstone Press
Johnny Tremain	Z	HF	250+	Forbes, Esther	Bantam Doubleday Dell
Journal of Patrick Seamus Flaherty, The	Z	HF	250+	White, Ellen Emerson	Scholastic
Keeping Days, The	Z	HF	250+	Johnston, Norma	Puffin Books
King of Shadows	Z	F	250+	Cooper, Susan	McElderry
Kingdom of Kush, The	Z	I	3395	Leveled Readers	Houghton Mifflin
Kurt Cobain	Z	B	250+	Rock Music Library	Capstone Press
Lady with the Hat, The	Z	HF	250+	Orlev, Uri	Penguin Group
Land, The	Z	HF	250+	Taylor, Mildred D.	Penguin Group
*Leaving Home	Z	RF	250+	Keillor, Garrison	Penguin Group
*Leaving Home: 15 Distinguished Authors Explore Personal Journeys	Z	RF	250+	Rochman, Hazel; McCampbell, Darlene	HarperTrophy
Letters to Cupid	Z	RF	250+	Lantz, Francess	Pleasant Company
Lifeboat in Space	Z	I	3358	Leveled Readers	Houghton Mifflin
*Lion Tamer's Daughter And Other Stories, The	Z	F	250+	Dickinson, Peter	Laurel-Leaf Books
Little Women	Z	HF	250+	Alcott, Louisa May	Aladdin
Lord of the Rings, The	Z	F	250+	Tolkien, J.R.R.	Houghton Mifflin
Louis Armstrong	Z	B	250+	Brown, Sandford	Franklin Watts
Make Lemonade	Z	RF	250+	Wolff, Virginia Euwer	Scholastic
Malka	Z	HF	250+	Pressler, Mirjam	Philomel Books
Mammoths: Ice-Age Giants	Z	I	250+	Agenbroad, Dr. Larry D.; Nelson, Lisa	Lerner Publishing
Mariel of Redwall	Z	F	250+	Jacques, Brian	Avon
Marlfox: A Novel of Redwall	Z	F	250+	Jacques, Brian	Ace Books
Mattimeo: A Tale from Redwall	Z	F	250+	Jacques, Brian	Avon
Memories of Vietnam: War in the First Person	Z	HF	250+	Weiss, Ellen	Scholastic
Memory Boy	Z	F	250+	Weaver, Will	HarperCollins
Millennium Prophecies	Z	I	250+	Innes, Brian	Steck-Vaughn
Miracle Worker, The	Z	B	250+	Gibson, William	Bantam
Miracle's Boys	Z	RF	250+	Woodson, Jacqueline	Penguin Group
Monster	Z	RF	250+	Myers, Walter Dean	HarperCollins
Mossflower	Z	F	250+	Jacques, Brian	Ace Books
Moves Make the Man, The	Z	RF	250+	Brooks, Bruce	HarperTrophy
My Name Is America	Z	HF	250+	White, Ellen Emerson	Scholastic
Mysteries of the Ancients	Z	I	250+	Innes, Brian	Steck-Vaughn
Mysteries of the Bermuda Triangle	Z	I	2348	Leveled Readers	Houghton Mifflin
Mysteries of UFOs, The	Z	I	250+	Innes, Brian	Steck-Vaughn
Mysterious Giant Squid, The	Z	I	2415	Leveled Readers	Houghton Mifflin
Mysterious Healing	Z	I	250+	Innes, Brian	Steck-Vaughn
Named, The	Z	F	250+	Curly, Marianne	Bloomsbury Children's Books
Never Cry Wolf	Z	B	250+	Mowat, Farley	Bantam
Newton's Laws	Z	I	2853	Leveled Readers Science	Houghton Mifflin
Night	Z	B	250+	Wiesel, Elie	Bantam Books
*Night Terrors, Stories of Shadow and Substance	Z	F	250+	Duncan, Lois	Aladdin
Night the White Deer Died, The	Z	HF	250+	Paulsen, Gary	Dell
Nine Man Tree	Z	RF	250+	Peck, Robert Newton	Random House
No Pretty Pictures: A Child of War	Z	B	250+	Lobel, Anita	Greenwillow
No Promises in the Wind	Z	HF	250+	Hunt, Irene	Berkley Books
*Odder Than Ever	Z	F	250+	Coville, Bruce	Harcourt Trade

* Collection of short stories